FROMMER'S

BUDGET TRAVEL GUIDE

SPAIN '91-'92
ON $50 A DAY

by Darwin Porter
Assisted by Danforth Prince

Sherwood GOFF

Cannon

PRENTICE
HALL
PRESS

NEW YORK • LONDON • TORONTO • SYDNEY • TOKYO • SINGAPORE

FROMMER BOOKS

Published by Prentice Hall Press
A division of Simon & Schuster Inc.
15 Columbus Circle
New York, NY 10023

ISBN 0-13-326984-1
ISSN 1053-2439

Design by Robert Bull Design
Maps by Geografix Inc.

**PRENTICE
HALL
PRESS**

Manufactured in the United States of America

FROMMER'S SPAIN '91–'92 ON $50 A DAY
Editor-in-Chief: Marilyn Wood
Senior Editors: Judith de Rubini, Pamela Marshall, Amit Shah
Editors: Alice Fellows, Paige Hughes
Assistant Editors: Suzanne Arkin, Ellen Zucker
Contributing Editor: Lisa Renaud

CONTENTS

LIST OF MAPS

ABOUT THIS FROMMER GUIDE

What $-A-Day Means   The $-A-Day budget is meant to cover accommodations and meals only. Expect to spend at least half of the sum on accommodations. Obviously, if two of you are traveling together, it's easier to stay within our budget guidelines.

WHAT THE SYMBOLS MEAN

FROMMER'S FAVORITES—hotels, restaurants, attractions, and entertainments you shouldn't miss

SUPER-SPECIAL VALUES—really exceptional values

FROMMER'S SMART TRAVELER TIPS—hints on how to secure the best value for your money

IN HOTEL AND OTHER LISTINGS

The following symbols refer to the standard amenities available in all rooms:
A/C air conditioning   TEL telephone   TV television
MINIBAR refrigerator stocked with beverages and snacks

The following abbreviations are used for credit cards:
AE American Express   DISC Discover   EU Eurocard
CB Carte Blanche   ER enRoute   MC MasterCard
DC Diners Club   V VISA

TRIP PLANNING WITH THIS GUIDE

Use the following features:
What Things Cost in . . . to help you plan your daily budget
Calendars of Events . . . to plan for or avoid
Suggested Itineraries . . . for seeing the regions or cities
What's Special About Checklist . . . a summary of each region or city's highlights—which lets you check off those that appeal most to you
Easy-to-read Maps . . . walking tours, city sights, hotel and restaurant locations
Distances and Transportation Information . . . at the beginning of each town
Fast Facts . . . all the essentials at a glance: currency, emergencies, embassies, and more

OTHER SPECIAL FROMMER FEATURES

Cool for Kids—hotels, restaurants, and attractions
Did You Know . . . ?—offbeat, fun facts
Famous People—the nation's greats
Impressions—what others have said
In Their Footsteps—tracking the lives of famous residents

INVITATION TO THE READERS

In researching this book, I have come across many wonderful establishments, the best of which I have included here. I am sure that many of you will also come across wonderful hotels, inns, restaurants, guesthouses, shops, and attractions. Please don't keep them to yourself. Share your experiences, especially if you want to comment on places that have been included in this edition that have changed for the worse. You can address your letters to:

Darwin Porter
Frommer's Spain '91–'92 on $50 A Day
c/o Prentice Hall Press
Travel Books
15 Columbus Circle
New York, NY 10023

A DISCLAIMER

Readers are advised that prices fluctuate in the course of time and travel information changes under the impact of the varied and volatile factors that affect the travel industry. Neither the author nor the publisher can be held responsible for the experiences of readers while traveling. Readers are invited to write to the publisher with ideas, comments, and suggestions for future editions.

SAFETY ADVISORY

Whenever you're traveling in an unfamiliar city or country, stay alert. Be aware of your immediate surroundings. Wear a moneybelt and keep a close eye on your possessions. Be particularly careful with cameras, purses, and wallets, all favorite targets of thieves and pickpockets.

CHAPTER 1

GETTING TO KNOW SPAIN

Since Franco died in 1975, Spain has been celebrating a vibrant political and cultural renaissance. This *movida* has rapidly turned its two major cities, Madrid and Barcelona, into exciting, energetic, and sophisticated European capitals where the bars and cafés hum until dawn. In every aspect of life—from politics and the economy to fashion and the arts—you can feel Spain's pride and prosperity and a newfound national self-confidence.

Outside the major cities, the old, traditional Spain still exists, a country of extreme contrasts, characterized by both passionate hotbloodedness and unconcerned indolence. In the remoter regions you can still find the Spain of your dreams—secluded castles, Roman ruins, jeweled Moorish palaces, sun-drenched beaches, terraced vineyards, sleepy fishing villages, and the rituals of the bullfight and flamenco.

1. GEOGRAPHY, HISTORY & POLITICS

GEOGRAPHY

Three times the size of Illinois, with a population of only 37 million, Spain faces the Atlantic Ocean and the Bay of Biscay to the north and the Mediterranean Sea to the south and east. Portugal borders on the west while the high Pyrénées mountain range separates Spain from France and the rest of Europe. The southern coastline is only a few sea miles from the north coast of Africa.

One finds it almost impossible to generalize about Spain because it is composed of so many regions—50 provinces in all—each with its own physical makeup, history, and culture. Though the country may look like a single geographical unit, the topography divides it into many different regions; the Cantabrian Mountains in the north, those of Cuenca in the east, and the Sierra Morena in the south mark off a high central tableland that itself is cut across by other hills.

THE REGIONS IN BRIEF

The Central Plateau Madrid stands at the center, ringed by such cities as Toledo, Segovia, and Salamanca. Stretching southwest to the Portuguese border is Extremadura, arid hilly country.

Andalusia and the Costa del Sol This is the Spanish south, including Córdoba, Seville, Málaga, and Granada. The heartland of traditional and Moorish Spain, it's famous for the Sierra Nevada mountains and also for its beaches.

The Levante This is the name given to the Mediterranean coastline of Murcia and Valencia, the latter region famous for its oranges.

The Northeast and the Balearic Islands Barcelona, capital of Catalonia, is the gateway to the Costa Brava and to the Balearics (Majorca, Ibiza, and Minorca).

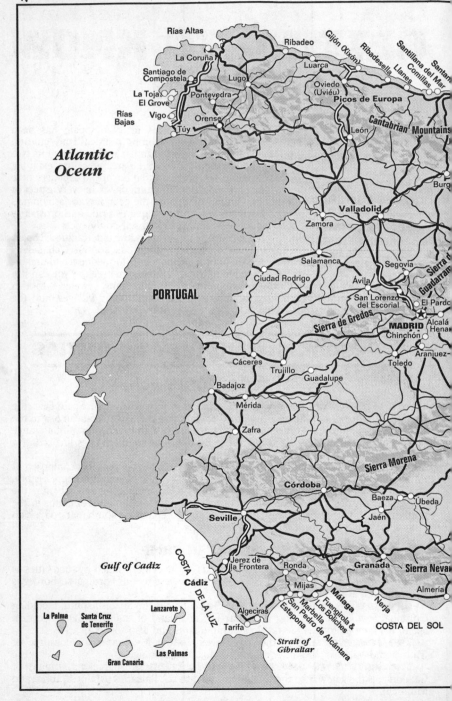

SPAIN

Bay of Biscay

FRANCE

Laredo
Castro-
Urdiales
Bermeo
Guernica
Lekeitio
Ondarroa
Guetaria
Zarauz
Fuenterrabia
Bilbao
San Sebastián/
Donostia
Vitoria/
Gasteiz
Haro
Nájera
Logroño
Calahorra
Estella
Olite
Sos del Rey
Católico
Tudela
Roncesvalles
Pamplona
Sangüesa
Jaca
Huesca
Tarazona
Calatayud
Zaragoza
Nuévalos
Piedra
Pyrenees
ANDORRA
Gulf of
Lions
Figueras
Girona
Cadaqués
COSTA
BRAVA
Tossà de Mar
Lloret de Mar
Montserrat
Barcelona
Sitges
Tarragona
COSTA DORADA
Cuenca
Teruel
COSTA DEL AZAHAR
Balearic Sea
Valencia
Gulf of Valencia
Elche
Benidorm
Alicante
Murcia
COSTA BLANCA
Cartagena
COSTA CALIDA

Mediterranean Sea

ALGERIA

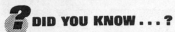

DID YOU KNOW . . . ?

- Spain is the only country on which the United States dropped four hydrogen bombs—it was an accident and they didn't explode.
- The Duchess of Alba, not the Queen of England, is the world's most titled woman.
- Spanish painter Pablo Picasso was the world's most profilic painter: 13,500 paintings or sketches, 34,000 illustrations, 300 sculptures, and 100,000 etchings.
- A Spaniard, Josep Grugués, cooked the world's largest sausage, measuring 3 miles long.
- A recent survey revealed that 60% of the Spanish population have no interest in bullfighting.
- The palm was introduced into Europe by Muslim monarch Abderraman I, who planted seedlings on the palace grounds at Córdoba.
- The body of the Duchess of Alba was exhumed in 1945 to "prove" she did not pose for Goya's *Naked Maja* in 1797.
- In 1762 Charles III ordered that all nudes in the royal collection be burned. Court painter Anton Raphael Mengs didn't obey, thereby rescuing many masterpieces for posterity.
- Ernest Hemingway himself never ran in the *encierro* (running of the bulls) held during the festival in Pamplona.

The North This region incorporates Navarre and Aragón; the inland cities of Valladolid, Burgos, and Zaragoza; the Basque country, famous for its cuisine and its summer capital, San Sebastián; and Cantabria, with its attractive beaches.

The Northwest Wrapping around the northern boundary of Portugal, this region includes Galicia, León, and Asturias. The prime attraction is Santiago de Compostela in Galicia.

Andorra This is a separate principality in the Pyrénées.

HISTORY & POLITICS
ANCIENT TIMES

Ancestors of the Basques may have been the first settlers in Spain 10,000 to 30,000 years ago, followed, it is believed, by Iberians from North Africa. They, in turn, were followed by Celts who crossed the Pyrénées around 600 B.C. After many intertribal battles these groups were melded into a Celtic-Iberian people who inhabited central Spain.

Others coming to the Iberian Peninsula in prehistoric times were the Phoenicians, who took over coastal areas on the Atlantic beginning in the 11th century B.C. Cádiz, originally the ancient Phoenician settlement of Gades, is perhaps the oldest town in Spain. Cartagena was settled by people from the Phoenician city of Carthage. Perhaps half a millennium after the Phoenicians, the Greeks came, lured by the gold and silver found in the peninsula. The Greeks set up colonies before they were conquered by the Carthaginians from North Africa.

Around 200 B.C. the Romans vanquished the Carthaginians and laid the foundations of the present Latin culture. Traces of Roman civilization can still be seen today. By the time of Julius Caesar, Spain (Hispania) was under Roman law and began a long period of peace and prosperity.

BARBARIAN INVASIONS, THE MOORISH KINGDOM, AND THE RECONQUEST

When Rome fell in the 5th century, Spain was overrun first by the Vandals, then by the Visigoths from eastern Europe. The chaotic rule of the Visigothic kings lasted about 300 years, but the barbarian invaders did adopt the language of their new country and tolerated Christianity as well.

Early in the 8th century Spain attracted the attention of the Moors, who were advancing along the north coast of Africa. In A.D. 711 Moorish warriors led by Tarik, crossed over to Spain and conquered the disunited country. By 714 they controlled most of it except for a few mountain regions like Asturias. For eight centuries, until 1492, the Moors occupied the land and imprinted their culture on the Spanish people.

The Moors, with Córdoba as their capital, called their new land "al-Andalus," or Andalusia. A great intellectual center, Córdoba became the scientific capital of Europe; notable advances were made in agriculture, industry, literature, philosophy, and medicine. The Jews were welcomed by the Moors, often serving as administrators, ambassadors, and financial officers. But the Moors quarreled with one another, and soon the few Christian strongholds in the north advanced south to eventually overpower them.

The Reconquest, the name given to the Christian efforts to rid the peninsula of the Moors, lasted more than 700 years. Intermittent battles between Christians and Moors slowly reduced the size of the Muslim holdings, with Catholic monarchies forming small kingdoms in the northern areas. By the middle of the 13th century, the kingdom of Granada was the only Muslim possession left on the Iberian Peninsula. By the time of Alfonso I of Aragón (1104–34), the final push began to rid the land of Islam. The three powerful kingdoms of Aragón, Castile, and León were joined in 1469, when Ferdinand of Aragón married Isabella. Catholic Kings, as they were called, launched the final attack on the Moors and completed the Reconquest in 1492 by capturing Granada.

That same year Columbus, the Genoese sailor, discovered the West Indies, laying the foundations of the far-flung empire that brought wealth and power to Spain during the 16th and 17th centuries.

Under Ferdinand and Isabella, the Spanish Inquisition was created to eradicate all heresy and firmly secure the primacy of Catholicism. Non-Catholics, Jews, and Moors, who had lived in Spain for centuries, were mercilessly persecuted.

In 1492, when given the choice of converting to Christianity or leaving the country, most Jews left, but the majority of Moors remained, converting to Catholicism and becoming known as the Moriscos. (They were nonetheless driven out of Spain in 1609–11, under inexorable pressure from the Inquisition.)

THE GOLDEN AGE AND THE LATER DECLINE

Columbus's discovery of America and its subsequent exploration by the conquistadores launched Spain into its Golden Age.

In the first half of the 16th century, Balboa discovered the Pacific Ocean, Cortés seized Mexico for Spain, Pizarro took Peru, and a Spanish ship (which had started out under the command of the Portuguese Magellan, who was killed during the voyage) circumnavigated the globe. The conquistadores took Catholicism to the New World and shipped masses of gold back to Spain. The Spanish Empire extended all the way to the Philippines. Spanish ships ruled the seas, and Spanish armies were feared all over Europe.

Charles V, the grandson of Ferdinand and Isabella, was the most powerful prince in Europe—king of Spain and Naples, Holy Roman Emperor and lord of Germany, Duke of Burgundy and the Netherlands, and ruler of the new-world territories. But much of Spain's wealth and human resources were wasted in religious and secular conflicts. Spain itself was neglected.

First Jews, then Muslims, and finally Moriscos were driven out—and with them much of the country's prosperity. When Philip II came to the throne in 1556, Spain could indeed boast vast possessions—the new-world colonies; Naples, Milan, Genoa, Sicily, and other portions of Italy; the Spanish Netherlands (modern Belgium and the Netherlands); and portions of Austria and Germany—but the seeds of decline had already been planted.

Philip, a fanatic Catholic, devoted his energies to subduing the Protestant revolt in the Netherlands and to becoming the standard bearer for the Counter-Reformation. He tried to return England to Catholicism, first by marrying Mary I (Bloody Mary) and later by wooing her half sister, Elizabeth I, who rebuffed him. When in 1588 he resorted to sending the Armada, it was ignominiously defeated—an event that signaled the decline of Spanish power, which continued through the 17th century.

In 1700 a Bourbon prince, Philip V, became king and the country fell under the influence of France. Philip V's right to the throne was challenged by a Hapsburg archduke of Austria, this giving rise to the War of the Spanish Succession. When it ended, Spain had lost Flanders, its Italian possessions, and Gibraltar (still held by the British today).

During the 18th century Spain's direction changed with each sovereign. Charles III (1759–88) developed the country economically and culturally. Charles IV became embroiled in wars with France, and the weakness of the Spanish monarchy allowed Napoleon to place his brother Joseph Bonaparte on the throne in 1808. Even after Napoleon's defeat, when Spain's rightful kings were restored to the throne, the country continued to decline.

THE 19TH AND 20TH CENTURIES

Although Britain and France had joined forces to restore the Spanish monarchy, the European conflicts encouraged the overseas Spanish colonists to rebel. Ultimately, this led to the United States' freeing the Philippines, Puerto Rico, and Cuba from Spain in 1898.

In Spain republican ideas agitated the country throughout the 19th century, and in 1876 it became a constitutional monarchy. But labor unrest, disputes with the Catholic Church, and war in Morocco combined to create political chaos. Conditions eventually became so bad that the Cortes, or Parliament, was dissolved in 1923 and Gen. Miguel Primo de Rivera formed a military directorate. Early in 1930 Primo de Rivera resigned but unrest continued.

On April 14, 1931, a revolution occurred, a republic was proclaimed, and King Alfonso XIII and his family were forced to flee. Initially the liberal constitutionalists ruled, but soon were pushed aside by the socialists and anarchists, who adopted a constitution separating church and state, secularizing education, and containing several other radical provisions (for example, agrarian reform and the expulsion of the Jesuits).

The extreme nature of these reforms fostered the growth of the conservative Falange party, modeled after Italy's and Germany's fascist parties. By the 1936 elections the country was equally divided between left and right, and political violence was common. On July 18, 1936, the army, supported by Mussolini and Hitler, seized power, igniting the Civil War. Gen. Francisco Franco, coming from Morocco to Spain, led the Nationalist (rightist) forces in the two years of fighting that ravaged the country. Towns were bombed and many atrocities committed. Early in 1939 Franco entered Barcelona and went on to Madrid; thousands of republicans were executed. Franco became chief of state, remaining so until his death in 1975.

Although Franco adopted a neutral position during World War II, his sympathies obviously lay with Germany and Italy. Both countries had helped him attain power, so Spain gave aid to the Axis as a nonbelligerent. This action intensified the diplomatic isolation into which the country was forced after the war's end—in fact, it was excluded from the United Nations until 1955.

Before his death General Franco selected as his successor Juan Carlos de Borbón y Borbón, to be king of Spain. After the 1977 elections a new constitution, approved by the electorate and the king, guaranteed human and civil rights, as well as free enterprise, and canceled the status of the Roman Catholic Church as the church of Spain. It also granted limited autonomy to several regions, including Catalonia and the Basque Provinces, both of which are still clamoring for complete autonomy. Under the new regime, Spain has advanced economically. In 1986 it gained entry to the European Community, and is now one of the fastest-growing economies in Europe.

DATELINE

- **13th–6th c. B.C.** Original Iberians enter Spain.
- **11th c. B.C.** Phoenicians settle Spain's coasts.

(continues)

2. FAMOUS SPANIARDS

Rodrigo Díaz de Vivar, or **El Cid** (ca. 1043–99) Known in Spain as Campeador, or winner of battles, El Cid was immortalized in a 12th-century epic poem bearing his name. After winning battles against the Moors, he was exiled in 1081 and became chief political adviser to the

Arabs. Later reconciling with Castile, he overthrew the Moorish kingdom at Valencia in 1089. Upon his death he left control of Valencia to his wife, who could not hold it.

Manuel de Falla (1876–1946) Famous composer of the opera *La Vida Breve* and the ballet *El Amor Brujo*. In 1907 he moved to Paris, where he was influenced by Claude Debussy and Maurice Ravel. Falla retired to Granada in 1922, writing mostly Spanish folk music and flamenco until 1939, when he moved to Argentina. He died before completing the dramatic cantata *L'Atlantida*.

Antoni Gaudí i Cornet (1852–1926) The most famous name in Catalán architecture. Gaudí studied in Barcelona, developing his talents in the art nouveau style. He designed apartment houses and office buildings along the Passeig de Gràcia between 1905 and 1907. A deeply religious man, he is best remembered for his uncompleted cathedral, Sagrada Familia.

El Greco (1541–1614) Born in Crete and named Doménikos Theotokópoulos, he trained in Italy under Titain. He became one of Spain's greatest artists, painting his masterpiece *The Burial of Count Orgaz* in Toledo in 1577.

Isabella La Católica (1451–1504) Better known as Isabella I, this powerful monarch ruled Castile and León. Her greatest accomplishment was the financing Columbus's expedition to America; she even sold her own jewels to do this. She also launched the Spanish Inquisition against Muslims, Jews, and Protestants, thus tainting her historical reputation and making her one of the most notorious bigots in history.

Moses ben Maimon, Maimonides (1135–1204) Born to a wealthy Jewish family, Maimonides fled to Morocco when the Almohades invaded Córdoba in 1148. Settling in Egypt, he became the leader of Egyptian Jewry and later court physician to Saladin. He wrote a summary of Jewish oral law in Hebrew entitled *Mishneh Torah,* and was also famed for his knowledge of medicine, theology, and philosophy. He wrote *Guide to the Perplexed,* which influenced both Jewish and Christian scholars.

Francisco Pizarro (ca. 1476–1541) A conquistador from Extremadura, he conquered Peru in 1533, using cunning and treachery.

Fray Gabriel Téllez, or **Tirso de Molina** (1584–1648) Often compared to Shakespeare, he ranked with Lope de Vega and Calderón de la Barca as a dramatist, writing more than 300 plays (the famous being *El Burlador de Sevilla* and *El Condenado por Desconfiado*).

St. Teresa of Ávila (1515–82) A mystic who founded a convent that observed the original rules of the Carmelite Order. After her death in Ávila, it is said, a violet and fragrant oil emanated from her tomb. The tomb was opened and one of the brothers cut off her hands, alleging they could work miracles. Relic seekers continued to desecrate her corpse over the years. Pope Gregory XV beatified her in 1622.

Tomás de Torquemada (1420–98) Inquisitor-general to Ferdinand and Isabella. As their confessor, he

DATELINE

- **650 B.C.** Greeks colonize the east.
- **600 B.C.** Celts cross Pyrénées; settle in Spain.
- **6th–3rd c. B.C.** Carthaginians make Cartagena their colonial capital. They drive out the Greeks.
- **218–201 B.C.** Second Punic War: Rome defeats Carthage.
- **2nd c. B.C.–2nd c. A.D.** Rome controls most of Iberia. Christianity spreads.
- **5th c.** Vandals, then Visigoths, invade Spain.
- **8th c.** Moors conquer most of Spain.
- **10th c.** Córdoba becomes center of learning under Moors.
- **1214** More than half of Iberia regained by Catholics.
- **1469** Ferdinand of Aragón marries Isabella of Castile.
- **1492** Catholic monarchs conquer last Moorish stronghold, Granada. Columbus discovers New World.
- **1519** Cortés seizes Mexico. Charles I crowned Holy Roman Emperor, as Charles V.
- **1556** Philip II inherits throne, launches Counter-Reformation.

(continues)

pushed for the expulsion of the Jews and Moriscos from Spain. At least 2,000 people were executed at his behest. According to legend, Torquemada never ate unless the tongue of a scorpion was placed beside his plate.

Miguel de Unamuno (1864–1936) Of Basque heritage, Spain's greatest scholar became a professor of Greek at the University of Salamanca, but was fired for political reasons in 1914. Regaining his position, he was made "rector for life" in 1931, but was fired again in 1936 and died under "house confinement." *Paz en la Guerra,* published in 1897, was considered the first real existential novel. His masterpiece, *The Tragic Sense of Life,* was written in 1913.

3. SOME CULTURAL BACKGROUND

ART

Spain's contributions to art range from the ancient carvings and cave paintings of Altamira (which, sadly, are no longer open to the public) to the works of some of the world's foremost artists.

After El Greco (1541–1614), not Spanish-born but a 40-year resident of the country, the great name of the Golden Age was Diego Velázquez (1599–1660), court painter to Philip IV and a portraitist of rare skills. Other top artists of the seventeenth century included Ribera, Zurbarán, and Murillo.

During the reigns of Charles III and Charles IV, neoclassical art flourished in Madrid, with Francisco de Goya (1746–1828) at the top of the list. You can view his frescoes depicting Madrid at the Pantéon de Goya (Goya's Tomb).

Among 19th-century painters, Joaquín Sorolla (1883–1923) doesn't enjoy the international reputation he deserves, but his work is displayed in his own museum in Madrid.

Madrid can't claim the Spanish genius of 20th-century art: Pablo Picasso was born in Málaga. But he left Madrid his most famous and controversial work, *Guernica,* which depicts the horrors of the Spanish Civil War. Spain was also the birthplace of Gris, Miró, and Dalí.

To name even the most outstanding Spanish artists and their works would demand more space than allotted, but I urge visitors to visit the Prado in Madrid and other places in Spain where famous artworks can be seen.

ARCHITECTURE

Spanish architecture might well have mirrored that of other European countries, had it not been for the Muslims' long dominance of most of the Iberian Peninsula. Because they lived for the present rather than planning and building for the future, their architecture tended to be lavishly decorated on the surface, but with a flimsy substructure. Therefore, not many complete examples are left of the monumental Saracenic structures of those centuries. But enough exist, including great mosques, minarets, and palaces, to show the lasting influence of various types of arches, colonnades, reflecting pools, and filigree ornamentation.

The Alhambra at Granada and the Alcázar at Seville are the most outstanding examples of Moorish architecture extant in Spain. Both these complexes evolved during various caliphates and periods of Muslim architecture and Mudejar art. The latter name refers to works fashioned in the Spanish Muslim tradition after the Reconquest, by either Moors or converted Muslims (or their trainees). A Mudejar style is still followed in Spain, especially in the villages, although it only dimly recalls the grandeur of Muslim art of old.

For truly original design, visitors should see the work of the controversial Catalonia-born Antoni Gaudí, especially in Santander and Barcelona.

DATELINE

neutral in World War II, but Franco favors Germany.

- **1955** Spain joins United Nations.
- **1969** Franco names Juan Carlos his successor.
- **1975** Juan Carlos becomes king.
- **1978** New constitution initiates reform.
- **1982** Socialists sweep to power after 43 years of right-wing rule.
- **1986** Spain joins European Community.

LITERATURE

The epic poetry of the late Moorish period and the popular poems composed by wandering minstrels were followed by romantic ballads and Italian-influenced poetry. The 15th century saw the greater dominance of prose biography, novels, and treatises, these forms continuing into the next century's so-called Golden Age, which was marked principally by religious and humanist writings, picaresque novels (the protagonist being a *picaro*, or rogue), pastoral novels, histories, books of chivalry, and plays. The most familiar figure to Americans from this era is probably the "Man of La Mancha," Don Quixote, created by Cervantes.

During the Civil War many writers heroically defended the Second Republic—the most famous being Federico García Lorca, Rafael Alberti, Jorge Guillen, and Luís Cernuda.

Four Spaniards have won the Nobel Prize for Literature since it was originated in 1901: the playwrights José Echegaray (1904) and Jacinto Benavente (1922), and the poets Juan Ramón Jiménez (1956) and Vicente Aleixandre (1977).

✪ **The Nobel Prize for literature has been won by a Spaniard four times.**

MUSIC

To North Americans, the best-known Spanish musicians are composer Manuel de Falla, pianist José Iturbi, classical guitarist Andrés Segovia, cellist Pablo Casals, and operatic tenor Plácido Domingo.

The first written music of Spain sprang from the early Christian era, when the

IMPRESSIONS

I thought that I should never return to the country I love more than any other, except for my own.
—ERNEST HEMINGWAY

Three Spaniards, four opinions.
—OLD SPANISH PROVERB

liturgy evolved into the Visigothic chant (or Moorish chant). Before the Arab invasion, music was flourishing in Toledo, Zaragoza, and Seville, and it continued as Christian Spain developed hymns and liturgical chants in the monasteries.

The conquerors from Africa brought with them many interesting instruments, including square tambourine (*adufe* in Spanish), standard tambourine (*panderete*), drum (*atabal*), psaltery (*canón*), and metal castanets (*sonajas de azófar*). During the Renaissance, instrumental music became an important art form. This was specially true of pieces written for an early six-string guitar called the *vihuela,* replaced by the five-string guitar in the 17th century.

Opera, emerging in the 17th century, was strongly influenced by the Italians. But the *zarzuela,* an 18th-century light musical entertainment similar to the Gilbert and Sullivan operettas (later a sort of variety show), was truly Spanish.

DANCE

From the lowliest *taberna* to the poshest nightclub, you are likely to hear heel clicking, foot stamping, castanet rattling, hand clapping, and the sound of sultry guitar music. This is flamenco. Its origins lie deep in Asia, but the Spanish gypsy has given it an original and unique style. It is a dance dramatizing inner conflict and pain. Performed by a great artist, flamenco can tear your heart out.

Flamenco has no story line. The leader sets the pace, drawing each of the performers forward. He or she lurks behind and around the group at all times, trying to infuse them with rhythm. It can be contagious, so don't be surprised if you end up with the castanets yourself.

Other regional dances include the *sardana* of Catalonia, the *muineira* of Galicia, and the fiery, colorful dances of León, Castile, and Valencia. The *jota* of Aragón is also renowned. When this dance is presented in a more sensuous Arabic fashion, it is transformed into the *fandango.* The *seguidilla* has much in common with the jota and fandango. Described by Cervantes as "the quicksilver of all senses," the seguidilla gave birth to the *bolero,* popular in the taverns of the 18th and 19th centuries.

Today, the most popular dance (especially in Madrid) is the *sevillana.* In the classic tradition, one or two flamenco guitars accompanies the steps, but now anything goes, even a mariachilike brass band or conga drums. Of course, all these dances end with *Ole!*

FIESTAS

Every month and every town has a fiesta. Almost all are religiously inspired, but combine the religious aspect with such popular entertainments as bullfights, parades, and exhibits.

Fiestas vary. A *romería,* which you may see along the road, is a pilgrimage (often overnight) to a particular historic site; a *verbena,* held in a city or town, is a nighttime festivity, with special emphasis on folk dancing; a *feria* (literally, fair) is a riot of song and dance—and an event dear to the Spanish soul, the most popular being the Feria of Seville.

To find out about fiesta times and locations, get a copy of the *Tourist Calendar*—listing more than 3,000 events—available at tourist offices. For our highlights of the year, see "Spain—Calendar of Events" in Chapter 2.

BULLFIGHTS — THE SPECTACLE OF DEATH

Many consider bullfighting to be cruel and shocking. But as Ernest Hemingway pointed out in *Death in the Afternoon,* "The bullfight is not a sport in the Anglo-Saxon sense of the word, that is, it is not an equal contest or an attempt at an equal contest between a bull and a man. Rather it is a tragedy; the death of the bull, which is played, more or less well, by the bull and the man involved and in which there is danger for the man but certain death for the bull " Hemingway, of course, was an aficionado.

When the symbolic drama of the bullfight is acted out some think it reaches a higher plane. Some people argue that it is not a public exhibition of cruelty at all, but rather a highly skilled art requiring great human qualities: survival, courage, showmanship, and gallantry.

Regardless of how you view it, this spectacle is an authentically Spanish experience, and as such has much to reveal about the character of the land and its people.

SEASON & TICKETS

The season of the *corridas* (bullfights) lasts from early spring until mid-October or earlier. Fights are held in a plaza de toros (bullring), ranging in location from the oldest ring in remote Ronda to the big-time Plaza de Toros in Madrid. Sunday is corrida day in most major Spanish cities, although Madrid and Barcelona may also have fights on Thursday.

Tickets fall into three classifications: *sol* (sun), the cheapest; *sombra* (shade), the most expensive; and *sol y sombra* (a mixture of sun and shade), the medium-priced range.

THE FIGHT ITSELF

The corrida begins with a parade. For many viewers, this may be the high point of the afternoon's festivities, as all the bullfighters are clad in their *trajes de luce,* or "suits of light."

Bullfights are divided into *tercios* (thirds). The first is the *tercio de capa* (cape), during which the matador tests the bull with various passes and gets acquainted with him. The second portion, the *tercio de varas* (sticks), begins with the lance-carrying *picadores* on horseback, who weaken, or "punish," the bull by jabbing him in the shoulder area. The horses are sometimes gored, even though they wear protective padding, or the horse and rider may be tossed into the air by the now infuriated bull. The picadores are followed by the *banderilleros,* whose job it is to puncture the bull with pairs of boldly colored darts.

In the final *tercio de muleta* the action narrows down to the lone fighter and the bull. Gone are the fancy capes. Instead, the matador uses a small red cloth known as a *muleta,* which, to be effective, requires a bull with lowered head. (The picadores and banderilleros have worked to achieve this.) Using the muleta as a lure, the matador wraps the bull around himself in various passes, the most dangerous of which is the *natural;* here, the matador holds the muleta in his left hand, the sword in his right. Right-hand passes pose less of a threat, since the sword can be used to spread out the muleta, making a larger target for the bull. After a number of passes, the time comes for the kill, the "moment of truth." A truly skilled fighter may dispatch the bull in one thrust.

After the bull dies, the highest official at the ring may award the matador an ear from the dead bull, or perhaps both ears, or ears and tail. For a really extraordinary performance, the hoof is sometimes added. The bullfighter may be carried away as a hero, or if he has displeased the crowd, be chased out of the ring by an angry mob. At a major fight six bulls are usually killed by three matadors in one afternoon.

IMPRESSIONS

Now you have two homes.
—TRADITIONAL SPANISH FAREWELL

Idiocy proliferates in Spain, from politics to culture.
—NOBEL PRIZE-WINNER CELA.

4. FOOD & DRINK

The food in Spain is varied, the portions immense, and the prices moderate by North American standards. Whenever possible, try the regional specialties, particularly when you visit the Basque country or Galicia. Many of these regional dishes, including Andalusian gazpacho and Valencian paella, have transcended their region and have become great dishes of the world.

FOOD

MEALS

Breakfast   In Spain the day starts with a continental breakfast of hot coffee, hot chocolate, or tea, with assorted rolls, butter, and jam. A typical Spanish breakfast consists of *churros* (fried fingerlike doughnuts) and a hot chocolate that is very sweet and thick. The coffee is usually strong and black, served with hot milk. Some Americans consider it too strong and bitter for their tastes, and therefore ask for instant coffee.

Lunch   An important meal in Spain, comparable to the farm-style noonday "dinner" in America. It usually includes three or four courses, beginning with a choice of soup or several dishes of hors d'oeuvres called *entremeses*. Often a fish or egg dish is served after this, then a meat course with vegetables. Wine is always on the table. Dessert is usually pastry, custard, or assorted fruit; this is followed by coffee. Lunch is served from 1 to 3:30 pm, with "rush hour" at 2pm.

Tapas   After the early-evening promenade, many Spaniards head for their favorite *tascas*, or bars, where they drink wine and sample assorted *tapas*, such as bits of fish, eggs in mayonnaise, or olives.

Dinner   Another extravaganza. A typical meal starts with a bowl of soup, followed by a second course, often a fish dish, and by another main course, usually veal, beef, or pork, accompanied by vegetables. Again, desserts tend to be fruit, custard, or pastries.

Wine is always available. Afterward, you might have a demitasse and a fragrant Spanish brandy. The chic dining hour, even in one-donkey towns, is 10 or 10:30pm. (In well-touristed regions and hardworking Catalonia, you can usually dine by 8pm). In most middle-class establishments, people dine no later than 9:30pm. Your choice.

DINING CUSTOMS

Hours   Most restaurants in Spain close on Sunday, so be sure to check ahead. Hotel dining rooms are generally open seven days, and there's always a food dispenser open in big cities like Madrid and Barcelona, or well-touristed areas like the Costa del Sol.

Reservations   Generally, reservations are not necessary, except at popular, top-notch restaurants.

For money-saving hints, including the *menú turístico* and *menú del día,* as well as the cafeterias, see Chapter 2.

SOME HEALTH/DIET TIPS

North Americans who plunge wholeheartedly into this routine may experience digestive trouble, particularly if they also drink more wine than usual. By the third day they will invariably be in the grip of "Toledo belly." To stop this malady, purchase Tanagel, sold in all pharmacies.

Two heavy Spanish meals a day are definitely not recommended. For lighter fare, patronize the cafeterias that are not self-service.

As a final caution, if you do eat a large lunch, don't rush out into the noonday sun for a round of sightseeing. Do as the Spaniard does: Take a siesta. Or, take your large meal at lunch and have a light snack at a tapas bar in the evening.

THE CUISINE

Soups and Appetizers Soups are usually served in big bowls. Cream soups, such as asparagus and potato, can be fine; sadly, however, they are too often made of powdered envelope soups such as Knorr and Liebig. The chilled gazpacho, on the other hand, is tasty. Served year round, it is particularly refreshing during the hot months. The combination is pleasant: olive oil, garlic, ground cucumbers, and raw tomatoes with a sprinkling of croûtons. Spain also offers several varieties of fish soup—*sopa de pescado*—in all of its provinces, and many of these are superb. In the *paradores* (government-run hostelries) and top restaurants, as many as 15 tempting hors d'oeuvres are served. In lesser-known places avoid these entremeses, which often consist of last year's sardines and shards of sausage left over from the Moorish Conquest.

Eggs These are served in countless ways. A Spanish omelet, a *tortilla española*, is made with potatoes. A simple omelet is called a *tortilla francesa*. A *tortilla portuguésa* is similar to the American Spanish omelet.

Fish Spain's fish dishes tend to be outstanding and vary from province to province. One of the most common varieties is hake (*merluza*)—sweet and white. *Langosta,* a variety of lobster, is seen everywhere and it's a treat, but terribly expensive. The Portuguese in particular, but some Spaniards too, go into raptures at the mention of barnacles. Gourmets relish their seawater taste; others find them tasteless. *Rape* is the Spanish name for monkfish, a sweet, wide-boned ocean fish with a scalloplike texture. Also try a few dozen half-inch baby eels. They rely heavily on olive oil and garlic for their flavor, but they're great-tasting. Squid cooked in its own ink is suggested only to those who want to go native. The charcoal-broiled sardines however, are a culinary delight—a particular treat in the Basque Provinces. Trout Navarre is one of the most popular fish dishes, usually stuffed with bacon or ham.

Paella You can't go to Spain without trying its celebrated paella. Flavored with saffron, paella is an aromatic rice dish usually topped with shellfish, chicken, sausage, peppers, and local spices. Served authentically, it comes steaming hot from the kitchen in a metal pan called a *paellera*. (Incidentally, what is known in America as Spanish rice isn't Spanish at all. If you ask an English-speaking waiter for Spanish rice, he'll serve you paella.)

Meats Don't expect Kansas City steak, but do try the spit-roasted suckling pig, so sweet and tender it can often be cut with a fork. The veal is also good, and the Spanish *lomo de cerdo,* a loin of pork, is unmatched anywhere. As for chicken, it will sometimes qualify for the Olympics in that it is stringy and muscular. Spit-roasted chicken, however, often can be flavorful.

Vegetables and Salads Except in summer, Spanish vegetables are not the greatest. In some places fresh green vegetables are hard to come by, and the diner is often served canned string beans, peas, or artichokes. Potatoes are also a staple, but avoid them mashed. Salads are usually fresh, made with crisp lettuce and vine-ripened tomatoes in summer.

Desserts The Spanish do not emphasize dessert. Flan, a home-cooked egg custard, appears on all menus—sometimes with a burnt-caramel sauce. Ice cream appears on nearly all menus as well. But the best bet is to ask for a basket of fresh fruit, which you can wash at your table. Homemade pastries are usually moist and not too sweet. As a dining oddity, many restaurants serve fresh orange juice for dessert. Madrileños love it!

Olive Oil and Garlic Olive oil is used lavishly in Spain. You may not want it in all dishes. If, for example, you prefer your fish grilled in butter, the word is *mantequilla.* In some instances, you'll be charged extra for the butter. Garlic is also an integral part of the Spanish diet, and even if you love it, you may find the Spaniard loves it more than you do, and uses it in the oddest dishes.

DRINK
NONALCOHOLIC

Water It is safe to drink in all major cities and tourist resorts. If you're traveling in remote areas, play it safe and drink bottled water. One of the most popular noncarbonated bottled drinks in Spain is Solares. Nearly all restaurants and hotels have it. If you'd like your water with a little kick, then ask for *agua mineral con gas.* Note that bottled water often costs more than the regional wine.

Soft Drinks In general, avoid the carbonated citrus drinks on sale everywhere. Most of them never saw an orange, much less a lemon. If you want a citrus drink, order old, reliable Schweppes. An excellent noncarbonated drink for the summer is called Trĭ-Naranjus and comes in lemon and orange flavors. Your cheapest bet is a liter bottle of *gaseosa,* which comes in various flavors. In summer you should also try a drink I've never had outside Spain, *horchata,* a nutty, sweet milklike beverage made of tubers called *chufas.*

Coffee Even if you are a dedicated coffee drinker, you may find the *café con leche* (coffee with milk) a little too strong. I suggest *leche manchada,* a little bit of strong, freshly brewed coffee in a glass, filled with lots of frothy hot milk.

Milk In the largest cities you get bottled milk, but it loses a great deal of its flavor in the process of pasteurization. In all cases, avoid untreated milk and milk products. About the best brand of fresh milk is called Lauki.

ALCOHOLIC

Beer Although not native to Spain, beer (*cerveza*) is now drunk everywhere. Domestic brands include San Miguel, Mahou, Aguila, and Cruz Blanka.

Wine Sherry (*vino de Jerez*) has been called "the wine with a hundred souls." Drink it before dinner (try the topaz-colored *finos,* a very pale sherry) or whenever you drop in to some old inn or bodega for refreshment; many of them have rows of kegs with spigots. Manzanilla, a golden-colored, medium-dry sherry, is extremely popular. The sweet cream sherries (Harvey's Bristol Cream, for example) are favorite after-dinner wines (called *olorosos*). While the French may be disdainful of Spanish table wines, they can be truly noble, especially two leading varieties, Valdepeñas and Rioja, both from Castile. If you're fairly adventurous and not too demanding in your tastes, you can always ask for the *vino de la casa* (wine of the house) wherever you dine. The Ampurdan of Catalonia is heavy. From Andalusia comes the fruity Montilla. There are also some good local champagnes (*cava*) in Spain, such as Freixenet. One brand, Benjamin, also comes in individual-size bottles.

Sangría This is the all-time favorite refreshing drink in Spain. It is red-wine punch that combines wine with oranges, lemons, seltzer, and sugar.

Whisky and Brandy Imported whiskies are available at most Spanish bars, but at a high price. If you're a drinker, switch to brandies and cognacs, where the Spanish reign supreme. Try Fundador, made by the Pedro Domecq family in Jerez de la Frontera. If you're seeking a smooth cognac, ask for "103" white label.

5. RECOMMENDED BOOKS, FILMS & RECORDINGS

BOOKS
ECONOMIC, POLITICAL AND SOCIAL HISTORY

Historically, Spain's Golden Age lasted from the late 15th to the early 17th century, a period when the country reached the height of its prestige and influence. This era is well surveyed in J. H. Elliot's *Imperial Spain 1469–1716* (New American Library, 1977).

Most accounts of the Spanish Armada's defeat are written from the English point of view. For a change of perspective, try David Howarth's *The Voyage of the Armada* (Penguin, 1981).

The story of the Spanish Inquisition is told by Edward Peters in his *Inquisition* (University of California Press).

One of the best accounts of Spain's earlier history is found in Joseph F. O'Callaghan's *History of Medieval Spain* (Cornell University, 1983).

In the 20th century the focus shifts to the Spanish Civil War, recounted in the classic by Hugh Thomas, *The Spanish Civil War* (Harper & Row, 1977). For a personal account of the war, read George Orwell's *Homage to Catalonia* (Harcourt Brace Jovanovich, 1969). The poet García Lorca was killed during the Civil War; the best account of his death is found in Ian Gibson's *The Assassination of Federico García Lorca* (Penguin, 1983).

If you like more contemporary history, read John Hooper's *The Spaniards* (Penguin, 1987). Hooper provides insight into the events of the post-Franco era, when the country came to grips with democracy after years of fascism.

THE ARTS

The Moors contributed much to Spanish culture, leaving Spain with a distinct legacy that is documented in Titus Burckhardt's *Moorish Culture in Spain* (McGraw Hill, 1972).

Antoni Gaudí is the Spanish architect who most excites visitors' curiosity. Among the many illustrated books on his work, *Gaudí* (Escudo de Oro's "Collection of Art in Spain," 1990) contains 150 photographs. It is sold at most newsstands along the Ramblas in Barcelona.

Spain's most famous artist was Pablo Picasso. The most controversial recent book about the late painter is *Picasso, Creator and Destroyer* by Arianna Stassinopoulos Huffington (Simon & Schuster, 1988).

Spain's other headline-grabbing artist was Salvador Dalí. In *Salvador Dalí: A Biography* (E. P. Dutton, 1986), author Meryle Secrest asks: Was he a mad genius or a cunning manipulator?

Andrés Segovia: An Autobiography of the Years 1893–1920 (Macmillan, 1976), with a translation by W. F. O'Brien, is worth seeking out.

For the most intimate glimpse into the world of a Spanish film director, read *Mi Último suspiro* (*My Last Sigh*), the autobiography of Luís Buñuel, whose films mirrored the social, political, and religious conflicts that have torn Spain apart in the 20th century.

FICTION AND BIOGRAPHY

Denounced by some as superficial, James A. Michener's *Iberia* (Random House, 1968) remains the classic travelogue on Spain. The *Houston Post* claimed this book "will make you fall in love with Spain."

The most famous Spanish novel is *Don Quixote* by Miguel de Cervantes. It deals with the conflict between the ideal and the real in human nature. It's readily available.

The collected works of the famed dramatist of Spain's golden age, Pedro Calderón de la Barca, can be read in *Plays* (University Press of Kentucky, 1985).

The major works of pre–Civil War playwright, Federico García Lorca, can be enjoyed in *Five Plays: Comedies and Tragicomedies* (New Directions, 1964).

Ernest Hemingway completed many works on Spain, none more notable than his

---

IMPRESSION

I also love the Spaniard, for he is a type in his own right, a copy of no one.
STENDHAL

novels of 1926 and 1940, respectively, *The Sun Also Rises* (Macmillan, 1987) and *For Whom the Bell Tolls* (Macmillan, 1988), the latter based on his experiences in the Spanish Civil War. Don Ernesto's *Death in the Afternoon* (various editions) remains the English-language classic on bullfighting.

For a very different, but dated, view of Spain, read W. Somerset Maugham's *Don Fernando* (Ayer, 1977; originally issued in 1935), with the famed English author's comments on everything from the Spanish diet to *Don Quixote*.

For travelers to Granada and the Alhambra, the classic is *Tales of the Alhambra* (Sleepy Hollow Press, 1982) by Washington Irving. If you're visiting Majorca, read George Sand's *A Winter in Majorca* (Academy Chicago Publications, 1978), detailing the troubled time she spent with Chopin at Valldemossa. Many translations (the best one is by Robert Graves) are for sale on Majorca.

The Life of Saint Teresa of Ávila by Herself (Penguin, 1987) is reputedly the third most widely read book in Spain, after the Bible and *Don Quixote*. Some parts are heavy going, but the remainder is lively. The translation is by J. M. Cohen.

FILM

The first Spanish feature film, *Los Guapos del Parque* (The Dandies of the Park), directed by Segundo de Chomon, was released in 1903, seven years after the film industry began in Barcelona.

Film studios opened in Madrid in 1920, and by 1926 Spain was producing some 30 feature films a year. Before World War II the biggest name was Florian Rey, who made both silents and talkies, his most notable work being *Le Aldea Maldita* (The Damned Village) in 1929.

After the Civil War and under Franco, Spain produced a lot of mediocre films. Even General Franco, using a pseudonym, wrote a propaganda piece called *Raza* (The Race) in 1941.

In the 1950s Spanish film achieved world recognition mainly because of two directors, Luís García Berlanga and Juan Antonio Bardem. Both made satirical films about social conditions in Spain, sometimes incurring the government's wrath. During the filming of *Death of a Cyclist*, in fact, Bardem was arrested and imprisoned. Upon his release, he finished the film which won acclaim at Cannes.

One of the big names in Spanish cinema is Luís Buñuel, whom some regard as the genius of Spanish cinema. In 1928 Salvador Dalí and Buñuel cooperated on the director's first movie, *Un Chien Andalou* (An Andalusian Dog), considered the most important surrealist film. Two years later, sadistic scenes in *L'Age d'Or* (The Golden Age)—again written with Dalí's help—led to riots in some movie houses. Buñuel also directed *La Mort en ce Jardin* (Death in the Garden) with Simone Signoret (1957). In 1960 he made *Viridiana*, which subsequently won the prize for best picture at Cannes, even though Franco banned the film in Spain.

Today's enfant terrible is Pedro Almódovar, whose *Women on the Verge of a Nervous Breakdown* won an Academy Award nomination in 1990. Ostensibly, the film is the story of a woman's abandonment, but its madcap proceedings deal with everything from spiked gazpacho to Shiite terrorists. An iconoclast like Almódovar, who has publicly declared his homosexuality, flourishes in the contemporary liberal Spain, which abolished censorship in 1977.

In 1982 José Luís García became the first Spaniard to win an Oscar for best foreign film, with *Volver a Empezar* (To Begin Again), even though local critics considered the film inferior to his earlier *Asignatura Pendiente* (Anticipated Assignation). *Volver a Empezar* takes a look at an exiled writer's homecoming to Spain.

One of the biggest box-office hits in Spanish film history (and still available in video) is *El Crimen de Cuenca* (The Crime in Cuenca), directed by Pilar Miró, who went on to become "chief of state of television." The film, which details Civil Guard torture, caused a furor when it was released and was suppressed until the coup attempt of 1981.

The Basque problem reached the movie screens in 1983 with *La Muerte de Mikel*

(Michael's Death), which dramatizes the tortured love story of a young Basque nationalist and a transvestite from Bilbao.

In 1988 Carlos Saura, whom many regard as the natural heir to Buñuel, produced *El Dorado*, the most expensive film ever produced in Spain. The critics panned it, audiences stayed away, but you can judge for yourself.

RECORDINGS
CLASSICAL

Don Odilo Cunill directs the Cor Monastic de Abadía de Montserrat in *Cants Gregorians de la Missa Per Els Fidels Missa Orbis Factor,* Gregorian chants recorded in the chapel of the monastery at Montserrat.

In the album *Andrés Segovia, España,* the late master plays guitar versions of fandangos and *tonadillas.* In a more classical vein, the same artist plays Bach, Scarlatti, and also music by the Czech composer Benda (1722–95) in *Recital Íntimo.*

The Orquesta de Conciertos de Madrid performs Falla's *El Amor Brujo* and *El Sombrero de Tres Picos.* The same group, conducted by Enrique Jorda, can be heard in Albéniz's *Suite Española* and *Dos Piezas Españoles.*

FOLK/ETHNIC

Isabel Pantoja, widow of the late bullfighter, sings soulful interpretations of Andalusian ballads in *Se Me Enamora el Alma.* Rocio Jurado renders them smolderingly in *Punto de Partida* and *Canciones de España.*

Carlos Cana performs popular interpretations of Spanish Argentinian tangos, habaneras, and sevillanas on Luna de Abril. In *Canalla,* Antonio Cortés Chiquetete is heard in 19th-century folk melodies. Felipe Campuzano gives piano interpretations of Andalusian folk music in *Cádiz: Andalucía Espiritual.*

Pasodobles Famosos, performed by the Gran Banda Taurina, is popular with older Spaniards, partly for its nostalgia value. This was the music played until very recently at every Spanish gathering, from bullfights to weddings to christenings.

In *Siroca,* Paco de Lucía combines traditional flamenco guitar in its purest form with modern influences, including tangos, *bulerías,* and *tanquillos.* You can also hear Paco de Lucía on *Fantasía Flamenca,* interpreting authentic *flamencas* in a traditional manner.

The brilliance of late virtuoso Narciso Yepes can be heard on *Música Española para Guitarra,* performing traditional favorites.

CONTEMPORARY

Ana Belén sings contemporary love ballads in *A la Sombra de un León.*

In Madrid, an outstanding local band is called *Radio Futura.* They have been called "the Einsteins of Spanish rock music." Reviewers usually cite the *Mecano,* a Madrid band, as "pretty boys." They're sort of a Spanish version of New Kids on the Block, and they sell records by the ton. Borrowing a name from a famous old German movie, the *Gabinete Caligari,* in the words of one reviewer, is a band that represents "macho Hispano-pop." From Catalonia comes a duo with a unique sound, a band recording rock music as *El Ultimo de la Fila.*

One of the biggest record sellers in Spain is Joan Manuel Serrat, a singer-songwriter recording more traditional popular music in both Catalán and Castilian.

In Madrid, traditional Spanish music is also offered by singer-songwriter Luís Eduardo Aute, who has thousands of fans in the Spanish-speaking world.

In current Spanish jazz, Tete Montoliu's recordings represent some of the best the country has to offer. All, or most, of these records are available at Spanish music stores in the United States. They are available throughout Spain as well.

CHAPTER 2

BEFORE YOU GO

This chapter is devoted to the where, when, and how of your trip—the advance planning required to get it together and take it on the road.

After they've decided where to go, most people have two fundamental questions: What will it cost? and How do I get there? This chapter will not only answer both those questions but also address such other important issues as when to go, whether or not to take a tour, what alternative travel vacations to consider, what pretrip health precautions to take, what additional insurance coverage to investigate, where to obtain more information about the destination, and so on.

---

1. INFORMATION, ENTRY REQUIREMENTS & MONEY

SOURCES OF INFORMATION

At least three months before you go, get in touch with the **National Tourist Office of Spain,** 665 Fifth Ave., New York, NY 10022 (tel. 212/759-8822), which can provide sightseeing information, calendars of events, train/ferry schedules, maps, and much, much more.

Other useful sources are newspapers and magazines. To find the latest articles that have been published on your destination, go to your library, ask for the *Guide to Periodical Literature,* and look under the city/country for listings.

You may also want to contact the State Department for their background bulletins. Write to the **Superintendent of Documents, U.S. Government Printing Office,** Washington, DC 20402 (tel. 202/783-3238).

A good travel agent can also be a good source of information. If you use one, make sure he or she is a member of the American Society of Travel Agents (ASTA). If you get poor service from a travel agent, write to ASTA's **Consumer Affairs Department,** P.O. Box 23922, Washington, DC 20006.

And finally, we come to the best source of all—friends and other travelers who have just returned from your destination.

ENTRY REQUIREMENTS
PASSPORTS

A valid passport is all an American, British, Canadian, Australian, or New Zealand citizen needs to enter Spain, and can be secured as follows.

In the United States Citizens 18 or older who meet the requirements may obtain a 10-year passport. Applications are available from post offices, court offices, and passport agencies. There are passport agencies in 13 cities—New York,

Washington, D.C., Stamford (Conn.), Seattle, Philadelphia, San Francisco, New Orleans, Boston, Honolulu, Chicago, Los Angeles, Miami, and Houston.

First-time applicants over 18 pay $42. Youths under 18 are granted a 5-year passport. Children under 13 must have a parent or a guardian apply on their behalf; teenagers 13 to 16 must have a parent's or a guardian's permission to apply for a passport. The fee for applicants under 18 is $27.

If your expired passport is 12 or more years old, or if it was granted to you before your 16th year, you must apply in person. Otherwise, you may apply by mail.

Your passport application must be accompanied by proof of U.S. citizenship—a certified copy of your birth certificate or naturalization papers, or an old passport (provided it's not more than 12 years old). A driver's license or employee ID card with photo is also acceptable. If none of these proofs is available, you may have someone who has known you at least two years (who has ID) accompany you and vouch for your identity. You'll also need two identical and recent color or black-and-white passport-size (2″ × 2″) photographs.

You'll wait the longest to receive your passport between mid-March and mid-September; in winter it usually takes about two weeks by mail. Passports can sometimes be issued quickly in an emergency, provided you present a plane ticket with a confirmed seat.

In Canada   Citizens may go to one of nearly two dozen regional offices located in major cities. Alternatively, you can mail your application to the Passport Office, Section of External Affairs, Ottawa, ON, K1A 0G3. Post offices have application forms. Passports cost $25 (Canadian), and proof of Canadian citizenship is required, along with two signed identical passport-size photographs. Passports are valid for 5 years.

In Great Britain   Citizens may apply at one of the regional offices in Liverpool, Newport, Glasgow, Peterborough, and Belfast, or else in London if they reside there. You can also apply in person at a main post office. Documents required include a marriage certificate or a birth certificate; two photos must accompany the application. The fee is £15, and the passport is good for 10 years.

In Australia   Citizens apply at the nearest post office. Provincial capitals and major cities have passport offices, where a passport valid for 10 years can be had for a fee of $66 (Australian).

In New Zealand   Citizens may go to their nearest consulate or passport office to obtain an application, which may be filed in person or by mail. To obtain a 10-year passport, proof of citizenship is required, plus a fee of $49.50 (New Zealand).

VISAS

Visas are not needed by U.S., Canadian, or British citizens for visits of less than three months. Citizens of Australia, New Zealand, and South Africa do need to obtain a visa, and should apply in advance at the Spanish Consulate in their home countries.

CUSTOMS

You can take into Spain most personal effects and the following items duty free: two still cameras and 10 rolls of film per camera; one movie camera; tobacco for personal use; one liter each of liquor and wine; a portable radio; a tape recorder; a typewriter; a bicycle; sports equipment; fishing gear; and two hunting weapons with 100 cartridges each.

Returning to the United States from Spain, you may bring in $400 worth of merchandise duty free, provided you have not made a similar claim within the past 30 days. Remember to keep your receipts for purchases made in Spain.

MONEY

To give you an idea of what Spain costs, consult the two "What Things Cost" charts, below.

CASH/CURRENCY

The basic unit of Spanish currency is the peseta (abbreviated pta.), currently worth about 94¢ in U.S. currency. One U.S. dollar is worth about 106.65 pesetas. Coins come in 1, 5, 25, 50, 100, 200, and 500 pesetas. Notes are issued in 500, 1,000, 5,000, and 10,000 pesetas.

All world currencies fluctuate, so you should be aware that the amounts appearing in this book are not exact. Currency conversions are presented only to give you a rough idea of the price you'll pay in U.S. dollars. There is no way to predict exactly what the rate of exchange will be when you visit Spain. Check the newspaper or ask at your bank for last-minute quotations.

Be advised that rates of exchange vary, depending on where you convert your money. Your hotel will offer the worst rate of exchange. In general, banks offer the best rate, but even banks charge a commission for the service, often $2 or $3, depending on the transaction.

TRAVELER'S CHECKS

Before leaving home, purchase traveler's checks and obtain some ready cash (about $200 worth). Change about $50 into pesetas, obtainable from major banks, so that you can avoid waiting in long lines at the currency-exchange offices upon arrival in Spain.

American Express (tel. toll free 800/221-7282 in the U.S. and Canada) is the most widely recognized traveler's check abroad; the agency imposes a 1% commission. Checks are free to members of the American Automobile Association. **Bank of America** (tel. toll free 800/227-3460 in the U.S.; 415/624-5400, collect, in Canada) also issues checks in U.S. dollars for a 1% commission everywhere but California. **Citicorp** (tel. toll free 800/645-6556 in the U.S.; 813/623-1709, collect, in Canada) issues checks in U.S. dollars, British pounds, and German marks. **MasterCard International** (tel. toll free 800/223-9920 in the U.S.; 212/974-5696, collect, in Canada) issues checks in about a dozen currencies. **Barclays Bank** (tel. toll free 800/221-2426 in the U.S. and Canada) issues checks in U.S. or Canadian dollars and in British pounds. **Thomas Cook** (tel. toll free in the U.S. 800/223-7373; 212/974-5696, collect, in Canada) issues checks in U.S. or Canadian dollars and in British pounds.

Each of these agencies will refund your checks if they are lost or stolen, provided you produce sufficient documentation. Keep a list of check numbers in a place separate from your checks. When purchasing checks from one of the banks listed, ask about refund hotlines; American Express and Bank of America have the most offices around the world.

Purchase checks in a variety of denominations—$20, $50, and $100—and divide them up in your luggage to avoid losing everything if you are robbed.

Foreign banks may charge up to 5% to convert your checks into Spanish pesetas. Note that you'll get the best rate if you cash traveler's checks at the banks issuing them: VISA at Barclays, American Express at American Express, and so forth.

THE PESETA AND THE DOLLAR

At this writing $1 equals approximately 106.65 ptas (or 1 pta. = 94¢), and this was the rate of exchange used to calculate the dollar values given in this book. This rate fluctuates from time to time and may not be the same when you travel to Spain. Therefore, the following table should be used only as a guide:

Ptas.	U.S.	Ptas.	U.S.
5	.05	1,000	9.40
10	.09	1,500	14.10
15	.14	2,000	18.80
20	.19	2,500	23.50
25	.24	3,000	28.20
30	.28	3,500	32.90
40	.38	4,000	37.60
50	.47	4,500	42.30
75	.71	5,000	47.00
100	.94	5,500	51.70
150	1.41	6,000	56.40
200	1.88	6,500	61.10
250	2.35	7,000	65.80
500	4.70	7,500	70.50

CREDIT CARDS

Credit cards are useful in Spain. **American Express, VISA,** and **Diners Club** are widely recognized. If you see the **Eurocard** or **Access** sign on an establishment, it means it accepts **MasterCard.**

WHAT THINGS COST IN MADRID   U.S. $

Taxi from airport to Puerto del Sol	16.90
Bus from airport to Plaza de Colón	2.35
Local telephone call	.15
Double room at Palace Hotel (very expensive)	389.55
Double room at Hotel Residencia Carlos V (moderate)	94.00
Double room at Hostal Principado (budget)	40.40
Continental breakfast	2.80
Dinner for one, without wine, at Cabo Mayor (expensive)	61.10
Dinner for one, without wine, at Sobrino de Botín (moderate)	20.70
Dinner for one, without wine, at Tienda de Vinos (budget)	7.50
Coca-Cola in restaurant	1.15
Cup of coffee	.95
Glass of wine	.95
Glass of beer	.65 to 1.40
Admission to Prado	3.75
Roll of Kodacolor film, 24 exposures	7.90
Car rental	47.00
Liter of gasoline	.74

WHAT THINGS COST IN SALAMANCA	U.S. $
Taxi from train station to cathedral	1.30
Local telephone call	.15
Double room at Gran Hotel (expensive)	122.20
Double room at Emperatriz (moderate)	47.00
Double room at Mindanao (budget)	28.20
Continental breakfast	1.30
Dinner for one, without wine, at Venecia (expensive)	42.30
Dinner for one, without wine, at El Candil (moderate)	18.80
Dinner for one, without wine, at any *tapas* bar (budget)	6.60
Coca-Cola in restaurant	.75 to 1.15
Cup of coffee	.60 to .80
Glass of wine	.45
Glass of beer	.55 to .70
Admission to Universidad museum	.95
Roll of Kodacolor film, 24 exposures	6.10
Car rental	47.00
Liter of gasoline	.74

Credit cards can save your life when you're abroad. With American Express and VISA, for example, not only can you charge purchases in shops and restaurants that take the card, but you can also withdraw pesetas from bank cash machines at many locations in Spain. Check with your credit-card company before leaving home.

Keep in mind that the price of purchases is not converted into dollars until notification is received in the United States, so the price is subject to fluctuations in the dollar. If the dollar declines by the time your bill arrives, you'll pay more for an item than you expected. But those are the rules of the game. It can also work in your favor it the dollar should rise.

2. WHEN TO GO — CLIMATE, HOLIDAYS & EVENTS

CLIMATE

May and October are the best months weatherwise and crowdwise.

In summer it's hot, hot, and hot again, with the cities of Castile (Madrid) and Andalusia (Seville and Córdoba) stewing up the most scalding brew. Madrid has dry heat; the temperature can hover around 84°F in July, 75° in September. Seville has the dubious reputation of being about the hottest part of Spain in July and August, often baking under temperatures that average around 93°.

Barcelona is humid. The temperature in Majorca in high summer often reaches 91°. The overcrowded Costa Brava has temperatures around 81° in July and August. The Costa del Sol has an average of 77° in summer. The coolest spot in Spain is the

Atlantic coast from San Sebastián to La Coruña, with temperatures in the 70s in July and August.

(In spite of attempts to change it, August remains the major vacation month in Europe. The traffic from France to Spain becomes a veritable migration, and low-cost hotels are almost fully booked along the coastal areas, with top prices in effect. To compound the problem, many restaurants and shops also decide it's time for a vacation, thereby limiting the visitor's selections for both dining and shopping.)

Spring and fall are ideal times to visit nearly all of Spain, with the possible exception of the Atlantic coast, which experiences heavy rainfall in October and November.

In winter the coast from Algeciras to Málaga is most popular, with temperatures reaching a warm 60° to 63°. It gets cold in Madrid, as low as 34°. Majorca is warmer, usually in the 50s, but often dipping into the 40s. Some of the mountain resorts have extreme cold.

Spain's Average Monthly Temperatures

		Jan	Feb	Mar	Apr	May	June	July	Aug	Sept	Oct	Nov	Dec
Barcelona	High (°F)	55	57	60	65	72	78	82	82	77	69	62	56
	Low (°F)	43	45	48	52	57	65	69	69	66	58	51	46
Seville	High (°F)	59	63	69	74	80	90	90	98	90	78	68	60
	Low (°F)	42	44	48	52	56	63	63	67	64	57	50	44
N. Coast	High (°F)	50	55	59	61	66	70	75	75	69	60	55	53
	Low°F)	39	40	42	43	43	59	59	59	53	45	48	42
Alicante	High (°F)	61	64	68	73	78	84	90	89	83	75	68	63
	Low (°F)	43	43	47	50	55	62	67	68	64	57	50	45

HOLIDAYS

Holidays include January 1 (New Year's Day), January 6 (Feast of the Epiphany), March 19 (Feast of St. Joseph), Good Friday, Easter Monday, May 1 (May Day), June 10 (Corpus Christi), June 29 (Feast of St. Peter and St. Paul), July 25 (Feast of St. James), August 15 (Feast of the Assumption), October 12 (Spain's National Day), November 1 (All Saints' Day), December 8 (Immaculate Conception), and December 25 (Christmas).

No matter how large or small, every city or town in Spain also celebrates its local saint's day. In Madrid it's May 15 (St. Isidro). You'll rarely know what the local holidays are in your next destination in Spain. Don't use up all your money, because you may arrive in town only to find banks and stores closed. In some cases intercity bus services are suspended on holidays.

SPAIN CALENDAR OF EVENTS

Be aware that the dates given below may not always be precise. Sometimes the exact days are not announced until six weeks before the actual festival. Check with the Spanish National Tourist Office if you're planning to attend a specific event.

JANUARY

- **Granada Reconquest Festival,** Granada. The whole of Granada celebrates the taking of the town from the Moors in 1492. The highest tower at the Alhambra is open to the public on Jan 2. For information, contact the Tourist Office of Granada, Plaza de Mariana Pineda, 10, 18009 Granada (tel. 958/22-66-88). Jan 1–2.
- **Día de los Reyes (Parade of the Three Kings),** all over Spain. Parades are held throughout the country on the eve of the Festival of the Epiphany. Various "kings" dispense candies to children. Jan. 6.
- **St. Anthony's Day (La Puebla),** Majorca. Bonfires, dancing, revelers dressed as devils, and other riotous events honor St. Anthony on the eve of his day. Jan 17.

FEBRUARY

- **Bocairente Festival of Christians and Moors,** Bocairente (Valencia). Fireworks, colorful costumes, parades, and a reenactment of the struggle between Christians and Moors mark this exuberant festival. A stuffed effigy of Mohammed is blown to bits. Feb 1–15
- **Carnivales de Cádiz,** Cádiz. The oldest and best-attended carnival in Spain has been called "rampant madness." Costumes, parades, strolling troubadours, drum beating—it's all fun and games. Feb 22–Mar 4.

MARCH

- **Fallas de Valencia,** Valencia. Going back to the 1400s, this fiesta sees the burning of papier-mâché effigies of winter demons. Burnings are preceded by bullfights, fireworks, and parades. Mar 19.

APRIL

- ✪ *FERIA DE SEVILLA (SEVILLE FAIR)* *This is the most celebrated week of revelry in all of Spain, with all-night flamenco dancing, merrymaking in casetas, bullfights, horseback riding, flower-decked coaches, and dancing in the streets.*
  Where: Seville. When: Mid-Apr. How: Make hotel reservations early. For information, contact the Seville Office of Tourism, Avenida de la Constitución, 21B, 41004 Sevilla (tel. 95/422-14-04).
- ✪ *SEMANA SANTA (HOLY WEEK)* *From Holy Thursday until Easter Sunday, a series of processions with hooded penitents moves to the piercing wail of the saeta, a love song to the Virgin or Christ. Pasos (heavy floats) bear images of the Virgin or Christ.*
  Where: Seville. When: Apr 8–15. How: Make hotel reservations early. For information, contact the Seville Office of Tourism, Avenida de la Constitución, 21B, 41004 Sevilla (tel. 95/422-14-04).

MAY

- **Festival de los Patios,** Córdoba. At this famous fair residents flamboyantly decorate their patios with cascades of flowers. Visitors wander from patio to patio. First 2 weeks in May.
- **Romería del Rocío (Pilgrimage of the Virgin of the Dew),** El Rocío (Huelva). The most famous pilgrimage in Andalusia, attracting a million people. Fifty men carry the statue of the Virgin 9 miles to Almonte for consecration. May 11–14.
- **Jerez Horse Fair,** Jerez de la Frontera. "Horses, wine, women, and song," according to the old Andalusian ditty, make this a stellar event at which some of the greatest horses in the world are on parade. May 13–20.

JUNE

○ *INTERNATIONAL MUSIC AND DANCE FESTIVAL* *In its 40th year (1991), this prestigious program of dance and music attracts international artists who perform at the Alhambra and other venues. It's a major event on the cultural calendar of Europe.*
Where: Granada. When: Mid- to late June. How: Make reservations as early as possible. For information, contact the Festival Office, City of Granada, Gracía, 21, 18002 Granada (tel. 958/267-442).

☐ **Corpus Christi,** all over Spain. A major holiday on the Spanish calendar, this event is marked by big processions, especially in such cathedral cities as Toledo, Málaga, Seville, and Granada. June 14.

☐ **Verbena de Sant Joan,** Barcelona. This traditional festival occupies all Cataláns. Barcelona literally "lights up"—fireworks, bonfires, and dances until dawn. The highlight of the festival is its culmination at Montjuïc with fireworks. June 24.

○ *FESTIVAL DE CINE DE BARCELONA* *Expanded since 1987, this increasingly prestigious event brings filmmakers from all over Europe. Awards are presented to outstanding films, and screenings of new movies take place. Retrospectives are also presented.*
Where: Barcelona. When: June. How: Get tickets at Rambla de Catalunya and Carrer Aragó (tel. 215-24-24).

JULY

☐ **Festival of St. James,** Santiago de Compostela. Pomp and ceremony mark this annual pilgrimage to the tomb of St. James the Apostle in Galicia. Galician folklore shows, concerts, parades, and the swinging of the *botafumeiro* (a mammoth incense burner) mark the event. Mid- to late July.

☐ **San Sebastián Jazz Festival,** San Sebastián. Celebrating its 26th year (1991), this festival brings together the jazz greats of the world at the pavilion of the Anoeta Sport Complex. Other programs takes place al fresco at the Plaza de Trinidad in the old quarter. Last 2 weeks in July.

○ *FIESTA DE SAN FERMÍN* *Torn from the pages of The Sun Also Rises, the "running of the bulls" through the streets of Pamplona is the most popular celebration in Spain. The running is the most photographed event, but the celebration also includes wine tasting, fireworks, and, of course, bullfights.*
Where: Pamplona. When: July 7-14. How: Make reservations months in advance ("Papa" Hemingway paid a man a yearly stipend to secure the best tickets and hotel rooms). For more information, such as a list of hotel accommodations, write the Office of Tourism, Duque de Ahumada, 3, 31002 Pamplona (tel. 948/22-07-41).

AUGUST

☐ **Santander International Festival of Music and Dance,** Santander. A repertoire of classical music, ballet, contemporary dance, chamber music, recitals, and much more. Most performances are staged at the Plaza de la Porticada. All month.

☐ **The Mystery Play of Elche,** Elche. In the 17th-century Basilica of Santa María in Elche (Alicante), this sacred drama is reenacted. It represents the Assumption and the Crowning of the Virgin. Tickets may be obtained from the Office of Tourism, Passeig de l'Estacío, 03203 Elche (tel. 96/545-27-47). Aug 11-15.

SEPTEMBER

- □ **Diada,** Barcelona. This is considered the most significant festival in all of Catalonia. It celebrates the glory of autonomy from the rest of Spain, following years of repression under the dictator Franco. Demonstrations and other "flag-waving" events take place. The *senyera,* the flag of Catalonia, is much in evidence. Not your typical tourist fare, but interesting nevertheless. September 11.
- □ **Cádiz Grape Harvest Festival,** Jerez de la Frontera. The major wine festival in Andalusia (which means Spain as well) honors the famous sherry of Jerez, with 5 days of processions, flamenco dancing, bullfights, livestock on parade, and, of course, sherry drinking. Mid-Sept (dates vary).
- □ **International Film Festival San Sebastián.** The premier film festival of Spain takes place in the Basque capital, often at the Victoria Eugenia Theater, a Belle Epoque extravaganza. Retrospectives are often featured, and weeklong screenings are shown. Second half of Sept (dates vary).
- □ **Setmana Cran,** Barcelona. As the summer draws to an end, Barcelona stages week-long *verbenas* and *sardana* dances to honor its patron saint, the Virgin of Merced. Parades, concerts, various theatrical and musical events at venues throughout the city, even sports competitions, mark this event dear to the heart of Catalonia. Bullfights are also part of the festival. Look for the "parade of giants" through the streets, culminating at Placa de Sant Jaume in front of the city hall.

OCTOBER

- □ **Mostra de Valencia Film Festival,** Valencia. A week of cinema—complete with homages and retrospectives—is staged at various venues in this Levante city. Tickets and information are available from Palau de la Música, Paseo de la Alameda, 46010 Valencia (tel. 96/360-33-56). Dates vary.
- □ **St. Teresa Week,** Ávila. *Verbenas* (carnivals), parades, singing, and dancing honor the patron saint of this walled city. Dates vary.

NOVEMBER

- □ **All Saints' Day,** all over Spain. This public holiday is reverently celebrated, as relatives and friends lay flowers on the graves of the dead. Nov 1.

DECEMBER

- □ **Día de los Santos Inocentes,** all over Spain. This equivalent of April Fools' Day is an excuse for people to do "loco" things. Dec 28.

MADRID
CALENDAR OF EVENTS

FEBRUARY

- □ **ARCO 91.** The best in contemporary art from Europe and America is lavishly presented. Exhibitions are held at IFEMA (the Madrid Trade Fair Organization), Avenida de Portugal, daily noon to 9pm. Metro: Lago. Dates vary.
- □ **Madrid Carnival.** The carnival kicks off with a big parade along the Paseo de la Castellana, culminating in a masked ball at the Círculo de Bellas Artes the following night. Fancy-dress competitions last until Feb 28, when the festivities end with a tear-jerking "burial of a sardine" at the Fuente de los Pajaritos in the Casa de Campo. This is followed that evening by a concert in the Plaza Mayor. Dates vary.

MAY

✪ **FIESTAS DE SAN ISIDRO** Madrileños run wild with a 10-day celebration honoring their patron saint. Food fairs, Castilian folkloric events, street parades, parties, music, dances, bullfights, and other festivities mark the occasion.
Where: Madrid. **When:** May 12–21. **How:** Make hotel reservations early. Expect crowds and traffic (beware of pickpockets). For information, contact the Office of Tourism in Madrid, Princesa, 1, 28008 Madrid (tel. 91/541-23-25).

JULY

☐ **Veranos de la Villa.** Called "the summer binge" of Madrid, this summerlong program presents folkloric dancing, pop music, classical music, zarzuelas, and flamenco at various venues throughout the city. Open-air cinema is a feature in the Parque del Retiro. Ask at the various tourist offices for complete details (which change every summer). Sometimes admission is charged, but often these events are free.

AUGUST

☐ **Fiestas of Lavapiés and La Paloma.** These two fiestas—the most traditional in Madrid—begin with the Lavapiés on Aug 1 and continue through the hectic La Paloma celebration on Aug 15, the day of the Virgen de la Paloma. Tens of thousands of residents and visitors race through the narrow streets. Apartment dwellers above hurl buckets of cold water onto the crowds below to cool them off. Children's games, floats, music, flamenco, and zarzuelas, along with street fairs, mark the occasion.

OCTOBER

✪ **AUTUMN FESTIVAL** Both Spanish and international artists participate in this cultural program, with a series of operatic, ballet, dance, music, and theatrical performances. From Strasbourg to Tokyo, this event is a premier attraction, yet tickets are reasonable in price, costing from 1,500 pesetas ($14.10) per event.
Where: Madrid. **When:** Usually Oct. **How:** Make hotel reservations early, and write for tickets to the Festival de Otoño, Paseo de la Castellana, 101, 28046 Madrid (tel. 91/556-24-12).

3. HEALTH & INSURANCE

HEALTH PREPARATIONS

Spain should not pose any major health hazards. Many travelers suffer from diarrhea, generally caused by the overly rich cuisine—garlic, olive oil, and wine. Take along some antidiarrhea medicine, moderate your eating habits, and, even though the water in most parts of Spain is considered safe, consume mineral water only. Milk and milk products are pasteurized and generally considered safe. The Mediterranean, a horrendously polluted sea, washes up on Spain's shores, and fish and shellfish from it should only be eaten cooked. Try to make sure it is fresh. Sometimes inadequate refrigeration of fish and shellfish, especially in the hot summer months, can lead to what some foreign visitors to Spain call "the Toledo trot," the equivalent of Mexico's "Montezuma's revenge."

Sometimes travelers find that the change of diet in Spain leads to constipation. If this occurs, eat a high-fiber diet and drink plenty of mineral water. Avoid large lunches and dinners with wine. Consult your doctor before you go about taking Colace, a stool softener, or Metamucil.

If you need a doctor, ask your hotel to locate one for you. You can also obtain a list of English-speaking doctors in Spain from the **International Association for Medical Assistance to Travelers (IAMAT),** in the United States at 417 Center St., Lewiston, NY 14092 (tel. 716/754-4883); in Canada, at 188 Nicklin Rd., Guelph, ON, N1H 7L5 (tel. 519/836-0102). Getting medical help in Spain is relatively easy, compared to many countries, and competent doctors are found in every part of the country.

If your medical condition is chronic, always talk to your doctor before taking an international trip. He or she may have specific advice to give you. For conditions such as epilepsy, a heart condition, diabetes, and some other afflictions, wear a Medic Alert Identification Tag, which will immediately alert any doctor as to the nature of your condition. It also provides the number of Medic Alert's 24-hour hotline, so that a foreign doctor can obtain medical records for you. For a lifetime membership, the cost is a well-spent $25. Contact the **Medic Alert Foundation,** P.O. Box 1009, Turlock, CA 95381-1009 (tel. toll free 800/432-5378).

Take along an adequate supply of any prescription drugs that you need and prescriptions that use the generic name—not the brand name—of the drugs as well. Carry all vital medicines and drugs (the legal kind only) with you in your carry-on luggage, in case your checked luggage is lost.

Also, take your own personal medical kit. Include first-aid cream, insect repellent, aspirin, nose drops, and Band-Aids. If you're subject to motion sickness on a plane or train, remember to bring along motion-sickness medicine as well.

It's also a good idea to take along a good sunscreen, one that has a high enough protection factor to block out most of the dangerous ultraviolet rays of the sun, which can be intense in the south of Spain. In case you do find yourself overexposed to the sun, have some liquid solution of the aloe plant with you for soothing relief.

VACCINATIONS

You aren't required to have any particular inoculations to enter Spain (except for yellow fever if you're arriving from an infected area).

INSURANCE

Before purchasing any additional insurance, check your homeowner, automobile, and medical insurance policies. Also check the membership contracts issued by automobile and travel clubs and by credit-card companies. If, after close examination, you feel you still need insurance, consider the following.

HEALTH/ACCIDENT

Many credit-card companies insure their users in case of a travel accident, provided a ticket was purchased with their card. Sometimes fraternal organizations have policies that protect members in case of sickness or accidents abroad.

The best policies provide advances in cash or transferrals of funds so that you won't have to dip into your travel funds to settle any medical bills you might incur while away from home.

To submit a claim, you'll need documentation from a medical authority that you did suffer the illness for which you are seeking compensation.

Another insurance option is **Travel Assistance International,** 1133 15th St. NW, Suite 400, Washington, DC 20005 (tel. 800/821-2828), which offers travel coverage up to $5,000 for urgent hospital care and medical evacuation back to the United States if necessary. For an additional fee you can be covered for trip cancellation, lost baggage, and accidental death and dismemberment. The fee depends on how long you plan to stay. Fees begin at $40 per person ($60 for family) for a one- to eight-day trip. You can call a 24-hour "hotline" number (tel. 202/347-7113 in Washington; toll free 800/368-7878 in the U.S. and Canada) that will put you in touch with agents all over Europe, including Spain.

LOSS/THEFT

Many homeowner insurance policies cover theft of luggage during foreign travel and loss of documents—your Eurailpass, your passport, or your airline ticket, for instance. Coverage is usually limited to about $500 (U.S.). To submit a claim on your insurance, you'll need police reports that you did in fact suffer the loss for which you are seeking compensation. Such claims can be filed only when you return from Spain.

CANCELLATION

If you've booked a charter fare, you will probably have to pay a cancellation fee if you cancel a trip suddenly, even if it is due to an unforeseen crisis. It's possible to get insurance against such a possibility. Some travel agencies provide this coverage, and often flight insurance against a canceled trip is written into tickets paid for by credit cards from such companies as VISA or American Express. Many tour operators or insurance agents provide this type of insurance.

Insurers

Among the companies offering such health, loss, and cancellation policies are:
   Travel Guard International, 1100 Center Point Dr., Stevens Point, WI 54481 (tel. toll free 800/634-0644 in Wisconsin, 800/826-1300 outside Wisconsin), which offers a comprehensive seven-day policy that covers basically everything.
   Access America, Inc. (an affiliate of Blue Cross/Blue Shield), 600 Third Ave., New York, NY 10163 (tel. 212/490-5345; toll free 800/851-2800), which writes coverage for single travelers or families, including medical, trip cancellation, and lost luggage.
   Health Care Abroad, 243 Church St. NW, Vienna, VA 22180 (tel. 703/255-9800; toll free 800/237-6616), which offers accident and illness coverage on trips lasting 10 to 90 days, charging $3 per day for $100,000 coverage. Luggage loss and trip cancellation can be added to this policy.

4. WHAT TO PACK

Always pack as light as possible. Sometimes it's hard to get a porter or a baggage cart at rail and air terminals. And airlines are increasingly strict about how much luggage you can take along, not only as carry-on but also as checked baggage.
   It depends on where you are going in Spain and at what time of year, but as a general rule, pack the same clothes that you might wear in the southeastern United States. That is, dress as if you were visiting Virginia or the Carolinas at the same time of year as your trip to Spain. Buildings in Spain tend not to be very well heated, so you might want to take an extra sweater.

Dress is casual in Spain. A jacket and tie are required in only first-class establishments. For special occasions, men should pack a suit. For women, skirts and sweaters, suits, simple dresses, and dress slacks are never out of place.

For sightseeing, casual clothes and comfortable shoes (two pairs) are best. When touring churches and cathedrals, dress appropriately: Head coverings are not required, but you'll be denied entry if you're wearing shorts. After sunning at the beach, both men and women should wear a cover-up when on the street. If you plan to visit a casino or nightclub, dress up—casual but chic is best.

Finally, pack only items that travel well. Don't count on being able to get your clothes pressed at hotels, especially budget hotels. Take clothes that you can wash out in your bathroom sink and hang up to dry overnight. Pack a plastic bag for clothes that are still damp when you move on to your next destination.

5. TIPS FOR THE DISABLED, SENIORS, SINGLE TRAVELERS & STUDENTS

FOR THE DISABLED

Because of its many hills and endless flights of stairs, getting around Spain can be difficult for the disabled. Despite the lack of adequate services, more and more disabled travelers are taking on the challenge of Spain, and conditions are slowly improving.

The newer hotels are more sensitive to the needs of the disabled, and in general, the more expensive restaurants are wheelchair-accessible. However, since most places have very limited, if any, facilities for the disabled, it would be best to consider an organized tour specifically designed to accommodate the disabled.

For information, contact the **Travel Information Service,** Moss Rehabilitation Hospital, 12th Street and Tabor Road, Philadelphia, PA 19141 (tel. 215/329-5715). You can request information on three cities, countries, or special interests. Packages cost $5.

You might want to subscribe to *The Itinerary,* P.O. Box 2012, Bayonne, NJ 07002-2012 (tel. 201/858-3400), a bimonthly magazine with news about travel aids for the disabled, special tours, and so on. The cost is $10 per year. The government publishes *Air Transportation of Handicapped Persons* for free; write to **U.S. Department of Transportation,** Distribution Unit, Publications Division, M-4332, Washington, DC 20590, and ask for Free Advisory Circular No. AC12032.

Tours for the disabled are offered by a variety of companies. One such company is **Whole Person Tours,** P.O. Box 1084, Bayonne, NJ 07002-1084 (tel. 201/858-3400). You might want to consider joining the **Federation of the Handicapped,** 211 W. 14th St., New York, NY 10011 (tel. 212/206-4200), which offers summer tours for members. The annual fee is $4. The names and addresses of other tour operators can be obtained from the **Society for the Advancement of Travel for the Handicapped,** 26 Court St., Brooklyn, NY 11242 (tel. 718/858-5483). Yearly membership dues are $40 ($25 for seniors and students). Send a self-addressed stamped envelope.

The best source for information for the vision-impaired is the **American Foundation for the Blind,** 15 W. 16th St., New York, NY 10011 (tel. 800/232-5463), which issues ID cards for the legally blind for $6.

FOR SENIORS

Many discounts are available for seniors, but often you need to be a member of an association to obtain them.

For information, write away for *Travel Tips for Senior Citizens* (publication no. 8970), distributed for $1 by the **Superintendent of Documents, U.S. Government Printing Office,** Washington, DC 20402 (tel. 202/783-3238). Another booklet—this one distributed free—is called *101 Tips for the Mature Traveler.* Write or phone **Grand Circle Travel,** 347 Congress St., Suite 3A, Boston, MA 02210 (tel. 617/350-7500; toll free 800/221-2610).

One of the most dynamic travel organizations for seniors is **Elderhostel,** 75 Federal St., Boston, MA (tel. 617/426-7788), established in 1975, which operates an array of programs throughout Europe, including Spain. Most courses last around three weeks, and represent good value, since they include airfare, accommodations in student dormitories or modest inns, all meals, and tuition. Courses involve no homework, are ungraded, and are often liberal arts–oriented. These are not luxury vacations, but they are fun and fulfilling. Participants must be at least 60 years old; however, if two members go as a couple, only one member need be "of age." Write or call for a free newsletter and a list of upcoming courses and destinations.

SAGA International Holidays is also well known for its all-inclusive tours for seniors. The company prefers that joiners be at least 60 years old. Tours encompass dozens of locations in Europe, and usually last for an average of 17 nights. Contact SAGA International Holidays, 120 Boylston St., Boston, MA 02116 (tel. toll free 800/669-7242).

In the United States, the best organization to belong to is the **American Association of Retired Persons,** 1909 K St. NW, Washington, DC 20049 (tel. 202/872-4700). Members are offered discounts on car rentals, hotels, and airfares, even sightseeing in some cases. Its affiliate, **AARP Travel Service,** 1000 N. Sepulveda Blvd., Suite 1020, El Segundo, CA 90024 (tel. toll free 800/227-7737), offers tours and, for those traveling independently, a list of discounts available on the road.

Information is also available from the **National Council of Senior Citizens,** 925 5th St. NW, Washington, DC 20005 (tel. 202/347-8800). A nonprofit organization, the council charges $10 per person to join (couples pay $14), for which you receive a monthly newsletter that is in part devoted to travel tips. Reduced discounts on hotel and auto rentals are previewed.

FOR SINGLE TRAVELERS

It's no secret that the travel industry caters to people who are not traveling alone. Double rooms, for example, are usually much more reasonably priced than singles. One company has made heroic efforts to match single travelers with like-minded companions. Founder Jens Jurgen charges $36 to $66 for a six-month listing in his well-publicized records. New applicants desiring a travel companion fill out a form stating their preferences and needs. They then receive a list of people who might be suitable. Companions of the same or opposite sex can be requested. For an application and more information, write to **Jens Jurgen, Travel Companion,** P.O. Box P-833, Amityville, NY 11701.

Singleworld, 444 Madison Ave., New York, NY 10022 (tel. 914/967-3334; toll free 800/223-6490), is a travel agency that operates tours geared to solo traveling. Two basic types of tours are available, youth-oriented tours for people under 35 and jaunts for any age. Annual dues are $20.

Since single supplements on tours usually carry a hefty price tag, a way to get around paying the supplement is to find a travel agency that allows you to share a room. One company offering a "guaranteed-share plan" is **Cosmos,** with offices at 9525 Queens Blvd., Rego Park, NY 11374 (tel. toll free 800/221-0090), and at 150 S. Los Robles Ave., Pasadena, CA 91101 (tel. 818/449-0919; toll free 800/556-5454).

FOR STUDENTS

Students can avail themselves of a number of discounts in travel. The most wide-ranging travel service for students is the **Council on International Educa-**

tional Exchange (CIEE), 205 E. 42nd St., New York, NY 10017 (tel. 212/661-1414). This service provides details about budget travel, study abroad, working permits, insurance, and much more. It also sells a number of helpful publications, including the *Student Travel Catalogue* ($1).

To keep costs bone-trimmed, membership in the **International Youth Hostel Federation (IYHF)** is recommended. Many countries have branch offices, including **AYH (American Youth Hostels),** P.O. Box 37613, Washington, DC 20013-7613 (tel. 202/783-6161). Membership costs $25 annually ($10 under 18).

6. EDUCATIONAL/ADVENTURE TRAVEL

Offbeat, alternative modes of travel often cost less and can be an enriching way to travel.

EDUCATIONAL TRAVEL
LEARNING VACATIONS

An international series of programs for persons over 50 years of age who are interested in combining travel and learning is offered by **Interhostel,** developed by the University of New Hampshire. Each program lasts two weeks, is led by a university faculty or staff member, and is arranged in conjunction with a host college, university, or cultural institution. Participants may stay longer if they wish. Interhostel offers programs in Spain that consist of cultural and intellectual activities, with field trips to museums and other centers of interest. For information, contact the **University of New Hampshire, Division of Continuing Education,** 6 Garrison Ave., Durham, NH 03824 (tel. 603/862-1147).

STUDYING SPANISH IN SPAIN

Your trip to Spain will be enriched and made easier by a basic understanding of the language.

Salinter, Calle Toro, 34-36, 37002 Salamanca (tel. 23/21-18-08; fax 23/26-02-63), conducts courses in Spanish, with optional courses in business Spanish, translation techniques, and Spanish architecture. Classes contain no more than 10 persons. The school can arrange housing with Spanish families, or in furnished apartments shared with other students. The school can also arrange excursions and walking tours to the surrounding region. For reservations and information, write or fax them at the address or number above.

A good source of information about courses in Spain is the **American Institute of Foreign Study (AIFS),** 102 Greenwich Ave., Greenwich, CT 06830 (tel. 203/869-9090; toll free at 800/727-2437). This organization can set up transportation and arrange for summer courses, with bed and board included.

The biggest organization dealing with higher education in Europe is the **Institute for International Education,** 809 United Nations Plaza, New York, NY 10017 (tel. 212/883-8200). Some of its booklets are free, but for $22.95 you can purchase the more definitive *Vacation Study Abroad.*

For more information about study abroad, contact the **Council on International Educational Exchange (CIEE),** 205 E. 42nd St., New York, NY 10017 (tel. 212/661-1414).

HOMESTAYS

The **Friendship Force** is a nonprofit organization existing for the sole purpose of fostering and encouraging friendship among people around the world. Group visits are arranged to a given host country, where each participant is required to spend two weeks—one of those weeks with a family. For more information, contact the Friendship Force, 575 South Tower, 1 CNN Center, Atlanta, GA 30303 (tel. 404/522-9490).

Servas, 11 John St., New York, NY 10038 (tel. 212/267-0252)—the name means "to serve" in Esperanto—is a nonprofit, nongovernmental, international, interfaith network of travelers and hosts whose goal is to help promote world peace, goodwill, and understanding. Servas travelers stay at people's homes without charge for up to two days. Visitors pay a $45 annual fee, fill out an application, and undergo an interview for suitability. They then receive a Servas directory listing the names and addresses of Servas hosts.

The **International Visitors Information Service,** 733 15th St. NW, Suite 300, Washington, DC 20005 (tel. 202/783-6540), will mail you a booklet listing opportunities for contact with local residents in foreign countries. For example, they can tell you how to find lodgings with a Spanish-speaking family whose members grow grapes and produce wine. Checks in the amount of $5 should be made out to Meridian/IVIS.

HOME EXCHANGES

One of the most exciting breakthroughs in modern tourism is the home exchange, whereby the Diego family of Ávila can exchange their home with the Brier family's in North Carolina. Sometimes the family automobile is included. Of course, you must be comfortable with the idea of having relative strangers in your home, and you must be content to spend your vacation in one place.

Home exchanges cut costs. You don't pay hotel bills, and you can also save money by shopping in markets and eating in. One potential problem, though, is that you may not get a home in the area you request. For instance, you might want to stay in Galicia, but be offered something in the Valencia area instead.

World Wide Exchange, 1344 Pacific Ave., Suite 103, Santa Cruz, CA 95060 (tel. 408/425-0531), is one of several home-exchange agencies. For $45 per year you can place an ad or list your home, in addition to receiving three booklets of listings. **Vacation Exchange Club,** 12006 111th Ave., Suite 12, Youngstown, AZ 85363 (tel. 602/972-2186), has around 100 listings for Spain. The annual dues of $24.70 entitle subscribers to receive spring and winter listings; they can also place a listing in one of these directories. Subscribers can pay $16 for the booklets only. **International Home Exchange Service,** Box 3975, San Francisco, CA 94119 (tel. 415/435-3497), charges $35 for three directories annually. The fee includes a listing in one of them. Seniors get a 20% discount.

ADVENTURE TRAVEL

THE COSTA BLANCA BY WAGON TRAIN

Every July horse-drawn carts form a caravan and make a six-day journey to remote mountain towns in what is called the **Vuelta en Carro.** Its purpose is to rediscover the past, when everybody in Spain traveled this way. The caravan stops for meals along the way as it passes citrus groves, vineyards, agricultural towns, and mountain villages. This odyssey, which always attracts amused onlookers along the trail, is definitely not for those more comfortable with the luxury hotels of nearby Benidorm. The trail is rough and hot, but many participants sign up for next year. For reservations, contact **Jaime Bordes Casa de Cultura,** Benissa (tel. 96/573-00-58), by June 15.

SADDLING UP IN SPAIN

Perhaps there is no better way to see the Spanish countryside than on horseback, and several outfits throughout the land offer this experience. Be advised that the terrain can be rugged and that riders often spend 7 to 8 hours on the trail. Bed and board, in most cases, is arranged.

Almansur Equestrian Trips, José Luís García Saullo, Glorieta Puente de Segovia, 3B, 28011 Madrid (tel. 91/463-59-62), offers excursions of 4 to 21 days in Extremadura. Lodgings are usually at paradors or first-class hotels.

Cabalgar, Rutas Alternativas, Carretera de Capileira, Bubíon (Granada), arranges a number of 1- to 10-day excursions, many in the Sierra Nevada in the south of Spain. Treks are even made through the Almería desert. Guests, for the most part, are lodged in typical Andalusian inns, farmhouses, or second-class hotels. If you're staying on the Costa del Sol, you can make reservations through **Viajes Málaga Internacional,** Avenida de la Aurora, 9, Málaga (tel. 952/347-75-00), which lies behind the El Corte Inglés department store in the center of Málaga.

MONASTIC RETREATS

Many people like to visit old monasteries and convents when they travel in Europe, and in Spain it's easy to do so, since many of them have been turned into deluxe *paradores.* But if you want a taste of the true monastic life in a tranquil retreat, you can experience that too. Most monasteries allow men only, but some accept women as well, and a few take women only. You don't need to be Catholic, but you must respect the peaceful monastic atmosphere and a few easy-to-follow rules. Even though you are free at most retreats to come and go as you please, don't use the monastery as you would a hotel or inn, that is, as a place to leave your gear while you go off sightseeing.

Accommodations include private rooms with bath, good heating, and modern plumbing, plus healthful meals. You take care of your own bedroom during your stay. Some of the monasteries and convents charge a small fee for room and board; others request a donation. For more information, contact the **National Tourist Office of Spain,** 665 Fifth Ave., New York, NY 10022 (tel. 212/759-8822).

CHAPTER 3

ARRIVING IN SPAIN

- **1. GETTING THERE**
- **• FROMMER'S SMART TRAVELER: AIRFARES**
- **2. GETTING AROUND**
- **3. SUGGESTED ITINERARIES**
- **4. ENJOYING SPAIN ON A BUDGET**
- **• FAST FACTS: SPAIN**

L ike the previous chapter, this chapter helps you prepare for your arrival in Spain. I explore the various options for getting to Spain, treating not only the obvious choices, but also some that you may not have thought of. I also discuss different ways of getting around Spain, and provide suggested itineraries for visiting different regions of the country. Capping off the chapter is a quick-reference list of facts about Spain.

1. GETTING THERE

BY PLANE

Flights from the U.S. East Coast take 6 to 7 hours, depending on the season and prevailing winds. The major airlines servicing Madrid from North America are Iberia, Trans World Airlines, and American Airlines.

BEST-VALUE FARES

Most airlines divide their year roughly into seasonal slots, with the least expensive fares between November 1 and March 14. The shoulder season (spring and early fall) is only slightly more expensive, and includes October, which many veteran tourists consider the ideal time to visit Spain. Summer, of course, is the most expensive time.

FROMMER'S SMART TRAVELER— AIR FARES

1. Shop all the airlines that fly to your destination.
2. Always ask for the lowest-priced fare, not just for a discount fare.
3. Keep calling the airline—availability of cheap seats changes daily. Airlines would rather sell a seat than have it fly empty. As the departure date nears, additional low-cost seats become available.
4. Ask about frequent-flyer programs when you book a flight.
5. Check bucket shops for last-minute discounts even greater than their advertised slashed fares.
6. Ask about discounted land arrangements. Sometimes they are cheaper when booked with an air ticket.
7. Ask if standby fares are offered.
8. Fly for free or at a heavy discount as a courier.
9. Look for special promotional fares offered by major carriers or airlines struggling to gain a foothold in the market.

APEX Most carriers offer a consistently popular **advance-purchase excursion (APEX)** fare that often requires a 30-day advance payment and an obligatory stay of between 7 and 21 days, depending on the carrier. In most cases this ticket is not completely refundable if you change flight dates or destination. At TWA, for instance, you'll lose 60% of the value of the ticket.

Iberia Airlines (tel. toll free 800/772-4642), the national carrier of Spain, offers more routes into and within Spain than any other carrier. It offers daily nonstop service to Madrid from New York, Chicago, Miami, and Los Angeles, and nonstop service to Barcelona (continuing on the same aircraft to Málaga) from New York several times a week. Tickets are cheapest if you reserve an APEX ticket at least 14 days in advance and schedule your return 7 to 60 days after your departure, and if you leave and return between Monday and Thursday. From June to September, tickets cost $776 round trip, plus $16 tax. If you fly Friday to Sunday, it costs an additional $50. Los Angeles to Madrid costs $986, plus $16 tax, with a $50 supplement for weekend travel. Fares are subject to change.

Trans World Airlines (tel. toll free 800/221-2000) operates one daily nonstop flight to Madrid from New York. Its cheapest APEX fare, with tax included, currently costs $827 in high season, with restrictions similar to Iberia's.

American Airlines (tel. 800/433-7300) has daily nonstop service to Madrid from Dallas. With a 14-day advance purchase, and a scheduled return of 7 to 60 days after your departure, American's least expensive high-season round-trip ticket from Dallas to Madrid costs $1,006. American charges a $50 supplement for weekend travel. It also charges a $100 penalty for any changes in itinerary once the ticket is issued.

Unlike Iberia or TWA, American offers a youth fare (for ages 12 to 24) of $491 one way (with a $25 surcharge each way for weekend travel). Not substantially less than the APEX fare, it at least favors last-minute departures, since its restrictions bypass the usual 14-day advance booking requirement. The youth fare cannot be reserved more than 3 days before departure in either direction.

Important news from American includes a proposed daily nonstop route from Miami to Madrid, as well as the possibility of a daily nonstop route from Dallas/Fort Worth to Barcelona, scheduled to begin before 1993.

Special Promotional Fares Since they are now deregulated, expect airlines to announce promotional fares to Europe. This means that you'll have to have a good travel agent, or do a lot of shopping or calling around yourself to learn what's available at the time of your intended trip.

Charter Flights A charter flight is one reserved months in advance for a one-time-only transit to a predetermined destination. For reasons of economy, some travelers choose this option.

Before paying for a charter, check the restrictions on your ticket or contract. You may be asked to purchase a tour package and pay far in advance. You'll pay a stiff penalty (or forfeit the ticket entirely) if you cancel. Charters are sometimes canceled if the tickets don't sell out. In some cases the charter-ticket seller will offer you an insurance policy for your own legitimate cancellation (hospital certificate, death in the family, for example).

There is no way to predict whether a charter or a bucket-shop flight will be cheaper. You'll have to investigate this at the time of your trip.

Among charter flight operators is the **Council on International Educational Exchange (Council Charters)**, 205 E. 42nd St., New York, NY 10017 (tel. 212/661-0311; toll free 800/223-7402). This outfit can arrange charter seats on regularly scheduled aircraft.

Bucket Shops "Bucket shops"—or "consolidators," as they are also called—exist in many shapes and forms. In their purest sense, they act as a clearinghouse for blocks of tickets that airlines discount and consign during normally slow periods of air travel. Charter operators and bucket shops used to perform separate functions, but today many perform both functions.

Ticket prices vary, sometimes going for as much as 35% off full fare. Terms of payment can be anywhere from 45 days before departure to the last minute.

Bucket shops abound from coast to coast, but just to get you started, here are some recommendations. (Look also for ads in your local newspaper's travel section.) **Maharaja Travel,** 393 Fifth Ave., New York, NY 10016 (tel. 212/213-2020; toll free 800/223-6862), has been around for some 20 years, offering tickets to 400 destinations worldwide, including Spain. **Access International,** 101 W. 31st St., Suite 1104, New York, NY (tel. 212/333-7280; toll free at 800/825-3633), may be the largest consolidator in the United States. It specializes in thousands of discounted tickets to the capitals of Europe, including Spain.

Standbys A favorite with spontaneous travelers who have absolutely no scheduled demands on their time, a standby fare leaves them dependent on the whims of fortune—and hoping that a seat will remain open at the last minute. Not all airlines offer standbys.

Going as a Courier This cost-cutting technique has lots of restrictions, and tickets may be hard to come by; so it's not for everybody. Basically, you travel as both an airline passenger and a courier. Couriers are hired by overnight air-freight firms hoping to skirt the often tedious Customs hassles and delays that face regular cargo on the other end. With a courier, the checked freight sails through Customs just as quickly as the passenger's luggage. Don't worry—the courier service is absolutely legal; you won't be asked to haul in illegal drugs, for example. For performing this service, the courier gets a great discount on airfare, and sometimes even flies for free.

You're allowed one piece of carry-on luggage only (your usual baggage allowance is used by the courier firm to transport its cargo). As a courier, you don't actually handle the merchandise you're "transporting" to Europe; you just carry a manifest to present to Customs. Upon arrival, an employee of the courier service will reclaim the company's cargo.

Incidentally, you fly alone, so don't plan to travel with anybody. A friend may be able to arrange a flight as a courier on a consecutive day, but don't count on it. Most courier services operate from Los Angeles or New York, but some operate out of other cities, such as Chicago or Miami.

Courier services are often listed in the *Yellow Pages* or in advertisements in travel sections or newspapers. One such firm is **Halbart Express,** 147–05 176th St., Jamaica, NY 11434 (tel. 718/656-8189 from 10am to 3pm daily). Another is **Now Voyager,** 74 Varick St., Suite 307, New York, NY 10013 (tel. 212/431-1616). Call daily to speak with someone from 11:30am to 6pm; at other times you'll get a recorded message.

REGULAR FARES

If your schedule does not permit you one of the options discussed above, you can opt for a regular fare. Economy class is the cheapest regular fare, followed by business class, and then by first class, the most expensive ticket. In first class, increased amenities are the rule, the food is better, and the seats extend backward into something resembling a bed; drinks are free. You ll also get free drinks and better meals in business class, while in economy class, meals are free but you pay for alcoholic beverages. All three of these fares have one thing in common: You can book them at the last minute, and can depart and return when you wish. Of course, you'll pay more for the lack of restrictions.

BY TRAIN

If you're already in Europe, you may want to go to Spain by train, especially if you have a Eurailpass. Even if you don't, the cost is moderate, depending on where you are. Rail passengers who visit from Britain or France should make couchette and sleeper reservations as far in advance as possible, especially during the peak summer season.

Since Spain's rail tracks are of a wider gauge than those used for French trains (except for the TALGO and Trans-Europe-Express trains), it's therefore necessary to change trains at the border. For long journeys on Spanish rails, seat and sleeper reservations are mandatory.

The most comfortable and the fastest trains in Spain are the TER, TALGO, and Electrotren. However, you pay a supplement to ride on these fast trains. Both first- and second-class fares are sold on Spanish trains. Tickets can be purchased in either the United States or Canada at the nearest office of FrenchRail Inc. or from any reputable travel agent. Confirmation of your reservation will take about a week.

If you want your car carried, you must travel Auto-Expreso in Spain. This type of auto transport can be booked only through travel agents or rail offices once you arrive in Europe.

BY BUS

Bus travel to Spain is possible, but not popular—it's slow. Coach services do operate regularly from major capitals of Western Europe, however, heading for Spain, usually Madrid or Barcelona.

The busiest routes are from London. Two companies there that book such passages are **SSS International,** 138 Eversholt St., London NW1 (tel. 071/388-1732), and **Euroways Express Coaches Ltd.,** 52 Grosvenor Gardens, London SW1 (tel. 071/730-8235). You might also try **Miracle Bus Company,** 408 The Strand, London WC2 (tel. 071/379-60-55), with connections to both Madrid and Lisbon.

BY CAR

If you're touring Europe in a rented car, you might, for an added cost, be allowed to drop off your vehicle in a major city such as Madrid or Barcelona.

Motor approaches to Spain are across France on expressways. The most popular border crossing is near Biarritz, but there are 17 other border stations between Spain and France. If you're planning to visit the north or west of Spain (Galicia), the Hendaye–Irún border is the most convenient frontier crossing. If you're going to Barcelona or Catalonia and along the Levante coast (Valencia), take the expressway in France to Toulouse, then the A61 to Narbonne, and then the A9 toward the border crossing at La Junquera. You can also take the RN20, with a border station at Puigcerda.

If you're driving from Britain, make sure you have a cross-Channel reservation, as traffic tends to be very heavy in summer. The major ferry crossings connect Dover and Folkestone with Dunkirk. Newhaven is connected with Dieppe, and the British city of Portsmouth with Roscoff. One of the fastest crossings is by Hovercraft from Dover to Boulogne or Calais. It costs more than the ferry, but it takes only about half an hour.

PACKAGE TOURS

Some people prefer that a tour operator take care of all their travel arrangements. There are many such companies, each offering transportation to and within Spain, prearranged hotel space, and such extras as a bilingual tour guide and lectures. Many of these tours to Spain include excursions to Morocco or Portugal.

American Express Vacations, P.O. Box 5014, Atlanta, GA 30302 (tel. toll free 800/637-6200 in Ga., 800/241-1700 outside Ga.), offers some of the most comprehensive programs available. If the company doesn't have what you want, you can ask the staff to package a tour especially designed for you.

Trafalgar Tours, 21 E. 26th St., New York, NY 10010 (tel. 212/689-8977; toll free 800/854-0103), has an exceptional schedule of moderately priced 14- to 32-day tours to Spain. (Two go to Morocco as well.) Ask about the CostSaver tours, which book you in tourist-class hotels to keep costs trimmed.

For tours geared to Americans who speak Spanish, try **Ibero Travel,** 109–19 72nd Rd., Forest Hills, NY 11375 (tel. 718/263-0200; toll free 800/882-6678 in N.Y., 800/654-2376 outside N.Y.). Guided sightseeing, good hotels, and meals at regional restaurants are included. Tours range from Cantabria and Galicia in the north to Andalusia in the south. Ask about the one-week vacation plan on the Costa del Sol, which comes with an apartment and a car.

Sun Holidays, 26 Sixth St., Stamford, CT 06905 (tel. 800/637-8747 in Conn., 800/243-2057 outside Conn.), sometimes offers very reasonable discount packages to both Spain and Portugal. The company regularly schedules fully escorted motorcoach tours of the peninsula, and recently featured winter tours to Spain for retired Americans at amazingly low prices. Ask about its low-cost charter program, "Spain on Sale."

One of the best fly-drive operations currently available is from **Kemwell Car Rental,** 106 Calvert St., Harrison, NY 10528-3199 (tel. 800/678-0-678). If you fly round trip transatlantic on Iberia Airlines, you can qualify for an added bonus of a free one-week car rental, including unlimited mileage—a saving of about $230. Of course, this offer could be withdrawn at any time. You can call **Iberia Airlines** year round about its fly-drive programs in Spain (tel. 800/772-4642).

Hispanidad Holidays, 99 Tulip Ave., Floral Park, NY 11001 (tel. 516/488-4700; toll free 800/274-4400), offers a number of attractive features on its tours. These include car rentals, accommodations at *paradores,* prepackaged and independent travel options, and "stay-put" land and air vacations at resort areas. It offers escorted motorcoach tours as well. Its fly-drive program—called "A la Carte"—allows travel to anywhere in Spain for those wishing to make their own itineraries. Compact budget cars are included in the program. Hotels or apartments can be arranged along the Costa del Sol, as well as in the Balearic or Canary Islands.

2. GETTING AROUND

BY PLANE

Two major airlines operate within Spain, **Iberia** and the smaller **Aviaco** (call either toll free in the U.S. at 800/772-4642). By European standards, domestic flights are inexpensive. If you plan to travel to a number of cities and regions, Iberia's **"Visit Spain" ticket** at $249 makes flying even more economical. It is valid for unlimited travel within the Spanish mainland and the Balearic Islands if round-trip transatlantic passage is purchased at the same time. You must choose the cities where you want to stop and the order of these stops; no changes can be made in the order of stops after the ticket has been issued. The exact dates and times of the actual flights, however, can be determined or changed without penalty once you arrive in Spain. If an optional-passage journey to the Canary Islands is added to the ticket, the price rises to a still-reasonable $299. Children under 2 travel for 10% of the adult fare, and children from 2 to 12 are half price. The ticket is valid for up to 60 days after your arrival in Spain.

BY TRAIN

If you plan to travel a great deal on the European railroads, it's worth securing the latest copy of the *Thomas Cook Continental Timetable of European Railroads*. It's available exclusively in North America from **Forsyth Travel Library,** P.O. Box 2975, Shawnee Mission, KS 66201 (tel. toll free 800/FORSYTH), for $19.95, plus $3 shipping.

The most economical way to travel in Spain is on the **Spanish State Railways (RENFE).** Most main long-distance connections are served with night express trains having first- and second-class seats as well as beds and bunks. There are also comfortable high-speed daytime trains of the TALGO, TER, Corail, and Electrotren types. There is a general fare for these trains; bunks, beds, and certain superior-quality trains cost extra. Nevertheless, the Spanish railway is one of the most economical in Europe, so that in most cases this is the best way to go.

Direct trains connect Madrid with Paris and Lisbon, and Barcelona with Paris and Geneva; and international connections are easily made on the frontiers, at Valencia de Alcantara–Marvão (Portugal), Irún–Hendaye, and Port Bou–Cerbère (France). There is also a direct express from Algeciras to Hendaye.

In addition, RENFE operates cultural tours throughout Spain that make stops for sightseeing, meals, guided tours, and leg stretching. In the months of May, June, September, and October, the train runs between Seville and Málaga, stopping at Córdoba and Granada. Depending on accommodation, season, and length of itinerary, the trip costs from $850 to $1,600. In July and August the train travels between Santiago de Compostela and Barcelona, stopping en route at Burgos, León and Pamplona or Haro. The trip costs from $1,100 to $1,500. For reservations and information, call **Donna Brunstad Associates,** 25 Sylvan Rd. S, Suite Y, Westport, CT 06880 (tel. toll free 800/992-3976).

RAIL PASSES

Spain Flexipass and Spain Railpass   RENFE, the national railways of Spain, offers both a Spain Flexipass and a Spain Railpass, both economical options that allow you to see all of the country by train. The choice is among hundreds of daily trains (including the super-speed TALGO rail cars).

A 4-day Flexipass ($75 economy; $99 first class) can be used over a 15-day period, whereas an 8- ($105 economy; $145 first class) or 15-day ($165 economy; $235 first class) Railpass is to be used consecutively. You must buy these passes in the United States prior to your departure. For more information, consult a travel agent or **FrenchRail Inc.,** 230 Westchester Ave., White Plains, NY 10604 (tel. 914/682-2999), or 610 Fifth Ave., Suite 501, New York, NY 10020 (tel. 212/582-2816).

Eurailpass   Many in-the-know travelers take advantage of the great travel bargain, the Eurailpass, which permits unlimited first-class travel in any country in Western Europe, except the British Isles (good in Ireland). The Eurailpass also entitles you to discounts on some bus and steamship lines. Passes are available for 15 days or as long as three months, and are strictly nontransferable.

Here's how it all works. Sold only outside Europe and North Africa, and only to residents of countries outside those areas, the passes cost $320 (15 days), $398 (21 days), $498 (one month), $698 (two months), and $860 (three months). Children under 4 travel free unless they occupy a separate seat (then they pay half fare), and children 5 to 12 travel for half price. The advantages are tempting: With no tickets and no supplements to worry about, you simply show the pass to the ticket collector. Seat reservations are required on some trains.

Those under the age of 26 can purchase a **Eurail Youthpass,** entitling them to one month's unlimited second-class transportation for only $360; for two months it's $470.

Eurail Saverpass provides discounted 15-day travel for groups of three people traveling continuously together between April and September, or two people between October and March. The price of a Saverpass, valid all over Europe and good for first class only, is $230 per person.

Eurail Flexipass is a time-flexible Eurailpass for 9 days of travel that can be used either consecutively or otherwise in 17 countries within a 21-day period.

Travel and railway agents in such major cities as New York, Montréal, Los Angeles, and Chicago sell the various passes. It's also available at the offices of CIT Travel Service, the French National Railroads, the German Federal Railroads, and the Swiss Federal Railways.

BY BUS

Buses in Spain are extensive, low-priced, and comfortable enough for short distances. You'll rarely encounter a bus terminal in Spain. The "station" might be a café, a bar, the street in front of a hotel, or simply a spot at an intersection.

The trip from Madrid to Toledo (44 miles; 70km) costs 380 pesetas ($3.55) one way; the trip from Madrid to Segovia (54 miles; 87km), 490 pesetas ($4.60).

BY CAR

A car offers the greatest flexibility while you're touring, even if you limit your explorations to the environs of Madrid. Don't, however, plan to drive in Madrid—it's too congested. Theoretically, rush hour is Mon-Sat 8–10am, 1–2pm, and 4–6pm. In fact, it is always busy.

CAR RENTALS

Many of North America's biggest car-rental companies, including Avis, Budget, and Hertz, maintain offices throughout Spain. Though several Spain-based car-rental companies will try to entice you with their business, letters from readers have shown that the resolution of billing irregularities and insurance claims tends to be less complicated with the U.S.-based car-rental firms.

Avis has almost a hundred branches throughout Spain, including several within Madrid. If you reserve a car by telephone at least two days before you leave for Spain, you'll qualify for Avis's best rate (around $240 per week, plus 12% tax) for an Opel Corsa Swing. For reservations and information within North America, call Avis toll free at 800/331-2112.

For its smallest car (a Ford Fiesta or an Opel Corsa), **Hertz** charges $241 per week, plus 12% tax. Like Avis, Hertz requires a two-day advance reservation and a minimum rental of between five and seven days. For reservations and information within North America, call Hertz toll free at 800/654-3001.

Your least expensive car rental will probably be from **Budget Rent-a-Car,** which offers more lenient insurance policies than those automatically included at both Avis and Hertz. (Budget's insurance options are worth investigating.) Budget's least expensive car, a Seat Marbella, rents for a rock-bottom price of around $151.57 per week in midsummer (slightly less in wintertime), plus 12% tax. For reservations and information within North America, call Budget's international department toll free at 800/472-3325.

GASOLINE

Gas is easily obtainable—and expensive—throughout Spain, with regular fuel being normally used in rented cars. The average Spanish vehicle gets close to 45 miles per gallon.

DRIVING RULES

Spaniards drive on the right side of the road. Drivers should pass on the left; local drivers sound their horns when passing another car. Autos coming from the right have the right-of-way.

Spain's express highways are known as *autopistas,* which charge a toll, and *autovías,* which don't. To exit in Spain, follow the *salida* sign, except in Catalonia, where the word is *sortida.* On most express highways, the speed limit is 75 m.p.h. (120kmph). On other roads speed limits range from 56 m.p.h. (90kmph) to 62 m.p.h. (100kmph).

Most accidents in Spain are recorded along the notorious Costa del Sol highway, the Carretera de Cádiz.

If you must drive through a Spanish city, try to do so between 3 and 5pm, when many motorists are having a siesta. Never park your car facing oncoming traffic, as that is against the law. If you are fined by the highway patrol (Guardia Civil de Tráfico), you must pay on the spot. Penalties for drinking and driving are very stiff.

MAPS

For the best overview of the Iberian Peninsula (both Spain and Portugal), obtain a copy of Michelin map no. 990. For closer looks at Spain, the Michelin series of seven maps (no. 441 to no. 447) is ideal.

For extensive touring, purchase *Mapas de Carreteras*—España y Portugal, published by Almax Editores and available at most leading bookstores in Spain. This detailed book of road maps provides an overview of the country itself, followed by detailed maps of the major cities of Spain.

BREAKDOWNS

These can be a serious problem. If you're driving a Spanish-made vehicle, you'll probably be able to find spare parts, if needed. But if you have a foreign-made vehicle, you may be stranded. Have the car checked out before setting out on a long trek through Spain. On a major motorway you'll find strategically placed emergency phone boxes. On secondary roads, call for help by asking the operator to locate the nearest Guardia Civil, who will put you in touch with a garage that can tow you to a repair job.

BY RV

In Spain many campgrounds are supplied with recreational-vehicle hookups. For the budget traveler in particular, RVs will save many, many pesetas on food and lodging; kitchen utensils are supplied as part of the rental agreement. But, regrettably, rental is very expensive. Gasoline is also extremely expensive in Spain.

Spanish rental companies offer mainly vans or minibuses with a raised roof. Other kinds of recreational vehicles tend not to be available. However, such RVs are offered in across-the-border France, where many visitors rent them and then drive on to Spain.

If you want a customized van for Spain, refer to the recommendations of major car-rental companies (see above). However, if you want to rent an RV in France, then make arrangements as far in advance with one of the following: **Europe by Car,** 1 Rockefeller Plaza, New York, NY 10020, or 9000 Sunset Blvd., Los Angeles, CA 90069 (tel. 212/581-3040 in N.Y.; toll free 800/252-9401 in Calif.; 800/223-1516 elsewhere in the U.S.); or **Avis Rent-a-Car,** 6128 E. 38th St., Tulsa, OK 74135 (tel. toll free 800/331-1084, ext. 7719).

BY FERRY

Travel by ferry is not normally associated with Spain; however, this method of transportation might be convenient at times. For example, the least expensive way to travel from Spain to Morocco is by ferry connections from the Spanish port of Algeciras. Several other boat links also exist between Spain and Tangier, and between mainland Spain and the Spanish enclave in Morocco, Ceuta.

There are also good connections by sea from Málaga (capital of the Costa del Sol) to Tangier, as well as to the Canaries. Many boat and ferry links connect mainland Spain and the Balearics (Majorca, Minorca, and Ibiza).

For specific details about these various ferry or boat transportation options, refer to the "Getting There" section in the chapter containing the port or island you're visiting.

HITCHHIKING

Even though people still do it and it is technically legal, hitchhiking is not tolerated as much as it used to be. And I don't recommend sticking out your thumb in the presence of the Guardia Civil. Most important, hitchhiking is an increasingly unsafe way to travel. Take the bus or train—it's safer, easier, and faster.

3. SUGGESTED ITINERARIES

The number of places and sites to see in Spain are staggering. It takes at least two months to see all the major cities, and even that calls for some fast moving. Most of us don't have so much time, however, and will want to get the most out of Spain in a shorter time.

The following 10 cities are particularly worth visiting: Barcelona, Córdoba, El Escorial, Granada, Madrid, Salamanca, Santiago de Compostela, Segovia, Seville, and Toledo.

IF YOU HAVE 1 WEEK

Days 1–2   Madrid (one to recover from the flight or drive there, another to see the sights, including the Prado).

Day 3   Leave Madrid and drive south to Aranjuez to see its Palacio Real (Royal Palace), then on to Toledo for the night.

Day 4   A full day and night in Toledo, seeing its cathedral, El Greco paintings, and Alcázar.

Day 5   Leave Toledo and drive north toward Madrid, taking the bypass west to reach El Escorial, Philip II's giant palace. Spend the night there.

Day 6   Proceed west from El Escorial to the walled city of Ávila for an overnight stay.

Day 7   Leave Ávila and drive northeast toward Segovia to visit its Alcázar and Roman aqueduct. Spend the night there before returning to Madrid. (If time remains the next morning, see the Bourbon summer palace at La Granja before returning to Madrid.)

IF YOU HAVE 2 WEEKS

Days 1–2   Spend these days as outlined above.

Day 3   While still based in Madrid, take a trip to Toledo, with a possible stopover in the morning at Aranjuez.

Day 4   Make a morning visit to El Escorial and spend the afternoon at Segovia.

Day 5   Drive south to Córdoba, arriving in time to view its world-famous mosque.

Day 6   Leave Córdoba and drive west to Seville, the capital of Andalusia, for an overnight stay.

Day 7   Go south to the sherry town of Jerez, perhaps pressing on to the Atlantic seaport of Cádiz for the night.

Day 8   Drive on to Algeciras, east of Cádiz, with an afternoon visit to Gibraltar.

Day 9   From either port, you could spend a day in Tangier.

Days 10–11   Bask in the sun at one of the resorts, such as Marbella, along the Costa del Sol.

Days 12–13   Drive inland north to Granada and its magnificent Alhambra.

Day 14   Return to Madrid, or travel to Málaga and catch a flight there.

IF YOU HAVE 3 WEEKS

Days 1–3   Fly directly to Barcelona and spend the first day recovering. The next day see some of the many attractions of Barcelona itself. While still based in Barcelona, make a day's pilgrimage to the monastery of Montserrat, 35 miles northwest.

Day 4   Drive south along the coast, stopping at Sitges to look at its art museums and have lunch, then head for the ancient Roman city of Tarragona for the night.

Day 5   Leave Tarragona and continue south to Valencia, city of El Cid and paella. Stay overnight there.

Day 6   After exploring Valencia in the morning, continue south to Alicante and explore its old quarter and castle before turning in.

Days 7–8   Leave Alicante and head west over mountain roads to Granada for two nights. You'll spend most of the first day driving there. You can see the Alhambra and Generalife on the second day.

Day 9   Drive south from Granada to the Mediterranean, then head west to Nerja, where you can explore its famous caves. Continue on Málaga or Torremolinos for one night on the Costa del Sol.

Day 10   The next day travel the Costa del Sol highway (be careful—it's the most dangerous in Spain) until you reach Gibraltar or Algeciras. Stay overnight in either place.

Day 11   Take a day trip across the channel to Tangier, spending the night there.

Day 12   After the ferry boat delivers you back to Algeciras, head north for an overnight stopover in Jerez to explore its sherry bodegas.

Days 13–14   Continue north for two nights in Seville, the capital of Andalusia and one of the cities in Spain most preferred by visitors.

Day 15   Drive northeast to Córdoba for the night and a visit to its famed mosque.

Day 16   Proceed north from Córdoba all the way to Toledo for an overnight stop.

Day 17   See what sights you didn't see on Day 16, then head north toward Madrid, bypassing that city and going west to El Escorial, Philip's II's giant palace. Stay overnight.

Day 18   Drive west from El Escorial to the walled city of Ávila for another overnight stay.

Day 19   Leave Ávila and drive northeast toward Segovia to visit its Alcázar and Roman aqueduct. Spend the night there.

Days 20–21   From Segovia, visit the nearby Bourbon palace at La Granja before heading to Madrid for two nights. Visit the Prado and take at least two of our walking tours before returning home.

A THEMED ITINERARY — ST. JAMES'S WAY

Six centuries ago pilgrims used to make the 500-mile trek from the Pyrénées to the shrine of St. James in Santiago de Compostela. The original route, suggested in the 1130 guidebook, *Liber Sancti Jacobi,* can't be followed anymore, so here is a modern-day itinerary from the Basque country to Santiago de Compostela.

Day 1   Cross from the Basque country of France and drive into Spain. Before Irún, cut south on C-133 to Pamplona, the capital of the old kingdom of Navarre and the setting of the famous "running of the bulls" (see "Calendar of Events" in Chapter 2).

Day 2   After an overnight stay in Pamplona, drive northwest to San Sebastián, a Belle Epoque resort just 12 miles (19km) from the French border.

Day 3   After a swim at the Playa de la Concha, and a panoramic view from Monte Iqueldo, continue west to Ondárroa—perhaps the most attractive fishing village in Spain—for lunch. In the afternoon continue west to Guernica, subject of Picasso's famous painting. Guernica lies 52 miles (83km) from San Sebastián. After a visit there, drive to Bilbao for the night.

Days 4–5   After a morning visit to Bilbao, drive west to Santander and relax in the afternoon at El Sardinero beach, 1½ miles (2½km) from the capital. Santander is a resort city of summer festivals. The next day, while still based at Santander, drive 18 miles (29km) southwest to visit Santillana del Mar, a medieval village near the site of the prehistoric cave paintings of Altamira. Return to Santander.

Day 6   Drive west from Santander to Oviedo, capital of the province of Asturias and the center of several excursions. Stay overnight.

Day 7   Drive all the way from Oviedo to Santiago de Compostela, revered as the burial site of St. James, patron saint of Spain. Spend as much time as you have. There are daily flights to Madrid, plus train and bus service; otherwise, it's a 390-mile (625km) drive.

4. ENJOYING SPAIN ON A BUDGET

For years Spain was a great budget destination, less expensive than most other European countries. Recently, however, its popularity, its entry into the European Community, and its concomitant flourishing economy have radically altered Spain's price structure. In the past, bargains were easy to find, but today they have to be sought out. This book aims to help you find them.

THE $50-A-DAY BUDGET

This daily budget covers the basic living costs of three meals a day and the price of a room. Naturally, the costs of sightseeing, transportation, shopping, and entertainment are extra, but in this section I'll discuss how to keep those expenses trimmed too.

The $50-a-day budget breaks down roughly this way: $26 per person (based on double occupancy) for a room and a continental breakfast, $8 for lunch, and $16 for dinner. Of course, for those who can afford more, I've included some hotels and restaurants that are worth the extra bucks.

SAVING MONEY ON ACCOMMODATIONS

BEST BUDGET BETS

Spain offers a variety of accommodations, but the best budget bets are described below.

Three- and Two-Star Hotels   The Spanish government rates hotels from one to five stars, and these represent modest but decent establishments. The stars appear on a blue sign by the door.

Hostals   Not to be confused with a hostel for students, a *hostal* is a modest hotel without services, where you can save money by carrying your own bags, etc. You'll know it's a hostal if a small *s* follows the capital letter *H* on the blue plaque by the door. A hostal with three stars is about the equivalent of a hotel with two stars.

Pensions   These are among the least expensive accommodations, but you are required here to take full board (three meals) or demi-pension, which is breakfast plus either lunch or dinner. The latter is the best option.

Casas Huespedes and Fondas: These are the cheapest places in Spain and can be recognized by the light-blue plaques at the door displaying *CH* and *F,* respectively. These are invariably basic but respectable establishments.

Youth Hostels   Spain has about 140 hostels (*alberques de juventud*). In theory, people 25 or under have the first chance at securing a bed for the night, but these places are certainly not limited to young people. Some of them are even equipped for the physically disabled. Most hostels impose an 11pm curfew. For information, write **Red Española de Alberques Juveniles,** Calle José Ortega y Gasset, 71, 2806 Madrid (tel. 91/401-13-00, ext. 319-625).

SEASONAL AND OTHER DISCOUNTS

In theory, the maximum rate established by a hotel for its rooms is charged for its better rooms during peak season, but in fact the maximum rate is often in effect all year. At some resorts in the slow season, rates may be lowered by the management to attract business. Always ask for a discount if you sense that business is slow.

OTHER MONEY-SAVING STRATEGIES

On your $50-a-day budget you will often be able to secure a room with private bath or else a tub or shower, but you'll save substantially if you ask for a room with washbasin only and a bathroom down the hall. In most establishments the shared baths are adequate if you don't use them during the peak hours, 7:30 to 9am and 6 to 8pm.

If there are three or more in your party, ask for an additional bed in your room. In a single an extra bed usually costs 60% or less than the maximum price for the room; in a double, 35% or less.

If you're traveling on a budget, don't expect to roll into a city after dark and secure the bargains—they will already have been grabbed by the early birds.

Rent a Place If you rent a home or apartment, you can save money on accommodations and dining and still take daily trips to see the surrounding area.

Apartments in Spain generally fall into two different categories: *hotel apartamientos* and *residencia apartamientos.* The hotel apartments have full facilities, with chamber service, equipped kitchenettes, and often restaurants and bars. The residencia apartments, also called *apartamientos turisticos,* are fully furnished with kitchenettes but lack the facilities of the hotel complexes. They are cheaper, however.

Companies in the United States arranging such rentals include **At Home Abroad,** 405 E. 56th St., Suite 6H, New York, NY 10022 (tel. 212/421-9165). A $50 registration fee is required, and two weeks is the minimum rental time. Most of this company's offerings are along the overbuilt Costa del Sol. Fortunately for the budget traveler, many of these rentals are low-cost, although some tend to be deluxe with swimming pools.

Rent a Vacation Everywhere (RAVE), 328 Main St. E, Suite 526, Rochester, NY 14604 (tel. 716/454-6440), includes not only the Costa del Sol in its rentals but other coasts as well, including the Costa del Ahazar (Valencia), Costa Dorada (south of Barcelona), Costa Brava (north of Barcelona), and perhaps some listings for the Balearic Islands. Minimum rental here is one week.

SAVING MONEY ON MEALS

The Spanish tend to eat large midday and evening meals. Below are ways to save money on meals.

BEST BUDGET BETS

Among the variety of budget eating options, these are your best bets.

Menú del Día and Cubierto Order the menú del día (menu of the day) or the *cubierto,* both fixed-price menus based on what is fresh at the market that day. They are the finest dining bargains in Spain. Usually each will include a first course, such as fish soup or hors d'oeuvres, followed by a main dish, plus bread, dessert, and the wine of the house. Though you won't have a large choice, you will dine well. The *menú turistico* is a similar fixed-price menu, but for many it's too large, especially at lunch. Only those with large appetites will find it the best bargain.

Cafeterias These are not self-service establishments, but restaurants serving light, often American, cuisine. Go for breakfast instead of dining at your hotel, unless it's included in the room price. Some cafeterias offer no hot meals, but many feature combined plates of fried eggs, french fries, veal, lettuce-and-tomato salad, which make adequate meals, or light fare like hot dogs and hamburgers.

Tapas If you wish, you can dine well at lunch and stop by a *tasca* for an evening meal of appetizer-size *tapas*—eggs in mayonnaise, potato omelets, codfish salad, cured ham, Russian salad, octopus in garlic mayonnaise sauce, grilled mushrooms, stuffed peppers, croquettes, etc.

OTHER MONEY-SAVING STRATEGIES

Don't overtip. Follow the local custom. Theoretically, service is included in the price of your meal, but it's customary to leave 10% additional.

For more details on dining (such as when and what to eat) see the "Food and Drink" section in Chapter 1.

SAVING MONEY ON SIGHTSEEING
SPECIAL DISCOUNTS/PASSES

Senior Citizens   Many discounts are offered to seniors, but sometimes to get these discounts you must be a member of a senior-citizen organization. One of the best known of these organizations is the **American Association of Retired Persons (AARP)**, open to anyone 50 or over (and you don't have to be retired). Its travel programs are geared for seniors—and loaded with discounts. Dues are only $5 annually, including a spouse. For information, contact AARP, 1909 K St. NW, Washington, DC 20049 (tel. 202/347-8800). The company also runs **AARP Travel Service**, P.O. Box 29233, Los Angeles, CA 90009 (tel. 213/322-7323; toll free 800/227-7737).

The **National Council of Senior Citizens,** also concerned with keeping travel expenses down, offers several annual tours. It will also arrange individual trips for its members, securing the most discounts possible for independent travel. Membership is open to everyone for $12 per person, rising to $16 per couple. Its headquarters are at 925 15th St. NW, Washington, DC 20005 (tel. 202/347-8800).

Students   The most commonly accepted form of identification is also an "open sesame" to bargains. An **International Student Identity Card (ISIC)** gets you such benefits as special student airfares to Europe, international medical insurance, and many special discounts. In Spain this card secures you free entrance to state museums, monuments, and archeological sights. Domestic train fares in Spain are also reduced for students. The card, which costs only $10, is available at several college and university travel offices. Proof of student status and a photograph (2″ × 2″) are necessary. One place to obtain the card is the **Council on International Educational Exchange (CIEE)**, 205 E. 42nd St., New York, NY 10017 (tel. 212/661-1414).

FREE DAYS

Throughout Spain many museums and cathedrals charge no admission. Some museums that do charge entrance fees offer a free day. The two major sightseeing attractions of Madrid—the art-stuffed Prado and the Palacio Real (Royal Palace)—are free on Wednesday.

SAVING MONEY ON SHOPPING
BEST BUYS

Some of the best purchases in Spain are suede coats, leather bags, shoes, handcrafts, antiques, jewelry, and art objects. The country offers excellent buys in ceramics from almost every province; collectors view Lladró figurines as lifetime treasures. Majorica pearls, which are made in Spain, carry a 10-year guarantee.

SALES

Major sales occur twice annually—after Christmas (usually the first week of January) and in summer. The large summer sales, called *rebajas,* begin in July. The best prices are found during the first three weeks of August, when stores try to rid their shelves of summer merchandise to make way for their fall offerings.

FLEA MARKETS

You'll find flea markets all over Spain, from Madrid to Barcelona, from Galicia to Andalusia. These places, such as El Rastro in Madrid, are probably your best bet for bringing home reasonably priced yet attractive souvenirs.

DUTY-FREE — WORTH IT OR NOT?

Before you leave home, check the regular retail price of items that you're most likely to buy. Duty-free prices vary from one country to another and from item to item. Sometimes you're better off purchasing an item in a discount store at home. If you don't remember Stateside prices, you can't tell when you're getting a good deal.

RECOVERING LOCAL TAXES

If you buy goods worth more than 10,000 pesetas ($94), as a nonresident of Spain you're entitled to a refund, which, depending on the internal sales tax (IVA), will be between 6% and 12%. To get this refund, you must fill out a form (three copies) detailing the value and nature of your purchase. If you're a citizen of a non-EC country, show the purchase and the form to the Spanish Customs Office. The government will refund the amount due in five to six weeks.

BARGAINING

The days of bargaining are, for the most part, long gone. Most stores have what is called *precio de venta al público* **(PVP),** a firm retail price not subject to negotiation.

With street vendors and with flea markets (see above), it's a different story. Here, haggling *à la española* is expected. However, you'll have to be very skilled to get the price reduced a lot, as most of these street-smart vendors know exactly what the price of their merchandise is worth and are old hands at getting it.

SAVING MONEY ON TRANSPORTATION

For more information on budget transportation tips, see "Getting Around," above, in this chapter.

TRAIN

On the train you can take advantage of the international passes like Eurailpass or the national train passes, which have been discussed earlier in this chapter.

BUS

Bus is the cheapest mode of transportation, but it's not really feasible for distances of more than 100 miles. On long hauls, buses are slow and often uncomfortable. Another major drawback might be a lack of toilet facilities, although rest stops are frequent. Bus travel is best for one-day excursions into the environs of a major tourist center such as Madrid. In the rural areas of the country, bus networks are more extensive than the railway system, as they go virtually everywhere, connecting every village. In general, a bus ride between two major cities in Spain, such as from Córdoba to Seville, is about two-thirds the price of a train ticket.

CAR

Car Rentals Saving on rentals is not easy. Always shop around before you leave home, as well as at the destination itself. Sometimes the major companies have special advance-purchase discounts; sometimes you can save by renting downtown instead of at the airport; sometimes you'll get a better deal by renting from a local company. See "Getting Around . . . By Car," above, for details.

Insurance   Always check your insurance policy. Sometimes credit card companies provide international coverage.

Tax   See "Recovering Local Taxes," above for information on how to get a tax refund on your rental.

Gas   Gasoline tends to be extremely expensive in Spain, and the price is always subject to seasonal variations. Arrange an itinerary and set up hotels along the way so that you won't have to empty the tank while looking for a room. Try to leave early in the day to avoid the endless traffic lines that form on major arteries of Spanish cities during rush hours. And remember that you'll get far better mileage if you drive at a steady, reasonable speed.

Maps   The AAA (American Automobile Association) publishes a regional map of Spain available free to members in most AAA offices throughout the United States. For $5.95, the AAA will sell you a 65-page guide, *Motoring in Europe*. Incidentally, the AAA has reciprocity in Spain with the **Real Automóvil Club de España,** José Abascal, 10, Madrid (tel. 91/447-32-00). This office can provide much helpful information about road conditions in Spain, including tourist and travel data. Only limited road service (emergencies only) is provided in case of breakdowns.

SAVING MONEY ON SERVICES & OTHER TRANSACTIONS

TIPPING

Don't overtip. The government requires hotels and restaurants to include their service charges—usually 15% of the bill. However, that doesn't mean you should skip out of a place without dispensing some extra pesetas. Following are some guidelines.

Hotel Staff   Porter—50 pesetas (45¢) per bag and never less than 100 pesetas (95¢), even if you have only one small suitcase. Maid—75 pesetas (70¢) per day. Doorman—100 pesetas (95¢) for assisting with baggage, 25 pesetas (25¢) for calling a cab. Concierge—in top-ranking hotels the concierge will often submit a separate bill, showing charges for newspapers, etc.; if he or she has been particularly helpful, tip extra.

Cab Drivers   Add about 10% to 15% to the fare as shown on the meter. However, if the driver personally unloads or loads your luggage, add 25 pesetas (25¢) per bag.

Porters   At airports such as Barajas in Madrid and major terminals, the porter who handles your luggage will present you with a fixed-charge bill, usually 75 to 110 pesetas (70¢ to $1.05) per bag.

Waiters   In both restaurants and nightclubs, a 15% service charge is added to the bill. To that, add another 3% to 5%, depending on the quality of the service. Waiters in deluxe restaurants and nightclubs are accustomed to the extra 5%, which means you'll end up tipping 20%. If that seems excessive, you must remember that the initial service charge reflected in the fixed price is distributed among all the help.

Services   Barbers and hairdressers expect 10% to 15%. Tour guides expect 200 pesetas ($1.90), although it's not mandatory. Gas station attendants get 25 to 50 pesetas (25¢ to 45¢). Theater/bullfight ushers get from 25 to 50 pesetas (25¢ to 45¢).

MONEY-CHANGING AND CREDIT CARDS

For the best exchange rate, always change your money at a bank, not at the hotel or a store. If you use a credit card, remember that you'll be billed at a later date. Whether the rate of exchange goes up or down is a bit of a gamble—you may end up paying more than you expected.

TELEPHONE CALLS

Make local and national long-distance calls from public phone booths. For international calls, the cheapest place to make them is from a post office.

FAST FACTS   *SPAIN*

Business Hours Banks are open Mon–Fri 9:30am–2pm, Sat 9:30am–1pm. Most **offices** are open Mon–Fri 9am–5 or 5:30pm; the longtime practice of early closings in summer seems to be dying out. In **restaurants,** lunch is usually 1–4pm and dinner 9–11:30pm or midnight. There are not set rules for the opening of **bars** and **taverns,** many opening at 8am, others at noon; most stay open until 1:30am or later. Major **stores** are open Mon–Sat 9:30am–8pm; smaller establishments, however, often take a siesta, doing business 9:30am–1:30pm and 4:30–8pm. Hours can vary from store to store.

Climate See "When to Go" in Chapter 2.

Currency See "Information, Entry Requirements, and Money" in Chapter 2.

Customs See "Information, Entry Requirements, and Money" in Chapter 2.

Driving Rules See "Getting Around," above, in this chapter.

Drugstores To find a drugstore outside normal hours, check the list of stores open for business posted on the door of any drugstore. The law requires drugstores to operate on a rotating system of hours so that there's always a drugstore open somewhere, even Sunday at midnight.

Electricity Most establishments have 220 volts AC. Some older places have 110 and 125 volts. Carry your adapter with you and always check at your hotel desk before plugging in any electrical appliance. It's best to travel with battery-operated equipment.

Embassies and Consulates If you lose your passport, fall seriously ill, get into legal trouble, or have some other serious problem, your embassy or consulate will probably have the means to provide assistance. The Madrid addresses and hours follow. The **United States Embassy,** Serrano, 75 (tel. 576-34-00; Metro: Núñez de Balboa), is open Mon–Fri 9:30am–1pm. The **Canadian Embassy,** Núñez de Balboa, 35 (tel. 431-43-00; Metro: Núñez de Balboa), is open Mon–Fri 9am–1pm. The **United Kingdom Embassy,** Fernando el Santo (tel. 319-02-00; Metro: Rubén Darío), is open Mon–Fri 10am–1pm. The **Republic of Ireland** has an embassy at Claudio Coello, 73 (tel. 576-35-00; Metro: Núñez de Balboa), open Mon–Fri 10am–1pm. The **Australian Embassy,** Paseo de la Castellana, 143 (tel. 279-85-04; Metro: Cuzco), is open Mon–Fri 10am–1pm. Citizens of **New Zealand** should contact the U.K. Embassy for assistance or advice.

Emergencies The police emergency number is **092** (but make sure it's a genuine emergency). The national emergency number for Spain (except the Basque country) is **006;** in the Basque country it is **088.**

Etiquette Women often kiss each other once on both cheeks when they meet. Men extend a hand when introduced; if they are good friends, they will often embrace. In general, women (except young moderns) expect men to open doors for them and to rise when they enter a room. The elderly are often treated with great respect and courtesy.

When it comes to lining up for something—say, for a bus—you should step forward or you may find yourself the last one on.

As a foreign guest, avoid all unfavorable references to Spain. Spanish nationalist pride often asserts itself vigorously in the face of criticism by a foreigner.

Film Negra makes both black-and-white and color film. Valca is another popular brand.

Holidays See "When to Go" in Chapter 2.

Information See "Information, Entry Requirements, and Money" in Chapter 2, as well as individual city chapters for local information offices.

Language The official language in Spain is Spanish (Castilian, actually), the third most widely spoken language in the world after Chinese and English. Although Spanish is spoken in every province of Spain, local tongues are beginning to reassert themselves. After years of being outlawed during the Franco dictatorship, Catalan has returned to Barcelona and Catalonia, even appearing on street signs; this language (or its derivatives) is also spoken in the Valencia area and in the Balearic Islands, including Majorca. The Basque language is widely spoken in the Basque region (the northeast, near France), which is seeking independence from Spain. Likewise, the Gallego language is enjoying a renaissance in Galicia (the northwest). Of course, English is spoken in most hotels, restaurants, and shops. The best **phrase book** is *Spanish for Travellers* by Berlitz; this pocket dictionary has a menu supplement and a 12,500-word glossary of both English and Spanish.

Laundry In most top hotels, fill out your laundry and dry-cleaning list and present it to your maid or valet. Same-day service usually costs from 25% to 50% more. To save money, go to a Laundromat; your hotel reception desk can advise you of the nearest one. Sometimes these establishments are self-service; others request that you drop off your laundry and pick it up later. See major cities for listings of Laundromats.

Liquor Laws The legal drinking age is 18. Bars, taverns, and cafeterias usually open at 8am, and many serve alcohol until around 1:30am or later. Generally, you can purchase alcoholic beverages in almost any market.

Mail To send an airmail letter to Canada or the United States costs 68 pesetas (65¢) for 15 grams and 58 pesetas (55¢) for a postcard. Allow about a week for delivery of an airmail letter or postcard. Rates change frequently, so check at your hotel before mailing anything. As for surface mail, forget it. Chances are, you'll be home long before your letter or postcard.

Maps See "Getting Around . . . By Car" in Chapter 2. See Chapters 6 and 13 and for specific recommendations of stores in Madrid and Barcelona. If you'd like a map before your trip to plan your itinerary, you can obtain one from Rand McNally, Michelin, or the AAA. These are sold at bookstores all over America. **Rand McNally** has retail stores at 150 E. 52nd St., New York, NY 10022 (tel. 212/758-7488); at 23 E. Madison, Chicago, IL 60602 (tel. 312/332-4627); and at 595 Market St., San Francisco, CA 94105 (tel. 415/777-3131). The U.S. headquarters of **Michelin** is at P.O. Box 3305, Spartanburg, SC 29304 (tel. 803/599-0850; toll free 800/423-0485).

Newspapers/Magazines Most newsstands along the Gran Vía in Madrid, as well as kiosks at the major hotels, carry the latest edition of the *International Herald Tribune*. The *Iberian Daily Sun* is an English-language newspaper of interest to expatriates and visitors. So, too, is *Lookout* magazine, focused primarily on Spain's Costa del Sol.

Passports See Information, Entry Requirements, and Money" in Chapter 2.

Pets It's best to leave them at home. If you don't, you must bring any licenses and proof of vaccinations to your nearest Spanish consulate before you leave. Normally, pets aren't welcome in public places; certain hotels will accept them, however. But these arrangements should be made in advance. Don't forget to check quarantine regulations affecting your animal upon your return. Guide dogs, however, are always excluded from such rigid rules. For the pamphlet "Pets," write the **U.S. Customs Service,** P.O. Box 7407, Washington, DC 20044, or call 202/566-8195 for a recorded message concerning Customs rules about pets.

Police The national emergency number is **006** throughout Spain, except in the Basque country, where it is **088.**

Radio/TV Every television network broadcasts in Spanish, but on radio you can listen to the voice of the American Armed Forces—news, music, sports, and local weather.

Rest Rooms In Spain they're called *aseos* and *servicios,* and labeled *caballeros* for men and *damas* or *señoras* for women. If you can't find any, go into a bar, but you should order something.

Safety Whenever you're traveling in an unfamiliar city or country, stay alert. Be aware of your immediate surroundings. Wear a moneybelt and keep a close eye on your possessions. Be particularly careful with cameras, purses, and wallets, all favorite targets for thieves and pickpockets.

Taxes   The internal sales tax (known in Spain as IVA) ranges between 6.12% and 33%, depending on the commodity being sold. Food, wine, and basic necessities are taxed at 6.12%; most goods and services (including car rentals) at 12%; luxury items (jewelry, all tobacco, imported liquors) at 33%; and luxury hotels at 12%, budget hotels at 6%. For more information about refunds see "Recovering Local Taxes" in Section 4 of this chapter.

Telephones   If you don't speak Spanish, you'll find it easier to telephone from your hotel, but remember that this is often very expensive, as hotels impose a surcharge on every operator-assisted call. On the street, phone booths (known as *cabinas*), have dialing instructions in English; local calls can be made by inserting two 5-pesetas (5¢) coins for 3 minutes. In Spain many of the smaller establishments, especially bars, discos, and a few low-cost restaurants, don't have phones. Further, many summer-only bars and discos secure a phone for the season only, then get a new number the next season. Many sightseeing attractions, such as small churches or even minor museums, have no staff to receive inquiries from the public.

Time   Spain is 6 hours ahead of Eastern Standard Time in the United States. Daylight Saving Time is in effect from the last Sunday in March to the last Sunday in September.

Tipping   See "Saving Money on Services and Other Transactions" in Section 4 of this chapter.

Tourist Offices   See "Information, Entry Requirements, and Money" in Chapter 2. See also specific cities.

Visas   See "Information, Entry Requirements, and Money" in Chapter 2.

Water   See "Food and Drink" in Chapter 1.

CHAPTER 4

GETTING TO KNOW MADRID

After years of stagnation and repression under Franco, Madrid has burst into bloom under King Juan Carlos. The city used to be a place where travelers went with a sense of duty and gloom—largely to see the Prado. That's all changed in the Madrid of today, since the creative explosion—*la movida*—that followed Franco's death in 1975. The city is now sought out as a destination unto itself—a bright, vibrant place in which to have fun.

The social life of Madrid, even more than its organized cultural offerings, is intriguing to visitors. It's literally a street scene, with locals enjoying the *terrazas* (open-air cafés) and *tascas* (taverns), and whole families dining at local inns where the tables spill out onto the sidewalks.

Nights are long in Madrid. Long after London has "gone to bed," Madrileños are just getting started in the cafés, jazz joints, dance clubs, and certainly the terrazas, which often don't close until dawn. Many club owners will tell you that the crowd doesn't really start pouring in until 2am.

The EC has designated Madrid as the Cultural Capital of Europe for the Year in 1992, a distinction due largely to the effects of la movida. This cultural awakening has brought profound changes to the capital in film, music, painting, and fashion. Madrid has regained a joie de vivre.

1. FROM A BUDGET TRAVELER'S POINT OF VIEW

BUDGET BESTS AND DISCOUNTS
PUBLIC TRANSPORTATION

You can save money on public transportation by purchasing a 10-trip ticket for the **Metro** (subway) for 430 pesetas ($4.05) at any Metro station. Metrotur tickets for 576 pesetas ($5.40) for three days, or 950 pesetas ($8.95) for five days, are also available. The center of the system is the **Puerta del Sol;** call 435-22-66 for more information.

For 430 pesetas ($405) you can also purchase a 10-trip ticket (but without transfers) for Madrid's **bus** system. It's sold at **Empresa Municipal de Transportes,** Plaza de la Cibeles (tel. 401-99-00), where you can also purchase a guide to the bus routes. Open daily from 8am to 8:30pm.

ENTERTAINMENT

In summer Madrid becomes a virtual free festival, as the city sponsors a series of plays,

WHAT'S SPECIAL ABOUT MADRID

Museums

☐ The Prado, the number-one attraction in Spain.

☐ Museum of Lazaro Galdiano, filled with old masters, many from the Golden Age.

☐ Convento de las Descalzas Reales, a 16th-century royal convent, with many art treasures.

Parks and Gardens

☐ Parque del Retiro, a place to relax in the heart of Madrid.

Architectural Highlights

☐ Plaza Mayor, the main square of the old town and quintessential Hapsburg Madrid.

☐ Palacio Real, Philip V's colossal palace, with 2,000 opulent rooms.

Shopping

☐ El Rastro, an open-air flea market, best visited on Sunday morning.

☐ Mercado Puerta de Toledo, a shopping mall with 150 of Spain's most glamorous names.

Events/Festivals

☐ The *corrida* (bullfight), a spectacle of death, celebrated in art and literature and also condemned. At the Plaza de Toros.

☐ Fiesta de Sant Isidro, 10 days of fairs, parades, and bullfights honoring the city's patron saint.

Cool for Kids

☐ Casa de Campo, a festive funpark filled with amusements.

After Dark

☐ Flamenco, the incomparable Spanish art form, at dozens of clubs late at night.

Literary Shrines

☐ Casa de Lope de Vega, home of the Shakespeare of the Spanish-speaking world.

---

concerts, and films—all gratis. Pick up a copy of the **Guía del Ocio** (available at most newsstands) for listings of these events. This guide also provides information about occasional discounts for commercial events, such as the concerts that are given in Madrid's parks. Also check the program of the **Fundación Juan March,** Castelló, 77 (tel. 435-42-40; Metro: Núñez de Balboa), which frequently stages free concerts.

Flamenco in Madrid is geared mainly to tourists with fat wallets, and nightclubs are expensive. But since Madrid is preeminently a city of song and dance, you can often be entertained at very little cost—in fact, for the price of a glass of wine or beer, if you sit at a bar with live entertainment. **Cambalache,** San Lorenzo (tel. 410-07-01; Metro: Tribuna), is one such place. Once inside, you can order a beer or sherry and watch live tangos. The club is open daily from 10pm to 5am.

Like flamenco clubs, discos tend to be expensive, but they often open for what is erroneously called "afternoon" sessions (from 7 to 10pm). Although discos charge entry fees, at an "afternoon" session the cost might be as low as 250 pesetas ($2.35), rising to 1,500 pesetas ($14.10) and beyond for a "night" session—that is, one beginning at 11:30pm and lasting until the early-morning hours. Therefore, go early, dance till 10, then go on to dinner (you'll be eating at the fashionable hour).

ACCOMMODATIONS

To keep your accommodations costs as low as possible, consider staying in a **hostal** (not hostel) in the old part of Madrid. There are dozens of these low-cost lodgings, which might be called the Madrid version of boarding houses. Sometimes they compete with one another in the same building, but on different floors. These are not always the cleanest, safest, or most elegant places to stay, but they *are* cheap.

If you'd like to search out lodgings even cheaper than the standard budget places recommended in this guide, walk along the **Calle del Príncipe** (running off the Plaza de Canalejas) and, a block away, the **Calle de Echegaray,** where there areseveral pensions and *residencias* that sell doubles without private bath for 2,130 ptas ($20) per night (or 1,065 ptas.; $10 per person).

Keep in mind that the price you pay for a hotel room depends on its plumbing. A room with a shower is cheaper than one with a private bathtub. Even cheaper is a room with a sink and a shared corridor bath.

Parents should always ask if children can stay free or at a reduced rate.

Paying cash will sometimes secure a reduction in price.

DINING

Your best bet is to go to one of the **cafeterias** or bars offering a *menú del día,* is a fixed-price menu consisting of three courses, bread, a small carafe of house wine, and service. Sometimes restaurateurs will also offer a *cubierto,* an even cheaper fixed-price meal, with no choice of dishes allowed. Enjoy one of these meals at lunch and visit one or two **tapas bars** in the evening, sampling a wide selection of appetizer-size snacks (usually already prepared), and you will have eaten as inexpensively as you can in the Spanish capital. (That is, other than purchasing food from street vendors.)

Look for the *platos del días,* or daily specials. They're usually fresh and often cheaper than the à la carte listings.

Wine is part of a meal in Madrid. But remember to ask for the *vino de la casa,* or house wine—it's only a fraction of the cost of bottled wines.

Patronize the famous budget-restaurant streets of Madrid: **Calle del Barco, Ventura de la Vega,** and **Calle de Echegaray.** Also check out the **Calle San Leonardo,** right off the Plaza de España behind the deluxe Hotel Plaza.

In Madrid you can judge the price of a restaurant by its forks—or lack of them. If only one fork is displayed outside, that indicates that the place is a *restaurante económico.*

If you shop carefully enough, you can find meals in Madrid for 1,000 pesetas ($9.40).

MISCELLANEOUS TIPS

Visit the Prado and the Royal Palace on Wednesday, when admission is free; otherwise, you'll spend from 400 to 500 pesetas ($3.75 to $4.70).

Do your serious shopping during the summer sales (called *rebajas*) in late July and August, when merchandise is heavily discounted.

FOR SENIORS

The biggest discounts for seniors are the half-price fares on all train travel from the city, cutting the price of day trips to Toledo and Segovia. For organizations offering discounted travel arrangements for seniors, see Chapter 2.

FOR STUDENTS

Students should possess an **International Student Identity Card** because it entitles them to discounts on travel, lodging, and admission to museums. However, if you don't have the card, and you are a bona fide student with identification to prove it, you can go to **TIVE,** José Ortega y Gasset, 71, 28006 Madrid (tel. 401-90-11; Metro: Becerra), where for a fee you can obtain the card plus information about discount opportunities for students in Madrid. This office also provides a list of cheap accommodations in the city.

2. ORIENTATION

ARRIVING

BY PLANE

Barajas, Madrid's international airport, has two terminals—one international, the other domestic. A shuttle bus runs between the two. For **Barajas Airport information,** call 408-52-00; for **Iberia Airlines,** call 411-25-45.

Air-conditioned yellow **airport buses** take you from the arrival terminal to the underground bus depot under the Plaza de Colón. You can also get off at stops along the way, provided your baggage isn't stored in the hold. The fare is 250 pesetas ($2.35), and the buses leave every 20 minutes, either to or from the airport.

If you go into town by **taxi,** it will cost 1,800 to 2,100 pesetas ($16.90 to $19.75), plus surcharges (in either direction) for the trip to the airport and for baggage handling. If you take an unmetered limousine, negotiate the price in advance.

BY TRAIN

Madrid has three major railway stations: **Atocha,** Glorieta del Emperador Carlos V (Metro: Atocha). for trains to Lisbon, Toledo, Andalusia, and Extremadura; **Chamartín,** in the northern suburbs at Agustín de Foxa (Metro: Chamartín), for trains to and from Barcelona, Asturias, Cantabria, Castilre–León, the Basque country, Aragón, Catalonia, Levante (Valencia), Murcia, and the French frontier; and **Norte (Príncipe Pío),** (Metro: Norte), is for trains to and from northwest Spain (Salamanca and Galicia). For railway information, call 552-05-18.

Warning: When leaving Madrid or taking an excursion, don't wait to buy your rail ticket or to make a reservation at the train station. There may be no tickets left. Go to the principal office of **RENFE,** Alcalá, 44 (tel. 733-30-00; Metro: Banco de España). The office is open Monday through Friday from 9am to 3pm and 4 to 7:30pm, on Saturday from 9am to 1:30pm.

BY BUS

Madrid has at least eight major bus terminals, including the large **Estación Sur de Autobuses,** Canarias, 17 (tel. 468-42-00; Metro: Palos de Moguer). Buses to the environs of Madrid, such as Toledo and Segovia, leave from numerous other stations; it's best to call 401-99-00 for current information about departures.

BY CAR

The following are the major highways into Madrid.

Route	From	Distance to Madrid
N-I	Irún	315 miles (505km)
N-II	Barcelona	389 miles (622km)
N-III	Valencia	217 miles (347km)
N-IV	Cádiz	400 miles (640km)
N-V	Badajoz	253 miles (405km)
N-VI	Galicia	374 miles (598km)

TOURIST INFORMATION

The most convenient tourist office is on the ground floor of the 40-story **Torre de Madrid,** Plaza de España (tel. 91/241-23-25; Metro: Plaza de España); open Monday through Friday from 9am to 7pm and on Saturday from 9:30am to 1:30pm.

Ask for a street map of the next town on your itinerary, especially if you're driving. The staff here can give you a list of hotels and hostales, but cannot recommend any particular establishment.

CITY LAYOUT

MAIN ARTERIES AND SQUARES

In modern Spain all roads, rails, and telephone lines lead to Madrid. The capital has outgrown all previous boundaries and is branching out in all directions.

Every new arrival must find the **Gran Vía,** which cuts a winding pathway across the city beginning at the **Plaza de España,** where you'll find one of Europe's tallest skyscrapers, the Edificio España. On this principal avenue is the largest concentration of shops, hotels, restaurants, and movie houses in the city. The **Calle de Serrano,** is a runner-up.

South of the avenue lies the **Puerta del Sol.** All road distances within Spain are measured from this square. However, its significance has declined, and today it is a prime hunting ground for pickpockets and purse snatchers. Here the **Calle de Alcalá** begins and runs for 2½ miles.

The **Plaza Mayor** is the heart of Old Madrid, an attraction in itself with its mix of French and Georgian architecture. (Again, be wary, especially late at night.) Pedestrians pass under the arches of the huge square onto the narrow streets of the old town, where you can find some of the capital's most intriguing restaurants and tascas. On the colonnaded ground level of the plaza are shops, many selling souvenir hats of turn-of-the-century Spanish sailors or officers in the kaiser's army.

The area south of the Plaza Mayor—known as *barrios bajos*—merits exploration. The narrow cobblestone streets are lined with 16th- and 17th-century architecture. Directly south of the plaza is the **Arco de Cuchilleros,** a street packed with street markets, restaurants, flamenco clubs, and taverns.

The Gran Vía ends at the Calle de Alcalá, and at this juncture lies the **Plaza de la Cibeles,** with its fountain to Cybele, the mother of the gods, and what has become known as "the cathedral of post offices." From Cibeles, the wide **Paseo de Recoletos** begins a short run to the **Plaza de Colón.** From this latter square rolls the serpentine **Paseo de la Castellana,** flanked by sophisticated shops, apartment buildings, luxury hotels, and foreign embassies.

Back at Cibeles again: Heading south is the **Paseo del Prado,** where you'll find Spain's major attraction, the Museo del Prado, as well as the Jardín Botánica (Botanical Garden). The paseo also leads to the Atocha Railway Station. To the west of the garden lies the **Parque del Retiro,** once reserved for royalty, with restaurants, nightclubs, a rose garden, and two lakes.

FINDING AN ADDRESS

Finding an address in Madrid can be a problem. The city is noted for its long boulevards, one stretching 2½ miles, so knowing the street number and cross street is very important.

The rule about street numbers is that there is no rule. Most streets begin their numbering on one side, running in order until the end, then running back in the opposite direction on the other side. Therefore, no. 50 could be opposite no. 308. But there are many exceptions to this, so be prepared.

NEIGHBORHOODS IN BRIEF

Madrid can be divided into three principal districts—Old Madrid, which holds the most tourist interest; Ensanche, the new district, often with the best shops and hotels; and the periphery, which is of little interest to visitors.

Plaza Mayor/Puerta del Sol This is the heart of Old Madrid, often called "the tourist zone." Filled with taverns and bars, it is bounded by the Carrera de San Jerónimo, Calle Mayor, Cava de San Miguel, Cava Baja, and Calle de la Cruz.

From the Plaza Mayor, the Arco de Cuchilleros is filled with Castilian restaurants and taverns; more cuevas lie along the Cava de San Miguel, Cava Alta, and Cava Baja. To the west of this old district is the Manzanares River. Muslim Madrid centers on the present-day Palacio de Oriente and Las Vistillas. What is now the Plaza de la Paja was the heart of the city and its main marketplace during the medieval and Christian period. In 1617 the Plaza Mayor became the hub of Madrid, and it remains the nighttime center of tourist activity, more so than the Puerta del Sol.

The Salamanca Quarter Ever since Madrid's city walls came tumbling down in the 1860s, the district of Salamanca to the north has been a fashionable address. The Calle de Serrano cuts through it, a street lined with stores and boutiques. The U.S. Embassy is also here.

Gran Vía/Plaza de España The Gran Vía is the city's main street, lined with cinemas, department stores, and the headquarters of banks and corporations. It begins at the Plaza de España, with its bronze figures of Don Quixote and his faithful Sancho Pancho.

Argüelles/Moncloa The university area is bounded by Pintor Rosales, Cea Bermúdez, Bravo Murillo, San Bernardo, and Conde Duque. Students haunt its famous ale houses.

Chueca An old and decaying area north of the Gran Vía. Its main streets are Hortaleza, Infantas, Barquillo, and San Lucas. It is the center of gay nightlife, with many clubs and cheap restaurants. It can be dangerous at night, however.

Castellana/Recoletos/Paseo del Prado Not a real city district, this is Madrid's north–south axis, its name changing along the way. The Museo del Prado and some of the city's more expensive hotels are found here. Many restaurants and other hotels are located along its side streets. In summer the several open-air terraces are filled with animated crowds. The most famous café is the Gran Café Gijón (see Chapter 5).

STREET MAPS

Arm yourself with a good map before setting out. The best is published by **Falk,** and it's available at most newsstands and kiosks in Madrid. Those given away free by tourist offices and hotels aren't adequate, as they don't list the maze of little streets.

3. GETTING AROUND

Getting around Madrid is not easy, because everything is spread out. Even many Madrileño taxi drivers are unfamiliar with their own city once they're off the main boulevards.

BY SUBWAY

The Metro system is easy to learn. The central converging point is the Puerta del Sol. Fares start at 65 pesetas (60¢). The Metro operates from 6am to 1:30am. Avoid rush hours. For information, call 435-22-66.

BY BUS

A bus network also services the city and suburbs, with routes clearly shown at each stop on a schematic diagram. Buses are fast and efficient because they travel along special lanes. Red buses charge 65 pesetas (60¢) per ride; yellow minibuses also charge 65 pesetas (60¢).

BY TAXI

Even though cab fares have risen recently, they're still so reasonable that taxis are recommended. When you flag down a taxi, the meter should register 125 pesetas

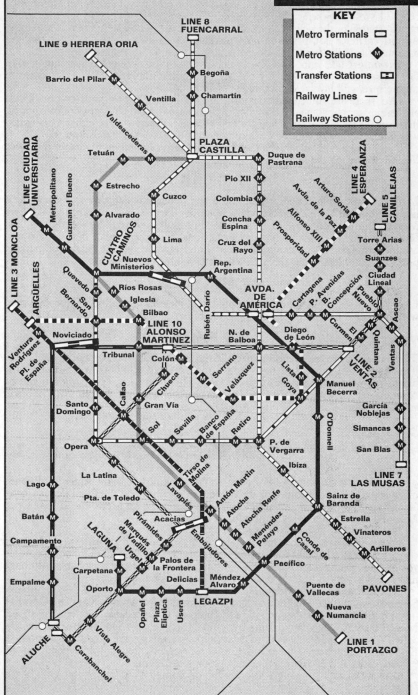

($1.15)—but that fare may have increased by the time of your visit. An average ride costs 500 to 600 pesetas ($4.70 to $5.65). A supplement is charged for trips to the railway station or the bullring, as well as on Sundays and holidays. The ride to Barajas Airport carries a 150-peseta ($1.40) surcharge, plus 20 pesetas (20¢) per bag. It's customary to tip at least 10% of the fare.

Warning: Make sure that the meter is turned on when you get into a taxi. Otherwise, some drivers will "assess" the cost of the ride, and their assessment, you can be sure, will involve higher mathematics.

Also, there are unmetered taxis that hire out for the day or the afternoon. These are legitimate, but some drivers will operate as gypsy cabs. Since they're unmetered, they can charge high rates. They are easy to avoid, though—take either a black taxi with horizontal red bands or a white one with diagonal red bands instead.

If you take a taxi outside the city limits, the driver is entitled to charge you twice the rate shown on the meter.

BY CAR

Driving is impossible in congested Madrid and potentially dangerous. It always feels like rush hour in Madrid (theoretically, hours are 8 to 10am, 1 to 2pm, and 4 to 6pm Monday through Saturday). Parking is also impossible. Save your car rentals (see "Fast Facts: Madrid," below) for one-day excursions from the capital. If you drive into Madrid from another city, ask at your hotel for the nearest garage or parking possibility, and leave your vehicle there until you're ready to leave.

BY BICYCLE

Ever wonder why you see so few people riding bicycles in Madrid? Those that tried were overcome by the traffic pollution. It's better to walk.

ON FOOT

The perfect way to see Madrid, especially the ancient narrow streets of the old town. If you're going to another district—and chances are that your hotel will be outside the old town—you can take the bus or Metro. For such a large city, Madrid can be covered amazingly well on foot, because so much of what will interest a visitor lies in various clusters.

 FAST / **_MADRID_**

American Express   For your mail or banking needs, the American Express office is located at the corner of the Marqués de Cubas and the Plaza de las Cortes (across the street from the Palace Hotel) (tel. 91/429-57-75; Metro: Gran Vía). Open Mon–Fri 9am–5:30pm, Sat until noon.

Area Code   For Madrid it is 91.

Baby-sitters   Most major hotels can arrange for baby-sitters. Usually, the concierge keeps a list of reliable nursemaids, and will contact them for you, provided you give adequate notice. Rates vary considerably but are fairly reasonable. Although many baby-sitters in Madrid speak English, don't count on it.

Bookstores Aguilar,   Calle de Serrano, 24 (tel. 577-36-74; Metro: Serrano), which sells English and Spanish editions, has two other outlets: Goya, 18 (tel. 575-06-40; Metro: Velázquez), and Paseo de la Castellana, 154 (tel. 259-09-67; Metro: Cuzco). Open daily 10am–1pm and 5–8pm; closed Sun. **Turner's,** Génova, 3 (tel. 410-43-59; Metro: Alonso Martínez), has one of the largest collections of English and French titles in Madrid. Lots of touring aids are available. Open Mon–Fri 9:30am–2pm and 5–8pm, Sat 9:30am–2pm; closed Sun.

Car Rentals   For more information on renting a car before you leave home, see "Getting Around" in Chapter 3. Should you want to rent one while in Madrid, you'll have several choices. In addition to its office at Barajas Airport, (tel. 205/85-32), **Avis** has a main office downtown at Gran Vía, 60 (tel. 247-20-48). **Hertz,** too, has an office at Barajas Airport (tel. 205-8452), and another in the heart of Madrid in the Edificio España, Gran Vía, 88 (tel. 240-58-03). **Budget Rent-a-Car,** also at Barajas Airport (tel. 100-560), maintains its headquarters at Gran Vía, 49 (tel. 248-90-40).

Climate   See "When to Go" in Chapter 2.

Crime   See "Safety," below.

Currency Exchange   The currency exchange at **Chamartín railway station** (Metro: Chamartín) is open 24 hours and gives the best rates in the capital. If you exchange money at a bank, ask about the minimum commission charged.

Dentist   For an English-speaking dentist, contact the **American Embassy,** Serrano, 75 (tel. 276-34-00).

Doctor   See "Dentist," above.

Drugstores   For a late-night pharmacy, dial **098** or look in the daily newspaper under **Farmacias de Guardia** to learn what drugstores are open after 8pm. Another way to find out is go to any pharmacy, even if it's closed—it will always post a list of nearby pharmacies that are open late that day. Try **Farmacia Gayoso,** Arenal, 2 (tel. 521-28-60; Metro: Puerta del Sol); or **Farmacia del Globo,** Atocha, 46 (tel. 239-46-00; Metro: Tirso de Molina).

Embassies and Consulates   See "Fast Facts: Spain" in Chapter 3.

Emergencies   **Fire,** 080; **police,** 091; **ambulance,** 252-32-64.

Eyeglasses   A reasonably priced place to purchase eyeglasses (prescription variety) or have eyeglasses repaired is **Visionlab,** Orense, 24 (tel. 556-44-15; Metro: N. Ministerios). Open Mon–Fri 10am–9pm, Sat 10am–3pm.

Hairdressers/Barbers   A good hairdresser for women is **Galico,** Velázquez, 89 (tel. 563-47-63; Metro: Núñez de Balboa). Open Mon–Sat 10am–5:30pm. Call for an appointment. For men, a fine choice is **Jacques Dessange,** O'Donnell, 9 (tel. 435-32-20; Metro: Príncipe de Vergara). Open Mon–Sat 10am–6:30pm. All the **El Corte Inglés** department stores have good barbershops. (See "Department Stores" under "Savvy Shopping" in Chapter 6.)

Holidays   See "When to Go" in Chapter 2.

Hospitals   The **British-American Medical Unit,** Conde de Aranda, 1 (tel. 435-18-23; Metro: Usera) has a staff of doctors, dentists, and even optometrists. However, this is not an emergency clinic, although someone is available on the staff all the time. The daily hours are 9am–8pm. For a real medical emergency, call **252-32-64** for an ambulance.

Information   See "Tourist Information," above, in Section 2 of this chapter.

Laundry   Try **Lavandería Marcenado,** Marcenado, 15 (tel. 416-68-71; Metro: Prospieridad), a full-service Laundromat. Open Mon–Fri 9:30am–1:30pm and 4:30–8pm, Sat 9:30am–1:30pm. Or try a self-service facility, **Lavandería Donoso Cortés,** Donoso Cortés, 17 (tel. 446-96-90; Metro: Quevedo). Open Mon–Fri 8:30am–7:30pm, Sat 8:30am–1pm.

Libraries   A large selection of American magazines and other material is available at the **Washington Irving Center,** Marqués de Villamagna, 8 (tel. 435-6922; Metro: Rubén Darío). Open Mon–Fri noon–7pm. The **British Cultural Center,** Almagro, 5 (tel. 419-12-50; Metro: Alonso Martínez), also has a large selection of English reading material. Open Mon–Fri 9am–1pm and 3–6pm.

Lost Property   If you've lost something on a Madrid bus, go to the **office at Alcantará, 26** (tel. 401-31-00; Metro: Goya). Open Mon–Fri 9am–2pm, Sat 9am–1pm. If you've lost something on the Metro, go anytime to the **Cuatro Caminos station** (tel. 233-20-00). For objects lost in taxis, go to Plaza de Legazpi, 6 (tel. 228-4806; Metro: Legazpi). Open Mon–Fri 9am–2pm, Sat 9am–1pm. For objects lost anywhere else, go to the **Palacio de Comunicaciones** at the Plaza de la Cibeles (Metro: Banco de España). Open Mon–Fri 9am–2pm, Sat 9am–1pm. Don't call—show up in person.

Luggage Storage/Lockers   These can be found at both the **Atocha**

and Chamartín railway terminals, as well as the major bus station at the **Estación Sur de Autobuses,** Calle Canarias, 17. Storage is also provided at the **air terminal** underneath the Plaza de Colón.

Newspapers/Magazines   The *Guidepost* is printed especially for visitors, and the *Iberian Daily Sun* is an English-language newspaper that always has interesting features. The Paris-based *International Herald Tribune* is sold at most major newsstands in the tourist districts. *Guía del Ocio,* a little magazine, contains entertainment listings and addresses (but in Spanish only) and sells at newsstands for 75 pesetas (70¢).

Photographic Needs   Kodak and other popular brands of film are sold in Madrid, but they're much more expensive than in the United States. For a Spanish film, try Valca (black and white) or Negra (black and white or color). Ask before photographing in churches or museums, as photography is often not permitted.

Police   Dial **091.**

Post Office   If you don't want to receive your mail at your hotel or the American Express office, direct it to **Lista de Correos** at the central post office in Madrid. To pick up mail, go to the window marked "Lista," where you'll be asked to show your passport. Madrid's central office is in "the cathedral of the post offices" at the Plaza de la Cibeles (tel. 221-81-95).

Radio/TV   During the day on shortwave **radio** you can hear the Voice of America and the BBC. An English-language radio program in Madrid called *"Buenos Días"* (Good Morning) airs many useful hints for visitors; broadcast Mon–Fri 6–8am on 657 megahertz. Radio 80 broadcasts news in English, Mon–Sat 7–8am, on 89 FM. Some **TV** programs are broadcast in English in the summer months. Many hotels—but regrettably not most of our budget ones—also bring in satellite TV programs in English.

Religious Services   Most churches in Madrid are **Catholic,** and they're all over the city. Catholic masses in English, however, are given at Alfonso XIII, 165. For information, call 233-20-32 in the morning. The British Embassy **Church of St. George** is at Núñez de Balboa, 43 (call 274-51-55 for worship hours). The interdenominational **Protestant Community Church,** Padre Damian, 34 (tel. 723-04-41), offers weekly services in the Colegio de los Sagrados Corazones, while the **Immanuel Baptist Church** offers English-speaking services at Hernández de Tejada, 4 (tel. 407-43-47). A **Christian Science church** is at Alonso Cano, 63 (tel. 259-21-350), and you'll find a **Jewish synagogue** at Balmes, 3 (tel. 445-98-35); services Fri 7:30pm, Sat 9:30am.

Rest Rooms   Some public rest rooms are available, including those in the Parque del Retiro and on the Plaza de Oriente across from the Palacio Real. Otherwise, you can always go into a bar or tasca, but you should order something. The major department stores, such as Galerías Preciados and El Corte Inglés, have good, clean rest rooms.

Safety   Because of an increasing crime rate in Madrid, the American Embassy has warned visitors to leave passports and valuables in a hotel safe or other secure place when going out. The embassy advises against carrying purses and suggests that you keep valuables in front pockets and carry only enough cash for the day's needs. Be aware of those around you and keep a separate record of your passport number, traveler's check numbers, and credit-card numbers.

Purse snatching is common, and the criminals often work in pairs, grabbing purses from pedestrians, cyclists, and even from cars. A popular scam involves one miscreant smearing the back of the victim's clothing, perhaps with mustard or ice cream. An accomplice pretends to help clean up the mess, while picking all the victim's pockets.

Every car can be a target, parked or just stopped at a light, so don't leave anything in sight in your car. If a vehicle is standing still, a thief may open the door or break a window in order to snatch a purse or package, even from under the seat. Place valuables in the trunk when you park, and always assume that someone is watching you to see whether you're putting something away for safekeeping. Keep the car locked while you're driving.

Shoe Repairs   In an emergency, go to one of the "Mister Minit" shoe repair centers at any **El Corte Inglés** department store. The flagship store of this chain is on the Calle Preciados (tel. 232-81-00), near the Puerta del Sol (also the Metro stop). Open daily 10am–9pm; closed Sun.

Taxes   There are no special city taxes for tourists, except for the **VAT** (central government tax) levied nationwide on all goods and services, ranging from 6% to 33%. In Madrid the only city taxes are for home and car owners, which need not concern the visitor.

Taxis   See "Getting Around," above, in this chapter.

Telegrams/Telex/Fax   Cables may be sent at the **central post office building** in Madrid at the Plaza de la Cibeles (tel. 221-81-95). However, the number for international telegrams is 241-33-00. In Spain it's cheaper to telephone within the country than to send a telegram. You can send telex and fax messages from the same central post office and from all major hotels.

Telephone   To make calls in Madrid, follow the instructions in "Fast Facts: Spain" in Chapter 3. However, for long-distance calls, especially transatlantic ones, it may be best to go to the main telephone exchange, **Locutorio Gran Vía,** Gran Vía, 10; or **Locutorio Recoletos,** Paseo de Recoletos, 37-41. You may not be lucky enough to find an English-speaking operator, but you can fill out a simple form that will facilitate the placement of a call.

Transit Information   For Metro information, call **435-22-66.**

---

4. NETWORKS & RESOURCES

FOR STUDENTS

Contact **TIVE,** Calle José Ortega y Gasset, 71 (tel. 401-9501; Metro: Becerra), which provides data on low-cost transportation in Spain and also Europe. Always check their discounts against those of other airlines to see just how great a reduction you're getting. For more data, refer to "Budget Bests and Discounts" earlier in this chapter.

FOR GAY MEN & LESBIANS

Before you go to Spain, you can order *Spartacus,* the international gay guide ($24.95), from **Giovanni's Room,** 1145 Pine St., Philadelphia, PA 19107 (tel. 215/923-2960; toll free 800/222-6996 outside Pa.).

Madrid is now one of the gay capitals of Europe. Besides Madrid, the major gay centers in Spain are Barcelona, Sitges (virtually the Fire Island of Spain), and Torremolinos on the Costa del Sol (although that resort attracts every known sexual persuasion). Madrid's gay life centers on the **Chueca district,** north of the Gran Vía, where the bar life begins around 11pm and often lasts until dawn.

In Madrid the Gay Switchboard is **Solidaridad Gay,** Tortosa, 4 (tel. 468-50-32), and it's open 24 hours a day with support, legal advice, and information. The best source for gay travel in Spain is **Sky Tours,** S.A., Mayor, 80 (tel. 241-04-03; Metro: Ópera or Puerta del Sol). Open Monday through Saturday from 9am to 2pm and 4:30 to 8pm.

Lesbians traveling abroad may want to order a copy of *Gaia's Guide International-al,* although this book is concerned primarily with the United States. It, too, can be ordered from Giovanni's Room.

Lesbian life remains much more underground in Spain than does male gay life. However, there is much activity—the problem is in finding it. The best source of information about Madrid is the **Librería de Mujeres** (see below). This feminist bookshop provides much useful data. The best women's entertainment center in Madrid (attracting men too) is **No Sé Los Digas a Nadie** ("Don't Tell Mama"), which will be recommended in Chapter 6.

FOR WOMEN

The **Women's Medical Hotline** in Madrid is at 419-94-41, receiving calls Mon–Fri 3:30–6:30pm.

A women's center is the **Librería de Mujeres,** San Cristóbal, 17 (tel. 521-70-43), near the Plaza Mayor (Metro: Puerta del Sol). Poetry readings, concerts, talks, and a good international bookstore with some English-language editions are part of the activities and offerings of this group. Open daily from 10am to 2pm and 5 to 8pm; closed Sun.

CHAPTER 5

MADRID ACCOMMODATIONS AND DINING

When it comes to **accommodations,** for the most part my suggestions are on the Gran Via, which abounds in pensions, many of them quite good. Some of the hotels are a block or so off the avenue, which many people find a plus, since they are farther away from the noise and traffic.

Another good hunting ground is the Plaza de la Cibeles, where the Paseo de Recoletos runs into the Paseo de la Castellana, a wide boulevard winding north. West of the paseo another wide boulevard, the Calle de Velazquez, also contains some good bargains.

Madrid's pensions, or *hostales,* are by and large superior to the hotels that the government rates one or two stars. Most occupy one large floor in an office or apartment building and all are conveniently located in the middle of the city. Some serve breakfast only, while others offer three meals a day.

Don't forget to ask if the quoted price for your room includes taxes.

Most of my **dining** recommendations are in the heart of Madrid, although dozens of restaurants have recently sprouted up in the suburbs. In the city you'll find restaurants offering every kind of cuisine.

The Calle del Barco is a great find if you're on a budget. Look for the SEPU department store on Gran Via, then walk 1 block up Calle Jimenez de Quesada, which becomes the Calle del Barco, or "bistro alley." The Ventura de la Vega, in the heart of Madrid, also features cheap eateries. In fact, it is the most popular budget-restaurant location in Madrid.

One caveat before you head out: Watch for August closings.

1. WHERE TO STAY

DOUBLES FOR LESS THAN 4,500 PTAS. ($42.30)

NEAR AMERICAN EXPRESS

HOSTAL RESIDENCIA ROSO, Plaza de las Cortes, 3, 28014 Madrid. Tel. 91/429-83-29. 12 rms (3 with bath). **Metro:** Sevilla.

$ Rates: 1,850 ptas. ($17.40) single without bath, 2,200 ptas. ($20.70) single with shower; 3,600–4,100 ptas. ($33.85–$38.55) double with shower. No credit cards.

Across the street from American Express, on the sixth floor of a 1920s elevator building, is the Hostal Residencia Roso. It is both tidy and well run. Set a few paces from the House of Parliament, it stands across the street from the posh Palace Hotel. There are seven bedrooms offering showers but no toilets, and two have no facilities at all. No breakfast is served.

HOSTAL PRINCIPADO, Zorrilla, 7, 28014 Madrid. Tel. 91/429-81-87. 15 rms with bath. **Metro:** Puerta del Sol, Sevilla, or Banco de España.
$ Rates: 3,000 ptas. ($28.20) single; 4,300 ptas. ($40.40) double. AE, MC, V.

The two-star Hostal Principado is a real find. In a well-kept townhouse, it is run by a gracious owner who keeps everything clean and renovated. New tiles, attractive bedspreads, and curtains give it a fresh look.

PENSION AGUADULCE, Plaza de las Cortés, 3, 28014 Madrid. Tel. 91/429-83-65. 10 rms with bath. **Metro:** Puerta del Sol or Sevilla.
$ Rates: 3,500 ptas. ($32.90) single; 4,500 ptas. ($42.30) double. No credit cards.
A family-run establishment, the Pension Aguadulce stands on the sixth floor of a grand circa-1920 building. There's a view of the Plaza de las Cortes from the windows of the communal TV room. No meals are served.

ON OR NEAR THE GRAN VÍA

HOSTAL-RESIDENCIA VENECIA, Gran Vía, 6, 28004 Madrid. Tel. 91/522-46-51. 8 rms without bath. **Metro:** Gran Vía.
$ Rates: 1,800 ptas. ($16.90) single; 2,000 ptas. ($18.80) double. Breakfast 300 ptas. ($2.80) extra. No credit cards.
Located on the upper floors of an older building on the Gran Vía, the Venecia is reached by an old-fashioned elevator. A bevy of scrubbing and polishing maids keeps the place extremely clean.

HOTEL ALCÁZAR REGIS, Gran Vía, 61, 28013 Madrid. Tel. 91/247-93-17. 25 rms without bath. **Metro:** Plaza de España or Santo Domingo.
$ Rates: 1,800 ptas. ($16.90) single without bath; 2,200 ptas. ($20.70) double without bath. Breakfast 250 ptas. ($2.35) extra. AE.
Conveniently perched on a corner in the midst of Madrid's best shops is this post–World War II building, complete with a circular Greek-style temple as its crown. In a captivating atmosphere, you'll find long and beautiful rooms, wood paneling, leaded-glass windows, parquet floors, crystal chandeliers, and graciously proportioned bedrooms, each with hot and cold running water.

HOTEL COSTA VERDE, Gran Vía, 61, 28013 Madrid. Tel. 91/541-91-41. 10 rms. **Metro:** Callao.
$ Rates: 1,800 ptas. ($16.90) single without bath; 3,200 ptas. ($30.10) double without bath, 3,500 ptas. ($32.90) double with shower (no toilet). No credit cards.
On the ninth floor of a turn-of-the-century building, this is an enclave of somewhat shabby but very clean charm. Set behind frosted-glass doors, rooms are simple but comfortable; six of them are doubles. An elevator services the little hotel, which isn't air-conditioned but is kept cool in summer by its high ceilings. No breakfast served.

HOSTAL MARGARITA, Gran Vía, 50, 28013 Madrid. Tel. 91/247-35-49. 8 rms (6 with bath or shower). **Metro:** Callao or Gran Vía.
$ Rates: 2,500 ptas. ($23.50) single without bath, 3,000 ptas. ($28.20) single with shower; 3,500 ptas. ($32.90) double with shower, 3,800 ptas. ($35.70) double with bath. Breakfast 300 ptas. ($2.80) extra. No credit cards.

The owners of this clean and friendly two-star hostal have furnished it with tasteful Spanish pieces. *Café con leche* (coffee with milk), along with fresh bread and butter, is offered in the kitchen, where guests can use the refrigerator for storing food.

HOSTAL LORENZO, Infantas, 26, 28004 Madrid. Tel. 91/521-30-57. 17 rms with bath. **Metro:** Gran Vía.

$ Rates: 3,000 ptas. ($28.20) single; 4,500 ptas. ($40.40) double. Breakfast 275 ptas. ($2.60) extra. No credit cards.

An attractive hostal frequented by several readers, the Lorenzo is housed on the third floor of an elegantly curving, brick corner building with white shutters and iron railings, 2 blocks from the Gran Vía and 3 from the Calle de Alcalá. Parquet floors lead to the comfortably old-fashioned bedrooms, which are well maintained. Depending on your room, you're likely to have a serpentine dressing table or rows of flowerpots on your terrace.

A "Casa" of Budget Hotels

At Gran Vía 44, close to many of Madrid's shops and restaurants, is a 19th-century building filled almost exclusively with small hotels and pensions. Some of the rooms are small, but for the pilgrim who hops off the train in tourist-packed Madrid—armed only with luggage and no reservation—this house of hotels is a good bet.

HOSTAL-RESIDENCIA TANGER, Gran Vía, 44, 28013 Madrid. Tel. 91/ 221-75-85. 6 rms (3 with bath). **Metro:** Callao.

$ Rates: 1,900 ptas. ($17.85) single without bath; 3,200 ptas. ($30.10) double with bath. Breakfast 275 ptas. ($2.60) extra. No credit cards.

On the top-floor roost, the Tanger has a quiet and sunny disposition. The lobby is small but tasteful, and there is pleasant old-fashioned furniture in the rooms. The owner's passion for knickknacks softens the rough edges, imbuing the Tanger with a homelike touch. Breakfast is the only meal served.

HOSTAL-RESIDENCIA MIAMI, Gran Vía, 44, 28013 Madrid. Tel. 91/ 221-14-64. 8 rms (2 with bath). **Metro:** Callao.

$ Rates: 2,100 ptas. ($19.75) single without bath; 2,900 ptas. ($27.25) double without bath. 3,600 ptas. ($33.85) double with bath. No credit cards.

The Miami, which enjoys the view from the eighth floor, is a good bet for peseta watchers. Although somewhat cluttered, the residencia is clean and has a helpful staff. No breakfast served.

HOSTAL-RESIDENCIA CONTINENTAL, Gran Vía, 44, 28013 Madrid. Tel. 91/521-46-40. 29 rms with bath. TEL **Metro:** Callao.

$ Rates: 3,200 ptas. ($30.10) single; 4,200 ptas. ($39.50) double. Breakfast 250 ptas. ($2.35) extra. AE, DC, MC, V.

Sprawling handsomely over the third and fourth floors of Gran Vía, 44, this hostal is a bit more expensive than the other accommodations in the building, but the rooms are comfortable, tidy, and newly renovated. The desk clerk speaks English.

NEAR THE PLAZA MAYOR

HOSTAL LA PERLA ASTURIANA, Plaza de Santa Cruz, 3, 28012 Madrid. Tel. 91/266-46-00. 30 rms with bath. **Metro:** Puerta del Sol.

$ Rates: 3,200 ptas. ($30.10) single with bath; 4,200 ptas. ($39.50) double with bath. Breakfast 275 ptas. ($2.60) extra. MC, V.

Ideal for those who want to stay in the heart of old Madrid (1 block off the Plaza Mayor and 2 blocks from the Puerta del Sol), this small family-run establishment has a courteous staff member at the desk 24 hours a day for security convenience. You can socialize in the small, comfortable lobby adjacent to the reception desk. The

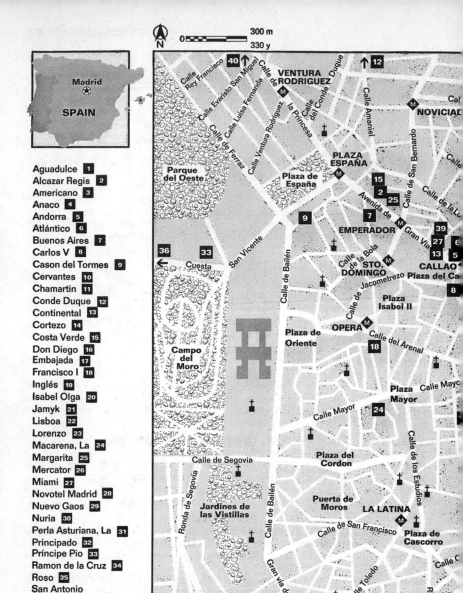

Madrid

SPAIN

Aguadulce **1**
Alcazar Regis **2**
Americano **3**
Anaco **4**
Andorra **5**
Atlántico **6**
Buenos Aires **7**
Carlos V **8**
Cason del Tormes **9**
Cervantes **10**
Chamartin **11**
Conde Duque **12**
Continental **13**
Cortezo **14**
Costa Verde **15**
Don Diego **16**
Embajada **17**
Francisco I **18**
Inglés **19**
Isabel Olga **20**
Jamyk **21**
Lisboa **22**
Lorenzo **23**
Macarena, La **24**
Margarita **25**
Mercator **26**
Miami **27**
Novotel Madrid **28**
Nuevo Gaos **29**
Nuria **30**
Perla Asturiana, La **31**
Principado **32**
Príncipe Pio **33**
Ramon de la Cruz **34**
Roso **35**
San Antonio
   de la Florida **36**
Santa Barbara **37**
Santander **38**
Tanger **39**
Tirol **40**
Tryp Lar **41**
Tryp Velázquez **42**
Venecia **43**

MADRID ACCOMMODATIONS

17 37 Calle de Genova

↑ 11   16 42 ↑   ↗

SERRANO
Calle de Goya   28
Ⓜ   34

Plaza de   Plaza
la Villa   de Colón
                COLÓN Ⓜ

Calle Fernando VI

Jardines
del
Descubrimiento

Calle Bárbara
de Braganza

Calle de
Gravina   del Almirante   Ⓜ CHECA

Calle de Fuencarral

Calle de Valverde

Calle de Hortaleza

30
Calle de Augusto Figueroa

Calle de Prim

paseo Recoletos

Plaza de la
Independencia

Calle de Serrano

GRAN VÍA Ⓜ

Red. de
San Luis

23

43

Avenida de Gran Vía

Calle de Barquillo

Plaza de
la Cibeles   Calle de Alcalá

41
4

Calle Montera

Ⓜ SEVILLA

Ⓜ BANCO
DE ESPAÑA
Calle de Montalbán

SOL Ⓜ

3

Calle de Alcalá

Calle de la Cruz

Carrera de San Jerónimo

21 32
1 35   20

Paseo del Prado

Plaza de
la Lealtad

Calle A. Maura

Calle de Alfonso XII

Plaza
de las
Cortes

38
19
ⓘ

Plaza C.
del Castillo

Calle del Prado

Calle de
Cervantes

22 10

Paseo del Prado

Calle Atocha

Calle de las Huertas

DE
OLINA   14

Calle de la Magdalena
✉

Calle de la Cabeza

ALONSO
MARTINEZ Ⓜ

Calle de Gobernador

Calle Atocha

Jardín
Botánico

Calle de Espalter

Calle de Alfonso XII

Calle Jesús y María Levapiés

Calle del Amparo

Calle Mesón de Paredes

Calle de Santa Isabel

26

✉

Ⓜ ATOCHA

Paseo de la Infanta Isabel

Plaza
Lavapies

Ⓜ LAVAPIES

Calle Miguel Servet

✉

Estación
de Atocha

Calle de Embajadores

Ronda de Atocha

Sta. María de la Cabeza

✉

Church ✝

Post Office ✉

Information ⓘ

FROMMER'S SMART TRAVELER—HOTELS

VALUE-CONSCIOUS TRAVELERS SHOULD TAKE ADVANTAGE OF THE FOLLOWING:

1. Reductions in rates for rooms without private bath. Usually a room with a shower is cheaper than a room with a private bath, and even cheaper is a room with a basin only.
2. Reductions at some hotels if you pay cash instead of with a credit card.
3. Long-term discounts if you're planning to spend more than one week in Madrid.

QUESTIONS TO ASK IF YOU'RE ON A BUDGET

1. If there's a garage, what is the parking charge? You might want to try to find a parking place on the street (hard to come by).
2. Is there a surcharge for local or long-distance telephone calls? Usually there is, and it can be as high as 40%. Make your calls at the nearest post office instead.
3. Is service included or will it be added to your final bill. Likewise, are all taxes included, or will you be billed extra?
4. Is a continental breakfast included in the rate? After a stay of 3 or 4 days, the cost of breakfast alone can make a big difference in your final bill.

---

bedrooms are clean, with fresh towels supplied daily. Many inexpensive restaurants and *tapas* bars are nearby.

HOSTAL LA MACARENA, Cava de San Miguel, 8, 28005 Madrid. Tel. 91/265-92-21. 18 rms with bath. **Metro:** Puerta del Sol, Ópera, or La Latina.
$ Rates: 3,200 ptas. ($30.10) single; 4,500 ptas. ($42.30) double. Breakfast 325 ptas. ($3.05) extra. MC, V.

Known for its reasonable prices and praised by readers for the warmth of its reception, this unpretentious, clean hostal is run by the Ricardo González family. Its 19th-century façade ornamented with Belle Epoque patterns offers an ornate contrast to the chiseled simplicity of the ancient buildings facing it. The location is one of the hostal's assets: on a street (admittedly noisy) immediately behind the Plaza Mayor, near one of the best clusters of *tascas* (bars) in Madrid.

NEAR THE PUERTA DEL SOL

HOTEL LISBOA, Ventura de la Vega, 17, 28014 Madrid. Tel. 91/429-98-94. 23 rms with bath. **Metro:** Puerta del Sol.
$ Rates: 3,500 ptas. ($32.90) single; 4,500 ptas. ($42.30) double. Breakfast 275 ptas. ($2.60) extra. AE, DC, MC, V.

The Lisboa, on Madrid's most famous restaurant street, can be a bit noisy, but that's my only complaint. The hotel is a neat, modernized townhouse with compact rooms, and central heating in the cooler months. The staff speaks five languages. The Lisboa has no restaurant, but it is surrounded by budget dining rooms and tascas.

DOUBLES FOR LESS THAN 7,000 PTAS. [$65.80]

NEAR AMERICAN EXPRESS

HOSTAL RESIDENCIA ISABEL OLGA, Zorrilla, 13, 28014 Madrid. Tel. 91/429-78-87. 20 rms (18 with bath). **Metro:** Sevilla.
$ Rates: 1,800 ptas. ($16.90) single without bath, 2,500 ptas. ($23.50) single with

bath; 3,200 ptas. ($30.10) double without bath, 4,800 ptas. ($45.10) double with bath. Breakfast 275 ptas. ($2.60) extra. No credit cards.
Located in a secure area behind the Cortes (Spain's House of Deputies) is this clean and well-managed family-run hostal. It's a bit timeworn, but the price is right.

HOSTAL CERVANTES, Cervantes, 34, 28014 Madrid. Tel. 91/429-27-45. 16 rms with bath. **Metro:** Banco de España.
$ Rates: 4,000 ptas. ($37.60) single; 5,000 ptas. ($47) double. No credit cards.
One of Madrid's most pleasant family-run hotels, the Cervantes has been widely appreciated by our readers for years. Take a tiny birdcage-style elevator to the immaculately maintained second floor of this stone-and-brick building. Each accommodation contains a bed, Spartan furniture, and a private bath. No breakfast is served, but the Alfonsos will direct you to a nearby café. The establishment is convenient to the Prado, Retiro Park, and oldest sections of Madrid.

PENSION JAMYK, Plaza de las Cortes, 4, 28013 Madrid. Tel. 91/429-0068. 18 rms (10 with bath). **Metro:** Sevilla.
$ Rates: 2,350 ptas. ($22.10) single without bath, 4,000 ptas. ($37.60) single with bath; 5,250 ptas. ($49.35) double with bath. Breakfast 300 ptas. ($2.80) extra. DC, MC, V.
A former private apartment in a well-located building from the turn of the century, the seventh-floor pension is reached by elevator. Rooms are clean and functional. Breakfast only.

ON OR NEAR THE GRAN VÍA

HOTEL NURIA, Fuencarral, 52, 28004 Madrid. Tel. 91/531-92-08. 57 rms (25 with bath). TEL **Metro:** Gran Vía or Tribunal.
$ Rates (including continental breakfast): 3,000 ptas. ($28.20) single without bath, 3,800 ptas. ($35.70) single with bath; 4,400 ptas. ($41.35) double without bath, 5,000 ptas. double ($47) with bath. AE, DC, MC, V.
Three blocks from the Gran Vía, the Hotel Nuria has bedrooms with interesting views of the capital. Renovated in the late '60s, it offers home-style food—a complete luncheon or dinner is 1,500 pesetas ($14.10). Rooms are spotless.

HOTEL RESIDENCIA SANTANDER, Echegaray, 1, 28014 Madrid. Tel. 91/429-95-51. 38 rms with bath. TV TEL **Metro:** Puerta del Sol.
$ Rates: 4,500 ptas. ($42.30) single; 5,500 ptas. ($51.70) double. Breakfast 275 ptas. ($2.60) extra. No credit cards.
A snug little hotel just off the Puerta del Sol, the Santander is a refurbished 1930 house with adequate rooms. Although it's on a teeming street, you might appreciate the local atmosphere.

FRANCISCO I, Arenal, 15, 28013 Madrid. Tel. 91/248-02-04. 57 rms with bath. **Metro:** Puerta del Sol or Ópera.
$ Rates: 4,200 ptas. ($39.50) single; 6,500 ptas. ($61.10) double. Breakfast 350 ptas. ($3.30) extra. MC, V.
The Francisco I offers modern, clean rooms, as well as a lounge, a bar, and a comfortable rustic restaurant on the sixth floor, where a set meal costs 2,000 pesetas ($18.80). Some bedrooms have air conditioning.

HOSTAL NUEVO GAOS, Mesonero Romanos, 14, 28012 Madrid. Tel. 91/532-71-07. Fax 91/522-70-98. 23 rms with bath. A/C MINIBAR TV TEL **Metro:** Callao.
$ Rates (including continental breakfast): 5,800 ptas. ($54.50) single; 7,000 ptas. ($65.80) double. AE, DC, MC, V.
On the second, third, and fourth floors of a building just off the Gran Vía, this residencia offers guests the chance to enjoy a comfortable standard of living at moderate rates. The place lies directly north of the Puerta del Sol, across the street from the popular flamenco club Torre Bermejas.

ANACO, Tres Cruces, 3, 28013 Madrid. Tel. 91/522-46-04. Fax 91/531-64-84. 39 rms with bath. TV TEL **Metro:** Gran Vía, Callao, or Puerta del Sol.
$ Rates: 4,700 ptas. ($44.20) single; 8,200 ptas. ($77.10) double; 11,000 ptas. ($103.40) triple. Breakfast 475 ptas. ($4.45) extra. AE, DC, MC, V.
This modern hotel just off the Gran Vía opens onto a tree-shaded plaza. The bedrooms are compact, with built-in headboards, reading lamps, and lounge chairs. Ask for one of the five terraced rooms on the top floor, as there is no extra charge. English is spoken, and there's a municipal garage nearby.

HOTEL TRYP LAR, Valverde, 16, 28004 Madrid. Tel. 91/521-65-92. 80 rms with bath. TEL **Metro:** Gran Vía.
$ Rates (including continental breakfast): 4,800 ptas. ($45.10) single; 5,800 ptas. ($54.50) double. AE, DC, MC, V.
Just off the Gran Vía, the Hotel Tryp Lar offers personal attention and clean rooms (some air-conditioned). There is a small sunken lobby, but no dining room; continental breakfast is available, however. The hotel has a garage.

NEAR THE NORTH STATION

TIROL, Manuel de Urquijo, 4, 28008 Madrid. Tel. 91/248-19-00. 93 rms with bath. A/C TEL **Metro:** Argüelles.
$ Rates: 5,800 ptas. ($54.50) double. Breakfast 275 ptas. ($2.60) extra. MC, V.
A short walk from the Plaza de España and the swank Meliá Madrid, the three-star Tirol makes a good choice, though it offers doubles only. Furnishings are simple and functional. In the downstairs cafeteria you can order a light meal. There's also a garage in the building.

SAN ANTONIO DE LA FLORIDA, Paseo de la Florida, 13, 28008 Madrid. Tel. 91/247-14-00. Fax 91/559-09-51. 96 rms with bath. TV TEL **Metro:** Norte.
$ Rates: 4,200 ptas. ($39.50) single; 6,500 ptas. ($61.10) double. Breakfast 400 ptas. ($3.75) extra. DC, MC, V.
A lot depends on the room you get here—I prefer those overlooking the Manzanares River and the Casa de Campo. The front rooms face a wide, traffic-heavy avenue, across from the North Station, and are less desirable. All accommodations are fairly modern and functionally furnished, however, and some have air conditioning; balconies add extra charm. Among the warm, contemporary public rooms, the dining room is particularly inviting. There's a cocktail lounge, plus a grill for light meals. For those who don't mind being slightly out of the center, or for motorists (there's a garage), the San Antonio might be ideal.

NEAR THE PLAZA MANUEL BECERRA

RAMÓN DE LA CRUZ, Don Ramón de la Cruz, 94, 28006 Madrid. Tel. 91/401-72-00. Fax 91/402-21-26. 103 rms with bath. **Metro:** Manuel Becerra.
$ Rates: 4,000–4,600 ptas. ($37.60–$43.15) single; 5,600–6,800 ptas. ($52.65–$63.90) double. Breakfast 300 ptas. ($2.80) extra. MC, V.
The relatively quiet, modern Ramón de la Cruz is just off the Plaza Manuel Becerra, reached from the Parque del Retiro via the Calle de Alcalá. The fairly large rooms are styled with English reproductions—mainly mahogany pieces such as chests and armchairs. Elevators service the eight floors, and there's a small breakfast room, plus an air-conditioned public lounge (no restaurant).

AT PLAZA DE SANTA BÁRBARA

SANTA BÁRBARA, Plaza de Santa Bárbara, 4, 28004 Madrid. Tel. 91/446-23-45. 14 rms with bath. TEL **Metro:** Alonso Martínez.
$ Rates: 4,500 ptas. ($42.30) single; 6,200–6,800 ptas. ($58.30–$63.90) double. Breakfast 275 ptas. ($2.60) extra. No credit cards.
Occupying the third floor of a building on a tree-lined street, the Santa Bárbara has

been renovated, and the bedrooms—many furnished with antique beds—are for the most part of generous size. All have balconies. There is a bright and airy breakfast/TV room.

NEAR THE PUERTA DEL SOL

HOSTAL RESIDENCIA AMERICANO, Puerta del Sol, 11, 28013 Madrid. Tel. 91/522-28-22. 43 rms with bath. TEL **Metro:** Puerta del Sol.
$ Rates: 3,300 ptas. ($31) single; 5,000 ptas. ($47) double. No credit cards.
The Hostal Residencia Americano, on the third floor of a five-floor building, is suitable for those who want to be in the Puerta del Sol. Owner/manager A. V. Franceschi has refurbished all rooms, most of them outside chambers with balconies facing the street. Mr. Franceschi promises hot and cold running water 24 hours a day. No breakfast served.

HOTEL INGLÉS, Echegaray, 8, 28014 Madrid. Tel. 91/429-65-51. Fax 91/420-24-23. 58 rms with bath. TEL **Metro:** Puerta del Sol or Sevilla.
$ Rates (including continental breakfast): 4,600 ptas. ($43.25) single; 6,800 ptas. ($63.90) double. AE, DC, MC, V.
You'll find the Hotel Inglés on a central street lined with tascas. It's perhaps more modern and impersonal than when Virginia Woolf made it her address in Madrid. Behind its red-brick façade you'll find unpretentious and contemporary bedrooms, each well maintained. The comfortable armchairs in the TV lounge are likely to be filled with avid soccer fans. Motorists will appreciate the adjacent garage.

DOUBLES FOR LESS THAN 10,000 PTAS.
[$94]
NEAR THE ATOCHA STATION

RESIDENCIA MERCÁTOR, Atocha, 123, 28012 Madrid. Tel. 91/429-05-00. 90 rms with bath. MINIBAR TV TEL **Metro:** Atocha.
$ Rates: 6,000 ptas. ($56.40) single; 8,000 ptas. ($75.20) double. Breakfast 500 ptas. ($4.70) extra. AE, DC, MC, V.
Only yards from the Reina Sofía Art Center, a 3-minute stroll from the Prado, and within walking distance of the Iberia air terminal and American Express, the residencia is modern, orderly, and clean, with enough comforts and conveniences to please the weary traveler. Some rooms are more inviting than others, especially those with desks and armchairs; several also have air conditioning. The Mercátor offers breakfast, and has a bar and cafeteria serving light meals. There is an adjacent parking lot.

NEAR THE GLORIETA QUEVADO

CONDE DUQUE, Plaza Conde Valle de Suchil, 5, 28015 Madrid. Tel. 91/447-70-00. 138 rms with bath. TEL **Metro:** San Bernardo.
$ Rates: 6,500 ptas. ($61.10) single; 9,800 ptas. ($92.10) double. Breakfast 500 ptas. ($4.70) extra. AE, DC, MC, V.
The modern three-star Conde Duque, near a branch of the Galerías Preciados department store, opens onto a tree-filled plaza in a residential neighborhood near the Glorieta Quevado. The hotel is located 12 blocks north of the Plaza de España, off the Calle de San Bernardo, which starts at the Gran Vía—too long to walk, but a subway stop is nearby. The furnishings include modern built-in headboards and reproductions of 19th-century English pieces. There are bedside lights and telephones.

ON OR NEAR THE GRAN VÍA

HOSTAL BUENOS AIRES, Gran Vía, 61, 28013 Madrid. Tel. 91/542-22-50. 25 rms with bath. TEL **Metro:** Plaza de España.

...ptas. ($50.75) single; 7,200 ptas. ($67.70) double. Breakfast 350 ...0) extra. MC, V.

...o reach this place, you pass through a marble-covered street-floor lobby within a 1935 building, then take the elevator to the second floor. The freshly decorated hostal occupies two floors. One of its best features is a wood-sheathed café bar, open daily from 8am to midnight. Bedrooms are comfortable, modern, and clean.

HOTEL RESIDENCIA CARLOS V, Maestro Vitoria, 5, 28013 Madrid. Tel. 91/531-41-00. Fax 91/531-41-00. 67 rms with bath. A/C TV TEL **Metro:** Puerta del Sol or Callao.

$ **Rates** (including continental breakfast): 7,800 ptas. ($73.50) single; 10,000 ptas. ($94) double. AE, DC, MC, V.

The Hotel Residencia Carlos V has long been a favorite of mine—I stayed here when I researched the original *Spain on $5 a Day* back in the 1960s. The seven-story art nouveau building, dating from 1904, has been altered over the years. Rooms have been upgraded and now contain such amenities as music and personal safes; bathrooms have been modernized. What hasn't changed is the unbeatable location: around the corner from the Galerías Preciados and just a short walk from the Gran Vía and the Puerta del Sol. The lobby retains its air of elegance.

HOTEL ATLÁNTICO, Gran Vía, 38, 28013 Madrid. Tel. 91/522-64-80. 63 rms with bath. MINIBAR TEL **Metro:** Gran Vía.

$ **Rates** (including continental breakfast): 6,500 ptas. ($61.10) single; 9,300 ptas. ($87.40) double; 12,400 ptas. ($116.55) triple. AE, DC, MC, V.

Newly refurbished, this hotel occupies the third and fourth floors of a grand turn-of-the-century building on a corner of Madrid's major artery. Established in 1989 as a Best Western affiliate, it offers security boxes in its well-furnished bedrooms. Off the third-floor lobby, where you register, is an English-inspired bar open 24 hours a day. Snacks are also available.

NEAR THE PLAZA DE ESPAÑA

CASÓN DEL TORMES, Río, 7, 28013 Madrid. Tel. 91/541-97-46. Fax 91/541-18-52. 61 rms with bath. A/C TV TEL **Metro:** Plaza de España.

$ **Rates:** 5,400 ptas. ($50.75) single; 7,800 ptas. ($73.30) double. Breakfast 450 ptas. ($4.25) extra. MC, V.

An unusually attractive three-star hotel around the corner from the Royal Palace and the Plaza de España, the Casón del Tormes is a four-story red-brick structure with stone-trimmed modern windows overlooking a quiet one-way street. The lobby, which fills most of the ground floor, is graced with lots of grained vertical paneling, a Spanish refectory table, and glass display cases containing silver and copper serving dishes. Breakfast tables are set up on the marble floors, and there is a bar. Public parking available in the nearby Plaza de España.

PRÍNCIPE PÍO, Cuesta de San Vincente, 16, 28008 Madrid. Tel. 91/247-08-00. Fax 91/541-11-17. 160 rms with bath. A/C TV TEL **Metro:** Plaza de España.

$ **Rates** (including continental breakfast): 6,500 ptas. ($61.10) single; 9,000 ptas. ($84.60) double. AE, MC, V.

The whizzing traffic heard in the front rooms of the Príncipe Pío doesn't appeal to some, while the location—within a short walk to the Royal Palace, the Plaza de España, and the Gran Vía—makes it perfect for others. The bedrooms, all with private bath (many singles and doubles with shower, but no bathtub), are comfortable and clean; furnishings are modern. A lunch or dinner costs 2,200 pesetas ($20.70). The hotel has its own garage.

NEAR THE PUERTA DEL SOL

HOTEL RESIDENCIA CORTEZO, Doctor Cortezo, 3, 28012 Madrid. Tel.

91/239-38-00. Fax 91/239-69-22. 90 rms with bath. A/C MINIBAR TV TEL **Metro:** Tirso de Molina.
$ Rates: 5,500 ptas. ($51.70) single; 8,000 ptas. ($75.20) double. Breakfast 475 ptas. ($4.45) extra. AE, MC, V.

Just off the Calle de Atocha, which leads to the railroad station of the same name, the hotel is a short walk from the Plaza Mayor and the Puerta del Sol. The accommodations are comfortable and attractive, with contemporary baths. The beds are springy, the colors well chosen, the furniture pleasantly modern; often there is a sitting area with a desk and armchair. The public rooms match the bedrooms in freshness.

IN THE SALAMANCA DISTRICT

HOSTAL RESIDENCIA DON DIEGO, Velázquez, 45, 28801 Madrid. Tel. 91/435-07-60. 58 rms with bath. TEL **Metro:** Velázquez.
$ Rates: 5,500 ptas. ($51.70) single; 7,800 ptas. ($73.30) double. Breakfast 425 ptas. ($4) extra. AE, V.

The Hostal Residencia Don Diego, convenient to many of the city's monuments, is on the fifth floor of an elevator building whose vestibule contains an elegant winding staircase with iron griffin heads supporting its balustrade. The place is inviting, filled with leather couches and comfortable furniture. There's a bar in the main sitting room where businesspeople usually gather.

WORTH THE EXTRA BUCKS

HOSTAL EMBAJADA, Santa Engracía, 5, 28010 Madrid. Tel. 91/447-33-00. 65 rms with bath. TEL **Metro:** Alonso Martínez.
$ Rates: 6,000 ptas. ($56.40) single; 10,000 ptas. ($94) double. Breakfast 475 ptas. ($4.45) extra. V.

Housed in a 1920s building, the Embajoda is a clean, pleasant three-star hostal a block from the Plaza Alonso Martínez, a distinguished residential area, and near the Puerta del Sol. The rooms are tastefully decorated. There's a modest lounge with no bar.

GRAND HOTEL TRYP VELÁZQUEZ, Velázquez, 62, 28001 Madrid. Tel. 91/575-28-00. Fax 91/575-28-00. 144 rms with bath. A/C MINIBAR TV TEL **Metro:** Velázquez.
$ Rates (including continental breakfast): 10,700 ptas. ($100.60) single; 14,000 ptas. ($131.60) double. AE, DC, MC, V.

The façade of the Grand Hotel Tryp Velázquez, facing an affluent street in the city center off the Paseo de la Castellana, qualifies as pure art deco. The interior is filled with well-upholstered furniture and richly grained paneling. Several public rooms are lined with marble and contain 19th-century bronzes; one of these rooms includes a bar with a reproduction of a 17th-century hunting scene. As for the individualized

 FROMMER'S COOL FOR KIDS
HOTELS

Most Madrid hotels are designed for adults. Scant attention is paid to kids. There is one exception, notably: **Novotel Madrid** (see p. 76). Children under 16 stay free in their parents' room, where the sofa converts into a comfortable bed. Kids delight in the open-air swimming pool and the offerings of the breakfast buffet.

accommodations, some are large enough for entertaining. Guests will find parking available on the premises. Expensive for our budget but very reasonable for its four-star status, this is one of the most attractive medium-size hotels in Madrid, offering both comfort and convenience.

NOVOTEL MADRID, Albacete, 1, 28027 Madrid. Tel. 91/405-46-00. Fax 91/404-11-05. 236 rms with bath. A/C MINIBAR TV TEL **Metro:** Concepción.
$ Rates (including continental breakfast): 12,000 ptas. ($112.80) single; 14,300 ptas. ($134.40) double. Children under 16 stay free in parents' room. AE, DC, MC, V.

The Novotel Madrid, at the corner of Avenida Badajoz, was intended to service a cluster of multinational corporations nearby. But its rooms are so comfortable and its prices so reasonable that sightseers have begun to stay here as well. One of the newer hotels in town, with an enthusiastic staff, it's a bit removed from the center of town; late-arriving motorists, however, find its location beside the M30 a viable alternative to the maze of Madrid's inner-city streets. (Exit from the M30 at the Barrio de la Concepción/Parque de las Avenidas, just before the city limits of central Madrid.) Each of the comfortably furnished bedrooms offers a color TV with in-house movies, a well-designed bathroom, radio, and access to an English-speaking reception desk. There's an attractive indoor/outdoor restaurant ringed with lattices, a cozy bar, and a swimming pool.

HOTEL CHAMARTÍN, Estación de Chamartín, 28036 Madrid. Tel. 91/733-90-11. Fax 91/733-02-14. 378 rms with bath. A/C MINIBAR TV TEL **Metro:** Chamartín.
$ Rates (including buffet breakfast): 11,000 ptas. ($103.40) single; 14,700 ptas. ($138.20) double. AE, DC, MC, V.

This nine-story hotel, part of the transportation and shopping complex in the modern train station, is owned by RENFE (the government railroad system) and operated by Entursa Hotels. The Chamartín is the first of the company's budget properties. It's 15 minutes from the airport and 5 minutes from the city's major business and sightseeing areas. Each room features a radio, safe, and specially insulated windows for maximum quiet and privacy. There are a coffee bar serving a buffet breakfast daily, a bar off the main lobby, and room service. Guests can dine at a variety of restaurants in the Chamartín complex. Among the extensive facilities and services are 13 shops, four movie theaters, a roller-skating rink, a disco, and ample parking. Especially oriented to the business traveler, the Chamartín also offers a currency exchange, travel agency, bank, car rental, and complete communication services.

2. WHERE TO EAT

Note: A list of **restaurants by cuisine** appears in the Index.

MEALS FOR LESS THAN 1,500 PTAS. ($14.10)

CHUECA

LA ARGENTINA, Válgame Dios, 8. Tel. 531-91-17.
Cuisine: INTERNATIONAL. **Reservations:** Not required. **Metro:** Chueca.
$ Prices: Appetizers 300–400 ptas. ($2.80–$3.75); main dishes 400–700 ptas. ($3.75–$6.60); fixed-priced menu 1,050 ptas. ($9.85). No credit cards.
Open: Lunch Tues–Sun noon–4pm; dinner Tues–Sun 9pm–12:45am. **Closed:** Aug.

S Two blocks away from Nuevo Oliver, at the corner of Calle Gravina, La Argentina is run under the watchful eye of its owner, Andrés Rodríguez. The restaurant has only 16 tables, but the food is tops. The best bets are cannelloni Rossini, noodle soup, creamed spinach, and meat dishes, including entrecote or roast veal. Chicken Villaroy is another special. All dishes are served with mashed or french-fried potatoes. For dessert, have a baked apple or rice pudding. The decor is simple and clean, and you're usually served by one of the two waitresses who have been here for years.

EL INCA, Gravina, 23. Tel. 532-77-45.
  Cuisine: PERUVIAN. **Reservations:** Recommended. **Metro:** Chueca.
  $ Prices: Appetizers 250–400 ptas. ($2.35–$3.75); main dishes 500–800 ptas. ($4.70–$7.50). AC, DC, MC, V.
  Open: Lunch daily 1:30–4pm; dinner Mon–Sat 9pm–midnight. **Closed:** Last 2 weeks in Aug.

S For a taste of South America, try El Inca, decorated with Incan motifs and artifacts. Since it opened a decade ago, it has hosted its share of diplomats and celebrities, although you're more likely to see families and local office workers. The house cocktail is a deceptively potent *pisco* sour—the recipe comes straight from the Andes. Many of the dishes contain potatoes, the national staple of Peru. The potato-and-black-olive salad is given an unusual zest with a white-cheese sauce. Other specialties are the *cebiche de merluza* (raw hake marinated with onions) and *aji de gallina* (a chicken-and-rice dish made with peanut sauce), a Peruvian favorite.

TIENDA DE VINOS, Augusto Figueroa, 35. Tel. 521-70-12.
  Cuisine: SPANISH. **Reservations:** None. **Metro:** Chueca.
  $ Prices: Appetizers 250–350 ptas. ($2.35–$3.30); main dishes 550–750 ptas. ($5.15–$7.05). No credit cards.
  Open: Breakfast/lunch Mon–Sat 9am–4:30pm; dinner Mon–Sat 8:30pm–midnight.
Officially, this restaurant is known as Tienda de Vinos, but in-the-know Madrileños have inexplicably dubbed it *"El Communista."* This rather rickety old wine shop, with a few tables in the back, is quite fashionable with actors and journalists looking for Spanish fare without frills. There is a menu, but no one ever thinks of asking for it—just ask what's available. Nor do you get a bill; you're just told how much. You sit at wooden tables and on wooden chairs and benches placed around the walls, which are decorated with old posters, calendars, pennants, and clocks. Start with garlic or vegetable soup or lentils, followed by lamb chops.

TABERNA CARMENCITA, Libertad, 16. Tel. 531-66-12.
  Cuisine: SPANISH. **Reservations:** Recommended. **Metro:** Chueca.
  $ Prices: Appetizers 600–800 ptas. ($5.65–$7.50); main dishes 800–1,800 ptas. ($7.50–$16.90); fixed-priced menu 950 ptas. ($8.95). AE, DC, V.
  Open: Lunch Mon–Sat noon–5pm; dinner Mon–Sat 8pm–midnight.

S Carmencita is a street-corner enclave of old Spanish charm, filled with 19th-century detailing and tilework that witnessed the conversations of a former patron, the poet Federico García Lorca. Meals might include entrecote with a green-pepper sauce, escalope of veal, braised mollusks with port, filet of pork, codfish with garlic, and Bilbao-style hake. Every Thursday the special dish is a complicated version of the famous *cocido* (stew) of Madrid.

ARRUMBAMBAYA, Libertad, 23. Tel. 521-72-24.
  Cuisine: SPANISH. **Reservations:** Not required. **Metro:** Chueca.
  $ Prices: Appetizers 450–650 ptas. ($4.25–$6.10); main dishes 1,300–1,550 ptas. ($12.20–$14.55); fixed price menu 1,000 ptas. ($9.40). V.
  Open: Lunch Wed–Mon 1–4pm; dinner Wed–Sun 8:30–11:30pm.
Arrumbambaya is a Galician establishment on a street of relatively undiscovered budget restaurants. In its heyday it was frequented by the Spanish writer Federico García Lorca. You pass through a bar to enter the dining room, with its rectangular stone masonry, brick arch, and timbered ceiling. If the atmosphere today is a bit

contrived, the reception is still warm. You might want to try the famed *caldo gallego* (potatoes-and-greens broth from Galicia); however, the cook doesn't make it every day. Other main dishes include *bacalao a pil-pil* (hake in either Basque or Galician style) and trout Navarre style. A *zarzuela* of shellfish is a popular item, as is the roast lamb.

NEAR THE EUROBUILDING

CHEZ LOU CRÊPERIE, Pedro Murguruza, 6. Tel. 250-34-16.
   Cuisine: FRENCH. **Reservations:** Recommended. **Metro:** Plaza de Castilla.
$ **Prices:** Appetizers 200–400 ptas. ($1.90–$3.75); crêpes 450–700 ptas. ($4.25–$6.60). AE, DC, MC, V.
   Open: Lunch Sun, Tues–Fri 1–4pm; dinner Tues–Sun 8pm–1am.
Chez Lou stands near a huge mural by Joan Miró, which alone would be worth the trek. This cozy little place evokes a small French inn and appeals to an international crowd. In this intimate setting you'll get well-prepared and reasonably priced French food. The restaurant serves pâté as an appetizer, then a large range of crêpes with many different fillings—one will make a perfectly adequate main course. I've sampled several variations, finding the ingredients nicely blended, yet each retaining a distinct identity. A favorite is the large crêpe stuffed with minced onions, cream, and smoked salmon. The ham-and-cheese variety is also tasty. This is the place to go if you want a light supper—when it's too hot for a full Spanish meal.

NEAR THE GLORIETA DE QUEVEDO

HOLLYWOOD, Magallanes, 1. Tel. 448-91-65.
   Cuisine: AMERICAN. **Reservations:** Recommended Sat–Sun. **Metro:** Quevedo.
$ **Prices:** Appetizers 250–400 ptas. ($2.35–$3.75); main dishes 550–1,200 ptas. ($5.15–$11.30). AE, DC, MC, V.
   Open: Sun–Thurs 1pm–1am, Fri–Sat 1pm–2am.
A popular hangout for locals and visiting Yanks—a place both for eating and for being seen—is Hollywood. This fashionable California-style hamburger joint serves the best *yanqui* food in Madrid. The terrace, one of the city's most comfortable, is great for people watching. Inside, it's nostalgia time, with bentwood chairs and many framed photographs and posters. Hamburgers weigh in at a half pound, including one with cheese, bacon strips, and Russian dressing; they are served with french fries and salad. Other treats: chili con carne, homemade apple pie, cheesecake, and, as reported in the *New York Times,* "probably the best onion rings in the world."

NEAR THE GOYA PANTHEON

CASA MINGO, Paseo de la Florida, 2. Tel. 247-10-98.
   Cuisine: SPANISH. **Reservations:** None. **Metro:** Norte, then a 15-minute walk.
$ **Prices:** Main dishes 450–800 ptas. ($4.25–$7.50). No credit cards.
   Open: Daily 11am–midnight.
Casa Mingo has been known for decades for its Asturian cider, both still and bubbly. The perfect accompanying tidbit is a piece of the local Asturian *cabrales* (goat cheese), but the roast chicken is the specialty of the house, with an unbelievable number of helpings served daily. There's no formality here, as customers share big tables under the vaulted ceiling in the dining room. In summer the staff places some tables and wooden chairs outdoors on the sidewalk.

NORTH OF THE GRAN VÍA

KUOPIN RESTAURANTE CHINO, Valverde, 6. Tel. 532-34-65.
   Cuisine: CHINESE. **Reservations:** Not required. **Metro:** Gran Vía.
$ **Prices:** Appetizers 200–350 ptas. ($1.90–$3.30); main dishes 400–750 ptas.

FROMMER'S SMART
TRAVELER—RESTAURANTS

VALUE-CONSCIOUS TRAVELERS SHOULD CONSIDER THE FOLLOWING:

1. Most budget restaurants offer a *cubierto* or *menú del día*. It's not very adventurous, and limited in selections, but in most cases it is at least 30% cheaper than ordering à la carte.
2. Often major restaurants will offer a *menú del día* at lunch—the Madrid equivalent of a businessperson's lunch—but will revert to expensive à la carte listings in the evening. Check the menu offerings posted outside the restaurant.
3. Patronize the *tascas* (local taverns), and order 2 or 3 *tapas* (hors d'oeuvres). Most portions are generous, and you can dine for one quarter of the price you'd pay in most restaurants.
4. Look for the *platos del días* (daily specials). They're invariably fresh, and usually carry a much lower price tag than regular à la carte listings.
5. Ask for the *vino de la casa* or house wine. This wine is served in a carafe and is only a fraction of the cost of bottled wines.
6. Anything consumed standing up at a counter or sitting on a bar stool is cheaper than at a table.
7. Patronize the famous budget restaurant streets of Madrid: Calle del Barco, Ventura de la Vega, and Calle Echegaray.

($3.75–$7.05); fixed-priced menu 750 ptas. ($7.05).
Open: Lunch daily noon–4pm; dinner daily 8pm–midnight.
Kuopin has conventional Chinese decor including the usual large lanterns. Many of your fellow diners will be Chinese—a fairly good gauge of authenticity and value. The chef's special budget dinner features egg-drop soup, sweet-and-sour pork, and ice cream, with bread and beverage included. A la carte temptations are sweet corn, egg, and chicken soup; Cantonese shrimp; and roast pork.

CAPRI, Barco, 27. Tel. 522-12-80.
Cuisine: SPANISH. **Reservations:** Not required. **Metro:** Gran Vía.
$ Prices: Appetizers 200–400 ptas. ($1.90–$3.75); main dishes 450–750 ptas. ($4.25–$7.05); fixed-priced menu 1,000 ptas. ($9.40).
Open: Lunch Mon–Sat 1–4pm; dinner Mon–Sat 8:30–11pm.
This is the Spanish equivalent of a French bistro. Foreigners are welcomed, but not catered to in the way more commercially oriented establishments treat their new customers. The restaurant is housed in a glass-fronted section of an old townhouse. The chef's *sopa de mariscos* (seafood soup) costs less than anywhere else in Madrid. The roast half chicken is a good buy, as are the freshly sliced tomatoes ordered as a salad. Best bet—select your main dish from Capri's plates of the day.

PAGASARRI, Barco, 7. Tel. 532-68-89.
Cuisine: SPANISH. **Reservations:** Recommended. **Metro:** Gran Vía.
$ Prices: Appetizers 200–400 ptas. ($1.90–$3.75); main dishes 450–750 ptas. ($4.25–$7.05); fixed-price menu 900 ptas. ($8.45). V.
Open: Lunch Tues–Sun 1–4pm; dinner Tues–Sat 8:30–11pm.
There's likely to be a line waiting outside for the 1pm opening of this family-style restaurant (air-conditioned). You are often asked to share tables. Paella is served as an appetizer on certain days, and the chef prepares a dozen different varieties of omelets.

MESÓN LAS MEIGAS, Barbieri, 6. Tel. 532-85-76.
Cuisine: SPANISH. **Reservations:** Recommended. **Metro:** Banco de España.

Abanico Gastronómico, El **1**
Alfredo's Barbacoa **2**
Anciano Rey de los Vinos, El **3**
António Sánchez **4**
Argentina, La **5**
Aroca **6**
Arrumbambaya **7**
Bilbaino, El **8**
Bola, La **9**
Burger King **10**
Café de l'Oriente **11**
Callejón, El **12**
Capri **13**
Casa Ciriaco **14**
Casa Mingo **15**
Casa Paco **16**
Casa Sierra **17**
Casablanca **18**
Cervecería Alemania **19**
Cervecería Santa Barbara **20**
Charlot Food Shop **21**
Chata, La **22**
Chez Lou Crêperie **23**
Corte Inglés Cafeteria **24**
Cuchi, El **25**
Cuevas del Duque, Las **26**
Dolores, La **27**
Edelweiss **28**
El Inca **29**
Embassy Tearoom **30**
Espejo, El **31**
Fast Pizza **32**
Galayos, Los **33**
Galette, La **34**
Helen's **35**
Hollywood **36**
Hylogui **37**
Kentucky Fried Chicken **38**
Kuopin Restaurant Chino **39**
Lacon, El **40**
Lhardy **41**
Luarques **42**
Mallorca Food Shop **43**
McDonald's **44**
Mesón d'a Morrina **45**
Meson las Descalzas **46**
Meson las Meigas **47**
Motivos, Los **48**
Nabucco **49**
Paellería Valenciana **50**
Pagasarri **51**
Pazo de Monterrey, El **52**
Pizza King **53**
Platerías Comedor **54**

Plaza, La **55**
Ríofrío **56**
Rodilla Food Shop **57**
Schotis, El **58**
Sobrino de Botín

Taberna Carmencita **60**
Taberna del Alabardero **61**
Taberna Toscana **62**

Tienda de Vinos **63**
Trucha, La **64**
V.I.P. **65**
Vera Cruz **66**

MADRID DINING

$ Prices: Appetizers 550–650 ptas. ($3.30–$6.10); main dishes 1,200–1,450 ptas. ($11.30–$13.65); fixed-priced menu 950 ptas. ($8.95). MC, V.
Open: Lunch Tues–Sat 1–4pm; dinner Tues–Sun 8pm–midnight.

Las Meigas is on a short street of tascas and low-priced restaurants—none of which live up to this *mesón*. The front room is like that of a country inn, with hanging garlic strings, sausages, and smoked hams. The dining room in the rear continues with the same rural ambience: hay forks, oxen yokes, and an open fireplace with an iron crane for pots of Galician soup. In all, it's a comfortable atmosphere, with spirited waiters who chop off hunks of whole-grain crusty bread, serving them with a jug of wine at your table. I recommend the caldo gallego, hearty with greens and potatoes. Another regional specialty is the *lacón con grelos* (boiled hamhock with greens). The *mariscada* special, a huge plate of shellfish, can be served for two, four, or six people. An appropriate beverage is the *sangría de vino ribeiro*.

NEAR THE PLAZA DEL CALLAO

MESÓN LAS DESCALZAS, Postigo San Martín, 3. Tel. 522-72-17.
   Cuisine: SPANISH. **Reservations:** Recommended. **Metro:** Callao.
$ Prices: Appetizers 450–650 ptas. ($4.25–$6.10); main dishes 1,300–1,500 ptas. ($12.20–$14.10); fixed-price menu, 1,000 ptas. ($9.40). AE, DC, MC, V.
   Open: Daily 10am–midnight.

Las Descalzas, a recommended tavern-style restaurant, sits behind a red façade accented with a black metal sign. Inside, you'll be greeted with a massive tapas bar, often crowded at night. Behind a glass-and-wood screen is the restaurant section, its specialties including kidneys with sherry, sopa castellana, seafood soup, Basque-style hake, crayfish, shrimp, oysters, clams, and paella with shellfish. For entertainment, there is folk music.

NEAR THE PLAZA DE COLÓN

RÍOFRÍO, Centro Colón, Plaza de Colón, 1. Tel. 419-29-77.
   Cuisine: SPANISH. **Reservations:** Not required. **Metro:** Colón.
$ Prices: Appetizers 350–750 ptas. ($3.30–$7.05); main dishes 600–1,300 ptas. ($5.65–$12.20).
   Open: Lunch daily noon–4:30pm; dinner daily 7:30pm–1:30am.

Ríofrío is an ideal central place for on-the-run snacks and drinks. Its terrace, overlooking the "Columbus Circle of Madrid," is favored on sunny days; otherwise, there is a more formal interior where you can get substantial meals, as well as a self-service section. You can order club sandwiches or perhaps an appetizing combination plate. The Spanish coffee is good here (but different), and you can also drop in just to order a refreshing drink, alcoholic or otherwise.

GRAN CAFÉ DE GIJÓN, Paseo de Recoletos, 21. Tel. 521-54-25.
   Cuisine: CAFE. **Reservations:** None. **Metro:** Banco de España, Colón, or Recoletos.
$ Prices: Meals from 2,000 ptas. ($18.80); drinks from 550 ptas. ($5.05).
   Open: Daily 9–1am; meals Mon–Sat 1–4pm and 9pm–midnight.

All old European capitals have a coffeehouse that traditionally attracts the literati—in Madrid it's the Gijón, which opened in 1890 in the heyday of the city's Bella Epoca. Artists and writers still patronize this venerated old café, many of them spending hours over one cup of coffee. The place has open street windows looking out onto the wide paseo, as well as a large terrace for sun worshipers and birdwatchers. Along one side of the café is a stand-up bar, and on the lower level is a restaurant. A set menu consists of two dishes, bread, wine or beer, and dessert, with main dishes varying daily. In summer you can sit in the garden, enjoying a *blanco y negro* (black coffee with ice cream) or mixed drinks.

AT THE PLAZA DE CUZCO

ALFREDO'S BARBACOA, Juan Hurtado de Mendoza, 11. Tel. 457-85-56.

Cuisine: AMERICAN. **Reservations:** Recommended. **Metro:** Cuzco.
$ Prices: Appetizers 425–550 ptas. ($4–$5.15); main dishes 725–1,200 ptas. ($6.80–$11.30). AE, DC, MC, V.
Open: Lunch Mon–Thurs and Sun 1–4:30pm, Fri 1–5pm; dinner Mon–Thurs and Sat 8:30pm–midnight, Fri 8:30pm–1am.

Alfredo's is a popular rendezvous for Americans longing for home-style food other than hamburgers. Al directs his bar/restaurant wearing boots, blue jeans, and a ten-gallon hat; his friendly welcome has made the place a center for both his friends and newcomers to Madrid. You *can* have hamburgers here, but they are of the barbecued variety, and you might prefer the barbecued spareribs or chicken. The salad bar is an attraction. And it's a rare treat to be able to have corn on the cob. The original Alfredo's Barbacoa, Lagasca, 5 (tel. 276-62-71), is still in business, also under Al's auspices.

NEAR THE PLAZA DE ESPAÑA

VERA CRUZ, San Leonardo, 5. Tel. 247-54-41.
 Cuisine: SPANISH. **Reservations:** Not required. **Metro:** Plaza de España.
$ Prices: Appetizers 250–450 ptas. ($2.35–$4.25); main dishes 450–750 ptas. ($4.25–$7.05); fixed-price menu 750 ptas. ($7.05). No credit cards.
Open: Daily 9am–1am.

S Behind the Plaza de España, with its landmark Edificio España, you'll find this old standby for hungry budget-minded visitors. It's a simple *económico,* but the food is acceptable and the service polite. The *menú del día* usually includes soup or hors d'oeuvres, followed by a meat or fish dish, then cheese or fruit, plus bread and wine. The Vera Cruz also has daily specials like paella or cocido, a typical Madrid dish made of chick peas, sausage, cabbage, and potatoes.

MESÓN D'A MORRIÑA, Leganitos, 33. Tel. 247-10-62.
 Cuisine: SPANISH. **Reservations:** Recommended. **Metro:** Plaza de España.
$ Prices: Appetizers 550–700 ptas. ($5.15–$6.60); main dishes 800–1,100 ptas. ($7.50–$10.35); fixed-priced menu 1,200 ptas. ($11.30). AE, DC, MC, V.
Open: Lunch daily 1–4pm; dinner daily 8:30pm–midnight.

A Galician restaurant near the Plaza de España and the Gran Vía, Mesón d'a Morriña lies on a nondescript street behind a stone façade lightened by a big window displaying the dried meats and fish you might eventually find served on your plate. Against one wall there's a long stand-up bar where you can have a preprandial glass of sherry. From your vantage point in front of an awesome array of tapas (the more exotic of which you may want to avoid), you'll see hanging garlands of garlic and a full assortment of hams. The restaurant section is decorated tavern style, with overhead beams, red tablecloths, and an occasional troupe of musicians who complement the welcome and service with their singing, mandolins, and guitars. Specialties include roast lamb, rabbit, Galician-style hake, roast suckling pig, and paella with shellfish.

NEAR THE PLAZA SANTA ANA

EL BILBAÍNO, Ventura de la Vega, 11–13. Tel. 429-76-06.
 Cuisine: SPANISH. **Reservations:** Not required. **Metro:** Puerta del Sol or Sevilla.
$ Prices: Appetizers 450–1,800 ptas. ($4.25–$16.90); main dishes 425–2,100 ptas. ($4–$19.75). AE, V.
Open: Lunch Mon–Sat 1–4pm; dinner Mon–Sat 8:45–11:30pm.

This restaurant is known in the neighborhood as a comfortable, unpretentious place that serves generous portions at reasonable prices. It contains a trio of long and narrow dining rooms accented with granite floors and mahogany paneling and trim. Vested waiters give good service. Although the cuisine reflects the national Spanish repertoire, it concentrates on Basque dishes. Specialties include filet of veal, fresh filet of tuna *vizcaína, calamares* (deep-fried squid), and a full choice of grilled meats.

HYLOGUI, Ventura de la Vega, 3. Tel. 429-73-57.
   Cuisine: SPANISH. **Reservations:** Recommended. **Metro:** Sevilla.
$ **Prices:** Appetizers 250–750 ptas. ($2.35–$7.05); main dishes 650–1,200 ptas. ($6.10–$11.30). No credit cards.
   Open: Lunch daily 1–4:30pm; dinner Mon–Sat 9pm–midnight.
Hylogui is one of the largest dining rooms along Ventura de la Vega, but there are many arches and nooks for privacy. One globe-trotting American wrote enthusiastically that he took all his meals here in Madrid, finding the soup pleasant and rich, the flan soothing, the regional wine dry. The food is old-fashioned Spanish home-style cooking.

EL LACÓN RESTAURANTE, Manuel Fernández González, 8. Tel. 429-60-42.
   Cuisine: SPANISH. **Reservations:** Recommended. **Metro:** Sevilla.
$ **Prices:** Appetizers 600–800 ptas. ($5.65–$7.50); main dishes 850–950 ptas. ($8–$8.95); fixed-price menu 1,200 ptas. ($11.30). No credit cards.
   Open: Lunch Thurs–Tues noon–4pm; dinner Thurs–Tues 8pm–1am.
El Lacón is a large, colorful country-inn restaurant with good food, a rustic atmosphere, and moderate prices, considering that it's been so expensively created. Rough white beams, hanging hams, lanterns, crude tables, and an antique-gun collection adorn the interior. Before dining on the mezzanine, order tapas in an old-world-style bar in the cellar. One of the chef's specialties is *bacalao vizcaína* (codfish Basque style). The clams in a marinara sauce are also tasty, as are the shrimp with garlic and the hamhock with greens.

LUARQUÉS, Ventura de la Vega, 16. Tel. 429-61-74.
   Cuisine: SPANISH. **Reservations:** None. **Metro:** Sevilla.
$ **Prices:** Appetizers 550–650 ptas. ($5.15–$6.10); main dishes 1,400–1,600 ptas. ($13.15–$15.05); fixed price-menu 1,500 ptas. ($14.10). No credit cards.
   Open: Lunch daily 1–4:30pm; dinner Mon–Sat 9–11:30pm. **Closed:** Aug.
Open since 1966, Luarqués dishes up some of the most savory meals on this street. It's not the cheapest place, offering a set meal of four *platos,* plus bread and wine for 1,500 pesetas ($14.10); but considering what you get, it's a fair buy. The restaurant serves all the standard dishes that are the hallmark of the Spanish cuisine: gazpacho, paella, flan, sopa de pescado (fish soup), and roast chicken.

NEAR THE PRADO

LA PLAZA, La Galería del Prado, Plaza de las Cortes. Tel. 429-65-37.
   Cuisine: SPANISH. **Reservations:** Not required. **Metro:** Sevilla.
$ **Prices:** Appetizers 250–500 ptas. ($2.35–$4.70); main dishes 600–750 ptas. ($5.65–$7.05). AE, MC, V.
   Open: Mon–Fri 10am–11pm; Sat 10am–1pm.
Its location amid the marble walls of Madrid's most sophisticated shopping complex eliminates the possibility of windows. Nevertheless, this is one of the best choices for light, refreshing meals in an expensive neighborhood. It is also handy for quick meals if you're spending a day at the Prado. Some of its tables spill into the rotonda of the shopping mall; most diners, however, sit within a glossy series of lattices whose rooms form a garden-inspired enclave near a well-stocked salad bar (visits here are priced according to the portions you take). You might begin with Serrano ham or a mountain-fermented goat cheese, perhaps a homemade pâté. Daily specials include such dishes as ragoût of veal. Platters of pasta also make a zesty way to fill up.

NEAR THE PUERTA DEL SOL

CASA CIRIACO, Calle Mayor, 84. Tel. 248-50-66.
   Cuisine: SPANISH. **Reservations:** Recommended. **Metro:** Puerta del Sol.
$ **Prices:** Appetizers 350–600 ptas. ($3.30–$5.65); main dishes 650–1,100 ptas. ($6.10–$10.35).
   Open: Lunch Thurs–Tues 1–4pm; dinner Thurs–Tues 8pm–midnight. **Closed:** Aug.

A special restaurant in one of the most romantic parts of Old Madrid, Casa Ciriaco enjoys associations with the Spanish painter Ignacio Zuloaga. The Casa's definitely not out for the tourist traffic—in fact, foreigners are still regarded with a certain curiosity around here. The chef features dishes from Navarre and Andalusia, but Castilian specialties predominate. Gazpacho makes a fine opener, then you can order Navarre-style trout or tender slices of veal.

NEAR THE RETIRO PARK

LA GALETTE, Conde de Aranda, 11. Tel. 576-06-41.
   Cuisine: VEGETARIAN. **Reservations:** Recommended. **Metro:** Retiro.
$ **Prices:** Appetizers 250–300 ptas. ($2.35–$2.80); main dishes 450–650 ptas. ($4.25–$6.10); fixed-price menu 1,800 ptas. ($16.90). No credit cards.
   Open: Lunch Mon–Sat 2–4pm; dinner Mon–Sat 9pm–midnight.
Madrid doesn't have many vegetarian restaurants, but La Galette remains one of the best. Small and charming, it lies in the Salamanca district, near the Plaza de la Independencia. The kitchen prepares a number of dishes for meat eaters, but vegetarians can enjoy baked stuffed peppers, omelets, eggplant croquettes, and even a vegetarian "hamburger." Some dishes are macrobiotic. La Galette is noted for its mouthwatering pastries.

MEALS FOR LESS THAN 2,800 PTAS. ($26.30)

CHUECA

NABUCCO, Hortaleza, 108. Tel. 410-06-11.
   Cuisine: ITALIAN. **Reservations:** Recommended. **Metro:** Alonso Martínez.
$ **Prices:** Pizzas 500–680 ptas. ($4.70–$6.40); appetizers 400–700 ptas. ($3.75–$6.60); main dishes 725–1,300 ptas. ($6.80–$12.20). AE, DC, MC, V.
   Open: Lunch Mon–Thurs 1:30–4pm; dinner Mon–Thurs 9pm–midnight; lunch Fri–Sat 1:30–4pm; dinner Fri–Sat 9pm–1am.
In a neighborhood of Spanish restaurants, the Italian format comes as a welcome change. The decor resembles a postmodern update of an Italian ruin, complete with trompe-l'oeil walls painted like marble. Roman portrait busts and a prominent bar lend a dignified air. Menu choices include cannelloni, a good selection of veal dishes, and such main courses as osso buco. You might begin your meal with a selection of antipasti, and for dessert, try the chocolate mousse.

IN MEDIEVAL MADRID

LA CHATA, Cava Baja, 24. Tel. 266-14-58.
   Cuisine: SPANISH. **Reservations:** Recommended. **Metro:** La Latina.
$ **Prices:** Appetizers 700–2,800 ptas. ($6.60–$26.30); main dishes 1,100–2,600 ptas. ($10.35–$24.45). No credit cards.
   Open: Lunch Mon, Wed–Sat 12:20–5pm; dinner Sun–Mon, Wed–Sat 8pm–midnight or 2am.
The cuisine here is Castilian, Galician, and northern Spanish. Set behind a heavily ornamented tile façade, the place has a stand-up tapas bar at the entrance and a formal restaurant in a side room. Many locals linger at the darkly paneled bar, which is framed by hanging Serrano hams, cloves of garlic, and photographs of bullfighters. Full meals might include such specialties as roast suckling pig, roast lamb, *calamares en su tinta* (squid in its own ink), grilled filet of steak with peppercorns, and omelets flavored with strips of eel.

AROCA, Plaza de los Carros, 3. Tel. 265-26-26.
   Cuisine: SPANISH. **Reservations:** Recommended. **Metro:** La Latina.
$ **Prices:** Appetizers 900 ptas. ($8.45); main dishes, 1,500–2,000 ptas. ($14.10–$18.80); fixed-price menu 2,300 ptas. ($21.60).
   Open: Lunch Mon–Sat 2–4pm; dinner Mon–Sat 9pm–midnight. **Closed:** Aug.

About a 10-minute walk southwest of the Plaza Mayor, this simple tavern refuses to be swept up in modern fads. Its allure lies in the fact that almost no changes have occurred in its cooking techniques in a century. The place dates from the 1880s, when it was established as a wine shop. Each generation of the Aroca family has staffed it since, including today's head chef, María Aroca. The never-varying food is often served with Rioja wines. Begin with a chunky version of seafood soup, perhaps going on to boiled prawns with an aromatic mayonnaise, lamb cutlets, fried chicken, or (when available) Galician oysters. On the side, you can have a simple but refreshing tomato-and-lettuce salad or an order of *croquetas* (fried dumplings studded with morsels of ham).

NORTH OF THE GRAN VÍA

PAELLERÍA VALENCIANA, Caballero de Gracia, 12. Tel. 531-17-875.
    Cuisine: SPANISH. **Reservations:** Recommended. **Metro:** Gran Vía.
$ Prices: Appetizers 450–650 ptas. ($4.25–$6.10); main dishes, 850–1,800 ptas. ($8–$16.90); fixed-price menu 2,500 ptas. ($23.50). V.
    Open: Lunch Tues–Sun 1–4pm.
This lunch-only restaurant ranks as one of the best in the city for value. The specialty is paella, which you must order by phone in advance. Once you arrive, you might begin with a homemade soup or the house salad, then follow with the paella, served in an iron skillet. At least two must order this rib-sticking fare. The choice of desserts includes the chef's special pride, razor-thin orange slices flavored with rum, coconut, sugar, honey, and raspberry sauce. A carafe of house wine comes with the set menu, and after lunch the owner comes around dispensing free cognac.

LAS CUEVAS DEL DUQUE, Duque de Liria, 9. Tel. 248-50-37.
    Cuisine: SPANISH. **Reservations:** Recommended. **Metro:** Ventura Rodríguez.
$ Prices: Appetizers (not offered); main dishes 900–1800 ptas. ($8.45–$16.90). AE, DC, MC, V.
    Open: Lunch daily 1–4pm; dinner daily 8pm–midnight.
In front of the Duke of Alba's palace, a short walk from the Plaza de España, is Las Cuevas del Duque, with an underground bar and a small, 10-table mesón that serves such simple Spanish fare as roast suckling pig, sirloin, lamb cutlet, and a few seafood dishes, including fish cooked in salt. In fair weather a few tables are set outside, beside a tiny triangular garden. Other tables line the Calle de la Princesa side and make an enjoyable roost for an afternoon drink.

NEAR THE ÓPERA

LA BOLA, Bola, 5. Tel. 247-30-90.
    Cuisine: SPANISH. **Reservations:** Recommended. **Metro:** Ópera.
$ Prices: Appetizers 500–975 ptas. ($4.75–$9.15); main dishes 900–1,600 ptas. ($9.40–$15.05). Fixed-price menu 1,850 ptas. ($17.40). No credit cards.
    Open: Lunch Mon–Sat 1:15–4:30pm; dinner Mon–Sat 9–11pm.
Just north of the Teatro Real, La Bola dates from 1870. If you'd like to savor 19th-century Madrid, then this is an inspired choice: soft, traditional atmosphere, polite waiters, Venetian crystal, and aging velvet. A specialty is sopa Wamba, made with ham and rice and sprinkled with chopped hard-boiled eggs. The *pollo asado* (roast chicken) is always reliable, as is the sole meunière.

TABERNA DEL ALABARDERO, Felipe V, 6. Tel. 541-51-92.
    Cuisine: SPANISH. **Reservations:** Required (for restaurant only). **Metro:** Ópera.
$ Prices: Tapas (in the bar) 350–750 ptas. ($3.30–$7.05); glass of house wine 75 ptas. (75¢). Appetizers (in the restaurant) 400–975 ptas. ($3.75–$9.20); main dishes 1,000–1,800 ptas. ($9.40–$16.90). AE, DC, V.
    Open: Lunch daily 1–4pm; dinner daily 8:30pm–midnight.

Because of its proximity to the Royal Palace, most patrons visit this little Spanish gem for its selection of tasty tapas, ranging from squid cooked in wine to fried potatoes dipped in hot sauce. Photographs of former patrons, including Nelson Rockefeller and race-car driver Jackie Stewart, line the walls. The restaurant in the rear is said to be one of the city's "best-kept secrets." Decorated in typical tavern style, it serves a savory Spanish Basque cuisine with market-fresh ingredients.

ALONG THE PASEO DE LA CASTELLANA

HELEN'S, Paseo de la Castellana, 204. Tel. 458-63-77.
  Cuisine: SPANISH. **Reservations:** Required for lunch. **Metro:** Plaza de Castilla.
$ Prices: Sandwiches (in the bar) from 500 ptas. ($4.70). Appetizers (in the restaurant) 600–700 ptas. ($5.65–$6.60); main dishes 1,200–2,000 ptas. ($11.30–$18.80). AE, MC, V.
  Open: Daily 8am–11:30pm.
If you're staying near the Chamartín train station, you'll find Helen's a popular neighborhood bar with a restaurant in the back. In the front café/bar section, you can enjoy drinks, coffee, and a simple selection of sandwiches. If you go on from the bar to the inner room, you can order a delectable fish soup, stuffed pimientos, filet mignon, and a wide array of fish, veal, and steaks. Fresh sardines will be brought to your table as an appetizer.

NEAR THE PLAZA DE CALLAO

EL CALLEJÓN, Ternera, 6. Tel. 522-54-01.
  Cuisine: SPANISH. **Reservations:** Recommended. **Metro:** Callao.
$ Prices: Appetizers 400–975 ptas. ($3.75–$9.15); main dishes 850–1,800 ptas. ($8–$16.90); fixed-price menu 1,500 ptas. ($14.10). AE, DC, MC, V.
  Open: Lunch daily 1–4pm; dinner daily 8:15–11:30pm. **Closed:** Sat in summer.
Hemingway's "other favorite" lies on a tiny street in the heart of Madrid, off the Gran Vía near the Galerías Preciados department store. Hemingway, called "Don Ernesto" by the waiters, came here for paella after a bullfight. Opened in 1944, El Callejón still attracts sportsmen, diplomats, and bullfighters. It features regional dishes on set days of the week. On Tuesday and Saturday you can order stewed veal, but you have to go here on Thursday for the Spanish soul-food dish, red beans with rice. Openers might include the classic garlic soup or shrimp Bilbao style. Among the main courses, the special steak and the calf's sweetbreads cost considerably more than the eggs Callejón and the roast chicken (half). Roman-style squid is popular, as is Navarre-style trout. For dessert, try the cherries with fresh cream or the fried bananas.

NEAR THE PLAZA MAYOR

EL CUCHI, Cuchilleros, 3. Tel. 266-44-24.
  Cuisine: SPANISH/MEXICAN/BRAZILIAN. **Reservations:** Recommended.
  Metro: Ópera.
$ Prices: Appetizers 420–1,350 ptas. ($3.95–$12.70); main dishes 950–3,000 ptas. ($8.95–$28.20). AE, DC, MC, V.
  Open: Lunch daily 1–4pm; dinner daily 8pm–midnight.
A few doors down from Hemingway's favorite restaurant (Botín), El Cuchi defiantly claims that "Hemingway never ate here." But about everybody else has, attracted both to its low prices and to its labyrinth of dining rooms. A European link in Mexico's famous Carlos 'n' Charlie's chain, the Madrid restaurant stands off a corner of the Plaza Mayor. Ceiling beams and artifacts suggest rusticity. Menu specialties include black-bean soup, ceviche, guacamole, quail Mozambique, "pregnant" trout, and roast suckling pig (much cheaper than that served at Botín).

LOS GALAYOS, Botoneras, 5. Tel. 266-30-28.

Cuisine: SPANISH. **Reservations:** Recommended. **Metro:** Puerta del Sol.
$ Prices: Appetizers 700–1,500 ptas. ($6.60–$14.10); main dishes, 2,200–3,000 ptas. ($20.70–$28.20); fixed-priced menu 2,200 ptas. ($20.70). AE, DC, MC, V.
Open: Lunch daily noon–3pm; dinner daily 8pm–1am.

⭐ Just off the Plaza Mayor, Los Galayos attracts both foreigners and loyal locals. In fair weather you can dine at sidewalk tables screened off by shrubbery. In cooler months you'll pass through a stand-up tapas bar—decorated with strings of garlic, country hams, and ornate beer tapas—en route to the upstairs country-style dining room with its leaded-glass windows. The owner serves such Castilian specialties as roast suckling pig and tender baby lamb; also offered are Basque-style hake, grilled shrimp, and grilled veal chops on a sizzling hot platter with roasted pimientos and crunchy potatoes. Many guests prefer to begin their meal with the fresh green beans cooked with Serrano ham. Fine Spanish wines also available.

CASA PACO, Puerto Cerrada, 11. Tel. 266-31-66.
Cuisine: SPANISH. **Reservations:** Not accepted. **Metro:** Puerta del Sol.
$ Prices: Appetizers 1,000–1,200 ptas. ($9.40–$11.30); main dishes 2,500–3,200 ptas. ($23.50–$30.10); fixed-priced menus 1,200–1,600 ptas. ($11.30–$15.05). DC, V.
Open: Lunch Mon–Sat 1:30–3:45pm; dinner Mon–Sat 8:30–11:45pm. **Closed:** Aug.

⭐ Just beside the Plaza Mayor, Casa Paco has been here for decades. Despite its popularity, the owners have kept up the quality of the food and the efficiency of the service. The restaurant is actually an old tavern, with both downstairs and upstairs dining rooms. Señor Paco was the first Madrid restaurateur to seal steaks in boiling oil before serving them on plates so hot that the almost-raw meat continued to cook, preserving the natural juices. You could start with fish soup and proceed to grilled sole, baby lamb, Casa Paco cocido, or *callos* (tripe) *à la madrileña,* but most people still come here for the deliciously thick steaks, priced according to weight and served sizzling hot—nowadays on a wooden board. You might top it off with a luscious dessert, but you can't have coffee here: Casa Paco won't serve it because customers used to linger over their cups, keeping tables occupied while people were turned away for lack of space.

NEAR THE PLAZA SANTA ANA

LA TRUCHA, Manuel Fernández González, 3. Tel. 532-82-02.
Cuisine: SEAFOOD. **Reservations:** Recommended. **Metro:** Sevilla.
$ Prices: Appetizers 250–375 ptas. ($2.35–$3.50); main dishes 750–1,500 ptas. ($7.05–$14.10). No credit cards.
Open: Lunch Mon–Sat 1–4pm; dinner Mon–Sat 8pm–midnight. **Closed:** Aug.
With its Andalusian tavern ambience, La Trucha boasts a street-level bar and small dining room—the arched ceiling and whitewashed walls festive with hanging braids of garlic, dried peppers, and onions. On the lower level the walls of a second bustling area are covered with eye-catching antiques, bullfight notices, and bric-a-brac. The specialty is fish, and there's a complete à la carte menu including *trucha* (trout); *verbenas de ahumados* (literally, a "street party" of smoked delicacies); a stew called *fabada* ("glorious"; made with beans, Galician ham, black sausage, and smoked bacon); and a *comida casera rabo de toro* (home-style oxtail). No one should miss nibbling on the *tapas variadas* in the bar.

NEAR THE PUERTA DEL SOL

EL PAZO DE MONTERREY, Alcalá, 4. Tel. 532-82-80.
Cuisine: SEAFOOD. **Reservations:** Recommended. **Metro:** Puerta del Sol.
$ Prices: Appetizers 700–1,100 ptas. ($6.60–$10.35); main dishes 1,500–2,800 ptas. ($14.10–$26.30); fixed-price menu 2,200 ptas. ($20.70). AE, DC, MC, V.
Open: Daily noon–midnight.
There's a lobster tank in the window of this stone-faced building. Many of the

restaurant's clients prefer the long stand-up tapas bar, one of the area's most popular gathering places. The dining room is upstairs, although about 20 tables are set up on the ground floor if you want to stay there for a view of the crowd. This is primarily a shellfish restaurant, but the bill won't paralyze you if you order carefully—and all portions are generous. À la carte meals do cost more if you order shellfish, but less if you stick to meat dishes. Specialties include seafood soup, seafood casserole, sea crab, barnacles, scampi, oysters, Bilboa eels, baked salmon, fried red squid, and such regional dishes as roast lamb Segovia style, fabada beans, and Madrid-style tripe. A dessert spectacular is baked Alaska.

PUERTA DEL TOLEDO

EL ABANICO GASTRONOMICO, Mercado Puerta de Toledo. Tel. 265-15-11.
    Cuisine: SPANISH. **Reservations:** Not required. **Metro:** Puerta de Toledo.
$ **Prices:** Appetizers 250–375 ptas. ($2.35–$3.50); main dishes 750–1,500 ptas. ($7.05–$14.10). MC, V.
    Open: Tues–Sat 11am–1am; Sun 11am–3pm.
The Culinary Fan, its English name, operates out of Madrid's most fashionable shopping mall, combining a restaurant with a deli and market. You can stop in at a marble-countered bar, order a selection of tapas, and have a drink in the outdoor café; or perhaps order a more formal meal in the restaurant section, which has not only private tables but also a 30-seat "family table." The deli sells everything from canned goods to 700 varieties of wines and liquors.

MEALS FOR LESS THAN 3,800 PTAS.
[$35.70]

IN MEDIEVAL MADRID

EL SCHOTIS, Cava Baja, 11. Tel. 265-32-30.
    Cuisine: SPANISH. **Reservations:** Recommended. **Metro:** Ópera.
$ **Prices:** Appetizers 1,000–1,200 ptas. ($9.40–$11.30); main dishes 2,500–3,200 ptas. ($23.50–$30.10). AE, DC, MC, V.
    Open: Lunch Tues–Sun 1–4pm; dinner Tues–Sun 9pm–midnight. **Closed:** Aug.
Casa Paco's rival, 2 blocks down, El Schotis is equally famous for its *churrasco* (barbecued steak) its entrecote Schotis (large veal chop).

NEAR THE PLAZA DE LA CIBELES

EL ESPEJO, Paseo de Recoletos, 31. Tel. 308-23-47.
    Cuisine: FRENCH. **Reservations:** Recommended. **Metro:** Colón.
$ **Prices:** Appetizers 950–1,500 ptas. ($8.95–$14.10); main dishes 1,800–2,800 ptas. ($16.90–$26.25). AE, DC, MC, V.
    Open: Lunch daily 1–4pm; dinner daily 9:30pm–midnight.
    El Espejo offers good food in one of Madrid's most perfectly crafted art nouveau decors: tile maidens with vines and flowers entwined in their hair, Belle Epoque lighting fixtures, sculptured plaster, brass railings, and bentwood chairs. You'll pass through a charming café/bar, where many visitors linger before heading to the spacious and alluring dining room. Dishes include vichyssoise, codfish omelet, shellfish terrine, grilled sole, *escargots bourguignons*, and crêpes Suzette. Weather permitting, you can also sit at one of the outdoor tables, served by a battery of uniformed waiters who carry food across the busy street to a green area flanked by trees and strolling pedestrians.

NEAR THE PLAZA DE LAS CORTES

EDELWEISS, Jovellanos, 7. Tel. 521-03-26.
    Cuisine: GERMAN. **Reservations:** None. **Metro:** Sevilla.
$ **Prices:** Appetizers 400–600 ptas. ($3.75–$5.65); main dishes 1,500–2,000 ptas. ($14.10–$18.80). V.

Open: Lunch Mon–Sat 12:30–4pm; dinner Mon–Sat 8:30pm–midnight. **Closed:** Aug.

This noteworthy German restaurant, in a corner building near the American Express office, offers a welcome respite from Spanish cuisine. And there are other good reasons why this place is always crowded: big portions, friendly waiters, and efficient service. Soups are hearty and homemade, and roast veal and goulash are featured among the main-course selections. The specialty is *eisbein* (pigs' knuckles German style), served with sauerkraut and mashed potatoes. For dessert, I'd suggest the apple tart with whipped cream.

LHARDY, Carrera de San Jerónimo, 8. Tel. 521-33-85.
   Cuisine: SPANISH. **Reservations:** Recommended. **Metro:** Puerta del Sol.
$ Prices: Appetizers 1,000–1,700 ptas. ($9.40–$16); main dishes 3,000–3,200 ptas. ($28.20–$30.10).
   Open: Lunch Mon–Sat 1–3:30pm; dinner Mon–Sat 9–11:30pm. **Closed:** Late July–early Sept.

Open since 1839, Lhardy has a great reputation as a gathering place for Madrid's literati. Upstairs is an expensive restaurant, but downstairs there's a deli shop selling some of the delicacies you can taste at the bar. It's traditional to come here for a glass of sherry or for a cup of consommé from a large silver samovar. Specialties of the house include roast beef and the best-known dish of Madrid, cocido. These might be served with wines from an excellent cellar.

NEAR THE PLAZA MAYOR

SOBRINO DE BOTÍN, Cuchilleros, 17. Tel. 266-42-17.
   Cuisine: SPANISH. **Reservations:** Required. **Metro:** Ópera.
$ Prices: Appetizers 850–1,250 ptas. ($8–$11.75); main dishes 1,800–2,800 ptas. ($16.90–$26.30); fixed-priced menu (seasonal) 3,200 ptas. ($30.10). AE, DC, MC, V.
   Open: Lunch daily 1–4pm; dinner daily 8pm–midnight.

Founded in 1725, Sobrino de Botín is the most famous restaurant in Spain. It has a prime location near the Plaza Mayor, in an old building with beautifully preserved and imaginatively furnished rooms. Don't miss the early-18th-century oven, out of which comes the justly praised roast suckling pig, or if you prefer, *cordero asado* (roast baby lamb). A set menu, offered only in autumn and winter, includes garlic soup with egg, roast suckling pig, melon, and a small pitcher of wine or a glass of beer (mineral water if you prefer). There's also a limited but well-chosen selection of fish dishes, including fried Cantabrian hake, baby squid in its own ink, and baby eels. At a small Andalusian-style bodega downstairs, you can also order a complete meal. The service is tops. Don Antonio, one of the owners, speaks English.

NEAR THE PLAZA DEL REY

CASABLANCA, Barquillo, 29. Tel. 521-15-68.
   Cuisine: INTERNATIONAL. **Reservations:** Recommended. **Metro:** Alonso Martínez.
$ Prices: Appetizers 800–900 ptas. ($7.50–$8.45); main dishes 1,500–2,200 ptas. ($14.10–$20.70). AE, DC, MC, V.
   Open: Lunch daily 1:30–4pm; dinner daily 9pm–1am.

Dick Angstadt took over Bogui (Spanish for Humphrey Bogart) in 1979. To follow the cinematic motif and to correspond with the old movie posters scattered around the restaurant, the Panama-born Angstadt changed the establishment's name to Casablanca; today it's the best restaurant in a rapidly developing neighborhood. The Moroccan theme fits in well with the salmon-colored walls and the art deco decor. Specialties are northern Spanish, continental, and Japanese, including duck à l'orange, lamb brains in a *fines herbes* mustard sauce, filet mignon with garlic and lemon, pepper steak, red peppers stuffed with hake, spinach and Roquefort crêpes, and kiwi mousse.

AT THE PLAZA DE SANTA ANA

PLATERÍAS COMEDOR, Plaza de Santa Ana, 11. Tel. 429-70-48.
  Cuisine: SPANISH. **Reservations:** Recommended. **Metro:** Puerta del Sol.
$ Prices: Appetizers 1,000–1,250 ptas. ($9.40–$11.75); main dishes 1,800–2,800 ptas. ($16.90–$26.30). AE, DC, MC, V.
  Open: Lunch Mon–Sat 1:30–4pm; dinner Mon–Sat 9pm–midnight.

One of the most charming dining rooms in Madrid, Platerías Comedor has richly brocaded walls evocative of 19th-century Spain. Despite the busy socializing on the plaza outside, this serene oasis makes few concessions to the new generation in its food, decor, or formally attired waiters. Specialties include beans with clams, stuffed partridge with cabbage and sausage, magret of duckling with pomegranates, duck liver with white grapes, tripe à la Madrid, veal stew with snails and mushrooms, and guinea hen with figs and plumbs. You might follow with a passionfruit sorbet.

NEAR THE ROYAL PALACE

CAFÉ DE ORIENTE, Plaza de Oriente, 2. Tel. 247-15-64 (café/bar), 248-20-10 (restaurant).
  Cuisine: SPANISH/FRENCH. **Reservations:** Recommended (restaurant only).
  Metro: Ópera.
$ Prices: In the café—pizzas 750 ptas. ($7.05); coffee 400–650 ptas. ($3.45–$6.10). In the restaurant—fixed-price lunch 1,250 ptas. ($11.75); fixed price dinner 4,000 ptas. ($37.60). AE, DC, MC, V.
  Open: Lunch daily 1–4pm; dinner daily 9pm–midnight.

The Oriente is a café and restaurant complex, the former being one of the most popular in Madrid. The dining rooms—Castilian upstairs, French Basque downstairs—are quite expensive at night, but offer reasonably priced luncheon menus. Typical of the refined cuisine are vichyssoise, fresh vegetable flan, and many savory meat and fresh-fish offerings; the service is excellent. Most visitors, however, patronize the café, trying if possible to get an outdoor table for a "ringside" view of the Royal Palace. The café is decorated in turn-of-the-century style, with banquettes and regal paneling, as befits its location. Pizza, tapas, and drinks (including Irish, Viennese, Russian, and Jamaican coffees) are served.

 FROMMER'S COOL FOR KIDS
Restaurants

Children visiting Spain will delight in patronizing any of the restaurants at the Parque de Atracciones in the **Casa de Campo** (see "Cool for Kids" in Chapter 6). Another good idea is to go on a picnic (see "Picnic Fare and Where to Eat It" in this chapter).

For a taste of home, there are always the fast-food chains like McDonald's, Burger King, and Kentucky Fried Chicken. Remember, though, that because Spain is a foreign country, everything may have a slightly different taste.

Try taking the family to a local tasca, where children are bound to find something they like from the wide selection of tapas. One tasca that is appropriate for the entire family is:

La Dolores (see p.92) There is an especially good selection of tapas here.

SPECIALTY DINING

LOCAL BUDGET BETS

Tasca Hopping

If you think you'll starve waiting for Madrid's fashionable 9:30 or 10pm dinner hour, you've been misinformed. Throughout the city you'll find tascas, bars that serve wine and platters of tempting hot and cold hors d'oeuvres known as tapas: mushrooms, salads, baby eels, shrimp, lobster, mussels, sausage, ham—and in one establishment at least, bull testicles. Keep in mind that you can often save pesetas by ordering at the bar.

EL ANCIANO REY DE LOS VINOS, Bailén, 19. Tel. 248-50-52.
   Cuisine: TAPAS. **Metro:** Ópera.
   $ Prices: Tapas 75–350 ptas. (70¢–$3.30). No credit cards.
   Open: Thurs–Tues 10am–3pm and 5:30–11pm.
The bar here is jammed during most of the day with crowds of Madrileños out for a glass (or a carafe) of one of the four house wines, which range from dry to sweet and start at 80 pesetas (75¢) per glass. Beer is also served.

CERVECERÍA ALEMANIA, Plaza de Santa Ana, 6. Tel. 429-70-33.
   Cuisine: TAPAS. **Metro:** Alonso Martín or Sevilla.
   $ Prices: Beer 85 ptas. (80¢); tapas 80–800 ptas. (75¢–$7.50). No credit cards.
   Open: Wed–Thurs, Sun–Mon 10am–12:30pm; Fri–Sat 10am–1:30am.
Hemingway used to frequent this casual spot with the celebrated bullfighter Luís Miguel Domínguín—ask the waiter to point out "Hemingway's table." Opening directly onto one of the liveliest little plazas of Madrid, it clings to its turn-of-the-century traditions. Young Madrileños are fond of stopping in for a mug of draft beer. You can sit at one of the tables, leisurely sipping beer or wine, since the waiters make no attempt hurry you along. To accompany your beverage, try the fried sardines or a Spanish omelet.

TABERNA TOSCANA, Ventura de la Vega, 22. Tel. 429-60-31.
   Cuisine: TAPAS. **Metro:** Puerta del Sol or Sevilla.
   $ Prices: Glass of wine 85 ptas. (80¢); tapas 100–1,200 ptas. (95¢–$11.30). No credit cards.
   Open: Daily noon–4pm and 8pm–midnight.
Many Madrileños begin their nightly tasca crawl here. The aura is that of a village inn, far removed from 20th-century Madrid. You sit on crude country stools under time-darkened beams from which hang sausages, pimientos, and sheaves of golden wheat. The long tile tasca bar is loaded with tasty tidbits, including the house specialties: *lacón y cecina* (boiled ham), *habas* (broad beans) with Spanish ham, and *chorizo* (a red-pepper and pork sausage)—almost meals in themselves. Especially delectable are the kidneys in sherry sauce and the snails in hot sauce.

LA DOLORES, Jesús de Medinaceli, 4. Tel. 468-59-30.
   Cuisine: TAPAS. **Reservations:** Not required. **Metro:** Atocha.
   $ Prices: Glass of house wine 80 ptas. (75¢); tapas 160–200 ptas. ($1.50–$1.90). No credit cards.
   Open: Daily 10am–midnight.
In business since the 1920s, this is one of the best-patronized tascas in the old city. A ceramic tile announces the wine specialty, *vinos de Valdepeñas*, one so beloved by matadors and their aficionados. As a decor note, beer cans "from all over" are stacked against the walls. However, La Dolores offers only one choice, Mahou, although its wine list is extensive. Many various tapas are served, and frankly, you can make a full meal by sampling two or three of these. Try smoked salmon on bread with cheese.

CERVECERÍA SANTA BARBÁRA, Plaza de Santa Bárbara, 8. Tel. 419-04-49.
   Cuisine: TAPAS. **Metro:** Alonso Martínez.
$ **Prices:** Beer 110–120 ptas. ($1.05–$1.15); tapas 185–250 ptas. ($1.75–$2.35). No credit cards.
   Open: Daily 11am–11pm.
Unique in Madrid, Cervecería Santa Bárbara is an outlet for a beer factory, and the management has spent a lot to make it modern and inviting. Hanging globe lights and spinning ceiling fans create an attractive ambience, as does the black-and-white marble checkerboard floor. You go here for beer of course: *cerveza negra* (black beer) or *cerveza dorada* (golden beer). The local brew is best accompanied by homemade potato chips or by fresh shrimp, lobster, crabmeat, or barnacles. You can either stand at the counter or go directly to one of the wooden tables for waiter service.

ANTONIO SÁNCHEZ, Mesón de Parades, 13. Tel. 239-78-25.
   Cuisine: SPANISH. **Metro:** Tirso de Molina.
$ **Prices:** Tapas (in the bar) 200–600 ptas. ($1.90–$5.65). Appetizers (in the restaurant) 200–350 ptas. ($1.90–$3.30); main dishes 650–1,200 ptas. ($6.10–$11.30). V.
   Open: Daily noon–4pm; Mon–Sat 8pm–midnight.
Named in 1850 after the founder's son, who was killed in the bullring, Antonio Sánchez is full of bullfighting memorabilia, including the stuffed head of the animal that gored young Sánchez. Also featured on the dark paneled walls are three works by the Spanish artist Zuloaga, who had his last public exhibition in this restaurant near the Plaza Tirso de Molina. A limited array of tapas, including garlic soup, are served with Valdepeñas wine drawn from a barrel, although many guests ignore the edibles in favor of smoking cigarettes and arguing the merits of this or that bullfighter. A restaurant in the back serves Spanish food with a vaguely French influence.

LOS MOTIVOS, Ventura de la Vega, 10. Tel. 429-67-29.
   Cuisine: TAPAS. **Metro:** Puerta del Sol.
$ **Prices:** Glass of wine 60 ptas. (55¢); tapas 325–1,400 ptas. ($3.05–$13.16). No credit cards.
   Open: Mon–Sat noon–4pm and 8pm–midnight.
Los Motivos offers two dozen different platters of tasty tapas every evening. It's one of the most frequented bars in Madrid, and its smart, sophisticated crowd starts filing in nightly around 8pm. It's decorated like an old tavern: hand-hewn beams, strings of garlic, wine bottles hanging from the ceiling, and crude wood stools and tables. The food at the bar is under glass—so it's most sanitary. Should you wish to stay on for dinner, the cubierto of the day goes for 900 pesetas ($8.45).

CASA SIERRA, Gravina, 1. Tel. 521-12-90.
   Cuisine: TAPAS. **Metro:** Chueca.
$ **Prices:** Beer 85 ptas. (80¢); tapas 375 ptas. ($3.55). No credit cards.
   Open: Thurs–Tues noon–4pm and 8pm–midnight.
The smoke stains on its 19th-century frescoed ceiling, the zinc bar, and the dozens of oak barrels of vintage sherries and ports make this one of the most atmospheric gathering places in town. You won't find any tables or chairs, only a sawdust-covered floor.

Cafeterias

EL CORTE INGLÉS, Preciados, 3. Tel. 532-81-00.
   Cuisine: SPANISH. **Metro:** Callao.
$ **Prices:** Buffet 1,800 ptas. ($16.90). AE, DC, MC, V.
   Open: Mon–Sat 12:30–4pm.
El Corte Inglés will be recommended later as one of the most prestigious department stores in Madrid. Every in-the-know shopper also knows that it offers some of the best food values around at its buffet on the seventh floor, featuring 70 different plates. Come here if you have a gargantuan appetite.

V.I.P., Gran Vía, 41. Tel. 411-60-44.
   Cuisine: SPANISH. **Reservations:** Not required. **Metro:** Callao.
$ **Prices:** Appetizers 350–625 ptas. ($3.30–$5.90); main dishes 515–800 ptas. ($4.85–$7.50). AE, DC, MC, V.
   Open: Daily 9am–3am.
This place looks like a bookstore emporium from the outside, but in back is a Formica-sheathed cafeteria serving fast food. You might begin with a cup of soothing gazpacho. There are at least 14 V.I.P.s scattered throughout Madrid, but this is the most central one. Hamburgers are the rage here.

Picnic Fare And Where To Eat It

On a hot day, do as the Madrileños do. Secure the makings of a picnic lunch and head for the Casa de Campo (Metro: El Batán), those once-royal hunting grounds in the west of Madrid across the Manzanares River. Children delight in this adventure, as they can also visit a boating lake, the Parque de Atracciones, and the Madrid Zoo.

Your best choice for picnic fare is **Mallorca,** Velázquez, 59 (tel. 431-99-00; Metro: Velázquez). This place has all the makings for a deluxe picnic. (See "Food and Wine" under "Savvy Shopping," Chapter 6.)

Another good bet is **Rodilla,** Preciados, 25 (tel. 522-57-01; Metro: Callao), where you can find sandwiches, pastries, and takeaway tapas. Sandwiches, including vegetarian, meat, and fish, range from 70 pesetas (65¢). It's open daily from 8:30am to 10:30pm.

Also try **Charlot,** Claudio Coello, 87 (tel. 276-67-40; Metro: Núñez de Balboa), where sandwich prices range from 70 pesetas (65¢). It's open Monday through Saturday from 10am to 4pm and 5 to 8pm; closed in August.

MADRID ATTRACTIONS

Madrid has changed drastically in recent years. No longer is it fair to say that it has only the Prado and after that, you should head for Toledo or El Escorial. As you will discover in the pages to come, Madrid has something to amuse and delight everyone.

1. SUGGESTED ITINERARIES

IF YOU HAVE ONE DAY

If you have just arrived in Spain after a long flight, don't tackle too much on your first day. Spend the morning at the **Prado,** one of the world's great art museums, arriving when it opens, at 9am (closed Mon). Have lunch and then visit the **Palacio Real (Royal Palace).** Have an early dinner near the Plaza Mayor.

IF YOU HAVE TWO DAYS

Spend day 1 as described above. On day 2 take a trip to **Toledo,** where you can visit El Greco's House and Museum, the Santa Cruz Museum, the Church of Santo Tomé, and the Alcázar. See the walking tour, below, in this chapter. Return to Madrid in the evening.

IF YOU HAVE THREE DAYS

Follow the suggestions for days 1 and 2. On day 3 take the train (1 hr.) to the **Monastery of San Lorenzo del Escorial,** in the foothills of the Sierra de Guadarrama. Return to Madrid in the evening.

IF YOU HAVE FIVE DAYS

Follow the suggestions for days 1 to 3, above. On day 4, be at the **Museum of Lázaro Galdiano** when it opens (10am). Afterward take one of the walking tours of Madrid (see below) and follow it with a late lunch in the old town. In the afternoon, either visit the **Goya Pantéon** and the **Convento de las Descalzas Reales** and end the day with another walking tour, or revisit the Prado.

On day 5 take a trip to **Segovia** in Old Castile. Be sure to see its Alcázar, Roman aqueduct, and cathedral. Sample the region's specialties at lunch and return to Madrid for dinner in the old town.

2. THE TOP ATTRACTIONS

MUSEO DEL PRADO, Paseo del Prado. Tel. 420-28-36.

★ With more than 7,000 paintings, the Prado is one of the most important repositories of art in the world. It began as a royal collection, and was enhanced by the Hapsburgs, especially Charles V, and later the Bourbons. In paintings of the Spanish school the Prado has no equal, and on your first visit, concentrate on the Spanish masters (Velázquez, Goya, El Greco, and Murillo).

Most major works are exhibited on the first floor. You'll see art by Italian masters—Raphael, Botticelli, Mantegna, Andrea del Sarto, Fra Angelico, and Correggio. Perhaps the most celebrated Italian painting here is Titian's voluptuous Venus being watched by a musician who can't keep his eyes on his work.

Don't miss the work of El Greco (1524–1614), the Crete-born artist who lived much of his life in Toledo. You can see a parade of "The Greek's" saints, Madonnas, Holy Families—even a ghostly *John the Baptist*.

In the five-star showcase that is the Prado, you'll find a splendid array of works by the incomparable Diego Velázquez (1599–1660). The museum's most famous painting, in fact, is his *Maids of Honor*, a triumph in the use of light effects. The faces of the queen and king are reflected in the mirror in the painting itself. The artist in the foreground? Velázquez, of course.

Rubens, who met Velázquez while in Spain, is represented by the peacock-blue *Garden of Love* and by the *Three Graces*. Don't miss the work of José Ribera (1591–1652), a Valencia-born artist and contemporary of Velázquez whose best painting is the *Martyrdom of St. Philip*. The Seville-born Bartolomé Murillo (1617–82)—often referred to as the "painter of Madonnas"—has three *Immaculate Conceptions* on display.

The Prado contains one of the world's outstanding collections of Hieronymus Bosch, the Flemish genius who died here in 1516. "El Bosco's" best-known work, *The Garden of Earthly Delights,* is here. You'll also see his *Seven Deadly Sins* and his triptych *The Hay Wagon*. Don't miss *The Triumph of Death* by another Flemish painter, Pieter Brueghel (the Elder), who carried on Bosch's ghoulish vision.

Francisco de Goya (1746–1828), ranks along with Velázquez and El Greco in the trio of great Spanish artists. Hanging here are his cruel portraits of his patron, Charles IV, and his family, as well as the *Clothed Maja* and the *Naked Maja*. You can also see the much-reproduced *Third of May* (1808), not to mention a series of Goya sketches (some of which, depicting the decay of 18th-century Spain, brought the Inquisition down on the artist) and his expressionistic "black paintings."

The painting that has stirred up the most excitement in recent years is Picasso's *Guernica*. Long banned in Spain, the work hung for years in the Museum of Modern Art in New York before it was returned to its homeland. The Prado houses it in one of its satellite museums, the Casón del Buen Retiro. Picasso's work reflects his sadness at Franco's bombing of the Basque town of the same name. The artist requested that

---

IN THEIR FOOTSTEPS

Diego Rodriguez de Silva Velázquez (1599–1660). Acclaimed as the greatest painter of the 17th century, who centuries later was to have great influence on Picasso, he was made court painter at age 25 to Philip IV. "I have found my Titian," the king declared. He was a master of atmospheric portraiture, making earth-shattering breakthroughs in use of color and light. His masterpiece, *Las Meninas*, hangs in the Prado. Velázquez painted his greatest works during the last two years of life, including the *Sinners*.

• **Resting Place:** A cross at Plaza del Ramal in Madrid marks the site of his burial at the former Church of San Juan.

❓ DID YOU KNOW . . . ?

- Casa Botín, a Hemingway favorite, claims to be the world's oldest restaurant. It was founded in 1725.
- The only public statue anywhere dedicated to the Devil stands in Madrid's Retiro Park.
- A Mexican composer wrote the unofficial anthem "Madrid, Madrid, Madrid," and he had never been to Madrid.

Guernica not be returned to Spain until the death of Franco and the "reestablishment of public liberties."

The Prado's display space has increased with the acquisition of the Villahermosa Palace, a 17th-century building across the Plaza Canovas del Castillo from the museum's main premises. For at least the next 10 years the palace will house one of the most important privately owned art collections in the world, that of Baron Hans Heinrich Thyssen-Bornemisza. The collection includes works by El Greco, Velázquez, Goya, Hals, Memling, Rubens, Rembrandt, Sebastiano del Piompo, Watteau, Canaletto, and John of Flanders, as well as the only privately owned Dürer painting, *Christ Among the Doctors*. Picasso's *Harlequin with Mirror* is here, as are works by such impressionist and postimpressionist painters as Degas, Renoir, Sisley, van Gogh, Gauguin, Chagall, Monet, Cézanne, Toulouse-Lautrec, and Gris. Modern art is represented by expressionists such as Vlaminck, Pechstein, Heckel, Kirchner, Feininger, Nolde, and Kandinsky. The baron's recent acquisitions are primarily American. His collection is slated to open in 1991, but check for specifics with the tourist office or the Prado's main reception area.

Admission: 400 ptas. ($3.75).

Open: Tues–Sat 9am–7pm, Sun 9am–2pm. **Closed:** Good Friday, Dec 25, and Jan 1. **Metro:** Banco de España and Atocha. **Bus:** 10, 14, 27, 34, 37, or 45.

PALACIO REAL (Royal Palace), Plaza de Oriente, Bailén, 2. Tel. 248-74-04.

⭐ This huge palace was begun in 1737 on the site of the Madrid Alcázar, which burned to the ground in 1734. Some of its 2,000 rooms—which that "enlightened despot" Charles III called home—are open to the public, while others are still used for state business. The palace was last used as a royal residence in 1931, before King Alfonso XIII and his wife, Victoria Eugénie, fled Spain.

You'll be taken on a guided tour of the palace—say "Inglés" to the person who takes your ticket, so you'll get an English-speaking guide. The tour includes the Reception Room, the State Apartments, the Tapestry Gallery, the Armory, the Library, and the Royal Pharmacy.

The Reception Room and State Apartments should get priority here if you're rushed. They embrace a rococo room with a diamond clock; a porcelain salon; the Royal Chapel, used whenever a new cardinal is sent to Spain; the Banquet Room, where receptions for heads of state are held; and the Throne Room.

The rooms are literally stuffed with art treasures and antiques—salon after salon of monumental grandeur, with no apologies for the opulence of damask, mosaics, stucco, Tiepolo ceilings, gilt and bronze, chandeliers, and paintings. The miles and miles of Flemish and Spanish tapestries in the Tapestry Gallery comprise an impressive collection numbering in the hundreds, many from the 15th century.

In the Armory, you'll see the finest collection of weaponry in Spain. Many of the items—powder flasks, shields, lances, helmets, saddles—are from the collection of Charles V (Charles I of Spain). From here, the comprehensive tour takes you into the Library and the less interesting Pharmacy.

You may want to visit the **Carriage Museum,** also at the Royal Palace, to see some of the grand old relics used by Spanish aristocrats. Afterward, stroll through the Campo del Moro, the gardens of the palace.

Admission: 500 ptas. ($4.70); 100 ptas. (95¢) for Carriage Museum alone.

Open: Mon–Sat 9:30am–12:45pm and 4–5:15pm, Sun 9:30am–12:15pm.

Metro: Ópera or Plaza de España.

MUSEO DE LA REAL ACADEMIA DE BELLAS ARTES DE SAN FERNANDO (Fine Arts Museum), Alcalá, 13. Tel. 232-15-46.

easy stroll from the Puerta del Sol, the Fine Arts Museum is considered by second only to the Prado as the leading Spanish museum. It is located in the red and remodeled 17th-century baroque palace of Juan de Goyeneche. The ction—more than 1,500 paintings and 80 sculptures, ranging from the 16th century to the present—was started in 1744 during the reign of King Philip V. It emphasizes works by Spanish, Flemish, and Italian artists. You can see masterpieces by El Greco, Rubens, Velázquez, Zurbarán, Ribera, Cano, Coello, Murillo, Goya, and Sorolla.

Admission: 200 ptas. ($1.90).
Open: Tues–Sat 9am–7pm, Sun–Mon 9am–2pm. **Metro:** Puerta del Sol or Sevilla.

PANTEÓN DE GOYA (Goya's Tomb), Glorieta de San Antonio de la Florida. Tel. 542-07-22.

In a remote part of town beyond the North Station lies Goya's tomb, containing one of his masterpieces—an elaborately beautiful fresco depicting the miracles of St. Anthony on the dome and cupola of the little hermitage of San Antonio de la Florida. The tomb and fresco are in one of the twin chapels (visit the one on the right) that were built in the latter part of the 18th century. Discreetly placed mirrors will help you see the ceiling better.

Admission: Free.
Open: Tues–Fri 10am–2pm and 4–8pm, Sat–Sun 10am–2pm. **Metro:** Norte.
Bus: 46

MUSEO TAURINO (Bullfighting Museum), Plaza de Toros de las Ventas, Alcalá, 237. Tel. 255-18-57.

This museum might serve as a good introduction to bullfighting for those who want to see the real event. Here you'll see the death costume of Manolete, the *traje de luces* (suit of lights) that he wore when he was gored to death at age 30 in Linares's bullring.

Other memorabilia evoke the heyday of Juan Belmonte, the Andalusian who revolutionized bullfighting in 1914 by performing close to the horns. Other exhibits include a Goya painting of a matador, as well as photographs and relics that trace the history of bullfighting in Spain from its ancient origins to the present day.

Admission: Free.
Open: Tues–Fri and Sun 9am–3pm. **Metro:** Ventas.

MUSEUM OF LÁZARO GALDIANO, Serrano, 122. Tel. 261-60-84.

Imagine 37 rooms in a well-preserved 19th-century mansion bulging with artworks—including many by the most famous old masters of Europe. Most visitors take the elevator to the top floor and work down, lingering over such artifacts as 15th-century handwoven vestments, swords and daggers, royal seals, 16th-century crystal from Limoges, Byzantine jewelry, Italian bronzes from ancient times to the Renaissance, and medieval armor.

IN THEIR FOOTSTEPS

Francisco José de Goya y Lucientes (1746–1828). One of the greatest artists of all time, Goya became a pupil of Francisco Bayeu in Madrid. In 1773, he married Bayeu's sister. In 1789, he was appointed court painter to King Carlos IV. The works of his early years combined elements of neoclassicism with rococo flamboyance, in contrast to the "Black Paintings" of his declining years. A mysterious illness in 1794 left him deaf in both ears. The Inquisition summoned him in 1803, wanting him to "explain" why he created the first painting in the history of art to show a woman's pubic hair. In Bordeaux, where he died in exile, he created lithography.

• **Resting Place:** Pantheon of Goya, Madrid.

Two paintings by Bosch evoke his own peculiar brand of horror, his canvases peopled with creepy fiends devouring human flesh. A portrait of Saskia signed by Rembrandt adorns a wall nearby. The Spanish masters are the best represented—El Greco, Velázquez, Zurbarán, Ribera, Murillo, and Valdés-Leal.

One section is devoted to works by the English portrait and landscape artists Reynolds, Gainsborough, and Constable. Italian artists exhibited include Tiepolo and Guardi. Salon 30—for many, the most interesting—is devoted to Goya and includes some paintings from his "black period," as well as a portrait of the weak Charles IV and his voluble, amorous queen, Maria Louisa.

Admission: 300 ptas. ($2.80).
Open: Tues–Sun 10am–2pm. **Closed:** Aug. **Metro:** Rubén Darío. **Bus:** 9, 16, 19, 51, or 89.

CONVENTO DE LAS DESCALZAS REALES, Plaza de las Descalzas Reales. Tel. 248-74-04.

In the mid-16th century, aristocratic women—either disappointed in love or "wanting to be the bride of Christ"—stole away to this convent to take the veil. All of them brought a dowry, making this one of the richest convents in the land. By the mid-20th century the convent sheltered mostly poor women. True, it still contained a priceless collection of art treasures, but the sisters were forbidden to auction anything; in fact, they were literally starving. The state intervened, and the pope granted special dispensation to open the convent as a museum. Today the public can look behind the walls of what was once a mysterious edifice on one of the most beautiful squares in Old Madrid.

An English-speaking guide will show you through. In the Reliquary are the noblewomen's dowries, one of which is said to contain bits of wood from Christ's Cross; another, some of the bones of St. Sebastian. The most valuable painting is Titian's *Caesar's Money*. The Flemish Hall shelters other fine works, including paintings by Hans van Baker, Brueghel the Elder, and Bernardino Luini. Many of the tapestries were based on Rubens's cartoons, displaying his chubby matrons.

Admission: 300 ptas. ($2.80). Free on Wednesday.
Open: Tues–Sat 10:30am–12:30pm and 4–5:15pm, Sun 11am–1:15pm. **Closed:** Summer, Mon; Fri afternoon. **Metro:** Puerta del Sol, Callao, or Ópera. **Directions:** From Plaza del Callao, off Gran Vía, walk down Postigo de San Martín to Plaza de las Descalzas Reales; convent is on left.

REAL FÁBRICA DE TAPICES (Royal Tapestry Factory), Fuenterrabía, 2. Tel. 551-34-00.

At this factory, the age-old process of making exquisite (and very expensive) tapestries is still carried on with consummate skill. Nearly every tapestry is based on a cartoon of Goya, who was the factory's most famous employee. Many of these patterns—such as *The Pottery Salesman*—are still in production today. (Goya's original cartoons are in the Prado.) Many of the other designs are based on cartoons by Francisco Bayeu, Goya's brother-in-law.

Admission: 50 ptas. (45¢).
Open: Mon–Fri 9:30am–12:30pm. **Closed:** Aug. **Metro:** Menéndez Pelayo.

---

3. MORE ATTRACTIONS

MAINLY MUSEUMS

CHURCH OF SAN FRANCISCO EL GRANDE, Plaza de San Francisco El Grande, San Buenaventura, 1. Tel. 265-38-00.

Ironically, Madrid, the capital of cathedral-rich Spain, does not itself possess a famous cathedral. But it does have an important church, with a dome larger than that

Madrid
★

SPAIN

MADRID ATTRACTIONS

Church ✝   Post Office ✉   Information ℹ

FROMMER'S FAVORITE
MADRID EXPERIENCES

Tasca Hopping The quintessential Madrid experience and the fastest way for a visitor to tap into the local scene. *Tascas* are Spanish pubs serving tantalizing appetizers (*tapas*). You can go from one to the other, sampling the special dishes and wines in each tavern.

Eating "Around Spain" The variety of gastronomic experiences is staggering: You can literally restaurant hop from province to province— without ever leaving Madrid.

Viewing the Works of Your Favorite Artist Spend an afternoon at the Prado, savoring the works of your favorite Spanish artist, devoting all your attention to his work.

Bargain Hunting at El Rastro Madrid has one of the greatest flea markets in Europe, if not the world. Wander through its many offerings, discovering that hidden treasure you've been searching for for years.

A Night of Flamenco Flamenco folk songs (*cante*) and dances (*baile*) are an integral part of the Spanish experience. Spend at least one night in a flamenco tavern, listening to the heartrending laments of gypsy sorrows, tribulations, hopes, and dreams.

Outdoor Café Sitting This is a famous Madrid experience for the summertime, when *madrileños* come alive again on their *terrazas*. The drinking and good times can go on until dawn. From glamorous hangouts to lowly street corners, the café scene takes place mainly along an axis shaped by the Paseo de la Castellana, Paseo del Prado, and Paseo de Recoletos.

of St. Paul's in London. This 18th-century church is filled with a number of ecclesiastical works, notably a Goya painting of St. Bernardinus of Siena. A guide will show you through.
Admission: 50 ptas. (45¢).
Open: Winter, Tues–Sat 11am–1pm and 4–7pm; summer, Tues–Sat 11am–1pm and 5–8pm. **Metro:** La Latina. **Bus:** 3.

MUSEO ARQUEOLÓGICO NACIONAL, Serrano, 13. Tel. 577-79-12.
This stately mansion is a storehouse of artifacts from the prehistoric to the

---

IN THEIR FOOTSTEPS

Miguel de Cervantes Saavedra (1547–1616). This reigning figure of Spanish letters led a life filled with more adventure than his fictional characters. In 1575 he was captured by pirates and sold into slavery in Algiers. Ransomed at great cost in 1580, he wrote 20 to 30 plays, only two of which survived. Joining the Invincible Armada in Seville, he was in great financial trouble and was imprisoned twice in 1590 and 1597. In 1600 he began his tale of a man chasing windmills across the plains of La Mancha, and his *Don Quixote* brought him immortality.
 • **Birthplace:** Alcalá de Henares.
 • **Favorite Haunt:** The plains of La Mancha.
 • **Resting Place:** The Trinitarian Convent in Calle de Cantarranas in Madrid.

baroque. One of the prime exhibits here is the Iberian statue *The Lady of Elche,* a piece of primitive carving (probably 4th century B.C.), discovered on the southeastern coast of Spain. Finds from Ibiza, Paestum, and Rome are on display, including statues of Tiberius and Livia. There are also collections of Spanish Renaissance lusterware, Talavera pottery, Retiro porcelain, and some rare 16th- and 17th-century Andalusian glassware.

Many of the exhibits are treasures that were removed from churches and monasteries. A much-photographed choir stall from Palencia dates from the 14th century. Also worth a look are the reproductions of the Altamira cave paintings (chiefly of bison, horses, and boars), discovered near Santander in northern Spain in 1868.

Admission: 200 ptas. ($1.90).

Open: Tues–Sun 9:15am–8:30pm. Caves: Tues–Sun 9:30am–1:30pm. **Metro:** Colón.

MUSEO SOROLLA, General Martínez Campos, 37. Tel. 410-15-84.

From 1912, painter Joaquín Sorolla and his family occupied this elegant madrileño townhouse off the Paseo de la Castellana. His widow turned it over to the government, and it is now maintained as a memorial. Much of the house remains as Sorolla left it, right down to his stained paintbrushes and pipes. In the museum wing a representative collection of his works is displayed.

Although Sorolla painted portraits of Spanish aristocrats, he was essentially interested in the common people, often depicting them in their native dress. And don't miss the artist's self-portrait, and the paintings of his wife and their son. Sorolla was especially fond of painting beach scenes of the Costa Blanca.

Admission: 200 ptas. ($1.90).

Open: Tues–Sun 10am–2pm. **Closed:** Aug. **Metro:** Iglesia. **Bus:** 5, 16, or 61.

MUSEO MUNICIPAL, Fuencarral, 78. Tel. 522-57-32.

After years of restoration, the Museo Municipal is now open, displaying collections on local history, archeology, and art, with an emphasis on the Bourbon Madrid of the 18th century. Paseos with strolling couples are shown on huge tapestry cartoons. Paintings from the royal collections are here, plus period models of the best-known city squares and a Goya that was painted for the Town Hall.

Admission: Free.

Open: Tues–Sat 10am–1:45pm and 5–8:45pm, Sun 10am–2:15pm. **Metro:** Tribunal.

MUSEO ROMÁNTICO, San Mateo, 13. Tel. 448-10-45.

Attracting those seeking the romanticism of the 19th century, the museum is housed in a mansion decorated with numerous period pieces—crystal chandeliers, faded portraits, oils from Goya to Sorolla, opulent furnishings, and porcelain. Many exhibits date from the days of Isabella II, the high-living, fun-loving queen who was forced into exile and eventual abdication.

Admission: 200 ptas. ($1.90).

Open: Tues–Sun 10am–3pm. **Closed:** Aug–Sept 15. **Metro:** Alonso Martínez.

TEMPLO DE DEBOD, Paseo de Rosales.

This Egyptian temple near the Plaza de España once stood in the Valley of the Nile, 19 miles from Aswan. When the new dam threatened the temple, the Egyptian government dismantled and presented it to Spain. Taken down stone by stone in 1969 and 1970, it was shipped to Valencia and taken by rail to Madrid, where it was reconstructed and opened to the public in 1971. Photos upstairs depict the temple's long history.

Admission: Free.

Open: Mon–Sat 10am–1pm and 4–7pm, Sun 10am–3pm. **Metro:** Plaza de España.

MUSEO DEL EJÉRCITO (Army Museum), Méndez Núñez, 1. Tel. 531-46-24.

This museum, in the Buen Retiro Palace, houses outstanding exhibits from military history, including the original sword of El Cid, which Isabella carried when she took Granada from the Moors. In addition, you can see the tent used by Charles V in Tunisia, relics of Pizarro and Cortés, and an exceptional collection of armor. Look for the piece of the cross that Columbus carried when he discovered the New World.

Admission: 50 ptas. (45¢).
Open: Tues–Sat 10am–2pm, Sun 10am–1:30pm. **Metro:** Banco de España.

MUSEO NAVAL, Paseo del Prado, 5. Tel. 521-04-19.

The history of nautical science and the Spanish navy comes alive at the Museo Naval. The most fascinating exhibit is the map made by the *Santa Maria's* first mate to show the Spanish monarchs the new discoveries. There are also souvenirs of the Battle of Trafalgar.

Admission: Free.
Open: Tues–Sun 10:30am–1:30pm. **Closed:** Aug. **Metro:** Banco de España.

MUSEO NACIONAL DE ARTES DECORATIVAS, Montalbán, 12. Tel. 532-64-99.

In 62 rooms spread over several floors, this museum near the Plaza de la Cibeles displays a rich collection of furniture, ceramics, and decorative pieces. Emphasizing the 16th and 17th centuries, the eclectic collection includes Gothic carvings, alabaster figurines, festival crosses, elaborate dollhouses, elegant baroque four-poster beds, a chapel covered with leather tapestries, and even kitchens from the 17th century.

Admission: 200 ptas. ($1.90).
Open: Tues–Fri 10am–2:30pm; Sat–Sun 10am–2pm.

PARKS & GARDENS

PARQUE DEL RETIRO

This famous park, originally a royal playground for the Spanish monarchs and their guests, sprawls over 350 acres. The huge palaces that once stood there were destroyed in the early 19th century, and only the former dance hall, the Casón del Buen Retiro (housing the modern works of the Prado, including Picasso's *Guernica*) and the building containing the Army Museum remain. The park boasts numerous fountains and statues, plus a large lake. There are also two exposition centers, the Velázquez and Crystal palaces (built to honor the Philippines in 1887), and a lakeside monument, erected in 1922 in honor of King Alfonso XII. In summer the rose gardens are worth a visit, and you'll find several places where you can have inexpensive snacks and drinks.

Admission: Free.
Open: 24 hours (safest 7am–8:30pm). **Metro:** Retiro.

JARDÍN BOTÁNICO (Botanical Garden), Plaza de Murillo, 2. Tel. 420-35-68.

Across the Calle de Alfonso XII, at the southwest corner of the Retiro, the celebrated Botanical Garden (founded in the 18th century) contains more than 100 species of trees and 200 types of plants. Also on the premises are an exhibition hall and a library specializing in botany.

Admission: 75 ptas. (70¢).
Open: Daily 10am–8pm. **Metro:** Atocha. **Bus:** 10, 14, 19, 32, or 37.

CASA DE CAMPO

Try to visit these former royal hunting grounds, miles of parkland lying south of the Royal Palace, across the Manzanares River. You can see the gate through which the kings rode out of the palace grounds—either on horseback or in carriages—on their way to the park. The Casa de Campo has a variety of trees and a lake, usually filled with rowers. You can have drinks and light refreshments around the water, or go swimming in an municipally operated pool. Children will love both the zoo and the Parque de Atracciones (see "Cool for Kids," below).

Admission: Free.
Open: Daily 8am–9pm. **Metro:** Lago or Batán.

4. COOL FOR KIDS

MUSEO DE LAS FIGURAS DE CERA (Wax Museum), Paseo de Recoletas, 41. Tel. 419-22-82.

The kids will enjoy seeing a lifelike wax Columbus calling on Ferdinand and Isabella, as well as Jackie O. having champagne at a supper club. The 400 wax figures also include heroes and villains of World War II. Besides two galleries displaying Romans and Arabs from the ancient days of the Iberian Peninsula, a new show in multivision gives a 30-minute recap of Spanish history from the Phoenicians to the present.

Admission: 500 ptas. ($4.70) adults, 300 ptas. ($2.80) children.
Open: Daily 10:30am–1:30pm and 4–8pm. **Metro:** Colón.

THE ZOO, Casa de Campo. Tel. 711-99-50.

This modern, well-organized facility allows you to see the wildlife of Africa, Asia, and Europe, with about 2,500 animals on display. Most are in a simulated natural habitat, with moats separating them from the public. There's also a petting zoo for the kids.

Admission: 875 ptas. ($8.20) adults, 650 ptas. ($6.10) ages 3–8.
Open: Daily 10am–7pm. **Metro:** Batán. **Directions:** Exit on right side for park, turn left, and walk up to Plaza de España, which takes you directly to zoo.

TELEFERICO. Tel. 241-19-97.

Madrid's cable car departs from the Paseo Pintor Rosales at the eastern edge of the Parque del Oeste (at the corner of the Calle Marqués de Urquijo) and carries you high above two parks, railway tracks, and over the Manzanares River to a spot near a picnic ground and restaurant in the Casa de Campo. Weather permitting, there are good views of the Royal Palace along the way. The ride takes 11 minutes.

Price: 400 ptas. ($3.75) round trip, 275 ptas. ($2.55) one way. Children under 5 ride free.
Service: Mar–Oct daily noon–9pm; Nov–Feb Mon, Thurs, Fri noon–2pm and 4–7pm, Sat and Sun noon–7pm. **Metro:** Arqüelles. **Bus:** 1.

PARQUE DE ATRACCIONES, Casa de Campo. Tel. 463-29-00.

The park was created in 1969 to amuse the young at heart with an array of rides and concessions. The former include a toboggan slide, a carousel, pony rides, an adventure into "outer space," a walk through a transparent maze, a visit to "jungleland," a motor-propelled series of cars disguised as a tail-wagging dachshund puppy, and a gyrating whirligig clutched in the tentacles of an octopus named "El Pulpo." The most popular rides are a pair of roller coasters named "7 Picos" and "Jet Star."

The park also has many diversions for adults. See "Evening Entertainment," below, for details.

Admission: 150 ptas. ($1.40) adults, 50 ptas. (45¢) children under 9. Most rides cost 1 to 5 tickets to board, at 50 ptas. (45¢) each. An all-inclusive ticket—good for all rides—is 1,200 ptas. ($11.30).
Open: July–Aug Tues–Fri 6pm–1am, Sat 6pm–2am, Sun noon–1am; Sept–Mar

Sat–Sun noon–8pm; Apr–June Tues–Fri 3–9 or 11pm, Sat–Sun noon–8 or 9pm.
Directions: Take cable car (see above). At end of ride, "micro-buses" await to take you rest of way. Alternatively, take the suburban train from Plaza de España, stopping near entrance to park (Entrada del Batán).

AQUAPOLIS, Villanueva de la Canada, Carretera de El Escorial. Tel. 815-69-86.
Sixteen miles northwest of Madrid lies a watery attraction where the kids can cool off. Scattered amid shops, a picnic area, and a barbecue restaurant are water slides, wavemaking machines, and tall slides that spiral children into a swimming pool below.
Admission: 1,400 ptas. ($13.15) adults, 900 ptas. ($8.45) children.
Open: Summer, daily 10am–8pm. **Directions:** Free bus runs every hour during park's open hours, leaving Madrid from Calle de los Reyes, next to Coliseum Cinema, on eastern edge of Plaza de España.

PLANETARIUM, Tierno Galvan Park, Méndez Alvaro. Tel. 467-34-61.
This planetarium has a projection room with optical and electronic equipment— including a multivision system—designed to reproduce outer space.
Admission: 260 ptas. ($2.45) adults, 230 ptas. ($2.15) children.
Open: Tues–Fri 5:30 and 7pm, Sat–Sun 11:30am, 1, 5, 6:30, and 8pm. **Metro:** Méndez Alvaro.

5. SPECIAL-INTEREST SIGHTSEEING

FOR THE LITERARY ENTHUSIAST

CASA DE LOPE DE VEGA, Cervantes, 11. Tel. 429-92-16.
This prolific Madrid-born author dramatized Hapsburg Spain as no one ever had before, earning a lasting position in Spanish letters. A reconstruction of his medieval house stands on a narrow street, ironically named for Cervantes, his competitor for the title of the greatest writer of the Golden Age of Spain, and a bitter enemy. The dank, dark house is furnished with relics of the period, although one can't be sure that any of the furnishings or possessions actually belonged to this 16th-century genius.
Admission: 75 ptas. (70¢).
Open: Tues and Thurs 11am–2pm. **Metro:** Antón Martín.

HEMINGWAY HAUNTS

CHICOTE, Gran Vía, 12. Tel. 532-67-37.
Hemingway used Chicote as a setting for his only play, *The Fifth Column*. He would sit here night after night, gazing at the *putas* (it was a famed hooker bar back then) as he entertained friends with such remarks as "Spain is a country for living and not for dying." The bar still draws a lively crowd.
Prices: 650 ptas. ($6.10) for whisky and soda.
Open: Mon–Sat 1:30pm–2:45am. **Metro:** Gran Vía.

MUSEO DEL PRADO, Paseo del Prado. Tel. 420-28-36.
Of the Prado, A. E. Hotchner wrote in his *Papa Hemingway:* "Ernest loved the Prado. He entered it as he entered cathedrals." More than any other, one picture held him transfixed, Andrea del Sarto's *Portrait of a Woman*. (For admission, etc., see "The Top Attractions," above.).

SOBRINO DE BOTÍN, Cuchilleros, 17. Tel. 266-42-17.
In the final two pages of his novel *The Sun Also Rises,* Jake invites Brett here for

the Segovian specialty, roast suckling pig, washed down with Rioja Alta. In another book, *Death in the Afternoon,* Hemingway told his mythical "Old Lady": "I would rather dine on suckling pig at Botín's than sit and think of casualties my friends have suffered." Since that time, thousands upon thousands of Americans have visited Botín (see Chapter 5 for details). It is a perennial favorite of all visiting Yankees.

EL CALLEJÓN, Ternera, 6 Tel. 522-54-01.

Hemingway's "other favorite" was this restaurant, right in the heart of Madrid, and you can still visit it today (see Chapter 5). The author loved the baby eels, paella, and roast lamb served here, accompanied by some fine Valdapeñas red wine. He'd always arrive smiling from a *corrida.* A round table in the corner of the first dining room, where he always sat, is decorated with photos and clippings as a tribute to his memory.

FOR THE ARCHITECTURE ENTHUSIAST

PLAZA MAYOR

⭐ In the heart of Madrid, this famous square was known as the Plaza de Arrabal in medieval times, when it stood outside the city wall.

The original architect of the Plaza Mayor itself was Juan Gómez de Mora, who worked during the reign of Philip III. Under the Hapsburgs, the square rose in importance as the site of public spectacles, including the gruesome autos-da-fé, in which "heretics" were burned. Bullfights, knightly tournaments, and festivals were also staged here.

Three times the buildings on the square burned—in 1631, 1672, and 1790—but each time the Plaza Mayor bounced back. After the last big fire, it was completely redesigned by Juan de Villanueva.

Nowadays a Christmas fair is held around the equestrian statue of Philip III (dating from 1616) in the center of the square. On summer nights the Plaza Mayor becomes the virtual living room of Madrid, as tourists sip *sangría* at the numerous cafés and listen to music, which is often spontaneous.

PUERTA DE TOLEDO

The Puerta de Toledo is one of the two surviving town gates (the other is the Puerta de Alcalá). Constructed during the brief and unpopular rule of Joseph I Bonaparte, this one marks the spot where citizens used to set out for the former imperial capital of Toledo. On an irregularly shaped square, it stands at the intersection of the Ronda de Toledo and the Calle de Toledo. Its original purposed was as a triumphal arch to honor Napoleon Bonaparte. In 1813 it became a symbol of Madrid's fierce independence and the loyalty of its citizens to their Bourbon rulers, who had been restored to the throne in the wake of the Napoleonic invasion.

Metro: Puerta de Toledo.

6. WALKING TOURS

You'll need public transportation to get around New Madrid, as it sprawls for miles in all directions, but walking is the best way to savor the unique charms of Old Madrid.

WALKING TOUR 1 —— Medieval Madrid

Start: Plaza de la Villa.
Finish: Plaza de Puerta Cerrada.
Time: 2½ hours.
Best Time: Any sunny day.

The oldest part of the city was a flourishing Muslim area before Madrid became the capital. Begin your tour at:

1. **Plaza de la Villa,** which stands beside the Calle Mayor, between the Palacio Real (Royal Palace) and the Puerta del Sol. In the center, note the bronze statue of Don Alvaro de Bazán, an admiral under Philip II, best remembered for defeating the Turks at Lepanto. With your back to the Calle Mayor, you will see the red-brick 17th-century façade of the:
2. **Ayuntamiento de Madrid (Town Hall)** on your right. It was originally built as a prison and today houses the Museo Municipal (see "More Attractions," above). On the square's south side rises the depressingly somber stone-and-brick façade of the 15th-century:
3. **Torre de los Lujanes,** a tower whose simple granite entrance is one of Madrid's few remaining examples of Gothic architecture. Beside the tower, behind a Gothic-Mudejar archway, lies the tomb of Beatriz Galindo, nicknamed La Latina because she taught Latin to the adolescent Isabella I. With your back to the Calle Mayor, you'll see two narrow streets stretching parallel to one another to the south. Take the one on the left (Calle del Cordón) and walk for about 1 short block to the:
4. **Plaza del Cordón.** (You won't see any street signs here). You'll find yourself amid a complex of unmarked 16th- and 17th-century municipal buildings, protected and patrolled by uniformed guards. Turn left at the entrance to the Plaza del Cordón, walk about 50 feet, and notice the convex, semicircular entrance to the baroque:
5. **The Church of San Miguel,** San Justo, 4, built by Giacomo Bonavia in the 18th century. A few steps farther, flanking the right side of the church, is a narrow alley, the Pasadizo del Panecillo, where 17th-century priests distributed bread to hungry paupers. Facing the front of the church is one of the oldest houses in Madrid, a grim, rather dingy-looking stone building. Look for the heraldic shields carved into its fortresslike façade. Historical sources report that the legendary Isidro, patron saint of Madrid, worked as a servant in this baronial, now much-faded residence, which today contains private apartments. Its address, although you probably won't see a street sign until you reach the bottom of the hill, is Calle del Doctor Letamendi. Descend this cobblestone street. You'll have to walk back about 10 feet and enter it from an edge of the Plaza del Cordón. Follow it 1 block and cross busy Calle de Segovia.
   Turn right and walk about 3 blocks (the street will now ascend sharply). Look down the Costanilla San Pedro, to your left, and notice the Mudejar tower of the:
6. **Church of San Pedro el Viejo (Old St. Peter's),** which marks the border of Madrid's Muslim quarter. The church's mid-14th-century tower is one of the few remnants of medieval architecture in Madrid. The church itself, however, dates from the 17th century; it was severely looted in 1936.
   Walking 1 more block along the Calle de Segovia, ascending it to the Costanilla San Andrés. Although houses in this neighborhood look small, they are considered among the most chic and expensive in Madrid. Across the Calle de Segovia, note the:
7. **Plaza de la Cruz Verde,** whose centerpiece is a 19th-century baroque fountain commemorating the end of the Spanish Inquisition. In the background you'll see the massive brick tower of the:
8. **Inglesia del Sacramento,** where memorial services for soldiers killed in war or by terrorists are performed. Continue ascending the steep cobblestones of the Costanilla San Andrés. Around you is the:
9. **Arab Quarter.** Many buildings that were erected during the past two centuries were built upon foundations of Muslim buildings. Very shortly, you'll reach the triangular and steeply sloping grounds of the:
10. **Plaza de la Paja,** whose lovely trees and calm give no hint that this was once the most important produce market in the region. Today the neighborhood waits

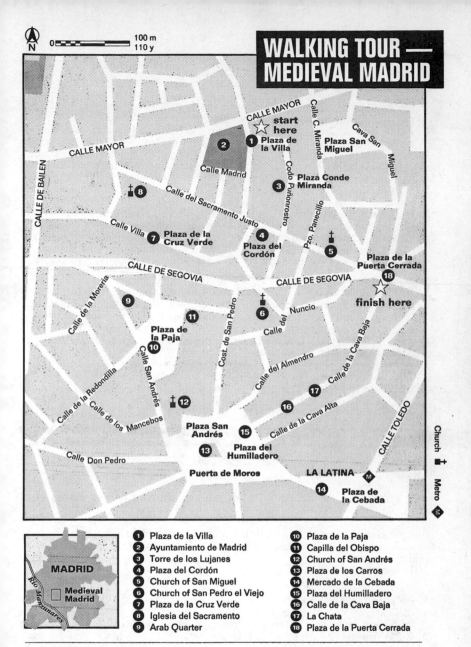

N
0   100 m
    110 y

CALLE MAYOR

start here

CALLE MAYOR

Calle C. Miranda

Cava San Miguel

Plaza de la Villa

Plaza San Miguel

CALLE MAYOR

CALLE DE BAILEN

Calle Madrid

Plaza Conde Miranda

Calle del Sacramento Justo

Pzo. Panecillo

Calle Villa

Plaza de la Cruz Verde

Plaza del Cordón

Plaza de la Puerta Cerrada

CALLE DE SEGOVIA

CALLE DE SEGOVIA

Calle de la Moreria

finish here

Cost. de San Pedro

Calle del Nuncio

Plaza de la Paja

Calle

Calle de la Cava Baja

Calle San Andrés

Calle del Almendro

Calle de la Redondilla

Calle de los Mancebos

Plaza San Andrés

Plaza del Humilladero

Calle de la Cava Alta

CALLE TOLEDO

Calle Don Pedro

Puerta de Moros

LA LATINA

Plaza de la Cebada

Church

Metro

MADRID

Rio Manzanares

Medieval Madrid

1. Plaza de la Villa
2. Ayuntamiento de Madrid
3. Torre de los Lujanes
4. Plaza del Cordón
5. Church of San Miguel
6. Church of San Pedro el Viejo
7. Plaza de la Cruz Verde
8. Iglesia del Sacramento
9. Arab Quarter
10. Plaza de la Paja
11. Capilla del Obispo
12. Church of San Andrés
13. Plaza de los Carros
14. Mercado de la Cebada
15. Plaza del Humilladero
16. Calle de la Cava Baja
17. La Chata
18. Plaza de la Puerta Cerrada

sleepily in the intense sunlight for night to bring business to the several famous restaurants that ring its perimeter. To your left as you climb the square is the:

11. Capilla del Obispo (Bishop's Chapel), entered from the Plaza de la Paja. The mortal remains of San Isidro were interred here from 1518 to 1657. Notice its Renaissance doors. The high altar is considered a masterpiece of Plateresque (the late Gothic style of Castile). At the top of the square, follow the continuation of the Costanilla San Andrés to the right side of the chapel. You'll discover that it abuts the back of the more imposing:

12. Church of San Andrés, Plaza de San Andrés. In one of the most colorful parts of the old town, the church dates from medieval times, but was rebuilt in the 17th century. A fire in 1936 destroyed its greatest treasures. Keep walking and you'll come to the fountains of the:

13. Plaza de los Carros, the first of four interconnected squares, each with its own name and allure. Descend the steps at the far edge of the Plaza de los Carros, and turn left onto the Plaza de Puerta de Moros. Diagonally across the street, you'll soon notice the modern brick-and-concrete dome of the:

14. Mercado de la Cebada. Contained within its echoing interior are open-air markets, open Monday to Saturday from 8am to 2pm and 5 to 8pm. The square has by this time changed its name to:

15. Plaza del Humilladero. Directly in your path are two streets. The one that forks to the left is the:

16. Calle de Cava Baja (the other is Calle la Cava Alta). Six hundred years ago these streets defined the city limits of Madrid. Take the Calle de Cava Baja, which is filled with some of the most typical cafés, bars, and restaurants in Madrid.

REFUELING STOP · 17. La Chata, Cava Baja, 24 (tel. 266-1458), has a restaurant in back, but its stand-up bar up front is more popular. Here, local residents chatter amid hanging Serrano hams and photographs of famous bullfighters. On a hot day, order a glass of beer, or perhaps some tapas. The bar is open Wednesday to Saturday and Monday from noon to 5pm and Wednesday to Monday from 8pm to midnight.

The tour ends at the end of the Calle de Cava Baja, at the:

18. Plaza de la Puerta Cerrada, with its simple white stone cross.

WALKING TOUR 2 —— Hapsburg Madrid

Start: Southeastern corner of the Palacio Real.
Finish: Calle del Arenal.
Time: 3 hours.
Best Time: Saturday or Sunday, when you can also visit the flea market of El Rastro.

This tour encompasses 16th- and 17th-century Madrid, including the grand plazas and traffic arteries that the Hapsburg families built to transform a quiet town into a world-class capital.
　　The tour begins at the:

1. Palacio Real (Royal Palace), at the corner of the Calle de Bailén and the Calle Mayor. The latter was built by Philip II in the 1560s to provide easy access from the palace to his preferred church, San Jerónimo el Real. Walk east on the:

2. Calle Mayor, on the south side of the street. Within a block, you'll reach a black bronze statue of a kneeling angel, erected in 1906 to commemorate the aborted assassination of King Alfonso XIII (grandfather of the present king, Juan Carlos). Across the street from the kneeling angel is the:

3. Palacio de Abrantes, Calle Mayor, 86, today occupied by the Italian Institute of Culture. On the same side of the street as the kneeling angel, to the statue's left, is the:

4. Palacio de Uceda, Calle Mayor, 79, today the headquarters of Spain General

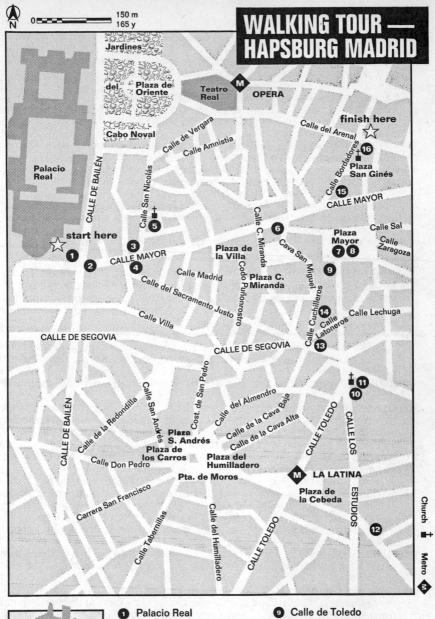

WALKING TOUR — HAPSBURG MADRID

N

0 — 150 m
0 — 165 y

Jardines
del Plaza de Oriente

Cabo Noval

Teatro Real

M OPERA

finish here ☆

Calle del Arenal

Calle de Vergara

Calle Amnistia

Calle San Nicolás

Palacio Real

Palacio Real

CALLE DE BAILÉN

Calle Bordadores

16

Plaza San Ginés

15

CALLE MAYOR

start here ☆

1

2

CALLE MAYOR

3

4

Plaza de la Villa

Calle C. Miranda

6

Cava San Miguel

Plaza Mayor

7 **8**

Calle Sal

Calle Zaragoza

Calle Madrid

Codo Puñonrostro

Plaza C. Miranda

9

Calle del Sacramento Justo

Calle Villa

CALLE DE SEGOVIA

CALLE DE SEGOVIA

Calle Cuchilleros

Calle Latoneros

14

Calle Lechuga

13

CALLE DE BAILÉN

Cost. de San Pedro

Calle San Andrés

Calle de la Redondilla

Calle del Almendro

Calle de la Cava Baja

Calle de la Cava Alta

11

10

CALLE TOLEDO

CALLE LOS

Plaza S. Andrés

Plaza de los Carros

Plaza del Humilladero

M LA LATINA

Calle Don Pedro

Pta. de Moros

Plaza de la Cebeda

ESTUDIOS

Carrera San Francisco

Calle Tabernillas

Calle del Humilladero

CALLE TOLEDO

12

Church ✝

Metro **M**

MADRID

Río Manzanares

☐ Hapsburg Madrid

1 Palacio Real
2 Calle Mayor
3 Palacio de Abrantes
4 Palacio de Uceda
5 Church of San Nicolás
6 Plaza de San Miguel
7 Plaza Mayor
8 Café Bar Los Galayos

9 Calle de Toledo
10 Catedral de San Isidro
11 Colegio Imperial
12 El Rastro
13 Calle de Segovia
14 Calle de Cuchilleros
15 Calle Bordadores
16 Church of San Ginés

Military. Both of these palaces are considered among the best examples of 17th-century civil architecture in Madrid. Walk half a block east, crossing to the north side of the Calle Mayor and detouring about 20 yards to the left, down the narrow Calle de San Nicolás. You'll come to the somber facade of the oldest church in Madrid, the 12th-century:

5. Church of St. Nicolás, Plaza de San Nicolás. Only a brick tower remains from the original building, one of the few examples of the Mudejar style in the capital. The reredos at the high altar is the work of Juan de Herrera, also the architect of El Escorial.

Retrace your steps to the Calle Mayor. Turn left and continue to walk east. You'll pass the Plaza de la Villa on your right, and, 1 block later, the:

6. Plaza de San Miguel, an iron-canopied meat-and-vegetable market. You might stock up on ingredients for a picnic here. (The market is open Mon–Fri 9am–2pm and 5–8pm, Sat 9am–2pm.)

Leave the Plaza de San Miguel by Ciudad Rodrigo (there might not be a sign), which leads under a soaring granite archway and up a sloping street to the northwestern corner of the:

7. Plaza Mayor, the landmark square that is at the heart of Old Madrid.

REFUELING STOP   8. Café Bar Los Galayos, Plaza Mayor, 1 (tel. 165-62-22), has long been one of the best places for tapas along this square. If you're taking the walking tour during the day, you may want to return to this café/bar at night, as it is most lively then. In summer you can select one of the outdoor tables for your drinks and tapas.

Stroll through the Plaza Mayor, crossing it diagonally, exiting at the closer of its two southern exits. A dingy steep flight of stone stairs leads down to the beginning of the:

9. Calle de Toledo. Note in the distance the twin domes of the yellow-stucco and granite:

10. Catedral de San Isidro, legendary burial place of Madrid's patron saint and his wife, Santa María de La Cadeza. The church will lose its status as a cathedral in 1992, when the honor goes to the larger Church of La Almudena. Adjacent to San Isidro is the baroque façade of the:

11. Colegio Imperial, which was also run by the Jesuits. Lope de Vega, Calderón, and many other famous men studied at this institute.

If your tour takes place on a Saturday or Sunday before 3pm, visit:

12. El Rastro, Madrid's world-famous flea market. Continue along the Calle de Toledo, then fork left onto the Calle Estudios and proceed to the Plaza de Cascorro, named after a hero of the Cuban wars. El Rastro begins here.

If your tour takes place Monday to Friday, skip the Rastro neighborhood. Instead, turn right onto the:

13. Calle de Segovia, which intersects the Calle de Toledo just before it passes in front of the Catedral de San Isidro. Walk 1 block and turn right onto the first street, the:

14. Calle de Cuchilleros. Follow it north past 16th- and 17th-century stone-fronted houses. Within a block, a flight of granite steps forks to the right. Climb the steps (a sign identifies the new street as the Calle Arco de Cuchilleros) and you'll pass one of the most famous *mesones* (typical Castilian restaurants) of Madrid, the Cueva de Luís Candelas.

Once again you will have entered the Plaza Mayor, this time on the southwestern corner. Walk beneath the southern most arcade and promenade counterclockwise beneath the arcades, walking north underneath the square's eastern arcade. Then walk west beneath its northern arcade. At the northwest corner, exit through the archway onto the Calle 7 de Julio. Fifty feet later, cross the Calle Mayor and take the right-hand narrow street before you. This is the:

15. Calle Bordadores, which during the 17th century housed Madrid's embroidery workshops, staffed exclusively by men. As you proceed, notice the 17th-century brick walls and towers of the:

16. Church of San Ginés, Arenal, 15. The church of one of Madrid's oldest parishes owes its present look to the architects who reconstructed it after a devastating fire in 1872. At the end of this tour, you'll find yourself on the traffic-congested Calle del Arenal, at the doorstep of many interesting old streets.

WALKING TOUR 3 — Bourbon Madrid

Start: Puerta de Alcalá.
Finish: Plaza de Oriente.
Time: 3 hours.
Best Time: Early morning or late afternoon in summer (or any sunny day in winter).

By the time the Bourbons came to power in Spain, Madrid was firmly ensconced as a political and cultural center, proud of its role as head of a centralized government. This tour shows off the broad boulevards, spectacular fountains, and interconnected plazas that put Madrid on a par architecturally with other European capitals. Much of this tour goes through neighborhoods planned by Charles III in the 18th century. Begin at the:

1. Puerta de Alcalá (Alcalá Gate), Plaza de la Independencia. One of the grand landmarks of Madrid, the Alcalá Gate was designed by Francesco Sabatini from 1769 to 1778. In neoclassical style, it replaced a baroque arch that used to mark the entry into the city; with its five arched passages, it soon became a symbol of the new Bourbon "enlightenment" that swept over Madrid. Today it guards the approach to the major artery leading to northwest Spain and on to France.

Walk west, slightly downhill, along the Calle de Alcalá to the:

2. Plaza de la Cibeles, the most beautiful square in Madrid. In the center of the square is the Fuente de Cibeles, showing the Roman goddess Cybele driving an elaborate chariot pulled by two docile lions, which symbolize elegance and harmony. José Hermosilla and Ventura Rodríguez, architects of Paseo del Prado (see below), designed the fountain. To your left, on the corner of the Calle de Alcalá and Plaza de la Cibeles, is the most magnificent post office in Europe, the Palacio de Comunicaciones. Its lavish embellishments give it the air of an ecclesiastical palace. It dates from 1904.

From the Plaza de la Cibeles you'll see two monuments—the pink-sided Palacio de Buenavista, the army headquarters of Spain, on the right side of the square; and immediately opposite you on the far side of the square, the Banco de España. You are now at the beginning of the most monumental part of Bourbon Madrid. Promenade beneath the leafy canopy of the:

3. Paseo del Prado, which incorporates two busy one-way streets separated by a wide pedestrian's promenade. Walk south down the world-famed promenade, passing shrubbery, trees, and benches. The Paseo del Prado links the Plaza de la Cibeles with the Plaza del Emperador Carlos V, site of the Atocha Train Station, the paseo's southern terminus. It is part of the busy north–south axis of the city. This whole section, called the Salón del Prado, incorporates more world-class art masterpieces than any other area of similar size in the world.

On your left, as you head south toward the Plaza de la Lealtad, you'll pass the:

4. Museo Naval, Paseo del Prado, 5. Adjacent to it, behind a gracefully angled row of neoclassical columns, stands the Madrid stock exchange (La Bolsa), dating from the 19th century. Continue down the Paseo del Prado to the:

5. Monument to the Heroes of the Second of May. This 19th-century obelisk, on your left behind a barrier of trees, honors the "unknown soldiers" who fell in the Napoleonic wars of independence. To your right, a few paces later, is the:

6. **Palace de Villahermosa,** Plaza Cánovas del Castillo, slated to open in 1991. This neoclassical palace holds one of the world's greatest artistic bequests. In the center of the Plaza Cánovas del Castillo (also called the Plaza de Neptuno) is a fountain dedicated to the Roman god Neptune. Continue walking south until you reach the:

7. **The Prado,** Paseo del Prado, one of the world's great art museums. The original core of its paintings, which came from royal palaces throughout Spain, were hugely increased in the 19th century by private bequests. Much of the museum's layout results from the efforts of Charles III in the late 1700s. He commissioned the construction of a neoclassical brick-and-stone palace to house a Natural History Museum, named El Prado de San Jerónimo (St. Jerome's Meadow). It had barely been completed before Napoleon's troops sacked and burned it. Under Ferdinand VII, the museum was restored and finally opened to the public in 1819. Continue south along the Paseo del Prado to the:

8. **Jardín Botánico,** a fine oasis on a hot day.

Head back up the Paseo del Prado, crossing the street. When you reach the Plaza Cánovas del Castillo, turn left toward the ancient heart of Madrid along the Calle de las Cortes, which leads into the:

9. **Carrera de San Jerónimo** (its name will briefly be the Plaza de las Cortes). Walk along the right side. On your left you'll pass the façade of the deluxe Palace Hotel. Turn around and look behind you for a distant view of the Gothic spire of the Iglesia de San Jerónimo.

Keep walking uphill. On your right you'll pass the Corinthian columns and bronze twin lions, flanking the entrance to the Spanish Parliament, built around 1850. Facing it in a small three-sided park is a statue of Cervantes.

At this point, the street will narrow considerably, funneling itself into the:

10. **Plaza Canalejas,** around which sit several charming late-19th- and early-20th-century buildings. On the left side of the square, notice the twin spires of one of the neighborhood's most whimsically appealing structures. Built around 1920, it was designed as an eclectic combination of 17th-century styles, including shells, neoclassical obelisks, and heraldic lions holding shields.

Pass along this square back onto the Carrera de San Jerónimo, by now a busy, congested, and commercial street lined with stores.

REFUELING STOP   11. Lhardy, Carrera de San Jerónimo, 8 (tel. 521-33-85), opened its doors in 1839. It soon became the gathering place of Madrid's literati, political leaders, and executives. Today this place has a decor called "Isabella Segundo," and gives off an aura of another era. Upstairs is a restaurant, but for refueling you can stop downstairs, as have thousands of visitors before you, and enjoy a cup of consommé from a large silver samovar; or in summer, a soothing gazpacho. Each cup costs 150 ptas. ($1.40). It's open Monday to Saturday from 1 to 3:30pm and 9 to 11:30pm.

Continue along the Carrera de San Jerónimo to the geographical heart of Spain, the:

12. **Puerta del Sol.** Two-thirds of the way along its half-moon–shaped expanse, you'll come upon a small brass plaque from which all the distances in Spain are measured, placed immediately in front of a red-brick municipal building called Comunidade de Madrid, on the southern edge of the square.

REFUELING STOP   13. La Mallorquina, Puerta del Sol, 8 (tel. 521-12-01), is the most famous pastry shop in Madrid, occupying a position at the

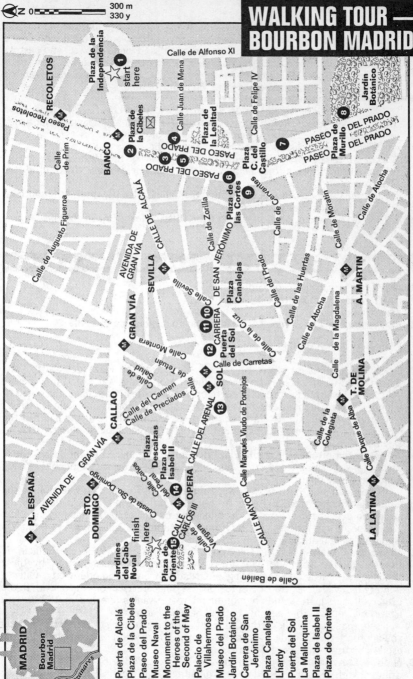

WALKING TOUR — BOURBON MADRID

Z 0 300 m / 330 y

Calle de Alfonso XI

1 Plaza de la Independencia — start here

RECOLETOS
Paseo Recoletos
Calle de Prim
Calle de Augusto Figueroa

2 Plaza de la Cibeles
BANCO

PASEO DEL PRADO
Calle Juan de Mena

3 **4** **5** **6** Plaza de la Lealtad
Plaza de las Cortes

Plaza C. del Castillo
7
8 Jardín Botánico
PASEO DEL PRADO
Plaza de Murillo

Calle de Felipe IV

9 Calle de Cervantes

CALLE DE ALCALÁ
AVENIDA DE GRAN VÍA
SEVILLA
GRAN VÍA

Calle de Zorilla
Calle de Sevilla
CARRERA DE SAN JERÓNIMO

Calle del Prado
Calle de las Huertas
Calle de Atocha

Calle de Moratín
A. MARTÍN

10 **11** Plaza Canalejas
12 Puerta del Sol
SOL
Calle de Carretas
Calle de la Cruz

Calle de la Magdalena
T. DE MOLINA

CALLAO
Calle del Carmen
Calle de Preciados
Calle de Tetuán
Calle de Montera
Calle de la Salud

13 CALLE DEL ARENAL
Calle Marqués Viudo de Pontejos

Calle de la Colegiata
Calle Duque de Alba
LA LATINA

PL. ESPAÑA
AVENIDA DE GRAN VÍA
STO. DOMINGO

Plaza Descalzas
Plaza de Isabel II
OPERA

Cuesta de Sto. Domingo
Calle del Peral
Calle Caños

14 CARLOS III
15 CALLE
Calle de Vergara

Jardines del Cabo Noval — finish here
Plaza de Oriente

CALLE MAYOR
Calle de Bailén

Post Office ⊠   Metro Ⓜ

MADRID
Bourbon Madrid
Río Manzanares

1 Puerta de Alcalá
2 Plaza de la Cibeles
3 Paseo del Prado
4 Museo Naval
5 Monument to the Heroes of the Second of May
6 Palacio de Villahermosa
7 Museo del Prado
8 Jardín Botánico
9 Carrera de San Jerónimo
10 Plaza Canalejas
11 Lhardy
12 Puerta del Sol
13 La Mallorquina
14 Plaza de Isabel II
15 Plaza de Oriente

southwest corner of the Puerta del Sol. It was founded before the turn of the century and became known for one specialty, a Napoletana, filled with cream and studded with almond slices. You can order sandwiches, coffee, and pastries on the ground floor, or head upstairs, where there's sit-down service. A Napoletana costs 100 ptas. (95¢) upstairs, but only 50 ptas. (45¢) at the downstairs bar. It is open daily from 9am to 9:15pm.

At the far end of the Puerta del Sol are two main streets, the Calle Mayor and the Calle del Arenal, forking off to the right. Take Arenal, passing the red-brick neoclassical façade of the Iglesia de San Ginés on your left.
Within a short distance, you'll come upon the:

14. Plaza de Isabel II, graced with a bronze statue of the 19th-century music-loving queen whose efforts helped construct an opera house for Madrid, the Teatro Real.
Follow the Calle del Arenal, now called the Calle Carlos III, around the southern edge of the opera house to the:

15. Plaza de Oriente, with its view of the Palacio Real (Royal Palace).

WALKING TOUR 4 — Grandeur: Past & Present

Start: Gran Vía at Plaza del Callao.
Finish: Plaza de la Encarnación.
Time: 3 hours.
Best Time: Any day except Monday, when collections are closed.

The tour begins on the:

1. Gran Vía, the major street of central Madrid, at the Plaza del Callao. The shop-flanked Gran Vía was opened at the end of World War I, and long before deluxe hotels started to sprout up north on the Paseo de la Castellana, the hotels of Gran Vía were the most expensive and elegant in the Spanish capital. The street runs from the Calle de Alcalá to the Plaza de España, and is at the heart of the modern city, with banks, department stores, and office blocks, plus an array of cinemas.
Begin your promenade at the Plaza del Callao, dominated by the Palacio de la Prensa (press), dating from 1924, and the Capitol, the most fashionable-looking building, dating from 1931.
From Gran Vía, head west toward the Plaza de España. This section of the Gran Vía is considered the most American in inspiration. The architects of the Gran Vía at that time were much influenced by the 1930s style sweeping New York, especially as reflected by the Roxy and Paramount buildings. The Gran Vía comes to an end at the:

2. Plaza de España, with its two tower blocks from the 1950s, the Edificio de España and the Torre de Madrid. This vast square, overshadowed by these skyscrapers, is at a hub separating old Madrid from the modern city. Once a military barracks, it is now one of the busiest traffic intersections in Madrid. In the center of the square stands a monument to Cervantes (erected in 1928), with figures of Don Quixote and his faithful Sancho Panza.
From the square, walk up the Calle de la Princesa, turning to your left (south) as you approach the Calle de Ventura Rodríguez, where you'll come upon one of the esoteric treasure houses of Madrid, the:

3. Museo Cerralbo, Ventura Rodríquez, 17 (tel. 247-36-46). This town house, dripping with the gilt and red-velvet romanticism of the 19th century, was once inhabited by the family of the marquis of Cerralbo, who filled its every nook and cranny with decorative bric-a-brac and art treasures. Note the crystal chandeliers

WALKING TOUR — GRANDEUR: PAST & PRESENT

0 — 200 m
0 — 220 y

N

TRIBUNAL

Calle de la Palma

Calle Amaniel

Travesia Conde Duque

Calle de San Bernardino

Calle de la Princesa

San Bernardo

NOVICIADO

Calle Jesús del Valle

Calle de

Calle del Pez

PL. ESPAÑA

Plaza de España

Calle de San Vicente

AVENIDA DE GRAN VÍA

Calle de la Luna

Corredera Baja de San Pablo

Calle de Fuencarral

Calle de Hortaleza

Calle de

STO. DOMINGO

Calle de Torija

Leganitos

Calle de Sto. Domingo

Plaza de Callao

finish here

Calle de la Bola

CALLAO

AVENIDA DE GRAN VÍA

GRAN VÍA

Plaza Encarnación

Cuesta de Sto.

Calle del Carmen

Calle Montera

Plaza de Oriente

Calle de Bailén

Calle del Arenal

Calle de Alcalá

Jardines del Cabo Noval

SOL

Puerta de Sol

Calle de San Jerónimo

Calle Mayor

Metro

Church

MADRID

Río Manzanares

1. Gran Vía
2. Plaza de España
3. Museo Cerralbo
4. Plaza de Oriente
5. Café de l'Oriente
6. Convento de la Encarnación

---

and the fashionable, opulently colored glass imported from Venice. The Cerralbo clan were art collectors as well, purchasing well-known works from Zurbarán, Ribera, and El Greco. Especially intriguing is the library and study of the late marquís, preserved just as he left it. Admission costs 200 ptas. ($1.90). It's open September through July Tuesday to Sunday from 10am to 3pm. (Metro: Plaza de España or Ventura Rodríguez.)

Returning to the Plaza de España, go to the southeastern corner of the square and head down the Calle de Bailén to the semicircular:

4. Plaza de Oriente, created in 1840, one of the most famous squares in Spain, and the setting of the Palacio Real. The square was designed to provide a harmonious panoramic vista between the Royal Palace and the Puerta del Sol. At the overthrow of the Napoleonic dynasty, work ended and the square was not completed until the reign of Isabella II. An equestrian statue of Philip IV stands in the center of the square, the work, based on drawings by Velázquez, of Italian sculptor Pietro Tacca.

REFUELING STOP **5. Café de l'Oriente,** Plaza de Oriente, 2 (tel. 241-3974), gives you a chance to have a drink and *tapas* with a view of the Royal Palace. The café's entrance is a well-marked doorway set behind a shaded sidewalk tables and a turn-of-the-century decor.

From the Plaza de Oriente take a tiny side street to the northeast of the square, the Calle de Pavia, which will lead to:

6. Convento de la Encarnación, Plaza de la Encarnación, (tel. 247-05-10), on one of the most charming squares in Madrid. The convent and adjoining church were completed in 1616. A Spanish-speaking guide will show you around, pointing out the most important ecclesiastical paintings and Ribera's *St. John the Baptist.* Other works include a gory Christ with serpentine hair by Gregorio Fernández. The cloisters are filled with richly decorated chapels, one in the Pompeiian style. Admission is 300 ptas. ($2.80). The convent is open Tuesday to Thursday and Saturday from 10:30am to 1pm and 4 to 5:30pm; Friday from 10:30am to 1pm; and Sunday from 11am to 1:15pm. (Metro: Opera).

7. ORGANIZED TOURS

A large number of agencies in Madrid book organized tours and excursions. One of the leaders in this field is **Viajes Marsans,** San Nicolás, 15 (tel. 542-55-00). Half-day tours of Madrid include an artistic tour costing 3,350 pesetas ($31.50), which covers entrance to museums, and a panoramic half-day tour for 2,150 pesetas ($20.20). Both of these leave Monday through Saturday at 8:30am from in front of Plaza de Oriente, 8.

Toledo is the most popular full-day excursion, costing 5,500 pesetas ($51.70), leaving daily at 8:30am (same departure point). You can, if you wish, take an abbreviated morning tour of Toledo for only 3,550 pesetas ($33.35). The second most popular tour is to the monastery at El Escorial, including the Valley of the Fallen. The cost is 3,500 pesetas ($32.90) for a half day, with departures Tuesday through Sunday at 8:30am. Daily tours, leaving at the same time, also depart for the walled city of Ávila, Segovia, and the Bourbon summer palace at La Granja, costing 7,100 pesetas ($66.75); with lunch, the ticket is 8,500 pesetas ($79.90).

8. SPORTS & RECREATION

SPECTATOR SPORTS

THE BULLFIGHT

PLAZA MONUMENTAL DE TOROS DE LAS VENTAS, Alcalá, 237. Tel. 246-22-00.

Madrid draws the finest matadors in Spain. If a matador hasn't proved his worth in the major ring in Madrid, he just hasn't been recognized as a top-flight artist. The major season begins during the Fiestas de San Isidro, patron saint of Madrid, on May 15. This is the occasion for a series of fights, during which talent scouts help make up the audience. Matadors who distinguish themselves in the ring are signed up for Majorca, Málaga, and other places.

For tickets to this biggest bullfight stadium in Madrid, go to its box office. Many hotels also have good seats that you can buy. Front-row seats are known as *barreras. Delanteras*—third-row seats—are available in both the *alta* (high) and *baja* (low) sections. The cheapest seats sold, *filas,* afford the worst view and are in the sun (*sol*) during the entire performance. The best seats are in the shade (*sombra*). Bullfights are held on Sunday and holidays at 7pm from Easter to October; in late September and October they often begin at 5pm. Fights by neophyte matadors are sometimes staged on Saturday at 11pm, and admission is cheaper.

On the day of the fight, arrive early to avoid the crowds. You'll want to leave the fight before the very end, again to avoid the crush.

Admission: 250 ptas.–10,000 ptas. ($2.35–$94).

Open: Box office, Mon–Sat 10am–2pm and 4–8pm. **Metro:** Ventas.

HORSE RACING

HIPÓDROMO DE LA ZARZUELA, Carretera de la Coruña. Tel. 207-01-40.

There are two seasons—spring (February through June) and fall (mid-September to early December). Races, often six or seven, are generally held on Sunday and holidays (11am), with a series of night races (11pm) held on weekends in July and August. A restaurant and bar are at the hippodrome, which is 11 miles (18km) from the center of Madrid (N-VI).

Admission: 400 ptas. ($3.75).

Directions: Take free bus, leaving from Moncloa, across from Air Ministry.

SOCCER

Futbol is played with a passion all year in Madrid. League matches, on Saturday or Sunday, run from September to May, culminating in the annual summer tournaments. Madrid has two teams in the top division.

REAL MADRID, Estadio Santiago Bernabéu, Concha Espina, 1. Tel. 250-06-00.

Tickets can be obtained at the stadium.

Prices: From 600 ptas. ($5.65).

Metro: Concha Espina.

ATLÉTICO DE MADRID, Estadio Vicente Calderón, Paseo de la Virgen del Puerto, 6. Tel. 266-47-07.

Tickets can be obtained at the stadium.

Prices: From 600 ptas. ($5.65).

Metro: Pirámides.

RECREATION

FITNESS CENTERS

Although Madrid has scores of gyms, bodybuilding studios, and aerobic-exercise centers, many of them are private. For one open to the public, try **Atenas,** Victor de la Serna, 37 (tel. 457-85-85; Metro: Colombia). This facility for men and women has an indoor swimming pool, workout equipment, a sauna, and such personal services as massage. Open: Mon–Sat 7:30am–9:30pm.

JOGGING

The **Parque del Retiro** and the **Casa de Campo** both have jogging tracks. For details on how to get there, see below and also refer to "Parks and Gardens" in Section 3 of this chapter.

SWIMMING AND TENNIS

The best swimming and tennis facilities are found at the **Casa de Campo,** Avenida del Angel (tel. 463-00-50; Metro: Lago), a 4,300-acre former royal hunting preserve that lies on the right bank of the Manzanares River. Today it is a public park, serving as a playground for madrileños.

9. SAVVY SHOPPING

Seventeenth-century playwright Tirso de Molina called Madrid "a shop stocked with every kind of merchandise," and it's true—its estimated 50,000 stores sell everything from high-fashion clothing to flamenco guitars to art and ceramics.

If your time is limited, go to one of the big department stores (see below). They all carry a "bit of everything."

THE SHOPPING SCENE
SHOPPING AREAS

The Center   The sheer diversity of shops in Madrid's center is staggering. Their densest concentration lies immediately north of the Puerta del Sol, radiating out from the Calle del Carmen, the Calle Montera, and Calle Preciados.

Calle Mayor and Calle del Arenal   Unlike their more stylish neighbors to the north of the Puerta del Sol, shops in this district to the west tend toward the small, slightly dusty enclaves of coin and stamp dealers, family-owned souvenir shops, clockmakers, sellers of military paraphernalia, and an abundance of stores selling musical scores.

Gran Vía   Conceived, designed, and built in the 1910s and 1920s as a showcase for the city's best shops, hotels, and restaurants, the Gran Vía has since been eclipsed by other shopping districts. Its art nouveau/art deco glamour still survives in the hearts of most Madrileños, though. The bookshops here are among the best in the city, as are outlets for fashion, shoes, jewelry, furs, and handcrafted accessories from all regions of Spain.

El Rastro   It's the biggest flea market in Spain, drawing collectors, dealers, buyers, and hopefuls from throughout Madrid and its suburbs. The makeshift stalls are at their most frenetic on Sunday morning. For more information, refer to the "Markets" section, below.

Plaza Mayor   Under the arcades of the square itself are exhibitions of lithographs and oil paintings, and every weekend there's a loosely organized market for stamp and coin collectors. Within 3 or 4 blocks in every direction you'll find more than the average number of souvenir shops.

On the Calle Marqués Viudo de Pontejos, which runs east from the Plaza Mayor, is one of the city's headquarters for the sale of cloth, thread, and buttons. Also running east, on the Calle de Zaragoza, are silversmiths and jewelers. On the Calle Postas you'll find housewares, underwear, soap powders, and other household items.

Near the Carrera de San Jerónimo   Several blocks east of the Puerta del Sol is Madrid's densest concentration of gift shops, craft shops, and antiques dealers—a decorator's delight. Its most interesting streets include the Calle del Prado, the Calle de las Huertas, and Plaza de las Cortes. The neighborhood is pricey—don't expect bargains here.

Northwest Madrid   A few blocks east of the Parque del Oeste is an upscale neighborhood well stocked with luxury goods and household staples. The Calle de la

Princesa, its main thoroughfare, has shops selling shoes, handbags, fashion, gifts, and children's clothing. Thanks to the presence of the university nearby, there's also a dense concentration of bookstores, especially on the Calle Isaac Peral and the Calle Fernando el Católico, several blocks north and northwest, respectively, from the subway stop of Argüelles.

Salamanca District   It's known throughout Spain as the quintessential upper-bourgeois neighborhood, uniformly prosperous, and its shops are correspondingly exclusive. They include outlets run by interior decorators, furniture shops, fur and jewelry shops, several department stores, and design headquarters whose output ranges from the solidly conservative to the high-tech. The main streets of this district are the Calle de Serrano and the Calle de Velázquez. The district lies northeast of the center of Madrid, a few blocks north of the Retiro Park. Its most central Metro stops are Serrano and Velázquez.

HOURS AND SHIPPING

Major stores are open (in general) Monday through Saturday from 9:30am to 8pm. Many small stores take a siesta between 1:30 and 4:30pm. Of course, there is no set formula, and hours can vary greatly from store to store.

   Many establishments will crate and ship bulky objects. Any especially large item, such as a piece of furniture, should probably be sent by ship. Every antiques dealer in Spain has lists of reputable maritime shippers; one reliable option is **Emery Ocean Freight,** c/o Grupinsa, Goya, 115–5, 28009 Madrid (tel. 402-91-49).

   For most small and medium-size shipments, air freight isn't much more expensive than ship. **Iberia** offers shipping service from Spain to New York, Miami, Chicago, or Los Angeles. At those gateways, Iberia can arrange to have the cargo transferred to other airlines.

   A shipment under 99 pounds (45kg) costs around $2.88 per pound. The price goes down as the weight increases, reaching $1.05 per pound for shipments more than 1,100 pounds (500kg). For an additional fee, Iberia will pick up your package. For a truly precious cargo, ask the seller to make a crate for it.

   For information within Spain about air-cargo shipments, call Iberia's cargo division at Madrid's Barajas Airport (tel. 205-4650 or 205-4090, ext. 2671 or 2679). In Barcelona, call Iberia at the Barcelona Airport (tel. 401-3426).

   Remember that your air-cargo shipment will need to clear Customs after it's brought into the United States. This involves some additional paperwork and perhaps trip to the airport near where you live. It's usually easier to hire a commercial customs broker to do the work for you. **Emery Worldwide,** a division of CF Freightways, can

---

 ## FROMMER'S SMART TRAVELER—SHOPPING

1. Read the section on tax refunds (*see page 122*). There's red tape, but refunds can mean substantial savings.
2. Tune your haggling skills in the open-air flea market of Madrid (El Rastro). You can come up with some good buys with strong, steady, firm bargaining.
3. If you pay cash some smaller stores will lower the price.
4. Look for the July and August sales, when merchandise is slashed in price.
5. Don't assume that because a certain product is "made in Spain" that it's cheaper in Spain. It pays to know what something costs at home before you make a substantial purchase.

clear your goods for around $100 for most shipments. For information, you can call toll free in the U.S.: 800/443-6379.

TAX AND HOW TO RECOVER IT

If you are a nonresident and make purchases in Spain worth more than 10,000 pesetas ($94), you can get a tax refund. (The internal tax, known as VAT in most of Europe, is called IVA in Spain.) Depending on the goods, the rate usually ranges from 6% to 12% of the total worth of your merchandise.

To get this refund, you must complete three copies of a form that the store will give you, detailing the nature of your purchase and its value. Citizens of non-EC countries show the purchase and the form to the Spanish Customs Office. The shop is supposed to refund the amount due you. Inquire at the time of purchase how they will do so, and discuss in what currency your refund will arrive.

TRADITIONAL SALES

The best sales are usually in summer. Called *rebajas,* they start in July and go through August. As a general rule, merchandise is marked down even more in August to make way for the new fall wares in most stores.

BEST BUYS & WHERE TO FIND THEM

Spain has always been known for its craftspeople, many of whom still work in the time-honored and labor-intensive traditions of their grandparents. It's hard to go wrong if you stick to the beautiful handcrafted Spanish objects—handpainted tiles, ceramics, and porcelain; handwoven rugs, handmade sweaters, and intricate embroideries—the creation of skilled Spanish workers. And, of course, Spain produces some of the world's finest leather. Jewelry, especially gold set with Majorca pearls, represents good value and unquestioned luxury.

Some of Madrid's art galleries are known throughout Europe for discovering and encouraging new talent. Antiques are sold in highly sophisticated retail outlets. Better suited to the budgets of many travelers are the weekly flea markets.

Spain continues to make inroads into the fashion world. Its young designers are regularly featured in the fashion magazines of Europe. Excellent shoes are available, some highly fashionable. But be advised that prices for shoes and quality clothing are generally higher in Madrid than in the United States.

ANTIQUES

These are sold at the flea market (see El Rastro, below) and at the Puerta de Toledo (see "Shopping Malls," below).

CENTRO DE ARTE Y ANTIGÜEDADES, Serrano, 5. Tel. 576-96-82.
Housed in a mid-19th-century building are several unusual antiques dealers (and a large carpet emporium as well). Each establishment maintains its own schedule, although the center itself has overall hours. Open: Mon–Sat 10:30am–2pm and 3–5:30pm. Metro: Retiro.

CENTRO DE ANTICUARIOS LAGASCA, Lagasca, 36.
You'll find about a dozen shops here—each specializing in antique furniture. Open: Mon–Sat 10am–1:30pm and 5–8pm. Metro: Serrano or Velázquez.

ART GALLERIES

CALCOGRAFÍA NACIONAL, Alcalá, 13. Tel. 532-15-43.
Here you'll find Goya prints from the artist's original plates, as well as many other engravings and etchings. Open: Tues–Fri 10am–2pm, Sat 10am–1:30pm. Metro: Sevilla.

GALERÍA KREISLER, Hermosilla, 8. Tel. 431-42-64.

One highly successful entrepreneur on Madrid's art scene is Ohio-born Edward Kreisler, whose Galería Kreisler occupies two different locations. This branch specializes in relatively conservative paintings, sculptures, and graphics. Open: Mon–Fri 10:30am–1:30pm and 4:30–7:30pm, Sat 10:30am–1pm. Metro: Serrano.

JORGE KREISLER GALERÍA, Calle Prim. Tel. 522-05-34.
Far less conservative than Galería Kreisler, this place displays the sculptures, paintings, and graphics of avant-garde artists. Metro: Chueca.

CAPES

CAPAS SESEÑA, Cruz, 23. Tel. 531-55-10.
Founded shortly after the turn of the century, this shop manufactures and sells wool capes for both women and men. The wool comes from the mountain town of Béjar, near Salamanca. Prices begin at 55,000 ptas. ($517) for men and at around 35,000 ptas. ($329) for women. Open: Mon–Fri 9:30am–1:30pm and 5–8pm, Sat 9:30am–1:30pm. Metro: Tirso de Molina.

CERAMICS

ANTIGUA CASA TALVERA, Isabel la Católica, 2. Tel. 247-34-17.
"The first house of Spanish ceramics" has wares that include a sampling of regional styles from every major area of Spain, including Talavera, Toledo, Manises, Valencia, Puente del Arzobispa, Alcora, Granada, and Seville. Sangría pitchers, dinnerware, tea sets, plates, and vases are all handmade. Inside one of the showrooms is an interesting selection of tiles, painted with reproductions of scenes from bullfights, dances, and folklore. There's also a series of tiles depicting famous paintings in the Prado. At its present location for more than 80 years, the shop is only a short walk from the Plaza de Santo Domingo. Open: Mon–Fri 10am–2pm and 4:30–7:30pm, Sat 10am–1:30pm. Metro: Santo Domingo.

CRAFTS

ARTESPAÑA, Plaza de las Cortes, 3. Tel. 429-12-51.
Handmade objects can be purchased in virtually every neighborhood in Madrid, but one of the city's most stylish outlets is sponsored by the Spanish government as a showcase for the best of its national designs. Artespaña, near the Palace Hotel and the Prado, exhibits Spanish ceramics, furniture, and household items. Open: Mon–Fri 10am–1:30pm and 4:30–8pm, Sat 10am–1:30pm. Metro: Cibeles.

DEPARTMENT STORES

EL CORTE INGLÉS, Calle Preciados, 3. Tel. 232-81-00.
This flagship of the largest and most glamorous department-store chain in Madrid sells hundreds of souvenirs and Spanish handcrafts—damascene steelwork from Toledo, flamenco dolls, embroidered shawls. Some astute buyers report that it also sells glamorous fashion articles such as Pierre Balmain designs for about a third less than equivalent items in most European capitals. Services include interpreters, currency-exchange windows, and parcel delivery either to a local hotel or overseas. Open: Mon–Sat 10am–9pm. Metro: Puerta del Sol.

GALERÍAS PRECIADOS, Plaza del Callao, 1. Tel. 522-47-71.
Right off the Gran Vía, this is really two stores connected by an underground passageway. Good buys include the suede jackets and the coats and capes. There is a moderately priced selection of clothing for men, women, and children, with a tailoring department on the second floor where men can have a suit made to order. Top-floor restaurant and snack bar. Open: Mon–Sat 10am–8pm. Metro: Callao.

EMBROIDERIES

CASA BONET, Núñez de Balboa, 76. Tel. 575-09-12.

The intricately detailed embroideries produced in Spain's Balearic Islands (especially Majorca) are avidly sought for bridal chests and elegant dinner settings. A few examples of the store's extensive inventory are displayed on the walls. Open: Mon–Fri 9:45am–2pm and 5–8pm, Sat 10:15am–2pm. Metro: Núñez de Balboa.

ESPADRILLES

CASA HERNANZ, Toledo, 18. Tel. 266-54-50.

A brisk walk south of the Plaza Mayor delivers you to this store, in business for 150 years. In addition to espadrilles, they sell shoes in other styles, as well as hats. Open: Mon–Fri 9am–1:30pm and 4:30–8pm, Sat 10am–2pm. Metro: Puerta del Sol, Ópera, or La Latina.

FANS AND UMBRELLAS

CASA DE DIEGO, Puerta del Sol, 12. Tel. 522-56-43.

Here you'll find a wide inventory of fans, ranging from plain to fancy, from plastic to exotic hardwood, from cost-conscious to lavish. Open: Mon–Sat 9:45am–1:30pm and 4:30–8pm. Metro: Puerta del Sol.

FASHIONS FOR MEN

For the man on a budget who wants to dress reasonably well, the best outlet for off-the-rack men's clothing is one of the branches of the **Corte Inglés** department-store chain (see above). Most men's boutiques in Madrid are very expensive, and may not be worth the investment.

FASHIONS FOR WOMEN

DON CARLOS, Serrano, 92. Tel. 575-75-07.

Don Carlos has a limited but tasteful array of clothing for women (and a somewhat smaller selection for men). Open: Mon–Sat 10am–2pm and 5–8:30pm. Metro: Núñez de Balboa.

HERRERO, Preciados, 16. Tel. 521-29-90.

The sheer size and buying power of this popular retail outlet for women's clothing make it a reasonably priced choice as well. Additional outlets can be found on the same street, at no. 7 (same phone) and no. 23 (tel. 527-27-22). Open: Mon–Sat 10:45am–2:15pm. Metro: Puerta del Sol or Callao.

JESÚS DE POZO, Almirante, 28. Tel. 531-66-76.

The fabrics are beautiful and the garments expensive, but when they make you look gorgeous, it may be worth it. Open: Mon–Sat 10am–1:30pm and 5–8pm. Metro: Colón.

MODAS GONZALO, Gran Vía, 43. Tel. 247-12-39.

This boutique's baroque, gilded atmosphere evokes the 1940s, but its fashions are strictly up-to-date and well made. Open: Mon–Sat 10am–1:30pm and 4:30–8pm. Metro: Callao or Puerta del Sol.

FOOD AND WINE

MALLORCA, Velázquez, 59. Tel. 431-99-09.

Madrid's best-established gourmet shop opened in 1931 as an outlet selling a pastry called *ensaimada,* and this is still one of the store's most famous products. Tempting arrays of cheeses, canapés, roasted and marinated meats, sausages, and about a dozen kinds of pâté—these accompany a spread of tiny pastries, tarts, and chocolates. Don't overlook the displays of Spanish wines and brandies. A stand-up tapas bar is clogged with clients three deep, sampling the wares before they buy larger portions to take home. Tapas cost from 100 pesetas (95¢) to 200 pesatas ($1.90) per *ración* (portion). Open: Daily 9am–9pm. Metro: Velázquez. Other branches are at Serrano, 6 (tel. 577-18-59; Metro: Serrano); Calle Juan Pérez, Zuñiga, 39 (tel. 448-9749; Metro: Concepción); Comandante Zorita, 39 (tel. 253-5102; Metro: Calle Caminos); and Alberto Alcocer, 48 (tel. 458-7511; Metro: Cuzco or Colombia).

HATS AND HEADGEAR

CASA YUSTAS, Plaza Mayor, 30. Tel. 266-50-84.
Founded in 1894, this extraordinary hat emporium is very popular. Want to see yourself as a Congo explorer, a Spanish sailor, an officer in the kaiser's army, or even Napoleon? Hats begin at 600 pesetas ($5.65). Open: Mon–Fri 9:45am–1:30pm and 4:30–8pm, Sat 9:45am–1:30pm. Metro: Puerta del Sol.

JEWELRY

YANNES, Goya, 37. Tel. 435-31-05.
Madrid has more than its share of predictably upscale jewelers, but this establishment is noted for producing relatively inexpensive jewelry with taste and whimsy. Open: Mon–Sat 10am–1:30pm and 5–8:30pm. Metro: Velázquez.

LEATHER

LOEWE, Gran Vía, 8. Tel. 577-60-56.
Since 1846 this has been the most elegant leather store in Spain. Its gold-medal-winning designers have always kept abreast of changing tastes and styles, but the inventory still retains a timeless chic. The store sells luggage, handbags, and jackets for men and women (in leather or suede). Open: Mon–Sat 9:30am–2pm and 4–8:30pm. Metro: Banco de España.

PATRICIA, Lagasca, 45. Tel. 276-23-30.
Less expensive than Loewe is Patricia, which specializes in purses, handbags, and leather clothes and shoes. Open: Mon–Sat 10am–1:30pm and 5–8pm. Metro: Serrano.

EL RASTRO, Plaza Cascorro and Ribera de Curtidores.
Foremost among markets is El Rastro (translated as either flea market or thieves' market), occupying a roughly triangular district of streets and plazas a few minutes' walk south of the Plaza Mayor. Its center is the Plaza Cascorro and the Ribera de Curtidores. This market will delight anyone attracted to a mishmash of fascinating junk interspersed with bric-a-brac and paintings. But thieves are rampant here (hustling more than just antiques), so secure your wallet carefully, be alert, and proceed with caution. Metro: La Latina. Bus: 3 or 17.

MUSICAL INSTRUMENTS

REAL MUSICAL, Carlos III. Tel. 241-30-09.
You'll find the best selection here—everything from a Spanish guitar to a piano, along with string and wind instruments. The place also has excellent Spanish records and sheet music. Open: Mon–Fri 9:30am–2pm and 5–8pm, Sat 9:30am–2pm. Metro: Ópera.

PERFUMES

PERFUMERÍA PADILLA, Preciados, 17. Tel. 522-66-83.
The Perfumería Padilla sells a large and competitively priced assortment of Spanish and international scents for women. Open: Mon–Fri 9:45am–1:45pm and 5–8pm, Sat 10am–2pm. Metro: Puerta del Sol.

URGUIOLA, Calle Mayor. Tel. 521-59-05.
Urguiola has one of the most complete stocks of perfume in Madrid—both

national and international brands. It also has a wide, tasteful selection of gifts and costume jewelry. Open: Mon–Fri 10am–2pm and 4:45–8:30pm. Metro: Puerta del sol.

PORCELAIN

KREISLER, Serrano, 19. Tel. 276-53-38.
Many shops sell Lladró porcelain, but Kreisler is especially well suited to the tastes of foreign visitors. An official distributor of both Lladró and Nao porcelains, it also sells Majorca pearls, damascene jewelry from Toledo, and a selection of Spanish soaps and perfumes. Open: Mon–Sat 10:30am–2pm and 5–9pm. Metro: Serrano.

LLADRÓ, Quintana, 2. Tel. 247-71-47.
An even more imposing outlet for Lladró porcelain is this store, devoted almost exclusively to its distribution. The staff can usually tell you about new designs and releases the Lladró company is planning for the near future. Open: Mon–Fri 10am–2pm and 5–8pm, Sat 10am–2pm. Metro: Argüelles.

SHOPPING MALLS

GALERÍA DEL PRADO, Plaza de las Cortes, 7.
Spain's top designers are represented in this marble-sheathed concourse below the Palace Hotel. It opened in 1989 with 47 different shops, many featuring *moda joven* (fashions for the young). Merchandise changes with the season, but you will always find a good assortment of fashions, Spanish leather goods, cosmetics, perfumes, and jewelry. You can also eat and drink in the complex. The entrance to the gallery is in front of the hotel, facing the broad tree-lined Paseo del Prado across from the Prado itself. Open: Mon–Sat 10am–9pm. Metro: Banco de España or Atocha.

MERCADO PUERTA DE TOLEDO.
One of Spain's most upscale, ambitious, and architecturally unusual shopping malls is the Mercado Puerta de Toledo, with 150 of the most glamorous names in Spain housed in a slightly run-down neighborhood just southeast of the historic center. Antiques and name-brand fashions especially are featured here, an unusual contrast for a building that served until very recently as Madrid's central fish market; it rises five floors above a sunny courtyard. You won't go hungry between shopping binges because of the many restaurants, tapas bars, and cafés within its premises. Each of the shops is open Monday through Saturday. Hours are 10am–8:30pm. Metro: Puerta de Toledo.

---

10. EVENING ENTERTAINMENT

Madrid abounds with dance halls, tascas, cafés, theaters, movie houses, music halls, and nightclubs. You'll have to proceed carefully through this maze, as many of these offerings are strictly for the residents or for Spanish-speakers.

Because dinner is served late in Spain, nightlife doesn't really get under way until after 11pm, and it generally lasts till around 3am—madrileños are so fond of prowling around at night that they are known around Spain as *gatos* (cats). If you arrive at 9:30pm at a club, you'll probably find that you have the place all to yourself.

In most clubs a one-drink minimum is the rule: Feel free to nurse one drink through the entire evening's entertainment.

THE ENTERTAINMENT SCENE

Nightlife is so plentiful in Madrid that the city can be roughly divided into "night zones."

Plaza Mayor/Puerta del Sol The most popular areas from both the standpoint of tradition and tourist interest, they can also be dangerous, so explore them with caution, especially late at night. They are filled with tapas bars and *cuevas* (drinking "caves"). Here it is customary to begin a tasca crawl, going to tavern after tavern, sampling the wine in each, along with a selection of tapas. The major streets for such a crawl are the Cava de San Miguel, Cava Alta, and Cava Baja. You can order *pinchos y raciones* (tasty snacks and tidbits).

Gran Vía Confined mainly to cinemas and theaters. Most of the after-dark action takes place on little streets branching off the Gran Vía.

Plaza de Isabel II/Plaza de Oriente This is another area much frequented by tourists. Many restaurants and cafés flourish here, including the famous Café de Oriente.

Chueca Embracing such streets as Hortaleza, Infantas, Barquillo, and San Lucas, this is the gay nightlife district, with many clubs. Cheap restaurants, along with a few female striptease joints, are also found here. This area can also be dangerous at night. Watch for pickpockets and muggers.

Argüelles–Moncloa For university students, this part of town sees most of the action. Many discos are found here, along with ale houses and fast-food joints. The area is bounded by Pintor Rosales, Cea Bermúdez, Bravo Murillo, San Bernardo, and Conde Duque.

THE PERFORMING ARTS

There are within Madrid a number of theaters, opera companies, and dance companies. To discover where and when specific cultural events are being performed, pick up a copy of *Guía del Ocio* for 75 pesetas (70¢) at any city newsstand. The sheer volume of cultural offerings might stagger you; for a highly distilled presentation, see below.

Tickets to dramatic and musical events usually range in price from 700 to 1,500 pesetas ($6.60 to $14.10), with discounts of up to 50% granted on certain days of the week (usually Wednesday and early performances on Sunday).

The concierge at most major hotels can usually get you tickets to specific concerts, if you are clear about your wishes and needs. He or she will, of course, charge a considerable markup, part of which will be passed along to whichever agency originally booked the tickets. You'll save money if you go directly to the box office to buy tickets. In the event your choice is sold out, you may be able to get tickets (with a considerable markup) at the **Galicia Localidads** at the Plaza del Carmen (tel. 531-27-32; Metro: Puerta del Sol). This agency also markets tickets to bullfights and sports events. It is open Tuesday through Sunday from 10am to 1pm and 4:30 to 7:30pm.

MAJOR CONCERT/PERFORMANCE HALLS	
AUDITORIO NACIONAL DE MÚSICA	337-02-00
AUDITORIO DEL REAL CONSERVATORIO DE MÚSICA	337-01-00
CENTRO CULTURAL DE LA VILLA	573-60-80
TEATRO CALDERÓN	239-13-33
TEATRO DE LA COMEDIA	521-49-31
TEATRO ESPAÑOL	429-62-97
TEATRO MARÍA GUERRERO	419-47-69
TEATRO REAL	248-14-05

Here follows a grab bag of nighttime diversions that might amuse and entertain you. First, the cultural offerings:

THEATER

Madrid offers many different theater performances, useful to you only if your Spanish is very fluent. If it isn't, check the *Guía del Ocia* for performances by English-speaking companies on tour from Britain, or select a concert or subtitled movie instead.

In addition to the major ones listed below, there are at least 30 other theaters, including one devoted almost entirely to children's plays, the **Sala La Bicicleta,** in the Ciudad de los Niños at the Casa de Campo. Dozens of other plays are staged by nonprofessional groups in such places as churches.

TEATRO CALDERÓN, Atocha, 18. Tel. 239-1333.
This is the largest theater in Madrid, with a seating capacity of 1,700. It's known for its popular revues, performances of popular Spanish plays, and flamenco. Metro: Tirso de Molina.

TEATRO DE LA COMEDIA, Príncipe, 14. Tel. 521-4931.
Site of the Compañía Nacional de Teatro Clásico. Here, more than anywhere else in Madrid, you're likely to see performances from the classic repertoire of great Spanish drama. Metro: Sevilla.

TEATRO ESPAÑOL, Príncipe, 25. Tel. 429-6297.
The company is funded by Madrid's municipal government, its repertoire a time-tested assortment of great and/or favorite Spanish plays. Metro: Sevilla.

TEATRO MARÍA GUERRERO, Tamayo y Baus, 4. Tel. 419-4769.
Also funded by the government, it works in cooperation with the Teatro Español (see above) for performances of works by such classic Spanish playwrights as Lope de Vega and García Lorca. The theater was named after a much-loved Spanish actress. Metro: Banco d'España or Colón.

CLASSICAL MUSIC

AUDITORIO NACIONAL DE MÚSICA, Príncipe de Vergara, 136, Tel. 337-0200.
Sheathed in slabs of Spanish granite, marble, and limestone, and capped with Iberian tiles, this hall is the ultramodern home of both the National Orchestra of Spain and the National Chorus of Spain. Standing just north of Madrid's Salamanca district, it ranks as a major addition to the competitive circles of classical music in Europe. Inaugurated in 1988, it is devoted exclusively to the performances of symphonic, choral, and chamber music. In addition to the Auditorio Principal (Hall A), whose capacity is almost 2,300, there's a hall for chamber music (Hall B), as well as a small auditorium (seating 250) for intimate concerts. Metro: Cruz del Rayo.

AUDITORIO DEL REAL CONSERVATORIO DE MÚSICA, Plaza Isabel II. Tel. 337-0100.
A few steps from the Palacio Real and the Teatro Real, this conservatory presents performances by its students in admission-free concerts. More regularly, however, there are performances by both Spanish and visiting musical ensembles. This 400-seat auditorium is sometimes sold out long in advance. Metro: Ópera.

THE FUNDACIÓN JUAN MARCH, Castelló, 77. Tel. 435-4240.

This foundation sometimes holds free concerts at lunchtime. The advance schedule is difficult to predict. Metro: Núñez de Balboa.

AUDITORIO DEL PARQUE DE ATRACCIONES, Casa de Campo.

The schedule of this 3,500-seat facility might include everything from punk rock musical groups to the more highbrow warm-weather performances of visiting symphony orchestras.

OPERA

TEATRO REAL [ROYAL THEATER], Plaza de Isabel II. Tel. 248-14-05).

Opera in Madrid has traditionally been performed at this neoclassical opera house facing the Royal Palace behind an ornate bronze statue of the music-loving Queen Isabella II, who inaugurated it in 1850. Ongoing renovations are transforming this elegant but antiquated building into one of the finest and most acoustically sophisticated opera houses in Europe, all the while retaining the neoclassical opulence for which the building is famous. Metro: Ópera.

BALLET

CENTRO CULTURAL DE LA VILLA, Plaza de Colón. Tel. 573-60-80.

Ballet, Spanish style, is presented at this cultural center. Tickets go on sale five days before the event of your choice, and performances are usually presented at two different evening shows (8 and 10:30pm). Metro: Serrano or Colón.

LOCAL CULTURAL ENTERTAINMENT

FLAMENCO

CAFÉ DE CHINITAS, Torija, 7. Tel. 248-51-35.

One of the most expensive flamenco spots in town, the Café de Chinitas, in Old Madrid, between the Opera and the Gran Vía, features the dancer La Chunga and the guitarist Serranito. Go for dinner at about 9:30pm and stay for the flamenco. Prices: Meals from 9,000 ptas. ($84.60). Open. Mon–Sat 9:30pm–3:30am; shows at 11pm. Metro: Santo Domingo.

Admission: One-drink minimum 4,000 ptas. ($37.60).

CORRAL DE LA MORERÍA, Morería, 17. Tel. 265-84-46.

In the old town, the Morería—meaning "where the Moors reside"—sizzles with flamenco. Strolling performers, colorfully costumed, warm up the audience around 11pm; a flamenco show follows, with at least 10 dancers. It's much cheaper to eat somewhere else first, paying only the one-drink minimum. Open: Daily 9pm–3am. Metro: La Latina or Puerta del Sol.

Admission: One-drink minimum 2,700 ptas. ($25.28); 7,000 ptas. ($65.80) with dinner.

ZAMBRA, Hotel Wellington, Velázquez, 8. Tel. 435-51-64.

Some of the best flamenco singers and dancers of Spain appear here every night in front of enthusiastic audiences. Reservations are a good idea. If no one answers the telephone, call the reception desk at Hotel Wellington (tel. 275-44-00). Open: Mon–Sat 9:30pm–3am; show at 10:15pm. Metro: Velázquez.

Prices: 3,000 ptas. ($28.20) show; 6,500 ptas. ($61.10) show and dinner.

ARCO DE CUCHILLEROS, Cuchilleros, 7. Tel. 266-58-67.

A good spot for flamenco is Arco de Cuchilleros, near the Botín restaurant. Lots of single men and women come here. All in all, it's fun if you don't take the proceedings

too seriously. Open: Daily 10:30pm–2:30am; shows 10:30pm and 12:30pm. Metro: Puerta del Sol.
   Admission: One drink minimum 2,800 ptas. ($26.30).

ZARZUELA

TEATRO NUEVO APOLO, Tirso de Molina, 1. Tel. 527-38-16.
   The Nuevo Apolo is the permanent home of the renowned Antología de la Zarzuela company. It is on the restored site of the old Teatro Apolo, where these musical variety shows were performed more than 50 years ago. Prices and times depend on the show. Open (box office): Daily 11:30am–1:30pm and 5–8pm; show times vary. Metro: Tirso de Molina.
   Prices: Usually 2,500 ptas. ($23.50) but varies.

TEATRO LIRICO NACIONAL DE LA ZARZUELA, Jovellanos, 4. Tel. 429-82-25.
   Near the Plaza de la Cibeles, this theater produces ballet and an occasional opera in addition to zarzuela. Open: Show times vary. Metro: Sevilla.
   Prices: Depend on the attraction.

THE CLUB & MUSIC SCENE

CABARET

LAS NOCHES DE CUPLE, La Palma, 51. Tel. 532-71-15.
   If you don't mind going to bed at sunrise, you might enjoy this updated version of a once-celebrated madrileño cabaret. Its entrance is on a narrow crowded street. Inside, in a long room with a vaulted ceiling and a tiny stage, Señora Olga Ramos conducts an evening of Iberian song. The charm of her all-Spanish act is increased by the discreet humor of an octogenarian accompanist with an ostrich-feather tiara and a fuchsia-colored boa. Open: Mon–Sat 9:30pm–2:30am; shows at midnight. Prices: Drinks from 900 ptas ($8.45); dinner 5,500 ptas. ($51.70). Metro: Noviciado.
   Admission: One-drink minimum 2,400 ptas. ($22.55).

JAZZ

CLAMORES, Albuquerque, 14. Tel. 445-79-38.
   With dozens of small tables and a huge bar in its dark interior, Clamores, the largest club in Madrid, specializes in the best Catalan champagne to accompany the music. Open: Daily 3pm–3am; shows at 11:30pm and 1:30am. Prices: Drinks 700 ptas. ($6.60); during performances, 300-peseta surcharge ($2.80) on first drink. Metro: Bilbao.

WHISKY JAZZ, Diego de León, 7. Tel. 261-11-65.
   Madrid's leading jazz center, Whisky lies off the Calle de Serrano near the American Embassy. There is no number on the oak door. The memorabilia on the walls reveal a reverence for jazz—letters and faded photographs of the greats from New Orleans, Kansas City, and Chicago. Jazz groups appear frequently; otherwise, the management plays jazz recordings. Open: Mon–Sat 9pm–3:30am. Prices: Drinks 800 ptas ($7.50). Metro: Núñez de Balboa.
   Admission: 800 ptas. ($7.50).

CAFÉ CENTRAL, Plaza del Angel, 10. Tel. 468-08-44.
   Off the Plaza de Santa Ana, beside the famed Hotel Victoria, the Café Central has a vaguely art deco interior, with an unusual series of stained-glass windows. Many of the customers read newspapers and talk at the marble-top tables during the day, but

the ambience is far more animated during the nightly jazz sessions. Open: Mon–Thurs 1pm–1:30am, Fri–Sun 1pm–2:30am; live jazz daily 10pm–2am. Prices: Drinks from 300 ptas. ($2.80). Metro: Antón Martín.

Admission: Cover charge Mon–Thurs 300 ptas. ($2.80), Fri–Sun 350 ptas. ($3.30).

CAFÉ BERLIN/OBA-OBA, Jacometrezo, 4.

This place is really two clubs in one. In the basement is Oba-Oba (tel. 531-0640), whose specialty is Caribbean- and Brazilian-inspired jazz, to which an animated clientele dances the *lambada,* the *salsa,* and an occasional *pasadoble.* Upstairs, the Café Berlin (tel. 531-0810) has live jazz. Open: Daily 6pm–4 or 5am. Prices: Drinks from 700 ptas. ($6.60). Metro: Callao.

CAFÉ POPULART, Huertas, 22. Tel. 429-8407.

This club is known for its exciting jazz groups, who encourage the audience to dance. Run by an engaging entrepreneur named Arturo, it specializes in Brazilian, Afro-bass, reggae, and "new African wave" music. When the music starts, prices of drinks are nearly doubled. Open: Daily 6pm–4 or 5am. Prices: Beer 350 ptas. ($3.30), whisky 500 ptas. ($4.70), when live music isn't playing. Metro: Antón Martín or Sevilla.

DISCOS

The Spanish disco takes its inspiration from those of other Western capitals. In Madrid most disco clubs are open from around 6pm to 9pm, reopening around 11pm. They generally start rocking at midnight or thereabouts.

BOCACCIO, Marqués de la Ensenada. Tel. 419-10-08.

Known for its clientele of show-biz entrepreneurs, this is considered one of the most elegant discos in Madrid. It seems more stylish art nouveau nightclub than rock-and-roll palace, with red-velvet and crescent-shaped banquettes and regally attired bartenders who become part of the show. Open: Daily 7pm–5am. Prices: Drinks 750 ptas. ($17.05). Metro: Colón.

Admission: 1,600 ptas. ($15.05).

JOY ESLAVA, Arenal, 11. Tel. 266-54-40.

This former movie theater has been converted into a high-tech nightspot, filled with an array of lights and sound equipment. Comfortable chaises longues are scattered throughout for those who don't feel like dancing. It's slightly more expensive on weekends, but that's when it's the most fun. Open: Daily 11:30pm–7am. Prices: Drinks 1,100 ptas. ($10.35). Metro: Puerta del Sol or Ópera.

Admission: 1,300 ptas. ($12.20).

MAU-MAU, Padre Damian. Tel. 457-94-23.

Mau-Mau, in the Eurobuilding complex, is a leading nightspot—anyone who's anyone will eventually show up or apply for membership in what is almost considered a private club, especially on those evenings when it's reserved for private parties. Management requires men to wear jackets and ties, except on Sunday and from July through September. Open: Daily midnight–5am. Prices: Drinks 2,000–3,000 ptas. ($18.80–$28.20). Metro: Colombia.

Admission: One-drink minimum.

THE BAR SCENE

PUBS AND BARS

MR. PICKWICK'S, Paseo Pintor Rosales, 48. Tel. 248-51-85.

For homesick English expatriates, no other establishment in Madrid better captures the pub atmosphere than Mr. Pickwick's, a 10-minute walk from the Plaza de España. On the walls hang framed prints of Dickens characters, brass hunting horns, and pewter and ceramic beer mugs. Loners can drink at the bar, or you can sit at one of the small tables, sinking into the soft sofas and armchairs. Open: Daily 6pm–1:30am. Prices: Drinks from 650 ptas. ($6.10). Metro: Argüelles.

SPORTSMAN BRITISH PUB, Alcalá, 65. Tel. 276-69-08.

One of the most attractive of Madrid's pubs (near the central post office), this beautifully paneled English-style club is ringed with banquettes and dotted with velvet. Near the entrance is a long bar area with comfortably padded elbow rests. Paddock, the restaurant in back, has a bulletin board that marks this as a gathering place of British expatriates in Madrid. Open: Mon–Fri 10–4am, Sat–Sun noon–4am. Prices: Beer 450 ptas. ($4.25); drinks 750 ptas. ($7.05). Metro: Retiro.

NUEVO OLIVER, Almirante. Tel. 529-01-47.

Nuevo Oliver, off the Paseo de la Castellana, is a hangout for show-biz people, with a good sprinkling of foreign personalities. The bar feels like a drawing room or library, and there are two club rooms, each with its own personality. The first floor has sofas and comfortable armchairs arranged for conversational gatherings. Reached by a graceful curving stairway, the downstairs room is softer, more secluded. On either side of the fireplace are shelves with an eclectic collection of records (you can pick the ones you want played), and books on theater, movies, and painting. Open: Daily 1pm–6am. Prices: Beer 600 ptas. ($5.50); drinks from 850 ptas. ($7.80). Metro: Chueca.

COCK, De la Reina, 16. Tel. 576-28-69.

This bar attracts some of the most visible artists, actors, models, and filmmakers in Madrid, among them award-winning Spanish director Pedro Almódovar. The decoration is elaborately antique, in contrast to the hip clientele. Open: Mon–Sat 9pm–3am. Prices: Drinks 600 ptas. ($5.65). Metro: Gran Vía.

VIVA MADRID, Manuel Fernández y González, 7. Tel. 467-46-45.

A congenial mix of students, artists, foreign tourists, and visiting Yanks crams into its turn-of-the-century interior, where tilework murals and carved animals contribute an undeniable charm. It's located in a neighborhood of narrow sheets near the Plaza de Santa Ana. Open: Sun–Fri noon–1:30pm, Sat noon–2am. Prices: Drinks from 500 ptas. ($4.70). Metro: Antón Martín.

BALNEARIO, Juan Ramón Jiménez, 37. Tel. 458-24-20.

Clients enjoy potent drinks in a setting with fresh flowers, white marble, and a stone bathtub that might have been used by Josephine Bonaparte. Near Chamartín Railway Station on the northern edge of Madrid, Balneario is one of the most stylish and upscale bars in the city. Tapas include endive with smoked salmon, asparagus mousse, and anchovies with avocado. Open: Mon–Sat noon–2:30pm. Prices: Drinks 350–700 ptas. ($3.30–$6.60); tapas 400–1,500 ptas. ($3.75–$14.10). Metro: Cuzco.

MARAVILLAS NEW AGE CENTER, San Vicente Ferrer, 33. Tel. 532-79-87.

At this new-wave bar youthful clients listen to occasional live concerts of folk music, pop, or jazz. The schedule is unpredictable, but it's always a good place to meet punk rockers. Open: Daily 10pm–5:30am. Prices: Drinks 550 ptas. ($5.15). Metro: Tribunal.

BALMORAL, Hermosilla, 10. Tel. 431-41-33.

Its exposed wood and comfortable chairs evoke a London club. The clientele tends toward journalists, politicians, army brass, owners of large estates, bankers, diplomats, and an occasional literary star. *Newsweek* magazine once dubbed it one of the "best bars in the world." No food other than tapas served. Open: Daily 7:30pm–2am. Prices: Beer 325 ptas. ($3.05); drinks 700 ptas. ($6.60). Metro: Serrano.

HISPANO, Paseo de la Castellana, 78. Tel. 411-48-76.

At the end of a workday, it's crowded with everybody from office workers to entrepreneurs, as well as a few stylishly dressed women. Open: Daily 7:30pm–3am. Prices: Drinks 800 ptas. ($7.50). Metro: Nuevos Ministerios.

LOS GABRIELES, Echegaray, 17. Tel. 429-62-61.

Los Gabrieles, in the heart of one of Madrid's pulsating nightlife centers, served throughout most of the 19th century as the sales outlet for a Spanish wine merchant. In the 1980s its two rooms were transformed into a bar and café, where you can admire lavishly tiled walls with detailed scenes of courtiers, dancers, and Andalusian maidens. Open: Daily 12:30pm–2am. Prices: Drinks 200–325 ptas. ($1.90–$3.05). Metro: Tirso de Molina.

GAY AND LESBIAN BARS

HANOI, Hortaleza, 81. Tel. 319-66-72.

Its setting is stylish and minimalist—stainless steel, curving lines, and sharp angles—and its clients are fun, young, attractive, and articulate. They include a bevy of male and female models who seem to be in constant attendance. The atmosphere is comfortable for both straights and gays. Eight video screens show films from long-defunct TV series, and the music is up-to-date; there is a small restaurant out back. After 1am the place becomes predominantly gay. Open: Daily 9:30pm–3:30am. Prices: Drinks from 600 ptas. ($5.50). Metro: Alonso Martínez.

NO SÉ LOS DIGAS A NADIE, Ventura de la Vega, 7. Tel. 420-29-80.

"Don't Tell Mama" defines itself as a women's entertainment center, although it seems to attract an almost equal number of men to its two floors, hidden behind a black garage door on this street of budget restaurants. Inside, there are an art gallery, a bar-café, a staff of mostly gay women with information on women's activities in Madrid, and live or recorded music every evening after 11pm. Open: Sun–Wed 7pm–1am, Thurs–Sat 7pm–2:30am. Prices: Drinks 700 ptas. ($6.60). Metro: Puerta del Sol.

BLACK AND WHITE, Gravina (corner of Libertad). Tel. 231-11-41.

This is the major gay bar of Madrid, located on a not-very-safe street in the center of the Chueca district. A guard will open the door to a large room—painted, as you might expect, black and white. There's a disco in the basement, but the street-level bar is the premier gathering spot. Old movies are shown against one wall. Open: Daily 8pm–2 or 4am. Prices: Drinks 350 ptas. ($3.30). Metro: Chueca.

CAFÉ FIGUEROA, Augusto Figueroa, 17 (corner of Hortaleza). Tel. 521-16-73.

This turn-of-the-century café attracts a diverse clientele, including a large number of gay men and women. It's one of the city's most popular gathering spots for drinks and conversations. Open: Daily 7:30pm–3:30am. Prices: Drinks 350 ptas. ($3.30). Metro: Chueca.

CRUISING, Perez Galdos, 5. Tel. 521-51-43.

This major gay bar has a vaguely permissive atmosphere, as its name suggests. In the heart of Chueca, it doesn't get lively until late at night. Open: Daily from 7:30pm–3:30am. Prices: Drinks 350 ptas. ($3.30). Metro: Chueca.

DUPLEX, Hortaleza, 64. Tel. 531-3792.

Attracting a young crowd of disco-loving gays, both men and women, this bar contains a modern decor, a disco with recent and very danceable music, and an amply stocked bar. Open: Daily 10pm–5am. Prices: Drinks 350 ptas. ($3.30). Metro: Chueca.

CAVE CRAWLING

To capture a peculiar Madrid joie de vivre of the 18th century, visit some mesones and cuevas, many found in the so-called *barrios bajos*. From the Plaza Mayor, walk down the Arco de Cuchilleros until you find a gypsylike cave that fits your fancy. Young people love to meet in the taverns and caves of Old Madrid for communal drinking and songfests. The sangría flows freely, the atmosphere is charged, the room usually packed; the sound of guitars wafts into the night air. Sometimes you'll see a strolling band of singing students (*tuna*) go from bar to bar, colorfully attired, with ribbons fluttering from their outfits.

MESÓN DE LA GUITARRA, Cava de San Miguel, 13. Tel. 248-95-31.

My favorite cueva in the area, Mesón de la Guitarra is loud and exciting any night of the week, and as warmly earthy as anything you'll find in Madrid. The decor combines terra-cotta floors, antique brick walls, hundreds of sangría pitchers clustered above the bar, murals of gluttons, old rifles, and faded bullfighting posters. Like most things in Madrid, the place doesn't get rolling until around 10:30pm, although you can stop in for a drink and tapas earlier. Don't be afraid to start singing an American song if it has a fast rhythm—60 people will join in, even if they don't know the words. Open: Daily 6:30pm–1:30am. Prices: Beer 225 ptas. ($2.10); wine 100 ptas. (95¢), tapas 400–600 ptas. ($3.75–$5.65). Metro: Puerta del Sol or Ópera.

MESÓN AUSTRIAS, Cava de San Miguel, 11. No phone.

One of several tapas bars just behind the Plaza Mayor, Mesón Austrias has a number of sit-down cells stretching off toward a second bar in the rear. Most customers prefer to stand near the front entrance. In winter the favorite spot is in front of the open fireplace in the front room, when a pitcher of sangría is the thing to order. There's often accordion music at night. Open: Daily 6:30pm–1:30am. Prices: Beer 225 ptas. ($2.10); pitcher of sangría 800 ptas. ($7.50); tapas from 400 ptas. ($3.75). Metro: Puerta del Sol or Ópera.

MESÓN DEL CHAMPIÑÓN, Cava de San Miguel, 17. Tel. 248-67-90.

The bartenders keep a brimming bucket of sangría behind the long stand-up bar as a thirst quencher for the crowd. The name of the establishment in English is Mushroom, and that is exactly what you'll see depicted in various sizes along sections of the vaulted ceilings. A more appetizing way to experience a *champiñón* is to order a ración of grilled, stuffed, and salted mushrooms, served with toothpicks and accompanied by beer, for 400 pesetas ($3.75). Two tiny, slightly dank rooms in the back are where Spanish families go to hear organ music performed. Unless you want to be exiled to the very back, don't expect to sit down here. Practically everybody prefers to stand. Open: Daily 6pm–2am. Prices: Sangría 800 ptas. ($7.50); tapas from 400 ptas. ($3.75). Metro: Puerta del Sol or Ópera.

SESAMO, Príncipe, 7. Tel. 429-65-24.

In a class by itself, this cueva, dating from the early 1950s, draws a clientele of young painters and writers with its bohemian ambience. Hemingway was one of those early visitors (a plaque commemorates him). At first you'll think you're walking into a tiny snack bar—and you are. But proceed down the flight of steps to the cellar. Here, the walls are covered with contemporary paintings and quotations. At squatty stools and tables, an international assortment of young people listens to piano music, and sometimes folk singing or guitar playing. Open: Daily 6pm–2am. Prices: Pitcher of sangría (for four) 800 ptas. ($7.50). Metro: Sevilla or Puerta del Sol.

MORE ENTERTAINMENT
MOVIES

Cinematic releases from Paris, New York, Rome, and Hollywood come quickly to Madrid, where an avid audience often waits in long lines for tickets. Most foreign films are dubbed into Spanish, unless they're indicated as *VO* (original version).

Madrid boasts at least 90 legitimate movie houses (many of which have several theaters under one roof), and many others with adult entertainment only. The premier theaters of the city are the enormous, slightly faded movie palaces of the Gran Vía, whose huge movie marquees announce in lurid colors whichever romantic or adventure *espectáculo* happens to be playing at the moment. For listings, see *Guía de Ocio, Guía de Diario 16* (also available at newsstands), or a newspaper.

If you want to see a film while in Madrid, one of the best places is the quadruplex **Alphaville,** Martín de los Heroes, 14 (tel. 248-72-33; Metro: Plaza de España). It shows English-language films with Spanish subtitles. The movie houses on the Gran Vía include the **Rex,** Gran Vía, 45 (tel. 248-1237); the **Palácio de la Música,** Gran Vía, 35 (tel. 521-62-09); and the **Coliseum,** Gran Vía, 78 (tel. 217-66-12). Metro: Gran Vía.

For classic revivals and foreign films, check the listings at Filmoteca in the **Cine Doré,** Santa Isabel, 3 (tel. 227-3866; Metro: Antón Martín). Movies here tend to be shown in their original language. Tickets cost around 200 pesetas ($1.90). There are a bar and a simple restaurant.

CHAPTER 7

EXCURSIONS FROM MADRID

Madrid makes a great base for excursions because it's surrounded by some of Spain's most exciting attractions. The day trips listed below, to both New Castile and Old Castile, range from 9 to 68 miles outside Madrid, allowing you to leave in the morning and be back by nightfall. If you choose to stay overnight, however, I've included the best budget hotels in each town. Three excursions—El Pardo, Alcalá de Henares, and Ávila—are included for those who have more than a day to spare.

SEEING THE ENVIRONS OF MADRID

A SUGGESTED ROUTE

The speed of the itinerary below can be achieved only by car. Using public transportation would take twice as long. Therefore, if you have only a week and don't have a car, travel by train or bus from Madrid, taking in only the most important attractions: Toledo, El Escorial, Segovia, and Ávila, in that order. Transportation links from Madrid to these cities are highlighted under the individual city listings in the pages that follow.

Day 1 Leave Madrid and drive south to Aranjuez, visiting the Bourbon palace and gardens and continuing southwest to Toledo for the night.

Day 2 Explore Toledo and spend the night.

Day 3 In the morning head northwest for Ávila, exploring its attractions in the afternoon. Stay overnight.

Day 4 Drive northeast to Segovia. Visit the city at leisure and stay overnight.

Day 5 Still in Segovia, spend the day at La Granja, then drive through the snowcapped Guadarrama Mountains.

Day 6 Head southeast toward Madrid. Spend the day exploring the monastery of San Lorenzo de El Escorial, with a side trip to the Valley of the Fallen. Stay overnight in El Escorial (limited accommodations) or return to Madrid.

1. TOLEDO

42 miles SW of Madrid, 85 miles SE of Ávila

GETTING THERE By Train RENFE trains depart frequently every day. Those departing Madrid's Atocha Railway Station for Toledo run from 8:15am to 8:55pm; those leaving Toledo for Madrid run daily from 6:25am to 9:50pm. Traveling time is approximately 90 minutes. For train information in Madrid, call 522-05-18; in Toledo, 22-12-71.

By Bus Buses are faster and more direct than trains. The Continental Auto Line (tel. 22-72-96) in Madrid runs about 30 different buses daily. They depart every half hour from 6:30am to 11:30pm from the lower level of Estación Sur de Autobuses,

WHAT'S SPECIAL ABOUT CASTILE

Great Towns/Villages
- ☐ Toledo, El Greco's hometown and religious center of Spain.
- ☐ Segovia, "a mirage of medieval Spain."
- ☐ Ávila, whose fairy-tale stone walls earned it the following nickname—Castilian "Disneylandia."

Ancient Monuments
- ☐ Roman aqueduct at Segovia, in use for 2,000 yeras.

Architectural Highlights
- ☐ Cathedral at Toledo.
- ☐ Monastery of San Lorenzo de El Escorial, a mammoth repository of paintings and tapestries.
- ☐ Alcázar at Segovia, the structure that inspired the romantic fantasy of "castles in Spain."

Grand Palaces
- ☐ Royal Palace at Aranjuez, spring and fall home of the Bourbons.
- ☐ La Granja, a miniature Versailles in Castile, summer palace of the Bourbons.

Film Locations
- ☐ Walled city of Ávila, where *The Pride and the Passion* was shot.

Religious Shrines
- ☐ Convent of St. Teresa at Ávila, dedicated to this much-adored reformer and tireless mystic.

Festivals/Events
- ☐ Chinchón's Easter Saturday Passion Play in ancient Plaza Mayor.
- ☐ Toledo's splendid Corpus Christi processions, most regal in Spain.

Canarías, 17. (Take the Metro to Palos de Moguer.) Buses take about 1¼ hours to complete the trip between Madrid and Toledo, and are usually marked "Santa Bárbara" or "Poligano." They will deposit you in Toledo's central square, the Plaza de Zocodover.

By Car   Exit Madrid via the Puerta del Toledo on the N-401 south.

ESSENTIALS   Toledo's area code is 925. The Tourist Information Office is at Puerta Nueva de Bisagra (tel. 925/22-08-43).

If you have only one day for an excursion outside Madrid, go to Toledo—a place made special by its blending of Arab, Jewish, Christian, even Roman and Visigothic elements. Declared a national landmark, the city that inspired El Greco in the 16th century has remained largely unchanged. You can still stroll through streets barely wide enough for a man and his donkey—much less an automobile.

Surrounded on three sides by a loop of the Tagus River, Toledo stands atop a hill overlooking the arid plains of New Castile—natural fortress in the center of the Iberian Peninsula. It was a logical choice for the capital of Spain, losing its political status to Madrid in the 1500s. But Toledo remains the country's religious center, as the seat of the Primate of Spain.

If you're driving, the spectacular **skyline** of Toledo will come into view about 3½ miles (6km) from the city. But the most awesome moment will follow later, when you cross the 14th-century Puente San Martín spanning the Tagus for a view of the city from its other bank. The scene is reminiscent of El Greco's moody, storm-threatened *View of Toledo,* which hangs in New York's Metropolitan Museum of Art. It is said that the artist painted that view from a hillside that is now the site of a government-owned *parador,* the Conde de Orgaz. If you arrive at the right time, you can enjoy an apéritif on the parador's terrace and watch one of the famous "violet sunsets" of Toledo.

One Toledan highlight that should not be missed is the **Carretera de Circunvalación,** the route that threads through the city and runs along the Tagus.

Clinging to the hillsides are rustic dwellings, the *cigarrales* of the Imperial City, immortalized by the 17th-century dramatist Tirso de Molina, who named his trilogy *Los Cigarrales de Toledo*.

WHAT TO SEE & DO

CATHEDRAL, Calle Arcos de Palacio. Tel. 22-22-41.

✪ Ranked among the greatest of Gothic structures, the cathedral actually reflects a variety of styles due to the more than 250 years it took to build, from 1226 to 1493. The portals have witnessed many historic events, including the proclamation of Joanna the Mad and her husband, Philip the Handsome, as heirs to the throne of Spain.

Among its art treasures, the *transparente* stands out—a wall of marble and florid baroque alabaster sculpture overlooked for years because the cathedral was too poorly lit. Sculptor Narcisco Tomé cut a hole in the ceiling, much to the consternation of Toledans, and now light touches the high-rising angels, a *Last Supper* in alabaster, and a Virgin in ascension.

The 16th-century Capilla Mozárabe, containing works by Juan de Borgona, is another curiosity of the cathedral. Mass is still held here using Mozarabic liturgy.

The Treasure Room has a 500-pound 15th-century gilded monstrance—allegedly made with gold brought back from the New World by Columbus—that is still carried through the streets of Toledo at the feast of Corpus Christi.

Other highlights of the cathedral include El Greco's *Twelve Apostles* and *Spoliation of Christ* and Goya's *Arrest of Christ on the Mount of Olives*.

Admission: 300 ptas. ($2.80).

Open: Summer, daily 10:30am–1pm and 3:30–7pm; winter, daily 10:30am–1:30pm and 3:30–7pm.

ALCÁZAR, Plaza de Zocodover, or General Moscardó, 4. Tel. 21-39-61.

The Alcázar, located at the eastern edge of the old city near the Plaza de Zocodover, dominates the Toledo skyline. It became world-famous at the beginning of the Spanish Civil War, when it underwent a 70-day siege that almost destroyed it. Today it has been rebuilt and turned into an army museum, housing such exhibits as a plastic model of what the fortress looked like after the Civil War, electronic equipment used during the siege, and photographs taken during the height of the battle. A walking tour gives a realistic simulation of the siege. Allow an hour for a visit.

Admission: 150 ptas. ($1.40); children under 9 free.

Open: Tues–Sun 9:30am–2pm.

MUSEUM OF SANTA CRUZ, Calle de Cervantes. Tel. 22-10-36.

A museum of art and sculpture today, it was originally a 16th-century Spanish Renaissance hospice, founded by Cardinal Mendoza—"the third king of Spain"—who helped Ferdinand and Isabella gain the throne. Look for El Greco's *The Assumption of the Virgin*. Goya and Ribera are also represented, along with a display of gold and opulent antique furnishings, Flemish tapestries, and Visigothic artifacts.

Admission: 200 ptas. ($1.90), including entrance to nearby Museo de los Concilios y de la Cultura Visigoda.

Open: Mon–Sat 10am–6:30pm, Sun 10am–2pm. **Directions:** Pass beneath granite archway piercing eastern edge of Plaza de Zocodover and walk about 1 block.

HOUSE OF EL GRECO, Calle de Samuel Leví. Tel. 22-40-46.

Located in Toledo's *antiguo barrio judio* (old Jewish quarter), a labyrinth of narrow streets on the old town's southwestern edge, the House of El Greco honors the great master painter. In 1585 the artist moved into one of the run-down palace apartments belonging to the marquis of Villena. Although he was to live at other Toledan addresses, he returned to the Villena palace in 1604, and remained there until

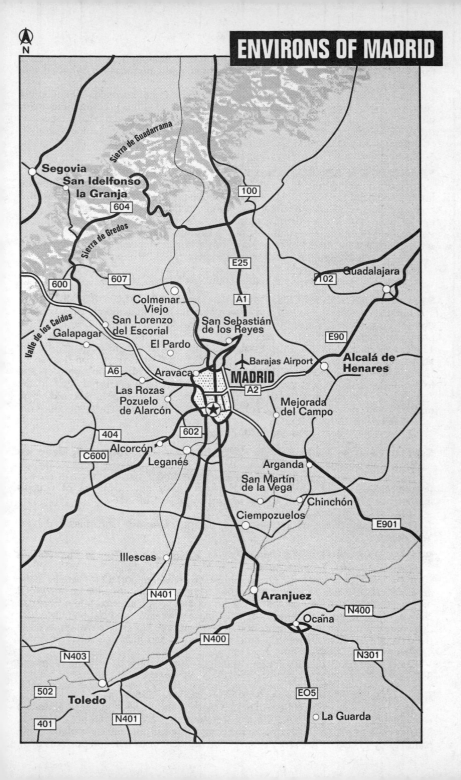

ENVIRONS OF MADRID

his death. Only a small part of the original residence was saved from decay. In time, this and a neighboring house became the El Greco museum; today it's furnished with authentic period pieces.

You can visit El Greco's studio, where one of his paintings hangs. The museum contains several more, including a view of Toledo and three portraits, plus many pictures by various 16th- and 17th-century Spanish artists. The garden and especially the kitchen also merit attention, as does a sitting room decorated in the Moorish style.
Admission: 200 ptas. ($1.90); children under 10 free.
Open: Tues–Sat 10am–7pm, Sun 10am–2pm.

TRÁNSITO SYNAGOGUE, Paseo del Tránsito. Tel. 22-36-65.

One block west of the El Greco home and museum stands this once-important house of worship for Toledo's large Jewish population. A 14th-century building, it is noted for its superb stucco Hebrew inscriptions, including psalms inscribed along the top of the walls and a poetic description of the Temple on the east wall. The synagogue is the most important part of the **Museo Sefardí (Sephardic Museum)**, which was opened in 1971 and contains art objects as well as tombstones with Hebrew epigraphy, some of which are dated before 1492.
Admission: 200 ptas. ($1.90).
Open: Tues–Sat 10am–2pm and 4–6pm, Sun 10am–2pm.

SAN JUAN DE LOS REYES, Reyes Católicos, 17. Tel. 22-38-02.

Founded by King Ferdinand and Queen Isabella to commemorate their triumph over the Portuguese at Toro in 1476, the church was started in 1477, according to the plans of architect Juan Guas. It was finished, together with the splendid cloisters, in 1504, dedicated to St. John the Evangelist, and used from the beginning by the Franciscan friars. A perfect example of Gothic-Spanish-Flemish style, San Juan de los Reyes has been restored since the damage caused during Napoleon's invasion and following its abandonment in 1835; since 1954 it has been entrusted again to the Franciscans. The church is located at the extreme western edge of the old town, midway between the Puente (bridge) of San Martín and the Puerta (gate) of Cambron.
Admission: 100 ptas. (95¢).
Open: Daily 10am–2pm and 3:30–6:45pm.

SANTO TOMÉ—EXPOSICIÓN ANEXA, Plaza del Conde, 4, Calle de Santo Tomé. Tel. 21-02-09.

This modest little 14th-century chapel, situated on a narrow street in the old Jewish quarter, might have been overlooked had it not possessed El Greco's masterpiece *The Burial of the Count of Orgaz,* created in 1586.
Admission: 85 ptas. (80¢).
Open: Daily 10am–1:45pm and 3:30–6:45pm. **Closed:** Christmas and New Year's Day.

SYNAGOGUE OF SANTA MARÍA LA BLANCA, Calle de los Reyes Católicos, s/n. Tel. 22-36-65.

In the late 12th century, the Jews of Toledo erected an important synagogue in the *almohade* style, which employs graceful horseshoe arches and ornamental horizontal moldings. Although by the early 15th century it had been converted into a Christian church, much of the original remains, including the five naves and elaborate Mudejar decorations—mosquelike in their effect. The synagogue lies on the western edge of the city, midway between the El Greco museum and San Juan de los Reyes.
Admission: 75 ptas. (70¢).
Open: Summer, daily 10am–2pm and 3:30–7pm; winter, daily 10am–2pm and 3:30–6pm.

HOSPITAL DE TAVERA, Paseo de Madrid. Tel. 22-04-51.

This 16th-century Greco-Roman palace north of the medieval ramparts of Toledo was originally built by Cardinal Tavera; it now houses a spectacular art collection. Titian's portrait of Charles V hangs in the banqueting hall, and the museum owns five paintings by El Greco: *The Holy Family, The Baptism of Christ,* and portraits of St.

Francis, St. Peter, and Cardinal Tavera. Ribera's *The Bearded Woman* also attracts many. The collection of books in the library is priceless. In the nearby church is the mausoleum of Cardinal Tavera, designed by Alonso Berruguete.

Admission: 150 ptas. ($1.40).

Open: Daily 10:30am–1:30pm and 3:30–6pm.

WHERE TO STAY

DOUBLES FOR LESS THAN 8,000 PTAS. ($75.20)

HOTEL IMPERIO, Cadenea, 5, 45001 Toledo. Tel. 925/22-76-50. 21 rms (all with bath). TEL

$ Rates: 2,600 ptas. ($24.45) single; 4,200 ptas. ($39.50) double; 5,350 ptas. ($50.30) triple. Breakfast 275 ptas. ($2.60) extra. DC, MC, V.

Just off the Calle de la Plata, 1 block west of the Plaza de Zocodover, the Imperio is the best bet for those on a tight budget. The rooms are clean and comfortable, but small. Most overlook a little church with a wall overgrown with wisteria.

HOTEL LOS CIGARRALES, Carretera Circunvalación, 32, 45001 Toledo. Tel. 925/22-00-53. Fax 925/21-55-46. 36 rms (all with bath). **Bus:** Chamartín from rail station.

$ Rates: 3,500 ptas. ($32.90) single; 5,000 ptas. ($47) double. Breakfast 350 ptas. ($3.25) extra. MC, V.

About a mile south of the city center, this hotel offers quiet seclusion. Built in the 1960s in traditional red brick, it looks like a private villa with a garden; the friendliness of the family owners adds to this feeling. Most of the interior is covered with blue and green tiles. The rooms are clean, sunny, and decorated with heavy Spanish furniture. The dining room offers meals for 1,300 pesetas ($12.20). From the flower-filled terrace of the cozy bar you can see the towers of medieval Toledo.

HOTEL MARAVILLA, Plaza de Barrio Rey, 7, 45001 Toledo. Tel. 925/22-33-00. 18 rms (all with bath). A/C TEL

$ Rates: 3,200 ptas. ($30.10) single; 5,300 ptas. ($49.80) double. AE, DC, MC, V.

If you enjoy hotels with lots of local color, then this little place will please you. It's only 1 block south of Plaza de Zocodover, and opens directly onto its own cobblestone plaza. Semi-modernized in 1971, the building has many bay windows; the bedrooms are modest but adequate, the furnishings so-so. You can hang your laundry on the roof and use an iron in the downstairs laundry room. Meals are available (see "Where to Eat," below).

LA ALMAZARA, Carretera de Piedrabuena, 47 (C-781), 48080 Toledo. Tel. 925/22-38-66. 21 rms (all with bath). TEL **Directions:** Follow the road to the Parador of Ciudad Real; then C-781 to Cuerva.

$ Rates: 3,200 ptas. ($30.10) single; 5,500 ptas. ($51.70) double. Breakfast 350 ptas. ($3.30) extra. AE, MC, V. **Closed:** *Dec.*–mid-Mar.

For readers who have a car or who don't mind one or two taxi rides a day, there are some excellent accommodations across the Tagus. Taking its name from an olive-oil mill that used to stand here, La Almazara offers some of the most offbeat accommodations around. Hidden away in the hills, this old-fashioned country villa, with its own courtyards and vineyards, offers a rare opportunity to soak up the atmosphere of old Spain, far removed from the pace of city life. It has an exceptional view of Toledo. You may be assigned either a spacious chamber in the main house or a bedroom in the annex. A continental breakfast is served.

HOTEL RESIDENCIA ALFONSO VI, General Moscardó, 45001 Toledo. Tel. 925/22-26-00. Fax 925/21-44-58. 88 rms. (all with bath). A/C TV TEL

$ Rates: 4,300 ptas. ($40.40) single, 6,500 ptas. ($61.10) double. Breakfast 425 ptas. ($4) extra. AE, DC, MC, V.

Although built in the early 1970s, this hotel has been kept up-to-date. It sits near a great concentration of souvenir shops in the center of the old city, at the southern perimeter of the Alcázar. Inside you'll discover a high-ceilinged, marble-trimmed decor with a scattering of Iberian artifacts, copies of Spanish provincial furniture, and dozens of leather armchairs. You can dine in the stone-floored dining room, where fixed-price meals are 1,800 pesetas ($16.90).

HOTEL CARLOS V, Plaza Horno de Magdalena, 1. 45001 Toledo. Tel. 925/22-21-00. 55 rms (all with bath). A/C TEL

$ Rates: 5,200 ptas. ($48.90) single; 6,800 ptas. ($63.90) double. Breakfast 425 ptas. ($4) extra. AE, DC, MC, V.

This old favorite midway between the Alcázar and the cathedral has a handsome, albeit somber, exterior. It looks more expensive than it is. The rooms are well appointed and the service is fine. Dining is available; lunch or dinner costs 1,800 pesetas ($16.90).

HOSTAL DEL CARDENAL, Paseo de Recaredo, 24, 45005 Toledo. Tel. 925/22-49-00. Fax 925/22-29-91. 27 rms (all with bath). A/C TEL **Bus:** 2 from rail station.

$ Rates: 5,000 ptas. ($47) single; 8,000 ptas. ($75.20) double. Breakfast 450 ptas. ($4.25) extra. AE, DC, MC, V.

The entrance to this unusual hotel is set into the stone fortifications of the ancient city walls, a few steps from the Bisagra Gate. Inside you'll find flagstone walkways, Moorish fountains, rose gardens, and cascading vines. To reach the hotel, you must climb a series of terraces to the top of the crenellated walls of the ancient fortress. There, grandly symmetrical and very imposing, is the former residence of the 18th-century cardinal of Toledo, Señor Lorenzana. The establishment has tiled walls, long, narrow salons, dignified Spanish furniture, and a splattering of antiques.

WORTH THE EXTRA BUCKS

PARADOR CONDE DE ORGAZ, Cerro del Emperador, 45000 Toledo. Tel. 925/22-18-50. Fax 925/22-51-66. 77 rms (all with bath). MINIBAR TV TEL **Directions:** Drive across Puente San Martín and head south for 2½ miles (4km).

$ Rates: 10,300 ptas. ($96.80) single; 13,000 ptas. ($122.20) double. Breakfast 900 ptas. ($8.45) extra. AE, DC, MC, V.

⭐ Make reservations well in advance for the Parador Conde de Orgaz, built on the ridge of a rugged hill where El Greco is said to have painted his View of Toledo. The main living room/lounge has fine furniture—old chests, brown-leather chairs, heavy tables—and leads to a sunny terrace overlooking the city. On chilly nights you can sit by the public fireplace. A stairway and balcony lead to dark oak-paneled doors opening onto the bedrooms, the most luxurious in all of Toledo. Spacious and beautifully furnished, they contain reproductions of regional antique pieces.

WHERE TO EAT

MARAVILLA, Plaza de Barrio Rey, 7. Tel. 22-33-00.
  Cuisine: SPANISH. **Reservations:** None.
$ Prices: Appetizers 450–600 ptas. ($4.25–$5.65); main dishes 750–1,200 ptas. ($7.05–$11.30); fixed-price menu 925 ptas. ($8.70). AE, DC, MC, V.
Open: Lunch Tues–Sun 1–4pm; dinner Tues–Sun 8–11pm.

Ⓢ Located in the Barrio Rey, a small square off the historic Plaza de Zocodover filled with budget restaurants and cafés that change their names so often it's virtually impossible to keep track, Maravilla offers the best all-round dining bargain.

EL EMPERADOR, Carretera del Valle, 1. Tel. 22-46-91.
  Cuisine: SPANISH. **Reservations:** Recommended. **Bus:** Carretera Valle.
$ Prices: Appetizers 450–600 ptas. ($4.25–$5.65); main dishes 900–1,100 ptas. ($8.45–$10.35); fixed-priced menu 900 ptas. ($8.45). V.
Open: Lunch Tues–Sat 1–4pm; dinner Tues–Sat 8–11:30pm.

Ⓢ A modern restaurant on the outskirts of Toledo, southwest of the historic core, El Emperador is reached via an arched bridge. Its terraces overlook the river and the towers of Toledo, while the tavern-style interior has leather and wooden chairs, heavy beams, and wrought-iron chandeliers. Service is attentive. The fixed-price menu might include a choice of soup (beef, vegetable, or noodle), followed by a small steak with french fries, then fresh fruit, plus wine.

HOSTAL DEL CARDENAL, Paseo Recaredo, 24. Tel. 22-49-90.
Cuisine: SPANISH. **Reservations:** Recommended. **Bus:** 2 from station.
$ Prices: Appetizers 650–850 ptas. ($7.10–$8); main dishes 900–1,200 ptas. ($8.45–$11.30). fixed-priced menu 2,200 ptas. ($20.70). AE, DC, MC, V.
Open: Lunch daily 1–4pm; dinner daily 8:30–11:30pm.

★ You may want to treat yourself to Toledo's best and most expensive restaurant, owned by the same people who run Madrid's Casa Botín, so beloved by Hemingway. The menu is very similar. You might begin with "quarter of an hour" (fish) soup or white-asparagus, then move on to curried prawns, baked hake, filet mignon, or smoked salmon. Arrive early and enjoy a sherry in the bar or in the courtyard.

VENTA DE AIRES, Circo Romano, 35. Tel. 22-05-45.
Cuisine: SPANISH. **Reservations:** Recommended.
$ Prices: Appetizers 650–900 ptas. ($7.10–$8.45); main dishes 900–1,600 ptas. ($8.45–$15.05); fixed-price menu 2,200 ptas. ($20.70). AE, DC, MC, V.
Open: Lunch daily 1–4pm; dinner daily 8–11pm.
Just outside the city gates, directly southwest of the Circo Romano (Roman Circus), this restaurant has served Toledo's pièce de résistance—*perdiz* (partridge)—since 1891, when the place was only a little roadside inn. On the à la carte menu, this dish is best eaten with the red wine of Méntrida, but if you want to keep your tab low, you'd better stick to the set menu. For dessert, try the marzipan, an institution in Toledo. On your way out, take note of former President Nixon's entry in the guest book (he dined here in 1963).

LA PARILLA, Horno de los Bizcochos, 8. Tel. 21-22-45.
Cuisine: SPANISH. **Reservations:** None.
$ Prices: Appetizers 250–450 ptas. ($2.35–$4.25); main dishes 900–1,200 ptas. ($8.45–$11.30); fixed-priced menus, 1,050–1,800 ptas. ($9.85–$16.90). AE, DC, MC, V.
Open: Lunch daily 1–4pm; dinner daily 8–11pm.
This classic Spanish restaurant, given a two-fork rating, stands on a cobbled street near the Alfonso VI Hotel, just east of the cathedral. The menu offers no surprises, but it's reliable. Likely inclusions on the bill of fare: roast suckling pig, spider crabs, Castilian baked trout, stewed quail, baked kidneys, and La Mancha rabbit.

AURELIO, Plaza del Ayuntamiento, 8. Tel. 22-77-16.
Cuisine: SPANISH. **Reservations:** Recommended.
$ Prices: Appetizers 450–700 ptas. ($4.25–$6.60); main dishes 1,000–1,300 ptas. ($9.40–$12.20); fixed-priced menu 1,900 ptas. ($17.85). AE, DC, MC, V.
Open: Lunch Wed–Mon 1–4pm; dinner Wed–Mon 8–11:30pm.
Centrally located by the northern edge of the cathedral, Aurelio is one of the best-value restaurants in Toledo, offering good food and efficient service. Begin with *sopa castellana,* then follow with grilled hake, *lubina à la sal* (white fish cooked in salt), fresh salmon, roast lamb, or, if you're feeling up to it, Toledo partridge or roast suckling pig.

SINAI, Reyes Católicos, 7. Tel. 22-56-23.
Cuisine: KOSHER. **Reservations:** Recommended. **Bus:** 2.
$ Prices: Appetizers 650–800 ptas. ($6.10–$7.50); main dishes 1,000–1,200 ptas. ($9.40–$11.30); fixed-price menu 1,200 ptas. ($11.30). AE, DC, MC, V.
Open: Lunch daily noon–5pm.
Considered one of the best Jewish restaurants in Spain, Sinai offers kosher-style

specialties, some derived from the Sephardic traditions of North Africa. Dishes include shaslik kebab, Tangier-style beefsteak, Moroccan couscous, roast chicken with plums, chopped chicken livers, and paella. The house Rioja wine is kosher. The restaurant is located on the western edge of the old town.

PARADOR CONDE DE ORGAZ, Cerro del Emperador. Tel. 22-18-50.
   Cuisine: CASTILIAN. **Reservations:** None. **Directions:** Drive across Puente San Martín and head south for 2½ miles (4km).
$ **Prices:** Appetizers 1,000–1,200 ptas. ($9.40–$11.30); main dishes 1,800–2,400 ptas. ($16.90–$22.55); fixed-priced menu 3,000 ptas. ($28.20). AE, DC, MC, V.
   Open: Lunch daily 1–4pm; dinner daily 8:30–11pm.

Some of the best Castilian regional cuisine is combined here with one of the most spectacular views from any restaurant in Europe. Located in a fine parador, the restaurant is on the crest of a hill—said to be the spot that El Greco selected for his *View of Toledo*. The fixed-price meal might include tasty Spanish hors d'oeuvres, hake, then perhaps either veal or beef grilled on an open fire, plus dessert. If you're dining lightly, try a local specialty, *tortilla española con magra* (potato omelet with ham or bacon). There is a bar on the upper level.

A TAPAS BAR

BAR LUDEÑA, Plaza de la Horn Madelena, 13, Corral de Don Diego, 10. Tel. 22-33-84.
   Cuisine: TAPAS. **Reservations:** None.
$ **Prices:** Tapas 100–500 ptas. (95¢–$4.70).
   Open: Thurs–Tues 10am–midnight.

Delectable combinations of *tapas* are served here to a loyal clientele. Sometimes glasses of wine are passed through a small window to clients who are standing outside enjoying the view of the square. The bar is little more than a narrow corridor, serving *raciones* of tapas that are so generous they make little meals, especially when served with bread. The roasted red peppers in olive oil are especially tasty, along with the stuffed crabs. Huge dishes of pickled cucumbers, onions, and olives are available. A tiny dining room behind a curtain at the end of the bar serves inexpensive fare.

---

2. ARANJUEZ

29 miles S of Madrid, 30 miles NE of Toledo

GETTING THERE   By Train   Trains run about every 20 minutes, to and from Madrid's Atocha Railway Station, (50 minutes). Trains run less often along the east–west route to and from Toledo (40 minutes). The Aranjuez station lies about a mile outside town. You can walk it in about 15 minutes, but taxis and buses line up on the Calle Stuart (2 blocks from the city tourist office). The bus that makes the run from the center of Aranjuez to the railway station is marked "N–Z."

By Bus   Autominibus Interurbaños, Paseo de las Delicias, 18 (tel. 230-46-070), operates buses that depart from Madrid's Estación Sur de Autobuses, Canarías, 17. Buses run about 7 times a day to and from Aranjuez from Madrid. They arrive and depart from the City Bus Terminal, Infantes, 8 (tel. 891-01-83), in Aranjuez.

By Car   Driving is easy and takes about 30 minutes once you reach the southern city limits of Madrid. To reach Aranjuez, follow the signs to Aranjuez and Granada, taking highway N-IV.

ESSENTIALS   The area code of Aranjuez is 91. The Tourist Information Office is at Plaza Santiago Rusiñol (tel. 91/891-04-27).

This Castilian town, at a confluence of the Tagus and Jarama rivers, was the spring and fall home of the Bourbon kings. With its manicured shrubbery, stately elms, fountains, and statues, it remains a regal garden oasis in what is otherwise an unimpressive agricultural flatland known for its strawberries and asparagus.

WHAT TO SEE & DO

On arrival in Aranjuez, purchase a ticket for 400 pesetas ($3.75), which allows you to visit the town's trio of attractions: the Palacio Real (Royal Palace), the Jardín de la Isla (Garden of the Island), and the Casita del Labrador (Little House of the Worker) in the Jardínes del Príncipe. The first sight visited will sell you the global ticket.

PALACIO REAL, Signposted off Carretera N-IV. Tel. 871-07-40.

As you enter the cobblestoned courtyard, you can tell just by the size of the palace that it's going to be spectacular. Ferdinand and Isabella, Philip II, Philip V, and Charles III all made their way through here at one time. The structure you see today dates from 1778 (the previous buildings were destroyed by fire). Its salons show the opulence of a bygone era, room after room of royal extravaganza. Many styles are blended: Spanish, Italian, Moorish, French. And of course, no royal palace would be complete without a room reflecting the rage for chinoiserie that once swept over Europe. The Porcelain Salon is also of special interest. A guide conducts you through the huge complex (tip expected).

Admission: Entrance included as part of global ticket (see above). Separate admission 300 ptas. ($2.80).

Open: Summer, daily 10am–12:30pm and 3:30–7pm; winter, daily 10am–1pm and 3:30–6pm. Bus: Routes from rail station converge at square and gardens at westernmost edge of palace.

JARDÍN DE LA ISLA, Palacio Real. Tel. 871-07-40.

After the tour of the Royal Palace, wander through the Garden of the Island, located directly northwest of the palace. The Spanish impressionist Santiago Rusiñol captured its evasive quality on canvas, and one Spanish writer said that you walk here "as if softly lulled by a sweet 18th-century sonata." A number of fountains are remarkable: the "Ne Plus Ultra" fountain, the black-jasper fountain of Bacchus, the fountain of Apollo, and the ones honoring Neptune (god of the sea) and Cybele (goddess of agriculture).

You may also stroll through the Jardín del Parterre, located in front of the palace. It's much better kept than the Garden of the Island, but not as romantic.

Admission: Entrance included as part of global ticket (see above). Separate admission 300 ptas. ($2.80).

Open: Summer daily 10am–12:30pm and 3:30–7pm; winter, daily 10am–1pm and 3:30–6pm.

CASITA DEL LABRADOR, Jardines del Príncipe. (No phone.)

The Little House of the Worker, modeled after the Petit Trianon at Versailles, was built in 1803 by Charles IV, who later abdicated in Aranjuez. The queen came here with her youthful lover, Godoy (whom she had elevated to the position of prime minister), and the feeble-minded Charles didn't seem to mind a bit. Surrounded by beautiful gardens, the "bedless" palace is lavishly furnished in the grand style of the 18th and 19th centuries. The marble floors represent some of the finest workmanship of that day, the brocaded walls emphasize the luxurious lifestyle, and the royal john is a sight to behold (in those days, royalty preferred an audience). The clock here is one of the treasures of the house. The *casita* lies half a mile east of the Royal Palace; those with a car can drive directly to it through the tranquil Jardín del Príncipe.

Admission: Entrance included as part of global ticket (see above). Separate admission 300 ptas. ($2.80).

Open: Daily 10am–sunset.

WHERE TO STAY

HOSTAL CASTILLA, Carretera Andalucia, 98, 28300 Aranjuez. Tel. 91/891-26-27. 15 rms (all with bath). A/C MINIBAR TV TEL

$ Rates: 2,500 ptas. ($23.50) single; 3,300 ptas. ($31) double. Breakfast 275 ptas. ($2.60) extra. AE, DC, MC, V.

On one of the town's main streets north of the Royal Palace and gardens, the Castilla consists of the ground floor and part of the first floor of a well-preserved early-18th-century house. Most of the accommodations overlook a courtyard with a fountain and flowers. The owner, Joaquín Suarez, speaks English fluently. There are excellent restaurants nearby, and the *hostal* has an arrangement with a neighboring bar for an inexpensive lunch. This is a good location from which to explore either Madrid or Toledo on a day trip.

HOSTAL INFANTAS, Avenida Infantas, 6, 28300 Aranjuez. Tel. 91/891-13-41. 40 rms (35 with bath). TEL **Bus:** Aisa bus line from rail station.

$ Rates: 1,800 ptas. ($16.90) single without bath; 3,600 ptas. ($33.85) double with bath. No credit cards.

⑤ A basic two-star hostal, the Infantas is well maintained and has reasonably up-to-date furnishings and modern plumbing. In a quiet area, with parking available, it's about a 6-minute walk from the Royal Palace. No meals are served, but you can enjoy a continental breakfast at the cafeteria nearby.

WHERE TO EAT

Note: Most of Aranjuez's tourist-financed restaurants—especially those along the river—charge high prices.

LA RANA VERDE, Reina, 1. Tel. 891-32-38.
   Cuisine: SPANISH. **Reservations:** Recommended.
$ Prices: Appetizers 450–600 ptas. ($4.25–$5.65); main dishes 750–1,500 ptas. ($7.05–$14.10). Fixed-price menu 2,000 ptas. ($18.80). No credit cards.
   Open: Daily noon–midnight.

The Green Frog, just east of the Royal Palace and next to a small bridge spanning the Tagus, is still the traditional choice for many. The restaurant looks like a summer house with its high-beamed ceiling and soft ferns drooping from hanging baskets. The preferred tables are in the nooks overlooking the river. As in all the restaurants of Aranjuez, asparagus is a special feature. Game, particularly partridge, quail, and pigeon, can be recommended in season; fish, too, including fried hake and fried sole, makes a good choice. Strawberries are served with sugar, orange juice, or ice cream.

CASA PABLO, Almibar, 42. Tel. 891-32-25.
   Cuisine: SPANISH. **Reservations:** Recommended.
$ Prices: Appetizers 600–800 ptas. ($5.65–$7.50); main dishes 1,200–1,600 ptas. ($11.20–$15.05); Fixed price menu (4 courses) 2,800 ptas. ($26.30). No credit cards.
   Open: Lunch daily 1–4:30pm; dinner daily 8pm–midnight. **Closed:** Aug.

A two-fork restaurant near the bus station in the town center, Casa Pablo offers good values. At tables set outside under a canopy, you can dine while enjoying the tree-lined street and the red and pink geraniums; in cooler weather you eat either upstairs or in the cozy and clean dining room in the rear. The fixed-price menu includes several courses, a carafe of wine, bread, and service. If it's hot and you don't want a heavy dinner, try a shrimp omelet or half a roast chicken; once I ordered just a plate of asparagus in season, accompanied by white wine. If you want a superb dish, try a fish called *mero* (Mediterranean pollack of delicate flavor), grilled over an open fire.

---

3. SAN LORENZO DE EL ESCORIAL

30 miles W from Madrid; 32 miles SE of Segovia

GETTING THERE By Train More than two dozen trains depart daily from Madrid's Atocha and Chamartín train stations. During the summer extra coaches are added. The railway station for San Lorenzo de El Escorial is located about a mile outside of town. The Herranz bus company meets all arriving trains with a shuttle bus that ferries arriving passengers to and from the Plaza Virgen de Gracia, about a block east of the entrance to the monastery.

By Bus   Madrid's Autocares Herranz, Reina Victoria, 3 (Tel. 890-41-22), runs about 15 buses daily to El Escorial from the capital. It leaves passengers at the Plaza Virgen de Gracia, about a block east of the entrance to the monastery. This same company also sells tickets for the single trip per day it makes between El Escorial's Plaza Virgen de Gracia and the Valley of the Fallen (see below). A round-trip ticket from El Escorial to this sight costs 425 pesetas ($4). Departure is at 3:15pm; return to El Escorial is at 5:30pm. Travel time is 20 minutes each way.

By Car   Follow the N-VI highway (on some maps marked as the A-6) from the northwest perimeter of Madrid, in the direction of Lugo, La Coruña, and San Lorenzo de El Escorial. After about a half-hour, fork left onto the C-505, in the direction of San Lorenzo de El Escorial. Driving time is about an hour.

ESSENTIALS   San Lorenzo de El Escorial's area code is 91. The Tourist Information Office is at Floridablanca, 10 (tel. 91/890-15-54).

Next to Toledo, the most important excursion from Madrid is the austere Royal Monastery of San Lorenzo de El Escorial. Philip II ordered the construction of this granite-and-slate rectangular monster in 1563, two years after he moved his capital to Madrid. Once the haunt of aristocratic Spaniards, El Escorial is now a summer resort where hotels and restaurants flourish in summer, as hundreds flock here to escape the heat of the capital. Despite the appeal of its climate, the town of San Lorenzo itself is not very noteworthy. But because of the monastery's size, you might decide to spend a night or two at San Lorenzo—or more if you have the time.

San Lorenzo makes an ideal base for visiting the cities and towns of nearby Segovia and Ávila, the royal palace at La Granja, the Valley of the Fallen—even the more distant university city of Salamanca.

WHAT TO SEE & DO

ROYAL MONASTERY OF SAN LORENZO DE EL ESCORIAL, José Antonio, 1. Tel. 890-50-11.

⭐ This huge granite fortress houses a wealth of paintings and tapestries, and also serves as a burial place for Spanish kings. Foreboding both inside and out because of its sheer size and institutional look, El Escorial took 21 years to complete, a remarkably fast time considering the bulk of the building and the primitive construction methods of the day. After his death, Juan Bautista de Toledo, the original architect, was replaced by Juan de Herrera, the greatest architect of Renaissance Spain, who completed the structure in the shape of a gridiron.

Philip II, who collected many of the paintings exhibited here in the New Museums, did not appreciate El Greco, and favored Titian instead. But you'll still find El Greco's *The Martyrdom of St. Maurice*, rescued from storage, and his *St. Peter*. Other superb works include Titian's *Last Supper* and Velázquez's *The Tunic of Joseph*.

The Royal Library houses a priceless collection of 60,000 volumes—one of the most significant in the world. The displays range from the handwriting of St. Teresa to medieval instructions on playing chess. See, in particular, the Muslim codices and a Gothic *Cantigas* from the 13th-century reign of Alfonso X ("The Wise").

You can also visit the Philip II Apartments, which are strictly monastic and which he called the "cell for my humble self" in this "palace for God." Philip became a religious fanatic and requested that his bedroom be erected overlooking the altar of the 300-foot-high basilica, which has four organs and whose dome is based on Michelangelo's drawings for St. Peter's. The choir contains a crucifix by Cellini. By comparison, the Throne Room is simple. On the walls are many ancient maps.

The Apartments of the Bourbon Kings are lavishly decorated, in contrast to Philip's preference for the ascetic. The tapestries look like paintings until examined closely.

Under the altar of the church you'll find one of the most regal mausoleums in the world, the Royal Pantheon, where most of Spain's monarchs—from Charles I to Alfonso XII, including Philip II—are buried. Nearby, on a lower floor, is the "Wedding Cake" tomb for children.

Ample visiting time is about 3 hours.

Admission: Comprehensive ticket 300 ptas. ($2.80) adults, 100 ptas. (95¢) children.

Open: Tues–Sun 9:30am–1pm and 3:30–6:30pm. **Directions:** Walk uphill from virtually any point in town.

CASA DE PRÍNCIPE (Prince's Cottage), Calle de la Reina s/n. Tel. 891-03-05.

This small but elaborately decorated 18th-century palace near the railway station was originally a hunting lodge built for Charles III by Juan de Villaneuva. Most visitors stay in El Escorial for lunch, visiting the cottage when it reopens in the afternoon.

Admission: 100 ptas. (95¢).

Open: Tues–Sat 10–1pm and 3:30–6:30pm.

VALLE DE LOS CAÍDOS (Valley of the Fallen) Tel. 890-56-11.

This is Franco's El Escorial, an architectural marvel that took two decades to complete, dedicated to those who died in the Spanish Civil War. Its detractors say that it represents the worst of neo-Fascist design; its admirers say they have found renewed inspiration by coming here.

A gargantuan cross, nearly 500 feet high, dominates the Rock of Nava, a peak of the Guadarrama Mountains. Directly under the cross is a basilica in mosaic, completed in 1959. Here José Antonio Primo de Rivera, the founder of the Falange party, is buried. When this Nationalist hero was buried at El Escorial, many, especially influential monarchists, protested that he was not a royal. Infuriated, Franco decided to erect another monument. Originally it was slated to honor the dead on the Nationalist side only, but the intervention of several parties led to a decision to include all the *caídos* (fallen). In time the mausoleum claimed Franco as well; his body was interred behind the high altar.

On the other side of the mountain is a Benedictine monastery that has sometimes been dubbed "the Hilton of monasteries" because of its seeming luxury.

Admission: 300 ptas. ($2.80).

Open: Tues–Sun 9:30am–7pm. **Directions:** Drive to valley entrance, about 5 miles (8km) north of El Escorial in heart of Guadarrama Mountains. Once there, drive 3½ miles (6km) along dusty road to west underground basilica. **Bus:** Autocares Herranz in El Escorial runs a bus here at 3:15pm, returning at 5:30pm; trip takes 15 minutes. Tour buses from Madrid usually include excursion to Valley of the Fallen on their one-day trips to El Escorial. **Funicular:** It extends from near entrance to basilica to base of gigantic cross erected on mountaintop above. Superb view at top. Price: 200 ptas. ($1.90). Open: 10:30am–1:15pm and 4–8:45pm.

WHERE TO EAT NEAR THE VALLEY OF THE FALLEN

HOSTELERIE VALLE DE LOS CAÍDOS, Valle de los Caídos. Tel. 890-55-11.

Cuisine: SPANISH. **Reservations:** None.

$ **Prices:** Appetizers 450–500 ptas. ($4.25–$4.70); main dishes 750–1,100 ptas. ($7.05–$10.35); fixed-price menu 1,000 ptas. ($9.40). No credit cards.

Open: Lunch daily 2–3:30pm; dinner daily 9–10pm.

This three-fork restaurant occupies a dramatic location halfway up to the Valley of the Fallen. Reachable only by car, it's a mammoth modern structure with wide terraces and floor-to-ceiling windows. The *menú del día* can include cannelloni Rossini as an opener, pork chops with potatoes, dessert, and wine.

WHERE TO STAY

DOUBLES FOR LESS THAN 6,400 PTAS. [$60.15]

HOSTAL MALAGON, San Francisco, 2, 28200 San Lorenzo de El Escorial. Tel. 91/890-15-76. 10 rms (none with bath).
$ Rates: 1,500 ptas. ($14.10) single; 2,300 ptas. ($21.60) double. Breakfast 275 ptas. ($2.60) extra. No credit cards.

A super bargain in the heart of town. The owner will welcome you into this very Spanish environment where rooms are plain and basic; doubles come with washbasins. In peak season you'll be asked to take one meal at the hostal, a filling repast for only 1,200 pesetas ($11.30).

HOSTAL CRISTINA, Juan de Toledo, 6, 28200 San Lorenzo de El Escorial. Tel. 91/890-19-61. 16 rms (all with bath).
$ Rates: 4,200 ptas. ($39.50) double. Breakfast 300 ptas. ($2.80) extra. Full board 4,500 ptas. ($42.30) per person. MC, V.
The best low-budget accommodation in the center of town offers clean, comfortable rooms and a helpful staff. No singles are available. With the food both good and plentiful, many Spanish visitors prefer to book on the full-board plan. There's also a small garden.

MIRANDA & SUIZO, Floridablanca, 18, 28200 San Lorenzo de El Escorial. Tel. 91/890-47-11. Fax 91/890-43-58. 47 rms (all with bath).
$ Rates: 4,500 ptas. ($42.30) single; 6,400 ptas. ($60.15) double. Breakfast 350 ptas. ($3.30) extra. AE, DC, MC, V.
On a tree-lined street in the heart of town, within easy walking distance of the monastery, this excellent middle-class establishment ranks as a leading two-star hotel. The Victorian-style building has good rooms, some with terraces. The furnishings are comfortable, the beds are often made of brass, and sometimes you'll find fresh flowers on the table. In summer, there is outside dining.

WORTH THE EXTRA BUCKS

HOTEL VICTORIA PALACE, Juan de Toledo, 4, 28200 San Lorenzo de El Escorial. Tel. 91/890-15-11. Fax 91/890-12-48. 87 rms (all with bath). TV TEL
$ Rates: 7,500 ptas. ($70.50) single; 10,000 ptas. ($94) double. Breakfast 600 ptas. ($5.65) extra. AE, DC, MC, V.
The Victoria Palace, with its view of El Escorial, is the finest hotel in town, a traditional establishment that has been modernized without losing its special aura of style and comfort. It is surrounded by beautiful gardens and has an outdoor swimming pool. The rooms, (some with private terrace) are well furnished and maintained. The rate—reasonable enough, and a bargain for a four-star hotel—also includes admission to El Escorial. The dining room serves some of the best food in town, with a meal averaging around 2,800 pesetas ($26.30).

WHERE TO EAT

MEALS FOR LESS THAN 1,400 PTAS. [$13.15]

CASTILLA, Plaza de la Constitución, 2. Tel. 890-52-19.
Cuisine: SPANISH. **Reservations:** None.
$ Prices: Appetizers 450–600 ptas. ($4.25–$5.65); main dishes 750–1,400 ptas. ($7.05–$13.15); fixed-price menu 1,050 ptas. ($9.85). No credit cards.
Open: Lunch Tues–Sun 1–3:30pm; dinner Tues–Sun 9:15–11pm.

Tables are placed outdoors in summer at this centrally located restaurant a few paces from the Town Hall. The featured dishes are typically Spanish, including paella and roast baby lamb.

MESÓN LA CUEVA (The Cave), San Antón, 4. Tel. 890-15-16.
   Cuisine: SPANISH. **Reservations:** Recommended.
$ Prices: Appetizers 650–750 ptas. ($6.10–$7.05); main dishes 950–1,200 ptas. ($8.95–$11.30). No credit cards.
   Open: Lunch daily 1–4pm; dinner daily 8:30–11pm.
Founded in 1768, this restaurant recaptures the world of Old Castile. A *mesón típico*, built around an enclosed courtyard, it boasts such nostalgic accents as stained-glass windows, antique chests, a 19th-century bullfighting collage, faded engravings, paneled doors, and iron balconies. The cooking is on target, the portions generous. Regional specialties include Valencian paella and *fabada asturiana* (pork sausage and beans), but fresh trout broiled in butter may be best of all. The menu's most expensive items are Segovian roast suckling pig and roast lamb (tender inside, crisp outside). Off the courtyard through a separate doorway is La Cueva's *tasca*, filled with Castilians quaffing their favorite before-dinner drinks.

WORTH THE EXTRA BUCKS

CHAROLES, Floridablanca, 24. Tel. 89-59-75.
   Cuisine: SPANISH/INTERNATIONAL. **Reservations:** Required.
$ Prices: Appetizers 950–1,800 ptas. ($8.95–$16.90); main dishes 2,000–2,800 ptas. ($18.80–$26.30); fixed-price menu 4,000 ptas. ($37.60). AE, DC, MC, V.
   Open: Lunch daily 1–4pm; dinner daily 9pm–midnight.
Its sunny terrace, air-conditioned interior, and impeccable service are reasons to seek this place out, but the best reason of all is the fresh meat and fish that owner Manolo Miguez imports daily from Madrid. The specials change daily depending on what's available, but outstanding past dishes have included shellfish soup; a *pastel* of fresh vegetables with crayfish; pepper steak; and herb-flavored baby lamb chops. Kiwi tart is a good choice for dessert.

---

4. SEGOVIA

54 to 63 miles NW of Madrid, 42 miles NE of Avila

GETTING THERE   By Train   About a dozen trains leave Madrid's Atocha Railway Station every day and arrive 2½ hours later in Segovia, where you can board bus no. 3, which departs every quarter hour for the Plaza Mayor. (Note that some maps and some residents still refer to the Plaza Mayor as the Plaza Franco.) The station lies on the Paseo Obispo Quesada s/n (tel. 42-07-74), a 20-minute walk southeast of the town center.

By Bus   Buses arrive and depart from the Estacionamiento Municipal de Auto-buses, Paseo de Equezuile González, 10 (tel. 42-77-25), near the corner of the Avenida Fernández Ladreda and the steeply sloping Paseo Conde de Sepúlveda. There are 8 or 9 buses a day to and from Madrid (which depart from the Paseo de la Florida, 11; Metro: Norte), and about 4 a day traveling between Ávila, Segovia, and Valladolid. One-way tickets from Madrid cost around 500 pesetas ($4.70).

By Car   Take the N-VI (on some maps its known as the A-6) or the Autopista del Nordeste northwest from Madrid, in the direction of León and Lugo. At the junction with Route 110 (signposted Segovia), turn northeast.

ESSENTIALS: Segovia's area code is 911. The Tourist Information Office is on Plaza Franco.

Less commercial than Toledo, Segovia, more than anywhere else, typifies the glory of Old Castile. Wherever you look, you'll see reminders of a golden era—whether it's the most spectacular Alcázar on the Iberian Peninsula or the well-preserved, still-functioning Roman aqueduct.

Segovia lies on the slope of the Guadarrama Mountains, where the Eresma and Clamores rivers converge. This ancient city lies in the center of the most castle-rich part of Castile. Isabella was proclaimed Queen of Castile here in 1474.

The narrow, winding streets of this hill city must be covered on foot to view the Romanesque churches and 15th-century palaces along the way.

WHAT TO SEE & DO

ALCÁZAR, Plaza de la Reina Eugenia. Tel. 43-01-76.

View the Alcázar first from below, at the junction of the Clamores and Eresma rivers. It is on the west side of Segovia, and you may not spot it when you first enter the city. But that's part of the surprise.

The castle dates back to the 12th century, but a large segment—notably its Moorish ceilings—was destroyed by fire in 1862. Restoration has continued over the years.

Royal romance is associated with the Alcázar. Isabella first met Ferdinand here, and today you can see a facsimile of her dank bedroom. Once married, she wasn't foolish enough to surrender her rights, as replicas of the thrones attest; both are equally proportioned. Philip II also married his fourth wife, Anne of Austria, here.

Walk the battlements of this once-impregnable castle, from which its occupants hurled down boiling oil onto the enemy below. Brave the hazardous stairs of the tower, originally built by Isabella's father as a prison, for a superb view of Segovia.

Admission: 225 pts. ($2.10) adults, 100 ptas. (95¢) children.

Open: Summer, daily 10am–7pm; winter, daily 10am–6pm. **Directions:** Take either Calle Vallejo, Calle de Velarde, Calle de Daoiz, or Paseo de Ronda.

ROMAN AQUEDUCT, near Plaza del Azoguejo.

This architectural marvel, built by the Romans almost 2,000 years ago, is still used to carry water. Constructed of mortarless granite, it consists of 118 arches, and in one two-tiered section it soars 95 feet to its highest point. The Spanish call it El Puente. It spans the Plaza del Azoguejo, the old market square, stretching nearly 800 yards. When the Moors took Segovia in 1072, they destroyed 36 arches, which were later rebuilt under Ferdinand and Isabella in 1484.

CATHEDRAL, Plaza Catedral, Calle Marqués del Arco. Tel. 43-53-25.

This 16th-century structure is supposedly the last Gothic cathedral built in Spain. Fronting the historic Plaza Mayor, it stands on the spot where Isabella I was proclaimed Queen of Castile. Affectionately called *la dama de las catedrales*, it contains numerous treasures, such as the Blessed Sacrament Chapel (created by the flamboyant Churriguera), stained-glass windows, elaborately carved choir stalls, 16th- and 17th-century paintings, including a reredos portraying the deposition of Christ from the cross by Juan de Juni. The cloisters are older than the cathedral, dating from an earlier church that was destroyed in the so-called War of the Communeros. Inside the cathedral museum you'll find jewelry, paintings, and a collection of rare antique manuscripts.

Admission: Cathedral free. Cloisters, museum, and chapel room 150 ptas. ($1.40).

Open: Daily 9:30am–7pm.

CHURCH OF VERA CRUZ, Carretera de Zamarramala. Tel. 43-14-75.

Built in either the 11th or 12th century by the Knights Templars, this is the most fascinating Romanesque church in Segovia. It stands in isolation outside the walls of the old town, overlooking the Alcázar. Its unusual 12-sided design is believed to have been copied from the Church of the Holy Sepulchre in Jerusalem. Inside you'll find a fascinating inner temple, rising two floors, where the knights conducted nightlong vigils as part of their initiation rites.

Admission: 50 ptas. (45¢).

Open: Summer, Tues–Sun 10:30am–1:30pm and 3:30–7pm; winter, Tues–Sun 10:30am–1:30pm and 3:30–6pm.

MONASTERY OF EL PARRAL, Calle del Marqués de Villena (across Eresma River). Tel. 43-12-98.

The recently restored Monastery of the Grape was established for the Hironymites by Henry IV, a Castilian king (1425–74) known as "The Impotent." The monastery's major art treasure is a large retable (1528) by Juan Rodriguez. A robed monk shows you through.

Admission: Free.

Open: Mon–Sat 10am–12:30pm and 4–6pm; Sun and holidays 10am–noon and 4–6pm. **Directions:** Take Ronda de Sant Lucía, cross Eresma River, and head down Calle del Marqués de Villena.

CHURCH OF ST. MARTIN, Plaza de las Sirenas. (No phone.)

Located in the center of Segovia, this church was once the most outstanding in Old Castile. The porticoes of the 12th-century Romanesque structure are especially striking, but except for the rare altar, the interior is less interesting. The square on which the church stands, the Plaza de las Sirenas, was modeled after the Piazza di Spagna in Rome. A fountain commemorates the legend of Juan Bravo, the hero of the War of the Communeros against Charles V. Nearby is the 15th-century Mansion of Arias Davila, one of the old houses of the Segovian aristocracy.

Admission: Free.

Open: Summer, daily 10:30am–1:30pm and 3:30–7pm; winter daily 10:30am–1:30pm and 3:30–6pm.

WHERE TO STAY

DOUBLES FOR LESS THAN 8,300 PTAS. ($78)

GRAN HOTEL LAS SIRENAS, Juan Bravo, 30, 40001 Segovia. Tel. 911/43-40-11. 39 rms (all with bath). A/C TEL

$ Rates: 3,800 ptas. ($35.70) single; 5,800 ptas. ($54.50) double. AE, DC, MC, V.

Standing on the most charming old plaza in Segovia, opposite the Church of St. Martín, this modest establishment ranks as one of the town's leading hotels. It attracts those with traditional tastes. Each room is well kept. No meals are served, but there are several cafés nearby.

HOTEL ACUEDUCTO, Avenida Padre Claret, 10. 40001 Segovia. Tel. 911/42-48-00. 8 rms (all with bath). TV TEL

$ Rates: 5,500 ptas. ($51.70) single; 7,500 ptas. ($70.50) double. Breakfast 550 ptas. ($5.15) extra. MC, V.

This bandbox-modern hotel, a block east of the aqueduct, was built in its shadow in 1963. Bedroom furnishings are streamlined. The dining room serves three complete Castilian-style meals a day, including a five-course luncheon or dinner from 1,800 pesetas ($16.90).

HOTEL LOS LINAJES, Dr. Velasco, 9, 40003 Segovia. Tel. 911/43-17-12. Fax 911/43-15-01. 55 rms (all with bath). TV TEL

$ Rates: 5,800 ptas. ($54.50) single; 8,300 ptas. ($78) double. Breakfast 525 ptas. ($4.95) extra. AE, DC, MC, V.

In the historical district of St. Stephen, at the northern edge of the old town, stands this hotel, the former home of a Segovian noble family. While the outside façade dates from the 11th century, the interior is modern except for some Castilian decorations. One of the best hotels in town, Los Linajes offers gardens and patios where guests can enjoy a panoramic view over the city. The hotel also has a bar/lounge, coffee shop, disco, and garage.

WORTH THE EXTRA BUCKS

PARADOR DE SEGOVIA, Carretera Valladolid s/n (N-601), 40003 Segovia. Tel. 911/43-04-62. Fax 911/43-73-62. 80 rms (all with bath). A/C MINIBAR TV TEL

$ Rates: 9,200 ptas. ($86.50) single; 11,500 ptas. ($108.10) double. Breakfast 900 ptas. ($8.45) extra. AE, DC, MC, V.

This 20th-century tile-roofed parador sits on a hill 2 miles northeast of Segovia (take N-601). The rooms are deluxe. The vast lawns and gardens contain two lakelike swimming pools, and there is also an indoor pool. Other facilities include saunas and tennis courts. You can eat in the dining room for 3,200 pesetas ($30.10) and up.

WHERE TO EAT

EL BERNARDINO, Cervantes, 2. Tel. 43-32-25.
   Cuisine: SPANISH. **Reservations:** Recommended.
$ Prices: Appetizers 350–600 ptas. ($3.30–$5.65); main dishes 950–1,400 ptas. ($8.95–$13.15); fixed-priced menus 1,300–2,300 ptas. ($12.20–$21.60). AE, DC, MC, V.
   Open: Lunch daily 1–4:15pm; dinner daily 7:30–11:15pm.

El Bernardino, a 3-minute walk west of the Roman aqueduct, is built like an old tavern. Lanterns hang from beamed ceilings, and the view over the red-tile rooftops of the city is delightful. The menú del día might include a huge paella, roast veal with potatoes, flan or ice cream, plus bread and wine. You might begin your meal with sopa castellana (made with ham, sausage, bread, egg, and garlic).

RESTAURANTE JOSÉ MARÍA, Cronista Lecea, 11. Tel. 43-44-84.
   Cuisine: SPANISH. **Reservations:** Recommended.
$ Prices: Appetizers 450–950 ptas. ($4.25–$8.95); main dishes 1,000–1,500 ptas. ($9.40–$14.10). AE, DC, MC, V.
   Open: Lunch daily 1–4pm; dinner daily 8–11:30pm. **Closed:** Nov.

This centrally located bar and restaurant, 1 block east of the Plaza Mayor, serves quality regional cuisine in a rustic stucco-and-brick dining room. Before dinner, locals crowd in for tapas at the bar, then move into the dining room for such Castilian specialties as roast suckling pig or some nouvelle cuisine dishes. Try the cream of crabmeat soup, roasted peppers, salmon with scrambled eggs, house-style hake, filet of sole, or a grilled veal steak. For dessert, try the ice-cream tart with whisky sauce.

CASA DUQUE, Cervantes, 12. Tel. 43-05-37.
   Cuisine: SPANISH. **Reservations:** Recommended.
$ Prices: Appetizers 350–600 ptas. ($3.30–$5.65); main dishes 1,400–1,800 ptas. ($13.15–$16.90). Fixed-priced menu 1,900 ptas. ($17.85). AE, DC, MC, V.
   Open: Lunch daily 12:30–5pm; dinner daily 8–11:30pm.

Duque—the *maestro asador*, as he calls himself—supervises the roasting of the pig, the house specialty. Waitresses, wearing the traditional garb of the mayoress of Zamarramala, will serve you other Segovian gastronomic specialties such as sopa castellana or a cake known as *ponche alcázar*. There is a tavern below so that you may enjoy a predinner drink.

MESÓN EL CORDERO, Carmen, 4. Tel. 43-51-96.
   Cuisine: SPANISH. **Reservations:** Recommended.
$ Prices: Appetizers 300–500 ptas. ($2.80–$4.70); main dishes 1,500–3,500 ptas. ($14.10–$32.90). AE, DC, MC, V.
   Open: Lunch daily 12:30–4:30pm; dinner daily 8–11:30pm.

Aficionados say this is *the* best place to sample *cordero lechal* (milk-fed baby lamb). An entire leg of tender lamb is served, bone included, seasoned with fresh herbs such as thyme. Many dishes are reasonably priced, but the meat dishes, especially the lamb, carry a high tariff. The service is good, and if you get a table near the corner window, you'll view the aqueduct, in whose shadow the restaurant stands.

MESÓN DE CÁNDIDO, Plaza del Azoguejo, 5. Tel. 42-59-11.

Cuisine: SPANISH. **Reservations:** Recommended.
$ **Prices:** Appetizers 550–750 ptas. ($5.15–$7.05); main dishes 1,600–2,400 ptas. ($15.05–$22.55); fixed priced menu 2,600 ptas. ($24.45). AE, DC, MC, V.
Open: Lunch daily 1–4:30pm; dinner daily 8–11:30pm or midnight.

For years this beautiful old Spanish inn, standing on the eastern edge of the old town, has maintained a monopoly on the tourist trade. The proprietor of The House of Cándido is known as *mesonero mayor de Castilla* (the major innkeeper of Castile). He's been decorated with more medals and honors than paella has grains of rice, and has entertained everyone from King Hussein to Hemingway. The restaurant's popularity can be judged by the flocks of hungry diners who fill every seat in the six dining rooms. It offers an à la carte menu that includes *cordero asado* (roast baby lamb) or *cochinillo asado* (roast suckling pig).

EVENING ENTERTAINMENT

A popular spot, next to the Roman aqueduct, **Disco Oky,** Carmen, 1-3 (tel. 43-21-28), offers weekly parties, where the music and program is varied. It's open daily from 9:30pm to 3:30am. Drinks cost 450 pesetas ($4.25).

5. ALCALÁ DE HENARES

18 miles E of Madrid

GETTING THERE By Train Trains travel between Madrid's Atocha or Chamartín station and Alcalá de Henares every day and evening.

By Bus Buses from Madrid depart from Avenida América, 18 (Metro: América), frequently throughout the day.

By Car Alcalá lies adjacent to the main national highway (N-11), connecting Madrid with eastern Spain. As you leave central Madrid, follow signs for Barajas Airport and Barcelona.

ESSENTIALS The area code for Alcalá de Henares is 91. The Tourist Information Office is at Callejón de Santa María, 1 (tel. 91/899-2694). It will provide a map locating all the attractions.

History has been unfair to this ancient town, which once flourished with colleges, monasteries, and palaces. When a university was founded here in the 15th century, Alcalá became a cultural and intellectual center. Europe's first polyglot Bible (supposedly with footnotes in the original Greek and Hebrew) was published here in 1517. But during the 1800s the town declined, the university moving to Madrid. Today, however, Alcalá is one of the main centers of North American academics in Spain, cooperating with the Fulbright Commission, Michigan State University, and Madrid's Washington Irving Center. Overall, the city has taken on new life. Commuters have turned it into a virtual suburb, dubbing it "the bedroom of Madrid."

WHAT TO SEE & DO

Visitors come for the day, mainly to see the birthplace of Spain's literary giant Miguel de Cervantes, the creator of *Don Quixote,* who may have been born here in 1547, at the **Casa de Cervantes,** Calle Mayor, 48. This 16th-century Castilian house was reconstructed in 1956 around a beautiful little courtyard that has a wooden gallery supported by pillars with Renaissance-style capitals, plus an old well. The house contains many Cervantes manuscripts and, of course, copies of *Don Quixote,* perhaps one of the most widely published books (in all languages) in the world. Admission is 100 pesetas (95¢), and the house is open Tuesday through Sunday from 10am to 1pm and 5 to 7pm.

Lope de Vega and other famous Spaniards studied at the **Colegio de San**

Idelfonso, which stands on the Plaza San Diego, adjacent to the main square of town, the Plaza de Cervantes. You can see some of their names engraved on plaques in the examination room. The old university's Plateresque façade dates from 1543. The great hall (*paraninfo*) is entered through a restaurant, Hostería del Estudiante (see below). The hall has a splendidly adorned Mudejar *artesonado* ceiling. From here you can walk across the Patio of the Philosophers to reach the Patio of the Three Languages (from 1557), where Greek, Latin, and Hebrew were once taught. Admission to the university is 100 pesetas (95¢). Between July 15 and September 15, it's open daily from 11am to 1pm and 6 to 8pm; the rest of the year, Saturday and Sunday only, from 11am to 1pm and 4 to 6pm.

Next door, visit the **Capilla de San Idelfonso,** Pedro Gumíelz, the 15th-century chapel of the old university. It also houses the Italian marble tomb of Cardinal Cisneros, the founder of the original university. This chapel also has an *artesonado* ceiling and intricately stuccoed walls. Admission is free, and the hours are the same as for the university (see above).

WHERE TO EAT

HOSTERÍA DEL ESTUDIANTE, Colegios, 3. Tel. 888-03-30.
   Cuisine: SPANISH. **Reservations:** Recommended.
$ Prices: Appetizers 600–900 ptas. ($5.65–$8.45); main dishes, 1,800–2,400 ptas. ($16.90–$22.55); fixed-price menu 3,200 ptas. ($30.10). AE, DC, MC, V.
   Open: Summer, lunch daily 1–4pm and dinner daily 8:30–11pm; winter, lunch Wed–Sun 1–4pm and dinner Wed–Sun 8:30–11pm.

Located within the university complex, this remarkable example of a 15th-century Castilian inn is an attraction in its own right. In the cooler months, if you arrive early you can lounge in front of a 15-foot open fireplace. Oil lamps hang from the ceiling; pigskins are filled with the locally made wine; and rope-covered chairs and high-backed carved settees capture the spirit of the past. Run by Spanish Parador System, the restaurant offers a tasty (and huge) three-course set-price lunch or dinner featuring such regional specialties as *cocido madrileño,* the hearty stew of Madrid, or trout Navarre style. For dessert, try the cheese of La Mancha.

---

6. EL PARDO

8 miles N of Madrid

GETTING THERE   By Bus   Local city buses depart every 15 minutes from Madrid's Calle Martín de los Heros (Metro: Moncloa).

By Car   Driving can be confusing on the minor roads. Head north from the city limits, following signs to La Coruña, then branch off to the west in the direction of "El Monte de El Pardo."

ESSENTIALS   The area code for El Pardo is 91. Spring and fall can be chilly, so dress accordingly. The Manzanares River flows nearby, but there are no convenient rail lines.

After visiting Alcalá de Henares, spend an afternoon in El Pardo. During the Civil War many Spaniards died here, and much of the town was destroyed during the famous advance toward University City. But there's no trace of destruction today, and the countryside, irrigated by the Manzanares River, is lush and peaceful. If possible, go to the top of the hill and take in the view.

WHAT TO SEE & DO

PALACIO DE EL PARDO, Avenida de La Guardia. Tel. 376-15-00.
   A royal residence since medieval times, this was Franco's home until his death, and

his body lay in state in front of the palace. When the palace was opened to the public in 1976, it quickly became one of the most popular sights around Madrid. The interior is lavishly furnished with Empire pieces, and Franco's ornate gilt throne reveals his royal pretensions. Many family mementoes are displayed, including an extensive wardrobe; make sure to see the 10 wax dummies modeling Franco's important state uniforms.

Highlights of the 45-minute tour include the Tapestry Room, many of its 18th-century pieces based on cartoons by Goya, Bayeu, Aguirre, and González Ruiz; and the Salon de Consejos, with its 19th-century coved ceiling and—Franco's most prized possession—a 15th-century sideboard that once belonged to Queen Isabella.

Behind the palace stands the 18th-century **Casita del Príncipe (Prince's Cottage),** a small hunting lodge built during the reign of Charles III. It was actually commissioned either by his son, the prince, or by his wife, who often needed trysting places. Designed by architect López Corona, the cottage is lavishly decorated with embroidered silk walls, eight paintings by Lucas Jordán, and Louis XV- and Louis XVI-style furniture. The Casita keeps the same hours as the main palace.

At the **Palacio de la Quinta,** taken over by the Crown in 1745 from the Duke of Arcos, you can view gardens and fountains and explore its elegant interior, where the Museo de Papeles Pintados is installed.

Admission: 400 ptas. ($3.75) adults, 125 ptas. ($1.20) children for main palace, Casita del Príncipe, and Palacio de la Quinta.

Open: Mon–Sat 9:30am–12:15pm and 3–6pm, Sun 9:30am–1pm.

WHERE TO EAT

LA MARQUESITA, Avenida de la Guardia, 4. Tel. 376-03-77.
 Cuisine: SPANISH. **Reservations:** Recommended.
 $ Prices: Appetizers 600–800 ptas. ($5.65–$7.50); main dishes 1,500–2,000 ptas. ($14.10–$18.80); fixed-priced menu 1,600 ptas. ($15.05). AE, DC, MC, V.
 Open: Lunch daily 1–5pm; dinner daily 8pm–midnight.

On the main boulevard across from the palace gardens, this restaurant offers al fresco dining in summer and cozy meals in front of a fireplace in winter. The front room functions as a tasca, where diners traditionally order a Tío Pepe before their meal. The decor is that of a typical Castilian inn—crude regional chairs, hams hanging from beamed ceilings, and an open kitchen. Dishes may include roast suckling pig, baby lamb, grilled entrecote, monkfish, grilled salmon, grilled wild rabbit, and braised venison in red wine.

---

7. CHINCHÓN

32 miles SE of Madrid, 16 miles NE of Aranjuez

GETTING THERE By Bus From Madrid's Place del Condé de Casal, buses run hourly to and from Chinchón, where the terminal is about 300 yards from the center of town. The bus trip takes about an hour each way, costing 250 pesetas ($2.35).

By Car Drive from Alcalá to Toledo, bypassing Madrid by taking the C-300 in a southwesterly arc around the capital. About halfway there, follow signs to the "Cuevas de Chinchón." Another option is to take the E-901 southeast of Madrid toward Valencia, turning southwest at the turnoff for Chinchón.

ESSENTIALS The area code for Chinchón is 91.

The main attraction of Chinchón is the **Cuevas (caves),** where Anis de Chinchón, an aniseed liqueur, is manufactured. You can buy bottles of the liqueur inexpensively in the Plaza Mayor, at the center of town.

Wander along the town's steep and narrow streets, past the houses with large bays and spacious carriageways. Although closed to the public, the 15th-century **Chinchón**

Castle, seat of the Condes of Chinchón, can be viewed from outside. The most interesting church, **Nuestra Señora de la Asunción,** dating from the 16th and 17th centuries, contains a painting by Goya.

WHERE TO STAY

PARADOR NACIONAL, Avenida Generalísimo, 1. Chinchón 28370 Madrid. Tel. 91/894-08-36. Fax 91/894-09-08. 38 rms (all with bath). A/C MINIBAR TV TEL

$ Rates: 9,400 ptas. ($88.35) single; 11,500 ptas. ($108.10) double. Breakfast 900 ptas. ($8.45) extra. AE, DC, MC, V.

This building in the center of town was originally installed in a restored 17th-century convent and has served as both a jail and a hall of justice. It has been handsomely converted, with a glass-walled hallway opening onto a Castilian courtyard. There are two bars and two dining halls, where a filling meal can be had for 3,200 pesetas ($30.10). Facilities include a swimming pool.

WHERE TO EAT

MESÓN CUEVAS DEL VINO, Benito Hortelano, 13. Tel. 894-02-06.
Cuisine: SPANISH. **Reservations:** Recommended.
$ Prices: Appetizers 900–1,500 ptas. ($8.45–$14.10); main dishes 1,800–2,500 ptas. ($16.90–$23.50). AE.
Open: Lunch daily 1–4pm; dinner daily 7:30–11:30pm.

This establishment is famous for its wine cellars, and you can sample the stock at lunch or dinner. Hams, hanging from the rafters, have been cured by the owners, and the flavorful spiced sausages are homemade. Chunks of the ham and sausage cooked in oil, plus olives and crunchy bread, are placed on the table when you sit down. The *morteruelo* (warm pâté) is a good beginning, and a popular dessert is *hojuelas* (soft pastry with honey). The wines, or the dry or sweet anisette that is the main export of Chinchón, help make the meal more enjoyable.

---

8. ÁVILA

68 miles NW of Madrid, 41½ miles SW of Segovia

GETTING THERE By Train There are more than two dozen trains leaving daily from Madrid for Ávila, about a 1½- to 2-hour trip each way. Depending on their schedule, trains depart from Chamartín, Atocha, and Príncipe (Norte) railway stations. The 8am train from Atocha, arriving in Ávila at 9:26am, is a good choice, considering all that there is to see. The Ávila station lies at Avenida Portugal, 17 (tel. 22-01-08), about a mile east of the old city.

By Bus Buses leave Madrid daily from Paseo Florida, 11 (Metro: Norte), in front of the Norte Railway Station. For information in Madrid, call 248-48-91. In Ávila the bus terminal (tel. 22-01-54) is at the corner of the Avenida Madrid and the Avenida Portugal, northeast of the center of town.

By Car Exit Madrid from its northwest perimeter, and head northwest on highway N-VI (A-6), in the direction of La Coruña, eventually forking southwest in the direction of Ávila. Driving time is around 1½ hours.

Taxis You can find taxis lined up in front of Ávila's railway station and at the more central Plaza Santa Teresa. For information, call 21-19-59 or 22-01-49.

ESSENTIALS The Ávila area code is 918. The Tourist Information Office is at Plaza Catedral, 4 (tel. 21-13-87). Emergency: Dial 091. Police: Avenida José Antonio, 3 (tel. 21-11-88). Bring warm clothes if you're visiting in the early spring.

The ancient city of Ávila is completely encircled by well-preserved 11th-century walls, which are among the most important medieval relics in Europe. The city has been declared a national landmark, and there is little wonder why. The walls aren't the only attraction, however. Ávila has several Romanesque churches, Gothic palaces, and a fortified cathedral.

Ávila's spirit and legend are most linked to St. Teresa, who was born here in 1515. This Carmelite nun, who helped defeat the Reformation and founded a number of convents, experienced visions of the devil and angels piercing her heart with burning hot lances. She was eventually imprisoned in Toledo. Many legends sprang up after her death, including the belief that a hand severed from her body could perform miracles. Finally, in 1622 she was declared a saint.

WHAT TO SEE & DO

WALLS OF ÁVILA

⭐ Begun on orders of Alfonso VI as part of the general reconquest of Spain from the Moors, the 11th-century walls, built over Roman fortifications, took nine years to complete. They average 33 feet in height, have 88 semicircular towers, and more than 2,300 battlements. Among the nine gateways, the two most famous are the St. Vincent and the Alcázar, both on the eastern side. In many respects the walls are best viewed from the west. Whatever your preferred point of view, you can drive along their entire length: 1½ miles.

CONVENT OF ST. TERESA, Plaza de la Santa. Tel. 21-10-30.
This 17th-century convent and neoclassical baroque church, 2 blocks southwest of the Plaza de la Victoria, is the site of St. Teresa's birth. It contains a number of relics, including a finger from her right hand. Look also for the fine sculpture by Gregorio Hernández.
Admission: Free.
Open: Daily 8:45–1:30pm and 3:30–7:30pm.

ÁVILA CATHEDRAL, Plaza Catedral. Tel. 21-16-41.
Built into the old ramparts of Ávila, this cold, austere cathedral and fortress (begun in 1099) bridges the gap between the Romanesque and the Gothic, and, as such, enjoys a certain distinction in Spanish architecture. One local writer compared it to a granite mountain. The interior is unusual, built with a mottled red-and-white stone.
Like most European cathedrals, Ávila's lost its purity of design through the years as new chapels and wings—one completely in the Renaissance mode—were added. A Dutch artist, Cornelius, designed the seats of the choir stalls, also in Renaissance style, and the principal chapel holds a reredos showing the life of Christ by Pedro Berruguete, Juan de Borgoña, and Santa Cruz. Behind the chapel the tomb of Bishop Alonso de Madrigal—nicknamed "El Tostado" ("The Parched One") owing to its brownish color—is Vasco de Zarza's masterpiece. The Cathedral Museum contains a laminated gold ceiling, a 15th-century triptych, a copy of an El Greco painting, as well as vestments and 15th-century songbooks. Note also *The Great Custodia* by Juan de Arfe (1572).
Admission: 100 ptas. (95¢) adults, 50 ptas. (45¢) children.
Open: Summer, daily 10am–1:15pm and 3–7pm; winter, daily 10am–1:30pm and 3–5pm.

BASILICA OF ST. VINCENT, Puerta de San Vincente. (No phone.)
Outside the city walls, at the northeast corner of the medieval ramparts, this Romanesque-Gothic church in faded sandstone encompasses styles from the 12th century to the 14th. It consists of a huge nave and a trio of apses. The eternal struggle between good and evil is depicted on a cornice on the southern portal. The western portal, dating from the 13th century, contains Romanesque carvings. Inside is the tomb of St. Vincent, martyred on this site in the 4th century. The tomb's medieval carvings, which depict his torture and subsequent martyrdom, are fascinating.
Admission: 30 ptas. (30¢).

Open: Summer, Mon–Sat 10am–1pm and 4–6pm, Sun 10:30am–noon; winter, Mon–Sat 10am–1pm and 4–6pm, Sun 10:30am–noon.

CHURCH AND MONASTERY OF ST. THOMAS, Plaza Granada. Tel. 22-04-00.

This 15th-century Gothic monastery was once the headquarters of the Inquisition in Ávila. For three centuries it housed the tomb of Torquemada, the first General Inquisitor, whose zeal in organizing the Inquisition made him a notorious figure in Spanish history. Legend has it that after the friars were expelled from the monastery in 1836, a mob of Torquemada-haters ransacked the tomb and burned the remains somewhere outside the city walls. His final burial site is unknown.

Prince John, the only son of Ferdinand and Isabella, was also buried here, in a sumptuous sepulchre in the church transept. The tomb was desecrated during a French invasion; now, only an empty crypt remains.

Visit the Royal Cloisters, in some respects the most interesting architectural feature of the place. In the upper part of the third cloister, you'll find the Museum of Far Eastern Art, which exhibits Vietnamese, Chinese, and Japanese art and handcrafts.

Admission: 50 ptas. (45¢).

Open: Daily 10am–1pm and 4–7pm. **Bus:** 1, 2, or 3.

CARMELITAS DESCALZAS DE SAN JOSÉ, Las Madres, 4. Tel. 22-21-27.

Also known as the Convento de las Madres (Convent of the Mothers), this is the first order founded by St. Teresa, who started the Reform of Carmel in 1562. Two churches are here—the primitive one, where the first Carmelite nuns took the habit; and the other, built by Francisco de Mora, architect of Philip III, after the saint's death. The museum displays many relics, including, of all things, St. Teresa's left clavicle.

Admission: 25 ptas. (25¢) for museum; Mon free.

Open: Daily 10am–1pm and 4–7pm. Directions: From Plaza de Santa Teresa and its nearby Church of San Pedro, follow Calle del Duque de Alba for about 2 blocks.

WHERE TO STAY

Ávila is a summer resort—a refuge from Castilian heat. The budget hotels are few in number, comfortable without being spectacular.

Warning: The Spanish book nearly all the hotel space in July and August. Make sure to have a reservation in advance.

HOTEL JARDÍN, San Saegundo, 38, 05001 Ávila. Tel. 918/21-10-74. 26 rms. TEL Bus: 3.

$ Rates: 1,900 ptas. ($17.85) single without bath, 2,100 ptas. ($19.75) single with shower; 2,800 ptas. ($26.30) double without bath, 3,000 ptas. ($28.20) double with shower. Breakfast 275 ptas. ($2.60) extra. MC, V.

A garden out front is refreshing to see in this town of narrow streets and stone buildings. The Jardín stands in a small parklike area near one of the old city gates (on the eastern side). The accommodations are utilitarian. Meals are served in a skylit dining room: 1,200 pesetas ($11.30) for either lunch or dinner.

EL RASTRO, Plaza del Rastro, 1, 05001 Ávila. Tel. 918/21-12-18. Fax 918/25-00-00. 19 rms (all with bath).

$ Rates: 1,900 ptas. ($17.85) single; 3,600 ptas. ($33.85) double. Breakfast 325 ptas. ($3.05) extra. AE, DC, MC, V.

Situated near the junction of the Calle Caballeros and the Calle Cepadas, this is the best choice for the bargain hunter. Few tourists know that they can spend the night at this old Castilian inn built, however, into the city walls. Rooms are basic and clean—some are doubles with a washbasin and a bathroom down the hall. El Rastro is one of my dining recommendations too (see below).

REY NIÑO, Plaza de José Tomé, 1, 05001 Ávila. Tel. 918/21-14-04. 24 rms (all with shower). TEL

$ Rates: 2,500 ptas. ($23.50) single; 4,000 ptas. ($37.60) double. MC, V.

Dating from 1840 but renovated in 1969, this hotel is ranked by some devotees as the best of Ávila's budget establishments. No frills here: Rooms are Spartan, though well kept and comfortable. For breakfast, you have to go to one of the nearby cafés. Rey Niño is located southwest of the cathedral, and convenient to most major attractions.

HOTEL REINA ISABEL, Avenida de José Antonio, 17, 05001 Ávila. Tel. 918/22-02-00. Fax 918/25-05-74. 20 rms (all with bath). TEL
$ Rates: 3,000 ptas. ($28.20) single; 4,500 ptas. ($42.30) double. Breakfast 275 ptas. ($3.55) extra. AE, DC, MC, V.

Near the railway station, outside the city proper, the Reina Isabel is a good middle-class hotel suitable for a night's stay. Bedrooms are simply furnished, clean, and comfortable.

PARADOR NACIONAL RAIMUNDO DE BORGOÑA, Marqués de Canales de Chozas, 16, 05001 Ávila. Tel. 918/21-13-40. Fax 918/22-61-66. 62 rms (all with bath). MINIBAR TV TEL
$ Rates: 7,800 ptas. ($73.30) single; 9,500 ptas. ($89.30) double. Breakfast 900 ptas. ($8.45) extra. AE, DC, MC, V.

This is another great parador, standing 2 blocks northwest of the Plaza de la Victoria. The place has a dignified entranceway, and most of its public lounges open onto a central courtyard with an inner gallery of columns. The furnishings are tasteful: tall stone fireplaces, highly polished tile floors, old chests, leather armchairs, paintings, and sculptures. The dining room, with its leaded-glass windows opening onto a terraced garden, serves tasty Castilian dishes. A large three-course dinner costs 3,000 pesetas ($28.20).

WHERE TO EAT

MESÓN EL SOL, Avenida 18 de Julio, 25. Tel. 22-02-11.
Cuisine: SPANISH. **Reservations:** Recommended. **Bus:** 12.
$ Prices: Appetizers 500–600 ptas. ($4.70–$5.65); main dishes 900–1,200 ptas. ($8.45–$11.30); fixed-price menu 1,500 ptas. ($14.10). AE, DC, MC, V.
Open: Lunch daily 1–4pm; dinner daily 8:30–11:30pm.

You may be distracted by the wonderful aromas emanating from the kitchen of one of the lowest-priced inns in Ávila—a place known for its good food, moderate prices, and efficient service. Full meals could include seafood soup, fried hake, veal with garlic, and house-style flan.

EL RASTRO, Plaza del Rastro, 1. Tel. 21-12-19.
Cuisine: SPANISH. **Reservations:** Required on weekends only.
$ Prices: Appetizers 350–600 ptas. ($3.30–$5.65); main dishes 950–1,600 ptas. ($8.95–$15.05); fixed-priced menu 1,300 ptas. ($12.20). AE, DC, MC, V.

S An old inn built into the 11th-century town walls, it serves typical Castilian dishes, with more attention given to freshness and preparation than to culinary flamboyance. Roast baby lamb and tender white veal are house specialties. Dessert recipes have been passed down from Ávila's nuns. Try, for example, the *yemas de Santa Teresa* (St. Teresa's candied egg yolk).

CHAPTER 8

CITIES OF THE HEARTLAND

- **WHAT'S SPECIAL ABOUT THE CITIES OF THE HEARTLAND**
- **1. SALAMANCA**
- **2. CIUDAD RODRIGO**
- **3. ZAMORA**
- **4. LEÓN**
- **5. VALLADOLID**
- **6. BURGOS**
- **7. CUENCA**

Spain owes much to Castile, Aragón, and León, for these three kingdoms helped forge the various regions of the country into a unified whole. Modern Spain was conceived when Isabella of Castile married Ferdinand of Aragón on October 19, 1469. Five years later she was proclaimed Queen of Castile and of León. The Moors were eventually driven out of Granada, the rest of Spain was conquered, and Columbus sailed to America—all during the reign of these two Catholic monarchs.

This proud and highly moral queen and her unscrupulous husband fashioned an empire whose influence extended throughout Spain, Europe, and the New World. The power once held by Old Castile shifted long ago to Madrid, but today there are many reminders of its storied past.

The ancient kingdom of León, which was eventually annexed to Castile, embraced three cities: Salamanca, Zamora, and the provincial capital of León. Today the district is known for its many castles.

In Old Castile I'll cover the inland provincial capital of Valladolid, where a brokenhearted Columbus died on May 19, 1506, and where Isabella married Ferdinand. From there I'll move on to Burgos, once the capital of Old Castile. Vivar, a small town near here, produced El Cid, Spain's greatest national hero, who conquered the Moorish kingdom of Valencia. Finally, I'll go on to Cuenca in New Castile—not because of any historical significance, but because of its amazing landscape.

SEEING THE CITIES OF THE HEARTLAND

GETTING THERE

The cities of Old Castile and León are best explored on overnight trips. Day trips from Madrid are possible, but you'll spend more time getting there and back than viewing the monuments.

All of these cities lie on fast and frequently serviced rail lines from Madrid. (See individual city listings for specific train connections.) Each city is also serviced by buses out of Madrid, which are usually slower than trains.

The only city with a major airport is Valladolid, with flights to Barcelona Monday through Friday.

Driving is easy thanks to the flat region and the good road connections. The main auto route, N-I, goes north from Madrid to the old capital at Burgos, and N-VI heads northwest from Madrid en route to Valladolid.

A SUGGESTED ROUTE

Those wishing to see the major capitals of the old provinces should head west from Madrid to Salamanca for two nights (**Days 1 and 2**). A good part of Day 1 will be spent getting there. On **Day 3**, head north to León, stopping for lunch at Zamora. Spend **Day 4** in León also. On **Day 5**, cut southeast to Valladolid for a one-night stay, then head northeast to Burgos for another overnight stopover (**Day 6**).

WHAT'S SPECIAL ABOUT THE CITIES OF THE HEARTLAND

Towns/Villages
- ☐ Salamanca, ancient university city, one of the most beautiful in Europe.
- ☐ León, old cathedral city, once the center of Christian Spain.
- ☐ Burgos, Gothic city of El Cid, Spain's national hero.

Architectural Highlights
- ☐ University at Salamanca, oldest in Spain, once the greatest in Europe.
- ☐ Cathedral at León, 13th-century early Gothic, known for its stained glass.
- ☐ Plaza Mayor, at Salamanca, the most beautiful public square in Spain.
- ☐ Cathedral at Burgos, in flamboyant Gothic style, which took 300 years to build.
- ☐ *Casas colgadas*, the cliff-hanging houses of Cuenca.

Natural Wonders
- ☐ Ciudad Encantada, 25 miles northeast of Cuenca, a "city" created from rocks and boulders.

Events/Festivals
- ☐ La Alberca celebrations at Salamanca (Aug 15–16), with crowds in folkloric dress converging on the Plaza Mayor.
- ☐ Carnival festivities at Ciudad Rodrigo (Feb), complete with running of the bulls, traditional dances, and costumes.

Great Museums
- ☐ Museum of Spanish Abstract Art at Cuenca, a galaxy of modern art in a cliff-hanging dwelling.
- ☐ National Museum of Sculpture at Valladolid, exhibiting the best of gilded polychrome sculpture.

As your week in Old Castile ends, either head back to Madrid or continue northeast to Basque Country.

Remote Cuenca, which is actually in New Castile, lies southeast of Madrid, and is best visited by those who plan to continue to Valencia on the eastern coast, as Cuenca lies midway between Madrid and Valencia. If you do visit Cuenca, you can return to Madrid from Burgos—our last stopover. You should stay overnight in Madrid. The next day go to Cuenca for at least a night's stopover.

Ciudad Rodrigo, west of Salamanca and the only town not mentioned on this tour, is not worth a special trip, but it makes a convenient overnight stop for those going from Madrid to Portugal.

---

1. SALAMANCA

127 miles NW of Madrid, 73 miles E of Portugal.

GETTING THERE   By Train. Only 3 trains travel directly from Madrid's North Station to Salamanca daily (3½ hours one way), arriving northeast of the center, on the

---

IMPRESSIONS

Now the traveller has re-entered the bald regions of Old Castile, and the best thing is to get out of them again as quickly as possible.
—RICHARD FORD, *A HANDBOOK FOR TRAVELLERS IN SPAIN*, 1855.

Paseo de la Estación de Ferrocarril (tel. 21-24-54). More frequent are the rail connections between Salamanca and Ávila and Ciudad Rodrigo (around 6 each per day) and to Valladolid (8 or 9 per day).

By Bus There are about 20 buses from Madrid every day. Salamanca's bus terminal is at Avenida Filiberto Villalobos, 79 (tel. 23-22-66), northwest of the center of town. There are also buses to and from Salamanca to Ávila, Zamora, Valladolid, León, and Caceres (2 to 13 per day, depending on destination).

By Car Salamanca is not located on a national highway, but there is a good network of roads that converge on Salamanca from such nearby cities as Ávila, Valladolid, and Ciudad Rodrigo. One of the most heavily trafficked highways is the 620, leading into Salamanca from both Barcelona and Portugal. From Madrid, take the N-VI northwest from the capital's periphery, forking off to Salamanca on the N-501.

ESSENTIALS Salamanca's area code is 923. The Tourist Information Office is at Gran Vía, 41 (tel. 923/24-37-30).

This ancient city, famous for the university founded here by Alfonso IX in the early 1200s, is well preserved, with turreted palaces, faded convents, Romanesque churches, and colleges that once attracted scholars from all over Europe. The only way to explore Salamanca conveniently is on foot. Arm yourself with a map and set out to explore the city. Nearly all the attractions are within walking distance of the Plaza Mayor.

WHAT TO SEE & DO

To start, spend some time in the Plaza Mayor, an 18th-century baroque square acclaimed as the most beautiful public plaza in Spain. No trip to the university city is complete unless you walk through the arcaded shops and feast your eyes on the honey-colored buildings. After this you'll understand why the Plaza Mayor (town square) is an integral part of Spanish life. If it's a hot day and you want what everybody else in the Plaza Mayor is drinking, stop in a café and order *leche helado*, an icy vanilla-and-almond milkshake—very refreshing and not too filling.

UNIVERSIDAD DE SALAMANCA, Patio de las Escuelas. Tel. 21-68-00.
The oldest university in Spain was once considered the greatest in Europe. In front of the plateresque facade of the building, a statue honors Hebrew scholar Fray Luís de León. Arrested for heresy, Fray Luís was detained for five years before being cleared. When he returned, he began his first lecture: "As I was saying yesterday . . ." Fray Luís's remains are kept in the chapel, which is worth a look. You can also visit a dim 16th-century classroom, cluttered with crude wooden benches, but the library upstairs is closed to the public. The university lies 2 blocks from the cathedral in the southern section of the old town.
Admission: 100 ptas. (95¢).
Open: Mon–Sat 9:30am–1:30pm and 4–7pm, Sun 10am–1:30pm.
Directions: Enter from Patio de las Escuelas, a widening of Calle de Libreros.

CATEDRAL NUEVA (New Cathedral), Plaza Juan XXII. Tel. 21-74-76.
The origins of this "new" cathedral date from 1513. It took over 200 years to complete it, so the edifice represents many styles; it's classified as late Gothic, but you'll see baroque and Plateresque features as well. Churriguera contributed some rococo elements too. The building has a grand gold-on-beige sandstone façade, elegant chapels, the best-decorated dome in Spain, and bas-relief columns that look like a palm-tree cluster. Unfortunately, its stained glass is severely damaged. The

cathedral lies in the southern section of the old town, about 5 blocks south of the Plaza Mayor at the edge of the Plaza de Anaya.
Admission: Free.
Open: Daily 10am–2pm and 4:30–7pm.

CATEDRAL VIEJA (Old Cathedral), Plaza Juan XXII. Tel. 21-74-76.

Adjoining the New Cathedral is this older Spanish Romanesque version, begun in the 12th century. Its simplicity provides a dramatic contrast to the ornamentation of its younger but bigger counterpart. After viewing the interior, stroll through the enclosed cloisters with their Gothic tombs of long-forgotten bishops. The chapels are of special architectural interest.
Admission: 200 ptas. ($1.90).
Open: Summer, daily 10am–2pm and 4:30–7pm; winter, daily 10am–1pm and 3:30–5pm.

CASA DE LAS CONCHAS (House of Shells), Calle Mayor and Calle de la Compañía.

The restored 1483 House of Shells is noteworthy for its façade of 400 simulated scallop shells. Count Santa Coloma of Madrid and Seville rents his casa to the city of Salamanca for the symbolic sum of one peseta a year. Admission is not permitted; the house can be viewed only from the outside while restoration continues. It stands within a plaza created by the junction of the Calle Mayor and the Calle de la Compañía, opposite the baroque façade of La Clericía (headquarters of the Pontifical University), about 1 block north of the New Cathedral.

MUSEO DE SALAMANCA (Casa de los Doctores de la Reina), Patio de las Escuelas, 2. Tel. 21-22-35.

Built in the late 15th century by Queen Isabella's physician, this structure, located near the university, is a fine example of the Spanish Plateresque style. The Fine Arts Museum is housed here, boasting a collection of paintings and sculptures dating from the 15th to the 20th century.
Admission: 200 ptas. ($1.90).
Open: Mon–Fri 8am–3pm, Sat–Sun 10am–4pm.

CONVENTO DE SAN ESTEBAN, Plaza del Concilio de Trento. Tel. 21-50-00.

Of all the old religious sites of Salamanca, St. Stephen's Convent is the best. The golden-brown Plateresque façade of this late-Gothic church competes with the Cathedral in magnificence. Inside, José Churriguera created a high altar that is one of Salamanca's greatest art treasures. The convent lies 2 blocks east of the New Cathedral on the opposite side of the busy Calle San Pablo at the southern terminus of the Calle de España (Gran Vía).
Admission: 100 ptas. (95¢).
Open: Mon–Fri 9am–1:30pm and 4–8pm, Sat–Sun 9:30am–1:30pm and 4–8pm.

LAS DUEÑAS CONVENTO, Plaza del Concilio de Trento. Tel. 21-54-42.

Across the Calle Buenaventura from San Esteban is one of the most popular sights of Salamanca. The cloisters date from the 16th century. Climb to the upper gallery for a close inspection of the carved capitals, which are covered with demons and dragons, saints and sinners, and animals of every description—some from the pages of the *Divine Comedy*. There is also a portrait of Dante.
Admission: 40 ptas. (40¢).
Open: Daily 10am–1pm and 4–7pm.

CASA-MUSEO DE UNAMUNO, Libreros, 11. Tel. 21-48-17.

The poet and philosopher—and one of the world's most renowned scholars—

lived from 1900 to 1914 in this 18th-century house beside the University. Here he wrote many of the works that made him famous. You can see some of his notebooks and library, along with many personal mementoes, including the small deck of cards he used to pay solitaire.

Admission: 25 ptas. (25¢).
Open: Mon–Fri 4–6pm, Sat 11am–1pm. **Closed:** Aug.

WHERE TO STAY

DOUBLES FOR LESS THAN 5,500 PTAS. [$51.70]

MINDANAO, Paseo de San Vicente, 2, 37007 Salamanca. Tel. 923/23-30-80. 35 rms (all with bath).
$ Rates: 2,500 ptas. ($23.50) single; 3,000 ptas. ($28.20) double. Breakfast 225 ptas. ($2.10) extra. V.
The Mindanao offers simply furnished bedrooms with private bathrooms. The place is clean and well run, often attracting many students and parents of students. You get no frills, but the welcome is nice. The hotel lies along the southwest edge of the busy traffic peripheral ringing Salamanca's center, just west of the city hospital, 10 pedestrian minutes from the historic core around the Plaza Mayor.

HOSTAL LAGUNA, Consuelo, 19, 37001 Salamanca. Tel. 923/21-87-06. 13 rms (none with bath).
$ Rates: 3,300 ptas. ($31) doubles only. Breakfast 200 ptas. ($1.90) extra. MC, V.
This good but modest place lies 2 blocks south of the Plaza Mayor and across from the Clavero Tower. This is in the monument district near the most popular *tascas,* where you can eat well on a "student budget." Its three-story façade, dotted with iron balustrades, shelters an unpretentious handful of double rooms, all of which are clean but spartan.

LOS INFANTES, Paseo de la Estación, 125, 37003 Salamanca. Tel. 923/25-28-44. 15 rms (all with bath).
$ Rates: 2,200 ptas. ($20.70) single; 3,800 ptas. ($35.70) double. Breakfast 300 ptas. ($2.80) extra. AE, DC, MC, V.
A small hotel, Los Infantes has basic but clean rooms, and it is one of the better bargains in town. Rooms lack such conveniences as phones, but they are well maintained. Summer nights are hot, and many guests don't return from the nearby tascas and bars until well after midnight, when the building has cooled down. Los Infantes is located northeast of the city center, between the peripheral highway and the rail station, beside the road leading from the train station to the town center.

HOTEL CLAVERO, Consuelo, 21, 37001 Salamanca. Tel. 923/21-81-08. 28 rms (all with bath). TEL
$ Rates: 2,800 ptas. ($26.30) single; 3,900 ptas. ($36.65) double. Breakfast 250 ptas. ($2.35) extra. MC, V.
This modern little hotel near the 15th-century Clavero Tower enjoys a top-notch location within walking distance of the city's major monuments. Lying just off a small tree-decked plaza, it's usually quiet and peaceful. A recent renovation was carried out with skill, and the bedrooms are tidy, with suitable furnishings, plus a sprinkling of antique reproductions. Dinner is available and usually costs 1,000 pesetas ($9.40).

LOS TORRES, Plaza Mayor, 26, 37002 Salamanca. Tel. 923/21-21-00. 29 rms (all with bath). AC MINIBAR TEL
$ Rates: 3,500 ptas. ($32.90) single; 5,500 ptas. ($51.70) double. Breakfast 275 ptas. ($2.60) extra. V.
Two flights up, this small one-star hotel combines comfort, low prices, and an unbeatable location. If you're lucky enough to get one of the six rooms overlooking

the Plaza Mayor, you're in for a treat. Downstairs is a large cafeteria bustling with activity in the evening. A lunch or dinner costs 1,200 pesetas. ($11.30). Food is served from 8 to 11am, 1 to 4pm, and 9 to 11pm. The restaurant is the only air-conditioned room.

WORTH THE EXTRA BUCKS

HOTEL ALFONSO X, Toro, 674, 37001 Salamanca. Tel. 923/21-44-01.
   66 rms (all with bath). TV TEL
$ **Rates:** 6,800 ptas. ($63.90) single; 8,600 ptas. ($80.85) double. Breakfast 550 ptas. ($5.15) extra. AE, DC, MC, V.
Attached to the more expensive Monterrey, this centrally located hotel just west of the tourist office, is a 4-minute walk from the Plaza Mayor. Rooms are old and traditionally furnished, but generally well kept. There's no restaurant.

PARADOR NACIONAL DE SALAMANCA, Teso de la Feria, 2, 37008 Salamanca. Tel. 923/26-87-00. Fax 923/21-54-38. 108 rms (all with bath). A/C MINIBAR TV TEL
$ **Rates:** 7,800 ptas. ($73.30) single; 10,500 ptas. ($98.70) double. Breakfast 900 ptas. ($8.45) extra. AE, DC, MC, V.
Situated just across the Tormes River from the center of the old city, the Parador Nacional, with its modern façade, looks like a space-age vacation village. Inside, subtly contrasting shades of polished stone accent the contemporary paintings and leather armchairs of the public areas. Each of the well-furnished and comfortable bedrooms has two or three framed lithographs, as well as a mirador-style balcony. Meals in the dining room go for 2,900 pesetas ($27.25). On the premises are a garden, a parking garage, and an outdoor swimming pool.

GRAN HOTEL, Plaza Poeta Iglesias, 5, 37001 Salamanca. Tel. 923/21-35-00. 100 rms (all with bath). AC TV
$ **Rates:** 9,500 ptas. ($89.30) single; 13,000 ptas. ($122.20) double. Breakfast 850 ptas. ($8) extra. AE, DC, MC, V.
A long-standing favorite, this traditional Victorian-style hotel at the southeast corner of the Plaza Mayor has always been sought out by bull breeders and matadors, as well as by many of the literati of this university town. Renovations have improved its decor a bit, although many of the authentic old pieces remain. All of the rooms are clean, and most are comfortable. Castilian-style meals are served in the Restaurante Feudal, costing from 2,800 pesetas ($26.30).

WHERE TO EAT

MEALS FOR LESS THAN 1,800 PTAS. [$16.90]

EL MESÓN, Plaza Poeta Iglesias, 10. Tel. 21-72-22.
   Cuisine: SPANISH. **Reservations:** Not required.
$ **Prices:** Appetizers 600–1,000 ptas. ($5.65–$9.40); main dishes 1,000–1,500 ptas. ($9.40–$14.10); fixed-priced menu 1,950 ptas. ($18.35). AE, V.
   Open: Lunch daily 1–4pm; dinner daily 8:45pm–midnight. **Closed:** Jan.
Two blocks south of the Plaza Mayor, just a short walk east of the Iglesia de San Martín, is one of the finest restaurants in the city, serving good Spanish cuisine in an inviting atmosphere. A set meal might include a choice of clam soup or gazpacho, followed by chicken cooked in its own juices or a breaded veal cutlet, and finally, fruit or flan, plus bread, wine, and service. Happy news: The Mesón is air-conditioned.

RÍO DE LA PLATA, Plaza del Peso, 1. Tel. 21-90-05.
   Cuisine: SPANISH. **Reservations:** Recommended.
$ **Prices:** Appetizers 850–1,500 ptas. ($8–$14.10); main dishes 1,500–1,800 ptas. ($14.10–$16.90); fixed-price menu 1,500 ptas. ($14.10). AE, V.
   Open: Lunch Tues–Sun 1:30–4pm; dinner Tues–Sun 8:45pm–midnight. **Closed:** July.

This centrally located restaurant, 2 blocks south of the Plaza Mayor on a small side square formed by the junction of the Plaza Poeta Iglesia and the Calle San Justo, uses only the freshest ingredients. The kitchen prepares a traditional *cocida castellana* (Castilian stew), house-style sole, roast baby goat, many varieties of fish, and pungently flavored sausages. The linen is crisply ironed, the service usually impeccable.

WORTH THE EXTRA BUCKS

RÍO CHICO, Plaza del Ejército, 4. Tel. 24-18-78.
   Cuisine: SPANISH. **Reservations:** Recommended.
$ Prices: Appetizers 900–1,100 ptas. ($8.45–$10.35); main dishes 1,200–2,200 ptas. ($11.30–$20.70); fixed-priced menu 2,800 ptas. ($26.30).
   Open: Lunch Mon–Sat 1:30–4pm; dinner Mon–Sat 9–11:30pm. AE, MC, V.

Marcelino Andrés may be one of the most creative chefs in Salamanca today. His cookery includes many traditional dishes (but always in his own style) and many imaginative new ones. Try, for example, his shellfish-stuffed peppers or his simpler hake in butter. Items are market fresh. In elegant, air-conditioned comfort, you can peruse the wine list, selecting some of the finest regional wines of Castile. Río Chico lies due north of the Plaza Mayor, alongside the peripheral beltway ringing the historic heart of Salamanca, at the junction of the Avenida de Alemania and the Avenida de Mirat.

A ONE-DAY EXCURSION

Admirers of St. Teresa may want to make the 11-mile (18km) pilgrimage southeast of Salamanca to visit the medieval village of **Alba de Tormes.** Cross a bridge with 22 arches spanning the Tormes River. Head between the Iglesia de San Pedro and the Basílica de Santa Teresa to the Plaza de Santa Teresa, where you will come upon the **Convento de las Carmelitas** and the **Iglesia de Santa Teresa.** The church is a medley of Gothic, Renaissance, and baroque styles. In its marble vault (over the altar) are the ashes of Spain's most beloved saint, St. Teresa of Ávila, who died here in 1582. A reliquary flanking the altar is said to contain an arm, another her heart. Opposite the entrance door in the rear of the church is a grating through which you can look at the cell in which she died. Pope John Paul II visited Alba de Tormes in 1982 on the occasion of the 400th anniversary of St. Teresa's death. Admission is free. The church is open daily from 9am to 2pm and 4 to 8pm.

---

2. CIUDAD RODRIGO

54 miles SW of Salamanca, 177 miles W of Madrid

GETTING THERE   **By Train**   There are 5 trains per day. The trip takes 1¾ hours from Salamanca. The station is about a 10-minute walk from the center of town.

By Bus   Seven buses per day depart Madrid for Ciudad Rodrigo. The trip takes 1¼ hours from Salamanca, 3½ hours from Madrid.

By Car   The A-620 is the town's main link to both Salamanca and Portugal. Driving time from Salamanca is about 1¼ hours.

ESSENTIALS   The area code for Ciudad Rodrigo is 923. The Tourist Information Office is at Arco de Amayuelas, 5 (tel. 923/46-05-61).

A walled town dating from Roman days, Ciudad Rodrigo is known for its 16th- and 17th-century townhouses, built by followers of the conquistadores. It was founded in the 12th century by Count Rodriguez González, and today has been designated a national monument. Near the Portuguese frontier, it stands high on a hilltop and is known for the familiar silhouette of the square tower of its 14th-century Alcázar.

The ramparts were built in the 12th century along Roman foundations. Several stairways lead up to a mile-long sentry path. You can wander these ramparts at leisure, and then walk through the streets with their many churches and mansions. It is not one chief monument that is the allure, but rather the city as a whole.

Its single chief attraction is its **cathedral,** Casco Viejo, built between 1170 and 1230. Subsequent centuries saw more additions. The Renaissance altar on the north aisle is a major work of ecclesiastical art; look also for the Virgin Portal, at the west door, which dates from the 1200s. For 50 pesetas (45¢), you'll be admitted to the cloisters, which have a medley of architectural styles, including a Plateresque door.

The **Plaza Mayor** is a showpiece of 17th-century architecture, with two Renaissance palaces. This is the main square of the city.

Your transportation in Ciudad Rodrigo will be your trusty feet, as it is the only way to "cover" the city. Pick up a map at the tourist office (see above).

WHERE TO STAY

A DOUBLE FOR 5,300 PTAS. [$49.80]

HOTEL CONDE RODRIGO, Plaza de San Salvador, 9, 37500 Ciudad Rodrigo. Tel. 923/46-14-04. 36 rms (all with bath). A/C TV
$ Rates: 4,000 ptas. ($37.60) single; 5,300 ptas. ($49.80) double. Breakfast 300 ptas. ($2.80) extra. AE, DC, MC, V.

Its central location next to the cathedral is one of this two-star hotel's advantages. Behind thick old walls of chiseled stone are simple but comfortable bedrooms. Each room contains a thoughtful bouquet of extras. Full meals in the hotel's popular restaurant go for 2,000 pesetas ($18.80).

WORTH THE EXTRA BUCKS

PARADOR NACIONAL ENRIQUE II, Plaza del Castillo, 1, 37500 Ciudad Rodrigo. Tel. 923/46-01-50. Fax 923/46-04-04. 28 rms (all with bath). A/C MINIBAR TV TEL
$ Rates: 8,200 ptas. ($77.10) single; 10,000 ptas. ($94) double. Breakfast 900 ptas. ($8.45) extra. AE, DC, MC, V.

Installed in a 15th-century fortress, this is one of the most handsome *paradores* in Spain. The Gothic entrance bears the royal coat-of-arms and a plaque in Gothic letters. Facilities include a garden and a foreign exchange. A complete lunch or dinner costs from 2,900 pesetas ($27.25). The food is well prepared, and the service is polite.

WHERE TO EAT

ESTORIL, Traversia Talavera, 1. Tel. 46-05-50.
Cuisine: SPANISH. **Reservations:** Recommended.
$ Prices: Appetizers 550–1,200 ptas. ($5.15–$11.30); main dishes 850–1,600 ptas. ($8–$15.05); fixed-priced menu 1,050 ptas. ($9.85). AE, MC, V.
Open: Lunch daily 1–4pm; dinner daily 8:30pm–midnight.

The Martín family will welcome you to their popular restaurant, which is decorated with bullfight photographs. Their cuisine is considered good for the price and includes scrambled eggs with shrimp, sea bream, and roast suckling pig, finished with the inevitable carmelized custard (flan). In air-conditioned comfort, you can select such wines as Cosechero Rioja. Estoril is within walking distance of the Plaza Mayor.

MAYTON, La Colada, 9. Tel. 46-07-20.
Cuisine: SPANISH. **Reservations:** Recommended.
$ Prices: Appetizers 400–900 ptas. ($3.75–$8.45); main dishes, 1,500–2,200 ptas. ($14.10–$20.70); fixed-priced menu 2,200 ptas. ($20.70). AE, MC.
Open: Lunch daily 12:30–3:30pm; dinner Tues–Sun 7:30pm–12:30am.

Many local critics will tell you that this is the best restaurant in town. In the center of the city, Mayton is situated in an antique and well-preserved bodega. The menu specializes in fresh fish and shellfish. Try the sopa castellana (Castilian soup) for an appetizer, followed by *merluza* (hake) in a green sauce. You can also order veal, as tender as that of Ávila. The place is air-conditioned.

3. ZAMORA

40 miles N of Salamanca, 148 miles NW of Madrid

GETTING THERE   By Train   There are 4 trains to and from Madrid every day, and 2 to and from La Coruña (3 and 6 hours, respectively). The railway station is at Calle Alfonso Pena (tel. 52-19-56), about a 15-minute walk from the edge of the old town. Follow the Avenida de las Tres Cruces northeast of the center of town.

By Bus   More than 12 connections a day from Salamanca make this the easiest way and easiest route in and out of town. Travel time between the cities is 1 hour. There are about 5 buses a day to Madrid and 3 per day to León. The town's bus station lies a few paces from the railway station, at Calle Alfonso Pena (tel. 52-12-81).

By Car   Zamora is at the junction of eight different roads and highways. Most of the traffic from northern Portugal into Spain comes through Zamora. Highways headed north to León, south to Salamanca, and east to Valladolid are especially convenient. From Madrid, take the A-6 superhighway northwest toward Valladolid, cutting west on the N-VI and west again at the turnoff onto 122.

ESSENTIALS   The area code for Zamora is 988. The Tourist Information Office is at Cortinas de San, 5 (tel. 988/53-64-70).

Little known to North American visitors, Zamora (pronounced "tha-mora") is perhaps the most representative city of Old Castile, blending ancient and modern, but noted mainly for its Romanesque architecture. In fact, Zamora is often called a "Romanesque museum." A medieval frontier city, it rises up starkly from the Castile flatlands, a reminder of an era of conquering monarchs and forgotten kingdoms.

You can explore Zamora's highlights in about 4 hours. Stroll along the main square, the dusty Plaza Canovas, cross the arched Romanesque bridge from the 1300s, and take in at least some of the Romanesque churches for which the town is known. Many of them date from the 12th century. The cathedral is the best example, but others include **Iglesia de la Magdelena,** Rua de los Francos, and **Iglesia de San Ildefonso,** Calle Ramos Carrión. You might also want to look at **Iglesia de Santa María La Nueva,** Plaza de Santa María, and **Iglesia de Santiago el Burgo,** Calle Santa Clara.

The crowning achievement, however, at the far west end of Zamora, is the **cathedral,** Plaza Castillo o Pio XII, open daily from 11am to 1pm. It is topped by a gold-and-white Eastern-looking dome. Inside, you'll find rich hangings, interesting chapels, two 15th-century Mudejar pulpits, and intricately carved choir stalls. Later architectural styles, including Gothic, have been added to the original Romanesque features, but this indiscriminate mixing of periods is typical of Spanish cathedrals. It costs 50 pesetas (45¢) to visit the cloisters.

Holy Week in Zamora is a celebration known throughout the country. Street processions, called *pasos*, are considered the most spectacular in Spain. If you plan to visit at this time, secure hotel reservations well in advance.

WHERE TO STAY

Since Zamora is not on the main tourist route, its hotel and restaurant facilities are behind the times. But that is changing, especially with the opening of the government parador.

DOUBLES FOR LESS THAN 4,000 PTAS. ($37.60)

CHIQUI, Benavente, 2, 49002 Zamora. Tel. 988/53-14-80. 10 rms (all with bath). A/C

$ Rates: 1,800 ptas. ($16.90) single; 2,800 ptas. ($26.30) double. AE, V.

If you're looking for a bargain and you don't mind a few minor inconveniences, try this simple second-floor pension. Rooms are spartan but clean. No breakfast is served, but cafés are within walking distance. It lies behind the post office in the northwest section of the old town, near a corner of the busy Calle Santa Clara.

TOARY, Benavente, 2, 49002 Zamora. Tel. 988/53-37-02. 12 rms (all with bath).

$ Rates: 2,000 ptas. ($18.80) single; 3,400 ptas. ($31.95) double. AE, V.

On the third floor of the same building as above, this hostal offers simply furnished, clean, and basic rooms. There is no restaurant, so you'll have to go to a local café for breakfast.

CUATRO NACIONES, Avenida de Alfonso IX, 7, 49002 Zamora. Tel. 988/53-22-75. 40 rms (all with bath). TEL

$ Rates: 3,000 ptas. ($28.20) single; 4,000–4,800 ptas. ($37.60–$45.10) double. Breakfast 300 ptas. ($2.80) extra. AE, DC, MC, V.

This relatively small two-star hotel is not inviting enough for more than an overnight stay, but furnishings are adequate and comfortable, and many of the rooms are spacious. The food is also acceptable, with a complete luncheon or dinner costing 1,500 pesetas ($14.10). The place is located at the northwest edge of the old town beside the peripheral avenue emptying into the Plaza Alemania.

WORTH THE EXTRA BUCKS

PARADOR NACIONAL CONDES DE ALBA Y ALISTE, Plaza de Viriato, 5, 49001 Zamora. Tel. 988/51-44-97. Fax 988/53-00-63. 27 rms (all with bath). MINIBAR TV TEL

$ Rates: 9,000 ptas. ($84.60) single; 11,000 ptas. ($103.40) double. Breakfast 900 ptas. ($8.45) extra. AE, DC, MC, V.

This magnificent government-run parador, 2 blocks south of the Plaza Mayor, near the junction of the Plaza de Viriato and the Calle Ramos Carrión, is one of the most impressive in Spain. A sumptuous old palace built in the late Middle Ages on the site of the Alcazaba and rebuilt in the 16th century, it has been tastefully decorated with splendid armor, antique furniture, tapestries, carpets, old mirrors and clocks, and plants. The paneled lounges and public rooms have fireplaces. In winter, glass partitions close off a large inner patio that contains a well. The dining room, where dinner costs 2,900 pesetas ($27.25), has been done in sumptuous rustic style, with a view of the swimming pool and surrounding countryside. There's also a cozy bar (open daily from 12:30 to 11pm).

WHERE TO EAT

RESTAURANT SERAFÍN, Plaza Maestro Haedo, 10. Tel. 53-14-22.
   Cuisine: SPANISH. **Reservations:** Not required.

$ Prices: Appetizers 500–800 ptas. ($4.70–$7.50); main dishes 1,000–2,000 ptas. ($9.40–$18.80); fixed-priced menu 1,600 ptas. ($15.05). AE, DC, MC, V.
   Open: Lunch daily 1–4:30pm; dinner daily 8:30pm–midnight.

At the northeast edge of the old town, about a block south of the busy traffic hub of the Plaza Alemania and the Avenida de Alfonso IX, this air-conditioned haven with an attractive bar makes a relaxing retreat from the sun. The specialties change with the season, but might include seafood soup Serafín, paella, fried hake, Iberian ham, and a savory *cocido* (stew).

RESTAURANT PARÍS, Avenida de Portugal, 34. Tel. 51-43-25.
   Cuisine: SPANISH. **Reservations:** Recommended.

$ Prices: Appetizers 1,000–1,400 ptas. ($9.40–$13.15); main dishes 1,500–2,500 ptas. ($14.10–$23.50); fixed-priced menu 1,650 ptas. ($15.50). AE, DC, MC, V.
Open: Lunch daily 1:30–4:30pm; dinner daily 8:30pm–midnight.

This elegantly decorated and air-conditioned restaurant with an affluent and sophisticated clientele, is known for its fish, often made with a regionally inspired twist. Well-prepared specialties include vegetable flan, braised oxtail, Zamora-style clams, and a delectable hake. Most critics rate this restaurant as number one in town. It is on the main traffic artery (Avenida de Portugal) that funnels traffic south to Salamanca.

EVENING ENTERTAINMENT

The **Calle Los Herreros,** or the "Calle de Vinos," contains more bars per square foot than any street in Zamora—about 16 of them. Each is willing to accommodate a stranger with a leisurely glass of wine or beer and a selection of *tapas*. The Calle Los Herreros is a narrow street at the southern end of the old town, about 2 blocks north of the Duero River, within the shadow of the Ayuntamiento Viejo (Old Town Hall), 1 block south of the Plaza Mayor.

---

4. LEÓN

203 miles NW of Madrid, 122 miles N of Salamanca

GETTING THERE   By Train   León has good rail connections to the rest of Spain—8 trains run to Madrid daily from León. The station, Estación del Norte, Avenida de Astorga, 2 (tel. 22-37-04), lies on the western bank of the Bernesga River. Cross the bridge near the Plaza de Guzmán el Bueno. The *rapido* train from Madrid takes 5 hours, the *talgo* only 4. There are around 4 trains per day from Barcelona, 20 from Valencia, 3 from La Coruña, and 1 and 2 trains per day, respectively, from Salamanca and Valladolid.

By Bus   Most of León's buses arrive and depart from Cardenal Lorenzana, 2 (tel. 22-62-00), off the Plaza Mayor. These include 4 per day from Madrid and Valladolid. Buses to and from Zamora and Salamanca (2 and 3 per day, respectively) depart from a different bus station, on the Avenida de Madrid, near the Parque de San Francisco.

By Car   León lies at the junction of five major highways coming from five different regions of Spain. From Madrid, head northwest from Madrid's periphery on the N-VI superhighway in the direction of La Coruña. At Benavente, bear right onto the N-630.

ESSENTIALS   León's area code is 987. The Tourist Information Office is at Plaza de Regla, 4 (tel. 987/23-70-82).

Once the leading city of Christian Spain, this old cathedral town was the capital of a centuries-old empire that declined after uniting with Castile. León today is the gateway from Old Castile to the northwestern routes of Galicia. It is a sprawling city, but nearly everything of interest to visitors—monuments, restaurants, and hotels—can be covered on foot, once you arm yourself with a good map.

WHAT TO SEE & DO

CATHEDRAL (Santa María de Regla), Plaza de Regla. Tel. 23-00-60.

The usual cathedral elements are virtually eclipsed here by the awesome stained-glass windows—some 125 windows (plus 57 *oculi*) in all, the oldest dating from the 13th century. They are so heavy they have strained the walls of the cathedral. Look for a 15th-century altarpiece depicting the Entombment in the Capilla Mayor, as well as a Renaissance *trascoro* by Juan de Badajoz. The nave dates from the 13th and 14th centuries; the Renaissance vaulting is much later. Almost as interesting as the stained-glass windows are the cloisters, dating in part from the 13th and 14th centuries and contain faded frescoes and Romanesque and Gothic tombs; some capitals are carved with starkly lifelike scenes. The cathedral is on the edge of the old city, 7 blocks east of the town's most central square, the Plaza de Santo Domingo.

Admission: Free to cathedral, 200 ptas. ($1.90) to cloisters.

Open: Cathedral daily 8:30am–1:30pm and 4–7pm; cloisters Mon 3–7pm, Tues–Sat 9:30am–7pm.

ROYAL PANTHEON OF ST. ISIDOR, Plaza San Isidoro. Tel. 22-96-08.
This church, just a short walk northwest of the cathedral, was dedicated to San Isidoro de Sevilla in 1063, and contains 23 tombs of Leonese kings. One of the first Romanesque buildings in León and Castile, it was later embellished by Ferdinand I's artists. The columns are magnificent, the capitals splendidly decorated; covering the vaults are murals from the 12th century. Unique in Spain, the Treasury holds rare finds—a 10th-century Scandinavian ivory, an 11th-century chalice, and an important collection of 10th- to 12th-century cloths from Asia. The Library contains many ancient manuscripts and rare books, including a Book of Job from 951, a Visigothic Bible, and an 1162 Bible, plus dozens of miniatures.

Admission: 150 ptas. ($1.40).

Open: Mon–Sat 10am–1:30pm and 2–4:30pm, Sun 10am–1:30pm.

WHERE TO STAY

DOUBLES FOR LESS THAN 6,300 PTAS. ($59.20)

GUZMÁN EL BUENO, López Castrillón, 6, 24003 León. Tel. 987/23-64-12. 30 rms (20 with bath). **Directions:** Walk up Calle Generalísimo from Plaza de Santo Domingo, turning left onto Calle de Cid. López Castrillón is a pedestrian-only street, branching off to the right.

$ Rates: 1,600 ptas. ($15.05) single without bath, 2,200 ptas. ($20.70) single with bath; 2,400 ptas. ($22.55) double without bath, 3,400 ptas. ($31.95) double with bath. Breakfast 200 ptas. ($1.90) extra. No credit cards.

⑤ The cheapest comfortable accommodation in León is the no-frills Guzmán El Bueno, on the second floor of a centrally located boarding house. Rooms are clean. In all, it's a safe destination, widely known among international student travelers drawn to its low prices. Some rooms have phones.

HOTEL QUINDÓS, Avenida José Antonio, 24, 24002 León. Tel. 987/23-62-00. Fax 987/24-22-01. 96 rms (all with bath). TV TEL

$ Rates: 4,200 ptas. ($39.50) single; 6,300 ptas. ($59.20) double. Breakfast 400 ptas. ($3.75) extra. AE, DC, MC, V.
This rather functional hotel has been tastefully decorated with modern paintings, which enhance the establishment considerably. The snug, comfortable, and well-maintained rooms are a good value. The Quindós lies 3 blocks south of the Plaza de San Marcos, in the central commercial district in the northwest quadrant of the old town.

WORTH THE EXTRA BUCKS

PARADOR SAN MARCOS, Plaza de San Marcos, 7, 24001 León. Tel. 987/23-73-00. Fax 987/23-34-58. 253 rms (all with bath). AC TV TEL

$ Rates: 11,500 ptas. ($108.10) single; 14,000 ptas. ($131.60) double. Breakfast buffet 900 ptas. ($8.45) extra. AE, DC, MC, V.

✪ A top tourist attraction, this 16th-century former monastery with its celebrated Plateresque façade is one of the most spectacular hotels in Spain. The government has remodeled it at great expense, installing extravagant authentic antiques and quality reproductions. The old "hostal" used to put up pilgrims bound for Santiago de Compostela, and still does today. The rooms are sumptuous. A complete dinner here runs to 3,200 pesetas ($30.10). The parador is located northwest of the cathedral on the outskirts of the old town on the east bank of the Bernesga River.

Note: Even if you don't stay at this five-star hotel, you can still visit it, since it contains a church with a scallop-shell façade and an archeological museum.

WHERE TO EAT

ALBINA, Condesa de Sagasta, 24. Tel. 24-16-51.
 Cuisine: SPANISH. **Reservations:** Recommended.
$ Prices: Appetizers 600–1,300 ptas. ($5.65–$12.20); main dishes 1,300–1,600 ptas. ($12.20–$15.05); fixed-priced menu 1,600 ptas. ($15.05). MC, V.
 Open: Lunch Tues–Sat 1–4:30pm; dinner Tues–Sun 8pm–midnight.
Outside the city center, a 10 to 15 minute walk northwest of the cathedral, beside the Parador San Marcos; is this local favorite. Albina Alonso, the owner, supervises the preparation of fresh fish and meat dishes based on local recipes, with updated and sometimes fanciful twists. The air conditioning is an added attraction.

CASA POZO, Plaza San Marcelo, 15. Tel. 22-30-39.
 Cuisine: SPANISH. **Reservations:** Recommended.
$ Prices: Appetizers 650–900 ptas. ($6.10–$8.46); main dishes 1,500–2,200 ptas. ($14.10–$20.70); fixed-priced menu 2,500 ptas. ($23.50). AE, MC, V.
 Open: Lunch Mon–Sat 1–4pm; dinner Mon–Sat 8:30–11:30pm.
 Closed: First 2 weeks of July; 2 weeks around Christmas.
Two blocks south of the busy traffic hub of the Plaza Santo Domingo, this unpretentious restaurant is a favorite with locals who appreciate its unassuming style and flavorful cuisine. Specialties, all made from fresh ingredients, include peas with salty ham, shrimp with asparagus, roast pork or lamb laden with herbs and spices, and a delicate smothered sole known as *estofado.*

EL RACIMO DE ORO, Caño Vadillo, 2. Tel. 25-75-75.
 Cuisine: SPANISH. **Reservations:** Recommended.
$ Prices: Appetizers 500–750 ptas. ($4.70–$7.05); main dishes 1,500–2,000 ptas. ($14.10–$18.80). fixed-priced menu 1,300 ptas. ($12.20). MC, V.
 Open: Lunch Wed–Sun 1:30–4pm; dinner Wed–Sat 8:30pm–midnight.
This bodega, beside the cathedral and behind the Plaza Mayor, dates from the 1100s, so a lot of food and wine have been consumed on this site. The building is what the Spanish call a *mesón típico* (house built in the regional style), and its tables overlook a Carvatian patio. The food is consistently good, with the owner specializing in a regional cuisine—*mollejas con rabo de toro* (oxtail), for example, or "hake *(merluza)* house style." You might begin with an appetizer of Serrano ham or else clams, then follow with one of the roast meats. Service is attentive.

EVENING ENTERTAINMENT

One of the liveliest places in the city is the **Barrio Humedo,** Plaza San Martín, where you'll find many regional restaurants and tapas bars, such as **El Racimo de Oro,** Plaza San Martín, 11, where the standard appetizer specialties are served amid a jostling and jovial crowd. Tapas usually run from 300 pesetas ($2.80). The same owner runs the previously recommended restaurant of the same name. The bar lies about 8 blocks north of the cathedral, 2½ blocks east of the Royal Pantheon of St. Isidor, in a narrow labyrinth of twisting streets enclosed on three sides by the ancient Roman walls of old León. Open: Daily 1–4pm and 6:30pm–midnight.

A ONE-DAY EXCURSION

The most popular excursion from León is to the **Caves of Valporquero,** 26 miles (42 km) north. Look for a signpost marking the trail near the Parador San Marcos. The ride takes an hour, and the last stretch of the trip covers twisting, steep mountain roads, so be careful. Wear hiking clothing, and once inside, be prepared for temperatures of 45° F. Only the hearty should explore inside the cave—even though you are guided through, there are many steep inclines, slippery steps, and damp clay paths. Look for a stalactite "star" hanging from the ceiling. At the end of the adventure, you'll be led along a narrow passage, about 5,000 feet in length, which has been tunneled out by underground waters. The admission fee is 250 pesetas ($2.35), and the cave is open from mid-May to October, daily from 10am to 1:30pm and 4 to 7pm.

---

5. VALLADOLID

125 miles NW of Madrid, 83 miles SE of León.

GETTING THERE By Air: Flights to Valladolid land at Vallanubla Airport (tel. 25-92-12), a 15-minute taxi ride from the center of town. Aviaco routes daily flights to and from Barcelona (there's no service to Madrid). The local Aviaco/Iberia office is at Comaza, 17 (tel. 30-26-39).

By Train Valladolid is well serviced by some two dozen daily trains to and from Madrid. Other cities with train links to Valladolid include Segovia and Salamanca (3 trains each per day) and Burgos and Zaragoza (2 trains each per day). The train station (Estación del Norte) is about 1 mile south of the historic center of town, 1 block southwest of the Campo Grande park. The phone number of the railway station is 22-33-57. There's a RENFE information and ticket office in the center, Divina Pastores, 6 (tel. 22-28-73).

By Bus The bus station lies within an 8-minute walk of the railway station, at Puente Colgante, 2 (tel. 23-63-08), at the southern edge of town. There are more than a dozen buses every day to and from Madrid, 2½ hours away, and 4 each to León, Segovia, Salamanca, and Seville. The 2 daily buses to Zaragoza provide connections to Barcelona.

By Car Valladolid lies at the center of the rectangle created by Burgos, León, Segovia, and Salamanca, and is interconnected to each with good highways. From Madrid, driving time is about 2¼ hours. Take superhighway A-6 northwest from Madrid, turning north on 403.

ESSENTIALS The area code for Valladolid is 983. The Tourist Information Office is at Plaza de Zorilla, 3 (tel. 983/35-18-01).

From the 13th century until its eventual decay in the early 17th century, Valladolid was a royal city and an intellectual center that attracted saints and philosophers. Isabella and Ferdinand were married here, Philip II was born here, and Columbus died here, on May 19, 1506, broken in spirit and body after Isabella had died and Ferdinand refused to reinstate him as a governor of the Indies.

Valladolid is bitterly cold in winter, sweltering in summer. Today after years of decline, the city is reviving economically and producing, among other things, flour, ironware, and cars. Consequently, it's polluted and noisy, and many of the old buildings have been replaced by utilitarian ones, although there are many, many attractions remaining.

From the tourist office (see above), you can pick up a map—*plano de la ciudad*—that marks all the major monuments of Valladolid. These attractions can be covered on foot, although you may want to take a taxi from the two most distant points recommended—the Museo Nacional de Escultura and the Museo Oriental.

WHAT TO SEE & DO

MUSEO NACIONAL DE ESCULTURA (National Museum of Sculpture), Colegio de San Gregorio, Calle Cadeñas de San Gregorio I. Tel. 26-79-67.
Located near the Plaza de San Pablo, the museum displays a magnificent collection

IMPRESSIONS

Valladolid, sovereign of infirmity. The priest's early death, the maggot's Compostela.
—GUILLEM DE LA GONAGAL

of gilded polychrome sculpture, an art form that reached its pinnacle in Valladolid. First, the figures were carved from wood, then painted with consummate skill and grace to assume lifelike dimensions. See, especially, the works by Alonso Berruguete (1480–1561), son of Pedro, one of Spain's great painters. From 1527 to 1532 the younger Berruguete labored over the altar of the Convent of San Benito—a masterpiece now housed here. In particular, see his *Crucifix with the Virgin and St. John* in Room II and his *St. Sebastian and the Sacrifice of Isaac* in Room III. Works by Juan de Juni and Gregorio Fernández are also displayed.

After visiting the galleries, explore the two-story cloisters. The upper level is florid, with jutting gargoyles and fleurs-de-lis. See the chapel where the confessor to Isabella I (Fray Alonso de Burgos) was buried—and don't miss the gruesome sculpture, *Death*.

Admission: 200 ptas. ($1.90).
Open: Tues–Sat 10am–2pm and 4–6pm; Sun 10am–2pm.

CATHEDRAL, Plaza de la Universidad. Tel. 30-43-62.

In 1580 Philip II commissioned Juan de Herrera, architect of El Escorial, to construct this monument in the city where he was born. When Philip II died in 1598, work came to a stop for 18 years. Alberto Churriguera resumed construction, drawing up more flamboyant plans, especially for the exterior, in an unharmonious contrast to the severe lines of his predecessor. The classical, even sober, interior conforms more with Herrera's designs. A highlight is the 1551 altarpiece in the main apsidal chapel, the work of Juan de Juni. Art critics have commented that his polychrome figures are "truly alive." The cathedral is in the heart of the city, east of the Plaza Mayor and north of the Plaza de Santa Cruz.

Admission: Cathedral free; museum 200 ptas. ($1.90).
Open: Cathedral daily 10am–2pm and 5–8pm; museum Tues–Fri 10am–1:30pm and 4:30–7pm; Sat–Sun 10am–2pm.

IGLESIA DE SAN PABLO, Plaza San Pablo, 4. Tel. 35-17-48.

Once a 17th-century Dominican monastery, San Pablo, with its Isabelline-Gothic façade, is very impressive. Flanked by two towers, the main entrance supports levels of lacy stone sculpture. The church lies 6 blocks north of the cathedral, 1 block south of the busy Avenida Santa Teresa.

Admission: Free.
Open: Daily 7:30am–1pm and 5–9:30pm.

MUSEO ORIENTAL, Paseo de Filipinos, 7. Tel. 30-68-00.

Located in the Royal College of the Augustinian Fathers, near the Campo Grande park, the museum has 13 rooms: 9 Chinese and 4 Filipino. It has the best collection of Asian art in Spain, with bronzes from the 7th century B.C. to the 18th century A.D., wooden carvings, 100 fine porcelain pieces, paintings on paper and silk from the 12th century to the 19th, and ancient Chinese coins, furniture, jade, and ivory. In the Filipino section, ethnological and primitive art is represented by shields and arms. Eighteenth-century religious art can be admired in extraordinary ivories, embroideries, painting, and silversmiths' work. Popular art of the 19th century includes bronzes, musical instruments, and statuary.

Admission: 200 ptas. ($1.90).
Open: Mon–Sat 4–7pm; Sun 10am–2pm.

CASA DE CERVANTES, Calle del Rastro s/n. Tel. 30-88-10.

Now a museum, this house was once occupied by Miguel de Cervantes, author of *Don Quixote,* who did much of his writing in Valladolid. Here the author remained

for the last years of his life; behind its white walls, the house is simply furnished as he left it. It lies half a block south of the cathedral, 2 blocks north of the city park, the Campo Grande.
Admission: 200 ptas. ($1.90).
Open: Tues–Sun 10am–3pm.

WHERE TO STAY

ENARA, Plaza de España, 5, 47001 Valladolid. Tel. 983/30-03-11. 26 rms (all with shower). TEL
$ **Rates:** 2,900 ptas. ($27.25) single with shower; 4,300 ptas. ($40.40) double with shower; 4,500 ptas. ($42.30) double with bath. Breakfast 275 ptas. ($2.35) extra. No credit cards.
About ¼ mile south of the cathedral, near the junction of the Avenida 2 de Mayo and the Paseo Miguel Iscar, is arguably the best budget accommodation in Valladolid. Its central location is backed up by contemporary, pleasantly furnished rooms. There is no restaurant, but you'll be near many budget dining rooms and cafés. However, a continental breakfast is offered.

HOTEL MELIÁ PARQUE, García Morato, 17, 47007 Valladolid. Tel. 983/47-01-00. Fax 983/47-50-29. 294 rms (all with bath). A/C TV TEL
$ **Rates:** 6,000 ptas. ($56.40) single, 9,500 ptas. ($89.30) double. Breakfast 750 ptas. ($7.05) extra. AE, DC, MC, V.
Completed in 1982, this modern chain hotel 2 blocks west of the rail station, lies on the city outskirts. It's popular with business travelers unwilling to negotiate the labyrinth of Valladolid's central streets. Rooms are comfortable and functionally furnished—no surprises, and few disappointments. The hotel has no restaurant, but it does offer a cafeteria featuring snacks and light meals.

FELIPE IV, Gamazo, 16, 47004 Valladolid. Tel. 983/30-70-00. Fax 983/30-86-87. 130 rms (all with bath). A/C TV TEL
$ **Rates:** 5,500 ptas. ($51.70) single; 9,500 ptas. ($89.30) double. Breakfast 550 ptas. ($5.15) extra. AE, DC, MC, V.
When it was built, the Felipe IV was considered one of the grandest hotels in the city. Each of its bedrooms was modernized in 1981, guaranteeing its position as one of Valladolid's solidly acceptable establishments. A garage provides parking for motorists. The hotel is south of the busy traffic hub of the Plaza de Madrid, a few blocks north of the rail station, near the eastern edge of the city park, the Campo Grande.

WHERE TO EAT

MESÓN CERVANTES, Rastro, 6. Tel. 30-61-38.
Cuisine: SPANISH. **Reservations:** Recommended.
$ **Prices:** Appetizers 800–1,000 ptas. ($7.50–$9.40); main dishes 1,200–2,000 ptas. ($11.30–$18.80); fixed-priced menu 2,400 ptas. ($22.55). AE, DC, MC, V.
Open: Lunch Mon–Sat noon–5pm; dinner Tues–Sun 9pm–1am. **Closed:** Aug.
The owner, Alejandro, works the dining room, capably complemented in the kitchen by his wife, Julia, and occasionally by his charming mother. Neighborhood residents favor this place for its lack of pretension and its delicious cuisine. Two particular favorites here are sole with pine nuts and seasonal river crabs. Many other fish dishes, including hake and monkfish are available. Roast suckling pig and roast lamb are also popular. The restaurant stands beside the Casa de Cervantes, ½ mile south of the cathedral.

MESÓN PANERO, Marina Escobar, 1. Tel. 30-16-73.
Cuisine: SPANISH. **Reservations:** Recommended.
$ **Prices:** Appetizers 700–1,500 ptas. ($6.60–$14.10); main dishes 1,700–2,500 ptas. ($16–$23.50). AE, DC, MC, V.
Open: Lunch daily 1:30–4pm; dinner Mon–Sat 9pm–midnight.
The chef of this imaginative restaurant, Angel Cuadrado, can turn even the most

austere traditional Castilian recipes into sensual experiences. Set near the water, the establishment lures diners with fresh fish, including a succulent brochette of sole and hake with fresh asparagus. Every week brings a featured favorite: cocida castellana, the famous regional stew. Roast lamb and suckling pig are also available, plus a selection of well-chosen wines. The Mesón Panero is near the Casa de Cervantes, just a short walk from the tourist office.

LA FRAGUA, Paseo de Zorilla, 10. Tel. 33-71-02.
   Cuisine: SPANISH. **Reservations:** Recommended.
$ Prices: Appetizers 700–1,500 ptas. ($6.60–$14.10); main dishes 1,800–2,200 ptas. ($16.90–$20.70); fixed-priced menu 3,300 ptas. ($31). AE, DC, MC, V.
   Open: Lunch daily 1–4pm; dinner Mon–Sat 9pm–midnight.
Amid rustic decor you'll enjoy beautifully prepared Castilian dishes, the best in town, at this restaurant just north of the rail station across the busy Paseo de Zorilla. You might begin with spicy sausage, followed by beef, chicken, or lamb, all carefully seasoned and served in a generous portion. A wide variety of fish is imported daily. The huge wine list offers many regional vintages, one of which the steward will choose for you if you request it. Dessert could include a cheese tart or a melt-in-your-mouth chocolate truffle. Owner Antonio Garrote proudly displays his culinary diplomas, as if to justify the price of the meals, which are worth it.

EVENING ENTERTAINMENT

A musically oriented pub with antique decor, **Recoletos,** Plaza de Recoletos, 11 (tel. 20-51-24), draws a lively crowd of drinkers. A DJ plays recently released music, but there's no dancing. Liquor is around 450 pesetas ($4.15), beer 150 pesetas ($1.40). Open daily from 12:30pm to 2:30am, Recoletos is just north of the railway station at the southeastern edge of the city park, the Campo Grande.

---

6. BURGOS

150 miles N of Madrid, 75 miles NE of Valladolid

GETTING THERE   By Train   Burgos is well connected to Madrid (8 trains per day; 3 to 6 hours), Barcelona (4 per day; 8 to 9 hours), the French border (10 per day), and Valladolid and Segovia (3 or 4 each per day). The Burgos railway station lies at the terminus of the Avenida de Conde Guadalhorce, ½ mile southwest of the center. To get there, head for the major traffic hub in the Plaza Castilla, then walk due south across the Arlazon River. For train information or a ticket, head for the RENFE office in the center of town, at Moneda, 21 (tel. 20-91-31), about a block northeast of the busy Plaza de Santo Domingo de Guzmán.

By Bus   There are 3 buses per day coming to and from Madrid and San Sebastián, and 2 per day to and from Barcelona and Santander. The bus depot in Burgos is on Calle Miranda, at no. 4-6 (tel. 26-28-00). The Calle Miranda intersects the large Plaza de Vega, due south of (and across the river from) the cathedral.

By Car   Burgos is well connected to its neighbors by a network of highways, but its routes to and from Barcelona (6 hours) are especially wide and modern. The road from Barcelona changes its name several times, from the A-2 to the A-68 to the E-4, but it is a superhighway all the way. From Madrid, the highway is fast but less dramatically modern than the route from Barcelona. From Madrid, follow the N-I north for about 3 hours.

ESSENTIALS   The area code for Burgos is 947. The Tourist Information office is at Plaza Alonso Martínez, 7 (tel. 947/20-31-25).

Founded in the 9th century, this Gothic city in the Arlazón River valley lives up to its reputation as the "cradle of Castile." Just as the Tuscans are credited with speaking the most perfect Italian, so the citizens of Burgos, with their distinctive lisp ("El Theed" for El Cid), supposedly speak the most eloquent Castilian.

El Cid Campeador, Spain's greatest national hero and immortalized in the epic *El Cantar de Mío Cid,* is forever linked to Burgos. He was born near here, and his remains lie in the city's grand cathedral.

Like all the great cities of Old Castile, Burgos declined seriously in the 16th century, only to be revived later. In 1936, during the Civil War, the right-wing city was Franco's Nationalist army headquarters.

WHAT TO SEE & DO

CATHEDRAL DE SANTA MARÍA, Plaza de Santa María. Tel. 20-47-12.

⭐ Begun in 1221, the cathedral became one of the most celebrated in Europe. Built in diverse styles, predominantly flamboyant Gothic, it took 300 years to complete. The three main doorways are flanked by ornamented 15th-century bell towers by John of Cologne. The 16th-century Chapel of Condestable, behind the main altar, is one of the best examples of Isabelline-Gothic architecture, richly decorated with heraldic emblems, a sculptured filigree doorway, figures of apostles and saints, balconies, and an eight-sided "star" stained-glass window.

Equally elegant are the two-story 14th-century cloisters, filled with fine Spanish Gothic sculpture. The cathedral's tapestries, including one well-known Gobelin, are rich in detail. In one of the chapels you'll see an old chest linked to the legend of El Cid—it was filled with gravel, but used as collateral by the warrior to trick moneylenders. The remains of El Cid himself, together with those of his wife, Doña Ximena, lie under Santa María's octagonal lanternlike dome. Finally, you may want to see the elaborate 16th-century Stairway of Gold in the north transept, the work of Diego de Siloé.

The cathedral is across the Arlazón River from the railway station, midway between the river and the Citadel.

Admission: 200 ptas. ($1.90) for chapels, cloisters, and treasury.

Open: Daily 10am–1pm and 4–6:30pm.

MONASTERIO DE LAS HUELGAS, Calle Compás de Adentro. Tel. 20-16-30.

This cloister outside Burgos has seen a lot of action. Built in the 12th century in a richly ornamented style, it was once "a summer place" for Castilian royalty, as well as a retreat for nuns of royal blood. Inside, the Gothic church is built in the shape of a Latin cross. Despite some unfortunate mixing of Gothic and baroque, it contains much of interest—notably some 14th- and 17th-century French tapestries. The tomb of the founder, Alfonso VIII, and his queen, daughter of England's Henry II, lies in the Choir Room.

Thirteenth-century doors lead to the cloisters, dating from that same century and blending Gothic and Mudejar styles. Despite severe damage to the ceiling, the remains of Persian peacock designs are visible. The beautiful Chapter Room contains the standard of the 12th-century Las Navas de Tolora (war booty taken from the Moors), while the Museo de Ricas Telas is devoted to 13th-century costumes removed from tombs. These remarkably preserved textiles give a rare look at medieval dress.

The monastery is 1 mile off the Valladolid Road (the turnoff is clearly marked). From the Plaza de José Antonio in Burgos, buses for Las Huelgas leave every 20 minutes.

Admission: 200 ptas. ($1.90); free Wed.

Open: Tues–Sun 11am–2pm and 4–6pm.

WHERE TO STAY

HOTEL ESPAÑA, Paseo del Espoleón, 32, 09003 Burgos. Tel. 947/20-63-40. Fax 947/20-13-30. 69 rms (all with bath). TEL

$ Rates: 3,600 ptas. ($33.85) single; 5,400 ptas. ($50.75) double. Breakfast 350 ptas. ($3.30) extra. MC, V.

The best budget choice lies a 5-minute walk southeast of the cathedral and a block south of the Plaza José Antonio, on a leafy promenade filled with sidewalk cafés and Castilians taking early-evening strolls. The bedrooms lack style and imagination, but are completely comfortable nonetheless. The management is extremely cooperative: When the España is full, they have been known to call other hostelries for stranded tourists. A lunch or dinner costs 1,800 pesetas ($16.90).

HOTEL NORTE Y LONDRES, Plaza de Alonso Martínez, 10, 09003 Burgos. Tel. 947/26-41-25. 50 rms (all with bath).
$ Rates: 3,500 ptas. ($32.90) single; 5,600 ptas. ($52.65) double. Breakfast 400 ptas. ($3.75) extra. AE, V.
Near the town's military headquarters and the tourist office, on a pleasant square a short walk northeast of the cathedral, this hotel has traces of faded grandeur with its stained glass, leaded windows, and crystal chandeliers. Bedrooms are of good size, with basic furnishings, and the large bathrooms come equipped with yesteryear's finest plumbing. Breakfast is the only meal served.

MESÓN DEL CID, Plaza de Santa María, 8, 09003 Burgos. Tel. 947/20-87-15. Fax 947/26-94-60. 29 rms (all with bath). TEL TV
$ Rates: 5,500 ptas. ($51.70) single; 10,000 ptas. ($94) double. Breakfast 700 ptas. ($6.60) extra. AE, DC, MC, V.
Built in 1983 by the Alzaga family, which still owns and operates it, this establishment stands in front of the cathedral and beside their restaurant (recommended below). The hotel is decorated like a 15th-century house, but it boasts 20th-century amenities, including extra-large beds in all rooms. A laundry and a garage are available.

WHERE TO EAT

The restaurants in the heart of Burgos—surrounding the cathedral—usually feature prices that soar as high as a Gothic spire. Every menu contains the roast lamb and suckling pig known throughout the area, or you might order *entremeses variados,* an appetizer sampler of many regional specialties.

MESÓN DE LOS INFANTES, Avenida Generalísimo, 2. Tel. 20-59-82.
  Cuisine: SPANISH. **Reservations:** Recommended.
$ Prices: Appetizers 800–900 ptas. ($7.50–$8.45); main dishes 1,000–1,500 ptas. ($9.40–$14.10); fixed-priced menu 1,500 ptas. ($14.10). AE, DC, MC, V.
  Open: Lunch daily 1–4:30pm; dinner daily 8pm–midnight.
Just below the gate leading into the Plaza de Santa María, this restaurant serves good food amid elegant Castilian decor. Dishes include the *olla podrida* (rotten pot) of Don Quixote, a Castilian stew containing lots of meats and vegetables; *zarzuela de mariscos* (shellfish); tripe cooked in the local style; and little snails called *caracoles.*

RINCÓN DE ESPAÑA, Nuño Rasura, 11. Tel. 20-59-55.
  Cuisine: SPANISH. **Reservations:** Required.
$ Prices: Appetizers 700–1,000 ptas. ($6.60–$9.40); main dishes 1,200–1,800 ptas. ($11.30–$16.90); fixed-priced menu 1,600 ptas. ($15.05). AE, DC, MC, V.
  Open: Lunch daily 1–4pm; dinner daily 8pm–midnight. **Closed:** Tues in winter.
This restaurant, about 1 block southwest of the cathedral, draws many discerning visitors. You can eat in a rustic dining room or outdoors under a large awning closed off by glass when the weather threatens. A daily menu might include an omelet, roast veal, flan, wine, and bread. The Spanish Corner also offers *platos combinados,* as well as a more extensive à la carte menu. The food here is good, the portions are large, and the vegetables are fresh.

CASA OJEDA, Vitoria, 5. Tel. 20-90-52.
  Cuisine: SPANISH. **Reservations:** Required.
$ Prices: Appetizers 750–1,000 ptas. ($7.05–$9.40); main dishes 1,800–2,400 ptas. ($16.90–$22.55); fixed-priced menu 3,400 ptas. ($31.95). AE, DC, MC, V.

Open: Lunch daily 1–4:30pm; dinner Mon–Sat 9–11:30pm.

This top-notch restaurant combines excellent Burgalese fare, cozy decor, attentive service, and moderate prices. Moorish tiles and low ceilings set an inviting ambience, enhanced by intimate nooks, old lanterns and fixtures, and intricate trelliswork. Upstairs the restaurant divides into two sections: one overlooking the street and the other, the Casa del Cordón, where Ferdinand and Isabella received Columbus after his second trip to America (1497). A *menú del día* might feature a Castilian soup, pork filets, dessert (ice cream, flan, or fruit), bread, and wine. A la carte dishes include roast lamb, Basque-style hake, sole Harlequin, and chicken in garlic. A house specialty: *alubias con chorizo y mirocilla* (small white beans with spicy sausages).

MESÓN DEL CID, Plaza de Santa María, 8. Tel. 20-87-15.
   Cuisine: SPANISH. **Reservations:** Required.
$ **Prices:** Appetizers 800–1,300 ptas. ($7.50–$12.20); main dishes 1,800–2,400 ptas. ($16.90–$22.95); fixed-priced menu 3,200 ptas. ($30.10). AE, DC, MC, V.
   Open: Lunch daily 1–4pm; dinner Mon–Sat 8pm–midnight.

Once the private home of the most powerful regional lords, today the Mesón del Cid is a restaurant serving delicious specialties concocted by José López Algaza (known to his clients as Pepín). Menu selections, always fresh, are prepared according to regional traditions. You might be tempted by one of the shellfish soups, roast baby lamb with aromatic herbs, roasted stuffed peppers, the fresh fish brought in daily, or a pork, veal, or chicken dish. Try codfish house style. The restaurant lies on the square flanking the main entrance of the cathedral.

A ONE-DAY EXCURSION

Some 42 miles (67.5km) west of Burgos, and easily visited on a day trip, lies **Santo Domingo de la Calzada.** The crowning achievement of the town, which grew as a stopover for pilgrims en route to Santiago de Compostela, is the 13th-century **cathedral,** a national landmark. For the most part Gothic in style, it nevertheless contains a hodgepodge of architectural elements—Romanesque chapels, a Renaissance choir, a freestanding baroque tower. The city is named after St. Dominic, who is buried in the crypt. A centuries-old legend attaches to the cathedral: Supposedly a rooster stood up and crowed after it had been cooked to protest the innocence of a pilgrim who had been accused of theft and sentenced to hang. To this day, a live cock and hen are kept in a cage up on the church wall, and you can often hear the rooster crowing at mass. The cathedral is open daily from 9am to 2pm and 4 to 8:30pm. Motorists can reach Santo Domingo de la Calzada by following either of the traffic arteries paralleling the river, heading east from the Burgos Cathedral until signs indicate N-120.

---

7. CUENCA

100 miles E of Madrid, 202 miles SW of Zaragoza

GETTING THERE   By Train   Trains leave Madrid's Atocha Railway Station about 8 times throughout the day, arriving at Cuenca's station at Avenida de la Estación, at the southern edge of the modern city.

By Bus   There are about 4 buses from both Madrid and Valencia every day. Buses from Madrid arrive at the Calle de Tervel (phone Auto-Res at 22-11-84 in Cuenca for information). Buses to and from Valencia use the Avenida Reyes Católicos, next to the town's bullring (phone the Alsina Bus Company at 22-04-96 for information). For schedules and routes to and from other cities, contact the tourist office.

By Car   Cuenca is the junction for several highways and about a dozen lesser roads that connect it to towns within its region. From Madrid, take the N-III to Tarancon, then the N-400, which leads directly into Cuenca. Driving time from Madrid is 2½ hours.

ESSENTIALS Cuenca's area code is 966. The Tourist Information Office is at Dalmacio García Izcarra, 8 (tel. 966/22-22-31).

This medieval town—once dominated by the Arabs—is a spectacular sight with its casas colgadas, the cliff-hanging houses set on multiple terraces that climb up the sides of a ravine. The Júcar and Huécar rivers meet at the bottom.

WHAT TO SEE & DO

The chief sight of Cuenca is Cuenca itself. Isolated from the rest of Spain, it requires a northern detour from the heavily traveled Valencia–Madrid road. Deep gorges give it an unreal quality, and eight old bridges spanning two rivers connect the ancient parts of town with the growing new sections. One of the bridges is suspended over a 200-foot drop.

Cuenca's streets are narrow and steep, often cobbled, and even the most athletic tire quickly. But you shouldn't miss it, even if you have to stop and rest periodically. At night you're in for a special treat when the casas colgadas are illuminated. Also, try to drive almost to the top of the castle-dominated hill. The road gets rough as you near the end, but the view makes the effort worthwhile.

CATHEDRAL, Plaza Pío XII.

Begun in the 12th century, the Gothic cathedral was influenced by England's Norman style. Part of it collapsed in this century, but it has been restored. A national monument filled with religious art treasures, the cathedral is a 10-minute walk from the Plaza Mayor, up the Calle Palafox.

Admission: Free.
Open: Daily 9am–1:30pm and 4:30–7:30pm.

MUSEO DE ARTE ABSTRACTO ESPAÑOL, Calle los Canónigos s/n. Tel. 21-29-83.

North of the Plaza Mayor, housed in a cliff-hanging dwelling, this ranks as one of the finest museums of its kind in Spain. It was conceived of by painter Fernando Zóbel, who donated it in 1980 to the Juan March Foundation. The most outstanding abstract Spanish painters are represented, including Rafael Canogar (especially his *Toledo*), Luís Feito, Zóbel himself, Tápies, Eduardo Chillida, Gustavo Torner, Gerardo Rueda, Millares, Sempere, Cuixart, Antonio Saura (see his grotesque Geraldine Chaplin and his study of Brigitte Bardot, a vision of horror, making the French actress look like an escapee from Picasso's *Guernica*).

Admission: 150 ptas. ($1.40).
Open: Tues–Fri 11am–2pm and 4–6pm; Sat 11am–2pm and 4–8pm, Sun 11am–2pm.

WHERE TO STAY

THE AVENIDA, Avenida José Antonio, 39, 16004 Cuenca. Tel. 966/21-43-43. 32 rms (27 with bath). TEL

$ Rates: 2,600 ptas. ($24.45) single; 3,900 ptas. ($36.65) double. Breakfast 210 ptas. ($1.95) extra. MC, V.

This two-star hostal-residencia, serving breakfast only, is a neat, tidy place with comfortable bedrooms (five of them air-conditioned) and a helpful staff. Generally conceded to be about the best value-for-money hotel in town, The Avenida lies in the modern part of the city, 1 block southwest of the Parque de San Julian.

HOTEL FIGÓN DE PEDRO, Cervantes, 15, 16004 Cuenca. Tel. 966/22-45-11. 28 rms (all with bath). TEL

$ Rates: 3,000 ptas. ($28.20) single; 4,200 ptas. ($39.50) double. Breakfast 300 ptas. ($2.80) extra. AE, V.

The Figón de Pedro lies south of the old city, a short walk north of both the bus and rail stations, and 1 block south of the landmark Plaza del Generalísimo. The hotel (with elevator) is immaculate but not stuffy, since the staff keeps the atmosphere pleasantly informal. On the second floor you'll find a lounge with TV, and the hotel boasts a country-style dining room, with a tasca in front. Wood beams, fresh linen on the tables, personal service—all make it an inviting place for meals.

POSADA DE SAN JOSÉ, Julian Romero, 4, 16001 Cuenca. Tel. 966/21-13-00. 24 rms (16 with bath). **Bus:** 1 or 2.

$ Rates: 1,800 ptas. ($16.90) single without bath; 3,200 ptas. ($30.10) single with shower; 5,600 ptas. ($52.65) double with shower. Breakfast 300 ptas. ($2.80) extra. DC, MC, V.

The Posada de San José stands in the oldest part of Cuenca, a short walk north of the cathedral. The 17th-century cells that used to shelter the sisters of this former convent now house overnight guests who consider its views of the old city the best in town. It sits atop a cliff, overlooking the forbidding depths of a gorge. Antonio and Jennifer Cortinas, the owners, renovated this place into one of the most alluring hotels of the region, with the bar perhaps the most charming of its well-decorated public rooms.

WHERE TO EAT

TOGAR, Avenida Republica Argentina, 3. Tel. 22-01-62.
  Cuisine: SPANISH. **Reservations:** Recommended.
$ Prices: Appetizers 600–800 ptas. ($5.65–$7.50); main dishes 650–1,200 ptas. ($6.10–$11.30); fixed-priced menu 1,300 ptas. ($12.20). AE, DC, MC, V.
  Open: Lunch Wed–Mon 1–4pm; dinner Wed–Mon 8–11pm.

This is one of the least expensive recommended restaurants in Cuenca, offering homemade cookery in a simple atmosphere. You can enjoy such classic dishes as fish soup, trout with ham, and loin of pork for a good, filling à la carte meal. Togar is located on the N-III to Madrid, on the southwest periphery of the city.

MESÓN CASA COLGADAS, Canónigos, 3. Tel. 21-18-22.
  Cuisine: SPANISH. **Reservations:** Recommended.
$ Prices: Appetizers 750–1,000 ptas. ($7.05–$9.40); main dishes 1,600–2,000 ptas. ($15.04–$18.80); fixed-priced menu 3,000 ptas. ($28.20). AE, DC, MC, V.
  Open: Lunch daily 1:30–4pm; dinner Mon–Sat 9–11pm.

One of the most spectacular dining rooms in Spain stands on one of the most precarious precipices in Cuenca. It's five stories high, with sturdy supporting walls and beams. Pine balconies and windows overlook the ravine below and the hills beyond. In fact, it's the most photographed "suspended house" in town, and dinner here is worth every *centímo*. The menu includes regional dishes and a wide variety of international cuisine. Preprandial drinks are served in the tavern room on the street level, so even if you're not dining here, you may want to drop in for a drink and the view. You'll find the Mesón Casa Colgadas just south of the cathedral and near the Museum of Spanish Abstract Art.

A ONE-DAY EXCURSION

If you're staying over in Cuenca—or otherwise have the time—you can easily visit what its citizens call their **Ciudad Encantada (Enchanted City),** Carretera de la Sierra, about 25 miles (40km) to the northeast. Storms and underground waters have created a city here out of large rocks and boulders, shaping them into bizarre designs: a seal, an elephant, a Roman bridge. Take CU-912, turning northeast onto CU-913. Ciudad Encantada is signposted.

CHAPTER 9
EXTREMADURA

- **WHAT'S SPECIAL ABOUT EXTREMADURA**
1. **GUADALUPE**
2. **TRUJILLO**
3. **CÁCERES**
4. **MÉRIDA**
5. **BADAJOZ**
6. **ZAFRA**

The westernmost region of Spain has always been known as "the land beyond the River Douro." It extends from the Gredos and Gata mountain ranges all the way to Andalusia, and from Castile to the Portuguese frontier. A land with a varied landscape, it has both plains and mountains, meadows with holm and cork oaks, and fields of stone and lime. Extremadura (not to be confused with the Portuguese province of Estremadura) includes the provinces of Badajoz and Cáceres.

Ancient civilizations were established here, including those of the Celts, Romans, and Visigoths, but the world knows Extremadura best as the land of the conquistadores. Famous natives included Cortés, Pizarro, Balboa, and many others less well known but also important, such as Francisco de Orellana and Hernando de Soto. Many of these men were driven from their homeland by economic necessity, finding it hard to make a living in this dry, sun-parched province. Many of these conquistadores sent back money to their native land to finance the building of mansions and public structures that stand today as monuments to their long-ago adventures in the Americas.

Many of Extremadura's previous conquerors have left enduring monuments as well, including, for example, the Roman ruins in Mérida. Arab ruins are found in Badajoz, and medieval palaces in Cáceres.

Many Spaniards come here to hunt. Fishing and water sports are also popular, as there are a large number of reservoirs. Horseback riding along ancient trails is another popular pastime.

Since summer is intensely hot, spring and fall make the best times to visit.

SEEING EXTREMADURA
GETTING THERE

Most visitors drive west to Extremadura after visiting Madrid or Toledo. It's also possible to swing northwest from Andalusia and explore the province before heading back to Madrid. The only **air** link is a small air base at Badajoz, 9 miles (14.5km) east at Talavera la Real (tel. 25-11-11), with Aviaco flights coming in from Madrid.

It's more popular to go by **train,** however. The main train depots are at Cáceres and Badajoz, with arrivals from Madrid and Seville (stops are made at smaller towns along the way; see individual city or town listings for more details).

There are many **bus** connections to Mérida, Badajoz, and Cáceres from either Madrid or Seville. Links also exist between Badajoz and Lisbon as well as Córdoba (Andalusia). The small towns of Extremadura are joined by buses to the bigger towns of Cáceres and Badajoz.

If you can afford it, explore Extremadura by **car,** as you'll see so much more scenery. The east–west run from Madrid to Lisbon (N-V) passes through Trujillo, Mérida, and Badajoz at the frontier. If you're visiting Cáceres from Madrid, travel the N-V to Trujillo (stopover suggested), then cut onto the N-521 to Cáceres. Some of the road connections between the cities or towns of Extremadura are difficult because of poor maintenance. An example is the N-523 linking Cáceres with Badajoz.

WHAT'S SPECIAL ABOUT EXTREMADURA

Great Towns/Villages
- ☐ Guadalupe, a village of great beauty known for its Gothic-Mudejar monastery.
- ☐ Cáceres, a national monument city encircled by old walls.
- ☐ Mérida, a miniature Rome, a treasure house of Roman antiquities.
- ☐ Zafra, a venerable white-walled town with a medieval castle.

Special Events/Festivals
- ☐ At Mérida, classical Greek and Latin drama performances in June at its Roman theater.

Architectural Highlights
- ☐ Monastery of Guadalupe, dating from the Gothic era, and filled with artistic treasures.

- ☐ Gothic and Renaissance seignorial mansions at Cáceres, unequaled in all of Spain.
- ☐ Plaza Mayor at Trujillo, with its irregular shape and seignorial mansions.

Great Museums
- ☐ Museo Nacional de Arte Romano at Mérida, housing the best collection of Roman artifacts in Spain.

Ancient Monuments
- ☐ Teatro Romano at Mérida, built by Agrippa in 24 B.C.
- ☐ Roman amphitheater, also at Mérida, dating from the 1st century B.C., an amphitheater once flooded for "sea battles."

A SUGGESTED ROUTE

Day 1   Drive southwest from Madrid or Toledo, planning an overnight stop at Guadalupe.

Day 2   Explore its monastery in the morning, then head west for Trujillo for the night, wandering at leisure through its old town.

Day 3   Make the short drive west from Trujillo to Cáceres, check into a hotel, see the sights, and spend the night.

Day 4   Drive south to Mérida and spend the night, after exploring its ancient Roman monuments.

Day 5   Those with a day to spare can head south to the town of Zafra for an afternoon's exploration and then an overnight stopover.

Day 6   Either continue southeast to Córdoba and the attractions of Andalusia or make for the border town of Badajoz, crossing into Portugal and driving toward the sights of Lisbon.

---

1. GUADALUPE

117 miles W of Toledo, 140 miles SW of Madrid

GETTING THERE   By Train   There are no trains coming into Guadalupe.

By Bus   There are 2 buses every day to and from Madrid's Estación Sur, a 3-hour ride away. The road is poor, but the route through the surrounding regions is savagely beautiful. In Guadalupe, the buses park on either side of the street, a few paces uphill from the Town Hall.

By Car   One narrow-highway goes through Guadalupe. Most maps don't give it a number; look on a map in the direction of the town of Navalmoral de la Mata. From Madrid, take the narrow, winding C-401 southwest from Toledo, turning north in the direction of Navalmoral de la Mata after seeing signs for Navalmoral de la Mata and

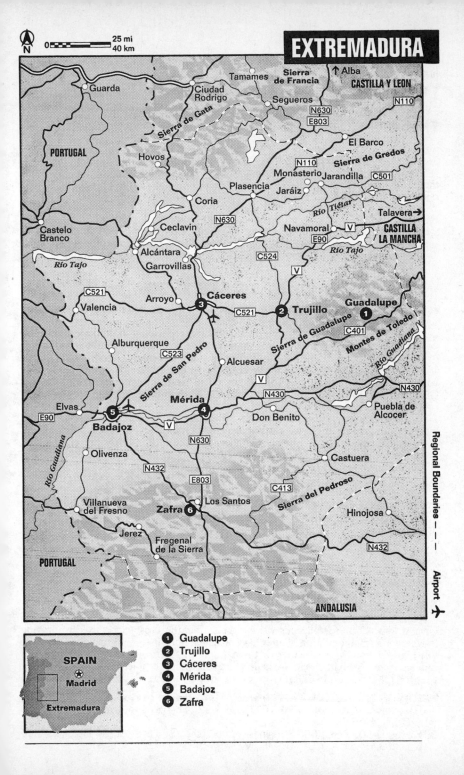

EXTREMADURA

N
0 ⸻ 25 mi
⸻ 40 km

CASTILLA Y LEON

Guarda
Ciudad Rodrigo
Tamames
Sierra de Francia
↑ Alba
Segueros
N630
E803
N110

PORTUGAL

Sierra de Gata
Hovos
El Barco
Sierra de Gredos
N110
Monasterio
Jarandilla
C501
Plasencia
Jaráiz
Coria
Río Tiétar
Talavera →
Castelo Branco
Ceclavin
N630
Navamoral
V
CASTILLA LA MANCHA
E90
Río Tajo
Río Tajo
Alcántara
Garrovillas
C524
V
C521
Valencia
Arroyo
Cáceres
③
C521
②
Trujillo
Guadalupe
①
Alburquerque
C523
Alcuesar
C401
Sierra de Guadalupe
Montes de Toledo
Río Guadiana
Sierra de San Pedro
V
Mérida
④
N430
Puebla de Alcocer
N430
Elvas
E90
Don Benito
⑤
Badajoz
V
N630
Olivenza
Castuera
N432
E803
C413
Sierra del Pedroso
Villanueva del Fresno
Zafra
⑥
Los Santos
Hinojosa
Jerez
Fregenal de la Sierra
N432
PORTUGAL

Río Guadiana

ANDALUSIA

Regional Boundaries − − −

Airport ✈

SPAIN
✪ **Madrid**
Extremadura

① Guadalupe
② Trujillo
③ Cáceres
④ Mérida
⑤ Badajoz
⑥ Zafra

Guadalupe. Driving time from Madrid is between 3½ and 4½ hours, depending on how well you fare with the bad roads.

ESSENTIALS   The area code for Guadalupe is 927.

Guadalupe lies in the province of Cáceres, 1,500 feet above sea level. The village has a certain beauty and much local color. Everything of interest lies within a 3-minute walk from the point where buses deposit you, at Avenida Don Blas Perez (tel. 36-70-06), also known as Carretera de Cáceres.

Around the corner and a few paces downhill is the Plaza Mayor, which contains the Town Hall (which is where many visitors go to ask questions in lieu of a tourist office).

The village is best visited in spring, when the balconies of its whitewashed houses burst into bloom with flowers. Wander at your leisure through the twisting, narrow streets, some no more than alleyways. The buildings are so close together that in summer you can walk in the shade of the steeply pitched sienna-colored tile roofs. The religious-souvenir industry views Guadalupe as one of its major outlets.

WHAT TO SEE & DO

MONASTERY OF GUADALUPE, Plaza de la Santa María de Guadalupe. Tel. 36-70-00.

⭐ In 1325 a shepherd searching for a stray lamb reportedly spotted a statue of the Virgin in the soil. In time, this statue became venerated throughout the world, honored in Spain by Isabella, Columbus, and Cervantes. Known as the Dark Virgin of Guadalupe, it is said to have been carved by St. Luke. A shrine was built to commemorate the statue, and tribute poured in from all over the world, making Guadalupe one of the wealthiest foundations in Christendom. You can see the Virgin in a small alcove above the altar.

The church is noted for the wrought-iron railings in its naves. Be sure to see the museum devoted to ecclesiastical vestments and to the choir books produced by 16th-century miniaturists. In the magnificently decorated sacristy are eight richly imaginative 17th-century masterpieces by Zurbarán. The 14th-century Gothic cloister is flamboyant, with two galleries, a patio, and coffered ceilings. The pièce de résistance is the stunning Mudejar cloister, with its brick-and-tile Gothic-Mudejar shrine dating from 1405; the Moorish fountain is from the 14th century.

Admission: Museum and sacristy 150 ptas. ($1.40) adults, 75 ptas. (70¢) children.

Open: Daily 9:30am–1pm and 3:30–6:30pm.

WHERE TO STAY

HOSPEDERÍA REAL MONASTERIO, Plaza Juan Carlos, 1, 10140 Guadalupe. Tel. 927/36-70-00. Fax 927/36-61-77. 40 rms (all with bath). TEL
$ Rates: 3,600 ptas. ($33.85) single; 5,200 ptas. ($48.90) double. Breakfast 400 ptas. ($3.75) extra. MC, V. **Closed:** Jan 15–Feb 15.

Once a way station for pilgrims visiting the shrine, the Hospedería used to provide lodging for a small donation. Times have changed, but the prices remain moderate at this two-star hotel in the center of town. Some of the rooms contain high-vaulted ceilings. There is a bar. Meals are generally good, and a complete luncheon or dinner goes for 1,900 pesetas ($17.85). Top it off with a home-brewed *licor de Guadalupe*.

PARADOR NACIONAL ZURBARÁN, Marqués de la Romana, 10, 10140 Guadalupe. Tel. 927/36-70-75. Fax 927/36-70-75. 40 rms (all with bath). A/C MINIBAR TV TEL
$ Rates: 7,000 ptas. ($65.80) single; 9,000 ptas. ($84.60) double. Breakfast 900 ptas. ($8.45) extra. AE, DC, MC, V.

In a scenic spot in the center of the village, the area's most luxurious accommodation is housed in a 16th-century building with a beautiful garden. Queen Isabella once stayed here, and the place often saw meetings between royal representatives and explorers setting out for the New World, who signed their contracts here. The house is named after Francisco de Zurbarán, the great 17th-century painter, who was born in the nearby town of Fuente de Cantos. There is a Zurbarán painting in one of the salons, along with ancient maps and engravings—many of them valuable works of art. In the attractive restaurant, good regional food, both lunch and dinner, is served for 2,900 pesetas ($27.25). Try such local dishes as herb-flavored roast kid or pork Mudejar style. Bedrooms are comfortable and decorated in part with reproduction medieval furnishings. Other facilities include a swimming pool, bar, garage, and tennis court.

WHERE TO EAT

Both of the hotels recommended above also have good restaurants.

MESÓN EL CORDERO, Calle Convento, 23. Tel. 36-71-31.
   Cuisine: SPANISH. **Reservations:** Recommended.
$ **Prices:** Appetizers 350–600 ptas. ($3.30–$5.65); main dishes 900–1,500 ptas. ($8.45–$14.10); fixed-priced menu 1,200 ptas. ($11.30). No credit cards.
   Open: Lunch Tues–Sun 1–4pm; dinner Tues–Sun 7–11pm. **Closed:** Feb.

Miguel and Angelita run Guadalupe's best independent restaurant, named for their specialty, *asado de cordero* (roast lamb flavored with garlic and thyme). You might begin with another of their specialties, *sopas guadalupanas,* then follow with partridge "from the countryside" if you have a taste for game. The house dessert is a creamy custard, *flan casero.*

---

2. TRUJILLO

152 miles SW of Madrid, 28 miles E of Cáceres

GETTING THERE   By Train   There are no trains to Trujillo.

By Bus   There are 14 buses per day to and from Madrid (3½ and 4½ hours, depending on whether it's local or *expreso*). There are also about a dozen buses running daily to Cáceres, 45 minutes away, and 5 each to both Badajoz and Mérida. Trujillo's bus station, Carretera à Badajoz (tel. 32-12-02), lies on the south side of town on a side street that intersects with the Calle de la Encarnación.

By Car   Trujillo lies at a network of large and small roads connecting it to Cáceres, via the N-521, and both Lisbon and Madrid, via the N-V superhighway. Driving time from Madrid is around 4 hours.

ESSENTIALS   The area code for Trujillo is 927. The Tourist Information Office is at Plaza de España (tel. 927/32-06-53).

Dating from the 13th century, the walled town of Trujillo is celebrated for the colonizers and conquerors born here. Among the illustrious natives were Francisco Pizarro, conqueror of Peru, whose family palace on the Plaza Mayor was built with gold from the New World, and Francisco de Orellana, the founder of Guayaquil and the first man to explore the Amazon. Other Trujillano history-makers were Francisco de las Casas, who accompanied Hernán Cortés in his conquest of Mexico and founded the city of Trujillo in Honduras; Diego García de Paredes, who founded Trujillo, Venezuela; Nuño de Chaves, founder of Santa Cruz de la Sierra in Bolivia; and several hundred others whose names are found throughout maps of North, Central, and South America. There is a saying that 20 American countries were "born" here.

Celts, Romans, Moors, and Christians have inhabited Trujillo. The original town, lying above today's modern one, was built on a granite ledge on the hillside. It is centered around the Plaza Mayor, one of the artistic landmarks of Spain. A Moorish castle and a variety of 16th- and 17th-century palaces, manor houses, towers, churches, and arcades encircle the plaza, and overlook a bronze equestrian statue of Pizarro by American artists Mary Harriman and Charles Runse. Steep, narrow streets and shadowy little corners evoke bygone times when explorers set out from here on their fantastic adventures.

WHAT TO SEE & DO

PLAZA MAYOR

The heart of Trujillo, one of the outstanding architectural sights in Extremadura, is dominated by a statue honoring Pizarro, who almost single-handedly destroyed the Inca civilization of Peru. The statue is an exact double of one standing in Lima. Many of the buildings on this square were financed with wealth brought back from the New World.

The most prominent structure on the square is the **Ayuntamiento Viejo** (Old Town Hall), with three tiers of arches, each tier more squat than the one below.

The **Iglesia de San Martín** stands behind the statue dedicated to Pizarro. This granite church, originally from the 15th century, was reconstructed in the 16th century in Renaissance style. Inside are an impressive nave, several tombs, and a rare 18th-century organ, still in working condition.

While you are on the square, observe the unusual façade of the **Casa de las Cadenas,** a 12th-century house across which a heavy chain is draped. This was a symbol that Philip II had granted the Orellana family immunity from heavy taxes.

You can then visit the **Palacio Duques de Carlos,** a 16th-century ducal residence turned into a convent. Ring the bell to gain entry any time daily from 9am to 1pm and 3 to 6pm. A donation is appreciated, and a resident nun will show you around; appropriate dress (no shorts) required. The façade has Renaissance sculptured figures, and a courtyard inside is even more impressive, built on two levels.

The **Palacio de la Conquista,** also on the square, is one of the most grandiose mansions in Trujillo. Originally constructed by Hernán Pizarro, the present structure was built by his son-in-law to commemorate the exploits of the explorer.

IGLESIA DE SANTA MARÍA, Calle de Ballesteros.

A Gothic building, this is the largest church in Trujillo, having been built over the ruins of a Moorish mosque. Ferdinand and Isabella once attended Mass in this church, with its outstanding Renaissance choir. Its proudest treasure is a retable with two dozen panels painted by Fernando Gallego (seen at the altar). Also here is the tomb of Diego García de Paredes, the "Samson of Extremadura," who is said to have single-handedly defended a bridge against an attacking French army with only a gigantic sword. To reach the church, go through one of the gates at the Plaza Mayor, the Puerta de San Andrés, and take the Calle de las Palomas through the old town.

CASTILLO, crowning the hilltop.

Constructed by the Arabs on the site of a Roman fortress, the castle stands at the summit of the granite hill on which Trujillo was founded. Once at the castle, you can climb its battlements and walk along the ramparts, enjoying a spectacular view of the austere countryside of Extremadura. Later, you can go below and see the dungeons. It is said that the Virgin Mary appeared here in 1232, giving the Christians renewed courage to free the city from Arab domination.

Admission: Free.

Open: No set hours; many visitors find it most dramatic at sunset.

WHERE TO STAY

LA CIGÜEÑAS, Carretera N-V, 10200 Trujillo. Tel. 927/32-12-50. 78 rms (all with bath). A/C TV

$ Rates: 4,000 ptas. ($37.60) single; 7,000 ptas. ($65.80) double. Breakfast 350 ptas. ($3.30) extra. AE, DC, MC, V.

Outside the city and better suited for motorists, this is the "second best" place to stay in Trujillo. Obviously, it doesn't have the charm of the Parador Nacional (see below), but it's definitely cheaper. A roadside hotel with a garden, it offers functional but clean and comfortable bedrooms. Its restaurant, specializing in regional cuisine, serves a complete meal for 1,900 pesetas ($17.85). There is also a bar. You'll find La Cigüeñas on the main highway from Madrid, 1 mile before Trujillo.

PARADOR NACIONAL DE TRUJILLO, Plaza de Santa Clara, 10200 Trujillo. Tel. 927/32-13-50. Fax 927/32-13-66. 45 rms (all with bath). A/C MINIBAR TV TEL
$ Rates: 8,000 ptas. ($75.20) single; 10,000 ptas. ($94) double. Breakfast 900 ptas. ($8.45) extra. AE, DC, MC, V.

⭐ Housed in the 16th-century Convent of Santa Clara, this centrally located *parador*, about 1 block south of the Avenida de la Coronación, is a gem of Trujillo-style medieval and Renaissance architecture, now faithfully restored. The beautifully decorated bedrooms, once nuns' cells, have canopied beds and spacious marble baths. The gardens and fruit trees of the Renaissance cloister are inviting, and there is a swimming pool in the courtyard of a new section that blends with the original convent architecture. You can have breakfast in the old refectory and dinner in what was once a long, vaulted chapel. A three-course Spanish meal costs 2,900 pesetas ($27.25)—try the *caldereta extremena*, a stew made with baby lamb or baby goat.

WHERE TO EAT

Both of the hotels recommended above also have good regional restaurants.

HOSTAL PIZARRO, Plaza Mayor, 13. Tel. 32-02-55.
Cuisine: SPANISH. Reservations: Recommended.
$ Prices: Appetizers 500–650 ptas. ($4.70–$6.10); main dishes 750–1,400 ptas. ($7.05–$13.15); fixed-priced menu 950 ptas. ($8.95). V.

Ⓢ Natives often cite this centrally located *hostal* as the best place to go for regional-style Extremaduran cookery. Local wines accompany meals that invariably include ham from acorn-fed pigs. You might begin with asparagus with a mayonnaise sauce, then follow with *asado de cordero* (roast lamb flavored with herbs and garlic). Also try Roman-style fried *merluza* (hake). The kitchen's game specialty is *estofado de perdices* (partridge casserole).

LA TROYA, Plaza Mayor, 10. Tel. 32-14-65.
Cuisine: SPANISH. **Reservations:** Recommended.
$ Prices: Fixed-priced menu 1,400 ptas. ($13.15). No credit cards.

Ⓢ Locals and visitors alike are drawn to this centrally located restaurant featuring the regional cuisine of Extremadura—and doing the province proud. Have a dry sherry in the bar, which was designed to resemble the façade of a Spanish house. This cozy provincial theme also flows into the dining rooms, with their white walls (decorated with ceramic plates), potted plants, and red tiles. Few people leave hungry after devouring the set menu, with its more than ample portions; food items change daily. Local dishes include *prueba de cerdo* (garlic-flavored pork casserole) and *carne con tomate* (beef cooked in tomato sauce). A table is always reserved for the village priest.

3. CÁCERES

185 miles SW of Madrid, 159 miles N of Seville

GETTING THERE   By Train   To and from Madrid, there are around 4 daily trains, traveling via Talavera (2 hours) and Navalmoral (3 hours). The train station in

Cáceres is on the Avenida Alemania (tel. 22-50-61), near the main highway heading south (Carretera de Sevilla). A green-and-white bus shuttles passengers about once an hour from the railway and bus stations (they lie across the street from one another; board it outside the bus station) to the busiest traffic junction in the new city, the Plaza de América. From there it's a 10-minute walk to the edge of the old town.

By Bus　Bus connections are more frequent than train. From the city bus station, on the busy Carretera de Sevilla (tel. 24-59-54), buses arrive and depart 7 times a day for Madrid and Seville (5 and 4½ hours, respectively). Other buses travel between 2 and 5 times a day to and from Guadalupe, Trujillo, Mérida, Valladolid, Córdoba, and Salamanca. For information on reaching the new town from the bus station, see "By Train," above.

By Car　Driving time from Madrid is about 5 hours. Most motorists approach Cáceres from eastern Spain via the N-V superhighway until they reach Trujillo. There, they exit onto the N-521, driving another 28 miles (45km) west to Cáceres.

ESSENTIALS　The area code for Cáceres is 927. The Tourist Information Office is at Plaza de España (tel. 927/24-63-47).

A national landmark and the capital of Extremadura, Cáceres is encircled by old city walls, and has several seignorial palaces and towers, many financed by gold sent from the Americas by the conquistadores. Allow about 2 hours to explore the city center.

WHAT TO SEE & DO

The modern city lies southwest of the old city, **Cáceres Viejo,** which is enclosed by ramparts. The heart of the old city lies between the **Plaza de Santa María** and, a few blocks to the south, the Plaza San Mateo. The Plaza Santa María, an irregularly shaped, rather elongated, square, is one of the major sights. On each of its sides are the honey-brown façades of buildings once inhabited by the nobility.

On the far side of the square rises the **Iglesia de Santa María,** which is basically Gothic in architecture, although the Renaissance era saw the addition of many embellishments. Completed some time in the 1500s, this church is the cathedral of Cáceres, and it contains the remains of many of the conquistadores. It has a trio of Gothic aisles of almost equal height. Look at the carved retable at the high altar, dating from the 16th century. (Insert coins to light it up.)

About 30 towers from the city's medieval walls remain, all of them heavily restored. Originally much taller, the towers reflected the pride and independence of their builders; when Queen Isabella took over, however, she ordered them "cut down to size." The largest tower is at the **Plaza del General Mola.** Beside it stands the **Estrella Arch** (Star Arch), constructed by Manuel Churriguera in the 18th century. To its right you'll see the **Torre del Horno,** a mud-brick adobe structure left from the Moorish occupation.

At the highest point of the old city and near its center is the 14th-century **Iglesia de San Mateo** (St. Matthew), which has a Plateresque portal and a rather plain nave (except for the Plateresque tombs, which add a decorative touch). The church lies at the edge of the Plaza San Mateo.

Next to it stands the **Casa de las Cigüeñas (Storks' House),** dating from the late 15th century. Its slender tower is all that remains of the battlements. Not open to the public, the building now serves as a military headquarters.

The **Church of Santiago** was begun in the 12th century and restored in the 16th. It possesses a reredos carved in 1557 by Alonso de Berruguete and a 15th-century figure of Christ. The church lies outside the ramparts, about a block to the north of Arco de Socorro (Socorro East Gate). To reach it, exit from the gate, enter the Plaza Socorro, then walk down the Calle Godoy. The Church of Santiago is on your right.

La Casa de los Toledo-Montezuma was built by Juan Cano de Saavedra with money from the dowry of his wife, the daughter of Montezuma. The house is set into the northern corner of the medieval ramparts, about a block to the north of the Plaza de Santa María.

On the site of the old Alcázar, the **Casa de las Veletas (Weather Vane House)**, Plaza Veletas (tel. 24-72-34), with its baroque façade, houses a provincial archeological museum. The building's ancient Moorish cistern, its five naves and horseshoe arches, and its patio and paneling from the 17th century, have been preserved. The museum holds a collection of Celtic and Visigothic remains, Roman and Gothic artifacts, and a numismatic collection. Admission is 200 ptas. ($1.90), and it's open Tuesday through Saturday from 9:30am to 2:30pm, on Sunday from 10:15am to 2:30pm.

WHERE TO STAY

HOTEL EXTREMADURA, Avenida Virgen de Guadalupe, 5, 10001 Cáceres. Tel. 927/22-16-00. 68 rms (all with bath). A/C TEL
$ Rates: 4,500 ptas. ($42.30) single; 7,000 ptas. ($65.80) double. Breakfast 475 ptas. ($4.25) extra. AE, DC, MC, V.

In the center of the modern city, north of the Plaza de América (a central and busy traffic hub), stands the Hotel Extremadura. Built in the mid-1950s and renovated in the '70s, it's a favorite with business and family travelers. A swimming pool has been set into the garden, and there is a parking garage. The well-kept rooms have modern furnishings and are reasonably comfortable, if short on style. The welcome is warm. In the good restaurant, lunch and dinner go for 1,850 pesetas ($17.40) per meal.

HOTEL ALCÁNTARA, Avenida Virgen de Guadalupe, 14, 10001 Cáceres. Tel. 927/22-89-00. Fax 927/28-943. 67 rms (all with bath). A/C MINIBAR TV TEL
$ Rates: 4,500 ptas. ($42.30) single; 7,000 ptas. ($65.80) double. Breakfast 475 ptas. ($4.25) extra. AE, DC, MC, V.

Located in the commercial city center, the Hotel Alcántara is still convenient to the old town. The rooms, most renovated in the 1970s, are tastefully decorated. There's a restaurant on the premises, serving meals for 1,850 pesetas ($17.40).

WHERE TO EAT

EL FIGÓN DE EUSTAQUIO, Plaza San Juan, 12. Tel. 24-81-94.
Cuisine: SPANISH. **Reservations:** Recommended.
$ Prices: Appetizers 600–800 ptas. ($5.65–$7.50); main dishes 1,600–2,000 ptas. ($15.05–$18.80); fixed-priced menu 1,450 ptas. ($14.65). AE, DC, MC, V.
Open: Lunch daily 1:30–4pm; dinner daily 8pm–midnight.

El Figón is a pleasant place that serves local Extremaduran cuisine. You'll notice the four Blanco brothers who run it doing practically everything. This includes preparing the amazingly varied dishes—for example, honey soup, *solomillo* (filet of beef), trout Extremaduran style, as well as typical Spanish specialties. The air-conditioned interior has a rustic decor. El Figon lies west of the western ramparts of the old city near the intersection of the Avenida Virgen de Guadalupe and the Plaza San Juan.

---

4. MÉRIDA

44 miles S of Cáceres, 35 miles E of Badajoz

GETTING THERE By Train Trains depart and arrive from the RENFE station on the Calle Cardero (tel. 31-81-09), about a half-mile north of the Plaza de España. There are 6 trains per day to and from Cáceres (the transit requires 1 hour); 6 trains per day from Madrid (4 hours), 1 daily train to and from Seville (4 hours), and 7 or 8 trains per day to and from Badajoz (1 hour).

By Bus   The bus station is on the Avenida de la Libertad (tel. 25-86-61), close to the train station. There are between 7 and a dozen buses every day to and from Madrid (5½ hours), 9 or 10 per day to and from Seville (3 hours), 3 or 4 per day to and from Cáceres (2 hours), and 8 per day to Badajoz (1 hour).

By Car   Take the N-V superhighway from Madrid or Lisbon. Driving time from Madrid is approximately 5 hours; from Lisbon, about 4½ hours. Park in front of the Roman theater and explore the town on foot.

ESSENTIALS   The area code for Mérida is 924. The Tourist Information Office is at Pedro María Plano (tel. 924/31-53-53).

Mérida, known as Augusta Emerita when it was founded in 25 B.C., lay at the crossroads of the Roman roads linking Toledo and Lisbon and Salamanca and Seville. At one time the capital of Lusitania (the Latin name for the combined kingdoms of Spain and Portugal), Mérida was considered one of the most splendid cities in Iberia, ranking as a town of major importance in the Roman Empire; in fact, it was once called a miniature Rome. Its monuments, temples, and public works make it the site of some of the finest Roman ruins in Spain, and as such, it is the tourist capital of Extremadura. Old Mérida can be covered on foot, the only way to see it. Pay scant attention to the dull modern suburb across the Guadiana River, which skirts the town with its sluggish waters.

WHAT TO SEE & DO

The **Roman bridge** over the Guadiana was the longest in Roman Spain—about half a mile—and consisted of 64 arches. It was constructed of granite under either Trajan or Augustus, then restored by the Visigoths in 686. Philip II ordered further refurbishment in 1610; work was also done in the 19th century. The bridge crosses the river south of the center of Old Mérida, its length increased because of the way it spans two forks of the river, including an island in midstream.

Another sight of interest is the old hippodrome, or **Circus Maximus,** which could seat about 30,000 spectators watching chariot races. The Roman masonry was carted off to use in other buildings, and today the site looks more like a parking lot. Excavations have uncovered rooms that may have housed gladiators. The site of the former circus lies at the end of the Avenida Extremadura, on the northeastern outskirts of the old town, about a half mile north of the Roman bridge and a 10-minute walk east of the railway station.

The **Arco Trajano (Trajan's Arch)** lies near the heart of the old town, beside the Calle Trajano, about a block south of the Parador Vía de la Plata. An unadorned triumphal arch, it measures 16 yards high and 10 yards across.

The **Acueducto de los Milagros** is the most intact of the town's two remaining Roman aqueducts, this one bringing water from Proserpina, 3 miles away. From the aqueducts, water was fed into two artificially created lakes, Cornalvo and Proserpina. The aqueduct is northwest of the old town, lying to the right of the road to Cáceres, just beyond the railway tracks. Ten arches still stand.

The latest monument to be excavated is the **Temple of Diana** (dedicated to Caesar Augustus). Squeezed between houses on a narrow residential street, it was converted in the 17th century into the private residence of a nobleman who used four of the original Corinthian columns in his architectural plans. The temple lies at the junction of the Calle Sagasta and the Calle Romero Léal in the center of town.

While in the area, you can also explore the 13th-century **Iglesia de Santa María la Mayor,** Plaza de España. It has a 16th century chapel, and is graced with Romanesque and Plateresque features. It stands on the west side of the square.

TEATRO ROMANO, José Ramon Melida s/n. Tel. 31-25-30.

⭐ The Roman theater, one of the best-preserved Roman ruins in the world, was built by Agrippa (Augustus's son-in-law) in 18 B.C. to house an audience of 6,000 people. Modeled after the great theaters of Rome, it was constructed by dry-stone methods, a remarkable achievement. In the reign of Hadrian (2nd century A.D.), a tall stage wall was adorned with statues and colonnades. Behind the stage, visitors of today can explore excavations of various rooms. In July they can enjoy a season of classical plays.

Admission: 200 ptas. ($1.90) adults; children free.

Open: Apr–Sept daily 8am–9:30pm; Oct–Mar daily 8am–6pm.

ANFITEATRO ROMANO, Calle José Rámon Melida s/n.

At the height of its glory, in the 1st century B.C., the amphitheater could seat 14,000 to 15,000 spectators. Chariot races were held here, along with gladiator combats and mock sea battles, for which the arena would be flooded. Many of the seats were placed dangerously close to the bloodshed. You can visit some of the rooms that housed the wild animals and gladiators waiting to go into combat.

Admission: 200 ptas. ($1.90).

Open: Apr-Sept daily 8am–9:30pm; Oct–Mar daily 8am–6pm.

MUSEO NACIONAL DE ARTE ROMANO, Calle José Rámon Melida s/n. Tel. 31-16-90.

The museum occupies a modern building adjacent to the ancient Roman amphitheater, to which it is connected by an underground tunnel. It contains more than 30,000 artifacts from Augusta Emerita, capital of the Roman province of Lusitania. Many of the sculptures came from the excavations of the Roman theater and amphitheater. You'll see displays of mosaics, figures, pottery, glassware, coins, and bronze objects. The museum is built of red brick in the form of a Roman basilica.

Admission: 200 ptas. ($1.90) adults; children free.

Open: Tues–Sat 10am–2pm and 4–6pm, Sun 10am–2pm.

ALCÁZAR, Plaza de España.

On the northern bank of the Guadiana River, beside the northern end of the Roman bridge (which it was meant to protect), stands the Alcázar, known as the Conventual or the Alcazaba. Built in the 9th century by the Moors, who used fragments left over from Roman and Visigothic occupations, the square structure was later granted to the Order of Santiago.

Admission: 100 ptas. (95¢).

Open: Apr–Sept Mon–Sat 8am–1pm and 4–7pm, Sun 9am–2pm; Oct–Mar Mon–Sat 9am–1pm and 3–6pm, Sun 9am–2pm.

MUSEO ARQUEOLÓGICO DE ARTE VISIGODO, Plaza de España.

In front of Trajan's Arch is this archeological museum, housing a treasure trove of artifacts left by the one-time conquering Visigoths. Look for the two statues of Wild Men in one of the alcoves.

Admission: Free.

Open: Mon–Fri 10am–2pm and 4–6pm.

WHERE TO STAY
DOUBLES FOR LESS THAN 6,500 PTAS. [$61.10]

HOTEL EMPERATRIZ, Plaza de España, 19, 06800 Mérida. Tel. 924/31-31-11. 45 rms (all with bath). TEL

$ Rates: 3,600 ptas. ($33.85) single; 6,500 ptas. ($61.10) double. Breakfast 375 ptas. ($3.30) extra. MC, V.

A former 16th-century palace, the Emperatriz has housed a long line of celebrated guests in its day, everybody from Kings Philip II and III of Spain to Queen Isabella of Portugal and Charles V, the Holy Roman Emperor. Its intricate tiled gallery foyer is in the Moorish style. All the rooms are functionally furnished and comfortable, but try to get one facing the plaza, where the people watching is great. (The rooftops around the square contain many storks nests, and these birds seem to take a similar interest in all the activity). You can have a complete meal for 1,950 pesetas ($18.35). Many intriguing specialties from Extremadura are served, including a soothing gazpacho made with white garlic and *tencas fritas* (fried tench), a typical fish of the region.

Later you can visit the Emperatriz's nightclub and bar. A garden stands in the center of this good-value three-star hotel, located in the center of town, just north of the ruins of the Alcazaba.

NOVA ROMA, Suárez Somonte, 42. Tel. 924/31-12-61. Fax 924/30-01-60. 28 rms (all with bath). A/C TEL
$ **Rates:** 4,000 ptas. ($37.60) single; 6,500 ptas. ($61.10) double. Breakfast 400 ptas. ($3.75) extra. AE, DC, MC, V.
Lacking the vintage charm of the Emperatriz (see above) or the Parador Vía de la Plata (see below), the Nova Roma wins hands down for those with more modern tastes. Clean, comfortable, and functionally furnished, it is considered a good value for this heavily frequented tourist town. The hotel also runs a reasonably priced restaurant, offering a lunch or dinner for 1,300 pesetas ($12.20), with many regional dishes. The Nova Roma is west of the Teatro Romano and north of the Plaza de Toros (bullring).

WORTH THE EXTRA BUCKS

PARADOR VÍA DE LA PLATA, Plaza de la Constitución, 3, 06800 Mérida. Tel. 924/31-38-00. Fax 924/30-03-76. 82 rms (all with bath). A/C MINIBAR TV TEL
$ **Rates:** 9,000 ptas. ($84.60) single; 11,500 ptas. ($108.10) double. Breakfast 900 ptas. ($8.45) extra. AE, DC, MC, V.
This parador is in the heart of town, across the street from the Plaza de la Constitución, in the former Convento de los Frailes de Jesus (16th century). A salon has been installed in the cloister, and a central garden is studded with shrubbery and flowers. Old stone stairs lead to the bedrooms. The place has had a long and turbulent history and was once a prison. In the 1960s two dictators met here: Franco of Spain and Salazar of Portugal. An elevator plummeted to the ground as El Caudillo was entertaining his Portuguese comrade—probably an assassination attempt on either Franco or Salazar (or both). In addition to its bar and garage, the parador has an excellent restaurant, serving both regional and national dishes, with meals costing from 2,800 pesetas ($26.30).

WHERE TO EAT

In addition to the independent restaurants listed below, the hotels recommended above have good restaurants.

BAR RESTAURANTE BRIZ, Félix Valverde Lillo, 5. Tel. 31-93-07.
Cuisine: SPANISH. **Reservations:** Not required.
$ **Prices:** Appetizers 200–350 ptas. ($1.90–$3.30); main dishes 450–750 ptas. ($4.25–$7.05); fixed-priced menu 850 ptas. ($8). No credit cards.
Open: Lunch daily 1:30–4pm; dinner daily 9–11:30pm.
ⓢ   There is almost universal agreement, even among the locals, that the set menu at Briz represents the best value in town—not only reasonable in price, but very filling. Unprepossessing in its exterior, Briz is known for its Extremaduran regional dishes. These include lamb stew (heavily flavored) and *perdiz in salsa* (a gamey partridge casserole), which might be preceded by an appetizer of peppery sausage mixed into a medley of artichokes. Strong, hearty wines accompany the dishes. A meal here will qualify you as an *extremeño*. You'll find Briz across from the post office.

RESTAURANTE NICOLAS, Félix Valverde Lillo, 13. Tel. 31-96-10.
Cuisine: SPANISH. **Reservations:** Recommended.
$ **Prices:** Appetizers 400–500 ptas. ($3.75–$4.70); main dishes 1,200–1,500 ptas. ($11.30–$14.10); fixed-priced menu 1,300 ptas. ($12.20). AE, DC, MC, V.
Open: Lunch daily 1–5pm; dinner Mon–Sat 9pm–midnight.
Transformed from an old run-down house, this ranks as one of the most charming restaurants in town. If the lower dining room isn't to your liking, you'll find seating upstairs, as well as a pleasant garden for outdoor repasts. Menu specialties are made

with care from fresh ingredients: You might enjoy an array of fresh shellfish, roast baby goat, carefully seasoned roast lamb, and flavorful concoctions of sole, salmon, and monkfish. Roast partridge is the game specialty. Nicolas is located opposite the post office.

---

5. BADAJOZ

57 miles SW of Cáceres, 39 miles E of Mérida, 254 miles SW of Madrid

GETTING THERE   By Train   There are 2 to 4 trains daily from Madrid (5 hours). Arrivals from Mérida are more frequent, 7 or 8 per day (1 hour). From Cáceres, there's 1 train daily (2½ hours). The railway station is situated at the terminus of Carolina Coronado in Badajoz, a 15-minute walk northwest of the center of town.

By Bus   From Madrid there are 7 daily buses (4 hours); from Seville, 5 daily buses (6½ hours). From Mérida, there are 6 buses daily (1 hour). The bus station at Badajoz lies at Calzadilla Maestre, south of town. Take Bus no. 4 to the town center, the Plaza de España.

By Car   Badajoz sits astride the superhighway N-V, which connects Madrid with Lisbon. The E-803 connects it with Seville. Driving time from Madrid is around 4 hours; from Seville, 6 to 7 hours.

ESSENTIALS   The area code for Badajoz is 924. The Tourist Information Office is at Pasaje de San Juan, 1 (tel. 924/22-27-63).

The capital of Spain's largest province, Badajoz stands on the banks of the Guadiana River near the once-turbulent Portuguese border. A Moorish fortress and an old Roman bridge are two reminders of the past. Sightseeing here is lackluster, but Badajoz does have some local color, provided mainly by its huge ramparts and its narrow medieval streets. Its fortified site is best appreciated if you drive to Badajoz from the north. Park outside and walk into town; along the way you'll pass the 13th-century Gothic cathedral.

WHERE TO STAY

HOTEL LISBOA, Avenida de Elvas, 13, 06006 Badajoz. Tel. 924/23-82-00. Fax 924/23-61-74. 176 rms (all with bath). A/C TV TEL
$ Prices: 4,800 ptas. ($45.10) single; 6,000 ptas. ($56.40) double. Breakfast 385 ptas. ($3.60) extra. MC, V.

One of Badajoz's major hotels, the Lisboa offers modern, comfortable rooms. It's at the edge of town, on the road to Lisbon, and is rated three stars by the government. There are both a garage and an economical restaurant, with lunch or dinner going for 1,200 pesetas ($11.30). There is also a disco.

HOTEL RÍO, Avenida Adolfo Diaz Ambrina s/n, 06006 Badajoz. Tel. 924/23-76-00. Fax 924/23-38-74. 86 rms (70 with bath). A/C TEL **Bus:** Urbano no. 2 or 6.
$ Prices: 4,700 ptas. ($44.20) single; 6,000 ptas. ($56.40) double. Breakfast 385 ptas. ($3.60) extra. AE, DC, MC, V.

Near a bridge on the highway connecting Lisbon and Madrid, the Hotel Río offers views of a eucalyptus grove and the river. Amenities include an outdoor pool, a parking garage, a disco pub/restaurant, and a garden; the functional rooms are comfortably furnished and well maintained. The hotel attracts many of the Portuguese who come over for the night for "a taste of Spain."

WHERE TO EAT

MESÓN EL TRONCO, Muñoz Torrero, 16. Tel. 22-20-76.
Cuisine: SPANISH. **Reservations:** Recommended.

$ Prices: Appetizers 250–400 ptas. ($2.35–$3.75); main dishes 650–1,000 ptas. ($6.10–$9.40); fixed-priced menu 950 ptas. ($8.95). AE, DC, MC, V.
Open: Lunch Mon–Sat 1–4pm; dinner Mon–Sat 8pm–midnight.

You might not suspect the existence here of an attractive restaurant when you encounter the popular bar near the front door, but the excellent tapas will hint at the delicacies available in the back room. The owner offers traditional Extremaduran dishes, as well as a changing repertoire of daily specials. Menu items include gazpacho, *cocido* (stew) of the region, and lamb cutlets, all at affordable prices and served in air-conditioned comfort. The Mesón el Tronco is in the center of town, 2 blocks west of the cathedral.

LOS GABRIELES, Vicente Barrantes, 21. Tel. 22-42-75.
   Cuisine: SPANISH. **Reservations:** Recommended.
$ Prices: Appetizers 600–800 ptas. ($5.65–$7.50); main dishes 900–1,200 ptas. ($8.45–$11.30); fixed-priced menu 1,300 ptas. ($12.20). AE, DC, MC, V.
Open: Lunch Mon–Sat 1:30–4pm; dinner Mon–Sat 9–11pm.

This restaurant, located 2½ blocks from the cathedral, is the personal domain of Gabriel Pelaez, whose father established the place 30 years ago. The extensive menu includes a range of carefully planned sauces and dishes, both traditional and unconventional, including soups, a regional stew, and other local specialties.

A ONE-DAY EXCURSION

Jerez de los Caballeros makes an interesting journey from either Badajoz (46½ miles [75km] south on the N-432) or Mérida (61½ miles [99km] southwest on the N-360). It's a small town of white houses clustered on a hillside, with the cathedral on the summit. The **birthplace of Balboa,** the first European to discover the Pacific, is nearby—a modest whitewashed house at Capitán Cortés, 10. A statue honors the explorer in one of the town's small squares. Jerez de los Caballeros, with many belfries and towers, including the **Torre Sagrienta** (Bloody Tower), takes its name, traditions, and ambience from the Caballeros del Templo (Knights Templars), who were given the town after it was taken from the Moors in 1230.

   Medellín, 25 miles (40km) east of Mérida and 62 miles (100km) east of Badajoz, is the little town where Hernán Cortés, conqueror of Mexico, was born. From the approach you'll see the old whitewashed buildings on the opposite side of the Guadiana River, with the ruins of medieval Medellín Castle dominating the skyline. A 17th-century stone bridge crosses the river into the town, where you'll find a monument to Cortés in the main cobblestoned plaza. From either Mérida or Badajoz, take the N-V superhighway, heading to Madrid, exiting at the C-520, the road into Medellín.

6. ZAFRA

38 miles S of Mérida, 107 miles N of Seville

GETTING THERE   By Train   From Seville, there are several trains daily, which pass through Huelva along the way. From Mérida there are also rail connections.

By Bus   Buses arrive from Mérida and Seville.

By Car   Zafra lies at the point where the highway from Seville (E-803) splits, heading east to Mérida and Cáceres and west to Badajoz. Driving there is easy. There's also a direct road to Córdoba.

ESSENTIALS   The area code for Zafra is 924. The Tourist Information Office is at Plaza de España (tel. 924/55-10-36).

One of the most interesting stopovers in Lower Extremadura, the white-walled town of Zafra is filled with old Moorish streets and squares. The cattle fair of San

Miguel, on October 4, draws cattle breeders from all over the region. The 1457 **castle** of the dukes of Feria, the most important in the province, boasts both a sumptuous 16th-century Herreran patio and the Sala Dorada, with its richly paneled ceiling. The place is now the government parador (see below). You'll want to spend time on the central square, the arcaded 18th-century **Plaza Mayor,** and its satellite, the 16th-century **Plaza Vieja (Old Square).** These are the two most important sights in Zafra, along with the **Neustra Señora de la Candelaria,** a church with nine panels by Zurbarán, displayed on the retable in a chapel designed by Churriguera. The church, constructed in the Gothic-Renaissance style, has a red-brick belfry. Admission is free. It's open Monday through Saturday from 10:30am to 1pm and 7 to 8:30pm, on Sunday from 11am to 12:30pm.

WHERE TO STAY AND EAT

PARADOR HERNÁN CORTÉS, Corazón de María, 7, 06300 Zafra. Tel. 924/55-02-00. A/C MINIBAR TV TEL
$ Rates: 8,500 ptas. ($79.90) single; 9,500 ptas. ($89.30) double. Breakfast 900 ptas. ($8.45) extra. AE, DC, MC, V.
Slated to reopen in the summer of 1991, this government-run parador, located in a restored castle midway between the Plaza de España and the Plaza de José Antonio, is named after Cortés, who stayed here with the dukes of Feria before his departure for the New World. The castle was originally built in 1457, on a square plan with four round towers. The interior of the parador, beautiful but restrained, contains the chapel of the Alcázar, with an octagonal Gothic dome. In addition to being decorated in splendid taste, the Hernán Cortés is quite comfortable; there are a patio, a garden, and a swimming pool. The magnificent-looking dining room offers regional meals for 2,200 pesetas ($20.70). Also on the premises: a bar and a large lounge.

HUERTA HONDA, Avenida López Azme, 36, 06300 Zafra. Tel. 924/55-08-00. Fax 924/55-08-00. 46 rms (26 with bath). A/C MINIBAR TV TEL
$ Rates: 4,000 ptas. ($37.60) single without bath, 6,300 ptas. ($59.20) single with bath; 8,200 ptas. ($77.10) double without bath, 11,000 ptas. ($103.40) double with bath. Breakfast 450 ptas. ($4.25) extra. AE, DC, MC, V.
Views of the citadel and the old town are available from the modern, recently renovated bedrooms of this Andalusian-style hotel in front of the Plaza del Alcázar. A sauna, gymnasium, and outdoor pool are only some of the amenities. There's even a disco, as well as a garden and a pretty patio for mid-afternoon drinks. The hotel also boasts one of the best restaurants in town, the Posada del Duque, offering meals from 1,800 pesetas ($16.90).

CHAPTER 10

ANDALUSIA

Andalusia, the wild, rugged tract of southern Spain, lives up to all the clichés you've heard about it: Silvery olive trees sway in the wind; the scent of orange blossoms is everywhere; women wearing mantillas and carnations in their hair run through the narrow streets on fiesta days; and Gypsies rattle their castanets in ancient caves.

This once-great stronghold of Muslim Spain is rich in history and tradition, containing some of the country's most celebrated sightseeing treasures: the world-famous Mezquita (mosque) in Córdoba, the Alhambra in Granada, and the great Gothic cathedral in Seville. It also has smaller towns just waiting to be discovered—Úbeda, castle-dominated Jaén, gorge-split Ronda, Jerez de la Frontera, and the gleaming white port city of Cádiz. Give Andalusia at least a week and you'll still have only skimmed the surface of its many offerings.

This dry, mountainous region also embraces the Costa del Sol (Málaga, Marbella, and Torremolinos), a popular strip of Spain that is dealt with separately in the following chapter. Go to the Costa del Sol for beach resorts, nightlife, and relaxation; visit Andalusia for its architectural wonders and its beauty.

Crime Alert: Anyone driving south into Andalusia and the Costa del Sol should be wary of thieves. Daylight robberies are commonplace, especially in Seville, Córdoba, and Granada. It is not unusual for a car to be broken into while tourists are enjoying lunch in a restaurant. Some establishments have hired guards (a service for which you should tip, of course). Under no circumstances should you ever leave passports and traveler's checks unguarded in a car.

SEEING ANDALUSIA

GETTING THERE

Most **air** traffic goes into Málaga, capital of the Costa del Sol (see next chapter), but there are also airports at Córdoba, Granada, Jerez de la Frontera, and Seville. If you want to visit Andalusia before the Costa del Sol, and wish to fly, consider Seville as your gateway, since it has the most domestic flights as well as a few international arrivals. Check with Iberia Airlines for information.

Getting to the major cities—Granada, Seville, and Córdoba—by **train** is the route preferred by most visitors. However, once you're there, buses are often best for travel between smaller towns.

The major cities are connected by **bus** links to other large cities of Spain, such as Valencia, Madrid, and Barcelona. These are long hauls, however, and the train is more comfortable. Once in Andalusia, the bus becomes the preferred link among the cities

WHAT'S SPECIAL ABOUT ANDALUSIA

Great Towns/Villages
- [ ] Seville, hometown of Carmen, Don Giovanni, and the Barber.
- [ ] Córdoba, the monument-filled capital of Muslim Spain.
- [ ] Granada, an old Moorish capital, number-one stop on the "romantic pilgrimage" tour of Spain.
- [ ] Ronda, an old aristocratic town known for its cliff-hanging houses.

Religious Shrines
- [ ] Spanish Renaissance cathedral at Granada, where Ferdinand and Isabella were buried.
- [ ] Grand Gothic cathedral at Seville, ranking in size with St. Peter's in Rome.

Events/Festivals
- [ ] Seville's April Fair, most famous *feria* in Spain—bullfights, flamenco, and folklore on parade.

- [ ] Holy Week in Seville, when wooden figures called *pasos* are paraded through streets with robed penitents.

Ancient Monuments
- [ ] Sinagoga at Córdoba, one of three pre-Inquisition synagogues remaining.
- [ ] Giralda Tower at Seville, erected as a minaret in the 12th century.
- [ ] Italica, ruins of ancient Roman city northwest of Seville.

Architectural Highlights
- [ ] Mezquita at Córdoba, mosque dating from the 8th century.
- [ ] Alcázar de los Reyes Cristianos at Córdoba, one of Spain's best examples of military architecture.
- [ ] Alcázar at Seville, Mudejar palace built in the 14th century by Pedro the Cruel.
- [ ] The Alhambra, Moorish palace made famous by Washington Irving.

---

of the province. Distances are usually much shorter by bus than by train, and you see more scenery—trains take time going through mountain tunnels.

By **car** from Madrid, you can take the superhighway N-IV to Andalusia, going by way of Córdoba and Seville, until it ends at Cádiz, an Atlantic seaport. Much of this *autopista* is toll free, except the A-4 from Seville to Cádiz, via Jerez de la Frontera.

A SUGGESTED ROUTE

Day 1 Leave Madrid in the morning and drive south to Andalusia, with an overnight stopover in Jaén.

Day 2 Explore Jaén in the morning, then drive to Baeza and Úbeda, two of the most charming towns in Andalusia. Return to Jaén for the night.

Day 3 Drive south from Jaén to Granada and check into a hotel, enjoying a night of gypsy flamenco.

Day 4 Still based in Granada, visit the Alhambra and the Generalife.

Day 5 Go northwest from Granada to Córdoba, arriving in the late afternoon for a visit to the Mezquita.

Day 6 Spend the morning exploring the sights of Córdoba before driving west in the afternoon to Seville. Stay there overnight.

Day 7 Still based in Seville, explore that city's many attractions, including its cathedral and Alcázar.

Day 8 Drive south to Cádiz for an overnight stopover, but en route have lunch and visit one of the sherry bodegas at Jerez de la Frontera.

Day 9 After exploring Cádiz, return to Madrid, or else drive to Algeciras and take the ferry over to Tangier in Morocco. Another alternative is to head east toward Algeciras, stopping at Gibraltar, before planning visits to some of the resort highlights along the Costa del Sol: Marbella, Torremolinos, Málaga, and Nerja.

1. JAÉN, BAEZA & ÚBEDA

The province of Jaén, with three principal cities—Jaén, the capital; Baeza; and Úbeda—is one of the most recently discovered tourist areas of Spain. For years visitors whizzed through Jaén on their way south to Granada, or bypassed it altogether on the southwest route to Córdoba and Seville. But the government is beefing up the province's hotel outlook with its excellent **paradores,** which now provide some of the best accommodations in Spain.

JAÉN

60 miles E of Córdoba, 60 miles N of Granada, 210 miles S of Madrid

GETTING THERE   By Train. It's easier to leave Jaén than it is to arrive there, because trains to Jaén run only from south to north. Northbound trains—including 4 daily to Madrid's Atocha Railway Station—arrive and depart from Jaén's RENFE station on the Paseo de la Estación (tel. 25-56-07), north of the center of town. If you're traveling from north to south, however, it isn't quite so easy. Most southbound trains from Madrid, and all trains heading south to Seville and the rest of Andalusia, stop only at a larger railway junction that lies inconveniently in the hamlet of Espeluy, 22 miles (35.5km) to the north. From Espeluy, trains are sometimes funneled a short ride to the east, to the railway junction midway between Linares (31 miles [50km] from Jaén) and Baeza (the Estación de Linares–Baeza). Consult the Jaén tourist office or the railway station for advice on your particular routing.

By Bus   The bus terminal is at Plaza Coca de la Piñera (tel. 25-01-06), 1 block south of the central Parque de la Victoria. Either directly or after a transfer at Baeza, 30 miles (48km) to the north, buses travel 10 times a day to Granada (2 hours), 8 times to Úbeda (1 hour), 7 times to Madrid (4½ to 5 hours), and 5 times to Seville (5 hours).

By Car   Four important highways, plus several provincial roads, converge upon Jaén from four directions. Driving time from Madrid is around 5 hours, almost all of which is spent on the N-IV superhighway.

ESSENTIALS   The area code for Jaén is 953. The Tourist Information Office is at Arquitecto Berges, 1 (tel. 953/22-27-37).

▌n the center of Spain's major olive-growing district, Jaén is sandwiched between Córdoba and Granada, and has always been considered a gateway between Castile and Andalusia. The Christian forces gathered here in 1492 before marching on Granada to oust the Moors.

Jaén's bustling modern section is of little interest to visitors, but the **Moorish old town,** where the narrow cobblestoned streets hug the mountainside, is reason enough to visit. A hilltop castle, now converted into a first-rate parador, dominates the city. On a clear day you can see the snow-covered peaks of the Sierra Nevada.

Jaén, the city, is at the center of a large province of 5,189 square miles, framed by mountains: the Sierra Morena to the north, the Segura and Cazoria ranges to the east, and those of Huelma, Noalejo, and Valdepeñas to the south. To the west, plains widen into the fertile Guadalquivir Valley. The landscape is rugged and irregular. Jaén province comprises three well-defined districts: the Sierra de Cazorla, a land of wild scenery: the plains of Bailén, Arjona, and Arjonilla, filled with wheat fields, vineyards, and old olive trees; and the valleys of the tributaries of the Guadalquivir.

WHAT TO SEE & DO

CATEDRAL, Plaza de la Catedral.
The formality and grandeur of Jaén's cathedral stand witness to the city's importance in days gone by. Begun in 1500 and completed in the 1800s, it is a honey-colored blend of Gothic, baroque, and Renaissance styles. The interior,

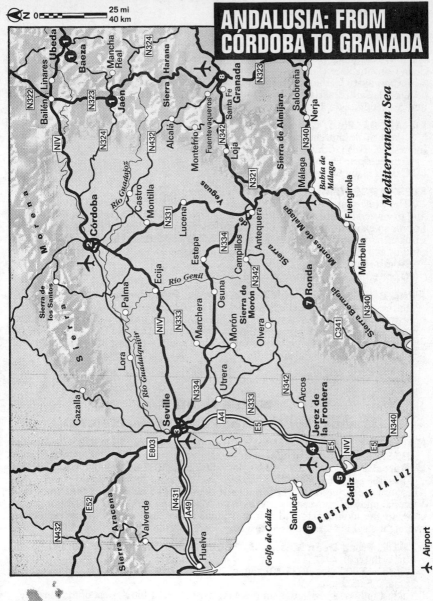

25 mi
40 km

N Z 0

Mediterranean Sea

Ubeda
Baeza
Mancha Real
N324
Sierra Harana
N322
N323
N324
Bailén
Linares
NIV
Jaén
N323
N432
Sierra Harana
N8
Granada
N323
Santa Fe
Sierra de Almijara
Salobreña
Alcalá
Montefrío
Fuentevaqueros
Loja
Nerja
N340
Montilla
Castro
Río Guadajoz
N331
Córdoba
Lucena
Vegas
N342
Antequera
Málaga
Bahía de Málaga
Fuengirola
N321
Estepa
N334
Campillos
Sierra
Marbella
Montes de Málaga
Ecija
Río Genil
Osuna
N342
Sierra de Morón
Ronda
N340
Sierra de los Santos
Palma
Marchena
Morón
Olvera
Sierra Bermeja
C341
Lora
Río Guadalquivir
Utrera
N342
Arcos
Cazalla
N334
Seville
N333
Jerez de la Frontera
E803
A4
E5
N340
E52
N431
Sanlúcar
Cádiz
COSTA DE LA LUZ
N432
Sierra Aracena
Valverde
A49
Golfo de Cádiz
Huelva

Airport

SPAIN
Madrid
Andalusia

1 Jaén, Baeza & Ubeda
2 Córdoba
3 Seville
4 Jerez de la Frontera
5 Cádiz
6 Costa de la Luz
7 Ronda
8 Granada

containing richly carved choir stalls, is dominated by a huge dome. The cathedral museum contains an important collection of historic objects in two underground chambers, including paintings by Ribera. The cathedral stands southwest of the Plaza de la Constitución.

Admission: Cathedral free; museum 75 ptas. (70¢).
Open: Cathedral daily 8am–1pm and 4:30–7pm; museum Mon–Sat 11am–1pm and 5–6:30pm, Sun 11am–1pm.

LA MAGDALENA, Calle de la Magdalena. Tel. 25-60-19.
Of the many churches worth visiting in Jaén, La Magdalena is the oldest and most interesting. This Gothic church was once an Arab mosque.

Admission: Free.
Open: Daily 6am–8pm.

MUSEO PROVINCIAL, Plaza de la Estación, 29.
The Provincial Museum's collection includes Roman mosaics, a Mudejar arch, and many ceramics from the early Iberian, Greek, and Roman periods. On the upper floor is an exhibition of Pedro Berruguete paintings, including *Christ at the Column*. Look also for the Paleo-Christian sarcophagus from Martos. The museum is between the bus and train stations.

Admission: 250 ptas. ($2.35).
Open: Tues–Sat 10am–2pm and 4–7pm.

ARAB BATHS, Palace of Villardompardo, Plaza Luisa de Marillac.
In the vicinity of the Calle San Juan and the Chapel of St. Andrew (San Andrés), underneath a palace, lies some of the finest Moorish architecture from the 11th century ever discovered—in fact, the most important Arab baths in Spain. You can visit the warm room, the hot room, and the cold room—the last having a barrel vault with 12 star-shaped chandeliers.

Admission: Free.
Open: Tues–Sun 10am–2pm and 4–7pm.

WHERE TO STAY

Doubles For Less Than 5,400 ptas. ($50.75)

HOTEL REY FERNANDO, Plaza Coca de la Piñera, 7, 23001 Jaén. Tel. 953/25-18-40. 36 rms (all with bath).
$ Rates: 2,800 ptas. ($26.30) single; 4,000 ptas. ($37.60) double. Breakfast 300 ptas. ($2.80). AE, DC, MC.
This fairly modern establishment rates two stars. One block south of the Parque de la Victoria, midway between the Avenida de Madrid and the Paseo de la Estación, it's close to the monuments and transportation center, and makes for a comfortable overnight stay. Plain but livable rooms.

XAUEN, Plaza Deán Mazas, 3, 23001 Jaén. Tel. 953/26-40-11. 35 rms (all with bath). A/C TEL
$ Rates: 3,800 ptas. ($35.70) single; 5,400 ptas. ($50.75) double. Breakfast 600 ptas. ($5.65) extra. V.
Breakfast only is served at this simple, family-run hotel 1 block west of the Plaza de la Constitución. The handcrafted detailing of the building, and its central location, make it an attractive choice. Rooms are simply furnished but comfortable. Motorists might have to park far away from the entrance.

Worth the Extra Bucks

PARADOR CASTILLO DE SANTA CATALINA, Castillo de Santa Catalina, 23000 Jaén. Tel. 953/26-44-11. Fax 953/22-39-30. 43 rms (all with bath). A/C MINIBAR TV TEL **Directions:** Follow Carretera al Castillo y Neveraol.
$ Rates: 9,000 ptas. ($84.60) single occupancy of double; 11,000 ptas. ($103.40) double. Breakfast 900 ptas. ($8.45) extra. AE, DC, MC, V.

⭐ This castle, 3 miles (4.8km) to the east on the hill overlooking the city, is one of the government's showplace paradors, and staying here is reason enough to visit Jaén. In the 10th century the castle was a Muslim fortress, surrounded by high protective walls and approached by a steep, winding road. When Christians did approach, the Moors were fond of throwing them over. The castle is still reached by the same road, but the hospitality has improved remarkably. Visitors enter through a three-story-high baronial hallway, and a polite staff shows them to their balconied bedrooms (doubles only), tastefully furnished and comfortable, with spick-and-span tile baths.

Dining at the castle is dramatic—the high-vaulted restaurant looks like a small cathedral with its wrought-iron chandeliers and stone arches, plus a raised hearth and a collection of copper kettles and ceramics. On either side of the lofty room, arched windows open onto a terrace or a fabulous view of Jaén. A luncheon or dinner here, at 2,900 pesetas ($27.25), includes typical Jaén dishes—usually made with the olives for which the area is famous—and regional wine.

WHERE TO EAT

Consider a meal in the luxurious hilltop parador commanding a view of the area (see above). It's worth the extra bucks.

THE JOCKEY CLUB, Paseo de la Estación, 20. Tel. 25-10-18.
Cuisine: SPANISH. **Reservations:** Required Fri and Sat (dinner).
$ **Prices:** Appetizers 350–500 ptas. ($3.30–$4.70); main dishes 650–1,600 ptas. ($7.10–$15.05); fixed-priced menu 1,850 ptas. ($17.40). AE, MC, V.
Open: Lunch daily 12:30–4pm; dinner daily 8:30–11:30pm.
The leading restaurant in town is the moderately priced Jockey Club, whose owner works hard to maintain a comfortable ambience and a well-prepared cuisine. Main dishes include *rape* (monkfish) "Jockey style," Milanese-style rice, salmon with green sauce, and a full range of meats and fish. You'll find the Jockey Club in the center of town, south of the Plaza de la Constitución.

NELSON, Paseo de las Estación, 33. Tel. 22-92-01.
Cuisine: SPANISH. **Reservations:** Required.
$ **Prices:** Appetizers 450–650 ptas. ($4.25–$7.10); main dishes 1,250–2,200 ptas. ($11.75–$20.70); fixed-priced menu 2,200 ptas. ($20.70). AE, DC, MC, V.
Open: Lunch Mon–Sat 1–4pm; dinner Mon–Sat 8:30–midnight. **Closed:** Aug.
On a pedestrian walkway near the railway station, the Plaza de las Batallas, and the Museo Provincial, this successful restaurant relies on fresh produce and the gruff charm of its owners, the Ordóñez brothers. An impressive array of *tapas* greets you at the bar, where you can pause for predinner drinks. In the air-conditioned dining room, full meals might include fish or a savory filet steak prepared "house style," with plenty of herbs.

BAEZA
28 miles NE of Jaén, 191 miles S of Madrid

GETTING THERE   By Train   The nearest important railway junction, receiving trains from Madrid and most of Andalusia, is the Estación Linares–Baeza, 8½ miles (14km) west of Baeza's center. For information about which trains arrive there, refer to "By Train" in the section on Jaén, above.

By Bus   Buses from Seville arrive several times a day at Avenida Puche y Pardo, 1; service is available from Madrid too.

By Car   Baeza lies east of the N-V, the superhighway linking Madrid with Granada. Hwy. 321/322, which runs through Baeza, links Córdoba with Valencia.

ESSENTIALS The area code for Baeza is 953. The Tourist Information Office is at Casa del Pópulo (tel. 953/74-04-44).

Historic Baeza (known to the Romans as Vilvatia), with its Gothic and Plateresque buildings and cobblestoned streets, is one of the best-preserved old towns in Spain. At twilight, lanterns hang on walls of plastered stone, flickering against the darkening sky and lighting the narrow streets. The town had its heyday in the 16th and 17th centuries, and in the Visigothic period it was the seat of a bishop.

WHAT TO SEE & DO

Entering Baeza from Jaén, you'll approach the main square, **Plaza de los Leones,** a two-story open colonnade—and a good point to begin exploring. The buildings here date in part from the 16th century. One of the most interesting houses the tourist office (see above), where you can obtain a map to help guide you through Baeza. Look for the fountain containing four half-effaced lions, the Fuente de los Leones, which may have been brought here from the Roman town of Cantulo.

Head south along the Cuesta de San Gil to reach the Gothic and Renaissance **cathedral,** Plaza de la Fuente de Santa María, constructed in the 16th century on the foundations of an earlier mosque. The Puerta de la Luna is in Arab-Gothic style. In the interior, remodeled by Andrés de Vandelvira and his pupils, look for the carved wood and the brilliant painted *rejas* (iron screens). The Gold Chapel is especially outstanding. Open daily from 10:30am to 1pm and 5 to 7pm.

After leaving the cathedral, continue up the Cuesta de San Felipe to the **Palacio de Jabalquinto,** a beautiful example of civil architecture in the flamboyant Gothic style. Juan Alfonso de Benavides, a relative of King Ferdinand, ordered it built. Its façade is filled with decorative elements, and there is a simple Renaissance-style courtyard with marble columns. Inside, two lions guard the stairway, heavily decorated in the baroque style.

WHERE TO STAY

HOTEL JUANITO, Plaza del Arca del Aqua s/n, 23400 Baeza. Tel. 953/74-00-40. Fax 953/74-23-24. 25 rms (all with bath). A/C TEL
$ Rates: 4,000 ptas. ($37.60) single; 5,000 ptas. ($47) double. Breakfast 450 ptas. ($3.25) extra. No credit cards.
This establishment, known mainly for its restaurant (see below), is also your best choice for an overnight stopover. Rooms (50% with TV) are unpretentious, but clean and comfortable. The Hotel Juanito stands on the outskirts of Baeza toward Úbeda.

WHERE TO EAT

SALI, Pasaje Cardenal Benavides, 15. Tel. 74-13-65.
Cuisine: SPANISH. **Reservations:** Not required.
$ Prices: Appetizers 350–400 ptas. ($3.30–$3.75); main dishes 750–1,200 ptas. ($7.05–$11.30); fixed-priced menus for 1,200 ptas. ($11.30). DC, MC, V.
Open: Lunch daily 1–4pm; dinner Thurs–Tues 8–11pm. **Closed:** Sept 18–Oct 10.

S A short walk north of the Plaza del Pópulo, you can dine in air-conditioned comfort on what many locals regard as the best and most reasonable set menu in town. The owners serve the cuisine of Andalusia, and are known for their fresh vegetables in summer. The atmosphere is relaxed, the service cordial; portions are generous. You won't leave here feeling hungry or overcharged.

CASA JUANITA, Plaza del Arca de Agua s/n. Tel. 74-00-40.
Cuisine: SPANISH. **Reservations:** Required Fri and Sat.
$ Prices: Appetizers 300–650 ptas. ($2.80–$6.10); main dishes 1,200–1,800 ptas. ($11.30–$16.90); fixed-priced menu 2,200 ptas. ($20.70). No credit cards.
Open: Lunch daily 1–3:30pm; dinner Mon–Sat 6:30–11:15pm. **Closed:** Nov 1–15.

Owners Juan Antonío and Luisa Salcedo serve regional specialties from Andalusia and La Mancha. Devotees of the "lost art" of Jaén cookery, they revive ancient recipes in their frequently changing "suggestions for the day." Game is served in season, and many vegetable dishes are made with ham. Among the savory and well-prepared menu items: *habas* beans, filet of beef with tomatoes and peppers, partridge in pastry crust, and codfish house style.

ÚBEDA
6 miles NE of Jaén, 194 miles S of Madrid

GETTING THERE **By Train** The nearest train station is the Linares–Baeza station. For information on trains to and from the station, refer to the Jaén section (see above).

By Bus There are buses several times daily to Baeza, less than 6 miles (9.6km) away, and to Jaén. Nine buses per day go to the busy railway station at Linares–Baeza, where a train can take you virtually anywhere in Spain. Bus service to and from Córdoba, Seville, and Granada (at least once a day) is also available. Úbeda's bus station lies in the heart of the modern town, on the Calle San José (tel. 75-21-57), where signs will point you on a downhill walk to the *zona monumental*.

By Car Turn off the Madrid–Córdoba road and head east for Linares, then on to Úbeda, a detour of 26 miles (42 km).

ESSENTIALS The area code for Úbeda is 953. The Tourist Information Office is at Plaza del Ayuntamiento, 2 (tel. 953/75-08-97).

A former stronghold of the Arabs, Úbeda, often called "the Florence of Andalusia," is a Spanish National Landmark filled with golden-brown Renaissance palaces and tile-roofed whitewashed houses. The best way to discover Úbeda's charm is to wander its narrow cobblestone streets.

The government has created a parador here in a renovated ducal palace—you might stop for lunch if you're pressed for time. Allow time for a stroll through Úbeda's shops, which sell, among other items, leathercraft goods and esparto grass carpets.

The palaces and churches of the city are almost endless. You might begin your tour at the centrally located **Plaza de Vázquez de Molina,** which is flanked by several mansions, including the Casa de las Cadenas, now the Town Hall. For centuries the mansions have been decaying, but many are now being restored. Most are not open to the public.

WHAT TO SEE AND DO

IGLESIA EL SALVADOR, Plaza de Vázquez de Molina.
One of the grandest examples of Spanish Renaissance architecture, this church was designed in 1536 by Diego de Siloé. The richly embellished portal is mere window dressing for the wealth of decoration inside the church, including a sacristy designed by Vandelvira and a single nave with gold-and-blue vaulting. Don't miss the many sculptures and altarpieces, or the spectacular rose windows.
Admission: Free.
Open: Daily 9am–1pm and 5–7pm.

IGLESIA SAN PABLO, Plaza 1 de Mayo.
This church, in the center of the old town near the Plaza del Generalísimo, is almost as fascinating as the Iglesia El Salvador. The Gothic San Pablo is famous for its 16th-century south portal in the Isabelline style, and its chapels.
Admission: Free.
Open: Daily 9am–1pm and 5–7pm.

HOSPITAL DE SANTIAGO, Calle Santiago.

On the western edge of town, off the Calle del Obispo Coros, stands the Hospital of Santiago, completed in 1575 and still in use. Built by Andrés de Vandelvira, "the Christopher Wren of Úbeda," over the years it has earned a reputation as the "Escorial of Andalusia."

Admission: Free.
Closed: For restoration.

SANTA MARÍA DE LOS REALES ALCÁZARES, Arroyo de Santa María.

Another intriguing Úbeda church is Santa María de los Reales Alcázares, on the site of a former Arab mosque. The cloisters, with their fan vaulting, are Gothic; the interior, with its tiled and painted ceiling, blends the Gothic and Mudejar styles. Also inside the church you'll find a gruesome statue of a mutilated Christ. Santa María is in the center of town, opposite the Ayuntamiento (Town Hall).

Admission: Free.
Open: Daily 9am–1pm and 5–7pm.

WHERE TO STAY

HOTEL CONSUELO, Avenida Rámon y Cajal, 12, 23400 Úbeda. Tel. 953/75-08-40. 39 rms (all with bath). A/C TV TEL
$ Rates: 2,000 ptas. ($18.80) single; 3,800 ptas. ($35.70) double. Breakfast 350 ptas. ($3.30) extra. V.

Frankly, if you can stay at the parador near the bus station (see below), there isn't much reason to go elsewhere—unless, of course, the parador's fully booked. In that case, head for this comfortable and utilitarian three-story building across from the Instituto Ensenanza Media. Rooms are basic but clean; some of them contain a minibar.

PARADOR NACIONAL DEL CONDESTABE DÁVALOS, Plaza de Vázquez de Molina, 1, 23400 Úbeda. Tel. 953/75-03-45. Fax 953/75-12-59. 26 rms (all with bath). A/C MINIBAR TV TEL
$ Rates: 9,500 ptas. ($89.30) double. Breakfast 900 ptas. ($8.45) extra. AE, DC, MC, V.

In the heart of town on the most central square, near the Town Hall, stands this 16th-century palace turned parador, which shares an old paved plaza with the Iglesia El Salvador and its dazzling façade. The formal entrance to the Renaissance palace leads to an enclosed patio, encircled by two levels of Moorish arches, where palms and potted plants stand on the tile floors. The bedrooms, doubles only, are nearly two stories high, with beamed ceilings and tall windows. Antiques and reproductions adorn the rooms, and the beds are comfortable.

Before lunch or dinner, stop in at the low-beamed wine cellar, with its stone arches, crude stools and tables, and giant kegs of wine. Dinner is served on the ground floor in a tastefully decorated room where a costumed staff serves traditional Spanish dishes. Lunch or dinner costs around 2,900 pesetas ($27.25), including wine and service.

WHERE TO EAT

The parador (see above) is the best place to eat for miles around. For dinner, try the stuffed partridge or baby lamb chops. The restaurants scattered around the Calle Rámon y Cajal are unremarkable.

---

2. CÓRDOBA

65 miles W of Jáen, 260 miles SW of Madrid

GETTING THERE **By Train** Córdoba is a railway junction for routes to the rest of Andalusia and the rest of Spain. There are about 5 Talgo and TER express trains daily between Córdoba and Madrid (4½ to 5 hours). Other, slower trains (*tranvías*) take 8 to 9 hours for the same transit. There are also trains from Seville every day (1½ hours). The railway station is on the town's northern periphery, on the Avenida de América, near the corner of the Avenida de Cervantes. For information, call 47-87-21. To reach the heart of the old town, head south on the Avenida de Cervantes or the Avenida del Gran Capitán. If you want to buy a ticket or to get departure times and prices only, you can go to the RENFE office at Ronda de los Tejares, 10 (tel. 47-58-84).

By Bus There are three different bus companies, each of which maintains a separate terminal. The town's most important bus terminal is operated by the Alsina-Graells Sur Company, Avenida Medina Azahara, 29 (tel. 23-64-74), on the western outskirts of town (just west of the gardens beside the Paseo de la Victoria).

From the bus terminal operated by the Transportes Urena, Avenida de Cervantes, 22 (tel. 47-23-52), a short walk south of the railway station, there are 3 buses per day to and from Seville (2 to 3 hours) and 5 daily buses to Jaén (3 hours).

The daily buses from Madrid (6 hours) drop you at the bus terminal operated by the Autocares Priego Company, Paseo de la Victoria, 29 (tel. 29-01-58), near the center of town.

By Car Córdoba lies astride the N-IV connecting Madrid with Seville. Driving time from Madrid is about 8 hours. Driving time from Seville is 2 to 3 hours.

ESSENTIALS The area code for Córdoba is 957. The Tourist Information Office is at Calle Torrijos, 10 (tel. 957/47-12-35). If you're driving, don't think of entering the complicated maze of streets in the old town by car. You'll invariably get lost and find no place to park.

Ten centuries ago Córdoba was one of the greatest cities in the world, with a population of 900,000. The capital of Muslim Spain, it was Europe's largest city, and a cultural and intellectual center. This seat of the Western Caliphate flourished with public baths, mosques, a great library, and palaces. But greedy, sacking hordes have since passed through, tearing down ancient buildings and carting off art treasures. Despite these assaults, Córdoba still retains traces of its former glory— enough to rival Seville and Granada as the most fascinating city in Andalusia.

Today this provincial capital is known chiefly for its mosque, but it abounds with other artistic and architectural riches, especially its domestic dwellings. The old Arab and Jewish quarters are famous for their narrow streets lined with whitewashed homes, their flower-filled patios and balconies, and it's perfectly acceptable to walk along gazing into the courtyards. This isn't an invasion of privacy: The citizens of Córdoba take pride in showing off their patios as part of the city's tradition. And don't forget to bring along a good pair of walking shoes, as the only way to explore the monumental heart of the city is on foot.

WHAT TO SEE & DO

The Mezquita, now a cathedral, is the principal reason for visiting Córdoba, but the old Alcázar, an ancient synagogue, museums, and galleries will round out your day (see below). There's a lot to absorb, and visitors with more time may want to spend at least two days here.

Don't miss Córdoba's **Roman bridge (Puente Romano)** believed to date from the time of Augustus. It's hardly Roman anymore, as none of its 16 supporting arches are original. The sculptor Bernabé Gómez del Río erected a statue of St. Raphael in the middle of the bridge in 1651. The Roman bridge crosses the Guadalquivir River about 1 block to the south of the Mezquita.

MEZQUITA, Torrijos, 1. Tel. 47-05-12.

Dating from the 8th century, the Mezquita was the crowning Muslim architectural achievement in the West, rivaled only by the mosque at Mecca. It is a fantastic labyrinth of red-and-white, peppermint-striped pillars. To the astonishment of visitors, a cathedral sits awkwardly in the middle of the mosque, disturbing the purity of the lines. The 16th-century cathedral, a blend of many styles, is impressive in its own right, with an intricately carved ceiling and baroque choir stalls. Additional ill-conceived annexes later turned the Mezquita into an architectural freak. Its most interesting feature is the *mihrab,* a domed shrine of Byzantine mosaics that once housed the Koran.

After exploring the interior, stroll through the Courtyard of the Orange Trees, which has a beautiful fountain. The hearty will climb a 16th-century tower built here on the base of a Moorish minaret to catch a panoramic view of Córdoba and its environs.

The Mezquita is south of the train station, just north of the Roman bridge.

Admission: 300 ptas. ($2.80) adults, 150 ptas. ($1.40) children.

Open: Daily 10:30am–1:30pm and 4–7pm.

ALCÁZAR DE LOS REYES CRISTIANOS, Amador de los Ríos s/n. Tel. 47-20-00.

Commissioned in 1328 by Alfonso XI ("The Just"), the Alcázar of the Christian Kings is a fine example of military architecture. Ferdinand and Isabella governed Castile from this fortress on the river as they prepared to reconquer Granada, the last Moorish stronghold in Spain. Columbus journeyed here to fill Isabella's ears with his plans for discovery.

Located 2 blocks southwest of the Mezquita, the quadrangular building is notable for powerful walls and a trio of towers—the Tower of the Lions, the Tower of Allegiance, and the Tower of the River. The Tower of the Lions contains intricately decorated ogival ceilings that are considered the most notable example of Gothic architecture in Andalusia.

The beautiful gardens, illuminated at night, and the Moorish are celebrated attractions. The Patio Morisco is a lovely spot, its pavement decorated with the arms of León and Castile. Be sure to seek out a distinguished Roman sarcophagus, representative of 2nd- and 3rd-century funeral art. The Roman mosaics are also outstanding—especially a unique piece dedicated to Polyphemus and Galatea.

Admission: 200 ptas. ($1.90) adults, 100 ptas. (95¢) children.

Open: May–Sept daily 9:30am–1:30pm and 5–8pm; Oct–Apr daily 9:30am–1:30pm and 4–7pm. Gardens illuminated May–Sept 10pm–midnight.

SINAGOGA, Calle de los Judíos.

In Córdoba you'll find one of Spain's few remaining pre-Inquisition synagogues, built in 1350 in the Barrio de la Judería (Jewish Quarter). The synagogue is noted particularly for its stucco work, and the east wall contains a large orifice where the Tabernacle was once placed (inside, the scrolls of the Pentateuch were kept). After the Jews were expelled from Spain, the synagogue was turned into a hospital, until it became a Catholic chapel in 1588. It is 2 blocks west of the northern wall of the Mezquita.

Admission: 75 ptas. (70¢).

Open: Tues–Sat 10am–2pm and 3:30–5:30pm, Sun 10am–1:30pm.

MUSEO BELLAS ARTES, Plazuela del Potro, 1. Tel. 47-33-45.

As you cross the Plazuela del Potro to reach the Fine Arts Museum, notice the fountain at one end of the square. Built in 1557, it is of a young stallion with forelegs raised, holding the shield of Córdoba. Housed in an old hospital on the plaza, the Fine Arts Museum contains medieval Andalusian paintings, examples of Spanish baroque art, and works by many of Spain's important 19th- and 20th-century painters, including Goya. The museum is east of the Mezquita, about a block south of the Church of St. Francis (San Francisco).

Admission: 250 ptas. ($2.35).

Open: May–Sept Tues–Sat 10am–2pm and 6–8pm, Sun 10am–1:30pm; Oct–Apr Tues–Sat 10am–2pm and 5–7pm, Sun 10am–1:30pm.

MUSEO DE JULIO ROMERO DE TORRES, Plazuela del Potro.

Across the patio from the Fine Arts Museum, this museum honors Julio Romero de Torres, a Córdoba-born artist who died in 1930. It contains his celebrated *Oranges and Lemons.* Other notable works include *The Little Girl Who Sells Fuel, Sin,* and *A Dedication to the Art of the Bullfight.* A corner of Romero's Madrid studio has been reproduced in one of the rooms, displaying the paintings left unfinished at his death. The museum is temporarily closed for restorations; check with the tourist office (see above) about its reopening dates.

MUSEO MUNICIPAL DE ARTE TAURINO, Plaza de las Bulas. Tel. 47-20-00.

Memorabilia of great bullfights are housed here in a 16th-century building in the Jewish Quarter, inaugurated in 1983 as an appendage to the Museo Municipal de Arte Cordobesas. Its ample galleries recall Córdoba's great bullfighters with "suits of lights," pictures, trophies, posters, even stuffed bulls' heads. You'll see Manolete in repose and the blood-smeared uniform of El Cordobés—both of these famous matadors came from Córdoba. The museum is located about a block northwest of the Mezquita, midway between the mosque and the synagogue.

Admission: 200 ptas. ($1.90).
Open: Tues–Sat 9:30am–1:30pm and 5–8pm, Sun 9:30am–1:30pm.

TOWER OF THE CALAHORRA, Avenida de la Confederación. Tel. 29-39-29.

Across the river, at the southern end of the Roman bridge, stands the Tower of the Calahorra. Commissioned by Henry II of Trastamara in 1369 to protect him from his brother, Peter I, it now houses a town museum where visitors can walk about on a self-guided tour with headsets. In the Mudejar-style chambers you'll find the three charters granted Córdoba by Ferdinand III, and displays honoring Gonzalo Fernández de Córdoba, the Gran Capitán. Don't miss the Hall of the Americas. One room houses wax figures of Córdoba's famous philosophers, including Averroës and Maimonides. Other rooms exhibit a miniature model of the Alhambra at Granada, complete with water fountains; a miniature Mezquita; and a display of Arab musical instruments. Finally, you can climb to the top of the tower for some excellent views of the Roman bridge, the river, and the cathedral/mosque.

Admission: Museum 250 ptas. ($2.35) adults, 150 ptas. ($1.40) children; multimedia presentation, 500 ptas. ($4.70).
Open: Daily 10am–2pm and 5:30–8:30pm.

MUSEO ARQUEOLÓGICO PROVINCIAL, Plaza Jerónimo Páez. Tel. 47-40-11.

Córdoba's Archeological Museum, 2 blocks northeast of the Mezquita, is one of the most important in Spain. Housed in a palace dating from 1505, it displays artifacts left behind by the various peoples and conquerors who have swept through the province—Paleolithic and Neolithic items; Iberian hand weapons and ceramics; and Roman sculptures, bronzes, ceramics, inscriptions, and mosaics. Especially interesting are the Visigothic artifacts. The most outstanding collection, however, is devoted to Arabic art and spans the entire Muslim occupation. Take a few minutes to relax in one of the patios, with its fountains and ponds.

Admission: 250 ptas. ($2.35).
Open: Tues–Sun 10am–2pm and Tues–Sat 4–7pm.

PALACIO DE LOS MARQUÉS DE VIANA, Plaza de Don Gome. Tel. 48-22-75.

The public has seldom had access to Córdoba's palaces, but that's changed with the opening of this newest museum. Visitors are shown into a carriage house where the elegant vehicles of another era are displayed. Note the intricate leather decoration on the carriages and the leather wall hangings, some of which date from the period of the Reconquest; there's also a collection of leather paintings. You can wander at leisure through the garden and patios. The palace lies 4 blocks southeast of the Plaza de Colón on the northeastern edge of the old quarter.

Admission: 300 ptas. ($2.80).
Open: June–Sept daily 10am–1pm; Oct–May Thurs–Tues 10am–1pm and 4–6pm.

A NEARBY EXCURSION

RUINAS DE MEDINA AZAHARA, Carretera Almodóvar.
This place, a kind of Moorish Versailles outside Córdoba, was constructed in the 10th century by Caliph Abd al-Rahman. He named it after the favorite of his harem, nicknamed "the brilliant." Thousands of workers and animals slaved to build this mammoth pleasure palace, said to have contained 300 baths and 400 houses. Over the years the site was plundered for building materials; in fact, it might have been viewed as a "quarry" for the region. Some of its materials, so it is claimed, went to build the Alcázar in Seville. The Royal House, rendezvous point for the ministers, has been reconstructed. The principal salon remains in fragments, though, and you have to imagine it in its majesty. Just beyond the Royal House lie the ruins of a mosque constructed to face Mecca. The Berbers sacked the place in 1013.
Admission: 110 ptas. ($1.05).
Open: Tues–Sun 10am–1:45pm and 4–5:45pm, Sun 10am–1:45pm. Bus: Leaves from station on Calle de la Bodega; lets you off about 2 miles from site, however.

WHERE TO STAY

Córdoba, at the peak of its summer season, has too few hotels to meet the demand—so reserve as far in advance as possible.

DOUBLES FOR LESS THAN 4,800 PTAS. ($45.10)

HOSTAL SENECA, Conde y Luque, 7, 14003 Córdoba. Tel. 957/47-32-34. 12 rms (none with bath).
$ Rates (including continental breakfast): 3,000 ptas. ($28.20) single; 4,000 ptas. ($37.60) double. No credit cards. **Closed:** 1 month around Christmas.
Fifteen minutes on foot from the train station in the old Jewish Quarter, you'll find the Hostal Seneca (built in 1864) on a narrow cobblestoned street. You enter a garden courtyard where ferns and cascades of vines are set off by blue and yellow tiles. Rooms, modest in appointments, are clean and well maintained. Breakfast only is served.

ANDALUCÍA, José Zorrilla, 3, 14008 Córdoba. Tel. 957/47-60-00. Fax 957/47-81-43. 40 rms (all with bath).
$ Rates: 2,500 ptas. ($23.50) single; 4,200 ptas. ($39.50) double. Breakfast 350 ptas. ($3.30) extra. AE, V.
This establishment has won many fans since opening in the late 1960s. Off the Gran Capitán, about a 15-minute walk north of the Mezquita and near the Civic Theater, it makes a presentable first impression with its admittedly modest trappings. You get a clean and comfortable double room for rock-bottom prices. Lunch or dinner goes for 950 pesetas ($8.95).

HOTEL RIVIERA, Plaza Aladreros, 5, 14008 Córdoba. Tel. 957/47-60-18. 30 rms (all with bath). A/C TEL
$ Rates: 2,800 ptas. ($26.30) single; 4,600 ptas. ($43.25) double. Breakfast 375 ptas. ($3.50) extra. AE, DC.
The genial owner of this modern hotel is likely to be behind the reception desk when you arrive. His establishment, set on a triangular plaza in a commercial section of town a short walk south of the train station, offers very clean "no-frills" accommodations. No main meals are served.

HOSTAL EL TRIUNFO, Cardenal González, 87, 14003 Córdoba. Tel. 957/47-55-00. Fax 957/48-68-50. 45 rms (all with bath). TEL
$ Rates (including continental breakfast): 3,000 ptas. ($28.20) single; 4,800 ptas. ($45.10) double. AE, DC, MC, V.

Opposite the mosque, 1 block from the northern bank of the Guadalquivir River, is a real find—a simple hotel with a formal entranceway, a pleasant white-walled lounge, and comfortable, well-furnished rooms. The service is polite and efficient, and in fact the only drawback is that the bells of the Mezquita church may make it difficult to sleep. Doubles for less than 7,500 ptas. ($70.50).

HOTEL GONZÁLEZ, Manríquez, 3, 14003 Córdoba. Tel. 957/47-98-19. 16 rms (all with bath). TEL
$ **Rates:** 7,000 ptas. ($65.80) single or double. Breakfast 375 ptas. ($3.50) extra. AE, DC, MC.

Very convenient, within walking distance of the major monuments of Córdoba, the González is a clean, decent hotel. Rooms are well kept and functionally furnished, most comfortable. In the hotel's restaurant, also excellent, you can sample both regional and national specialties. Readers have praised the staff's attitude. One claimed, "They solve problems like magicians, take your car to the parking lot and back, and even teach you Spanish."

HOTEL SELU, Eduardo Dato, 7, 14003 Córdoba. Tel. 957/47-65-00. Fax 957/47-83-76. 108 rms (all with bath). A/C MINIBAR TV TEL
$ **Rates:** 5,200 ptas. ($48.90) single; 7,500 ptas. ($70.50) double. Breakfast 350 ptas. ($3.30) extra. AE, DC, MC, V.

A modern hotel in a dusty commercial part of town near the Paseo de la Victoria, the Hotel Selu has made some laudable efforts to renovate the lobby; near the reception desk, masses of plants, dozens of velvet-covered armchairs, and a huge photograph of the Moorish columns of the Mezquita soften the angular lines. The hotel contains modern functional bedrooms, and there's an in-house parking garage. Breakfast only is served.

WORTH THE EXTRA BUCKS

HOTEL RESIDENCIA EL CALIFA, Lope de Hoces, 14, 14004 Córdoba. Tel. 957/29-94-00. 67 rms (all with bath). A/C TV TEL
$ **Rates:** 7,500 ptas ($70.50) single; 11,000 ptas. ($103.40) double. Breakfast 700 ptas. ($6.60) extra. V.

Attracting a mainly Spanish clientele, this centrally located hotel, a short walk northwest of the Mezquita, has russet-colored marble floors, velour wall coverings, a spacious lounge, and a TV set that seems to broadcasts soccer matches perpetually. There are a restaurant, a bar, and a parking garage. Rooms are reasonably comfortable and furnished in a functional modern style.

LOS GALLOS SOL, Avenida de Medina Azahara, 7, 14005 Córdoba. Tel. 957/23-55-00. 105 rms (all with bath). A/C TV TEL
$ **Rates:** 9,000 ptas. ($84.60) single; 11,500 ptas. ($108.10) double. Breakfast 750 ptas. ($7.05) extra. AE, DC, MC, V.

Half a block from a wide, tree-shaded boulevard on the western edge of town, this tasteful hotel stands eight floors high, crowned by an informal roof garden. The comfortable rooms have many extra comforts, such as balconies, and the outdoor swimming pool is a lifesaver during the summer. The hotel also offers a restaurant, a drinking lounge, and a spacious public lobby.

PARADOR NACIONAL DE LA ARRUZAFA, Avenida de la Arruzafa, 33, 14012 Córdoba. Tel. 957/27-59-00. Fax 957/28-04-09. 95 rms (all with bath). A/C MINIBAR TV TEL
$ **Rates:** 10,000 ptas. ($94) single; 13,000 ptas. ($122.20) double. Breakfast 900 ptas. ($8.45) extra. AE, DC, MC, V.

A few miles outside town in a suburb called El Brillante, this parador—named after an Arab word meaning palm grove—offers the conveniences and facilities of a luxurious resort hotel at reasonable rates. Occupying the site of a former caliphate palace, it's one of the finest paradores in Spain, with both a view and a swimming pool. The spacious rooms have been furnished with fine dark-wood pieces, and some have balconies for eating breakfast or relaxing over a drink. Meals cost 3,200 pesetas ($30.10). Try some of the specialties of the regional cuisine, which include *salmorejo* (a chilled vegetable soup, a variation of gazpacho), stewed oxtail, and a local cake called *pastel cordobés*.

HOTEL ADARVE, Magistral González Francés, 15, 14003 Córdoba. Tel. 957/48-11-02. Fax 957/47-50-79. 103 rms (all with bath). A/C TV TEL
$ Rates: 11,500 ptas. ($108.10) single; 17,500 ptas. ($164.50) double. Breakfast 900 ptas. ($8.45) extra. AE, DC, MC, V.

Built centuries ago as a private villa, the Adarve was tastefully renovated in 1986 into one of the most attractive hotels in town, with triple rows of stone-trimmed windows and ornate iron balustrades. It sits opposite an unused rear entrance to the Mezquita. The marble-and-granite lobby opens into an interior courtyard filled with seasonal flowers, a pair of splashing fountains, and a symmetrical stone arcade. The quality, size, and comfort of the bedrooms—each with a black-and-white marble floor—have earned the hotel four stars, the highest rating of any place in town. But for the added amenities, you also pay more for your bedroom. There's no restaurant, but a coffee shop and bar serve snacks and drinks.

WHERE TO EAT

By all means, shake free of your hotel for at least one meal a day in Córdoba. The restaurants are not just places at which to have a quick bite. Some combine food with flamenco—so make an evening of it.

LA ALMUDAINA, Plaza de los Santos Mártires, 1. Tel. 47-43-42.
Cuisine: SPANISH. **Reservations:** Required.
$ Prices: Appetizers 650–1,400 ptas. ($6.10–$13.15); main dishes, 1,000–2,200 ptas. ($9.40–$20.70); fixed-priced menu 1,800 ptas. ($16.90). AE, DC, MC, V.
Open: Lunch daily noon–4pm; dinner Mon–Sat 8:30pm–midnight.

The owners of this historic restaurant near the Alcázar deserve as much credit for their renovation of a decrepit 15th-century palace as they do for the excellent cuisine produced by their bustling kitchens. Fronting the river in what used to be the Jewish Quarter, La Almudaina is one of the most attractive eateries in Andalusia. You dine in one of the lace-curtained salons or on a glass-roofed central courtyard. Specialties include salmon crêpes, a wide array of fish such as hake with shrimp sauce, and meats such as pork loin in wine sauce. For dessert, try the not-too-sweet chocolate crêpe.

CIRO'S, Paseo de la Victoria, 19. Tel. 29-04-64.
Cuisine: SPANISH. **Reservations:** Recommended.
$ Prices: Appetizers 650–1,200 ptas. ($6.10–$11.30); main dishes 1,000–1,900 ptas. ($9.40–$17.85); fixed-priced menu 2,200 ptas. ($20.70). AE, DC, MC, V.
Open: Lunch daily 1–5pm; dinner daily 8pm–midnight.

Once a simple cafeteria, Ciro's has been transformed into an accommodating and comfortably air-conditioned restaurant. The proprietors mix good service with nouvelle and Andalusian-style cuisine. The menu includes such items as a salmon-and-anchovy pudding, stuffed sweet peppers, hake in shrimp sauce, veal in red wine, and an array of dessert sorbets. Ciro's lies directly south of the rail station, about ¼ mile northwest of the Mezquita.

EL CABALLO ROJO, Cardenal Herrero, 28, Plaza de la Hoguera. Tel. 47-53-75.
Cuisine: SPANISH. **Reservations:** Recommended.
$ Prices: Appetizers 650–1,400 ptas. ($6.10–$13.15); main dishes 1,000–2,200 ptas. ($9.40–$20.70); fixed-priced menu 3,000 ptas. ($28.20). AE, DC, MC, V.
Open: Lunch daily 1–4:30pm; dinner daily 8:30–midnight.

Having dinner at this atmospheric and most elegant restaurant in Córdoba means something of a splurge. Within walking distance of the Mezquita in the old town, it is down a long open-air passageway flanked with potted geraniums and vines. Stop in the restaurant's popular bar for a prepandial drink, then take the iron-railed stairs to the upper dining room; where a typical meal might include gazpacho, a main dish of chicken, then ice cream and *sangría*. (The ice cream, incidentally, is likely to be homemade pistachio.) Try a variation on the usual gazpacho—almond-flavored broth with apple pieces. In addition to Andalusian dishes, the chef offers both Sephardic and Mozarabic specialties, an example of the latter being the monkfish prepared with pine nuts, currants, carrots, and cream. The real aficionado comes here for the *rabo de toro* (stew made with the tail of an ox or a bull).

EL CHURRASCO, Romero, 16. Tel. 29-08-19.
  Cuisine: SPANISH. **Reservations:** Required.
$ Prices: Appetizers 650–1,000 ptas. ($6.10–$9.40); main dishes 1,200–2,400 ptas. ($11.30–$22.55); fixed-priced menu 2,200 ptas. ($20.70). AE, DC, MC, V.
  Open: Lunch Fri–Wed 1–4:30pm; dinner Fri–Wed 6:45pm–midnight.
Housed in an ancient stone-fronted building in the Jewish Quarter just northwest of the Mezquita, El Churrasco serves elegant meals on two tastefully decorated floors. You'll pass a bar and an open grill before reaching a ground-floor dining room that resembles a Moorish courtyard, with its rounded arches and splashing fountain. Upstairs a more formal dining room displays the owner's riveting collection of paintings. You can enjoy such specialties as grilled filet of beef with whisky sauce, succulent roast lamb, grilled salmon, monkfish in a pine-nut sauce—all accompanied by good service—but the signature dish here is the charcoal-grilled pork loin.

RESTAURANT OSCAR, Plaza de los Chirinos, 6. Tel. 47-43-63.
  Cuisine: SEAFOOD. **Reservations:** Recommended.
$ Prices: Appetizers 875–1,200 ptas. ($8.25–$11.30); main dishes 1,600–2,200 ptas. ($15.05–$20.70); fixed-priced menu 2,900 ptas. ($27.25). AE, DC, MC, V.
  Open: Lunch Mon–Sat 1:30–5pm; dinner Mon–Sat 8:30pm–midnight. **Closed:** Last 2 weeks of Aug.
Although hard to find even for seasoned residents of Córdoba—it's in a quiet neighborhood 1 block off the city's main boulevard, the Calle Cruz Conde—this ranks as *the* seafood restaurant in town. Before heading into the dining room, stop for a drink in the comfortable bar near the entrance, where many guests fill up on the tempting tapas. Full meals might include the likes of seafood soup, different concoctions of shrimp, sea bass baked in salt, deep-fried squid, grilled hake, and such meat dishes as veal scaloppine with Roquefort. Among the huge selection of appetizers are a savory seafood salad, smoked salmon, and fish soup.

SHOPPING

In Moorish times Córdoba was famous for its leather, known as "cordwainer." Highly valued in 15th-century Europe, this leather was studded with gold and silver ornaments, then painted with embossed designs (*guadamaci*). Large panels of it often served in lieu of tapestries. Today the industry has fallen into decline, and the market is filled mostly with cheap imitations.

However, one shop in Córdoba continues the old traditions. **Meryan,** Calleja de las Flores, 2 (tel. 47-59-02)—one of the most colorful streets in the city—is run by Angel López-Obrero and his two skilled sons. Here, in this 250-year-old building, you can see the artisans plying their craft. Most items must be custom-ordered, but there are some ready-made pieces for sale, including cigarette boxes, jewel cases, attaché cases, book and folio covers, and ottoman covers. Meryan is open Monday through Friday from 9am to 8pm, on Saturday from 9am to 2pm.

EVENING ENTERTAINMENT
BODEGAS AND BARS

BODEGA CAMPOS, Lineros, 32. Tel. 47-41-42.
  The most festive-looking old tavern and wine cellar in the old part of Córdoba,

Bodega Campos is accustomed to the foreigners who constantly seek it out. Ramble through the long-beamed room, exploring the rows of high-stacked barrels of aging wine. Then perhaps have a glass of sherry in the courtyard, with its balcony and trailing flowers and vines. The bar in the bodega offers tasty regional apéritifs. Maybe you'll be lucky enough to hear some spontaneous flamenco while you're there. Open: Daily 10am–2pm and 5–8pm. Prices: Wine per glass from 150 ptas. ($1.40).

BAR MEZQUITA, Cardenal Herrero, 24. Tel. 47-30-94.

One of the oldest and coziest bars in Córdoba, Bar Mezquita, on the northern boundary of the mosque, has served beer, wine, and a tasty collection of tapas to a loyal clientele for years. The decor, with its Andalusian tiles and battered wooden tables, evokes of another era. Open: Daily 9am–3pm and 5–10:30pm. Prices: Beer 100 ptas. (95¢); tapas 100–150 ptas. (95¢–$1.40).

LA CANOA, Ronda los Tejares, 18. Tel. 47-17-61.

The rustic interior decorated with wine-barrel tables and Carthusian cellar decor appeals to La Canoa's many customers. A glass of wine or beer here will probably be more of a rapid pick-me-up than something to linger over for hours. You can order a ration of Serrano ham or a hefty platter of cheese if you're hungry. La Canoa is between the Plaza de Colón and the Paseo de la Victoria. Open: Mon–Sat noon–4pm and 8pm–midnight. Closed: 2 weeks in Aug. Prices: Beer 75 ptas. (70¢); tapas 800–1,000 ptas. ($7.50–$9.40).

CASA RUBIO, Puerta de Almodóvar, 5. Tel. 29-00-64.

Push back a thick curtain to enter this dimly lit enclave of pre-Franco Spain. Once inside, you'll find a gruff but accommodating welcome at the rectangular bar or in one of a pair of rooms partially covered with Andalusian tiles. My preferred place is within a plant-festooned inner courtyard, where iron tables and a handful of chairs wobble only slightly on the uneven flooring. Open: Daily 6:30am–11pm. Prices: Wine per glass from 50 ptas. (45¢); tapas 90–300 ptas. (85¢–$2.80).

A DANCE CLUB

In the center of town, **Contactos** Eduardo Dato, 8 (tel. 29-24-66), is one of the most popular additions to the city's disco scene. It's set behind a modern blue-green tile façade on a narrow pedestrian street, and the entrance looks like a small art-movie theater. Admission is 1,000 to 2,000 pesetas ($9.40 to $18.80), and drinks cost 500 to 600 pesetas ($4.70 to $5.65). Contactos is open daily from 11pm to 2am.

---

3. SEVILLE

341 miles SW of Madrid, 135 miles NW of Málaga

GETTING THERE By Plane From Seville's San Pablo Airport, Calle Almirante Lobo (tel. 422-8901 or 421-8800), Iberia flies several times a day to and from Madrid (and elsewhere via Madrid). It also flies several times a week to and from Alicante, Grand Canary Island, Lisbon, Barcelona, Palma de Mallorca, Tenerife, Santiago de Compostela, and (once a week) to Zaragoza. The airport lies about 6 miles (9.6km) from the center of the city, along the highway leading to Carmona.

By Train Seville has two terminals. Trains to and from Cádiz (about 7 per day; 1½ to 2 hours), Granada, and Málaga use the Estación San Bernardo (also called the Estación de Cádiz), San Bernardo, 13 (tel. 423-22-55). It lies 1 block east of the prominent Calle Menéndez y Pelayo, on the southeast edge of town. Trains to and from most of the other cities of Spain (including about 6 daily from Madrid; 6 hours) use the station at Plaza des Armas, 56 (tel. 422-88-17). (To add to the confusion, this station is sometimes referred to as the Estación de Córdoba.) It lies on the western edge of town, near the banks of the river.

By Bus Although Seville confusingly has several satellite bus stations servicing

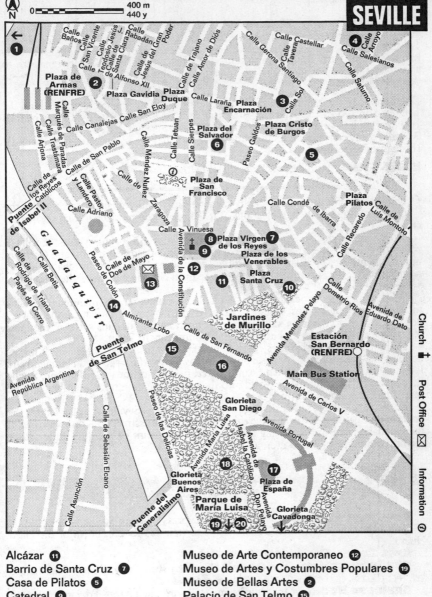

SEVILLE

0 — 400 m
440 y

Calle Baños
Calle San Vicente
Calle Leopoldo
Calle Jesús J.
Calle Santa Clara
Calle de Alfonso XII
Calle de Trajano
Calle Amor de Diós
Calle Habadánca
Calle del Gran Poder
Calle Jesús del Gran Poder
Calle Gerona Santiago
Calle Castellar
Calle Saturno
Calle Sol
Calle Salesianos
Calle Arroyo

Plaza de Armas (RENFRE)
Plaza Gavidia
Plaza Duque
Calle Laraña
Plaza Encarnación
Plaza Cristo de Burgos

Calle Marqués de Paradas
Calle Trastamara
Calle Arfona
Calle Canalejas
Calle San Eloy
Calle Tetuan
Calle San Pablo
Calle de los Reyes Católicos
Calle Pastor y Landero
Calle Adriano
Calle Méndez Núñez
Calle Sierpes
Plaza del Salvador
Paseo Galdos

Plaza de San Francisco
Plaza de San Francisco
Calle Condé de Ibarra
Plaza Pilatos
Calle de Luis Montoto
Calle Recaredo

Puente de Isabel II
Guadalquivir
Calle Betis
Calle de Rodrigo de Triana
Pagés del Corro
Paseo de Dos de Mayo
Calle de Vinuesa
Avenida de la Constitución
Paseo de Colón

Plaza Virgen de los Reyes
Plaza de los Venerables
Plaza Santa Cruz

Calle Almirante Lobo
Calle de San Fernando
Jardines de Murillo

Puente de San Telmo
Avenida República Argentina
Calle de Sebasián Elcano

Calle Domario Rios
Avenida de Eduardo Dato
Estación San Bernardo (RENFRE)
Main Bus Station
Avenida de Carlos V

Paseo de las Delicias
Glorieta San Diego
Avenida Portugal

Avenida María Luisa
Avenida de Isabel la Católica
Avenida de Don Pelayo

Glorieta Buenos Aires
Parque de María Luisa
Plaza de España
Glorieta Cavadonga

Puente del Generalísimo
Calle Asunción

Church ✝
Post Office ⊠
Information ⊝

small towns and nearby villages of Andalusia, most buses arrive and depart from the city's largest bus terminal, on the southeast edge of the old city, at Prado de San Sebastián, 1 (tel. 441-71-11), about 2 short blocks south of the San Bernardo train station. From there, buses from several different companies make frequent runs to Córdoba (2½ hours), Málaga (3½ hours), Granada (4 hours), and—3 daily—to Madrid (8 hours).

By Car   Several major highways converge upon Seville, connecting it with all the rest of Spain and Portugal. Driving time from Madrid is about 8 hours. During periods of heavy holiday traffic, the N-V from Madrid through Extremadura (which, at Mérida, connects with the southbound E-803) is usually less congested than the N-IV through eastern Andalusia.

ESSENTIALS   See "Fast Facts: Seville," below.

Sometimes a city becomes famous for its beauty and romance, and Seville, the capital of Andalusia, is such a place. It is indeed the most charming of Spanish cities.

Don Juan and Carmen—aided by Mozart and Bizet—have given Seville a romantic reputation. Perhaps because of the acclaim of *Don Giovanni* and *Carmen*, not to mention *The Barber of Seville*, debunkers have risen to challenge this reputation. But if a visitor can see only two Spanish cities in a lifetime, they should be Seville and Toledo.

All the images associated with Andalusia—orange trees, mantillas, lovesick toreros, flower-filled patios, castanet-rattling Gypsies—come to life in Seville. But it's not just a tourist city; it's a substantial river port, and it contains some of the most important artistic works and architectural monuments in Spain.

Unlike most Spanish cities, Seville has fared rather well under most of its conquerors—the Romans, Arabs, and Christians. Pedro the Cruel and Ferdinand and Isabella held court here. When Spain entered its 16th-century Golden Age, Seville funneled gold from the New World into the rest of the country. Columbus docked here after his journey to America.

Be warned, however, that driving here is a nightmare: Seville was planned for the horse and buggy rather than for the car, and nearly all the streets run one way toward the Guadalquivir River. Locating a hard-to-find restaurant or a hidden little square might require patience and even a little luck.

 SEVILLE

American Express   The American Express office in Seville is operated by **Viajes Alhambra,** Teniente Coronel Sequi, 3 (tel. 421-29-23), north of the Plaza Nueva.

Area Code   The area code for Seville is 95.

Bus Information   The **Central Bus Station,** Prado de San Sebastián, 1 (tel. 441-71-11), is the place to go for bus information.

Business Hours   Most **banks** in Seville are open Mon–Fri 9am–2pm and

---

IMPRESSIONS

Seville doesn't have an ambiance. It is ambiance.
—JAMES A. MICHENER

Seville is a pleasant city, famous for oranges and women.
—LORD BYRON

Sat 9am–noon. (Always conceal your money before walking out of a bank in Seville.) **Shops** are generally open Mon–Sat 9:30am–1:30pm and 4:30–8pm. Most **department stores** are open Mon–Sat 10am–8pm.

   Consulate   The **U.S. Consulate** is at Paseo de las Delicias, 7 (tel. 428-18-84). The **Canadian Consulate** is on the second floor at Avenida de la Constitución, 30 (tel. 422-94-13). The **consulate for the United Kingdom** is at Plaza Nueva, 8 (tel. 422-88-75).

   Hospital   For medical emergencies, go to the **Hospital Universitario y Provincial,** Avenida Doctor Fedriani (tel. 437-84-00).

   Information   The tourist office, **Oficina de Información del Turismo,** Avenida de la Constitución, 21B (tel. 95/422-14-04), is open Mon–Sat 9:30am–7:30pm.

   Laundromat   **Lavandería Robledo,** Calle Sánchez Bedoya, 18 (tel. 21-81-32), is open Mon–Fri 10am–2pm and 5–8pm, Sat 10am–2pm.

   Safety   With massive unemployment, the city has been hit by a crime wave in recent years. María Luisa Park is especially dangerous, as is the highway leading to Jerez de la Frontera and Cádiz. Dangling cameras and purses are especially vulnerable. Don't leave cars unguarded with your luggage inside.

   Police   The police station is located on the Plaza de la Gavidia (tel. 422-88-40).

   Post Office   The post office is at Avenida de la Constitución, 32 (tel. 422-88-80). Hours are Mon–Fri 9am–8pm, Sat 9am–1pm.

   Telephone/Telex   The telephone office is at Plaza Nueva, 3 (for telephone service information, call 003). To send wires by phone, call 422-20-00. If you want a radio taxi, call 425-08-59.

WHAT TO SEE & DO

Seville has an astonishing number of palaces, churches, cathedrals, towers, and historic hospitals. Since it would take a week or two to visit all of them, I have narrowed the sights down to the very top attractions. The only way to explore Seville is on foot, with a good map in hand.

CATHEDRAL, Plaza del Triunfo, Avenida de la Constitución. Tel. 421-28-00.

The year 1992 will bring the major event on the Sevillian calendar for the 20th century: the 500th-anniversary celebration of the discovery of America. Indeed, the theme of the **Universal Exposition Seville** will be "The Age of Discovery." Not just a reference to explorers' voyages, it is meant to suggest discovery in all areas of human endeavor—both past and future. Emphasis will be on trade and tourism.

Countries representing 90% of the world's population are expected to participate in Expo '92, including the United States, which will be represented with the largest pavilion. Many individual states will have their own exhibitions, including the "sister city" of Seville, Kansas City, which boasts a replica of the Giralda Tower.

It's going to be an extremely tight hotel situation.

★ This huge Gothic building ranks in size with St. Paul's in London and St. Peter's in Rome. Construction began in the late 1400s and took centuries to complete. Built on the site of an ancient mosque, the cathedral claims to contain the remains of Columbus, with his tomb mounted on four statues.

Works of art abound, many of them architectural, such as the 15th-century stained-glass windows, the iron screens (rejas) closing off the chapels, the elaborate 15th-century choir stalls, and the Gothic reredos above the main altar. During Corpus Christi and the Immaculate Conception observances, altar boys with castanets dance in front of the high altar. In the Treasury are works by Goya, Murillo, and Zurbarán; here, in glass cases, a touch of the macabre shows up in the display of skulls.

After touring the dark interior, emerge into the sunlight of the Patio of Orange Trees, with its fresh citrus scents and chirping birds.

Warning: Shorts and T-shirts are definitely not allowed.

Admission: 225 ptas. ($2.10); includes visit to Giralda Tower.

Open: Mon–Fri 11am–5pm, Sat 11am–4pm, Sun 2–4pm.

GIRALDA TOWER, Plaza del Triunfo.

★ Just as Big Ben symbolizes London, La Giralda conjures up Seville—this Moorish tower, next to the cathedral, is the city's most famous monument. Erected as a minaret in the 12th century, it has seen later additions, such as 16th-century bells. To climb it is to take the walk of a lifetime. There are no steps—you ascend an endless ramp. If you make it to the top, you'll have a dazzling view of Seville. Entrance is through the cathedral.

Admission: Free with admission to cathedral.

Open: Same hours as cathedral (see above).

ALCÁZAR, Plaza del Triunfo. Tel. 422-71-63.

★ This magnificent 14th-century Mudejar palace, north of the cathedral, was built by Pedro the Cruel. It is the oldest royal residence in Europe still in use: On visits to Seville, King Juan Carlos stays here. From the Dolls' Court to the Maidens' Court through the domed Ambassadors' Room, it contains some of the finest work of Sevillian artisans. In many ways, it evokes the Alhambra at Granada. Ferdinand and Isabella, who at one time lived in the Alcázar and influenced its architectural evolution, welcomed Columbus here on his return from America. On the top floor, the Oratory of the Catholic Monarchs has a fine altar in polychrome tiles made by Pisano in 1504.

The well-kept gardens, filled with beautiful flowers, shrubbery, and fruit trees, are alone worth the visit.

Admission: 150 ptas. ($1.40).

Open: Daily 9am–1pm and 3–5:30pm.

HOSPITAL DE LA SANTA CARIDAD, Temprado, 3. Tel. 422-32-22.

IN THEIR FOOTSTEPS

Ferdinand II of Aragón (1452–1516). A cruel and unfair ruler, Ferdinand married Isabella of Castile in 1469, and the two became known in history as *Los Reyes Católicos.* They ran Spain as an absolute monarchy, and disliked anything that wasn't Catholic. They expelled the Moors from Granada, conquered Navarre, and financed Columbus's expeditions, although Ferdinand broke many promises to the explorer. With Isabella, he produced a daughter who was insane. Upon the death of Isabella, he claimed the throne of Castile. In 1505 he married Germaine of Foix.

• **Favorite Haunt:** The Alcázar at Seville.
• **Resting Place:** Capilla Real in Granada.

This 17th-century hospital is intricately linked to the legend of Miguel Manara, portrayed by Dumas and Mérimée as a scandalous Don Juan. It was once thought that he built this institution to atone for his sins, but this has been disproved. The death of Manara's beautiful young wife in 1661 caused such grief that he retired from society and entered the "Charity Brotherhood," burying corpses of the sick and diseased as well as condemned and executed criminals. Today the members of this brotherhood continue to look after the poor, the old, and invalids who have no one else to help them.

Nuns will show you through the festive orange-and-sienna courtyard. The baroque chapel contains works by the 17th-century Spanish painters Murillo and Valdés-Leál. As you're leaving the chapel, look over the exit door for the macabre picture of an archbishop being devoured by maggots.

Admission: 125 ptas. ($1.20).
Open: Daily 9:30am–1:30pm and 4–7pm.

TORRE DEL ORO, Paseo de Cristóbal Colón. Tel. 422-24-19.

The 12-sided Tower of Gold, dating from the 13th century, overlooks the Guadalquivir River. Originally it was covered with gold tiles, but someone long ago made off with them. Recently restored, the tower has been turned into a maritime museum.

Admission: 50 ptas. (45¢).
Open: Tues–Sat 10am–2pm, Sun 10am–1pm.

CASA DE PILATOS, Plaza Pilatos, 1. Tel. 422-52-98.

A visit to an Andalusian palace in Seville is a must. This 16th-century home of the dukes of Medinaceli recaptures the splendor of the past, combining Gothic, Mudejar, and Plateresque styles in its courtyards, fountains, and salons. According to tradition, this is a reproduction of Pilate's House in Jerusalem. Don't miss the two old carriages, or the rooms filled with Greek and Roman statues. The collection of paintings includes works by Carreño, Pantoja de la Cruz, Sebastiano del Piombo, Lucas Jordán, Batalloli, Pacheco, and Goya. The palace lies about a 7-minute walk northeast of the cathedral on the northern edge of Barrio de Santa Cruz in a warren of labyrinthine streets whose traffic is funneled through the nearby Calle de Aguiles.

Admission: 400 ptas. ($3.75).
Open: May–Sept daily 9am–8pm; Oct–Apr daily 9am–6:30pm.

MUSEO DE BELLAS ARTES, Plaza de Museo, 9. Tel. 422-18-29.

This lovely old convent off the Calle de Alfonso XII houses one of the most important Spanish art collections. A whole gallery is devoted to two paintings by El Greco, and works by Zurbarán are exhibited; however, the devoutly religious paintings of the Seville-born Murillo are the highlights. An entire wing is given over to macabre paintings by the 17th-century artist Valdés-Leál. His painting of John the Baptist's head on a platter includes the knife—in case you didn't get the point. The top floor, which displays modern paintings, is less interesting.

Admission: 250 ptas. ($2.35).
Open: Tues–Fri 10am–2pm and 4–7pm, Sat–Sun 10am–2pm.

BARRIO DE SANTA CRUZ

What was once a ghetto for Spanish Jews, who were forced out of Spain in the 15th century in the wake of the Inquisition, is today the most colorful district of Seville. Near the old walls of the Alcázar, winding medieval streets with names like Vida (Life) and Muerte (Death) open onto pocket-sized plazas. Flower-filled balconies with draping bougainvillea and potted geraniums jut out over this labyrinth, shading you from the hot Andalusian summer sun. Feel free to look through numerous wrought-iron gates into patios filled with fountains and plants. In the evening it's common to see Sevillians sitting outside drinking icy sangría under the glow of lanterns.

Although the district as a whole is recommended for sightseeing, seek out in particular the **Casa de Murillo (Murillo's House)**, Santa Teresa, 8 (tel. 421-75-35). Bartolomé Esteban Murillo, the great Spanish painter known for his religious works, was born in Seville in 1617. He spent his last years in this house in Santa Cruz, dying in 1682. Five minor paintings of the artist are on display. The furnishings, though not owned by the artist, are period pieces.

Admission: 150 ptas. ($1.40).

Open: Tues–Fri 10am–2pm and 4–7pm, Sat–Sun 10am–2pm. **Directions:** To enter Barrio Santa Cruz, turn right after leaving Patio de Banderas exit of Alcázar. Turn right again at Plaza de la Alianza, going down Calle Rodrigo Caro to Plaza de Doña Elvira. Use caution strolling through the area, particularly at night; many robberies have occurred here.

PARQUE MARÍA LUISA

This park, dedicated to María Luisa, sister of Isabella II, was once the grounds of the Palacio de San Telmo, Avenida de Roma. Its baroque façade visible behind the deluxe Alfonso XIII Hotel, the palace today houses a seminary. The former private royal park is now open to the public.

Running south along the Guadalquivir River, the park attracts those who want to take boat rides, walk along paths bordered by flowers, jog, or go bicycling. The most romantic way to traverse it is by rented horse and carriage, but this can be expensive, depending on your negotiation with the driver.

In 1929 Seville was to host the Spanish American Exhibition, and many pavilions from other countries were erected here. The worldwide depression put a damper on the exhibition, but the pavilions still stand.

Exercise caution while walking through this park. Many muggings have been reported.

PLAZA DE ESPAÑA

The major building left from the exhibition at the Parque María Luisa (see above) is a magnificent half-moon–shaped structure in Renaissance style, set on this landmark square of Seville. The architect, Anibal González, not only designed but supervised the building of this immense structure; today it is a government office building. At a canal here you can rent rowboats for excursions into the park; or else you can walk across bridges spanning the canal. Set into a curved wall are alcoves, each focusing on characteristics of one of Spain's 50 provinces, as depicted in tile murals.

PLAZA DE AMÉRICA

Another landmark Sevillian square, the Plaza de América represents city planning at its best: Here you can walk through gardens planted with roses, enjoying the lily ponds and the fountains, and feeling the protective shade of the palms. And here you'll find a trio of elaborate buildings left over from that world exhibition which never materialized—in the center, the home of the government headquarters of Andalusia; on either side, two minor museums worth visiting only if you have time to spare.

The **Museo Arqueológico Provincial,** Plaza de América s/n (tel. 423-24-01), contains many artifacts from prehistoric times and the days of the Romans, Visigoths, and Moors. It's open Tuesday to Sunday from 10am to 2pm and from 7 to 8pm. Admission is 250 pesetas ($4.35).

Also opening onto the square is the **Museo de Artes y Costumbres Populares,** Plaza de América s/n (tel. 423-25-76), displaying folkloric costumes, musical instruments, *cordobán* saddles, weaponry, and farm implements, documenting the life of the Andalusian people. It's open Tuesday to Saturday from 10am to 2pm and from 4 to 7pm. Admission is 250 pesetas ($2.35). It's closed in August.

REAL FÁBRICA DE TABACOS, Calle San Fernando.

When Carmen waltzed out of the tobacco factory in the first act of Bizet's opera, she made its 18th-century original in Seville world famous. Many visitors arriving today, in fact, ask guides to take them to "Carmen's tobacco factory." The building, second-largest in Spain and located near the city's landmark luxury hotel, the Alfonso XII, is still there. But the Real Fábrica de Tabacos is now part of the Universidad de Sevilla. Look for signs of its former role, however, as reflected in the bas-reliefs of tobacco plants and Indians over the main entrances. You'll also see bas-reliefs of Columbus and Cortés. Then you can wander through the grounds for a look at student life, Sevillian style. The factory is directly south of the Alcázar gardens.

ARCHIVO GENERAL DE INDIAS, Avenida de la Constitución s/n. Tel. 421-12-34.

The great architect of Philip II's El Escorial outside Madrid, Juan de Herrera, was also the architect of the old Lonja (Stock Exchange), located next to the cathedral. Construction on the building lasted from 1584 to 1598. In the 17th century it was headquarters for the Academy of Seville, which was founded in part by the great Spanish artist Murillo. In 1758, during the reign of Charles III, the building was turned over for use as a general records office for the Indies. That led to today's Archivo General de Indias, said to contain some four million antique documents, even letters exchanged between patron Queen Isabella and explorer Columbus (he detailing his discoveries and impressions). These very rare documents are locked in air-conditioned storage to keep them from disintegrating. Special permission has to be acquired before examining some of them. Many treasure hunters come here, hoping to learn details of where Spanish galleons laden with gold went down off the coast of the Americas. On display in glass cases are fascinating documents in which the dreams of those early explorers come alive again.

Admission: 250 ptas. ($2.35).
Open: Mon–Fri 10am–1pm.

WHERE TO STAY

DOUBLES FOR LESS THAN 8,500 PTAS. ($79.90)

Seville's hotels, unlike its restaurants, are usually moderately priced. Antiquated but adequate, several of them have Andalusian charm and style.

HOSTAL GOYA, Mateus Gago, 31, 41004 Sevilla. Tel. 95/421-11-70. 20 rms (12 with bath).
$ Rates: 2,500 ptas. ($23.50) single without bath; 3,600 ptas. ($33.85) double with shower (no toilet), 3,900 ptas. ($36.65) double with bath. Breakfast 250 ptas. ($2.35) extra. No credit cards.

Its location in a narrow-fronted townhouse in the oldest part of the barrio is one of the Goya's strongest virtues. The building's gold-and-white façade, ornate iron railings, and picture-postcard demeanor are all noteworthy. Bedrooms are cozy and simple, without phones and TVs. Guests congregate in the marble-floored ground-level salon, where a skylight floods the couches and comfortable chairs with sunlight. Breakfast only is served. Reserve well in advance for this place: The word is out.

HOSTAL RESIDENCIA DUCAL, Plaza de la Encarnación, 19, 41003 Sevilla. Tel. 95/421-51-07. 51 rms (all with bath). A/C TEL
$ Rates: 3,600 ptas. ($33.85) single; 5,200 ptas. ($48.90) double. Breakfast 275 ptas. ($2.60) extra. AE, DC, MC, V.

In this fairly modern hotel the rooms are airy and spacious, with provincial and utilitarian furnishings. Each room has central heating for those cold Sevillian winters. A continental breakfast can be brought to your room, but no other meals are served. English is spoken. The location near the Corte Inglés department store is handy to many specialty shops.

HOTEL SIMÓN, García de Vinuesa, 19, 41001 Sevilla. Tel. 422-66-60. Fax 495/56-22-41. 48 rms (25 with bath). TEL
$ Rates: 2,500 ptas. ($23.50) single without bath, 3,900 ptas. ($36.65) single with bath; 4,500 ptas. ($42.30) double without bath, 5,500 ptas. ($51.70) double with bath. Breakfast 250 ptas. ($2.35) extra. No credit cards accepted.

This one-star hotel, located off the Avenida de la Constitución and near the Giralda Tower, is on what one reader called "the local drag strip for Vespa motor scooters." If you can stand that, you'll find this place an old-fashioned charmer, and there *are* some quiet rooms. Before its present reincarnation, the hotel was a private mansion, typical of those built here in the 18th and 19th centuries. The chandelier-lit dining room in the old Moorish style offers good food and excellent service.

BÉCQUER, Reyes Católicos, 4, 41001 Sevilla. Tel. 95/422-89-00. Fax 95/421-44-00. 126 rms (all with bath). A/C TEL
$ Rates: 5,500 ptas. ($70.50) double. Breakfast 400 ptas. ($3.75) extra. AE, DC, MC, V.
A short walk from the action of the Seville bullring (Maestranza), and only 2 blocks from the river, the Bécquer lies on a street of cafés where you can order tapas (appetizers) and drink Andalusian wine. The Museo de Bellas Artes (previously recommended) also lies nearby. Guests register in a wood-paneled lobby before being shown to one of the bedrooms, which are functionally furnished, well kept, and reasonably comfortable. The price is the attraction, the Bécquer being considered good value for Seville. Breakfast only. But you'll find a bar and lounge, as well as a garage.

RESIDENCIA Y RESTAURANT FERNANDO III, San José, 21, 41001 Sevilla. Tel. 95/421-77-08. Fax 95/422-02-46. 156 rms (all with bath). A/C TV TEL
$ Rates: 6,600 ptas. ($62.05) single; 7,600 ptas. ($71.45) double. Breakfast 475 ptas. ($4.45) extra. AE, DC, MC, V.
You'll find the Fernando III on a narrow, quiet street at the edge of the barrio, near the northern periphery of the Murillo Gardens. Its vast lobby and baronial dining hall are reminiscent of a wealthy South American hacienda; meals are served for 2,500 pesetas ($23.50). The building is modern, but constructed with richly textured marble and hardwood detailing; it is coolly and sparsely furnished with leather chairs, plants, and wrought-iron accents. Many of the accommodations—medium in size, comfortably furnished, and well maintained—offer private balconies filled with cascading plants. There are a TV salon and an attractively paneled bar.

RESIDENCIA SEVILLA, Daoiz, 5, 41003 Sevilla. Tel. 95/438-41-61. 29 rms (all with bath). A/C TEL
$ Rates: 5,300 ptas. ($49.80) single; 7,800 ptas. ($73.30) double. No credit cards.
A quiet, secluded, and inexpensive hotel on a little plaza in the city center, the Residencia Sevilla is typically Andalusian, with its central glass-covered courtyard, balconies, hanging vines, and plants. The entire first floor has an homey, old-fashioned ambience. The clean, traditionally furnished bedrooms open onto a large patio. No meals are served here.

RESIDENCIA MURILLO, Lope de Rueda, 9, 41004 Sevilla. Tel. 95/421-60-95. Fax 95/421-96-16. 61 rms (all with bath). TEL
$ Rates: 5,200 ptas. ($44.90) single; 8,500 ptas. ($79.90) double. Breakfast 300 ptas. ($2.80) extra. AE, DC, MC, V.
Tucked away on a narrow street in the heart of Santa Cruz, the old quarter, the Residencia Murillo (named after the artist who used to live in this district) is almost next to the gardens of the Alcázar. Inside, the lounges harbor some fine architectural characteristics and antique reproductions; behind a grilled screen is a retreat for drinks. Many of the rooms I inspected were cheerless and gloomy, so have a look before checking in. Like all of Seville's hotels, the Murillo is in a noisy area.
You can reach this residencia from the Menéndez y Pelayo, a wide avenue west of the Parque María Luisa, where a sign will take you through the Murillo Gardens on the left. Motorists should try to park in the Plaza de Santa Cruz. Then walk 2 blocks to the hotel, which will send a bellhop back to the car to pick up your suitcases. If

there are two in your party, station a guard at the car, and if you're going out at night, call for an inexpensive taxi to take you instead of strolling through the streets of the old quarter—it's less romantic, but a lot safer.

HOTEL ALCÁZAR, Menéndez y Pelayo, 10, 41004 Sevilla. Tel. 95/41-20-11. Fax 495/42-16-59. 93 rms (all with bath). A/C TV TEL
$ Rates: 6,500 ptas. ($61.10) single; 8,500 ptas. ($79.90) double. Breakfast 400 ptas. ($3.75) extra. AE, DC, MC, V.

On the wide and busy Boulevard Menéndez y Pelayo, across from the Murillo Gardens, this pleasantly contemporary hotel is sheltered behind a façade of brown brick. Slabs of striated gray marble cool the reception area in the lobby, next to which you'll find a Spanish restaurant and bar. Above, three latticed structures resemble a trio of *miradores*. The medium-sized rooms have modern, functional furniture, offering reasonable comfort for the price.

WORTH THE EXTRA BUCKS

HOTEL DOÑA MARÍA, Don Remondo, 19, 41004 Sevilla. Tel. 95/422-49-90. Fax 95/422-97-65. 61 rms (all with bath). A/C TV TEL
$ Rates: 9,500 ptas. ($89.30) single; 13,000 ptas. ($122.20) double. Breakfast 650 ptas. ($6.10) extra. AE, DC, MC, V.

Its location a few steps from the cathedral creates a dramatic view from the Doña María's rooftop terrace. This four-star hotel represents a worthwhile splurge, partly because of the tasteful Iberian antiques in the stone lobby and upper hallways. The ornate neoclassical entryway is offset with a pure-white façade and iron balconies, which hint at the building's origin in the 1840s as a private villa. Amid the flowering plants on the upper floor, you'll find a swimming pool ringed with garden-style lattices and antique wrought-iron railings. Each of the "one-of-a-kind" bedrooms is well furnished, stylishly appointed, and comfortable. A few have four-poster beds, others a handful of antique reproductions. Breakfast only is served.

HOTEL AMÉRICA, Jesús del Gran Poder, 2, 41002 Sevilla. Tel. 95/422-09-51. 100 rms (all with bath). A/C MINIBAR TV TEL
$ Rates: 8,500 ptas. ($79.90) single; 13,800 ptas. ($129.70) double. Breakfast 400 ptas. ($3.75) extra. AE, DC, MC, V.

Rooms here are small, but everything is spick-and-span. Superior features include wall-to-wall carpeting and, in winter, an individual heat control that works. Relax in the TV lounge or order a drink in the Duque Bar. Beside the hotel is a parking garage for 600 cars. There isn't a major restaurant, but the América does offer a tea room, cafeteria, and snack bar. The hotel is set on the northern side of the Plaza del Duque. One of Spain's major department stores, El Corte Inglés, opens onto the same square.

WHERE TO EAT

Nearly all the major restaurants known and frequented by visitors have increased their prices considerably in the past few years. That will be even truer with Expo '92. To avoid the high costs of formal dining, seek out a tapas bar or go to one of the fast-food places or cafeterias recommended. Avoid the cheap restaurants near the train station. They may not cost much, but they are not very hygienic.

MEALS FOR LESS THAN 2,500 PTAS. [$23.50]

LA RAZA, Avenida Isabel la Católica, 2. Tel. 423-38-50.
Cuisine: SPANISH. **Reservations:** Recommended.
$ Prices: Appetizers 650–1,000 ptas. ($6.10–$9.40); main dishes 900–1,800 ptas. ($8.45–$16.90). No credit cards.
Open: Lunch daily 1–4pm; dinner daily 8–11:30pm.

A terrace restaurant in the Parque María Luisa, La Raza is known both for its setting and its Andalusian specialties. Begin with gazpacho, then go one to one of the savory meat dishes. On Friday and Saturday there is often music to entertain guests, many of whom are American and Japanese tourists.

EL MESÓN, Dos de Mayo, 26. Tel. 421-30-75.
   Cuisine: SPANISH. **Reservations:** Not required.
   $ Prices: Appetizers 600–1,400 ptas. ($5.65–$13.15); main dishes 1,000–2,200 ptas. ($9.40–$20.70); fixed-priced menu 1,500 ptas. ($14.10). AE, DC, MC, V.
   Open: Lunch Tues–Sun 12:30–4:30pm; dinner Tues–Sun 8pm–midnight.

Many bullfighters frequent this establishment just off the river, and their presence is commemorated in the photographs and pictures decorating the walls. Look for American artist and bullfighter John Fulton, as well as Kenneth Vanderford, known as "the poor man's Hemingway." The restaurant owns several drawings of bulls and Spanish cowboys by Fulton. James Michener singled out the restaurant in his now-classic *Iberia*; in fact, a dessert favored by the novelist, *membrillo* (quince paste) and *manchego* cheese, is now called "The Michener Combination." You might begin your dinner here with a soothing bowl of gazpacho, then go on to hake Navarre style. Sometimes flamenco shows are presented.

RESTAURANT EL TENORIO, Mateus Gago, 11. Tel. 421-40-30.
   Cuisine: SPANISH. **Reservations:** Recommended.
   $ Prices: Appetizers 800–900 ptas. ($7.50–$8.45); main dishes 1,000–1,900 ptas. ($9.40–$17.85); fixed-priced menu 1,600 ptas. ($15.05). V.
   Open: Lunch Mon–Sat 11:30–4:30pm; dinner Mon–Sat 8pm–midnight.
Between the cathedral and the barrio, this white-fronted restaurant sits behind a row of orange trees. Its interior, dimly illuminated by a single window whose iron bars are festooned with ivy, is replete with copper pots and pans, heavy timbers, and Spanish artifacts. Menu items prepared in the aromatic kitchen include roast lamb, an array of fresh fish, and succulent pork and beef dishes.

HOSTERÍA DEL LAUREL, Plaza de los Venerables, 5. Tel. 422-02-95.
   Cuisine: SPANISH. **Reservations:** Recommended.
   $ Prices: Appetizers 600–1,400 ptas. ($5.65–$13.15); main dishes 1,500–2,000 ptas. ($14.10–$18.80); fixed-priced menu 2,500 ptas. ($23.50). AE, DC, MC, V.
   Open: Lunch daily 10:30–4pm; dinner daily 7:30pm–midnight.
Located in one of the most charming buildings on the tiny, difficult-to-find Plaza de los Venerables in the labyrinthian Barrio de Santa Cruz, this hideaway restaurant has iron-barred windows stuffed with plants. Inside, amid Andalusian tiles, beamed ceilings, and more plants, you'll enjoy good regional cooking. Many diners stop for a drink and tapas at the ground-floor bar before going into one of the dining rooms. The hostería is attached to a three-star hotel.

MESÓN DON RAIMUNDO, Argote de Molina, 26. Tel. 421-29-25.
   Cuisine: SPANISH. **Reservations:** Recommended.
   $ Prices: Appetizers 600–1,000 ptas. ($5.65–$9.40); main dishes 1,500–2,100 ptas. ($14.10–$19.75); fixed-priced menu 1,850 ptas. ($17.40). AE, MC, V.
   Open: Lunch daily noon–5pm; dinner daily 7pm–midnight.
Once a 17th-century convent, this is an attractively furnished restaurant whose entrance lies at the end of a flower-lined alleyway in the center of the Barrio de Santa Cruz. The interior contains lots of brick, terra-cotta, and carved columns, which support the beamed or arched high ceilings. Your meal might include fish stew or one of the six kinds of soup (including one with clams and pine nuts), then fresh grilled king shrimp, a casserole of partridge in sherry sauce, or wild rabbit casserole. Some of the recipes were adapted from old Arab-Hispanic cookbooks. In winter the central fireplace imparts a warm glow to the antique copper and wrought-iron art objects; in summer the place is comfortably air-conditioned.

RESTAURANT RÍO GRANDE, Betis, 70. Tel. 427-39-56.
   Cuisine: SPANISH. **Reservations:** Required.

$ Prices: Appetizers 800–1,800 ptas. ($7.50–$16.90); main dishes 1,500–2,100 ptas. ($14.10–$19.75); fixed-priced menu 2,850 ptas. ($26.80). AE, DC, MC, V.
Open: Lunch daily 1–5pm; dinner daily 8pm–1am.

This classic Sevillian restaurant is named for the Guadalquivir River, which its panoramic windows overlook. It sits against the bank of the river near the Plaza de Cuba in front of the Torre del Oro. Some diners come here just for a view of the city monuments, but they quickly fall under the spell of the well-prepared Andalusian cuisine. A meal here might include stuffed sweet pepper *flamenca*, fish-and-seafood soup seaman's style, the chef's fresh salmon, chicken-and-shellfish paella, bull tail Andalusian, garlic-chicken Giralda. You can also have a selection of fresh shellfish, brought in daily. Large terraces contain a snack bar, the Río Grande Pub, and a Bingo room. You can watch the frequent sports events on the river in this pleasant English-speaking spot.

ENRIQUE BECERRA, Gamazo, 2. Tel. 421-30-49.
  Cuisine: SPANISH. **Reservations:** Recommended.
$ Prices: Appetizers 750–1,400 ptas. ($7.05–$13.15); main dishes 1,600–2,200 ptas. ($15.05–$20.70). AE, DC, MC, V.
  Open: Lunch Mon–Sat 1–5pm; dinner Mon–Sat 8pm–midnight.

On my latest rounds, this restaurant off the Plaza Nueva and near the cathedral provided one of my best meals. A popular tapas bar and Andalusian dining spot, it offers an intimate setting and a hearty welcome that leaves you with the feeling that your business is really appreciated. While perusing the menu, you can sip dry Tío Pepe and nibble herb-cured olives with lemon peel. The gazpacho here is among the city's best, and the sangría is served ice cold. Specialties include hake *real,* sea bream Bilbaon style, and a wide range of meat and fish dishes. Many vegetarian dishes are also featured.

BODEGÓN EL RÍOJANA, Virgen de la Montañas, 12. Tel. 445-06-82.
  Cuisine: SPANISH. **Reservations:** Required.
$ Prices: Appetizers 750–1,200 ptas. ($7.05–$11.30); main dishes 1,800–2,000 ptas. ($16.90–$18.80); fixed-priced menu 3,300 ptas. ($31). AE, DC, MC, V.
  Open: Lunch daily 1:30–4pm; dinner daily 8:30pm–12:15am.

You'll be sure to get good-quality meat and shellfish in this restaurant across the Guadalquivir River about 1 mile southwest of the city center. The bar area here is always crowded with jovial devotees of seafood tapas. The adjacent two-fork restaurant section serves a delectable cuisine that includes *pimientos Ríojana,* Andalusian beefsteak, artichokes and mussels in green sauce, and several dessert soufflés.

LA ISLA, Arfe, 25. Tel. 421-53-76.
  Cuisine: SPANISH. **Reservations:** Recommended.
$ Prices: Appetizers 750–1,200 ptas. ($7.05–$11.30); main dishes 1,800–2,200 ptas. ($16.90–$20.70). AE, DC, MC, V.
  Open: Lunch Tues–Sun 1:30–4:30pm; dinner Tues–Sun 8pm–midnight.
  Closed: Aug.

Although extremely noisy, this air-conditioned restaurant is unquestionably popular. Once exclusively a working person's dining spot, the Isla now appeals to more formal diners also. Fresh seafood is flown in from Galicia. The cooking is good, including such typical dishes as sole covered with a tasty sauce, grilled liver, and chicken croquettes. At an appealing bar up front, guests can order a predinner sherry. The restaurant stands next to a food market, which makes for great people watching.

LA ALBAHACA, Plaza de Santa Cruz, 12. Tel. 422-07-14.
  Cuisine: SPANISH. **Reservations:** Recommended.
$ Prices: Appetizers 750–1,500 ptas. ($7.05–$14.10); main dishes 2,000–2,500 ptas. ($18.80–$23.50); fixed-priced menu 3,000 ptas. ($28.20). AE, DC, MC, V.
  Open: Lunch Mon–Sat 1–4pm; dinner Mon–Sat 8pm–midnight.

Located on a prominent square in the old Barrio de Santa Cruz, this restaurant with an open-air terrace offers a limited but savory menu that has become a favorite of Sevillians. Specialties include seafood soup, shellfish bisque, grilled lamb chops, partridge braised in sherry, salmon in papillote, and, for dessert, a chocolate pudding. The restaurant is in an antique seignorial home built by a well-known Spanish architect.

BEST BUDGET BETS — FAST FOOD

Lying directly east of the cathedral, the **Cervecería Giralda**, Calle Mateus Gago (tel. 422-74-35), is one of the least expensive dining spots in the "monumental center" (cathedral, Alcázar, and Giralda Tower). Residents and tourists alike eat here. You can make a meal from the selection of tapas (appetizers), 175 to 400 pesetas ($1.75 to $4.25), or order one of the *platos combinados* (combination plates), ranging from 450 to 1,200 pesetas ($4.25 to $11.30). The place is open daily from 9am to midnight.

On the same street, the **Pizzeria El Artesano**, Calle Mateus Gago (tel. 421-38-58), also lures customers in the vicinity of the cathedral. Here the feature is an Andalusian version of pizza, in the 350 to 600 peseta ($3.30 to $5.65) range. Daily hours are 12:30pm to 1am.

Lying on the "opposite side" of the Guadalquivir, away from the throngs of tourists, is the Barrio de Triana. This used to be its own little village community until Seville burst its seams and absorbed it. It still is the place to go to escape the high food tariffs on the cathedral side of the river.

El Puerto, Betis, 59 (tel. 427-17-25), stands next door to the famed Río Grande restaurant. It has multilevel al fresco terrace opening onto the river. You can get fresh seafood here, but the special buy is the chef's *cubierto* (menu of the house), costing 900 pesetas ($8.45). At the cafeteria bar, you serve yourself; inside is an inexpensive restaurant with waiter service. It's open Tuesday through Sunday: lunch from 1 to 4pm and dinner from 8:30pm to midnight.

Another way to keep costs trimmed is to eat at one of the tapas bars recommended below. Portions, called *raciones,* are usually generous, and many budget-minded tourists often eat standing at the bar, making a full meal out of two orders of tapas.

WORTH THE EXTRA BUCKS

SAN MARCO, Cuna, 6. Tel. 421-24-40.
   Cuisine: SPANISH. **Reservations:** Required.
$ **Prices:** Appetizers 950–1,400 ptas. ($8.95–$13.15); main dishes 1,900–2,400 ptas. ($17.85–$22.55); fixed-priced menu 4,000 ptas. ($37.60). AE, MC, V.
   Open: Lunch Mon–Sat 1:30–4pm; dinner Mon–Sat 8:30pm–midnight. Closed: Aug.

There are those Sevillian food critics who consider this the city's best restaurant; others rank it number two. At any rate, it's expensive and should be saved for that special occasion. It lies in the city center in a 19th-century house decorated in a restrained and tasteful style; elegance is the keynote here. The service ranks among the finest in town. Try a specialty such as rape (monkfish) with three different peppers, gratin of sole with mushrooms and spinach in a cream sauce, Iberian pork Stroganoff, or duck with port sauce and green peppers. The pasta dishes are homemade. The chef confirms his reputation every day with his sumptuous desserts.

EVENING ENTERTAINMENT

FLAMENCO

When the moon is high in Seville and the scent of orange blossoms is in the air, it's time to wander the alleyways of Santa Cruz in search of the sound of castanets. Or take a taxi to be on the safe side.

EL PATIO SEVILLANO, Paseo de Cristóbal Colón, 11. Tel. 421-41-20.

In central Seville on the riverbank between two historic bridges, El Patio Sevillano is a showcase for Spanish folksong and dance, performed by exotically costumed dancers. The presentation includes a wide variety of Andalusian flamenco and songs, as well as classical pieces by composers such as Falla, Albéniz, Granados, and Chueca. Open: Two shows nightly, 9:30pm and 11:30pm (occasionally also 7:30pm). Prices: Drinks 500 ptas. ($4.70).

Admission: 2,300 ptas. ($21.60), including cover and first drink.

EL TABLAO DE CURRO VÉLEZ, Rodó, 7. Tel. 421-64-92.

Locals enjoy the drinks and flamenco in this club, which features many types of dance. Open: Thurs–Tues 9:30pm–dawn. Closed: Feb. Prices: Drinks 600 ptas. ($5.65).

Admission: 2,400 ptas. ($22.55), including first drink.

DRINKS AND TAPAS

EL RINCONCILLO, Gerona, 40. Tel. 422-31-83.

El Rinconcillo has a 1930s ambience, partly because of its real age and partly because of its owners' refusal to change one iota of the decor—this has always been one of the most famous bars in Seville. Amid dim lighting, heavy ceiling beams, and iron-based, marble-topped tables, you can enjoy a beer or a full meal along with the rest of the easygoing clientele. The bartender will mark your tab in chalk on a well-worn wooden countertop. Look for the art nouveau tile murals. El Rinconcillo is at the northern edge of the Barrio de Santa Cruz, near the Santa Catalina Church. Open: Thurs–Tues noon–2am. Prices: Pitcher of sangría 350 ptas. ($3.30); complete meal around 2,000 ptas. ($18.80).

LA ALICANTINA, Plaza del Salvador, 2. Tel. 422-61-22.

It's not the decor that attracts clients here, but rather the best seafood tapas in town. Both the bar and the sidewalk tables are always filled to overflowing. The owner serves generous portions of clams marinara, fried squid, grilled shrimp, fried codfish, and clams in béchamel sauce. La Alicantina is about 5 blocks north of the cathedral. Open: Daily noon–3:30pm and 7–11:30pm. Prices: Tapas 850 ptas. ($7.05).

JOSÉ LUIS, Plaza de Cuba, 3. Tel. 427-96-49.

Located across the river from the cathedral, José Luis stresses its image as a cocktail bar rather than a pub—it's stylish and chic. There are comfortable wicker chairs on the sidewalk in front and a glossy interior designed to conjure up an English hunting ambience, with marble floors, horse prints, and lots of green leather. Red-vested waiters serve beer and a wide array of drinks. Open: Daily 9am–midnight. Prices: Beer 100 ptas. (95¢); drinks 370 ptas. ($3.50).

MODESTO, Cano y Cueto, 5. Tel. 441-68-11.

At the northern end of the Murillo Gardens, opening onto a quiet square with flowerboxes and an ornate iron railing, Modesto serves fabulous seafood tapas. The bar is air-conditioned, and you can choose your appetizers just by pointing. Upstairs there's a good-value restaurant, offering a meal for 1,200 pesetas ($11.30), including such dishes as fried squid, baby sole, grilled sea bass, and shrimp in garlic sauce. Open Thurs–Tues 8–2am. Prices: Drinks 375 ptas. ($3.55); tapas from 500 ptas. ($4.70).

CASA RAMÓN, Plaza des los Venerables. (No phone.)

Tapas are said to have originated in Andalusia, and this old-fashioned bar looks as if it has been dishing them up since day one. Definitely include this place on your *tasca*-hopping through the old quarter. At the deli counter in front you can make your selection; you might even pick up the fixings for a picnic in the Parque María Luisa. The Casa Ramón is in the Barrio de Santa Cruz. Open: Mon–Fri 9am–3pm and

5:30pm–12:30am; Sat–Sun 10am–3pm and 6:30pm–12:30am. Prices: Wine per glass 100 ptas. (95¢); tapas from 350 ptas. ($3.30).

A Seville Disco

Popular and often crowded, **El Coto,** Luís Montoto, 118 (tel. 457-62-03), is located in the basement of the Hotel Los Legreros Sol in the center of Seville. Admission, including one drink, is 1,000 pesetas ($9.40). The club is open daily from 7:30 to 10:30pm and 11:30pm to 5am. El Coto is located due south of the Estación de Cádiz, in the modern part of town.

A Special Bar

ABADES, Abades, 1. Tel. 421-50-96.

A converted mansion in the Barrio de Santa Cruz has been turned into an elegant rendezvous point that has been compared to "a living room in a luxurious movie set." In the heart of the old Jewish ghetto, it evokes the style of the Spanish Romantic era. The house dates from the 19th century, when it was constructed around a central courtyard with a fountain. Drinks and low-key conversations are the style here, and since its opening in 1980 all the visiting literati and glitterati have put in an appearance. Young men and women in jeans also patronize the place, enjoying the comfort of the sofas and wicker armchairs.

The ingredients of a special drink called *aqua de Sevilla* are a secret, but I suspect sparkling white wine, pineapple juice, and eggs (the whites and yolks mixed in separately, of course). Classical music is played in the background. Take a taxi to get here at night, as it might not be safe to wander late along the narrow streets of the barrio. Open: Summer, daily 9pm–4am; winter, daily 8pm–2:30am. Prices: Drinks from 275 ptas. ($2.35).

NEARBY EXCURSIONS

Carmona

An easy hour-long bus trip from the main terminal in Seville, Carmona is an ancient city dating from Neolithic times. Twenty-one miles (34km) east of Seville, it grew in power and prestige under the Moors, establishing ties with Castille in 1252.

Surrounded by fortified walls, Carmona has three Moorish fortresses, one of which has been turned into a luxurious parador (see below). The other two include the **Alcázar de la Puerta de Córdoba** and the **Alcázar de la Puerta de Sevilla.** The top attraction is the **Seville Gate,** with its double Moorish arch, opposite St. Peter's Church. Note too, the **Córdoba Gate** on the Calle Santa María de Gracia, which was attached to the ancient Roman walls in the 17th century.

The town itself is a virtual national landmark, filled with narrow streets, whitewashed walls, and Renaissance mansions. The **Plaza San Fernando** is the most important square, filled with elegant 17th-century houses. The most important church is dedicated to **Santa María,** and stands on the Calle Martín López. You enter a Moorish ablutionary patio before exploring the interior with its 15th-century white vaulting.

A **Roman necroplois and amphitheater** at Jorge Bonsor contain the remains of a thousand families who lived in and around Carmona 2,000 years ago. There is also an archeological museum on the site, which offers 45-minute tours Tuesday through Sunday from 9am to 2pm and 4 to 6 pm; admission is 200 pesetas ($1.90). Of the two important tombs, the Elephant Vault consists of three dining rooms and a kitchen. The other, the Servilia Tomb, was the size of a nobleman's villa. If you're driving to Carmona, exit from Seville's eastern periphery onto the N-V superhighway, following the signs to the airport, then to Carmona on the road to Madrid. The Carmona turnoff is clearly marked.

Where to Stay & Eat

**PARADOR NACIONAL ALCÁZAR DEL REY DON PEDRO, 41410
Carmona (Sevilla). Tel 95/414-10-10.** Fax 495/14-17-12. 59 rms (all with bath). A/C MINIBAR TV TEL
$ Rates: 9,200 ptas. ($86.50) single; 13,000 ptas. ($122.20) double. Breakfast 950 ptas. ($8.95) extra. AE, DC, MC, V.

★ Finding this parador amid the narrow Carmona streets that wind in and out of the ancient fortifications is part of the establishment's charm. By following strategically located signs, you'll see it clinging by diagonal stilts to the rock face of a forbidding cliff. After parking in the shadows of a medieval courtyard, you'll enter one of the most attractive paradors in Spain, built around an Andalusian patio whose monumental fountain is ringed with Moorish columns, potted geraniums, and intricate tiles. A hallway crafted from brick, stone, and wooden beams leads to a lattice-shaded breakfast room where views of the surrounding fertile farmland stretch for miles.

The parador, open since 1976, contains comfortable bedrooms with rustically detailed accessories. In most rooms, French doors open onto panoramic views. Special features include a flower garden, a tile-roofed gazebo, and a beautiful swimming pool set with herringbone patterns of blue and white tiles. A snack bar, 16 tile-roofed cabañas, and rose bushes surround it. Fixed-price meals, from 3,200 pesetas ($30.10), are served in the stone-vaulted restaurant.

Italica

Lovers of Roman history will flock to Italica (tel. 95/439-27-84), the ruins of an ancient city 5½ miles (9km) northwest of Seville, on the major road to Lisbon, near the small town of Santiponce.

After the battle of Ilipa, Publius Cornelius Scipio Africanus founded Italica in 206 B.C. Two of the most famous of Roman emperors, Trajan and Hadrian, were born here. Indeed, master builder Hadrian was to have a major influence on his hometown. In his reign the **amphitheater,** the ruins of which can be seen today, was among the largest in the Roman Empire. Lead pipes that carried water from the Guadalquivir River still remain. A small museum displays some of the Roman statuary found here, although the finest pieces have been shipped to Seville. Many mosaics, depicting beasts, gods, and birds, are on exhibit, and others are constantly being discovered. The ruins, including a Roman theater, can be explored Tuesday through Friday from 9am to 5:30pm, on Saturday and Sunday from 9am to 3pm. Admission is 250 pesetas ($2.35).

If you're driving, exit from the northwest periphery of Seville, following the signs for highway E-803 in the direction of Zafra and Lisbon. But if you don't have a car, take the bus marked "Calle de Santiponce" leaving from the Calle Marqués de Parada near the Córdoba Railway Station (Estación de Córdoba) in Seville. Buses depart every hour, and the trip takes about 30 minutes.

Where to Eat

MESÓN ALIJA, Reál, 88, Castilleja de la Cuesta, Italica. Tel. 954/16-08-58.
Cuisine: SPANISH. **Reservations:** Required Sat and Sun. **Bus:** Empresa Casals bus from Seville.
$ Prices: Appetizers 750–1,200 ptas. ($7.05–$11.30); main dishes 1,800–3,000 ptas. ($16.90–$28.20). AE, MC, V.
Open: Lunch daily 11am–5pm; dinner daily 8:30pm–1am.
Despite the difficulty they may have finding this out-of-the-way place, 3 miles (4.8km) outside Seville, many visitors feel that the culinary rewards are worth the effort. The chef prepares excellent seafood and meat specialties, each concocted with fresh ingredients (many displayed near the entrance). You might enjoy several versions of shrimp or crayfish; game dishes; succulent beef, lamb, or pork; or such grilled temptations as brochette of grouper and saffron-flavored, shellfish-studded paella—all

of which can be consumed beside the restaurant's blazing fireplace. In summer, meals are served on a flower-ringed outdoor terrace. The restaurant stands opposite the Convent of Irish Nuns on the main street.

---

4. JEREZ DE LA FRONTERA

54 miles S of Seville, 368 miles SW of Madrid, 21 miles NE of Cádiz

GETTING THERE   By Plane   Iberia and Aviaco offer flights to Jerez every Monday through Friday from Barcelona and Zaragoza; daily flights from Madrid; and several flights a week to and from Valencia, Tenerife, Palma de Mallorca, and Grand Canary Island. No international flights land at Jerez. The airport lies about 7 miles (11km) northeast of the city center (follow the signs to Seville). There's an Iberia ticketing and information office conveniently located in the center of Jerez at Plaza Reyes Católicos, 2 (tel. 33-99-08).

By Train   Trains from Madrid arrive daily (8 to 11 hours). The railway station in Jerez lies at Plaza de la Estación (tel. 34-96-12), at the eastern end of the Calle Medina.

By Bus   Bus connections are more frequent than train connections, and the location of the bus terminal is also more convenient. You'll find it on the Calle Medina, at the corner of the Calle Madre de Díos, a 12-minute walk east of the Alcázar. About 8 buses arrive daily from Cádiz (45 minutes) and 3 from Ronda (2½ hours). Seven buses a day arrive from Seville (1½ hours).

By Car   Jerez lies on the highway connecting Seville with Cádiz, Algeciras, Gibraltar, and the ferryboat landing for Tangier, Morocco. There's also an overland road connecting Jerez with Granada and Málaga.

ESSENTIALS   The area code for Jerez de la Frontera is 956. The Tourist Information Office is at Calle Alameda Cristina, 7 (tel. 956/31-05-37). To reach it from the bus terminals, take the Calle Medina to the Calle Honda and continue along as the road turns to the right. An English-speaking staff can provide directions, transportation suggestions, open hours, and so on, for any bodega you might want to visit. You will also be given a map pinpointing the location of various bodegas.

The charming little Andalusian town of Jerez made a name for itself in England for the thousands of casks of golden sherry it shipped there over the centuries. With origins going back nearly 3,000 years, Jerez is nonetheless a modern, progressive town with wide boulevards, although it does have an interesting old quarter. Busloads of visitors pour in every year to get those free drinks at one of the bodegas where wine is aged and bottled.

The town is pronounced both "Herez" and "Her-eth," in Andalusian and Castilian, respectively. The French and the Moors called it various names, including Heres and Scheris, which the English corrupted to Sherry.

WHAT TO SEE & DO

TOURING THE BODEGAS

Jerez is surrounded by vineyards, and the ideal time to visit is during the September grape harvest. However, visitors can count on the finest in hospitality all year round, since Jerez is widely known for the warm welcome it bestows.

There must be over a hundred bodegas in and around Jerez, where not only can you see how sherries are made, bottled, and aged, but where you can also get free samples. Among the most famous brands are Sandemán, Pedro Domecq, and González Byass, the maker of Tío Pepe.

On a typical visit to a bodega, you'll be shown through several buildings in which sherry and brandy are manufactured. In one building, you'll see grapes being pressed and sorted; in another, you'll see them being bottled; in a third, you'll see thousands of large oak casks. Then it's on to an attractive bar where various sherries—amber, dark gold, cream, red, sweet, and velvety—can be sampled. If either is offered, try the very dry La Ina sherry or the Fundador brandy, one of the most popular in the world. **Warning:** These drinks are more potent than you might expect.

Most bodegas are open Monday through Friday only, from 10:30am to 1:30pm. Regrettably, many of them are closed in July and August; many do reopen by the third week of August to prepare for the wine festival in early September.

Of the dozens of bodegas you can visit, the most popular are the following. Some of them charge an admission fee and require a reservation.

A favorite among British visitors is **Harveys of Bristol,** Arcos, 53 (tel. 34-60-00), which is one of the few Jerez bodegas that doesn't charge an admission fee or require a reservation. An English-speaking guide leads a 2-hour tour year round, except for the first three weeks of August. Another famous name is **González Byass,** Manuel María González, 12 (tel. 34-00-00); admission is 350 pesetas ($3.30), and reservations are required. Equally famous is **Domecq,** San Ildefonso, 3 (tel. 33-19-00), requiring a reservation and charging an admission of 350 pesetas ($3.30). The widely advertised **Sandemán,** Calle Pizarro s/n (tel. 33-11-00), requires no reservation but charges an admission of 250 pesetas ($2.35). Finally, you might also want to visit the lesser-known **Williams and Humbert,** Nuño de Cañas (tel. 34-59-72), which doesn't require a reservation, but charges an admission of 250 pesetas ($2.35).

THE DANCING HORSES OF JEREZ

A serious rival to Vienna's famous Spanish Riding School is the **Escuela Andaluza del Arte Ecuestre (Andalusian School of Equestrian Art),** Avenida Duque de Abrantes (tel. 31-11-11). In fact, the long, hard schooling that brings horse and rider into perfect harmony originated in this province. The Viennese school was started with Hispano-Arab horses sent from this region, the same steeds you can see today in Jerez. Every Thursday at noon, crowds come to admire the Dancing Horses of Andalusia perform in a show that includes local folklore. Admission is 1,280 pesetas ($12.05).

A NEARBY ATTRACTION

Since many people go to Jerez specifically to visit a bodega, August or weekend closings can be very disappointing. If this happens to you, make a trip to the nearby village of **Lebrija,** about halfway between Jerez and Seville, 8½ miles (14km) west of the main highway. Lebrija, a good spot to get a glimpse of rural Spain, is a local winemaking center where some very fine sherries originate. At one small bodega, that of Juan García, you are courteously escorted around by the owner. There are several other bodegas in Lebrija, and the local citizens will gladly point them out to you. It's all very casual—lacking the rigidity and formality attached to the bodegas of Jerez.

WHERE TO STAY

Jerez has no nightlife to speak of, and few hotels—most visitors come just for the day, pressing on to Cádiz by nightfall or heading back to Seville. There are a few good hotel choices however, listed below. One of the best streets for budget hotels is the Calle Higueras, off the Calle Fermín Aranda.

LAS PALOMAS, Higueras, 17, 11400 Jerez de la Frontera. Tel. 956/34-37-73. 43 rms (20 with shower).
$ Rates: 1,400 ptas. ($13.15) single without bath; 2,400 ptas. ($22.55) double without bath, 2,600 ptas. ($24.45) double with shower. Breakfast 275 ptas. ($2.35) extra. No credit cards.

⑤ Three blocks from the bus terminal is one of the least expensive hotels in town. Las Palomas is well run, most respectable, and very clean. Both the public bathrooms and the private showers are modern. Bedrooms have simple, functional furnishings. The decor, typically Andalusian, includes a plant-filled courtyard. Canaries sing out your welcome.

NUEVO HOSTAL, Caballeros, 23, 11400 Jerez de la Frontera. Tel. 956/33-16-00. 30 rms (15 with bath). TEL
$ Rates: 2,200 ptas. ($20.70) single without bath, 2,700 ptas. ($25.40) single with bath; 3,800 ptas. ($35.70) double without bath, 4,300 ptas. ($40.40) double with bath. Breakfast 300 ptas. ($2.80) extra. No credit cards.

This peseta-saver near the Church of St. Michael (San Miguel) is frequented mostly by Spaniards. The entrance has superb 12-foot-high doors, with grillwork like a townhouse. Inside, the lobby is three floors high and covered with Andalusian-style glass. The bedrooms are mostly large and pleasingly old-fashioned. A large lunch or dinner is available for 1,200 pesetas ($11.30).

HOSTAL ÁVILA, Ávila, 3, 11140 Jerez de la Frontera. Tel. 956/33-48-08. 30 rms (all with bath). A/C TEL
$ Rates: 3,500 ptas. ($32.90) single; 5,500 ptas. ($51.70) double. Breakfast 325 ptas. ($3.05) extra. MC, V.

One of the better bargains in Jerez, the Ávila is as comfortable as a three-star hotel. Don't judge it by its façade: Inside, its rooms are clean, comfortable, and well maintained. The Ávila is in the commercial center of town, near the post office and the Plaza del Arenal.

HOTEL SERIT, Higueras, 7, 11400 Jerez de la Frontera. Tel. 956/34-07-00. Fax 956/34-07-16. 35 rms (all with bath). A/C TV TEL
$ Rates: 6,300 ptas. ($59.20) single; 8,500 ptas. ($79.90) double. Breakfast 350 ptas. ($3.30) extra. AE, DC, MC, V.

The best choice is the new three-star Hotel Serit, where all rooms are well furnished and comfortable. There's a pleasant bar downstairs, plus a modern breakfast lounge. You'll find it near the Plaza de las Angustias.

HOTEL RESIDENCIA CAPELE, Corredera, 58, 11400 Jerez de la Frontera. Tel. 956/34-64-00. 48 rms (all with bath). A/C TV TEL
$ Rates: 7,500 ptas. ($70.50) single; 11,600 ptas. ($109.05) double. Breakfast 540 ptas. ($5.10) extra. AE, DC, MC, V.

Considered the second-best second-class hotel in town, the Residencia Capele, a contemporary structure, offers well-furnished bedrooms. The location is good, a block or so from the heart of Jerez, near the Plaza del Arenal. There is neither garage nor restaurant, but the place does serve continental breakfast.

WHERE TO EAT

RESTAURANTE TENDIDO 6, Circo, 10, Tel. 34-48-35.
   Cuisine: SPANISH. **Reservations:** Recommended.
$ Prices: Appetizers 600–950 ptas. ($5.65–$8.95); main dishes 1,100–1,800 ptas. ($10.35–$16.90). AE, DC, MC, V.
   Open: Lunch Mon–Sat 1–4pm; dinner Mon–Sat 8–11:30pm.
This combination restaurant and tapas bar has loyal clients who come from many walks of life. The chef creates a dignified regional cuisine that includes grilled

rumpsteak, fish soup, and a wide array of Spanish dishes. The Tendido is on the south side of the Plaza de Toros.

GAITÁN, Avenida Gaitán, 3. Tel. 34-58-59.
   Cuisine: SPANISH. **Reservations:** Recommended.
$ **Prices:** Appetizers 750–1,200 ptas. ($7.05–$11.30); main dishes 1,500–1,900 ptas. ($14.10–$17.85); fixed-priced menu 1,500 ptas. ($14.10). AE, DC, MC, V.
   Open: Lunch daily 1–4:30pm; dinner Mon–Sat 8:30–11:30pm. **Closed:** First 2 weeks in Aug.

This small restaurant near the Puerta Santa María is owned by Juan Hurtado, who has won acclaim for the food served here. Surrounded by walls displaying celebrity photographs, you can enjoy such Andalusian dishes as garlic soup, various stews, duck à la Sevillana, and fried seafood. For dessert, the almond tart is a favorite.

EL BOSQUE, Avenida Alcalde Alvaro Domecq, 26. Tel. 30-33-33.
   Cuisine: SPANISH. **Reservations:** Required.
$ **Prices:** Appetizers 600–1,200 ptas. ($5.65–$11.30); main dishes 1,800–2,200 ptas. ($16.90–$20.70). AE, MC, V.
   Open: Lunch Mon–Sat 1:30–5pm; dinner Mon–Sat 9pm–midnight.

The city's most elegant restaurant, near a park about a mile northeast of the center of Jerez, is a favorite of the sherry aristocracy, who like the homey ambience cultivated by owner. He has decorated the establishment with art that suggests a bullfight. You might order the excellent *rabo de toro* (bull's-tail stew), grilled monkfish brochette, or one of the numerous beef, pork, chicken, and fish dishes. The lemon mousse makes a wonderful choice for dessert, and the restaurant maintains a fine wine list.

A TAPAS BAR

LA VENECIA, Calle Larga, s/n. Tel. 33-72-94.
Many sherry producers maintain that this is the best place for tapas in the entire town. Of course, the drink to order here is sherry, as the *jerezanos* do—whether your tapas be meatballs, croquettes, meat-stuffed peppers, or even a bowl of stew. You can make an entire meal of these tapas, and do so relatively inexpensively.
   Prices: Tapas from 150–350 ptas. ($1.40–$3.30).
   Open: Mon–Sat 7:30am–11:30pm.

NEARBY EXCURSIONS
MEDINA SIDONIA

This survivor of the Middle Ages is one of the most unspoiled hillside villages of Spain, about 29 miles (46.5km) east of Cádiz and 22 miles (35.5km) southeast of Jerez de la Frontera. Motorists from Jerez should follow the 440 southeast.
   A village that time forgot, Medina Sidonia has cobblestoned streets, white tile-roofed buildings dotting the hillside, a Gothic church, a Moorish gate, and steep alleyways traveled by locals on donkeys. The Arab influence is everywhere. The surrounding countryside is wild and seldom visited. The pockets of fog that sometimes settle over the land will make you think you're on the Yorkshire moors.
   From Medina Sidonia, it's a 2½-hour drive to the port city of Algeciras, or you can take the Jerez road back to Seville.

ARCOS DE LA FRONTERA

Twenty miles (32km) east of Jerez de la Frontera, this old Arab town—now a national historic monument—was built in the form of an amphitheater. Sitting on a rock and surrounded by the Guadalete River on three sides, it contains many houses that have been hollowed out of this formation. From the old city, there's a high-in-the-clouds view that some visitors find without rival on the Iberian Peninsula.

The city is filled with whitewashed walls and narrow winding streets that disappear into steps. It holds a lot of historical interest, and has a beautiful lake complete with paddleboats and a Mississippi riverboat.

The most exciting attraction is the **view from the principal square,** the Plaza del Cabildo, a rectangular esplanade overhanging a deep river cleft. You can see a Moorish castle, but it is privately owned and cannot be visited by the public. You can, however, visit the main church, located on the main square—the **Iglesia de Santa María,** constructed in 1732, a blend of Gothic, Renaissance, and baroque. Its western front—and its most outstanding architectural achievement—is in Plateresque style. The second major church of town, **Iglesia de San Pedro,** standing on the northern edge of the old barrio (quarter), at the far end of the cliff, is known for its 16th- and 18th-century tower. This church, which grew up on the site of a Moorish fortress, owns works by Zurbarán and Murillo, among others. Check with the tourist office (see below) about gaining admission to these churches, as they are often closed for security reasons. Several art thefts have occurred in the area.

Even if you don't succeed in gaining entrance to the churches, it is reason enough to visit Arcos merely to wander its alleys and view its ruins from the Middle Ages. If you have to return to wherever you're going for the night, stay at least long enough to have a drink in the patio of the parador (recommended below) and take in that monumental view.

As there is no train service to this little bit of paradise, take the bus from Seville, Cádiz, or Jerez de la Frontera. From Jerez, motorists should follow the 342 east until they see the turnoff for Arcos.

The area code for Arcos de la Frontera is 956. The Tourist Information Office is at Calle Calderón de la Barca, 1 (tel. 956/21-13-13). To reach it, go along the Calle Antonio López.

Where to Stay & Eat

PARADOR CASA DEL CORREGIDOR, Plaza de España, 11630 Arcos de la Frontera. Tel. 956/70-05-00. Fax 956/70-11-16. 24 rms (all with bath). A/C MINIBAR TV TEL

$ Rates: 8,000 ptas. ($75.20) single; 11,000 ptas. ($103.40) double. Breakfast buffet 900 ptas. ($8.45) extra. AE, DC, MC, V.

The best place to stay is this government-run parador, in a restored palace in the heart of the old quarter. From the balconies, there are views of the Valley of Guadalete with its river, plains, and farms. In good weather you can take your meals on one of these balconies (try the pork with garlic); lunch or dinner costs 2,900 pesetas ($27.25). The decor consists of tiles and antiques. Bedrooms are handsomely furnished and beautifully maintained; perhaps you'll be assigned the one where Charles de Gaulle once stayed.

---

5. CÁDIZ

76 miles S of Seville, 388 miles SW of Madrid

GETTING THERE By Train Trains arrive at Cádiz from Seville (1½ to 2½ hours), Jerez de la Frontera, and Algeciras (3 hours). The train station is located on the Avenida del Puerto (tel. 25-43-01), on the southeast border of the main port.

By Bus Passengers in transit to or from Madrid usually require a transfer in Seville. Buses in Cádiz arrive at two separate terminals. From Seville (8 per day; 1½-2½ hours), Jerez de la Frontera (12 per day), Málaga, Córdoba, and Granada, buses arrive at the Estación de Comes terminal, Plaza de la Hispanidad, 1 (tel. 21-17-63), on the north side of town, a few blocks west of the main port. Far less prominent is the terminal run by the Transportes Los Amarillos, Avenida Ramón de Carranta (tel. 28-58-52), several blocks to the south, which runs frequent buses to several nearby towns and villages, most of which are of interest only for local residents and workers.

By Car   Cádiz is connected to Seville via a wide and fast highway (1 hour) and to the other cities of the Mediterranean coast by a road that can at times be busy, especially during weekends and holidays.

ESSENTIALS   The area code for Cádiz is 956. The Tourist Information Office is at Calderón de la Barca, 1 (tel. 956/21-13-13).

The oldest inhabited city in the Western world, founded in 1100 B.C., this now modern, bustling Atlantic port is a kind of Spanish Marseille, a melting pot of Americans, Africans, and Europeans who are docking or passing through. The old quarter teems with native life, little dives, and seaport alleyways through which sailors from many lands wander in search of adventure. But despite its thriving life, the city does not hold major interest for tourists except for the diverse cultural strains that have helped shape it. Phoenicians, Arabs, Visigoths, Romans, and Carthaginians all passed through Cádiz and left their cultural imprints. Throughout the ages this ancient port city has enjoyed varyng states of prosperity, especially after the discovery of the New World.

At the end of a peninsula, Cádiz separates the Bay of Cádiz from the Atlantic, so from numerous sea walls around the town, you have views of the ocean. It was here that Columbus set out on his second voyage.

WHAT TO SEE & DO

Despite its being one of the oldest towns in Europe, Cádiz has few remnants of antiquity. It is still worth visiting, however, especially to wander through the old quarter, which retains a special charm.

The **Plaza de San Juan de Dios** is a wonderful place to sit at a sidewalk café and people watch in the shadow of the neoclassical Isabelline Ayuntamiento (Town Hall), with its outstanding chapter house. The **Oratory of San Felipe Neri,** where the Cortes (Parliament) met in 1812 to proclaim its constitution, has an important Murillo (*Conception*) and a history museum. Admission is free, and it's open August through June, daily from noon to 2pm and 5 to 7pm. The **Hospital de Mujeres (Women's Hospital)** has a patio courtyard dating from 1740 and a chapel with El Greco's *Ecstasy of St. Francis.*

MUSEO DE CÁDIZ, Calle Antonia López. Tel. 21-43-00.

This museum, now fully restored, contains one of Spain's most important Zurbarán collections, as well as paintings by Rubens and Murillo (including the latter's acclaimed picture of Christ). The archeology section displays Roman, Carthaginian, and Phoenician finds, while ethnology exhibits include pottery, baskets, textiles, and leather works.

Admission: 275 ptas. ($2.35).

Open: Tues–Fri 9:30am–1:30pm and 5:30–7:30pm, Sat 9:30am–1:30pm.

CATEDRAL DE CÁDIZ, Plaza Catedral.

This magnificent 18th-century baroque building by architect Vicente Acero has a neoclassical interior dominated by an outstanding apse. The tomb of Cádiz-born composer Manuel de Falla lies in its splendid crypt; music lovers from all over the world come here to pay their respects. Haydn composed *The Seven Last Words of Our Savior on the Cross* for this cathedral. The treasury/museum contains a priceless collection of Spanish silver, embroidery, and paintings by Spanish, Italian, and Flemish artists.

Admission: 125 ptas. ($1.20) adults; 75 ptas. (70¢) children.
Open: Mon–Sat 10am–1pm.

WHERE TO STAY

Cádiz has a number of budget accommodations, some of which are quite poor. However, for moderate tabs you can afford some of the finest lodgings in the city. Rooms are scarce during the February carnival season.

DOUBLES FOR LESS THAN 7,000 PTAS [$65.80]

IMARES, San Francisco, 9, 11004 Cádiz. Tel. 956/21-22-57. 37 rms (25 with bath). TEL
$ Rates: Single without bath 2,500 ptas. ($23.50), single with bath 3,300 ptas. ($31); double with bath 3,900 ptas. ($36.65). Breakfast 275 ptas. ($2.60) extra. No credit cards.
An older hotel with a large entrance patio, a marble staircase, and a balcony, the Imares has more Andalusian flavor than the other choices here. The rooms are large and well kept, and the staff offers good service. The only drawback is the noise level—all the rooms face the cavernous inside patio and noise reverberates through the whole building. Light sleepers, take note. The Imares is within walking distance of the Plaza de Juan de Dios.

REGIO 1, Ana de Viya, 11, 11009 Cádiz. Tel. 956/27-93-31. 40 rms (all with bath). TEL
$ Rates: 3,500 ptas. ($32.90) single; 6,000 ptas. ($56.40) double. Breakfast 375 ptas. ($3.55) extra. AE, DC, MC, V.
This is a modern hotel on the main avenue of town, east of the historic barrio, 1 block north of the Paseo Marítimo. The bedrooms have contemporary furniture and many conveniences. Breakfast is the only meal served.

HOTEL FRANCIA Y PARÍS, Plaza San Francisco, 1, 11004 Cádiz. Tel. 956/21-23-19. 69 rms (all with bath). TV TEL
$ Rates: 4,200 ptas. ($39.50) single; 6,200 ptas. ($58.30) double. Breakfast 420 ptas. ($3.95) extra. AE, DC, MC, V.
Only a 5-minute walk from the waterfront, west of the Plaza de Mina in the heart of the old town, this modern hotel is on one of Cadiz's attractive tree-filled squares. The medium-sized bedrooms are fairly comfortable, and most have windows fitted with awnings to keep out the strong sun (Cádiz is called the "City of Light"). There is a cozy, wood-paneled bar/lounge, but no restaurant. Many of the staff members speak English.

REGIO 2, Avenida Andalucía, 79, 11008 Cádiz. Tel. 956/25-30-08. 40 rms (all with bath). TEL
$ Rates: Singles 4,000 ptas. ($37.60); doubles 7,000 ptas. ($65.80). Breakfast 450 ptas. ($4.25) extra. AE, DC, MC, V.
This hotel is similar in character and comfort to the slightly newer Regio 1 (see above), and lies a short distance from the beach. Rooms are well furnished and kept—in fact, some travel agents rate this number two in the city. Breakfast only is served.

WORTH THE EXTRA BUCKS

HOTEL ATLÁNTICO, Duque de Nájera, 9, 11002 Cádiz. Tel. 956/22-69-05. Fax 956/21-45-82. 153 rms (all with bath). A/C MINIBAR TV TEL
$ Rates: 9,000 ptas. ($84.60) single; 11,000 ptas. ($103.40) double. Breakfast 900 ptas. ($8.45) extra. AE, DC, MC, V.
Actually a modern resort hotel, this national parador is built on one of the loveliest beaches of the Bay of Cádiz, at the western edge of the old town. The white six-story

building has a marble patio, a salon decked out in rattan and cane, and bedrooms that have balconies with tables and chairs for relaxed ocean viewing. The Atlántico's own swimming pool is surrounded by palm trees. The hotel also boasts a bar and a dining room known for its superb Andalusian cuisine, particularly the seafood. Meals cost from 2,900 pesetas ($27.25).

WHERE TO EAT

Head for the heart of the city, the Plaza de San Juan de Dios, for good economy dinners. But pick and choose carefully, since many restaurants in Cádiz are more used to serving a rough-and-ready fleet than tourists.

A MEAL FOR LESS THAN 1,065 PTAS. [$10]

LA ECONOMÍA, San Fernando, 2. Tel. 28-69-52.
   Cuisine: SPANISH. **Reservations:** Not required.
$ Prices: Appetizers 150–200 ptas. ($1.40–$1.90); main dishes 500–600 ptas. ($4.70–$5.65); fixed-priced menu 550 ptas. ($5.15). No credit cards.
   Open: Lunch Mon–Sat noon–4pm; dinner Mon–Sat 7:30–10:30pm.

⑤ A good budget choice, La Economía, at the northern edge of the old city, offers such fare as a plate of lentils, paella, macaroni, and fresh fish. A specialty is stewed bull's tail, and you might also try the seafood soup. The place has white tile walls and neon lights, and exudes a kind of budget charm all its own.

WORTH THE EXTRA BUCKS

EL ANTEOJO, Alameda de Apodaca, 22. Tel. 22-13-20.
   Cuisine: SPANISH. **Reservations:** Recommended.
$ Prices: Appetizers 750–1,200 ptas. ($7.05–$11.30); main dishes 1,400–2,000 ptas. ($13.15–$18.80). AE, DC, MC, V.
   Open: Lunch daily 1–5pm; dinner daily 8pm–midnight.
The ground-floor bar area here is so pleasantly decorated and the seafood tapas are so delicious that you might never get around to climbing upstairs to the dining room. There, however, the sea view proves to be only one of the pleasant surprises. The restaurant serves traditional Andalusian specialties, including tournedos, squid in its own ink, and a wide array of seafood. Dessert might be a chocolate soufflé. El Anteojo lies beside the seafront promenade flanking the northern edge of the old town, a short walk northwest of the Plaza de España.

MESÓN DEL DUQUE, 12 Paseo Marítimo, 12. Tel. 28-10-87.
   Cuisine: SPANISH. **Reservations:** Recommended.
$ Prices: Appetizers 650–1,000 ptas. ($6.10–$9.40); main dishes 1,500–2,100 ptas. ($14.10–$19.75); fixed-priced menu 1,500 ptas. ($14.10). AE, DC, MC, V.
   Open: Lunch daily 12:30–5:30pm; dinner daily 7:30pm–2am.
Within the rough-hewn walls of a corner of the Edificio Madrid, east of the old city and near the waterfront, guests at the air-conditioned Mesón del Duque enjoy what might be the most varied menu in Cádiz. Owner Arsenio Cueto makes daily visits to the town's food suppliers to secure the ingredients for his frequently changing house specialties, such as crayfish or dorado cooked in salt, crayfish with rice, and many other fish and meat dishes.

EVENING ENTERTAINMENT

BARS & A DISCO

EL PARISIÉN, Plaza San Francisco, 1. Tel. 22-18-30.

This turn-of-the-century bar near the Plaza de Mina is usually flooded with crowds of chattering locals enjoying well-prepared tapas and drinks. The kitchen prepares a delicious Russian salad and an *ensalada pescado* (fish salad). Open: Mon–Sat 9:30am–3pm and 5:30–10pm. Prices: Wine from 100 ptas. (95¢); tapas from 80–100 ptas. (75¢–95¢).

LA BOITE, Edificio Isecotel, Paseo Marítimo s/n. Tel. 26-13-16.
This is another one of those redecorated discos with recorded music that flourishes briefly throughout the south of Spain. This one is air-conditioned and draws a large crowd of Andalusian youth. It is in the old town on an avenue running alongside the Playa de la Victoria. Open: Daily 10pm–4am. Prices: Drinks 650 ptas. ($6.10).

LA CERVECERÍA DEL PUERTO, Zorrilla, 4. Tel. 22-18-37.
One of the most popular beer halls in town, La Cervecería del Puerto is usually loaded with an energetic crowd of drinkers who down large numbers of well-prepared tapas in addition to what is said to be the best brew in town. You'll find it west of the main port. Open: Thurs–Tues 11am–3:30pm and 7:30–11pm. Prices: Beer 100 ptas. (95¢); tapas from 100 ptas. (95¢).

EL MANTECA, Mariana Pineda, 66. Tel. 21-36-03.
This establishment's decor recalls the bullfight, as does that of many places in Cádiz. Homemade tapas are served, many made with fresh seafood. Open: Tues–Sat 8:30am–10pm; Sun–Mon 8:30am–4pm. Prices: Wine from 75 ptas. (70¢); tapas 100–300 ptas. (95¢–$2.80). **Bus:** 2 or 6.

---

6. COSTA DE LA LUZ

Isla Cristina, one of the coast's westernmost cities, lies 34 miles W of Huelva, 403 miles SW of Madrid; Tarifa, at the opposite end of the coast, lies 59 miles SE of Cádiz, 429 miles SW of Madrid

GETTING THERE By Train Huelva, the coast's most prominent city, is serviced by train from Seville (2 hours). From Huelva, trains continue on to Ayamonte and the rest of the Portuguese Algarve.

By Bus Buses run from Seville several times a day. From Seville, connections can be made to all parts of Spain. From Huelva, about 8 buses a day depart for Ayamonte and the Portuguese frontier.

By Car Huelva is easily reached from Seville, 55 miles (88.5km) to the east (1 hour), via a broad and modern highway, the E-01.

ESSENTIALS The area code for the Costa de la Luz is 955. The Tourist Information Office is in Huelva at Vázquez López, 5 (tel. 955/25-74-03).

West of Cádiz, near Huelva and the Portuguese frontier, lies the rapidly developing Costa de la Luz (Coast of Light), which hopes to pick up the overflow from the Costa del Sol. The Luz coast stretches from the mouth of the Guadiana River, forming the boundary with Portugal, to Tarifa Point on the Straits of Gibraltar. Dotting the coast are long stretches of sand, pine trees, fishing cottages, and lazy whitewashed villages.

The Huelva district forms the northwestern half of the Costa de la Luz. The southern half stretches from Tarifa to **Sanlúcar de Barrameda,** the spot from which Magellan, in 1519, embarked on his voyage around the globe. Columbus also made this his home port for his third journey to the New World. Sanlúcar today is widely known in Andalusia for its local sherry, Manzanilla, which you can order at any of the city's wine cellars (bodegas). If you make it to Sanlúcar, you'll find the Tourist Information Office at Calzada de Ejército, Paseo Marítimo, just 1 block inland from the beach. Do not count on a great deal of guidance, however. To travel between the northern and southern portions of the Costa de la Luz, you must go inland to Seville, since no roads go across the Coto Doñana and the marshland near the mouth of the Guadalquivir.

At **Huelva** a large statue on the west bank of the river commemorates the departure of Christopher Columbus on his third voyage of discovery; and about 4½ miles (7.2km) up on the east bank of the Tinto River, a monument marks the exact spot of his departure. His ships were anchored off this bank while they were being loaded with supplies.

South of Huelva is the **Monasterio de la Rabida** (tel. 35-04-11), in whose little white chapel Columbus prayed for success on the eve of his voyage. (The chapel may be visited.) Even without the connections to Columbus, the monastery would be worth a visit for its paintings and frescoes. A guide will show you around the Mudejar chapel and a large portion of the old monastery, which is open daily from 10am to 1pm and 4 to 7pm. Admission is free, but donations are accepted. The monastery lies on the east bank of the Tinto. Take bus no. 1 from Huelva.

WHERE TO STAY

The resort town of **Isla Cristina,** to the West of Huelva, is almost an island, surrounded as it is by the estuaries at the mouth of the Guadiana River. **Ayamonte,** even farther west, is the older resort—and the more interesting and colorful town. It was built on the slopes of a hill on which a castle stood. Both Isla Cristina and Ayamonte are full of beach high-rises, which, for the most part, contain vacation apartments for Spaniards in July and August. Judging by their license plates, most of these visitors come from Huelva, Seville, and Madrid, so the Costa de la Luz is more Spanish in flavor than the overrun and more international Costa del Sol.

Many readers find it hard to choose between Isla Cristina and Ayamonte. Both have clean, wide, sandy beaches, and the waves, for the most part, are calm. Portions of the beaches are even calmer because of sand bars some 55 to 110 yards from the shore, which become virtual islands at low tide.

The fishing harbor at Isla Cristina is uniquely beautiful, and the town is within walking distance of the beach, whereas in Ayamonte the town is miles from its beaches, Isla Canela and Moral. Accommodations are severely limited along the Costa de la Luz in summer, and it's crucial to arrive with a reservation. You can stay at a government-run parador east of Huelva in Mazagón (see below), at Isla Cristina, or at Ayamonte, near the Portuguese frontier. Where you are unlikely to want to stay overnight is in the dreary industrial port of Huelva itself.

HOTEL PATO AZUL, Gran Vía, 43, 21410 Isla Cristina. Tel. 955/31-12-50. 55 rms (all with bath). TEL
$ Rates: 4,600 ptas. ($43.25) single; 5,300 ptas. ($49.80) double. Breakfast 290 ptas. ($2.75) extra. AE, DC, MC, V.
The Pato Azul, near the town center in Isla Cristina, is quite comfortable, and the staff is pleasant. The rooms are basic, but inexpensive, and you'll enjoy the swimming pool. Open from May to September.

PARADOR NACIONAL CRISTÓBAL COLÓN, Carretera de Matalascañas s/n, 21130 Mazagón. Tel. 955/37-60-00. Fax 955/37-62-28. 43 rms (all with bath). A/C MINIBAR TV TEL **Directions:** Exit from Magazón's eastern sector, following the signs to the town Matalascañas. Take the coast road (highway 442) to the parador.
$ Rates: 9,300 ptas. ($87.40) single; 11,500 ptas. ($108.10) double. Breakfast 900 ptas. ($8.45) extra. AE, DC, MC, V.

One of the best accommodations in the area is 12 miles (19.3km) from Huelva and 4 miles (6.5km) from the center of Mazagón. A rambling modern structure, the parador has comfortable rooms with balconies and terraces overlooking a tranquil, expansive garden and pine groves that slope down to the white-sand beach of Mazagón. Swimmers and sunbathers can also enjoy the large pool. The dining room offers a set menu for 2,900 pesetas ($27.25).

PARADOR NACIONAL COSTA DE LA LUZ, El Castillito, 21400 Ayamonte. Tel. 955/32-07-00. 20 rms (all with bath). A/C MINIBAR TV TEL
Directions: From the center of Ayamonte, signs indicating the location of the parador will lead you up a winding road to the hilltop, about ½ mile southeast of the center.
$ Rates: 9,300 ptas. ($87.40) single; 11,500 ptas. ($108.10) double. Breakfast 900 ptas. ($8.45) extra. AE, DC, MC, V.

The leading accommodation in Ayamonte, this parador closed in 1990 for renovations, but is slated to reopen in 1991. Commanding a sweeping view of the river and the surrounding towns along its banks—don't miss the memorable sunsets here—the parador stands about 100 feet above sea level on the site of the old castle of Ayamonte. Built in a severe modern style, with Nordic-inspired furnishings, it numbers among its facilities a swimming pool, a garden, central heating, a dining room, and a bar. Good regional meals cost from 2,900 pesetas ($27.25). Try, if featured, the *raya en pimiento* (ray with red pepper); the *calamar relleno* (stuffed squid) is another specialty.

WHERE TO EAT

Isla Cristina has many bars and outdoor cafés serving tapas or desserts. But since most vacationers eat at their hotels or in their apartments, there are only a few restaurants.

RESTAURANTE ACOSTA, Plaza del Caudillo, 13, Isla Cristina. Tel. 33-14-20.
Cuisine: SPANISH. **Reservations:** Recommended.
$ Prices: Appetizers 650–1,000 ptas. ($6.10–$9.40); main dishes 1,200–1,900 ptas. ($11.30–$17.85); fixed-priced menu 1,000 ptas. ($9.40). AE, DC, MC, V.
Open: Lunch Tues–Sun 1:30–4pm; dinner Tues–Sun 9pm–midnight.

Near the village church in the town center is one of Isla Cristina's best restaurants for well-prepared seafood. Acosta specializes in seafood soup, oven-baked tuna, Andalusian meat stew, and several veal dishes. Service is polite and efficient.

7. RONDA

63 miles NE of Algeciras, 60 miles W of Málaga,
91 miles SE of Seville, and 367 miles S of Madrid

GETTING THERE   By Train   There are 3 trains daily from Málaga (2 hours), 2 per day from Seville (4½ hours), and 2 per day from Granada (4 hours). Most rail routes into Ronda require a change of train in the railway junction of Bobadilla, several miles to the northeast. Ronda's railway station lies in the western edge of the new city, on the Avenida Andalucía (tel. 87-16-73).

By Bus   There are 4 buses daily between Ronda and Seville (3 hours), 2 per day to Málaga (1 hour), 3 per day to Jerez de la Frontera (2½ hours), 6 per day to Marbella, and 1 daily to and from Cádiz. The bus station in Ronda lies on the western edge of the new town, at Avenida Concepción García Redondo, 2 (tel. 87-22-64).

By Car   Five highways converge on Ronda from all parts of Andalusia. All five head through mountainous scenery, but the road south to Marbella, through the Sierra

Palmitera, is one of the most winding and dangerous. Driving time to Marbella, depending on your nerves and the traffic, is between 1 and 1½ hours.

ESSENTIALS The area code for Ronda is 952. The Tourist Information Office is at Plaza de España, 1 (tel. 952/87-12-72).

This little town, high in the Serranía de Ronda Mountains (2,300 feet above sea level), is one of the oldest and most aristocratic places in Spain, but the main tourist attraction is the 500-foot **gorge,** spanned by a Roman stone bridge, Puente San Miguel, over the Guadelevín River. On both sides of this "hole in the earth" are cliff-hanging houses, which look as if—with the slightest push—they would plunge into the chasm.

Ronda is an incredible sight. The road there, once difficult to navigate, is now a wide highway with guard rails. The town and the surrounding mountains were legendary hideouts for bandits and smugglers, but today the Guardia Civil has almost put an end to that occupation.

The gorge divides the town into an older part, the Moorish and aristocratic quarter, and the newer section south of the gorge, built principally after the Reconquest. The old quarter is by far the more fascinating; it contains narrow, rough streets, and buildings with a marked Moorish influence (watch for the minaret). After the lazy resort living of the Costa del Sol, a side excursion to Ronda, with its unique beauty and refreshing mountain air, is a tonic.

Ronda is great for the explorer. Native children may attach themselves to you as guides. For a few pesetas it might be worth it, since it's difficult to weave your way in and out of the narrow streets.

WHAT TO SEE & DO

The still-functioning **Baños Arabes** are reached from the turnoff to the Puente San Miguel. Dating from the 13th century, the baths have glass roof-windows and hump-shaped cupolas. They are generally open Tuesday through Sunday from 10am to 1pm and 4 to 7pm. Admission is free, but you should tip the caretaker who shows you around.

The **Palacio de Mondragón,** El Campillo, was once the private home of one of the ministers to Charles III. Flanked by two Mudejar towers, it now has a baroque façade. Inside are Moorish mosaics. Posted hours are daily from 8am to 2pm, but be advised that the place is often closed. Admission is free.

The **Casa del Rey Moro,** Marqués de Parada, 17, is misnamed. The House of the Moorish King was actually built in the early 1700s. However, it is believed to have been constructed over Moorish foundations. The interior is closed, but from the garden you can take an underground stairway, called La Mina, which leads you to the river, a distance of 365 steps. Christian slaves cut these steps in the 14th century to guarantee a steady water supply in case Ronda came under siege.

On the same street you'll see the 18th-century **Palacio del Marqués de Salvatierra.** Still inhabited by a private family, this Renaissance-style mansion is open for guided tours. Tours depart every 30 minutes, provided half a dozen people are present. It's open Monday through Wednesday and Friday and Saturday from 11am to 2pm and 4 to 7pm, on Sunday from 11am to 1pm. Admission is 150 pesetas ($1.40).

Ronda has the oldest bullring in Spain. Built in the 1700s, the **Plaza de Toros** is the setting for the yearly Goyesque Corrida in honor of Ronda native son Pedro Romero, one of the greatest bullfighters of all time. If you want to know more about Ronda bullfighting, head for the **Museo Taurino,** reached through the ring, open daily from 10am to 2pm and 4 to 6pm, charging 200 pesetas ($1.90) for admission. Exhibits document the exploits of the noted Romero family. Francisco invented the killing sword and the *muleta,* and his grandson, Pedro (1754–1839), killed 5,600 bulls during his 30-year career. Pedro was the inspiration for Goya's famous *Tauromaquia* series. There are also exhibits devoted to Cayetano Ordóñez, the matador immortalized by Hemingway in *The Sun Also Rises*.

A NEARBY ATTRACTION

Near Benaoján, the **Cueva de la Pileta** (tel. 16-72-02), 15½ miles (25km) southwest of Ronda, plus a 1¼-mile (2km) hard climb, has been compared to the Caves of Altamira in northern Spain, where prehistoric paintings were discovered toward the end of the 19th century. In a wild, beautiful area known as the Serranía de Ronda, this cave was discovered in 1905 by José Bullón Lobato, grandfather of the present owners. More than a mile in length and filled with oddly and beautifully shaped stalagmites and stalactites, the cave was found to contain five fossilized human and two animal skeletons.

In the mysterious darkness, prehistoric paintings have been discovered, depicting animals in yellow, red, black, and ochre, as well as mysterious symbols. One of the highlights of the tour is a trip to the "chamber of the fish," containing a wall painting of a great black seal-like creature about 3 feet long. This chamber, the innermost heart of the cave, ends in a precipice that drops vertically nearly 250 feet.

In the valley just below the cave lives a guide who will conduct you around the chambers, carrying artificial light to illuminate the paintings. Plan to spend at least an hour here. The cost is a well-spent 300 pesetas ($2.80). Daily hours are 9am to 2pm and 4 to 7pm.

You can reach the cave most easily by car from Ronda, but those without private transport can take the train to Benaoján. The cave, whose entrance is at least 4 miles (6.5km) uphill, is located in the rocky foothills of the Sierra de Libar, midway between two tiny villages: Jimera de Libar and Benaoján. The valley that contains the cave is parallel to the valley holding Ronda, so the town of Ronda and the cave are separated by a steep range of hills, requiring a rather complicated detour either to the south or north of Ronda, then a doubling back.

WHERE TO STAY

HOSTAL BIARRITZ, Cristo, 7, 29400 Ronda. Tel. 952/87-29-10. 18 rms (5 with bath).

$ Rates: 1,400 ptas. ($13.15) single without bath, 2,800 ptas. ($26.30) single with bath; 2,200 ptas. ($20.70) double without bath, 2,800 ptas. ($26.30) double with bath. Breakfast 275 ptas. ($2.60) extra. No credit cards.

Despite its chic name, this is not an upscale hotel—rather, one of the better bargains in town. In the lobby an aquarium is the only adornment. The bedrooms are simple, plain, and well maintained, although lacking such amenities as phones and TVs. Meals, costing from 850 pesetas ($8), are also served. The Biarritz is located in the Mercadillo, the modern section of town.

HOSTAL RESIDENCIA ROYAL, Virgen de la Paz, 42, 29400 Ronda. Tel. 952/87-11-41. 29 rms (all with bath). A/C TEL

$ Rates: 2,400 ptas. ($22.55) single; 3,800 ptas. ($35.70) double. Breakfast 150 ptas. ($1.40) extra. AE, DC, MC, V.

A good value for those who want to spend the night in the modern section, the Residencia Royal stands near the old bull arena. Each of the comfortably conservative rooms is reasonably well furnished; bedrooms in the rear tend to be noisy. The staff is polite and helpful.

HOTEL RESIDENCIA POLO, Mariano Souvirón, 8, 29400 Ronda. Tel. 952/87-24-47. 33 rms (all with bath). TEL

$ Rates: 5,500 ptas. ($51.70) single; 7,500 ptas. ($70.50) double. Breakfast 450 ptas. ($4.25) extra. AE, DC, MC, V.

In the commercial, modern heart of Ronda, near a large shopping arcade, the Polo is run with professionalism. Its accommodations are pleasantly—not elegantly—decorated and maintained. Bedrooms are spacious, with even the closets and private bathrooms large enough for your needs. A good value.

HOTEL REINA VICTORIA, Paseo Dr. Fleming, 25, 29400 Ronda. Tel. 952/87-12-40. 88 rms (all with bath). A/C TEL
$ Rates: 6,500 ptas. ($61.10) single; 10,000 ptas. ($94) double. Breakfast 600 ptas. ($5.65) extra. AE, DC, MC, V.

Similar to an English country house, this hotel was in fact built by an Englishman in 1906. It's at the edge of town near the bullring, with terraces that hang right over the 490-foot precipice.

Hemingway frequently visited the hotel, suggesting that it was ideal for a honeymoon, "or if you ever bolt with anyone." But the Reina Victoria is known best as the place where poet Rainer Maria Rilke wrote *The Spanish Trilogy.* His third-floor room has been set aside as a museum, with first editions, manuscripts, photographs, and even a framed copy of his hotel bill. A life-size bronze statue of the poet stands in a corner of the hotel garden.

The bedrooms are big, airy, and comfortable, and some have complete living rooms with sofas, chairs, and tables. Many also have private terraces with garden furniture. The beds are sumptuous, and the bathrooms boast all the latest improvements.

Dining here can be recommended. The food is well prepared, and a set meal costs 2,500 pesetas ($23.50).

WHERE TO EAT

MESÓN SANTIAGO, Marina, 3. Tel. 87-15-59.
    Cuisine: SPANISH. **Reservations:** Not required.
$ Prices: Appetizers 600–1,200 ptas. ($5.65–$11.30); main dishes 1,400–2,000 ptas. ($13.15–$18.80); fixed-priced menu 1,600 ptas. ($15.05). AE, DC, MC, V.
    Open: Lunch daily noon–4:30pm.

Santiago Ruíz Gil operates one of the best budget restaurants in Ronda, serving lunch only. A three-course *menú del día,* with bread and wine, is not a bad deal, considering the price. If you order from the *especialidades de la casa,* count on spending more. Try the *caldo de cocido,* a savory stew with large pieces of meat cooked with such vegetables as garbanzos and white beans, almost a meal in itself. You might also like the tongue cooked in wine and served with potato salad. All the servings are generous. The more expensive à la carte menu is likely to include partridge, lamb, mountain trout, and regional meats. Fresh asparagus and succulent strawberries are also available in season. The Mesón Santiago is located near the Plaza del Socorro.

DON MIGUEL RESTAURANT, Villanueva, 4. Tel. 87-10-90.
    Cuisine: SPANISH. **Reservations:** Not required.
$ Prices: Appetizers 750–1,700 ptas. ($7.05–$16); main dishes 1,400–2,100 ptas. ($13.15–$19.75). AE, DC, MC, V.
    Open: Lunch daily 12:30–4pm; dinner daily 8–11pm. **Closed:** Last 2 weeks in Jan; Sun in summer; Wed in winter.

At the end of the bridge, facing the river, this restaurant allows visitors views of the upper gorge. It has enough tables set outside on two levels to seat 300 people, and in summer this is a bustling place. The food is good, the rest rooms are clean, and the waiters are polite and speak enough English to get by. There is also a pleasant bar for drinks and tapas. Try one of the seafood selections, or the house specialty, stewed bull's tail.

PEDRO ROMERO, Virgen de la Paz, 18. Tel. 87-10-61.

Cuisine: SPANISH. **Reservations:** Required on day of corrida.

$ Prices: Appetizers 750–1,200 ptas. ($7.05–$11.30); main dishes 1,400–2,100 ptas. ($13.15–$19.75). AE, DC, MC, V.

Open: Lunch daily 1–4pm; dinner daily 8–11pm.

Named after Francisco Romero, who codified the rules of bullfighting, this restaurant attracts aficionados. In fact, it stands opposite the ring and gets extremely busy on bullfight days, when it's almost impossible to get a table. (The location is also just down the way from the recommended Hostal Residencia Royal.) While seated under a stuffed bull's head, surrounded by photographs of young matadors, you might begin your meal with the classic garlic soup.

---

8. GRANADA

258 miles S of Madrid, 76 miles NE of Málaga

GETTING THERE By Plane Iberia flies to Granada once or twice daily from Barcelona and Madrid; several times a week from Palma de Mallorca; 3 times a week from Valencia; and every Thursday from Tenerife in the Canary Islands. To phone Iberia at Granada's airport, 10 miles (16km) west of the center of town, dial 23-33-22. A more convenient ticketing office lies 2 blocks east of the cathedral, at Plaza Isabel la Católica, 2 (tel. 22-14-52). A shuttle bus departs several times daily, connecting this office with the airport.

By Train Three trains connect Granada with Madrid's Atocha Railway Station daily (7 to 8½ hours). Trains run twice daily from Seville (5 hours). Many connections to the rest of Spain are funneled through the railway junction at Bobadilla, a 2-hour ride to the west. The train station (tel. 23-34-08) in Granada lies in the modern part of town, about 1 mile (1.6km) northwest of the cathedral, on the Avenida Andaluces (a short street radiating to the south of the very prominent Avenida Calvo Sotelo); bus no. 11 runs into the old city. For information and tickets, head for the RENFE office, Reyes Católicos, 63 (tel. 22-34-97), about 1 block south of the cathedral.

By Bus Most of Granada's long-range buses arrive and depart from the Bacoma Company's terminal, Avenida Andaluces, 12, a few steps from the train station. Buses arrive from Barcelona 3 times a day, from Valencia and Alicante 4 times a day, and from Madrid 5 times a day. Buses from closer destinations in Andalusia arrive at the Alsina Graells Company's terminal, Camino de Ronda, 97 (tel. 25-13-58), a small street radiating out from the larger Calle Emperatriz Eugenia. Buses arrive from Almería 4 times a day; from Córdoba 5 times a day; from Málaga about a dozen times a day; and from Seville about 8 times a day. Bus no. 11 services both stations.

By Car Granada is connected by superhighway to both Madrid, Málaga, and Seville. Driving time from Madrid is about 8 hours. Many sightseers prefer to make this drive in two days, rather than one. If that is your plan, Jaén makes a perfect stopover.

ESSENTIALS The area code for Granada is 958. The Tourist Information Office is at Plaza de Mariana Pineda, 10 (tel. 958/22-66-88). Granada lies 2,200 feet above sea level. It sprawls over two main hills, the Alhambra and the Albaicín, and it is crossed by two rivers, the Genil and the Darro.

CITY LAYOUT The **Cuesta de Gomérez** is one of the most important streets in Granada. It climbs uphill from the Plaza Nueva, the center of the modern city, to the Alhambra. At the Plaza Nueva the east–west artery, the **Calle de los Reyes Católicos,** goes to the heart of the 19th-century city and the towers of the cathedral. The main street of Granada is the **Gran Vía de Colón,** the principal north–south artery.

IMPRESSIONS

One should remember Granada as one should remember a sweetheart who has died.
—FEDERICO GARCÍA LORCA

The Calle de los Reyes Católicos and the Gran Vía de Colón meet at the circular **Plaza de Isabel la Católica,** graced by a bronze statue of the queen offering Columbus the Santa Fe agreement, which granted the rights to the epochal voyage to the New World.

Going west, the Calle de los Reyes Católicos passes near the cathedral and other major sights in the "downtown" section of Granada. The street runs to the **Puerta Real,** which is the commercial hub of Granada, with many stores, hotels, cafés, and restaurants.

This former stronghold of Moorish Spain, in the foothills of the snowcapped Sierra Nevada mountain range, is full of romance and folklore. Washington Irving (*Tales of the Alhambra*) used the symbol of this city, the pomegranate (*granada*), to conjure up a spirit of romance. In fact, the name probably derives from the Moorish word *Karnattah.* Some historians have suggested that it comes from Garnatha Alyehud, the name of an old Jewish ghetto.

Washington Irving may have helped publicize the glories of Granada to the English-speaking world, but in Spain the city is known for its ties to another writer: Federico García Lorca. Born in 1898, this Spanish poet and dramatist, whose masterpiece was *The House of Bernarda Alba,* was shot by soldiers in 1936 in the first months of the Spanish Civil War. During Franco's rule García Lorca's works were banned in Spain, but happily, that situation has changed and he is once again honored in Granada, where he grew up.

WHAT TO SEE & DO

Try to spend some time walking around Old Granada. Plan on about 3 hours to see the most interesting sights.

The **Puerta de Elvira** is the gate through which Ferdinand and Isabella made their triumphant entry into Granada in 1492. It was once a grisly place, with the rotting heads of executed criminals hanging from its portals. The quarter surrounding the gate was the Arab section (*morería*), until all the Arabs were driven out of the city after the Reconquest.

One of the most fascinating streets in Granada is the **Calle de Elvira,** west of which the Albaicín, or old Arab quarter, rises on a hill. In the 17th and 18th centuries, artisans occupied the shops and ateliers along this street and those radiating from it. Come here if you're looking for antiques.

Perhaps the most-walked street in Granada is the **Carrera del Darro,** running north along the Darro River. It was discovered by the Romantic artists of the 19th century; many of their etchings (subsequently engraved) of scenes along this street were widely circulated, doing much to spread the fame of Granada throughout Europe. You can still find some of these old engravings in the musty antique shops. The Carrera del Darro ends at the **Paseo de los Tristes (Avenue of the Sad Ones),** so named for the funeral cortèges that used to go by here on the way to the cemetery.

On the Calle de Elvira stands the **Iglesia de San Andrés,** begun in 1528, with its Mudejar bell tower. Much of the church was destroyed in the early 19th century. Inside are several interesting pieces of art, both paintings and sculptures. Another old church in this area is the **Iglesia de Santiago,** constructed in 1501 and dedicated to St. James, patron saint of Spain. Built on the site of an Arab mosque, it was damaged in the 1884 earthquake that struck Granada. The church contains the tomb of architect Diego de Siloé (1495–1563), who did much to change the face of Granada.

Despite its name, the oldest square in Granada is the **Plaza Nueva,** which, under the Muslims, was the site of the "bridge of the woodcutters." The Darro River was covered over here, but its waters still flow underneath the square (which in Franco's time was named Plaza del General Franco). On the east side of the Plaza Nueva is the 16th-century **Iglesia de Santa Ana,** built by Siloé. Inside its five-nave interior you can see a Churrigueresque reredos and coffered ceiling.

ALHAMBRA, Palacio de Carlos V. Tel. 22-75-25.

⭐ When you first see the Alhambra, you may be surprised by its somewhat somber exterior. You have to walk across the threshold to discover the true delights of this Moorish palace.

Tickets are sold in the office next to the uncompleted palace of the Habsburg king Charles V. Enter through the incongruous 14th-century Gateway to Justice. Most visitors do not need an expensive guide, but will be content to stroll through the richly ornamented open-air rooms, with their lacelike walls and their courtyards with fountains. Many of the Arabic inscriptions translate as "Only Allah is conqueror."

The most-photographed part of the palace is the Court of Lions, named after its highly stylized fountain. This was the heart of the palace, the most private section, where the sultan enjoyed his harem. Opening onto the court are the Hall of the Two Sisters, where the favorite of the moment was kept, and the Gossip Room, a factory of intrigue. In the dancing room in the Hall of Kings, entertainment was provided nightly to amuse the sultan's party. Eunuchs guarded the harem, but apparently not too well—one sultan, according to legend, beheaded 36 Moorish princes here because one of them was suspected of having been intimate with his favorite.

You can see the room where Washington Irving lived (in the chambers of Charles V) while he was compiling his *Tales of the Alhambra*—the best known of which is the legend of Zayda, Zorayada, and Zorahayda, the three beautiful princesses who fell in love with three captured Spanish soldiers outside "La Torre de las Infantas." Irving did more than any other writer to publicize the Alhambra to the English-speaking world.

Irving credits the French with saving the Alhambra for posterity, but in fact they were responsible for blowing up seven of the towers in 1812, and it was a Spanish soldier who cut the fuse before more damage could be done. When the Duke of Wellington arrived a few years later, he chased out the chickens, the Gypsies, and the transient beggars who were using the Alhambra as a tenement, and set up housekeeping here himself.

Charles V may have been horrified when he saw the cathedral placed in the middle of the great mosque at Córdoba, but he is responsible for architectural meddling here himself, building a Renaissance palace at the Alhambra—although it's quite beautiful, it's terribly out of place. Today it houses the **Museo Bellas Artes en la Alhambra** (tel. 22-48-43), open Monday through Friday from 10am to 2pm. It also shelters the **Museo Hispano-Musulman en la Alhambra** (tel. 22-62-79), devoted to Hispanic-Muslim art.

Admission: Comprehensive ticket, including Alhambra and Generalife, 475 ptas. ($4.45); Museo Bellas Artes 250 ptas. ($2.35); Museo Hispano-Musulman 250 ptas. ($2.35). Illuminated visits: 350 ptas. ($3.30).

Open: May–Aug Mon–Sat 9am–7:45pm; Sun 9am–6pm; Sept–Apr Mon–Sat 9:30am–6pm, Sun 9:30am–5:30pm. Illuminated visits: Wed and Sat 10pm–midnight. **Bus:** 2. **Directions:** Later enriched by Moorish occupants into a lavish palace, the Alhambra was originally constructed for defensive purposes atop a rocky outcropping on a hilltop above the Darro River. The modern city of Granada was built across the river from the Alhambra, about a half mile from its western foundations.

Many visitors opt for a taxi or bus no. 2. But some hardy souls enjoy the uphill climb from the cathedral, Plaza de la Lonja, to the Alhambra (signs indicate the winding roads and the steps that lead there). If you decide to walk, enter the Alhambra via the Cuesta de Gomérez, which, although steep, is the quickest and shortest pedestrian route. It begins at the Plaza Nueva, about 4 blocks east of the cathedral, and goes steeply uphill to the Puerta de las Granadas, the first of two gates to the Alhambra. The second, another 200 yards uphill, is the Puerta de la Justicia, which accepts 90% of the touristic visits to the Alhambra. Here you'll find a large parking lot, lots of Gypsies willing and able to guide you (or pick your pocket), lines of taxis, and some souvenir and refreshment stands.

GENERALIFE, Alhambra, Cerro de Sol. Tel. 22-75-32.

✪ The sultans used to spend their summers in this palace (pronounced hay-nay-rahl-ee-fay), safely locked away with their harems. Built in the 13th century to overlook the Alhambra, the Generalife depends for its glory on its gardens and courtyards. Don't expect an Alhambra in miniature: The Generalife was always meant to be a retreat, even from the splendors of the Alhambra. This palace was the setting for Irving's story of the prince locked away from love.

Admission: Comprehensive ticket, including Alhambra and Generalife, 475 ptas. ($4.45).

Open: See Alhambra, above. **Directions:** Exit from Alhambra via Puerta de la Justicia, then circumnavigate Alhambra's southern foundations until you reach gardens of summer palace, where Paseo de los Cipreses quickly leads you to main building of Generalife.

CATEDRAL AND CAPILLA REAL, Plaza de la Lonja, Gran Vía de Colón, 5. Tel. 22-29-59.

✪ This richly ornate Spanish Renaissance cathedral, with its spectacular altar, is one of the country's great architectural highlights, acclaimed for its beautiful façade and gold-and-white decor. It was begun in 1521 and completed in 1714.

Behind the cathedral (entered separately) is the flamboyant Gothic Royal Chapel (tel. 22-92-32), where lie the remains of Queen Isabella and her husband, Ferdinand. It was their wish to be buried in recaptured Granada, not Castile or Aragón. The coffins are remarkably tiny—a reminder of how short people used to be. Accenting the tombs is a wrought-iron grill, a masterpiece. Occupying much larger tombs are the remains of their daughter, Joan the Mad, and her husband, Philip the Handsome. The cathedral lies in the center of Granada, off two prominent streets, the Gran Vía de Colón and the Calle de San Jerónimo. The Capilla Real abuts the cathedral's eastern edge.

Admission: Cathedral 150 ptas. ($1.40); chapel 150 ptas. ($1.40).

Open: Cathedral and chapel, daily 10:30am–1pm and 4–7pm.

ALBAICÍN

This old Arab quarter, on one of the two main hills of Granada, doesn't belong to the city of 19th-century buildings and wide boulevards. It, and the surrounding Gypsy caves of Sacromonte, are holdovers from the past. The Albaicín once flourished as the residential section of the Moors, even after the city's reconquest, but it fell into decline when the Christians drove them out. This narrow labyrinth of crooked streets escaped the fate of much of Granada, which was torn down in the name of progress. Fortunately, it has been preserved, as have its cisterns, fountains, plazas, whitewashed houses, villas, and the decaying remnants of the old city gate. Here and there, one catches a glimpse of a private patio filled with fountains and plants, a traditional elegant way of life that continues.

Bus: 7 to Calle de Pagés.

LA CARTUJA, Carrera Alfacar, s/n. Tel. 20-19-32.

This 16th-century monastery, off the Albaicín on the outskirts of Granada, is sometimes called "the Christian answer to the Alhambra" because of its ornate stucco and marble and the baroque Churrigueresque fantasy in the sacristy. Its most notable paintings are by Bocanegra, its outstanding sculpture by Mora. The church of this

Carthusian monastery was decorated with baroque stucco in the 17th century. Don't miss the 18th-century sacristy, an excellent example of latter-day baroque style. Napoleon's armies killed St. Bruno here, and La Cartuja is said to be the only monument of its kind in the world. Sometimes one of the Carthusian monks will take you on a guided tour.

Admission: 150 ptas. ($1.40).

Open: Daily 10am–1pm and 4–7pm. **Bus:** No. 8 from cathedral.

HUERTA DE SAN VICENTE, Virgen Blanca, 6, Fuentevuaqueros. Tel. 25-84-66.

Poet Federico García Lorcá spent many happy summers with his family here at their vacation home. He had moved to Granada in 1909, a dreamy-eyed schoolboy, and he was endlessly fascinated with its life, including the Alhambra and the Gypsies, whom he was later to describe compassionately in his *Gypsy Ballads*. You can look out at the Alhambra from a balcony of the house, which is decorated with green trim and grillwork, and filled with family memorabilia, including furniture and portraits. Visitors may inspect the poet's upstairs bedroom and see his oak desk stained with ink. Look for the white stool that he carried to the terrace to watch the sun set over Granada. The house lies in the Fuentevaqueros section of Granada, near the airport.

Admission: 100 ptas. (95¢).

Open: Apr–Sept 10am–2pm and 6–9pm; Oct–Mar Tues–Sun 10am–1pm and 4–6pm. (*Warning:* Check with tourist office to see if it's open before going there.)

CASA MUSEO DE MANUEL DE FALLA, Antequeruela Alta, 11. Tel. 22-94-21.

The famous Spanish composer Manuel de Falla, known for his strongly individualized works, came to live in Granada in 1919, hoping to find a retreat and inspiration. He moved into a *carmen* (local dialect for a small white house) just below the Alhambra, and in time befriended García Lorca. In 1922 on the grounds of the Alhambra, they staged the Cante Jondo Festival, the purest expression of flamenco. Today visitors can walk through the gardens of the man who wrote such works as *Nights in the Gardens of Spain* and see his collection of handcrafts and ceramics, along with other personal memorabilia.

Admission: Free.

Open: Tues–Sun 10am–2pm and 4–6pm.

BAÑOS ARABES, Carrera del Darro, 31.

These Arab baths were called by the Moors the "baths of the walnut tree." Among the oldest buildings still standing in Granada, and among the best-preserved Muslim baths in Spain, they predate the Alhambra. Supposedly Visigothic and Roman building materials went into their construction. It is considered remarkable that they escaped destruction during the reign of the so-called Catholic Kings (Ferdinand and Isabella).

IN THEIR FOOTSTEPS

Federico García Lorca (1898–1936). The most written about Spanish writer since Cervantes, this playwright, poet, and musician was brutally murdered by Nationalist soldiers during the Spanish Civil War. A tortured homosexual, born in Granada, he worked in vagabond theater, called *La Barraca*. In 1928, he created his masterpiece *Gypsy Ballads*. He visited New York that year and wrote two famous works, *Nueva York* and *The Odes to the King of Harlem*. *The House of Bernarda Alba* brought him world fame. Lorca today, next to Cervantes, is the most translated Spanish writer of all time.

• **Favorite Haunt:** Huerta de San Vicente, Granada.

Admission: Free.
Open: Daily 9am–6pm.

CASA DE CASTRIL, Museo Arqueológico, Carrera del Darro, 41. Tel. 22-55-90.
This building has always been considered one of the handsomest Renaissance palaces in Granada. The Plateresque façade of 1539 has been attributed to Diego de Siloé. In 1869 it was converted into a museum with a collection of artifacts found in the area.
Admission: 150 ptas. ($1.40).
Open: Tues–Sun 10am–2pm.

WHERE TO STAY

DOUBLES FOR LESS THAN 9,500 PTAS. [$89.30]

HOSTAL CALIFORNIA, Cuesta de Gomérez, 37, 18009 Granada. Tel. 958/22-40-56. 10 rms (5 with bath). TEL **Bus:** 2.
$ Rates: 1,300 ptas. ($12.20) single without bath; 2,400 ptas. ($22.55) double without bath, 2,800 ptas. ($26.30) double with bath. Breakfast 250 ptas. ($2.35) extra. No credit cards.

S The Hostal California is often passed by as people whiz up the hill toward the Alhambra. But don't miss it (on your left) if you want an inexpensive and typically Spanish accommodation. It's run in an informal, familylike manner, totally unlike a hotel. The bedrooms, though simply furnished, are well kept. A set lunch or dinner is available for 750 pesetas ($7.05).

HOSTAL CARLOS V, Plaza de los Campos Eliseos, 4, 18009 Granada. Tel. 958/22-15-87. 28 rms (all with bath). TEL
$ Rates: 2,900 ptas. ($27.25) single; 4,900 ptas. ($46.05) double. Breakfast 350 ptas. ($3.30) extra. No credit cards.
This unpretentious, comfortable hotel on an upper floor has several rooms with balconies that provide spectacular views of the city. You're expected to have some meals in the hotel—1,200 pesetas ($11.30) for lunch or dinner. The owner says he has special accommodations for four people.

MACÍA, Plaza Nueva, 4. 18010 Granada. Tel. 958/22-75-36. 40 rms (all with bath). TEL
$ Rates: 3,800 ptas. ($35.70) single; 5,800 ptas. ($54.50) double. Breakfast 350 ptas. ($3.30) extra. AE, DC, MC, V.
An attractive modern hotel, at the bottom of the hill leading to the Alhambra, the Macía is a real bargain for what should be a three-star hotel. All rooms have heating, and are clean and functional. About 30% have air conditioning. Breakfast is the only meal served.

HOSTAL AMÉRICA, Real de la Alhambra, 53, 18009 Granada. Tel. 958/22-74-71. Fax 958/22-74-70. 13 rms (all with bath). TEL **Bus:** 2.
$ Rates: 4,500 ptas. ($42.30) single; 7,000 ptas. ($65.80) double. Breakfast 550 ptas. ($5.15) extra. **Closed:** Nov–Feb.
Located within the ancient Alhambra walls, this is one of the leading boarding houses of Granada. Walk through the covered entryway of this former villa into the shady patio—lively yet intimate, with large trees, potted plants, and ferns. Other plants cascade down the white plaster walls and entwine with the ornate grillwork. Garden chairs and tables are set out for home-cooked Spanish meals. The living room of this homey little retreat is graced with a collection of regional decorative objects; the bedrooms occasionally have Andalusian reproductions. Rooms are rented only with meals, lunch and dinner each going for around 1,500 pesetas ($14.10).

HOTEL KENIA, Molinos, 65, 18009 Granada. Tel. 958/22-75-06. 19 rms (all with bath). TEL **Bus:** 2.
$ Rates: 4,000 ptas. ($37.60) single; 7,800 ptas. ($73.30) double. Breakfast 600 ptas. ($5.65) extra. AE, DC, MC, V.

An Andalusian nugget, the Kenia sits behind a high wall in a residential neighborhood, amid a maze of sloping streets near the Alhambra. You pass through an ornate iron gate to enter the baroque gardens of this former 19th-century villa with an ornate tower. The bedrooms are sunny and quiet, decorated with dignified and conservative furniture. There are a formal parlor with a marble fireplace and Spanish versions of Eastlake period chairs; a dining room; and a graveled terrace where tables are placed in fair weather. Breakfast only is served.

HOTEL WASHINGTON IRVING, Paseo del Generalife, 2, 18009 Granada. Tel. 958/22-75-50. 68 rms (all with bath). TEL **Bus:** 2.
$ Rates: 5,500 ptas. ($51.70) single; 7,800 ptas. ($73.30) double. Breakfast 525 ptas. ($4.95) extra. MC, V.

Named after the famous American writer, this hotel is set at the edge of a winding road leading to the Alhambra. King Alfonso XII visited it at the turn of the century, when it was the only hotel in town. Today it's rated three stars by the government, occupying a dignified five-story building whose iron railings are festooned with vines. Its modernized lobby has tasteful dark-grained paneling, but the public rooms are at their baronial best in the pleasantly masculine bar and in the lavishly ornate Moorish dining room.

HOTEL RESIDENCIA CÓNDOR, Avenida de la Constitución, 6, 18012 Granada. Tel. 958/28-37-11. Fax 958/28-55-91. 104 rms (all with bath). A/C TV TEL **Bus:** 2.
$ Rates: 6,000 ptas. ($56.40) single; 8,000 ptas. ($75.20) double. Breakfast 550 ptas. ($5.15) extra. AE, DC, MC, V.

The attractive contemporary design of this hotel helps make it one of Granada's best. It's in the center of town, a 5-minute walk from the Alhambra and the cathedral. Many of the pleasant bedrooms have terraces, and all have attractive light-grained contemporary furniture. Only breakfast is served.

HOTEL GUADELUPE, Avenida de los Alijares, s/n, 18009 Granada. Tel. 958/22-34-23. Fax 958/22-37-98. 60 rms (all with bath). A/C MINIBAR TEL **Bus:** 2.
$ Rates: 4,800 ptas. ($45.10) single, 8,200 ptas. ($77.10) double. Breakfast 530 ptas. ($5) extra. AE, DC, MC, V.

Near a cluster of hotels and souvenir shops, the Guadelupe lies along the steep road beside the entrance to the gardens of the Generalife and the Alhambra. It was built in 1969, but with its thick stucco walls, rounded arches, and jutting beams, it seems older. The comfortably furnished bedrooms overlook the Alhambra. There's a fifth-floor à la carte restaurant, plus a pleasant bar in the lobby.

GRAN HOTEL BRASILIA, Recogidas, 7, 18005 Granada. Tel. 958/25-84-50. Fax 958/25-84-50. 68 rms (all with bath). A/C TV TEL
$ Rates: 5,600 ptas. ($52.65) single; 8,600 ptas. ($80.85) double. Breakfast 525 ptas. ($4.95) extra. DC, MC, V.

The rooms are well furnished in this centrally located hotel, where you'll find the staff efficient and polite (English spoken). In short, it's one of the best hotels in the city. Facilities include an American bar, a roof terrace, and a grill for light snacks. The location is fine for shopping too—only 3 blocks from the Puerta Real.

HOTEL VICTORIA, Puerta Real, 3, 18005 Granada. Tel. 958/25-77-00. Fax 958/26-31-08. 69 rms (all with bath). A/C TV TEL
$ Rates: 6,500 ptas. ($61.10) single; 9,500 ptas. ($89.30) double. Breakfast 550 ptas. ($5.15) extra. AE, DC, MC, V.

The Hotel Victoria, in the heart of Granada, has long been a favorite. Its domed tower and the elegant detailing around each of its windows evoke 19th-century Paris. You'll enter a circular salmon-and-cream marble lobby. The upper hallways have intricately geometric tilework, and on the second floor there's a graceful American bar with Ionic columns, as well as an attractively formal dining room. Many of the rooms have reproductions of antiques and walls upholstered in shades of terra-cotta.

WORTH THE EXTRA BUCKS

HOTEL ALHAMBRA PALACE, Peña Partida, 1, 18009 Granada. Tel. 958/22-14-68. Fax 958/22-64-04. 147 rms (all with bath). A/C MINIBAR TV TEL **Bus:** 2.

$ **Rates:** 11,500 ptas. ($108.10) single; 16,000 ptas. ($150.40) double. Breakfast 950 ptas. ($8.95) extra. AE, DC, MC, V.

Evoking a Moorish fortress, complete with a crenellated roofline, a crowning dome, geometric tilework, and a suggestion of a minaret, this legendary hotel is a splurge choice. It sits in a shady, secluded spot, midway up the slope between the Alhambra and the commercial center of Granada. Inside, amid a decor of ornate ceilings, chastened brass, Moorish arches, and green and blue tiles, you'll find a rather formal restaurant, a grillroom, two bars, and renovated bedrooms with lots of comfortable extras. Fixed-price lunches or dinners cost around 3,300 pesetas ($31).

PARADOR NACIONAL SAN FRANCISCO, Alhambra, 18009 Granada. Tel. 958/22-14-40. Fax 958/22-22-64. 39 rms (all with bath). A/C MINIBAR TV TEL **Bus:** 2.

$ **Rates:** 13,500 ptas. ($126.90) single; 17,000 ptas. ($159.80) double. Breakfast 950 ptas. ($8.95) extra. AE, DC, MC, V.

This is definitely romantic living, in some of the finest accommodations in Spain. It is imperative that you reserve weeks in advance, since it's always booked solid. Part of the greater Alhambra compound, the parador dates from the 15th century, when it was built as a convent after the Reconquest. Queen Isabella was buried here until her tomb in the Royal Chapel was completed. The large old Moorish-inspired patio is planted with time-aged vines and trees. The long gallery, opening onto the patio, must have been a chapel or a meeting hall; it is now a comfortable living room furnished with a mixture of antiques and upholstered pieces. The accommodations differ widely: Many are large antique-filled bedrooms, but there are also smaller and more simply furnished ones, in the newer wing. But from every window you get a picture-postcard view. As for the food, most of the excellent dishes served are native to the province—try to dine here even if you aren't staying at the parador.

WHERE TO EAT

MESÓN ANDALUZ, Elvira, 17. Tel. 22-73-57.
   Cuisine: SPANISH. **Reservations:** Not required.
$ **Prices:** Appetizers 450–950 ptas. ($4.25–$8.95); main dishes 750–1,200 ptas. ($7.05–$11.30); fixed-priced menu 950 ptas. ($8.95). AE, DC, MC, V.
   Open: Lunch daily 1–4pm; dinner daily 7:30–11:30pm.

Two blocks east of the cathedral, the Mesón Andaluz is the best pick on this street of budget restaurants. It's decorated in typical Andalusian style, and you get efficient and polite service along with good inexpensive food. A menu, printed in English, offers selections such as hake stew, rabbit hunter's style, brains Roman style, fried chicken with garlic, and, to finish off, a whisky ice-cream tart.

GALERÍAS PRECIADAS Carrera del Genil s/n. Tel. 22-35-83.
   Cuisine: SPANISH. **Reservations:** Not required.

$ Prices: Fixed-price menu 850 ptas. ($8). AE, DC, MC, V.
Open: Tues–Sun 10am–8pm.

You can get one of the best lunches in Spain in any Galerías Preciadas department store, and the one in Granada is no exception. For shoppers in a rush, it offers a low-priced express menu that is a terrific bargain. The meal begins with soup, followed by a main course such as breast of chicken and french fries. For one low price, you also get bread and wine (or beer or mineral water).

LA NUEVA BODEGA, Cetti Meriem, 9. Tel. 22-59-34.
  Cuisine: SPANISH. **Reservations:** Not required.
$ Prices: Platos combinados 750–900 ptas. ($7.05–$8.45); fixed-priced menus 940–1,500 ptas. ($8.85–$14.10). No credit cards.
  Open: Lunch daily 1–4pm; dinner daily 8–11pm.

This place seems to be everyone's favorite budget restaurant in Granada. You can enjoy both cafeteria and restaurant service, and even order food at the bar, which is cheaper than sitting at a table. The restaurant and cafeteria specialize in platos combinados (combined plates). This doesn't mean that you get everything on one plate. You might be served chicken soup, followed by an omelet, then swordfish Milanese style, along with bread and a simple dessert. In addition, the restaurant offers a selection of good-quality set menus that are both filling and well prepared. Specialties are from not only Andalusia but all of Iberia, including Portugal.

TORRES BERMEJAS, Plaza Nueva, 6. Tel. 22-31-16.
  Cuisine: SPANISH. **Reservations:** Recommended.
$ Prices: Appetizers 750–1,200 ptas. ($7.05–$11.30); main dishes 1,200–1,900 ptas. ($11.30–$17.85); fixed-priced menu 1,300 ptas. ($12.20). AE, DC, MC, V.
  Open: Lunch daily noon–4pm; dinner daily 8pm–midnight.

Opening onto one of the most charming squares of Granada, a short walk east of the cathedral at the bottom of the hill leading to the Alhambra, is a stylish bar area where you can have an apéritif before heading into the warmly contemporary dining room. Main dishes include such delectable specialties as grilled swordfish, roast lamb, tournedos Rossini, veal chops, and shrimps pil-pil.

POLINARÍO, Real de la Alhambra, 3. Tel. 22-29-91.
  Cuisine: SPANISH. **Reservations:** Not required. **Bus:** 2.
$ Prices: Complete buffet, including wine and service, 1,300 ptas. ($12.20) AE, DC, MC, V.
  Open: Daily 9am–7pm.

At this restaurant within the ancient walls of the Alhambra, across from the Palace of Charles V, the Spanish cooking is reasonably good, having earned the chef a two-fork rating for such Andalusian dishes as chilled gazpacho—always a favorite with the summer crowd who flit in and out of here with copies of Washington Irving's book. Main dishes include lamb chops, ragout, and hake fried Roman style. The inevitable but always-welcome flan is served for dessert. In summer, like the caliphs of old, diners eat in the garden.

CHIKITO, Plaza del Campillo, 9. Tel. 22-33-64.
  Cuisine: SPANISH. **Reservations:** Recommended.
$ Prices: Appetizers 450–950 ptas. ($4.25–$8.95); main dishes 1,450–1,900 ptas. ($13.65–$17.85); fixed-priced menu 1,500 ptas. ($14.10). AE, DC, MC, V.
  Open: Lunch Thurs–Tues 1–4pm; dinner Thurs–Tues 8–11:30pm.

Chikito sits across the street from the famous tree-shaded square where García Lorca met with other members of El Rinconcillo (The Little Corner), a dozen young men considered the best and the brightest in the 1920s, when they brought a brief but dazzling cultural renaissance to their hometown. The café where they met has now changed its name, but it's the same building. The present-day Chikito is both a bar and a restaurant. In fair weather, guests enjoy drinks and snacks on tables placed in the square; in winter they retreat inside to the tapas bars. There is also a complete restaurant facility, offering *sopa sevillana,* shrimp cocktail, Basque hake, baked tuna, ox tail, *zarzuela* (seafood stew), grilled swordfish, and Argentine-style veal steak.

LOS MANUELES, Zaragoza, 2-4. Tel. 22-34-13.

Cuisine: SPANISH. **Reservations:** Recommended.

$ Prices: Appetizers 650–950 ptas. ($7.10–$8.95); main dishes 1,500–1,900 ($14.10–$17.85); fixed-priced menu 1,600 ptas. ($15.05). AE, DC, MC, V.

Open: Lunch daily 1–4:30pm; dinner daily 7:30pm–midnight.

An old Granada standby since 1917, located on a narrow side street near the Town Hall and right off the central Puerta Real, this unpretentious restaurant has colorful tile walls and floors, and fans and lanterns suspended from the ceiling. Above the counter hang dozens of tempting Serrano hams. The king and queen of Spain have dined here. Sit in one of the two small dining rooms, or on the no-traffic street outside in the summer. A la carte specialties include tortilla (omelet) Sacromonte and *habas con jamón* (broad beans and Serrano ham). You might begin with *ajoblancos* (cold garlic soup)—and finish with strawberries and cream.

PARADOR DE SAN FRANCISCO, Alhambra. Tel. 22-14-40.

Cuisine: SPANISH. **Reservations:** Required. **Bus:** 2.

$ Prices: Appetizers 750–1,200 ptas. ($7.05–$11.30); main dishes 1,500–2,000 ptas. ($14.10–$18.80); fixed-priced menu 3,100 ptas. ($29.15). AE, DC, MC, V.

Open: Lunch daily 1–4pm; dinner daily 8–11pm.

Even if you can't afford to stay at this luxurious parador—the most famous in Spain—consider a meal here. It comes as close as anything to duplicating what the sultans enjoyed long ago in their kingdom. The dining room is spacious, the service is polite, and you gaze upon the rose gardens and a distant view of the Generalife. The same set menu—which changes daily—is repeated in the evening, although you can always order à la carte. At this 16th-century convent built by the Reyes Católicos, you get not only atmosphere, but also a cuisine that features regional dishes of Andalusia and Spanish national specialties. Lunch is the preferred time to dine here, because the terrace overlooking the palace is open then. A light outdoor lunch menu of sandwiches and salads can be ordered on the à la carte menu if you don't want to partake of the heavy major Spanish repast in the heat of the day. The lighter meal will run about 1,200 pesetas ($11.30).

RESTAURANTE CUNINI, Pescadería, 14. Tel. 26-37-01.

Cuisine: SEAFOOD. **Reservations:** Required.

$ Prices: Appetizers 750–1,800 ptas. ($7.05–$16.90); main dishes 1,600–2,400 ptas. ($15.05–$22.55); fixed-priced menu 1,500 ptas. ($14.10). AE, DC, MC, V.

Open: Lunch daily noon–4pm; dinner Mon–Sat 8pm–midnight.

The array of seafood specialties, perhaps a hundred selections, extends even to the tapas served at the long stand-up bar. Many guests move on after a drink or two, to the paneled ground-floor restaurant, where the cuisine reflects the whole of Spain, even the Basque country. Meals often begin with soup, such as sopa Cunini or sopa sevillana (with ham, shrimp, and whitefish). Also popular is a deep fry of small fish called a *fritura Cunini,* with other specialties including stuffed sardines, a zarzuela, smoked salmon, and grilled shrimp. Pescadería is adjacent to the Gran Vía de Colón.

RESTAURANTE SEVILLA, Oficios, 14. Tel. 22-12-23.

Cuisine: SPANISH. **Reservations:** Required.

$ Prices: Appetizers 750–1,200 ptas. ($7.05–$11.30); main dishes 1,700–2,100 ptas. ($16–$19.75); fixed-priced menu 2,000 ptas. ($18.80). AE, DC, MC, V.

Open: Lunch daily 1–4pm; dinner Mon–Sat 8–11pm.

Attracting a mixed crowd of all ages, the Sevilla is definitely *típico,* with an upbeat elegance. My most recent meal here included gazpacho, Andalusian veal, and dessert (selections included caramel custard and fresh fruit), plus bread and the wine of Valdepeñas. To break the gazpacho monotony, try *sopa virule,* made with pine nuts and chicken breast. For a main course, try the *cordero à la pastoril* (lamb with herbs and paprika). The best dessert is bananas flambé. You can dine inside, where it is pleasantly decorated, or have a meal on the terrace. Sevilla also has a bar. You'll find the place in the center of town opposite the Royal Chapel, near the Plaza Isabel la Católica.

SHOPPING

The Alcaicería, once the Moorish silk market, is next to the cathedral in the lower city. The narrow streets of this rebuilt village of shops are filled with vendors selling the arts and crafts of Granada province. For the souvenir hunter, the Alcaicería offers one of the most splendid assortments in Spain of tiles, castanets, and wire figures of Don Quixote chasing windmills. Lots of Spanish jewelry can be found here, comparing favorably with the finest Toledan work. For the window shopper, in particular, it makes a pleasant stroll.

EVENING ENTERTAINMENT
THE GYPSY CAVES OF SACROMONTE

These inhabited Gypsy caves are the subject of much controversy. Admittedly, they are a tourist trap, one of the most obviously commercial and shadowy rackets in Spain. Still, the caves are a potent enough attraction, if you follow some rules.

Once thousands of Gypsies lived on the "Holy Mountain," so named because of several Christians martyred here. However, many of the caves were heavily damaged in the floodlike rains of 1962, forcing hundreds of the occupants to seek shelter elsewhere. Nearly all the Gypsies remaining are in one way or another involved with tourism. (Some don't even live here—they commute from modern apartments in the city.)

When evening settles over Granada, loads of visitors descend on these caves near the Albaicín, the old Arab section. In every cave you'll hear the rattle of castanets and the strumming of guitars, while everybody in the Gypsy family struts his or her stuff. Popularly known as the *zambra,* this is intriguing entertainment only if you have an appreciation of the grotesque. Whenever a Gypsy boy or girl comes along with genuine talent, he or she is often grabbed up and hustled off to the more expensive clubs. Those left at home can be rather pathetic in their attempts to entertain.

One of the main reasons for going is to see the caves themselves. If you're expecting primitive living, you may be in for a surprise—many are quite comfortable, with conveniences like telephones and electricity. Often they are decorated with copper and ceramic items—and the inhabitants need no encouragement to sell them to you.

If you want to see the caves, you can walk up the hill by yourself. Your approach will already be advertised before you get there. Attempts will be made to lure you inside one or another of the caves—and to get money from you. Alternatively, you can book an organized tour, arranged by one of the travel agencies in Granada. Even at the end of one of these group outings—with all expenses theoretically paid in advance—there is likely to be an attempt by the cave-dwellers to extract more money from you. As soon as the zambra ends, hurry out of the cave as quickly as possible. Many readers have been critical of these tours.

During the zambra, refuse to accept a pair of castanets, even if offered under the friendly guise of having you join in the fun. If you accept them, the chances are that you'll later be asked to pay for them. Buying anything in these caves is not recommended. Leave your jewelry at your hotel, and don't take more money than you're prepared to lose.

The main access route to the caves is called the Camino del Sacromonte, intersecting and heading east from the Cuesta del Chapiz, which is the eastern boundary of the Albaicín. If you must go, better stick to an organized tour, as it's safer than wandering around on your own at night. Check the latest offerings from **Viajes Melía,** Calle de los Reyes Católicos (tel. 22-30-98).

FLAMENCO

The best flamenco show in Granada is staged at **Jardines Neptuno,** Calle Arabial s/n (tel. 25-11-12), nightly at 10pm and midnight. The acts are a bit racy, even though they have been toned down considerably for today's audiences. In addition to flamenco, performers attired in regional garb do folk dances and give guitar concerts. The show takes place in a garden setting. There's a high cover charge of 2,300 pesetas ($21.60), but it includes a drink that you can nurse all evening. Further drinks start at 500 pesetas ($4.70). It's best to take a taxi here.

CHAPTER 11

THE COSTA DEL SOL

Nowhere is the Spanish tourist boom more evident than on the Costa del Sol. The mild winter climate and almost guaranteed sunshine in summer have made this razzle-dazzle stretch of Mediterranean shoreline a year-round attraction. It begins at the western frontier harbor city of Algeciras and stretches east to the port city of Almería. Sandwiched between these two points is a steep, rugged coastline, with poor-to-fair beaches, set against the Sierra Nevada. You'll find sandy coves, whitewashed houses, olive trees, lots of new apartment houses, fishing boats, golf courses, souvenir stands, fast-food outlets, and a widely varied flora—both human and vegetable.

From June through October the coast is mobbed, so make sure you've nailed down a reservation. And keep in mind that October 12 is a national holiday; thus visitors should make doubly sure of their reservations at this time. At other times, chances are that the innkeeper will roll out the red carpet.

Many restaurants close around October 15 for a much-needed vacation. Remember, too, that many supermarkets and other facilities are closed on Sunday.

SEEING THE COSTA DEL SOL
GETTING THERE

Visitors to the Costa del Sol arriving by **plane** fly into Málaga, Almería, or Gibraltar on both scheduled and charter flights (see city listings for details). The airports also offer a network of domestic air links with the rest of Spain.

Málaga is linked by RENFE to **rail** connections from all the major Spanish cities, including Granada, Seville, Barcelona, and Madrid. From Málaga airport, there is local train service to take you to the resort of Fuengirola in the west, stopping at Benalmadena (near Torremolinos) and Los Boliches. These trains run daily every 30 minutes between 6am and 11pm.

It's also possible to take a **bus** to the Costa del Sol from all major cities in Spain. From Málaga, bus links to all satellite resorts are available.

By **car,** the main highway from the north to Andalusia is the N-IV from Madrid to Cádiz, via Córdoba and Seville (see Chapter 10). Once at Cádiz, cut east along the coastal road, the E-25, to Algeciras, where it becomes the E-26, connecting all the resorts along the Costa del Sol. This highway is also known as the Carretera de Cádiz. Establishments along this highway use distances from Cádiz as addresses (i.e., Carretera de Cádiz, km 68, means the establishment is 68 kilometers from Cádiz).

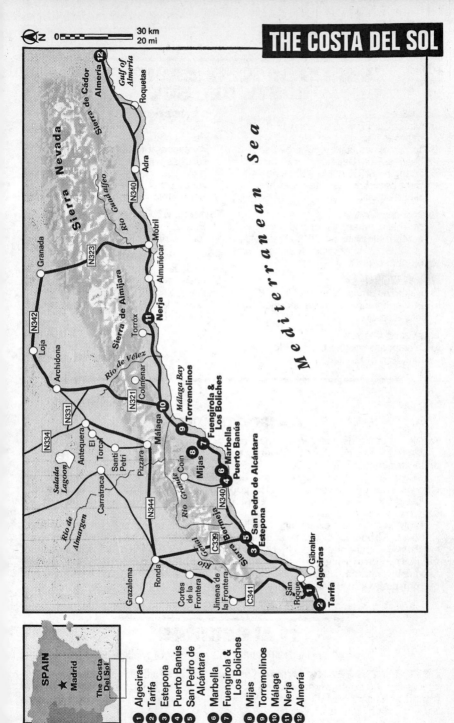

THE COSTA DEL SOL

30 km
20 mi

SPAIN
★ Madrid
The Costa Del Sol

1 Algeciras
2 Tarifa
3 Estepona
4 Puerto Banús
5 San Pedro de Alcántara
6 Marbella
7 Fuengirola & Los Boliches
8 Mijas
9 Torremolinos
10 Málaga
11 Nerja
12 Almería

WHAT'S SPECIAL ABOUT THE COSTA DEL SOL

Beaches
- ☐ Marbella, 17 miles of sandy beaches.
- ☐ Torremolinos, sandy but crowded beaches. Try Bajondillo or El Lido.
- ☐ Fuengirola, 3½ miles of beaches. Best bets: Las Gaviotas, Carrajal, Santa Amalja.

Great Resorts
- ☐ Marbella, where glitter and hype reach their pinnacle. Visit "the Golden Mile" strip of super-wealthy.
- ☐ Nerja, scenic resort.

Great Villages
- ☐ Mijas, an Andalusian *pueblo.*
- ☐ Nerja, fishing village transformed into a resort.

Historic Cities
- ☐ Málaga, former harbor for Moorish kingdom of Granada.

Architectural Highlights
- ☐ Marbella's old quarter, around Plaza de los Naranjos.
- ☐ Alcazaba at Málaga, 11th-century fortress with Hispano-Muslim garden.
- ☐ Alcabaza at Almería, 8th-century panoramic vistas from battlements.

Pocket of Posh
- ☐ Puerto Banús, yacht-clogged harbor for the rich.

Festivals/Special Events
- ☐ Málaga's major festivals on religious occasions. Big annual *feria* (fair) in August.
- ☐ Marbella's flamenco festival second half of June.

A SUGGESTED ROUTE

Allow about six days to explore the Costa del Sol.

Day 1 Begin at Algeciras. During the day, cross over to Gibraltar to see all the main attractions. Stay overnight in Algeciras.

Days 2–3 Leave Algeciras and drive west to Marbella. This will be your only chic stopover on the coast. Enjoy the good beaches, restaurants, bars, and discos.

Day 4 Continue east to Torremolinos for the night. For most of the year, the activity here is like a street festival.

Day 5 Leave Torremolinos and continue east to Málaga for an overnight stopover. Although Málaga is an ancient city, its sights can be covered in a day.

Day 6 Continue east to Nerja, the final overnight stopover, and visit the Cave of Nerja. If you're driving, you can continue your trip along the eastern coast all the way to Valencia and Barcelona. If you must leave, the best transportation links are found by returning west to Málaga.

---

1. ALGECIRAS

422 miles S of Madrid, 82 miles W of Málaga

GETTING THERE   By Train   The local RENFE office is at Calle Juan de la Cierva (tel. 66-36-46). From Madrid, there are 2 trains daily; from Málaga, 4 daily (running along most of the Costa del Sol, including Marbella and Torremolinos); from Seville, 3 daily; and from Granada, 2 daily.

By Bus   Various independent bus companies service Algeciras. Empresa Portillo, Avenida Virgen de Carmen, 15 (tel. 65-11-55), 1½ blocks to the right when you exit the port complex, runs nearly a dozen buses a day along the Costa del Sol to Algeciras from Málaga. It also sends 1 bus daily from Madrid and 2 from Granada. To make connections to or from Seville, use Empresa La Valenciana, Viajes Travimar, Avenida de la Marina s/n (tel. 65-36-61). Three buses a day go to Jerez de la Frontera and Seville. Empresa Comes, Hotel Octavio, Calle San Bernardo (tel. 65-34-56), sells tickets to La Línea (the border station for the approach to Gibraltar) for 140 pesetas ($1.30), and to Tarifa for 150 pesetas ($1.40), from which a ferry to Tangier can be arranged.

By Ferry   Most visitors are in Algeciras planning to cross to Tangier in Morocco. From April to October, Monday through Saturday, 4 ferries a day leave from the port complex in Algeciras, heading for Tangier; on Sunday, only 3 a day (in off-season, 2 a day all seven days). A Class A ticket costs 3,600 pesetas ($33.85) per person; Class B ticket, 2,900 pesetas ($27.25) per person. To transport a car, it costs from 9,000 pesetas ($84.60). Discounts are granted: 20% with a Eurailpass, 30% with an InterRail pass, and 50% for children.

By Car   The Carretera de Cádiz (E-26) makes the run from Málaga west to Algeciras. If you're driving south from Seville (or Madrid), take highway N-IV to Cádiz, then connect with the 340/E-25 southwest to Algeciras.

ESSENTIALS   The area code for Algeciras is 956. The Tourist Information Office is at Juan de la Cierva (tel. 956/60-09-11).

Algeciras is the jumping-off point for Africa—it's only 3 hours to Tangier or Spanish Morocco. If you're planning an excursion, there's an inexpensive baggage storage depot at the ferry terminal. Algeciras is also a base for day trips to Gibraltar. Check at the **Gibraltar Turismo office,** Avenida de la Marina (tel. 956/60-09-11), in Algeciras for the latest border-crossing situation—at one time this border could not be passed. If you don't have time to visit "the Rock," you can view it from Algeciras—it's only 6 miles away, out in the Bay of Algeciras.

WHERE TO STAY

HOTEL ALARDE, Alfonso XI, 4, 11201 Algeciras. Tel. 956/66-04-08. Fax 956/66-04-08. 68 rms (all with bath). A/C MINIBAR TV TEL
$ Rates: 4,800 ptas. ($45.10) single; 6,800 ptas. ($63.90) double. Breakfast 800 ptas. ($7.50) extra. AE, DC, MC, V.
If you want to get away from the port area, consider this three-star hotel near the Parque María Cristina—a central location in a quiet commercial section. The double rooms have balconies and Andalusian-style furnishings. There's a snack bar (no restaurant). During my most recent stay I was impressed with both the staff and the inviting atmosphere.

HOTEL AL-MAR, Avenida de la Marina, 2, 11201 Algeciras. Tel. 956/65-46-61. Fax 956/65-45-01. 192 rms (all with bath). A/C TV TEL
$ Rates: 4,500 ptas. ($42.30) single; 9,000 ptas. ($84.60) double. Breakfast 850 ptas. ($8) extra. AE, DC, MC, V.
The three-star Al-Mar, one of the best choices in town, stands near the port, where the ferries embark for Ceuta and Tangier. This large hotel boasts a blue-and-white Sevillian and Moorish decor, as well as three restaurants, a handful of bars, and lots of verdant hideaways. Rooms are well maintained, furnished in a slightly Andalusian style. From the fourth-floor drawing room, there's a panoramic view of the Rock.

HOTEL OCTAVIO, San Bernardo, 1, 11207 Algeciras. Tel. 956/65-24-61. Fax 956/65-28-02. 80 rms (all with bath). A/C MINIBAR TV TEL
$ Rates: 5,500 ptas. ($50.70) single; 9,500 ptas. ($89.30) double. Breakfast 800 ptas. ($7.50) extra. AE, DC, MC, V.
Conveniently located in the center of town near the railway station, the Octavio is

decorated with reproductions of English antiques, which contrast sharply with the building's angular, modern exterior. There's an American bar that serves international drinks, plus a restaurant, the Iris, that serves meals from 1,600 pesetas ($15.05). Rooms are nicely furnished and well maintained.

WHERE TO EAT

CASA ALFONSO, Juan de la Cierva, 4. Tel. 60-27-54.
   Cuisine: SPANISH. **Reservations:** Not required.
$ **Prices:** Appetizers 175–350 ptas. ($1.65–$3.30); main dishes 350–750 ptas. ($3.30–$7.05); *menú del día* 700 ptas. ($6.60).
   Open: Lunch Mon–Sat 1–4pm; dinner Mon–Sat 8pm–midnight.
   This simple, unpretentious bargain spot, which attracts lots of Morocco-bound students, is located near the tourist office. A menú del día here might include paella or bean soup, fried fish, beefsteak with potatoes, bread, wine, and fruit. Unnumbered buses from Cádiz and Seville stop nearby.

RESTAURANT MAREA BAJA, Trafalgar, 2. Tel. 66-36-54.
   Cuisine: SPANISH. **Reservations:** Required.
$ **Prices:** Appetizers 575–900 ptas. ($5.15–$8.45); main dishes 1,200–1,500 ptas. ($11.30–$14.10). AE, DC, MC, V.
   Open: Lunch Mon–Sat 1–4pm; dinner Mon–Sat 8pm–midnight.
At this centrally located restaurant near the Plaza Alta, specializing in fish and *mariscos* (shellfish), the owners often introduce creative recipes. A long *tapas* bar might whet your appetite before you select from the wide array of specialties, which include seafood crêpes, *rape* (monkfish), hake, and omelets.

---

2. TARIFA

14 miles W of Algeciras, 443 miles S of Madrid, 61 miles SE of Cádiz

GETTING THERE   By Bus   In Algeciras, Empresa Comes, Calle San Bernardo s/n (tel. 65-34-56), under the Hotel Octavio, runs buses to Tarifa, several leaving daily depending on the time of year (45 minutes) and costing 150 pesetas ($1.40).

By Car   Take the Cádiz highway, N-340, west from Algeciras.

ESSENTIALS   The area code for Tarifa is 956.

Instead of heading east from Algeciras along the Costal del Sol, I'd suggest a visit west to Tarifa, an old Moorish town that is the southernmost point in Europe. After leaving Algeciras, the roads climb steeply, and the drive to Tarifa is along one of Europe's most splendid coastal routes. In the distance you'll see Gibraltar, the straits, and the "green hills" of Africa—in fact, you can sometimes get a glimpse of houses in Ceuta and Tangier on the Moroccan coastline.

Tarifa, named for Tarik, a Moorish military hero, has retained more of its Arab character than any other town in Andalusia. Narrow cobblestoned streets lead to charming patios filled with flowers. The main square is the Plaza San Mateo.

Two factors have inhibited the development of Tarifa's beautiful white 3-mile beach, the Playa de Lances: It's still a Spanish military zone, and the wind never stops blowing (43% of the time). For windsurfers, though, the strong western breezes are unbeatable. Tarifa is filled with shops renting windsurfing equipment, as well as giving advice about the best locales.

Many visitors also come to see Tarifa's historical past and wander its crumbling ramparts. The town is dominated by the **Castle of Tarifa,** site of a famous struggle in 1292 between Moors and Christians. The castle was held by Guzmán el Bueno ("the Good"). When Christians captured his 9-year-old son and demanded surrender of the garrison, Guzmán tossed the Spanish a dagger for the boy's execution, preferring "honor without a son, to a son with dishonor." Sadly, the castle is not open to the public.

From Tarifa, it's possible to take a 9:30am hydrofoil to Tangier, returning at 4:30pm Spanish time or at 6:30pm Moroccan time (Spain is 2 hours ahead of Morocco). The trip takes 30 minutes. Tickets may be purchased at the embarkation kiosk on the quay, **Cia Transtour-Touráfrica,** Estación Marítima (tel. 68-47-51).

A NEARBY ATTRACTION

Eight miles (13km) beyond Tarifa lie the ruins of the ancient Roman town of **Baelo Claudio,** Carretera Nacional 340, off Rte. N-340 along the Algeciras–Cádiz highway. The town was founded in the 1st century A.D., and under Roman rule it flourished as a fishing town, with a population as high as 30,000. Then it was nearly forgotten for 1,500 years, until the archeological site was discovered shortly after World War I; excavations are still far from complete. Don't miss the old Roman theater. The site is open Tuesday through Saturday from 9am to 2pm and 4 to 6pm, on Sunday from 10am to 1pm. Admission is 250 pesetas ($2.35).

WHERE TO STAY & EAT

MESÓN DE SANCHO, 340 Carretera Cádiz–Málaga, km 94, 11380 Tarifa. Tel. 956/68-49-00. 45 rms (all with bath). TEL
$ Rates: 5,300 ptas. ($49.80) single; 6,000 ptas. ($56.40) double. Breakfast 390 ptas. ($3.65) extra. AE, DC, MC, V.

Ten miles (16km) southwest of Algeciras, and 6.5 miles (10.5km) northeast of Tarifa on the Cádiz road, stands an informal hacienda-style inn where you can swim in a pool surrounded by olive trees and terraces. The rooms are furnished in modest but contemporary style, and there is steam heating in the cooler months. In the provincial dining room, with its window walls overlooking the garden, a complete lunch or dinner goes for 1,600 pesetas ($15.05). Meals are available daily from 1 to 5pm and 8pm to midnight.

HOTEL BALCÓN DE ESPAÑA, La Pena, 2, Carretera Cádiz–Málaga, km 76, 11380 Tarifa. Tel. 956/68-43-26. Fax 956/68-43-26. 38 rms (all with bath). TEL
$ Rates: 5,300 ptas. ($49.80) single; 7,500 ptas. ($70.50) double. Breakfast 460 ptas. ($4.30) extra. AE, MC, V. **Closed:** Early Oct–mid-Apr.

The surrounding park adds a welcome calm to your stay at the Balcón de España, located 5 miles (8km) north of Tarifa. The hotel offers clean and well-kept accommodations, an outdoor pool, tennis courts, and a riding stable. Some guests prefer to stay in outlying bungalows. In the restaurant, meals are served daily from 1 to 4pm and 8 to 11pm.

---

3. ESTEPONA

53 miles W of Málaga, 397 miles S of Madrid, 28½ miles E of Algeciras

GETTING THERE   By Train   The nearest rail links are in Algeciras.

By Bus   Estepona is on the bus route from Algeciras to Málaga.

By Car   Drive east from Algeciras along the 340.

ESSENTIALS   The area code for Estepona is 952. The Tourist Information Office is at Paseo Marítimo Pedro Manrique (tel. 952/80-09-13).

A town of Roman origin, Estepona is a budding beach resort, less developed than Marbella or Torremolinos, but perhaps preferable for that reason. Estepona contains an interesting 15th-century parish church, with the ruins of an old aqueduct nearby (at Salduba). Its recreational port is an attraction, as are its **beaches:** Costa Natura, km 257 on the N-340, the first legal nude beach of its kind along the Costa del Sol; La Rada, 2 miles long; and El Cristo, only 600 yards. Estepona is also a **shopper's paradise,** offering some of the best bargains along the Costa del Sol. After the sun goes down, stroll along the Paseo Marítimo, a broad avenue with gardens on one side, the beach on the other.

In summer the cheapest places to eat in Estepona are the *merenderos,* little dining areas set up by local fishermen and their families right on the beach. Naturally, they feature seafood, including sole and sardine kebabs grilled over an open fire. You can usually order a fresh salad and fried potatoes; desserts are simple.

After your siesta, head for the tapas bars. You'll find most of them—called *freidurías* (fried-fish bars)—at the corner of the Calle de los Reyes and La Terraza. Tables spill onto the sidewalks in summer, and *gambas à la plancha* (shrimp) are the favorite (but not the cheapest) tapas to order.

WHERE TO STAY

LA MALAGUEÑA, Castillo, 1, 29680 Estepona. Tel. 952/80-00-11. 22 rms (3 with bath).
$ **Rates:** 1,500 ptas. ($14.10) single without bath; 2,400 ptas. ($22.55) double without bath. 2,800 ptas. ($26.30) double with bath. Breakfast 260 ptas. ($2.40) extra. No credit cards.

A modest low-budget hostal in the center of town, La Malagueña offers basic rooms that open onto either a three-story-high glassed-in courtyard with an Andalusian fountain or the Plaza de las Flores, with its border of orange trees.

EL PILAR, Plaza de las Flores, 29680 Estepona. Tel. 952/80-00-18. 16 rms (2 with bath).
$ **Rates:** Single without bath 1,500 ptas. ($14.10); double without bath 2,500 ptas. ($23.50), double with bath 2,900 ptas. ($27.25). No credit cards.

This modest two-story tile-roofed *hostal* opens onto the prettiest square in Estepona, with tables set out for refreshments amid orange trees and bougainvillea. The rooms are basic but clean. No breakfast is served, but there are many cafés nearby. And the beach is only 300 yards away.

BUENAVISTA, Avenida de España, 180, 29680 Estepona. Tel. 952/80-01-37. Fax 972/13-02-32. 38 rms (all with bath) A/C
$ **Rates:** 3,400 ptas. ($31.95) single; 4,500 ptas. ($42.30) double. Breakfast 260 ptas. ($2.45) extra. AE, MC, V.

This comfortable little residencia is right on the coastal road near the beach. It's recommended for an overnight stopover or a modest holiday. Rooms are clean, but likely to be noisy in summer because of heavy traffic nearby. Meals are served; lunch or dinner costs 1,000 pesetas ($9.40). Buses from Marbella stop nearby.

CARACAS, San Lorenzo, 32, 29680 Estepona. Tel. 952/80-08-00. 36 rms (all with bath). TEL
$ **Rates:** 4,300 ptas. ($40.40) single; 6,300 ptas. ($59.20) double. Breakfast 370 ptas. ($3.50) extra. MC, V. **Closed:** Jan 8–Feb 8.

Considered the best bet in town, this white five-story modern hotel with balconies and salmon-pink accents lies just off the coastal highway, 150 feet from the beach in the heart of Estepona. The modern rooms, though not very stylish, are comfortably large; the atmosphere is clean and bright. A complete lunch or dinner costs 1,800 pesetas ($16.90).

WHERE TO EAT

BENAMARA, Carretera de Cádiz, km 168. Tel. 78-11-48.
Cuisine: FRENCH-MOROCCAN. **Reservations:** Recommended.
$ **Prices:** Appetizers 350–750 ptas. ($3.30–$7.05); main dishes 750–1,000 ptas. ($7.05–$9.40). AE, V.

Open: Lunch Sun 1–4pm; dinner Tues–Sun 8pm–midnight.

Benamara consistently provides a good cuisine, especially to those who are tired of Andalusian fare. Several dishes have a French touch, but the chef excels in Moroccan dishes, notably couscous and lamb *mechoui*. For dessert, try one of the pastry *briques*. The place is located 8 miles (13km) northeast of Estepona.

COSTA DEL SOL, Calle San Roque. Tel. 80-11-01.
   Cuisine: FRENCH. **Reservations:** Recommended.
$ **Prices:** Appetizers 650–950 ptas. ($6.10–$8.95); main dishes 1,200–1,900 ptas. ($11.30–$17.85). AE, MC, V.
   Open: Lunch Tues–Sat noon–4pm; dinner Mon–Sat 7pm–midnight.

This is your best choice for a meal in the heart of the town, especially recommended for those depending on public transportation. You get French cookery with flair here. Try the bouillabaisse, different from that served on the French Riviera. You might also try the duck or a filet of beef with béarnaise sauce. If you order in advance, the chef will whip you up a soufflé.

---

4. PUERTO BANÚS

5 miles E of Marbella, 486 miles S of Madrid

GETTING THERE **By Bus** Fifteen buses a day connect Marbella to Puerto Banús.

By Car Drive east from Marbella along the 340.

ESSENTIALS The area code for Puerto Banús is 952.

A favorite resort for international celebrities, this marine village was created almost overnight in the traditional Mediterranean style. It's a dreamy place, a Disney World creation of what a Costa del Sol fishing village should look like. Yachts can be moored at your doorstep. Along the harborfront you'll find an array of sophisticated, expensive bars and restaurants. (There are no inns that I know of.) Wander through the quiet back streets past elegant archways and patios with grilles.

WHERE TO EAT

RED PEPPER, Muelle Ribera. Tel. 81-21-48.
   Cuisine: GREEK. **Reservations:** Recommended.
$ **Prices:** Appetizers 550–750 ptas. ($5.15–$7.05); main dishes 1,500–2,100 ptas. ($14.10–$19.75). AE, DC, MC, V.
   Open: Daily 11:30am–1am.

Run by an exuberant band of Cypriot expatriates, Red Pepper offers an array of Greek and Cypriot food in a sunny and sparsely furnished dining room. Selections include Hellenic chicken soup, moussaka, a variety of well-seasoned grilled meats, and honey-flavored Greek pastries. Full meals are usually accompanied by a selection of Greek and Spanish wines. You'll find the place in the center of the Paseo Marítimo.

DON LEONE, Muelle Ribera. Tel. 81-17-16.
   Cuisine: ITALIAN. **Reservations:** Recommended.
$ **Prices:** Appetizers 750–1,250 ptas. ($7.05–$11.75); main dishes 1,900–2,300 ptas. ($17.85–$21.60). No credit cards.
   Open: Lunch daily 1–4pm; dinner daily 8pm–12:30am. **Closed:** Nov 20–Dec 20.

Many residents in villas around Marbella drive to this dockside restaurant for dinner. Luxuriously decorated, it tends to get crowded at times. Begin with the house minestrone, then follow with a pasta in either a Bolognese or clam sauce; lasagne is also a regular. Meat specialties include veal parmigiana and roast baby lamb, while the fish dishes are also worth a try. The wine list is one of the best along the coast.

EVENING ENTERTAINMENT

THE BEST BARS

HOLLYWOOD BAR, Muelle Ribera. Tel. 81-68-12.
Linger over a drink and watch the yachts bobbing a few feet away. The green-and-white, terra-cotta–tiled interior is decorated with photo collages of yesteryear's Hollywood stars. Monroe and Chaplin mark the entrance to the rest rooms. You can order a "Hollywood Burger" with everything on it. Open: Daily 9–3am. Prices: Drinks 500 ptas. ($4.70); burger 650 ptas. ($6.10).

SINATRA BAR, Muelle Ribera. Tel. 81-48-25.
In this ideal spot for people watching, locals meet for late-night drinks. The preferred spot, in good weather, is out on the sidewalk a few feet away from rows of luxury yachts. Tables are usually shared, and the music is piped in. Menu selections include a hamburger plate. Open: Daily 9pm–4am. Prices: Drinks 650 ptas. ($6.10); burgers 650 ptas. ($6.10).

5. SAN PEDRO DE ALCÁNTARA

43 miles W of Málaga, 42½ miles E of Algeciras

GETTING THERE   By Bus   Service is every 30 minutes from Marbella.

By Car   Take the N-340 west from Marbella.

ESSENTIALS   The area code for San Pedro de Alcántara is 952.

Between Marbella and Estepona, this interesting village contains **Roman remains** that have been officially classified as a national monument. In recent years it has been extensively developed as a resort suburb of Marbella, and now offers some good hotels selections.

WHERE TO STAY

CORTIJO BLANCO, Carretera de Cádiz, km 172, 29670 San Pedro de Alcántara. Tel. 952/78-09-00. 162 rms (all with bath). TEL
$ Rates: 3,800 ptas. ($35.70) single; 5,500 ptas. ($51.70) double. Breakfast 575 ptas. ($5.40) extra. AE, V.
Just a few miles west of Marbella and only 600 yards from the beach, the Cortijo Blanco offers bedrooms overlooking miniature patios overgrown with bougainvillea, canna, and roses. The hotel, built in the Andalusian hacienda style, offers modern accommodations. Lunch is served under a long, covered garden pergola, and dinner in the more formal dining hall, with oil paintings on the walls and tables surrounded by high-backed gilt-and-red Valencian chairs. There's a large open-air swimming pool. Expect to pay more from mid-July to mid-September.

WHERE TO EAT

GARUDA DE ORO, Carretera de Cádiz, km 166.5. Tel. 782-743.
Cuisine: INDONESIAN. **Reservations:** Recommended.
$ Prices: Appetizers 550–750 ptas. ($5.15–$7.05); main dishes 1,300–1,900 ptas. ($12.20–$17.85). AE, DC, MC, V.
Open: Lunch Mon–Sat 1–4pm; dinner Mon–Sat 8–11pm.

Named after the mythical bird-dragon of the Spice Islands, the Garuda, this Indonesian restaurant serves *rijsstafel,* a special rice table brought to the West by Dutch settlers of Java. It includes between 18 and 25 different dishes, such items as *saté* (small shish kebabs) of pork, beef, and chicken—sometimes with a peanut sauce; chicken, egg, and lemon soup; and aromatic stews. Each is accompanied by rice from a large bowl whose contents are periodically replenished. Some Indian and Chinese dishes are also served.

---

6. MARBELLA

37 miles W of Málaga, 28 miles W of Torremolinos, 50 miles E of Gibraltar

GETTING THERE   By Bus   Nine buses run from Málaga to Marbella daily; 2 depart from Madrid daily.

By Car   Marbella is the first major resort as you head east on the N-340 from Algeciras.

ESSENTIALS   The area code for Marbella is 952. The Tourist Information Office is at Miguel Cano, 1 (tel. 952/77-14-42).

Although it's packed with tourists, ranking just behind Torremolinos in popularity, Marbella is still the most exclusive resort along the Costa del Sol—with such bastions of posh as the Marbella Club. Despite the tourists, Marbella remains a pleasant Andalusian town at the foot of the Sierra Blanca. Traces of the past are found in its palatial Town Hall, its medieval ruins, and its ancient Moorish walls. Marbella's most charming area is the **old quarter,** with narrow cobblestoned streets and Arab houses, centering around the Plaza de los Naranjos.

The biggest attractions in Marbella, though, are **El Fuerte** and **La Fontanilla,** the two main beaches. There are other, more secluded beaches, but you need your own transportation to get there.

WHERE TO STAY

Marbella's prices are sometimes 15% higher than those in other towns along the Costa del Sol, but you can still find excellent budget and moderately priced hotels.

NAGÜELES, Carretera de Cádiz, km 177, 29600 Marbella. Tel. 952/77-16-88. 17 rms (all with bath).

$ Rates: 2,400 ptas. ($22.55) single; 3,500–4,000 ptas. ($32.90–$37.60) double. Breakfast 325 ptas. ($3.05) extra. No credit cards. **Closed:** Mid-Oct–mid-Mar.

Two and a half miles (4km) west of Marbella and only 300 yards from the beach, the Nagüeles is near the luxurious Marbella Club and right on the main coastal road. Although its entrance and restaurant are on the busy highway, the whitewashed two-story brick hotel has bedrooms set back from the traffic and protected by orange and willow trees. Red bougainvillea vines crawl through the railings of the balconies. The rooms are simple and clean.

HOSTAL MUNICH, Virgen del Pilar, 5, 29600 Marbella. Tel. 952/77-24-61. 18 rms (all with bath). TEL

$ Rates: 3,000 ptas. ($28.20) single; 3,800 ptas. ($35.70) double. Breakfast 275 ptas. ($2.60) extra. No credit cards.

Set back from the street and shielded by banana and palm trees, this unassuming three-story hostal is just a short walk from the water and the bus station. Some rooms have balconies, all are simply furnished and well kept. A continental breakfast is the only meal served. The homey lounge and breakfast room are cluttered with knickknacks and a mixture of old and new furniture.

HOSTAL-RESIDENCIA ENRIQUETA, Joaquin Chinchilla, 18, 29600 Marbella. Tel. 952/77-00-58. 23 rms (all with bath). TEL
$ Rates: 2,200 ptas. ($20.70) single; 4,000 ptas. ($37.60) double. No credit cards. **Closed:** Jan–Feb.
No breakfast is served at the family-run Enriqueta, near the Plaza de los Naranjos, but if you're not driving the location couldn't be better for tours of the old town. Concealed in a maze of winding, traffic-free walkways, this well-maintained hotel contains a clean reception area filled with leather-upholstered chairs, plus a garden courtyard. Rooms are basic but clean.

EL CASTILLO, Plaza San Bernabé, 2, 29600 Marbella. Tel. 952/77-17-39. 27 rms (all with bath).
$ Rates: 2,500 ptas. ($23.50) single; 4,000 ptas. ($37.60) double. No credit cards.
At the foot of the castle in the narrow streets of the old town, this small but choice budget hotel opens onto a minuscule triangular square used by the adjoining convent and school as a playground. There's a small covered courtyard, and the second-floor bedrooms have only inner windows. The Spartan rooms are scrubbed clean, and contain white-tile baths. No morning meal is served, and not one word of English is spoken.

RESIDENCIA SAN CRISTÓBAL, Ramón y Cajal, 3, 29600 Marbella. Tel. 952/77-12-50. Fax 952/86-20-44. 96 rms (all with bath). TEL
$ Rates: 4,500 ptas. ($42.30) single; 5,800 ptas. ($54.50) double. Breakfast 350 ptas. ($3.30) extra. DC, MC, V.
In the heart of Marbella, 200 yards from the beach, this modern five-story hotel has long, wide terraces and flower-filled windowboxes. The bedrooms have walnut headboards, individual overhead reading lamps, and room dividers separating the comfortable beds from the small living-room areas. An added plus is the private terrace attached to each room—just right for a continental breakfast, the only meal served here.

RESIDENCIA FINLANDIA, Finlandia, 12, 29600 Marbella. Tel. 952/77-07-00. 11 rms (all with bath). TEL
$ Rates: 4,200 ptas. ($39.50) single; 6,000 ptas. ($56.40) double. Breakfast 250 ptas. ($12.35) extra. DC, V.
Situated in the Huerta Grande, a peaceful residential section, the Finlandia is only a 5-minute walk from the center of the old quarter, and a 2-minute walk from the Mediterranean. It's clean, modern, and well run, with spacious rooms and contemporary furnishings. Your bed will be turned down at night.

RESIDENCIA LIMA, Avenida Antonio Belón, 2, 29600 Marbella. Tel. 952/77-05-00. 64 rms (all with bath). TEL
$ Rates: 4,200 ptas. ($39.50) single; 6,000 ptas. ($56.40) double. Breakfast 425 ptas. ($4) extra. AE, DC, MC, V.
Tucked away in a residential section of Marbella, right off the N-340 and near the sea, this hotel is more secluded than the others just mentioned. The modern eight-story structure features bedrooms with Spanish provincial furnishings and private balconies.

EL RODEO, Victor de la Serna, s/n, 29600 Marbella. Tel. 952/77-51-00. Fax 952/82-33-20. 100 rms (all with bath). TEL
$ Rates: 5,000 ptas. ($47) single; 7,000 ptas. ($65.80) double. Breakfast 400 ptas. ($3.75) extra). AE, DC, MC, V.
Even though this modern hotel stands just off the main coastal road of Marbella—within walking distance of the bus station, the beach, and the old quarter—it is quiet and secluded. Facilities in the seven-story structure include a swimming pool, terrace, sunbathing area, solarium, and piano bar. Two elevators whisk you to the sunny, spacious second-floor lounges with country furnishings; there's also a bar with

tropical bamboo chairs and tables. Continental breakfast is the only meal served in the cheerful breakfast room. The bedrooms are functional, with several shuttered closets, lounge chairs, and white desks. Although the hotel is open all year, the highest rates are charged from April 1 to October 31.

HOTEL GUADALPÍN, Carretera 340 Cádiz–Málaga, km 186, 29600 Marbella. Tel. 952/77-11-00. 110 rms (all with bath). TEL
$ Rates: 6,800 ptas. ($63.90) single; 8,600 ptas. ($80.85) double. Breakfast 425 ptas. ($4) extra. AE, DC, MC, V.
This three-star hotel is right on the coast, only 300 yards from the beach and a mile from the center of Marbella. Guests relax around the two swimming pools, or walk along the fir-lined private pathway to the Mediterranean. The dining room has large windows that overlook the patio, while the ranch-style lounge boasts round marble tables and leather armchairs. There's also a bar. Most accommodations have two terraces, a living room, and a bedroom furnished in "new ranch" style and centrally heated during the cooler months.

LAS CHAPAS, Carretera de Cádiz, km 192, 29600 Marbella. Tel. 952/83-13-75. Fax 952/83-13-77. 117 rms (all with bath). A/C TEL
$ Rates: 9,000 ptas. ($84.60) single; 10,500 ptas. ($98.70) double. Breakfast 500 ptas. ($4.70) extra. MC, V.
Bedrooms have private balconies and picture windows overlooking pine trees, minigolf courses, tennis courts, and the Mediterranean across the main highway. Two swimming pools, a children's playground, and a private beach area complete the facilities. The lounges and bedrooms are informal and traditional. The restaurant offers good food; my most recent meal included an appetizer called simply "white garlic from Málaga," smoked salmon from the Bidasoa River, and fresh pineapple with Morella cherries. Las Chapas is located 5½ miles (9km) from the town center along the N-340. Take a "Portilla" bus from Marbella.

HOTEL EL FUERTE, Avenida del Fuerte s/n, 29600 Marbella. Tel. 952/ 77-15-00. Fax 952/82-44-11. 262 rms (all with bath). A/C TV TEL
$ Rates: 8,000 ptas. ($75.20) single; 15,000 ptas. ($141) double. Breakfast 800 ptas. ($7.50) extra. AE, DC, MC, V.
The best hotel in the town center, directly north of the Avenida Duque de Ahumada and a short walk from the Plaza Bajadilla, El Fuerte faces a sheltered lagoon and wide-open beach. A handful of terraces, some shaded by flowering arbors, provide hideaways for quiet drinks. There are two bars, a restaurant with a panoramic water view, and a coffee shop. The comfortable contemporary bedrooms have piped-in music, terraces, and sea views. Facilities include two palm-fringed swimming pools, a floodlit tennis court, minigolf, and a squash court.

WHERE TO EAT

Restaurant prices are high in Marbella, and in many instances your hotel remains a good bet.

MEALS FOR LESS THAN 1,900 PTAS. [$17.85]

CASA ELADÍO, Virgen Dolores, 6. Tel. 77-00-83.
Cuisine: SPANISH. **Reservations:** Recommended (accepted only before 8pm).
$ Prices: Appetizers 300–500 ptas. ($2.80–$4.70); main dishes 800–1,000 ptas. ($7.50–$9.40); fixed-priced lunch 950 ptas. ($8.95). AE, DC, MC, V.
Open: Lunch Fri–Wed 12:30–4pm; dinner Fri–Wed 7pm–midnight.
⑤ On a narrow street near the Plaza de los Naranjos, the Casa Eladío is Andalusian and elegant with its garden setting, blue, white, and yellow tiles, and trickling fountains. A series of brick arches surrounds an open-air

courtyard, where local pottery is set into wall niches. Rich aromas drift out from the kitchens, which prepare swordfish with tarragon, jewfish with pineapple, house pâté, spaghetti carbonara, and kidneys with sherry. This attractive place is less expensive than other nearby restaurants.

MESÓN DEL PASAJE, Pasaje, 5. Tel. 77-12-61.
   Cuisine: CONTINENTAL. **Reservations:** Required.
$ Prices: Appetizers 450–550 ptas. ($4.25–$5.15); main dishes 950–1,500 ptas. ($8.95–$14.10). No credit cards.
   Open: Lunch Wed–Sun 1–3pm; dinner Tues–Sun 7:30–11:30pm; **Closed:** Nov–mid-Dec.

A well-run restaurant in an old house in the ancient quarter, just off the Plaza de los Naranjos, this *mesón* is a maze of little dining rooms. Since word is out that the food is the best in the old town—for the price—the place invariably fills up. You can fill up on one of the excellent pastas, which are most reasonable, or else try the well-prepared, but more expensive, seafood and meat selections. The place has charm and good value.

PIZZERÍA SANREMO, Paseo Marítimo. Tel. 77-43-33.
   Cuisine: ITALIAN. **Reservations:** Not required.
$ Prices: Pizza and pasta 650–1,800 ptas. ($6.10–$16.90); fixed-priced menu 1,200 ptas. ($11.30). AE, MC, V.
   Open: Lunch Thurs–Tues 11am–4:30pm; dinner Thurs–Tues 7–11pm.

Right on the beach, this restaurant is for lovers of Italian cooking. Most diners prefer one of the pizza or pasta concoctions; the veal dishes, too, are well prepared. Or try the special couscous on Thursday. The raw-carrot salad is an unusual item for such a menu (printed in English).

CALYCANTO, Avenida Canovas del Castillo, 9. Tel. 77-19-59.
   Cuisine: CONTINENTAL. **Reservations:** Recommended.
$ Prices: Appetizers 550–750 ptas. ($5.15–$7.05); main dishes 1,200–1,900 ptas. ($11.30–$17.85). MC, V.
   Open: Lunch daily 1:30–4pm; dinner daily 8pm–midnight. **Closed:** Lunch July–Aug.

This restaurant, built in the *cortijo* style, is typical of the south. Summer meals are served in the garden, winter meals in a large room with a fireplace. The menu offers a number of good dishes, and the wine list is extensive. For your main course, select guinea fowl or an interesting fish dish with grapes. Vegetarians can enjoy vegetable mousse pudding and crisp salads. Also worth trying: the tagliatelle, asparagus mousse, and endives Roquefort.

LA TRICYCLETTE, Buitrago, 14. Tel. 77-78-00.
   Cuisine: CONTINENTAL. **Reservations:** Not required.
$ Prices: Appetizers 550–750 ptas. ($5.15–$7.05); main dishes 1,200–1,900 ptas. ($11.30–$17.85). AE, MC, V.
   Open: Dinner Mon–Sat 7:30–11:30pm.

One of the more popular dining spots in Marbella, this restaurant is in a converted home—courtyard and all—located on a narrow street in the old quarter near the Plaza de los Naranjos. Sofas in the bar area provide a living-room ambience, and a stairway leads to an intimate dining room with an open patio that is delightful in the warmer months. Start with crêpes with a soft cream-cheese filling or grilled giant prawns, then move on to a delectable main dish such as beef *en daube,* roast duck in beer, filet steak with a green-pepper sauce, or chicken breast Leone (cooked in breadcrumbs and topped with cheese and asparagus). The wine list is extensive and reasonable.

WORTH THE EXTRA BUCKS

LA GITANA, Calle Buitrago, 2. Tel. 77-66-74.
   Cuisine: INTERNATIONAL. **Reservations:** Recommended.

$ Prices: Appetizers 500–900 ptas. ($4.70–$8.45); main dishes 1,400–2,000 ptas. ($13.15–$18.80). AE, MC, V.
Open: Dinner daily 8–11:45pm.

La Gitana offers popular rooftop dining on a narrow street in the old pueblo off the Plaza de los Naranjos. It specializes in barbecued meats, including honey-glazed chicken, spareribs, sirloin steak, and even lamb. Other dishes, such as fresh fish, are also available.

GRAN MARISQUERÍA SANTIAGO, Paseo Marítimo, 5. Tel. 77-00-78.
Cuisine: SEAFOOD. **Reservations:** Recommended.
$ Prices: Appetizers 750–1,200 ptas. ($7.05–$11.30); main dishes 1,600–2,200 ptas. ($15.05–$20.70). AE, MC, V.
Open: Lunch daily 1–5pm; dinner daily 7pm–1am.

The bubbling lobster tanks give you an idea of the dishes available. The stand-up tapas bar, the summertime patio, and the fresh seafood dishes make this one of the more popular restaurants in town. On my last visit, I arrived so early for lunch that the mussels were just being delivered. The fish soup is well prepared, spicy, and savory. The sole in champagne comes in a large serving, and the turbot can be grilled or sautéed. On a hot day the seafood salad, garnished with lobster, shrimp, and crabmeat and served with a tangy sauce, is especially recommended. For dessert, I suggest a serving of *manchego* cheese. The restaurant is directly across from the Club Marítimo.

NEARBY DINING

EL REFUGIO, Carretera de Ojén C337. Tel. 88-10-00.
Cuisine: FRENCH. **Reservations:** Not required.
$ Prices: Appetizers 450–650 ptas. ($4.25–$6.10); main dishes 1,200–1,700 ptas. ($11.30–$16). AE, DC, MC, V.
Open: Lunch Tues–Sun 1–4pm; dinner Tues–Sat 8–11pm.

If the summer heat has you down, retreat to the Sierra Blanca, just outside Ojén, where motorists come to enjoy both the mountain scenery and the French cuisine at El Refugio. Meals are served in a rustic dining room, with an open terrace for drinks. The lounge has an open fireplace and comfortable armchairs, along with a few antiques and Oriental rugs.

EVENING ENTERTAINMENT
A MARBELLA TASCA CRAWL

No doubt about it—the best way to keep food costs low in Marbella is to do what the Spaniards do: Eat your meals in the tapas bars. You get plenty of atmosphere, lots of fun, good food, and low costs. Order a first course in one bar with a glass of wine or beer, a second course in another, and on and on as your stamina and appetite dictate. You can eat well in most places for around 600 pesetas ($5.65), and *tascas* are found all over town.

DANCE CLUBS

ANA MARÍA, Plaza del Santo Cristo, 4-5. Tel. 86-07-04.
The elongated tapas bar here is often crowded with locals, and a frequently changing collection of singers, dancers, and musicians performs everything from flamenco to popular songs. Open: Daily 11pm–4am. Closed: Mon Dec–Mar; Nov. Prices: Drinks 800 ptas. ($7.50).
Admission: 2,200 ptas. ($20.70).

PEPE MORENO, Carretera de Cádiz, km 186. Tel. 77-02-79.
A leading disco on the Costa del Sol, Pepe Moreno has a Spanish decor and ambience. The disc jockey always seems to play the right music at the right time. Open: Daily 11pm–4am. Prices: Drinks 800 ptas. ($7.50).
Admission: 1,800 ptas. ($16.90).

---

7. FUENGIROLA & LOS BOLICHES

20 miles W of Málaga, 64½ miles E of Algeciras, 356½ miles S of Madrid

GETTING THERE **By Train** From Torremolinos, take the Metro at La Nogalera station (under the RENFE sign). Trains depart every 30 minutes.

By Bus Fuengirola is on the main Costa del Sol bus route from either Algeciras in the west or Málaga in the east.

By Car Take the N-340 east from Marbella.

ESSENTIALS The area code for Fuengirola and Los Boliches is 952. The Tourist Information Office is at Plaza de España (tel. 952/47-85-00).

The twin fishing towns of Fuengirola and Los Boliches lie halfway between the more famous resorts of Marbella and Torremolinos. The promenade along the water stretches some 2½ miles, with the less developed Los Boliches just half a mile from Fuengirola. The towns don't have the facilities or drama of Torremolinos and Marbella. Fuengirola and Los Boliches are cheaper, though, and that has attracted a horde of budget-conscious European tourists.

On a promontory overlooking the sea, the ruins of **San Isidro Castle** can be seen. The **Santa Amalja, Carvajal,** and **Las Gaviotas beaches** are broad, clean, and sandy. Everybody goes to the big **flea market** at Fuengirola on Tuesdays.

WHERE TO STAY

HOSTAL SEDEÑO, Don Jacinto, 1. 29640 Fuengirola. Tel. 952/47-47-88. 34 rms (all with bath).
$ Rates: 2,500 ptas. ($23.50) single; 3,800 ptas. ($35.70) double. Breakfast 225 ptas. ($2.10) extra. No credit cards.

The Sedeño is three minutes from the beach, in the heart of town. Its modest lobby leads to a larger lounge furnished with antiques and reproductions. You pass a small open courtyard where stairs go up to the second- and third-floor balconied bedrooms. These overlook a small garden with fig and palm trees, plus a glassed-in breakfast room with terrace. There is no restaurant.

FLORIDA, Paseo Marítimo, s/n, 29640 Fuengirola. Tel. 952/47-61-00. Fax 952/58-15-29. 116 rms (all with bath). TEL
$ Rates: 4,000 ptas. ($37.60) single; 6,500 ptas. ($61.10) double. Breakfast 425 ptas. ($4) extra. AE, DC, MC, V.
There is a semitropical garden in front of the Florida, and guests can enjoy refreshments under a wide, vine-covered pergola. Most of the comfortable rooms have balconies overlooking the sea or mountains. The floors are of tile, and the furnishings, particularly in the lounge, make much use of plastic. It's a 10-minute walk from the train station.

WHERE TO EAT

DON PE', Cruz, 19, Fuengirola. Tel. 47-83-51.
Cuisine: CONTINENTAL. **Reservations:** Recommended (dinner).
$ Prices: Appetizers 550–750 ptas. ($5.15–$7.05); main dishes 1,200–1,900 ptas. ($11.30–$17.85). AE, DC, MC, V.
Open: Lunch Mon–Sat 1–3:30pm; dinner Mon–Sat 7–11:30pm. **Closed:** Lunch July–Sept.

In hot weather, visitors dine in the courtyard, whose roof can be adjusted to allow in light and air. In cold weather, a fire within the hearth illuminates the heavy ceiling beams and rustic accessories. The menu features a selection of game dishes: medallion of venison, roast filet of wild boar, duck with orange sauce. The ingredients are imported from the forests and plains of Andalusia. Don Pe' lies off the Avenida Ramón y Cajal.

EL JARDÍN ESCONDIDO, Avenida Acapulco, s/n, Los Boliches. Tel. 47-56-83.
   Cuisine: SPANISH/FRENCH. **Reservations:** Recommended. **Directions:** Head out on Paseo Marítimo to Playa de los Boliches.
$ Prices: Appetizers 650–900 ptas. ($5.65–$8.45); main dishes 1,200–1,900 ptas. ($11.30–$17.85). MC, V.
   Open: Lunch Mon–Sat 1:30–3:30pm; dinner Mon–Sat 7:30–11:30pm. **Closed:** Jan 15–Feb 15.
The restaurant is set within an Iberian chalet whose garden gate opens to reveal a charming oasis of comfort and gastronomic skill. Its owners are Dutch-born Dirk Simonsz and his partner, Louise Sutton, who almost single-handedly direct the kitchen and dining room. Every item is prepared to order, the ambitious menu including such temptations as cream of walnut and zucchini soup, filet of swordfish in a saffron cream sauce, and chicken breast rendered more pungent with a savory orange-and-ginger sauce.

EL TOMATE, El Troncon, 19, Fuengirola. Tel. 46-35-59.
   Cuisine: CONTINENTAL. **Reservations:** Recommended.
$ Prices: Appetizers 650–850 ptas. ($6.10–$8); main dishes 1,200–1,900 ptas. ($11.30–$17.85). AE, MC, V.
   Open: Dinner daily 7pm–midnight.
In a deep and narrow townhouse in the heart of Fuengirola, just around the corner from the old market, German-born owner Michael Lienhoop infuses his cuisine with the best traditions of southern and northern Europe: such dishes as succulent marinated salmon; fresh tomato soup laced with gin; filet of hake floating atop a sauce concocted of cream, mustard, and fresh dill; and a savory version of pork in a red-wine-and-mushroom sauce. You can even order the German favorite: Sauerkraut with bacon and sausage.

CEFERINO, Rotonda de la Luna, 1, Pueblo López, Fuengirola. Tel. 46-45-93.
   Cuisine: SPANISH. **Reservations:** Required.
$ Prices: Appetizers 750–950 ptas. ($7.05–$8.95); main dishes 1,500–2,100 ptas. ($14.10–$19.75). AE, MC, V.
   Open: Lunch daily 1–4pm; dinner daily 8pm–midnight. **Closed:** Jan.
The air-conditioned dining room can accommodate only about two dozen diners, who know they're getting the best food in Fuengirola. Against the backdrop of Iberian decor, chef Ceferino García Jiménez has prepared dinners for kings, statesmen, and resort guests. His specialties include an avocado-based gazpacho, stuffed crêpe Ceferino, and grilled turbot with roe. Braised duck is served with spinach pudding and pears. The restaurant lies off the Avenida de Suel, near the bus station.

DON BIGOTE, Francisco Cano, 39, Los Boliches. Tel. 47-50-94.
   Cuisine: SPANISH/CONTINENTAL. **Reservations:** Recommended. **Directions:** Take Paseo Marítimo to Playa de Los Boliches.
$ Prices: Appetizers 550–750 ptas. ($5.15–$7.05); main dishes 1,500–1,900 ptas. ($14.10–$17.85); fixed-priced menu 2,200 ptas. ($20.70). AE, MC, V.
   Open: Dinner Mon–Sat 7pm–midnight.
Once a deserted century-old sardine factory and a row of fishermen's cottages, Don Bigote (Mr. Mustache) was transformed into one of the most popular restaurants in

the area. In summer the garden patio with its splashing fountain is great for enjoying the well-prepared Spanish and continental fare. In cooler weather you can eat in one of the attractive regional-style dining rooms. You might enjoy a predinner drink under the rafters in the lounge bar.

8. MIJAS

18½ miles W of Málaga, 363 miles S of Madrid

GETTING THERE By Bus   There's frequent bus service from the terminal at Fuengirola.

By Car. At Fuengirola, take the Mijas road north.

ESSENTIALS   The area code for Mijas is 952.

Just 5 miles (8 km) north of coastal road N-340, this village is known as "White Mijas" because of its marble-white Andalusian-style houses. Mijas is at the foot of a sierra near the turnoff to Fuengirola, and from its lofty height, 1,476 feet above sea level, you get a panoramic view of the Mediterranean.

Celts, Phoenicians, and Moors, as well as today's intrepid tourists, visited Mijas, all of which is an attraction. The easiest way to get around its cobblestoned streets is to rent a burro taxi. If you find it overrun with souvenir shops, head for a park at the top of Cuesta de la Villa, where you'll see the ruins of a **Moorish fortress** dating from 833. If you're in Mijas for a fiesta, you'll be attending events in the country's only square bullring.

WHERE TO STAY

HOTEL MIJAS, Urbanización Tamisa, Carretera Benalmadena, 29650 Mijas. Tel. 952/48-58-00. Fax 952/48-58-25. 100 rms (all with bath). TV TEL
$ Rates: 9,500 ptsas. ($89.30) single; 12,500 ptas. ($117.50) double. Breakfast 975 ptas. ($9.15) extra. AE, DC, MC, V.

One of the most charming hotels on the Costa del Sol, it sits on a mountain slope in the town center. There is a flower patio, and the terrace has white wicker furniture. There is a tavern in the Andalusian style, replete with large kegs of wine. In the evening guests retreat to the handsome lounge, furnished with inlaid chests and antiques, including an interesting collection of fans. The bedrooms are stylish. Facilities include tennis courts, a swimming pool, sauna, gymnasium, boutique, hairdresser, and barber, plus a barbecue. Evening entertainment is provided (in summer), and during the day guests can play at the 18-hole Mijas golf course.

WHERE TO EAT

EL PADRASTRO, Paseo del Compás. Tel. 48-50-00.
Cuisine: INTERNATIONAL. **Reservations:** None.
$ Prices: Appetizers 550–700 ptas. ($5.15–$8.45); main dishes 900–1,500 ptas. ($8.45–$14.10); special budget meals 1,000–1,500 ptas. ($9.40–$14.10). AE, DC, MC, V.
Open: Fri–Wed noon–midnight.

Part of the fun of dining at El Padrastro is reaching the place. You go to the cliff side of town and, if you're athletic, walk up 77 steps; if you're not, take the elevator to the highest point. Once you get there, you'll discover that El Padrastro is the town's best dining spot, offering international cuisine on its terraces with their panoramic views of the Mediterranean coast. You can choose whether to eat inexpensively or elaborately. If it's the latter, make it chateaubriand with a bottle of the best Spanish champagne. If you stick to regional dishes, you'll save money.

EL CAÑUELO, Málaga, 32. Tel. 48-52-98.
Cuisine: INTERNATIONAL. **Reservations:** Not required.

$ Prices: Appetizers 375–800 ptas. ($3.55–$7.50); main dishes 995–1,650 ptas. ($9.35–$15.51). AE, MC, V.
Open: Lunch Tues–Sun 11:30am–3:30pm; dinner Tues–Sun 7:30–11pm.

Set within a renovated medium-sized house at the entrance to town, this restaurant contains a small bar and a pair of dining rooms where you can enjoy good food. Owned and managed by Alex Hunter and John Brians, it offers a frequently changing menu based on regionally available ingredients, such fare as fettuccine in a salmon-and-cream sauce, filet steak with green peppercorns or with a mushroom sauce, seafood crêpes, a Cajun-style fish kebab, chicken with barbecue sauce, and even a Texas-inspired chili.

RESTAURANTE EL CAPRICHO, Caños, 5. Tel. 48-51-11.
 Cuisine: INTERNATIONAL. **Reservations:** Recommended.
$ Prices: Appetizers 550–650 ptas. ($5.15–$6.10); main dishes 1,100–1,600 ptas. ($10.35–$15.05); fixed-priced menus 1,050–1,400 ptas. ($9.85–$13.15). AE, MC, V.
 Open: Lunch Thur–Tues 1–4pm; dinner Thurs–Tues 7–11:30pm.

El Capricho, located in what was once a private home in the town center, draws a large English-speaking clientele, and the varied menu is geared to their tastes. Appetizers include prawn cocktail, Serrano ham, omelets, corn on the cob, soups, and salads. Among main dishes are sole and trout, grilled swordfish, chicken Kiev, shish kebab, steak Diane, chicken Hawaii, and pheasant Capricho. You might prefer the paella Mijeña, which is excellent. Desserts range from flambéed concoctions to baked Alaska. The wine list offers good choices, including the house Valdepeñas.

9. TORREMOLINOS

9 miles W of Málaga, 353 miles S of Madrid

GETTING THERE By Air Málaga airport is nearby.

By Train Frequent departures from the terminal at Málaga.

By Bus Buses run frequently between Málaga and Torremolinos.

By Car Take the N-340 west from Málaga or the N-340 east from Marbella.

ESSENTIALS The area code for Torremolinos is 952. The Tourist Information Office is at La Nogalera, 517 (tel. 952/38-15-78). In winter the weather can get chilly; pack accordingly.

This Mediterranean beach resort is the most famous in Spain. It's a gathering place for international visitors, a melting pot of Europeans and Americans. Many relax here after a whirlwind tour of Europe—the living's easy, the people are fun, and there are no historical monuments to visit. Thus the sleepy fishing village of Torremolinos has been engulfed in a cluster of cement-walled resort hotels. Prices are on the rise, but it nevertheless remains one of Europe's vacation bargains.

WHERE TO STAY

HOTEL LOS ARCOS, Avenida Montemar, 192, 29620 Torremolinos. Tel. 952/38-08-22. 51 rms (all with bath). A/C TV TEL
$ Rates (including continental breakfast): 3,400 ptas. ($31.95) single; 3,800 ptas. ($35.70) double. AE, DC, MC, V.

Once a grand old villa, the Hotel Los Arcos is reminiscent of the Spanish-style houses built for movie stars in Beverly Hills in the 1920s. Eclectic furnishings are placed throughout, and the bedrooms are pleasant, each with a balcony and a garden view. Half of the rooms have minibars. A complete lunch or dinner is available for 1,500 pesetas ($14.10). The hotel stands 225 yards from the beach and ¾ mile from the town center.

HOTEL PLATA, Pasaje Pizarro, 1, 29620 Torremolinos. Tel. 952/38-00-70. 39 rms (all with bath). TEL Bus: 4.

$ Rates: 3,300 ptas. ($31) single; 4,000 ptas. ($37.60) double. Breakfast 300 ptas. ($2.80) extra. MC, V.

A centrally located hotel, right on the coastal road to Málaga, the Plata is surrounded by private terraces with folding chairs and tables set out for breakfast or drinks. The oddly shaped rooms are large; there's enough space to add extra beds if required. The air-conditioned dining room, which serves reasonably good meals, captures the Andalusian spirit with its beamed ceiling, crude yet comfortable chairs, and lots of bric-a-brac.

HOTEL EL POZO, Casablanca, 4, 29620 Torremolinos. Tel. 952/38-06-22. 28 rms (all with bath). TEL

$ Rates: 2,900 ptas. ($27.25) single; 4,400 ptas. ($41.35) double. Breakfast 275 ptas. ($2.35) extra. DC, MC, V.

This hotel isn't for light sleepers; It's in one of the liveliest sections of town, a short walk from the train station. The lobby-level bar has an open fireplace, heavy Spanish furniture, cool white tiles, and a view of a small courtyard. From your window or terrace you can view the promenades below. Rooms are furnished in a simple, functional style. The double rooms have TV.

HOSTAL LOS JAZMINES, Avenida del Lido, s/n, 29620 Torremolinos Tel. 952/38-50-33. Fax 952/37-27-02. 85 rms (all with bath). TEL

$ Rates: 4,700 pts. ($44.20) double. Breakfast 225 ptas. ($2.10) extra. AE, MC, V.

On one of the best beaches in Torremolinos, facing a plaza at the foot of the shady Avenida del Lido, this paradise for sunseekers is replete with terraces, lawns, and an odd-shaped swimming pool. Meals are served al fresco or inside the appealing dining room, furnished with Spanish reproductions. The bedrooms, all doubles, seem a bit impersonal, but they have their own little balconies, coordinated colors, and compact baths. From here it's a good hike up the hill to the town center.

HOTEL BLASÓN, Avenida de los Manantiales, 1, 29620 Torremolinos. Tel. 952/38-67-67. 48 rms (all with bath). TEL Bus: 4.

$ Rates: 4,200 ptas ($39.50) single; 4,800 ptas. ($45.10) double. Breakfast 300 ptas. ($2.80) extra. AE, DC, MC, V.

Those who want a simple, centrally located place to stay should try the Hotel Blasón. But beware of the noise: The hotel opens directly onto the Plaza de Costa del Sol, where there are outdoor tables for drinks and snacks. The bedrooms are furnished with reproductions of Spanish provincial pieces.

ALTA VISTA, Ma Barrabino s/n, 29620 Torremolinos. Tel. 952/38-76-00. Fax 952/38-78-34. 107 rms (all with bath). TEL

$ Rates (including continental breakfast): 3,800 ptas. ($35.70) single; 5,000 ptas. ($47) double. No credit cards.

A few minutes' walk from the beach, the Alta Vista is situated in the old marketplace, right in the heart of Torremolinos, surrounded by little lanes of boutiques and patios with coffee shops. The entire roof of the hotel is a tiled solarium with umbrella tables, lounge chairs, and a bar. Each of the bedrooms—furnished with ornate wrought-iron beds, reed-seated chairs, phones, and bedside reading lamps—has a balcony. Guests gather in the lounge or the bar. Lunch and dinner are served in a stylish dining room, with meals from 1,400 pesetas ($13.15).

HOTEL BRISTOL, Avenida Montemar, 112, 29620 Torremolinos. Tel. 952/38-28-00. 58 rms (all with bath). A/C TEL

$ Rates: 4,300 ptas. ($40.40) single; 5,000 ptas. ($47) double. Breakfast 225 ptas. ($2.10) extra. MC, V.

Each of the spacious rooms in this modern motel has a private balcony overlooking the swimming pool. On the western side of Torremolinos, the Bristol escapes the bedlam of the town center, but not the traffic roaring past its door. Off the N-340, the main coast road, it's on an embankment covered with bushes and flowers.

MIAMI, Aladino, 14, 29620 Torremolinos. Tel. 952/38-52-55. 27 rms (all with bath). TEL
$ Rates: 3,300 ptas. ($31) single; 5,000 ptas. ($47) double. Breakfast 250 ptas. ($2.35) extra. V.
Near the Carihuela section of town, 45 yards from the beach, the Miami offers rooms decorated with style, comfort, and traditional trappings; every room opens onto a balcony. Isolated by high walls, the house has a private garden, even a small swimming pool. In the rear patio, bougainvillea climbs over arches, and the tile terrace is used both for sunbathing and for serving refreshments. The country-rustic living room boasts a walk-in fireplace, plus lots of brass and copper. Continental breakfast is the only meal served.

HOTEL AMARAGUA, Los Nidos, 23, 29620 Torremolinos. Tel. 952/38-47-00. Fax 952/38-49-45. 198 rms (all with bath). TEL
$ Rates: 4,800 ptas. ($45.10) single; 7,000 ptas. ($65.80) double. Breakfast 550 ptas. ($5.15) extra. AE, DC, MC, V.
With the hotel right on the beach in the residential section of Montemar, all rooms have terraces with sea views. Facilities include lounges, television, a bar, three large swimming pools (one heated), gardens, water sports, a children's playground, parking facilities, and a tennis court.

HOTEL EDÉN, Avenida Las Mercedes, 24, 29620 Torremolinos. Tel. 952/38-46-00. 96 rms (all with bath). TEL
$ Rates (including continental breakfast): 4,200 ptas. ($39.50) single; 7,500 ptas. ($70.50) double. AE, DC, MC, V. **Closed:** Oct–Apr.
Built into a cliff, the Hotel Edén has an eighth-floor entrance. An elevator takes you down to the bedroom area, where private terraces overlook rooftops, a cultivated field, a stable (that rents riding horses), and the Mediterranean. The rooms are utilitarian and comfortable, although plumbing and maintenance may be shaky at times. On the lower level you'll find a swimming pool and an adjoining terrace. A veranda restaurant overlooks the sea. The hotel is near the train station.

SIDI LAGO ROJO, Miami, 1, 29620 Torremolinos. Tel. 952/38-76-66. Fax 952/38-08-91. 144 rms (all with bath). A/C TEL
$ Rates (including continental breakfast): 9,000 ptas. ($84.60) double. AE, DC, MC, V.
Located in the heart of the fishing village of La Carihuela, and the finest place to stay there, Sidi Lago Rojo stands only 150 feet from the beach and has its own gardens, swimming pool, terraces for sunbathing, and refreshment bar. It offers studio-style rooms, doubles only, tastefully decorated with contemporary Spanish furnishings and tile baths. All rooms have terraces with views; some have minibars, and TV is available upon request. Lunch and dinner are available for a set rate of 1,700 pesetas ($16). The bar is popular, and in the late evening there's dancing.

WHERE TO EAT

The cuisine in Torremolinos is more American and continental European than Andalusian. The hotels often serve elaborate four-course meals, but you may want to sample the local fast-food offerings. A good spot to try is the food court called **La Nogalera,** the major gathering place in Torremolinos, located between the coast road and the beach. Head down the Calle del Cauce to this compound of modern whitewashed Andalusian buildings. Open to pedestrian traffic only, it features a maze of passageways, courtyards, and patios for eating and drinking. If you're seeking anything from sandwiches to Belgian waffles to scrambled eggs to pizzas, you'll find it here.

EL GATO VIUDO, Nogalera, 8. Tel. 38-51-29.
Cuisine: SPANISH. **Reservations:** Not required.

$ Prices: Appetizers 350–500 ptas. ($3.30–$4.70); main dishes 650–1,300 ptas. ($6.30–12.20). AE, DC, MC, V.

Open: Lunch Thurs–Tues noon–3pm; dinner Thurs–Tues 6–11:30pm.

S This two-fork tavern-style restaurant off the Calle San Miguel offers sidewalk tables with tartan tablecloths and Kelly-green Spanish chairs. The chef specializes in Spanish cuisine, and the small but interesting à la carte menu (in English) includes shellfish soup, paella, and roast chicken. Fresh fruit is your best bet for dessert. The atmosphere is informal, and the international clientele shows up in all kinds of attire.

VIETNAM SUR, Bloque, 9. Tel. 38-67-37.
Cuisine: VIETNAMESE. **Reservations:** Recommended.
$ Prices: Appetizers 350–750 ptas. ($3.30–$7.05); main dishes 750–1,400 ptas. ($7.05–$13.25). No credit cards.
Open: Lunch Sun from 1–4pm; dinner Thurs–Tues 7pm–midnight.

The food is inexpensive here and it's best shared. Chopsticks are the norm as you begin with spring rolls served with mint and a spicy sauce for dipping. The chef's specials include fried stuffed chicken wings and beef with rice noodles. The wine list is short and moderately priced. With an outside dining terrace, the restaurant stands in the Playamar section near the beach.

RESTAURANT FLORIDA, Casablanca, 15, La Nogalera. Tel. 38-50-95.
Cuisine: DANISH. **Reservations:** Recommended.
$ Prices: Fixed-priced menu 795–1,500 ptas. ($7.45–14.10). AE, DC, MC, V.
Open: Lunch daily 1–4pm; dinner daily 7pm–midnight.

This is an international Danish restaurant on the lower level of a modern shopping complex near the Calle del Cauce. The decor is South Seas, and the spread is gargantuan—one of the best food values in Torremolinos. For a set price you can enjoy a vast array of dishes from this smörgåsbord; many diners linger late, making occasional forays to the table for fine herring, tasty salads, cold meats, and hot dishes. A spread of cheeses and fruits is offered along with desserts.

VIKING, Casablanca, 9. La Nogalera. Tel. 38-10-41.
Cuisine: INTERNATIONAL. **Reservations:** Recommended.
$ Prices: Appetizers 200–550 ptas. ($1.90–$5.15); main dishes 800–1,500 ptas. ($7.50–$14.10). AE, DC, MC, V.
Open: Daily 12:30–11:30pm.

S A popular budget restaurant, drawing an international crowd, Viking is located at the end of the Calle San Miguel (where you can stop at one of the tapas bars before dinner). The food is superior. Specialties include pork chops with red cabbage, chicken American style, snails in garlic, and cucumber salad.

EL CABALLO VASCO, Calle Casablanca, La Nogalera. Tel. 38-23-36.
Cuisine: BASQUE. **Reservations:** Recommended.
$ Prices: Appetizers 550–900 ptas. ($5.15–$8.45); main dishes 950–1,900 ptas. ($8.95–$17.85). AE, MC, V.
Open: Lunch Tues–Sun 1–4pm; dinner Tues–Sun 8pm–midnight.

Considered the best independent restaurant in Torremolinos, El Caballo Vasco is located on the top floor of a modern building complex in the dead-eye center of town (down the Calle del Cauce). Reached by an elevator, it has picture windows that open onto a terrace. Generous portions of tasty, deservedly popular Basque cuisine are served, include such dishes as prawns in garlic sauce, codfish, and pork shanks.

FRUTOS, Carretera de Cádiz, km 235, Urbanización Los Alamos. Tel. 38-14-50.
Cuisine: SPANISH. **Reservations:** Recommended.
$ Prices: Appetizers 550–750 ptas. ($5.15–$7.05); main dishes 950–1,800 ptas. ($8.95–$16.90); fixed-priced menu 1,400 ptas. ($13.15). AE, MC, V.
Open: Lunch daily 1–4:30pm; dinner year round Mon–Sat 8pm–midnight, July–Sept also Sun 8pm–midnight.

Malagueños frequent this place in droves, as they like its good old-style cooking—the cuisine is Spanish with a vengeance. Portions are large and service is hectic. Diners enjoy the "day's catch," perhaps *rape* (monkfish), angler fish, or the increasingly rare *mero* (grouper). Also available: the garlic-studded leg of lamb and the oxtail prepared in a savory ragoût. Frutos is located next to the Los Alamos service station, 1¼ miles (2km) from the town center.

MARRAHECH, Carretera de Benalmadena, 7. Tel. 38-21-69.

Cuisine: MOROCCAN. **Reservations:** Recommended.

$ Prices: Appetizers 450–850 ptas. ($4.25–$8); main dishes 950–1,800 ptas. ($8.95–$16.90). No credit cards.

Open: Lunch Mon and Wed–Sat 12:30–4:30pm; dinner Mon and Wed–Sat 7:30pm–midnight.

Excellent Moroccan cuisine is offered amid a rather garish decor of tiles and carved plaster. Some of the more famous dishes of the Maghreb served here include couscous, *tagine* (meat pies), and various kebabs, usually made with lamb. The stuffed pastries make a fitting dessert if you're Moroccan; otherwise, you might find them too sweet. Marrahech is located at the western edge of Torremolinos, 1¼ miles (2km) from the town center.

MESÓN CANTARRANAS, Avenida de Benalmadena, s/n. Tel. 30-15-77.

Cuisine: SPANISH. **Reservations:** Recommended. **Directions:** Head to Arroyo de la Miel and Benalmadena to the western end of the Torremolinos bypass.

$ Prices: Appetizers 550–750 ptas. ($5.15–$7.05); main dishes 950–1,800 ptas. ($8.95–$16.90). AE, MC, V.

Open: Lunch daily noon–4pm; dinner daily 8pm–midnight.

Dating from 1840 and housed in a former olive mill, this restaurant is set back from the Arroyo de la Miel–El Pinillo highway. Arrange for a table on the terrace overlooking the olive grove. You can order frogs' legs ("singing frogs" is the restaurant's English name), but perhaps you'll prefer a hefty portion of roast suckling pig or roast baby lamb. Daily specials are also featured, and they often come from the sea—squid cooked in its own ink or hake prepared Cantabrian style.

RESTAURANTE CANTON, Plaza de la Gamba Alegre. Tel. 38-21-17.

Cuisine: CHINESE. **Reservations:** Recommended. **Bus:** 4 to town center.

$ Prices: Appetizers 250–650 ptas. ($2.35–$6.10); main dishes 950–1,500 ptas. ($8.95–$14.10); fixed-priced menu 950 ptas. ($8.95). No credit cards.

Open: Lunch Wed–Mon 1–4pm; dinner Wed–Mon 7pm–midnight.

Near the main shopping center of Torremolinos, this is one of the resort's most reasonably priced restaurants. Its very popular set menu includes a spring roll, sweet-and-sour pork, beef with onions, steamed white rice, dessert, and a drink. You can also order à la carte, partaking of such specialties as Cantonese roast duck and grilled king prawn Chinese style. The staff is efficient and cordial.

SEAFOOD AT LA CARIHUELA

If you want to get away from the brash high-rises and honky-tonks, head to nearby Carihuela, the old fishing village on the western outskirts of Torremolinos, where some of the best bargain restaurants are found. You can walk down a hill toward the sea to reach it.

CASA PRUDENCIA, Carmen, 43. Tel. 38-14-52.

Cuisine: SEAFOOD. **Reservations:** Recommended.

$ Prices: Appetizers 450–600 ptas. ($4.25–$5.65); main dishes 750–1,500 ptas. ($7.05–$14.10); fixed-priced menu 1,200 ptas. ($11.30). AE, DC, MC, V.

Open: Lunch Tues–Sun 1–5pm; dinner Tues–Sun 7:30pm–midnight.

Tops with locals and visitors alike, this seaside restaurant 1¼ miles (2km) west of the center features gazpacho, lentils, shrimp omelet, swordfish, and shish kebab. Try the special paella for a main course, followed by strawberries with whipped cream (in the late spring) for dessert. The atmosphere is cordial and almost everyone sits together at long tables. If you want to splurge, order *lubina à la sal*—a huge, boneless fish packed under a layer of salt, which is then broken open at your table. It makes a singular gastronomical treat.

EL ROQUEO, Carmen, 35. Tel. 38-49-46.
   Cuisine: SEAFOOD. **Reservations:** Recommended.
$ **Prices:** Appetizers 450–750 ptas. ($4.25–$7.05); main dishes 1,200–1,900 ptas. ($11.30–$17.85). AE, MC, V.
   Open: Lunch Wed–Mon 1–4pm; dinner Wed–Mon 7pm–midnight. **Closed:** Nov.

Right in the heart of this fisherman's village, El Roqueo makes the perfect place for a seafood dinner near the sea. Begin with the savory *sopa de mariscos* (shellfish soup). Then try a specialty of the chef, fish baked in rock salt; you can also order grilled sea bass or shrimp. Top everything off with a soothing caramel custard for dessert. Some of the more expensive fish courses are priced by the gram, so order carefully.

EVENING ENTERTAINMENT
BARS AND TAPAS

BAR CENTRAL, Plaza Andalucía. Tel. 38-27-60.
This place offers coffee, brandy, beer, cocktails, sandwiches, and pastries—served, if you prefer, on the large covered terrace. Open: Daily 8am–midnight. Prices: Beer 70 ptas. (65¢); drinks 300 ptas. ($2.80). Bus: 4.

BAR EL TORO, San Miguel, 32. Tel. 38-65-04.
The bullfight theme is everywhere here, and kegs of beer, bar stools, and the sidewalk terrace on the main shopping street make it the perfect spot for a before-dinner sherry or an after-dinner beer. As a special attraction, the staff will prepare a bullfight poster with your name between those of two famous matadors—500 pesetas ($4.70). Open: Daily 8am–midnight. Prices: Beer 150 ptas. ($1.40); pitcher of *sangría* 380 ptas. ($3.55).

LA BODEGA, San Miguel, 38. Tel. 38-73-37.
You'll be lucky to find space at one of the small tables in La Bodega, since many consider the bar food filling enough for a meal. Once you begin to order the platters of fried squid, tuna, grilled shrimp, or tiny brochettes of sole, you might not be able to stop. Open: Daily noon–midnight. Prices: Beer 150 ptas. ($1.40); tapas 150–600 ptas. ($1.40–$5.65). Bus: 4.

DANCE CLUBS

PIPER'S CLUB, Plaza Costa del Sol, s/n. Tel. 38-29-94.
This fun subterranean spot, with ramps and tunnels connecting various grottoes, has music piped to several dance floors—each with strobe lighting and reflecting fountains and pools. There's also a swimming pool. The place is usually packed. Open: Daily 6–10:30pm and 11pm–4:30am. Bus: 4.
   Admission: 500 ptas. ($4.70) before 10:30, 1,000 ptas. ($9.40) after 11pm Sun–Thurs; 1,200 ptas. ($11.30) after 11pm Fri–Sat. Includes first drink.

GATSBY, Avenida Montemar, 68. Tel. 38-53-72.
Located on a traffic-choked boulevard off the N-340 at the western entrance to town, Gatsby provides a loud, distortion-free sound system, which plays the latest releases. There's private parking. Open: Daily 6–10:30pm; 11:30pm–4:30am.
   Admission: 500 ptas. ($4.70) 6–10:30pm, 1,000 ptas. ($9.40) 11:30pm–4:30am. Includes first drink.

LA CARIHUELA AFTER DARK

To avoid the frenzied uptown scene, head to the little fishing village and beach district of La Carihuela. The **Intermezzo Piano Club,** Plaza del Remo, 2 (tel. 38-32-67), by far the most sophisticated bar in La Carihuela, offers sea views from the front door, with the interior focusing around a shiny black piano. There's a small dance floor. It's open daily from 10pm to 3am, and drinks are 400 to 600 pesetas ($3.75 to $5.65).

THE GAY LIFE

Torremolinos has the largest cluster of gay life along the coast of southern Spain. Several bars huddle together in Pueblo Blanco, which is like a little village of its own. Although much gay life also sprawls across La Nogalera, the restaurants there tend to attract a mixed crowd.

El Comedor, Calle Casablanca s/n, Pueblo Blanco (tel. 38-38-51), serves Andalusian/Basque/international cuisine to a mix of straight and gay couples. Try the sole in a port-wine sauce or the codfish croquettes. The dessert specialty is *leche frita*—literally "fried milk," but actually a sort of sweet croquette. Prices for appetizers range from 550 to 750 pesetas ($5.15 to $7.05); for main dishes, from $1,200 to 1,900 pesetas ($11.30 to $17.85). Some major credit cards are accepted. The restaurant is open for dinner Thursday through Tuesday from 7pm to midnight; it's closed January 15 to March 1.

The leading gay disco is called **Bronx,** Edificio Centro Jardín (tel. 38-73-60). It's open nightly from 10pm to 6am, charging an entrance fee of 1,000 pesetas ($9.40), with beer going for 350 pesetas ($3.30).

One popular gay bar is **"Men's Bar,"** La Nogalera, 714 (tel. 38-42-05). Crowded most nights, it charges 350 pesetas ($3.30) for a beer. Another hot bar is **La Gorila,** Pueblo Blanco, 33 (no phone), which has good music and a congenial crowd. Open daily from 9pm to 3am, it charges 350 pesetas ($3.30) for a beer.

---

10. MÁLAGA

340 miles S of Madrid, 82 miles E of Algeciras

GETTING THERE   By Air   Most visitors to the Costa del Sol fly into Málaga airport. The biggest carrier is Iberia, the national airline of Spain, along with its affiliate, Aviaco. In addition to weekly flights from Europe and South America, Iberia/Aviaco has several daily flights from Barcelona and about a dozen via Madrid. Less frequent service into Málaga comes from such airports as Bilbao, Tenerife (Canary Islands), Palma de Mallorca, and Valencia. Most other cities in Spain transfer their domestic passengers through Madrid or Barcelona.

Many residents of the East Coast of North America opt for one of Iberia's frequent flights to Málaga from New York, usually with a brief touchdown in Barcelona. Other routings to Málaga, including some from New York and all the flights from Chicago, Boston, Dallas, Philadelphia, Los Angeles, Mexico City, and Miami, require a change of plane in either New York or Madrid.

In Málaga, Iberia's central ticketing and information office is at Molina Larío, 13 (for reservations, phone 213-731).

Málaga's airport, Rompedizio, lies 6 miles (9.5km) southwest of the city. Bus service runs between the airport and the cathedral every ½ hour, and there are also frequent train departures. If you're driving, follow coastal highway, the N-340, in the direction of Torremolinos. For airport information, dial 232-221.

By Train   RENFE has excellent rail connections between Málaga and the rest of Spain. It's main office in Málaga is at Strachan, 2 (tel. 21-31-22). From Madrid, there are 4 connections daily, the *expreso* and *talgo* trains. The latter is faster but more expensive. From Barcelona, there are 2 trains per day; from Seville, 1; and from Córdoba, 3.

By Bus Buses from all over Spain arrive at the terminal on the Paseo de los Tilos, in back of the RENFE offices. Málaga is linked by bus to all the major cities of Spain, including Madrid (3 a day), Barcelona (3 a day), and Valencia (1 a day).

By Car From the resorts in the west (such as Torremolinos or Marbella), head east along the N-340 to Málaga. If you're in the east at the end of the Costa del Sol (Almería), take the N-340 west of Málaga, with a recommended stopover at Nerja.

ESSENTIALS The area code for Málaga is 952. The Tourist Information Office is at Calle Marqués de Laríos, 5 (tel. 952/21-34-45).

Warning: Málaga has one of the highest crime rates in Spain. The most common complaint is purse-snatching, with an estimated 75% of the crimes committed by juveniles. Stolen passports are also a problem—if it happens to you, contact the U.S. Consulate, Edificio El Ancla, Calle Ramón y Cajal, Apt. 502, in nearby Fuengirola (tel. 952/47-48-91).

Málaga is a bustling commercial and residential center whose economy does not depend exclusively on tourism. Its chief attraction is the mild off-season climate—summer can be sticky.

The most festive time in Málaga is the first week in August, when the city celebrates its reconquest by Ferdinand and Isabella in 1487. This big **feria** (fair) is the occasion for parades and bullfights. A major tree-shaded boulevard of the city, the Paseo del Parque, is transformed into a fairground featuring amusements and restaurants.

Málaga's most famous citizen is Pablo Picasso, born here in 1881 at the Plaza de la Merced, in the center of the city. The co-founder of cubism, who would one day paint his *Guernica* to express his horror of war, unfortunately left little of his spirit in his birthplace, and only a small selection of his work.

WHAT TO SEE & DO

Unlike the rest of the Costa del Sol, Málaga has several historical sites of interest to the average visitor.

ALCAZABA, Plaza de la Aduana, Alcazabilla. Tel. 21-60-05.

The remains of this ancient Moorish palace are within easy walking distance of the city center, off the Paseo del Parque (plenty of signs point the way up the hill). The fortress was probably erected in the 9th or 10th century, although there have been later additions and reconstructions. Ferdinand and Isabella stayed here when they reconquered the city. The Alcazaba now houses an archeological museum, with exhibits of cultures ranging from Greek to Phoenician to Carthaginian. With government-planted orange trees and purple bougainvillea making the grounds even more beautiful, the view overlooking the city and the bay is among the best on the Costa del Sol.

Admission: 22 ptas. (20¢).

Open: Mon–Sat 10am–1pm and 5–8pm, Sun 10am–2pm.

MÁLAGA CATHEDRAL, Plaza Obsipo. Tel. 21-59-17.

This 16th-century Renaissance cathedral in Málaga's center, built on the site of a great mosque, suffered damage during the Civil War. But it remains vast and impressive, reflecting changing styles of interior architecture. Its most notable attribute: the richly ornamented choir stalls by Ortiz, Mena, and Michael. The cathedral has been declared a national monument.

Admission: Free.

Open: Mon–Sat 10am–1pm and 4–7pm.

CASTILLO DE GIBRALFARO, Cerro de Gibralfaro.

On a hill overlooking Málaga and the Mediterranean are the ruins of an ancient Moorish castle-fortress of unknown origin. It is near the government-run parador, and might easily be tied in with a luncheon visit.

Warning: Do not walk to Gibralfaro Castle from town. Readers have reported muggings along the way, and the area around the castle is dangerous. Take the bus (see below).

Admission: Free.

Open: Daylight hours. **Microbus:** H, leaving hourly from cathedral.

MUSEO DE BELLAS ARTES, San Agustín, 6. Tel. 21-83-82.

This former Moorish palace, located in back of the cathedral, houses a modest collection of paintings, including a gallery devoted to native son Pablo Picasso. In addition, it also displays works by Murillo, Ribera, and Morales, along with Andalusian antiques, mosaics, and sculptures.

Admission: 250 ptas. ($2.35).

Open: Mon–Fri 10:30am–1:30pm and 5–8pm, Sat–Sun 10:30am–1:30pm.

A NEARBY ATTRACTION

MUSEO HOLLANDER, Pizarra. Tel. 48-31-63.

Operated by New York natives Gino and Barbara Hollander, this museum in Pizzara (25 miles [40km] northwest of Málaga, near the village of Zalea) contains a wealth of exhibits—tools and weapons from Neolithic and Paleolithic sites in Spain; Iberian, Visigothic, and Roman artifacts; and historic clothing. The Hollanders built their own palatial home and museum here, using bricks, tiles, and carved ceiling beams from a 15th-century palace in Córdoba. The 40 massive doors date mostly from 1492. The museum can be visited by appointment, as the Hollanders take turns guiding visitors through the house and stables, where a series of small rooms and artisans' shops show what life was like in other days. Call for directions.

Admission: Free.

Open: By appointment

WHERE TO STAY

EL CENACHERO, Barroso, 5, 29001 Málaga. Tel. 952/22-40-88. 14 rms (8 with bath).

$ Rates: 2,400 ptas. ($22.55) single without bath; 4,000 ptas. ($37.60) double with bath. No credit cards.

Opened in 1969, this modest little hotel is 5 blocks from the park (near the harbor). Each of the nicely carpeted rooms is different; half of them have showers. Everything is kept clean. No meals served.

HOSTAL RESIDENCIA DERBY, San Juan de Dios, 1, 29015 Málaga. Tel. 952/21-13-01. 16 rms (all without bath). TEL

$ Rates: 2,600 ptas. ($24.45) single; 4,000 ptas. ($37.60) double. No credit cards.

The Derby is a real find. This fourth-floor boarding house right in the heart of Málaga, on a main square directly north of the train station, has some rooms with excellent views of the Mediterranean and the port of Málaga. The hostal is quite clean, and all rooms have hot and cold running water. No breakfast served.

HOSTAL RESIDENCIA CARLOS V, Cister, 6, 29015 Málaga. Tel. 952/21-51-20. 52 rms (all with bath). TEL **Bus:** 15 from the rail station.

$ Rates: 3,200 ptas. ($30.10) single; 4,500 ptas. ($42.30) double. Breakfast 300 ptas. ($2.80) extra. AE, MC, V.

This might serve as an emergency stopover if nothing else is available within the old city. It has a good central location near the cathedral, as well as an interesting façade decorated with wrought-iron balconies and *miradores*. The lobby is fairly dark, but this remains an old, safe haven. An elevator will take you to your room, furnished in a no-frills style.

ASTORIA, Avenida Comandante Benítez, 3, 29001 Málaga. Tel. 952/22-45-00. 61 rms (all with bath). A/C TEL

$ Rates: 4,000 ptas. ($37.60) single; 5,800 ptas. ($54.50) double. Breakfast 375 ptas. ($3.55) extra. MC, V.

If you need an inexpensive place to sleep near the railway station, and don't expect too much, the Astoria is for you. It's a 10-minute walk from the center of town. You'll find no lounge here, just a check-in counter. Rooms are simply furnished and clean.

PARADOR NACIONAL DE GIBRALFARO, Monte Gibralfaro, 29016 Málaga. Tel. 952/22-19-03. Fax 952/22-19-04. 12 rms (all with bath). A/C MINIBAR TV TEL **Directions:** Drive north along coastal road, Paseo de Reding, which becomes Avenida Casa de Pries, and later Paseo de Sancha. Turn left on Camino Nuevo, toward hill. **Microbus:** H from cathedral.

$ **Rates:** 8,000 ptas. ($75.20) single; 10,000 ptas. ($94) double. Breakfast 900 ptas. ($8.45) extra. AE, DC, MC, V.

Málaga's parador has everything you could possibly want in a Spanish accommodation: quality, economy, seclusion, history, and scenic location. High on a plateau near an old fortified castle, it overlooks the city and the Mediterranean, with views of the bullring, mountains, and beaches. Originally a famous restaurant, the parador has been converted into a fine hotel with two dining rooms. The bedroom suites, with their own entranceways, have private baths, living-room areas, wide glass doors opening onto private sun terraces with garden furniture. The rooms are tastefully decorated with modern furnishings and reproductions of Spanish antiques.

PARADOR NACIONAL DEL GOLF, Torremolinos, Apartado 324, 29080 Málaga. Tel. 952/38-12-55. Fax 952/38-21-41. 60 rms (all with bath). A/C MINIBAR TV TEL

$ **Rates:** 10,000 ptas. ($94) single; 13,000 ptas. ($122.20) double. Breakfast 900 ptas. ($8.45) extra. AE, DC, MC, V.

Another tasteful resort hotel created by the Spanish government, this hacienda-style parador is flanked by a golf course on one side and the Mediterranean on another. It's less than 2 miles (3.2km) from the airport, 6.5 miles (10.5km) from Malaga, and 2.5 miles (4km) from Torremolinos. Each bedroom has a private balcony, with a view of the golfing greens, the circular swimming pool, or the water. Furnishings are attractive. Long tile corridors lead to the air-conditioned public rooms: graciously furnished lounges, a bar, and a restaurant.

WHERE TO EAT

LA MANCHEGA, Marín García, 4. Tel. 22-21-80.
  Cuisine: SPANISH. **Reservations:** Not required. **Bus:** 7 or 9.
$ **Prices:** Appetizers 250–400 ptas. ($2.35–$3.75); main dishes 400–700 ptas. ($3.75–$6.60); fixed-priced menu 825 ptas. ($7.75). No credit cards.
  Open: Lunch daily 11:30am–4:30pm; dinner daily 7:30–11:30pm.

La Manchega is representative of the local bars and eateries on this popular pedestrians-only street in a downtown commercial area. Outside, there are sidewalk tables for drinking or dining; inside, a ground-floor bar with tile walls and a decorator's attempt to create an indoor Andalusian courtyard. A Salon Comedor offers additional space for dining on an upper floor. Specialties include shrimp omelets; Málaga-style soup; beans with Andalusian ham; snails; eels; and a full array of shellfish, including grilled shrimp, clams, and mussels. Try the fish soup.

MESÓN DANES (FAARUP), Barroso, 7. Tel. 22-74-42.
  Cuisine: DANISH/SPANISH. **Reservations:** None.
$ **Prices:** Appetizers 375–500 ptas. ($3.55–$4.70); main dishes 875–975 ptas. ($8.25–$9.15); fixed-priced menus 700–1,500 ptas. ($6.60–$14.10). V.
  Open: Lunch Mon–Sat 11am–4pm; dinner Mon–Sat 7:30–11:30pm. **Closed:** Aug.

Here you can enjoy Danish and Spanish snacks at low prices, with choices including Danish or Spanish soup, fish, and meat. Also available is a special Faarup plate with assorted food. The cheapest *menú del día* represents one of the best food values in Málaga. Mesón Danes is located near the bus station.

EL CORTE INGLÉS, Avenida de Andalucía, 4. Tel. 30-00-00.
  Cuisine: SPANISH. **Reservations:** Not required.

$ **Prices:** Appetizers 550–750 ptas. ($5.15–$7.05); main dishes 1,200–1,900 ptas. ($11.30–$17.85); fixed-priced menu 1,775 ptas. ($16.70). AE, DC, MC, V.
Open: Mon–Sat 10am–9pm.

There are two restaurants located in the Corte Inglés department store, in the center of Málaga. The more formal of the two, the top-floor Steak House, offers comfortable seating and a formally dressed staff that serves such specialties as green peppers stuffed with shellfish, filet of pork in a pepper cream sauce, and an array of temptingly seasoned brochettes, along with a complete wine list.

Immediately adjacent to the Steak House is a popular buffet, with over 70 dishes available for a set price of 1,775 pesetas ($16.70), half price for children under 6. Wine is extra.

REFECTORIUM, Avenue Juan Sebastián Elcano, 146. Tel. 29-45-93.
Cuisine: SPANISH. **Reservations:** Recommended.
Prices: Appetizers 550–750 ptas. ($5.15–$7.05); main dishes 1,200–1,900 ptas. ($11.30–$17.85). AE, DC, MC, V.
Open: Lunch Tues–Sun 1–4pm; dinner Tues–Sun 8pm–midnight.

It may involve a bit of searching, but it's worth the effort to find this place. Located outside of town near the Playa de El Palo beachfront, 3 miles (4.8km) east of the Plaza de Toros (bullring), the Refectorium stands on the east side of the bridge spanning the Arroyo Jaboneros. The restaurant offers dining in an ambience steeped in Spanish tradition, with brick-red floors, old wooden beams, and white stucco walls. The cuisine has an old-fashioned flair, and servings are generous. The typical soup of the Málaga area is *ajoblanco con uvas* (cold almond soup flavored with garlic and garnished with big muscatel grapes). For a classic opener, try a plate of garlic-flavored mushrooms seasoned with bits of ham. The fresh seafood is a delight, including *rape* (monkfish) and angler fish; lamb might be served with a saffron-flavored tomato sauce. Desserts are "like mama made," such as rice pudding.

RESTAURANTE ANTONIO MARTÍN, Paseo Marítimo, 4. Tel. 22-21-13.
Cuisine: SPANISH. **Reservations:** Required.
$ **Prices:** Appetizers 550–750 ptas. ($5.15–$7.05); main dishes 1,500–2,100 ptas. ($14.10–$19.75). AE, DC, MC, V.
Open: Lunch Tues–Sun 1–4pm; dinner Tues–Sun 8pm–midnight.

Although this tastefully designed brick building is close to a busy intersection near the Plaza de Toros, you'll hardly be aware of the traffic outside. Three dining rooms with natural brick walls are clustered under a peaked wooden ceiling. The most rustic of them, the Rincón de Ordóñez, honors one of Spain's top matadors. On the wall is the head of the last bull Ordóñez killed before retiring, and the suit he wore. In summer the shaded harborfront terrace makes an ideal place to dine. Menu items include stewed oxtail, grilled sirloin, kidneys in sherry sauce, leg of baby lamb, grilled salmon, mixed fried fish, grilled red mullet, fresh fried anchovies, shrimp cocktail, and shellfish soup. Service is both fast and attentive.

PARADOR GIBRALFARO, Monte Gibralfaro. Tel. 22-19-02.
Cuisine: SPANISH. **Reservations:** Not required. **Microbus:** H by cathedral.
$ **Prices:** Appetizers 450–750 ptas. ($4.25–$7.05); main dishes 1,500–1,900 ptas. ($14.10–$17.85). AE, DC, MC, V.
Open: Lunch daily 1–4pm; dinner daily 8:30–11pm.

This has long been the most panoramic restaurant in Málaga, enjoying a reputation for its seafood. From its hilltop location overlooking the city and the Mediterranean, it offers a choice of two dining rooms—one inside, with window walls opening onto the wide, covered terrace; the other in the open air, with garden chairs and tables.

PARADOR NACIONAL DEL GOLF, Apartado, 324. Tel. 38-12-55.
Cuisine: SPANISH. **Reservations:** Not required.
$ **Prices:** Appetizers 450–750 ptas. ($4.25–$7.05); main dishes 1,500–1,900 ptas. ($14.10–$17.85). AE, DC, MC, V.
Open: Lunch daily 1:30–4pm; dinner daily 8:30–11pm.

This government-owned restaurant is off the N-340 (6.5 miles [10.5km] west of Málaga). Its indoor/outdoor dining room opens onto a circular swimming pool, lawns, a golf course, and a private beach. The interior dining area, furnished with antique reproductions, has a refined country-club atmosphere. Before-lunch drinks at a modern bar tempt golfers and others, who then proceed to the covered terrace for their meals. You can make it an afternoon by using the pool, 700 pesetas ($6.60) Monday through Saturday, 900 pesetas ($8.45) on Sunday and holidays. There's a 50% discount on the pool charge if you order a meal.

TAPAS

EL BOQUERÓN DE PLATA, Alarcon Lujan, 6. Tel. 22-20-20.
Cuisine: TAPAS. **Reservations:** Not required.
$ Prices: Tapas 350 ptas. ($3.30); beer 100 ptas. (95¢). No credit cards.
Open: Daily 10am–3pm and 6–10pm.
One of the most famous bars of Málaga, behind the Alcazaba, this is the place for good Spanish wine and tapas. Most guests have a beer and a helping of prawns. The fish selection, invariably fresh, depends on the catch of the day.
Warning: There are two other places in the area using the same name.

LA TASCA, Marín García, 12. Tel. 22-20-82.
Cuisine: TAPAS. **Reservations:** Not required.
$ Prices: Tapas 350 ptas. ($3.30); beer 100 ptas. (95¢). No credit cards.
Open: Daily noon–1:30pm and 9–10:30pm.
Although just a hole in the wall, between the Calle Marqués de Larios and the Calle Nueva, La Tasca has style, conviviality, and a large staff. Among the array of tapas, try the *croquetas* (croquettes) and pungent shish kebabs laced with garlic and cumin. If you see an empty seat, grab it. There is beer from the tap, as well as wine.

BAR LOQÜENO, Marín García, 12. Tel. 22-30-48.
Cuisine: TAPAS. **Reservations:** Not required.
$ Prices: Tapas 350 ptas. ($3.30); wine 125 ptas. ($1.20) per glass. No credit cards.
Open: Daily noon–4pm and 7pm–midnight.
Bar Loqüeno offers basically the same tapas as its neighbor, La Tasca (see above). The entrance is behind a wrought-iron–and–glass door, leading into a stucco-lined room decorated in local tavern style. There are enough hams, bouquets of garlic, beer kegs, fish nets, and sausages to feed an entire village for a week. There's hardly room to stand, and you'll invariably be jostled by a busy waiter. You can eat at a table outside.

11. NERJA

32 miles E of Málaga, 104 miles W of Almería, 340 miles S of Madrid

GETTING THERE   By Bus   Nerja is well serviced by buses from Málaga, at least 10 per day (1½ hours). If you're coming from Almería in the east, there are 2 buses a day (3 hours).
   By Car   Head along the N-340 east from Málaga or take the N-340 west from Almería.

ESSENTIALS   The area code for Nerja is 952. The Tourist Information Office is at Puerta del Mar, 4 (tel. 952/52-15-31).

Nerja is known for its good beaches and small coves, its seclusion, its narrow streets and courtyards, and its whitewashed flat-roofed houses. Nearby is one of Spain's greatest attractions, the Cave of Nerja (see below).

At the mouth of the Chillar River, Nerja gets its name from an Arabic word, *narixa,* meaning "bountiful spring." Its most dramatic spot is the **Balcón de Europa,** a palm-shaded promenade that juts out into the Mediterranean. The sea-bordering walk was constructed in 1885 and named to honor Alfonso XIII, and it commands a panoramic coastline view. To reach the best beaches, go west from the Balcón and follow the shoreline.

A NEARBY ATTRACTION

The most popular outing from Málaga or Nerja is to the ✪ **Cueva de Nerja,** which scientists believe was inhabited from 100,000 to 40,000 B.C. This prehistoric stalactite-and-stalagmite cave lay undiscovered until 1959, when it was found by a handful of men on a routine exploring mission. When fully opened, it revealed a wealth of treasures left from the days of the cave dwellers, including Paleolithic paintings believed to be 15,000 years old. These depict horses and deer, but as of this writing they are not open to public view. The archeological museum in the cave contains a number of prehistoric artifacts; don't miss walking through its stupendous galleries. In the Hall of the Cataclysm, the ceiling soars to a height of 200 feet. From May 1 to September 1, daily hours are 9:30am to 9pm; during other months the cave is open from 10am to 1:30pm and 4 to 7pm. Admission is 150 pesetas ($1.40).

Nerja-bound buses leave from the Plaza Queipo de Llano in Málaga at 10am and again at noon, returning at 3 and 4:45pm. (The trip takes 2 hours each way, since the bus makes frequent stops.) Cave-bound buses leave from the center of Nerja hourly during the day, costing 50 pesetas (45¢).

WHERE TO STAY

DOUBLES FOR LESS THAN 8,500 PTAS. [$79.90]

HOSTAL MENA, Alemania, 15, 29780 Nerja. Tel. 952/52-05-41. 14 rms (8 with bath). TV TEL
$ Rates: 1,800 ptas. ($16.90) single without bath; 3,800 ptas. ($35.70) double with bath. No credit cards.

This modest little residencia near the Balcón de Europa serves no meals, but there's a lot of charm about the place, including the central hallway whose back walls are lined with hundreds of blue and white Andalusian tiles. The family running the hostal are very helpful. Bedrooms are plain and functional, but clean.

MONTESOL, Pintada, 130, 29780 Nerja. Tel. 952/52-00-14. 7 rms (2 with bath).
$ Rates: 2,800 ptas. ($26.30) double without bath, 3,800 ptas. ($35.70) double with bath. Breakfast 300 ptas. ($2.80) extra. AE, DC, MC, V. **Closed:** Oct–Apr.
Only two of the bedrooms of this humble guesthouse contain private facilities; the others have washbasins. Otherwise, the house is modern and well kept. It's located near the Balcón de Europa.

PEPE RICO APARTMENTOS, Almirante Ferrándiz, 28, 29780 Nerja. Tel. 952/52-02-47. 10 rms (all with bath).
$ Rates: 3,900–4,400 ptas. ($36.65–$41.35) double. No credit cards (accepted in restaurant only). **Closed:** Nov–Dec 20.
Pepe Rico gets an enthusiastic recommendation, both as a restaurant (see below) and as a secluded place to stay near the Balcón de Europa. These attractive, comfortable, recently remodeled apartments are priced on a daily basis, but no reservations are accepted for less than a week. Each double room has twin beds and a living room, with daily maid service. The lowest rates run from January through March, and rates peak in July, August, and September.

HOSTAL MIGUEL, Almirante Ferrándiz, 31, 29780 Nerja. Tel. 952/52-15-23. 9 rms (all with bath). MINIBAR TEL
$ Rates (including continental breakfast): 3,000 ptas. ($28.20) single; 4,000 ptas. ($37.60) double. AE, DC, MC, V.

The Miguel is a pleasant, unpretentious inn that contains only nine simply furnished rooms. They're housed in a 19th-century building with iron-rimmed balconies, situated on a quiet back street about a 3-minute walk from the Balcón de Europa, and across from the well-known Pepe Rico Restaurant. Breakfast is the only meal served.

CALA-BELA, Puerta del Mar, 8, 29780 Nerja. Tel. 952/52-07-00. 10 rms (with bath). TEL

$ Prices: 3,300 ptas. ($31) single; 4,200 ptas. ($39.50) double. Breakfast 300 ptas. ($2.80) extra. AE, DC, MC, V.

A recently improved miniature hotel just a 1-minute walk from the Balcón de Europa, the Cala-Bela has bedrooms opening onto the sea. They may be small, but they're clean—and what a view! The lounge is charming. In the seafront dining room, seated in a bone-white Valencian chair, you are served a fixed-price meal for 1,500 pesetas ($14.10). The food is good, so even if you're not staying at the hotel, you may want to give it a try. Enjoy the filet of pork in a sherry sauce, the chef's paella, grilled crayfish, or trout with cream.

HOSTAL FONTAINBLEAU, Calle Alejandro Bueno, 5, 29780 Nerja. Tel. 952/52-09-39. Fax 952/52-11-62. 22 rms (all with bath). A/C TEL

$ Rates: 3,500 ptas. ($32.80) single; 5,000 ptas. ($47) double or twin; 5,500 ptas. ($51.70) family room for three. Breakfast 480 ptas. ($3.50) extra. DC, MC, V.

A personal favorite, the Hostal Fontainbleau is owned by four young people from England. It's a 5-minute walk from the town center and 10 minutes from the Playa Burriana. Each of the pleasantly furnished rooms has wall-to-wall carpeting, local and Gibraltar radio, and tea- and coffee-making facilities. All rooms open onto an attractive fountain patio. You can order a continental breakfast there or have a cooked breakfast in the restaurant, which serves a fixed-priced lunch or dinner for 1,500 pesetas ($14.10). You can have drinks on the rooftop terrace from May to October, and in the Fountain Bar, which resembles a British pub, anytime; the Beefeater Steak Bar features English home-style cooking. The hostal has a clients' telephone booth for metered calls; laundry, drying, and ironing facilities; a TV lounge; and a currency exchange desk open seven days a week.

VILLA FLAMENCA, Andalucía, 1, 29780 Nerja. Tel. 952/52-18-69. Fax 952/52-21-96. 88 rms (all with bath). **Bus:** Alcina–Grat route.

$ Rates (including continental breakfast): 6,000 ptas. ($56.40) double. AE, DC, MC, V.

The villa is a modern building near the beach. The bedrooms have no particular style, but they are comfortable and well kept. No singles are available. A lunch or dinner costs 1,500 pesetas ($14.10).

HOTEL BALCÓN DE EUROPA, Paseo Balcón de Europa, 1, 29780 Nerja. Tel. 952/52-08-00. Fax 952/52-44-90. 105 rms (all with bath). A/C TV TEL

$ Rates: 6,500 ptas. ($61.10) single; 8,500 ptas. ($79.90) double. Breakfast 500 ptas. ($4.70) extra. AE, DC, MC, V.

Occupying the best position in town at the edge of the Balcón de Europa, the hotel offers rooms with private balconies overlooking the water and the rocks. At a private beach nearby, parasol-shielded tables offer a place for a peaceful vista. The comfortable bedrooms are decorated with modern furniture and terra-cotta floors. There's a private garage a few steps away.

WORTH THE EXTRA BUCKS

PARADOR NACIONAL DE NERJA, El Tablazo, s/n, 29780 Nerja. Tel. 952/52-00-50. Fax 952/52-19-97. 73 rms (all with bath). A/C MINIBAR TV TEL

$ Rates: 9,500 ptas. ($89.30) single; 12,000–13,500 ptas. ($112.80–$126.90) double. Breakfast 900 ptas. ($8.45) extra. AE, DC, MC, V.

This parador just outside town, above the Playa de Burriana, is worth saving up for. Like an elegant California motel, it blends modern concepts with traditional Spanish elements. Built on the edge of a cliff, the parador is surrounded by sprawling lawns and an outdoor swimming pool (or, if you prefer, an elevator will take you to the sandy beach below). The double bedchambers are (1) worthy of a honeymoon, (2) worthy of a second honeymoon, or (3) reason enough to get married in the first place! The more expensive doubles have Jacuzzis.

If you can't stay here, maybe you'll want to have dinner after viewing the nearby cave. The set price is 3,100 pesetas ($29.15), and a typical meal might include shrimp cocktail, veal accompanied by vegetables, and homemade cake. Before your meal you can go for a swim, for free if you're a guest.

WHERE TO DINE

EL COLONO, Granada, 6. Tel. 52-18-26.
   Cuisine: SPANISH. **Reservations:** Required.
$ **Prices:** Appetizers 395–1,000 ptas. ($3.70–$9.40); main dishes 895–1,750 ptas. ($8.40–$16.45); fixed-priced menus 2,100–3,200 ptas. ($19.75–$30.10). No credit cards.
   Open: In summer, dinner daily 8pm–midnight; in winter, dinner Wed–Sat 8pm–midnight.
A family place for a night of Spanish fun—that's El Colono, near the Balcón de Europa, a 3-minute walk from the main bus stop at Nerja. Guitar music and flamenco dancing account for the entertainment highlights, and you can also dine here in a tavern atmosphere, either à la carte or from set menus featuring local specialties. If you just want a glass of wine, you can still enjoy the shows (three an evening, from 8pm until "the wee hours").

CASA LUQUE, Plaza Cavana, 2. Tel. 52-10-04.
   Cuisine: INTERNATIONAL. **Reservations:** Required.
$ **Prices:** Appetizers 300–1,200 ptas. ($2.80–$11.30); main dishes 950–1,400 ptas. ($8.95–$13.15). AE, DC, MC, V.
   Open: Lunch Mon–Sat 12:30–3:30pm; dinner Mon–Sat 7:30–midnight.
With its impressive canopied and balconied façade, the Casa Luque looks like a dignified private villa. The interior has an Andalusian courtyard. Meals might include *pâté maison* with raspberry sauce, shoulder of ham, osso buco, pork filet, hot-pepper chicken Casanova, grilled meats, or a limited selection of fish, including grilled Mediterranean grouper.

PORTOFINO, Puerta del Mar, 4. Tel. 52-01-50.
   Cuisine: FRENCH. **Reservations:** Required.
$ **Prices:** Appetizers 350–750 ptas. ($3.30–$7.05); main dishes 1,000–1,500 ptas. ($9.40–$14.10); menú del día 1,600 ptas. ($15.05). MC, V.
   Open: Dinner daily 7–10:30pm. **Closed:** Dec–Feb.
For well-prepared food, a sweeping view of the sea, and a tasteful but whimsical decor, here is a gem. An open hearth surrounded by comfortable chairs greets you near the front entrance. You can dine either behind the shelter of large sheets of glass or on the open terrace at the edge of the bay. Specialties include *salade de chèvre chaude* (salad garnished with goat cheese and baked in an apple); red mullet with tomatoes, black olives, and anchovies; *entrecôte;* pork simmered in mustard sauce; filet of sole *à l'orientale;* and calves' kidneys sautéed in Madeira; plus such tempting desserts as *tarte tatin* (apple crumble enriched with butter and caramel) and *gratin de fruits* in a sweet sauce.

PEPE RICO RESTAURANT, Almirante Ferrándiz, 28. Tel. 52-02-47.
   Cuisine: INTERNATIONAL. **Reservations:** Required.
$ **Prices:** Appetizers 550–950 ptas. ($5.15–$8.95); main dishes 1,200–1,900 ptas. ($11.30–$17.85); fixed-priced menu 2,500 ptas. ($23.50). AE, DC, MC, V.
   Open: Dinner Wed–Mon 8–10:30pm. **Closed:** Nov–mid-Dec.
One of the finest restaurants in Nerja, near the Balcón de Europa, it's run by Robert and Kathy Holder, who also rent apartments (see above). Dining is in a half-paneled tavern room, with handmade wooden chairs, plaster upper walls, and ivy vines. These vines creep in from the patio, where you can order meals al fresco. The specialty of the

day on the international menu might be Spanish, German, Swiss, or French. Soups range from the Holders' own cold almond-and-garlic soup to Andalusian gazpacho, available only in summer. The hors d'oeuvres are impressive—Pepe Rico salad, smoked swordfish, pâté maison—and the main dishes include filet of sole Don Pepe, prawns Café de Paris, Zurich-style veal, and steak. Considering the quality of the food, the prices are reasonable.

CASA PACO Y EVA, Barrio, 50. Tel. 52-15-27.
　　Cuisine: SEAFOOD. **Reservations:** Required.
$ **Prices:** Appetizers 550–750 ptas. ($5.15–$7.05); main dishes 1,500–1,900 ptas. ($14.10–$17.85). MC, V.
　　Open: Lunch Thurs–Tues noon–4pm; dinner Thurs–Tues 7pm–midnight.
　　Closed: Nov.
The first things you'll notice in this air-conditioned tavern restaurant, on the ground floor of an apartment building 5 minutes from the Balcón de Europa, are the fresh flowers on the wooden tables. Many of the featured menu items are seafood and include a fish soup, crayfish, and a house salad. In autumn you can order pheasant with grapes. For dessert, try one of the house pastries.

RESTAURANT REY ALFONSO, Paseo Balcón de Europa, s/n. Tel. 52-01-95.
　　Cuisine: FRENCH/INTERNATIONAL. **Reservations:** Required.
$ **Prices:** Appetizers 550–950 ptas. ($5.15–$8.95); main dishes 1,500–2,000 ptas. ($14.10–$18.80). MC, V.
　　Open: Lunch Thurs–Tues 1–4pm; dinner Thurs–Tues 8–11pm.
Few visitors to the Balcón de Europa realize that they're standing directly above one of the best restaurants in town—you enter at the bottom of a flight of stairs skirting some of the most dramatic rock formations along the coast. The menu doesn't hold many surprises, but the view, ambience, and clientele make dining here worthwhile. Have a drink at the bar if you don't want a full meal. Specialties include *paella valenciana*, Cuban-style rice, five different preparations of sole (from grilled to meunière), several versions of tournedos and entrecôte, beef Stroganoff, *fondue bourguignonne*, crayfish in whisky sauce, and for dessert, crêpes Suzette.

---

12. ALMERÍA

106 miles SE of Granada, 340 miles S of Madrid

GETTING THERE　By Train　Almería is well serviced by RENFE, which runs 2 trains a day from Madrid, 1 from Barcelona, 2 from Granada, and 1 from Seville. The RENFE office (tel. 25-11-35) is across from the bus station at Plaza de Barcelona.

By Bus　This is a popular way to reach Almería if you're at one of the resorts in the western part of the Costa del Sol. Two buses a day arrive from Málaga (5½ hours). Two buses also arrive from Barcelona (a long 14 hours).

By Car　From Málaga, continue along the coastal road, the N-340, to Almería.

ESSENTIALS: The area code for Almería is 951. The Tourist Information Office is at Hermanos Machado, 4, Edificio Multiple (tel. 951/23-08-58).

Once known as Spanish Hollywood, in past years Almería has attracted a large colony of film people, who have made epics in and around the town. When the celluloid folk aren't here—and you don't see as much of them these days—Almería can be dull. At first it appears to belong to a stretch of North African landscape, but actually it lies at the far eastern stretch of the Costa del Sol, as frontier outpost for motorists traveling to and from Granada and Torremolinos.

　　Although it's the most Eastern-looking city in southern Spain, Almería still reflects its Andalusian heritage in its narrow streets and terraced white houses. Flowers grow abundantly, and orange groves and palm trees give the city a certain grace. The province is traversed by a series of high rugged mountains, separated by narrow valleys, and the coast is elevated and rocky.

WHAT TO SEE & DO

This hot provincial capital is dominated by the **Alcazaba,** its Moorish castle, and the **Castillo de San Cristóbal.** The former, the Arab fortress, dates from the 8th century and sprawls across 14 acres of dusty land, offering a panoramic vision of the Mediterranean. It is open daily from 10am to 2pm and 4 to 7pm, charging an admission of 75 pesetas (70¢).

Mini-Hollywood, Hwy. N-340 (tel. 36-52-36), lies in the small town of Tabernas between Almería and Murcia. Here such epics as *Conan the Barbarian* and *Lawrence of Arabia,* as well as portions of *Reds,* were filmed—not to mention some of the so-called spaghetti westerns. Now the western set, constructed years ago by Sergio Leone, has been transformed into a tourist attraction where desperadoes are thrown through barroom doors daily in regularly scheduled brawls. You can even rent a horse and costume and ride through the main street of the re-created town. Admission is 550 pesetas ($5.15) for adults, 350 pesetas ($3.30) for children, and daily hours are 9am to 9pm. Take the Almería–Tabernas bus, a 15½-mile (25km) run north.

WHERE TO STAY

RESIDENCIA NIXAR, Antonio Vico, 14, 04003 Almería. Tel. 951/23-72-55. 38 rms (all with bath). MINIBAR TV TEL
$ Rates: 2,000 ptas. ($18.80) single; 3,600 ptas. ($33.85) double. Breakfast 160 ptas. ($1.50) extra. V.

The Nixar supplies a warm welcome and adequate, clean rooms, each with bath. Breakfast only is served. For the price, this is about the best-value hotel in town. It's located near the Puerta de Purchena.

COSTASOL, Paseo de Almería, 58, 04001 Almería. Tel. 951/23-40-11. Fax 951/23-40-11. 55 rms (all with bath). A/C TV TEL
$ Rates: 4,500 ptas. ($42.30) single; 7,000 ptas. ($65.80) double. Breakfast 500 ptas. ($4.70) extra. AE, DC, MC, V.

A modern, functional hotel, the Costasol offers reasonable comfort. Although it doesn't have a restaurant, it does have a cafeteria and serves breakfast. The first-class hotel stands in the center of town, 260 yards from the beach.

WHERE TO EAT

IMPERIAL, Puerta de Purchena, 20. Tel. 23-51-65.
Cuisine: SEAFOOD. **Reservations:** Required on holidays.
$ Prices: Appetizers 400–1,500 ptas. ($3.75–$14.10); main dishes 650–2,200 ptas. ($6.10–$20.70); fixed-priced menu 1,600 ptas. ($15.05). AE, DC, MC, V.
Open: Lunch daily 1–4:30pm; dinner daily 8pm–midnight. **Closed:** Wed in winter.

This air-conditioned restaurant on the town's main square (at the junction of the Carretera de Granada and the Calle Maranon) has a *menú del casa,* or you can order à la carte if you don't mind spending more. The Imperial specializes in fish and shellfish. You might select as a main dish a large plate of squid, flounder, and a fried fish, unless you prefer the beef with red peppers or roast pork or veal. For dessert, I'd recommend the soufflé Imperial.

RINCÓN DE JUAN PEDRO, Federico de Castro, 2. Tel. 23-58-19.
Cuisine: SPANISH. **Reservations:** Recommended.
$ Prices: Appetizers 500–1,500 ptas. ($4.70–$14.10); main courses 1,200–1,800 ptas. ($11.30–$16.90); fixed-priced menu 750 ptas. ($7.05). AE, DC, MC, V.

Open: Lunch Mon–Sat 1–4pm; dinner Mon–Sat 8pm–midnight.
One of the best places to dine in town, the Rincón de Juan Pedro can be expensive, depending on what you order, but the atmosphere is inviting and pleasant. The rich, well-prepared regional cuisine relies heavily on a varied fish repertoire, with typical dishes served with olive oil and plenty of spices. In season, you might be able to order partridge, prepared in many different ways. The restaurant is located in the center near the Puerta de Purchena.

CHAPTER 12

VALENCIA & THE COSTA BLANCA

- **WHAT'S SPECIAL ABOUT VALENCIA & THE COSTA BLANCA**
1. **VALENCIA**
2. **BENIDORM**
3. **ALICANTE**
4. **ELCHE**
5. **MURCIA**
6. **CARTAGENA**

The third largest-city of Spain, Valencia, celebrated for oranges and paella, lies in the midst of a *huerta*—a fertile crescent of an alluvial plain irrigated by a system built centuries ago. As such, the area is a bread basket of Spain, a place where "the soil never sleeps."

For such a major city, Valencia is relatively unexplored by foreigners, but it provides an offbeat adventure for those who decide to seek out its treasures. The town has a wealth of baroque architecture, fine museums, good cuisine, and a proud but troubled history.

The Costa Blanca (White Coast) begins rather unappealingly at Valencia, but improves considerably as it winds its way south toward Alicante. The route is dotted with fishing ports and resorts known chiefly to Spanish and other European vacationers. The success of Benidorm, fitting for a long stay, began in the 1960s, when this fishing village was transformed into an international resort. Alicante, the official capital of the Costa Blanca, enjoys a reputation as a winter resort because of its mild climate. Murcia is inland, but on the main road to the Costa del Sol, so hordes of motorists pass through it.

WHAT'S SPECIAL ABOUT VALENCIA AND THE COSTA BLANCA

Beaches
- [ ] Benidorm, with 3½ miles of beach.
- [ ] Alicante, with its Postiguet Beach and balmy Mediterranean climate.

Great Towns/Cities
- [ ] Valencia, home of paella and El Cid.
- [ ] Alicante, capital of the Costa Blanca.
- [ ] Elche, touch of North Africa in Spain.

Architectural Highlights
- [ ] Cathedral at Valencia, said to possess the Holy Grail.
- [ ] Castillo de Santa Bárbara at Alicante, fortress dating from 3rd century B.C.

Ancient Ruins
- [ ] Sagunto, outside Valencia, the reason the Second Punic War began.

Natural Sights
- [ ] La Albufera, outside Valencia, land of rice paddies and reed-beds
- [ ] Palm grove at Elche, with some 600,000 trees started by Phoenician or Greek seafarers.

Festivals/Special Events
- [ ] Mystery play at Elche (August), oldest liturgy performed in Europe.
- [ ] Fallas of San José in Valencia (March), honoring spring's arrival.
- [ ] Holy Week celebration at Murcia, a mile-long procession with 3,000 tak ing part.

SEEING VALENCIA AND THE COSTA BLANCA

GETTING THERE

Flying is the best way, with international airports at both Valencia and Alicante. Valencia is the best choice if you want to land in the north, whereas Alicante is better if you'd like to begin in the south along the Costa Blanca.

Many arrive by **train,** with RENFE offering good service along the Barcelona–Alicante line. The Rapido Talgo Mare Nostrum begins its mid-morning run at the French frontier, getting you to Valencia in 6 hours. Stay on it for another 2½ hours and you'll be in Alicante. Most train passengers head for Valencia from Barcelona, the trip taking about 4 hours.

The Costa Levante is also well serviced by **buses,** with coaches arriving from Madrid and Barcelona, among other cities.

If you're **driving,** take the A-7 *autopista* (expressway) along the coast to the southern side of Alicante. It's expensive because of high tolls, but you avoid the slow-moving drive on the N-340 through the beach towns. Valencia can also be reached from Madrid via the N-III.

A SUGGESTED ROUTE

Day 1   Begin in Valencia, exploring its ancient monuments.

Day 2   Still based in Valencia, branch out on a day trip. Try going north to the old Roman ruins at Sagunto or south to the rice paddies of La Albufera.

Day 3   Head south along the coast for an overnight stop in Benidorm, a popular beach resort. You'll also find interesting stopovers in the coastal towns of Calpe and Denia, north of Benidorm.

Day 4   Make the short drive south to Alicante, where you can explore its monuments.

Day 5   While in Alicante, spend the day exploring the palm groves and the huerta around Elche.

Day 6   Drive to Murcia to see its attractions, usually taking 3 to 4 hours. Either stay in Murcia or continue on for a final stopover at the ancient port of Cartagena.

---

1. VALENCIA

218 miles SE of Madrid, 224 miles SW of Barcelona, 404 miles NE of Málaga.

GETTING THERE   By Plane   Iberia flies to Valencia from Barcelona, Madrid, Málaga, and many other destinations. There are also flights between Palma de Mallorca and Valencia. You land 9 miles (14.5km) southwest of the city, but bus no. 15 takes you to the terminal, leaving hourly and costing 90 pesetas (85¢). For flight information, call 153-02-11. In the city, the office of Iberia Airlines is at Paz, 14 (tel. 352-97-37).

By Train   Valencia is linked to all parts of Spain. The Estación del Norte (North Station) is close to the heart of the city, making a convenient arrival point. Its information office is at Jatíva, 15 (tel. 351-36-12); open daily from 7am to 10:30pm. Nine trains from Barcelona arrive daily, both the *talgo* (4 hours; faster and more

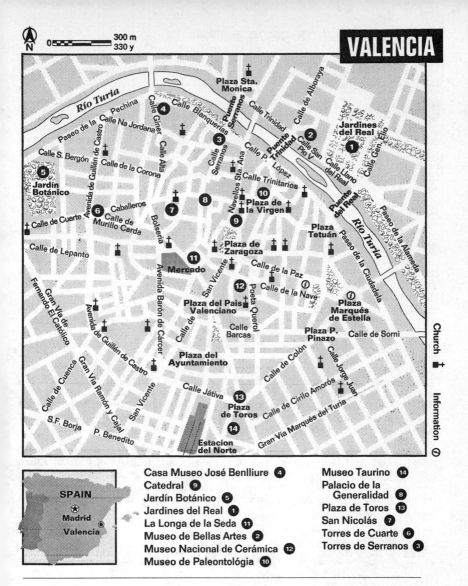

VALENCIA

Casa Museo José Benlliure ④
Catedral ⑨
Jardín Botánico ⑤
Jardines del Real ①
La Longa de la Seda ⑪
Museo de Bellas Artes ②
Museo Nacional de Cerámica ⑫
Museo de Paleontológia ⑩

Museo Taurino ⑭
Palacio de la Generalidad ⑧
Plaza de Toros ⑬
San Nicolás ⑦
Torres de Cuarte ⑥
Torres de Serranos ③

SPAIN
★ Madrid
◉ Valencia

Church ◾✝

Information ⓘ

expensive) and the *rápido* (6 hours). Seven trains daily connect Madrid to Valencia, the *ter* (5 hours; more expensive) and the *rápido* (7½ hours). It's also possible to take a train from Málaga on the Costa del Sol (9 hours).

By Bus   Valencia's Central Station, Avenida de Ménendez Pidal, 13 (tel. 349-72-22), is about a 30-minute walk northwest of the city's center, so you take bus no. 8 leaving from the Plaza del Ayuntamiento. Fifteen buses a day run from Madrid (5 hours), 8 buses from Barcelona (5 hours), and 4 buses from Málaga (11 hours).

By Ferry   You can take a ferry to and from the Balearic Islands. Ferries for Palma de Mallorca depart Monday through Saturday at 11:30pm. The all-night journey (9 hours) lets passengers off the next morning in Majorca. Travel agents in Valencia sell these tickets (see American Express, below), or else on the day of departure, go to the office at the port, Estación Marítima (tel. 367-39-72), to purchase them. To reach it, take bus no. 4 from the Plaza del País Valenciano.

By Car   The easiest route is the express highway (E-15) south from Barcelona. Connections are also made on a national highway, E-901, from Madrid, which lies northwest of Valencia. From Alicante, south of Valencia, an express highway, E-15, connects the two cities. If you're coming from Andalusia, the roads are longer and more difficult and not connected by express highways. You can drive from Málaga north to Granada and cut across southeastern Spain along the 342 which links with the 340 into Murcia. From there, take the road to Alicante for an easy drive into Valencia.

ESSENTIALS   See "Fast Facts: Valencia," below.

The charms of Valencia—or the lack of them—have been much debated. There are those who claim that the city where El Cid faced the Moors is one of the most beautiful on the Mediterranean. Others write it off as drab, provincial, and industrial. The truth lies somewhere in between.

Set in the midst of orange trees and rice paddies, Valencia seems to justify its reputation as a romantic city more by its past than by its present looks. Hidden between modern office buildings and monotonous apartment houses, remnants of that illustrious past do remain. However, floods and war have been cruel to Valencia, forcing Valencianos to tear down buildings that today would be considered architectural treasures.

Valencia also has a strong cultural tradition. Its most famous son was the writer Vicente Blasco Ibañez, best known for his novel about bullfighting, *Blood and Sand,* and for his World War I novel, *The Four Horsemen of the Apocalypse.* Both were filmed twice in Hollywood, with Rudolph Valentino starring in the first version of each. Joaquín Sorolla, the famous Spanish impressionist, was another native of Valencia. You can see his works at a museum dedicated to him in Madrid.

A Note on Language   Don't be surprised if you see signs in a language that's not Spanish—and not Catalan either. It is *valenciano,* a dialect of Catalan. Often you'll be handed a "bilingual" menu that is in Spanish Castilian and in *valenciano.* Of course, many citizens of Valencia are not caught up in this cultural resurgence, viewing the promotion of the dialect tongue as possibly damaging to the city's economic goals.

 VALENCIA

American Express   The local agency is **Viajes Melià,** Paz, 41 (tel. 352-69-73). Open: Mon–Fri 9:30am–1:30pm and 4:30–8pm, Sat 9:30am–1pm.

Area Code   The area code for Valencia is 96.

Buses   For information and tickets, go to the red-painted kiosk at Plaza del Ayuntamiento. Tickets: One ride 65 ptas. (60¢), 10 rides 420 ptas. ($3.95).

Consulate   The **U. S. Consulate** is at Ribera, 3 (tel. 351-69-73). Open: Mon–Fri 10am–1pm.

Emergency   Call 091.

First Aid   Go to Plaza de América, 5 (tel. 322-22-39).

Hospital Go to the **Provincal Hospital,** Avenida Cíd/Tres Cruces s/n (tel. 379-16-00).

Information The **Tourist Information Office** is at Playa del Ayuntamiento, 1 (tel. 96/351-04-17).

Laundromat Lying northwest of the rail terminus is **Lava Super,** Gran Vía Germanías, 35 (tel. 341-86-48). Open: Mon–Fri 9am–2pm and 5–8pm, Sat 9am–noon.

Post Office The main post office is at Plaza del Ayuntamiento, 1. Open: Mon–Fri 9am–2pm and 4–6pm, Sat 9am–2pm.

Taxis Call 370-32-04.

Telephone The local office is at Plaza del Ayuntamiento, 27 (tel. 003). Open: Mon–Sat 9am–1pm and 5–9pm. It's much cheaper to make a long-distance call from here than from your hotel room.

WHAT TO SEE & DO

CATEDRAL, Plaza de la Reina. Tel. 331-81-27.

For the past 500 years, the cathedral (called La Seo), has claimed to possess the Holy Grail, the chalice used by Christ at the Last Supper. The subject of countless legends, the Grail was said to have been used by Joseph of Arimathea to collect Christ's blood as it fell from the cross. It looms large in Sir Thomas Malory's *Morte d'Arthur,* Tennyson's *Idylls of the King,* and Wagner's *Parsifal.*

Although this 1262 cathedral represents a number of styles, such as Romanesque and baroque, Gothic predominates. Its huge arches have been restored, and in back is a handsome domed basilica. It was built on the site of a mosque torn down by the Catholic monarchs.

After seeing the cathedral, you can scale an uncompleted 155-foot-high Gothic tower—known as Miguelete—for a panoramic view of the city and the fertile huerta beyond, or visit the **Museo de la Catedral,** where works by Goya and Zurbarán are exhibited.

Admission: Cathedral free; Miguelete 100 ptas. (95¢); Museo de la Catedral free.

Open: Cathedral Mon–Sat 10am–1pm and 4–7pm; Miguelete Mon–Sat 10:30am–12:30pm and 5–7:30pm, Sun 10:30am–12:30pm; Museo de la Catedral Mon–Sat 10am–1pm and 4–7pm. **Bus:** 9, 27, 70, or 71.

PALACIO DE LA GENERALIDAD, Caballeros, 2. Tel. 386-61-00.

Located in the old aristocratic quarter of Valencia, this Gothic palace, built in the 15th and 16th centuries, is one of the most fascinating buildings in Spain, with its two handsomely restored square towers and its carved wooden gallery. It now serves as the headquarters of the regional government of Valencia, and is visited with permission of the Secretaría de la Diputación.

Admission: Free.

Open: Mon–Fri 9am–2pm. **Bus:** 5 from the station.

LA LONJA DE LA SEDA, Plaza del Mercado. Tel. 331-65-00.

This former silk exchange, completed in 1498, is the most splendid example of secular Gothic architecture in Spain. A beautiful building, La Lonja has twisted spiral columns inside and stained-glass windows.

Admission: Free.

Open: Tues–Fri 10am–2pm and 4–6pm, Sat–Sun 10am–1pm. **Closed:** Holidays. Bus: 7, 27, 4, 60, or 81.

MERCADO CENTRAL, Plaza del Mercado. Tel. 332-10-51.

Across the street from La Lonja is one of the most fascinating city markets you'll ever encounter, with about 1,200 stalls. It has everything: dried herbs, homemade soup, black-blood sausage, plucked chickens. You may never want to shop in a supermarket again. The Mercado Central is in a giant stained-glass building that dates from 1928.

Open: Mon–Sat 8am–2:30pm. **Bus:** 7, 27, 81, 4, or 60.

MUSEO NACIONAL DE CERÁMICA, Palacio del Marqués de Dos Aguas, Poeta Querol, 2. Tel. 351-63-92.
The National Ceramics Museum, the best in Spain, looks like a surrealist decorator's masterpiece: an 18th-century palace of rococo and Churrigueresque elements. It's not surprising that the architect died in an insane asylum. The rooms in this bizarre building compete with the vast collection of ceramics, some by Picasso. In addition, there are a Gallery of Humorists, with caricatures from Einstein on down, and a carriage display.
Admission: 200 ptas. ($1.90).
Open: Tues–Sat 10am–2pm and 4–7pm, Sun 10am–2pm. **Bus:** 24 or 27.

MUSEO DE BELLAS ARTES, San Pío V, 9. Tel. 360-57-93.
This treasure house of paintings and sculptures, which stands on the north bank of the Turia River, contains a strong collection of Flemish and native Valencian artworks (note particularly those by the 14th- and 15th-century Valencian "primitives"). The most celebrated painting is a 1640 self-portrait by Velázquez, and there is a whole room devoted to Goya. Other artists exhibited include Bosch, Morales, El Greco (*St. John the Baptist*), Ribera, Murillo, Pinturicchio, and Sorolla. Of special interest is a salon displaying the works of contemporary Valencian painters and an important sculpture by Mariano Benlliure. The archeological collection on the ground floor encompasses early Iberian, Roman, and early Christian finds, including an altar to a pagan Roman emperor.
Admission: Free.
Open: Tues–Sat 10am–2pm and 4–6pm, Sun 10am–4pm. Bus: 26 or 79.

INSTITUTO VALENCIANO DE ARTE MODERNO [IVAM], Guillén de Castro, 118. Tel. 386-30-00.
This giant complex, costing millions to build, consists of two sites—an ultramodern building and a 13th-century former convent. Its opening launched Valencia into prime status among the world's art capitals.
The **Julio González Center** is named for an avant-garde Spanish artist whose paintings, sculptures, and drawings form the nucleus of the institute's permanent collection. Much influenced by Picasso, González was a pioneer in iron sculpture.
The other site is the nearby **Center del Carme,** the old convent, with cloisters from both the 14th and 16th centuries. It contains three halls devoted to changing exhibitions of contemporary art. Other permanent exhibitions include works of Ignacio Pinazo, whose paintings and drawings mark the beginning of modernism in Valencia.
The institute is located on the western edge of the old quarter, near the Torres de Quart.
Admission: 250 ptas. ($2.35).
Open: Julio González Center Tues–Sun 11am–8pm; Center del Carmen Tues–Sun noon–2:30pm and 4:30–8:30pm.

WHERE TO STAY

DOUBLES FOR LESS THAN 8,900 PTAS. [$83.65]

HOSTAL RESIDENCIA BISBAL, Pie de la Cruz, 9, 46001 Valencia. Tel. 96/331-70-84. 17 rms (all with shower or bath). **Bus:** 7 or 27.
$ Rates: 1,900–2,500 ptas. ($17.85–$23.50) single; 2,800–3,900 ptas. ($26.30–$36.65) double. No credit cards.
Conveniently located in the old city, this husband-and-wife operation has clean and simply furnished rooms. English is spoken. No meals are served, but you'll find many bars and restaurants nearby.

HOTEL BRISTOL, Abadia San Martín, 3, 46002 Valencia. Tel. 96/352-11-76. 40 rms (all with bath). TEL **Bus:** 24 or 27.

$ Rates: 3,600–4,200 ptas. ($33.85–$39.50) single; 5,800–6,500 ptas. ($54.50–$61.10) double. Breakfast 275 ptas. ($2.60) extra. AE, DC, MC, V.

This clean, comfortable hotel stands on a secluded narrow street in the old city, near the Church of St. Martin (San Martín), only a 3-minute walk from the central shopping district. Rooms are simply furnished. The Bristol is said to offer the best value of any hotel in Valencia.

LLAR, Colón, 46, 46004 Valencia. Tel. 96/352-84-60. 50 rms (all with bath). A/C MINIBAR TEL **Bus:** 5, 8, or 70.

$ Rates: 5,000 ptas. ($47) single; 7,200 ptas. ($67.70) double. Breakfast 325 ptas. ($3.05) extra. AE, DC, MC, V.

The government has awarded this establishment three stars, but the rates are still reasonable. Built in 1967, it has since been renovated. The modern lounge is decorated with comfortable armchairs, and a carved wood divider separates it from the bar. Bedrooms are well maintained and comfortably furnished.

HOTEL METROPOL, Játiva, 23, 46002 Valencia. Tel. 96/351-26-12. 107 rms (all with bath). TEL **Bus:** 7 or 27.

$ Rates: 4,800 ptas. ($45.10) single; 7,200 ptas. ($67.70) double. Breakfast 350 ptas. ($3.30) extra. AE, DC, MC, V.

This three-star choice is near the railway station, directly opposite the bullring. The old-fashioned exterior, with its balconies and tall French doors, contrasts with the modern and well-organized interior. Many bedrooms are unusually large and well furnished; wall-to-wall draperies separate the sleeping area from the living room, with its upholstered pieces. The front of the Metropol has tables and chairs set out for drinks and meals.

SOROLLA, Convento de Santa Clara, 5, 46002 Valencia. Tel. 96/352-33-92. 50 rms (all with bath). A/C TEL

$ Rates: 4,200 ptas. ($39.50) single; 7,500 ptas. ($70.50) double. AE, MC, V.

In the city center, this modern hotel is named after Valencia's most famous artist. Bedrooms have narrow balconies and compact, utilitarian furnishings. Comfort, not style, is the key; everything, however, is clean. No meals are served. To reach the Sorolla, take any bus from the rail station.

HOTEL OLTRA, Plaza del Ayuntamiento, 4, 46002 Valencia. Tel. 96/352-06-12. 93 rms (all with bath). A/C TEL

$ Rates: 4,800 ptas. ($45.10) single; 8,000 ptas. ($75.20) double. Breakfast 395 ptas. ($3.70) extra. AE, DC, MC, V.

Most of the comfortably renovated bedrooms overlook Valencia's central square. There's no restaurant, but a cafeteria serves drinks and light meals. The Hotel Oltra lies north of the Estación del Norte.

HOTEL INGLÉS, Marqués de Dos Aguas, 6, 46002 Valencia. Tel. 96/351-64-26. Fax 96/394-02-51. 62 rms (all with bath). TV TEL **Bus:** 24 or 27.

$ Rates: 6,500 ptas. ($61.10) single; 8,900–11,000 ptas. ($83.65–$103.40) double. Breakfast 415 ptas. ($3.90) extra. AE, DC, MC, V.

This turn-of-the-century hotel, the former palace of the Duke and *Duchess of Cardona*, has aged well. In the heart of old Valencia, it stands opposite another, Churrigueresque palace. Most of its bedrooms, some of them air-conditioned, have views of the tree-lined street below, and offer old-fashioned comforts. The lounge and dining room have original decorating touches—chandeliers, gilt mirrors, provincial armchairs, and murals. Service is unobtrusive and elegant.

WORTH THE EXTRA BUCKS

HOTEL REINA VICTORIA, Barcas, 4, 46002 Valencia. Tel. 96/352-04-87. Fax 96/352-04-87. 92 rms (all with bath). A/C TV TEL

$ Rates: 14,500 ptas. ($136.30) single; 17,000 ptas. ($159.80) double. Breakfast 675 ptas. ($6.35) extra. AE, MC, V.

★ The "aristocrat of Valencia hotels," the Reina Victoria was reborn on its 75th anniversary. After opening in 1913, it served many distinguished guests: Alfonso XIII and Queen Victoria (its namesake), Dalí, Manolete, Picasso, Falla, García Lorca, and Miró. Now completely remodeled, with a neoclassical architectural style and a rich decor, it is once again a leading hotel of Valencia. Wrought-iron balconies and picture windows overlook the flower gardens and fountains of the central square, the Plaza del País Valenciano. Rooms are beautifully furnished and most comfortable. The Bar Inglés is a popular rendezvous spot, and the hotel restaurant, Levant, serves international and regional dishes. The rail station is 3 minutes away.

WHERE TO EAT

BARRACHINA, Plaza del País Valenciano, 2. Tel. 351-87-50.
   Cuisine: INTERNATIONAL. **Reservations:** Recommended.
$ **Prices:** Appetizers 275–750 ptas. ($2.60–$7.05); main dishes 900–1,400 ptas. ($8.45–$13.15); fixed-priced menu 1,250 ptas. ($11.75). AE, DC, MC, V.
   Open: Daily 1pm–1:30am.

⑤ The Barrachina, a super-deli and restaurant, has one of the best selections in all of Spain. It spreads of goodies mazelike over a whole block, and there are also outdoor café chairs and tables. Specialties include sweets and candies, croissants, apple tarts, *batidos* (milkshakes) in all flavors, and about 25 combination plates. Of course, there are *sangría* and *horchata* (for which Valencia is famous), hot dogs and sandwiches, cakes, and glazed fruit. The *mil-hojas* (napoleons) are good, as are the *palonatas* (eclairs with whipped-cream filling). In the restaurant proper, the least expensive paella is served with chicken; you'll pay more for the shellfish version. At the counter, there's a daily combination-plate special, which includes an omelet, veal steak with tomatoes and lettuce, plus bread, dessert, and wine, for 750 pesetas ($7.05). Barrachina lies north of the Estación del Norte.

LIONEL, Pizarro, 9. Tel. 351-65-66.
   Cuisine: INTERNATIONAL. **Reservations:** Required. **Bus:** 2, 3, or 13.
$ **Prices:** Appetizers 600–750 ptas. ($5.65–$7.05); main dishes 900–1,800 ptas. ($8.45–$16.90). AE, DC, MC, V.
   Open: Lunch Sun–Fri 1:30–4pm; dinner Mon–Sat 9–11:30pm.

⑤ Named after its owner, Lionel Tarzaon, this Belle Epoque–style air-conditioned restaurant is filled with antique lamps and accessories. Meals here are a good value and could include partridge, veal Orloff, steak tartar, and duckling or turkey. Daily specials available.

CASA CESÁREO, Guillén de Castro, 15. Tel. 351-42-14.
   Cuisine: SPANISH. **Reservations:** Required Sun night. **Bus:** 5.
$ **Price:** Appetizers 300–500 ptas. ($2.80–$4.70); main dishes 1,000–2,500 ptas. ($9.40–$23.50); fixed-priced menu 1,200 ptas. ($11.30). AE, DC, MC, V.
   Open: Lunch Tues–Sat 7am–5pm; dinner Sun 8–11pm.
You'll eat well in this old-world tavern, within walking distance of the railway station and near the Plaza de San Augustín. On the street level are counters and tables—if you order at a counter, prices are considerably cheaper than those of the *mesa* (table) menu. The counter *menú del día* includes three plates, plus bread and wine. Chef's specialties, which can be ordered only at the tables, include Valencian paella, grilled red mullet, and half a chicken cooked with garlic. Try also the lamb with apple fritters. The walls are tile, and the furnishings provincial.

MA CUINA, Gran Vía Germanías, 49. Tel. 341-77-99.
   Cuisine: SPANISH. **Reservations:** Recommended.
$ **Prices:** Appetizers 650–850 ptas. ($6.10–$8); main dishes 1,100–1,900 ptas. ($10.35–$17.85). AE, MC, V.
   Open: Lunch Mon–Sat 1:30–3:30pm; dinner Mon–Sat 9–11:30pm.
Ma Cuina is known for serving the best rice dishes in the city, and the steaming

platters are offered in air-conditioned comfort. You can also order fresh fish, such as *merlusa* (hake) or sole with a Roquefort sauce, or one of the Basque specialties. Paella and other dishes are cooked to order.

PALACE FESOL, Hernán Cortés 7. Tel. 352-93-23.
   Cuisine: INTERNATIONAL. **Reservations:** Recommended. **Bus:** 13.
$ Prices: Appetizers 900–1,500 ptas. ($8.45–$14.10); main dishes 1,100–2,000 ptas. ($10.35–$18.80); fixed-priced menu 2,000 ptas. ($18.80). AE, DC, MC, V.
   Open: Lunch Tues–Sun 1–3:30pm; dinner Tues–Sat 9–11:30pm.
More than 75 years ago the Palace Fesol, known as the "bean palace," became famous for its namesake specialty, lima beans. Today, of course, many more excellent dishes grace the menu, with typical Valencian paella high on the list at lunchtime. You can also order several chicken dishes served with rice that go under the general name paella, since they are cooked in paella pans. Dinner selections include *zarzuela de mariscos* (shellfish medley), grilled red mullet and baby hake, baby lamb cutlets, and chateaubriand. Photos of film stars, bullfighters, and other celebrities line the walls. The restaurant is cooled by old-fashioned ceiling fans, and is decorated with beamed ceilings, lanterns, and a hand-painted tile mosaic.

HORCHATERÍAS

Stop in one of Valencia's famous *horchaterías,* old-time cafés where Valencianos drink a milky, nut-flavored beverage called horchata. The two best-known horchaterías are **El Siglo,** Santa Catalina, 11 (tel. 331-84-66), a turn-of-the-century establishment where a horchata costs 90 pesetas (85¢) to 150 pesetas ($1.40), open daily from 8:30am to 9pm; and the **Horchatería Santa Catalina,** Santa Catalina, 6 (tel. 331-23-79), where a horchata costs 140 pesetas ($1.30), open daily from 9am to 1pm and 4 to 9pm.

EVENING ENTERTAINMENT
CULTURAL

The **Palau de la Música,** Plaza del Rey, 1 (tel. 232-22-89), is a contemporary concert hall constructed in a dried-out river bed of the Turia. Opened in 1987, it stands within a sort of Hispano-Muslim venue—palm trees, "temples," and reflecting pools—between the Aragón and Angel Custudio bridges. Call to find out the day's program, or you can ask at the tourist office (see "Fast Facts: Valencia," above). Details of major concerts are also published in the newspapers. Ticket prices vary.

THE BARS

BARCAS 7, Barcas, 7. Tel. 352-12-33.
Set among banks and office buildings in the heart of town, directly north of the Estación del Norte, Barcas 7 offers drinks and *tapas* (including small servings of paella) at the stand-up bar, and there is often live music at night. Despite the restaurant in back, where beef filet and veal dishes are house specialties, the establishment is more popular as a bar than as a restaurant. Open: Daily 7pm–1:30am. Prices: Drinks 375 ptas. ($3.55); tapas 150 ptas. ($1.40).

EVENING, Joaquín Costa, 3. Tel. 334-50-12.
The ambience here is heightened by South American and other kinds of recorded music. It's a popular pub, decorated in the English style, located near the Gran Vía Germanias and the Place Canovas. Open: Daily 5pm–2:30am. Prices: Beer 300 ptas. ($2.80); drinks 500 ptas. ($4.70).

BELLE EPOQUE, Cuba, 8–10. Tel. 341-64-66.
Located in the city center near the Estación del Norte, this is a place to drink, dance, and chatter with friends. On Saturday there's a show at 12:15am. Open: Mon–Sat 11pm–3:30am. Prices: Drinks 500 ptas. ($4.70).
   Admission: 2,500 ptas. ($23.50), including first drink.

ONE-DAY EXCURSIONS
LA ALBUFERA

Eleven miles (17.7km) south of Valencia lies La Albufera, a land of rice paddies and reed-beds. The largest wetland along the Mediterranean coast of Spain, it was called "an agreeable lagoon" in the writings of Pliny the Elder. Sand dunes separate the fresh water from the salt water.

La Albufera has been declared a national park, its lagoonlike lake being home to some 250 species of waterfowl, including a European version of the endangered flamingo. About waist deep at its center, it abounds with such fish as mullet, tench, and eel, still caught by ancient traps. You can rent an *albuferenc* (flat-bottomed boat) from local fishermen, but make sure to negotiate prices beforehand. As you go about the lake, you can see *barracas,* whitewashed houses with thatched and steeply pitched roofs. Some of these barracas, which stand on stilts, can be reached only by boat.

La Albufera gave the world paella, and nearly all the restaurants in the area serve this classic dish. Try **Raco de l'Olla** (tel. 161-00-72), 9 miles (14.5km) south of Valencia on the El Saler road near the turnoff to El Palmer. It's open Tuesday through Sunday at lunch (1–3:30pm). It's also customary to stop in the town of El Palmer to order a plate of *alli al pebre* (garlic-flavored eels), before heading north to Valencia or south to Alicante.

SAGUNTO

Another popular excursion is to Sagunto, 15½ miles (25km) north of Valencia, reached by bus or rail connections. Sagunto is known for holding out nine months against Hannibal's conquering Carthaginian soldiers in 219 B.C. The Iberians set themselves on fire rather than surrender. In time, the Romans discovered the town, and later it was taken by the Visigoths and the Muslims.

Its **Roman ruins** today are just that: ruins. But it makes an interesting stopover. In the 2nd century A.D. it had an amphitheater seating 8,000, in the remains of which theatrical performances are still staged. It also has an old **Acrópolis**—*castillo* (castle)—and the remains of its Moorish walls and ramparts stretch for about a half mile. The letters FORV suggests that a Roman forum once stood on the spot. The **Museo Arqueológico** on the hill has artifacts of the early Romans, including some mosaics. Admission is 255 pesetas ($2.40) to the castle, with the museum and theater free. The ruins are open to view Tuesday through Saturday from 10am to 2pm and 4 to 6pm, on Sunday from 10am to 2pm.

The best place for food is right at the castle: **L'Armeler,** Subida del Castillo, 4 (tel. 266-43-82). Meals cost 2,500 pesetas ($23.50); open Tuesday through Saturday from 1 to 4pm and 8 to 11pm. You can get both French and Spanish food in the ambience of a *vieja mansión* (old mansion). Try one of the splendid pâtés, perhaps salmon or sole in a truffle sauce. A terrace opens onto a view.

---

2. BENIDORM

27 miles NE of Alicante, 84 miles S of Valencia

GETTING THERE   By Train   From Alicante, departures are hourly.

By Bus   Buses connecting Valencia and Alicante with Benidorm leave almost hourly.

By Car   Take the E-15 expressway south from Valencia or north from Alicante.

ESSENTIALS   The area code for Benidorm is 96. The Tourist Information Office is at Avenida Martínez Alejos, 16 (tel. 96/585-13-11).

Before its 3½ miles of beach were discovered by tourists, Benidorm was the tiniest of fishing villages. But now summer vacationers pour in apace, and it seems as if a new concrete hotel were being built every day. With its heavy European influence and its topless beach, Benidorm has become the most sophisticated town this side of Torremolinos.

WHERE TO STAY

Make sure you reserve in advance between mid-June and September. If you arrive without a reservation, you're out of luck. During this time most hotel managers slap the full-board requirement onto their rates. The way to beat this is to book into one of the rare *residencias* in Benidorm. I've avoided mentioning the hotels along the coastal road, after having spent sleepless nights in them listening to the rumbling traffic outside.

DOUBLES FOR LESS THAN 8,500 PTAS. ($79.90)

RESIDENCIA BRISTOL, Avenida de Martínez Alejos, 1, 03500 Benidorm. Tel. 96/854-40-28. 30 rms (all with bath). TEL

$ Rates: 2,500 ptas. ($23.50) single; 3,200 ptas. ($30.10) double. Breakfast 280 ptas. ($2.65) extra. No credit cards. **Closed:** Nov–Mar.

⑤ A one-star pension in the heart of Benidorm, directly north of the Playa de Levante, this modernized elevator building contains fairly comfortable bedrooms. The best of them, parceled out on a first-come, first-served basis, are the ones with the front view. Some rooms have private baths; others have showers.

RESIDENCIA DON JOSÉ, Carretera del Alt, 2, 03500 Benidorm. Tel. 96/585-50-50. 62 rms (all with bath).

$ Rates: 2,000 ptas. ($18.80) single; 3,500 ptas. ($32.90) double. Breakfast 300 ptas. ($2.80) extra. MC, V. **Closed:** Oct–Mar.

Just a short walk from the seashore and north of the Playa de Levante, this white-brick balconied building is a rare Benidorm residencia. Breakfast is the only meal served, but some of the best budget restaurants are nearby (and some intriguing, but touristy, shops). The Don José is neat and clean; bedrooms (some with private phones) are up-to-date and attractively furnished.

HOTEL BRISA, Playa de Levante, 03500 Benidorm. Tel. 96/585-54-00. 70 rms (all with bath). TEL

$ Rates: 3,000 ptas. ($28.20) single; 5,200 ptas. ($48.90) double. Breakfast 300 ptas. ($2.80) extra. No credit cards.

On its beachfront perch, the Brisa looks spotless. It's reasonably priced, with bright and airy rooms (some have minibars), plus a swimming pool. Dining is available; you can order one main meal a day for 1,800 pesetas ($16.90).

HOTEL LA PEÑA, Avenida Gerona, s/n, 03500 Benidorm. Tel. 96/851-06-94. 95 rms (all with bath). TEL

$ Rates: 4,000 ptas. ($37.60) single; 5,500 ptas. ($51.70) double. Breakfast 300 ptas. ($2.80) extra. No credit cards.

This modern six-story hotel, 3 minutes north of the Playa de Levante, offers balconied rooms and sea views. The comfortable, streamlined accommodations have furnishings inspired by Spanish antiques, large built-in wardrobes, and functional, attractive baths. The lounge area is at once tasteful, spacious, and cool. A terrace opens onto a long private swimming pool.

HOTEL CANFALI, Plaza de San Jaime, 5, 03500 Benidorm. Tel. 96/585-08-18. Fax 96/585-47-16. 37 rms (all with bath). TEL

$ Rates: 5,500 ptas. ($51.70) single with full board; 8,500 ptas. ($79.90) double with full board. No credit cards.

A seaside villa between the Playa de Levante and the Playa de Poniente, the Canfali ranks as one of the best small hotels in town. Its position is a scene-stealer—on a low cliff at the end of the esplanade, with a staircase winding down to the beach. The more expensive rooms have balconies with sea views. Although the hotel is spacious and comfortable, its decor is undistinguished, its bedrooms functional. Terraces overlook the sea, a perfect spot for morning coffee.

WORTH THE EXTRA BUCKS

DON PANCHO, Avenida del Mediterráneo, 39, 03500 Benidorm. Tel. 96/585-29-50. Fax 96/586-77-79. 251 rms (all with bath). A/C TV TEL
$ Rates: 7,600 ptas. ($71.45) single; 11,000 ptas. ($103.40) double. Breakfast 600 ptas. ($5.65) extra. AE, DC, MC, V.

One of the best hotels in Benidorm, Don Pancho is a high-rise set a short walk from the beach, directly north of the Avenida de Madrid. Its inviting lobby has a Spanish-colonial/Aztec decor, and each of the well-furnished, well-maintained bedrooms opens onto a small balcony. Facilities include a swimming pool and lighted tennis court.

HOTEL CIMBEL, Avenida de Europa, 1, 03500 Benidorm. Tel. 96/585-21-00. Fax 96/586-06-61. 144 rms (all with bath). A/C TV TEL **Bus:** 1, 2, 3, 4, or 5.
$ Rates: 6,500 ptas. ($61.10) single; 13,000 ptas. ($122.20) double. Breakfast 500 ptas. ($4.70) extra. AE, DC, MC, V.

Since this hotel stands on one of the most popular beaches in town, it has tremendous appeal for sun-worshippers, who step from the lobby virtually onto the sand. At this glamorous address, rooms are well furnished and comfortable. Guests will enjoy the swimming pool and disco.

WHERE TO EAT

DON LUIS, Edificio Zeus, Avenida Dr. Orts Llorca, s/n. Tel. 585-46-73.
Cuisine: INTERNATIONAL. **Reservations:** Required.
$ Prices: Appetizers 550–650 ptas. ($5.15–$6.10); main dishes 1,200–1,900 ptas. ($11.30–$17.85). AE, DC, MC, V.
Open: Lunch daily 1–4pm; dinner daily 7:30pm–midnight. **Closed:** Jan.

This modern, stylish restaurant north of the Playa de Levante has a sun-flooded outdoor terrace for dining al fresco, or, if you prefer, an air-conditioned interior. Increasingly appreciated for his Italian specialties, the chef uses fresh produce delivered daily from local markets. A dinner might include chilled salmon mousse, confit of duckling, homemade pasta such as ravioli or fettuccine, and a wide choice of Spanish and Italian wines.

I FRATELLI, Edificio Principado, Avenida Dr. Orts Llorca, 21. Tel. 585-39-79.
Cuisine: ITALIAN. **Reservations:** Recommended.
$ Prices: Appetizers 500–1,250 ptas. ($4.70–$11.75); main dishes 1,800–2,200 ptas. ($16.90–$20.70). AE, DC, MC, V.
Open: Lunch daily 1–4pm; dinner daily 7:30pm–midnight. **Closed:** Nov.

I Fratelli competes with its neighbor, Don Luis, as the best Italian eatery in town. Its menu is similar to that of a sophisticated restaurant in Italy. Dishes include fresh grilled peppers stuffed with Mediterranean seafood, delicious homemade pastas, grilled meats, saltimbocca, and tempting calorie-laden Italian desserts. You can dine on the outdoor terrace or in the air-conditioned dining room.

PÉRGOLA, Acantilado-Edificio Coblanca, Rincón de Loix, 25. Tel. 585-38-00.
Cuisine: SPANISH. **Reservations:** Required.
$ Prices: Appetizers 1,000–1,500 ptas. ($9.40–$14.10); main dishes 2,000–2,500 ptas. ($18.80–$23.50). AE, MC, V.
Open: Lunch daily 1–4pm; dinner daily 7:30pm–midnight. **Closed:** Mid-Dec–mid-Feb.

One of the attractions here is the sweeping view of the bay, visible from the flower-strewn outdoor terrace. The food is skillfully prepared, including such fresh specialties as seafood crêpes with clams, stuffed crabs, stewed codfish with a confit of garlic, breast of duck with pears, and rack of beef with a mustard sauce.

WHERE TO STAY AND EAT IN NEARBY CALPE

PARADERO DE IFACH, Explanada del Puerto, 50, 03710 Calpe. Tel. 96/583-03-00. Fax 96/583-03-00. 29 rms (all without bath). TEL **Bus:** Ubesa line from Benidorm.
$ Rates: 2,800 ptas. ($26.30) single; 5,500 ptas. ($51.70) double. Breakfast 300 ptas. ($2.80) extra. AE.

Thirteen miles (21km) north of Benidorm, and set back 2 miles (3.2km) from the Valencia–Alicante highway, this establishment is close to the giant Rock of Ifach, Alicante's Gibraltar. The hotel is built in the white flat-roofed North African style, offering sun-terrace living at moderate rates. Most of the bedrooms are handsomely designed. You can have a drink in a beam-ceilinged room (complete with an open fireplace) or in the sun-room greenhouse, with its red-tile floors, plants, cages of singing birds, and arched windows overlooking the sea. The hotel's restaurant is closed.

EL CLAUSTRO, RESIDENCIA LA COMETA, Urbanización La Cometa III. Tel. 583-11-20.
Cuisine: INTERNATIONAL. **Reservations:** Required. **Bus:** "La Camela."
$ Prices: Appetizers 350–800 ptas. ($3.30–$7.50); main dishes 850–1,700 ptas. ($8–$16); fixed-priced menu 1,550 ptas. ($14.55). V.
Open: Fri–Wed 7pm–1am. **Closed:** Mid–Nov–mid-Dec, Jan 10–mid-March.

Built on the site of the former cloisters of an old nunnery, this restaurant overlooks Calpe. It has been converted into a mirrored dining room with a lounge and cocktail bar, where diners can relax on plush divans while they order their meals. The extensive menu includes such offerings as snails in pastry and salmon in orange sauce to start, followed by the likes of shrimp aspic, pigeon salad, and smoked salmon with crabmeat mousse. Your main dishes might be fish in pastry, steak with goose liver, pork Wellington, trout with almonds, or veal kidneys in mustard sauce. A good wine list complements the menu.

EVENING ENTERTAINMENT

CASINO COSTA BLANCA, Carretera Nacional, km 114. Tel. 589-27-12.
This is the spot for gambling and good food. Admission is charged for the gaming rooms, but many come here just for the restaurant, off the casino's huge foyer. Appetizers include cream of crab soup and salad of baby eels and lobster, while main dishes feature sole with truffles, turbot, and hake with creamy chopped-clam sauce. A small but excellent dessert list and good wines add to the pleasure. If you prefer, try the buffet just inside the entrance. Open: Casino daily 8pm–4am; restaurant daily 9pm–1am. Prices: Complete meal 4,500 ptas. ($42.30); Fri-Sat buffet 2,200 ptas. ($20.70); Bus: Alicante–Valencia route.
Admission: Casino 650 ptas. ($6.10), plus a passport.

BENIDORM PALACE, Carretera de Circunvalación s/n. Tel. 585-16-60.
One of the best dance clubs in the region, located in the Rincón de Loix, the Benidorm Palace features the latest music and a large dance floor. There are an outdoor garden, expansive bars, and ample seating. Open: Daily 9:30pm–1:30am. Prices: Drinks 500 ptas. ($4.70).
Admission: 2,500 ptas. ($23.50).

INTERNATIONAL CLUB DE BENIDORM, Avenida Alcoy, 7 (Edificio Iberia). Tel. 585-31-21.
The nautical decor of this pub is appropriate to its setting at the edge of the water. It's only a few minutes' walk from the center of town and likely to be filled with a crowd enjoying Irish coffee and an array of cocktails. Snacks available. Open: Daily 10am–midnight. Prices: Beer 125 ptas. ($1.20); drinks 450 ptas. ($3.85).

3. ALICANTE

50 miles N of Murcia; 25 miles S of Benidorm; 107 miles
S of Valencia by the coast; 259 miles SE of Madrid

GETTING THERE   By Plane   Alicante's El Altet Airport (tel. 528-50-11) is 12 miles (19.3km) from the city, with usually 2 daily flights from Alicante to Madrid, Barcelona, and Seville. By transfering from one of those three cities, you can reach virtually any place in Europe from Alicante. There are also 3 flights weekly from Ibiza and Málaga (Costa del Sol). Twelve buses daily connect the city to the airport, the fare costing 50 pesetas (45¢). The Iberia Airlines ticket office is at Calle C.F. Soto, 9 (tel. 521-85-10).

By Train   From Valencia, there are 4 trains a day (3 hours); from Barcelona, 3 trains a day (11 hours); and from Madrid, 7 trains a day (9 hours). The RENFE office is at the Estación Término, Avenida Salamanca s/n (tel. 522-01-27).

By Bus   Different bus lines from various parts of the coast converge at the terminus, corner of Calle Portugal and Calle Italia (tel. 522-07-00). There is frequent service—almost hourly—from Benidorm (see above) and from Valencia (4 hours). From Murcia (see below), there is daily bus service (1½ hours). Buses also run from Madrid (5 to 6 hours).

By Car   Take the E-15 expressway south along the coast from Valencia. The espressway and the N-340 run northeast from Murcia.

By Ferry   There are ferry connections 4 times a day by Trasmediterránea, Esplanada de Espana, 2 (tel. 520-61-09), to Ibiza (3 hours). Marítima de Formentera offers service to Ibiza and Formentera 2 times weekly (7 hours to Ibiza, 10 hours to Formentera).

ESSENTIALS   The area code for Alicante is 96. The Tourist Information Office is at Explanada de España, 2 (tel. 96/521-22-85). The telephone office is at Avenida de la Constitución, 10 (tel. 004), open daily from 9am to 10pm. For medical assistance, go to the Hospital Provincial, Calle General Elizaicín (tel. 520-10-00). Phone numbers: ambulance, 521-17-050; emergency, 091; city police, 528-47-65.

Alicante, capital of the Costa Blanca, is be considered the best all-around city in Spain by many, since it's popular in both summer and winter. As you walk its esplanades, you almost feel as if you're in Africa: Women in caftans and peddlers hawking carvings from Senegal or elsewhere often populate the waterfront.

WHAT TO SEE & DO

With its wide, palm-lined avenues, this town was made for walking. The magnificent **Explanada de España,** extending around part of the yacht harbor, includes the great promenade of mosaic sidewalks under the palms. All the boulevards are clean and lined with unlimited shopping facilities, including Alicante's leading department store, **Galerías Preciadas,** where you can find bargains without being trampled by mobs, as in Madrid. Traffic is easygoing, so you can wander leisurely about the city. You'll come upon beautiful parks and gardens and apparently endless lines of palms. You'll also find several plazas, some paved with marble.

The impressive **Castillo de San Fernando** has a panoramic view and can be visited during the day. High on a hill, the more awesome **Castillo de Santa Bárbara** (tel. 520-51-00) towers over the bay and provincial capital. The Greeks called the fort Akra Leuka (White Peak). Its original defenses were probably erected by the Carthaginians in 400 B.C. and were later used by the Romans and the Arabs. The grand scale of this fortress is evident in its moats, drawbridges, tunneled entrances, guardrooms, bakery, cisterns, underground storerooms, hospitals, batteries, powder stores, barracks, the Matanza Tower and the Keep, high breastworks, and deep dungeons. From the top of the castle there's an impressive view over land and sea (reachable by road or an elevator that is boarded at the Explanada de España). Admission is 90 pesetas (85¢) by elevator, 55 pesetas (50¢) by road. In winter the castle is open from 9am to 7pm; in summer, from 9am to 9pm.

On the slopes of the Castillo de Santa Bárbara is the **Barrio de Santa Cruz.** Lying behind the cathedral and forming part of the **Villa Vieja** (as the old quarter of Alicante is called), it is a colorful section with wrought-iron grilles on the windows, banks of flowers, and a view of the entire harbor.

Alicante isn't all ancient. Although the **Museo de la Asegurada** (Casa de la Asegurada, facing the Iglesia Santa María at the east end of the Calle Mayor) is housed in the city's oldest building—constructed as a granary in 1685—it contains works by Miró, Calder, Cocteau, Vasarely, Dalí, Picasso, and Tápies. Notable foreign artists include Braque, Chagall, Giacometti, Kandinsky, and Zadkine. You'll also see a musical score by Manuel de Falla. The museum was formed in 1977 from the donation of a private collection by the painter/sculptor Eusebi Sempere, whose works are also on display. Admission is free, and you can visit Tuesday through Saturday from 10am to 1pm and 5 to 8pm, on Sunday from 10am to 1pm.

Just north of the entrance to Santa Bárbara, catch a 58-mile narrow-gauge train that will take you along the beautiful rocky, beach-lined coast to **Denia,** passing through Villajoyosa, Benidorm, Altea, and 26 other stations, almost all of which are worth a visit. Now a lively tourist center, Denia stretches from the slopes of a hill to the seashore. It was inhabited by the Greeks, its name deriving from an ancient temple dedicated to the goddess Diana (fragments of the temple are displayed in the early-16th-century Town Hall). You'll also find the remnants of an old Iberian settlement and a great Moorish castle. Denia has fine beaches, and its fishing port is one of the region's best.

San Juan, the largest beach in Alicante, lies a short distance from the capital. It's lined with villas, hotels, and restaurants. The bay of Alicante has two capes, and on the bay is **Postiguet Beach.** The bay stretches all the way to the **Cape of Santa Pola,** a town with two good beaches, a 14th-century castle, and several seafood restaurants.

WHERE TO STAY

PORTUGAL, Portugal, 26, 03003 Alicante. Tel. 96/522-32-44. 18 rms (5 with bath).
$ Rates: 1,400 ptas. ($13.15) single with sink; 2,400 pta. ($22.55) double with sink, 3,200 ptas. ($30.10) double with bath. Breakfast 300 ptas. ($2.80) extra. No credit cards.

The Portugal is a two-story hotel, 1 block from the bus station, about 4 blocks from the railway station, and a 3-minute walk from the harbor. The accommodations, furnished in tasteful modern style, are immaculate.

RESIDENCIA NAVAS, Navas, 26, 03001 Alicante. Tel. 96/520-40-11. 37 rms (7 with bath). TEL
$ Rates: 1,800 ptas. ($16.90) single with sink; 2,800 ptas. ($26.30) double with sink, 3,500 ptas. ($32.90) double with bath. Breakfast 300 ptas. ($2.80) extra. AE, MC, V.

Built in 1965, this hotel gets but one star from the government, since breakfast is the only meal served and most rooms have washbasins instead of private baths. However, the accommodations are clean, comfortable, and fairly handsome, most with their own balconies. The Navas is located near the Teatro Principal.

HOTEL RESIDENCIA SAN REMO, Navas, 30, 03001 Alicante. Tel. 96/520-95-00. 28 rms (all with bath). TEL **Bus:** D, E, or F.
$ Rates: 3,200 ptas. ($30.10) single; 5,000 ptas. ($47) double. Breakfast 300 ptas. ($2.80) extra. AE, DC, MC, V.

A white-plastered seven-floor building, the San Remo offers clean, unpretentious, comfortable rooms, some with their own balconies. Only breakfast served. The welcome is warm, the price right.

CRISTAL, López Torregrosa, 11, 03002 Alicante. Tel. 96/520-96-00. 54 rms (all with bath). A/C TEL
$ Rates: 4,700 ptas. ($44.20) single; 5,800 ptas. ($54.50) double. Breakfast 350 ptas. ($3.30) extra. MC, V.
This seven-story glass structure is one of the best-designed hotels in town. In cooler months there is central heating. The spacious reception lounge has comfortable furnishings arranged on hand-loomed circular rugs. While the Cristal doesn't have a restaurant, there are both a bar and a snack bar. Built in the heart of Alicante, off the Rambla Méndez Núñez, the hotel is a 5-minute walk from the inner harbor and the esplanade. Rooms are clean and functionally furnished.

HOTEL RESIDENCIA COVADONGA, Plaza de los Luceros, 17, 03004 Alicante. Tel. 96/520-28-44. 83 rms (all with bath). A/C TV TEL **Bus:** C.
$ Rates: 3,800 ptas. ($35.70) single; 6,200 ptas. ($58.30) double. Breakfast 380 ptas. ($3.60) extra. AE, DC, MC, V.
Centrally located to attractions, the railway station, buses, and the airport, the Covadonga also offers comfortable, spacious rooms and good service. The public rooms are large and inviting. There's no restaurant, but you'll find many eating places nearby.

PALAS, Cervantes, 5, 03002 Alicante. Tel. 96/520-92-11. 49 rms (all with bath). A/C TEL
$ Rates: 5,200 ptas. ($48.90) single; 8,000 ptas. ($75.20) double. Breakfast 420 ptas. ($3.95) extra. AE, DC, MC, V. **Closed:** Nov.
Although a bit pricier, this charmer has a lot of old-fashioned style. Many guests like its location—near the seafront at the eastern end of the Explanada de España—along with its personal service. Several public areas are graced with chandeliers and antiques. The bedrooms are well furnished and maintained. The hotel also offers a good restaurant, serving meals from 1,800 pesetas ($16.90).

WHERE TO EAT

The characteristic dish of Alicante is rice, served in many different ways. The most typical sauce is *aioli,* a kind of mayonnaise made from oil and garlic. Dessert selections offer the greatest variety on the Costa Blanca, with *turrón de Alicante* (Spanish nougat) the most popular of all.

PACHÁ, Haroldo Parres, 6. Tel. 521-19-38.
Cuisine: SPANISH. Reservations: Required. **Bus:** 6.
$ Prices: Appetizers 800–1,000 ptas. ($7.50–$9.40); main dishes 1,000–2,000 ptas. ($9.40–$18.80); fixed-priced menus 1,500–3,000 ptas. ($14.10–$28.20). AE, DC, MC, V.
Open: Lunch Thurs–Tues 1–5:30pm; dinner Thurs–Tues 8pm–midnight.
At the edge of the Plaza Estrella in the old city, this pleasantly decorated restaurant has only a dozen or so tables. The owner/chef prepares the house specialties, variations on rice dishes dressed with meat, seafood, and shellfish. You might also order Catalan spinach, eggplant in cream sauce, or entrecote pizzaiola as an accompaniment.

QUO VADIS, Plaza Santísma Faz, 3. Tel. 521-66-60.
Cuisine: SPANISH. **Reservations:** Required.
$ Prices: Appetizers 700–1,000 ptas. ($6.60–$9.40); main dishes 1,000–1,500 ptas. ($9.40–$14.10); fixed-priced menus 1,650–2,000 ptas. ($15.50–$18.80). AE, DC, MC, V.
Open: Lunch daily 1–5pm; dinner daily 8pm–midnight.
Considered one of the best restaurants in town, Quo Vadis is located north of the Explanada de España. You'll first pass through a sidewalk café and popular bar before reaching the air-conditioned dining room. Amid a dignified country decor,

you'll be able to watch your food prepared with touches of culinary theater. There's also an intimate terrace, open from May to October. Specialties of the house include a wide array of fresh seafood, such as *dorada, besugo à la Bilbaina, lubina à la sal* (encrusted in salt, removed after baking), and flambéed fish, as well as roast suckling pig. A dessert specialty is *nueces flambé*—whipped cream, ice cream, and chocolate flambéed with Grand Marnier and sprinkled with grated almonds.

RESTAURANT LA DÁRSENA, Muelle del Puerto (Explanada de España). Tel. 520-75-89.

Cuisine: SPANISH. **Reservations:** Required at lunch.

$ **Prices:** Appetizers 475–2,500 ptas. ($4.45–$23.50); main dishes 1,300–1,900 ptas. ($12.20–$17.85); fixed-priced menu 3,300 ptas. ($31). AE, DC, MC, V.

Open: Lunch Tues–Sun 1–4pm; dinner Tues–Sat 8pm–midnight.

At this popular place, located off the Explanada de España, paella is the best choice on the menu. Some 20 other rice dishes are commendable as well—for example, *arroz con pieles de bacalao* (rice with dried codfish). Try the crab soup flavored with Armagnac or a tart made with tuna and spinach.

RESTAURANT EL JUMILLANO, César Elquezábal, 64. Tel. 521-17-64.

Cuisine: SPANISH. **Reservations:** Recommended. **Bus:** D or F.

$ **Prices:** Appetizers 500–1,000 ptas. ($4.70–$9.40); main dishes 1,400–2,000 ptas. ($13.15–$18.80); fixed-priced menu 3,000 ptas. ($28.20). AE, DC, MC, V.

Open: Lunch Mon–Sat 1–4pm; dinner Mon–Sat 8pm–midnight.

This was a humble wine bar when it opened in 1936 near the old city. The original wine-and-tapas bar is still going strong, but the food has improved immeasurably. Today the sons of the original owner (Juan José and Miguel Pérez Mejías) offer a cornucopia of succulent food, including an array of fresh fish laid out in the dining room on the sun-bleached planks of an antique fishing boat. Many of the menu items are derived from locally inspired recipes. The specialties of the house include a "festival of canapés," slices of cured ham served with fresh melon, shellfish soup with mussels, Alicante stew, pig's trotters, a savory filet of beef seasoned with garlic, and a full gamut of grilled hake, sea bass, and shellfish.

EVENING ENTERTAINMENT

NOU MANOLIN, Villegas, 3. Tel. 520-03-68.

This beer hall in back of the Teatro Principal is a favorite spot. Many residents come here for the tapas and never get around to dining in the adjoining restaurant. Open: Daily 1–4pm and 8:30pm–midnight. Prices: Wine by the glass 140 ptas. ($1.30), tapas 500–1,000 ptas. ($4.70–$9.40).

BUGATTI, San Fernando, 37. Tel. 521-06-46.

Near the port off the Rambla Méndez Núñes, this ranks as one of the most modern dance clubs on the Costa Blanca. The music is up-to-date, and the entrepreneur/owner has become a regular fixture on the regional night scene. Open: Daily 7–10pm and 11:30pm–5:30am. Prices: Drinks 700 ptas. ($6.60).

Admission: Before 11pm, 500 ptas. ($4.70), including one drink; after 11pm, 1,000 ptas. ($9.40), including one drink.

---

4. ELCHE

13 miles SW of Alicante; 35 miles NE of Murcia; 252 miles SE of Madrid

GETTING THERE **By Train** The central train station is the Estación Parque, Plaza Alfonso XII. Trains arrive almost hourly from Alicante.

By Bus The bus station is at Avenida de la Libertat. Buses travel between Alicante and Elche on the hour.

By Car Take the N-340 highway from Alicante and proceed southwest.

ESSENTIALS: The area code for Elche is 96. The Tourist Information Office is at Passeig de l'Estació (tel. 545-27-47).

Between Alicante and Murcia, the little town of Elche is famous for its age-old mystery play, its lush groves of date palms, and its shoe- and sandal-making. The play is reputedly the oldest dramatic liturgy performed in Europe. On August 14 and 15 for the last six centuries, the *☉Mystery of Elche* has celebrated the Assumption of the Virgin. Songs are performed in an ancient form of Catalan. Admission is free but it's hard to get a seat unless you book in advance through the tourist office (see above). The play is performed at the Church of Santa María, dating from the 17th century.

Unless you visit at the time of the mystery play, the town's date palms will hold the most appeal. The palm forest is unrivaled in Europe—some 600,000 trees said to have been originally planted by Phoenician (perhaps Greek) seafarers. The Moors created the irrigation system 1,000 years ago. Stroll through the **Huerto del Cura (Priest's Grove),** open daily from 9am to 6pm, to see the palm garden and collection of tropical flowers and cacti. In the garden look for the Palmera del Cura (Priest's Palm), some 150 years old and having seven branches sprouting from its trunk. In the grove you will see one of the most famous ladies of Spain, *La Dama de Elche.* This is a replica, the original limestone bust (500 B.C.) being on display in the National Archeological Museum in Madrid. It was discovered in 1897.

WHERE TO STAY

DON JAIME, Primo de Rivera, 7, 03203 Elche. Tel. 96/545-38-40. 64 rms (all with bath). TEL

$ Prices: 4,000 ptas. ($37.60) single; 5,000 ptas. ($47) double. Breakfast 300 ptas. ($2.80) extra. V.

Totally lacking the glamor of the parador Huerto del Cura (see below) and rated only two stars by the government, this hotel is much easier on the purse. It's located near the town center. Bedrooms are comfortable and well maintained rather than stylish. During performances of the *Mystery of Elche,* prices here rise about 25%. There's no restaurant, but there are a number of places to eat nearby.

HUERTO DEL CURA, Porta de La Morera, 14, 03200 Elche. Tel. 96/545-80-40. Fax 96/542-19-10. 70 rms (all with bath). A/C MINIBAR TV TEL

$ Rates: 8,500 ptas. ($79.90) single; 11,500 ptas. ($108.10) double. Breakfast 800 ptas. ($7.50) extra. AE, DC, MC, V.

The Huerto del Cura stands in the so-called Priest's Grove, and from your bedroom you'll have lovely views of the palm trees. The privately owned parador consists of a number of cabins in the grove. Although the rates are high, staying here proves a unique experience—everything beautifully furnished and immaculately kept, the service impeccable. A swimming pool under the palms separates the cabins from the main hotel building. There is an attractive bar, and in the upstairs dining room, the four-fork Els Capellans, the food is well prepared and the wine list extensive. Dinner costs around 2,800 pesetas ($26.30).

WHERE TO EAT

PARQUE MUNICIPAL, Paseo Alfonso XIII, s/n. Tel. 545-34-15.
Cuisine: SPANISH. **Reservations:** Recommended.
$ Prices: Appetizers 250–500 ptas. ($2.35–$4.70); main dishes 1,000–1,400 ptas. ($9.40–$13.15); fixed-priced menu 1,050 ptas. ($9.85). MC, V.
Open: Lunch daily 1–4pm; dinner daily 8–11pm.

A large open-air restaurant and café right in the middle of a public park, the Parque Municipal is a good place to go for decent food and relaxed service. Many regional dishes appear on the menu; try one of the savory rice dishes as a main course, followed by "cake of Elche."

RESTAURANTE LA FINCA, Carretera Perleta, 1–7. Tel. 545-60-07.
  Cuisine: SPANISH. **Reservations:** Recommended.
$ Prices: Appetizers 800–1,600 ptas. ($7.50–$15.05); main dishes 1,300–1,600 ptas. ($12.20–$15.05); fixed-priced menu 3,900 ptas. ($36.65). AE, DC, MC, V.
  Open: Lunch Tues–Sun 1–5pm; dinner Tues–Sat 8:30pm–midnight.

In the campo near the Elche football stadium, 3 miles south of town along the Carretera de El Alted, La Finca opened in 1985 and has attracted customers ever since with its good food. As an appetizer, enjoy a *table de quesos y pâtés* (a selection of cheeses such as brie, cream herb, and *manchego* with homemade pâté) or smoked fish. Specialties are striped bass in pastry stuffed with diced Serrano ham and pimientos, roast baby lamb, pheasant in port wine with cream of chestnuts, and pigeon stuffed with its own giblets. The paella is good, the several different varieties including *marinera* (with shellfish), *valenciana* with rabbit and snails, and vegetable. A rich dessert is *tarta de trufas,* or you may settle for one of the sherbets made with seasonal fruit.

---

5. MURCIA

52 miles SW of Alicante; 245 miles SE of Madrid; 159 miles SW of Valencia

GETTING THERE By Train From Alicante, 12 trains arrive daily (1½ hours); from Barcelona, 1 daily (11 hours); and from Madrid, 3 daily (7 hours). From the Estación del Carmen, Calle Industría s/n (tel. 26-37-36), take bus no. 11 to the heart of the city.

By Bus From Valencia, 3 buses arrive daily; from Granada, 3; and from Seville, 1. If you're coming from Almería, there are 2 connections daily. Buses come into the terminal at Plaza de Casanova. Call 29-22-11 for information.

By Car Take the N-340 southwest from Alicante.

ESSENTIALS: The area code for Murcia is 968. The Tourist Information Office is at Alejandro Seiquier, 4 (tel. 968/21-37-16).

This ancient Moorish city of sienna-colored buildings is an inland provincial capital on the main road between Valencia and Granada. With a population of some 300,000, it lies on the Segura River.

The **Holy Week celebration** at Murcia is an ideal time to visit. Its processions are spectacular, with about 3,000 people taking part, and some sculptures of Salzillo (see below) are carried through the streets. Musicians blow horns so big they have to be carried on wheels.

WHAT TO SEE & DO

Although it suffered much from fire and bombardment during the Spanish Civil War, the city abounds in grand houses built in the 18th century. But the principal artistic treasure is the **cathedral,** Plaza Cardenal Belluga (tel. 21-63-44), a bastardized medley of Gothic, baroque, and Renaissance. Begun in the 1300s, its bell tower was built at four different periods by four different architects. You can climb the tower for a view of Murcia and the enveloping fertile huerta (plain). The Capilla de los Vélez, off the ambulatory, is the most interesting chapel. You can see works by the famous local sculptor, Francisco Salzillo (1707–83), as well as the golden crown of the Virgen de la Fuensanta, patroness of Murcia. To reach the museum, go through the north transept. You can visit it daily from 10am to noon and 5 to 7:30pm for an admission of 60 pesetas (55¢). The cathedral and bell tower keep the same hours.

The other major sight is the **Museo de Salzillo,** San Andrés, 1 (tel. 29-18-93). The son of an Italian sculptor and a Spanish mother, Salzillo is the last famous name in Spanish polychrome wood sculpture. This museum displays his finest work, plus many terra-cotta figurines based on Biblical scenes. It is open Monday through Saturday from 9:30am to 1pm and 4 to 7pm, on Sunday from 10am to 1pm. Admission is 100 pesetas (95¢).

Another attraction is the **Museo de Arqueología,** Alfonso X el Sabio, 7 (tel. 23-41-30), considered one of the best in Spain. Through artifacts—mosaics, fragments of pottery, Roman coins, ceramics, and various other objects—it traces life in Murcia province from prehistoric times. The two most important collections are devoted to objects from the Hispano-Moorish period of the 12th to 14th centuries and to Spanish ceramics of the 17th and 18th centuries. In summer the museum is open Monday through Saturday from 9am to 2pm; closed holidays. In winter it is open Tuesday through Friday from 10am to 2pm and 6 to 8pm; on Saturday and Sunday from 11am to 2pm. Admission is 75 pesetas (70¢).

WHERE TO STAY

DOUBLES FOR LESS THAN 10,000 PTAS. [$94]

HISPANO 1, Trapería, 8, 30001 Murcia. Tel. 968/21-61-52. Fax 968/21-68-59. 46 rms (all with bath). TV TEL
$ Rates: 4,500 ptas. ($42.30) single; 5,500 ptas. ($51.70) double. Breakfast 700 ptas. ($6.60) extra. AE, DC, MC, V.
An older version of Hispano 2 (see below), run by the same people, this hotel is still reliable after all these years. It stands right at the cathedral. Rooms are functional, comfortable, and well kept. There are no dining facilities, but you'll find a number of cafés and restaurants nearby. Although Hispano I is considered good value, its singles tend to be expensive.

HOTEL MAJESTI, Plaza San Pedro, 5, 30007 Murcia. Tel. 968/21-47-41. 68 rms (all with bath). TEL
$ Rates: 4,000 ptas. ($37.60) single; 7,200 ptas. ($67.70) double. Breakfast 300 ptas. ($2.80) extra. No credit cards.
If you're looking for an unpretentious, centrally located hotel, the Majesti, which adjoins the open-air market, may be the place. Rooms are simply furnished, but comfortable and well maintained. Doubles have air conditioning.

HOTEL CONDE DE FLORIDABLANCA, Corbalán, 7, 30002 Murcia. Tel. 968/21-46-24. Fax 968/21-32-15. 60 rms (all with bath). A/C MINIBAR TV TEL
$ Rates: 6,500 ptas. ($61.10) single; 9,000 ptas. ($84.60) double. Breakfast 700 ptas. ($6.60) extra. AE, DC, MC, V.
In the center of the Barrio del Carmen, near the cathedral, this hotel is ideally situated for explorations of the old city. The building is attractively decorated, the neighborhood fairly quiet at night. Rooms are comfortable and appealing—among the best in town. The hotel serves breakfast only, but restaurants are found nearby.

HOTEL HISPANO 2, Calle Lucas, 3, 30001 Murcia. Tel. 968/21-61-52. Fax 968/21-68-59. 35 rms (all with bath). A/C MINIBAR TV TEL
$ Rates: 8,000 ptas. ($75.20) single; 10,000 ptas. ($94) double. Breakfast 900 ptas. ($8.45) extra. AE, DC, MC, V.
The older Hispano 1 proved so successful that the owners inaugurated this version in the late 1970s. Bedrooms are comfortably furnished. Family run, the hotel has good tapas in its bar, plus a restaurant offering well-prepared regional food.

WORTH THE EXTRA BUCKS

RESIDENCIA RINCÓN DE PEPE, Plaza de Apóstoles, 34, 30002 Murcia. Tel. 968/21-22-39. Fax 968/22-17-44. 115 rms (with bath). A/C TV TEL **Bus:** 3, 4, or 8.
$ Rates: 10,500 ptas. ($98.70) single; 13,200 ptas. ($124.10) double. Breakfast 950 ptas. ($8.95) extra. AE, DC, MC, V.
This modern hotel hidden on a narrow street in the heart of the old quarter is a delight. Once beyond its entranceway, accented with marble, glass, and plants, you'll

discover a good-sized lounge as well as a bar. The comfortable bedrooms are up-to-date with many built-in conveniences; some have minibars. The Rincón de Pepe is also my finest dining recommendation (see below).

WHERE TO EAT

RINCÓN DE PEPE, Plaza de Apóstoles, 34. Tel. 21-22-39.
    Cuisine: SPANISH/INTERNATIONAL. **Reservations:** Recommended. **Bus:** 3, 4, or 8.
$ Prices: Appetizers 650–3,600 ptas. ($6.10–$33.85); main dishes 850–3,000 ptas. ($8–$28.20); fixed-priced menu 3,000 ptas. ($28.20). AE, DC, MC, V.
    Open: Lunch daily noon–5pm; dinner Mon–Sat 8pm–midnight. **Closed:** Sun June–Aug.

⭐   Many won't leave town without going to this culinary landmark set up in the mid-1920s. It rates as the best restaurant in town, and you can dine here at a wide range of price levels, depending on what you order. Specialties change frequently, since every effort is made to produce a menu with seasonal variations. You might enjoy a dish such as pig's trotters and white beans, spring lamb kidneys in sherry, or white beans with partridge. The excellent shellfish selection includes Carril clams, a platter of assorted grilled seafood and fish, and grilled red prawns from Aguilas. Among the meat and poultry specialties: roast spring lamb Murcian style and duck in orange sauce.

ACUARIO, Plaza Puxmaria, 1. Tel. 21-99-55.
    Cuisine: SPANISH. **Reservations:** Recommended.
    Open: Lunch Mon–Sat 1–4pm; dinner Mon–Sat 8pm–midnight.
Long respected for its excellent Murcian cuisine, this restaurant located near the cathedral offers a savory menu in air-conditioned comfort. Begin with the pâté of salmon, following with merluza (hake) in sherry sauce. You can also order a tender tournedos. The lemon soufflé is delectable.

TAPAS

Good tapas are served at **La Tapa,** Plaza Flores (tel. 21-13-17), from 7am to 8pm. In addition to being an unusual end to a walk through the old city (it's located on one of oldest town squares), La Tapa offers beer on tap as well as its savory selection of appetizers, from 150 pesetas ($1.40).

---

6. CARTAGENA

30 miles S of Murcia; 275 miles S of Madrid; 68 miles SW of Alicante

GETTING THERE   **By Train**   RENFE runs 4 trains a day from Murcia (1 hour).

By Bus   Buses run hourly between Murcia and Cartagena.

By Car   Take the 301 south from Murcia.

ESSENTIALS   The area code for Cartagena is 968. The Tourist Information Office is at Plaza Castellini, 5 (tel. 968/50-75-49).

Today this ancient Carthaginian port city is Spain's naval base for the Mediterranean. For centuries it has been known for its copper, zinc, iron, lead, and silver mines. Along the 110-mile (177km) Murcian shoreline, rocks rich in these ores are found in profusion.

WHAT TO SEE & DO

Two forts guard the entrance to the harbor at Cartagena: the **Castillo de San Juan** and the **Castillo de las Galeras.** Another castle or fortress, the **Castillo de la**

Concepción, constructed in the late 11th century by Henry III, stands on a hill overlooking the city. Today this former fort serves as a public garden, the **Parque Torres,** from which you get the best overview of the harbor and the deep bay sheltered by promontories. The ruins of the 13th-century Gothic cathedral of **Santa María de la Vieja,** which came under heavy shelling in the Spanish Civil War, can also be seen.

Stroll along the port. Notice the monument to the men who died in the Spanish-American War. You will also see a submarine, one of the first in the world, built by a local inventor, Issac Peral, in 1888. Its 72 feet long and weighs 85 tons.

Scattered Roman ruins, including those of an amphitheater, can also be found throughout the city.

The **Museo Nacional de Arqueología Marítima,** Ramón y Cajal, 45, lies 2 miles (3.2km) from the center of Cartagena at Dique de Navidad, Puerto de Cartagena (tel. 50-84-15). It includes a full-sized model of a Roman galley among many exhibits from the Roman era. The museum is open Tuesday through Friday from 10am to 1pm and 4 to 6pm; on Saturday and Sunday from 10am to 1pm. Admission is 115 pesetas ($1.10). Take the Mazarrón road and watch for signs.

WHERE TO STAY

ALFONSO XIII, Paseo Alfonso XIII, 30, 30290 Cartagena. Tel. 968/52-00-00. Fax 968/50-05-02. 224 rms (all with bath). A/C TEL
$ Prices: 3,600 ptas. ($33.85) single; 5,400 ptas. ($50.75) double. Breakfast 450 ptas. ($4.25) extra. AE, DC, MC, V.
The hotel, dating from 1976 and named for the king who abdicated and sailed into exile from Cartagena in 1931, is considered "second best." Rooms are comfortable and well maintained, some opening onto a view. The hotel also has a restaurant specializing in both regional and national dishes, with meals costing from 1,200 pesetas ($11.30). Its located near the port at the edge of town.

CARTAGONOVA, Marcos Redondo, 3, 30290 Cartagena. Tel. 968/50-42-00. Fax 968/50-05-02. 126 rms (all with bath). A/C TV TEL
$ Prices: 4,500 ptas. ($42.30) single; 7,500 ptas. ($70.50) double. Breakfast 500 ptas. ($4.70) extra. AE, DC, MC, V.
This hotel *is* the best in town but still moderate in price. Rooms are nicely furnished with a number of amenities, and each is comfortable and well maintained. Facilities include a parking garage. Breakfast only is served, but restaurants and cafés are nearby.

WHERE TO EAT

BARLOVENTO, Cuatro Santos, 33. Tel. 50-66-41.
Cuisine: SPANISH. **Reservations:** Recommended.
$ Prices: Appetizers 450–675 ptas. ($4.25–$6.35); main dishes 1,200–2,650 ptas. ($11.30–$24.90); fixed-priced menu 1,550 ptas. ($14.55). MC, V.
Open: Lunch Tues–Sun 11am–4pm; dinner Tues–Sun 8–11pm.
Some of the best food in the town is served at this air-conditioned restaurant in the center near the port. Enjoy regional wines of the Murcia district, and also sample a local version of paella. Most diners prefer the mixed fish and shellfish platter—each succulent morsel from the Mediterranean grilled to perfection. The chef also prepares an excellent cheese tart.

CHAPTER 13
GETTING TO KNOW BARCELONA

Barcelona has long had a reputation for being the most European of Spanish cities. Third-largest port on the Mediterranean, it has rediscovered itself following the long, dank slumber of the Franco dictatorship, which seemed determined to wipe out a proud Catalonian culture. Barcelona may still be the "second city of Spain" (Madrid gives it stiff competition), but it is very much a "first" city in many respects.

Blessed with richly fertile soil, an excellent harbor, and a hardworking population, Barcelona has always shown a talent for transforming dreams into art and dialogue into commerce. It has always been one of Spain's most prosperous cities, with more wealth distributed among greater numbers of people (especially during the 19th century) than anywhere else in Spain.

Barcelona was a powerful and richly diverse capital when Madrid was still a dusty and unknown Castilian backwater. Exploited by several different empires, Barcelona turned to the Mediterranean for inspiration and linguistic roots, inspired more by the cultures to the east than the arid plains of Iberia.

As if the attractions of Barcelona weren't enough, it stands on the doorstep of some of the great playgrounds and vacation retreats of Europe: the Balearic Islands to the east; the Costa Brava (Wild Coast) to the north and the Pyrénées even beyond, the Penedés wine country, resorts such as Sitges on the Costa Dorada to the south, the old Roman city of Tarragona, and the monastery of Montserrat.

Despite its allure, Barcelona shares the problems of hundreds of other cities: an increasing polarization between rich and poor, a rising rate of delinquency and drug abuse, and an upsetting frequency of crime. In fairness, however, the city authorities have, with some degree of success, managed to combat much of the crime—at least within the tourist zones—in reaction to a rash of negative publicity.

As the 20th century ends, a revitalized Barcelona eagerly prepares to welcome you and thousands of other visitors as part of the 1992 Olympic Games. But the action doesn't stop there. Barcelona is planning to turn its multimillion-dollar Olympic building projects into permanently expanded facilities for sports and tourism. As its new $150-million terminal at El Prat de Llobregat Airport gears up to receive 12 million passengers a year, the restructuring of Barcelona is called "Post Olympica"—a race to the 21st century.

1. SOME CULTURAL BACKGROUND

Barcelona (which was described in the Middle Ages as "the head and trunk of Catalonia") has always thrived on contacts and commerce with countries beyond

WHAT'S SPECIAL ABOUT BARCELONA

Museums
- ☐ Museu Picasso, Barcelona's most popular attraction, focusing on artist's early period.
- ☐ Fundació Joan Miró at Montjüic, paying tribute to Catalonia's master of surrealism.
- ☐ Museu d'Art de Catalunya, with its renowned collection of Romanesque and Gothic art from many small churches.

Architectural Highlights
- ☐ Cathedral of Barcelona, begun in 1298, exemplary monument to Mediterranean Gothic.
- ☐ Gaudí's works—surrealistic imagination running rampant, as exemplified by his church, La Sagrada Familia.

Promenades
- ☐ Les Rambles, single most famous promenade in Spain, five separate sections extending from city's main square to its harbor.

Parks and Gardens
- ☐ Montjuïc, south of the city—great museums, re-created Spanish village, and site of 1992 Olympic Games.

- ☐ Parc Güell, a Gaudí dream unfulfilled, but a fascinating preview of what might have been.
- ☐ Parc de la Ciutadella, former citadel, with everything from a lake to a zoo to a modern art museum.

Panoramas
- ☐ Tibidabo Mountain, where Satan is said to have taken Christ to tempt him with the world.
- ☐ Columbus Monument, with view of one of Mediterranean's most famous harbors.

Districts
- ☐ Barri Gòtic (Gothic Quarter), filled with buildings constructed between 13th and 15th centuries.
- ☐ Eixample, studded with late 19th- and early 20th-century architecture unequaled in Europe. Many works by Gaudí.

Spain's borders. From its earliest days, the city has been linked more closely to France and the rest of Europe than to Iberia. And each of the military and financial empires that swept through and across the collective consciousness of Catalonia left its cultural legacy.

ARCHITECTURE

Like many other cities in Spain, Barcelona has its share of Neolithic dolmens and ruins from the Roman and Moorish periods. Monuments survive from the Middle Ages, when the Romanesque solidity of no-nonsense barrel vaults (sometimes with ribbing), narrow windows, and a fortified design were widely used. In fact, as early as the 10th century, Catalonian churches were among the first to use the stone barrel vault.

In the 11th and 12th centuries, a religious fervor swept through Europe and pilgrims began to flock through Barcelona on their way west to Santiago de Compostela, bringing with them the influence of French building styles and a need for new and larger churches. The style that developed had softer lines, more ornamentation (columns with decorative capitals), and an understood freedom for the stonemason to carve, within limits, in whatever manner he felt the most inspired. This eventually led to a richly ornate, very dignified style called Catalonian Gothic. Appropriate for both civic and religious buildings, it called for ogival (pointed) arches, intricate stone carvings, very large interior columns, exterior buttresses, and large rose windows set with colored glass. One of Barcelona's purest and most-loved examples of this style is the Church of Santa María del Mar, north of the city's harborfront.

Oddly, certain 16th- and 17th-century styles that swept over other regions of Spain made little impression in Barcelona. Notably absent were the baroque (with the exception of the façade of the Palau de la Generalitat) and the Plateresque movements, the latter featuring elaborate designs in low relief carved onto extensive surfaces of stone façades. The result mimicked the heavily detailed work of the era's silversmiths.

In the 1700s the neoclassical movement was popular, thanks to the promotional efforts of its strongest proponent, Charles III. While Madrid is full of this style, Barcelona boasts only a few great examples, most notably the Plaça Reial, a few steps east of Les Rambles (spelled with an *e* in Catalan).

The Barcelona that visitors best remember, however, is the Barcelona of Modernism, a movement that, from about 1860 to 1910, put the city on the architectural map of the world. From the minds of a highly articulate school of Catalan architects came a blend of Pre-Raphaelite voluptuousness and Catalonian romanticism, heavily laced with a yearning for the curved lines and organic forms easily recognized in nature.

The movement's most visible architect was Antoni Gaudí, who usually preferred a curved over a straight line. The chimneys of his buildings look like half-melted mounds of chocolate twisted into erratic spirals, and his horizontal lines flow, rather than lie, over their vertical supports. Some of Gaudí's most distinctive creations include the Casa Milà, the Casa Batlló, Parc Güell and the neighborhood around it, and the landmark Temple Expiatori de la Sagrada Familia (never completed).

Other modernist architects looked to Romanesque and medieval models for inspiration, particularly the fortified castles and sculpted gargoyles and dragons of the 12th-century Counts of Barcelona. Examples include Domènech i Montaner and Puig i Cadafalch, whose elegant mansions and concert halls seemed perfectly suited to the enlightened and sophisticated prosperity of the 19th-century Catalonian bourgeoisie. Fortunately, a 19th-century economic boom neatly coincided with the profusion of geniuses who suddenly emerged in the building business. Some of the elaborately beautiful villas of Barcelona and the nearby resort of Sitges were commissioned by entrepreneurs whose fortunes had been made in the fields and mines of the New World.

Contemporary with the buildings designed by the modernist architects was the expansion—first initiated in 1858—of Barcelona into the northern Eixample district. Its gridwork pattern of streets was intersected, in surprisingly modern motifs, with broad diagonals. Though opposed by local landowners, and never manifested with the detail of its original design, it provided a carefully planned and elegant path in which a growing city could showcase its finest buildings.

Consistent with the general artistic stagnation of Spain during the Franco era (1939 to 1975), the 1950s saw a tremendous increase in the number of anonymous housing projects around the periphery of Barcelona. Since the death of Franco, the renaissance of the much-discussed *la movida* (the movement) has enhanced all aspects of Spain's

IMPRESSION

. . . although the great adventures that befell me there occasioned me no great pleasure, but rather much grief, I bore them the better for having seen the city [Barcelona].

—DON QUIXOTE

artistic life, and new and more creative designs for buildings are once again being executed.

ART

From the cave paintings discovered at Lérida to the giants of the 20th century, such as Picasso, Dalí, and Miró, Catalonia has had a long artistic tradition. It is said to be the center of the plastic arts in Spain.

Barcelona entered the world art pages with its Catalonian Gothic sculpture, which held sway from the 13th century to the 15th and produced such renowned masters as Bartomeu and Pere Johan. Sculptors working with Italian masters brought the Renaissance to Barcelona, but few great Catalonian legacies remain from this period. The rise of baroque art in the 17th and 18th centuries saw Catalonia filled with several impressive examples, but nothing worth a special pilgrimage.

In the neoclassical period of the 18th century, Catalonia, and particularly Barcelona, arose from an artistic slumber. Art schools opened in the city and foreign painters arrived, exerting considerable influence. The 19th century produced many Catalonian artists who, it might be said, followed the general European trends of the time without forging any major creative breakthroughs.

The 20th century brought renewed artistic ferment in Barcelona, as reflected by the arrival of Málaga-born Pablo Picasso (the city today is the site of a major Picasso museum). The great surrealist painters of the Spanish school, Joan Miró (who also has a museum in Barcelona devoted to his works) and Salvador Dalí (whose museum is along the Costa Brava, north of Barcelona), also came to the Catalonian capital.

Many Catalan sculptors also achieved acclaim in this century, including Casanovas, Llimon, and Blay. The Spanish Civil War brought a cultural stagnation, yet against all odds many a Catalan artist continued to make bold statements. Tàpies was a major artist of this period (one of the newest museums in Barcelona is devoted to his work). Among the various schools formed in Spain at the time was the neofigurative band, which included such artists as Vázquez Díaz and Pancho Cossio. Antonio López, dubbed a hyperrealist, went on to international acclaim.

Today, toward the end of the 20th century, many Barcelona artists are making major names for themselves, and their works are sold in the most prestigious galleries of the Western world.

LITERATURE AND LANGUAGE

Catalonia, a region lying midway between France and Castilian Spain, is united by a common language, Catalan. The linguistic separateness of the region is arguably the single most important element in the sometimes obsessive independence of its people. Modern linguists attribute the earliest division of Catalan from Castilian to two phenomena: The first was the cultural links and trade ties between ancient Barcina and the neighboring Roman colony of Provence, which shaped the Catalan tongue along Provençal and Languedocian models. The second major event was the invasion of the eastern Pyrénées by Charlemagne in the late 800s and the designation of Catalonia as a Frankish march (buffer zone) between Christian Europe and a Moorish-dominated Iberia.

Contemporaneous with the troubadour tradition of courtly love so popular in Provence and neighboring Languedoc during the 1100s and the 1200s, a handful of courtly minstrels composed similar poems in Catalan and recited them at banquets for the amusement of the lords of Barcelona. By the late 1200s, Catalonia's literature became better defined, thanks to the works of Peter the Ceremonious, Desciot, Mutaner, and the religious treatises of Arnau de Vilanova. The best-remembered of them all was a socially prominent physician and mystic theologican, a true Renaissance man born 200 years too soon, Ramón Llull. In addition to poetry and the composition of a scientific encyclopedia, he worked in what has been called an early form of the novel, describing a medieval urban landscape filled with what later generations would have labeled bourgeois characters. Llull also coined many words of his own (or recorded existing words for the first time), thereby enriching the Catalan language.

The most prolific period of Catalan literature flourished during the late 1300s and early 1400s, a period that critics view as an early articulate expression of the humanism that later swept through the rest of Europe in better-developed forms. Authors from this period include Bernat Metge, Febrer, Ausias March, Ruís de Corella, and Jordi de Sant Jordi. About a century later, Catalan literature received a tremendous boost from the most important and venerated writer in Spanish history, Miguel de Cervantes (1547–1616), who lavishly praised a Catalan epic written about a century before his birth—the chivalric poem *Tirant lo Blanch* by Joanot Martorell.

From about 1500 to about 1810, Catalan literature was severely eclipsed by the brilliant works being written in Castilian. The capital of the Spanish Empire shifted to Madrid, and it was both fiscally and politically expedient to mimic Castilian, rather than Catalan, models. A more cynical view suggests that this era marked the beginning of the suppression of Catalonian culture, with the simultaneous relegation to obscurity of works that otherwise might have been celebrated.

The 19th century, however, brought economic prosperity to a hardworking Catalonia, where the bourgeois middle class enjoyed a financial boom that made it the envy of Spain. Prosperity and the resulting *renaixença* (renaissance) of Catalonian culture produced a form of romanticism exemplified by Jacint Verdaguer and Ángel Guimerà (in dramatics), Milà i Fontanals (in poetry), Narcís Oller (described as a naturalist), and Santiago Rusiñol (described as a modernist). Writing was considered inappropriate for women at this time, but Catalonia nevertheless produced a female novelist, Caterina Albert, who wrote under the pseudonym Victor Catala.

During the early 20th century, there was a strong emphasis on literary style and form. In the same way that the Parisians applauded the sophistication of a Proust, Catalans read and appreciated such stylists as Eugeni d'Ors, poets such as Carles Riba (*Elégies de Bierville*) and Salvat-Papasseit.

In the 1950s, despite the suppression of the Catalonian language by Franco, such works as *Béarn* by Lorenc Villalonga, *La Plaça del Diamant* by Mercé Rodoreda, and *Els Payesos* by Josep Plá were enthusiastically received by international critics.

MUSIC AND DANCE

The Counts of Barcelona, so we are told, were great music lovers, and the Catalan appreciation of music continues to this day, as exemplified by the city's superb 19th-century opera house, the Gran Teatre del Liceu. Richard Strauss arrived to dedicate the second major musical center, the Palau de la Música Catalana, in 1908.

In addition to importing the great talents of Europe for its listening pleasure, the people of Catalonia also create music. Many of their own artists and composers have gone on to international acclaim in their fields, Pablo Casals being the most notable figure.

But few artistic traditions enjoy the renown of the *sardana,* the national dance of the Catalans. This is really a street dance, accompanied by *coblas* (brass bands). You can perform a sardana almost anywhere and at any time, provided you get some like-minded people to join you. Age doesn't matter—everybody joins in the spontaneous outburst. The roots of the dance are not known. Some claim that it originated in one of the Greek islands and was brought to Barcelona by seafarers; others, that it came from the Italian island of Sardinia, which would at least account for its name. To see this dance, go to the Plaça de Sant Jaume in the Gothic Quarter of Barcelona on a Sunday morning.

2. FROM A BUDGET TRAVELER'S POINT OF VIEW

FOR EVERYONE

TRANSPORTATION

To save money on public transportation, buy one of the two-card transportation cards, each good for 10 trips. **Tarjeta T-1,** costing 390 pesetas ($3.65), is good for the Metro, bus, Montjuïc funicular, and Tramvia Blau, which runs from the Passeig de Sant Gervasi/Avinguda del Tibidabo to the bottom part of the funicular to Tibidabo. **Tarjeta T-2,** for 325 pesetas ($3.05), is good on everything but the bus.

In the summer you'll also save by buying one-, three-, and five-day **passes** for 275 pesetas ($2.60), 775 pesetas ($7.30), and 1,100 pesetas ($10.35), respectively. These allow unlimited travel on buses and the Metro system. To make the most use of these, obtain a copy of *Guía del Transport Públic,* distributed free at the tourist office or at the transportation office (see below).

Passes (*abonos temporales*) are available at the office of **Transports Metropolita de Barcelona,** Plaça de Catalunya, open Monday to Friday from 8am to 7pm and on Saturday from 8am to 1pm.

To save money on sightseeing tours during the summer, take a ride on **Tourist Bus No. 100,** which passes by a dozen of the most popular sights. You can get on and off the bus as you please, and also ride the Tibidabo funicular and the Montjuïc cable car and funicular for the price of a single ticket. Tickets are 600 pesetas ($5.65) for one day; 1,200 pesetas ($11.30) for three days. Tickets may be purchased on the bus or at the transportation booth at Plaça de Catalunya.

ENTERTAINMENT

In the summer you'll have plenty of free entertainment just by walking the streets. You'll see everything from opera to monkey acts. The Rambles are a particularly good place to watch.

For more formal entertainment, consult "La Semana de Barcelona" in the *Guía del Ocio,* a guide to the weekly happenings in the city. It's sold at all newsstands along the Rambles for 60 pesetas (55c). Another publication, *Vivir en Barcelona,* also has listings of restaurants, museums, nightspots, and other diversions. You're sure to find some inexpensive entertainment in these papers. Or call 010 for information on special events, many of which are free.

Museums are free in Barcelona. The tourist office (see below) can give you a complete list of museums.

There is almost always a **festival** happening in the city, and many of the events can be enjoyed for free. The tourist office can give you details of when and where.

Some **theaters** advertise discount or half-price nights. Check in the weekly *Guía del Ocio.*

If you want to go to a **disco,** but don't want to spend a lot of money, look for an "afternoon" session, presented from 7 to 10pm by many of the clubs. Admission might be as little as 250 pesetas ($2.35) instead of the usual 1,500 pesetas ($14.10) for a night session beginning at around 11:30pm.

SHOPPING

Watch for summer **sales** (*rebajas*) in late July and August. Merchandise is often heavily discounted by stores getting rid of their summer stock before fall.

ACCOMMODATIONS

To keep costs down, consider staying in a **hostal** (not hostel) in the old quarter of Barcelona. There are dozens of these low-cost lodgings, sometimes several in one building. Pick and choose carefully—they are not all equally clean and safe. Hostals tend to fill up quickly with Spaniards and tourists alike. If all of the rooms are taken, the owners will probably direct you to a comparable place, perhaps owned by a friend or relative. To keep costs low in hostals, *residencias,* and pensions, ask for a double room without a private bath.

In general, it is cheaper to stay and eat in the Barri Gòtic (Gothic Quarter) than in the more modern parts of Barcelona. The best hostals are in the Eixample, which is safer at night than the Gothic Quarter but slightly more expensive too.

RESTAURANTS

To keep food costs low in this expensive city, seek out a **cafeteria** or a **tasca** and order from the *menú del día*. This set menu will consist of three courses, with bread and house wine included. Sometimes the proprietor will offer the even cheaper *cubierto,* also a fixed-price meal, but with no options allowed. You might have a cubierto for lunch and then have a dinner of a couple of *tapas* (hors d'oeuvres) at a tasca. Some tapas are big enough to be a meal.

The Gothic Quarter is the place to find budget restaurants. Many feature menus for about 650 pesetas ($6.10). Try, for example, the Carrer d'Avinyó or Carrer Gignàs.

In Barcelona, the price of an establishment is indicated by the number of forks on its sign. One fork means that the place is a *restaurante económico.*

FOR STUDENTS

It's best to arrive in Barcelona with an **International Student Identity Card** in hand, which entitles you to discounts on travel, museums, and lodging. If you arrive without one, go to **TIVE,** Officine de Turisme Juvenil, Gravina, 1 (tel. 302-06-82; Metro: Catalunya), 1 block from the Plaça de la Universitat. Hours are Monday through Friday from 9am to 1pm and from 4 to 5:30pm. Ask about discounted fares on trains and buses.

FOR SENIORS

Seniors travel for half price on all trains from the city. In most cases your passport will be proof enough of age. You can also purchase a RENFE **"golden card"** at any train station.

---

3. ORIENTATION

ARRIVING

BY PLANE

Iberia, the national airline of Spain, is your best bet for flights into Barcelona because of the frequency of its departures and arrivals. Iberia flies nonstop to Barcelona from dozens of cities within Europe and North Africa. From North America, service to Barcelona is especially easy because of carefully timed connections in Madrid, and because of **Iberia's** five or six weekly nonstop flights to Barcelona from JFK. Residents of the American Northeast invariably depart from New York. Residents of the American Southwest often select a flight on another carrier, **American,** which flies daily from Dallas/Fort Worth to Madrid, after which connections are made on Iberia to Barcelona. Passengers in other parts of the New World can fly nonstop to Madrid on Iberia's daily flights from Los Angeles, Chicago, and Miami, after which connections can be made as frequently as every quarter hour to Barcelona.

Within Spain, Iberia flies between Barcelona and Madrid every 15 minutes during peak travel times, and every 40 minutes at others. In addition, dozens of flights converge on Barcelona from all parts of Spain. If you don't mind changing aircraft in Madrid, you can get to Barcelona from even the smallest airports of Spain.

El Prat de Llobregat, the Barcelona airport, lies 7½ miles (12km) southwest of the city. The route to downtown Barcelona is carefully signposted. A train runs between the airport and Barcelona's Estació Central de Sants every half hour between 6am and 11pm (10:30pm is the last city departure; 6:30am is the first airport departure). The trip takes about a quarter hour and costs 150 pesetas ($1.40). If your hotel lies near the Plaça de Catalunya, you might opt instead for the Bus EA, which runs every 40 or 45 minutes between 7:15am and 7:15pm. The fare ranges from 80 to 95 pesetas (75¢ to 90¢), depending on the day of the week. A taxi from the airport into central Barcelona will cost approximately 1,600 to 2,000 pesetas ($15.05 to $18.80).

Within Barcelona, clients can arrange ticketing at one of four Iberia offices. The easiest to find lies a few blocks north of the sprawling Plaça de Catalunya, at Passeig de Gràcia, 30 (tel. 401-33-84; Metro: Plaça de Catalunya).

BY TRAIN

A train called Barcelona-Talgo provides rail lines between Paris and Barcelona in 11½ hours. For many other connections from the mainland of Europe, it will be necessary to change trains at Port Bou. Most trains issue seat and sleeper reservations.

All RENFE trains in Barcelona pass through the **Estació Central de Sants,** Plaça de Països Catalanes (tel. 322-41-42; Metro: Sants-Estació). From this station you can book tickets to many of the major cities of Spain: Madrid (3 *talgos,* 9 hours; and 3 *rápidos,* 10 hours), Seville (3 per day, 13 hours), and Valencia (12 per day, 4 hours).

RENFE also maintains two minor terminals: Plaça de Catalunya (Metro stop of the same name) and Passeig de Gràcia (also the name of the Metro stop) at Passeig de Gràcia and Carrer d'Aragó. The latter station handles the traffic from mainland Europe on trains that had to change at Port Bou.

For general RENFE information, call 490-02-02.

BY BUS

Many visitors from mainland Europe arrive by bus, but it's a long, tedious haul. For example, the daily bus from London takes 25 hours; from Paris, 15 hours; and from Rome, 20 hours. For these continental connections in Barcelona, contact **Iberbus,** Paral.lel (tel. 242-33-00; Metro: Paral.lel). The most frequently used bus connection by visitors to Barcelona is the bus to Montserrat (see Chapter 16). Departures are from **Auto Transporte Julià,** Plaça de la Universitat, 12 (tel. 317-04-76). You can make bus connections for Andorra at **Alsina Graells,** Ronda de la Universitat, 4 (tel. 302-40-86; Metro: Plaça de Catalunya).

For bus travel to one of the beach towns along the Costa Brava, see **Sarfa,** Plaça de Duc de Medinaceli (tel. 318-94-34; Metro: Drassanes). About a dozen buses a day leave Barcelona for the Costa Brava (see Chapter 17; your best resort bet is Tossà de Mar).

BY CAR

From France (the usual road approach to Barcelona), the major access route is at the eastern end of the Pyrénées. You have a choice of the express highway (E-15) or the more scenic coastal road. Be forewarned, however, that if you take the scenic coastal road in July and August, you will often encounter bumper-to-bumper traffic. From France, it is possible to approach Barcelona also via Toulouse. Cross the border into Spain at Puigcerdá (frontier stations are there), near the principality of Andorra. From there, take the N-152 to Barcelona.

From Madrid, take the N-2 to Zaragoza, then the A-2 to El Vendrell, followed by the A-7 motorway to Barcelona. From the Costa Blanca or Costa del Sol, take the E-15 north from Valencia along the eastern Mediterranean coast.

TOURIST INFORMATION

A conveniently located tourist office is the **Patronat de Turisme,** Gran Via de les Corts Catalanes, 658 (tel. 93/301-74-43; Metro: Urquinaona or Plaça de Catalunya). It's open Monday through Friday from 9am to 7pm, on Saturday from 9am to 2pm. There's also an office at the airport, **El Prat de Llobregat** (tel. 93/325-58-29), which you'll pass as you clear Customs. In summer it's open Monday through Saturday from 9:30am to 8:10pm; in winter, Monday through Saturday from 9:30am to 8pm; on Sunday, year round from 9:30am to 3pm.

There's another office at the **Estació Central de Sants** (tel. 93/410-25-94; Metro: Sants-Estació), open daily from 8am to 8pm, and at **Molle de la Fusta** (tel. 93/310-37-16; Metro: Drassanes), open in summer daily from 8am to 8pm, in winter daily from 9am to 3pm.

At these offices, you can pick up maps and information.

CITY LAYOUT

MAIN SQUARES, STREETS, AND ARTERIES

The **Plaça de Catalunya** (Plaza de Cataluña in Spanish) is the city's heart; the world-famous **Rambles** are its arteries. The Rambles begin at the **Plaça Portal de la Pau,** with its 164-foot-high monument to Columbus and a superb view of the port, and stretch north to the Plaça de Catalunya, with its fountains and trees. Along this wide promenade you'll find bookshops and newsstands, stalls selling birds and flowers, and benches or café tables and chairs, where you can sit and watch the passing parade.

At the end of the Rambles is the **Barri Xinés** (Barrio Chino in Spanish, Chinese Quarter in English), which has enjoyed notoriety as a haven of prostitution and drugs, populated in Jean Genet's *The Thief's Journal* by "whores, thieves, pimps, and beggars." Still considered a dangerous district, it is best viewed during the day, if at all.

Off the Rambles lies the **Plaça Reial** (Plaza Real in Spanish), the most harmoniously proportioned square in Barcelona. Come here on Sunday morning to see the stamp and coin collectors peddle their wares.

The major wide boulevards of Barcelona are the **Avinguda** (Avenida in Spanish) **Diagonal** and **Passeig de Colom,** and the elegant shopping street—the **Passeig de Gràcia** (Paseo de Gràcia in Spanish).

A short walk from the Rambles will take you to the newly developed **Passeig del Moll de la Fusta,** a waterfront promenade with some of the finest (but not the cheapest) restaurants in Barcelona. If you can't afford the high prices, come here at least for a drink in the open air and take in a view of the harbor.

To the east is the old port of the city, called **La Barceloneta,** dating from the 18th century. This strip of land between the port and the sea has traditionally been a good place for seafood.

The **Barri Gòtic** (Barrio Gótico in Spanish, Gothic Quarter in English) lies to the east of the Rambles. This is the site of the city's oldest buildings, including the cathedral.

Moving north of the Plaça de Catalunya, the **Eixample** unfolds. An area of wide boulevards, in contrast to the Gothic Quarter, it contains two major roads leading out of Barcelona, the previously mentioned Avinguda Diagonal and Gran Via de les Corts Catalanes. Another major area, Gràcia, lies north of the Eixample.

Montjuïc, one of the mountains of Barcelona, begins at the Plaça d'Espanya, a traffic rotary. This will be the setting for the 1992 Olympic Games. The other mountain is **Tibidabo,** in the northwest, offering views of the city and the Mediterranean. It contains a fun-fair park.

FINDING AN ADDRESS/MAPS

Finding an address in Barcelona can be a problem. The city is characterized by long boulevards and a complicated maze of narrow, twisting streets. Therefore, knowing the street number is all-important. If you see the designation s/n, it means that the building is without a number. Therefore, it's crucial to learn the cross street if you're seeking a specific establishment.

The rule about street numbers is that there is no rule. On most streets, numbering begins on one side and runs up that side until the end, then runs in the opposite direction on the other side. Therefore, number 40 could be opposite 408. But there are many, many exceptions to this. Sometimes street numbers on buildings in the older quarters have been obscured by the patina of time.

Arm yourself with a good map before setting out. Those given away free by tourist offices and hotels generally aren't adequate, since they don't label the little streets. The best map for exploring Barcelona is published by **Falk,** available at most bookstores and newsstands, such as those found along the Rambles. This pocket map includes all the streets, with an index of how to find them.

NEIGHBORHOODS IN BRIEF

Barri Gòtic The glory of the Middle Ages lives on here. The section rises to the north of the Passeig de Colom, with its Columbus Monument, and is bordered on its east by a major artery, the Via Laietana, which begins at La Barceloneta at the Plaça d'Antoni López and runs north to the Plaça d'Urquinaona. The Rambles are the western border of the Gothic Quarter and on the northern edge is the Ronda de Sant Pere, which intersects with the Plaça de Catalunya and the Passeig de Gràcia. The heart of the quarter is the Plaça de Sant Jaume, which was a major crossroads in the old Roman city. Many of the structures in the old section are ancient, including the ruins of a Roman temple dedicated to Augustus. Antiques stores, restaurants, cafés, museums, some hotels, and bookstores fill the place today. It is also the headquarters of the Generalitat, seat of the Catalan government.

Les Rambles The most famous promenade in Spain, ranking with Madrid's Paseo del Prado, was once a drainage channel. That was long ago filled in, however, much to the delight of today's street entertainers, flower vendors, news vendors, café patrons, and strollers. Les Rambles (spelled with an "e" in Catalan) is actually composed of five different sections, each a particular Ramble, with names like Ramble de Canaletes, Ramble dels Estudis, Ramble de Sant Josep, Ramble dels Caputxins, and Ramble de Santa Mònica. The pedestrian esplanade is shaded, as it makes its way from the Plaça de Catalunya to the port—all the way to the Columbus Monument. Along the way you'll pass the Gran Teatre del Liceu, Ramble de Caputxins, 61, at Sant Pau, 1, one of the most magnificent opera houses in the world. Miró did a sidewalk mosaic at the Plaça de la Boqueria. During the stagnation of the Franco era, this street grew seedier and seedier. But the opening of the Ramada Renaissance hotel and the restoration of many buildings have brought new energy and hope for the street.

Barri Xinés This isn't "Chinatown," as most people assume from the name—and it never was. For decades it has had an unsavory reputation, known for its houses of prostitution. Franco outlawed prostitution in 1956, but apparently no one ever got around to telling the denizens of this district of narrow, often murky, old streets and dark corners. Petty thieves, drug peddlers, purse snatchers, and other "fun types" form just part of the parade of humanity that flows through the district.

Nighttime can be dangerous, so exercise caution. Still, most visitors like to take a quick look to see what all the excitement is about. Just off Les Rambles, the area lies primarily between the waterfront and the Carrer de l'Hospital.

Barri de la Ribera Another *barrio* that stagnated for years but is now having a renaissance, the Barri de la Ribera lies alongside the Barri Gòtic, going east to the Passeig de Picasso, which borders the Parc de la Ciutadella. The centerpiece of this district is the Museu Picasso, housed in the 15th-century Palau Agüilar, Montcada, 15. Many art galleries have opened around the museum, and the old quarter is beginning to become fashionable. Many mansions in this area were built at the time of one of the major maritime expansions and trading explosions in Barcelona's history, principally in the 1200s and 1300s. Many of these grand homes still stand along the Carrer de Montcada and nearby streets.

La Barceloneta and the Harborfront Although Barcelona was founded on a seagoing tradition, its waterfront was allowed to decay for years. Today it is alive again and bursting with activity, as exemplified by the newly built waterfront promenade, the Passeig del Moll de la Fusta. The best way to get a bird's-eye view of this section is to take an elevator to the top of the Columbus Monument in the Plaza Portal de la Pau.

In the vicinity of the monument were the Reials Drassanes, or royal shipyards, a booming place of industry during Barcelona's maritime heyday in the Middle Ages. Years before Columbus discovered the New World, ships sailed around the world from here, flying the traditional yellow-and-red flag of Catalonia.

To the east lies a mainly artificial peninsula called La Barceloneta (Little Barcelona), formerly a fishing district, dating mainly from the 18th century. It's now filled with seafood restaurants. The blocks here are long and surprisingly narrow— architects planned it that way so that each room in every building fronted a street. Many bus lines terminate at the Passeig Nacional here, site of the Barcelona Aquarium.

Eixample/Ensanche To the north of the Plaça de Catalunya lies the Eixample, or Ensanche, where avenues form a grid of perpendicular streets cut across by a majestic boulevard, the Passeig de Gràcia, a posh shopping street ideal for leisurely promenades. This is the section of Barcelona that grew beyond the old medieval walls. This great period of "extension," or enlargement (Eixample in Catalan), came mainly in the 19th century. The area's main traffic artery is the Avinguda Diagonal, which links the expressway and the heart of this congested city.

The Eixample possesses some of the most original buildings any architect ever designed—not just those by Gaudí, but by other notable achievers as well. Of course, Gaudí's Sagrada Familia is one of the major attractions of the area, which was the center of Barcelona modernism. This cultural renaissance began in 1814, and reached its greatest heights of expression in the Eixample, where you'll want to walk, perhaps live or dine, while visiting Barcelona.

Montjuïc and Tibidabo These mountains form two of the most enduring attractions of Barcelona. Montjuïc, called Hill of the Jews after a Jewish necropolis there, gained prominence in 1929 as the site of the World's Fair. Today work is under way for the 1992 Olympic Games. Its major attraction is the Poble Espanyol (Spanish Village), a 5-acre site constructed for the World's Fair, with examples of Spanish art and architecture displayed against the backdrop of a traditional Spanish village. Tibidabo (1,650 feet) may be where you'll want to go for your final look at Barcelona. On a clear day you can see the mountains of Majorca (the most famous of the Balearic Islands). Reached by train, tram, and cable car, Tibidabo is the most popular Sunday excursion in Barcelona.

Pedralbes Pedralbes is where the wealthy people live, some in stylish blocks of apartment houses, others in 19th-century villas behind ornamental fences, and others still in structures erected during the heyday of modernism. Set in a park, the Palau de Pedralbes, Avinguda Diagonal, 686, was constructed in the 1920s as a gift from the city of Barcelona to Alfonxo XIII, the last king of Spain, who was forced to abdicate (he was the grandfather of today's Juan Carlos). Regrettably, the king fled in 1931 and never made much use of the palace. Today it has a new life, housing a museum of carriages and a collection of European paintings, grouped under the name of Colecció Cambó.

4. GETTING AROUND

For money-saving information on subway and bus transportation, see "Budget Bests and Discounts," above.

BY SUBWAY

Barcelona's underground railway system is called the **Metro.** Consisting of five main lines, it crisscrosses the city more frequently and with greater efficiency than the bus network. Two commuter trains also service the city, fanning out to the suburbs. Service is Monday through Friday from 5am to 11pm, on Saturday from 5am to 1am, and on Sunday and holidays from 6am to 1am. The one-way fare is 60 pesetas (55¢) Monday through Friday, rising to 65 pesetas (60¢) on Saturday, Sunday, and holidays. Entrances to Metro stations are marked with a red diamond. The major station for all subway lines is Plaça de Catalunya.

BY BUS

Some 50 bus lines traverse the city, and as always, you don't want to ride them at rush hour. The driver issues a ticket as you board at the front. Most buses operate daily from 6:30am to 10pm; some night buses go along the principal arteries from 10pm to 4am. Buses are color-coded—red ones cut through the city center during the day, and blue ones do the job at night.

BY TAXI

Taxis bear the letters *SP (servicio público)* on both their front and rear. A lit green light on the roof and a "Libre" sign in the window indicate that a taxi is free to pick up passengers. Taxis are painted yellow and black. The basic rate begins at 210 pesetas ($1.95). Check to make sure you're not paying the fare of a previously departed passenger; taxi drivers have been known to "forget" to turn back the meter. For each additional kilometer in the slow-moving traffic, you are assessed 52 pesetas (50¢). Supplements might also be added—40 pesetas (40¢) for a big suitcase, for instance, Rides to terminals also carry a surcharge: 150 pesetas ($1.40) to the airport, 55 pesetas (50¢) from a train station. For a taxi, call 330-08-04, 300-38-11, or 386-50-00.

BY BICYCLE

Ever wonder why you see so few people ever riding a bicycle in Barcelona? Heavy pollution from traffic and pedestrian-clogged narrow streets of the inner city make riding a bicycle very difficult. It's better to walk.

BY CAR

Driving is next to impossible in congested Barcelona and potentially dangerous. Besides, it is unlikely that you would find a place to park. Try other means of getting around. Save your car rentals for one-day excursions from the Catalonian capital to such places as Sitges and Tarragona in the south, Montserrat in the west, or the resorts of the Costa Brava in the north.

In that case, you may want to rent a car. All the major U.S. firms are represented,

BARCELONA METRO

Mediterranean Sea

N

0 — 1 km
.6214 mi

Rio Besòs

MERIDIANA

AVINGUDA

LINE 1 STA. COLONNA
Baró de Viver
Trinitat Vella

LINE 4 PEP VENTURA
Gorg
Sant Roc
Joan XXIII
Verneda

Torras i Bages
Sant Andreu
Fabra i Puig
Sagrera
Navas
La Pau

LINE 4 ROQUETES
Llucmajor
Maragall
Vilapicina
Congrés
Guinardó
Camp de l'Arpa
Clot
Glòries

Besòs
Besòs Mar
Selva de Mar
Poblenou
Llacuna
Bogatell
Ciutadella

GRAN VIA

LINE 5 HORTA
Virrei Amat
Alfons X
Hospital de Sant Pau
Sagrada Família
Marina

LINE 3 MONTBAU
Vall d'Hebron
Penitents
Vallcarca
Lesseps
Fontana

Girona
Passeig de Gràcia
Urquinaona
Arc de Triomf
Jaume I
Barceloneta

Joanic
Verdaguer
Diagonal

Provença
Universitat
Catalunya
Liceu
Drassanes

AVINGUDA DIAGONAL

Hospital Clínic
Entença
Urgell
Paral·lel

Maria Cristina
Les Corts
Plaça de Centre
Sants-Estació
Tarragona
Rocafort

LINE 3 ZONA UNIVERSITÀRIA
Palau Reial

GRAN VIA DE CARLES III

Plaça de Sants
Hostafrancs
Espanya
Poble Sec

Pubilla Cases
Can Vidalet

GRAN VIA

LINE 5 CORNELLÀ
Gavarra
Sant Ildefons
Can Boixeres
Collblanc
Badal
Mercat Nou
Sta. Eulàlia

LINE 1 TORRASSA

To Airport

Legend

- Metro Terminals
- Metro Stations
- Transfer Stations
- Railway Lines —
- Funicular ◆◆◆
- Telefèric ■■■
- Tramvia Blau ┼┼┼

along with the major Spanish firm (Atesa) and some European ones. Rental companies include **Atesa,** Balmes, 141 (tel. 237-81-40), open Monday through Friday from 9am to 1:30pm and 4 to 7:30pm, on Saturday from 9am to 12:30pm; **Avis,** Casanova, 209 (tel. 209-95-33), open Monday through Friday from 8am to 8pm, on Saturday from 8am to 7pm, and on Sunday from 8am to 1pm; and **Hertz,** Tuset, 10 (tel. 237-37-37), open Monday through Friday from 8am to 8pm, on Saturday from 8am to 1pm and 4 to 8pm, and on Sunday from 9am to 1pm.

These firms also operate kiosks at the airport. If you plan to rent a car, however, it's best—and often more economical—to arrange the rental before leaving the U.S. by calling one of the car-rental firm's toll-free numbers. Refer to the section on car rentals under "Getting Around" in Chapter 3.

FUNICULARS AND RAIL LINKS

At some point in your journey, you may want to visit both Montjuïc and Tibidabo. There are various links to these mountaintops.

A train called **Tramvia Blau (Blue Streetcar)** goes from the Passeig de Sant Gervasi/Avinguda del Tibidabo to the bottom of the funicular to Tibidabo every 3 to 15 minutes. It operates Monday through Saturday from 7am to 10pm, on Sunday and holidays from 7am to 10:30pm. The fare is 55 pesetas (50¢) Monday through Saturday, rising to 60 pesetas (55¢) on Sunday and holidays. At the end of the run, you can continue the rest of the way by **funicular** to the top, at 1,600 feet, for an amazing view of Barcelona. The funicular operates every half hour Monday through Friday from 7:45am to 9:45pm, on Saturday from 7:15am to 9:45pm, and on Sunday and holidays from 7:15 to 10:15am and 8:45 to 9:45pm. During peak visiting hours (10:15am to 8:45pm) service is increased, with a funicular departing every 15 minutes. A round-trip fare is 250 pesetas ($2.35).

Montjuïc, site of the 1992 Summer Olympic Games, can be reached by the Montjuïc funicular, linking up with subway Line 3 at Paral.lel. The funicular operates in summer daily from 11am to 10pm, charging a fare of 70 pesetas (65¢) Monday through Friday, 75 pesetas (70¢) on Saturday and Sunday. In winter it operates on Saturday, Sunday, and holidays from 11am to 8:15pm.

A **cable car** linking the upper part of the Montjuïc funicular with the castle is in service June to September, daily from noon to 3pm and 4 to 8:30pm; the one-way fare is 150 pesetas ($1.40). In off-season it operates only on Saturday, Sunday, and holidays from 11am to 2:45pm and 4 to 7:30pm.

To get to these places, you can board the **Montjuïc telefèric,** which runs from La Barceloneta to Montjuïc. Service June to September is daily from 11am to 9pm; the fare is 500 pesetas ($4.70) round trip, 400 pesetas ($3.75) one way. Off-season hours are Monday through Saturday from 11:30am to 6pm, on Sunday and holidays from 11am to 6:45pm.

 BARCELONA

American Express   For your mail or banking needs, the American Express office in Barcelona is at Passeig de Gràcia, 101 (tel. 217-00-70; Metro: Diagonal), near the corner of Carrer del Rosselló. Open: Mon–Fri 9:30am–6pm, Sat 10am–noon.

Area Code   The area code for Barcelona is 93.

Baby-sitters   Most major hotels can arrange for baby-sitters with adequate notice. Rates vary considerably, but tend to be reasonable. You'll have to make a special request for an English-speaking baby-sitter.

Bookstores   The best selection of English-language books, including travel maps and guides, is **LAIE,** Pau Claris, 85 (tel. 318-17-39; Metro: Plaça de Catalunya or Urquinaona), 1 block from the Gran Via de les Corts Catalanes. Open: Mon–Sat 10am–8pm.

Climate   See Chapter 3.

Consulates (For embassies, refer to Chapter 4, "Fast Facts: Madrid"). The **U.S. Consulate** is at Via Laietana, 33 (tel. 319-95-50; (Metro: Jaume I), 4th floor. Open: Mon–Fri 9am–12:30pm and 3–5pm. The **Canadian Consulate** is at Via Augusta, 125 (tel. 209-06-34; Metro: Passeig de Gràcia). Open: Mon–Fri 9am–1pm. The **U.K. Consulate** is at Avinguda Diagonal, 477 (tel. 322-21-51; Metro: Diagonal). Open: Mon–Fri 9am–1pm and 3:15–4:15pm, Sat 9:45am–noon.

Currency Exchange Most banks will exchange currency Mon–Fri 8:30am–2pm, Sat 8:30am–1pm. A major *oficina de cambio* (exchange office) is operated at the **Estació Central de Sants,** the principal rail station for Barcelona. Open: Mon–Sat 8:30am–10pm, Sun 8:30am–2pm and 4:30–10pm. Exchange offices are also available at Barcelona's airport, **El Prat de Llobregat.** Open: Daily 7am–11pm.

Dentist Dr. Angel Salesi, Casanoves, 209 (tel. 200-70-11; Metro: Guinardo), 2nd floor. Call for an appointment.

Doctors See "Hospitals," below.

Drugstores The most central one is **Farmacía Manuel Nadal i Maso,** Ramble de Canaletes, 121 (tel. 317-49-42; Metro: Plaça de Catalunya). Open: Mon–Fri 9am–1:30pm and 4:30–8pm, Sat 9am–1:30pm. After hours, various pharmacies take turns staying open at night. Pharmacies not open post the names and addresses of pharmacies in the area that are open.

Emergencies Fire, 080; **police,** 092; **ambulance,** 300-20-20.

Eyeglasses Complete service is provided by **Optica 2000,** Santa Anna, 2 (tel. 302-12-47; Metro: Plaça de Catalunya. Open: Mon–Sat 9:30am–2pm and 4:30–8pm.

Hairdresser A few steps from the Rambles, **Santos,** Santa Anna, 6 (tel. 317-54-87; Metro: Plaça de Catalunya), is for both *señoras y caballeros.* Located one floor above street level, the shop receives men 9am–2pm and 4–8pm; women 10am–7pm. Open: Mon–Fri 9am–8pm, Sat 2–8pm.

Hospitals If you need medical attention in a hurry, call 212-85-85. Otherwise, Barcelona has many hospitals, including the **Hospital Evangelico,** Alegre de Dalt, 87-93 (tel. 219-71-00; Metro: Passeig de Gràcia).

Information: See "Tourist Information," in Section 3, above.

Laundromats Ask at your hotel for the one nearest you, or try one of the following. **Lavandería Brasilia,** Avinguda Meridiana, 322 (tel. 352-72-05; Metro: Plaça de Catalunya). Open: Mon–Fri 9am–2pm and 4–8pm, Sat 9am–2pm. Also centrally located is **Lava Super,** Carme, 63 (tel. 329-4368; Metro: Liceu, at the Rambles), which keeps the same hours as the establishment listed above.

Libraries There's an English-language library at the **Instituto de Estudios Norteamericanos,** Via Augusta, 123 (tel. 227-31-45), with many U.S. newspapers and magazines. There's also a reference section. Open: Mon–Fri 11am–1:30pm and 4–8pm. Closed: Aug. Take the FFCC commuter train to the Plaça de Molina.

Lost Property To recover lost property, go to **Objetos Perdidos,** Ajuntament (ground floor), Plaça de Sant Jaume (tel. 301-39-23; Metro: Jaume I). Open: Mon–Fri 9:30am–1:30pm. If you've lost property on public transport, contact the office in the Metro station at Plaça de Catalunya (tel. 318-52-93).

Luggage Storage/Lockers The train station, **Estació Central de Sants** (tel. 322-41-42), has lockers for 125 pesetas ($1.20) daily. Open: Daily 7am–11pm.

Mail The **main post office** is at Plaça d'Antoni López (tel. 318-38-31; Metro: Jaume I). Open: Mon–Fri 8:30am–10pm, Sat 9am–2pm, Sun and holidays 10am–noon. Other post offices are open Mon–Fri 9am–2pm.

Newspapers/Magazines The *International Herald-Tribune* is sold at major hotels and nearly all the news kiosks along the Rambles. Sometimes you can also obtain copies of *USA Today,* or one of the London newspapers, such as *The Times.* The two leading daily newspapers of Barcelona, which often list cultural events, are *El Periódico* and *La Vanguardia.*

Police See "Emergencies," above.

Post Office See "Mail," above.

Radio/TV If your hotel room has a TV set (unlikely in budget accommodations), you can often get Britain's BBC World Service. If you're listening to radio, tune in the Spanish music program, "Segunda Programa," with everything from classical music to jazz—nights only. Otherwise, what you'll see in the TV lounges of most budget hotels are Spanish broadcasts of international soccer and rugby competitions and perhaps a bullfight. Two national TV channels (1 and 2) transmit broadcasts in Spanish, and two regional channels (3 and 33) broadcast in Catalan. By the time of your arrival, some private TV channels will also be broadcasting.

Religious Services Nearly all of the churches of Barcelona are Roman Catholic, holding mass on Sunday between 7am and 2pm and 7 and 9pm. For a mass in English, attend **Paroisse Française,** Anglí, 15 (tel. 204-49-62; Metro: Sarrià), at 10:30am on the first and third Sunday of every month. An Anglican Mass (in English) is held at 11am on Sunday and 11:30am on Wednesday at **Saint George Church,** Sant Joan de la Salle, 41 (tel. 417-88-67; Metro: Putxet).

Rest Rooms Some public rest rooms are available, including those at popular tourist spots, such as Tibidabo and Montjuïc. You'll also find rest rooms at the major museums of Barcelona, at all train stations and airports, and at Metro stations. The major department stores, such as Galerías Preciados, also have good rest rooms. Otherwise, out on the streets you may be a bit hard-pressed. Sanitation is a bit questionable in some of the public facilities. If you use the facilities of a café or tavern, it is customary to make a small purchase at the bar, even if only a glass of mineral water.

Safety Whenever you're traveling in an unfamiliar city or country, stay alert. Be aware of your immediate surroundings. Wear a moneybelt and keep a close eye on your possessions. Be particularly careful with cameras, purses, and wallets, all favorite targets of thieves and pickpockets; particularly on the world-famous Rambles. The southern part of the Rambles, near the waterfront, is the most dangerous section, especially at night. Proceed with caution.

Shoe Repairs **Simago,** Ramble dels Estudis, 113 (tel. 302-48-24; Metro: Plaça de Catalunya or Liceu), in the basement. Open: Mon–Sat 9am–8pm.

Taxes See "Shopping" in Chapter 6 for details on VAT.

Taxis See "Getting Around," above.

Telegrams/Telex These can be sent at the **main post office** (see "Mail," above). You can send telex and fax messages at all major and many budget hotels.

Telephone Dial 003 for local operator information within Barcelona. For elsewhere in Spain, dial 009. Most local calls cost 25 pesetas (25¢). Hotels impose various surcharges on phone calls, especially long-distance, either in Spain or abroad. It's cheaper to go to the **central telephone office** at Fontanella, 4, off the Plaça de Catalunya (Metro: Plaça de Catalunya). Open: Mon–Sat 8:30am–9pm.

Transit Information For general **RENFE** (train) information, dial 490-02-02. For details about **public transportation** within Barcelona, dial 360-00-00.

5. NETWORKS AND RESOURCES

FOR STUDENTS

Try the previously recommended **TIVE—Oficina de Turisme Juvenil,** Gravina, 1 (tel. 302-06-82; Metro: Plaça de Catalunya), off the Plaça de la Universitat. Hours are 9am to 1pm and 4 to 5:30pm Monday through Friday. Ask about flight discounts, but check fares with other airlines to learn just how much a reduction you are getting. Also, ask the staff about the best deals on traveling within Spain.

FOR GAY MEN AND LESBIANS

For gay men, Barcelona is a mecca for those who practice safe sex. A wide assortment of gay establishments, ranging from discos to saunas, from restaurants to bars, await the visitor. And if you get bored with the gay scene in Barcelona, it's just a half hour by train to the sands of Sitges, the premier gay resort of Europe.

The best source of information about gay life in Barcelona is provided by **Sextienda,** Rauric, 11 (tel. 318-86-87; Metro: Liceu). It's open Monday through Saturday from 10am to 8:45pm. This is the premier gay pornography shop in Spain, located on a street with some gay bars. The English-speaking staff will give you a free map pinpointing the bars, restaurants, discos, and other places catering to gay men. It's called *Plano Gay de Barcelona y Sitges,* and it's revised every year.

A feminist bookstore and café is found at **La Sale Bar y Biblioteca Feminista,** València, 226 (tel. 323-17-98; Metro: Passeig de Gràcia). This shop will also give you a list of all women's centers in Spain and supply data about bars in the country that cater to women.

FOR WOMEN

Women traveling alone should avoid the area near the port at night. See the Plaça Reial during the day, but go elsewhere at night. There have been attacks on women in this area. Women who have been the victim of an attack or rape should call the crisis service—**Informaciones i Urgencies de Les Dones,** Comerç, 44 (tel. 319-00-42; Metro: Jaume I).

FOR SENIORS

For seniors in Barcelona, a good organization to know about is **Travel Assistance International,** 1133 15th St. NW, #400, Washington, DC 20005 (tel. 800/821-2828), which has a "hotline" to agents all over Europe, including Spain. This outfit—not just for senior citizens—charges a membership fee, but rates vary, depending on how long you plan to stay abroad. They are experts in offering health assistance in case of a medical emergency, and they can even arrange transatlantic medical transport. You'll also learn about their insurance program and, if necessary, a cash-advance scheme.

CHAPTER 14

BARCELONA ACCOMMODATIONS & DINING

1. WHERE TO STAY

2. WHERE TO EAT

• **FROMMER'S COOL FOR KIDS: RESTAURANTS**

Although there are plenty of **accommodations** in Barcelona, few top-notch modern establishments fall into our price range. The best hotels possible on our budget offer good value and are comfortable, but they tend to be a bit faded.

Safety is an important factor in choosing a hotel in Barcelona. Some of the least expensive hotels are not in good locations. My recommendations are safe first and foremost, and sometimes that has meant going a little over our budget. In Barcelona, you may just have to accept that you're going to spend a little more.

A popular area for the budget traveler is the Barri Gòtic, located in the heart of town. You'll live and eat less expensively here than in any other part of Barcelona. But you should be especially careful when returning to your hotel late at night.

More modern, but also more expensive, accommodations can be found north of the Rambles and the Barri Gòtic in the Eixample district, centered around the Metro stops Plaça de Catalunya and Universitat. Many of the buildings are in the modernist style (that is, turn-of-the-century art nouveau), and sometimes the elevators and plumbing tend to be of the same vintage. The Eixample is a desirable and safe neighborhood, especially along its wide boulevards. Noise is the only problem you might encounter.

Farther north still, above the Avinguda Diagonal, you'll enter the Gràcia area, where you can enjoy Catalan neighborhood life. You'll be a bit away from the main attractions, but they can be reached by public transportation.

For tips on saving money on accommodations, see Frommer's Smart Traveler: Hotels (*p.70*).

Finding a cheap **restaurant** in Barcelona is easier than finding a cheap, safe hotel. There are sometimes as many as eight places per block, if you include *tapas* bars as well as restaurants. Reservations are seldom needed, except in the most expensive and popular places.

The Barri Gòtic offers the cheapest meals. There are also many low-cost restaurants in and around the Carrer de Montcada, site of the Picasso museum. Dining rooms in the Eixample tend to be more formal, more expensive, and less adventurous.

For tips on saving money on dining, see Frommer's Smart Traveler: Restaurants (*p.79*).

1. WHERE TO STAY

DOUBLES FOR LESS THAN 5,000 PTAS.
[$47]
IN THE BARRI GÒTIC

HOSTAL LEVANTE, Baixada de Sant Miguel, 2, 08002 Barcelona. Tel. 93/317-95-65. 38 rms (all with shower). **Metro:** Liceu or Jaume I.
$ Rates: 1,300 ptas. ($12.20) single; 2,200 ptas. ($20.70) double. Breakfast 275 ptas. ($2.60) extra. No credit cards.

Ⓢ In my opinion, this is one of the nicest and most reasonably priced places to stay in Barcelona. In a quiet, imposing building more than two centuries old, it stands just a short distance from the Plaça de Sant Jaume, in the center of the Barri Gòtic. Units are clean and comfortable, and there is central heating. The staff speaks English.

LAYETANA, Plaça de Ramón Berenguer el Gran, 2, 08002 Barcelona. Tel. 93/319-20-12. 20 rms. (none with bath). **Metro:** Jaume I.
$ Rates: 1,400 ptas. ($13.15) single without bath; 2,200 ptas. ($20.70) double without bath. Breakfast 300 ptas. ($2.80) extra. No credit cards.

✪ Centrally located within the Barri Gòtic, this well-run little hotel stays reasonably quiet at night. It is in a 19th-century structure, and some of its windows open onto a view of the old Roman wall. The simply furnished rooms are clean and comfortable. Breakfast only is served.

HOTEL INGLÉS, Boquer, 17, 08002 Barcelona. Tel. 93/317-37-70. Fax 93/98-215. 28 rms (all with bath). TEL **Metro:** Jaume I.
$ Rates: 2,600 ptas. ($24.45) single; 4,200 ptas. ($39.50) double. Breakfast 350 ptas. ($3.30) extra. AE, DC, MC, V.
A small, modest hotel in the Barri Gòtic, it is located on a narrow street off the Rambles, a few minutes' walk from the heart of the city. The management is helpful, the rates are moderate, and the rooms are fair. The level of cleanliness is adequate.

ON PASSEIG DE GRÀCIA

RESIDENCIA MONTSERRAT, Passeig de Gràcia, 114, 08008 Barcelona. Tel. 93/217-27-00. 39 rms (all with bath). TEL **Metro:** Diagonal.
$ Rates: 2,000 ptas. ($18.80) single; 3,500 ptas. ($32.90) double. Breakfast 300 ptas. ($2.80) extra. No credit cards.

Ⓢ This hotel lies in one of Barcelona's most desirable central neighborhoods. Although the façade is ornately handsome, the rooms on the fourth-floor *residencia* are serviceable and clean—but drab. Some have terraces, and all have some sort of bath.

ALONG THE RAMBLES

HOSTAL NEUTRAL, Ramble de Catalunya, 42, 08007 Barcelona. Tel. 93/318-73-70. 35 rms (all with bath). TEL **Metro:** Plaça de Catalunya.
$ Rates: 2,000 ptas. ($18.80) single; 3,100 ptas. ($29.15) double with shower, 3,800 ptas. ($35.70) double with complete bath. Breakfast 300 ptas. ($2.80) extra. No credit cards.

Ⓢ An older pension, but very recommendable, the *hostal* has a reputation for its cleanliness and efficiency. As the name suggests, the rooms here are neutral— but comfortable nevertheless. English is spoken.

DOUBLES FOR LESS THAN 7,500 PTAS. ($70.50)

IN THE BARRI GÒTIC

HOTEL CORTÉS, Santa Anna, 25, 08002 Barcelona. Tel. 93/301-33-96.
Fax 93/301-31-35. 46 rms (all with bath). TEL **Metro:** Plaça de Catalunya.
$ Rates (including continental breakfast): 3,900 ptas. ($36.65) single; 6,500 ptas. ($61.10) double. AE, DC, MC, V.

⭐ A short walk from the cathedral, the hotel has an attractive, functional decor. Half the bedrooms are above a quiet courtyard and half overlook the street. Guests can take breakfast in the bar that is connected to the hotel, and in the evening they can enjoy a *cerveza* (beer) here. There's a small salon on the ground floor, with another, slightly larger one upstairs.

ON PASSEIG DE GRÀCIA

HOSTAL RESIDENCIA URBIS, Passeig de Gràcia, 23, 08007 Barcelona.
Tel. 93/317-27-66. 58 rms (all with bath). TEL **Metro:** Plaça de Catalunya.
$ Rates: 5,800 ptas. ($54.50) single; 7,000 ptas. ($65.80) double. Breakfast 400 ptas. ($3.75) extra. AE, DC, MC, V.

⭐ More than 100 years old and once the private palace of a marquis, this building became a hotel in the 1970s. It has traditional styling, and spreads out across four floors. Rooms are comfortably furnished and well maintained; if you prefer quiet, ask for one in the rear. The Urbis, lying in a main shopping center, offers a snack bar and restaurant.

ALONG THE RAMBLES

HOTEL SAN AGUSTÍN, Plaça de San Agustín, 3, 08001 Barcelona. Tel. 93/318-16-58. Fax 93/317-29-28. 71 rms (all with bath). TEL **Metro:** Plaça de Catalunya.
$ Rates: 3,800 ptas. ($35.70) single; 5,800 ptas. ($54.50) double. Breakfast 400 ptas. ($3.75) extra. MC, V.
This tastefully renovated five-story hotel stands in the center of the old city—near the covered produce markets overlooking the brick walls of an unfinished Romanesque church. Bedrooms are comfortable and modern. The hotel also runs a good restaurant, offering reasonably priced meals for 1,350 pesetas ($12.70).

HOTEL CONTINENTAL, Ramble de Canaletes, 138, 08002 Barcelona.
Tel. 93/301-25-70. Fax 93/302-73-60. 32 rms (all with bath). MINIBAR TV TEL **Metro:** Plaça de Catalunya.
$ Rates (including continental breakfast): 5,500 ptas. ($51.70) single; 6,900 ptas. ($64.85) double. AE, DC, V.
This hotel lies on the upper two floors of a commercial building in a safer section of the upper Rambles. The flowery, slightly faded reception area is clean and accented with 19th-century statues. Of the 32 pleasant and modern rooms, 10 of them have semicircular balconies overlooking the Rambles. A buffet breakfast is served daily from 8am to noon.

HOTEL INTERNACIONAL, Rambles, 78-80, 08002 Barcelona. Tel. 93/302-25-66. Fax 93/302-25-66. 62 rms (all with bath). TEL **Metro:** Plaça de Catalunya.
$ Rates: 5,800 ptas. ($54.50) single; 7,300 ptas. ($68.60) double. Breakfast 375 ptas. ($3.50) extra. AE, MC, V.
If your heart is set on staying on the Rambles, you'll find the Internacional at the upper, and slightly safer, end. The detailed peach-and-gray baroque façade is exquisite, but the interior has been renovated into a modern style. The high-ceilinged bedrooms contain functional furniture. There are a bar and a breakfast room. Since the place is a favorite with tour groups, make sure you have a reservation.

IN PLAÇA DE CATALUNYA

HOTEL LLEÓ, Pelai, 24, 08001 Barcelona. Tel. 93/318-13-12. Fax 93/412-26-57. 42 rms (all with bath). A/C TV TEL **Metro:** Plaça de Catalunya.
$ Rates: 5,000 ptas. ($47) single; 7,500 ptas. ($70.50) double. Breakfast 275 ptas. ($2.60) extra. AE, DC, MC, V.
Solid and conservative, this hotel has recently been renovated. It's on a busy commercial street, and has a restaurant on one of the upper floors. Dimly lit hallways lead to clean bedrooms, each equipped with a safe and comfortable, functional furniture.

MESÓN CASTILLA, Valldonzella, 5, 08001 Barcelona. Tel. 93/318-21-82. Fax 93/412-40-20. 56 rms (all with bath). TEL **Metro:** Plaça de Catalunya.
$ Rates: 5,000 ptas. ($47) single; 7,500 ptas. ($70.50) double. Breakfast 425 ptas. ($4) extra. AE, MC, V.
This two-star hotel has a lavish façade, with a wealth of art nouveau detailing, and the high-ceilinged lobby is filled with cabriole-legged chairs. Owned and operated by the Spanish hotel chain HUSA, the Castilla is clean, charming, and well maintained. The rooms are comfortable—beds have ornate Catalan-style headboards—and 28 of them have air conditioning. Breakfast only is served.

DOUBLES FOR LESS THAN 15,000 PTAS.
[$141]

IN THE BARRI GÒTIC

HOTEL REGENCIA COLÓN, Sagristans, 13-17, 08002 Barcelona. Tel. 93/318-98-58. Fax 93/317-28-22. 55 rms (all with bath). A/C MINIBAR TV TEL **Metro:** Urquinaona.
$ Rates: 6,500 ptas. ($61.10) single; 10,500 ptas. ($98.70) double. Breakfast 550 ptas. ($5.15) extra. AE, DC, MC.
⭐ This stately stone building stands directly behind the more prestigious (and more expensive) Hotel Colón—both in the shadow of the cathedral. The formal lobby seems bit dour, but the rooms are well-maintained and comfortable, if somewhat small. All have piped-in music. The hotel's location at the edge of the Barri Gòtic is a plus.

RIALTO, Ferran, 41, 08002 Barcelona. Tel. 93/318-52-12. Fax 93/315-38-19. 129 rms (all with bath). A/C TV TEL **Metro:** Jaume I.
$ Rates: 7,500 ptas. ($70.50) single; 10,800 ptas. ($101.50) double. Breakfast 525 ptas. ($4.95) extra. AE, DC, MC, V.
One of the best choices in the Barri Gòtic, this hotel is part of the Gargallo chain, which also owns the Hotel Suizo (see below). The three-star Rialto is furnished with Catalan flair and style; completely overhauled in 1985, it offers clean, well-maintained, and comfortably furnished bedrooms. There is a cafeteria.

HOTEL SUIZO, Plaça de l'Àngel, 12, 08010 Barcelona. Tel. 93/315-41-11. Fax 93/315-38-19. 48 rms (all with bath). A/C MINIBAR TV TEL **Metro:** Jaume I.
$ Rates: 7,500 ptas. ($70.50) single; 14,000 ptas. ($131.60) double. Breakfast 525 ptas. ($4.95) extra. AE, DC, MC, V.
⭐ A few blocks from the cathedral in a 19th-century building, the Hotel Suizo has an elaborate Belle Epoque–style bar, where drinks and snacks are served. The reception area is pleasantly modern. Bedrooms have antique-patterned wallpaper and Spanish furniture. The staff is polite and helpful.

BARCELONA

 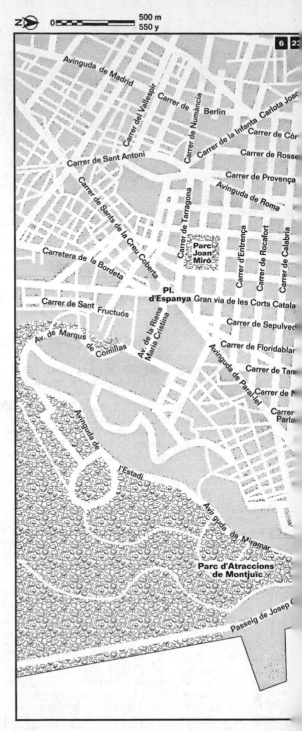

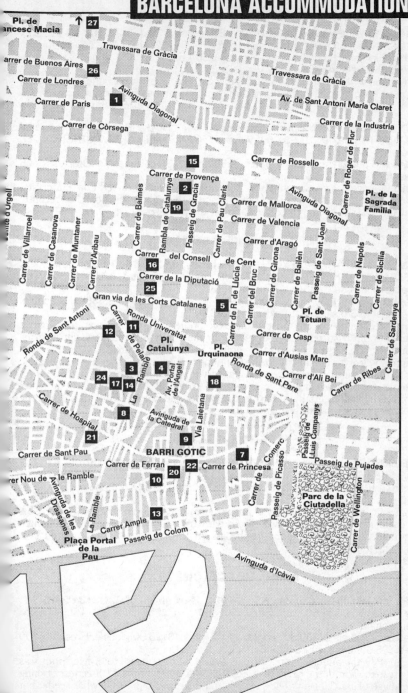

BARCELONA ACCOMMODATIONS

Pl. de ncesc Macia

↑ 27

Travessara de Gràcia

Travessara de Gràcia

rrer de Buenos Aires

26

Carrer de Londres

Av. de Sant Antoni Maria Claret

Carrer de Paris

1

Avinguda Diagonal

Carrer de la Industria

Carrer de Còrsega

Carrer de Roger de Flor

Carrer de Rossello

15

Carrer de Provença

Pl. de la
Sagrada
Familia

2

Avinguda Diagonal

19

Carrer de Mallorca

Carrer de Balmes

Rambla de Catalunya

Passeig de Gràcia

Carrer de Pau Claris

Carrer de Valencia

Carrer d'Aragó

Carrer

del Consell

Passeig de Sant Joan

Carrer de Napols

Carrer de Sicilia

16

de Cent

Carrer de Villarroel

Carrer de Casanova

Carrer de Muntaner

Carrer d'Aribau

Carrer de la Diputació

Carrer de R. de Llúcia

Carrer del Bruc

Carrer de Girona

Carrer de Bailèn

25

Gran via de les Corts Catalanes

5

Pl. de
Tetuan

Carrer de Sardenya

nte a Urgell

Ronda de Sant Antoni

Carrer de Pelaio

Ronda Universitat

11

Pl.
Catalunya

Carrer de Casp

12

Pl.
Urquinaona

Carrer d'Ausias Marc

Carrer de Ribes

3

4

Av. Portal
de l'Angel

18

Ronda de Sant Pere

Carrer d'Ali Bei

24 17 14

La Rambla

Via Laietana

Carrer de Hospital

8

Avinguda de
la Catedral

Passeig de Lluis Companys

21

9

Passeig de Pujades

Carrer de Sant Pau

BARRI GOTIC

7

Carrer de Comerç

Parc de la
Ciutadella

Carrer de Ferran

10 20 22

Carrer de Princesa

er Nou de le Ramble

Passeig de Picasso

Carrer de Wellington

La Rambla

13

Carrer Ample

Avinguda de les Drassanes

Plaça Portal
de la
Pau

Passeig de Colom

Avinguda d'Icàvia

ALONG THE RAMBLES

TURÍN, Pintor Fortuny, 9, 08001 Barcelona. Tel. 93/302-48-12. Fax 93/302-10-05. 60 rms (all with bath). A/C TV TEL **Metro:** Plaça de Catalunya.
$ Rates (including continental breakfast): 5,500 ptas. ($51.70) single; 8,500 ptas. ($79.90) double. AE, DC, MC, V.
This neat and well-run three-star hotel is in a terra-cotta grillwork building located in a shopping district. It offers small, streamlined accommodations with balconies. An elevator will take you to your room. The Turín also offers a restaurant.

MONTECARLO, Ramble dels Estudis, 124, 08002 Barcelona. Tel. 93/ 317-58-00. Fax 93/317-57-50. 77 rms (all with bath). A/C MINIBAR TV TEL **Metro:** Plaça de Catalunya.
$ Rates: 6,500 ptas. ($61.10) single; 9,500 ptas. ($89.30) double. Breakfast 425 ptas. ($4) extra. AE, DC, V.
The main lounge has an elaborately detailed ceiling, stylized carved doors, a crystal chandelier, and a baronial fireplace. The furniture throughout the hotel has recently been upgraded, and there is a coffee shop on the premises.

IN PLAÇA DE CATALUNYA

GRANVIA, Gran Via de les Corts Catalanes, 642, 08007 Barcelona. Tel. 93/318-19-00. Fax 93/318-99-97. 48 rms (all with bath). A/C MINIBAR TEL **Metro:** Plaça de Catalunya.
$ Rates: 6,400–7,600 ptas. ($60.15–$71.45) single; 9,500 ptas. ($89.30) double. Breakfast 475 ptas. ($4.45) extra. AE, DC, MC, V.
A grand hotel on one of the most fashionable boulevards in Barcelona, the Granvia has public rooms that reflect the opulence of the 1860s—chandeliers, gilt mirrors, French provincial furniture—and a grand balustraded staircase. Although the traditional bedrooms contain interesting antique reproductions, they are comfortable rather than luxurious. The courtyard, graced with a fountain and palm trees, is set with tables for al fresco drinks; in the garden room off the courtyard, continental breakfast is served. Centrally heated in the winter, the hotel has one drawback: the noise. Street sounds might disturb the light sleeper.

IN SANT GERVASI

HOTEL ZENIT, Santaló, 8, 08021 Barcelona. Tel. 93/209-89-11. Fax 93/414-59-65. 61 rms (all with bath). A/C TV TEL **Metro:** Muntaner.
$ Rates: 10,200 ptas. ($95.90) single; 12,500 ptas. ($117.50) double. Breakfast 550 ptas. ($5.15) extra. AE, DC, MC, V.
This unpretentious and efficiently managed member of Spain's nationwide HUSA hotel chain shares its bottom two floors with the headquarters of the Catalonian Automobile Club. The balconied bedrooms are clean and simple, decorated in a bland international style.

NEAR BARCELONETA

HOTEL METROPOL, Ample, 31, 08002 Barcelona. Tel. 93/315-40-11. Fax 93/319-12-76. 68 rms (all with bath). A/C MINIBAR TV TEL **Metro:** Barceloneta.
$ Rates: 9,500 ptas. ($89.30) single; 13,500 ptas. ($126.90) double. Breakfast 700 ptas. ($6.60) extra. AE, DC, MC, V.
In 1989 the antique Hotel Torelló closed and the new Hotel Metropol was created, right in the heart of Barcelona, just north of the 18th-century fishing village of Barceloneta. The surrounding district may be somewhat seedy, but this ranks as one of the city's finest three-star hotels. It offers style and comfort, with

sleek, modern furnishings in both bedrooms and public rooms. The staff is helpful. Breakfast only.

IN SARRIÀ

HOTEL TRES TORRES, Calatrava, 32, 08017 Barcelona. Tel. 93/417-73-00. Fax 93/418-98-34. 61 rms (all with bath). A/C MINIBAR TV TEL **Metro:** Tres Torres.
$ Rates: 14,000 ptas. ($131.60) double. Breakfast 550 ptas. ($5.15) extra. AE, DC, MC, V.
The Tres Torres is in the northern Sarrià district, a neighborhood of lush gardens and expensive apartments. This unpretentious five-story hotel contains tasteful, conservative public rooms and clean, comfortable bedrooms. All rooms are doubles.

IN THE EIXAMPLE

HOTEL ASTORIA, París, 203, 08036 Barcelona. Tel. 93/209-83-11. Fax 93/202-30-08. 115 rms (all with bath). A/C MINIBAR TV TEL **Metro:** Diagonal.
$ Rates: 11,500 ptas. ($108.10) single; 15,000 ptas. ($141) double. Breakfast 950 ptas. ($8.95) extra. AE, DC, MC, V.

⭐ One of my favorite hotels, the Astoria has an art-deco-inspired façade that makes it appear older than it is. The high ceilings, geometric designs, and brass-studded detailings in the public rooms could be Moorish or Andalusian. Each of the comfortable bedrooms is soundproofed; half have been renovated with slick international louvered closets and glistening white paint. The more old-fashioned rooms have warm textures of exposed cedar and elegant, pristine modern accessories.

HOTEL WILSON, Avinguda Diagonal, 568, 08021 Barcelona. Tel. 93/209-25-11. Fax 93/200-83-70. 55 rms (all with bath). A/C MINIBAR TV TEL **Metro:** Diagonal.
$ Rates (including continental breakfast): 10,000 ptas. ($94) single; 15,000 ptas. ($141) double. AE, DC, MC, V.
Set in a neighborhood rich with architectural curiosities, this comfortable hotel is a member of the nationwide HUSA chain. The small lobby isn't indicative of the rest of the building, which on the second floor opens into a large and sunny coffee shop/bar/TV lounge. Rooms are well kept.

WORTH THE EXTRA BUCKS

HOTEL HESPERÍA, Los Vergos, 20, 08017 Barcelona. Tel. 93/204-55-51. Fax 93/204-43-92. 139 rms (all with bath). A/C MINIBAR TV TEL **Metro:** Tres Torres.
$ Rates: 17,500 ptas. ($164.50) double. Breakfast 1,000 ptas. ($9.40) extra. AE, DC, MC, V.
This hotel on the northern edge of the city, a 12-minute taxi ride from the center, is surrounded by the verdant gardens of one of Barcelona's most pleasant residential neighborhoods. You'll pass a Japanese rock garden to reach the stone-floored reception area, with its adjacent bar. Sunlight floods the monochromatic interiors of the bedrooms—all doubles. The uniformed staff offers fine service.

HOTEL REGENTE, Ramble de Catalunya, 76, 08008 Barcelona. Tel. 93/215-25-70. Fax 93/487-32-27. 78 rms (all with bath). A/C MINIBAR TV TEL **Metro:** Plaça de Catalunya.
$ Rates: 13,600 ptas. ($127.85) single; 19,500 ptas. ($183.30) double. Breakfast 800 ptas. ($7.50) extra. AE, DC, MC, V.
Despite the hotel's extensive renovations, its grand art nouveau façade, famous picture windows, and traditional lobby have been preserved. The Regente's Scotch Bar-Restaurant is elegant, and the rooftop terrace with swimming pool and sun deck provides panoramic views of the area from Montjuïc to the harbor. Situated amid fine shops and restaurants, the hotel is easily accessible to city sights.

HOTEL CONDES DE BARCELONA, Passeig de Gràcia, 75, 08008 Barcelona. Tel. 93/215-06-16. Fax 93/216-08-35. 100 rms (all with bath). A/C MINIBAR TV TEL **Metro:** Passeig de Gràcia.

$ Rates: 16,500 ptas. ($155.10) single; 22,000 ptas. ($206.80) double. Breakfast 1,100 ptas. ($10.35) extra. AE, DC, MC, V.

Located off the architecturally splendid Passeig de Gràcia, this four-star hotel, originally designed to be a private villa (1895), is one of Barcelona's most glamorous. It boasts a unique neomedieval façade, influenced by Gaudí's modernist movement. During recent renovation, just enough hints of high-tech furnishings were added to make the lobby exciting, but everything else has the original opulence. The curved lobby-level bar and its adjacent restaurant add a touch of art deco. The comfortable salmon-, green-, or peach-colored bedrooms all contain marble baths, reproductions of Spanish paintings, and soundproof windows.

RAMADA RENAISSANCE, Pintor Fortuny, 2, 08002 Barcelona. Tel. 93/318-62-00. Fax 93/301-77-76. 203 rms (all with bath), 7 suites. A/C MINIBAR TV TEL **Metro:** Liceu.

$ Rates: 25,000 ptas. ($235) single; 35,000 ptas. ($329) double. Breakfast 1,800 ptas. ($16.90) extra. AE, DC, MC, V.

⭐ There may not be a better hotel in all of Barcelona. A remake of the old Hotel Manila, the Ramada Renaissance, lying right off the Rambles, is a medley of pastels and tasteful decorating. Its rooms are spacious and comfortable, with amenities such as extra-large beds, heated bathroom floors, eight TV channels, three in-house videos, hairdryers, and two phones in each room; all rooms facing the street have double windows. The Renaissance Club provides extra amenities, including private check-ins.

The chic lobby bar, open from 7 to 11pm, has live piano music. El Patio restaurant, nearby, serves fine continental and Catalan cuisine.

Other facilities include a business center and private meeting rooms, and limousine service is available. Some of the most celebrated visitors to Barcelona, including Michael Jackson, have stayed here.

---

2. WHERE TO EAT

Note: A list of **restaurants by cuisine** appears in the Index.

MEALS FOR LESS THAN 1,500 PESETAS [$14.10]

IN THE BARRI GÒTIC

CASA JOSÉ, Plaça de Sant Josep Oriol, 10. Tel. 302-40-20.
Cuisine: CATALAN. **Reservations:** Not required. **Metro:** Liceu.
$ Prices: Appetizers 200–600 ptas. ($1.90–$5.65); main dishes 400–800 ptas. ($3.75–$7.50); fixed-priced menu 550 ptas. ($5.15). No credit cards.
Open: Lunch Mon–Sat 1–4pm; dinner Mon–Sat 8–11pm.

Ⓢ In my opinion, the Casa José is the best spot for rock-bottom economy dining in Barcelona. This corner bistro overlooks the back of the old Church of Santa María del Piño, a 3-minute walk up the Cardenal Casañas and Carrer Boqueria. The diners are mostly locals. The well-prepared prix-fixe menu might include spaghetti to start with, lamb stew, plus bread and dessert. A popular meal is roast chicken, french fries, salad, bread, and dessert. For the same price, you can order paella, although you must wait about half an hour for it to be prepared. More expensive meals are also available.

PJTARRA, Avinyó, 561. Tel. 301-16-47.
Cuisine: CATALAN. **Reservations:** Required. **Metro:** Liceu.

$ Prices: Appetizers 300–800 ptas. ($2.80–$7.50); main dishes 550–1,800 ptas. ($5.15–$16.90). AE, DC, MC, V.
Open: Lunch Mon–Sat 1–4pm; dinner Mon–Sat 8:30–11pm.

Ⓢ Founded in 1890, this restaurant was named after a 19th-century Catalan playwright whose works were performed here in the back room. Try the grilled fish chowder or a Catalan salad, followed by grilled sirloin or squid Málaga style. Valencian paella is another specialty.

CASA CUELLERETES, Quintana, 5. Tel. 317-30-22.
Cuisine: CATALAN. **Reservations:** Recommended. **Metro:** Liceu.
$ Prices: Appetizers 350–950 ptas. ($3.30–$8.95); main dishes 625–1,200 ptas. ($5.85–$11.30). No credit cards.
Open: Lunch Tues–Sun 1:30–4pm; dinner Tues–Sat 9–11pm. **Closed:** July.

Ⓢ Founded in 1786 as a *pastelería*, this oldest of Barcelona restaurants still retains many original architectural features. All three dining rooms are decorated in Catalan style, with tile dadoes and wrought-iron chandeliers. The well-prepared food features authentic dishes of northeastern Spain, including sole Roman style, *zarzuela à la marinara* (shellfish medley), canalones, and paella. From October to January, special game dishes are available, including *perdiz* (partridge). Signed photographs of celebrities, flamenco artists, and bullfighters who have visited this *casa* decorate the walls.

LA CUINETA, Paradis, 4. Tel. 315-01-11.
Cuisine: CATALAN. **Reservations:** Recommended. **Metro:** Jaume I.
$ Prices: Appetizers 750–2,900 ptas. ($7.05–$27.25); main dishes 975–2,000 ptas. ($9.15–$18.80); Fixed-priced menu 1,500 ptas. ($14.10). AE, DC, MC, V.
Open: Lunch daily 1–4pm; dinner daily 8pm–midnight.
A well-established restaurant near the center of the Catalan government, this is a culinary highlight of the Barri Gòtic. The restaurant is decorated in typical regional style and favors local cuisine. The fixed-price menu represents good value, or you can order à la carte. The most expensive appetizer is *bellota* (acorn-fed ham), but I suggest you settle instead for a market-fresh Catalan dish.

ON PASSEIG DE GRÀCIA

C'AN TRIPAS, Sagues, 16. Tel. 200-85-40.
Cuisine: CATALAN/SPANISH. **Reservations:** Recommended. **Metro:** Muntaner.
$ Prices: Appetizers 250–400 ptas. ($2.35–$3.75); main dishes 350–800 ptas. ($3.30–$7.50). No credit cards.
Open: Lunch daily 1–4pm; dinner daily 9–11pm.
This well-known no-frills budget restaurant has a certain charm, even if it is located on a block of adult nightclubs. There's sawdust on the floor, tables are covered with oilcloths, arc lights shine, racks of bottles line the poster-covered walls, and a TV set plays in the background. Among the menu choices that might make up a full meal are fish soup, beef with brussels sprouts, brook trout, and Spanish melon. Or sample the most classic dish of Barcelona, the regional stew called *escu della i carn d'olla* (broad beans, sausages, meatballs, and herbs).

ON AND OFF THE RAMBLES

GARDUÑA, Morera, 17-19. Tel. 302-43-23.
Cuisine: CATALAN. **Reservations:** Recommended. **Metro:** Liceu.
$ Prices: Appetizers 210–1,100 ptas. ($1.95–$10.35); main dishes 470–1,600 ptas. ($4.40–$15.05); fixed-priced menu 675–875 ptas. ($6.35–$8.25). MC, V.
Open: Lunch Mon–Sat 1–4pm; dinner Mon–Sat 8pm–midnight.

Ⓢ This is the most famous eatery in La Boqueria, the old market right off the Rambles, near the Gran Teatre del Liceu. A bit ramshackle, it's at the back of the market; you can dine either downstairs or (more formally) upstairs. The ingredients are market fresh (the chef doesn't have far to go for produce). Begin by selecting one of the "hors d'oeuvres of the sea," or else *canalones* (cannelloni) Rossini, followed by, perhaps, filet of steak with green peppercorns, seafood rice, or a zarzuela of fresh fish with spices.

EGIPTE, Jerusalem, 3. Tel. 317-74-80.
Cuisine: CATALAN. **Reservations:** Recommended. **Metro:** Liceu.
$ Prices: Appetizers 550–850 ptas. ($5.15–$7.50); main dishes 750–1,200 ptas. ($7.05–$11.30); fixed-priced menu 825 ptas. ($7.75). MC, V.
Open: Lunch Mon–Sat 1–4pm; dinner Mon–Sat 8:30pm–12:30am.

⑤ A favorite among the locals, this tiny place, located right behind the central marketplace, jumps day and night. The excellent menu includes spinach vol-au-vent (traditionally served with an egg on top), *lengua de ternera* (tongue), and *berengeras* (stuffed eggplant), a chef's specialty. Ingredients are fresh and the price is right.

RESTAURANTE D'ESPAÑA, Sant Pau, 9-11. Tel. 318-17-58.
Cuisine: SPANISH. **Reservations:** Not required. **Metro:** Liceu.
$ Prices: Appetizers 500–1,000 ptas. ($4.70–$9.40); main dishes 850–2,000 ptas. ($8–$18.80); fixed-priced dinner 1,200 ptas. ($11.30). AE, DC, MC, V.
Open: Lunch daily 12:30–2:30pm; dinner daily 8:30–11:30pm.

This two-star hotel/restaurant, just off the Rambles in the Barri Xinés area, has a late-medieval feel with a touch of art nouveau Gothic, which includes an interior patio and mosaic floors. The large dining hall has huge chandeliers, bentwood chairs, and tile walls. A fixed-priced dinner might include hors d'oeuvres or salad, paella or hake, followed by a grilled veal steak and ending with ice cream, fruit, or caramel custard.

AMAYA, Ramble de Santa Mònica, 20. Tel. 302-61-38.
Cuisine: SPANISH/BASQUE. **Reservations:** Not required. **Metro:** Drassanes.
$ Prices: Tapas 365–1,790 ptas. ($3.45–$16.85); fixed priced menu 1,400 ptas. ($13.15). AE, MC, V.
Open: Daily 9am–1pm.

This recommendation is not the expensive restaurant but its attached tapas outlet. Tapas lovers can sit at the long bar and select their favorites from a well-stocked display case. There are also *platos del día* (plates of the day). The cuisine might include rice with chicken, pesto *bilbaino* (a Basque dish), cannelloni Rossini, ham with melon, two kinds of paella, and grilled sardines.

NEAR BARCELONETA

SIETE PUERTAS, Passeig d'Isabel II, 14. Tel. 319-30-46.
Cuisine: SEAFOOD. **Reservations:** Required. **Metro:** Barceloneta.
$ Prices: Appetizers 190–1,500 ptas. ($1.80–$14.10); main dishes 615–2,200 ptas. ($5.80–$20.70). AE, DC, MC, V.
Open: Daily 1pm–midnight.

This is a lunchtime favorite for businesspeople and an evening favorite for in-the-know clients who have made it their preferred restaurant in Catalonia. It's been going since 1836. Regional dishes include fresh herring with onions and potatoes, a different paella daily (sometimes with shellfish, for example, or with rabbit), and a wide array of fresh fish, succulent oysters, and a herb-laden stew of black beans with pork or white beans with sausage.

IN THE EIXAMPLE

EL BODEGÓN, Mallorca, 197. Tel. 253-10-17.
Cuisine: CATALAN. **Reservations:** Recommended. **Metro:** Hospital Clinic.
$ Prices: Appetizers 300–500 ptas. ($2.80–$4.70); main dishes 700–1,400 ptas. ($6.60–$13.15).
Open: Lunch Mon–Fri 1–4:30pm; dinner Mon–Fri 8pm–midnight.

The best dishes in this cozy bistrolike restaurant are the seafood and the tapas. Usually included on the à la carte menu: *besugo* (sea bream), kidneys in sherry, partridges (in season) served with fresh mushrooms, and a civet of boar, also a seasonal dish. There are two dining rooms, each with plastic chairs and paper tablecloths, where sometimes a local guitarist will serenade you.

ALONG MOLL DE LA FUSTA

GAMBRINUS, Passeig del Moll de la Fusta. Tel. 310-55-77.
   Cuisine: SEAFOOD. **Reservations:** Required. **Metro:** Drassanes.
$ **Prices:** Appetizers 550–1,200 ptas. ($5.15–$11.30); main dishes 550–3,500 ptas. ($5.15–$32.90). AE, DC, MC, V.
   Open: Daily 10am–2:30am.
On a restored pier near the Columbus Monument, this seafront restaurant is decorated with a giant lobster designed by the creator of the Olympic mascot, Javier Mariscal. In summer, outdoor tables enable you to dine in the open air shaded by umbrellas. There are several price levels, lobster being the most expensive item. The chef prepares a selection of *platos del día,* including shellfish paella. You can order fried squid, fresh oysters, and various grilled fish, depending on the day's catch. There's also a boat-shaped bar.

BLAU MARI, Passeig del Moll de la Fusta. Tel. 310-10-15.
   Cuisine: CATALAN. **Reservations:** Recommended. **Metro:** Drassanes.
$ **Prices:** Appetizers 450–950 ptas. ($4.25–$8.95); main dishes 650–1,850 ptas. ($6.10–$17.40). MC, V.
   Open: Drinks, snacks daily 1pm–2 or 3am; lunch daily 1–4pm; dinner daily 9pm–midnight.
My favorite waterfront eatery, Blau Mari serves superb cuisine in a relaxed environment. A Catalan version of bouillabaisse, studded with shellfish, is prepared for two persons or more. Although formal service is provided, you can have snacks, coffee, or drinks, plus a tasty selection of tapas, throughout the day. It's refreshing to come here in the afternoon and sit out at the *chiringuito* (open-air bar). The owners also own one of Barcelona's best restaurants, Roig Robi (see below).

IN THE BARRI DE LA RIBERA

NOU CELLER, Princesa, 16. Tel. 310-47-73.
   Cuisine: CATALAN/SPANISH. **Reservations:** Recommended (not accepted in summer). **Metro:** Jaume I.
$ **Prices:** Appetizers 250–400 ptas. ($2.35–$3.75); main dishes 350–800 ptas. ($3.30–$7.50); fixed-priced menu 1,300 ptas. ($12.20). AE, DC, MC, V.
   Open: Sun–Fri 8am–midnight.
Near the Picasso Museum, this establishment is perfect for either a bodega-type meal or a cup of coffee. Country artifacts hang from the beamed ceiling and plaster walls. The back entrance, at Barra de Ferro, 3, is at the quieter end of the place, where dozens of original artworks are arranged into a collage. The dining room offers fish soup, Catalan soup, *zarzuela* (a medley of seafood), paella, hake, and other classic dishes.

MEALS FOR LESS THAN 2,000 PTAS.
($18.80)
IN THE BARRI GÒTIC

LLIVIA, Copons, 2. Tel. 318-10-78.
   Cuisine: INTERNATIONAL. **Reservations:** Recommended. **Metro:** Urquinaona.
$ **Prices:** Appetizers 500–800 ptas. ($4.70–$7.50); main dishes 1,000–1,400 ptas. ($9.40–$13.15); *menu del día* 1,000 ptas. ($9.40). No credit cards.

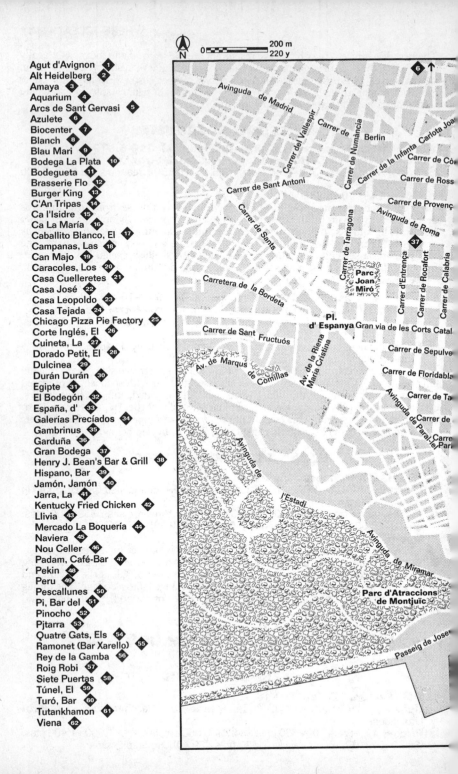

BARCELONA DINING

Open: Lunch Mon–Sat 1–4pm; dinner Mon–Sat 7–11pm.

A small restaurant with only eight tables, Llivia is located near the cathedral. The white tiled bar makes a comfortable place to enjoy a drink while waiting to be seated. The market-fresh menu includes vichyssoise, fish soup, goat cutlets, entrecote, barbecued partridge, and Basque-style hake.

RESTAURANT AQUARIUM, Cardenal Casañas, 15. Tel. 302-30-84.

Cuisine: CATALAN. **Reservations:** Required. **Metro:** Liceu.

$ Prices: Appetizers 500–1,000 ptas. ($4.70–$9.40); main dishes 1,000–2,000 ptas. ($9.40–$18.80); *cubierto* 1,500 ptas. ($14.10). AE, MC, V.

Open: Lunch Tues–Sun 1–4pm; dinner Tues–Sun 8–11pm. **Closed:** June.

S This small, inviting restaurant decorated with Spanish ceramics offers one of the biggest and best cubiertos available in a Barcelona bistro. A typical meal might include fish soup, Cuban-style rice, veal filet and tomatoes, dessert, bread, and wine. The chef's specialties on the à la carte menu are snails with crab and a zarzuela of shellfish.

CASA LEOPOLDO, Sant Rafael, 24. Tel. 241-30-14.

Cuisine: SEAFOOD. **Reservations:** Required. **Metro:** Liceu.

$ Prices: Appetizers 850–1,500 ptas. ($8–$14.10); main dishes 1,800–3,500 ptas. ($16.90–$32.90); fixed-priced lunch 1,000 ptas. ($9.40). AE, MC, V.

Open: Lunch Tues–Sun 1–4pm; dinner Tues–Sat 9–11pm. **Closed:** Aug.

An excursion through the seedy streets of the Barri Xinés is part of the experience of coming to this restaurant. At night, though, it's safer to come by taxi. This colorful restaurant (founded in 1939) has some of the freshest seafood in town and caters to a loyal clientele. There's a popular stand-up tapas bar in front, then two dining rooms, one slightly more formal than the other. Specialties include eel with shrimp, barnacles, cuttlefish, seafood soup with shellfish, and deep-fried inch-long eels.

IN PLAÇA DE CATALUNYA

ELS QUATRE GATS, Montsió, 3. Tel. 302-41-40.

Cuisine: CATALAN. **Reservations:** Required Sat–Sun. **Metro:** Plaça de Catalunya.

$ Prices: Appetizers 500–1,200 ptas. ($4.70–$11.30); main dishes 1,000–2,000 ptas. ($9.40–$18.80); fixed-priced menu 1,300 ptas. ($12.20). MC, V.

Open: Lunch daily 1–5pm; dinner daily 9pm–midnight.

A Barcelona legend, The Four Cats was the favorite of Picasso and other artists. In their heyday, their works decorated the walls of the avant-garde café on a narrow cobblestoned street near the cathedral. It was the setting for poetry readings by Maragall, piano concerts by Albéniz and Granados, and murals by Ramón Casa.

Today a *tertulia* bar in the heart of the Barri Gòtic, it has recently been restored, but retains its fine old look. The fixed-price meal, offered every day but Sunday, rates as one of the best bargains in town, considering the locale. The good food is prepared in an unpretentious style of Catalan cooking called *cuina de mercat* (based on whatever looked fresh at the market that day). The constantly changing menu reflects the seasons.

AT OR NEAR BARCELONETA

EL TÚNEL, Ample, 33-35. Tel. 315-27-59.

Cuisine: CATALAN. **Reservations:** Recommended for lunch. **Metro:** Barceloneta.

$ Prices: Appetizers 500–1,000 ptas. ($4.70–$9.40); main dishes 1,000–2,000 ptas. ($9.40–$18.80). AE, DC, MC, V.

Open: Lunch Tues–Sun 1:30–4pm; dinner Tues–Sat 9–11:30pm.

This established and prestigious restaurant features a delectable fish soup, cannelloni with truffles, kidney beans with shrimp, roast goat, fish stew, and filet of beef with peppers. The service is eager, the wine cellar extensive.

RAMONET [BAR XARELLO], Maquinista, 17. Tel. 319-30-64.
    Cuisine: SEAFOOD. **Reservations:** Recommended. **Metro:** Barceloneta.
$ Prices: Appetizers 1,000–3,000 ptas. ($9.40–$28.20); main dishes 1,000–3,500 ptas. ($9.40–$32.90). AE, DC, MC, V.
    Open: Lunch Tues–Sun 1–4pm; dinner Tues–Sun 8:30–11:30pm.
Located in an Andalusian-style villa near the seaport, this rather expensive restaurant serves a large variety of fresh seafood. The front room, with stand-up tables for seafood tapas, beer, and regional wine, is often crowded. In the two dining rooms in back, lined with wooden tables, you can choose from a wide variety of fish—shrimp, hake, and monkfish are almost always available. Other specialties include a portion of pungent anchovies, grilled mushrooms, braised artichokes, and a tortilla with spinach and beans. Mussels "from the beach" are also sold.

RESTAURANT PERÚ, Passeig Nacional, 10. Tel. 310-37-09.
    Cuisine: SPANISH. **Reservations:** Not required. **Metro:** Barceloneta.
$ Prices: Appetizers 300–1,500 ptas. ($2.80–$14.10); main dishes 1,000–3,500 ptas. ($9.40–$32.90); fixed-priced menu 1,100 ptas. ($10.35). AE, MC, V.
    Open: Lunch Tues–Sun 1–5pm; dinner Tues–Sun 8pm–midnight.
The fare at this seafood restaurant is served in generous portions. Specialties include paella with shellfish and a distinctly Catalan bouillabaisse. Cannelloni makes a good appetizer.

IN THE EIXAMPLE

PEKIN, Rosselló, 202. Tel. 215-01-77.
    Cuisine: CHINESE. **Reservations:** Recommended. **Metro:** Entença.
$ Prices: Appetizers 175–1,700 ptas. ($1.65–$16); main dishes 850–2,500 ptas. ($8–$23.50). MC, V.
    Open: Lunch Mon–Sat 1–4pm; dinner Mon–Sat 8pm–midnight.
Service is efficient and understated in this minimalist, high-tech Chinese restaurant, where you can order such tasty dishes as fish soup, hake with ginger, "five weeping willows" sole, and veal with oyster sauce.

MEALS FOR LESS THAN 3,000 PTAS.
[$28.20]
IN THE BARRI GÒTIC

BRASSERIE FLO, Jonqueras, 10. Tel. 317-80-37.
    Cuisine: FRENCH. **Reservations:** Recommended. **Metro:** Urquinaona.
$ Prices: Fixed-priced menu 1,400 ptas. ($13.15); appetizers 700–850 ptas. ($6.60–$8); main dishes 1,500–2,000 ptas. ($14.10–$18.80). AE, DC, MC, V.
    Open: Lunch daily 1–4pm; dinner daily 8:30pm–1am.
The art deco dining room here has been compared to one on a transatlantic steamer at the turn of the century—it's spacious, palm-filled, comfortable, and air-conditioned. The food isn't overlooked either, and you might begin with fresh foie gras. The specialty is a large plate of *choucroûte* (sauerkraut) served with a steamed hamhock. Also good: the shrimp in garlic, salmon tartare with vodka, and stuffed sole with spinach.

LOS CARACOLES, Escudellers, 14. Tel. 302-31-85.
    Cuisine: CATALAN/SPANISH. **Reservations:** Required. **Metro:** Drassanes.
$ Prices: Appetizers 650–900 ptas. ($6.10–$8.45); main dishes 1,500–2,000 ptas. ($14.10–$18.80). AE, DC, MC, V.
    Open: Daily 1pm–midnight.
Set in a labyrinth of narrow cobblestoned streets, this ranks as one of the port's most colorful and popular restaurants, and has been since 1835. It has won acclaim for its spit-roasted chickens and for its namesake, snails. A long angular bar is located up front, with a two-level restaurant in back. You can watch the busy preparations in the kitchen, where dried herbs, smoked ham shanks, and garlic

bouquets hang from the ceiling. In summer, tables are placed outside in the "cat alley," with the spit. The excellent food features all sorts of Spanish and Catalan specialties. Everybody from John Wayne to Richard Nixon has stopped in.

RESTAURANT PESCALLUNES, Magdalenes, 23. Tel. 318-54-83.
   Cuisine: FRENCH. **Reservations:** Required for lunch. **Metro:** Urquinaona.
$ **Prices:** Appetizers 500–700 ptas. ($4.70–$6.60); main dishes 1,500–2,000 ptas. ($14.10–$18.80). MC, V.
   Open: Lunch Mon–Fri 1–3:30pm; dinner Mon–Fri 8:30–11pm.
With the look, feel, and menu of a French bistro, this 10-table restaurant is a short walk from the cathedral. An elaborate street lantern marks the entrance. Specialties are *rape* with clams and tomatoes, a smooth vichyssoise, chateaubriand with béarnaise sauce, sole cooked in cider, steak tartare, and dessert crêpes with Cointreau. Specials change daily.

NEAR PASSEIG DE GRÀCIA

RESTAURANTE BLANCH, Diputació, 269. Tel. 302-40-24.
   Cuisine: INTERNATIONAL. **Reservations:** Not required. **Metro:** Passeig de Gràcia.
$ **Prices:** Appetizers 650–900 ptas. ($6.10–$8.45); main dishes 1,500–3,000 ptas. ($14.10–$28.20); fixed-price menu 950 ptas. ($8.95). AE, DC, MC, V.
   Open: Lunch Mon–Fri 1–4pm; dinner Mon–Fri 8:30–11pm.
This cozy place offers a good lunch special, including a big bowl of soup or a mixed salad; paella, ravioli, sardines, or hors d'oeuvres; wienerschnitzel, a quarter chicken, or a steak. You end with dessert, and beer or a half bottle of wine is included. Portions are so large you can hardly finish. For dinner, choose from an array of international specialties.

ALONG THE RAMBLES

NAVIERA, Ramble de Canaletas, 127. Tel. 301-92-25.
   Cuisine: CATALAN. **Reservations:** Not required. **Metro:** Plaça de Catalunya.
$ **Prices:** Appetizers 600–1,900 ptas. ($5.65–$17.85); main dishes 1,300–2,900 ptas. ($12.20–$27.25). AE, DC, MC, V.
   Open: *Cervecería* daily 9am–2pm; restaurant, lunch daily 2–4pm; dinner 8pm–2am.
In this two-in-one establishment, you'll find a popular cervecería (beerhall) downstairs, with sidewalk tables spilling out onto the Rambles, and a more formal sit-down restaurant upstairs. If you'd like to eat cheaply, order a beer and some tapas downstairs, beginning at 350 pesetas ($3.30). Upstairs is much more expensive, especially if you have a shellfish dish. Try grilled hake, grilled sole, entrecote, or *zarzuela de pescado* (fish and shellfish medley).

IN PLAÇA DE CATALUNYA

CA LA MARÍA, Tallers, 76. Tel. 318-89-93.
   Cuisine: CATALAN. **Reservations:** Recommended on Sat–Sun. **Metro:** Universitat.
$ **Prices:** Appetizers 600–1,000 ptas. ($5.65–$9.40); main dishes 1,500–2,500 ptas. ($14.10–$23.50). AE, DC, MC, V.
   Open: Lunch Tues–Sun 1:30–4pm; dinner Tues–Sat 8:30–11pm.
This small blue-and-green–tiled bistro (only 18 tables) is on a quiet square opposite a Byzantine-style church near the Plaça de la Universitat. Menu items include roast goat, veal scaloppine, *rape* (monkfish) in a pimiento-cream sauce, sole with orange, and codfish in a garlic-cream sauce. There are also daily specials that change frequently.

IN SANT GERVASI

ARCS DE SANT GERVASI, Santaló, 103. Tel. 201-92-77.

Cuisine: CATALAN. **Reservations:** Recommended. **Metro:** Muntaner.
$ Prices: Appetizers 675–925 ptas. ($6.35–$8.70); main dishes 1,500–1,800 ptas. ($14.10–$16.90). AE, DC, MC, V.
Open: Lunch daily 1–4pm; dinner daily 8:30–11:30pm.

North of the old town, Arcs de Sant Gervasi is sleekly decorated with such trappings as black-lacquer chairs. The walls are filled with pictures from a nearby gallery that are for sale. To begin, try the cream of crab soup or Palafrugell "black rice." For a main dish, order tender slices of veal served with wild mushrooms in a delectable cognac-flavored sauce; the kid cutlets are also juicy and superb. For dessert, try the scooped-out pineapple filled with chopped fresh fruit and *crema catalana*. The restaurant is open every day of the year.

DURÁN DURÁN, Alfons-XII, 39-41. Tel. 201-35-13.
    Cuisine: CATALAN/FRENCH. **Reservations:** Required. **Metro:** Plaça de Molina.
$ Prices: Appetizers 750–1,500 ptas. ($7.05–$14.10); main dishes 1,500–3,500 ptas. ($14.10–$32.90). AE, DC, MC, V.
    Open: Lunch Mon–Sat 1–4pm; dinner Mon–Sat 9–11:30pm. **Closed:** last 2 weeks in Aug.

This stylish bar/restaurant has minimal but elegant decor, dramatic lighting, and a warm atmosphere. Begin your meal with an appetizer such as fresh foie gras of duckling or smoked salmon and apple salad. The main course may be brochette of filet of pork, *rape* (monkfish) with a crab-cream sauce, or four different kinds of *entrecôte*. Another specialty: roast leg of lamb. The coffee and tea selection is exceptional.

NEAR BARCELONETA

CAN MAJO, Almirante Aixada, 23. Tel. 310-14-55.
    Cuisine: SEAFOOD. **Reservations:** Recommended. **Metro:** Barceloneta.
$ Prices: Appetizers 450–750 ptas. ($4.25–$7.05); main dishes 1,300–2,000 ptas. ($12.20–$18.80). AE, MC, V.
    Open: Lunch Tues–Sun 1:30–4pm; dinner Tues–Sun 9–11:30pm. **Closed:** Aug.

Located in the old fishing quarter of Barceloneta, it attracts many people from the fancier quarters who journey down here for a great seafood dinner. The Suárez-Majo family welcome you; they're still operating a business where their grandmother first opened a bar. Try a house specialty, *pelada* (Catalan for paella), perhaps starting with *entremeses* (hors d'oeuvres), from which you can select barnacles, oysters, prawns, whelks, clams, and crab—virtually whatever was caught that day. The clams with white beans are recommended. The classic all-vegetable gazpacho comes with fresh mussels and shrimp.

IN THE EIXAMPLE

ROIG ROBI, Séneca, 20. Tel. 218-92-22.
    Cuisine: CATALAN/FRENCH. **Reservations:** Required. **Metro:** Diagonal.
$ Prices: Appetizers 850–3,200 ptas. ($8–$30.10); main dishes 1,200–2,550 ptas. ($11.30–$23.95). AE, DC, MC, V.
    Open: Lunch Mon–Sat 1–4pm; dinner Mon–Sat 9pm–midnight.

Excellent food from an imaginative kitchen and a warm welcome keep patrons coming back. Begin by ordering an apéritif from the L-shaped oaken bar. Then head down a long corridor to a pair of flower-filled dining rooms. In warm weather, glass doors open onto a walled courtyard, ringed with cascades of ivy and shaded with willows and mimosa. Menu items include fresh beans with a pine-nut sauce, codfish salad with pintos, lobster salad, ravioli stuffed with spring herbs, three different preparations of hake, chicken stuffed with foie gras, and a cockscomb salad.

EL CABALLITO BLANCO, Mallorca, 196. Tel. 253-10-33.
    Cuisine: SEAFOOD. **Reservations:** None. **Metro:** Hospital Clinic.

$ Prices: Appetizers 400–600 ptas. ($3.75–$5.65); main dishes 1,500–2,500 ptas. ($14.10–$23.50). V.

Open: Lunch Tues–Sat 1–3:45pm; dinner Tues–Sat 9–10:45pm. **Closed:** Aug. This old Barcelona standby, famous for its seafood, has long been popular among locals. The fluorescent-lit dining area does not offer much atmosphere, but the food is good, varied, and relatively inexpensive. The Little White Horse, in the Passeig de Gràcia area, features a huge selection, including *rape*, mussels marinara, and shrimp with garlic. If you don't want fish, try the grilled pork cutlets. Several different pâtés and salads are offered. There's a bar to the left of the dining area.

NEAR PARAL.LEL

CA L'ISIDRE, Les Flors, 12. Tel. 241-11-39.
Cuisine: CATALAN. **Reservations:** Required. **Metro:** Paral.lel.
$ Prices: Appetizers 1,000–3,000 ptas. ($9.40–$28.20); main dishes 1,500–3,500 ptas. ($14.10–$32.90). AE, MC, V.
Open: Lunch Mon–Sat 1:30–3:30pm; dinner Mon–Sat 8:30–11:30pm. **Closed:** Sat night in summer.

This is perhaps the most sophisticated Catalan bistro in Barcelona, drawing such patrons as King Juan Carlos and Queen Sophia. Opened in 1970, it has also been visited by Julio Iglesia and the famous Catalan band leader Xavier Cugat. Isidre Gironés, helped by his wife, Montserrat, is known for his market-fresh Catalonian cuisine. Flowers decorate the restaurant, along with artwork, and the array of food is beautifully prepared and served. Try spider crabs and shrimp, a gourmand salad with foie gras, sweetbreads with port and flap mushrooms, or a carpaccio of veal Harry's Bar style. Sometimes *espardenyes,* that increasingly rare sea creature, is served here. The selection of Spanish and Catalan wines is excellent.

SPECIALTY DINING

LOCAL BUDGET BETS

Tascas

ALT HEIDELBERG, Ronda Universitat, 5. Tel. 318-10-32.
Cuisine: TAPAS. **Metro:** Universitat.
$ Prices: Tapas 400–800 ptas. ($3.75–$7.50); combination plates 900 ptas. ($8.45). No credit cards.
Open: Daily 8am–2am.
For more than half a century this has been an institution in Barcelona, offering German beer on tap, a good selection of German sausages, and Spanish tapas. You can also enjoy meals here.

BAR DEL PI, Plaça Sant Josep Oriol, 1. Tel. 302-21-23.
Cuisine: TAPAS. **Metro:** Jaume I.
$ Prices: Tapas 175 ptas. ($1.65). No credit cards.
Open: Mon–Fri 9am–10pm, Sat 10am–3pm, Sun 5–9:30pm.
One of the most famous bars in the Barri Gòtic, this establishment lies midway between two medieval squares, opening onto Església del Pi. You can sit inside at one of the cramped bentwood tables or stand at the crowded bar. In warm weather, take a table beneath the single plane tree on this landmark square. Tapas are limited; most visitors come to drink coffee, beer, or wine.

BAR HISPANO, Passeig Nacional, 21. Tel. 319-02-97.
Cuisine: TAPAS. **Metro:** Barceloneta.
$ Prices: Tapas 400–1,000 ptas. ($3.75–$9.40). AE, DC, MC, V.
Open: Sun–Sat 9am–midnight.

You'll find this strictly unpretentious place—you'll dine at simple Formica tables—beside the harborfront road in a colorful area known as Platja Barceloneta. The array of food is so complete that neighborhood families arrive in large groups, camping out for a full meal of the delectably seasoned tapas, of which there are at least 30 kinds. These include tuna chunks, croquettes of minced fish, squid, Russian salad, and anchovies.

BAR TURÓ, Tenor Viñas, 1. Tel. 200-69-53.
   Cuisine: TAPAS. **Metro:** Muntaner.
$ **Prices:** Tapas 400–900 ptas. ($3.75–$8.45). No credit cards.
   Open: Daily 9am–1am.
Set in an affluent residential neighborhood north of the old town, this establishment serves some of the best tapas in town. In summer you can either sit outside or retreat to the narrow confines of the inside bar. There you can select from about 20 different kinds of tapas, including Russian salad, fried squid, and Serrano ham.

BODEGA LA PLATA, Mercè, 24. Tel. 315-10-09.
   Cuisine: TAPAS. **Metro:** Barceloneta.
$ **Prices:** Tapas 125 ptas. ($1.20). No credit cards.
   Open: Mon–Sat 8:30am–11pm.
Part of a trio of famous bodegas on this narrow medieval street, La Plata occupies a corner building whose two open sides allow richly aromatic cooking odors to permeate the neighborhood. This bodega contains a marble-topped bar and overcrowded tables. The culinary specialty is *raciones* (small plates) of deep-fried sardines (head and all). You can make a meal with two servings of these, coupled with the house's tomato, onion, and fresh anchovy salad.

BODEGUETA, Ramble de Catalunya, 100. Tel. 215-48-94.
   Cuisine: TAPAS. **Metro:** Diagonal.
   Open: Mon–Sat 8am–2am.
Founded in 1940, this old wine tavern specializes in Catalan sausage meats.

CAFÉ BAR PADAM, Rauric, 9. Tel. 302-50-62.
   Cuisine: TAPAS. **Metro:** Liceu.
$ **Prices:** Tapas 250–475 ptas. ($2.35–$4.45). No credit cards.
   Open: Mon–Sat 9am–1am.
The tapas served here are derived from time-honored Catalan culinary traditions, but the clientele and decor are modern, hip, and often gay. The café/bar lies on a narrow street in the Ciutat Vella, about 3 blocks east of the Ramble dels Caputxins. The only color in the black-and-white rooms comes from fresh flowers and modern paintings. Tapas include fresh anchovies and tuna, grilled squid, and cheese platters.

LAS CAMPANAS (Casa Marcos), Mercè, 21. Tel. 315-06-09.
   Cuisine: TAPAS. **Metro:** Barceloneta.
$ **Prices:** Tapas 175 ptas. ($1.65). No credit cards.
   Open: Thurs–Tues noon–2am.
No sign announces its name—from the street it looks like a storehouse for cured hams and wine bottles. At a long and narrow stand-up bar, patrons flock here for a *chorizo* (spicy sausage), which is then pinioned between two pieces of bread. Sausages are usually eaten with beer or red wine. The place opened in 1952, and nothing has changed since then. A tape recorder plays everything from Edith Piaf to the Andrew Sisters.

CASA TEJADA, Tenor Viñas, 3. Tel. 200-73-41.
   Cuisine: TAPAS. **Metro:** Muntaner.
$ **Prices:** Tapas 400–1,000 ptas. ($3.75–$9.40). No credit cards.
   Open: Thurs–Tues 7am–2am.
Covered with rough stucco and decorated with hanging hams, the Casa Tejada (established in 1964) offers some of Barcelona's best tapas. Arranged behind a glass display case, they include such specialties as marinated fresh tuna, German-style potato salad, five preparations of squid (including one that's stuffed), and ham salad.

For variety, quantity, and quality, this place is hard to beat. There's outdoor dining in summer.

GRAN BODEGA, València, 193. Tel. 318-85-77.
   Cuisine: TAPAS/CATALAN. **Metro:** Tarragona.
   $ Prices: Tapas 350 ptas. ($3.30); appetizers 600–1,700 ptas. ($5.65–$16); main dishes 1,550–1,950 ptas. ($14.55–$18.35). No credit cards.
   Open: Bar, Mon–Sat 8am–12:30am. Restaurant, lunch Mon–Sat 1–4pm; dinner Mon–Sat 9pm–midnight. **Closed:** Holidays.
This tapas bar, restaurant, deli, and food shop is an unusual place in the Eixample district. In business for half a century, it was once a wine tavern, as evidenced by the casks and bottles that are now part of the decor, along with a chandelier made from *porrones* (old glass wine jars with long spouts). The tapas, including seafood salad, octopus in a garlic mayonnaise sauce, cod fritters, and croquettes, are among the best in town. Two specialties: omelets cooked with zucchini, eggplant, spinach, and mushrooms; and anchovies from the port town of La Escala. In the back restaurant you can order full meals, sitting at either private or communal tables. The menu of skillfully prepared Catalan cuisine lists a number of daily specials. Main dishes include anglerfish Costa Brava style, duck with port wine, and veal cutlet bordelaise.

JAMÓN JAMÓN, Mestre Nicolau, 4. Tel. 209-41-03.
   Cuisine: TAPAS. **Metro:** Muntaner.
   $ Prices: Tapas 1,100–1,300 ptas. ($10.35–$12.20). No credit cards.
   Open: Mon–Sat 9am–4pm and 6pm–1am.
Located north of the Avinguda Diagonal, near the Plaça de Francesc Maria, this establishment has a modern interior of gray granite and chrome, a deliberate contrast to the traditional pork products that are the tasca's specialty. Entire hams from Heulva, deep in the south of Andalusia, are impaled upon steel braces, evoking the Spanish Inquisition. The ham is laboriously carved and trimmed before you into paper-thin slices.

LA JARRA, Mercè, 9. Tel. 315-17-59.
   Cuisine: TAPAS. **Metro:** Barceloneta.
   $ Prices: Tapas 175 ptas. ($1.65). No credit cards.
   Open: Thurs–Tues 10:30am–2am.
La Jarra occupies a tile-covered L-shaped room that's somewhat bleak in appearance, yet residents claim it is one of the most authentic tapas bars in the old town. You can order a ración of marinated mushrooms or well-seasoned artichokes Rioja style, but the culinary star is the ever-present haunch of *jamón canario* (Canary Island ham), which is carved before your eyes into lean, succulent morsels served with boiled potatoes, olive oil, and lots of salt. It resembles roast pork in flavor and appearance.

PINOCHO (Bar Kiosco), Mercat de la Boqueria. Tel. 317-17-31.
   Cuisine: TAPAS. **Metro:** Liceu.
   $ Prices: Tapas 250 ptas. ($2.35). No credit cards.
   Open: Mon–Sat 6am–6pm. **Closed:** 2 weeks in Aug.
This famous little hole-in-the-wall occupies a narrow stall (no. 66-67) among the fruit and vegetable vendors beneath the soaring iron roof of the most colorful marketplace of Barcelona. Owner Juan Bayan and his sister María serve filling portions of flavorful food, including *ensaladilla rusa* (Russian salad), freshly grilled sardines served with freshly baked bread, aromatic slices of *pa amb tomàquet* (bread rubbed with garlic and tomatoes), anchovy and avocado salad with pine nuts and raisins, and batter-fried artichokes. Enter the marketplace from the Rambles and turn right at the second alleyway.

REY DE LA GAMBA. Passeig Nacional, 46. Tel. 310-30-96.
   Cuisine: TAPAS. **Metro:** Barceloneta.
   $ Prices: Tapas 300 ptas. ($2.80). No credit cards.
   Open: Fri–Wed 11am–1am.
The name of this place means King of the Prawns, but it could also be called House of

Mussels since it sells even more of that shellfish. In the old fishing village of Barceloneta, dating from the 18th century, this place packs them in, especially on weekends. A wide array of seafood is sold, along with cured ham—the combination is considered a tradition.

FAST FOOD/CAFETERIAS

For those travelers who miss good ol' American food, don't fret—there are plenty of fast-food joints. It may not be as adventurous as trying authentic Spanish cuisine, but you'll definitely please the kids!

Burger King, Ramble de Canaletes, 135 (tel. 302-54-29; Metro: Plaça de Catalunya), is open Monday through Thursday from 10am to midnight; on Friday and Saturday from 10:30am to 1:30am; and on Sunday from 11am to midnight.

The **Chicago Pizza Pie Factory,** Carrer de Provença (tel. 215-94-15; Metro: Passeig de Gràcia), offers meals for around 1,400 to 1,800 pesetas ($13.35 to $16.90). It's open daily from noon to 1:30pm; happy hour runs from 5 to 7pm.

Viena, Ramble dels Estudis (tel. 317-1492; Metro: Plaça de Catalunya), is Barcelona's most elegant fast-food place. Waiters wearing Viennese vests serve croissants with Roquefort for breakfast and, later in the day, Bikinis (toasted ham sandwiches), hamburgers with onions, and pasta with tomato sauce. Meals cost from 500 pesetas ($4.70). Service is daily from 9am to 1am.

Kentucky Fried Chicken, Ferran, 2 (tel. 412-51-54; Metro: Drassanes), is open daily from 11am to midnight.

FOR THE SWEET TOOTH

DULCINEA, Via Petrixol, 2. Tel. 302-68-24.
   Cuisine: CHOCOLATE. **Metro:** Plaça de Catalunya or Liceu.
$ **Prices:** Cup of chocolate 200 ptas. ($1.90). No credit cards.
   Open: Mon–Sat 9am–1pm and 4:30–9pm.
At this, the most famous chocolate shop in Barcelona, the specialty is *melindros* (sugar-topped soft-sided biscuits), which the regulars who flock here love to dunk into the very thick hot chocolate—so thick, in fact, that imbibing it resembles eating a melted chocolate bar.

DEPARTMENT-STORE DINING

El Corte Inglés, Plaça de Catalunya, 14 (tel. 302-12-12; Metro: Plaça de Catalunya), and Avinguda Diagonal, 617 (tel. 322-40-11), offers combination plates and a buffet, with complete meals for 2,500 pesetas ($23.50).

Getting a table may be more of an adventure in **Galerías Preciados,** Avinguda Portal de l'Àngel, 19 (tel. 317-00-00; Metro: Plaça de Catalunya). Meals cost around 2,500 pesetas ($23.50). Both store restaurants have buffets Monday through Saturday from 12:30 to 4p.m.

AMERICAN

HENRY J. BEAN'S BAR AND GRILL, La Granada de Penedés, 14-16. Tel. 218-29-98.
   Cuisine: AMERICAN. **Reservations:** None. **Metro:** Diagonal.
$ **Prices:** Appetizers 600–950 ptas. ($5.65–$8.95); main dishes 1,000–1,800 ($9.40–$16.90). AE, DC, MC, V.
   Open: Daily 12:30pm–1am.
Food is cheap, plentiful, and savory, in this unassuming restaurant filled with Americana. Have a great smokehouse burger. Also available are chili con carne, stuffed mushrooms, nachos, and an array of barbecued beef and chicken. No meal is

complete without pecan or mud pie for dessert. Half-price drinks are de rigueur during happy hour, between 5 and 8pm.

VEGETARIAN

BIOCENTER, Pintor Fortuny, 24. Tel. 302-35-67.
   Cuisine: VEGETARIAN. **Reservations:** Not required. **Metro:** Liceu.
$ Prices: Appetizers 150–350 ptas. ($1.40–$3.30); main dishes 300–600 ptas. ($2.80–$5.65); fixed-priced menu 750 ptas. ($7.05). No credit cards.
   Open: Mon–Sat 1–5pm.
Off the Rambles, this vegetarian restaurant is intimate and inviting, the food a notch above most such fare. Diners help themselves to a salad bar, and they can then order hot main dishes.

GAY RESTAURANTS

TUTANKHAMON, Rauric, 12. Tel. 412-52-01.
   Cuisine: CATALAN. **Reservations:** Recommended. **Metro:** Liceu.
$ Prices: Appetizers 150–450 ptas. ($1.40–$4.25); main dishes 500–1,200 ptas. ($4.70–$11.30); fixed-priced menu 850–1,300 ptas. ($8–$12.20). MC, V.
   Open: Lunch Wed–Mon 1–4:30pm; dinner daily 7:30pm–1:30am.
This leading gay restaurant is on a narrow street near Sextienda, Rauric, 11, where you can find the gay information center and the first gay sex shop in Spain. At Tutankhamon you can order from a set menu or à la carte. Try the eggplant salad, shish kebab, grilled fish, or a shrimp dish. The place is attractively decorated with a granite bar, Andalusian chairs, and a tile floor. After dinner, you can drink in a number of bars nearby, many of which have a large gay clientele.

PICNIC FARE & WHERE TO EAT IT

The best place in all of Barcelona to buy the makings of your picnic is **Mercat de la Boqueria,** lying in the center of the Rambles (Metro: Liceu). This is the old marketplace of Barcelona. You'll jostle elbows with butchers and fishermongers in bloodied smocks and see saleswomen selling cheeses and sausages. Much of the food is uncooked, but hundreds of items are already prepared and you can even buy a bottle of wine or mineral water.

For choice ingredients, go to **Gran Bodega,** València, 193 (tel. 318-85-77; Metro: Terragona). Your food will be packaged and wrapped. (See "Specialty Dining," above.)

 # FROMMER'S COOL FOR KIDS
RESTAURANTS

Fast-Food Places Burger King (see p. 351), **Chicago Pizza Pie Factory** (see p. 351), and **Kentucky Fried Chicken** (see p. 351) are good bets for fast food.

Henry J. Bean's Bar and Grill (see p. 351) This place has sit-down meals that the kids will love.

Dulcinea (see p. 351) This makes a great refueling stop any time of the day—guaranteed to satisfy any chocoholic.

Poble Espanyol (see p. 361) A good introduction to Spanish food. All the restaurants here serve comparable food at comparable prices—let the kids choose what to eat.

A cheaper suggestion is stop in at a **Kentucky Fried Chicken,** Ferran, 2 (tel. 412-51-54; Metro: Drassanes), lying at the southern end of the Rambles.

Now for where to have your picnic. Right in the heart of Barcelona is the **Parc de la Ciutadella** (see "Parks and Gardens" in Chapter 15), at the southeast section of the district known as the Barri de la Ribera, site of the Picasso Museum. After lunch, take the kids to the park zoo and later go out on the lake in a rented rowboat.

It's more scenic to picnic in **Montjuïc,** site of the 1992 Olympics. After your picnic, you can enjoy the amusement park or walk through the Poble Espanyol, a re-created Spanish village.

WORTH THE EXTRA BUCKS

AGUT D'AVIGNON, Trinitat, 3. Tel. 302-60-34.
   Cuisine: CATALAN. **Reservations:** Required. **Metro:** Jaume I.
$ **Prices:** Appetizers 950–1,500 ptas. ($8.95–$14.10); main dishes 1,800–2,500 ptas. ($16.90–$23.50). AE, MC, V.
   Open: Lunch daily 1–3:30pm; dinner daily 9–11:30pm.

One of my favorite restaurants in Barcelona, it's located near the Plaça Reial, in a tiny alleyway (the cross street is Calle d'Avinyó, 8). A small 19th-century vestibule leads to the multilevel dining area that has two balconies and a main hall. You might need help translating the Catalan menu, which includes chilled cream of crabmeat soup, shrimp in cognac sauce, clams marinara, stuffed squid, monkfish stew, tournedos in a green-pepper sauce, entrecote with Roquefort, and a delectable sole with orange sauce.

EL DORADO PETIT, Dolors Monserdà, 51. Tel. 204-51-53.
   Cuisine: MEDITERRANEAN. **Reservations:** Required. **Metro:** Reina Elisenda.
$ **Prices:** Appetizers 1,000–2,800 ptas. ($9.40–$26.30); main dishes 2,000–3,000 ptas. ($18.80–$28.20); fixed-priced menu 3,000 ptas. ($28.20). AE, DC, MC, V.
   Open: Lunch Mon–Sat 1:30–4pm; dinner Mon–Sat 9pm–midnight. **Closed:** 2 weeks in Aug.

Located in a former private 19th-century villa, this restaurant serves a nouvelle, cuisine that's the rage of Barcelona. Very imaginative dishes are offered— carpaccio à la Harry's Bar, brochette of crayfish, lasagna of fresh asparagus and salmon, peppers stuffed with pâté of *rascasse* (Mediterranean fish), and original variations of pork, lamb, and fish dishes. Diners can sit in either the enclosed courtyard or the high-ceilinged champagne-colored dining room.

AZULETE, Via Augusta, 281. Tel. 203-59-43.
   Cuisine: INTERNATIONAL. **Reservations:** Required. **Metro:** Reina Elisenda.
$ **Prices:** Appetizers 975–1,500 ptas. ($9.15–$14.10); main dishes 2,500–3,000 ptas. ($23.50–$28.20). AE, DC, MC, V.
   Open: Lunch Mon–Fri 2–4pm; dinner Mon–Sat 9–11pm. **Closed:** Aug 1–15.
This is one of the more expensive restaurants listed, but also one of the best. It sits in a beautifully restored beaux arts house with a glassed-in garden and a ground-level salon that has been turned into one of the most elegant bars around. The menu is eclectic. You might begin with an artfully arranged fresh garden salad or with artichokes stuffed with crab. For a main course, try monkfish in champagne sauce or breast of duck in a honey sauce laced with sherry vinegar. You can also order lamb medallions on thyme cake, Catalan-style saddle of rabbit, and Peking-style lamb brains.

BARCELONA ATTRACTIONS

Barcelona, long a Mediterranean center of commerce, is fast emerging as one of the focal points of world tourism to Europe, a role that will reach its zenith at the 1992 Summer Olympic Games. Spain's second-largest city is also its most cosmopolitan and avant-garde.

Because its rich historical past extends back centuries into history, it is filled with landmark buildings and world-class museums offering many sightseeing opportunities. These include Antoni Gaudí's Church of the Holy Family, the Picasso Museum, Barcelona's Gothic cathedral, and Les Rambles, the famous tree-lined promenade cutting through the heart of the old quarter.

The capital of Catalonia, Barcelona sits at the northeast end of the Costa Brava, Spain's gateway on the Mediterranean, and a half-hour flight east will land you in one of the Balearic Islands—Majorca, Ibiza, or Minorca. You can also branch out from Barcelona to one of the cities of historic interest in its environs, including the old Roman city of Tarragona or the monastery at Montserrat.

To begin with, however, you will want to take in the artistic and intellectual aura of the unique seafaring city of Barcelona. The people take justifiable pride in their Catalan heritage, and they are eager to share it with you. Many of these sights can be covered on foot, and I have included a number of walking tours.

The multifaceted array of nightlife (Barcelona is a *big* bar town), shopping possibilities, and sports programs are also covered in this chapter, along with some organized tours, special events, and trips to the wine country of Catalonia. It makes for some hefty sightseeing, and you'll need plenty of time to take it all in, with or without the Olympic Games.

1. SUGGESTED ITINERARIES

IF YOU HAVE ONE DAY

Spend the morning following my walking tour of the **Gothic Quarter,** taking in all of the highlights of this ancient district. In the afternoon visit Antoni Gaudí's unfinished cathedral, **La Sagrada Familia,** before returning to the heart of the city for a walk down the Rambles. To cap your day, take the funicular to the spectacular fountains at **Montjuïc,** or go to the top of **Tibidabo** Mountain for an outstanding view of Barcelona and its harbor.

IF YOU HAVE TWO DAYS

Spend day one as described above. On day 2 visit the **Picasso Museum,** housed in two Gothic mansions. Then stroll through the district, the **Barri de la Ribera,** filled with Renaissance mansions. Follow this with a ride to the top of the **Columbus Monument** for a spectacular view of the harborfront. Have a seafood lunch at La Barceloneta, and in the afternoon stroll up the Rambles again. In the afternoon explore Montjuïc and visit the **Museu d'Art de Catalunya.** End the day with a meal at Los Caracoles, the most famous restaurant in the city, just off the Rambles.

IF YOU HAVE THREE DAYS

Spend days one and two as described above. On day three, make a pilgrimage to the monastery of **Montserrat** to see the venerated Black Virgin and a host of artistic and scenic attractions. Try to time your visit to hear the 50-member boys' choir.

IF YOU HAVE FIVE DAYS

Spend your first three days as described above. On day 4 take a morning walk in modernist Barcelona, and have lunch at a restaurant on the pier called Moll de la Fusta. In the afternoon visit Montjuïc again to tour the **Joan Miró museum** and walk through the **Poble Espanyol,** a miniature village created for the 1929 World's Fair. On day five take another excursion from the city. If you're interested in history, visit the former Roman city of **Tarragona** to the south. If you want to **unwind on a beach,** head south to Sitges or north to the Costa Brava to Tossà de Mar.

---

2. THE TOP ATTRACTIONS

LA SAGRADA FAMILIA, Mallorca, 401. Tel. 255-02-47.

⭐ Gaudí's incomplete masterpiece is one of the more idiosyncratic artworks of Spain—if you have time to see only one Catalan landmark, make it this one. Begun in 1882, and still incomplete at Gaudí's death in 1926, this incredible cathedral—the Church of the Holy Family—rates as one of the bizarre wonders of Spain. The lanquid, amorphous structure embodies the essence of Gaudí's style, which some have described as art nouveau run rampant. Work continues on the structure, but without any sure idea of what Gaudí intended. Some say that the cathedral will be completed in the mid-21st century.

Admission: 300 ptas. ($2.80), including 12-minute video about religious and secular works of Gaudí. Elevator takes you to top (about 200 feet) for additional 75 ptas. (70¢).

Open: July 1–Sept daily 9am–8pm; Oct–June daily 9am–7pm. **Metro:** Sagrada Família.

CATHEDRAL OF BARCELONA, Plaça de la Seu, s/n. Tel. 315-35-55.

⭐ Barcelona's cathedral stands as a celebrated example of Catalonian Gothic. Except for the 19th-century west façade, the basilica was begun at the end of the 13th century and completed in the mid-15th century. The three naves, recently cleaned and illuminated, have splendid Gothic details. With its large bell towers, its blending of medieval and Renaissance styles, its beautiful cloister, high altar, side chapels, sculptured choir, and Gothic arches, it ranks as one of the most impressive cathedrals in Spain. Vaulted galleries in the cloister surround a charming garden of magnolias, medlars, and palm trees; the galleries are further enhanced by exquisitely forged iron grilles. The historian Cirici called this place the loveliest oasis in Barcelona. The cloister, effectively illuminated on Saturdays and fiesta days, also

BARCELONA

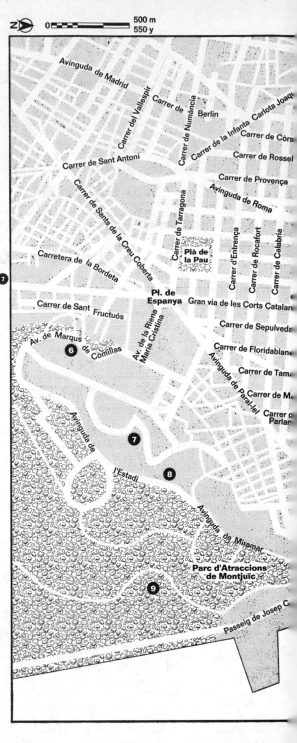

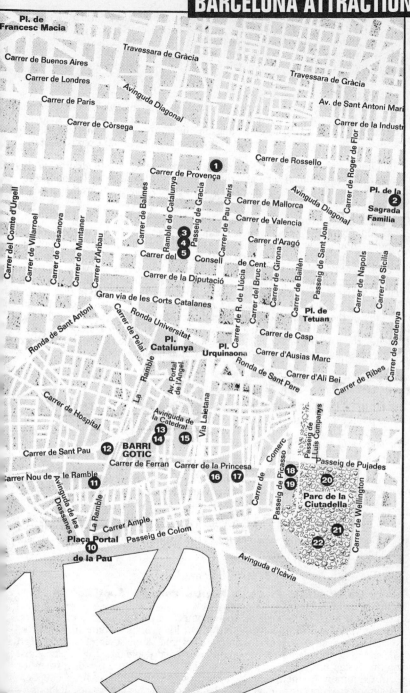

Pl. de Francesc Macia

Carrer de Buenos Aires

Travessara de Gràcia

Carrer de Londres

Travessara de Gràcia

Carrer de Paris

Avinguda Diagonal

Av. de Sant Antoni Mari

Carrer de Còrsega

Carrer de la Industr

Carrer de Rossello

Carrer de Roger de Flor

❶ Carrer de Provença

Avinguda Diagonal

Pl. de la ❷

Carrer de Balmes

Rambla de Catalunya

Passeig de Gracia

Carrer de Pau Claris

Carrer de Mallorca

Sagrada Familia

Carrer de Valencia

Carrer d'Aragó

Passeig de Sant Joan

Carrer de Napols

Carrer de Sicilia

Carrer del Comte d'Urgell

Carrer de Villarroel

Carrer de Casanova

Carrer de Muntaner

Carrer d'Aribau

❸ ❹ ❺

Consell

Carrer del

de Cent

Carrer de Girona

Carrer del Bruc

Carrer de Bailen

Carrer de la Diputació

Carrer de R. de Llúcia

Gran via de les Corts Catalanes

Carrer de Sardenya

Ronda de Sant Antoni

Carrer de Pelai

Ronda Universitat

Pl. Catalunya

Pl. de Tetuan

Carrer de Casp

Pl. Urquinaona

Carrer d'Ausias Marc

La Ramble

Av. Portal de l'Angel

Ronda de Sant Pere

Carrer d'Ali Bei

Carrer de Ribes

Carrer de Hospital

Avinguda de la Catedral

Via Laietana

❶❸ ❶❹ ❶❺

BARRI GOTIC

Carrer de Sant Pau

❶❷

Passeig de Pujades

Carrer de Ferran

Carrer de la Princesa

Passeig de Comerc

Passeig de Luis Companys

Carrer Nou de le Ramble

❶❻ ❶❼

Carrer de

❶❽

❷⓿

La Ramble

Avinguda de les Drasanes

❶❶

Carrer Ample

❶❾

Passeig de Picasso

Parc de la Ciutadella

Carrer de Wellington

Plaça Portal

Passeig de Colom

❷❶

❶⓿

de la Pau

❷❷

Avinguda d'Icàvia

contains a museum of medieval art. The most notable work displayed is the 15th-century *La Pietat* of Bartolomé Bermejo. At noon on Sunday you can see a *sardana*, the Catalonian folk dance, performed in front of the cathedral.

Admission: Cathedral free; museum 25 ptas. (25¢).

Open: Cathedral 7:30am–1:30pm and 4–7:30pm; cloister museum 11am–1pm. **Metro:** Jaume I.

BARRI GÒTIC

This is the old aristocratic quarter of Barcelona, parts of which have survived from the Middle Ages. Spend at least two or three hours exploring its narrow streets and squares; start by walking up the Carrer del Carme, east of the Rambles. A nighttime stroll takes on added drama, but you should exercise extreme caution.

The buildings, for the most part, are austere and sober, the cathedral being the crowning achievement. Roman ruins and the vestiges of 3rd-century walls add further interest. This area is intricately detailed and filled with many attractions that are easy to miss. For a tour of the Barri Gòtic, see Walking Tour 1, below.

MUSEU PICASSO, Montcada, 15-19. Tel. 319-63-10.

Two old converted palaces on a medieval street have been turned into a museum housing works by Pablo Picasso, who donated some 2,500 of his paintings, engravings, and drawings to the museum in 1970. Picasso was particularly fond of Barcelona, the city where he spent much of his formative youth. In fact, some of the paintings were done when Picasso was 9. One portrait, dating from 1896, depicts his stern aunt, Tía Pepa. Another, completed at the turn of the century when Picasso was 16, depicts *Science and Charity* (his father was the model for the doctor). Many of the works, especially the early paintings, show the artist's debt to van Gogh, El Greco, and Rembrandt; a famous series, *Las Meninas* (1957), is said to "impersonate" the work of Velázquez. From his blue period, the *La Vie* drawings are perhaps the most interesting. His notebooks contain many sketches of Barcelona scenes.

Admission: 400 ptas. ($3.75).

Open: Tues–Sat 9am–8pm. **Metro:** Jaume I.

MUSEU D' ART DE CATALUNYA, Parc de Montjuïc. Tel. 423-18-24.

At some point during your visit to the park, take in the Museum of Catalonian Art at the National Palace. Catalonian Gothic retables (including examples by the Serras), wood carvings, and paintings; a huge collection of religious works from the Spanish and European Renaissance; and an impressive collection of Romanesque murals—all are featured. Particular works of note are a 12th-century painted altarpiece depicting a saint being tortured and other Bosch-like scenes of horror; fragments of 12th-century decorative murals from the Church of Santa María de Taüll (Lérida); *God the Majesty*, a 12th-century concave fresco from San Clemente de Taüll, considered by some to be the pinnacle of 12th-century art.

You can also find an interesting alabaster 15th-century Virgin; Jaume Cirera's well-known painting of *Angels and Demons* (1433); and pictures by Lluís Dalmau, Jaume Huguet, and El Greco.

Admission: 400 ptas. ($3.75).

Open: Tues–Sun 9am–2pm. **Metro:** Espanya.

FUNDACIÓ JOAN MIRÓ, Plaça de Neptu, Parc de Montjuïc. Tel. 329-19-08.

Born in 1893, Joan Miró went on to become one of Spain's greatest painters, known for his whimsical abstract forms and his brilliant colors. Some 10,000 works by this Catalan surrealist, including paintings, graphics, and sculptures, have been collected here. The foundation building has been greatly expanded in recent years, following the design of Catalan architect Josep Lluís Sert, a close personal friend of Miró's. An exhibition in a new wing charts (in a variety of media) Miró's complete artistic evolution from his first drawings at the age of 8 to his last works. Temporary exhibitions on contemporary art are also frequently shown.

Admission: 300 ptas. ($2.80).
Open: Tues–Sat 11am–8pm, Sun 10:30–2:30pm. **Bus:** 61 at Plaça d'Espanya.

3. MORE ATTRACTIONS

MAINLY MUSEUMS

MUSEU FREDERIC MARÉS, Plaça de Sant Iú, s/n. Tel. 310-58-00.
　　One of the biggest repositories of medieval sculpture in the region is the Frederic
Marés Museum, located just behind the cathedral. It's housed in an ancient palace
whose interior courtyards, chiseled stone, and soaring ceilings are impressive in their
own right, an ideal setting for the hundreds of polychrome sculptures. The art dates
from pre-Roman times to the 19th century.
　　Admission: 200 ptas. ($1.80).
　　Open: Tues–Sun 9am–2pm, Tues–Sat 4–7pm. **Metro:** Jaume I.

MUSEU MARÍTIM, Portal de la Pau, 1. Tel. 301-18-31.
　　At the edge of the harbor near the southern end of the Rambles, this maritime
museum, with its stone-vaulted ceilings, displays figureheads and nautical instruments

FROMMER'S FAVORITE
BARCELONA EXPERIENCES

A Walk Through the Barri Gòtic *(see p. 365)* Fifteen centuries of
history in one district.

Watching the Sardana, The national dance of Catalonia is performed
at noon at the Plaça de San Jaume, in front of the cathedral.

A Trip to the Top of Montjuïc Enough amusement to fill three days.

Soaking Up Bar Culture Bars in all shapes and sizes are the chic places
to go at night. Barcelona has more bars than any other city in Spain.

Drinking Cava in a Xampanyería Enjoy a glass of bubbly—Barcelona
style. The wines are excellent, and Catalans swear that they taste better than
French champagne.

A Tour of Barcelona's Harbor From the pier in front of the
Columbus Monument to the breakwater. Call 310-03-82 for information.

Museu Picasso *(see p. 358)* This museum allows you to see the birth of a
genius from the age of 14.

La Sagrada Família *(see p. 355)* Gaudí's "sandcastle cathedral"—a
testimony to the architect's talent and religious belief.

Museu d'Art de Catalunya *(see p. 358)* One of the world's great
collections of medieval art, all rescued from crumbling old churches in
Catalonia.

Fundació Joan Miró *(see p. 358)* A museum on a mountain (Montjuïc),
housing drawings, tapestries, paintings, and sculptures of this Catalan master.

Poble Espanyol *(see p. 361)* An artificial village, to be sure, but a chance
to see the architecture of all of Spain without leaving Barcelona.

and artifacts. The most outstanding exhibition here is a reconstruction of *La Galería Real* of Don Juan of Austria, a lavish royal galley. As of this writing, no one is permitted to go aboard. Another special exhibit features a map by Gabriel de Vallseca that was owned by explorer Amerigo Vespucci. The nautical displays are housed in a 14th-century royal boatyard, called Drassanes Reials.

Admission: 100 ptas. (95¢).
Open: Tues–Sat 9:30am–1pm and 4–7pm, Sun 9:30am–1pm. **Closed:** Holidays. **Metro:** Drassanes.

FUNDACIÓ ANTONI TÀPIES, Aragó, 299. Tel. 487-00-09.

When this museum opened in 1990, it became the third museum in Barcelona devoted to the work of a single artist. In 1984 the Catalan artist Antoni Tàpies set up the foundation bearing his name, and the city of Barcelona donated an ideal site: the old Montaner i Simon publishing house near the Passeig de Gràcia in the 19th-century Eixample. One of the landmark buildings of Barcelona, the brick-and-iron structure was built between 1881 and 1884 by that exponent of Catalan modernism, architect Lluís Domènech i Montaner. The core of the museum is a collection of works by Tàpies (most contributed by the artist himself), covering the different stages of his career as it evolved into abstract expressionism. Here you can see his entire spectrum of mediums: painting, assemblage, sculpture, drawing, and ceramics. His associations with Picasso and Miró are apparent. The largest of all of Tàpies' works is on top of the building itself: a gigantic sculpture made from 9,000 feet of metal wiring and tubing, entitled *Cloud and Chair*.

Admission: 400 ptas. ($3.75).
Open: Tues–Sun 11am–8pm. **Metro:** Passeig de Gràcia.

MUSEU D'ART MODERN, Plaça d'Armes, Parc de la Ciutadella. Tel. 319-57-28.

This museum shares a wing of the Palau de la Ciutadella with the Catalonian Parliament. Constructed in the 1700s, it once formed part of the Barcelona's defenses, as it was used as an arsenal. In time it became a royal residence before being turned into a museum early in this century. Its collection of art focuses on the early 20th century and features the work of Catalan artists, including Martí Alsina, Vayreda, Casas, Fortuny, and Rusiñol. The collection also encompasses some 19th-century Romantic and neoclassical works, as well as modernist furniture (including designs by the architect Puig i Cadafalch).

Admission: 400 ptas. ($3.75).
Open: Mon 3–7pm; Tues–Sat 9am–7:30pm, Sun 9am–2pm. **Metro:** Arc de Triomf.

MONESTIR DE PEDRALBES, Baixada Monestir, 9. Tel. 203-92-82.

One of the oldest buildings in Pedralbes (the city's wealthiest residential area) is this monastery founded in 1326 by Elisenda de Montcada, queen of Jaume II. Still a convent, the establishment is also the mausoleum of the queen, who is buried in its Gothic church. Walk through the cloisters, with nearly two dozen arches on each side, rising three stories high. A small chapel contains the chief treasure of the monastery, murals by Ferrer Bassa, who was considered the major artist of Catalonia in the 1300s.

Admission: 200 ptas. ($1.90).
Open: Tues–Sun 9:30am–2pm. **Bus:** 22, 64, or 75.

MUSEU PALAU REIAL DE PEDRALBES, Avinguda Diagonal, 686. Tel. 203-75-01.

Set in a beautiful park, this palace was constructed as a municipal gift to King Alfonso XIII. He didn't get to make much use of it, however, as he was forced into exile in 1931. Many of its furnishings and objets d'art were imported from Italy. Much personal memorabilia of the royal family remains. Some local visitors come here just to walk through the gardens, which have ornamental statues and charming

fountains. There's a **Museo de las Carrozas** on the grounds, with some antique carriages.
Admission: 200 ptas. ($1.90).
Open: Tues–Fri 10am–1pm and 4–6pm, Sat–Sun 10am–1:30pm. **Metro:** Palau Reial.

PALAU REIAL, Plaça del Rei. Tel. 315-09-57.

Former palace of the Counts of Barcelona, this later became the residence of the kings of Aragón—hence, the name of its plaza (Kings' Square). It is believed that Columbus was received here by Isabella and Ferdinand when he returned from his first voyage to the New World. Here, some believe, the monarchs got their first look at a Native American. Columbus may have been received in the Saló del Tinell, a banqueting hall with a wood-paneled ceiling held up by half a dozen arches. The hall dates from the 14th century. Rising five stories above the hall is the Torre del Reí Martí, a series of porticoed galleries.
Admission: 200 ptas. ($1.90).
Open: Mon–Sat 9am–8pm, Sun 9am–1:30pm. **Bus:** 16, 17, 19, 22, or 45.

MUSEU D'HISTÒRIA DE LA CIUTAT, Plaça del Rei. Tel. 221-01-44.

Connected to the Royal Palace (see above), this museum traces the history of the city from its early days as a Carthaginian seaport to its up-and-coming role as the city of the Olympics. The museum is housed in a Catalan Mediterranean mansion from the 1400s called the Padellás House. Many of the exhibits date from Roman days, with much else from the time of the Muslims and various relics from the Middle Ages.
Admission: 300 ptas. ($2.80).
Open: Mon–Sat 9am–8pm, Sun 9am–1:30pm. **Bus:** 16, 17, 19, 22, or 45.

MUSEU ARQUEOLÒGIC, Lérida, Parc de Montjuïc. Tel. 233-21-49.

This museum at Montjuïc occupies the former Palace of Graphic Arts built for the 1929 World's Fair. It reflects the long history of this Mediterranean port city, beginning with prehistoric Iberian artifacts. The collection includes articles from the Greek, Roman (glass, ceramics, mosaics, bronzes), and Carthaginian periods. Some of the more interesting relics were excavated in the ancient Greco-Roman city of Empúries in Catalonia, and other parts of the collection came from the Balaeric Islands.
Admission: 200 ptas. ($1.90).
Open: Tues–Sat 9:30am–1pm and 4–7pm, Sun 9:30am–2pm. **Metro:** Espanya.

POBLE ESPANYOL, Marqués de Comillas, Parc de Montjuïc. Tel. 325-78-66.

In this re-created Spanish village, built for the 1929 World's Fair, various regional architectural styles—from the Levante to Galicia—are reproduced. At the entrance-way, for example, stands a facsimile of the gateway to the walled city of Ávila. The center of the village has an outdoor café where you can sit and have drinks. Numerous shops sell crafts and souvenir items from all of the provinces, and in some of them, you can see artists at work, printing fabric and blowing glass. The village also has restaurants and bars, daily concerts, and an audiovisual presentation about the town.
Admission: 400 pesetas ($3.75).
Open: Daily 9am–4am (when last bars close). **Metro:** Espanya, then free red double-decker bus.

MONUMENT A COLOM, Portal de la Pau. Tel. 302-52-34.

This monument to Christopher Columbus was erected at the harborfront of Barcelona on the occasion of the Universal Exhibition of 1888. It is divided into three parts, the first being a circular structure, raised by four stairways (19½ feet wide) and eight iron heraldic lions. On the plinth are eight bronze bas-reliefs depicting the principal feats of Columbus. (The originals were destroyed—the present ones are copies.) The second part is the base of the column, consisting of an eight-sided polygon, four sides of which act as buttresses; each side contains sculptures. The third part is formed by the column itself, Corinthian in style and rising 167 feet. The capital boasts representations of Europe, Asia, Africa, and America—all linked together. Finally, over a princely crown and a hemisphere recalling the newly discovered part of the globe, is a 25-foot-high bronze statue of Columbus himself by Rafael Ataché. Inside the iron column, an elevator ascends to the mirador. From there, a panoramic view of Barcelona and its harbor unfolds.

Admission: 175 ptas. ($1.65).
Open: Daily 10am–2pm and 3:30–6:30pm. **Metro:** Drassanes.

PARKS & GARDENS

Barcelona isn't about dark and stuffy museums. Much of its life takes place outside, in its parks and gardens through which you'll want to stroll. Each one is different.

PARC GÜELL, Carrer del Carmel. Tel. 214-64-46.

Begun by Gaudí as a real-estate venture for a wealthy friend, Count Eusebi Güell, a well-known Catalan industrialist of his day, this development was never completed. Only two houses were constructed, but it makes for an interesting excursion nonetheless. The city took over the property in 1926 and turned it into a public park.

One of the houses, **Casa Museo Gaudí** (tel. 317-52-21), contains models, furniture, drawings, and other memorabilia of the architect. Gaudí, however, did not design the house. Ramón Berenguer took that honor. Admission is 125 pesetas ($1.20). The museum can be visited Sunday through Friday from 10am to 2pm and 4 to 6pm.

Gaudí completed several of the public areas, which today look like a surrealist Disneyland, complete with a mosaic pagoda and a lizard fountain spitting water. Originally, Gaudí planned to make this a model community of 60 dwellings, somewhat like the arrangement of a Greek theater. A central grand plaza with its market below was built, as well as an undulating bench decorated with ceramic fragments. The bizarre Doric columns of the would-be market are hollow, part of Gaudí's drainage system.

Admission: Free.
Open: Summer, daily 9am–8pm; winter, daily 10am–6pm. **Metro:** Lesseps.

TIBIDABO MOUNTAIN

At the top of Tibidabo Mountain, at 1,600 feet, you'll have a spectacular view of Barcelona. The ideal time to visit this summit north of the port (the culmination of the Sierra de Collcerola), is at sunset, when the city lights are on. An amusement park—with Ferris wheels swinging over Barcelona—has been opened here. There's also a church in this carnival-like setting, called Sacred Heart, plus restaurants and mountaintop hotels. From the Plaça de Catalunya, take a bus to the Avinguda del Tibidabo, where you can board a special bus that will transport you to the funicular. You can hop aboard and scale the mountain.

Admission: Tibidabo funicular 250 ptas. ($2.35) round trip.
Open: See "Cool for Kids," below, for details on the Parc d'Atraccions.

MONTJUÏC

Located in the south of the city, the mountain park of Montjuïc (Montjuch in Spanish) has splashing fountains, gardens, outdoor restaurants, and museums, making for quite an outing. The re-created village, the Poble Espanyol, and the Joan Miró Foundation are also within the park. There are many walks and vantage points for viewing the Barcelona skyline.

The park will be the site of several events during the 1992 Olympics. An impressive illuminated fountain display, the Fuentes Luminosas at Plaça de la Font Màgica, near the Plaça d'Espanya, is on view from 8 to 11pm every Saturday and Sunday from

October to May, and from 9pm to midnight on Thursday, Saturday, and Sunday from June to September.

Open: See individual attractions in the park for various hours of opening. **Bus:** 61 from Plaça d'Espanya, or Montjuïc funicular.

PARC DE LA CIUTADELLA, at edge of Barri de la Ribera.

This is called the Park of the Citadel because it is the site of a former fortress that defended the city. After winning the War of the Spanish Succession (Barcelona was on the losing side), Philip V got his revenge. He ordered that the "traitorous" residential suburb be leveled. In its place rose a citadel. In the mid-19th century it, too, was leveled, though some of the architectural evidence of that past remains in a governor's palace and an arsenal. Today most of the park is filled with lakes, gardens, and promenades, including a zoo (see "Cool for Kids," below) and the Museu d'Art Modern (see "Other Attractions," above). Gaudí is said to have contributed to the monumental "great fountain" in the park when he was a student.

Admission: Free.

Open: Daily 24 hours (but don't go wandering around here late at night). **Metro:** Ciutadella.

PARC DE JOAN MIRÓ

Lying in the vicinity of the Plaça d'Espanya, this park, dedicated to Joan Miró, one of the most famous artists of Catalonia, occupies a whole city block. One of Barcelona's newest parks and one of its most popular, it is often called Parc de l'Escorxador (slaughter house), a reference to what the park used to be. Its main features are an esplanade and a pond from which a spectacular sculpture by Miró, *Woman and Bird,* rises up. Palm, pine, and eucalyptus trees, as well as playgrounds and pergolas, complete the picture.

Open: Throughout the day. **Metro:** Espanya.

4. COOL FOR KIDS

The Catalans have a great affection for children, and although many of the attractions of Barcelona are for adults only, there is an array of amusements designed for the young or the young at heart.

PARC ZOOLOGIC, Parc de la Ciutadella. Tel. 309-25-00.

Modern, with barless enclosures, this ranks as Spain's top zoo. One of the most unusual attractions is the famous albino gorilla, Snowflake (Copito de Nieve), the only one of its kind in captivity in the world. The main entrances to the Ciutadella Park are via the Passeig de Pujades and Passeig de Picasso.

Admission: Mon–Sat 600 ptas. ($5.65); children under 3 free.

Open: Summer, daily 9:30am–7:30pm; winter, 10am–5pm. **Metro:** Ciutadella.

PARC D'ATRACCIONS, Parc de Montjuïc. Tel. 242-31-75.

This place becomes a festival in summer, with open-air concerts and more than three dozen rides for the kiddies. Everything is set against a spectacular view of Barcelona and its harbor. Children love the nightly illuminated fountain displays and the music.

Admission: 300 ptas. ($2.80); ticket for all rides 1,200 ptas. ($11.30).

Open: Summer, Tues–Fri 6pm–midnight, Sat 6pm–1am, Sun noon–midnight (hours subject to change); winter, Sat–Sun noon–8pm. **Transportation:** Metro to Paral.lel, then funicular.

PARC D'ATRACCIONS, Cumbre del Tibidabo. Tel. 211-79-42.

On top of Tibidabo, Ferris wheels swing out over Barcelona 1,600 feet above sea level. There's even an *aeroplano* from the 1920s. In summer the place takes on a carnival-like setting.
Admission: 350 ptas. ($3.30) with three attractions included; ticket for all rides 1,300 ptas. ($12.20). **Transportation:** Ferrocarrils de la Generalitat to Tramvia Blau (Blue Streetcar), then the funicular.
Open: Apr–Sept, Mon–Sat 4:30pm–12:30am, Sun and holidays noon–12:30am; Oct–Mar, Sat–Sun 11am–8pm.

POBLE ESPANYOL, Marqués de Comillas, Parc de Montjuïc. Tel. 325-78-66.
Kids compare a visit here to a Spanish version of Disneyland (see Section 3 of this chapter). Frequent fiestas enliven the place, and it's fun for everybody, young and old.

5. SPECIAL-INTEREST SIGHTSEEING

FOR THE ARCHITECTURE ENTHUSIAST

The **Casa Milà,** Passeig de Gràcia, 92 (tel. 215-33-98; Metro: Passeig de Gràcia), commonly called La Pedrera, is the most famous apartment house complex in Spain. Antoni Gaudí's imagination went wild in planning its construction; he even included vegetables and fruit shapes in his sculptural designs. Controversial and much criticized upon its completion, today it stands as a classic example of modernist architecture. The ironwork around the balconies forms an intricate maze, and the main gate has windowpanes shaped like eggs. The rooftop is filled with phantasmagorical chimneys known in Spanish as *espantabrujas* (witch-scarers). Tours of the famous rooftops are available hourly Monday through Friday from 10am to 1pm and 4 to 5pm, on Saturday from 10am to noon, and on alternate Sundays from 11am only. From the rooftop, you'll also have a view of Gaudí's unfinished cathedral, La Sagrada Familia.

The **Casa Lleó Morera,** Passeig de Gràcia, 35 (tel. 255-44-77; Metro: Passeig de Gràcia), lying between the Carrer del Consell de Cent and the Carrer d' Aragó, is one of the most famous buildings of the modernist movement. It comprises one of the trio of structures called the Mançana de la Discòrdia (Block of Discord), an allusion to the mythical judgment of Paris. Three of the most famous modernist architects of Barcelona, including Gaudí, competed with their various works along this block. In florid modernist design, the Casa Lleó, designed by Domènech i Montaner in 1905, was considered extremely revolutionary in its day. Perhaps that assessment still stands. Today the building is the headquarters of Patronato de Turismo. Go inside for a look at the florid stairwell.

Constructed in a cubical design, with a Dutch gable, the **Casa Amatller,** Passeig de Gràcia, 41 (tel. 216-01-75; Metro: Passeig de Gràcia), was created by Puig i Cadafalch in 1900. It stands in sharp contrast to its neighbor, the Gaudí-designed Casa Batlló. The architecture of the Casa Amatller, actually imposed on an older structure, is a vision of ceramics, wrought iron, and sculptures. Admission to the Gothic-style interior is free, anytime Monday through Friday from 10am to 2pm and 4 to 8pm.

Next door to the Casa Amatller, the **Casa Batlló,** Passeig de Gràcia, 43 (tel. 204-52-50; Metro: Passeig de Gràcia), was designed by Gaudí in 1905. With "sensuous" curves in iron and stone, the architect created a lavish baroque exuberance in the façade. The balconies have been compared to "sculptured waves." The upper part of the façade evokes animal forms, and delicate tiles spread across the design. A polychromatic exterior extraordinaire. The downstairs building is the headquarters of an insurance company. Although visitors are not always welcome, many tourists walk inside for a view of Gaudí's interior, which is basically as he designed it. Since this *is* a place of business, be discreet.

The **Casa de la Ciutat Ayuntamiento,** Plaça de Sant Jaume (Metro: Jaume I), originally constructed at the end of the 14th century, is considered one of the best examples of Gothic civil architecture in the Catalan Mediterranean style. Across this landmark square from the Palau de la Generalitat, it has been endlessly renovated and changed since its original construction. Behind a neoclassical façade, the building has a splendid courtyard and staircase. Its major architectural highlights are the 15th-century Salón de Ciento (Room of the 100 Jurors) and the *Salón de las Cronicas* (Room of the Chronicles), the latter decorated with black marble. The Salón de Ciento, in particular, represents a medley of styles. You can enter the building Monday through Saturday from 9:30am to 1:30pm and 4:30 to 7:30pm; it is closed from mid-December to mid-January.

6. WALKING TOURS

You'll need public transportation to see all of Barcelona, since it sprawls for miles in all directions. But along the harborfront, in the Gothic Quarter, and in the 19th-century Eixample, on foot is the best way to go.

WALKING TOUR 1 — Gothic Quarter

Start: Plaça Nova

Finish: Plaça de la Seu.

Time: 3 hours.

Best Time: Any sunny day.

Begin at the:

1. **Plaça Nova,** set within the shadow of the cathedral. This is the largest open-air space in the Gothic Quarter and the usual site of the Barcelona flea market. Opening onto this square is the Portal del Bisbe, a gate flanked by two round towers that have survived from the ancient Roman wall that once stood here. From the Plaça Nova, climb the incline of the narrow asphalt-covered street (Carrer del Bisbe) lying between these massive walls. On your right, notice the depth of the foundations, which indicates how much the city has risen since the wall was constructed.

    At the approach of the first street, the Carrer de Santa Llúcia, turn left, noticing the elegant simplicity of the corner building with its Romanesque façade, the:

2. **Capilla de Santa Llúcia,** open daily from 8am to 1:30pm and 4 to 7:30pm. Its solidly graceful portal and barrel-vaulted interior were completed in 1268. Continue down the Carrer de Santa Llúcia a few paces, noticing the:

3. **Casa d'Ardiaca (Archdeacon's House),** constructed in the 15th century as a residence for Archdeacon Despla. The Gothic building has sculptural reliefs with Renaissance motifs. In its cloisterlike courtyard are a fountain and a palm tree. Notice the mail slot, where five swallows and a turtle carved into stone await the arrival of important messages. Since 1919 this building has been home to the **Municipal d'Història de la Ciutat (Municipal Institute of the History of the City).** As you exit the Archdeacon's House, continue in the same direction several steps until you reach the:

4. **Plaça de la Seu,** the square in front of the main entrance to the **Cathedral of Barcelona** (see "Top Attractions," above). Here you can stand and admire the façade of Mediterranean Gothic architecture. On each side of the Plaça de la Seu, you can see the remains of Roman walls. After touring the cathedral, exit from the door you entered and turn right onto the Carrer des Comtes, admiring the gargoyles along the way. In about 100 paces, you'll approach the:

5. Museu Frederic Marés on Plaça de Sant Iú. On the lower floors are Punic and Roman artifacts, but most of the museum is devoted to the works of this Catalan sculptor. Exit through the same door you entered and continue your promenade in the same direction. You'll pass the portal of the cathedral's side where the heads of two rather abstract angels flank the throne of a seated female saint. A few paces farther, notice the stone facade of the:

6. Arxiu de la Carona d'Aragó, the archives building of the crown of Aragón. Formerly called Palacio del Lugarteniente (Deputy's Palace), this Gothic building was the work of Antonio Carbonell. On some maps it also appears as the Palacio de los Virreyes (Palace of the Viceroys). The palace contains medieval and royal documents. Enter its courtyard, admiring the century-old grape vines. Then climb the 11 monumental steps to your left, facing a modern bronze sculpture by a Catalan artist. It represents with a rather abstract dateline and map, the political history and imperial highlights of Catalonia.

As you exit from the courtyard, you'll find yourself back on the Carrer des Comtes. Continue in the same direction, turning left at the intersection of the Baixada de Santa Clara. This street, in 1 short block, will bring you to one of the most famous squares of the Gothic Quarter, the:

7. Plaça del Rei. The Great Royal Palace, an enlarged building of what was originally the residence of the Counts of Barcelona, stands at the bottom of this square. Here at the King's Square you can visit both the **Palau Reial** and the **Museu d'Història de la Ciutat** (see "Other Attractions," above). On the right side of the square stands the **Palatine Chapel of Santa Àgata,** a 14th-century Gothic temple that is part of the Palau Reial. In this chapel is preserved the altarpiece of the Lord High Constable, a 15th-century work by Jaume Huguet.

Retrace your steps up the Baixada de Santa Clara, crossing the Carrer des Comtes, and continue straight to the Carrer de la Pietat, which will skirt the semicircular, massively buttressed rear of the cathedral. With the buttresses of the cathedral's rear to your right, pass the 14th-century:

8. Casa del Canonge (House of the Canon), opening onto the Calle Arzobispo Irurita, s/n. This building was erected in the Gothic style and restored in 1929; escutcheons from the 15th and 16th centuries remain. Notice the heraldic symbols of medieval Barcelona on the building's stone plaques—twin towers supported by winged goats with lion's feet. On the same façade, also notice the depiction of twin angels. The building today is used as a women's training school, the Escola Professional per a la Doña.

Continue walking along the Carrer de la Pietat, which makes a sudden sharp left. Notice the carved *Pietà* above the Gothic portal leading into the rear of the cathedral. Continue walking straight. One block later, turn left onto the Carrer del Bisbe and continue downhill. Your path will lead you beneath one of the most charming bridges in Spain. Carved into lacy patterns of stonework, it connects the Casa del Canonge with the Palau de la Generalitat.

Continue walking until the Carrer del Bisbe opens into the:

9. Plaça de Sant Jaume, in many ways the political heart of Catalan culture. Across this square, constructed at what was once a major junction for two Roman streets, race politicians and bureaucrats intent on Catalonian government affairs. On Sunday evenings you can witness the dance of the sardana, the national dance of Catalonia. Many bars and restaurants stand on side streets leading from this square. Standing in the square, with your back to the street you just left (Carrer del Bisbe), you'll see, immediately on your right, the Doric portico of the **Palau de la Generalitat,** the parliament of Catalonia. With its large courtyard and open-air stairway, along with twin arched galleries, this exquisite work in the Catalonian Gothic style began construction in the era of Jaume I. A special feature of the building is the Chapel of St. George, built in flamboyant Gothic style between 1432 and 1435, and enlarged in 1620 with the addition of vaulting and a cupola with hanging capitals. The back of the building encloses an orangery courtyard begun in 1532. In the Salón Dorado, the Proclamation of the

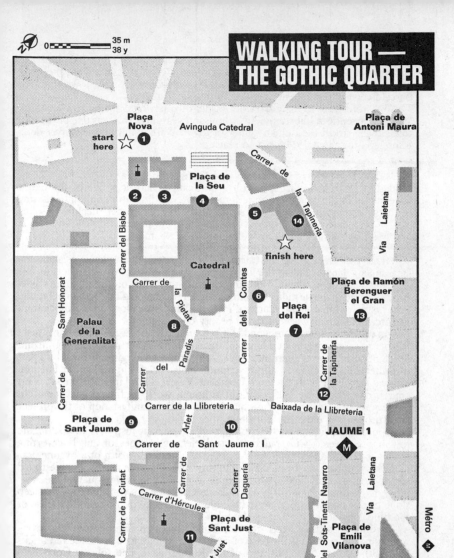

WALKING TOUR — THE GOTHIC QUARTER

0 ‖‖‖‖‖‖‖ 35 m
‖‖‖‖‖‖‖ 38 y

Plaça Nova

start here ☆ ❶

Avinguda Catedral

Plaça de Antoni Maura

❷ ❸

Plaça de la Seu

❹

Carrer de la Tapineria

❺

❶④

Via Laietana

Carrer del Bisbe

finish here ☆

Catedral

Carrer de la Pietat

Comtes

❻

Plaça de Ramón Berenguer el Gran

Sant Honorat

❽

Plaça del Rei

❼

❶③

Palau de la Generalitat

Carrer dels

del Paradis

Carrer

Carrer de la Tapineria

Carrer de

Carrer de la Llibreteria

❶②

Baixada de la Llibreteria

Plaça de Sant Jaume ❾

Arlet

❶⓪

JAUME 1 Ⓜ

Carrer de Sant Jaume I

Carrer de la Ciutat

Carrer de

Carrer Dagueria

Carrer del Sots-Tinent Navarro

Via Laietana

Métro Ⓜ

Carrer d'Hércules

✝

Plaça de Sant Just

❶①

Palma de Sant Just

Carrer dels Lledó

Plaça de Emili Vilanova

Church ✝

BARCELONA

The Gothic Quarter

❶	Plaça Nova	❽	Casa del Canonge
❷	Capilla de Santa Llúcia	❾	Plaça de Sant Jaume
❸	Casa de'Ardiaca	❶⓪	Mesón del Café
❹	Plaça de la Seu	❶①	Plaça de Sant Just
❺	Museu Frederic Marés	❶②	Carrer de la Tapinería
❻	Arxiu de la Carona d'Aragó	❶③	Plaça de Ramón Berenguer el Gran
❼	Plaça del Rei	❶④	Roman Walls

Republic was signed. The palace bell tower houses a carillon on which both old and popular music is played each day at noon. Across the square are the Ionic columns of the **Casa de la Ciutat/Ayuntamiento,** the Town Hall of Barcelona (see "For the Architecture Enthusiast," above).

With your back to the Carrer del Bisbe, turn left onto the narrow and very ancient Carrer de la Llibreteria. Two thousand years ago, this was one of the two roads that marked the Roman center of town. Walk uphill on the Carrer de la Llibreteria for about 1½ blocks to reach a:

REFUELING STOP 10. Mesón del Café, Llibreteria, 16 (tel. 315-07-54), founded in 1909. Specializing in coffee and cappuccino, it is one of the oldest coffeehouses in the neighborhood, sometimes crowding 50 people into its tiny precincts. Some regulars perch on stools at the bar and order breakfast. Coffee costs 70 pesetas (65¢) and a cappuccino goes for 150 pesetas ($1.40). The café is open Monday through Saturday from 7am to 12:45am.

Retrace your steps along the Carrer de la Llibreteria and enter once again the Plaça de Sant Jaume. Facing the Town Hall, take the street that parallels its left side, the Carrer de la Ciutat. Note the elegant stonework on the building's side, which is carved in a style radically different from the building's neoclassical façade. At the first left, turn onto the Carrer d'Hercules, and walk along it for 1 block until you enter the quiet, somewhat faded beauty of the:

11. Plaça de Sant Just, dominated by the entrance to the Església dels Sants Just i Pastor. You can enter the building on Saturday and Sunday from 9am to 1pm and 5 to 8:30pm. Above the entrance portal, an enthroned Virgin is flanked by a pair of protective angels. The Latin inscription hails her as Virgo Nigra et Pulchra, Nostra Patrona Pia (Black and Beautiful Virgin, Our Holy Patroness). This church dates from the 14th century, although work continued into the 16th. Some authorities claim that this church—an earlier manifestation of the present structure—is the oldest in Barcelona.

Opposite the façade of the church, at Plaça de Sant Just, 4, is an aristocratic townhouse covered with faded but still elegant frescoes of angels cavorting among garlands, an example of the artistry, taste, and wealth of a bygone era.

With your back to the black Virgin, turn right onto the narrow cobblestoned street, the Carrer del Lledo, which begins at the far end of the square. One short block later, turn left onto the Baixada de Cassador. As you descend the steep slope of this narrow street, notice the blue-and-white covering of the House of the Blue Tiles at the bottom of the hill.

Turn left onto the Carrer del Sots Tinent Navarro. The massive gray-stone wall rising on your left is the base of an ancient Roman fort. Note the red bricks of a 13th-century palace on top of the Roman wall. The solitary Corinthian column rising from the base is another reminder of Barcelona's Roman past.

Continue on to the Plaça d'Emili Vilanova. Near the top of the Roman wall, note the pair of delicate columns of a Gothic window. Continue another block to the cross street, the Carrer Jaume I. Cross it and approach the Plaça de l'Àngel. Continue walking to the:

12. Carrer de la Tapineria. In medieval times, this was the street of the shoemakers. (In fact, the industry is so entrenched that there is even a museum devoted to footwear, the **Museu del Calçat Antic,** Plaça Sant Felip Neri (tel. 302-26-80). It is open Tuesday through Sunday from 11am to 2pm, with admission at 100 pesetas (95¢).

In 1 short block the Carrer de la Tapineria leads to the:

13. Plaça de Ramón Berenguer el Gran. An equestrian statue dedicated to this hero (1096–1131) is ringed with the gravel of a semicircular park whose backdrop is formed by the walls of the ancient Roman fort and, nearby, a Gothic tower.

Traverse the park, crossing in front of the equestrian statue, until you once again reach the edge of the Roman wall as you head toward the park's distant end. There the Carrer de la Tapineria will lead you on a path parelleling the ancient:

14. Roman Walls, one of Barcelona's most important treasures from its past. The walls, known as *Las Murallas* in Spanish, were constructed between 270 and 310. The perimeter of the walls was 1,389 yards. They followed a rectangular course, and were built so that their fortified sections would face the sea. By the 11th and 12th centuries, Barcelona had long outgrown their confines. Jaume I ordered the opening of the Roman walls, and the burgeoning growth that ensued virtually destroyed them, except for the foundations you see today.

Continue your promenade, but turn left at the narrow Baixada de la Canonja. A short walk down this cobblestoned alleyway will return you to the **Plaça de la Seu,** not far from where you began this tour.

WALKING TOUR 2 —— Les Rambles

Start: Plaça Portal de la Pau.

Finish: Plaça de Catalunya.

Time: 1½ hours.

Best Time: Any time except midnight to dawn, which might be unsafe.

This most famous promenade in Spain was laid out in the 18th century. Begin at the

1. Plaça Portal de la Pau, with its Columbus Monument, which you can scale for a view of the harbor. (See under "Other Attractions," above). You can also book a harbor cruise of the port here or even take a horse-and-carriage ride.

Near the port you can also board a replica of the *Santa María,* which Columbus sailed to the New World. It is anchored opposite the monument honoring him. Admission is 150 pesetas ($1.40). Daily hours in the summer are 9am to 9pm; in winter, 9am to 6pm.

With your back to the monument to Columbus, head up Les Rambles, the first of which is the:

2. Ramble de Santa Mònica, where it is recommended that you walk with care late at night, as this Ramble borders the Barri Xinés, long known as a center of drugs, prostitution, and criminal activity. Hookers, pimps, beggars, transvestites, and various immigrants live in this quarter along with some hardworking, respectable poor people. If you have children with you (or even if you don't), you may want to turn right at the Passatge de la Banca and visit the:

3. Museu de Cera, a wax museum with some 300 figures—past and present—in Barcelona's history. Admission is 360 pesetas ($4.40) for adults, 180 pesetas ($1.70) for children aged 5 to 11; open daily from 11am to 8pm.

REFUELING STOP **4. Café Opera,** Les Rambles, 74 (tel. 317-75-85). In warm weather, its tables spill out onto the Rambles, but for most of the year clients pack into a narrow stand-up area beside a marble-topped bar or head to the tables in back. Everywhere, reminders of the café's Belle Epoque past sheath the slightly seedy room with its tarnished crystal chandeliers and turn-of-the-century frescoes. International gays mingle with unionists, trade leaders, anarchists, vacationing American students, and French schoolteachers. It is the most famous café along Les Rambles. Waiters in black vests bring beer costing from 190 pesetas ($1.80) or other drinks to the tables either inside or outside. The café is open daily from 8am to 3pm.

The next Ramble is the:

5. Ramble dels Caputxins, which begins at the Plaça del Teatre. This was once the heart of the old theater district, but only the rather bleak Teatro Principal survives. Philip II launched this area on its theatrical career when he granted permission for the construction of a playhouse here to raise money for the city. In the Plaça del Teatre you can see a monument to Serafí Pitarra, considered "the father" of contemporary theater in Catalonia.

Turn left here to reach the:

6. Museu de les Artes de l'Espectable, Nou de La Rambla, 3 (tel. 317-39-74). Also known as the Güell Palace (it was constructed for Gaudí's patron Eusebi Güell in the 1880s), this is considered one of the masterpieces of Antoni Gaudí. His tastes, although essentially Gothic, show even Moorish influences in this strange building. The main hall is usually open to the public, who can wander in and look about—and up. Its perforated cupola is adorned with broken fragments of ceramic tiles, and crowned with a curious mélange of balustrades, multiform chimneys, and crenels. The building houses theatrical archives containing such items as memoirs of Catalan literary figures, props left over from long-forgotten hits of yesteryear, and interesting antique theater posters. The archives are open Monday through Saturday from 11am to 2pm and 5 to 8pm, charging 100 pesetas (95¢) for admission.

Walking back to Les Rambles, continue up the promenade but veer right onto the Carrer de Colom on the other side of the esplanade, entering the landmark:

7. Plaça Reial (Royal Square). At first you'll think you've been transported to Andalusia. Constructed in a neoclassical style during the 19th century, this plaza has palms and elaborate façades, even ocher-painted arcades, and in the center is a fountain dedicated to the Three Graces. The lampposts are attributed to the young Gaudí. You'll see old men sunning themselves on the beaches in this square, which was built on the site of a former Capuchin monastery, one of many religious edifices that lined the Rambles until they were suppressed in 1835. Sunday morning brings out a coin and stamp market.

Returning to Les Rambles, continue north from the harbor until you reach, on the left side, the:

8. Gran Teatre del Liceu, Sant Pau, 1 bis (tel. 318-92-77), the second-largest opera house in Europe, which you can enter around the corner from its main façade fronting the Rambles. This magnificent theater, originally constructed in 1846 and restored after a devasting fire, is the most important cultural venue in the entire province of Catalonia. Here you can buy tickets to attend a performance. Thirty-minute guided tours (some in English) are offered Monday through Friday at 11:30am and at 12:15pm. The tour fee is 200 pesetas ($1.90).

Back on Les Rambles once more, continue north along the:

9. Ramble de Sant Josep, also known as Ramble de les Flors. Flower stands line this part of Les Rambles. This Ramble begins at the Plaça de la Boqueria, where you can visit the centuries-old market that bears the same name as the square.

At Ramble de Sant Josep, 99, stands the neoclassical Palau de la Virreina dating from 1778, named after a vicereine of Peru. Frequent contemporary exhibitions are staged here.

Next comes the:

10. Ramble dels Estudis, beginning at the Carrer del Carme. The esplanade of the students takes its name from a university that once stood there until Philip V converted it into army barracks. Because so many birds are sold here, some people call this (in Spanish) the Rambla de los Pajaros (Boulevard of the Birds).

The final Ramble is the:

11. Ramble de Canaletes, which begins at the Carrer del Santa Anna. This Ramble takes its name from a famous fountain. If you take a drink from it, it is said you will never leave Barcelona. The fountain stands near the intersection of the Ramble and the Carrer del Pelai.

WALKING TOUR — LES RAMBLES

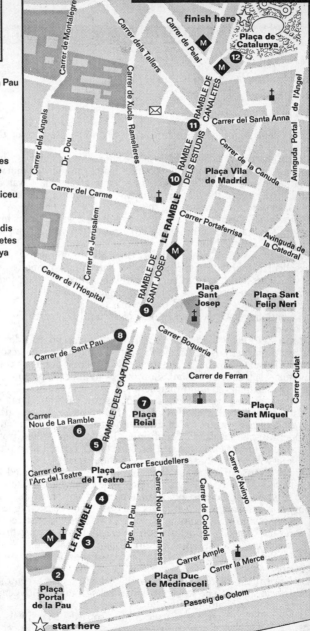

1. Plaça Portal de la Pau
2. Ramble de Santa Mónica
3. Museu de Cera
4. Café Opera
5. Ramble dels Caputxins
6. Museu de les Artes de l'Espectable
7. Plaça Reial
8. Gran Teatre del Liceu
9. Ramble de Sant Josep
10. Ramble dels Estudis
11. Ramble de Canaletes
12. Plaça de Catalunya

BARCELONA

Les Rambles

0 ____ 100 m / 110 y

finish here

start here

Church †

Post Office ⊠

Métro

At the end of this promenade you will have arrived at the:

12. Plaça de Catalunya, with its fountains, shade trees, benches, chairs, and, most important, a public toilet.

WALKING TOUR 3 —— Barcelona Harborfront

Start: Plaça Portal de la Pau.

Finish: Parc de la Ciutadella.

Time: 2 hours.

Best Time: Any sunny day.

This tour begins near the harborfront at the end of the Rambles in the shadow of the Columbus Monument at the:

1. Plaça Portal de la Pau. Here at the base of the Columbus Monument, look at the quartet of nymphs seeming to offer laurel garlands to whoever approaches. If you haven't already done so, you may want to take the elevator to the top for a bird's-eye view of the harborfront you are about to traverse.

Afterward, head east along the

2. Passeig de Colom, which, at this point, is raised on stilts high above a yacht basin. The waterside promenade adjacent to the yacht basin, far below you on your right, is called the:

3. Passeig del Moll de la Fusta, originally the timber wharf. It stands as an excellent symbol of the recovery of Barcelona's formerly seedy waterfront. Several bars and restaurants enliven this balcony over the Mediterranean, from which one can descend via bridges to the level of a pedestrian wharf where palm trees arise from the cobbled pavement.

Continue along the Passeig de Colom until you reach the slightly faded but very grand:

4. Plaça del Duc de Mendinaceli, on the inland (left) side of the boulevard. When traffic permits, cross the Passeig de Colom, perhaps resting a moment on one of the park benches in the square, whose focal point is a column ringed with mermen (half fish, half men). Continue walking east, passing pigeons, children, and grandparents sunning themselves.

You can now begin a brisk 7-block stroll eastward along the left side (the inland one) of the Passeig de Colom. After about 2½ blocks, glance to your right at an enormous sculpture of a lobster waving a claw from atop the low-slung modern restaurant called Gambrinus. The lobster, crafted from fiberglass by a local sculptor, has become one of Barcelona's conversation pieces.

You will eventually reach a monumental square the:

5. Plaça d'Antoni López, whose northern end is dominated by the Barcelona Post Office (Correos y Telegrafos). Cross the Carrer de la Fustería, heading toward the front side of the post office, then pass in front of the building, traversing the busy Via Laietana, which borders the post office's eastern edge.

Continue to walk in straight, always east. The quiet street you'll enter is the Carrer del Consolat del Mar, more interesting than the broader Passeig d'Isabel II, which runs parallel and a short distance to the right. Walk east along the Carrer del Consolat del Mar. The neoclassical doorway on your right marks the entrance to:

6. La Lonja, the stock exchange of Barcelona. It has a central courtyard with allegorical statues. The stock exchange dates from the 14th century. Once it was a fine arts school attended by Picasso and Miró.

A half block later, the Carrer del Consolat del Mar opens onto the:

7. Plaça del Palau, a gracefully proportioned square reminiscent of another era's political and cultural glory.

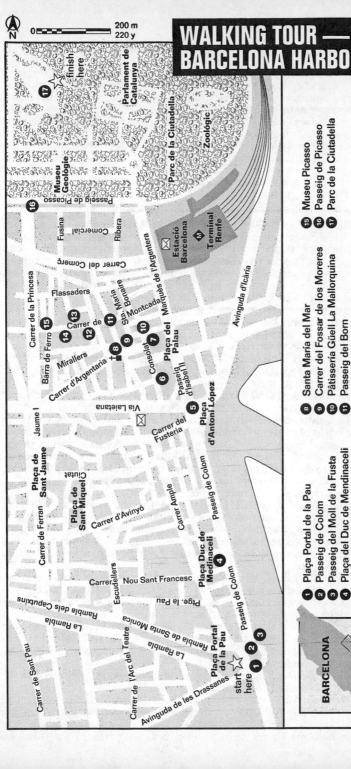

WALKING TOUR — BARCELONA HARBORFRONT

0 ⊨⊨⊨⊨⊨⊨⊨ 200 m
                220 y

N

① Plaça Portal de la Pau
② Passeig de Colom
③ Passeig del Moll de la Fusta
④ Plaça del Duc de Mendinaceli
⑤ Plaça d'Antoni López
⑥ La Lonja
⑦ Plaça del Palau

⑧ Santa María del Mar
⑨ Carrer del Fossar de los Moreres
⑩ Pâtisseria Güell La Mallorquina
⑪ Passeig del Born
⑫ Carrer de Montcada
⑬ Galeria Maeght
⑭ Museu Textil i d'Indumentaria

⑮ Museu Picasso
⑯ Passeig de Picasso
⑰ Parc de la Ciutadella

 Metro   ⊠ Post Office   ✝ Church

BARCELONA

Barcelona Harborfront

finish here

start here

Midway down the length of this square, head north (left) on the Carrer de l'Espasería, at the end of which you'll come upon:

8. **Santa María del Mar,** in Plaça de Santa María, a Catalonian Gothic church with a soaring interior dating from the 14th century. After your visit, turn left as you exit, then left again, so that your footsteps along the Carrer de Santa María flank the southern exterior of the church.

A half block later, the Carrer de Santa María opens onto one of the most bizarre monuments in Barcelona, the:

9. **Carrer del Fossar de los Moreres.** Occupying most of the medieval square that contains it, the plaza incorporates a sprawling and steeply inclined red-brick pavement, fronted by a low wall of reddish porphyry, inscribed with a memorial to Catalonian martyrs who died in an uprising against Castilian Spain in 1714. As you enter the square, note on your left a narrow street leading to our:

REFUELING STOP   10. Pâtissería Güell La Mallorquina, Plaça de Les Oiles (tel. 319-38-83), established in 1878 in a 16th-century building. Sample the *llunes,* half-mooned shaped pastries filled with almonds and sprinkled with powdered sugar. Or take out an order of *coques,* sprinkled with sugar and topped with pine nuts. All pastries are made on the premises, and the dough is rolled out on marble tables. You can stop in here and buy pastries Wednesday through Monday from 8am to 2:30pm and from 5 to 8:30pm.

Return to the square of the martyrs and continue walking along the Carrer de Santa María until you reach the rear of the Church of Santa María del Mar, where you'll notice the massive buttresses. You have arrived at the:

11. **Passeig del Born,** one of the colorful old squares of Barcelona and the residence of some appealing and nostalgic bars. But this square doesn't come alive until much later at night.

Turn left after 1 very short block onto the Placeta de Montcada, which after about 30 paces becomes more narrow and changes its name to the:

12. **Carrer de Montcada,** which represents the aristocratic heart of Barcelona during the height of its prestige and power. Notice the semifortified palace at no. 20, which served during the 18th century as the Barcelona residence of the Catalonian ambassador from Great Britain. Also note the nine gargoyles adding visual interest to the fourth and uppermost floor of the palace, whose forbidding exterior seems even more severe because of the narrow street containing it.

A few steps later, on your right, is the:

13. **Galería Maeght,** Montcada, 25 (tel. 310-42-45), established by the children of the couple who created one of the most famous museums of modern art in Europe, the Galerie Maeght in St-Paul-de-Vence in France. Many well-known and unknown painters are exhibited under the gallery's brick vaults, and works are for sale. The showrooms are open Tuesday through Saturday from 9:30am to 2pm and 3 to 8pm.

As you leave the gallery, turn right and continue walking until you reach the:

14. **Museu de Textil i d'Indumentaria,** Montcada, 12 (tel. 210-45-16), occupying two 13th-century Gothic palaces. Many of the articles in this textile and costume museum are Egyptian and Hispano-Muslim. Textiles range from the Gothic era to the 20th century; many of the garments are liturgical. In summer the museum is open Tuesday through Sunday from 10am to 2pm and 4:30 to 7pm; in winter, Tuesday through Sunday from 9am to 2pm and 4 to 7pm. Admission is 200 pesetas ($1.90).

After exiting the museum, turn left and continue walking until you reach the most visited museum in Barcelona; the:

15. **Museu Picasso,** Montcada, 15-19 (tel. 319-63-10), ensconced in two Gothic mansions. (See "Top Attractions," above, for more details). Exit from the museum and turn right along the Carrer de Montcada. In 1 short block, turn right again onto the Carrer de la Princesa and walk straight for 4 blocks,

traversing a confusing five-way intersection. You'll soon arrive at the wide and busy Carrer del Comerç, which you should cross. Continue walking along the Carrer de la Princesa until it dead-ends at the:

16. Passeig de Picasso, designed by architects Amadó and Domènech. A sculpture by Tàpies, *Homage to Picasso,* is the central piece. Cross the Passeig de Picasso and notice the ornate wrought-iron gates guarding the entrance to the:

17. Parc de la Ciutadella, which was the site of the 1888 Universal Exposition. (See "Parks and Gardens", above, for more details.) If you enter the park through its main entrance on the Passeig Lluís Companys, you can still see some of the relics from that great fair. The park is filled with museums, a zoo, and many attractions. Since it covers a large area, these attractions are signposted, and you can follow the directions and take in whatever interests you—or whatever you have time to explore.

WALKING TOUR 4 —— Modernist Barcelona

Start: Plaça de Catalunya.

Finish: Plaça de Catalunya.

Time: 2 hours.

Best Time: Any sunny day.

Much of the Barcelona's worldwide reputation is based on the architectural works found in the 19th-century Eixample (Ensanche) section, an urban expansion plan dating mostly from 1860. This barrio was filled with a Catalonian art nouveau style of architecture called *modernisme.* Its most famous monument is Antoni Gaudí's Sagrada Familia, his unfinished cathedral. Many other architects worked in this area as well, including Domènech i Montaner, Puig i Cadafalch, and Josep Vilaseca. Most of these buildings are still occupied as businesses and apartments.

Begin your tour at the symbolic center of Barcelona, the sprawling and traffic-clogged:

1. Plaça de Catalunya, site of everything from Catalonian song and dance festivals to political protests. This square is a potent symbol of Barcelona's cultural independence from the rest of Spain. Exit onto the plaza's northernmost boulevard, the Passeig de Gràcia. Keep the city's largest department store, El Corte Inglés, on your right.

As you ascend the Passeig de Gràcia, you'll be heading north. Walk along its east (right) sidewalk and notice the dozens of bookstands patronized by an avidly literate Catalan market. You'll reach:

2. Gran Via de les Corts Catalanes, a major boulevard intersecting the Passeig de Gràcia. Traverse this intersecting boulevard and continue to walk straight to the north to the Carrer de la Disputació. Turn right. After going 1 block east, notice that the 19th-century city planners designed their intersections like miniature plazas, rounding off the edges of each of the corner buildings. Turn left at the Carrer de Pau Claris and walk on the east (right) side of the street, heading north. Note in about a half block the private passageway (reserved for residents only) of the:

3. Passatge de Permanyer, whose wrought-iron gates and sculpted cherubs guard an entrance reserved for the occupants of 19th-century villas and gardens lining either side. (There's likely to be a surly-looking guard blocking your entrance to the gate.) Some consider the Passatge de Permanyer the most charming little street of Barcelona.

Continue walking a few paces to the next boulevard, Carrer del Consell de Cent, where you should go right, crossing it at the Hotel Diplomatic. Walk east along the north (left) side of the Carrer del Consell de Cent. At the intersection with Carrer de Roger de Llúria, turn left. Walk 1 block north. When you reach Carrer d'Aragó, cross it and turn right. A few steps later, you'll see the massively buttressed 14th-century Església de la Concepció, Aragó, 299, which seems to host an elaborate wedding every weekend.

Continue to walk east on Aragó until you reach the Carrer del Bruc. Observe the Consell Municipal on Carrer del Bruc's far side. Designed by the noted Catalan architect Pere Falques i Urpi in 1893, it is considered a neighborhood landmark and a good example of Neo-Romanesque Catalonian architecture. Note its wrought-iron gates, the oak-leaf clusters carved into the Romanesque capitals, and the coat-of-arms over the third floor.

Turn left (north) onto the Carrer del Bruc, which has dozens of plane trees lining the sidewalk. Notice the massive stones of the building on your right. The entrance to this famous structure is at the next street corner, at the intersection of the Carrer de València. The building is the Conservatorio Superior Municipal de Música.

Turn left (heading west) onto the Carrer de València. A landmark building stands at:

4. **Carrer de València, 296,** on the street's north (right-hand side). Considered one of the city's most distinguished examples of wrought ironwork and *modernisme,* it has twin towers, jutting bay windows, and a bit of romantic fantasy—as though an urban château had been crafted with grace and style. Like many other buildings in this neighborhood, it houses private apartments and cannot be visited.

Continue walking west along the Carrer de València until you reach the corner of the Carrer de Roger de Llúria, where virtually every building at the intersection is architecturally noteworthy. Turn right onto the Carrer de Roger de Lluría and walk 1 block. At the Carrer de Mallorca, detour for half a block to the right to admire the:

5. **Casa Tómas,** Mallorca, 291, one of Barcelona's most famous 19th-century buildings. Designed by Domènech i Montaner, it is now the home of a design firm. Retrace your steps for half a block, heading west until you reach the Carrer de Mallorca. Across the intersection is the Neo-Byzantine:

6. **Delegación del Gobierno,** Mallorca, 278. The tilework here is among the best of its kind in Barcelona. Through an iron fence, you can admire the building's garden as well.

From your position on the Carrer de Mallorca, turn right at the Carrer de Roger de Llúria. Within half a block on the right-hand side, you'll see:

7. **Carrer de Roger de Llúria, 112,** a charming building and a good example of the many beautiful art nouveau structures whose builders and architects are barely remembered. This particular example contains private apartments. A half block later, turn left on the Carrer de Provença. Continue walking straight 2 blocks, crossing the intersection of the Carrer de Pau Claris. One block later, on the right side (at the corner of the Passeig de Gràcia), you'll pass one of the most famous apartment buildings in the world, the:

8. **Casa Milà,** known as La Pedrera (The Quarry). Its serpentine front and "organically" inspired iron balconies represent Gaudí at his most distinctive. (Note that the Casa Milà's address is Carrer Provença, 261-265, or Passeig de Gràcia, 92.) Admire the Casa Milà from both the Carrer Provença and the Passeig de Gràcia, observing the womblike slabs of chiseled stone. Now, traverse the busy Passeig de Gràcia, stopping on the far (west) side for a view of the building's twisted chimneys, which are the best examples of their highly bizarre kind.

You will now descend the gentle slope of one of Europe's most famous boulevards, the:

9. **Passeig de Gràcia.** At the first intersection, the Carrer de Mallorca, notice the red brick and gray stone of the Hotel Condes de Barcelona, Passeig de Gràcia, 75. Built in 1895 as the private home of a Catalan nobleman, it was designed by the master architect Vilaseca, who used many medieval decorative touches (crenellations, heraldic shields, palm-shaped columns) that later helped define the

WALKING TOUR — MODERNIST BARCELONA

0 ⊟⊟⊟⊟⊟ 150 m
165 y

Carrer de Provença

Avinguda Diagonal

Ramble de Catalunya

CARRER DE ROGER DE LLÚRIA

Carrer del Bruc

Carrer de Girona

⑧

⑦

⑤

Carrer de Mallorca ⑥

⑨

⑩

④

PASSEIG DE GRÀCIA

CARRER DE VALENCIA

Carrer Pau Claris

Carrer d'Aragó ⑪

Carrer d'Aragó

Carrer del Consell de Cent

PASSATGE DE
PERMANYER

⑫

③

PASSEIG DE GRÀCIA

Ramble de Catalunya

Carrer de la Diputacio

⑬
⑭

DE LLÚRIA

Jardins
Reina Victoria

② GRAN VIA DE LES CORTS CATALANES

Carrer de Pau Claris

CARRER DE ROGER DE

Carrer del Bruc

Carrer de Girona

Ronda Universitat

finish here Plaça de
⭐ Catalunya

① ⭐ start here

Ronda de Sant Pere

BARCELONA

Modernist
Barcelona

① Plaça de Catalunya
② Gran Via de les
  Corts Catalanes
③ Passatge de Permanyer
④ Carrer de Valencia, 296
⑤ Casa Tómas
⑥ Delegació del Gobierno
⑦ Carrer de Roger de Llúria

⑧ Casa Milà
⑨ Passeig de Gràcia
⑩ El Drugstore
⑪ Fundació Antoni Tàpies
⑫ Casa Amatller y Casa Batlló
⑬ Casa Lléo Morera
⑭ Passeig de Gràcia, 27

modernist movement. Today, rescued from destruction and restored, it is one of Barcelona's best hotels.

Continue your walk down the western (right) slope of the Passeig de Gràcia.

REFUELING STOP   **10. El Drugstore,** Passeig de Gràcia, 71 (tel. 215-70-74), is a complex with a snack bar and cafeteria, boutiques, record shops, and a tearoom. Combination plates are available, and you can order these plus a wide variety of drinks, sitting out at sidewalk tables if you prefer. It's ideal for people watching. If it's lunchtime, you'll find a *menú del día* offered for only 850 pesetas ($8). The place stays open 24 hours.

When you reach the Carrer d'Aragó, turn right and walk to the:

11. Fundació Antoni Tàpies, Aragó, 255, one of Barcelona's newest museums (see "Other Attractions," above). The building was designed by one of Barcelona's most admired modernist architects, Domènech i Montaner. The façade was not changed during the building's transformation into a museum of modern art.

Turn left to retrace your steps back to the Passeig de Gràcia. As you go downhill along the boulevard, two buildings merit your attention (both are described under "For the Architecture Enthusiast"), the:

12. Casa Amatller, Passeig de Gràcia, 41, and the **Casa Batlló,** Passeig de Gracia, 43, the former by Puig; Cadafalch, the latter by Gaudí.

A few steps farther, you'll encounter the:

13. Casa Lléo Morera (see "For the Architecture Enthusiast," above), another building by Domènech i Montaner, dating from 1905. Today it houses the Patronato de Turismo. Step inside to admire the vestibule. One block farther at:

14. Passeig de Gràcia, 27, is a magnificently embellished building, with eagles, laurel branches, and floral garlands carved in high relief into the stone.

Shortly after, after having seen some of the more stunning examples of modernisme, you'll find yourself back at the northern edge of the Plaça de Catalunya, where you started.

---

7. ORGANIZED TOURS

Pullmantur, Gran Via de les Corts Catalanes, 635 (tel. 317-12-97), offers a number of tours and excursions (with English-speaking guides) — both in Barcelona and its environs. For a preview of the city, you can take a morning tour departing from the company's terminal at the above address at 9:30am, taking in the cathedral, the Gothic Quarter, the Rambles, the monument to Columbus, and the Spanish Village. An afternoon tour leaves at 3:30pm, with visits to some of the most outstanding architectural examples in the Eixample, including Gaudí's Sagrada Familia, and a stop at the Picasso Museum. Each of these tours costs 2,600 pesetas ($24.45).

---

8. SPECIAL EVENTS

OLYMPIC GAMES

The big news in Barcelona is the 1992 Olympic Games, whose centerpiece will be the Olympic Stadium at Montjuïc. Facilities there will hold 70,000 spectators for the track-and-field competitions and also for the opening and closing ceremonies. The games are scheduled to take place from July 29 to August 9.

Worldwide distribution of some 6.7 million entrance tickets to the games began in early 1991. In the United States, tickets are sold by **Olson Travelworld,** 100 North

Sepulveda Blvd., El Segundo, CA 90245 (tel. toll free 800/US4-1992). There will be a total of 526 events, each with three entrance prices. The games will take place in 44 competition venues in or near Barcelona.

9. SPORTS/RECREATION

BULLFIGHTING

The Catalans of Barcelona do not pursue this "art" with as much fervor as do the Castilians of Madrid. Nevertheless, you may want to attend one of the *corridas*. Bullfights are held from March to September, usually on Sunday at 5:30pm at the **Plaça de Toros Monumental,** Gran Via de les Corts Catalanes (tel. 245-58-04). It's recommended that you purchase tickets in advance. Go to the office at Muntaner, 24 (tel. 253-38-21).

FITNESS CENTER

You can use the facilities of **Piscina Bernardo Picornell** at Montjuïc (tel. 325-92-81). See "Swimming," below.

GOLF

A local course, **Club de Golf Vallromanas,** Afueras, s/n, Vallromanas (Barcelona) (tel. 568-03-62), accepts nonmembers. It's 20 minutes by car from Barcelona in the suburb of Vallromanas. Nonmembers are welcomed from 2 to 9pm only, as mornings are reserved for members. The cost for 18 holes is 4,500 pesetas ($42.30) Monday through Friday, rising to 9,000 pesetas ($84.60) on Saturday and Sunday. To rent clubs costs another 1,500 pesetas ($14.10).

JOGGING

In the heart of Barcelona, the **Parc de la Ciutadella** (see "Parks and Gardens," above) is the jogger's favorite. You can also use the paths surrounding Montjuïc.

SQUASH

Squash Club Barcelona, Doctor Gregoria Maranon, 17 (tel. 334-02-58); (Metro: Universitat), accepts nonmembers and is open daily from 8:30am to 2am. Squash courts can be rented by anyone for 980 pesetas ($9.20) per half hour of play time. There are 15 courts in all. The swimming pool and gym, however, are reserved for members.

SWIMMING

Esportiu Can Carelleu, Desportes, s/n (tel. 203-78-74), has an indoor pool open throughout the year and an outdoor pool open only from June to September. Daily hours for both pools are 10am to 4pm, with an entrance charge of 175 pesetas ($1.65). Take bus no. 94 to get there.

You can also swim where the 1992 Olympics will take place, at **Piscina Bernardo Picornell** (tel. 352-92-81), on Montjuïc in the vicinity of the principal arena. It is open June to September, daily from 10am to 5pm, charging an admission of 175 pesetas ($1.65). From the Plaça d'Espanya a free double-decker shuttle bus goes back and forth.

TENNIS

Barcelona has several tennis clubs, but they are all private. You'll have to taxi 3½ miles (5.6km) beyond the airport in the direction of Sitges to Castel de Fels, where there are several tennis clubs that accept nonmembers. Look for the signs directing you to the most popular one: **Club Open** (tel. 379-42-46).

10. SAVVY SHOPPING

Barcelonans look more to Paris than to Madrid for their fashions and style and, of course, create much of their style themselves. *Moda joven* (young fashion) is all the rage in Barcelona.

If your time and budget are limited, you may want to patronize the two major department stores, El Corte Inglés or Galerías Preciadas, for an overview of Catalan merchandise at reasonable prices. Barcelona is filled with boutiques, but clothing is an expensive item here, even though the city has been a textile center for centuries.

Markets (see below) are very popular in Barcelona, and a good place to find good buys.

THE SHOPPING SCENE

If you're a window shopper, stroll along the **Passeig de Gràcia** from the Avinguda Diagonal to the Plaça de Catalunya. Along the way, you'll see some of the most elegant and expensive shops in Barcelona, along with an assortment of splendid turn-of-the-century buildings and cafés, many with outdoor tables.

Another shopping expedition is to the **Mercat de la Boqueria,** just off the Rambles near the Carrer del Carme, open all day. Here you'll see a wide display of straw bags and regional products, along with a handsome display of the food you are likely to be eating later in a local restaurant: fruits, vegetables (beautifully displayed), breads, cheeses, meats, and fish.

In the **old quarter** the principal shopping streets are all five of the Rambles, plus the Carrer del Pi, Carrer de la Palla, and Avinguda Portal de l'Àngel, to cite only some of the major ones. Moving north in the Eixample are the Passeig de Catalunya, Passeig de Gràcia, and Ramble de Catalunya. Going even farther north, the Avinguda Diagonal is a major shopping boulevard. Other prominent shopping streets include Bori i Fontesta, Via Augusta, Carrer Muntaner, Travessera de Gràcia, and Carrer de Balmes.

HOURS & SHIPPING IT HOME

In general, hours are Monday through Saturday from 9am to 9pm. Some smaller shops close from 1:30 to 4pm.

The American **Visitors Bureau,** Gran Via, 591 (tel. 301-01-50), between the Ramble de Catalunya and the Calle de Balmes, will pack and ship your purchases and gifts, and even handle excess luggage and personal effects. It's open Monday through Friday from 9am to 1:30pm and 4 to 7pm, on Saturday from 9am to 1pm.

TAXES & SALES

For information on **taxes,** including recovering the IVA (VAT), and sales, see "Saving Money on Shopping," Chapter 3.

BEST BUYS AND WHERE TO FIND THEM

Barcelona, a city of design and fashion, offers a staggering wealth of shopping opportunities. In general, prices tend to be slightly lower than in London, Paris, and Rome.

In addition to modern, attractively designed, and stylish clothing, shoes and decorative objects are often good buys. In the city of Miró, Tàpies, and Picasso, art is a major business, and the reason so many gallery owners from around the world come to visit. You'll find dozens of galleries, especially in the Barri Gòtic and around the Picasso Museum. Barcelona is also noted for its flea markets, where good purchases are always available if you search hard enough.

Antiques abound here, but rising prices have put them beyond the means of the average shopper. However, I've listed some shops where you can look, if nothing else. Most shoppers from abroad settle happily for handcrafts, and the city is rich in offerings, ranging from simple pottery to handmade furniture. Barcelona has been in the business of creating and designing jewelry for 300 years, and its offerings in this field are of the widest possible range—as are the prices.

What follows is only a limited selection of some of the hundreds of shops in Barcelona.

ANTIQUES

ARTUR RAMÓN ANTICUARIO, Palla, 25. tel. 302-59-70.

One of the finest antiques stores in Barcelona is this three-level emporium with high ceilings and a medieval kind of grace. Set on a narrow flagstone-covered street near the Plaça del Pi (the center of the antiques district), it stands opposite a tiny square, the Placeta al Carrer de la Palla, whose foundations were laid by the Romans. The store, which has been operated by four generations of men named Artur Ramón, contains everything from Romanesque works to Picasso. Prices are high, as you'd expect, for items of quality and lasting value. Open: Mon–Fri 9am–1:30pm and 5–8pm, Sat 9am–1:30pm. Metro: Jaume I.

EL BULEVARD DES ANTIQUARIS, Passeig de Gràcia, 55 (no central phone).

This 70-unit shopping complex just off one of the town's most aristocratic avenues has a huge collection of art and antiques, assembled in a series of boutiques. There's a café/bar on the upper level. Some boutiques keep "short" hours. Open: Summer, Mon–Fri 9:30am–8:30pm; winter, Mon 4:30–8:30pm, Tues–Sat 10:30am–8:30pm. Metro: Passeig de Gràcia.

URBANA, Còrsega, 258. Tel. 218-70-36.

Urbana sells a bewildering array of architectural remnants (usually from torn-down mansions), antique furniture, and reproductions of brass hardware. There are antique and reproduction marble mantlepieces, wrought-iron gates and garden seats, even carved wood fireplaces with the modernist look. It's an impressive, albeit costly, array of merchandise rescued from the architectural glory of yesteryear. Open: Mon–Sat 10am–2pm and 4:30–8pm. Metro: Hospital Sant Pau.

CAMERAS

CASA ARPI, Ramble dels Caputxins, 40. Tel. 301-74-04.

This is one of the most famous camera shops in Spain. A multilingual staff will guide you to the best buys in new and used cameras, including familiar brand-name products. The firm also does quality processing, ready within 24 to 48 hours. Open: Mon–Sat 9:30am–1:30pm and 4:30–8pm. Metro: Liceu.

DEPARTMENT STORES

EL CORTE INGLÉS, Plaça de Catalunya, 14. Tel. 302-12-12.

The largest and most glamorous department store chain in Spain. The store sells a wide variety of merchandise, ranging from Spanish handcrafts to high-fashion items, from Spanish or Catalan records to food. The store also has restaurants and cafés, and offers a number of consumer-related services, such as a travel agent. It has a department that will arrange for the mailing of purchases back home. Open: Mon–Fri 10am–8pm, Sat 10am–9pm. Metro: Plaça de Catalunya.

GALERÍAS PRECIADAS, Avinguda Portal de l'Àngel, 19-21. Tel. 317-00-00.

The other major department store in Barcelona. It has much the same merchandise as El Corte Inglés, but with perhaps a larger selection of more cut-rate items. It, too, has a travel agent and a number of other consumer-related services of interest to visitors. There are also catering facilities if you'd like food on the run. Open: Mon–Fri 10am–8pm, Sat 10am–9pm. Metro: Urquinaona.

DESIGNER HOUSEWARES

BD EDICIONES DE DISEÑO, Mallorca, 291. Tel. 258-69-09.
Housed in one of the Belle Epoque's most famous buildings, a modernist creation by Llúis Domènech i Montaner, is this showcase of Catalan design. The "Bd" stands for Barcelona design. The emporium's two floors of showrooms contain housewares, furniture, and utilitarian household aids whose unifying element is a style-conscious flair brought to the design. Some of the merchandise, such as chairs, are copies of pieces by such masters as Gaudí. A catalog shows photographs and prices of everything in inventory; only a fraction of the offerings are displayed in the showrooms. Famous designer names from abroad include Alvar Aalto of Finland and Le Corbusier of France. The store can arrange to ship purchases abroad. Open: Mon–Fri 10am–1:30pm and 4–8pm, Sat 10am–1:30pm. Closed: Aug. Metro: Verdaguer.

VINCON, Passeig de Gràcia, 96. Tel. 215-60-50.
Fernando Amat's Vincon is the best in the city, with 10,000 products—everything from household items to the best in Spanish contemporary furnishings. Housed in the former home of artist Ramón Casas, with gilded columns and mosaic-inlaid floors, the showroom is filled with the best Spain has, with each item personally selected because of its quality and craft. You pay for what you get here, and you get the best. The window display alone is worth the trek there: Expect *anything*. Open: Mon–Sat 10am–1:30pm and 5–8pm. Metro: Passeig de Grácia.

FABRICS AND WEAVINGS

COSES DE CASA, Plaça de Sant Josep Oriol, 5. Tel. 302-73-28.
Appealing fabrics and weavings are displayed in this 19th-century store. Many are handwoven in Majorca (Balearic Islands), their boldly geometric patterns inspired by the Arabs centuries ago. The fabric, for the most part, is 50% cotton, 50% linen; much of it would make excellent upholstery material. One of the store's best buys; an array of Vasarely-inspired quilts made of Indian silk, handcrafted works of pop-art beauty. Open: Mon–Sat 9:45am–1:30pm and 4:30–8pm. Metro: Jaume I.

FASHION

BEVERLY FELDMAN, Mallorca, 259. Tel. 487-03-83.
Stylish shoes are offered here, all designed by Feldman herself. An American, she has lived and worked in Spain for many years. The shop is in the Eixample. Open: Mon–Sat 10am–2pm and 4:30–8:30pm. Metro: Passeig de Gràcia.

GROC, Ramble de Catalunya. Tel. 215-74-74.
Designs for both women and men—clothes by Toni Miró and jewelry by Chelo Sastre. One of the most stylish shops in Barcelona, it is expensive but filled with high-quality apparel made from the finest of natural fibers selected by the designer himself. The men's store is downstairs, the women's store one flight up. Open: Mon–Sat 10am–2pm and 4:30–8pm. Closed: Aug; men's department closed Mon 10am–2pm, women's department closed Sat 4:30–8pm. Metro: Plaça de Catalunya.

ROSER-FRANCESC, Roger de Llúria, 87. Tel. 215-78-67.
This outstanding shop for men's fashion stocks the work of a designer whose influence is felt beyond the borders of Catalonia. Clothes are sold from two levels of a narrow storefront in the Eixample district. For the most part, they are casually elegant cotton garments, ideal for such resorts as Sitges, south of Barcelona. Open: Mon–Sat 10:30am–2pm and 5–8:30pm. Metro: Urquinaona.

FURNITURE AND ACCESSORIES

ARTESPAÑA, Ramble de Catalunya, 75. Tel. 215-61-46.
Part of a nationwide government-owned chain, Artespaña sells Spanish-made artifacts from throughout the country. This particular branch specializes in furniture

and household accessories, along with some gift items—not the country-style, handmade products you might expect, but elegantly crafted and styled pieces. They will ship your purchase home if you wish. Open: Mon–Sat 10am–1:30pm and 5–8pm. Metro: Passeig de Gràcia.

GALLERIES

ART PICASSO, Tapineria, 10. Tel. 310-49-57.
Here you can get good lithographs of works by Picasso, Miró, and Dalí, as well as T-shirts emblazoned with the designs of these masters. Tiles sold here often carry their provocatively painted scenes. Open: Mon–Sat 9:30am–8pm, Sun 9:30am–3pm. Metro: Jaume I.

SALA PARÉS, Petroxol, 5. Tel. 318-70-20.
Established in 1840, this is the finest art gallery in the city, recognizing and promoting the work of many Spanish and Catalan painters and sculptors who have gone on to acclaim. The Maragall family has been the "talent" who recognized all this budding talent. Paintings are displayed in a two-story amphitheater, whose high-tech steel balconies are supported by a quartet of steel columns evocative of Gaudí. Exhibitions of the most avant-garde art in Barcelona change about every three weeks. Open: Mon–Sat 10am–1:30pm and 4–8pm, Sun 11am–1:30pm. Metro: Plaça de Catalunya.

GIFTS

BEARDSLEY, Petritzol, 12. Tel. 301-05-76.
Named after the Victorian English illustrator, this store lies on the same street where the works of Picasso and Dalí were exhibited before they became world-famous. The sophisticated array of gifts, perhaps the finest selection in Barcelona, includes a little bit of everything from everywhere—dried flowers, Mexican pottery, writing supplies, silver dishes, unusual bags and purchases, and lots more. Open: Mon–Fri 10am–1:30pm, Sat 10am–2pm and 5–8:30pm. Metro: Plaça de Catalunya.

LEATHER

LOEWE, Passeig de Gràcia. Tel. 216-04-00.
The biggest branch in Barcelona of this prestigious nationwide leather-goods chain. Everything is top-notch, from the elegantly spacious showroom to the expensive merchandise to the gracious salespeople, who operate out of one of the most celebrated modernist buildings in the city. The company exports its goods to branches throughout Asia, Europe, and North America. Open: Mon–Sat 9:30am–2pm and 4:30–8pm. Metro: Passeig de Gràcia.

MARKETS

El Encants antiques market is held every Monday, Wednesday, Friday, and Saturday in the Plaça de les Glóries Catalanes (Metro: Glóries) (no specific times—go any time during the day to survey the selection).

The open-air **Mercado Gótico de Antiquedades (Gothic Antiques Market),** Plaça Nova (tel. 317-19-96; Metro: Jaume I), takes place next to the cathedral every Thursday, except in August, from 9am to 8pm. Here you can bargain with abandon if you find something that appeals to you.

Coins and postage stamps are traded and sold in the **Plaça Relal** on Sunday from 10am to 2pm. The location is off the southern flank of the Rambles (Metro: Drassanes).

A book-and-coin market is held at the **Ronda Sant Antoni** every Sunday from 10am to 2pm (Metro: Universitat).

MUSIC

CASA BEETHOVEN, Rambles, 97. Tel. 301-48-26.

Probably the most complete collection of sheet music in town. In a narrow store established in 1920, the collection naturally focuses on the works of Spanish and Catalan composers. Music lovers might make some rare discoveries here. Open: Mon–Fri 9am–1:30pm and 4–8pm, Sat 9am–1:30pm. Metro: Liceu.

PORCELAIN

KASTORIA 2, Avinguda Catedra, 6-8. Tel. 310-04-11.

This large store near the cathedral carries many kinds of leather goods, including purses, suitcases, coats, and jackets. But most people come here to look at its famous Lladró porcelain—they are authorized dealers and have a big selection. Open: Mon–Sat 10am–2pm and 4–8pm. Metro: Plaça de Catalunya.

POTTERY

ARTESANA I COSES, Placeta de Montcada, 2. Tel. 319-54-13.

Here you'll find pottery and porcelain from every major region of Spain. Most of the pieces are heavy and thick-sided—designs in use in the country for centuries. Open: Mon–Sat 10am–2pm and 4–8pm. Metro: Jaume I.

ITACA, Ferran, 26. Tel. 301-30-44.

A wide array of handmade pottery, not only from Catalonia but from Spain, Mexico, and Morocco. The merchandise has been selected for its basic purity, integrity, and simplicity. Open: Mon–Fri 10am–1:30pm and 4:30–8pm, Sat 10am–2pm and 5–8:30pm. Metro: Liceu.

SHOPPING MALLS

EL BULEVARD ROSA, Passeig de Gràcia, 55. Tel. 309-06-50.

In some 100 stores you'll find a wide display of merchandise. Upstairs is the previously recommended antiques gallery, El Bulevard des Antiquaris, with some 70 shops. Open: Mon–Sat 10:30am–8:30pm. Metro: Passeig de Gràcia.

DIAGONAL CENTER, Avinguda Diagonal, 584. Tel. 209-65-97.

One of the leading shopping malls of Barcelona, with 60-odd stores displaying a wide range of merchandise. Some of it is geared mainly to local consumers, but casual shoppers from abroad will also find items of interest here to take home. Open: Mon–Sat 10:30am–2pm and 4:30–8:30pm. Metro: Diagonal.

POBLE ESPANYOL

This is not technically a shopping mall but a "village" (see "More Attractions," above) with about 35 stores selling typical folk crafts from every part of Spain: glassware, leather goods, pottery, paintings, carvings—you name it. Stores keep various hours, but you can visit any time during the day. Transportation: Metro to Espanya; from there, free red double-decker bus to Montjuïc.

STRAW PRODUCTS

LA MANUEL ALPARGATERS, Aviño, 7. Tel. 301-01-72.

In addition to its large inventory of straw products, such as hats and bags, this shop is known mainly for its footwear, called *espadrilles* (*alpargatas* in Spanish). This basic rope-soled shoe (said to go back 1,000 years) is made on the premises. Some Catalans wear only espadrilles when performing the sardana, their national dance. To find La Manuel Alpargaters, turn off the Rambles at the Carrer Ferran, walk two blocks, and make a right. Open: Mon–Sat 9:30am–1:30pm and 4:30–8pm. Metro: Jaume I.

UMBRELLAS

JULIO GOMEZ, Ramble de Sant Josep, 104 (also called Ramble de les Flors). **Tel. 301-33-26.**

For over 100 years, Julio Gomez has rung up umbrella sales here. In a workshop out back, women labor over these unique umbrellas or lace-trimmed silk or cotton parasols. There are also Spanish fans, walking sticks capped with silver, and other memorabilia—all adding up to an evocative piece of nostalgia in shopping. Open: Mon–Sat 9:30am–1:30pm and 4–8pm. Metro: Liceu.

11. EVENING ENTERTAINMENT

Barcelona comes alive at night—the funicular ride to Tibidabo or the illuminated fountains of Montjuïc are especially popular. In the Franco era the center of club life was the cabaret-packed district near the south of the Rambles, an area incidentally known for nighttime muggings—so use caution if you go there. But the most fashionable clubs long ago deserted this seedy area and have opened in nearly every major district of the city.

Your best source of local information is a little magazine selling for 60 pesetas (55¢)—*Guía del Ocio*, which previews "La Semana de Barcelona" (This Week in Barcelona). It's in Spanish, but most of its listings will probably be comprehensible. The magazine is sold at virtually every news kiosk along the Rambles.

Nightlife begins for Barcelonans with a promenade (*paseo*) along the Rambles in the early evening, usually from 5 to 7pm. Then things quiet down a bit, until a second surge of energy brings out the Rambles crowds again, from 9 to 11pm. After that the esplanade clears out quite a bit.

If you've been scared off by press reports of the Rambles between the Plaça de Catalunya and the Columbus Monument, you'll feel safer along the Ramble de Catalunya, in the Eixample, north of the Plaça de Catalunya. This street and its offshoots are lively at night, with many cafés and bars.

The array of nighttime diversions in Barcelona is staggering. There is something to interest almost everyone, and to fit most pocketbooks. For families, the amusement parks are the most-frequented venues. Sometimes locals opt for an evening in the *tascas* (taverns) or pubs, perhaps settling for a bottle of wine at a café, an easy and inexpensive way to spend an evening people watching. Serious drinking in pubs and cafés begins by 10 or 11pm. But for the most fashionable bars and discos, Barcelonans delay their entrances until at least 1am.

Cultural events are big in the Catalonian repertoire, and the old-fashioned dance halls, too, still survive in some places. Although disco has waned in some parts of the world, it is still going strong in Barcelona. Decaying movie houses, abandoned garages, long-closed vaudeville theaters, whatever, have been taken over and restored to become nightlife venues for *movida*, that after-dark movement that sweeps across the city until dawn.

Flamenco isn't the rage here that it is in Seville and Madrid, but it still has its devotees. The city is also filled with jazz aficionados. And, best of all, the old tradition of the music hall lives forever in Barcelona.

MAJOR CONCERT/PERFORMANCE HALLS

La Fábrica	257-44-17
Gran Teatre del Liceu	318-92-77
Mercat de los Flors	416-18-75
Palau de la Música Catalán	301-11-04
Teatre Lliure	218-92-51
Teatre Poliorama	317-75-99

THE PERFORMING ARTS

Culture is deeply ingrained in the Catalan soul. The performing arts are strong here—some, in fact, taking place on the street, especially along the Rambles. Crowds will often gather around a singer or mime. A city square will suddenly come alive on Saturday night with a spontaneous festival—"tempestuous, surging, irrepressible life and brio," is how Rose MacCauley wrote about it.

Long a city of the arts, Barcelona experienced a cultural decline during the Franco years, but now is filled once again with the best opera, symphonic, and choral music.

OPERA AND CLASSICAL MUSIC

GRAN TEATRE DEL LICEU, Ramble dels Caputxins, 61. Tel. 318-92-77.

A monument to Belle Epoque extravagance, this 2,700-seat 19th-century opera house, opening onto the Rambles, is one of the grandest theaters in the world. Designed by Catalan architect Josep Oriol Mestves, it presents a classical repertoire of ballets, concerts, and operas. Front-row and box tickets are extremely expensive—and sometimes virtually impossible to obtain. After restoration, the theater is scheduled to reopen the beginning of 1992.

The opera season lasts from early in February until June; ballet is usually presented in October and November. Open: Box office Mon–Fri 10am–1pm and 4–7pm, Sat 10am–1pm. Evening performances begin at 9pm, with matinees at 5pm. Metro: Liceu.

Prices: Opera, 550–8,500 ptas. ($5.15–$79.90); ballet, 320–5,000 ptas. ($3–$47).

PALAU DE LA MÚSICA CATALÁN, Amadeu Vives, 1. Tel. 301-11-04.

In a city of architectural highlights, this one stands out. In 1908 Lluís Domènech i Montaner, a Catalan architect, designed this structure, including stained glass, ceramics, statuary, and ornate lamps among other elements. It stands today—restored—as a classic example of modernism. Concerts and leading recitals are presented here. In February and March you can often attend performances by the Orquestra Ciutat de Barcelona. Open: Box office Mon–Fri 10am–1pm and 4–7pm, Sat 10am–1pm.

Prices: Tickets 500–3,900 ptas. ($4.70–$36.65).

THEATER

Theater is presented in the Catalan language, and therefore will not be of interest to most visitors. However, for those who speak the language, or perhaps who are fluent in Spanish, the following venues are recommended.

TEATRE LLIURE, Leopold Alas, 2. Tel. 218-92-51.

This self-styled free theater is the leading Catalan-language theater in Barcelona. Once a workers' union, the building today is the headquarters of a theater cooperative, and has been since 1976. Its leader is Fabià Puigserver, famous in Barcelona for the bold presentations here, including works by Bertolt Brecht, Luigi Pirandello, Jean Genet (who wrote about Barcelona), and even Molière and Shakespeare. New dramas by Catalan playwrights are also presented. The house seats from 200 to 350. Metro: Fontana.

Prices: Tickets 600–1,000 ptas. ($5.65–$9.40).

COMPANYIA FLOTATS, Teatre Poliorama, 115, Ramble dels Estudis, 115. Tel. 317-75-99.

This leading company is directed by Josep Maria Flotats, an actor-director who trained at the Comédie Française in Paris. It generally presents lighter programs than does the Lliure. Metro: Liceu.

Prices: Tickets 600–1,200 ptas. ($5.65–$11.30).

MERCAT DE LES FLORS, Lleida, 59. Tel. 416-18-75.

Housed in a building constructed for the 1929 International Exhibition at Montjuïc is this other major Catalan theater. Peter Brook first used it as a theater for a 1983 presentation of *Carmen*. Innovators in drama, dance, and music are showcased here, as are modern dance companies from Europe, including troupes from Italy and France. The 999-seat house also has a restaurant overlooking the rooftops of the city. Metro: Espanya.

Prices: Tickets 800–1,000 ptas. ($7.50–$9.40).

DANCE

LA FÁBRICA, Perill, 10. Tel. 257-44-17.

A former textile factory, this venue is now the leading place in Catalonia for experimental dance. It was founded in 1980 by María Antonia Gelabert and Norma Axenfelt-Pereira as part of the movida sweeping Barcelona in the years following Franco's death. During the day it's a dance studio, but at night it witnesses adventurous performances staged by some of Catalonia's leading choreographers. Metro: Diagonal.

Prices: Tickets 600–1,000 ptas. ($5.65–$9.40).

LOCAL CULTURAL ENTERTAINMENT
Flamenco Shows

TABLAO FLAMENCO CORDOBÉS, Les Rambles, 35. Tel. 317-66-53.

At the southern end of the Rambles, a short walk from the harborfront, you'll hear the strum of a guitar, the sound of hands clapping rhythmically, and the haunting sound of the flamenco. Head upstairs to an Andalusian-style room where performances take place with the traditional *cuadro flamenco*—singers, dancers, and guitarist. Cordobés is said to be the best showcase for flamenco in Barcelona. Open: Nightly at 10 and 11:45pm. Reservations: Required. Closed: Jan–Feb. Metro: Drassanes.

Prices: 2,750–3,000 ptas. ($25.85–$28.20), including one drink.

EL TABLAO DE CARMEN, Poble Espanyol, Montjuïc. Tel. 325-68-95.

This club provides a highly rated flamenco cabaret in the re-created village. You can go early and explore the village if you wish and even have dinner here. This place has long been a tourist favorite. Open: Tues–Sun 9pm–3am; dinner shows Tues–Thurs 10:30pm and 12:30am, Fri–Sat 11pm and 1am, Sun 6:30pm and 10:30pm. Reservations: Recommended. Bus: From Plaça d'Espanya (free).

Prices: Dinner and show 4,200 ptas. ($39.50); drink and show 2,500 ptas. ($23.50).

THE CLUB AND MUSIC SCENE
CABARET

BODEGA BOHEMIA, Lancaster, 2. Tel. 302-50-61.

This cabaret extraordinaire, off the Rambles, is a Barcelona institution, and everybody who is anybody has been here. The Bodega Bohemia rates as high camp—a talent showcase for theatrical personalities whose joints aren't so flexible, but who perform with bracing dignity. Curiously, most audiences fill up with young people, who cheer, boo, catcall, and scream with laughter—and the old-timers on stage love it. The show stretches on forever. In all, it's an incredible entertainment bargain if your tastes lean slightly to the bizarre. The street outside is none too safe; take a taxi right to the door. Open: Daily 10:30pm–3am. Metro: Liceu.

Prices: No cover, but 600 ptas. ($5.65) first drink Sun–Fri; 700 ptas. ($6.60) Sat.

EL MOLINO, Vila Vila, 99. Tel. 241-63-83.

This long-standing *café-concierto* features variety shows. Most of the entertainment is pretty bad, but fun to watch nonetheless—especially the give-and-take between audience (often sailors and locals) and performers. You sit in regular theater chairs. Open: Tues–Sun 6–8pm and 11pm–2am; showtimes 6pm and 11pm. Metro: Paral.lel.

Admission: Matinees 900 ptas. ($8.45), including first drink (beer); evening shows 2,000–2,500 ptas. ($18.80–$23.50), including first drink (beer).

BARCELONA DE NOCHE, Tàpies, 5, in Barri Xinés. Tel. 241-11-67.

The cabaret/mime/dance routines here are mostly performed by men in drag. Spaniards go for the exotic, and maybe you will too. This well-known place has been around for a long time. The nightly show is at midnight. Open: Thurs–Tues 11pm–4am. Metro: Paral.lel.

Admission: 2,500 ptas. ($23.50), including entrance, show, and first drink.

BELLE EPOQUE, Muntaner, 246. Tel. 209-73-85.

The opulent crystal chandeliers and plush accessories provide an appropriate backdrop for the glamour and glitter. The sophisticated amplification system plus some of the most advanced lighting tricks in Barcelona add to the quality of the old-time music-hall shows. Open: Mon–Sat 11:30pm–2:15am. Metro: Diagonal.

Admission: Mon–Thurs 3,200 ptas. ($30.10); Fri–Sat 3,700 ptas. ($34.80).

ARNAU, Avinguda del Paral.lel, 60. Tel. 242-28-04.

A variety of cabaret, comedy, and music-hall acts are presented here, and usually to enthusiastic crowds. Open: Sun–Fri 6:30–11pm, Sat 10:30pm–1:15am. Metro: Paral.lel.

Admission: 2,500 ptas. ($23.50), including first drink.

DANCE CLUBS/DISCOS

UP AND DOWN, Numancia, 179. Tel. 204-88-09.

The chic atmosphere of this disco attracts the elite of Barcelona, spanning a generation gap. The more mature patrons, specifically the black-tie, post-opera crowd, head for the upstairs section, leaving the downstairs to the loud music and "flaming youth." Up and Down is the most cosmopolitan disco in Barcelona, with a carefully planned ambience, impeccable service, and a welcoming atmosphere. Every critic who comes here comments on the piquant, sassy antics of the waiters, whose theatricality is part of the carnival-like atmosphere prevading this place. The disco is enhanced by audiovisual techniques; the decor is black and white. Dress can be your own selection, but men must always—regardless of their outfit—wear a tie. Technically, this is a private club and you can be turned away at the door. Open: Daily 11pm–4am. Metro: Sants Estació.

Admission: 2,800 ptas. ($26.30), including first drink.

ESTUDIO 54, Avinguda del Paral.lel, 54. Tel. 329-54-54.

When New York's Studio 54 died, energy seems to have crossed the Atlantic. Barcelona's version of the place lies on the opposite side of the Barri Xinés from the Rambles. If you look as if you can afford the price of a drink, you'll probably be admitted into an enormous room—and partially mesmerized by several different light and slide shows. The dance floor will probably be filled by some of the more offbeat members of Barcelona's night scene. Open: Matinees Sat–Sun 6:30–10pm; Fri–Sun 10:30pm–4am. Closed: Mon–Thurs. Metro: Paral.lel.

Admission: 500 ptas. ($4.70) for the "matinee," 900 ptas. ($8.45) at night.

DON CHUFO, Avinguda Diagonal, 618. Tel. 209-28-31.

This is one of the best-known clubs in town. During the early hours it's a youth-oriented dance club, and late at night it becomes a cabaret that sometimes features well-known singers and comedians. The service is polite and people usually have a good time. Open: Mon–Sat 11pm–4am. Metro: Diagonal.

Admission: 1,500 ptas. ($14.10), including first drink.

2001, Passeig Sant Joan, 49. Tel. 245-00-84.

This is a two-level disco plus a terrace restaurant. Live music and shows are presented to a young crowd. Open: Tues–Sun 7pm–4am. Prices: Drinks 700 ptas. ($6.60). Metro: Girona.
   Admission: 900 ptas. ($8.45).

DANCE HALLS

Those feeling nostalgic may want to drop in on **La Paloma,** Tigre, 27 (tel. 301-68-97; Metro: Universitat), the most famous dance hall of Barcelona. It was young in 1914. Remember the fox trot? The mambo? If not, learn about them at La Paloma, where they're still danced, along with the tango, the cha-cha, and the bolero. Tuesday is boxing night: A boxing match actually takes place in a ringed-off area of the dance floor. Live orchestras provide the music for this old hall with its faded but flamboyant trappings, including gilded plaster angels, crystal chandeliers, and opera-red draperies. Admission is 300 to 500 pesetas ($2.80 to $4.70). "Matinees" are from 6 to 9:30pm; night dances, from 11:30pm to 3:30am.

THE BAR SCENE
PUBS/BARS

PUB 240, Aribau, 240. Tel. 209-09-67.
   This elegant bar, which bears absolutely no resemblance to an English pub, is arranged in three sections: a bar, a small amphitheater, and a lounge for talking and listening to music. Rock and South American folk music are played here, and the place is jammed every night. Open: Daily 7pm–4:30am.
   Admission: 1,000–1,800 ptas. ($9.40–$16.90).

IDEAL COCKTAIL BAR, Aribau, 89. Tel. 253-10-28.
   This is a pleasant drinking spot in an area that has lots of nightlife. Decorated with paneling, stained-glass windows, comfortable leather-covered chairs, and original artworks, the bar has a 19th-century air. It is one of the few places in town that specializes in vodka cocktails—try the Beso Cosaca (vodka with Grand Marnier and lemon juice). It also has the largest selection of malt whiskies in the country, with some 60 labels. Open: 12:30pm–2:30am. Prices: Drinks 650 ptas. ($6.10). Metro: Universitat.

LA COVA DEL DRAC, Tuset, 30. Tel. 217-56-42.
   This pleasant neighborhood bar features jazz every night between October and June. If you want just coffee, a beer, or a drink, you're welcome. Light meals cost from 650 pesetas ($6.10). Someone will serve you in a setting of medium-green walls, art nouveau iron-base marble tables, original artworks, and tropical rattan chairs. Sidewalk tables are available too. Open: Mon–Sat 8pm–2am. Prices: Beer 125 ptas. ($1.20). Metro: Diagonal.
   Admission: Jazz sessions 700–1,200 ptas. ($6.60–$11.30), including first drink.

DIRTY DICK'S, Marc Aureli, 2. Tel. 200-89-52.
   An English-style pub behind an inwardly curving bay window in a residential part of town, Dirty Dick has an interior of dark paneling and exposed brick, with banquettes for quiet conversation. If you sit at the bar, you'll be faced with a tempting array of tiny sandwiches that taste as good as they look. The pub is set at the corner of the Via Augusta, a main thoroughfare leading through the district. Open: Daily 6pm–2am. Prices: Beer 275 ptas. ($2.60); drinks 475 ptas. ($4.45). Metro: Muntaner.

COCKTAIL BAR BOADAS, Tallers, 1. Tel. 318-95-92.
   This small, cozy, intimately conservative bar is usually filled with regulars. Established in 1933, and lying near the top of the Rambles, it is the domain of its proprietor, María Dolors, daughter of the original owner and author of a collection of favorite recipes for cocktails and *tapas*. Many visitors use this place for a predinner drink and snack before wandering to one of the district's many restaurants. You can choose among a wide array of Caribbean rums, Russian vodkas, and English gins; the

skilled bartenders know how to mix them all. The place is especially well known for its daiquiris. Open: 12:30pm–2:30am. Prices: Drinks 500 ptas. ($4.70). Metro: Plaça de Catalunya.

EL BORN, Passeig del Born, 26. Tel. 319-53-33.

Facing a rural-looking square, this place once a fish store, has been cleverly converted. There are a few tables near the front, but my preferred spot is the inner room, decorated with rattan furniture, ceramic jugs, books, and modern paintings. Music here could be anything from Louis Armstrong to Steely Dan. Dinner can also be had at the upstairs buffet. The room is somewhat cramped, but there you'll find carefully laid out, a simple but tasty collection of fish, meat, and vegetable dishes; a full dinner without wine costs around 2,000 pesetas ($18.80). Open: Daily 6:30am–2:30am. Prices: Beer 300 ptas. ($2.80); tapas 700–1,300 ptas. ($6.60–$12.20). Metro: Jaume I.

SPECIALTY BARS
Champagne Bars

The growing popularity of champagne bars during the 1980s is an indication of Spain's increasing cosmopolitanism. The Catalans call their own version of champagne *cava*. In Spanish, champagne bars are called *champanerías,* and in Catalan the name is *xampanyerías*. These Spanish wines are often excellent, said by some to be better than their French counterparts. With more than 50 companies producing cava in Spain, and with each bottling up to a dozen different grades of wine, the best way to learn about Spanish champagne is either to visit the vineyard or to sample the products at a xampanyería.

Champagne bars usually open at 7pm and stay open into the wee hours of the morning. Tapas are served, ranging from caviar to smoked fish to frozen chocolate truffles. Most establishments sell only a limited array of house cavas by the glass—you'll be offered a choice of *brut* or *brut nature* (brut is slightly sweeter). More esoteric cavas must be purchased by the bottle. The most acclaimed brands include Mont-Marçal, Gramona, Mestres, Parxet, Torello, and Recaredo.

LA XAMPANYERÍA, Provença 236. Tel. 253-74-55.

The oldest, best-established, and perhaps most popular champagne bar in town, this tavern has a wine list that includes more than 50 Catalan cavas and a few French champagnes. Sorbets and chocolates are served. Patrons enjoy their drinks at one of two levels—at the long, curved bar or at marble-topped tables. Open: Mon–Thurs 7pm–12:30am, Fri–Sat 7pm–3am. Closed: Aug. Prices: Cava 425–475 ptas. ($4–$4.45). Metro: Provença.

LA CAVA DE OLIMPIA, Loreto, 10. Tel. 239-10-73.

Vintners' memorabilia, ceramic murals of a grape harvest, and rows of champagne bottles create the ambience here. Seventy different cavas are available, as are fresh oysters, anchovies, and an array of cheeses to go with your drinks. Open: Daily 7pm–2:30am. Prices: Cava 425–500 ptas. ($4–$4.70). Metro: Muntaner.

XAMPÚ XAMPANY, Gran Via de les Corts Catalanes, 702. Tel. 232-07-16.

At the corner of the Plaça de Tetuan, this champanería offers a variety of hors d'oeuvres in addition to the wine. Abstract paintings, touchs of high tech, bouquets of flowers, and a pastel color scheme create the decor. Open: Sun–Thurs 6:30pm–2:30am, Fri–Sat 6:30pm–4am. Prices: Cava 350–425 ptas. ($3.30–$4). Metro: Girona.

LA CAVA DEL PALAU, Verdaguer i Callis, 10. Tel. 310-09-38.

Located in an old part of Barcelona, this large champagne bar is a favorite of the after-concert crowd (the Palace of Music is just around the corner). Live music is sometimes presented, accompanied by a wide assortment of cheeses, cold cuts, pâtés, and fresh anchovies—the best in Europe, they say. Open: Mon–Sat 7pm–2:30pm. Prices: Cava 425 ptas. ($4). Metro: Urquinaona.

XAMPANYERÍA CASABLANCA, Bonavista, 6. Tel. 237-63-99.

Someone had to fashion a champagne bar after the Bogart-Bergman film, and this is it. Potted palms, ceiling fans, and wicker chairs are what it's all about—as well as four kinds of house cava served by the glass. The staff also serves a good selection of tapas, especially pâtés. The Casablanca is close to the Passeig de Gràcia. Open: Sun–Thurs 6:45pm–2:30am, Fri–Sat 6:45pm–3am. Prices: Cava 550–650 ptas. ($5.15–$6.10); tapas 400–800 ptas. ($3.75–$7.50). Metro: Passeig de Gràcia.

Grand Chic Bars

In Barcelona they speak of a "bar boom"—the weekly entertainment guide, *Guía del Ocio,* has estimated that 500 new bars have opened in just four years. A staff writer said, "The city has put her ambition and energy into designing bars and hopping from bar to bar. The inauguration of a new watering hole interests people more than any other social, cultural, or artistic event." The bars are stylishly and often daringly avant-garde in design—more so than any you are likely to find in Paris or London. We'll sample only a few of the better ones, but know that there are literally hundreds more.

NICK HAVANNA, Rosselló, 208. Tel. 215-65-91.

Its soaring ceiling is supported by vaguely ecclesiastical concrete columns, off which radiate four arms like a high-tech cathedral. There's a serpentine-shaped curve of two different bars upholstered in black-and-white cowhide, plus a bank of at least 20 different video scenes. To keep patrons in touch with world events between drinks, a Spanish-language teletype machine chatters out news events. Some women have admitted to detouring to the men's room for a view of the famous mirrored waterfall cascading into the urinal. This has become one of Barcelona's most-talked-about and -frequented watering holes. It's hip and happening—so dress accordingly and go late or you'll have the place to yourself. Open: Sun–Thurs 8pm–3am, Fri–Sat 8pm–4am. Prices: Drinks 700–1,500 ptas. ($6.60–$14.10). Metro: Diagonal.

TICKTACKTOE, Roger de Llúria, 40. Tel. 318-99-47.

In the Eixample district, this bar/restaurant is one of the most-talked-about rendezvous points in the city. The decor is definitely tongue-in-cheek—everything from a marble whale to a bar in the form of a female breast. Frequented by TV personalities, Ticktacktoe draws a yuppie crowd, most of whom are under 35. The restaurant offers smooth service and a French Cordon Bleu menu. At the snooker tables and the billiards tables, regular competitions are held. Open: Mon–Thurs 7pm–2:30am, Fri–Sat 7pm–3am. Closed: Aug. Prices: Drinks 700 ptas. ($6.60). Metro: Passeig de Gràcia.

VELVET, Balmes, 61. Tel. 227-67-14.

In the Eixample section of Barcelona, in a modernist building, this is both a night bar and a disco. The intimate dance floor is often overly populated—part of its charm—and the music covers a range of at least 30 years. The walls are covered with magnificent ceramics and marble, while the men's room with its waterfall is considered a local sightseeing attraction on the after-dark circuit, regardless of whether you are male or female. Often flamboyantly attired patrons anchor at one of the bar stools shaped to fit your buttocks. Open: Mon–Thurs 7:30pm–4:30am, Fri–Sat 7:30pm–5am, Sun 7pm–4:30am. Prices: Drinks 900 ptas. ($8.45). Metro: Provença.

ZSA ZSA, Roselló, 156. Tel. 253-85-66.

This is a favorite bar with journalists, writers, and advertising executives, who mingle, drink, converse, and make or break deals. A light system creates endlessly different patterns that seem to change with the mood of the crowd. Chrome columns capped with stereo speakers dot the room like a high-tech forest. Open: Sun–Thurs 7pm–2:30am, Fri–Sat 7pm–3am. Prices: Beer 450 ptas. ($4.15); drinks 650 ptas. ($6.10). Metro: Provença.

OTTO ZUIZ, Lincoln, 15. Tel. 238-07-73.

Glorifying a neoindustrial decor, this ultimately hip nightspot is facetiously named after a German optician. The recipient of millions of pesetas of interior drama, it sits behind a façade that used to house a textile factory. Inside, a labyrinth of metal staircases carries visitors between several levels of rooms decorated in shades of black, sometimes accented with motifs of cerulean-blue clouds. One of the rooms contains a scattering of pool tables. Above the longest bar a Cinerama-size mural shows what might be taken for a bombed-out Berlin in 1945. Don't even think of showing up before midnight. Open: Daily 11pm–4:30am. Prices: Drinks 700 ptas. ($6.60). Metro: Passeig de Gràcia or Fontana.

Admission: 2,000 ptas. ($18.80).

DON TORRES, Via Augusta, 300. Tel. 203-98-99.

One of the most sophisticated and fashionable late-night bars in Barcelona, Dos Torres is located in the affluent northern edge of the city, amid gardens that surround the private villas and expensive apartments of the Sarrià district. In every season except winter, its triangular forecourt is filled to overflowing with well-dressed, articulate young men and women. The minimalist decor, with its art deco accents, unusual lithographs, and a long and dramatically illuminated bar, is in the salon area of this former private villa. Open: Mon–Sat 1pm–3am. Prices: Beer 500 ptas. ($4.70); drinks 700 ptas. ($6.60). Metro: Passeig de Gràcia.

Nostalgia Bars

BAR PASTIS, Santa Mònica, 4. Tel. 318-79-80.

Just off the southern end of the Rambles, this tiny bar was opened in 1947 by Carme Pericás and Quime Ballester, two *valencianos*. They made it a shrine to Edith Piaf, and her songs are still played on an old phonograph in back of the bar. If you look at the dusty art in this dimly lit place, you'll see some of Piaf. But mainly the decor consists of paintings by Quime Ballester, who had a dark, rather morbid vision of the world. You can order four different kinds of *pastis* in this "corner of Montmartre." Outside the window, check out the view, usually a parade of transvestite hookers. The crowd is likely to include almost anyone, especially people who used to be called "bohemians"; they live on in this bar of yesterday. Go after 11:30pm. Open: Mon–Thurs 7:30pm–2am, Fri–Sat 7:30pm–3am, Sun 6:30pm–1:30am. Prices: Pastis 250 ptas. ($2.35); beer 300 ptas. ($2.80); drinks 500 ptas. ($4.70). Metro: Drassanes.

ELS QUATRE GATS, Montsió, 3. Tel. 302-41-40.

The Four Cats has been called "the best bar in Barcelona." (See restaurant listing, Chapter 14.) In 1897 Pere Romeu and three of his friends, painters Ramón Casas, Santiago Rusiñol, and Miguel Utrillo, opened a café for artists and writers at the edge of the Barri Gòtic. Early in the history of the café, they staged a one-man show for a young artist, Pablo Picasso, but he didn't sell one painting. However, Picasso stayed around to design the art nouveau cover of the menu. The café folded in 1903, becoming a private club and art school, and attracting Joan Miró.

In 1978 two Catalans, Pero Notó and Ricard Alsina, reopened the café in the Casa Martí, a building designed by Josep Puig i Cadafalch, one of the leading architects of *modernisme*. The café displays works by major modern Catalan painters, including Tàpies. You can come in to drink coffee at the café, try some wine, eat a full meal—and even try, if you dare, a potent Marc de Champagne, an *eau de vive* distilled from the local cava. Open: Café daily 1pm–1am. Prices: Drinks 175 ptas. ($1.65). Metro: Urquinaona.

Gay Bars

MARTIN'S DISCO, Passeig de Gràcia, 130. Tel. 218-71-67.

Behind a pair of unmarked doors, in a neighborhood of art nouveau buildings, this is one of the more popular gay discos in Barcelona. Within a series of all-black rooms, you'll wander through a landscape of men's erotic art, upended oil drums (used as cocktail tables), and the disembodied front-end chassis of yellow cars set amid the angular surfaces of the drinking and dancing areas. Another bar supplies drinks to a large room where films are shown. Open: Sun–Thurs midnight–4:30am; Fri–Sat midnight–5am. Prices: Beer 400 ptas. ($3.75). Metro: Passeig de Gràcia.

Admission: 800–1,000 ptas. ($7.50–$9.40), including first drink; beer 400 ptas. ($3.75).

CHAPS, Avinguda Diagonal, 365. Tel. 215-53-65.

Gay residents of Barcelona refer to this saloon-inspired bar as the premier leather bar of Catalonia. But in fact, the dress code usually steers more toward boots and jeans than leather and chains. Set behind a pair of swinging doors evocative of the old American West, Chaps contains two different bar areas. Open: Mon–Thurs 7pm–2:30am, Fri–Sun 7pm–3am. Prices: Beer 300 ptas. ($2.80). Metro: Diagonal.

MONROE'S, Lincoln, 3. Tel. 237-56-78.

Honoring everybody's favorite goddess, this gay bar is one of the best decorated and most chic in town. As you go about your business, the eyes of Marilyn will follow you everywhere. The club has a pool table and a garden out back, and attracts a friendly, relaxed crowd of mostly young men. Open: Daily 7pm–3am. Prices: Beer 300 ptas. ($2.80). Metro: Muntaner.

SANTANASSA, Aribau, 27. Tel. 451-00-52.

As a welcoming gesture, a plate of cookies and apples is placed at the front door. Up front you'll find a bar, and at the disco in back is a *homo erectus* mural. In back, too, look for the pop-art large-hipped black woman, one of the treasures of modern art in the city. The clientele is predominantly gay, but many single women also come here. Open: 11pm–3am. Prices: Beer 300 ptas. ($2.80). Metro: Provença.

MORE ENTERTAINMENT

MOVIES

Recent cinematic releases from Paris, New York, Rome, Hollywood, and even Madrid come quickly to Barcelona, where an avid audience often waits in long lines for tickets. Most foreign films are dubbed into Catalan, unless they're indicated as *VO* (original version). Movie listings are published in *Guía de Ocio,* available at any newsstand along the Rambles.

If you're a movie buff, the best time to be in Barcelona is June and early July for the annual film festival.

Filmoteca, Traversera de Gràcia, 63 (tel. 201-19-06; Metro: Fontana), presents various film retrospectives throughout the year, sometimes the work of only one director, or the best offerings from a specific country. Cult films, classics, and other offerings are screened here. Admission is 225 ptas. ($2.10). For show times, consult *Guía de Ocio.*

CASINOS

On the way to Sitges, 24½ miles (39.5km) south of Barcelona, stands the **Gran Casino de Barcelona,** Sant Pere de Ribes, s/n (tel. 893-36-66). The major casino in all of Catalonia, it is housed in a villa from the 1800s. Against an elegant backdrop, the place also attracts restaurant- and disco-goers. A set menu in the restaurant (reservations recommended) costs 3,000 pesetas ($28.20), and drinks go for 700 pesetas ($6.60). Cabaret performances are presented in summer in the open air. For admission, you need 600 pesetas ($5.65) plus a passport. The casino is open June to August, daily from 6pm to 5am; September to May, Sunday through Thursday from 5pm to 4am, on Friday and Saturday from 5pm to 5am.

12. EASY EXCURSIONS

The major one-day excursions, such as to the monastery of Montserrat or to the resorts north along the Costa Brava, are covered in Chapters 16, "Catalonia and Andorra." However, if you've got a day to spare, you might also want to consider the following jaunt.

PENEDÉS WINERIES

From the Penedés wineries comes the famous cava (Catalan champagne), which can be sampled in the champagne bars of Barcelona. You can see where this wine originates by journeying 25 miles (40 km) from Barcelona via highway A-2, Exit 27. There are also daily trains to Sant Sadurní d'Anoia, home to 66 cava firms. Trains depart from Barcelona Sants.

The firm best equipped to receive visitors is **Codorniu,** the largest producer of cava—some 40 million bottles a year. Codorniu is ideally visited by car because of unreliable public transportation. However, it's sometimes possible to get a taxi from the station at Sant Sadurní d'Anoia.

Groups are welcomed at Codorniu (there must be at least four). It's not necessary to make an appointment before showing up. Tours are presented in English, among other languages, and take 1½ hours; they visit some of the 10 miles of underground cellars by electric cart. Take a sweater, even on a hot day. A former pressing section has been turned into a museum, exhibiting wine-making instruments through the ages. The museum is housed in a building designed by the great modernist architect, Puig i Cadafalch.

King Juan Carlos has declared the plant a national historic and artistic monument. The tour ends with a cava tasting. Tours are conducted Monday through Thursday from 8 to 11:30am and 3 to 5:30pm, on Friday from 8 to 11:30am. The ideal time for a visit is for the autumn grape harvest. Codorniu is closed in August.

CARDONA

Another popular excursion from Barcelona is to Cardona, 60 miles (97km) northwest of Barcelona or 370 miles (596km) northeast of Madrid. Take the N-11 west, then north on Rte. 150 to Manresa. Cardona, reached along Rte. 1410, lies northwest of Manresa, a distance of 20 miles (32km).

The home of the dukes of Cardona, the town is known for its canonical church, **Sant Vicenç de Cardona,** placed inside the walls of the castle. The church was consecrated in 1040. The great Catalan architect Josep Puig i Cadafalch wrote, "There are few elements in Catalan architecture of the 12th century that cannot be found in Cardona, and nowhere better harmonized." The church reflects the Lombard style of architecture. The castle (now the parador—see below) was the most important fortress in Catalonia.

WHERE TO STAY AND EAT

PARADOR NACIONAL DUQUES DE CARDONA, 08261 Cardona. Tel. **93/869-12-75.** Fax 93/869-16-36. 60 rms (all with bath). A/C TV TEL
$ Rates: 7,000 ptas. ($65.80) single; 9,000 ptas. ($84.60) double. Breakfast 900 ptas. ($8.45) extra. AE, DC, MC, V.

Sitting atop a cone-shaped mountain that towers 330 feet above Cardona, this restored castle opened as a four-star parador in 1976. Once the seat of Ludovici Pio (Louis the Pious) and a stronghold against the Moors, it was later expanded and strengthened by Guifré el Pilós (Wilfred the Hairy). In the 9th century the palace went to Don Ramón Folch, nephew of Charlemagne. The massive fortress castle proved impregnable to all but the inroads of time, and several ancient buildings in this hilltop complex have been authentically restored and made part of the parador.

The spacious accommodations, some with minibars, are furnished with handcarved wooden canopied beds and woven bedspreads and curtains. The bedrooms command superb views. The public rooms are decorated with antique furniture, tapestries, and paintings of various periods. The bar is in a former castle dungeon, with meals served in the lone stone-arched medieval dining room where the counts once took their repasts. Regional dishes are offered on the menu costing 2,700 pesetas ($25.40). Try the Catalan bouillabaisse, accompanied by wines whose taste would be familiar to the Romans. Service is daily from 1 to 4pm and 8 to 10:30pm.

CHAPTER 16
CATALONIA & ANDORRA

- **WHAT'S SPECIAL ABOUT CATALONIA & ANDORRA**
1. **MONTSERRAT**
2. **TARRAGONA**
3. **SITGES**
4. **ANDORRA**

From Barcelona you can take several one- and two-day excursions. The most popular excursion is to the Benedictine monastery of Montserrat, northwest of Barcelona. To the south, the Roman city of Tarragona has been neglected by visitors, but is particularly interesting to those who appreciate history, while beach lovers should head for the resort of Sitges. Andorra, a principality in the Pyrénées, can be reached in a day from Barcelona, but you should definitely plan on spending the night before heading back.

Catalonia has about six million residents, and twice that many visitors annually. It is one of the "playgrounds" of Europe, with its beaches along the Costa Brava (see Chapter 17) and the Costa Dorada, centered around Sitges. Tarragona is the capital of its own province, and Barcelona, of course, is the major center of Catalonia (see Chapters 13–15).

The province of Catalonia forms a triangle bordered by the French frontier to the north, the Mediterranean Sea to the east, and the ancient province of Aragón to the west. The northern part is a rugged coastline, whereas the Costa Dorada is flatter, with miles of sandy beaches as well as a mild, sunny climate.

Andorra is not part of Catalonia, but I have included it in this chapter because it makes an easy excursion from the area. To visit it, you must face customs formalities at both the Spanish and French borders, and you must have a valid passport. If you're driving a rented car, make sure you have a green card and the necessary identification papers.

Pilgrims may go to Montserrat for its scenery and religious associations, and history buffs to Tarragona for its Roman ruins, but foreigners and locals alike head for the Costa Dorada just for fun. This seashore, named for its strips of golden sand, extends sometimes unbroken along the coastlines of Barcelona and Tarragona provinces. The most avid beach explorers sometimes traverse the entire coast.

One popular stretch is called La Maresme, extending from Río Tordera to Barcelona, a distance of 40 miles (64.5km). Allow at least 2½ hours to cross it without stopovers. The Tarragonese coastline extends from Barcelona to the Ebro River, a distance of 120 miles (193km); a trip along it will take a whole day. Highlights along this coast include Costa de Garraf, a series of creeks skirted by the corniche road after Castelldefels; Sitges; and Tarragona. One of the most beautiful stretches of the coast is Cape Salou, lying south of Tarragona in a setting of pinewoods.

We'll begin our tour through this history-rich part of Catalonia by going not along the coast but rather inland to the Sierra de Montserrat, which has more spectacular views than any place along the coast. Wagner used it as the setting for his opera *Parsifal*. The serrated outline made by the pinnacles of the sierra's steep cliffs led the

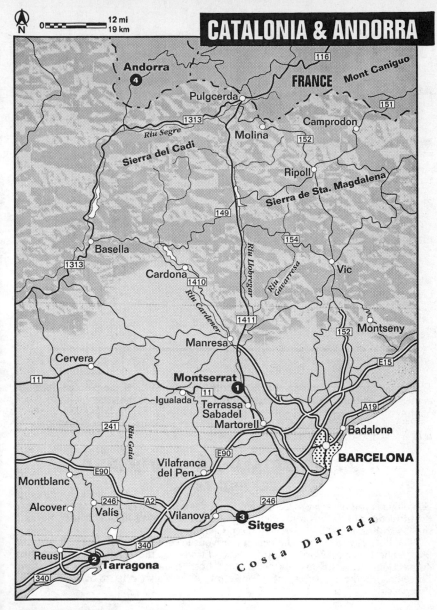

CATALONIA & ANDORRA

12 mi
19 km

N

1 Montserrat
2 Tarragona
3 Sitges
4 Andorra

Andorra **4**

116

FRANCE

Mont Caniguo

Pulgcerda

1313

Riu Segre

Molina

Camprodon

151

152

Sierra del Cadi

Ripoll

Sierra de Sta. Magdalena

149

154

Basella

Riu Llobregar

Riu Gavarresa

Vic

1313

Cardona

1410

Riu Cardener

1411

152

Montseny

Manresa

Cervera

Montserrat

E15

11

11

1

A19

Igualada

Terrassa

Sabadel

Martorell

Badalona

241

Riu Gaia

E90

BARCELONA

Vilafranca
del Pen.

Montblanc

E90

Alcover

246

A2

Vilanova

246

Valís

3 Sitges

Reus

340

2 Tarragona

Costa Daurada

340

Catalonia &
Andorra
⊛
Madrid

SPAIN

WHAT'S SPECIAL ABOUT CATALONIA & ANDORRA

Beaches
- ☐ Sitges, with miles of golden beaches—from family favorites to nudist spots.

Great Towns/Villages
- ☐ Tarragona, one-time home of Julius Caesar.
- ☐ Nearby Montblanch, living museum from the Middle Ages.
- ☐ Sitges, gay resort mecca. Famous early-20th-century colony for artists and writers.
- ☐ Andorra, little principality tucked away in the Pyrénées—nowadays a shopper's paradise.

Ancient History
- ☐ Museum Nacional Arqueològic at Tarragona, with golden-age relics from the Roman Empire. Celebrated *Head of Medusa*.

- ☐ Passeig Arqueològic, at Tarragona, a walk along ancient Roman ramparts.

Pilgrimage Centers
- ☐ Monastery at Montserrat, legendary home of the Black Virgin, patron saint of Catalonia.

Scenic Views
- ☐ Monastery road to Montserrat, with eerie rock formation.
- ☐ Mountain road into the Pyrénées—from Barcelona to Andorra.

Special Events/Festivals
- ☐ Carnaval at Sitges, celebrated before Lent, complete with floats and fancy dress.

Catalonians to call it *montserrat* (sawtooth mountain). It is the premier religious center of Catalonia. Thousands of pilgrims annually visit its monastery with its Black Virgin.

The Monestir de Poblet in Tarragona is the other major monastery of Catalonia. It, too, is a world-class attraction.

SEEING CATALONIA & ANDORRA

GETTING THERE

Barcelona is your gateway to Catalonia. From this city you can consider visiting any of the attractions in the environs, including not only the towns in this chapter, but also the Costa Brava, north of Barcelona (see Chapter 17).

The best way to explore the region is at your leisure by **car.** Failing that, you can use public transportation. For Sitges and Tarragona, the **train** is best, but **bus** connections are also possible. There are both train and bus connections from Barcelona to the monastery at Montserrat. A bus also runs to Andorra in the Pyrénées.

A SUGGESTED ROUTE

Day 1   From Barcelona visit Montserrat. Return to Barcelona in the evening.

Day 2   Head south from Barcelona for a day at Sitges. (If you have an extra day, spend it on the beach). Based in Sitges, you can visit Tarragona. Or go to Tarragona and spend the night.

Day 3   Head for Tarragona, either as a day trip (from Barcelona) or as an overnight excursion. You'll need all the time you can spare in Tarragona, as it offers many monuments.

Day 4   Drive to Andorra, the principality in the Pyrénées.

Day 5   Spend the day exploring this tiny mountain land.

---

1. MONTSERRAT

35 miles NW of Barcelona, 368 miles E of Madrid

GETTING THERE   By Train   The best and most exciting way to go is via the Catalan railway—Ferrocarrils de la Generalitat de Catalunya (Manresa line), with 5 trains a day leaving from the Plaça d'Espanya in Barcelona. The central office is at Plaça de Catalunya, 1 (tel. 205-15-15). The train connects with an aerial cableway (Aeri de Montserrat), included in the rail passage. Expect to spend around 975 pesetas ($9.15) round trip.

By Bus   The **Empresa Julià Company,** Plaça de la Universitat, 12 (tel. 318-38-95), operates morning buses (8 and 9am) from Barcelona. The return is at 5 and 6pm. Round-trip tickets cost 600 pesetas ($5.65).

By Car   Take the N-2 southwest of Barcelona toward Tarragona, turning west at the junction with the N-11. The signposts and exit to Montserrat will be on your right. From the main road, it's 9 miles (14.5km) up to the monastery through dramatic Catalan scenery, with eerie rock formations. Parking is available at the monastery for 200 pesetas ($1.90).

ESSENTIALS   The area code for Montserrat is 93. The Tourist Information Office is at Plaça de la Creu (tel. 93/835-02-51).

Avoid visiting Montserrat on Sunday, if possible. Thousands of locals pour in then, especially if the weather is nice. Remember that the winds blow cold at Montserrat. Even in summer, visitors should take along warm sweaters, jackets, or coats. In winter, thermal underwear might not be a bad idea.

WHAT TO SEE & DO

Montserrat, sitting atop an impressive 4,000-foot mountain 7 miles (11km) long and 3.5 miles (5.5km) wide, is one of the most important pilgrimage spots in Spain, ranking with Zaragoza and Santiago de Compostela. Thousands travel here every year to see and touch the 12th-century statue of La Moreneta (The Black Virgin), the patron saint of Catalonia. So many newly married couples flock here for her blessings that Montserrat has become Spain's Niagara Falls.

The 50-member **cathedral boys' choir** (*escolanía*) is one of the oldest and most renowned in Europe, dating from the 13th century. At 1pm daily you can *usually* hear them singing the hymn of Montserrat in the basilica. The basilica, at Plaça de Santa María, is open daily from 6 to 10:30am and noon to 6:30pm; admission free. To view the Black Virgin statue, enter the church through a side door to the right.

At the Plaça de Santa María you can also visit the **Museu de Montserrat,** known for its collection of ecclesiastical paintings, including works by Caravaggio and El Greco. Modern Spanish and Catalan artists are also represented (see Picasso's early *El Viejo Pescador,* dating from 1895). The collection of biblical artifacts is also interesting; look for the crocodile mummy at least 2,000 years old. Charging 225 pesetas ($2.10) admission, the museum is open July through October, daily from 10:30am to 2pm and 3 to 7pm. Off-season hours are daily from 10:30am to 2pm and 3 to 6pm.

The 9-minute funicular ride to the 4,119-foot-high peak, **Sant Jeroni,** makes for an exciting trip. The funicular operates April through October, daily from 10am to 6:40pm, about every 20 minutes. The cost is 510 pesetas ($4.80) round trip. From the top, you'll see not only the whole of Catalonia, but also the Pyrénées and the islands of Majorca and Ibiza.

You can also make an excursion to **Sant Cova (Holy Grotto),** the alleged site of the discovery of the Black Virgin. The grotto dates from the 17th century, and was built in the shape of a cross. Many famous Catalan artists, such as Puig i Cadafalch and Gaudí, exhibited religious works on the road to the shrine. You go halfway by funicular, but must complete the trip on foot.

The chapel is open April to October, daily from 9am to 6:30pm; off-season from 10am to 5:30pm. The funicular operates from April to October only, every 20 minutes from 10am to 7pm, charging 225 pesetas ($2.10) round trip.

WHERE TO STAY & EAT

Few people spend the night here, but most visitors will want at least one meal. If you don't want to spend a lot, purchase a picnic in Barcelona, or ask your hotel to pack a meal.

ABAT CISNEROS, Plaça de Monestir, 08691 Montserrat. Tel. 93/835-02-01. Fax 93/828-40-06. 41 rms (all with bath). TEL
$ Rates: 4,000 ptas. ($37.60) single; 6,500 ptas. ($61.10) double. Breakfast 500 ptas. ($4.70) extra. AE, DC, MC, V.
This three-star hotel located in the main square is the best in town—simple, comfortable, and attractively furnished. Meals here cost from 1,800 pesetas ($16.90).

---

2. TARRAGONA

60 miles S of Barcelona, 344 miles E of Madrid

GETTING THERE By Train There are 32 trains a day to and from the Barcelona Sants station (1½ hours). The trip costs 450 pesetas ($4.25) one way. There are 4 trains per day (8 hours) from Madrid and there are 3 per day from Valencia (4 hours). In Tarragona, the RENFE office is at Ramble Nova, 40 (tel. 23-28-61).

By Bus From Barcelona, there are 18 buses per day to Tarragona (1½ hours). The cost is 370 pesetas ($3.50) one way.

By Car Take the A-2 southwest from Barcelona to the A-7, then take the N-340. The route is well signposted. This is a fast toll road, costing about 600 pesetas ($5.70) to reach Tarragona.

ESSENTIALS The area code for Tarragona is 977. The Tourist Information Office is at Fortuny, 4 (tel. 977/20-18-59). The American Express representative is Viajes Eurojet, Ramble Nova, 30 (tel. 23-36-23), open Monday through Saturday from 8am to 1pm and 4 to 7pm. In an emergency, dial 091; to summon the police, 23-33-11.

The ancient Roman port city of Tarragona, on a rocky bluff above the Mediterranean, is one of the grandest, but most neglected, sightseeing centers in Spain. Despite its Roman and medieval remains, it is however, the "second city" of Catalonia.

The Romans captured Tarragona in 218 B.C., and during their rule the city sheltered one million people behind its 40-mile-long city walls. One of the four capitals of Catalonia when it was an ancient principality, Tarragona today consists of an old quarter filled with interesting buildings, particularly the houses with connecting balconies. The upper walled town is mainly medieval, whereas the town below is newer.

In the new town, walk along the Ramble Nova, a wide and fashionable boulevard, the main artery of life in modern Tarragona. Running parallel with the Ramble Nova, and lying to the east, is the Ramble Vella, which designates the beginning of the old town. The city has a bullring, good hotels, and beaches. The Romans were the first to launch Tarragona as a resort.

After seeing the attractions listed below, cap off your day with a stroll along the **Balcó del Mediterrani,** with especially beautiful vistas at sunset.

WHAT TO SEE & DO

PASSEIG ARQUEOLÒGIC, Plaça del Pallol.

At the far end of Plaça del Pallol, an archway leads to this half-mile walkway along the ancient ramparts, built by the Romans on top of cyclopean boulders. The ramparts have been much altered over the years, especially in medieval times and in the 1600s. There are pleasant view from many points along the way.

Admission: 100 ptas. (95¢).

Open: July–Sept daily 10am–8pm; Oct–Jan Mon–Sat 10am–1pm and 3–5pm, Sun 10am–2pm; Feb–June daily 10am–1pm and 3–6:30pm.

CATHEDRAL, Plaça de la Seu. Tel. 23-34-12.

Situated at the highest point of Tarragona is this 12th-century cathedral, whose architecture represents the transition from Romanesque to Gothic. It has an enormous vaulted entrance, fine stained-glass windows, Romanesque cloisters, and an open choir. In the main apse, observe the altarpiece of St. Thecia, patron of Tarragona, carved by Pere Johan in 1430. Two flamboyant doors open into the chevet. In the east gallery is the Museu Diocesà, with a collection of Catalan art.

Admission: Cathedral, free; museum, 150 ptas. ($1.40).

Open: Apr–Oct daily 10am–7pm; Nov–Mar daily 10am–1pm and 4–6pm.

ROMAN AMPHITHEATER, Milagro Park.

At the foot of Milagro Park, and dramatically carved from the cliff that rises from the beach, the Roman amphitheater recalls the days in the 2nd century when thousands of Romans gathered here for amusement.

Admission: Free.

Open: Apr–Sept Sun–Fri 10am–2pm, Sat 10am–8pm; Nov–Mar Mon–Sat 10am–6pm, Sun 10am–2pm.

NECROPOLIS, Passeig de la Independéncia. Tel. 21-11-75.

This is one of the most important burial grounds in Spain, having been used by the Christians from the 3rd century through the 5th. It stands outside town next to a tobacco factory whose construction led to its discovery in 1923. While on the grounds, visit the **Museu Paleocristià,** which contains a number of sarcophagi and other objects discovered during the excavations.

Admission: Necropolis plus museum 100 ptas. (95¢).

Open: Mid-May–mid-Sept Mon–Sat 10am–1pm and 4:30–8pm, Sun 10am–2pm; mid-Sept–mid-May Mon–Sat 10am–1:30pm and 4–7pm, Sun 10am–2pm.

MUSEU NACIONAL ARQUEOLÒGIC, Plaça del Rei. Tel. 23-62-06.

The archeology museum, overlooking the sea, houses a collection of Roman relics—mosaics, ceramics, coins, silver, sculpture, and more. Don't miss the outstanding *Head of Medusa,* with its penetrating stare.

Admission: 100 ptas. (95¢).

Open: July–Sept Tues–Sat 10am–1pm and 4:30–8pm, Sun 10am–2pm; Oct–June Tues–Sat 10am–1:30pm and 4–7pm, Sun 10am–2pm.

WHERE TO STAY

NURÍA, Via Augusta, 217, 43007 Tarragona. Tel. 977/23-50-11. 61 rms (all with bath). TEL **Bus:** Playa Travesada from the center.

$ Rates: 3,200 ptas. ($30.10) single; 5,000–5,200 ptas. ($47–$48.90) double. Breakfast 350 ptas. ($3.30) extra. AE, DC, MC, V. **Closed:** Oct–Apr.

Built near the beach in 1967, this five-floor modern building offers neat, pleasant rooms, most with balconies. You can dine in the sunny restaurant, where a meal goes for 1,300 pesetas ($12.20); even cheaper is a tourist menu with paella for 800 pesetas ($7.50). The Nuría's specialty is *romesco,* a kind of *zarzuela* (seafood medley).

HOTEL ASTARI, Via Augusta, 95, 43003 Tarragona. Tel. 977/23-69-00. 83 rms (all with bath). TV TEL **Bus:** From station to Via Augusta.
$ Rates: 4,500 ptas. ($42.30) single; 6,500 ptas. ($61.10) double. Breakfast 350 ptas. ($3.30) extra. AE, DC, MC. **Closed:** Oct–May.

In-the-know travelers in search of peace and quiet on the Mediterranean come here. This five-story resort hotel on the Barcelona road offers fresh and airy, but rather plain, accommodations, a swimming pool, and a solarium. The Astari has long balconies and terraces, one favorite spot being the outer flagstone terrace with its umbrella tables set among willows, orange trees, and geranium bushes. There are both a cafeteria and a cocktail lounge. This is the only hotel in Tarragona with garage space for each client's car.

HOTEL PARÍS, Maragall 4, 43003 Tarragona. Tel. 977/23-60-12. Fax 977/23-86-54. 45 rms (all with bath). TEL
$ Rates: 4,500 ptas. ($42.30) single; 6,500 ptas. ($61.10) double. Breakfast 400 ptas. ($3.75) extra. AE, DC, MC, V.

Opening onto an attractive landmark square, the Plaça de Berdaguer, this hotel with simply furnished but clean rooms rates as one of your best bets. There is no restaurant, but you can order a continental breakfast.

HOTEL URBIS, Reding, 20 bis, 43001 Tarragona. Tel. 977/21-01-16. 44 rms (all with bath). A/C MINIBAR TV TEL
$ Rates: 5,000 ptas. ($47) single; 7,500 ptas. ($70.50) double. Breakfast 425 ptas. ($4) extra. AE, MC, V.

Rooms at this hotel off the Plaça de Corsini are three-star quality and much improved in recent years, with such added amenities as safes. The place doesn't have a restaurant, but many are within walking distance. The nearby tourist office will give you a map for exploring Tarragona.

WHERE TO EAT

LEMAN, Ramble Nova, 27. Tel. 23-42-33.
Cuisine: CATALAN. **Reservations:** Recommended.
$ Prices: Appetizers 300–450 ptas. ($2.80–$4.25); main dishes 400–1,600 ptas. ($3.75–$15.05). V.
Open: Lunch 1–3:30pm; dinner daily 8–11pm.

Reputed to be one of the best restaurants in town, Leman has a menu that reflects what is available at the market—specialties such as seafood stew, bourride of *rape* (monkfish), tropical salad, and an array of well-prepared beef and fish dishes.

CAFETERÍA ARIMANY, Ramble Nova, 43-45. Tel. 23-79-31.
Cuisine: CATALAN. **Reservations:** Not required.
$ Prices: Appetizers 500–1,000 ptas. ($4.70–$9.40); main dishes 1,200–2,100 ptas. ($11.30–$19.75); fixed-priced menu 1,500 ptas. ($14.10). AE, DC, MC, V.
Open: Breakfast daily 8–11am; lunch daily 1–4pm; dinner Mon–Sat 8–11pm.

When this central and popular cafeteria opens its doors at 8am, visitors and locals alike pour in for breakfast. Others come back for lunch, and some finish with a good-value dinner. You can eat here inexpensively or for more money, depending on your appetite. The shrimp in garlic oil is outstanding. Try the fresh fish of the day, based on the local catch, or else squid cooked Roman style.

LA GALERÍA, Ramble Nova, 16. Tel. 23-61-43.
Cuisine: CATALAN. **Reservations:** Recommended.
$ Prices: Appetizers 650–950 ptas. ($6.10–$8.95); main dishes 1,600–2,100 ptas. ($15.05–$19.75); fixed-price menu 1,500 ptas. ($14.10). AE, DC, MC, V.
Open: Lunch Mon–Sat 1–4pm; dinner Thurs–Sat and Mon–Tues 8–11pm.

Right on the most famous esplanade of Tarragona, the Tomás brothers, sons of the more famous Tomás brothers who run the Sol-Ric, operate this centrally located establishment. Friendly and intimate, it has many Belle Epoque touches in its decor. Fish and seafood get the most attention on the menu, with some excellent paellas also served. You can dine either in air-conditioned comfort or out on the terrace.

SOL-RIC, Via Augusta, 227. Tel. 23-20-32.
   Cuisine: CATALAN. Reservations: Not required.
$ Prices: Appetizers 500–750 ptas. ($4.70–$7.05); main dishes 1,700–2,000 ptas. ($16–$18.80). AE, MC, V.
   Open: Lunch Tues–Sun 1–4pm; dinner Tues–Sat 8:30–11pm. **Closed:** Mid-Dec to mid-Jan.

Many guests remember the service here long after memories of the good cuisine have faded. Dating from 1859, the place has a rustic ambience, replete with antique farm implements hanging from the walls. There are also an outdoor terrace and a central fireplace, usually blazing in winter. The chef prepares oven-baked *dorado* with potatoes, tournedos with Roquefort, seafood stew, and several exotic fish dishes, among other specialties.

EXCURSIONS FROM TARRAGONA

If you have a car, you can visit two star sightseeing attractions within a 30- to 45-minute drive from Tarragona. The first stop is the **Monestir de Poblet** (tel. 87-02-54), 29 miles (46.5km) northwest of Tarragona, one of the most intriguing monasteries in Spain. Its most exciting feature: the oddly designed tombs of the old kings of Aragón and Catalonia. Constructed in the 12th and 13th centuries, and still in use, Poblet's cathedral-like church reflects a mixture of Romanesque and Gothic architecture styles. Cistercian monks live here, passing their days writing, studying, working a printing press, farming, and helping to restore the building that suffered heavy damage during the 1835 revolution. Admission to the monastery is 300 pesetas. ($2.80). It's open Monday through Friday from 10am to 12:30pm and 3 to 6pm, on Saturday and Sunday from 10am to 12:30pm and 2:35 to 5pm.

About 3 miles (4.8km) farther, you can explore a fascinating, unspoiled medieval Spanish town, **Montblanch.** At its entrance, a map pinpoints the principal artistic and architectural treasures—and there are many. Walk. Don't drive along the narrow, winding streets.

---

3. SITGES

25 miles S of Barcelona, 370 miles E of Madrid

GETTING THERE By Train RENFE runs trains from Barcelona Sants to Sitges (50 minutes). Call 322-41-42 for information about schedules. A round-trip same-day ticket costs 420 pesetas ($3.85). Two trains leave Barcelona per hour.

By Car Sitges lies a 45-minute drive from Barcelona along the C-246, a coastal road. An express highway, the A-7, is scheduled to open in 1991. (Check before setting out.) The coastal road is more scenic, but it can be extremely slow on weekends because of all the heavy traffic, as Barcelona heads for the beaches.

ESSENTIALS The area code for Sitges is 93. The Tourist Information Office is at Passeig Villafranca (tel. 93/094-12-30).

Sitges is one of the most frequented resorts of southern Europe, the brightest spot on the Costa Dorada. It is crowded in summer, mostly with affluent young northern Europeans, many of them gay. For years the resort was patronized largely by prosperous middle-class industrialists from Barcelona. But those rather staid days have gone; Sitges is as live today as Benidorm and Torremolinos down the coast, but nowhere near as tacky.

Sitges has long been known as a city of culture, thanks in part to resident artist, playwright, and Bohemian mystic Santiago Rusiñol. The 19th-century modernist movement largely began at Sitges, and the town remained the scene of artistic encounters and demonstrations long after modernism waned. Sitges continued as a resort of artists, attracting such giants as Salvador Dalí and poet Federico García Lorca. Then the Spanish Civil War (1936–39) erased what has come to be called the "golden age" of Sitges. Although other artists and writers arrived in the decades to follow, none had the name or the impact of those who had gone before.

The **Carnaval** at Sitges is one of the outstanding events on the Catalan calendar. For more than a century, the town has celebrated the days prior to the beginning of Lent. Fancy dress, floats, feathered outfits, and sequins all make this an exciting event. The party begins on the Thursday before Lent with the arrival of the king of the "Carnestoltes" and ends with the "Burial of a Sardine" on Ash Wednesday. Activities reach their flamboyant best on Sant Bonaventura, where gays hold their own celebrations.

WHAT TO SEE & DO

The old part of Sitges used to be a fortified medieval enclosure. The castle is now the seat of the town government. The local parish church, called La Punta (the point) and built next to the sea on top of a promontory, presides over an extensive maritime esplanade where people parade in the early evening. Behind the side of the church are the Museu Cau Ferrat and the Museu Mar i Cel (see below).

It is the beaches that attract most visitors to Sitges. They have showers, bathing cabins, and stalls. Kiosks rent such items as motorboats and air cushions for fun on the water. Beaches on the eastern end and those inside the town center are the most peaceful, such as **Aiguadolc** and **Els Balomins.** The **Playa San Sebastián, Fragata Beach,** and the **"Beach of the Boats"** (under the church and next to the yacht club) are the area's family beaches. Most young people go to the **Playa de la Ribera,** in the west.

All along the coast women can go topless. Farther west are the most solitary beaches, where the scene grows more kinky, especially along the **Playas del Muerto,** where two tiny nude beaches lie between Sitges and Vilanova i la Geltrú. A shuttle bus runs between the cathedral and Golf Terramar. From Golf Terramar, go along the road to the old Guardia Civil headquarters, then walk along the railway. The first beach draws nudists of every sexual persuasion, and the second is almost solely gay. Be advised that lots of action takes place in the woods in back of these beaches.

Beaches aside, Sitges has some interesting museums.

MUSEU CAU FERRAT, Carrer del Fonollar. Tel. 894-03-64.

Catalan artist Santiago Rusiñol combined two 16th-century cottages to make this house, where he lived and worked and which he willed upon his death (1931) to Sitges along with his art collection. More than anyone else, Rusiñol made Sitges popular as a resort. The museum collection includes two paintings by El Greco and several small Picassos, including *The Bullfight.* A number of Rusiñol's works are also on display.
Admission: 100 ptas. (95¢).
Open: Tues–Sat 10am–1pm and 4–6pm, Sun 10am–2pm.

MUSEU MAR I CEL, Carrer del Fonollar. Tel. 894-03-64.

This museum, opened by the king and queen of Spain in 1970, contains art donated by Dr. Jesús Pérez Rosales. The palace, owned by American Charles Deering when it was built right after World War I, is in two parts connected by a small bridge. The museum has a good collection of Gothic and Romantic paintings and sculptures, as well as many fine Catalan ceramics. There are three noteworthy works by Rebull and an allegorical painting of World War I by Sert.
Admission: 100 ptas. (95¢).
Open: Tues–Sat 10am–1pm and 4–6pm, Sun 10am–2pm.

MUSEU ROMÀNTIC, Sant Gaudenci, 1. Tel. 894-29-69.

This museum re-creates the daily life of a Sitges landowning family in the 18th and

19th centuries. The family rooms, furniture, and household objects are most interesting. You'll also find wine cellars, an important collection of musical instruments, and a collection of antique dolls (upstairs).

Admission: 100 ptas. (95¢).
Open: Tues–Sat 10am–1pm and 4–6pm, Sun 10am–2pm.

WHERE TO STAY

In spite of a building spree, Sitges is unprepared for the large numbers of tourists who come here, especially during July and August. Furthermore, the town is caught in a spiral of rising prices that place many of its major hotels beyond the means of the average budget traveler. But I have managed to scare up a number of bargains for those willing to nail them down with reservations. By mid-October just about everything, including hotels, restaurants, and bars, slows down considerably or closes altogether.

HOTEL EL CID, San José, 39, 08870 Sitges. Tel. 93/894-18-42. 88 rms (all with bath). TEL
$ Rates (including continental breakfast): 3,200 ptas. ($30.10) single; 4,800 ptas. ($45.10) double. AE, DC, MC, V. **Closed:** Oct 21–Apr.
Its exterior suggests Castile and inside, appropriately enough, you'll find beamed ceilings, natural stone walls, heavy wrought-iron chandeliers, and leather chairs. The same theme is carried out in the rear dining room and in the pleasantly furnished bedrooms. A fine meal costs 1,400 pesetas ($13.15). The hotel has a top-floor swimming pool and solarium. El Cid lies off the Passeig de Vilanova in the center of town.

HOTEL RESIDENCIA ALEXANDRA, Pasaje Termes, 1, 08870 Sitges. Tel. 93/894-15-58. 26 rms (12 with bath). TV TEL
$ Rates (including continental breakfast): 3,100 ptas. ($29.15) single without bath, 4,000 ptas. ($37.60) single with bath; 4,100 ptas. ($38.55) double without bath, 5,000 ptas. ($47) double with bath. AE, DC, MC, V. **Closed:** Oct to May.
Hidden on a narrow and unfashionable street off the central Plaça d'Espanya, a short stroll from the beach, this brick building looks nondescript except for its canopied balconies. The rooms are compact, with up-to-date bathrooms. The only meal served: continental breakfast, for an extra charge.

SITGES PARK HOTEL, Jesús, 16, 08870 Sitges. Tel. 93/894-02-50. Fax 93/894-08-39. 88 rms (all with bath). TEL
$ Rates: 3,200 ptas. ($30.10) single; 5,200 ptas. ($48.90) double. Breakfast 290 ptas. ($2.75) extra. DC, MC, V. **Closed:** Dec–Jan.
Outside, it has an 1880s red-brick façade. Inside, past the desk, a beautiful garden with palm trees and a swimming pool. This, in fact, was once a private villa, owned by a family who made their fortune in Cuba. You'll find a good restaurant downstairs, and you can have your coffee or drinks indoors or outdoors at the café-bar, surveying the landmark Catalan tower on the premises. The hotel is about 50 yards from the bus station.

HOTEL MONTSERRAT, Espalter, 27, 08870 Sitges. Tel. 93/894-03-00. 28 rms (all with bath). TEL
$ Rates: 3,500 ptas. ($32.90) single; 5,500 ptas. ($51.70) double. Breakfast 360 ptas. ($3.40) extra. No credit cards accepted. **Closed:** Nov–May.
A rather bland building located on a street near the beach and lined with shops and restaurants, the Montserrat features spacious and reasonably comfortable rooms. For 1,400 pesetas ($13.15), you can take lunch or dinner here. In fair weather, diners enjoy the rooftop.

HOTEL SITGES, Sant Gaudenci, 5, 08870 Sitges. Tel. 93/894-00-72. 52 rms (all with bath). TEL

$ Rates: 3,500 ptas. ($32.90) single; 5,500 ptas. ($51.70) double. Breakfast 350 ptas. ($3.30) extra. V. **Closed:** Oct–May.

S This hotel lies on a narrow residential street in the center of town, 3 blocks from the beach. Behind a façade of modern gray tiles, it welcomes guests into its stone terrazzo lobby. The bedrooms in this one-star choice are furnished simply, but are reasonably comfortable. No full meals here, but the Sitges does maintain a snack service.

HOTEL DON PANCHO, San José, 12, 08870 Sitges. Tel. 93/894-16-62. 85 rms (all with bath). TEL
$ Rates (including continental breakfast): 6,000 ptas. ($56.40) double. **Closed:** Oct to mid-May.
A modern white stucco corner hotel, near the beach, with wraparound balconies, the Don Pancho has a Scandinavian interior with natural woods, a raised fireplace, and rush-seated dining chairs. The rooms, doubles only, are a good size and recently renovated. A restaurant and terrace on the top floor open onto views of the sea and mountains.

HOTEL ROMÀNTIC DE SITGES, Sant Isidre, 33, 08870 Sitges. Tel. 93/894-06-43. 55 rms (all with bath).
$ Rates: 3,800 ptas. ($35.70) single; 6,000 ptas. ($56.40) double. Breakfast 450 ptas. ($4.25) extra. AE, DC, MC, V. **Closed:** Mid-Oct to mid-Apr.
Made up of three beautifully restored 1882 villas, the hotel lies only a short walk from both the beach and the train station. The bar and public rooms are filled with artworks. You can have breakfast either in the hotel's dining rooms or in the garden filled with mulberry trees. The hotel's romantic bar is an international rendezvous point. Overflow guests are housed in a nearby annex, Renaixenca.

EL GALEÓN, Sant Francesc, 44, 08870 Sitges. Tel. 93/894-06-12. Fax 93/894-63-35. 47 rms (all with bath). TEL
$ Rates: 3,500 ptas ($32.90) single; 6,200 ptas. ($58.30) double. Breakfast 310 ptas. ($2.90) extra. V. **Closed:** Oct 20–Apr.
A leading three-star hotel only a short walk from both the beach and the Plaça d'Espanya, this well-styled hostelry blends a bit of the old Spain with the new. The small public rooms feel cozy, while the good-sized bedrooms, accented with woodgrain, have a more streamlined aura. There are a swimming pool and a patio in the rear. Advance reservations necessary.

HOTEL FLORIDA, Espalter, 16, 08870 Sitges. Tel. 93/894-21-00. 12 rms (all with bath). TV
$ Rates (including continental breakfast): 4,800 ptas. ($45.10) single; 7,500 ptas. ($70.50) double. MC. **Closed:** Oct–May.
The focus of this renovated hotel near the beach is the large dining patio, surrounded by 25-foot-high ivy-covered walls and shaded by flowering trees—you'll feel that you're in a separate little enclave. The Florida also has a swimming pool and a solarium. All of its rooms lack decorative flair, but are good-sized and offer simple comfort. Breakfast only is offered.

HOTEL PLATJADOR, Passeig de la Ribera, 35, 08870 Sitges. Tel. 93/894-50-54. 59 rms (all with bath).
$ Rates (including continental breakfast): 4,800 ptas. ($45.10) single; 8,000 ptas. ($75.20) double. MC, V. **Closed:** Oct 21–Apr.
One of the best hotels in town, the Platjador, on the esplanade fronting the beach, has comfortably furnished bedrooms, many with big French doors opening onto balconies and sea views. The dining room, facing the beach, is known for its good cuisine, including gazpacho, paella, fresh fish, and dessert flan. For 1,400 pesetas ($13.15) you can enjoy a set menu.

HOTEL SUBUR, Passeig de la Ribera, s/n, 08870 Sitges. Tel. 894-00-66.
Fax 93/894-69-86. 95 rms (all with bath). TEL
$ Rates: 6,250 ptas. ($58.75) single with half board; 10,860 ptas. ($102.10) double with half board. AE, DC, MC, V.
The first hotel built in Sitges (in 1916), the Subur was later torn down and reconstructed in 1960. Today, as always, it occupies a prominent position in the center of town on the seafront. Its rooms are well furnished, with balconies opening onto the Mediterranean; some accommodations contain minibars and air conditioning. The dining room, decorated with fine woods, lays a bountiful table of both regional and international dishes.

WHERE TO EAT

ELS 4 GATS, Sant Pau, 13. Tel. 894-19-15.
Cuisine: CATALAN. **Reservations:** Recommended.
$ Prices: Appetizers 500–1,500 ptas. ($4.70–$14.10); main dishes 550–2,400 ptas. ($5.15–$22.55); fixed-priced menu 950 ptas. ($8.95). AE, DC, MC, V.
Open: Lunch Thurs–Tues 1–3:30pm; dinner Thurs–Tues 8–11pm.

S Named after a famous old café frequented by Picasso, Nonell, Casas, and others at the beginning of the century, The 4 Cats is an intimate restaurant decorated with paintings, paneled-wood ceiling, and provincial wooden chairs. Typical dishes include garlic soup, lamb cutlets, roast chicken, and kidneys in sherry sauce. The carrer Sant Pau intersects with the beachfront Passeig de la Ribera.

OLIVER'S, Isla de Cuba, 39. Tel. 894-35-16.
Cuisine: CATALAN. **Reservations:** Required.
$ Prices: Appetizers 450–1,600 ptas. ($4.25–$15.05); main dishes 650–1,950 ptas. ($6.10–$18.35). MC, V.
Open: Dinner Tues–Sun 8pm–midnight.
Lying on the northern fringe of the old town, directly south of the Plaça de Maristany, this angular bistro-style establishment is decorated like a regional tavern with local paintings. It makes a good choice for dinner, unless you insist on being on the beachfront esplanade. The wines are reasonably priced, and the chef features daily specials. Try grilled salmon, entrecote flavored with herbs of Provence, grilled goat cutlets, and a daily soup prepared with fresh ingredients of the market.

FRAGATA, Passeig de la Ribera, 1. Tel. 894-10-86.
Cuisine: SEAFOOD. **Reservations:** Recommended.
$ Prices: Appetizers 475–1,700 ptas. ($4.45–$16); main dishes 700–2,800 ptas. ($6.60–$26.30). AE, DC, MC, V.
Open: Lunch Fri–Wed 1–4pm; dinner Fri–Wed 8–11pm. **Closed:** Nov–Dec.
Although its simple interior offers little more than well-scrubbed floors, tables with crisp napery, and air conditioning, some of the most delectable seafood specialties in town are served here, and hundreds of loyal customers come to appreciate the fresh, authentic cuisine. Specialties include seafood soup, grilled turbot, mussels marinara, several preparations of squid and octopus, plus some flavorful meat dishes such as grilled lamb cutlets.

CHEZ JEANETTE, Sant Pau, 23. Tel. 894-00-48.
Cuisine: CATALAN. **Reservations:** Recommended.
$ Prices: Appetizers 450–795 ptas. ($4.25–$7.50); main dishes 925–1,700 ptas. ($8.70–$16); fixed-priced menu 910 ptas. ($8.55). No credit cards.
Open: Lunch Fri–Wed 1–4pm; dinner Fri–Wed 7:30–11:30pm.

S Although Jeanette is no longer with us, this place continues to lure patrons in an atmosphere of roughly textured stucco walls and regional tavern decor. Set back on a restaurant-flanked street a short walk from the beach, it draws both straight and gay clients. The food features *platos del día* (plates of the day). From the standard menu, you can order such dishes as onion soup, *rape* (monkfish) with whisky, and entrecote with Roquefort sauce.

MARE NOSTRUM, Passeig de la Ribera, 60. Tel. 894-33-93.
   Cuisine: SEAFOOD. **Reservations:** Recommended.
   $ Prices: Appetizers 650–1,300 ptas. ($6.10–$12.20); main dishes 950–2,800 ptas. ($8.95–$26.30); fixed-priced menu 1,600 ptas. ($15.05). DC, MC, V.
   Open: Lunch Thurs–Tues 1–4pm; dinner Thurs–Tues 8–11pm. **Closed:** Dec 15 to Jan 20.
This place has been around so long (some 40 years) that it's a landmark. The dining room has a waterfront view, and in warm weather tables are placed outside. The menu includes a full range of seafood dishes, among them grilled fish specialties and steamed hake with champagne. The fish soup is particularly delectable. Next door the restaurant's café—resting under a blue beamed ceiling—serves ice creams, milk shakes, sandwiches, a selection of *tapas,* and three varieties of *sangría,* including one with champagne and fruit.

EL VELERO, Passeig de la Ribera, 38. Tel. 894-20-51.
   Cuisine: SEAFOOD. **Reservations:** Recommended.
   $ Prices: Appetizers 550–1,300 ptas. ($5.15–$12.20); main dishes 950–3,000 ptas. ($8.95–$28.20). AE, DC, MC, V.
   Open: Lunch Tues–Sun 1:30–4pm; dinner Tues–Sun 8:30–11:30pm.
This is one of the leading restaurants of Sitges, occupying a position along the beachfront promenade. The most desirable tables are found on the "glass greenhouse" terrace, opening onto the esplanade, although there is a more glamorous restaurant inside. Try a soup such as clam and truffle or white fish, followed by a main dish such as paella marinara (with seafood) or suprême of salmon in a pine-nut sauce. The restaurant is named after a type of pleasure boat.

LA MASÍA, Paseo Vilanova 164. Tel. 894-10-76.
   Cuisine: CATALAN. **Reservations:** Recommended.
   $ Prices: Appetizers 675–750 ptas. ($6.35–$7.05); main dishes 1,200–2,000 ptas. ($11.30–$18.80); fixed-priced menu 1,200 ptas. ($11.30). AE, MC, V.
   Open: Lunch daily 1–4pm; dinner daily 8:30–11:30pm.
The provincial decor complements the imaginative regional specialties for which this place is known. They include codfish, roast suckling lamb well seasoned with herbs, a wide array of fresh fish and shellfish, and the legendary local dessert, *crème catalán.* If you prefer to dine outdoors, you can sit in the pleasant garden adjacent to the main dining room.

EVENING ENTERTAINMENT

One of the best ways to spend the night in Sitges is to walk the waterfront esplanade, have a leisurely dinner, then retire at about 11pm to one of the open-air cafés for a nightcap and some serious people-watching. Few local dives can compete with "the scene" taking place on the streets.
   If you're straight, you'll have to look carefully for a bar that isn't gay. There are so many gay bars, in fact, that a map is distributed pinpointing their locales. Most of them are concentrated on Sant Bonaventura in the center of town, a 5-minute walk from the beach (near the Museu Romàntic); there are nine gay bars in this small district alone. If you grow bored with the action in one place, you just have to walk down the street to find another. Drink prices run about the same in all the clubs.

RICKY'S DISCO, Sant Pau, 25. Tel. 894-39-93.
   This is the town's most popular straight disco. In business for some 20 years, it is set back from the beach on a narrow little street noted for such favorite restaurants as Els 4 Gats. The music is recorded, and the crowd is international. Don't overlook the comfortable annex high above the dance floor. Open: Daily 11:15pm–5am. Prices: Drinks 800 ptas. ($7.50). Closed: Nov.

MEDITERRÁNEO, Sant Bonaventura, 6. No phone.

The leading—also the largest—gay disco and bar in Sitges has a formal Iberian garden and sleek modern styling. And upstairs in this restored 300-year-old house just east of the Plaça d'Espanya, there are pool tables and a covered terrace. The club, which on a summer night can be filled to overflowing, is open only from mid-April to November. Open: Mon–Thurs 10pm–3am, Fri–Sat 10pm–3:30am. Prices: Beer 250 ptas. ($2.35); drinks 450 ptas. ($4.25).

---

4. ANDORRA

136 miles N of Barcelona, 388 miles NE of Madrid

GETTING THERE By Plane The mountaintop airport at Seu d'Urgell (Seo de Urgel in Spanish), lies 7 miles (11km) across the border in Spain. It's not well used because of uncertain weather conditions.

By Train From Barcelona, trains go as far as Puigcerdá, where connections for Andorra have to be made the rest of the way by bus.

By Bus The **Alsina Graells** line operates buses from Barcelona (4 hours). Buses leave from Ronda Universitat, 4, in Barcelona (tel. 302-40-86) daily at 6:30am and 2:45pm.

By Car The drive will take you through some of the finest mountain scenery in Europe, with peaks, vineyards, and rushing brooks. From Barcelona, drive via Puigcerdá to Seu d'Urgell. Allow about 4 hours because of poor road conditions. Take Rte. 152 north of Barcelona toward France. The turnoffs from Andorra are clearly signposted.

ESSENTIALS The area code for Andorra is 9738. The Tourist Information Office is at Carrer Dr. Vilanova, s/n (tel. 202-14). The official language of Andorra is Catalan.

Charlemagne gave the "country" its independence in 784, and, with amused condescension, Napoleon let Andorra keep its autonomy. The principality of Andorra is now ruled by two co-princes, the president of France and the Spanish archbishop of Seo de Urgel.

Andorra, less than 200 square miles in size, is a storybook land of breathtaking scenery—cavernous valleys and snowcapped peaks, rugged countryside and pastureland, deep gorges. It's popular for summer excursions and recently has been gaining as a winter ski resort as well.

Perhaps because of its isolation—sandwiched between France and Spain high in the eastern Pyrénées—Andorra retained one of the most insular peasant cultures in Europe as late as 1945. But since the late 1950s tourists have increased from a trickle to a flood—12 million in fact. This has created havoc with Andorra's economy, although opinions are sharply divided on what the deluge has done to the country overall.

Some suggest that Andorra has ruined its mountain setting with urban sprawl, as taxis, crowds, and advertising have transformed the once-rustic principality into a busy center of trading and commerce. At first glance, the route into the country from Spain looks like a used-car lot, and traffic jams are legendary. New hotels and hundreds of shops have opened in the past decade to accommodate the French and Spanish pouring across the frontiers to buy duty-free merchandise. A magazine once called Andorra "Europe's feudal discount shopping center." In addition, there is cheap gasoline in Andorra.

Warning: Border guards check very carefully for undeclared goods.

GETTING AROUND ANDORRA

Most people make their base in the capital, **Andorra-la-Vella** (in Spanish, Andorra-la-Vieja) or the adjoining town, **Les Escaldes,** where there are plenty of shops, bars, and hotels. Shuttles run between the towns, but most shoppers prefer to walk. Most of the major hotels and restaurants are on the main street of Andorra-la-Vella (**Avinguda Meritxell**) or on the main street of Les Escaldes (**Avinguda Carlemany**). French francs and Spanish pesetas may be used interchangeably, and hotel, restaurant, and shop prices are quoted in both currencies.

But unless you've come just to shop, you will want to leave the capital for a look at this tiny principality. Two nearby villages, **La Massana** and **Ordino,** can be visited by car or by bus (leaving about every 30 minutes). Buses don't have numbers. They cross the country from south to north and vice versa. Buses branching off the main line are marked with the name of the place where they are heading.

WHERE TO STAY IN LES ESCALDES

HOTEL ESPEL, Plaça de la Creu Blanca, 1, Les Escaldes. Tel. 9738/20-855. Fax 9738/280-56. 102 rms (all with bath). TV TEL
$ Rates (including continental breakfast): 3,600 ptas. ($33.85) single; 5,000 ptas. ($47) double. No credit cards.

Conveniently located about 225 yards from the shopping center and 15 minutes from the ski slopes, this modern hotel has two TV lounges, a bar, and a restaurant, as well as a parking area opposite the building and a small private garage. Hot thermal baths are offered. Rooms are well furnished and comfortable.

LA GRANDALLA, Avinguda Carlemany, 14, Les Escaldes. Tel. 9738/21-125. 44 rms (all with bath). TEL
$ Rates (including continental breakfast): 3,000 ptas. ($28.20) single; 5,500 ptas. ($51.70) double. AE, DC, MC, V.

Although the modern interior of this hotel lacks charm, it is nonetheless a centrally located, clean, safe haven. Rooms are simply furnished, and the hotel operates a restaurant, charging 1,400 pesetas ($13.15) for lunch or dinner.

LES CLOSES, Avinguda Carlemany, 93, Les Escaldes. Tel. 9738/28-311. 44 rms (all with bath). TV TEL
$ Rates: 5,000 ptas. ($47) double; 6,500 ptas. ($61.10) triple. Breakfast 400 ptas. ($3.75) extra. DC, MC, V.

This little budget find on the principal street in Les Escaldes resembles a comfortable, well-run French pension. The rooms are adequate, and breakfast is served.

HOTEL ROC BLANC, Plaça dels Coprinceps, 5, Les Escaldes. Tel. 9738/21-486. Fax 9738/602-44. 240 rms (all with bath). MINIBAR TV TEL
$ Rates: 10,000 ptas. ($94) single; 14,000 ptas. ($131.60) double. Breakfast 1,100 ptas. ($10.35) extra. AE, DC, MC, V.

Built in the 1960s to accommodate the many spa patients who come here for thermal treatments and health reasons, the hotel has many facilities—swimming pool, sauna, gym, and tennis court. There are also several convention rooms, plus a garage. The bedrooms are conservatively but comfortably furnished. The in-house restaurant, El Pi, is listed separately below. You can also dine at a second restaurant, L'Entrecôte.

WHERE TO EAT IN LES ESCALDES

PIZZA ROMA, Avinguda Carlemany, 95. Tel. 28-538.
Cuisine: FRENCH/ITALIAN. **Reservations:** Not required.
$ Prices: Appetizers 350–500 ptas. ($3.30–$4.70); main dishes 400–1,800 ptas. ($3.75–$16.90). AE, DC, MC, V.
Open: Lunch daily 1–3:30pm; dinner daily 8–11:30pm.

Pizza is not the only item served here, although it is delicious. Also available are fresh pastas, an array of salads, onion tarts, grilled beef and pork, and osso buco. You'll find a good selection of beer and wine. The dining room is air-conditioned and tastefully decorated, and you can also eat out on the flower-decked terrace. Pizza Roma lies on the main bus route.

EL PI, Hotel Roc Blanc, Plaça dels Coprinceps, 5. Tel. 21-486.
   Cuisine: FRENCH/SPANISH. **Reservations:** Recommended.
$ Prices: Appetizers 800–1,000 ptas. ($7.50–$9.40); main dishes 1,500–2,500 ptas. ($14.10–$23.50); fixed-priced menu 3,800 ptas. ($35.70). AE, DC, MC, V.
   Open: Lunch daily 12:30–3:30pm; dinner daily 8–10:30pm.
This restaurant lies one floor above street level in the Hotel Roc Blanc, on the main street near the bus station. The best regional dishes of France and Spain are served here, along with wines from both countries. Your meal might consist of duckling pâté, *entrecôte* with Roquefort, crayfish in cream sauce, or filet of beef Stroganoff.

WHERE TO STAY IN ANDORRA-LA-VELLA

L'ISARD, Avinguda Meritxell, 36, Andorra-la-Vella. Tel. 9738/20-092.
   Fax 9738/283-29. 55 rms (all with bath). A/C TEL
$ Rates (including continental breakfast): 4,800 ptas. ($45.10) single; 6,400 ptas. ($60.15) double. AE, DC, MC, V.
In winter this centrally located hotel caters to the skiers who come to the Pyrénées, while summer guests can take advantage of the outdoor pool, the garden, and the tennis courts. The rooms are well furnished; some have minibars, and TV is available upon request. The hotel restaurant serves complete meals for 1,750 pesetas ($16.45). You'll find L'Isard on the main bus route in the center of town.

HOTEL MERCURE ANDORRA, Avinguda Meritxell, 58, Andorra-la-Vella.
   Tel. 9738/20-773. Fax 9738/290-18. 67 rms (all with bath). MINIBAR TV TEL
$ Rates: 10,000 ptas. ($94) single; 12,000 ptas. ($112.80) double. Breakfast 950 ptas. ($8.95) extra. AE, DC, MC, V.
Designed in the successful chain-hotel format, this establishment (located on the main bus route) is loaded with facilities: outdoor pool, tennis courts, gym, disco, sauna, and parking garage. Rooms are furnished with streamlined furniture, and each has a balcony. The hotel offers two dining choices: La Truita, serving meals at a costly 4,200 pesetas ($39.50); or the less expensive La Brasserie, with meals costing from 2,600 pesetas ($24.45).

ANDORRA PALACE, Prat de la Creu, s/n, Andorra-la-Vella. Tel. 9738/
   21-072. Fax 9738/290-18. 140 rms (all with bath). MINIBAR TV TEL
$ Rates: 11,000 ptas. ($103.40) single; 14,000 ptas. ($131.60) double. Breakfast 950 ptas. ($8.95) extra. AE, DC, MC, V.
Located in the congested center of town near the Casa Lavall and many of the city's most interesting bars and restaurants, this hotel offers a pleasant garden, tennis courts, a gym, and a sauna. Each of the well-furnished rooms has its own balcony. The hotel has two dining choices, the expensive La Truita and the less expensive La Brasserie. The Hotel Mercure Andorra also has two restaurants with the same names.

WHERE TO EAT IN ANDORRA-LA-VELLA

CAN MANEL, Carrer Mestre Xavier Plana, s/n. Tel. 223-97.
   Cuisine: ANDORRAN. **Reservations:** Required.
$ Prices: Appetizers 650–950 ptas. ($6.10–$8.95); main dishes 1,200–2,000 ptas. ($11.30–$18.80). AE, DC, MC, V.
   Open: Lunch Thurs–Tues 1–3pm; dinner Thurs–Tues 8–10pm. **Closed:** Late June to mid-July.
This is another excellent choice for regional fare, accompanied by the wine of the Pyrénées. Informal and relaxed, the place resembles a regional tavern. You get good, honest, filling fare here. Try the spicy civet of hare, chamois, or wild goat in season. Service is unpretentious. The restaurant lies on a back street off Via Carrer Ciutat de Valls in the old quarter.

HOSTAL CALONES, Antic Carrer Major. Tel. 21-312.

Cuisine: ANDORRAN. **Reservations:** Recommended.

$ **Prices:** Appetizers 650–950 ptas. ($6.10–$8.95); main dishes 1,200–2,000 ptas. ($11.30–$18.80). AE, DC, MC, V.

Open: Lunch daily 1–3pm; dinner Mon–Sat 8:30–10:30pm. **Closed:** 2 weeks in June, 2 weeks in Nov.

Miguel Canturri is said to offer the best regional cooking in Andorra. Here, in the heart of the old quarter, you get the fare of the Pyrénées, often original recipes handed down through generations. Pork has always figured prominently in the menu of these mountains, and the chef prepares at least a dozen pork dishes, including a locally prized head cheese, *brinquera.* One of the most robust dishes is *trinxat,* made with potatoes and cabbage, then topped with bacon. Try the dried eel (which became popular in the days when fresh fish was out of the question because of transportation) or the honey- and vinegar-flavored mountain hams.

VERSALLES, Cap del Carrer, 1. Tel. 2-13-31.

Cuisine: FRENCH. **Reservations:** Recommended.

$ **Prices:** Appetizers 750–900 ptas. ($7.05–$8.45); main dishes 1,800–2,500 ptas. ($16.90–$23.50). AE, MC, V.

Open: Lunch Fri–Tues 1–3pm; dinner Thurs–Tues 8:30–10:30pm.

Claudi Martí comes from Carcassonne, that walled French city across the border, and he brought all his culinary secrets with him when he opened this restaurant. Many food critics consider this intimate spot the finest dining room in the country. Begin with one of his delectable pâtés (offered both hot and cold) or one of his superb fresh salads, some with crab or duck. Your main course might be filet mignon, saffron-flavored monkfish, or confit of duck with flap mushrooms. Versalles is located on a pedestrian alley off the Plaça de Princeps de Benlloch.

CHAPTER 17

GIRONA & THE COSTA BRAVA

- **WHAT'S SPECIAL ABOUT GIRONA & THE COSTA BRAVA**
1. **GIRONA**
2. **LLORET DE MAR**
3. **TOSSÀ DE MAR**
4. **FIGUERES**
5. **CADAQUÉS**

The Costa Brava (Wild Coast) is that 95-mile (153-km) stretch of coastline—the most northern Mediterranean seafront in Spain—that begins north of Barcelona at Blanes and stretches toward the French border. Visit in May, June, September, or October and avoid July and August when tour groups from northern Europe book virtually all the bedrooms.

Undiscovered little fishing villages along the coast long ago burst into resort towns. Tossà de Mar is perhaps the most delightful of these resorts. Lloret de Mar is also immensely popular, but perhaps too commercial for many tastes. The most unspoiled spot is remote Cadaqués. Some of the smaller villages also make excellent stopovers.

If you want to visit the Costa Brava but simply cannot secure space in high season, consider either taking a day trip by car from Barcelona or booking one of the daily organized tours that leave from that city. Allow plenty of time for driving. In summer the traffic jams can be fierce, the roads between towns difficult and winding.

If you visit the coast in summer without a hotel reservation, you'll stand a fair chance of getting a room in Girona, the capital of the province and one of the most interesting medieval cities in Spain.

SEEING GIRONA & THE COSTA BRAVA

GETTING THERE

The main **airport** for the Costa Brava is in the provincial capital, Girona, where most of the package tours from northern Europe land. Most North Americans arrive first at Barcelona's Prat de Llobregat airport, explore that city, then head north for the Costa Brava.

Some parts of the area can be toured using the **train.** Girona lies on the main rail link between Barcelona and the French frontier. Local train service from Barcelona also covers the coast to the French border, with Figueres the best hub. Coastal resorts reached by train are Blanes in the south and Port Bou in the north (not covered here).

All the small coastal resorts have local **bus** service. There is, as well, service from both Barcelona and Girona to all the major resorts, such as Tossà de Mar.

The north–south *autopista* A-17 is the fastest way to travel the coast by **car,** but expect high tolls. The N-11 also runs north and south, but it's slower and more crowded. At the coast, the C-253 runs from Blanes to Palamós. You get great views but sometimes dangerous turns and curves. Some of the roads connecting coastal resorts are unclassified.

A SUGGESTED ROUTE

Day 1 Drive north from Barcelona, stopping at the coastal town of Blanes to see the famous botanical gardens designed by botanist Karl Faust. Leave Blanes and drive to Lloret de Mar or Tossà de Mar for a two-day stopover.

✓ WHAT'S SPECIAL ABOUT GIRONA & THE COSTA BRAVA

Beaches
☐ Tossà del Mar, with two sandy beaches and plenty more in the environs; for beach lovers who enjoy a "Cézanne landscape."

☐ Lloret de Mar, the so-called fun house of the Costa Brava, with area's longest beach (it's packed).

Great Towns/Villages
☐ Tossà de Mar, with its battlements and towers, former hideaway for writers and artists.

☐ Cadaqués, select retreat on this rugged coast so beloved by Salvador Dalí.

☐ Girona, capital of province; medieval city with centuries-old Jewish ghetto.

Museums
☐ Dalí Museum at Figueres, outranked only by Prado in attendance, is pure surrealist theater.

Gardens and Parks
☐ Blanes, where you can wander through gardens originally planted by famed German botanist Karl Faust—more than 3,000 Mediterranean plants and trees.

Ancient Monuments
☐ Arab baths at Girona—Romanesque civic architecture at its best and site of many movie backdrops.

Special Events/Festivals
☐ International Music Festival at Cadaqués—Tuesday and Friday in late July and August. Attracts some of world's finest musicians.

Day 2 While based in Tossà or Lloret, explore the environs if you have a car, or stay and enjoy the joie de vivre of these fun-loving towns. If you're staying at Lloret, go to Tossà to explore its old quarter.

Day 3 Leave Tossà or Lloret and continue to drive along the coast to Figueras to see the Dalí Museum, one of the most popular attractions in Spain. Stay overnight in the gourmet citadel of Figueras, or drive over to Cadaqués on the far eastern coast, where Dalí used to live, and spend the night there.

Day 4 Drive south again on the N-11 or the A-17 to the provincial capital of Girona. See what you can before nightfall, and the following morning take a walk through the monumental district.

Day 5 Return to Barcelona, continue into the Pyrénées to Andorra, or go north to France.

---

1. GIRONA

60 miles NE of Barcelona, 56 miles S of the French city of Perpignan

GETTING THERE By Train Two trains run daily from Barcelona Sants station; also two trains daily from Figueras.

By Bus From the Costa Brava, you can take one of the SARFA buses to Girona. Two per day depart from Tossà de Mar and 16 per day from Palafrugell. Fills de Rafael Mas, another bus company, makes 3 to 5 runs per day between Girona and Lloret de Mar. You can also travel here by bus from Barcelona's Estació de Vilanova (tel. 232-04-59 in Barcelona for schedules).

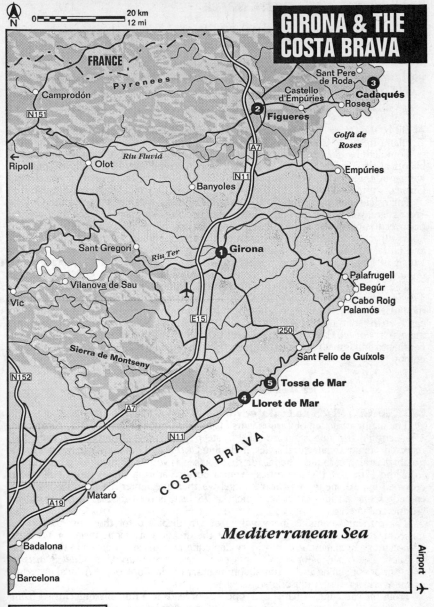

GIRONA & THE COSTA BRAVA

0 |=====| 20 km
12 mi

N

FRANCE

Pyrenees

Camprodón

N151

Ripoll →

Olot

Riu Fluvià

Banyoles

Sant Gregori

Riu Ter

Vilanova de Sau

Vic

E15

Sierra de Montseny

N152

A7

N11

COSTA BRAVA

A19

Mataró

Badalona

Barcelona

Sant Pere
de Roda

Castello
d'Empúries

2 **Figueres**

A7

N11

Empúries

Golfà de
Roses

3 **Cadaqués**

Roses

1 **Girona**

Palafrugell
Begúr
Cabo Roig
Palamós

250

Sant Felío de Guíxols

5 **Tossa de Mar**

4 **Lloret de Mar**

Mediterranean Sea

Airport ✈

Girona & the
Costa Brava

⊛
Madrid

SPAIN

1 Girona
2 Lloret de Mar
3 Tossà de Mar
4 Figueres
5 Cadaqués

By Car From Barcelona or the French border, connect with the main north–south route (A-7), taking the turnoff to Girona. From Barcelona, take the A-2 north to reach the A-7.

ESSENTIALS: The area code for Girona is 972. The Tourist Information Office is at Ramble de la Libertat (tel. 972/20-26-79).

Split by the Onyar River, this sleepy medieval city attracts crowds of tourists darting inland from the Costa Brava for the day.

Founded by the Romans, Girona is considered one of the most important historical sites in Spain. Later, it was a Moorish stronghold. Later still, it reputedly withstood three invasions by Napoleon's troops (1809). For that and other past sieges, Girona is often called La Ciudad de los Sitios (The City of a Thousand Sieges).

For orientation purposes, go to the ancient stone footbridge across the Onyar. From there, you'll have the finest view. Bring good walking shoes, as the only way to discover the particular charm of this medieval city is on foot. You can wander for hours through the **Call,** the labyrinthine old quarter, with its narrow, steep alleyways and lanes, its ancient stone houses, which form a rampart chain along the Onyar. Much of Girona can be appreciated from the outside, but it does contain some important attractions you'll want to see on the inside.

The Jews of Girona form part of its cultural heritage. From 890 to 1492, they were a strong community in the city. It is believed that early settlers from Jerusalem formed the nucleus of the first colony. They were forced to live ghetto style in the Call, their early settlements grouped around the Plaça dels Apòstols. Carrer de la Força was the main artery of the Call. In 1492, the year Columbus discovered America, his patrons, Ferdinand and Isabella, expelled all Jews from Spain, thus ending this once-flourishing colony.

WHAT TO SEE AND DO

CATHEDRAL, Plaça de la Catedral.
The major attraction of Girona is its magnificent cathedral, reached by climbing a 17th-century baroque staircase of 90 steep steps. The 14th-century cathedral represents many architectural styles, including Gothic and Romanesque, but it is most notably Catalan baroque. The façade that you see as you climb those long stairs dates from the 17th and 18th centuries; from a cornice atop it, there rises a bell tower crowned by a dome with a bronze angel weathervane. Enter the main door of the cathedral, and go into the nave, which, at 75 feet, is the broadest in the world of Gothic architecture.

The cathedral contains many works of art, displayed for the most part in its museum. Its prize exhibit is a tapestry of the creation, a unique piece of 11th- or 12th-century Romanesque embroidery depicting humans and animals in the Garden of Eden. The other major work displayed is the 10th-century *Códex del Beatus,* a manuscript containing an illustrated commentary on the Book of the Apocalypse, one of the world's rarest manuscripts.

From the cathedral's Chapel of Hope a door leads to a Romanesque cloister from the 12th and 13th centuries, with an unusual trapezoidal layout. The cloister gallery, with a double colonnade, has a series of biblical scenes that are considered the prize jewel of western Catalan Romanesque art. From the cloister you can view the Torre de Carlemany (Charlemagne's Tower), from the 12th century.

Admission: Cathedral and museum 150 ptas. ($1.40).
Open: Cathedral and museum—summer, daily 9:30–8pm; winter, daily 9:30am–7pm.

MUSEU D'ART, Pujada de la Catedral, 12. Tel. 20-95-36.
In a former Romanesque and Gothic episcopal palace (Palau Episcopal) next to the

cathedral, this museum displays artworks spanning 10 centuries (once housed in the old Diocesan Museum and the Provincial Museum). Stop in the throne room to view the altarpiece of Sant Pere of Púbol by Bernat Martorell, and that of Sant Miguel de Crüilles by Lluís Borrassa. Both of these works, from the 15th century, are considered exemplary pieces of Catalan Gothic painting. The museum is also proud of its altar stone of Sant Pere de Roda, which dates from the 10th and 11th centuries; this work in wood and stone, depicting figures and legends, was once covered in embossed silver. The 12th-century *Crüilles Timber* is a unique piece of Romanesque polychrome wood. *Our Lady of Besalú,* from the 15th century, is considered one of the best Virgins carved in alabaster.

Admission: 100 ptas. (95¢).

Open: Tues–Sat 10am–1pm and 4:30–7pm, Sun 10am–1pm.

BANYS ARABS, Pujada dei Bei Mart.

In the old quarter of the city are the 12th-century Arab baths, an example of Romanesque civic architecture. Visit the *caldarium* (hot bath), with its paved floor, and the *frigidarium* (cold bath), with its central octagonal pool surrounded by pillars that support a prismlike structure in the overhead window. The Moorish baths were heavily restored in 1929, but they give you an idea of what the old ones were like.

Admission: 100 ptas. (95¢).

Open: Summer, Tues–Sat 10am–1pm and 4:30–7pm, Sun 10am–1pm; winter, Tues–Sat 10am–1pm.

MUSEU ARQUEOLÒGIC, Sant Pere de Galligants, Santa Llúcia, 1. Tel. 20-26-32.

Housed in a Romanesque church and cloister from the 11th and 12th centuries, this museum illustrates the history of the city from the Paleolithic to the Visigothic period, using artifacts discovered in nearby excavations. The monastery itself ranks as one of the best examples of Catalan Romanesque architecture. In the cloister, note some Hebrew inscriptions from gravestones of the old Jewish cemetery.

Admission: 100 ptas. (95¢).

Open: Tues–Sat 10am–1pm and 4:30–7pm, Sun 10am–1pm.

MUSEU D'HISTÓRIA DE LA CUITAT, Força, 13. Tel. 20-91-60.

Housed in the old 18th-century Capuchin Convent de Sant Antoni, this collection dates from the time of Puig d'en Roca (Catalonia's oldest prehistoric site) to the present. It includes Girona's (and Spain's) first electric streetlights.

Admission: 200 ptas. ($1.90).

Open: Tues–Sat 10am–2pm and 5–7pm, Sun 10am–2pm.

ESGLÉSIA DE SANT FELIU, Plaça de Sant Feliu.

This 14th- to 17th-century church was built over what may have been the tomb of Feliu of Africa, martyred during Diocletian's persecution at the beginning of the 4th century. Important in the architectural history of Catalonia, the church has pillars and arches in the Romanesque style and a Gothic central nave. The bell tower, one of the Girona skyline's most characteristic features, has eight pinnacles and one central tower, each supported on a solid octagonal base. The main façade of the church is baroque. The interior contains some exceptional works, including a high altarpiece from the 16th century and an alabaster *Reclining Christ* from the 14th century. Notice the eight pagan and Christian sarcophagi set in the walls of the presbytery, the two oldest of which are from the 2nd century. One shows Pluto carrying Proserpina off to the depths of the earth.

Admission: Free.

Open: Daily 10am–1pm and 6–8:15pm.

WHERE TO STAY

CONDAL, Joan Maragall, 10, 17002 Girona. Tel. 972/20-44-62. 39 rms (all with bath).

$ Rates: 2,050 ptas. ($19.25) single; 4,000 ptas. ($37.60) double. No credit cards.

⑤ Located near the police station west of the old town, this place is a bargain. Although rated third class, it manages to be both modern and pristine. The lounge and reception area are small, there is no service elevator, and no meals (not even breakfast) are served—but these prove minor concerns. The bedrooms are good and comfortable, and some have nice views.

HOTEL PENINSULAR, Nou 3, 17001 Girona. Tel. 972/20-38-00. Fax 972/21-04-92. 67 rms (all with bath).
$ Rates: 3,500 ptas. ($32.90) single; 5,000 ptas. ($47) double. Breakfast 300 ptas. ($2.80) extra. AE, DC, MC, V.

A leading second-class hotel in Girona, this comfortable but characterless structure in the old quarter is near the Cathedral and the river. Its rooms are traditional and comfortably furnished. The Peninsular is better suited for stopovers than longer stays. It has no restaurant, and serves continental breakfast only on order.

HOTEL ULTONIA, Avinguda Jaume I, 22, 17001 Girona. Tel. 972/20-38-50. Fax 972/20-33-34. 45 rms (all with bath). A/C TV TEL
$ Rates: 5,500 ptas. ($51.70) single; 7,800 ptas. ($73.30) double. Breakfast 450 ptas. ($4.25) extra. AE, DC, MC, V.

A three-star hotel just a short walk from the Plaça de la Independència, the Ultonia has recently been restored and is now better than ever. Ever since the 1960s it has been a favorite with business travelers, but today it attracts more tourists, as it lies close to the historical district. Bedrooms are compact and furnished in modern style; soundproof double-glazed windows keep out the noise. Some of the rooms opening onto the avenue have tiny balconies. In just 8 to 12 minutes, you can cross the Onyar into the medieval quarter. Across the street, garages offer parking for a fee. Guests enjoy a breakfast buffet in the morning, but no other meals are served.

COSTABELLA, Avinguda de Francia, 61, 17007 Girona. Tel. 972/20-25-24. Fax 972/20-22-03. 50 rms (all with bath). A/C MINIBAR TV TEL
$ Rates: 6,500 ptas. ($61.10) single; 8,800 ptas. ($82.70) double. Breakfast 600 ptas. ($5.65) extra. AE, DC, MC, V.

Lying north off the N-11 in the direction of Figueres (across from the General Alvarez de Castro Hospital), this hotel with sleek modern styling is one of the area's best. Rooms offer ample amenities and such extras as piped-in music and remote control for the TV. Most bedrooms are a medley of pastels. A generous breakfast buffet greets guests.

SOL GIRONA, Carretera de Barcelona, 112, 17003 Girona. Tel. 972/24-32-32. Fax 972/24-32-33. 114 rms (all with bath). A/C MINIBAR TV TEL
Directions: Take Exit 6 or 7 off A-7 (hotel is signposted from there).
$ Rates: 8,500 ptas. ($79.90) single; 10,500 ptas. ($98.70) double. Breakfast 850 ptas. ($8) extra. AE, DC, MC, V.

A four-star choice and the best in town, yet reasonable in price, Sol Girona was inaugurated in 1989 in the western part of the city. It attracts many motorists traveling the route between Barcelona and Perpignan in France. This chain hotel is well maintained, with bedrooms comfortably furnished in a compact, functional, modern style with all the amenities. It has a bar and a good restaurant, offering meals for 1,800 pesetas ($16.90).

NOTOTEL GIRONA, Carretera del Aeropuerto, s/n, 17467 Riudellots de la Selva. Tel. 972/47-71-00. Fax 972/47-72-96. 81 rms (all with bath). A/C TV TEL
$ Rates: 9,500 ptas. ($89.30) single; 11,500 ptas. ($108.10) double. Breakfast 850 ptas. ($8) extra. AE, DC, MC, V.

Its easy accessibility and garden-style surroundings make this efficient modern hotel a favorite with visitors who want to explore the surrounding resorts of the Costa Brava. It lies near Exit 8 (Girona airport) on the A-17. Only a meadow and a well-placed copse of birches and pines separate it from the busy autoroute, but despite its location, it has the feel of a country hotel. Comfortable leather couches, plants, and airy lattices fill the public rooms; there are an exposed-brick hideaway bar and a spacious room for watching the wide-screen TV. The bedrooms are efficiently designed with built-in furniture. Meals served in the dining room cost 2,200 pesetas ($20.70). There's a swimming pool on the premises, plus a gift shop that sells well-crafted leather goods.

WHERE TO EAT

BRONSOMS, Avinguda de Sant Francesc, 7. Tel. 21-24-93.
Cuisine: CATALAN. **Reservations:** Recommended.
$ **Prices:** Appetizers 550–950 ptas. ($5.15–$8.95); main dishes 1,200–1,900 ptas. ($11.30–$17.85); fixed-priced menus 900–1,000 ptas. ($8.45–$9.40). DC, MC, V.
Open: Lunch daily 1–4pm; dinner Mon–Thurs 9–10:30pm. **Closed:** 2 weeks in Aug.

Ⓢ This bustling family-owned restaurant in the heart of Girona caters to a nicely integrated crowd of locals and visitors, mostly European. You can get some of the best food in town at this modest spot. The chef makes good-tasting vegetable soup, served in large bowls; another favorite is veal with mushrooms, a hearty dish that might fortify you for your climb up those 90 steps to Girona's cathedral. Other specialties include typical fish dishes, steamed beef ragout, roast leg of lamb, and paella. There's also a bar.

L'HOSTALET DEL CALL, Batlle y Prats, 4. Tel. 21-26-88.
Cuisine: CATALAN. **Reservations:** Recommended.
$ **Prices:** Appetizers 450–750 ptas. ($4.25–$7.05); main dishes 1,200–1,900 ptas. ($11.30–$17.85). V.
Open: Lunch Tues–Sun 1–4pm; dinner Tues–Sat 8–11pm.
Taking its name from the old Jewish ghetto, this intimate restaurant lies near the cathedral in a house that dates from the Middle Ages. Many of its dishes are based on centuries-old recipes, including *fava* (broad beans prepared Sephardic style with spicy lamb). Try duck with pears or veal with "mushrooms from the country."

2. LLORET DE MAR

62 miles S of the French border, 42 miles N of Barcelona

GETTING THERE By Train and Bus From Barcelona, take a train to Blanes, then take a bus 5 miles (8km) to Lloret.

By Car Head north from Barcelona along the A-19.

ESSENTIALS The area code for Lloret de Mar is 972. The Tourist Information Office is at Plaça de la Vila, 1 (tel. 972/36-57-88).

Although it has a good half-moon–shaped sandy beach, Lloret is neither chic nor sophisticated, and most of the people who come here are low-income Europeans. The competition for cheap rooms is fierce.

Lloret de Mar has grown at a phenomenal rate from a small fishing village with just a few hotels to a bustling resort with more hotels than anyone could count. And more keep opening up, although there are never enough in July and August. The accommodations are typical of the Costa Brava towns, running the gamut from impersonal modern box-type structures to vintage whitewashed, flowerpot-adorned buildings on the narrow streets of the old town.

The area has rich vegetation, scenery, and a mild climate.

WHERE TO STAY

Many of the hotels—particularly the three-star establishments—are booked solidly by tour groups. Here are some bargains if you reserve in advance.

HOTEL METROPOL, Plaça de la Torre, 2, 17310 Lloret de Mar. Tel. 972/36-41-62. 86 rms (all with bath). TEL
$ Rates (including continental breakfast): 3,000 ptas. ($28.20) single; 4,600 ptas. ($43.25) double. No credit cards. **Closed:** Nov to Apr.

Ⓢ This eight-story concrete hotel stands 1 block from the beach. The efficiently designed rooms are clean and have built-in furniture; a few of them have private terraces, although views are obstructed. A contemporary bar and dining room are on the premises.

HOTEL SANTA ROSA, Senia del Barral, 31, 17310 Lloret de Mar. Tel. 972/36-43-62. Fax 972/37-01-96. 138 rms (all with bath). TEL
$ Rates: 3,800 ptas. ($35.70) single; 4,800 ptas. ($45.10) double. Breakfast 425 ptas. ($4) extra. V.

Ⓢ The roof terrace, with its swimming pool, semi-enclosed bar, music, potted flowers, and chaise longues, is the social center of the Santa Rosa. Some of the comfortable bedrooms have balconies with views of the sea (100 yards away). This is one of the handful of hotels in town that accepts individual travelers, and receives them from April to October.

XAINE HOTEL, Vila, 55, 17310 Lloret de Mar. Tel. 972/36-50-08. Fax 972/37-11-68. 88 rms (all with bath).
$ Rates (including continental breakfast): 3,200 ptas. ($30.10) single; 5,200 ptas. ($48.90) double. V. **Closed:** Nov to Apr.
Small and compact, this modern hotel is right in the noisy center of town, 3 blocks from the beach. Many of its above-average rooms have their own balconies.

HOTEL EXCELSIOR, Passeig Mossèn Jacinto Verdaguer, 16, 17310 Lloret de Mar. Tel. 972/36-41-37. 45 rms (all with bath). TEL
$ Rates: 4,200 ptas. ($39.50) single; 7,800 ptas. ($73.30) double. Breakfast 435 ptas. ($4.10) extra. AE, DC, MC, V.
This glorified beach clubhouse is right on the esplanade, perfect if you want to go for an early-morning dip before your coffee. Although you can easily get a room during the off-season, chances are slim in July and August. The accommodations are comfortable, although furnished with uninspired modern furniture. A complete luncheon or dinner costs 1,600 pesetas ($15.05) extra; board is obligatory from July to September. The hotel receives guests from April to October.

HOTEL CLUAMARSOL, Passeig Mossèn Jacinto Verdaguer, 7, 17310 Lloret de Mar. Tel. 972/36-57-50. Fax 972/37-16-37. 87 rms (all with bath). TEL
$ Rates: 4,800 ptas. ($45.10) single; 8,800–12,500 ptas. ($82.70–$117.50) double. Breakfast 900 ptas. ($8.45) extra. AE, DC, MC, V. **Closed:** Nov through Jan.
This small modern brick hotel on a public square near the town's seaside promenade is one of the few places in town that accepts individual bookings during the high season. Occupying the ground floor are a Victorian-style bar with comfortable leather-covered armchairs and a dining room that overlooks the palm-treed plaza. A glass-enclosed pool is found on the sixth-floor rooftop. The rooms are comfortably furnished.

WHERE TO EAT

RECO CATALÁ, Vila, 55. Tel. 36-50-08.
Cuisine: CATALÁN. Reservations: Not required.
$ Prices: Appetizers 400–900 ptas. ($3.75–$8.45); main dishes 1,300–1,800 ptas. ($12.20–$16.90); fixed-priced menu 1,000 ptas. ($9.40). MC, V.
Open: Lunch daily 1–3:30pm; dinner daily 8–11pm.

Ⓢ This ground floor restaurant 2 blocks from the beach offers a low-priced set menu that won't disappoint. A typical menu might consist of cream of mushroom soup, York ham with mashed potatoes, a French omelet, and dessert (drinks are extra). Lamb is a specialty. The view of the passing parade outside is worthwhile.

EL TRULL, Cala Canyelles, s/n. Tel. 36-49-28.
  Cuisine: SEAFOOD. **Reservations:** Not required.
$ **Prices:** Appetizers 300–600 ptas. ($2.80–$5.65); main dishes 1,600–1,900 ptas. ($15.05–$17.85); fixed-priced menu 1,350 ptas. ($12.70). AE, DC, MC, V.
  Open: Lunch daily 1–4pm; dinner daily 8–11pm.

⑤ Located about 1.5 miles (2.5km) outside town in the suburb of Urbanización Playa Canyelles, this rustic-looking restaurant makes the trip worthwhile. There are also a swimming pool and a pleasant garden nearby. The seafood-inspired house specialties include fish soup, a fish stew heavily laced with lobster, an omelet surprise (the waiter will tell you the ingredients if you ask him), and clams Trull.

EVENING ENTERTAINMENT

HOLLYWOOD, Carretera Tossà-Hostalrich, s/n. Tel. 36-74-63.
  This dance club at the edge of town is the place to be and be seen. Look for it on the corner of Carrer Girona. Open: Daily 11pm–4am. Prices: Drinks 600 ptas. ($5.65).

CASINO LLORET DE MAR, Carretera de Tossà, s/n. Tel. 36-65-12.
  Games of chance include French and American roulette, blackjack, and chemin de fer, among others. There are a restaurant, buffet dining room, bar-boîte, and dance club, along with a swimming pool. Bring your passport. The casino lies southwest of Lloret de Mar, beside the coastal road leading to Blanes and Barcelona. Drive or take a taxi at night. Open: Mon–Fri 5pm–4am; Sat–Sun 5pm–4:30am. Prices: Drinks 700 ptas. ($6.60).
  Admission: 550 ptas. ($5.15).

---

3. TOSSÀ DE MAR

56 miles N of Barcelona, 7½ miles NE of Lloret de Mar

GETTING THERE By Bus Direct bus service is offered from Blanes and Lloret. Tossà de Mar is also on the main Barcelona–Palafruggel route.

By Car Head north of Barcelona along the A-19.

ESSENTIALS The area code for Tossà de Mar is 972. The Tourist Information Office is at Carretera de Lloret, Edificio Terminal (tel. 972/34-01-08).

This gleaming white town, with its 12th-century walls and labyrinthine old quarter, fishing boats, and fairly good sands, is the most attractive base for a Costa Brava vacation. It seems to have more joie de vivre than its competitors. The battlements and towers of Tossà were featured in the 1951 Ava Gardner and James Mason movie, *Pandora and the Flying Dutchman.*

In the 18th and 19th centuries Tossà survived as a port center, growing rich on the cork industry. But that declined in the 20th century, and many of its citizens emigrated to America. But by the 1950s, thanks in part to the Ava Gardner movie, tourists began to discover the charms of Tossà and a new industry was born.

To experience these charms, walk through the 12th-century walled old town, known as **Vila Vella**, built on the site of a Roman villa from the 1st century A.D. The Vila Vella is entered through the Torre de les Hores.

Tossà was once a secret haunt for artists and writers, and Marc Chagall called it a blue paradise. It has two main beaches: **Mar Gran** and **La Bauma.** The coast near Tossà—north and south—offers even more possibilities.

As one of few resorts to have withstood exploitation and retained most of its allure, Tossà enjoys a broad base of international visitors—so many, in fact, that it can no longer shelter them all. In spring and fall, finding a room may be a snap, but in summer it's next to impossible.

WHERE TO STAY

HOTEL TONET, Plaça de l'Església, 1, 17320 Tossà de Mar. Tel. 972/32-02-37. 36 rms (all with bath).
$ Rates (including half board): 3,500 ptas. ($32.90) single; 6,000 ptas. ($56.40) double. AE, DC, MC, V.

On a central plaza surrounded by narrow streets, this hotel has a country-inn atmosphere. It is built with terraces on its upper floors where guests can relax or have breakfast amid potted vines and other plants. The rooms are rustically simple, with natural Spanish wooden headboards and rush-seated chairs. Classified as one-star, the Tonet deserves a far higher rating.

L'HOSTELET, Plaça de l'Església, 4, 17320 Tossà de Mar. Tel. 972/34-00-88. Fax 972/34-18-65. 36 rms (all with bath). TV TEL
$ Rates (including continental breakfast): 3,000 ptas. ($28.20) single; 4,000 ptas. ($37.60) double. AE, DC, MC, V. **Closed:** Nov to Apr.

On the same plaza as the Tonet, this modern-looking hotel has an open garden terrace in the front, plus a patio shaded by lemon trees. The **hostal** is sometimes known as the House of the American Student because of the number of Americans who stay here. All of the rooms are basic, some much more inviting than others.

HOTEL AVENIDA, Avinguda de sa Palma, 5, 17320 Tossà de Mar. Tel. 972/34-07-56. Fax 972/34-01-60. 50 rms (all with bath).
$ Rates (including continental breakfast): 3,000 ptas. ($28.20) single; 5,500 ptas. ($51.70) double. MC, V. **Closed:** Nov to Easter.

This pleasant, clean four-story hotel, located near the village church, about 1 block from the beach, is one of the best values in town. The lobby level contains a sunny dining room and a modern bar. The comfortable bedrooms have private terraces.

HOTEL VORA LA MAR, Avinguda de sa Palma, 14, 17320 Tossà de Mar. Tel. 972/34-03-54. 63 rms (all with bath). TEL
$ Rates: 5,500 ptas. ($51.70) double. Breakfast 400 ptas. ($3.75) extra. AE, DC, MC, V.
On a quiet street a block away from the beach, this hotel was built in the '50s and renovated in the '70s. It has an outdoor café, a garden, and a dining room. The terrazzo-floored bedrooms, doubles only, are comfortable, and many have balconies.

HOTEL NEPTUNO, La Guardia, 52, 17320 Tossà de Mar. Tel. 972/34-01-43. Fax 972/34-19-33. 126 rms (all with bath).
$ Rates (including continental breakfast): 3,900 ptas. ($36.65) single; 5,600 ptas. ($52.65) double. AE, DC, MC, V. **Closed:** Nov to Apr.

This is my favorite hotel in Tossà, on a quiet residential hillside northwest of Vila Vella, somewhat removed from the seaside promenade. Inside, antiques are mixed in with modern furniture, creating a personalized decor; the beamed-ceiling dining room is charming, and the bedrooms are tastefully lighthearted, modern, and sunny. A small swimming pool with its own terraced garden has a view of the sloping forest next door.

HOTEL CAP D'OR, Passeig de Vila Vella, 17320 Tossà de Mar. Tel. 972/34-00-81. 11 rms (all with bath).
$ Rates (including continental breakfast): 3,800 ptas. ($35.70) single; 6,200 ptas. ($58.30) double. MC, V. **Closed:** Nov through Mar.
Perched on the waterfront on a quiet edge of town, this 200-year-old building,

originally a fish store, nestles against the stone walls and towers of the village castle. Built of rugged stone itself, the Cap d'Or is like an old country inn and seaside hotel combined. It is both neat and well run. The old-world dining room, with its ceiling beams and ladderback chairs, has a pleasant sea view and food that is far above the average. Outsiders are welcome to come in for a complete meal, served daily from 12:30 to 3:30pm and 7 to 10:30pm.

HOTEL ANCORA, Avinguda de sa Palma, 25, 17320 Tossà de Mar. Tel. 972/34-02-99. 58 rms (all with bath). TEL
$ Rates: 5,500 ptas. ($51.70) single; 6,400 ptas. ($60.15) double. Breakfast 400 ptas. ($3.75) extra. AE, DC, MC, V.
About 70 yards from the beach, this hotel is really a pair of architecturally dissimilar buildings, the older one constructed in 1950. Inside, there's a large art deco bar near the reception desk, as well as an elegant courtyard restaurant. Many rooms have terraces with views either of the sea or of a narrow tree-lined canal. There is an in-house garage.

HOTEL DIANA, Plaza de España, 10-12, 17320 Tossà de Mar. Tel. 972/34-18-86. Fax 972/34-11-03. 21 rms (all with bath).
$ Rates: 4,400 ptas. ($41.35) single; 6,500 ptas. ($61.10) double. Breakfast 500 ptas. ($4.70) extra. No credit cards. **Closed:** Nov to Apr.
Set back from the esplanade, this two-star hotel is a former villa designed in part by students of Gaudí's. It boasts the most elegant fireplace on the Costa Brava. The inner patio—with its towering palms, its vines and flowers, and its fountains—is almost as popular with guests as the sandy "frontyard" beach. The spacious rooms contain fine furnishings; many open onto private balconies.

MAR MENUDA, Paraje Mar Menuda, 17320 Tossà de Mar. Tel. 972/34-10-00. Fax 972/34-00-87. 50 rms (all with bath).
$ Rates: 5,000 ptas. ($47) single; 9,000 ptas. ($84.60) double. Breakfast 625 ptas. ($6.10) extra. AE, DC, MC, V. **Closed:** Oct to mid-Apr.
On the premises of this rustically decorated Mediterranean-style hotel are a pool, tennis courts, a garden, and a big parking lot. A restaurant serves competently prepared meals. Rooms are pleasant and comfortably furnished 10 of them with air conditioning, minibars, TVs, and phones (naturally these are booked first).

WHERE TO EAT

CAN TONET, Plaça de l'Església, 2. Tel. 34-05-11.
   Cuisine: CATALAN. **Reservations:** Not required.
$ Prices: Appetizers 350–650 ptas. ($3.30–$6.10); main dishes 900–1,800 ptas. ($8.45–$16.90). AE, DC, MC, V.
   Open: Lunch daily 1–4pm; dinner daily 8–11:30pm. **Closed:** Nov–Feb.
Situated on one of the most secluded charming old squares of Tossà, this restaurant has an extensive menu that includes soup Tonet, paella, sole Tonet, Tossà crayfish, grilled shrimp, and *zarzuela* (fish stew). At night the chef keeps the pizza oven going. Diners can eat at outside café tables or in the tavernlike dining room with its old beams and brass chandeliers.

ES MOLÍ, Tarull, 5. Tel. 34-14-14.
   Cuisine: CATALAN. **Reservations:** Required.
$ Prices: Appetizers 425–1,350 ptas. ($4–$12.70); main dishes 1,200–2,750 ptas. ($11.30–$25.85); fixed-priced menu 2,500 ptas. ($23.50). AE, DC, MC, V.
   Open: May–Sept lunch daily 1–4pm, dinner daily 8pm–midnight; Apr and Oct lunch Wed–Mon 1–4pm, dinner Wed–Mon 8pm–midnight.
The most beautiful—and the best—restaurant in Tossà is behind the church, set in the courtyard of a stone-walled windmill built in 1856. You'll dine beneath one of three arcades, each of which faces a three-tiered fountain. There is also a cluster of iron tables near a garden for those who prefer the sunlight. Among the specialties are

an elaborately presented platter of local grilled fish, a delightful sole amandine, fisherman's cream soup, salad Es Molí (garnished with seaweed), hazelnut cream soup, hake and shrimp in garlic sauce, crayfish flambé with Calvados, chef's-style tournedos, and a long list of well-chosen wines. The impeccably dressed waiters serve with a flourish.

RESTAURANT BAHÍA, Passeig del Mar, 19. Tel. 34-03-22.
   Cuisine: CATALAN. **Reservations:** Recommended.
$ **Prices:** Appetizers 700–900 ptas. ($6.60–$8.45); main dishes 1,500–2,500 ptas. ($14.10–$23.50). AE, DC, MC, V.
   Open: Lunch Tues–Sun 1–4pm; dinner Tues–Sun 7:30–8:45pm. **Closed:** Nov–Mar.

Bahía is a well-known seaside restaurant with a much-awarded chef. Menu favorites include juicy chicken Marengo, an array of rice dishes containing everything from beef to salmon, seafood soup, and a classic zarzuela. There are frequently changing new dishes.

EVENING ENTERTAINMENT

In Tossà de Mar's fast-changing nightlife, there is little stability or reliability. However, one club that's been in business for a while is the **Ely Club,** Calle Pola (tel. 34-00-09). Devotees from all over the Costa Brava come here to dance to music that is among the most up-to-date in the region. Daily hours are 10pm to 4am. In July and August, admission is 1,000 pesetas ($9.40), which includes your first drink. From September to June, admission and your first drink cost only 800 pesetas ($7.50). The Ely Club is in the center of town between the two local cinemas.

4. FIGUERES

136 miles N of Barcelona, 23 miles E of Girona

GETTING THERE   By Train   RENFE has hourly train service between Barcelona and Figueres. All trains between Barcelona and France stop here.

By Bus   It's better and faster to take the train if you're coming from Barcelona. But if you're in Cadaqués (see below), there are 5 daily SARFA buses a day (45 minutes).

By Car   A 40-minute ride from Cadaqués. Take the excellent north–south highway, the A-7, either south from the French border at La Jonquera or north from Barcelona, exiting at the major turnoff to Figueres.

ESSENTIALS   The area code for Figueres is 972. The Tourist Information Office is at Plaça del Sol (tel. 972/50-31-55).

As the heart of Catalonia, Figueres once played a role in Spanish history. Philip V wed Maria Luisa of Savoy here in 1701 in the church of San Pedro, thereby paving the way for the War of the Spanish Succession. But that historical fact is relatively forgotten today: The town is better known as the birthplace of surrealist artist Salvador Dalí, in 1904.

There are two reasons for visiting Figueres—one of the best restaurants in Spain and the Dalí Museum.

The **Teatre Museu Dalí,** Plaça de Gala-Dalí, 5 (tel. 51-19-76), is filled with works by the late artist. The internationally known Dalí was as famous for surrealist and often erotic imagery as he was for flamboyance and exhibitionism. At the Figueres museum you'll find his paintings, watercolors, gouaches, charcoals, and pastels, along with graphics and sculptures, many of them rendered with seductive and meticulously detailed imagery. His wide-ranging subject matter encompassed everything from putrefaction to castration. You'll see, for instance, *The Happy Horse,* a grotesque and lurid purple beast that the artist painted during one of his long exiles at Port Lligat. A tour of the museum will be an experience. When a catalog was prepared, Dalí said with a perfectly straight face, "It is necessary that all of the people who come out of the museum have false information." The museum is open July through September, daily from 9am to 8:15pm; during the rest of the year, it is open daily from 11:30am to 5:15pm. Admission is 400 pesetas ($3.75). The museum stands in the center of town beside the Ramble.

WHERE TO STAY

HOTEL PIRINEOS, Ronda de Barcelona, 1, 17600 Figueres. Tel. 972/ 50-03-12. Fax 972/50-07-66. 56 rms (all with bath). TEL
$ **Rates:** 4,200 ptas. ($39.50) single; 5,000 ptas. ($47) double. Breakfast 400 ptas. ($3.75) extra. AE, DC, MC, V.
This pleasant hotel, near the main road leading to the center of town, is a 5-minute walk from the Dalí Museum. The hotel's restaurant takes up most of the ground floor, and there's also a bar. Many of the comfortable rooms have balconies. Parking available.

HOSTAL BON RETORN, Carretera Nacional II, 17600 Figueres. Tel. 972/50-46-23. 65 rms (all with bath). TV TEL **Directions:** Take the A-17 to Exit 4—Figueres south; head toward town on Carretera Nacional II, or else take a taxi from rail station.
$ **Rates:** 3,000 ptas. ($28.20) single; 6,000 ptas. ($56.40) double. Breakfast 530 ptas. ($5) extra. AE, MC, V. **Closed:** Mid-Nov to mid-Dec.
Located near the edge of the national highway (not the autoroute), 1.5 miles (2.5km) south of Figueres, this family-owned hotel features a large and relaxing bar, a children's garden, and a sunny restaurant with an outdoor terrace where fixed-priced meals go for 1,800 pesetas ($16.90). The hotel has a private enclosed garage. The rooms are rustically furnished and comfortable, and some of them have air conditioning and minibars.

WHERE TO EAT

DURÁN, Lasauca, 5, 17600 Figueres. Tel. 972/50-12-50. Fax 972/50-26-09.
Cuisine: CATALAN. **Reservations:** Required.
$ **Prices:** Appetizers 575–700 ptas. ($5.40–$6.60); main dishes 1,000–2,000 ptas. ($9.40–$18.80); fixed-priced menu 1,300 ptas. ($12.20). AE, DC, MC, V.
Open: Lunch daily 12:15–3:30pm; dinner daily 8:15–11:30pm.

IN THEIR FOOTSTEPS

Salvador Dalí (1904–89).
• **Birthplace:** Figueres.
He became the leading exponent of Surrealism, depicting irrational imagery of dreams and delirium in a meticulously detailed style. Famous for his eccentricity, he was called "outrageous, talented, relentlessly self-promoting, and unfailingly quotable." At his death at 84, he was the last survivor of the famous *enfants terribles* of Spain (García Lorca and Luis Buñuel being the other two). His partner was the Russian-born Gala, his neurotic and ambitious wife. The first volume of his autobiography was called *The Secret Life of Salvador Dalí*, published in 1942.
• **Favorite Haunt:** Port Lligat on the Costa Brava.

S This popular place for a top-notch meal in the provinces had Dalí as a loyal patron. You can start with the salad Catalan, made with radishes, boiled egg, ham pâté, tuna fish, tomato, and fresh crisp salad greens. Other specialties include steak with Roquefort, zarzuela (Catalan fish stew), and *filetes de lenguado à la naranja* (sole in orange sauce). Like the Ampurdán (see below), the Durán also specializes in game. Try, if available, the grilled rabbit on a plank, served with white wine. The french fries here, unlike those in most of Spain, are crisp and excellent. Finish off with a rich dessert or at least an espresso.

You can also stay at the Durán in one of its 67 well-furnished rooms, each with private bath and phone. A single costs 4,600 pesetas ($43.25), a double 6,500 pesetas ($61.10). Breakfast is another 425 pesetas ($4).

AMPURDÁN, Antigua Carretera de Francia, s/n (N-11), 17600 Figueres. Tel. 972/50-05-62. Fax 972/50-93-58.
Cuisine: CATALAN. **Reservations:** Required.
$ Prices: Appetizers 600–1,900 ptas. ($5.65–$17.85); main dishes 1,200–4,800 ptas. ($11.30–$45.10). AE, DC, MC, V.
Open: Lunch daily 12:45–3:30pm; dinner daily 8:30–10:30pm.

At this restaurant, you'll probably have your finest meal in Catalonia. Don't judge the place by its appearance, which is ordinary, if not institutional-looking. But not the cuisine, as all the food-loving French who cross the border to dine here will tell you. This family-run restaurant, half a mile from the center of town, also gained a reputation early on among U.S. servicemen in the area for subtly prepared game and fish dishes. In time, it was to win devotees in Salvador Dalí (who wrote his own cookbook) and Josep Pla, perhaps the country's greatest 20th-century writer. The appetizers are the finest along the Costa Brava, including such selections as duck foie gras with Armagnac, warm pâté of *rape* (monkfish) with a garlic mousseline, and fish soup with fennel. The outstanding fish dishes include cuttlefish in a Catalan sauce, suprême of sea bass with a flan made with fennel and anchovy, and filet of red mullet with basil. Among the meat selections are the chef's special roast duck, beef filet in a red-wine sauce with an onion marmalade, and goose in a delectable mushroom sauce.

The Ampurdán also rents 42 well-furnished bedrooms, each with private bath, air conditioning, television, and phone. Some also contain minibars. Prices are 6,800 pesetas ($63.90) for a single, rising to 10,500 pesetas ($98.70) for a double. Breakfast is another 750 pesetas ($7.05).

---

5. CADAQUÉS

122 miles N of Barcelona, 19 miles E of Figueres

GETTING THERE   By Bus   The only public transportation to Cadaqués is a bus that leaves 5 times daily from Figueres, Mendez Nuñez, 14. The last bus back to Figueres is at 5pm.

ESSENTIALS   The area code for Cadaqués is 972. The Tourist Information Office is at Cotche, 2A (tel. 972/25-83-15).

This little village is still amazingly unspoiled and remote, despite the publicity it received when Salvador Dalí lived in the next village of Lligat in a split-level house surmounted by a giant egg. There are, as yet, no high-rise apartments or garish fast-food joints. The last resort on the Costa Brava before reaching the French border, Cadaqués is reached by a small winding road, twisting over the mountains from Rosas, the nearest major center. When you get to Cadaqués, you really feel you're off the beaten path. The village winds around half a dozen small coves, with a narrow street running along the water's edge. This street has no railing, so exercise caution.

Scenically, Cadaqués is a knockout, with crystal-blue water, fishing boats on the sandy beaches, old, whitewashed houses, narrow, twisting streets, and a 16th-century parish up on a hill. At times the place is reminiscent of Venice—complete with all the parking problems of that city.

WHERE TO STAY

HOSTAL MARINA, Riera Sant Vicente, 3, 17488 Cadaqués. Tel. 972/25-81-99. 27 rms (23 with bath).

$ **Rates:** 2,500 ptas. ($23.50) single without bath, 3,000 ptas. ($28.20) single with bath; 5,000 ptas. ($47) double with bath. Breakfast 350 ptas. ($3.30) extra. AE, MC, V. **Closed:** Nov.

This simple, centrally located hotel close to the beach is the oldest in town. It offers clean no-frills bedrooms at a good price. A fixed-priced meal in the flagstone-floored dining room costs 1,400 pesetas ($13.15).

HOSTAL S'AGUARDA, Carretera de Port Lligat, 28, 17488 Cadaqués. Tel. 972/25-80-82. Fax 972/25-87-56. 27 rms (all with bath). TEL

$ **Rates:** 4,500 ptas. ($42.30) single; 5,900 ptas. ($55.45) double. Breakfast 425 ptas. ($4) extra. AE, DC, MC, V. **Closed:** Nov.

Situated on the road winding above Cadaqués on the way to Port Lligat, this hostal has a lovely view of the village's harbor and medieval church. Each of the modern, airy accommodations opens onto a flower-decked terrace. The rooms have tile floors and simple furniture. Meals are served for 1,450 pesetas ($13.60).

HOTEL PORT LLIGAT, Carretera de Port Lligat, s/n, 17488 Cadaqués. Tel. 972/25-81-62. 30 rms (all with bath). A/C

$ **Rates:** (including continental breakfast): 6,500 ptas. ($61.10) double without balcony; 7,200 ptas. ($67.70) double with balcony to the sea. No credit cards. **Closed:** Nov.

Many visitors find the relative isolation of this hotel—at the end of a winding gravel road a half mile outside Cadaqués—to be its most alluring point. The terrace overlooks an idyllic harbor and an unusual house once occupied by Salvador Dalí. The gallery adjoining the reception lobby features a changing series of surrealist paintings. Also on the premises are a swimming pool with cabañas, a restaurant, and a snack bar. The airy bedrooms, all doubles, have tile floors, exposed wood, and balconies.

HOTEL PLAYA SOL, Platja Pianch, 3, 17488 Cadaqués. Tel. 972/25-81-00. Fax 972/25-80-54. 50 rms (all with bath). TEL

$ **Rates:** 5,800–7,500 ptas. ($54.50–$70.50) single; 8,900–11,000 ptas. ($83.65–$103.40) double. Breakfast 650 ptas. ($6.10) extra. AE, DC, MC, V. **Closed:** Jan 10–Feb

In a relatively quiet section of the port along the bay, this 1950s hotel has, arguably, the best view of the stone church at the distant edge of the harbor. The balconied building is constructed of brick and terra-cotta tiles. Its bedrooms are comfortably furnished, and each is well maintained by the Lladó family management. The hotel doesn't have a restaurant but it does offer a cafeteria.

WHERE TO EAT

LA GALIOTA, Narciso Monturiol, 9. Tel. 25-81-87.
Cuisine: CATALAN/FRENCH. **Reservations:** Required.

$ **Prices:** Appetizers 600–1,000 ptas. ($5.65–$9.40); main dishes 1,200–1,500 ptas. ($11.30–$14.10); fixed-priced menu 1,600 ptas. ($15.05). AE, DC, MC, V. **Open:** Lunch daily 2–3:30pm; dinner daily 9–11pm. **Closed:** Nov–May except Sat and Sun.

Dozens of surrealist paintings adorn the walls of this award-winning restaurant, the finest in town. Located on a sloping street below the cathedral, the place has a downstairs sitting room, and a dining room converted from what was a private house.

SA GAMBINA, Riba Nemesio Llorens, s/n. Tel. 25-81-27.

Cuisine: CATALAN. **Reservations:** Recommended.

$ **Prices:** Appetizers 800–1,100 ptas. ($7.50–$10.35); main dishes 1,200–2,000 ptas. ($11.30–$18.80); fixed-priced menu 1,300–1,500 ptas. ($12.20–$14.10). AE, DC, MC, V.

Open: Lunch daily noon–4pm; dinner daily 7–11pm.

Ⓢ This restaurant, with its regional ambience and its cavelike dining room, is located on the waterfront and serves reasonably good food at moderate prices. A Catalan salad (tomato, lettuce, peppers, *butifarra*, onions, and olives) is a good choice, as is the paella or the fish soup. The shrimp (*gambas*), for which the place was named, are always reliable. You might also try the fish soufflé.

ES TRULL, Port Ditxos, s/n. Tel. 25-81-96.

Cuisine: SEAFOOD. **Reservations:** Recommended.

$ **Prices:** Appetizers 500–800 ptas. ($4.70–$7.50); main dishes 1,500–2,000 ptas. ($14.10–$18.80); fixed-priced menus 1,000–1,500 ptas. ($9.40–$14.10). MC, V.

Open: Lunch daily 12:30–4pm; dinner daily 7:30–11pm. **Closed:** Oct–Easter.

On the harborside street in the center of town, this cedar-shingled cafeteria is named for the ancient olive press that dominates the interior. Two filling fixed-price meals are served. According to the chef, if it comes from the sea and can be eaten, he will prepare it with that special Catalan flair.

DON QUIJOTE, Avinguda Caridad Seriñana, 6. Tel. 25-81-41.

Cuisine: CATALAN. **Reservations:** Recommended.

$ **Prices:** Appetizers 650–750 ptas. ($6.10–$7.05); main dishes 1,500–2,200 ptas. ($14.10–$20.70). AE, DC, MC, V.

Open: Lunch Tues–Sun 1–4pm; dinner Tues–Sun 8–11:30pm. **Closed:** Nov–Mar.

Located on the road leading into the village, this pleasant, intimate bistro has a large vine-covered garden in front. You can dine either inside or al fresco. The à la carte specialties include lamb chops, pepper steak, zarzuela (seafood stew), and gazpacho. The Don Quijote cup, a mixed dessert, is the best way to end a meal.

EVENING ENTERTAINMENT

L'HOSTAL, Paseo, 8. Tel. 25-80-00.

This distinctive place has attracted some of the most glamorous names of the art and music worlds. Some music critics have called it the second-best jazz club in Europe, and it certainly rates as the best club along the coast. It's a Dixieland bar par excellence, run by the most sophisticated entrepreneurial team in town. Habitués still remember when Salvador Dalí escorted Mick Jagger here, much to the delight of Colombian writer Gabriel García Marquez. In fact, the bar's logo, which is not only on the matchbooks but on the doorstep (in mosaic), was designed by Dalí himself. Heightening the ambience are the dripping candles, the high ceilings, and the heavy Spanish furniture. The best music is usually performed late in the evening. Open: Daily noon–4am. Prices: Beer 250 ptas. ($2.35); drinks 700 ptas. ($6.60).

ES PORRÓ, Portal de la Font, 1. Tel. 25-80-82.

Although small, Es Porró is popular, thanks to its in-house video shows and warm ambience. At times it becomes a piano bar. Open: Daily 11pm–4:30am. Prices: Drinks 700 ptas. ($6.60).

CHAPTER 18

ARAGÓN

- **WHAT'S SPECIAL ABOUT ARAGÓN**
1. **ZARAGOZA**
2. **TARAZONA**
3. **CALATAYUD**
4. **NUÉVALOS/PIEDRA**
5. **SOS DEL REY CATÓLICO**

Landlocked Aragón, which along with Navarre forms the northeastern quadrant of the country, is an ancient land. It is composed of a trio of seldom-visited provinces, including Zaragoza; remote Teruel, farther south; and Huesca, in the north as you move toward the Pyrénées. These are also the names of the provinces' major cities. Most of Aragón constitutes terra incognita for the average tourist.

Long neglected by most visitors, Aragón is one of the most history-rich regions of Spain. You can visit it as an extension of your trip to Castile in the west or an extension of your trek through Catalonia in the east. Huesca, being close to the mountains, is ideal for a summer visit unlike most of Aragón, especially the fiercely hot south—considered Spain's worst climate. Winter is often bitterly cold. Spring and autumn are ideal.

Aragón is known best for two of its former residents: Catherine of Aragón, who foolishly married Henry VIII of England, and Ferdinand of Aragón, whose marriage to Isabella, queen of Castile and León in the 15th century, led to the unification of Spain.

Aragón is also noted for its notable Mudéjar architecture, which owes a debt to the Muslims, and for its tradition of bull fighting. In September many villages in the region have their own *encierros*, in which bulls run through the streets. What they don't have is the world promotion that Hemingway gave the festival at Pamplona. On the other hand, they aren't plagued with all the wine-drunk foreigners, the curse of the Pamplona festival. In folklore, Aragón is known for a dance, the *jota*, a bounding, leaping dance performed by men and women since at least the 1700s.

Aragón's capital, Zaragoza, is the most visited city because it lies on the main route between Madrid and Barcelona. If you're driving from Madrid to Barcelona (or vice versa), I suggest a detour to Zaragoza. If you get interested in Aragón there, you may want to stick around to explore more of the old land.

SEEING ARAGÓN
GETTING THERE

The easiest way to reach Zaragoza is by **plane.** Aviaco has several daily weekday flights from both Barcelona and Madrid. International connections are made through either Barcelona or Madrid.

It's also easy to take the **train,** as RENFE offers frequent service to Zaragoza from both Barcelona and Madrid. The *talgo* express makes the fewest stops. Daily express trains from Madrid continue past Zaragoza to targets in the north, such as Huesca and Jaca, the gateway to the Pyrénées.

Zaragoza is also provided with **bus** links daily from both Madrid and Barcelona. Once at Zaragoza, you can make bus connections—and sometimes rail—to the chief sightseeing goals in the province.

For motorists, Zaragoza lies on the main **auto** route between Madrid and Barcelona. The A-68 Basque–Aragón highway links Bilbao with coastal Tarragona in

WHAT'S SPECIAL ABOUT ARAGÓN

Great Towns/Villages

☐ Zaragoza, provincial capital—vital, alive, and action-packed, with two famous cathedrals.

☐ Tarazona, Mudejar city, former abode of Aragonese kings and known for its Muslim-influenced architecture.

☐ Albarracín, near Teruel, unspoiled gem of a medieval town.

☐ Sos del Rey Católico, birthplace of King Ferdinand, with its medieval architecture declared a national landmark.

Historic Castles/Monasteries

☐ Castillo de Loarre, showpiece of Aragón, one of Europe's most perfectly preserved medieval fortresses.

☐ San Juan de la Peña, outside Jaca, pantheon of kings and nobles of Aragón and Navarre.

Parks and Gardens

☐ Parque Nacional de Ordesa y Monte Perdido in the Pyrénées— incomparable natural beauty, rich in flora and fauna.

☐ Monasterio de Piedra outside Nuévalos—roaring waterfalls, dancing cascades, everything from a reflecting lake to Diana's bath.

Special Events/Festivals

☐ Pilar festivities beginning October 12 in Zaragoza—bullfights, jota dancing, and panoramic processions to extol the Virgin.

☐ Folklore Festival of the Pyrénées, late July to mid-August (odd years) in Jaca, drawing international array of top-notch music and dance groups.

Catalonia, and provides easy access to Zaragoza if you're coming north from Basque country.

A SUGGESTED ROUTE

Days 1–2 Travel to Zaragoza from either Madrid or Barcelona, arriving late in the afternoon. Sample some of the *tascas* (taverns) and nightlife of the city before retiring. In the morning, take a stroll around Zaragoza and visit its major monuments. In the afternoon, if you have a car, consider at least one of the "Easy Excursions" from Zaragoza.

Day 3 If you're driving, strike out on "the Mudejar trail," visiting Tarazona to the west of Zaragoza and driving on to Calatayud. If time remains, visit Nuévalos and spend the night at the Monasterio de Piedra (reservation required). If not, there are other accommodations in the area.

Day 4 Head south toward Teruel and spend the night there, but stop first at Daroca for about 2 hours of sightseeing.

Day 5 After an overnight stay in Teruel, drive west to the medieval village of Albarracín, have lunch there, and continue back north to Zaragoza for the night. Those with more time to spare can then begin their exploration of North Aragón.

Day 6 Journey to Huesca, either by car or public transportation, and rest overnight there. If you arrive in time, visit its attractions in the afternoon.

Day 7 If you have a car, visit one of the star attractions of Spain, the Castillo de Loarre, near Huesca. After seeing the castle, continue north along the N-240 to Jaca, where you will need at least two nights.

Day 8 Jaca, which has a few attractions of its own, is mainly a launching pad for excursions into the national park of the Spanish Pyrénées and to some ancient monasteries nearby.

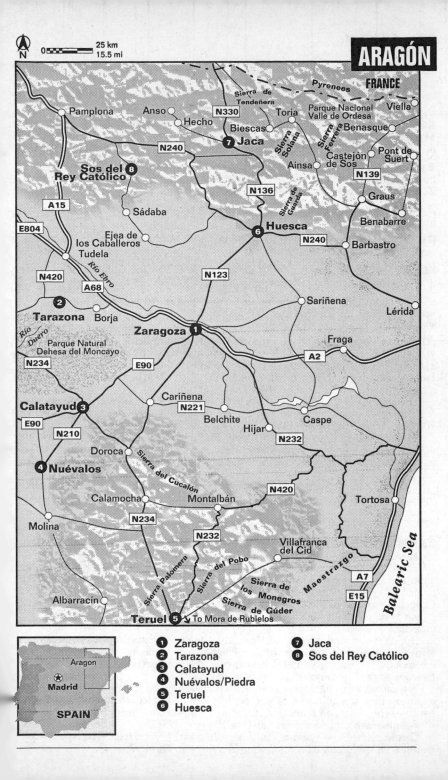

1. ZARAGOZA

200 miles W of Madrid, 190 miles E of Barcelona

GETTING THERE By Plane Aviaco has direct flights to Zaragoza from Madrid and Barcelona. From the airport in Zaragoza, you can get a bus to the Plaza de San Francisco. The Iberia office is at Canfranc, 22-24 (tel. 21-11-66) in Zaragoza.

By Train From Barcelona, 16 trains arrive daily, and from Madrid 14 per day (4½ hours from either city). The RENFE office in Zaragoza is at San Clemente, 13 (tel. 22-65-98), lying just off Paseo de la Independencia.

By Bus There is one direct bus a day running between Zaragoza and Barcelona (7 hours).

By Car Zaragoza is easily reached on the E-90 (A-2) east from Madrid or west from Barcelona.

ESSENTIALS The area code for Zaragoza is 976. The Tourist Information Office is at Torreón de la Zuda-Glorieta Pío XII (tel. 976/39-35-37).

Zaragoza ("Tha-ra-go-tha") is halfway between Madrid and Barcelona. This big provincial capital, the seat of the ancient kingdom of Aragón, is a bustling, newly prosperous, commercial city of wide boulevards and arcades.

Zaragoza has not one, but two, cathedrals, and ranks with Santiago de Compostela in Galicia as a pilgrimage center. According to legend, the Virgin Mary appeared to St. James, patron saint of Spain, on the banks of the Ebro River, and ordered him to build a church there.

Zaragoza (Saragossa in English) lies in the center of a rich *huerta*. Its history goes back to the Romans, who called it Caesar Augusta. Today, Zaragoza is a city of 700,000 people, slightly less than 75% of the population of Aragón.

Some 40,000 students at the University of Zaragoza have brought a new joie de vivre to the once-staid old city. Cafés, theaters, restaurants, music bars, and tascas have boomed in recent years, and more monuments have been restored and opened to the public.

The city's big festivities take place the week of October 12, with top-name bullfighters, religious processions, and general merriment.

WHAT TO SEE & DO

CATEDRAL DE NUESTRA SEÑORA DEL PILAR, Plaza de las Catedrales. Tel. 39-74-97.

This 16th- and 17th-century basilica, on the banks of the Ebro River, is in an almost Oriental style with its domes and towers. Thousands of the faithful travel here annually to pay homage to the tiny statue of the Virgin del Pilar, placed in the Holy Chapel. The name of the cathedral, El Pilar, comes from the pillar upon which the Virgin is supposed to have stood when she asked Santiago (St. James) to build the church.

During the second week of October, the church is a backdrop for an important festival devoted to Our Lady of the Pillar, which combines parades, bullfights, fireworks, flower offerings, and street dancing. Also of interest within the church are frescoes painted by Goya, who was born nearby.

You can also visit the Museo del Pilar, which houses the jewelry collection used to adorn the Pilar statue, as well as sketches by Goya and other artists, including Bayeu. Much of the collection is ancient, including an 8th-century ivory horn.

Admission: Cathedral free; museum 100 ptas. (95¢).

Open: Cathedral—summer, daily 8am–2pm and 4–7pm; winter, daily 9am–2pm and 4–6pm. Museum, daily 9am–2pm and 4–6pm. **Bus:** 22 or 23.

LA SEO DEL SALVADOR, Plaza de la Seo. Tel. 29-12-38.
This Gothic-Mudejar church, built between 1380 and 1550, is more impressive than El Pilar, but has been closed for restoration. It has a rich baroque and Plateresque façade and is a particularly fine example of Aragonese Gothic architecture. Among its more important features are the main altar and a fine collection of French and Flemish tapestries from the 15th to the 17th century. The baroque cupolas in the Temple of Pilar were decorated by Goya and Bayeu.
Ask at the tourist office for the church's scheduled reopening.

PALACIO DE LA ALJAFERÍA, Aljafería, Calle Los Diputados. Tel. 43-56-18.
This most unusual sight, a Moorish palace in Aragón, has been restored by the government and preserved as a national monument. Reminiscent of *cordobán* architecture, the palace was built in the 11th century for Moorish kings, but has seen considerable alterations and additions since then, particularly when Ferdinand and Isabella lived here.
Admission: Free.
Open: Tues–Sat 10am–2pm and 4–8pm, Sun 10–2pm. **Bus:** 21 or 36.

MUSEUM OF ZARAGOZA, Plaza de los Sitios, 6. Tel. 22-21-81.
This museum is installed in a 1908 building that has 10 ground-floor rooms devoted to exhibits from the prehistoric to the Muslim period. The Roman legacy (rooms 4 to 8) has sculptures (see the head of Augustus), mosaics, and ceramics. The fine arts section includes paintings by Goya (room 20); see his self-portrait. In the next room you'll find his drawings of *Los Caprichos* (The Whims). Also displayed is a Goya portrait of Carlos IV and his wife. The museum lies directly north of the Paseo de Marino Moreno.
Admission: 250 ptas. ($2.35).
Open: Tues–Sun 9am–4pm.

MUSEO CAMÓN AZNAR, Espoz y Mina, 23. Tel. 39-73-28.
One block from El Pilar, occupying a Renaissance palace, this museum has three floors and 23 rooms, each filled with artwork. On the second floor is a sketch of María Sarmiento that Velázquez made for his masterpiece *Las Meninas,* (The Maids of Honor), hanging in the Prado in Madrid. The Bayeu brothers (Francisco and Ramón) are represented by several works, as is Goya. His collection includes an important self-portrait, a version of his *Los Caprichos* (The Whims), *La Tauromaquia* (The Tauromachy), *Los Desastres de la Guerra* (The Disasters of War), and *Los Disparates* (The Follies).
Admission: 35 ptas. (35¢).
Open: Tues–Fri 10am–2pm, Sat 10am–1pm, Sun 11am–2pm.

PABLO GARGALLO MUSEO, Plaza de San Felipe, 3. Tel. 39-20-50.
The museum honors eponymous sculptor Pablo Gargallo, born in Maella in 1881. It is installed in a beautiful Aragonese Renaissance-style palace (1659) that was declared a national monument in 1963. Gargallo, influential in the art world of the 1920s, is represented by 100 original works, ranging from *Dr. Petit's Fireplace* (1904) to *Great Prophet,* a bronze piece from 1933. The museum is located in the center, a 5-minute walk south of El Pilar.
Admission: Free.
Open: Tues–Sat 10am–1pm and 5–9pm, Sun 11am–4pm.

WHERE TO STAY

Hemingway and one of his biographers, A. E. Hotchner, stayed at the Gran when they were in Zaragoza. But on a $50-a-day budget, you should consider one of the following choices.

HOTEL LAFUENTE, Valenzuela, 7, 50003 Zaragoza. Tel. 976/22-48-06.
58 rms (25 with bath). TEL **Bus:** 22.

$ Rates: 3,200 ptas. ($30.10) single; 4,200 ptas. ($39.50) double. Breakfast 325 ptas. ($3.05) extra. No credit cards.

At the corner of a quiet, charming square not far from an old church, this somewhat bleak-looking hotel is a bit dated, but it does offer good budget accommodations. The high-ceilinged lobby has wrought-iron accents and there is an unusual art deco bar. The rooms are spacious and clean.

HOTEL SAUCE, Espoz y Mina, 33, 50003 Zaragoza. Tel. 976/39-01-00. 20 rms (all with bath). A/C TV TEL **Bus:** 22.

$ Rates: 6,500 ptas. ($61.10) double. Breakfast 375 ptas. ($3.55) extra. AE, V.

Lying in the historic and artistic old town, right off the Calle de Don Jaime I, this rates as one of the best bargains in a high-priced city. The decor is cozy, the staff helpful. Rooms, doubles only, are small but comfortably furnished and well maintained.

HOTEL ORIENTE, Coso, 11, 50003 Zaragoza. Tel. 976/39-80-61. Fax 976/39-83-02. 87 rms (all with bath). A/C MINIBAR TV TEL **Bus:** 22.

$ Rates: 5,200 ptas. ($48.90) single; 9,500 ptas. ($89.30) double. Breakfast 550 ptas. ($5.15) extra. AE, DC, MC, V.

This hotel has been completely renovated and given three stars by the government. The lobby has been modernized, and the attractive, comfortable bedrooms have been considerably upgraded. It's in a good location—about 1 block from the Plaza de España and the Plaza de Salamero.

REY ALFONSO I, Coso, 17-19, 50003 Zaragoza. Tel. 976/39-48-50. Fax 976/39-48-50. 117 rms (all with bath). A/C TV TEL **Bus:** 22.

$ Rates: 7,500 ptas. ($70.50) single; 10,500 ptas. ($98.70) double. Breakfast 600 ptas. ($5.70) extra. AE, DC, MC, V.

This clean, efficient place is a favorite with businesspeople, who prefer its location in the commercial heart of town. A prominent arcade marks the entrance. The hotel has a popular countertop-service snack bar and, in the basement, a comfortably modern restaurant. A helpful crew of veteran and good-natured doormen help visitors with their luggage. The rooms are furnished with comfortable modern furniture; some come with minibars.

HOTEL GOYA, Cinco de Marzo, 5, 50004 Zaragoza. Tel. 976/22-93-31. Fax 976/23-47-05. 148 rms (all with bath). A/C TV TEL **Bus:** 22.

$ Rates: 8,500 ptas. ($79.90) single; 12,000 ptas. ($112.80) double. Breakfast 600 ptas. ($5.70) extra. AE, DC, MC, V.

Just off the Paseo de la Independencia, near the Plaza de España in the city center, this hotel (rebuilt in 1986) has excellent bedrooms that in some respects equal the much more expensive accommodations at the Gran. True to its namesake, the hotel displays copies of Goya's paintings throughout the multilevel lobby, which is decorated in black marble and wood paneling.

WHERE TO EAT

FAUSTINO'S, Plaza San Francisco, 3. Tel. 35-68-68.
Cuisine: ARAGONESE. **Reservations:** Recommended.

$ Prices: Appetizers 375–500 ptas. ($3.55–$4.70); main dishes 635–1,100 ptas. ($5.95–$10.35); fixed-priced menu 1,200 ptas. ($11.30). AE, DC, MC, V.
Open: Lunch daily 12:30–5pm; dinner daily 7pm–1am.

This starkly modern building near the football stadium is on the corner of one of the largest squares in town. At a sidewalk café and a metallic bar, you can choose from a selection of *tapas*. One flight down you'll find the Bodega, one of Zaragoza's most charming restaurants. The heavy ceiling beams, stone floors, and enormous copper still nestled in the stairwell create a unique ambience. Grilled specialties include veal chops, spicy sausages, entrecote, and filet of pork. Dessert might be a temptingly caloric slice of whisky-flavored tart. Enjoy an array of local wines, poured from oak-sided casks placed behind the bar.

LA RINCONADA DE LORENZO, La Salle, 3. Tel. 55-51-08.
 Cuisine: ARAGONESE. **Reservations:** Required. **Bus:** 40 or 45.
$ **Prices:** Appetizers 375–500 ptas. ($3.55–$4.70); main dishes 800–1,100 ptas. ($7.50–$10.35). AE, DC, MC, V.
 Open: Lunch Tues–Sun 1–4pm; dinner Tues–Sun 8–11:30pm. **Closed:** Holy Week; Aug; national holidays.

This restaurant, one of the best in town, offers such unusual dishes as fried rabbit with snails. Oven-roasted lamb or lamb hock can be ordered in advance, but lamb skewers are always available. The chef prepares several versions of *migas* (fried breadcrumbs), flavored with a number of different ingredients, including ham. Giant asparagus spears are often served. If you care to go local, try the beans with pig's ear and sausage.

MESÓN DEL CARMEN, Hernán Cortés, 4. Tel. 21-11-51.
 Cuisine: ARAGONESE. **Reservations:** Required. **Bus:** 22.
$ **Prices:** Appetizers 650–850 ptas. ($6.10–$8); main dishes 1,200–1,900 ptas. ($11.30–$17.85); fixed-priced menu 1,200 ptas. ($11.30). AE, DC, MC, V.
 Open: Lunch Mon–Sat 1–4pm; dinner Mon–Sat 8:30–11:30pm.
This unusually fine Aragonese restaurant is a local landmark, with an almost endless bar where tapas of all kinds are proudly displayed beneath glass cases. In the rear dining rooms, replete with wagon-wheel chandeliers and rustic wood and iron accessories, specialties include Aragonese vegetable soup, duckling with tomatoes, rabbit with garlic, and codfish with garlic.

COSTA VASCA, Teniente Coronel Valenzuela, 13. Tel. 21-73-39.
 Cuisine: BASQUE/ARAGONESE. **Reservations:** Required. **Bus:** 30.
$ **Prices:** Appetizers 650–950 ptas. ($6.10–$8.95); main dishes 1,200–1,900 ptas. ($11.30–17.85). AE, DC, MC, V.
 Open: Lunch Mon–Sat 1–4pm; dinner Mon–Sat 8:30–11pm.
Some of the city's best food is served here, including a number of Basque and Aragonese specialties, in an elegantly restrained setting. The elaborate set menu is expensive, but many à la carte items are reasonable. Dishes include spider-crab crêpes, roast lamb, hake with cider, sole filet with smoked salmon, and cold lemon soufflé.

EVENING ENTERTAINMENT

EL PLATA, Cuatro 4 de Agosto, s/n. Tel. 29-32-15.
 Located at the Plaza de España, this is one of the last *café-cantantes* left in Spain. The good-sized café, popular with all types of people, has a bar at the entrance and an old, musty stage at the other end of the room. Three times daily a wobbly three-piece orchestra whoops up the tunes, and a scantily dressed dancer comes out to warble a love song and do a couple of bumps and grinds. It's all hilariously simple and authentic. Open: Shows Thurs–Tues 3, 8:30, and 10:45pm. Prices: Drinks 250 ptas. ($2.35).
 Admission: 500 ptas. ($4.70).

CASA LUIS, Romea, 8. Tel. 29-11-67.
 This tiled-and-oak bar is one of the more interesting places in the barrio of La Magdalena. The array of tapas served here—some of the best around—includes fresh oysters, shrimp, and razor clams "in little bundles." Open: Daily 1–4pm and 7–11pm. Prices: Glass of wine 30 ptas. (30¢); tapas 80–350 ptas. (75¢–$3.30). Bus: 22.

CASA AMADICO, Jordan de Urries, 3. Tel. 29-10-41.
 This popular hangout is located near the Plaza del Pilar, on one of the smallest streets in the city. Local government workers and businesspeople come here after work for the tasty seafood tapas. Oysters come in three different sizes, or perhaps you'll be tempted by the smoked salmon, lobster, or Serrano ham. Open: Tues–Sun 12:30–4pm and 7pm–midnight. Prices: Glass of wine 40 ptas. (40¢); tapas 100–300 ptas. (95¢–$2.80). Bus: 22.

SALÓN OASIS, Boggiero, 28. Tel. 44-10-62.
This former theater transformed into a cabaret/music hall features a variety of artists who perform to a predominantly local crowd. Open: Tues–Thurs 11pm–end of show; Fri 11pm–1am and 1:30am–end of show; Sat 7–10:30pm and 11pm–1am. **Admission:** 1,100 ptas. ($10.35).

EASY EXCURSIONS

Goya aficionados (male ones) can visit the **Cartuja de Aula Dei,** a 16th-century Carthusian monastery lying 7 miles (11km) north of Zaragoza in Montañana. The young Goya, an Aragonese, completed one of his first important commissions here in 1774, a series of 11 murals depicting scenes from the lives of Christ and Mary. In the Napoleonic invasion, the murals suffered badly, but restoration has since been done. In this strictly run Carthusian community, only men are admitted. Visiting times are Wednesday and Saturday from 10am to 1pm and 3 to 7pm. From Zaragoza you can drive or take a local bus. Buses to Cartuja are run by **Autocares Teodoro Marrón,** Reconquista, 11 (tel. 29-59-90), in Zaragoza; check the schedules carefully.

Goya fans—this time male *and* female—can also go east from Zaragoza to the little village of **Fuendetodos,** birthplace of Goya. The small two-room cottage where he was born in 1746 was restored and turned into a museum, **Casa de Goya,** in 1985. You're shown transparencies of his most important works. In summer, daily hours are 10am to 1pm and 4 to 8pm; in winter, 3 to 6pm. Admission is free. From Muel, go 11 miles (18km) to Villanueva del Huerve, then continue east for 5 miles (8km) to Fuendetodos on the C-221.

---

2. TARAZONA

54½ miles W of Zaragoza, 182 miles NE of Madrid

GETTING THERE   By Bus   From Zaragoza, 4 buses leave daily for Tarazona (1½ hours).

By Car   Drive west from Zaragoza along the A-68, connecting with the N-122 to Tarazona.

ESSENTIALS   The area code for Tarazona is 976. The Tourist Information Office is at Iglesias, s/n (tel. 976/64-00-74).

To call this town the Toledo of Aragón may be a bit much, but it does deserve the name Mudejar City. Lying about halfway along the principal route connecting Zaragoza to the province of Soria, it is laid out in tiers above the quays of the Queiles River. Once the kings of Aragón lived here, and before that the place was known to the Romans. You can walk through the old barrio with its tall façades and narrow medieval streets.

Tarazona's major attraction is its Gothic **cathedral,** begun in 1152 but essentially reconstructed in the 15th and 16th centuries. However, the Aragonese Mudejar style is still much in evidence, especially as reflected by the lantern tower and belfry. Its dome resembles that of the old cathedral in Zaragoza. Daily visiting hours are 11am to 1pm and 4 to 6pm. Admission is free.

The town is also known for its 16th-century **Ayuntamiento (Town Hall),** which has reliefs across its façade depicting the retaking of Granada by Ferdinand and Isabella. The monument stands on the Plaza de España in the older upper town, on a hill overlooking the river. Take the Ruta Turística from here up to the church of Santa Magdalena, with a Mudejar tower that forms the chief landmark of the town's skyline; its mirador opens onto a panoramic view. Continuing up the hill, you reach **La Concepción,** another church with a narrow brick-built tower.

WHERE TO STAY & EAT

BRUJAS DE BECQUER, Carretera de Zaragoza, s/n, 50500 Tarazona. Tel. 976/64-04-04. Fax 976/64-01-98. 60 rms (all with bath). A/C TEL
$ Rates: 2,800 ptas. ($26.30) single; 4,800 ptas. ($45.10) double. Breakfast 300 ptas. ($2.80) extra. DC, MC, V.

Ⓢ Half a mile southeast of town on the road to Zaragoza is Tarazona's best place for both rooms and meals. The two-star hotel offers immaculately kept and comfortable accommodations for a moderate cost. The dining room serves lunch and dinner for 900 pesetas ($8.45), daily from 1 to 4pm and 8 to 10:30pm. Reservations are rarely needed.

---

3. CALATAYUD

53 miles W of Zaragoza, 146 miles NE of Madrid

GETTING THERE   By Train   Calatayud lies on the main rail line linking Madrid to Zaragoza. There are 12 trains a day from Madrid, 9 from Zaragoza, and 3 from Barcelona.

By Bus   There are 3 to 4 buses a day from Zaragoza (1¼ hours).

By Car   Calatayud is on the E-90 linking Madrid with Zaragoza.

ESSENTIALS   The area code for Calatayud is 976. The Tourist Information Office is at Plaza del Puerte, s/n (tel. 976/88-13-14).

The Romans founded the town, only to abandon it some time during the 2nd century, and it wasn't until the arrival of the Muslims in the 8th century that it was repopulated. The Moors were routed in 1120 by the conquering Catholic forces, who allowed some of the inhabitants to stay. But they were made virtual slaves and forced to live in a *morería* (Moorish ghetto). Some of the Moorish influence can still be seen in the town today. Many 14th- and 15th-century church towers in Calatayud are reminiscent of minarets.

The major attraction of Calatayud is **Santa María la Mayor,** Calle de Opispo Arrué, a brick church built in an Aragonese style, with an ornate Plateresque-Mudejar façade and an exceptionally harmonious octagonal belfry. Nearby, on the Calle Datao, the **Iglesia de San Pedro de los Francos** might be called the leaning tower of Calatayud. This is a fine example of the Mudejar style.

A walk along the Calle Unión leads to **La Parraguía de San Andrés,** with an elegant and graceful Mudejar belfry.

Strike a path through the old Moorish quarter up the hill to the ruins of the castle that dominated Qal'at Ayyub (the old Arab name for the town). Once you're there, a panoramic view unfolds.

East of Calatayud, excavations continue to uncover the **Roman city of Bibilis,** lying on the Merida–Zaragoza highway. It was the birthplace of Roman satirist Martial (ca. A.D. 40–104).

WHERE TO STAY

HOTEL CALATAYUD, Carretera Madrid–Zaragoza, km 237, 50300 Calatayud. Tel. 976/88-13-23. 63 rms (all with bath). A/C TEL
$ Rates: 4,000 ptas. ($37.60) single; 6,000 ptas. ($56.40) double. Breakfast ($3.55) extra. AE, V.

Of a lackluster lot, this is your best bet. Rooms are comfortable and acceptable, and the service is good. The hotel has a garden and a garage. Complete lunches and dinners are served, with meals costing from 1,500 pesetas ($14.10). The Hotel Calatayud is on the Carretera N-11, 1 mile (1.6km) east of Calatayud.

WHERE TO EAT

LISBOA, Paseo Cortes de Aragón, 10. Tel. 88-25-35.
   Cuisine: ARAGONESE. **Reservations:** Recommended.
$ **Prices:** Appetizers 400–650 ptas. ($3.75–$6.10); main dishes 900–1,500 ptas. ($8.45–$9.40); fixed-priced menu 1,000 ptas. ($9.40). AE, DC, MC, V.
   Open: Lunch daily 1–4pm; dinner Tues–Sun 8:30–11:30pm.

David Asenjo serves the best cuisine in town. In such a sleepy backwater as Calatayud, the Lisboa comes as a surprise, offering not only good food at reasonable prices, but also professional service administered in air-conditioned comfort. Try the hake Basque style with baby eels or perhaps the roast lamb Aragón style. The combination of green beans and spicy sausage makes a delectable dish. For dessert, try the specialty, *biscuit glacé.* The Lisboa is in the center near the train station.

EASY EXCURSIONS

From Calatayud, take the N-234 25 miles (40km) southeast to **Daroca.** Once a Roman military outpost known as Agiria, it was eventually taken by the Moors, who called it Kalat-Daruca. Moorish clans fought the town bitterly, paving the way for its eventual takeover in 1122 by King Alfonso I of Aragón. Daroca is a gem of an Aragonese town, known for its architecture, including Roman, Mudejar, Romanesque, and Gothic. It is visited mainly for the ruins of its walls, with 114 towers. An attempt in the 15th century to restore them was abandoned due to the enormity of the task. Some of the gates are in better shape, particularly the impressive Puerta Baja, flanked by twin towers and bearing the coat-of-arms of Carlos I. Other attractions include a beautiful fountain, Fuente de Veine Caños (20 spouts), lying just outside the walls, and a half-mile tunnel carved into a mountain to carry off flood waters, an unusual feat of engineering for the 16th century.

For lunch, head for **El Ruejo,** Mayor, 112 (tel. 80-03-35), right in the center and easy to find. The bar is rather unappealing, but the large dining room upstairs is inviting and air-conditioned. Order regional food and drink here, especially the herb-flavored roast lamb. Meals cost from 1,200 pesetas ($11.30), and the service is daily from 1 to 4pm and 8 to 10:30pm. Reservations aren't required. Daroca can be visited easily from Calatayud by train (2 daily). The station is 1¼ miles from town. The bus from Calatayud, however, delivers you to the center.

---

4. NUÉVALOS/PIEDRA

73 miles W of Zaragoza, 143 miles E of Madrid

GETTING THERE **By Train** From Madrid, train connections reach Alhama de Aragón. Take a taxi from there to the monastery.

By Car From Calatayud, head west along N-11. At the little town of Ateca, take the left turnoff, which is signposted for Nuévalos and the Monasterio de Piedra. If you're driving from Madrid, turn east at the spa town of Alhama de Aragón. From Zaragoza, turn left at Calatayud and drive 14 miles (22.5km).

ESSENTIALS The area code for Nuévalos/Piedra is 976.

The town of Nuévalos with its one paved road isn't much of a lure, but thousands of visitors from all over the world flock to the **Monasterio de Piedra,** called the garden district of Aragón.

Piedra means rock in Spanish, and after the "badlands" of Aragón, you expect bleak, rocky terrain. Instead, you have a virtual Garden of Eden, with a 197-foot waterfall. It was here in 1194 that Cistercian monks built a charter house on the banks of the Piedra River. The monks are long gone, having departed in 1835, and their former quarters have been reconstructed and turned into a hotel (see below).

Two pathways, marked in either blue or red, meander through the grounds. Views are offered from any number of levels. Tunnels and stairways date from the 19th century, the work of Juan Federico Mutadas, who created a park here. Slippery steps lead down to an iris grotto, just one of many quiet, secluded retreats. It is said that the original monks inhabited the site because they wanted a "foretaste of paradise." To be honest, they were also escaping the court intrigues at the powerful Monestir de Poblet in Tarragona province. The monastery at Piedra lies only 2 miles (3.2km) from the hillside village of Nuévalos. You can wander through the monastery grounds daily from 9am to 6pm for an admission charge of 300 pesetas ($2.80).

Either for rooms or meals, **Monasterio de Piedra**, 50201 Nuévalos (tel. 84-90-11), is one of the showplaces of Aragon, and a meal in the great hall is a medieval event. The room has been tastefully decorated, and is a perfect backdrop for the good-tasting Aragonese meals. Meals cost from 2,200 pesetas ($20.70), and service is daily from 1 to 4pm and 7:30 to 10pm. On weekends, the dining room can get crowded. The grounds include a swimming pool, tennis courts, and, naturally, a garden, with little log bridges and masses of flowering plants and trees. The beautifully maintained bedrooms (all doubles), for which you should reserve well in advance, have phones but no other amenities. Some open onto terraces.

---

5. SOS DEL REY CATÓLICO

262 miles N of Madrid, 37 miles SW of Pamplona

GETTING THERE By Bus   From Zaragoza to Sos, there is a daily bus at 6:30pm, returning at 7am the next morning (2¼ hours).

By Car   From Huesca, take Rte. 240 to Pamplona, but turn south at the cutoff to Sanquesa.

ESSENTIALS   The area code for Sos del Rey Católico is 948.

In northern Aragón, Sos del Rey Católico formed one of the Cinco Villas of Aragón, stretching along a 56-mile (90km) frontier with Navarre. The far-distant part of northern Aragón, these villages included Tauste, Ejea, Uncastillo, and Sabada. Despite their small size, they were raised to the status of towns by Philip V, who was grateful for their assistance and loyalty in the War of Spanish Succession (1701–13).

The most visited town is Sos del Rey Católico, so named because it was the birthplace of Ferdinand, El Rey Católico, who was born here in 1452 and later entered the world's history books, especially after his marriage to Isabella of Castile and León. Locals will point out the Palacio de Sada, where the future king was alleged to have been born. The town is more interesting than its minor monuments, and you can explore it at will, wandering its narrow cobbled streets and stopping at any place that attracts your fancy. The kings of Aragón fortified this village on the border with Navarre with a thick wall. Much of that medieval character has been preserved today—enough so that the village has been declared a national monument.

WHERE TO STAY & EAT

PARADOR FERNANDO DE ARAGÓN, Sianz de Vicuna, 1, 50680 Sos del Rey Católico. Tel. 948/88-80-11. Fax 948/88-81-00. 65 rms (all with bath). A/C MINIBAR TV TEL

$ Rates: 6,500 ptas. ($61.10) single; 8,000 ptas. ($75.20) double. Breakfast 900 ptas. ($8.45) extra. AE, DC, MC, V.

A three-star choice in the center of town, this parador is in a much-restored Aragonese palace. From its windows, spectacular views open onto the country. Rooms are handsome and comfortable, and beautifully kept in the best parador tradition. Hearty Aragonese fare is served in the restaurant, with meals costing from 2,000 pesetas ($18.80). Service is daily from 1 to 4pm and from 8 to 10:30pm.

CHAPTER 19

NAVARRE & LA RIOJA

The ancient land of Navarre (Navarra in Spanish; Nafarroa in Basque) shares an 81-mile (130km) frontier with France and nine different crossing points. As such, it is an important link between Iberia and the rest of the continent. Lying east of Castile, Navarre is a single province with a strong Basque tradition. Unlike most provinces of Spain, it elected to keep its old name, Navarre, instead of using the name of the major city, Pamplona, for the province.

When the Muslims ruled from Córdoba, Navarre was one of the four Catholic kingdoms of northern Spain. Its history has always been linked to that of its neighbors, the Basques. Basque language and customs are still very important here, but the Navarrese tend to be very conservative, rejecting for the most part the extremists and terrorists of the more radical Basque parties.

As a border region, Navarre has had a rough time in history, and to this day the remains of lonely castles and fortified walled towns bear witness to that. But somehow this kingdom, one of the most ancient on the peninsula, has managed to preserve its own government and identity. Romans, Christians, Muslims, and Jews have all influenced Navarre, and its architecture is as diverse as its landscape. It is also a province rich in folklore. Pagan rites were blended into Christian traditions to form a mythology that lives even today in Navarre's many festivals. Dancers and singers wear the famous red beret; the *jota* is the most celebrated folk dance; and the best known sport is *pelota*, sometimes called *jai alai* elsewhere in the world.

The Pyrenean scenery of Navarre is unmatched in Spain. However, mountain scenery gives way to rather arid and brown flatlands in the south as the province moves closer to the great Castilian *meseta*. The landscape is dotted with monasteries and churches, dating from the days when it lay on the main pilgrim's path from France to the shrine of St. James in Santiago de Compostela in Galicia.

Navarre is rich in natural attractions, although most foreign visitors miss them when they visit just for the Fiesta de San Fermín in July, the running of the bulls through the streets of Pamplona, Navarre's capital and major city. Even if you do visit just for the festival, try to stay on to explore some of the panoramic Pyrenean landscapes of Navarre.

Adjoining Navarre is La Rioja, the smallest region on mainland Spain—bordered not only by Navarre but by Castile and Aragón. Extending along the Ebro River, this little province has far greater influence than its tiny dimensions would suggest, since it is one of the most important wine-growing districts of Europe. The land is generally split into two sections: Rioja Alta, which gets a lot of rainfall and has a mild climate, and Rioja Baja, which is much hotter and more arid, more like Aragón. The capital of the province, Logroño, a city of some 200,000, provides the link between the two regions.

WHAT'S SPECIAL ABOUT NAVARRE & LA RIOJA

Great Towns/Villages

☐ Pamplona, most important city of Spanish Pyrénées, immortalized in *The Sun Also Rises.*

☐ Estella, unspoiled historic town on pilgrims' route to Santiago de Compostela.

☐ Haro, best center for visiting La Rioja's famous bodegas and sampling its wines.

Ancient Monuments

☐ Monastery of San Salvador of Leyre, 11th-century spiritual center of Navarre, whose crypt is Spain's major piece of Romanesque architecture.

☐ Monastery of the Oliva, one of first Cistercian monasteries built by French monks outside France.

Historic Castles

☐ Javier Castle, built around birthplace of St. Francis Xavier, who is said to have converted two million Buddhists to Christianity.

☐ Castle of kings of Navarre at Olite—preferred residence of Navarrese royalty in a "Gothic town."

Major Cathedrals

☐ Cathedral at Pamplona, with 14th- and 15th-century Gothic cloisters; built in front of ancient city wall.

☐ Cathedral at Tudela, dating from 12th century and in traditional Romanesque-Gothic style; famous for its Doorway of the Last Judgment.

Special Events/Festivals

☐ Fiesta de San Fermín at Pamplona, with running of the bulls through the streets. July 6–14.

☐ Battle of Wine at Haro, mock contest in which opposing teams get doused with the precious stuff. June 29.

☐ Wine Harvest Festival throughout La Rioja—dances, parades, music, bullfights. Sept. 15–30.

In the 1980s long overdue recognition came to La Rioja's vineyards, as its wines gained increasing recognition on the tables of the world. The popularity of the district grows, and, of course, this has led to much tourist activity in the area—mainly by those wishing to visit the wineries.

The smallest *autonomía,* or government department, of Spain, La Rioja boasts only a quarter of a million inhabitants—and a lot of grapes. Its name comes from a river, Río Oja, compressed into one word: Rioja. The Ebro River is the backbone of the district, and major towns cluster in its seven tributary valleys.

The most visited towns are the capital of Logroño and Hang, the latter known for its wineries. Santo Domingo de la Calzada was considered a major stop on the pilgrim's route, and Nájera was once the capital of the kings of Navarre. Now, little more than a village, it lies long the Najerilla River. From that river's valleys comes about a third of all Rioja wine production.

SEEING NAVARRE & LA RIOJA
GETTING THERE

Several **flights** arrive weekdays, via Aviaco Airlines, from Madrid and Barcelona, from which air connections to the rest of the world can be made. Pamplona also has flights to and from Santander on the northern coast. There is no commercial airport in La Rioja. However, any of the airports at Pamplona, Zaragoza, Bilbao, even Madrid, can be used as a gateway to La Rioja. From one of those cities, you can take either the bus or the train, or else drive to La Rioja.

Pamplona has the best **rail** links to the Basque country to its north, including Irún, from which you can transfer onto French rail lines. Pamplona is also linked by rail to

Barcelona and Zaragoza. From Madrid, you can take an overnight express pulling out of Chamartín Station and be in Pamplona in 10 hours.

The best rail link to La Rioja is via Zaragoza (Aragón) or Bilbao in the Basque country. Most visitors, however, take a RENFE-operated *talgo* express from Madrid, going first to Miranda de Ebro, where a change of trains is necessary to reach the capital of Logroño. You can also continue by bus from Miranda de Ebro to the major towns of La Rioja.

Pamplona has **bus** links with Madrid in the south and San Sebastián in the north, and many other cities as well, including Logroño in La Rioja. You can also take the bus from Irún near the French frontier. The Conda bus company services the Ebro Valley area, including Logroño. For villages in the north of Navarre, take the Montañesa line.

To reach La Rioja by **car** from Madrid, take Rte. N-1, going east on the A-1 expressway or else east on the N-1 to Miranda de Ebro. You can go on to Logroño via the A-68. If you're north in the Basque country, take the A-68 south from Bilbao to reach La Rioja.

Pamplona can be reached by major toll roads, including the A-68 Basque country–Aragón expressway, which links Bilbao with Tarragona on the Mediterranean coast. Of the major N roads in the district, the most vital link is the east–west Barcelona–Madrid highway, the N–11.

A SUGGESTED ROUTE

The major center for visitors will be Pamplona. If you have a car, you need never leave Pamplona to check out all the tourist highlights of the province. But if you're dependent on public transportation, you may want to stay in various towns and villages.

Days 1–2   Spend Day 1 in Pamplona. On your second day, drive west to the town of Estella, returning by nightfall to Pamplona.

Day 3   Head south to visit the towns of Olite and Tudela, planning an overnight · stopover in either place.

Day 4   Continue east to the town of Sangüesa and visit the Javier Castle and the Monastery of San Salvador of Leyre in its environs.

Day 5   For a look at the pass made famous by the *Song of Roland* (Roncesvalles), continue east to the French border, enjoying the scenery. Stay overnight there.

Day 6   If you have time, drive to Logroño, a province in the west bordering Navarre, and spend the night.

Day 7   Head north to Haro, which has the most wineries in the province. Here you can learn about wine making and sample a vintage yourself.

Days 8–9   For a tour of the historic monuments of La Rioja, make either Santo Domingo de la Calzada or Nájera your base. From either, you can easily explore all the major attractions in the area, including the monasteries of Yuso and Suso.

1. PAMPLONA (IRUÑA)

56 miles SE of San Sebastián, 239 miles NE of Madrid, 104 miles NE of Zaragoza

GETTING THERE   By Plane   The gateway for air travel to Navarre is Pamplona. The city is served by several weekday Aviaco flights from both Madrid and Barcelona; international connections can be made from either city.

BY TRAIN   Two trains a day arrive from Madrid (6 hours) and 3 from Barcelona (6½ hours). Pamplona also maintains rail links with San Sebastián in the north (4 per day; 1 hour) and with Zaragoza in the south (6 per day; 2½ hours).

By Bus   Buses connect Pamplona with several major Spanish cities: 2 per day from

Madrid (5½ hours), 1 per day from Barcelona (5½ hours), 8 per day from Zaragoza (3¼ hours), and 3 per day from San Sebastián (2¾ hours).

By Car   The A-15 Navarra national highway begins on the outskirts of Pamplona, and runs south and joins the A-68, midway between Zaragoza and Logroño. Rte. 240 connects San Sebastián with Pamplona.

ESSENTIALS   The area code for Pamplona is 948. The Tourist Information Office is at Duque de Ahumada, 3 (tel. 948/22-07-41).

More than 60 years have passed since Ernest Hemingway wrote *The Sun Also Rises*. But the book's glamour remains undiminished for foreigners who read the novel, then rush off to Pamplona to see the running (*encierro*) of the bulls during the Fiesta de San Fermín. Attempts to outlaw this world-famed ceremony have failed so far, and it remains a superstar attraction, particularly among aficionados. The riotous festival of San Fermín usually begins on July 6 and lasts through the 14th. Fireworks and Basque flute concerts are only some of the spectacles that give added color to the fiesta, where the wine flows.

Nobody sleeps, which is just as well—accommodations are virtually impossible to find. You can bed down in a sleeping bag in an emergency, or, like most, stay up carousing with the drunks around the clock. Those who want to know they'll have a bed after watching the encierro should reserve years in advance at one of the city's handful of hotels or boarding houses, or stay in San Sebastián or some other neighboring town and visit Pamplona during the day. After all, one visit to Pamplona will probably be enough to satisfy your curiosity.

Pamplona is more than just a city where an annual festival takes place. Long the most significant town in Spain's Pyrenean region, it was also a major stopover for those traveling either of two frontier roads: the Roncesvalles Pass and the Velate Pass. Once a fortified city, it was for centuries the capital of the ancient kingdom of Navarre.

In its historical core, the Pamplona of legend lives on, but the city has been engulfed by modern real-estate development. The saving grace of "new Pamplona" is La Taconera, a spacious "green lung" of fountain-filled gardens and parkland, lying west of the old quarter, where you will often see students from the University of Navarre.

Pamplona became the capital of Navarre in the 10th century. Its golden age was the reign of Charles III (called "the Noble"), who gave it its cathedral, in which he was eventually buried. Over the years the city has been the scene of many battles, with various factions struggling for control. Those who lived in the old quarter, the Navarrería, wanted to be allied with Castile, whereas those on the outskirts favored a French connection. Obviously, Castile eventually won out, although some citizens of Navarre today want Pamplona to be part of a newly created country of the Basque lands.

WHAT TO SEE & DO

The heart of Pamplona is the **Plaza del Castillo,** built in 1847. It was the former Plaza de Toros (bullring). Expanded in 1932, it is today the seat of the provincial government, which has a certain amount of autonomy. This elegant-tree lined *paseo* becomes a virtual communal bedroom during the Festival of San Fermín.

The narrow streets of the old quarter extend from three sides of the square. The present bullring, the **Plaza de Toros,** lies just east and south of this square alongside the Paseo Hemingway. Running parallel to the east of the square is the **Calle Estafeta,** a narrow street that is the site of the running of the bulls. With its bars and *tascas,* it attracts university students and is lively all year, even without a festival. During the festival it is the most frequented place in town next to the Plaza del

Castillo. The bulls are also run through the barricaded streets of Santo Domingo and Mercaderes.

FIESTA DE SAN FERMÍN

★ Beginning at noon on July 6 and continuing nonstop through July 14, the running of the bulls is one of the most attended events in Europe, drawing thousands of tourists who overtax the severely limited facilities of Pamplona.

Get up early (or don't go to bed in the first place)—the bulls run every day at 8am sharp. To watch, be in position behind the barricades along the Calle Estafeta no later than 6am. Only the able-bodied and sober should plan to run. Women are not permitted to run. (Many defy this ban each year.)

There simply aren't enough beds or bullfight tickets to go around, and scalpers have a field day. Technically, tickets for a good seat in the ring go on sale at 8pm the night before the *corrida* and tickets for standing room go on sale at 4pm on the day of the bullfight. But all of the tickets are sold out, and since it is impossible to obtain them through a travel agent beforehand, tourists have to use scalpers. At the festival of 1990, scalper prices for seats in the shade ranged from 6,000 to 15,000 pesetas ($56.40 to $141).

The fiesta draws half a million visitors, many of whom camp in the city parks. Temporary facilities are set up, but there are never enough beds. Hotel reservations should be confirmed at least six months beforehand. If you look respectable, some Pamplonicos will probably rent you a room. Expect to pay about 2,000 pesetas ($18.80). To arrange a home stay, call 948/12-44-24. If you can't find a room, check your valuables at the bus station on the Calle Conde Oliveto (where there are also showers—free, but cold).

As for bars and restaurants, ignore all of the times given below. Most establishments operate around the clock at this time.

A Couple of Warnings: (1) Some people go to the festival not to watch the bulls, but to pick pockets. (2) Don't take needless risks, such as leaping from a building in the hope that friends below will catch you. Many people do this each year, and not all are caught.

CATHEDRAL, Plaza de la Catedral.

The most important sight in Pamplona is the cathedral, dating from the late 14th century on the site of a former Romanesque basilica. The present facade, a mix of neoclassical and baroque, was the work of Ventura Rodríguez, architect to Charles III. The interior is Gothic, with lots of fan vaulting. In the center is the alabaster tomb of Charles III and his Castilian wife, Queen Leonor, the work of Flemish sculpture Janin de Lomme in 1416. The 14th- and 15th-century Gothic cloisters are a highlight of the cathedral. The Barbazán Chapel, off the east gallery, is noted for its vaulting. Housed in the cathedral's refectory and kitchen, the Museo Diocesano displays religious objects.

Admission: 150 ptas. ($1.40).

Open: Mid-May–mid-Oct daily 9am–2pm.

MUSEO DE NAVARRA, Santa Domingo, s/n.

Close to the river, housed in a 16th-century hospital, the Nuestra Señora de la Misericordia is the major museum of Pamplona. It has rich collections of both Roman artifacts, including some 2nd-century mosaics, and Romanesque art, plus an important Goya portrait of the Marqués de San Adrián. Gothic and Renaissance paintings are on the second floor. Murals from the 13th century are also a highlight.

Admission: 150 ptas. ($1.40).

Open: Tues–Sun 10am–2pm.

PELOTA (JAI ALAI)

Three miles outside Pamplona, along the Avenida de Francia, you can watch professional pelota (jai alai) being played at the Frontón Euskal Jai Berri. Four matches are usually played on game days, and tickets can be purchased at any time during the sets. Betting is for aficionados only.

Admission: Bleachers 800–1,000 ptas. ($7.50–$9.40).

Game Times: Thurs and Sat–Sun 4pm.

WHERE TO STAY

During the Festival of San Fermín, prices are two or three times higher than those listed below. Some owners charge pretty much what they think they can get, and they can get a lot. Therefore, agree on the price when making a reservation, if you've been able to get a reservation in the first place. At the time of the festival, you can check with the tourist office about getting a room in a private home, as these prices remain reasonable. The locals prefer that you do that instead of joining the drunken revelers who sleep free in their gardens at night as unwanted guests. At other times of the year, Pamplona is a reasonably priced tourist destination.

LA PERLA, Plaza del Castillo, 22, 31001 Pamplona. Tel. 948/22-77-04. 67 rms (all with bath). TEL
$ Rates: 4,800 ptas. ($45.10) single; 6,800 ptas. ($63.90) double. Breakfast 475 ptas. ($4.45) extra. AE, MC, V.
Inaugurated in 1880 and last renovated in 1970, this is not the most prepossessing hotel in town—far from it. But at the festival it becomes the most desirable place to stay, since it opens onto the main square of Pamplona and overlooks the Calle Estafeta, the straightaway of the encerrio through which the bulls run. Rooms are basic, moderate in comfort, and at the festival you'll certainly be in the eye of the hurricane.

RESIDENCIA ESLAVA, Plaza Virgen de la Q, 7, 31001 Pamplona. Tel. 948/22-22-70. 28 rms (all with bath). TV TEL **Bus:** 9.
$ Rates: 3,800 ptas. ($35.70) single; 7,500 ptas. ($70.50) double. Breakfast 400 ptas. ($3.75) extra. AE, DC, MC, V.
Located right off the Plaza del Cardenal Ilundain, this renovated hotel manages to combine the spirit of old and new Spain. Its small living room resembles the drawing room of a distinguished Spanish house. The rooms are an average size, and all are tastefully decorated; some have balconies with views of the city walls and the balconies beyond. There is a cellar lounge offering drinks.

MAISONNAVE, Nueva, 20, 31001 Pamplona. Tel. 948/22-26-00. Fax 948/22-01-66. 152 rms (all with bath). A/C MINIBAR TV TEL
$ Rates: 7,200 ptas. ($67.70) single; 8,400 ptas. ($78.95) double. Breakfast 800 ptas. ($7.50) extra. AE, DC, MC, V. **Parking:** 800 ptas. ($7.50).
In the old barrio of Pamplona, west of the Plaza del Castillo and within easy walking distance of the tascas and restaurants in old town, this place is solidly booked for the fiesta. You must reserve at least six months in advance—and then say a prayer. Rooms have been completely renovated, each well furnished, well maintained, and comfortable. The hotel also offers a Navarrese restaurant, serving a regional and Spanish national cuisine, with meals beginning at 2,200 pesetas ($20.70).

HOTEL YOLDI, Avenida San Ignacio, 11, 31002 Pamplona. Tel. 948/22-48-00. 48 rms (all with bath). TV TEL
$ Rates: 5,000 ptas. ($47) single; 8,500 ptas. ($79.90) double. Breakfast 500 ptas. ($4.70) extra. AE, DC, MC, V.
You'll be close to the bullring in the centrally located Yoldi, whose well-furnished bedrooms were recently renovated. This hotel has long been a favorite of visiting matadors, and aficionados gather here to discuss bullfights.

HOTEL ORHI, Leyre, 7, 31002 Pamplona. Tel. 948/22-85-00. 55 rms (all with bath). MINIBAR TV TEL **Bus:** 9.
$ Rates: 6,500 ptas. ($61.10) single; 9,000 ptas. ($84.60) double. Breakfast 600 ptas. ($5.65) extra. AE, DC, MC, V.
This hotel, conveniently located in the town center a few steps from the bullring, is popular with both matadors and aficionados. Each of the high-ceilinged rooms, although modernized, retains its 1930s atmosphere. A few contain minibars. Breakfast is the only meal served, but many cafés are nearby.

AVENIDA, Avenida de Zaragoza, 5, 31000 Pamplona. Tel. 948/24-54-54. Fax 948/23-23-23. 24 rms (all with bath). A/C MINIBAR TV TEL
$ Rates: 6,400 ptas. ($60.15) single, 9,400 ptas. ($88.35) double. Breakfast 800 ptas. ($7.50) extra. AE, DC, MC, V.

One of the best inns in town, and also one of the newest, this small, well-run place was inaugurated in 1989. The bedrooms are well furnished and maintained; some are even better than the inn's three-star rating suggests. Furnishings tend toward the sleekly modern, and local watercolors add a warming touch. At the restaurant, known for its regional cuisine, you can order a full lunch or dinner for 2,900 pesetas ($27.25). At a balcony café you can enjoy snacks or refreshing cold drinks.

HOTEL SANCHO RAMÍREZ, Sancho Ramírez, 11, 31008 Pamplona. Tel. 948/27-17-12. Fax 948/17-11-43. 85 rms (all with bath). A/C TV TEL **Bus:** 7.
$ Rates: 6,200 ptas. ($58.30) single; 11,500 ptas. ($108.10) double. Breakfast 450 ptas. ($4.25) extra. AE, DC, MC, V.

Built in 1981, the Sancho Ramírez has quickly drawn business away from its older competitors. Each of the reasonably priced units has a streamlined and contemporary decor. Some rooms contain minibars.

WHERE TO EAT

ESTAFETA, Estafeta, 57. Tel. 22-16-05.
Cuisine: NAVARRESE. **Reservations:** None.
$ Prices: Appetizers 150–250 ptas. ($1.40–$2.35); main dishes 350–750 ptas. ($3.30–$7.05); fixed-priced menu 750 ptas. ($7.05). No credit cards.
Open: Lunch Sun–Tues and Thurs–Sat noon–4pm; dinner Mon–Tues and Thurs–Sat 8:30–11:30pm.

⑤ At the festival this self-service cafeteria west of the Plaza del Castillo seems to be everybody's favorite budget restaurant. It's cheap and clean. Go as early as possible in the evening—the dishes are cooked at the same time and everything tastes fresher and better the earlier you dine. Drawing everybody from young American students to retired pensioners in Pamplona, the Estafeta is a relaxed, informal place with wholesome and filling food.

CASA MARCELLIANO, Mercado, 7–9. Tel. 22-14-26.
Cuisine: NAVARRESE. **Reservations:** Required.
$ Prices: Appetizers 400–600 ptas. ($3.75–$5.65); main dishes 600–1,200 ptas. ($5.65–$11.30); fixed-priced menu 1,300 ptas. ($12.20). AE, DC, MC, V.
Open: Lunch daily 1–5pm; dinner daily 8pm–12:30am.

⑤ Hemingway immortalized the Casa Marcelliano in *The Sun Also Rises,* and his favorite dishes are still being served: trout Navarre style (stuffed with ham) and roast lamb with a *chilindrón* sauce of fresh tomatoes and sweet red peppers. Since 1908 this place, located near the Plaza del Castillo, has been wining and dining fiesta revelers, and is perhaps the most patronized establishment in Pamplona during the running of the bulls; it is packed about 20 out of every 24 hours. Your hosts are Irene Arraztoa and her brother Tomás. Main dishes include *merluza* (hake) Koskera and bull stew, which seems to be everybody's favorite dish at the festival. Seating areas are on two floors. The wine list contains some of the region's best vintages, including Castillo de Tiebas and Rioja Bordón. Many visit only the bar to enjoy the wine and *tapas.*

HARTZA, Juan de Labrit, 19. Tel. 22-45-68.
Cuisine: NAVARRESE. **Reservations:** Recommended.
$ Prices: Appetizers 250–550 ptas. ($2.35–$5.15); main dishes 1,300–2,800 ptas. ($12.20–$26.30); fixed-priced menu 3,000 ptas. ($28.20). AE, DC, MC, V.
Open: Lunch Tues–Sun 1:30–3:30pm; dinner Tues–Sun 9–11pm. **Closed:** July 15–Aug 10.

A popular and much-honored restaurant, this establishment near the bullring is almost unbeatable in Pamplona for its cuisine and its tranquil setting. The portions are generous (and expensive) and specialties change with the season. Menu items might include a steamy, well-seasoned vegetable soup, stuffed peppers, tournedos, hake and eel, and a selection of regional cheeses. The interior is air-conditioned during the hottest summer months, and there is a summer garden.

SHANTI, Castillo de Maya, 39. Tel. 23-10-04.
   Cuisine: NAVARRESE. **Reservations:** Recommended. **Directions:** From Plaza del Catillo, take Avenida Carlos III.
$ **Prices:** Appetizers 650–950 ptas. ($6.10–$8.95); main dishes 1,500–1,900 ptas. ($14.10–$17.85). AE, DC, MC, V.
   Open: Lunch daily 1–4pm; dinner Tues–Sat 9pm–midnight. **Closed:** July.
This is one of the most dependable restaurants in town. As you walk in, there is a tapas bar where you can linger over a drink and an appetizer. The cuisine in the adjacent restaurant is straightforward, honest, and fresh, featuring grilled hake, pig's-feet stew, roast lamb, and shellfish rice. The restaurant has a good selection of fresh vegetables.

LAS POCHOLAS, Paseo de Sarasate, 6. Tel. 22-22-14.
   Cuisine: INTERNATIONAL. **Reservations:** Required.
$ **Prices:** Appetizers 550–750 ptas. ($5.15–$7.05); main dishes 1,600–2,200 ptas. ($15.05–$20.70).
   Open: Lunch Mon–Sat 1–3:30pm; dinner Mon–Sat 9–11pm. **Closed:** Mid-Aug.
This restaurant west of the Plaza del Castillo is well known for its good food and elegant dining salons. You can enjoy salt-cured cod with lobster chunks in a garlic sauce, sea bass baked in red wine, a champagne-laden filet of sole, seasonal game dishes, a superb roast pork, and temptingly elaborate desserts. The restaurant is air-conditioned.

EVENING ENTERTAINMENT

CAFÉ IRUÑA, Plaza de Castillo, 44. Tel. 22-42-93.
   This art deco bar and café, dating from 1888, has an outdoor terrace that is popular in summer. The winter crowd is likely to congregate around the bar, ordering combination plates and snacks in addition to drinks. Open: Daily 9am–1am. Prices: Beer 225 ptas. ($2.10).

CAFETERIA EL MOLINO, Avenida Bayona, 13. Tel. 25-10-90.
   This cafeteria, centrally located in the commercial Barrio San Juan, doubles as a popular tapas bar. Late in the evening its ambience becomes more youthful, lighthearted, and animated. The huge assortment of tapas includes fried shrimp, squid, anchovies, fish croquettes, and Russian salad. Open: Daily 8am–1am. Closed: Aug. Prices: Beer 125 ptas. ($1.20); tapas 100–125 ptas. (95¢–$1.20).

BAR LA PAPA, Estafeta, 46. Tel. 22-52-58.
   Honoring Hemingway, this bar stands on the bull-running street of Pamplona. It might be considered the town's best all-around "fast-food" outlet. Known for its pizzas and good-tasting pasta dishes, it reaches a frenetic pace at the time of the festival, but is always a good choice for a drink or a light meal. The price is right too. Open: Daily 11am–midnight. Prices: Pizzas and pasta 550–750 ptas. ($5.15–$7.05).

---

2. OLITE

27 miles S of Pamplona, 229 miles N of Madrid

GETTING THERE   **By Train**   Olite is connected by rail to Pamplona.

By Bus   Three buses a day make the run from Pamplona.

By Car   Take the expressway highway, the A-15, directly south from Pamplona.

ESSENTIALS   The area code for Olite is 948. The Tourist Information Office is at the castle (tel. 948/74-00-35).

A historical city, Olite sits in a rich agricultural belt with a Mediterranean climate of short winters and long hot summers. Cornfields and vineyards, along with large villages, pepper the countryside. It is also the center of a wine-making industry carried on by cooperative cellars. These wine merchants hold a local festival each year from September 14 to 18.

WHAT TO SEE & DO

In the 15th century, this "Gothic town" was a favorite address of the kings of Navarre. Charles III put Olite on the map, ordering that a **castillo** be built in 1406. The oldest part of the castle is now a government parador (see below). Each summer the castle/palace sponsors theater and music festivals held at various times (check with the tourist office for the year's schedule). You can tour the newer section of the castle; towers and lookouts make visiting it a bit of an adventure. Daily hours in summer are 10am to 1pm and 6 to 8pm. In winter, hours are 10am to 2pm and 4 to 6pm. Admission is 150 pesetas ($1.40) for adults, 75 pesetas (70¢) for children.

Next to the castle stands the Gothic church of **Santa María la Real,** with its splendid 12th-century doorway decorated with flowers. It also has a notable altarpiece. This church owes its cloister to the inspiration of Doña Leonor, queen of Charles III. The façade is an outstanding example of the Navarrese Gothic style.

Wander through the town taking a look at many of its stately houses, some dating from the 14th to the 18th century. Calle Mayor, beginning at the square in front of the castle, is the main artery.

Since the area is known for its wines, you might visit the **Bodegas Carricas,** Rúa Romana, 11 (tel. 74-01-06), which can be arranged by appointment only. Most hotels will make arrangements for you.

WHERE TO STAY & EAT

PARADOR PRINCIPE DE VIANA, Plaza de los Teobaldos, 2, 31390 Olite. Tel. 948/74-00-00. Fax 948/74-02-01. A/C MINIBAR TV TEL
$ Rates: 8,500 ptas. ($79.90) single; 10,500 ptas. ($98.70) double. Breakfast 900 ptas. ($8.45) extra. AE, DC, MC, V.
This parador in the center of town is located in the wings of the Castle of Olite, which dates from the 12th and 13th centuries. It is encircled by well-preserved walls with impressive towers and galleries. The modern facilities of the parador blend in with the medieval characteristics of the whole place. The bedrooms, both well furnished and well maintained, have a lot of charm. Even if you're visiting just for the day, consider a meal here, which might include a dish such as grilled ribs or rabbit with snails. The chef takes pride in his regional offerings. Meals cost from 2,800 pesetas ($26.30). Open daily from 1 to 4pm and 8 to 10:30pm.

ONE-DAY EXCURSIONS

High up on a mountain of the same name, **Ujúe,** a short drive east along a secondary road from Olite, appears as if from the Middle Ages. Built as a defensive town, it has cobblestoned streets and stone houses clustered around its fortress **Church of Santa María,** dating from the 12th to the 14th century. The heart of King Charles II ("the Bad") was placed to rest here. The church towers open onto views of the countryside, extending to Olite in the west and the Pyrénées in the east.

On the Sunday after St. Mark's Day (April 25), Ujúe is an important pilgrimage center for the people of the area, many of whom wear tunics and go barefoot, and carry large crosses. They come to Ujúe to worship Santa María, a Romanesque statue dating from 1190. It was plated in silver in the second half of the 15th century.

Motorists may want to consider yet another excursion from Olite, to the **Monastery of the Oliva,** 21 miles (34km) south of Olite. It was founded by King García Ramírez in 1143 and is an excellent example of Cisterian architecture. This monastery, one of the first to be constructed by French monks outside of France, once had great influence; its most notable feature is its 14th-century Gothic cloisters. The church dates from the late 12th century and is even more impressive than the cloisters. It has a distinguished portal and two rose windows. Pillars and pointed arches fill its interior. In summer it's open daily from 9am to 8pm; October through March, it's open daily from 9am to 6pm.

3. TUDELA

52 miles S of Pamplona, 196 miles N of Madrid

GETTING THERE By Train Tudela lies on the southern rail line south of Pamplona.

By Bus There is a daily bus service linking Pamplona and Tudela.

By Car Take the expressway highway, the A-15, south from Pamplona.

ESSENTIALS The area code for Tudela is 948. The Tourist Information Office is at Plaza de los Fueros (tel. 948/82-15-39).

In the center of the food belt of the Ribera or Ebro valley, the ancient city of Tudela, with a population of only 26,000, is the second largest in Navarre. Lying on the right bank of the Ebro, it had a long history as a city where Jews, Arabs, and Christians lived and worked together. The Muslims made it a dependency of the Caliphate at Córdoba, a period of domination that lasted until 1119. The city had a large Moorish quarter, the *morería,* and many old brick houses are in the Mudejar style. King Sancho VII ("the Strong"), who defeated the Saracens, chose Tudela as his favorite residence in 1251. It has been a bishopric since the 18th century.

WHAT TO SEE & DO

Begin your exploration at the central Plaza de los Fueros, from where you can wander through a maze of narrow alleys that were laid out during the Moorish occupation. At the square, visit Tudela's most important monument, the **Catedral de Santa Ana,** which is open daily from 9am to 1pm and 5 to 8pm. Constructed in the 12th and 13th centuries, it has an outstanding work of art on its façade, the Doorway of the Last Judgment, with about 120 groups of figures. Creation is depicted, but the artisans showed their true inspiration in showing the horrors of hell. The church contains many Gothic works of art, such as choir stalls from the 1500s. Several chapels are richly decorated, including one dedicated to Our Lady of Hope, with masterpieces from the 15th century. The main altar contains an exceptional retablo painted by Pedro Díaz de Oviedo. The small but choice cloisters, however, are the highlight of the tour. Dating from the 12th and 13th centuries, they contain many Romanesque arches. Capitals on the columns include scenes from the New Testament.

WHERE TO STAY

HOSTAL TUDELA, Avenida Zaragoza, 56, 31500 Tudela. Tel. 948/41-07-78. Fax 948/41-09-72. 15 rms (all with bath). A/C MINIBAR TV TEL
$ Rates: 6,500 ptas. ($61.10) single; 9,000 ptas. ($84.60) double. Breakfast 350 ptas. ($3.30) extra. AE, MC, V.

Located in front of the bullring (Plaza de Toros), the Tudela was completely restored in 1989 and is now one of the best hotels in the area. Today it is modern and functional, although very small. Rooms contain TVs with satellite reception and video movies, and the bathrooms are thoughtfully filled with a number of extra little conveniences.

MORASE, Paseo de Invierno, 2, 31500 Tudela. Tel. 948/82-17-00. 11 rms (all with bath). A/C MINIBAR TV TEL
$ Rates: 9,000 ptas. ($84.60) single; 12,500 ptas. ($117.50) double. Breakfast 750 ptas. ($7.05) extra. AE, DC, MC, V.
This is not only one of the best places to stay in town, but it's also the leading restaurant (see below). Built in 1963 and completely renovated in 1983, it is small but very comfortable. Rooms are furnished in a modern style and have many conveniences.

WHERE TO EAT

HOSTAL TUDELA, Avenida Zaragoza, 50. TEL. 41-07-78.
   Cuisine: NAVARRESE. **Reservations:** Recommended.
$ Prices: Appetizers 700–900 ptas. ($6.60–$8.45); main dishes 1,700–2,100 ptas. ($16–$19.75). AE, MC, V.
   Open: Lunch daily 1:15–3:30pm; dinner Mon–Sat 9–11:30pm. **Closed:** Aug.
Previously recommended as a place to stay, this is also one of the leading restaurants in the city. It offers typical and fresh products of the Ribera region, along with some magnificent fish and grilled meat. Try the omelet with codfish or the baked monkfish. You can also order beefsteak, followed by homemade pastries and desserts. And sample such wines as Viña Magaña. You can dine in air-conditioned comfort, and will find parking on the premises.

MORASE, Paseo de Invierno, 2. Tel. 82-17-00
   Cuisine: NAVARRESE. **Reservations:** Recommended.
$ Prices: Appetizers 750–950 ptas. ($7.05–$8.95); main dishes 1,750–2,200 ptas. ($16.45–$20.70); fixed-priced menu 2,000 ptas. ($18.80). AE, DC, MC, V.
   Open: Lunch daily 1–4pm; dinner Mon–Sat 8pm–midnight. **Closed:** Aug.
Considered the finest dining room in town, the Morase is a special delight when the first of the asparagus comes in, as the region's product is praised by gastronomes all over Spain. Specialties sound conventional, but are well prepared, including a "pastel" of vegetables and hake baked with garlic. The lamb from Navarre is delectable. Set on the banks of the Ebro, the restaurant offers a garden, an air-conditioned dining room, and adequate parking.

4. SANGÜESA

253 miles N of Madrid, 29 miles SE of Pamplona

GETTING THERE   By Bus   Sangüesa buses leave from Pamplona at the rate of 4 per day (45 minutes).

By Car   Take the 240, a secondary road, to Sangüesa.

ESSENTIALS   The area code for Sangüesa is 948. The Tourist Information Office is at Mercado, 2 (tel. 87-03-29).

On the left bank of the Aragón River, Sangüesa stands at the Aragonese frontier. If after visiting the town, you want to spend the night in the area, drive 9 miles (14.5km) across the border south to Sos del Rey Católico, one of the most charming towns of Aragón; the town has an excellent parador. Pilgrims crossing northern Spain to Santiago de Compostela stopped at Sangüesa. With fewer than 5,000 inhabitants, it is the largest town on the eastern side of the middle zone of Navarre.

Sangüesa was long a trading center, as mountain sheep passed through on their route to the south of Navarre to spend the winter. Today it is the hub of a large agricultural area, where grapes and cereals are produced on irrigated land. Sangüesa, a "monumental town" in its own right, also serves as base for a number of excursions in the area, including visits to some of Navarre's major attractions, such as the monastery at Leyre and Javier Castle.

Long known to the Romans, Sangüesa was also involved in the battle against Muslim domination in the 10th century. It has known many wars, including occupation by supporters of Archduke Charles of Austria in 1710, and many a skirmish occurred during the Carlist struggles of the 19th century. On several occasions, it has been the seat of the Parliament of Navarre.

WHAT TO SEE & DO

The **Iglesia de Santa María** stands at the far end of town beside the river. Begun in the 12th century, it has a doorway from the 12th and 13th centuries that is considered one of the outstanding works of Romanesque art. The south portal, filled with remarkably carved sculptures, is Santa María's most outstanding feature. The vestry contains a 4½-foot-high processional monstrance from the 15th century.

The nearby **Iglesia de Santiago** is a late traditional Romanesque structure from the 12th and 13th centuries. It has a battlemented tower and contains an impressive array of Gothic sculpture, which was discovered under the church only in 1964. Look for the bizarre statue of St. James atop a big conch.

WHERE TO STAY & EAT

YAMAGUCHY, Carretera de Javier, s/n, 31400 Sangüesa. Tel. 948/87-01-27. 40 rms (all with bath). A/C TEL

$ Prices: 3,500 ptas. ($32.90) single; 6,000 ptas. ($56.40) double. Breakfast 600 ptas. ($5.65) extra. AE, MC, V.

The best place to stay (of an extremely limited choice) is this hotel lying ¼ mile outside town on the road to Javier. In summer its most attractive feature is a swimming pool. Bedrooms are in a functional modern style, but clean and comfortable. Meals cost from 2,250 pesetas ($21.15), and are available daily from 1 to 4pm and 8 to 10:30pm. The many Navarrese dishes served here include lamb stew and steak. The local wine cellars produce red and rosé wines that have won many prizes, and you can sample some of them here.

EASY EXCURSIONS

The **Monastery of San Salvador of Leyre** lies 10 miles (16km) east of Sangüesa, perched on the side of a mountain of the same name, overlooking the Yesa Dam. Of major historical and artistic interest, the main body of the monastery was constructed between the 11th and 15th century on the site of a primitive Pre-Romanesque church; in time, it became the spiritual center of Navarre. Many kings, including Sancho III, made it their pantheon. Its crypt, consecrated in 1057, ranks as one of the country's major works of Romanesque art.

When the church was reconstructed by the Cistercians in the 13th century, they kept the bays of the old Romanesque church. The 12th-century west portal is outstanding and richly adorned. Called the Porta Speciosa, it is covered with intricate carvings; in one section, Jesus and the disciples are depicted atop mythical creatures. Some of the other artistic treasures this once-great monastery displayed at the Museum of Navarre in Pamplona.

When Navarre joined with Aragón, the power of Leyre declined. Finally, in the 19th century, the monastery was abandoned. Not until 1954 did a Benedictine order come here and begin the difficult restoration.

The monastery lies 2½ miles (4km) from Yesa, which itself is on the major road linking Pamplona with Huesca. The church opens daily at 8pm, and vespers are held at 7pm just before the church closes. Admission is free.

At Leyre you'll also find one of the most unusual accommodations in Navarre, the **Hospedería,** Monasterio de Leyre, 31410 Leyre (tel. 948/88-41-00), which is open only from March to October. This 30-room (each with private bath and air conditioning) two-star inn was created from the annexes constructed by the Benedictines in the 1700s. Rooms open onto views of the Yesa Reservoir. Rates are 3,000 pesetas ($28.20) for a single, 5,600 pesetas ($52.64) for a double, with breakfast costing another 500 pesetas ($4.70). The restaurant of the hotel serves good Navarrese dishes in a rustic setting. A meal is offered daily for 1,700 pesetas ($16) from 1 to 4pm and 8 to 10:30pm. AE, DC, V.

The second major excursion possible in the area is to **Javier Castle,** 5 miles (8km) from Sangüesa, and dating from the 11th century. It owes its present look to restoration work carried out in 1952. Francisco Javier (Xavier), patron of Navarre, was born here on April 7, 1506. Along with Ignatius Loyola, he founded the order of the Society of Jesus (the Jesuits) in the mid-16th century. The castle houses a magnificent 13th-century crucifix, and thousands of the faithful congregate at Javier on two consecutive Sundays in March. This is one of the most popular pilgrimages in Navarre. Known as the Javierada, it pays homage to Francisco Javier, who was canonized in 1622.

Guided tours of the castle take you through the oratory, the guard chamber, the great hall, and the saint's bedroom. The most interesting art is pointed out on the tour, including a 15th-century fresco, *The Dance of Death.* Hours are 10am to 1pm and 4 to 7pm. Admission is 150 pesetas ($1.40).

5. RONCESVALLES

277 miles N of Madrid, 29 miles E of Pamplona

GETTING THERE   By Bus   Roncesvalles itself has no bus or rail connections. A bus leaves Pamplona for Burguete, 2 miles (3.2km) away, Monday through Saturday at 6pm (2 hours).

ESSENTIALS   The area code for Roncesvalles is 948.

Memories of the early 12th-century *Song of Roland,* the first French epic poem, live on here. This was the site where in 778 the Basques of Navarre massacred the rear guard of Charlemagne's army as it was returning to France through the pass in the Pyrénées. The Navarrese were angered at the razing of Pamplona's walls by the troops of Charlemagne, even though the French forces had routed the Moors. Some historians suggest that the actual battle occurred more to the east, but in legend Roland's last hours were at Roncesvalles, and monuments throughout the town commemorate the legendary warrior.

A monastery that stood here marked the beginning of the pilgrims' route to the tomb of St. James at Santiago de Compostela. Monks were said to have rung bells constantly to guide pilgrims through the pass in foul weather.

WHAT TO SEE & DO

Visit the **Royal Collegiate Church,** consecrated in 1219 and one of the first Gothic churches built in Spain. Architecturally, it seems to reflect a transition from Romanesque to Gothic. Over the years it has been the victim of some unfortunate restoration. Its major treasure is the *Madonna de Roncesvalles,* a legendary wooden sculpture of the Virgin and Child plated in silver, dating from the 13th or 14th century. It is said to have appeared miraculously in the mountains, where it was discovered by a stag with a star shining from its antlers. Be sure to see the Gothic chapter house, lying off the cloisters. It contains the tomb of the founder of the church, Sancho VII (1154–1234). The church is open daily from 8:30am to 7pm.

In the adjoining monastery, converted from the old stables, visit the **Museum of Roncesvalles.** Here many articles left by the pilgrims who risked their lives in fogs and blizzards to cross through the pass are on display. The museum is open from June to September, daily from 11am to 1:30pm and 4 to 6pm. Admission is 150 ptas. ($1.40).

Burguete, 2 miles (3.2km) south of Roncesvalles, is a Basque town made famous by Ernest Hemingway, who fished for trout there after he watched the bullfights at Pamplona.

WHERE TO STAY & EAT

LA POSADA, Colegiata de Roncesvalles, 31650 Roncesvalles. Tel. 948/76-02-25. 11 rms (all with bath).

$ Rates: 4,000 ptas. ($37.60) double. Breakfast 350 ptas. ($3.30) extra. No credit cards.

This simple mountain inn, situated near the major ecclesiastical buildings of the village, is suitable for either food or lodging. It has a certain charm and enjoys a tranquil location, but can receive only a few guests because of its small size. Rooms, doubles only, are well maintained and comfortable. The hotel also has a good restaurant serving Pyrenean mountain fare. Meals cost 1,250 pesetas ($11.75), and service is daily from 1 to 4pm and 8 to 10:30pm. The Posada is closed in November.

6. LOGROÑO

205 miles N of Madrid, 57 miles W of Pamplona

GETTING THERE   By Train   There are 4 RENFE trains from Barcelona per day (6 to 7 hours), and 1 a day from Madrid (5½ hours). From Bilbao in the north, 4 trains arrive per day (3 hours).

By Bus   There are good bus connections from Pamplona 4 times per day (2 hours) and from Madrid twice a day (5 hours). From San Sebastián, 2 buses arrive daily (3½ hours).

By Car   The A-68 expressway from Bilbao runs south of Logroño. Take the N-1 from Madrid connecting with the A-1 expressway directly south of Burgos. Head northeast from there.

ESSENTIALS: The area code is 941. The Tourist Information Office is at Calle M. Villaneuva, 10.

The capital of the province of La Rioja, Logroño is also the major distribution center for the area's wines and agricultural products. Because La Rioja is so small, Logroño could be your base for touring all the major attractions of the province. Although much of Logroño is modern and dull, it does have an old quarter known to the pilgrims crossing this region to visit the tomb of St. James at Santiago de Compostela.

WHAT TO SEE & DO

The **Catedral de Santa María de la Redonda,** Plaza del Mercado, has vaulting from the 1400s, but the baroque façade dates from 1742. Inside, you can visit its 1762 Chapel of Our Lady of the Angels, built in an octagonal shape with rococo adornments. Constructed on top of an earlier Romanesque church, today's cathedral is known for its broad naves and twin towers.

From the square on which the cathedral sits, walk up the Calle de la Sagasta until you reach the 12th-century **Iglesia de Santa María de Palacio,** Marqués de San Nicolás, once part of a royal palace. The palace part dates from 1130, when Alfonso VII offered his residence to the Order of the Holy Sepulchre. Most of what he left is long gone, of course, but there is still a pyramid-shaped spire from the 13th century.

Walk through the heart of Logroño, exploring the gardens of the broad **Paseo del Espolón.** In the late afternoon, all the residents turn out for their paseo.

While in Logroño, you can visit the **Bodegas Olarra,** Poligono Independencia de Cantabria, s/n (tel. 23-52-99), open Monday through Friday from 10am to 1pm and 4 to 6pm. It produces wines under the Otonal and Olarra labels.

WHERE TO STAY

LA NUMANTINA, Sagasta, 4, 26000 Logroño. Tel. 941/25-14-11. 17 rms (all with bath). TEL

$ Rates: 3,300 ptas. ($31) single; 4,000 ptas. ($37.60) double. No credit cards. **Closed:** Dec 24–Jan 8.

Viewed as one of the bargains of town, this well-run hotel lies on a street central to both the historic core and the commercial district. Its basic rooms are clean and reasonably inviting. No breakfast is served, but you can buy pastries at a shop across the street.

PARIS, Avenida de La Rioja, 8, 26000 Logroño. Tel. 941/22-87-50. 36 rms (all with bath). TEL

$ Rates: 3,500 ptas. ($32.90) single; 5,500 ptas. ($51.70) double. No credit cards.

One of the town's bargain accommodations, this agreeable and well-run hotel near the police station attracts many wine makers who are in Logroño on business. Rooms are furnished in a basic modern style. No meals are served, but many cafés populate the area.

HOTEL MURRIETA, Avenida Marqués de Murrieta, 1, 26000 Logroño. Tel. 941/22-41-50. Fax 941/24-35-02. 113 rms (all with bath). A/C TV TEL

$ Rates: 5,000 ptas. ($47) single; 6,800 ptas. ($63.90) double. Breakfast 475 ptas. ($4.45) extra. **Parking:** 800 ptas. ($7.50). MC, V.

Directly west of the center, off the N-232 leading in from Vitoria, is this three-star choice run by the same people who manage the more expensive Carlton Rioja. Rooms are furnished in a basic modern style, each well maintained and comfortable. The hotel has one of the best restaurants in town, El Figón, serving regional meals for 1,300 pesetas ($12.20) except on Saturday night and Sunday.

WHERE TO EAT

CASA EMILIO, Pérez Galdós, 18. Tel. 25-88-44.
Cuisine: RIOJANA. **Reservations:** Recommended.
$ Prices: Appetizers 650–780 ptas. ($6.10–$7.35); main dishes 800–1,600 ptas. ($7.50–$15.05). AE, DC, MC, V.
Open: Lunch Mon–Sat 9am–midnight. **Closed:** Aug.

There is an ample bar set at the entrance to the dining room, which serves a cuisine based primarily on roasts, especially goat and beef. In air-conditioned comfort, you can also enjoy peppers stuffed with codfish or baked hake. From the well-stocked wine cellar come some of the finest Rioja wines. The Casa Emilio lies south of the old town directly west of the major boulevard, Vara de Rey.

LAS CUBANAS, San Agustín, 17. Tel. 22-00-50.
Cuisine: RIOJANA. **Reservations:** Recommended.
$ Prices: Appetizers 400–650 ptas. ($3.75–$6.10); main dishes 1,000–1,500 ptas. ($9.40–$14.10). No credit cards.
Open: Lunch Mon–Sat 1–4pm; dinner Mon–Fri 9–11:30pm. **Closed:** Sept.

In the center of the old town west of the police station and 3 minutes from the cathedral is this family-owned establishment, which succeeds in maintaining a happy balance between quality and price. The cuisine is based on the use of fresh seasonal ingredients. Try the veal with mushrooms. The dessert specialty is *leche frita* (fried milk). The restaurant is air-conditioned.

MESÓN LORENZO, Marqués de San Nicolás, 136. Tel. 25-91-40.
   Cuisine: RIOJANA. **Reservations:** Recommended.
$ **Prices:** Appetizers 700–900 ptas. ($6.60–$8.45); main dishes 1,300–1,800 ptas. ($12.20–$16.90). AE, MC, V.
   Open: Lunch Mon–Sat 1–3:45pm; dinner Mon–Sat 9–11:15pm. **Closed:** Jan 7–31, July 1–15.

This place has the ambience of a *Riojana bodega,* with a cuisine based primarily on regional produce. Naturally it has an excellent wine list, with the emphasis on regional vintages. In an air-conditioned interior, try such dishes as codfish cooked with wine. The lamb cutlets are also good. You'll find the restaurant in the old town.

ASADOR LA CHATA, Carnicerías, 3. Tel. 25-12-96.
   Cuisine: RIOJANA. **Reservations:** Recommended.
$ **Prices:** Appetizers 550–750 ptas. ($5.15–$7.05); main dishes 1,450–1,800 ptas. ($13.65–$16.90); fixed-priced menu 2,000 ptas. ($18.80). AE, MC, V.
   Open: Lunch Tues–Sat 1:30–4pm; dinner Tues–Sun 9–11:30pm. **Closed:** Jan 7–23, July 5–20.

Founded in 1821, this is one of the most delightful dining choices in Logroño. Housed within a charming antique buildings, it's an *asador,* which means that it specializes in wood-roasted meat dishes, including pig, goat, and baby lamb. Many of the roasts are prepared early in the day, and they are succulently tender, having cooked long and slowly before you arrive. The interior is air-conditioned.

7. HARO
223 miles N of Madrid, 30 miles NE of Logroño

GETTING THERE   **By Train**   Six trains a day run from Logroño to Haro (45 minutes).

By Bus   There are 4 buses per day from Logroño to Haro (40 minutes).

By Car   Take the A-68 expressway (south of Logroño) northwest to the turnoff for Haro.

ESSENTIALS   The area code for Haro is 941. The Tourist Information Office is at Plaza Hermanos Florentino Rodríguez, s/n (tel. 941/31-27-26).

Center of the wine tours of the Rioja Alta district, this region has been compared to Tuscany. Come here to taste the wine at the bodegas, as the international wine merchants do every year.

WHAT TO SEE & DO

The town itself deserves a look before you head for the bodegas. Its old quarter is filled with mansions, some from the 16th century; the most interesting ones lie along the **Calle del Castillo.** The major architectural monument of town is the 16th-century **Iglesia de San Tomás,** Plaza de la Iglesia, the center of the old quarter. With its wedding-cake tower and its Plateresque south portal, the 16th-century church is the major town landmark. The interior is Gothic.

    You could spend at least three days touring the wineries in the town, but chances are a few visits will satisfy your curiosity. The **Bodegas Muga,** Avenida Vizcaya, s/n (tel. 31-04-98), near the rail station, offers tours (usually in Spanish) of its wine cellars. It's open Monday through Friday from 10:30am to 1pm.

You can also visit the **Compañia Vinícola del Norte de España,** Avenida Costa del Vino, 21 (tel. 31-06-50), which is open Monday through Friday from 9am to 1pm and 3 to 6:30pm. It dates from the 1870s, and its cellars have some vintages more than 100 years old.

You can also visit **Rioja Alta,** Avenida Vizcaya, s/n (tel. 31-03-46), not far from the Muga, which is open Monday through Friday from 11am to 1pm.

Many of the bodegas are closed in August and the first two weeks in September. If you arrive in Haro when they are closed, settle instead for drinking wine in the *tascas* that line the streets between Parroquía and the Plaza de la Par. After a night spent there, you'll forget all about the bodega tours. Some of the finest wines in Spain are sold at these tascas, along with tapas—all at reasonable prices.

WHERE TO STAY

ITURRIMURRI, Carretera N-232, s/n, 26200 Haro. Tel. 941/31-12-13. Fax 941/31-07-21. 36 rms (all with bath). A/C TV TEL
$ **Rates:** 4,000 ptas. ($37.60) single; 7,000 ptas. ($65.80) double. Breakfast 400 ptas. ($3.75) extra. AE, V.
Lying a half mile southeast of the city on the highway, this is the "second choice" hotel for Haro. The comfortable rooms are attractively furnished, and many of them have impressive views. There is an animated cafeteria, as well as a large dining room serving regional meals for 1,950 pesetas ($18.35). Ample parking facilities are also provided. In summer the garden and swimming pool are compelling reasons to stay here.

LOS AGUSTINOS, San Agustín, 2, 26200 Haro. Tel. 941/31-13-08. 62 rms (all with bath). A/C TV TEL
$ **Rates:** 10,000 ptas. ($94) double. Breakfast 600 ptas. ($5.65) extra. AE, MC, V.
A former Augustinian convent has been turned into a four-star hotel in the center of Haro. Since its restoration and reopening in 1990, it has become the most desirable place to stay in a town that has always had too few accommodations. Owned by a Basque chain of hotels, it lies in a "zone of tranquility." The bedrooms, all doubles, are well appointed and offer much comfort. Good-tasting regional meals, with a well-stocked cellar of Rioja wines, are offered Tuesday through Sunday for 1,850 pesetas ($15.50).

WHERE TO EAT

TERETE, Lucrecia Arana, 17. Tel. 31-00-23.
Cuisine: RIOJANA. **Reservations:** Recommended.
$ **Prices:** Appetizers 550–750 ptas. ($5.15–$7.05); main dishes 1,200–1,800 ptas. ($11.30–$16.90); *menu dégustation* 2,825 ptas. ($26.55). V.
Open: Lunch Tues–Sun 1:15–4pm; dinner Tues–Sat 8–11pm. **Closed:** Oct.
This place has been a *horno asado* (restaurant specializing in roasts) since 1867 and is beloved by locals. The service is discreet, the food both savory and succulent—the kitchen has had a long time to learn the secrets of roasting meats. They are all prepared according to traditional regional recipes. When the fresh asparagus comes in, that is reason enough to dine here. The local peaches in season make the best dessert. Naturally, the finest of Rioja wines are served. Terete is located in the center of Haro.

BEETHOVEN I Y II, Santo Tomás, 3. Tel. 31-11-81.
Cuisine: RIOJANA/BASQUE. **Reservations:** Required in summer.
$ **Prices:** Appetizers 500–750 ptas. ($4.70–$7.05); main dishes 1,400–2,000 ptas. ($13.15–$18.80). MC, V.
Open: Lunch Wed–Sun 1:30–4pm; dinner Wed–Mon 9–11:30pm. **Closed:** Feb.
In the center of town is the premier restaurant of Haro—actually two restaurants, standing beside each other. Both offer good food and value. One of them is a large old house where a bar has been installed. Have a drink here, then perhaps move next door to sample the more modern restaurant, Beethoven II, which was recently renovated.

The place is justifiably famous for its platters of wild mushrooms, which owner Carlos Aquirre raises himself. Try the stuffed filet of sole, vegetable stew, or wild pheasant, finishing off with an apple tart. The interior is air-conditioned.

8. NÁJERA

201 miles N of Madrid, 17 miles W of Logroño

GETTING THERE **By Bus** Buses from Logroño to Santo Domingo de la Calzada (see below) stop at Nájera.

By Car From Logroño, take the secondary cross-country road (Rte. 120) toward Burgos. Nájera lies along this road.

ESSENTIALS The area code for Nájera is 941.

The major sight in Nájera is the **Iglesia de Santa María la Real,** Plaza Santa María la Real, founded in 1052 by King García. In all, more than 30 kings, queens, and princes of the crowns of Navarre, León, and Castile were buried here, including Blanca, wife of Sancho III, who died in 1158. Built on the site of a grotto where an early king purportedly found a statue of the Virgin, the church has a lovely cloister with a flamboyant Gothic tracery. The choir stalls, dating from 1495 and also flamboyant Gothic, were considered heretical by many of the devout because of their irreverent scenes. They are truly works of art. The church is open daily from 9:30am to 12:30pm and 4:30 to 7:30pm. Admission is 150 pesetas ($1.40).

Nájera was a main stop on the pilgrims' route to Santiago de Compostela. A bridge had to be built over the Najerilla River to accommodate the huge numbers.

WHERE TO STAY

SAN FERNANDO, Paseo de San Julián, 1, 26300 Nájera. Tel. 36-77-00.
48 rms (all with bath). TEL
$ Rates: 5,000 ptas. ($47) double. Breakfast 400 ptas. ($3.75) extra. MC, V.

The best place to stay in the area is the San Fernando, located in the center of town on the major boulevard near the Najerilla River. It's only one part of an entertainment complex, containing a restaurant, cafeteria, catering hall and disco. The owners are also the managers. Rooms, doubles only, contain basic furnishings, but are well kept and clean.

WHERE TO EAT

MESÓN DUQUE FORTE, Calvo Sotelo, 16. Tel. 36-35-20.
Cuisine: CASTILIAN. **Reservations:** Recommended.
$ Prices: Appetizers 350–750 ptas. ($3.30–$7.05); main dishes 1,000–1,600 ptas. ($9.40–$15.05); fixed-priced menu 1,000 ptas. ($9.40). V.
Open: Lunch daily 1–3:30pm; dinner Wed–Mon 8–11:30pm.

The owner of this place in the center of Nájera is María Pilar-Busto, who bought it in 1986 and turned it into a well-run Castilian-style restaurant. Many claim that hers is the best place around. Specialties include a flan of leeks and crayfish, followed by peppers stuffed with tuna, and perhaps roast beef marinated in red wine. You get good value here for your money.

LOS PARRALES, Mayor, 52. Tel. 36-37-35.
Cuisine: RIOJANA. **Reservations:** Recommended.
$ Prices: Appetizers 350–650 ptas. ($3.30–$6.10); main dishes 1,200–1,700 ptas. ($11.30–$16); fixed-priced menu 850 ptas. ($8). V.
Open: Lunch daily 1–4pm; dinner Tues–Sun 8:30pm–midnight.
This restaurant in the town center has a bar and a dining room of small but pleasing dimensions. It serves family-style regional food in ample portions. In summer the

outdoor terrace makes an agreeable place to dine. The dining room inside is air-conditioned. Specialties of the chef include a stew of hake and eels and roast loin of veal, followed by a selection of homemade desserts. The wine list represents very good value.

ONE-DAY EXCURSIONS

Motorists can take a detour south of Nájera for 10½ miles (17km) through the countryside of Sierra de la Demanda to the village of **San Millán de la Cogolla,** which grew up around two ancient monasteries, **Suso** and **Yuso,** of which Suso is the more interesting.

The church at Suso, built in the Mozarabic style (horseshoe arches), was dug into the mountain about 1½ miles (2.5km) above the town to house the 12th-century tomb of San Millán, around whom a cult was formed. Hours for visiting Suso are 10am to 1pm and 4 to 7pm Tuesday through Sunday. Admission is 200 pesetas ($1.90).

Yuso, down below, has been rather ambitiously dubbed "El Escorial of La Rioja." This Benedictine abbey was founded in the 11th century and reconstructed in the 16th. Its chief artistic treasures are ivories from two 11th-century reliquaries. Yuso was constructed by King García in 1053 over the remains of an early monastery, which was once an important center of learning, and even today is known for its library of valuable manuscripts. Guided tours are conducted Wednesday through Sunday from 10am to 12:30pm and 4:30 to 7pm. Admission is 200 pesetas ($1.90).

9. SANTO DOMINGO DE LA CALZADA

126 miles N of Madrid, 29 W of Logroño

GETTING THERE **By Bus** Two buses a day leave Logroño for Burgos in Castile, stopping at Santo Domingo de la Calzada.

By Car Head west of Logroño along secondary cross-country Rte. 120, which passes by Santo Domingo de la Calzada.

ESSENTIALS The area code for Santo Domingo de la Calzada is 941.

This town was one of the most important stopovers on the pilgrims' route to Santiago de Compostela in Galicia. The name honors an 11th-century monk named Dominic, who devoted his life to helping pilgrims and working to build a bridge over the Oca River. The name of the town means Saint Dominic of the Causeway.

The town is the setting for a famous legend in Spain concerning an alleged miracle. A cock is said to have stood up and crowed on the governor's plate after it had been roasted to testify to the innocence of a pilgrim who had been accused of theft and hanged after he resisted the unwanted advances of the innkeeper's daughter. The hanged man was found to be alive, and the governor allowed him to go free.

To this day, a white cock and hen are kept in the town **cathedral** to remind visitors of this miracle. With some minor Romanesque features, the cathedral is essentially Gothic, with a baroque tower dating from the 18th century. The saint's tomb rests under a 1513 baldachin in the south transept. The retable at the high altar is from 1538, representing the last work of Damián Forment. The cathedral is open daily from 8am to 2pm and 4 to 8pm.

WHERE TO STAY

EL CORREGIDOR, Zumalacárregui, 14–16, 26250 Santo Domingo de la Calzada. Tel. 941/34-21-28. 32 rms (all with bath).

$ Rates: 6,500 ptas. ($61.10) single; 8,500 ptas. ($79.90) double. Breakfast 400 ptas. ($3.75) extra. AE, MC, V.

Lying in the center, yet situated in one of the town's most tranquil corners, this hotel opened in 1989. It stands next door to the Hotel Peregrino, which is owned by the same family. Rooms are comfortable and well maintained. Facilities include a garden, a garage, and a parabolic antenna for TV reception.

PARADOR NACIONAL SANTO DOMINGO DE LA CALZADA, Plaza del Santo, 3, 26250 Santo Domingo de la Calzada. Tel. 941/34-03-00. Fax 941/34-03-35. 27 rms (all with bath). A/C TV TEL

$ Prices: 7,500 ptas. ($70.50) single; 9,500 ptas. ($89.30) double. Breakfast 800 ptas. ($7.50) extra. AE, MC, V.

Originally, this site on the plaza in front of the Church of Santo Domingo was a hospital for the hundreds of pilgrims who passed through here on their way to Santiago de Compostela. Filled with medieval history, it is the most desirable place to stay in the area. Now a fashionable parador on two floors, it looks out over the main square. With all this medieval allure, modern comforts and conveniences have not been neglected. The restaurant is one of the finest around, specializing in a regional cuisine and offering meals for 2,900 pesetas ($27.25). Ample parking is provided.

WHERE TO EAT

EL RINCÓN DE EMILIO, Plaza de Don Bonifacio Gil, 7. Tel. 34-09-90.
   Cuisine: RIOJANA. **Reservations:** Recommended.
$ Prices: Appetizers 450–650 ptas. ($4.25–$6.10); main dishes 1,200–1,600 ptas. ($11.30–$15.05); fixed-priced menu 1,350 ptas. ($12.70). No credit cards.
   Open: Lunch daily 1:30–4:30pm; dinner daily 8:30pm–12:30am. **Closed:** Feb; Tues Oct–June.

This solidly prestigious, centrally located establishment has been well tested by time and hundreds of dinners. You can enjoy the garden and terrace or else retreat to the air-conditioned interior. Regional fare is prepared with a certain flair here. Begin with the vegetable soup, then go on to stuffed peppers, or pig's trotters if you want something more local. The caramel custard makes a smooth finish.

EL PEREGRINO, Zumalacárregui, 18. Tel. 34-02-02.
   Cuisine: RIOJANA. **Reservations:** Recommended.
$ Prices: Appetizers 450–650 ptas. ($4.25–$6.10); main dishes 1,300–2,000 ptas. ($12.20–$18.80); fixed-priced menu 1,450 ptas. ($13.65). AE, MC, V.
   Open: Daily 9am–midnight.

This restaurant in the center of town has a very large and long bar, as well as a cocktail salon for predinner drinks. In the dining room, care goes into the serving of the regional cuisine, with everything backed up by the large supply of Rioja wines. A main dish specialty—for aficionados only—is a platter of merluza (hake) heads, prepared for two persons only. Perhaps you'll settle happily for the delectable roast lamb instead. The dessert specialty is leche frita (fried milk). A car park and garden are part of the facilities.

---

10. CALAHORRA

198 miles N of Madrid, 34 miles E of Logroño

GETTING THERE   By Train   Calahorra lies on the rail line heading southeast from the capital of Logroño.

By Bus   Five buses a day leave Logroño heading for Calahorra.

By Car   From Logroño, take the A-68 (an expressway) southeast to Zaragoza, exiting at the Calahorra turnoff.

ESSENTIALS   The area code for Calahorra is 941.

An ancient episcopal center, Calahorra dates from dimly recorded times when it was an Iberian settlement. Later, under the Romans, it was known as Calagurris Nassica, and was the birthplace of authors Quintilian and Prudentius. Its worst moment came when Pompey laid seige to the town in his war against Sertorius. Sources claim that the locals were so starved that they turned to eating human flesh.

At the edge of town is its major monument, the **cathedral,** a Gothic structure from the 13th to the 15th century, with a façade from the 18th century. Visit the chapels, the choir, and the splendid sacristy.

In the town center the major monument is the **Iglesia de San Andrés,** a Gothic building from the 14th century.

Note also as you walk around the town the remains of the Roman walls.

WHERE TO STAY

MONTSERRAT, Maestro Falla, 1. 26500 Calahorra. Tel. 941/13-00-17.
25 rms (all with bath). A/C TEL
$ Rates: 2,500 ptas. ($23.50) single; 4,000 ptas. ($37.60) double. Breakfast 250 ptas. ($2.35) extra. AE, DC, MC, V.

⑤ This is the town's bargain hotel—a centrally located modern building. Room furnishings are basic, but everything is clean and comfortable. The hotel itself doesn't operate a restaurant, but in the same building is one of the best restaurants in town, **Montserrat 2** (tel. 13-00-17), offering good-tasting regional meals for 1,400 pesetas ($13.15).

PARADOR NACIONAL MARCO FLAVIO QUINTILIANO, Paseo Mercadal, s/n. 26500 Calahorra. Tel. 941/13-03-58. Fax 941/13-51-39. 63 rms (all with bath). A/C TV TEL
$ Rates: 7,200 ptas. ($67.70) single; 9,000 ptas. ($84.60) double. Breakfast 900 ptas. ($8.45) extra. AE, DC, MC, V.
Named for the famous Roman orator, this three-star parador is the best place to stay in the area. Surrounded by gardens, the three-floor modern structure stands on a hill overlooking the Ebro River valley. Its location away from town gives sleepers more tranquility. Each room has many modern amenities and is most comfortable, furnished in a fashionable rustic style. Families like the children's playground and public park nearby. The restaurant specializes in a good regional cuisine, with a fine list of Rioja wines.

WHERE TO EAT

CASA MATEO, Quintiliano, 15. Tel. 13-00-09.
Cuisine: RIOJANA. **Reservations:** Recommended.
$ Prices: Appetizers 450–750 ptas. ($4.25–$7.05); main dishes 1,200–1,500 ptas. ($11.30–$14.10). No credit cards.
Open: Lunch only Mon–Sat 1–4:30pm. **Closed:** Aug 29–Sept 20.
Known for its fair prices and good quality, the Casa Mateo is an inviting and appealing choice. It prides itself on its excellent selection of fresh vegetables. Specialties include many different preparations of hake, a vegetable ragoût, and (on occasion) a wild rabbit. Desserts are homemade.

LA TABERNA DE LA CUARTA ESQUINA, Cuastro Esquinas, 16. Tel. 13-43-55.
Cuisine: RIOJANA. **Reservations:** Recommended.
$ Prices: Appetizers 750–1,200 ptas. ($7.05–$11.30); main dishes 1,200–2,000 ptas. ($11.30–$18.80). AE, DC, MC, V.
Open: Lunch Wed–Mon 1:30–3:30pm; dinner Wed–Mon 8:30–11:30pm.
Closed: July 10–31.
This is the finest dining choice in town, although its specialties are a bit expensive if you gravitate toward foie gras and *gambas* (shrimp). You'll enjoy dining in air-conditioned comfort on meals prepared by the owner himself. Selections might include roast loin of beef with peppers, truffles in a cream sauce, and crayfish with garlic sauce. The restaurant is centrally located.

BASQUE COUNTRY

The Basques are the oldest traceable ethnic group in Europe. Their language, called Euskera, predates any of the commonly spoken Romance languages, and its origin, like that of the Basque race itself, is lost in obscurity. Perhaps the Basques were descended from the original Iberians, who lived in Spain before the arrival of the Celts some 3,500 years ago. Conqueror after conqueror, Roman to Visigoth to Moor, may have driven these people into the vastness of the Pyrénées, where they stayed and carved out a life for themselves—filled with tradition and customs still practiced to this day.

The region is called Euskadi, which in Basque means "collection of Basques." In a very narrow sense it refers to three provinces of Spain, Guipuzcoa (with its capital San Sebastian, the number-one sightseeing target in Euskadi), Viscaya, (whose capital is industrial Bilbao), and Alava (with a capital at Vitoria). But to Basque nationalists, who dream of forging a new nation that will one day unite all the Basque lands, Euskadi also refers to the northern part of Navarre and three provinces in France, including the famed resort of Biarritz.

The three current Basque provinces occupy the eastern part of the Cantabrian Mountains, lying between the Pyrénées and the valley of the Nervión. They maintained a large degree of independence until the 19th century, when they finally gave in to control from Castile, which recognized their ancient rights and privileges until 1876.

As a badge of pride, Basques wear a *boina*, a beret of red, blue, or white woolen cloth. Today, more than ever, the wearing of the boina is also a political statement. In recent years, more and more graffiti have appeared. You'll see such slogans as "Euskadi Ta Askatasuna" ("Freedom for Basques") painted virtually everywhere. Most of the people are friendly, hospitable, and welcoming, but a small but violent minority has given the land much bad publicity. Politics, however, rarely needs to concern the foreign traveler intent on having a vacation in these lands, which remain some of the most beautiful in Spain.

SEEING BASQUE COUNTRY
GETTING THERE

The three Basque provinces are a major gateway into Spain from Europe via France, and public transportation is excellent. The busiest **airport** is Sandira, outside Bilbao. There's a smaller airport at Fuenterrabía, about 11 miles (18km) northeast of San Sebastián. If you're already in Spain, domestic connections can be arranged through Iberia Airlines, offering daily service to both Bilbao and Fuenterrabía (1 hour). Planes are small, so reserve far in advance.

The Basque lands are also easily reached by **train.** The most notable run is RENFE service from Chamartín Station in Madrid, heading for Irún and the French border. Many frontier-bound trains stop at San Sebastián. RENFE also runs trains to Bilbao, plus overnight service from Barcelona to San Sebastián and to Bilbao.

✓ WHAT'S SPECIAL ABOUT BASQUE COUNTRY

Beaches

☐ Playa de la Concha at San Sebastián, one of Spain's best-loved and most popular stretches of sand.

☐ Fuenterrabía, widest sandy stretch of beach in Guipúzcoa province. Known for its calm waters.

Great Towns/Villages

☐ San Sebastián, fashionable Belle Epoque resort, with Basque coast's choicest sands.

☐ Fuenterrabía, near French border, with many well-preserved villas in its medieval quarter.

☐ Lekeitio, in Vizcaya, an old fishing town, now a resort, visited for its fish restaurants and marine life.

☐ Ondárroa—for some, the ultimate symbol of the picture-postcard Costa Vasca fishing village.

Pilgrimages

☐ Guernica, immortalized by Picasso; living symbol of federation of Basque towns.

☐ Loyola, birthplace of St. Ignatius of Loyola, founder of Jesuit order. Family home now a monument.

Panoramic Vistas

☐ Jaizkibel Road, west of Fuenterrabía, winner of "spectacular at sunset" sweepstakes.

☐ Costa Vasca, or Basque coast— string of fishing villages spread along Bay of Biscay.

Special Events/Festivals

☐ International Film Festival at San Sebastián, drawing stars from around the world in September.

☐ Semana Grande at San Sebastián in mid-August, with fun fairs, fireworks, concerts, and sports competitions.

☐ Jazzaldia, jazz festival at San Sebastián, second half of July.

Bus links are also possible from major cities of Spain (see individual city or town listing for connections).

For those **driving** from Madrid, access to the Basque country is on the N-1 to Burgos and Miranda de Ebro, then the A-68 to Bilbao (if that is your gateway). If you're coming from France, take the A-8 running inland along the coast to your desired turnoff.

A SUGGESTED ROUTE

Most visitors arrive from France, crossing the border at Irún.

Days 1–2   Spend two nights in San Sebastián, enjoying its beaches and lively after-dark *tapas* crawls through the old quarter. The following day take one or two day trips, such as to Fuenterrabía.

Days 3–4   Leave San Sebastián and spend two nights in one of the little fishing villages along the Costa Vasca, or Basque coast. The most desirable places are Bermeo and Ondárroa. Using one of the villages as your center, explore the other ones outlined in this chapter. Allow time for a morning or afternoon visit south to Guernica, made famous by Picasso.

Day 5   Bilbao, the "Chicago of Spain," deserves a day. This sturdy bastion of Basque industrial might is surprisingly light in historic monuments.

Day 6   If time remains, explore Vitoria, capital of Alava, in the south, the most neglected of the three Basque provinces.

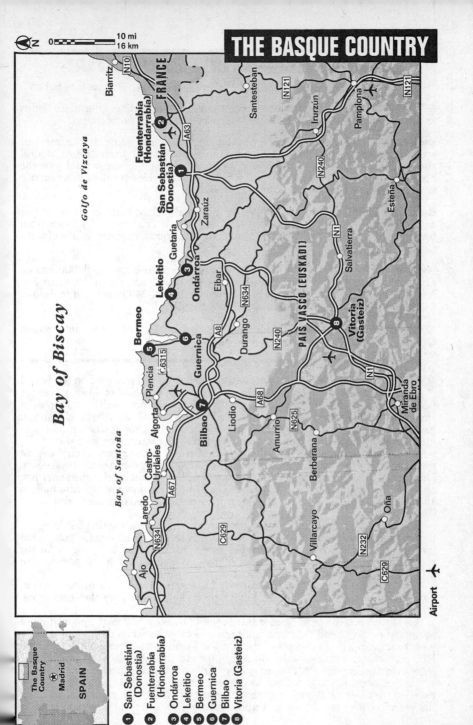

THE BASQUE COUNTRY

0 | 10 mi / 16 km

Bay of Biscay

Golfo de Vizcaya

Bay of Santoña

FRANCE

Biarritz

Fuenterrabia (Hondarrabia) ②

San Sebastián (Donostia) ①

Santesteban

Irurzún

Pamplona

Esteña

Zarauz

Guetaria

Lekeitio ④

Ondárroa ③

Eibar

Salvatierra

Bermeo

Guernica ⑥

Durango

PAÍS VASCO (EUSKADI)

Vitoria (Gasteiz) ⑧

Plencia

Algorta

Castro-Urdiales

Bilbao ⑦

Liodio

Amurrio

Berberana

Miranda de Ebro

Laredo

Ajo

Villarcayo

Oña

SPAIN

The Basque Country

Madrid

① San Sebastián (Donostia)
② Fuenterrabia (Hondarrabia)
③ Ondárroa
④ Lekeitio
⑤ Bermeo
⑥ Guernica
⑦ Bilbao
⑧ Vitoria (Gasteiz)

Airport

1. SAN SEBASTIÁN [DONOSTIA]

13 miles W of the French border, 300 miles N of Madrid, 62 miles E of Bilbao

GETTING THERE   By Plane   From Madrid, Iberia Airlines offers daily flights to San Sebastián (1 hour). The domestic airport is at nearby Fuenterrabía.

By Train   From Madrid, RENFE runs trains to the French border at Irún, many of which stop in San Sebastián (6 to 7 hours). An overnight train from Paris to Madrid also stops in San Sebastián—just in time for breakfast. (San Sebastián's cafes serve the best croissants south of the Pyrénées.) RENFE also provides overnight train service from Barcelona to San Sebastián and on to Bilbao.

By Bus   San Sebastián is well linked by a bus network to many of Spain's major cities. Fourteen buses a day connect it to Bilbao (1¼ hours); 1 bus per day arrives from Barcelona (7 hours); 5 per day from Pamplona (1½ hours). If you're in Madrid, it's more convenient to take a train.

By Car   From Madrid, take the N-1 toll road north to Burgos and Miranda de Ebro, continuing on the A-68 north to Bilbao, then along the A-8 east to San Sebastián and the French border. From Pamplona, the N-240 runs north to Tolosa, where the N-1 route will take you into San Sebastián.

ESSENTIALS   The area code for San Sebastián is 943. The Tourist Information Office is at Reina Regente, s/n (tel. 943/42-10-02).

San Sebastián (Donostia in Basque), ideally situated on a choice spot on the Bay of Biscay, surrounded by green mountains, is the summer capital of Spain, where the Belle Epoque lives on. From June to September the population swells as hundreds of Spanish bureaucrats escape the heat and head for this capital city. A tasteful resort, it has few of the tawdry trappings associated with major beachfront cities. It is also an ideal excursion center for trips to some of Spain's most fascinating towns.

Queen Isabella II put San Sebastián on the map as a tourist resort when she spent the summer of 1845 there. In time it became the summer residence of the royal court. On July 8, 1912, Queen María Cristina inaugurated the grand hotel named after her, and the resort became the pinnacle of fashion. In what is now the city hall, built in 1887, a casino opened, and here European aristocrats gambled in safety during World War I.

San Sebastián is the capital of the province of Guipúzcoa, the smallest in Spain, tucked in the far northeastern corner, bordering France. It is said that Guipúzcoa has preserved Basque customs better than any other province. Half of the *donostiarras* speak Euskera. It is also a major seat of Basque nationalism, so be advised that protests, sometimes violent, are frequent.

San Sebastián contains an old quarter, **La Parte Vieja** with narrow streets, hidden plazas, and medieval houses, but it is primarily a modern city of elegant shops, wide boulevards, sidewalk cafés, and restaurants.

La Concha is the most famous beach, where it seems half of the population of Spain and France spend their days under striped canopies when they're not dashing into the refreshingly cool waters of the bay. Shell-shaped La Concha is half encircled by a promenade, where crowds mill during the evening. The adjoining beach is the **Playa de Ondarreta.** Its climate is more Atlantic than Mediterranean.

San Sebastián has a good, but insufficient, choice of hotels in summer, and an excellent number of Basque restaurants, most of which are expensive. Its chief drawback is overcrowding—it is overpopulated in July, and there is no space at all in August.

Bullfights, art and film festivals, sporting events, and cultural activities keep San Sebastián hopping during the season.

WHAT TO SEE & DO

Two weeklong events draw visitors from around the world. From August 13 to 20, San Sebastián stages its annual carnival, **Aste Nagusia,** a joyous celebration of traditional Basque music and dance, along with fireworks, cooking competitions, and sports events. From September 15 to 23, the San Sebastián **International Film Festival** draws luminaries from America and Europe. Actual dates of these festivals vary from year to year, so check with the tourist office.

People come to San Sebastián for fun and to take a promenade along the Paseo de la Concha. The monuments, such as they are, can easily be viewed before lunch.

The **Museo de San Telmo,** Plaza Ignacio Zuloaga, housed in a former Dominican monastery, contains an impressive collection of Basque artifacts dating from unrecorded Iberian times. Paintings and display include works by Zuloaga (his *Torreillos en Turégano,* for example), Golden Age artists such as El Greco and Ribera, and a large number of Basque painters. The museum stands in the old town at the base of Monte Urgull. The museum is open Tuesday through Saturday from 10am to 1:30pm and 3:30 to 5:30pm. Admission is 60 pesetas (55¢).

The **Paseo Nuevo** is a wide promenade that almost encircles **Monte Urgull,** one of the two mountains between which San Sebastián is nestled (Monte Igueldo is the other one). A ride along this promenade opens onto panoramic vistas of the Bay of Biscay. The *paseo* comes to an end at the **Palacio del Mar** (tel. 42-19-05), an oceanographic museum and aquarium. Here you can see the skeleton of the last whale caught in the Bay of Biscay, in 1878. The museum is open in summer from 10am to 2pm and 3:30 to 8:30pm. Admission is 125 pesetas ($1.20).

Other sights include the **Palacio Miramar,** which stands on its own hill opening onto La Concha. In the background is the residential district of Antiguo. Queen María Cristina, after whom the grandest hotel in the north of Spain is named, opened this palace in 1893, but by the turbulent 1930s it had fallen into disrepair. The city council took it over in 1971, and renovations continue. You can visit in summer from 9am to 9pm and in winter from 10am to 5pm. Since you can't go inside the palace, you must settle for a look at the lawns and gardens. The palace stands on land splitting the two major beaches of San Sebastián: Playa de la Concha and Playa de Ondarreta.

Another palace of interest is the **Palacio de Ayete,** which was constructed by the duke of Bailéen in 1878 and which became the summer home of King Alfonso XII and his queen, María Cristina, until their own Palacio Miramar (see above) was completed. Standing in 250,000 square feet of parkland, the palace also served as the summer home of Franco from 1940 until 1975. The residence remains closed to the public, but you can wander through the beautiful grounds in summer from 10am to 5pm. To reach it, take bus 19 to Ayete from the Plaza de Guipúzcoa.

Finally, for the best view of the city, take the funicular for 55 pesetas (50¢) to the top of **Monte Igueldo,** where from the belvedere you get a fabulous view of the bay and the Cantabrian coastline. The funicular operates in season from 10am to 10pm. It's also possible to drive up. In spring the air is scented with honeysuckle.

WHERE TO STAY

If you book space well in advance, you'll find many good hotel values, but in season most hoteliers will insist that you take full or at least half board (breakfast, plus one main meal).

DOUBLES FOR LESS THAN 8,700 PTAS. [$81.80]

HOSTAL BAHÍA, San Martín, 54, 20007 San Sebastián. Tel. 943/46-10-83. Fax 943/47-17-30. 59 rms (all with bath). TEL

$ **Rates:** 5,000 ptas. ($47) single; 6,000 ptas. ($56.40) double. Breakfast 375 ptas. ($4.55) extra. MC, V.

A good-value little hotel just 1 block from the beach near a string of other hotels, the Bahía features bedrooms of varying sizes: Some are large enough to contain sofas and armchairs; others fall into the cubicle category. Many North

Americans stay at the *hostal* and take public transportation to Pamplona for the running of the bulls.

CODINA, Avenida Zumalacarregui, 21, 20008 San Sebastián. Tel. 943/ 21-22-00. Fax 943/21-25-23. 77 rms (all with bath). TV TEL **Bus:** 5
$ Rates: 6,000 ptas. ($56.40) single; 8,000 ptas. ($75.20) double. Breakfast 500 ptas. ($4.70) extra. AE, DC, MC, V. **Closed:** Feb.
Near an attractive residential district and close to a beach, this modern building is designed so that all of the comfortably furnished, compact rooms have a view of the bay. On the wide, busy boulevard you'll find a popular café and bar. Basque lunches and dinners cost 1,500 pesetas ($14.10).

AVENIDA, Carretera Subida a Igueldo, 22, 20008 San Sebastián. Tel. 943/21-20-22. 47 rms (all with bath). TEL **Bus:** Igueldo
$ Rates: 6,500 ptas. ($61.10) single; 8,500 ptas. ($79.90) double. Breakfast 525 ptas. ($5) extra. AE, DC, MC, V. **Closed:** Nov to Mar.
This hotel sits on the edge of San Sebastian, on the road up to Monte Igueldo. Accommodations are tasteful and comfortable. The lounge, with its French provincial pieces, has a view of the hills beyond. Guests enjoy watching sunrises and sunsets from April through October.

RESIDENCIA PARMA, General Jáuregui, 11, 20002 San Sebastián. Tel. 943/42-88-93. 21 rms (all with bath). TEL
$ Rates: 4,800 ptas. ($45.10) single; 8,500 ptas. ($79.90) double. Breakfast 525 ptas. ($5) extra. No credit cards.
A modern, clean hotel in the center of town, where many of the accommodations have beautiful views of the ocean, the Parma has up-to-date rooms cozily furnished in wood, with good, modern bathrooms. There are also a downstairs snack bar and a pleasant TV lobby, with armchairs and sofas. Breakfast only is served.

NIZA, Zubieta, 56, 20007 San Sebastián. Tel. 943/42-66-63. Fax 943/42-66-63. 41 rms (all with bath). TV TEL
$ Rates: 4,300 ptas. ($40.40) single; 8,700 ptas. ($81.80) double. Breakfast 450 ptas. ($4.25) extra. AE, DC, MC, V.
This little hotel, which opens onto the Playa de la Concha, has character and is favored by those who like to be near the beach and the esplanade. It has Scandinavian modern furnishings in the bedrooms and antiques in the public lounges. The petit salon, for example, contains an Oriental rug, Directoire chairs, a tall grandfather clock, and a rosewood breakfront. In direct contrast are the basic rooms, with wooden headboards, white walls, and wall-to-wall carpeting. There's a pizzeria in the cellar.

WORTH THE EXTRA BUCKS

MONTE IGUELDO, Monte Igueldo, 20008 San Sebastián. Tel. 943/21-02-11. Fax 943/21-50-28. 125 rms (all with bath). TV TEL **Bus:** Igueldo
$ Rates: 10,000 ptas. ($94) single; 12,500 ptas. ($117.50) double. Breakfast 725 ptas. ($6.80) extra. AE, DC, MC, V.
On the top of the mountain overlooking San Sebastián, this first-class hotel perches like a castle. The public rooms, bedrooms, and pool terrace all boast a panoramic view of the Cantabrian coast. Each of the streamlined, modern rooms has a private balcony. Ample parking is provided. The hotel stands only a 10-minute drive from the center of town.

HOTEL SAN SEBASTIÁN, Avenida Zumalacárregui, 20, 20008 San Sebastián. Tel. 943/21-44-00. Fax 943/21-72-99. 92 rms (all with bath). MINIBAR TV TEL Bus: 5.
$ Rates: 8,000 ptas. ($75.20) single; 13,000 ptas. ($122.20) double. Breakfast 800 ptas. ($7.50) extra. AE, DC, MC, V.
Only a short distance from the beach, near the edge of the city on the main road to Bilbao and Madrid, this Belle Epoque hotel has a swimming pool in a pleasant

garden, as well as an informal restaurant, a disco, and a bar. Rooms are comfortably and attractively furnished. A garage is provided.

WHERE TO EAT

MEALS FOR LESS THAN 2,600 PTAS. [$24.45]

LA OKA, San Martín, 43. Tel. 46-38-84.
  Cuisine: BASQUE. **Reservations:** Not required.
$ Prices: Appetizers 300–450 ptas. ($2.80–$4.25); main dishes 450–900 ptas. ($4.25–$8.45). V; fixed-priced menu 850 ptas. ($8).
  Open: Lunch Thurs–Tues 1–3:30pm; dinner Fri–Sat 8:30–11pm.

⭐ Don't come to La Oka, near the beach in the center of town, looking for glamour. If on the other hand, you're looking for an inexpensive self-service cafeteria, you might enjoy this place. Some critics, in fact, rate it the best self-service cafeteria in Spain. Most of the diners represent a cross section of the city's office workers. The Basque cooking is hearty and plentiful.

GURE ARKUPE, Letra D. Iztingorra, 7. Tel. 21-15-09.
  Cuisine: BASQUE. **Reservations:** Recommended.
$ Prices: Appetizers 500–850 ptas. ($4.70–$8); main dishes 1,300–2,000 ptas. ($12.20–$18.80); fixed-priced meals 1,500 ptas. ($14.10). AE, DC, MC, V.
  Open: Lunch daily 1–4pm; dinner 8:30pm–midnight. **Closed:** Dec.

⭐ An intimate beachside restaurant that is popular for its flavorful, unpretentious food. You can feast on seafood such as shrimp with salmon or a *zarzuela* (shellfish stew), as well as other fish dishes. Other specialties are homemade pâté, duckling with orange sauce, and juicy veal dishes. My preferred dessert is thin crêpes stuffed with cream.

SALDUBA, Pescadería, 6. Tel. 42-56-27.
  Cuisine: BASQUE. **Reservations:** Recommended.
$ Prices: Appetizers 800–1,200 ptas. ($7.50–$11.30); main dishes 1,500–1,900 ptas. ($14.10–$17.85); fixed-priced menu 3,500 ptas. ($32.90). AE, DC, MC, V.
  Open: Lunch Mon–Sun 1–4pm; dinner Mon–Sat 8–11pm. **Closed:** Nov.
Opened shortly after the end of World War II, this well-established restaurant owes much of its popularity to the owners, who oversee the cooking. Specialties include Basque hake, herb-laden fish soup, a confit of duckling, filet of beef, and a platter stacked high with the "fruits of the sea," as well as succulent beef, veal, and pork dishes and various desserts. There are several dining rooms. Salduba lies on edge of the old town, 5-minute walk from the beach.

PATXIKU KINTANA, San Jerónimo, 22. Tel. 42-63-99.
  Cuisine: BASQUE. **Reservations:** Required.
$ Prices: Appetizers 800–1,500 ptas. ($7.50–$14.10); main dishes 1,600–2,600 ptas. ($15.05–$24.45). AE, DC, MC, V.
  Open: Lunch Thurs–Tues 1–3:30pm; dinner Thurs–Mon 8:30–11:30pm.
This well-known restaurant in the heart of the old city off 31 de Agosto has hosted many celebrities during its time. The menu contains many good old traditional standbys that are prepared with subtle Basque variations. Among them you might find *cocido* (a stew), *merluza* (hake) stew, squid in its own ink, and many veal, pork, and beef dishes.

JUANITO KOJUA, Puerto, 14. Tel. 42-01-80.
  Cuisine: SEAFOOD. **Reservations:** Required.
$ Prices: Appetizers 1,000–1,500 ptas. ($9.40–$14.10); main dishes 1,800–2,400 ptas. ($16.90–$22.55); fixed-priced menu 2,300 ptas. ($21.60). AE, DC, MC, V.
  Open: Lunch Mon–Sun 1–3:30pm; dinner Mon–Sat 8:30–11:30pm. **Closed:** Sun night.
This little seafood restaurant in the old town, off the Plaza de la Constitución, has no decor to speak of, but it has become famous throughout Spain. There's always a wait, but it's worth it. There are two dining areas on the main floor, behind a narrow bar

(perfect for an appetizer while you're waiting for your table), plus one downstairs—all of them air-conditioned in summer. Specialties may include paella, *pisto,* half a *besugo* (sea bream), *rape* (monkfish) *l'americana,* and *lubina* (sea bass). Meats are good too, but it's best to stick to the fresh fish dishes.

SPECIALTY DINING

In the summer, walk along the **Fishermen's Harbor** in San Sebastián and order a plate of charcoal-broiled sardines. At several bistros, rustic wooden tables and chairs have been placed outside rough-and-tumble restaurants.

EVENING ENTERTAINMENT

The best evening entertainment in San Sebastián is to go tapa-tasting in the old quarter of town. Throughout the rest of Spain this is known as a *tapeo,* or tapas crawl. In San Sebastián it's called a *poteo-ir-de pinchos,* or searching out morsels on cocktail sticks. Groups of young people often spend their evenings on some 20 streets in the old town, each leading toward Monte Urgull, the port, or La Brecha marketplace. The Alameda del Bulervar, the "popular grove," is the most upscale of these streets, the Calle Fermín Calveton one of the most popular. You'll find plenty of these places on your own, but here are some to get you going.

CASA ALCALDE, Mayor, 19. Tel. 42-62-16.

The tasty tapas served here, just a 5-minute walk from the Parque Alderdi Eder, are thinly sliced ham, cheeses, and shellfish dishes. The different varieties are all neatly displayed. You can also have full meals in a small restaurant at the back, for 1,350 pesetas ($12.70) to 2,200 pesetas ($20.70). Open: Daily 10am–11pm. Prices: Tapas 100–200 ptas. (95¢–$1.90).

BAR ASADOR GAMBARA, San Jerónimo, 21. Tel. 42-25-75.

Decorated with a sophisticated flair in light-colored wood, this is a tapas lover's delight. Dishes are well prepared, using market-fresh ingredients. Try the house specialty and the chef's pride: small croissants made of melt-in-your-mouth dough, filled with cheese, egg, bacon, and Serrano ham. Try also the spider crab and prawns with mayonnaise. The Calle San Jerónimo runs at right angles to the Calle Fermín Calveton. Open: Tues–Sun 10am–1am. Prices: Tapas 200–650 ptas. ($1.90–$6.10); drinks 125 ptas. ($1.20).

BAR ORNAZABAL, 31 de Agosto, 22. Tel. 42-99-07.

This is one of the oldest tapas bars in San Sebastián, lying at the northern edge of the old town. The favorite drink is the Basque wine *taxcolo.* Try such specialties as a salt-cod casserole or calf's cheek. The croquettes—known as *bolas*—use bechamel sauce as a base and are often served with egg or prawns. Open: Tues–Sun 10am–1am. Prices: Tapas 150–500 ptas. ($1.40–$4.70); drinks 125 ptas. ($1.20).

BATI JAI, Fermín Calveton, s/n. Tel. 42-77-37.

Here at the bar counter you can make your selection among what are said to be the finest fish and shellfish tapas in town. The house specialty is *txangurro* (baked spider crab), but your eyes may also be tempted by prawns of all sizes, crayfish, or octopus dressed with olive oil, red pepper, vinegar, and onions. Many dishes, such as mushrooms, are cooked and served in earthenware pots. Bati Jai is near the Alameda del Bulevar. Open: Wed–Sun 9am–1am. Prices: Tapas 300–550 ptas. ($2.80–$5.15); beer 125 ptas. ($1.20).

EL ASTELENA, Plaza de la Constitución. Tel. 42-62-75.

This bar lies in the very heart of San Sebastián, which is the center of many cultural and political events, including protests. The Plaza de la Constitución, lined with houses with tall arcades and balconies, was once the scene of bullfights, and the tapas served in this much-patronized bar are often called *banderillas,* which means bullfighting darts. They include a favorite Basque specialty, calf's cheek, but you may opt instead for a cheese croquette. Salt cod with onions and green peppers is the eternal favorite. Open: Tues–Sun 10am–1am. Prices: Tapas: 150–500 ptas. ($1.40–$4.70); drinks 125 ptas. ($1.20).

EL BARTOLO, Fermín Calveton, s/n. Tel. 42-17-43.

This is both a bar and restaurant, serving a cuisine prepared in earthenware dishes, along with grilled fresh fish and savory meat dishes. Step inside the wood-paneled room and up to the bar to place your order. An *asador* (barbecue) is in back. As a change of pace, you might ask for a bottle of cider or else *txacoli,* a popular Basque wine. Try codfish with garlic and olive oil, quail in a savory sauce, or peppers stuffed with *bacalao* (salt cod). Open: Wed–Sun 10am–5pm and 7pm–1am. Prices: Tapas 100–500 ptas. (95¢–$4.70); drinks 125 ptas. ($1.20).

LA CEPA, 31 de Agosto, 9. Tel. 42-63-94.

✪ Many locals say that the best tapas in town are found at La Cepa, on the northern edge of the old town, and the Jabugo ham is one proof of this claim. Try the grilled squid or a salt-cod–and–green-pepper omelet. You can also order dinner here—a daily changing menu costs 1,200 pesetas ($11.30). The owner, a former bullfighter known as Barberito, is usually on the scene visiting with his many friends. Open: Thurs–Tues 11am–midnight. Prices: Tapas 100–200 ptas. (95¢–$1.90); glass of wine 40 ptas. (40¢).

CASA VALLES, Reyes Católicos, 10. Tel. 45-22-10.

The variety of tapas and wines offered here seems endless. Go to hang out with the locals and feast on tidbits guaranteed to spoil your dinner. You'll find it in the center behind the cathedral. Open: Thurs–Tues 8:30–11:30pm. Closed: Late June, late Dec. Prices: Tapas 75–150 ptas. (70¢–$1.40); beer 90 ptas. (85¢); glass of wine 25 ptas. (20¢).

NEARBY EXCURSIONS
TWO FISHING VILLAGES

One of the reasons for coming to San Sebastián is to use it as a base for touring the environs. Driving is best because bus connections are awkward or nonexistent.

On the east bank of a natural harbor 6.5 miles (10.5km) from San Sebastián, **Pasai Donibane** is one of the most typical of Basque fishing villages. Once it was known by its Spanish name, Pasajes de San Juan. Many visitors come here to dine. The village, with its codfish-packing factories, is on a sheltered harbor; fishing boats are tied up at the wharf. The architecture is appealing: five- and six-story balconied tenementlike buildings in different colors.

Victor Hugo lived here in the summer of 1846 (it hasn't changed much since) at building no. 63 on the narrow main street, San Juan.

In summer, don't take a car into the village. Parking is difficult, the medieval streets are one-way, and the wait at traffic signals is long, for all southbound traffic has to clear the street before northbound motorists have the right of way.

A bus leaves every 15 minutes from the Calle Aldamar in San Sebastián for **Pasajes de San Pedro,** Pasai Donibane's neighboring fishing village. It's also possible to walk from Pasai Donibane. Buses head back to San Sebastián from Pasajes de San Pedro, at a quarter to the hour all day long.

Where to Eat

TXULOTXO, San Juan, 71, Pasai Donibane. Tel. 52-39-52.

Cuisine: BASQUE. **Reservations:** Recommended.

$ **Prices:** Appetizers 850–1,400 ptas. ($8–$13.15); main dishes 1,400–1,800 ptas. ($13.15–$16.90). AE, DC, MC, V.

Open: Lunch Wed–Mon noon–5pm; dinner Wed–Mon 8–11pm. **Closed:** Mid-Oct to mid-Nov.

Right on the waterfront, this old stone building with a glass-enclosed dining room overlooking the harbor is one of the most authentic and typical of Basque restaurants. The house specialties are made from fish that is delivered daily.

LOYOLA

Surrounded by mountain scenery, Loyola, about 34 miles (55km) southwest of San Sebastián, is the birthplace of St. Ignatius, founder of the Jesuits. He was born in 1491, died in 1556, and was canonized in 1622. The sanctuary at Loyola is the most-visited attraction outside the city.

There are large pilgrimages to Loyola for an annual celebration on St. Ignatius Day, July 31. The activity centers around the **Monastery of San Ignacio de Loyola,** a immense structure built by the Jesuits in the 1700s around the Loyola family manor house near Azpeitia. An International Festival of Romantic Music is held here during the first week of August.

The **basilica** was the work of Italian architect Fontana. Surrounded by a 118-foot-high cupola by Churriguera, it is circular in design.

From 12:30 to 3:30pm daily, visitors can enter the **Santa Casa,** site of the former Loyola manor house, with its 15th-century tower. The rooms in which the saint was born and in which he convalesced have been converted into richly decorated chapels. At the entrance you can rent a tape detailing Loyola's life, and dioramas are shown at the end of the tour.

Six buses a day leave from Plaza Guipúzcoa, 2, San Sebastián, for Loyola (the first departing at 8:30am and the last at 8pm). Buses return about every two hours.

2. FUENTERRABÍA (HONDARRIBÍA)

14 miles E of San Sebastián, 317 miles N of Madrid,
11 miles W of St-Jean-de-Luz (France)

GETTING THERE   By Train   Irún is the "end of the line" for trains in northern Spain. East of Irún, you must board French trains. Irún is about 3 miles (4.8km) from Fuenterrabía.

By Bus   Buses running every 20 minutes from San Sebastián connect that city with Fuenterrabía (1 hour).

By Car   Take the A-8 east to the French border, turning toward the coast at the exit sign for Fuenterrabía.

ESSENTIALS   The area code for Fuenterrabía is 943.

A big seaside resort and fishing port, Fuenterrabía (Hondarribía in Basque) lies near the French frontier, and for that reason it has been subject to frequent attacks over the centuries. In theory, it was supposed to guard the access to Spain, but sometimes it didn't perform that task too well.

WHAT TO SEE & DO

The most interesting part of town is the **medieval quarter** in the upper market. Some of the villas here date from the early 17th century. The fishing district, in the lower part of town, is called **La Marina;** old homes, painted boats, and the general marine atmosphere attract many visitors. Since restaurants in Fuenterrabía tend to be very expensive, you can fill up here on seafood tapas in the many taverns along the waterfront. The beach at Fuenterrabía is wide and sandy, and many prefer it to the more famous ones at San Sebastián.

Wander for an hour or two around the old quarter, taking in the Calle Mayor, Calle Tiendas y Pampinot, and Calle Obispo. The **Castillo de Carlos V,** standing at the Plaza de las Armas, has been turned into one of the smallest and desirable *paradores* in Spain (see below). It's hard to get a room here unless you reserve well in advance, but you can visit the well-stocked bar over the entrance hall.

Sancho Abarca, a king of Navarre in the 10th century, is supposed to have founded the original castle that stood on this spot. The present look owes more to Charles V in the 16th century. You can still see the battle scars on the castle that date from the time of the Napoleonic invasion of Spain.

The most impressive church in the old quarter is the **Iglesia de Santa María,** a Gothic structure that was vastly restored in the 17th century and given a baroque tower. The proxy wedding of Louis XIV and the Infanta María Teresa took place here in June 1660.

If you have a car, you can take some interesting trips in the area, especially to **Cabo Higuer,** a promontory with spectacular views, reached by going 2½ miles (4km) north. Leave by the harbor and beach road. You can see the French coast and the town of Hendaye from this cape.

You can also head west out of town along the **Jaizkibel Road,** which many motorists prefer at sunset. After going 3 miles (4.8km), you'll reach the shrine of the Virgin of Guadalupe, where a magnificent view unfolds. From here you can see the French Basque coast. Even better views await you if you continue along to the Hostal Jaizkibel. If you stay on this road, you will come to the little fishing village of Pasai Donibane (see excursions from San Sebastián), 11 miles (18km) away.

WHERE TO STAY

GUADALUPE, Nafarroa, s/n, 20280 Fuenterrabía. Tel. 943/64-16-50. 36 rms (all with bath). TV TEL

$ Rates: 4,400 ptas. ($41.35) single; 7,300 ptas. ($68.60) double. Breakfast 350 ptas. ($3.30) extra. MC, V.

This Basque-owned hotel, a 10-minute walk from the beach, is considered one of the bargains of the town. It has a pretty garden and a swimming pool for those wanting to remain close to home. Each room is comfortably furnished. The Guadalupe does not have a restaurant, and it is open only from June to September.

JÁUREGUI, San Pedro, 28, 20280 Fuenterrabía. Tel. 943/64-14-00. Fax 943/64-44-04. 53 rms (all with bath). TV TEL

$ Rates: 5,500 ptas. ($51.70) single; 8,000 ptas. ($75.20) double. Breakfast 400 ptas. ($3.75) extra. AE, DC, MC, V.

Opened in 1981 in the center of the old village is this moderately priced choice for accommodations. The modern interior boasts comfortable accessories, and the hotel also has a garage—a definite plus, since parking in Fuenterrabía is virtually impossible. Each of the rooms is well furnished and maintained; thoughtful extras include a hairdryer in each bathroom and a shoeshine machine on each floor.

PARADOR NACIONAL EL EMPERADOR, Plaza de las Armas, 20280 Fuenterrabía. Tel. 943/64-21-40. Fax 943/64-21-53. 16 rms (all with bath). TEL

$ Rates: 9,000 ptas. ($84.60) single; 11,000 ptas. ($103.40) double. Breakfast 900 ptas. ($8.45) extra. AE, DC, MC, V.

⭐ This beautifully restored 10th-century castle situated on a hill in the center of the old town was once used by Emperor Charles V as a border fortification. The building itself is impressive, and so are the taste and imagination of the restoration: Antiques, old weapons, and standards hang from the high-vaulted ceilings. Some of the comfortable provincial-style rooms open onto the Bay of Biscay. Breakfast only is served. It's best to reserve well in advance. Ample parking available out front.

WHERE TO EAT

SEBASTIÁN, Mayor, 7. Tel. 64-01-67.
Cuisine: BASQUE. **Reservations:** Required.
$ Prices: Appetizers 650–1,200 ptas. ($6.10–$11.30); main dishes 1,700–2,500 ptas. ($16–$23.50). AE, MC, V.
Open: Lunch Tues–Sun 1–3:30pm; dinner Tues–Sat 8:30–11pm. **Closed:** Nov.

Lying within the oldest district of Fuenterrabía, close to the castle, this restaurant offers modern, sophisticated cuisine, well presented and using top-notch ingredients appropriate to the season. On two different floors, the milieu is a sheltering one, with thick masonry walls; among them are scattered an array of 18th-century paintings. Mari José directs the highly agreeable service. Try one of the specialties: foie gras of duckling Basque style, terrine of fresh mushrooms, or medallions of sole and salmon with a seafood sauce.

3. ONDÁRROA

30 miles W of San Sebastián, 38 miles E of Bilbao, 265 miles N of Madrid

GETTING THERE By Bus From San Sebastián, Ondárroa is serviced by buses that run along the Costa Vasca.

By Car Head west from Zarauz along the coastal road.

ESSENTIALS The area code for Ondárroa is 94.

Ondárroa is described as a *pueblo típico,* a typical Basque fishing village. It is also the area's largest fishing port. Lying on a spit of land, it stands between a hill and a loop of the Artibay River. Laundry hangs from the windows of the little plant-filled balconied Basque houses, and most of the residents are engaged in canning and fish salting, if not fishing. The local church looks like a ship's prow at one end. Around the snug harbor you'll find many little places to drink and dine, after a stroll through the village.

WHERE TO STAY & EAT

HOTEL/RESTAURANT VEGA, Avenida de la Antigua, 8, 48700 Ondárroa. Tel. 947/683-00-02. 30 rms (all with bath). TEL
$ Rates: 6,800 ptas. ($63.90) single; 10,200 ptas. ($95.90) double. Breakfast 350 ptas. ($3.30) extra. AE, DC, MC, V.
In the center of town is a real find, offering comfortable and simple rooms for reasonable prices. It is the only hostal of note in town, and the setting is pleasant. The dining room serves well-prepared meals for around 2,200 pesetas ($20.70). Veal, fish, fried beef, and fish soup are typical items. The restaurant is open daily from 1:30 to 3:30pm and 8 to 11pm (Friday through Wednesday in winter), and is closed for the month of October. The hotel stays open all year.

RESTAURANT PENALTY, Eribera, 32. Tel. 683-00-00.
Cuisine: SEAFOOD. **Reservations:** Required.
$ Prices: Appetizers 750–1,200 ptas. ($7.05–$11.30); main dishes 1,400–2,200 ptas. ($13.15–$20.70). No credit cards.
Open: Lunch Thurs–Tues 1:30–3:30pm; dinner daily Thurs–Tues 8:30–11:30pm.
Closed: Dec and Jan.
This small restaurant, with a limited number of tables, stands at a crossroads at the edge of town. Meals might include a house recipe for hake that is simply heavenly, plus other fish specialties. The *sopa de pescado* (fish soup) invariably makes a good choice as an appetizer.

4. LEKEITIO

38 miles W of San Sebastián, 37 miles E of Bilbao, 280 miles N of Madrid

GETTING THERE By Bus Six buses a day connect Lekeitio with Bilbao (1½ hours), and 4 buses a day run from San Sebastián (1½ hours).

By Car From Ondárroa, take the coastal road northwest along the Costa Vasca.

ESSENTIALS The area code for Lekeitio is 94.

This unspoiled Basque fishing village that everybody talks about is most often visited on a day trip. There are those who consider it "more authentic" than Ondárroa, the more obvious choice. At the foot of Mount Calvario, Lekeitio opens onto a deeply indented bay. Queen Isabella II first gave the town prominence when she spent time here in the 19th century. Fishing may have diminished in recent years, but Lekeitio is still home to some of the Basque coast's trawlers. The island of San Nicolás converts the bay into a naturally protected harbor, a phenomenon that led to the village's growth.

A beach lies across from the harbor, but the one at Carraspio, farther along the bay, is considered safer. Note the **church** from the 15th century "guarding" the harbor. Three tiers of flying buttresses characterize this monument, which has a baroque belfry. Go inside to the third south chapel, of the right nave, to see a remarkable altarpiece, *The Road to Calvary,* which was erected in a flamboyant Gothic style.

The town is noted for its **festivals,** including the feast day of SS. Peter and Paul on June 29, at which a *Kaxarranca,* a Basque folk dance, takes place. A dancer leaps about on top of a trunk carried through the streets by some hearty Basque fishermen. Even better known is the controversial Jaiak San Antolín, or goose festival, September 1 to 8. A gruesome custom, it involves hanging live geese in the harbor. Youths leap from row boats to grab the greased necks of the geese. Both youth and goose are dunked into the water, using a system of pulleys, until the youth cries uncle or the neck of the goose is wrenched off. Perhaps you'll want to skip this one. The candlelit march through the streets, with everyone dressed in white, does not mourn the unfortunate geese but signals the end of the festival.

WHERE TO EAT

RESTAURANTE EGAÑA, Santa Catalina, 4. Tel. 684-01-03.
   Cuisine: SEAFOOD. **Reservations:** Not required.
$ **Prices:** fixed-priced menu 750 ptas. ($7.05). Appetizers 350–500 ptas. ($3.30–$4.70); main dishes 450–1,200 ptas. ($4.25–$11.30). No credit cards.
   Open: Lunch daily 1–4pm; dinner daily 8–10:30pm.

In a spacious, breezy dining room on the upper side of the village, devotees of Basque seafood get their fill. Portions are large and generous, and the price is right. The place is unfussy and unpretentious: You are here to eat without frills. The menu depends on the catch of the day. Try the Basque-style hake.

---

5. BERMEO

60 miles W of San Sebastián, 20 miles E of Bilbao, 268 miles N of Madrid

GETTING THERE   By Bus   Bermeo lies along the coastal bus route connecting the Costa Vasca fishing villages with either Bilbao or San Sebastián.

By Car   From Lekeitio, take the coastal route west to Bermeo. From Bilbao, go along the C-6313.

ESSENTIALS   The area code for Bermeo is 94.

This is the major inshore fishing port on the Cantabrian coast. Visit the narrow streets of the **fishing quarter** along the harbor, one of the most charming of such barrios along the Costa Vasca. An early-morning fish auction is held quayside, but even more interesting—only if you're lucky enough to be there when it happens—is the return of the fishing fleet to port. Bermeo and its neighbor, Mundaca, have an ongoing dispute over the ownership of the Isle of Izaro, and a regatta staged yearly on June 22 attempts to settle the dispute.

The town has an early Gothic church, the **Iglesia Juaadera de Santa Eufernía,** where back in the Middle Ages the kings of Castile vowed to uphold ancient Biscay privileges. If you have time, pay a visit to the **Museo del Arrantxale,** housed in the grim, granite Torre de Ercilla, located at Toorrontero Emparaza, 1, and open from 10am to 2pm and 5 to 7pm; admission is free. *Arrantxale* is a Basque word meaning fishermen, and this museum displays artifacts from Bermeo's history as a fishing port, which dates from the 11th century. The beach at Bermeo is far from the best along the coast.

Most of the city's *tascas* border the Parque de Ercilla. At these small taverns you can sample memorable tapas of fresh *bonita* (tuna) or succulent, fresh anchovies.

WHERE TO EAT

PILI, Parque de Ercilla, 1. Tel. 688-18-50.
   Cuisine: SEAFOOD. **Reservations:** Recommended.
$ **Prices:** Appetizers 450–850 ptas. ($4.25–$8); main dishes 1,100–1,900 ptas. ($10.35–$17.85); fixed-priced menu 1,400 ptas. ($13.15). AE, V.
   Open: Lunch daily 1–3:30pm; dinner daily 8:30–11pm.
This restaurant has been restored, enlarged, and modernized, and today is one of the most inviting places at the port for fresh fish and shellfish. You can enjoy air conditioning when it gets too muggy outside. Try many different preparations of hake or fresh tuna. You can also order such specialties as scrambled eggs with spinach and shrimp. The chef also has a winning way with beefsteak.

JOKIN, Eupeme Deuna, 13. Tel. 688-40-89.
   Cuisine: SEAFOOD. **Reservations:** Recommended on weekends.
$ **Prices:** Appetizers 650–950 ptas. ($6.10–$8.95); main dishes 1,200–2,200 ptas. ($11.30–$20.70); fixed-priced menu 1,600 ptas. ($15.05), served Mon-Fri. AE, V.
   Open: Lunch Tues–Sun 1–4pm; dinner Tues–Sun 8:30–11pm.
You come here not just for the view of the harbor, but for the ever-changing repertoire of Basque fish and seafood dishes, including grilled sea bream *(besugo)* and merluza (hake) prepared in various ways. A specialty is a brochette of monkfish and large prawns. Meat dishes aren't ignored: You can even order a well-prepared filet mignon.

6. GUERNICA

266 miles N of Madrid, 52 miles W of San Sebastián

GETTING THERE   By Train   From San Sebastián, trains run 3 times daily to Guernica. Change at Amorebieta.

By Bus   Vascongados, Estación de Amara in San Sebastián, runs buses to Bilbao, with connections to Guernica. Inquire at the station.

By Car   Guernica is a 20-minute drive beyond Bermeo on the C-6315.

ESSENTIALS   The area code for Guernica is 94.

The subject of Picasso's most famous painting (returned to Spain from the United States, and displayed at the Casón del Buen Retiro in Madrid), Guernica, the spiritual home of the Basques and the seat of Basque nationalism, was destroyed in a Nazi air raid on April 26, 1937. It was the site of a revered oak tree, under whose branches Basques had elected their officials since medieval times. No one knows how many died during the 3½-hour attack—estimates range from 200 to 2,000. The bombers reduced the town to rubble, but a mighty symbol of independence had been born.

The town has been attractively rebuilt, close to its former style. The chimes of a church ring softly, and laughing children play in the street. In the midst of this peace, however, you'll suddenly come upon a sign: "Souvenirs . . . Remember."

WHAT TO SEE & DO

The former Basque parliament, the **Casa de Juntas** (or *Juntetxea*), is the principal attraction in the town, containing a historical display of Guernica. It is open daily from 10am to 2pm and 4 to 7pm in summer (to 6pm in winter). Admission is free. Outside are the remains of the ancient communal oak tree, symbol of Basque independence; it was not uprooted by Hitler's bombs. From the train station, head up the Calle Urioste.

WHERE TO EAT

RESTAURANTE ZALDUA, Sabino Arana, 10. Tel. 687-08-71.
  Cuisine: BASQUE. **Reservations:** Required on weekends in summer.
$ **Prices:** Appetizers 800–1,200 ptas. ($7.50–$11.30); main dishes 1,500–1,800 ptas. ($14.10–$16.90); fixed-priced menu 1,900 ptas. ($17.85). AE, DC, MC, V.
  Open: Lunch daily 1:30–3:30pm; dinner daily 9–11pm. **Closed:** mid-Dec to Jan 31.
Most of the specialties served here come from the blazing grill, whose turning spits are visible from the dining room. A wide array of seafood and fish is also available, some dishes baked to a flaky goodness in a layer of rock salt. The restaurant lies outside the center of town on the road to Bermeo.

FAISÁN DE ORO, Adolfo Urioste, 4. Tel. 685-10-01.
  Cuisine: BASQUE/INTERNATIONAL. **Reservations:** Required.
$ **Prices:** Appetizers 1,200–1,500 ptas. ($11.30–$14.10); main dishes 1,600–2,200 ptas. ($15.05–$20.70); fixed-priced menu 1,900 ptas. ($17.85). AE, DC, MC, V.
  Open: Lunch Thurs–Tues 1–3:30pm; dinner Thurs–Mon 8:30–11pm.
In this congenial sun-filled dining room, located near the church in the town center, such dishes as steamed fish, asparagus in an orange-cream sauce, and entrecôte with béarnaise sauce are served. You can also order beef in a Roquefort sauce and vegetable flan. The namesake pheasant (*faisán*) is also offered in hunting season.

---

7. BILBAO

246 miles N of Madrid, 62 miles W of San Sebastián

GETTING THERE By Plane Sandira Airport (tel. 453-13-50) lies 5 miles (8km) north of the city, near the town of Erandio. From the airport into town take red bus no. 23. Flights arrive from Madrid, Barcelona, Vigo, London, Las Palmas, and Tenerife. Iberia's main booking office in Bilbao is at Ercilla, 20 (tel. 424-43-00). British Airways has a booking office in the center at Gran Vía, 38 (tel. 416-78-66).

By Ferry Ferryboats leave for the Canary Islands from Compañia Transmediterránea, Buenos Aires Bajo, 2 (tel. 442-18-50).

By Train The RENFE station, Estación de Abando (tel. 423-86-36), is on the Hurtado de Amézaga, just off the Plaza de España. From here, you can catch trains to most parts of Iberia. From this station, 3 trains a day run to and from Madrid (9 hours), and 2 trains per day to and from Barcelona (11 hours). Five trains a day arrive from San Sebastián (3 hours), but leave from another station: Estación de Atxuri (tel. 433-00-88).

By Bus PESA, Urazurrutia, 7 (tel. 416-46-10), operates 4 buses per day to San Sebastián (1¼ hours). If you want to take an excursion to Guernica, you can take a Vascongadas bus, leaving from Plaza Encarnación, 7 (tel. 433-12-79). Ten buses a day make the 45-minute run. You can also visit the Basque coast from Bilbao on a

Vascongadas bus from Plaza Encarnación, 7, and going to Lekeitio (a good center for exploring the coast). Six buses a day make the run to Lekeitio (1½ hours).

By Car   Bilbao lies beside the A-8, linking the cities of Spain's northern Atlantic seacoast to the western edge of France. It is connected by superhighway to both Barcelona and Madrid.

ESSENTIALS   The area code for Bilbao is 94. The Tourist Information Office is at Alameda Mazzarredo, s/n (tel. 94/423-64-30), near the corner of the Calle Ercilla, off the Gran Vía, 2 blocks from the Plaza de España and the RENFE station. The Post Office is at Alameda de Urquijo, 15. The post building with telephone booths is nearby at Buenos Aires, 10.

Bilbao is often described as an "ugly, gray, decaying, smokestack city," and so it is—in part. But it has a number of interesting secrets to reveal, as well as a good-quality cuisine, and it is a rail hub and a center for exploring some of the best attractions in the Basque country if you're dependent on public transport. Most of its own attractions can be viewed in a day.

It is Spain's sixth-largest city, its biggest port (with hundreds of skycranes), the industrial hub of the north, and the political capital of the Basques. Shipping, shipbuilding, and steelmaking have made it prosperous. Many bankers and industrialists live here. Its commercial heart contains skyscrapers and hums with activity. Among cities of the Basque region, it has the highest population (around 450,000); the metropolitan area, including the suburbs and many surrounding towns, takes in one million inhabitants.

Bilbao has a wide-open feeling, extending more than 5 miles across the valley of the Nervión River, one of Spain's most polluted waterways. Many buildings wear a layer of grime. Some visitors compare Bilbao to England—not the England of hills and vales, but rather the sooty postindustrial sprawl of an English port town. (Because of the interconnected interests of coal and iron, in fact, there has always been English commerce here, and even English schools and pubs.) Surrounding the city's central core are slums and heavily polluting factories. There's a feeling of decay here, not to mention political unrest from the Basque separatist movement. These factors, plus the frequent rainfall, do not place Bilbao on the major touristic maps of Europe, or even of Spain.

The city was established by a charter dated June 15, 1300, which converted it from a village (*pueblo*), ruled by local feudal duke Don Diego López de Haro, into a city. Aided by water power and the transportation potential of the Nervión River, it grew and grew, most of its fame and glory coming during the industrial expansion of the 19th century. Many grand homes and villas for industrialists were constructed at that time. (Its wealthiest suburb is Neguri.) The most famous son of Bilbao was Miguel de Unamuno, the writer and educator, more closely associated with Salamanca.

The hardworking Basques of Bilbao, who have a rough-and-ready, no-nonsense approach to life, like to have a good time. **Festivals** often fill the calendar, the biggest and most widely publicized being La Semana Grande, dedicated to the Virgin of Begoña and lasting from mid-August until early September. During this time, the Nervión River is the site of many flotillas and regattas. July 25 brings the festival of Bilbao's patron saint, Santiago (St. James), whereas July 31 is the holiday devoted to the region's patron saint, St. Ignatius.

CITY LAYOUT

The River Nervión meanders through Bilbao, whose historic core was built inside one of its loops, with water protecting it on three sides. Most of the important shops, banks, and tourist facilities lie within a short walk of the **Gran Vía,** running east–west through the heart of town. The old quarter lies east of the modern commercial center, across the river. It and the shop-flanked Gran Vía on the western edge form an east–west axis upon which are located most of the major attractions.

WHAT TO SEE & DO

MUSEO DE BELLAS ARTES, Parque de Doña Casilda de Iturriza, s/n. Tel. 441-95-36.

This is considered one of Spain's most important art museums, containing both medieval and modern works of art, including paintings by Velázquez, Goya, Zurburán, and El Greco. Among the works of non-Spanish artists is *The Money Changers* by the Flemish painter Quentin Metsys. In its modern wing, the museum contains works by Gauguin, Picasso, Léger, Sorolla, and American Mary Cassatt. The gallery is particularly strong in 19th- and 20th-century Basque artists, the foremost of which is the modern sculptor Chillida, who created a massive piece entitled *Monument to Iron.* If you tire of looking at the art, you can walk in the English-inspired gardens around the museum.

Admission: Free.

Open: Tues–Sat 10am–1:30pm and 4:30–7:30pm, Sun 11am–2pm.

EUSKAL ARKEOLOGIA, ETNOGRAFIA ETA KONDAIRI-MUSEOA, Cruz, 4–6. Tel. 415-54-23.

In the center of the old quarter, south of the Calle Esperanza Ascao, this museum—devoted to Basque archeology, ethnology, and history—is contained within a centuries-old Jesuit cloister. Some of the exhibits showcase Basque commercial life during the 16th century. You see everything from ship models to shipbuilding tools, along with reconstructions of rooms illustrating political and social life. Basque gravestones are also on view. You'll also see the equipment used to play the popular Basque game of *pelota.*

Admission: Free.

Open: Tues–Sat 10:30am–1:30pm and 4–7pm; Sun 11am–2pm.

CASCO VIEJO (Old Quarter), east side of Nervión River.

Despite Bilbao's establishment around 1300, it is curiously scarce in medieval monuments. It does have this old quarter, however, site of its most charming bars and restaurants. The custom is to go here at night and bar-hop, ordering small cups of beer or wine. A small glass of wine is called a *chiquiteo.*

The old quarter of Bilbao is connected by four bridges to the much larger modern section on the opposite bank. A few paces north of the old quarter's center lie the graceful arches, 64 in all, enclosing the Plaza Nueva, also called the Plaza de los Martires, completed in 1830.

The entire barrio has been declared a national landmark. It originally defined an area around seven streets, but it long ago spilled beyond that limitation. Every Sunday at 8am a flea market is held on the streets of the old quarter. Its most important church is the **Church of St. Nicolás.** Behind this church you'll find an elevator on the Calle Esperanza Ascao, which, if working, carries sightseers to the upper town. You can also climb 64 steps from the Plaza Unamuno. From there it's a short walk to the **Basílica de Begoña,** built largely in the early 1500s. Inside the dimly lit church, there is a brightly illuminated depiction of the Virgin, dressed in long, flowing robes. She is the patroness of the province. Also displayed are some enormous paintings by Lucas Giordano.

While in the old town, you might also visit the **Cathedral of Santiago,** Plaza Santiago, which was originally built in the 14th century, then restored in the 16th century after a fire. The façade was later rebuilt in the 19th century.

To reach the old town on foot, the only way to explore it, take the Puente del Arenal from the Gran Vía, the main street of Bilbao.

WHERE TO STAY

ROQUEFER, Lotería, 2–4, 48005 Bilbao. Tel. 94/415-07-55. 10 rms (none with bath).

$ Rates: 3,000 ptas. ($28.20) double. Breakfast 225 ptas. ($2.10) extra. No credit cards.

Ⓢ If you'd like to live in the old quarter and avoid the high prices of the businesspeople's hotels, this is a winning candidate. Rooms, doubles only, are simple and furnished in a functional style, but they are clean and inviting. The hospitable family who runs the place extends a nice welcome. You're in the center of the tasca and restaurant district for nighttime prowls. To reach the hotel, take the bridge, the Puente del Arenal, across the river to the old town.

AVENIDA, Avenida Zumalacárregui, 40, 48007 Bilbao. Tel. 94/412-43-00. 116 rms (all with bath). TV TEL

$ Rates: 6,500 ptas. ($61.10) single; 8,500 ptas. ($79.90) double. Breakfast 660 ptas. ($6.20) extra. AE, MC, V.

For those who want to be away from the center and don't mind a taxi ride or two, this is a welcoming choice set near one of the major religious monuments of Bilbao, the Basílica de Begoña. Rooms, furnished in a sober, functional modern style, are well kept and maintained. The hotel has a garden and a helpful staff. During special fairs in Bilbao, rates are increased by at least 10%.

HOTEL NERVIÓN, Paseo del Campo de Volantín, 11, 48007 Bilbao. Tel. 94/445-47-00. 351 rms (all with bath). A/C MINIBAR TEL

$ Rates: 6,500 ptas. ($61.10) single; 9,000 ptas. ($84.60) double. Breakfast 650 ptas. ($6.10) extra. No credit cards.

This is a functional modern hotel, its bedrooms opening onto views of the river. Close to the Town Hall, it attracts many tour groups and conventions, but also caters to individual clients. Rooms are clean and satisfactory. From here, you can head south along the Calle Esperanza Ascao to reach the bars and restaurants of the old quarter.

WHERE TO EAT

MEALS FOR LESS THAN 2,500 PTAS. [$23.50]

RESTAURANT BEGOÑA, Virgen de Begoña, s/n. Tel. 412-72-57.
   Cuisine: BASQUE. **Reservations:** Recommended.
$ Prices: Appetizers 450–950 ptas. ($4.25–$8.95); main dishes 1,600–2,500 ptas. ($15.05–$23.50). AE, MC, V.
   Open: Lunch Mon–Sat 1:30–3:30pm; dinner Mon–Sat 9–11pm. **Closed:** Aug.
At this tranquil choice–near the famous Basílica de Begoña, lying on the eastern bank of the river, the chef combines classic dishes with those of the modern repertoire, and does so in imaginative ways. Specialties include stuffed onions, loin of pork, and sea bass with *fines herbes*. The relation of food quality to price is correct, and the wine cellar offers prestigious vintages at competitive rates. Service is attentive.

GREDOS, Alameda de Urquijo, 50. Tel. 443-50-01.
   Cuisine: BASQUE. **Reservations:** Recommended.
$ Prices: Appetizers 450–750 ptas. ($4.25–$7.05); main dishes 1,700–2,300 ptas. ($16–$21.60); fixed-priced menu 925 ptas. ($8.70). AE, MC, V.
   Open: Lunch daily 1–4pm; dinner daily 8:30pm–midnight. **Closed:** Sept 15 to Oct 15.

Ⓢ This restaurant, located about 3 blocks south of the Gran Vía, has an agreeable ambience, with excellent service and a menu dependent on the seasons and the availability of good, fresh ingredients. The interior was recently restored, and guests today dine in air-conditioned comfort. Specialties include a savory sauté of fresh vegetables, roast goat, and hake stuffed with spider crab. The set menu is one of the dining bargains of Bilbao.

WORTH THE EXTRA BUCKS

MACHIMBENTA, Ledesma, 26. Tel. 424-84-85.
   Cuisine: BASQUE. Reservations: Required.
$ Prices: Appetizers 750–1,500 ptas. ($7.05–$14.10); main dishes 1,900–2,700 ptas. ($17.85–$25.40). AE, DC, MC, V.
   Open: Lunch Mon–Sat 1–3:30pm; dinner Mon–Sat 8–11:30pm.

Serving some of the finest Basque food in the city, Machimbenta, 1 block north of the Gran Vía, is popular for business luncheons or dinners. Specialties include fresh tuna in a piquant tomato sauce and a local version of French ratatouille known as *piperada*. You can also order veal cutlets cooked in port wine, finishing with a mint-flavored fresh-fruit cocktail. Service is excellent.

GURIA, Gran Vía de López de Haro, 66. Tel. 441-05-43.
   Cuisine: BASQUE. **Reservations:** Required.
$ **Prices:** Appetizers 950–1,500 ptas. ($8.95–$14.10); main dishes 2,200–3,200 ptas. ($20.70–$30.10). AE, DC, MC, V.
   Open: Lunch Mon–Sat 1:30–4pm; dinner Mon–Sat 8:30pm–midnight. **Closed:** Last week of July, first week of Aug.

One of the most venerated restaurants of Bilbao, the air-conditioned Guria is expensive—and worth it, say its devotees. The skilled chef, Génaro Pildain, shows care and concern for his guests, serving only market-fresh ingredients. He is celebrated for his bacalao (codfish), which he prepares in many different ways. Try his sea bass with saffron as an alternative, or perhaps loin of beef cooked in sherry. A slightly caloric but divine dessert is *espuma de chocolat*.

---

8. VITORIA (GASTEIZ)

41 miles S of Bilbao, 71 miles SW of San Sebastián, 218 miles N of Madrid

GETTING THERE   By Plane   Forondona Airport (tel. 27-33-00), 5 miles (8km) northwest of the center of town, has domestic air links from Madrid. The sales office for Iberia Airlines is at Avenida Gasteiz, 50biz (tel. 22-82-50).

By Train   From San Sebastián, 11 trains run daily (2 hours).

By Bus   From San Sebastián, 5 buses leave daily (2½ hours). Bus connections are also possible through Bilbao (8 per day; 1½ hours).

By Car   Take the N-1 north from Madrid to Burgos, cutting northwest until you see the turnoff for Vitoria.

ESSENTIALS   The area code for Vitoria is 945. The Tourist Information Office is at Parque de la Florida (tel. 945/13-13-21).

Quiet and sleepy until the early 1980s, Vitoria was chosen as headquarters of the Basque region's autonomous government. In honor of that occasion, it revived the name Gasteiz, by which it was known when founded in 1181 by King Sancho of Navarre. Far more enduring, however, has been the name Vitoria, a battle site revered by the English. On June 21, 1813, Wellington won here against the occupying forces of Napoleon. A statue dedicated to the Iron Duke stands today on the neoclassical Plaza de la Virgen Blanca.

Shortly after its founding, the city became a rich center for the wool and iron trades, and this wealth paid for the fine churches and palaces in the medieval quarter. The citys buildings are all made of gray-gold stone. There is a university here, whose students keep the taverns rowdy until the wee hours.

WHAT TO SEE & DO

The most important sight in Vitoria is the **medieval district,** whose Gothic buildings were built on a series of steps and terraces. Most of the streets are arranged in concentric ovals, and are named after medieval artisan guilds. The northern end is marked by the Cathedral of Santa María, its southern flank by the Church of San Miguel.

One of the barrio's most interesting streets is the **Calle Cuchillería,** which contains many medieval buildings. You can enter the courtyard at no. 24, the Casa del

Cordón, which was constructed in different stages from the 13th to the 16th century. Number 58, the Bendana Palace, built in the 15th century, has a fine ornate staircase set into its courtyard.

The **Cathedral of Santa María** (the "old" cathedral), Calle Fray Zacaras, was built in the 14th century in the Gothic style. It contains a good art collection, with paintings that imitate various schools, including those of van Dyck, Caravaggio, and Rubens, as well as several tombs carved in a highly decorated Plateresque style. Santa María lies at the northern edge of the old town.

This cathedral is not to be confused with the town's enormous "new" cathedral on the Avenida Magdalena, lying just north of the Jardines la Florida, and built in a Neo-Gothic style.

The major historic square is the **Plaza de la Virgen Blanca,** a short walk south of the Gothic quarter. Its neoclassical balconies overlook the statue of Wellington. The square is named after the late-Gothic polychrome statue of the Virgen Blanca (the town's patron) that adorns the portico of the 13th-century **Church of San Miguel,** which stands on the square's upper edge. The 17th-century altarpiece inside was carved by Gregoria Hernández.

At the **Plaza de España** (also known as the Plaza Nueva), a satellite square a short walk away, the student population of Vitoria congregates to drink.

Vitoria has some minor museums, which are free. The **Museo de Arqueología,** Correría, 116, behind a charming half-timbered façade, exhibits artifacts such as pottery shards and statues, unearthed from digs in the area. Some of these are from Celto-Iberian days as well as from the Roman era. The museum is open Tuesday through Friday from 10am to 2pm and 5 to 7pm, on Saturday from 11am to 2pm.

The **Museo de Bellas Artes,** Palacio de Agustín, Plaza Fray Francisco, 8, has a collection of several unusual weapons, a *Crucifixion* by Ribera, as well as his portraits of SS. Peter and Paul, and a triptych by the Master of Ávila. Open Tuesday through Friday from 11am to 2pm and 5 to 7pm, on Saturday from 11am to 2pm.

For a week in early August, usually beginning on the 4th, the Festival of the Virgen Blanca is presented. Tradition dictates that every resident of town light a cigar the moment the chimes of the Church of San Miguel signal the beginning of the festival. Bullfights, street dances, and gaiety are the order of the day.

WHERE TO STAY

HOTEL DATO, Eduardo Dato, 28, 01005 Vitoria. Tel. 945/23-23-20. 14 rms (all with bath). TEL

$ Rates: 3,500 ptas. ($32.90) single; 4,500 ptas. ($42.30) double. Breakfast 500 ptas. ($4.70) extra. AE, DC, MC, V.

Ⓢ Lying 3 blocks south of the southern extremity of the old town in the pedestrian zone, this hotel has firmly established itself as the best budget establishment in town. It has modern decor and amenities, but only a few bedrooms—so reservations are wise.

ACHURI, Rioja, 11, 01005 Vitoria. Tel. 945/25-58-00. 40 rms (all with bath). TEL

$ Rates: 3,300 ptas. ($31) single; 5,000 ptas. ($47) double. Breakfast 325 ptas. ($3.05) extra. DC, V.

Ⓢ This is an attractively priced modern hotel without any particular style. A short walk from the train station, it offers tidy and comfortably furnished bedrooms. Breakfast is the only meal available, but you'll find several places serving food in the vicinity.

HOTEL GENERAL ALAVA, Avenida de Gasteiz, 79, 01009 Vitoria. Tel. 945/22-22-00. Fax 945/24-83-95. 40 rms (all with bath). TV TEL

$ Rates: 5,400 ptas. ($50.75) single; 8,500 ptas. ($79.90) double. Breakfast 550 ptas. ($5.15) extra. AE, DC, MC, V.

Considered one of the best and most classic hotels in town, the General Alava attracts many businesspeople. Its rooms are well furnished and maintained. The hotel doesn't have a restaurant, but there is a cafeteria on the premises—a 10-minute walk west of the center of town, near the junction of the Calle Chile.

WHERE TO EAT

As in Bilbao, tasca-hopping before dinner, with the consumption of many small glasses (chiquiteos) of beer or wine at many different bars and taverns, is popular and fun. There are a number of places on the Avenida de Gasteiz.

OLEAGA, Adrinao VII, 16. Tel. 24-54-05.

Cuisine: BASQUE. **Reservations:** Recommended.

$ Rates: Appetizers 450–950 ptas. ($4.25–$8.95); main dishes 1,100–2,000 ptas. ($10.35–$18.80); fixed-priced menu 750 ptas. ($7.05) (bar only). AE, V.

Open: Lunch Tues–Sun 1–3:30pm; dinner Tues–Sat 9–11:30pm. **Closed:** Aug.

Oleaga's owner, Jesus Oleaga, is a professional restaurateur who pays particular attention to the wines served within his bodega. Many guests come in only for drinks at the stand-up bar. The tapas, called *pinchos* here, make a tasty prelude to a dinner. You can also order one of the most reasonably priced fixed-priced menus at this bar. In the restaurant, try stuffed onions filled with minced pork and covered with a green sauce or else foie gras of duckling with grapes and an onion sauce.

MESA, Chile, 1. Tel. 22-84-94.

Cuisine: BASQUE. **Reservations:** Recommended.

$ Prices: Appetizers 450–750 ptas. ($4.25–$7.05); main dishes 1,400–1,700 ptas. ($13.15–$16); fixed-priced menu 1,400 ptas. ($13.15). AE, MC, V.

Open: Lunch Thurs–Tues 1–3:30pm; dinner Thurs–Tues 9–11:30pm. **Closed:** Aug 10 to Sept 9.

For price and value, this ranks as one of the most competitive and worthwhile restaurants in town. In air-conditioned comfort you can partake of a number of Basque specialties, none better than the notable merluza (hake), the fish so beloved by Basque chefs. Fresh fish and a well-chosen selection of meats are presented nightly, and the service is attentive.

EL PORTALÓN, Correría, 151. Tel. 14-27-55.

Cuisine: BASQUE. **Reservations:** Recommended.

$ Prices: Appetizers 650–1,500 ptas. ($6.10–$14.10); main dishes 1,700–2,200 ptas. ($16–$20.70); fixed-priced menu 2,000 ptas. ($18.80). AE, MC, V.

Open: Lunch Mon–Sat 1–3:30pm; dinner Mon–Sat 9–11pm. **Closed:** Aug.

The premier dining choice in town, and worthy of a splurge, this antique inn was originally built for the many merchants who sold their wares here in the 15th century. Today the Basque owners present traditional and regional dishes of fine quality, served with style. Try a salad of endive with shellfish and seasonal vegetables, the vegetarian crepes, or one of many different fish and shellfish dishes. The interior is air-conditioned.

CHAPTER 21

CANTABRIA & ASTURIAS

Part of "Green Spain," the provinces of Cantabria and Asturias remain relatively undiscovered by many foreign tourists, lured by the charms of the south. But these historic old lands are filled with attractions, ranging from the fishing villages of the Cantabrian and Asturian coastlines to the Picos de Europa, a magnificent stretch of snow-capped mountains.

Cantabria, an ancient land settled in prehistoric times, was heavily colonized by the Romans. The Muslims were less successful in their invasion. Many Christians, protected by the mountains, found refuge here during the long centuries of Moorish domination. Much religious architecture remains from this period, particularly Romanesque. Cantabria was once part of the Castilla y León district of Spain but is now an autonomous region with its own government.

Most of the tourism is confined to the northern coastal strip, whereas much of the mountainous area inland is poor and depopulated. If you venture away from the coast, which is serviced by buses, you'll usually need a rented car, as public transport is inadequate at best. Santander, a rail terminus, makes the best center for touring the province; it also has the most tourist facilities. From Santander, you can reach virtually anywhere in the province in a 3-hour drive.

The ancient principality of Asturias lies between Cantabria in the east and Galicia in the west. It reaches its scenic peak in the Picos de Europa, where the first Spanish national park was inaugurated. Asturias is a land for all seasons, with green valleys, fishing villages, and forests.

The coastline of Asturias constitutes one of the major sightseeing attractions of northern Spain. Once called the Costa Verde, it begins in the east at San Vicente de la Barquera and stretches about 88 miles (142km) to Gijón. Allow about 6 hours to drive it without stopovers. The western coast, beginning at Gijón, goes all the way to Ribadeo, a border town with Galicia—a distance of 112 miles (180km). This rocky coastline studded with fishing villages, and containing narrow estuaries and small beaches, is one of the most spectacular stretches of scenery in Spain. It takes all day to explore.

Asturias is an ancient land, as prehistoric cave paintings in the area demonstrate. Iron Age Celtic tribes resisted the Romans, as Asturians proudly point out even to this day. They also resisted the Moors, who subjugated the rest of Spain. The Battle of Covadonga in 722 represented the Moors' first major setback after their arrival in Iberia some 11 years previously.

The Asturians are still staunchly independent. In 1934 Francisco Franco, seen as a promising young general, arrived with his Moroccan troops to suppress an uprising by miners who had declared an independent Socialist Republic. His Nationalist forces returned again and again to destroy Asturian cities such as Gijón for their fierce resistance during the Spanish Civil War.

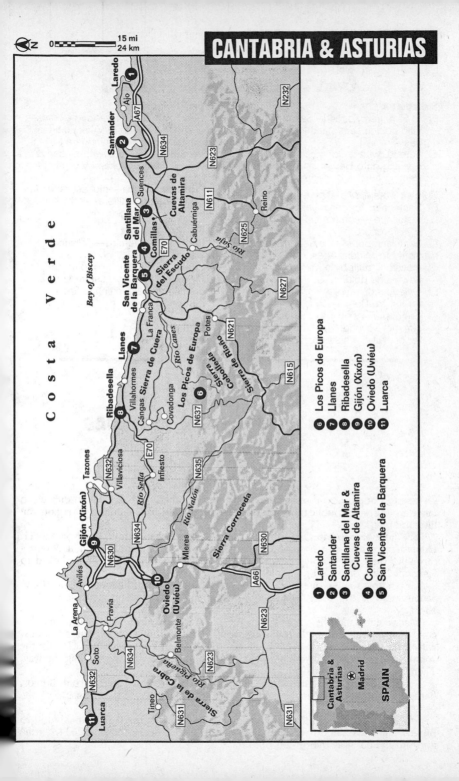

CANTABRIA & ASTURIAS

15 mi
24 km

N

Bay of Biscay

C o s t a   V e r d e

Laredo ❶
Ajo
Santander ❷
Suences
Santillana del Mar ❸
Cuevas de Altamira
Comillas ❹
Cabuérniga
San Vicente de la Barquera ❺
Sierra del Escudo
La Franca
Llanes ❼
Sierra de Cuera
Río Cares
Ribadesella ❽
Villahormes
Cángas
Covadonga
Los Picos de Europa
Sierra de Cabra?
Sierra de Riaño
Potes
❻
Reino
Tazones
Gijón (Xixón)
Villaviciosa
Río Sella
Infiesto
Gijón (Xixón) ❾
Avilés
Mieres
Río Nalón
Sierra Corroceda
Oviedo (Uviéu) ❿
Belmonte
Pravia
Soto
La Arena
Tineo
Río Piguena
Sierra de la Cabra
Luarca ⓫

Reino
Río Saja

N232
N67
N634
N623
N611
N625
E70
N627
N621
N615
N632
E70
N635
N637
N634
N630
N634
N632
N631
N631
N630
A66
N623

❶ Laredo
❷ Santander
❸ Santillana del Mar & Cuevas de Altamira
❹ Comillas
❺ San Vicente de la Barquera
❻ Los Picos de Europa
❼ Llanes
❽ Ribadesella
❾ Gijón (Xixón)
❿ Oviedo (Uviéu)
⓫ Luarca

Cantabria & Asturias
Madrid
SPAIN

WHAT'S SPECIAL ABOUT CANTABRIA & ASTURIAS

Beaches

☐ El Sardinero, outside Santander, with golden sands and lots of facilities.

☐ Laredo, with its long sandy beach opening onto Bay of Santoña, attracting hordes of people in summer.

Great Towns/Villages

☐ Santander, former royal summer residence—commercial city and stylish resort.

☐ Santillana del Mar, a gem preserved from the Middle Ages, with mansions built by adventurers using new-world gold.

☐ Oviedo, capital of Asturias, unique for its Pre-Romanesque architecture.

☐ Gijón, major port of Asturias and a summer vacation spot; its old quarter declared a historic zone.

Scenic Routes

☐ Coast of Cantabria—long expanses of sands cleaned by Atlantic tides.

☐ Costa Verde, from Unquera to Vegadeo—studded with estuaries and low cliffs, broken by sandy islets.

☐ Picos de Europa—highest range in Cantabrian Cordillera—snowcapped and split by gorges.

Cave Paintings

☐ Cuevas de Altamira—"Sistine Chapel of prehistoric art."

☐ Cueva de Tito Bustillo, outside Ribadesella, third-most important prehistoric cave-painting find in Europe.

SEEING CANTABRIA & ASTURIAS

GETTING THERE

Cantabria

Getting to Cantabria without a car is easy, but once there, you may find it difficult to move around, since public transportation is very poor. In this mountainous region, rail lines are few.

The only **airport** in Cantabria is at Parayas, 4 miles (6.5km) outside Santander. Domestic service from Madrid consists of a morning and evening flight Monday through Friday, with only one per day on weekends. Barcelona is also linked to Santander by a daily flight.

It's possible to take one of the twice-weekly **ferries** from Plymouth, England, to Santander. The trip takes 24 hours. For information in Plymouth, phone 752/22-13-21.

Madrid and Santander are linked by RENFE, with 5 **trains** a day. Daily trains also come in from Valladolid. Narrow-gauge FEVE trains link Bilbao and Santander daily, with continuing service to El Ferrol, north of La Coruña in Galicia. You can take the complete journey all the way in about 13 hours, or make stopovers along the way. There's an obligatory change of trains at Oviedo.

It's also possible to arrive at Santander by **bus,** with service from Burgos, Barcelona, and Bilbao. Once at Santander, you can take buses to the villages along the coast.

Santander lies about a day's **drive** from Madrid. Take the N-1 from Madrid to Burgos, then the 623 north to Santander. From Bilbao in the east, take the 624, cutting north to the coast at the turnoff onto the 623.

Asturias

Your gateway to Asturias is likely to be Gijón or Oviedo, either of which can be reached by **air** from Madrid on Iberia Airlines. Iberia flies into Ranón Airport, 12 miles (19.5km) from Oviedo and 26 miles (42km) from Gijón. After that, it's a long haul by taxi into either city, or a sometimes seemingly endless wait for a bus.

Therefore, many visitors opt for the **train.** From Madrid's Chamartín Station, two trains a day head for both Gijón and Oviedo. The *talgo* departs in the middle of the afternoon, whereas the Costa Verde sleeper express is an overnight train. Figure on about 8 hours to make either trip.

By **bus,** connections are usually convenient on one of the ALSA buses out of Madrid, about half a dozen daily, leaving early in the morning and late in the evening. You'll be in Oviedo in about 5½ hours on this bus. From Oviedo, ALSA buses also connect with other major towns. For example, you can make day trips to nearly all the recommended coastal towns if you time your schedule properly. From Oviedo, you can also take a bus to the Picos de Europa, although a car would be a lot more convenient.

It's a long **drive** from Madrid to Asturias, a hard day's work. From Cantabria, continue west along the N-634 coastal highway.

A SUGGESTED ROUTE

Cantabria can be part of a car or train ride across the northern rim of Spain. After visiting the Basque country in the east, you can head west to the Cantabrian coastline.

Day 1   Spend the day in Laredo, after a stop for lunch in Castro-Urdiales.

Days 2–3   Spend two nights in Santander. You'll need a day to explore the single most rewarding sightseeing target in the province: the medieval town of Santillana del Mar, with the nearby Cuevas de Altamira.

Day 4   Leave Santander and pay a morning visit to the seaside town of Comillas (to look at the Catalan *modernisme* architecture). Have a seafood lunch farther west at San Vicente de la Barquera, another seaside town. At Unquera, on the border between Cantabria and Asturias, begin a drive into the Picos de Europa. Take the N-621 through magnificent landscapes alongside the Deva River until you reach the town of Potes, 24 miles (39km) inland. Stay overnight in or around Potes.

Day 5   Continue your drive through the Picos de Europa, heading for the western section. Plan to spend the night either in the Picos district at Cangas de Ons or in the nearby coastal town of Ribadesella, which has more tourist facilities.

Day 6   Explore Ribadesella in the morning and visit the prehistoric cave paintings in its environs. Then take the N-632, a winding but scenic coastal road west to Gijón for another overnight stopover.

Day 7   Drive to Oviedo and spend the day exploring the capital of Asturias. Spend the night there.

Day 8   Head west from Oviedo along the N-634 to reach the old port city of Luarca. Have lunch there and, if time is up, conclude your tour and return to Oviedo, where rail and train connections can be made to Madrid. If time permits, continue west along the N-634 coastal road to Ribadeo, a border town between Galicia and Asturias, and a possible gateway to the province of Galicia.

---

1. LAREDO

37 miles W of Bilbao, 30 miles E of Santander, 265 miles N of Madrid

GETTING THERE   By Bus   Service is available from both Bilbao and Santander (1 hour).

By Car   From Castro-Urdiales, take the coastal route, the N-634, west to Laredo, 16 miles (26km).

ESSENTIALS The area code for Laredo is 942. The Tourist Information Office is at Alameda de Miramar, s/n (tel. 942/60-54-92).

To an American "the streets of Laredo" means the gun-slinging Old West. To a Spaniard it means an ancient maritime town on the eastern Cantabrian coast that has been turned into a major summer resort, with hundreds of apartments and villas along its 3 miles of beach. The Playa de la Salvé lies to the west and the Playa de Oriñón to the east.

On the last Friday of August, the annual **Battle of Flowers** draws thousands of visitors to watch bloom-adorned floats parade through the old town.

The medieval quarter, the **Puebla Vieja,** retains the traditional atmosphere of Laredo. It was walled on orders of Alfonso VIII of Castile, who wanted to protect the town from private raids along the coast. The hillside **Church of La Asunción,** dating from the 13th century, overlooks the harbor. It has five naves and rather bizarre capitals.

If you're driving west to Santoña, note the big monument honoring native son Juan de la Cosa, the cartographer who sailed with Columbus on his first voyage to America.

WHERE TO STAY

RISCO, La Arenosa, 2, 39770 Laredo. Tel. 942/60-50-30. 25 rms (all with bath). TEL
$ **Rates:** 5,400 ptas. ($50.75) single; 8,400 ptas. ($78.95) double. Breakfast 550 ptas. ($5.15) extra. AE, DC, MC, V.

On a hillside overlooking Laredo, a half mile southeast of the center of town, this hotel opens onto impressive views of the old town and also of one of the nearby beaches. It offers simple bedrooms, each clean and comfortable, as well as a garden in which scattered tables are placed for food service (see restaurant recommendation below). Ample parking is provided.

WHERE TO EAT

CAMAROTE, Avenida de la Vitoria, s/n. Tel. 60-67-07.
Cuisine: SEAFOOD. **Reservations:** Recommended.
$ **Prices:** Appetizers 450–950 ptas. ($4.25–$8.95); main dishes 1,200–1,800 ptas. ($11.30–$16.90); fixed-priced menu 2,000 ptas. ($18.80). AE, DC, MC, V.
Open: Lunch daily 1:30–4pm; dinner daily 8:30pm–midnight. **Closed:** Sun dinner in winter.

The owner of Camarote (in the center of town) is Felipe Manjarrés, his chef de cuisine is Ignacio Llorente, and their specialty is seafood, especially fish as opposed to shellfish. The decor is tasteful and attractive, and an outdoor terrace makes a pleasant alternative to an indoor dining room. Truly excellent are the spinach with crayfish and the cheese tarts. "Original recipes" are used for salads with ham and shrimp as well as for those with tuna and fresh fruit. Try the grilled sea bream or a filet steak Rossini.

RISCO, La Arenosa, 2. Tel. 60-50-19.
Cuisine: SEAFOOD. **Reservations:** Recommended.
$ **Prices:** Appetizers 650–950 ptas. ($6.10–$8.95); main dishes 1,400–2,200 ptas. ($13.15–$20.70); fixed-priced menu 1,600 ptas. ($15.05). AE, DC, MC, V.
Open: Lunch daily 1–4pm; dinner daily 8:30–11:30pm.

This is Laredo's most appealing restaurant, known for its innovative seafood dishes. Chef de cuisine Inés Merecen, assisted by a battery of helpers, prepares such items as *en panaché,* marinated salmon with pink peppercorns, scrambled eggs with lobster, and codfish "prepared in the style of the mountains." One of the more unusual dishes: peppers stuffed with minced pig's trotters or crabmeat. For dessert, try a fresh-fruit sorbet. Some tables are set up in the garden, or else you can dine in a traditional dining room with views of the sea. The restaurant is on the ground floor of the Risco hotel (see above).

2. SANTANDER

244 miles N of Madrid, 72 miles NW of Bilbao

GETTING THERE   By Air   Daily flights from Madrid and Barcelona land at Parayas Airport (tel. 25-10-07), a little more than 4 miles (6.5km) from the center, accessible by taxi only.

By Train   There are 5 trains daily from Madrid (6 to 7½ hours). Four trains a day arrive from Bilbao (3 hours).

By Bus   About 7 buses daily run from San Sebastián; from Madrid, 4 buses daily.

By Car   The N-634 continues west to Santander, with an N-635 turnoff to reach the resort.

ESSENTIALS: The area code for Santander is 942. The Tourist Information Office is at Plaza Porticada (tel. 942/31-07-08).

Santander has always been a rival of San Sebastián in the east, although it has never attained the premier status of that Basque resort. It did, however, become a royal residence from 1913 to 1930, after city officials presented an English-style Magdalena Palace to Alfonso XIII and his queen, Victoria Eugenia.

Franco has been "dethroned" in many parts of Spain, as streets and plazas once named after him have reverted to their older names. In contrast, in Santander a bronze statue of the dictator on horseback stands in the Plaza del Generalísimo, across from the Town Hall.

An ancient city, Santander was damaged by a 1941 fire that destroyed the old quarter and most of its dwellings. It was rebuilt along original lines, with wide boulevards, a waterfront promenade, sidewalk cafés, shops, restaurants, and hotels.

The **Music and Dance Festival** in August is considered one of the most important artistic events in Spain (accommodations are very hard to find then). At times, this festival coincides with religious celebrations honoring Santiago, the patron saint of Spain.

Santander is an education center in summer as well. Courses are offered at the once-royal palace, now the Menéndez Pelayo International University. Students and teachers from all over North America and Europe come here to study and enjoy the area.

Most visitors to Santander head for **El Sardinero,** a resort less than 1.5 miles (2.4km) from the city. Buses and trolleys make the short run between the city center and El Sardinero both day and night. Besides hotels and restaurants, Santander has three beaches, the **Playa de Castaneda,** the **Playa del Sardinero,** and the **Playa de la Concha,** where people stretch out under candy-striped umbrellas.

If these beaches get too crowded, take a 15-minute boat ride to **El Puntal,** a beautiful beach that is not crowded, even in August.

If you don't like crowds *or* beaches, go up to the lighthouse, a little more than a 1¼ mile from El Sardinero, where the views are spectacular. A restaurant serves both indoor and outdoor snacks. Here you can hike along the green cliffs, or loll in the lush grass.

WHAT TO SEE & DO

CATHEDRAL, Somorrostro, s/n.
Greatly damaged in the 1941 fire, this restored fortresslike 13th-century cathedral holds the tomb of historian/writer Marcelino Menéndez y Pelayo (1856–1912), Santander's most illustrious man of letters. The 12th-century crypt with a trio of low-slung aisles, untouched by fire, can be entered through the south portico. The

Gothic cloister was restored after the fire. Roman ruins were discovered beneath the north aisle in 1983.

Admission: Free.

Open: Daily 9:30am–12:30pm and 5:30–8:30pm.

MUSEO PROVINCIAL DE PREHISTORIA Y ARQUEOLOGÍA, Casimiro Sainz, 4.

This museum has some interesting artifacts discovered in the Cantabrian province—not only Roman but also some unusual prehistoric finds. Since it is unlikely that you'll be allowed to visit the Cuevas de Altimira (see Section 4, below), come here to see objects and photographs from these prehistoric caves with their remarkable paintings. Some of the displays date from 15,000 years ago.

Admission: Free.

Open: Tues–Sun 9am–2pm.

MUSEO MUNICIPAL DE BELLAS ARTES, Rubío, s/n. Tel. 23-94-87.

Located near the Ayuntamiento (Town Hall), the Municipal Museum of Fine Arts has some interesting Goyas, notably his portrait of Ferdinand VII, commissioned by the city, and his series of etchings called *Disasters of War*. You can also see some of his continuing series of *caprichos* (whims). See also Zurbarán's *Mystic Scene* and an array of works by Flemish, Spanish, and Italian artists, many of them contemporary.

Admission: Free.

Open: Mon–Sat 11am–1pm and 5–9pm.

BIBLIOTECA MENÉNDEZ Y PELAYO, Rubío, 4.

Located in the same building as the municipal museum is this 45,000-volume library amassed by Menéndez y Pelayo and left to Santander upon his death in 1912. Guided tours are available. Opposite the building is the Casa Museo, which displays this great man's study and shows how modestly he lived.

Admission: Free.

Open: Mon–Sat 9am–1:30pm.

WHERE TO STAY

Santander is loaded with bargains, from its year-round city hotels to its summer villas at El Sardinero. It gets crowded, so try to reserve in advance.

IN TOWN

HOTEL REX, Avenida de Calvo Sotelo, 9, 39002 Santander. Tel. 942/21-02-00. Fax 942/21-02-00. 56 rms (all with bath). TV TEL

$ Rates: 6,500 ptas. ($61.10) single; 9,500 ptas. ($89.30) double. Breakfast 450 ptas. ($4.25) extra. AE, DC, MC, V.

This seven-story establishment near the Town Hall was built at the turn of the century, when hotels were known for their comfort. The large doubles have recently been modernized. The oak-paneled lounge has comfortable groups of armchairs and couches.

AT EL SARDINERO

HOTEL RHIN, Avenida Reina Victoria, 156, 39005 Santander. Tel. 942/27-43-00. Fax 942/27-86-53. 95 rms (all with bath). A/C TV TEL **Bus:** 1, 2, 5, or 7.

$ Rates: 6,000 ptas. ($56.40) single; 9,000 ptas. ($84.60) double. Breakfast 450 ptas. ($4.25) extra. AE, DC, MC, V.

Built in the early 1970s, this hotel has panoramic views of the city's beaches. The rooms are comfortable and clean, and cheaper than many of the nearby accommodations. There are a cafeteria and a restaurant on the premises.

HOTEL ROMA, Avenida de los Hoteles, 5, 39005 Santander. Tel. 942/ 27-27-00. Fax 942/27-27-51. 47 rms (all with bath). TV TEL **Bus:** 1, 2, 5, or 7.
$ Rates: 5,500 ptas. ($51.70) single; 9,300 ptas. ($87.40) double. Breakfast 425 ptas. ($4) extra. DC, MC, V. **Closed:** Oct to May.
This turn-of-the-century hotel in the heart of El Sardinero, in the shadow of the once-grand casino, was built when life at Santander was lived on a much grander scale. Many of the original features remain—the crystal chandeliers, the great central staircase. Meals are served daily in the hotel's restaurant, and 24-hour room service is available. Guests can play tennis and enjoy the garden.

HOTEL MARÍA ISABEL, Avenida de García Lago, s/n, 39005 Santander. Tel. 942/27-18-50. 60 rms (all with bath). TEL **Bus:** 1, 2, 5, or 7.
$ Rates: 6,300 ptas. ($59.20) single; 10,000 ptas. ($94) double. Breakfast 450 ptas. ($4.25) extra. MC, V.
This renovated hotel on one of the beaches of El Sardinero offers expansive views of the ocean from most of its comfortably furnished rooms. Also available to guests are a swimming pool, and garden, late-night disco, parking lot, and several convention rooms.

HOTEL SARDINERO, Plaza de Italia 1, 39005 Santander. Tel. 942/27-11-00. Fax 942/27-89-43. 112 rms (all with bath). A/C TV TEL **Bus:** 1, 2, 5, or 7.
$ Rates: 9,000 ptas. ($84.60) single; 11,500 ptas. ($108.10) double. Breakfast 425 ptas. ($4) extra. AE, DC, MC, V.
The façade of this centrally located hotel near the beach and the casino is noteworthy for its architectural beauty. The dining room serves good meals starting at 1,800 pesetas ($16.90). There's also an in-house disco. The bedrooms, among the best at the beach for the price, are well furnished and comfortable.

WHERE TO EAT

Most visitors to Santander eat at their hotels or boarding houses, which offer better value for the money and more efficient service than any of the city's restaurants. For variety, though, here are a few budget suggestions.

MEALS FOR LESS THAN 3,200 PTAS. [$30.10]

BODEGA CIGALEÑA, Daoíz y Velarde, 19. Tel. 21-30-62.
Cuisine: CANTABRIAN. **Reservations:** None.
$ Prices: Appetizers 500–1,700 ptas. ($4.70–$16); main dishes 900–3,200 ptas. ($8.45–$30.10); fixed-priced menu 2,500 ptas. ($23.50). AE, DC, MC, V.
Open: Lunch Mon–Sat noon–4pm; dinner Mon–Sat 7:30pm–midnight. **Closed:** June 20 to 30; Oct 20 to Nov 20.
Popular with the young set of Santander, this Castilian bodega in the city center serves typical regional cuisine in a rustic decor—hanging hams, large wine kegs, provincial tables. The set menu changes every day. A sample meal might be *sopa de pescado* (fish soup), shellfish paella, the fruit of the season, bread, and wine. The Cigaleña offers a good choice of wines from an old Castilian town near Valladolid. Ask to see its Museo del Vino.

LA SARDINA, Doctor Fleming, 3. Tel. 27-10-35.
Cuisine: SEAFOOD. **Reservations:** Required. **Bus:** 1, 2, 5, or 7.
$ Prices: Appetizers 1,000–1,500 ptas. ($9.40–$14.10); main dishes 1,200–1,900 ptas. ($11.30–$17.85).
Open: Lunch Mon–Sun 1:30–4pm; dinner Mon–Sat 8:30pm–midnight.
In a warren of small streets in the center of the old city, this nautically designed restaurant serves an imaginative cuisine highlighted by several delicate sauces. Menu selections might include cheese mousse, beef filet with truffles and cognac, and an unusually seasoned fish salad. There is also an extensive wine list. Service is courteous.

CAÑADÍO, Gómez Oreña, 15. Tel. 31-41-49.

Cuisine: BASQUE. **Reservations:** Recommended Fri and Sat.

$ Prices: Appetizers 800–1,700 ptas. ($7.50–$16); main dishes 1,700–2,600 ptas. ($16–$24.45). AE, DC, MC, V.

Open: Lunch Mon–Sat 1–4pm; dinner Mon–Sat 9:15pm–midnight. **Closed:** Oct 15–31.

This pleasant centrally located restaurant off the Plaza Cañadío has a reputation for serving some of the best specialties in the region. Featured may be shrimp flan, hake in *cava* (Catalan champagne) sauce, and escalopes of ham with cheese. The bar, where drinks and light snacks are served, is open from 11am to midnight.

PIQUÍO, Plaza de las Brisas. Tel. 27-55-03.

Cuisine: SPANISH. **Reservations:** Recommended. **Bus:** 1, 2, 5, or 7.

$ Prices: Appetizers 1,200–1,900 ptas. ($11.30–$17.85); main dishes 2,000–2,500 ptas. ($18.80–$23.50); fixed-priced menu 2,300 ptas. ($21.60). AE, DC, MC, V.

Open: Lunch Tues–Sun 1–4pm; dinner Tues–Sun 9pm–midnight.

The panoramic view of the public gardens and the beach beyond offered by this restaurant is only one of many reasons to visit it. Specialties include a full array of fish and meat dishes, each well prepared. The chef uses market-fresh ingredients.

SPECIALTY DINING

In the evening, for a change of pace, walk or take a taxi to the fishing port, where three or four outdoor restaurants specialize in grilled sardines and other freshly caught seafood. Across the street, fishermen might be mending their nets. It's all part of the local color.

EVENING ENTERTAINMENT

LA BOHEMÍA, Daoíz y Velarde, 25. Tel. 22-69-53.

Near the cathedral is one of the most popular spots in town, especially with music lovers under 30. In a café/pub ambience, the management offers musical acts in addition to the piano playing.

Open: Tues–Sun 8:30pm–5:30am. Prices: Drinks 150–500 ptas. ($1.40–$4.70).

LISBOA, Plaza de Italia. Tel. 27-10-20.

Located within the city casino, this establishment draws all kinds of people—from gamblers taking a break from the tables to visitors looking for action of another sort. Beer and mixed drinks are served. In summer it's especially crowded. **Open:** Daily 8:30pm–3:30am. **Bus:** 1, 2, 5, or 7.

Prices: Drinks 200–500 ptas. ($1.90–$4.70).

GRAN CASINO DEL SARDINERO, Plaza de Italia. Tel. 27-60-54.

This is the most exciting nighttime diversion, offering such games as blackjack and chemin de fer. Be sure to bring your passport. The casino serves dinner from 9pm to 1am, costing 2,000 pesetas ($18.80). Open: Daily 7pm–4am. Bus: 1, 2, 5, or 7.

Admission: 400 ptas. ($3.75).

3. SANTILLANA DEL MAR & CUEVAS DE ALTAMIRA

18 miles SW of Santander; 244 miles N of Madrid

GETTING THERE By Bus From Santander, 7 buses leave the Plaza de las Estaciones daily.

By Car. Take the N-611 out of Santander to reach the C-6316 cutoff to Santillana.

ESSENTIALS The area code for Santillana del Mar is 942. The Tourist Information Office is at Plaza Mayor (tel. 942/81-82-51).

✪ Among the most perfectly preserved medieval villages in Europe, and a Spanish national landmark, **Santillana del Mar** was once famous as a place of pilgrimage. A monastery housed the relics of St. Juliana, a martyr in Asia Minor who refused to surrender her virginity to her husband. Pilgrims, especially the grandees of Castile, came to worship at this site. The name Santillana is a contraction of Santa Juliana. The "del Mar" is misleading, as Santillana is not on the water but inland.

Jean-Paul Sartre called Santillana "the prettiest village in Spain," and I wouldn't want to dispute his judgment. In spite of all the tour buses, Santillana still retains its medieval atmosphere and is still very much a village of dairy farmers. Milk is sold directly from the stable doors.

Wander on foot throughout the village, taking in its principal sites, including the **Plaza de Ramón Pelayo** (sometimes called the Plaza Mayor). Here the Parador Nacional Gil Blas (see below), named after the hero of the novel by 18th-century French writer Alain-René Lesage, has been installed in the old Barreda Bracho residence.

A 15th-century tower, facing the Calle de Juan Infante, is known for its pointed arched doorway. A walk along the Calle de las Lindas (Street of Beautiful Women) doesn't live up to its promise, but includes many of the oldest buildings in Santillana and two towers dating from the 14th and 15th centuries. The Calle del Ro gets its name from a stream running through town to a central fountain.

Visit the 800-year-old cathedral, the **Colegiata de Santillana,** Calle Santo Domingo, which shelters the tomb of the patron saint of the village, Juliana, and walk through its interesting cloister. Other treasures include 1,000-year-old documents and a 17th-century Mexican silver altarpiece. The cathedral is open daily from 9am to 12:30pm and 4 to 7:30pm. Admission, including entrance to the Convent of the Poor Clares, is 100 pesetas (95¢).

The 400-year-old Convent of the Poor Clares **(Museo Diocesano)** houses a rich art collection that was inspired by a Madrid art professor who encouraged the nuns to collect and restore religious paintings and statues damaged or abandoned during the Spanish Civil War. The collection is constantly growing. It's open daily from 9am to 12:30pm and 4 to 7:30pm.

WHERE TO STAY

HOSTAL-RESIDENCIA EMPERADOR, Avenida L'Dorat, 12, 39330 Santillana del Mar. Tel. 942/81-80-54. 5 rms (all with bath).

$ Rates: 5,200 ptas. ($48.90) single; 6,000 ptas. ($56.40) double. Breakfast 300 ptas. ($2.80) extra. No credit cards.

⑤ This residencia offers simply furnished but clean and reasonably comfortable rooms. For such a modest place, the hospitality is gracious. Because of the Emperador's small size, it can be difficult to get a room from June 15 to September 1.

HOTEL ALTAMIRA, Cantón, 1, 39330 Santillana del Mar. Tel. 942/81-80-25. Fax 942/84-01-36. 32 rms (all with bath). TV TEL

$ Rates: 4,000 ptas. ($37.60) single; 7,500 ptas. ($70.50) double. Breakfast 400 ptas. ($3.75) extra. AE, DC, MC, V.

This two-star hotel in the center of the village is a 400-year-old former palace. Though not as impressive as the government-run parador, it often takes the overflow in its comfortable, well-maintained bedrooms. At the large restaurant seating 300 and decorated in Castilian style, you can get a complete meal for 1,300 pesetas ($12.20).

LOS INFANTES, Avenida L'Dorat, 1, 39330 Santillana del Mar. Tel. 942/81-81-00. Fax 942/84-01-03. 30 rms (all with bath). TV TEL
$ Rates: 6,000 ptas. ($56.40) single; 8,000 ptas. ($75.20) double. Breakfast 425 ptas. ($4) extra. AE, DC, MC, V.

This three-star hotel, though not as charming as the Altamira, is modern and comfortable. Located on the main road leading into the village, the Infantes has successfully kept the old flavor of Santillana: beamed ceilings and lounges furnished with tapestries, antiques, clocks, and paintings. The rooms are pleasant and simple, with wall-to-wall carpeting. Two of them have small balconies.

PARADOR NACIONAL GIL BLAS, Plaza de Ramón Pelayo, 11, 39330 Santillana del Mar. Tel. 942/81-80-00. Fax 942/81-83-91. 56 rms (all with bath). MINIBAR TV TEL
$ Rates: 10,500 ptas. ($98.70) single; 13,000 ptas. ($122.20) double. Breakfast 900 ptas. ($8.45) extra. AE, DC, MC, V.

A 400-year-old former palace filled with many beautiful antiques, this parador is one of the most popular in Spain. The public rooms are elegantly informal. The hand-hewn plank floor, the old brass chandeliers, and the refectory tables with their bowls of fresh flowers enhance the atmosphere. Large portraits of knights in armor hang in a gallery. Four-course evening meals and luncheons are served in the great dining hall, a set meal costing 2,900 pesetas ($27.25). Most of the accommodations are unusually large, with windows on two sides; many have views of the garden. The rooms are decorated with antiques. The baths are large and contain all sorts of conveniences, including terrycloth dressing robes. **Note:** The third-floor rooms are very small.

WHERE TO EAT

LOS BLASONES, Plaza de la Gándara. Tel. 81-80-70.
Cuisine: CANTABRIAN. **Reservations:** Recommended.
$ Prices: Appetizers 450–1,200 ptas. ($4.25–$11.30); main dishes 800–1,500 ptas. ($7.50–$14.10); fixed-priced menu 1,800 ptas. ($16.90). AE, V, MC.
Open: Lunch daily 1–4pm; dinner daily 8–11pm. **Closed:** Dec–Feb.

Located in the center of town off the Calle del Cantón, this bar-cum-restaurant is a local hangout. It's in a rustic building made of stone. Barbecue specialties are featured. The chef's specialty is *solomillo al queso de Tresviso* (sirloin with cheese sauce).

A ONE-DAY EXCURSION

About 1.5 miles (2.5km) from Santillana del Mar are the **Cuevas de Altamira** (tel. 81-80-05), famous for prehistoric paintings dating from the end of the Ice Age, paintings that have led those caves to be called the "Sistine Chapel of prehistoric art."

These magnificent depictions of bison and horses, painted vividly in reds and blacks on the cave ceilings, were not discovered until the late 19th century. Once their authenticity was established, scholars and laypeople alike flocked to see these works of art, which provide a fragile link to our remote ancestors.

Severe damage was caused by the bacteria that so many visitors brought with them, so now the Research Center and Museum of Altamira allows only 10 visitors per day (no children under 13). If you wish to visit, write three months in advance asking permission to see the main cave, specifying the number in the party and the date desired, to: **Centro de Investigación y Museo de Altamira,** 39330 Santillana del Mar, Cantabria, Spain.

Reservations are not necessary for visits to the nearby **Cave of the Stalactites** and the little admission-free museum at the site, open Monday through Saturday from 10am to 1pm and 4 to 6pm, on Sunday from 10am to 1pm. There you can see reproductions of the caves' artwork and buy color slides that show the subtleties of color employed. You'll also see pictures of what the bacteria did to these priceless paintings. To reach the area, you need to go by car or on foot, as there is no bus service.

4. COMILLAS

30 miles W of Santander; 255 miles N of Madrid, 94 miles E of Oviedo

GETTING THERE By Bus Easy connections are made through Santander, with frequent service in summer. There are also bus connections with San Vicente de la Barquera (see below) and Santillana del Mar in the east.

By Car Continue west from Santander on the C-6316.

ESSENTIALS The area code for Comillas is 942. The Tourist Information Office is at Aldea, 6 (tel. 942/72-07-68).

The word most often used to describe this beachfront resort is "curious." Thanks to the interest of the Marqués de Comillas in the late 1880s, the town became a western outpost of the modernist architecture sweeping across Barcelona. The big names in this movement, including the inimitable Antoni Gaudí, transformed Comillas with a trio of buildings that still dominate it.

In time, the resort drew the Castilian aristocrats from Madrid and the Catalan aristocrats from Barcelona. Under Alfonso XII, the town was a royal residence, and it became the center of the Spanish court in summer. **El Capricho,** designed by Gaudí, has now been turned into the major restaurant of Comillas (see below). It has been compared to a Moorish optical illusion, with patterns of ceramics and bricks imbedded in its façade. Its large cylindrical tower is crowned by a dome that seems to "hang" in space. In typical Gaudí style, it also has jutting iron balconies in the form of balustrades. Standing next to El Capricho, a **summer palace** and former chapel for the Marqués de Comillas was designed by Gaudí's Catalan contemporary Joan Martorell. Looming over both of them is a Jesuit seminary, **Seminario Pontificia,** the Neo-Gothic statement of the celebrated Domènech i Montaner, also of Catalonia. Overall, these three buildings make a rather bizarre effect.

After viewing them, wander through the **old quarter** of Comillas, with its arcaded villas with overhanging second floors and its cobbled streets. Its Plaza Mayor is a delight.

The resort has two excellent beaches, the **Playa de Comillas,** which is just below the town, and the wider **Playa de Oyambre,** 3 miles (4.8km) to the west.

WHERE TO STAY

HOTEL CASAL DE CASTRO, San Jerónimo, s/n, 39520 Comillas. Tel. 942/72-00-36. 45 rms (all with bath).
$ Rates: 5,000 ptas. ($47) single; 6,500 ptas. ($61.10) double. Breakfast 450 ptas. ($4.25) extra. AE, MC, V.
Occupying a scenic spot on a hill near the center of town, the Casal de Castro is the best place to stay in the area, and it's also reasonable in price. Surrounding this beautiful building are grounds with a garden and a tennis court. Inside, the salons and public rooms contain some antiques. Bedrooms, some spacious, are well kept. The staff is cordial.

WHERE TO EAT

EL CAPRICHO DE GAUDÍ, Barrio de Sobrellano. Tel. 72-03-65.
Cuisine: INTERNATIONAL. **Reservations:** Recommended.
$ Prices: Appetizers 650–1,300 ptas. ($6.10–$12.20); main dishes 1,400–2,200 ptas. ($13.15–$20.70). AE, DC, MC, V.

Open: Lunch Tues–Sun 1–3:30pm; dinner Tues–Sun 8–11:30pm.

⭐ At this prestige choice for dining along the Cantabrian coast, you get to enjoy a historic building by Gaudí (described above), fine food, and attentive service—all for a good-value price. This palace in the Sobrellano section was restored in 1989 and the restaurant opened. A luxurious establishment, with decorations going back to 1883, El Capricho holds up to 300 persons (there's an outdoor parking lot). Specialties vary with the season, but are likely to include such dishes as crêpes of foie gras in a cider and apple sauce, thickly sliced hake with mushrooms, breast of duckling with sliced peppers, and a full array of homemade pastries for dessert.

5. SAN VICENTE DE LA BARQUERA

261 miles N of Madrid, 40 miles W of Santander, 87 miles E of Oviedo

GETTING THERE By Bus There are frequent connections in summer from Santander via Comillas.

By Car From Comillas, follow the road signs for 5 miles (8km) to La Revilla. There the C-6316 joins the N-634, the national route. Continue west for 2 miles (3.2km), crossing the Puente La Maza to reach San Vicente de la Barquera.

ESSENTIALS The area code for San Vicente de la Barquera is 942. The Tourist Information Office is at Avenida de Antonio Garelly, 9 (tel. 942/71-00-12).

W hen Holy Roman Emperor Charles I landed in Spain at this harbor, he demanded to see his first bullfight, and the inhabitants happily obliged.

The approach to the resort is scenic, as it appears marooned on both sides of the bay. To reach it, cross a bridge with 28 arches.

The town's most famous landmark is its 13th-century church on a once-fortified hill above San Vicente. Built in the Gothic style, with many Romanesque architectural features, **Nuestra Señora de los Angeles** contains the Renaissance tomb of Antonio Corro, the inquisitor.

Many old villas grace the town, and the Plaza Mayor has arcaded porticoes. Fairly good beaches lie a short drive either west or east of the center.

WHERE TO STAY

BOGA-BOGA, Plaza José Antonio, 10, 39540 San Vicente de la Barquera. Tel. 942/71-01-35. 18 rms (all with bath). A/C TEL

$ Rates: 4,500 ptas. ($42.30) single; 5,600 ptas. ($52.65) double. Breakfast 275 ptas. ($2.60) extra. AE, DC, MC, V.

Ⓢ Rated two stars, the Boga-Boga has simple and well-scrubbed rooms lying on the upper floors, but most of the attention is devoted to the restaurant (see below). The owner is also the manager. The place operates year round, with reservations imperative in July and August. It lies in the center of town facing the seaside promenade.

MIRAMAR, Paseo Barquera, s/n, 39540 San Vicente de la Barquera. 15 rms (all with bath). TV TEL

$ Rates: 4,400 ptas. ($41.35) single; 5,800 ptas. ($54.50) double. Breakfast 500 ptas. ($4.70) extra. AE, MC, V.

Ⓢ From March to mid-December, guests can enjoy rooms in a privileged location half a mile from the center where the river empties into the sea. Some of the simply but adequately furnished rooms open onto views of the bay or else the Picos de Europa. The setting is tranquil and comfortable. A commendable restaurant at the hotel serves meals for 1,700 pesetas ($16). Facilities include a garden and a parking lot.

WHERE TO EAT

BOGA-BOGA, Plaza José Antonio, 9. Tel. 71-01-35.
  Cuisine: CANTABRIAN. **Reservations:** Recommended.
$ **Price:** Appetizers 450–850 ptas. ($4.25–$8); main dishes 1,400–1,800 ptas. ($13.15–$16.90); fixed-priced menu 1,400 ptas. ($13.15). AE, DC, MC, V.
  Open: Lunch daily noon–4pm; dinner Wed–Mon 8–11:30pm. **Closed:** Dec 15 to Jan 15.
Jesús Santovenia makes an excellent ambassador for spreading the allure of Cantabrian cuisine. His faithful clients gravitate to such dishes as *marmita marinera*—called *sorropotun* in local dialect—a sailor's stew with tuna and fresh sardines. The kitchen turns out its own version of *merluza* (hake), and many of its succulent fish dishes are prepared on an open grill. Most of the catch comes directly from the Bay of Biscay. Dessert might be pears in red wine or else a homemade pastry.

MARUJA, Avenida Generalísimo, s/n. Tel. 71-00-77.
  Cuisine: SEAFOOD. **Reservations:** Recommended.
$ **Prices:** Appetizers 750–1,300 ptas. ($7.05–$12.20); main dishes 1,800–2,700 ptas. ($16.90–$25.40); fixed-priced menu 2,400 ptas. ($22.50). AE, DC, MC, V.
  Open: Lunch daily 1–4pm; dinner daily 8pm–midnight.
Since it was first established, three generations of the same family have maintained fine cookery at reasonable prices in this establishment near the town center. The dining room is comfortable, and the service attentive. You might try a time-tested dish such as the *zarzuela* of shellfish or the lobster salad. For those tired of fish, a house-style tournedos is available, and new dishes are always being added to the menu. A full array of reasonably priced wines are offered.

6. LOS PICOS DE EUROPA

Potes: 71 miles W of Santander, 247 miles N of Madrid
Cangas de Onís: 91 miles W of Santander, 260 miles N of Madrid

GETTING THERE   By Car   By far the best way to see this region is by car. Most drivers head into the region on the N-621 highway, heading southwest from Santander, or on the same highway northeast from the cities of north central Spain (especially León and Valladolid). This highway connects many of the region's best vistas in a straight line. It also defines the region's eastern boundary. If you're driving east from Oviedo, you'll take the N-6312, in which case the first town of any importance will be Cangas de Onís.

By Bus   Much less convenient, but possible if you have lots of time and have had your fill of the rich architecture of the Spanish heartland. The region's touristic hubs are the towns of Panes and Potes, both of which receive bus service (2 buses per day in summer, 1 per day in winter) from both Santander and León. More frequent buses (5 per day) come from the coastal town of Unquera (which lies along the coastal train lines) to Potes. From Oviedo, there are 2 buses daily to the district's easternmost town of Cangas; these continue a short distance farther southeast to Covadonga. Within the region, a small local bus runs once a day, according to an erratic schedule, along the northern rim of the Picos, connecting Cangas de Onís with Las Arenas. Frankly, bus service in this region is inconvenient and time-consuming.

These mountains are technically part of the Cordillera Cantábrica, which runs parallel to the northern coastline of Spain. In the narrow and vertiginous band known as Los Picos de Europa, they are by far at their most dramatic.

They are the most famous and most legend-riddled mountains in Spain. Rising more than 8,500 feet, they are not considered high by alpine standards, but their proximity to the sea makes their height especially awesome. During the Middle Ages, they were considered passable only with great difficulty. (Much earlier, the ancient

Romans constructed a north–south road whose stones are still visible in some places.) The abundance of wildlife, the medieval battles that occurred here, and the dramatically rocky heights have all contributed to the "twice-told tales" that are an essential part of the entire principality of Asturias.

The position of Los Picos defined the medieval borders between Asturias, Santander, and León. Covering a distance of only 24 miles at their longest point, they are geologically and botanically different from anything else in the region. Thousands of years ago, busy glaciers created massive and forbidding limestone cliffs that today challenge the most dedicated and intrepid rock climbers in Europe.

Even hill climbers should never underestimate the dangers of walking here. Many of the slopes are covered with loosely compacted shale, making good treads and hiking boots necessary. For amateurs, only well-established paths are safe: Setting out on their own for uncharted vistas has left many neophytes stranded. In summer, temperatures can get hot and humid, and sudden downpours sweeping in from the frequently rainy coastline are common in any season. Hiking is not recommended between October and May. Excursions by car and the walking tour contained in Motor Tour 3, below, are possible in any season.

The Picos are divided by swiftly flowing rivers into three different regions. From east to west, they are Andara, Urrieles, and Cornion.

MOTOR TOURS

If you have a car, the number and variety of tours within this region are almost endless, but for the purposes of this guide, I have organized the region into three different motor tours. Any of them, with their side excursions, could fill an entire day; if you're rushed and omit some of the side excursions, half a day.

MOTOR TOUR 1 — FROM PANES TO POTES
18 miles; 1 hour

This drive, except for one optional detour, extends entirely along one of the region's best roads, the N-621, which links Leon and Valladolid to Santander. The drive is most noteworthy for its views of the ravine containing the Deva River, a ravine so steep that direct sunlight rarely penetrates it.

About two-thirds of the way to Potes, signs will point you on a detour to the village of **Lebana,** a half mile off the main road. There you'll find the church of Nuestra Señora de Lebena, built in the 10th century in the Mozarabic style, surrounded by a copse of trees at the base of tall cliffs. Some people consider it the best example of "Arabized" Christian architecture in Europe, with Islamic-inspired geometric motifs. If it isn't open, knock at the door of the first house you see as you enter the village—the home of the guardian, who will unlock the church if she's around. For this, she will expect a tip. If she's not around, content yourself with admiring the church from the outside, noting its spectacular natural setting.

Continuing for about another 5 miles (8km), you'll reach the village of **Potes,** a charming place with well-kept alpine houses against a backdrop of jagged mountains.

Excursions From Potes

Two miles (3.2km) southwest of Potes, near Turiano, stands the **Monastery of Santo Toribio de Liébana,** dating from the 17th century. Restored to the style it enjoyed at the peak of its vast power, a transitional Romanesque, it contains what is reputed to be a splinter from the True Cross, brought from Jerusalem in the 8th century by the Bishop of Astorga. The monastery is also famous as the former home of Beatus de Liébana, the 8th-century author of *Commentary on the Apocalypse,* one of medieval Spain's most famous ecclesiastical documents. Today the building remains a functioning monastery. Ring the bell during daylight hours, and one of the brothers will probably let you enter if you are properly attired.

At the end of a winding and breathtakingly beautiful road to the west of Potes lies the **Parador de Fuente-Dé,** where you can spend the night or stop for lunch only.

The drive to Fuente-Dé will, for the most part, follow the path of the Deva River. Once you're there, a teleferic will carry you 2,000 feet up to an observation platform above a wind-scoured rock face. In summer the teleferic operates daily from 9am to 8pm; in winter, from 10am to 1pm and 3 to 6pm. Round-trip fare is 550 pesetas ($5.15). At the top you can walk 3 miles (4.8km) along a footpath to the rustic **Refugio de Aliva,** open between June 15 and September 15. A few bunks are available for 450 pesetas ($4.25). If you opt for just a meal or snack at the hostal's simple restaurant, remember to allow enough time to return to the teleferic before its last trip down.

MOTOR TOUR 2 — FROM POTES TO CANGAS DE ONÍS

93 miles; 4 hours

This tour includes not only the Quiviesa Valley and some of the region's most vertiginous mountain passes, but also some of its most verdant fields and most elevated pastures. You might stop at an occasional village, but most of the time you will be going through deserted countryside. Your route will take you under several tunnels, and high above mountain streams set deep into gorges. The occasional belvederes signposted along the way always deliver on their promise of spectacular views.

After a day of vistas, the first really important place you'll reach is **Cangas de Onís,** the westernmost town in the region, where you can get a clean hotel room and a solid meal after a trek through the mountains. The biggest attraction in Cangas de Onís is an ivy-covered **Roman bridge,** lying west of the center, spanning the Sella River. Also of interest is the **Capilla de Santa Cruz,** lying immediately west of the center. One of the earliest Christian sites in Spain (and probably a holy spot many centuries before that), it was originally built in the 8th century over a Celtic dolmen, and rebuilt in the 15th century.

A mile northwest of Cangas de Onís, beside the road leading to Arriondas, stands the Benedictine **Monastery of San Pedro,** in the village of Villanueva. The church that you see was originally built in the 17th century, when it enclosed within its premises the ruins of a much older Romanesque church. Combining a blend of baroque opulence and Romanesque simplicity, it has some unusual carved capitals showing the unhappy end of the medieval King Favila, supposedly devoured by a Cantabrian bear.

MOTOR TOUR 3 — FROM CANGAS DE ONÍS TO PANES

35 miles; 1 hour

This tour travels along the relatively straight C-6312 from the western to the eastern entrance to the Picos de Europa region. A number of unusual excursions could easily stretch this into an all-day outing.

From Cangas de Onís, heading west about 1 mile (1.6km), you'll reach the turnoff to the **El Buxu Cueva.** Inside the cave are a limited number of prehistoric rock engravings and charcoal drawings, somewhat disappointingly small. Only 25 persons per day are allowed inside (respiration erodes the drawings), so unless you get there early, you won't get in. It's open Tuesday through Sunday, except during November, from 10am to 12:30pm and 4 to 6:30pm. Admission costs 100 pesetas (95¢).

Four miles (6.5km) east, signs point south in the direction of **Covadonga,** revered as the birthplace of Christian Spain, about 6 miles (9.6km) off the main highway. A battle here in A.D. 718 pitted a ragged band of Christian Visigoths against a small band of Muslims. The resulting victory introduced the first niche of Christian Europe into a Moorish Iberia.

The town's most important monument is **La Santa Cueva,** a cave containing the sarcophagus of Pelayo, king of the Visigothic Christians (d. 737) and an enormous Neo-Romanesque basilica, built between 1886 and 1901, commemorating the Christianization of Spain. At the end of the long boulevard that funnels into the base of the church stands a statue of Pelayo.

Return to the highway and continue east. You'll come to the village of Las Estazadas; then after another 7 miles (11km), to **Las Arenas de Cabrales** (some maps refer to it as Arenas). This is the headquarters of a cheese-producing region whose Cabrales, a blue-veined cheese made from ewe's milk, is avidly consumed throughout Spain.

Drive 3 miles (4.8km) south from Arenas, following signs to the village of **Puente de Poncebos** (known on some maps as Poncebos). Here, the road ends abruptly (except perhaps for four-wheeled vehicles). This village is set several miles downstream from the source of Spain's most famous salmon-fishing river, the Cares, which flows from its source near the more southerly village of Cain through deep ravines.

A Trek Through The Divine Gorge

Beginning at Poncebos, a footpath has been cut into the ravine on either side of the Cares River. It is one of the engineering marvels of Spain, known for centuries at The Divine Gorge. It crosses the ravine many times over footbridges, and sometimes through tunnels chiseled into the rock face beside the water, making a hike along the banks of this river a memorable outing. You can climb up the riverbed from Poncebos, overland to the village of Cain, a total distance of 7 miles (11km). Allow between 3 and 4 hours. At Cain, you can take a taxi back to where you left your car in Poncebos if you don't want to retrace your steps.

After your trek up the riverbed, continue your drive on to the village of **Panes,** a distance of 14 miles (22km), to the eastern extremity of the Picos de Europa.

WHERE TO STAY & EAT

Accommodations are extremely limited in these mountain towns. If you're planning an overnight stopover, make sure you have a reservation. Most taverns will serve you food during regular opening hours without a reservation.

CANGAS DE ONÍS

RESTAURANT VENTURA, Avenida de Covadonga, s/n. Tel. 84-82-00.
   Cuisine: ASTURIAN. **Reservations:** Not required.
   $ **Prices:** Appetizers 450–750 ptas. ($4.25–$7.05); main dishes 1,000–1,500 ptas. ($9.40–$14.10). AE, DC, MC, V.
   Open: Lunch Tues–Sun 1–4pm; dinner Tues–Sun 8pm–midnight.
Just east of the center of town on the road to Covadonga is this well-managed restaurant/hotel. It is well stocked with many of the region's local delicacies, including salmon from mountain rivers and seasonal game dishes from the hills. You can also enjoy local cheeses, including the Roquefort-like Cabrales. A limited wine list is available. If you'd like to spend the night here, you'll find 53 comfortably furnished but very simple bedrooms, costing 4,600 pesetas ($43.25) for a single and 6,600 pesetas ($62.05) for a double, with breakfast an extra 350 pesetas ($3.30).

LA PALMERA, Soto de Cangas. Tel. 84-88-96.
   Cuisine: ASTURIAN. **Reservations:** Not required.
   $ **Prices:** Appetizers 550–950 ptas. ($5.15–$8.95); main dishes 1,300–2,100 ptas. ($12.20–$19.75). No credit cards.
   Open: Lunch daily 1–4pm; dinner daily 8pm–midnight.
When the weather is right, you can dine outside here, enjoying some mountain air with the mountain food. Sometimes this place is overrun, but on other occasions you can have a meal in peace. The menu features game from the surrounding mountains, along with filet of beef, lamb chops, and salmon in green sauce. Try the local mountain cheese. La Palmera lies 2 miles (3.2km) east of Cangas de Onís on the road to Covadonga.

COSGAYA

HOTEL DEL OSO, Carretera Espinama, s/n, 39539 Cosgaya. Tel. 73-04-18. 36 rms (all with bath). TEL **Directions:** From Potes, take the road signposted to Espinama 9 miles (14.5km) south.

$ Rates: 4,800 ptas. ($45.10) single; 6,400 ptas. ($60.15) double. Breakfast 375 ptas. ($3.55) extra. MC, V.

This well-run little hotel is set next to the banks of the Deva River, beside the road leading from Potes to the parador and cablecar at Fuente-Dé. The place is ringed with natural beauty. Its bedrooms are well furnished and maintained, and meals are taken at the Mesón del Oso (see below).

MESÓN DEL OSO, Carretera Espinama, s/n. Tel. 73-04-18.
   Cuisine: ASTURIAN. **Reservations:** Not required. **Directions:** From Potes, take the route south toward Espinama 9 miles (14.5km).
$ Prices: Appetizers 450–850 ptas. ($4.25–$8); main dishes 900–1,500 ptas. ($8.45–$14.10). MC, V.
   Open: Lunch daily 1–4pm; dinner daily 8–11pm.

Ⓢ   Open to the public since 1981, this stone-built place is named after the bear that supposedly devoured Favilia, an 8th-century king of Asturias. Here, at the birthplace of the Christian warrior king Pelayo, you can enjoy Liébana cuisine, reflecting the bounty of mountain, stream, and sea. Portions are generous. Try trout from the Deva River, grilled tuna, roast suckling pig, or a mountain stew called *cocida lebaniego,* whose recipe derives from local lore and tradition. Dessert might be a fruit-based tart. There's also an outdoor terrace.

COVADONGA

HOTEL PELAYO, 33589 Covadonga. Tel. 985/84-60-00. Fax 985/84-60-54. 43 rms (all with bath). TV TEL **Directions:** Take the road that leads into the national park.
$ Rates: 4,800 ptas. ($45.10) single; 8,300 ptas. ($78) double. Breakfast 450 ptas. ($4.25) extra. MC, V.

There's no street address for this place, but it lies in the shadow of the large 19th-century basilica that dominates the village. The view from its windows takes in a panoramic landscape. Guests come here to enjoy the mountain air, and many pilgrims check in while visiting religious shrines in the area. The place has a somewhat dated, but nevertheless appealing, family atmosphere. Rooms are comfortable and well furnished. Facilities include a parking lot, a garden, and a restaurant offering well-prepared meals for 1,900 pesetas ($17.85), lunch or dinner.

FUENTE-DÉ

PARADOR DEL RÍO DEVA, 39588 Espinama. Tel. 73-00-01. 78 rms (all with bath). TV TEL **Directions:** Drive 16 miles (26km) west of Potes.
$ Rates: 6,500 ptas. ($61.10) single; 8,000 ptas. ($75.20) double. Breakfast 900 ptas. ($8.45) extra. AE, DC, MC, V.

The finest place to stay in the area, this government-run parador opens onto panoramic vistas of the Picos de Europa. It lies at the end of the major road through the Liébana region. Hunters in autumn and mountain climbers in summer often fill its attractively decorated and comfortably furnished bedrooms. The place has a pleasant bar, and its restaurant serves good regional cuisine, with meals costing from 2,800 pesetas ($26.30). It also has parking space.

POTES

RESTAURANT MARTÍN, Roscabao, s/n. Tel. 73-02-33.
   Cuisine: ASTURIAN. **Reservations:** Not required.
$ Prices: Appetizers 350–500 ptas. ($3.30–$4.70); main dishes 1,000–1,500 ptas. ($9.40–$14.10); fixed-priced menu 850 ptas. ($8). MC, V.
   Open: Lunch daily 1–4:30pm; dinner daily 8:30–11:30pm. **Closed:** Jan.

ⓢ This family-run establishment in the center of Potes is filled with regional charm and spirit. They prepare garbanzos (chick peas) with bits of chorizo sausage. Other vegetables and the rich produce of the region appear on the seasonally adjusted menu, as well as game from the Picos and fish from the Cantabrian coast. The dessert choices comprise more than a dozen different tarts and pastries.

---

7. LLANES

282 miles N of Madrid, 69 miles E of Oviedo

GETTING THERE   By Train   FEVE, the independent narrow-gauge railroad, makes stops at Llanes. You can board this train in either Santander or Bilbao.

By Bus   Connections are possible from Oviedo (4 per day) and from Santander (5 per day).

By Car   From Santander, continue west along the 634 until you see the turnoff (AS-263) north to the coast and Llanes.

ESSENTIALS   The area code for Llanes is 985. The Tourist Information Office is at Nemesio Sobrino, 1 (tel. 985/40-01-64).

The capital of eastern Asturias, Llanes is both a fishing village and a resort known for at least two dozen beaches, principally **El Sabión.** In the 13th century the town was encircled by walls to fend off pirates' attacks from the sea, and the remains of those walls can still be seen.

You can visit the 14th-century **Church of Santa María,** part Gothic, part Romanesque. Many 17th-century houses were constructed in town by *los indianos,* the name given to adventurers who struck it rich in the New World. Many of their most ostentatious structures at Llanes are called follies; some contain heraldic coats-of-arms. Before sunset it is customary to promenade along the **Paseo de San Pedro,** which offers spectacular clifftop views of the bay and town.

Each July 16, Llanes celebrates the **Fiesta de San Roque,** with ancient dances like the *pericote* and traditional costumes.

WHERE TO STAY

LAS BRISAS, La Arquera, s/n, 33500 Llanes. Tel. 985/40-17-26. 35 rms (all with bath).
$ Rates: 6,000 ptas. ($56.40) single; 7,000 ptas. ($65.80) double. Breakfast 400 ptas. ($3.75) extra. DC, V.
This modern hotel (opened in 1988) is set in a tranquil place on the southern outskirts, a half mile from the center just off the N-634. Each bedroom is clean, comfortably furnished, and well kept. The hotel, which isn't air-conditioned, has a good restaurant, with both regional and national dishes. Complete meals cost 1,600 pesetas ($15.05).

HOTEL MONTEMAR, Genero Riestra, 8, 33500 Llanes. Tel. 985/40-01-00. Fax 985/41-20-73. 41 rms (all with bath). TV TEL
$ Rates: 5,300 ptas. ($49.80) single; 7,000 ptas. ($65.80) double. Breakfast 450 ptas. ($4.25) extra. AE, DC, MC, V.
This is the less expensive of two hotels owned by the same family. Near the beach, it stands close to the medieval walls that once surrounded Llanes. Each bedroom is comfortably furnished and well maintained. The hotel doesn't have a restaurant, but it does offer a cafeteria.

WHERE TO EAT

LA BOLERA, Muelle, s/n. Tel. 40-13-36.
Cuisine: SEAFOOD. **Reservations:** Recommended.
$ Prices: Appetizers 450–750 ptas. ($4.25–$7.05); main dishes 1,100–1,700 ptas. ($10.35–$16). AE, MC, V.
Open: Lunch daily 1:30–5:30pm; dinner daily 8:30pm–midnight.
You can drink at a street-level bar on the waterfront, then head upstairs to the smaller and somewhat calmer dining room. Displayed on the premises is a theatrically arranged exhibition of fresh fish and shellfish. Many fish dishes are on the menu, including salmon from the Bedrón River, white bream, and hake (served in a savory seafood sauce). Game selections, including rabbit-and-bean stew, come from the nearby Picos de Europa. A good array of wines is also offered in this air-conditioned dining room.

MIRADOR DE TORÓ, Avenida Toró, s/n. Tel. 40-08-82.
Cuisine: SEAFOOD. **Reservations:** Recommended.
$ Prices: Appetizers 450–750 ptas. ($4.25–$7.05); main dishes 1,100–1,700 ptas. ($10.35–$16). MC, V.
Open: Lunch daily 1–4pm; dinner daily 8pm–midnight.
This restaurant has a tasteful interior and big windows overlooking the town's most popular beach, the Playa de Toro. Fresh ingredients from the sea are handled with culinary skill, and portions are big. Try the chef's hake in champagne sauce or perhaps a zesty seafood stew. The "razor" clams are always beautifully fresh. As for dessert, the chef takes pride in his *arroz con leche* (rice pudding). Try a Rioja Bordón as a wine accompaniment to your meal.

---

8. RIBADESELLA

301 miles N of Madrid, 52 miles E of Oviedo, 79 miles W of Santander

GETTING THERE   By Train   FEVE, the independent narrow-gauge railroad that runs trains along the north coast of Spain, stops in Ribadesella. You can board this train either in Bilbao or Santander.

By Bus   Three buses per day run between Oviedo and Ribadesella.

By Car   From Llanes, drive west on the N-634 to the turnoff for Ribadesella.

ESSENTIALS   The **area code** for Ribadesella is 985. The Tourist Information Office is at Puente Rio Sella/Carretera de la Piconera, s/n (tel. 985/80-00-38).

Ribadesella is both a seaside resort with a splendid beach and a convenient base for exploring the Picos de Europa. It is strategically placed at the mouth of the Sella River. Its harbor, one of the most important in eastern Asturias, often serves as a refuge for transatlantic yachts.
   Ribadesella is home base for a fiesta, the **International Descent of the Sella River,** taking place the first Saturday in August. All-night revelry follows the canoeists for 11 miles (18km) down river from Arriondas. A special train filled with fans chugs along the banks of the river.
   Ribadesella straddles the wide Sella estuary. Once you reach the port side of town, you'll discover an array of *tascas* (taverns), *siderías* (Asturian cider bars), shops, and restaurants. You can easily spend about 2 hours wandering through its old quarter.

★ The major sight in the environs, other than the Picos de Europa, is **La Cueva de Tito Bustillo,** with prehistoric paintings, considered the third most important such cave in Europe. It is compared favorably with the more celebrated caves at Altamira and with those in Lascaux, France. In what must have been brilliant red and ocher pigments, deer, horses, and other animals were painted. You'll also see a vulva painted as a fertility symbol. The paintings are said to be some 15,000 to 20,000 years old. The caves, found in 1968, are named for their Asturian discoverer.

The caves consist of a trio of galleries. To see them, go early in the morning, as only 400 visitors a day are permitted. They're open April through September from 10am to 1pm and 3:30 to 6:30pm. They're closed Monday in April, May, June, and September, and Sunday in July and August. Admission is 150 pesetas ($1.40).

WHERE TO STAY

RIBADESELLA-PLAYA, Ricargo Cangas, 3, 33560 Ribadesella. Tel. 985/86-07-17. Fax 985/86-13-32. 17 rms (all with bath). TEL
$ **Rates:** 5,000 ptas. ($47) single, 7,000 ptas. ($65.80) double. Breakfast 300 ptas. ($2.80) extra. DC, MC, V.
From March to October, holidaymakers are received at this spacious old villa on the beach, right outside the center of Ribadesella. Furnishings are plain, but the place is comfortable and guests go to sleep listening to the sound of waves crashing against the breakers. The hotel also operates a commendable regional restaurant that serves meals from 1,500 pesetas ($14.10).

GRAN HOTEL DEL SELLA, Ricargo Cangas, 17, 33560 Ribadesella. Tel. 985/86-01-50. Fax 985/86-01-76. 82 rms (all with bath). TV TEL
$ **Rates:** 8,000 ptas. ($75.20) single; 10,800 ptas. ($101.50) double. Breakfast 550 ptas. ($5.15). AE, DC, MC, V.
This hotel next to the beach, the finest accommodation in the area for those willing to spend a little more, occupies the *dependencias* (outbuildings) of the art nouveau summer palace of the marquis of Argüelles. The original buildings have been enhanced, improved, and enlarged with a modern annex. On the premises is a good restaurant, as well as a bar designed to make you want to linger. Facilities include a swimming pool, a garden, tennis courts, and ample parking. Each of the bedrooms is well furnished and maintained, with TV reception that gets many channels. The hotel is open only from April to September.

WHERE TO EAT

EL REPOLLU, Santa María, 2. Tel. 86-07-34.
Cuisine: ASTURIAN. **Reservations:** Recommended.
$ **Prices:** Appetizers 450–750 ptas. ($4.25–$7.05); main dishes 1,000–1,700 ptas. ($9.40–$16). No credit cards.
Open: Lunch daily 1–4pm; dinner daily 9–11pm.
This is a crowded, boisterous tavern in the center of town, often with too many patrons and not enough waiters, but all the locals seem to love it. The fish prepared here is reason enough to wait, and everybody seems to have a good time, especially if they have enough cider to drink. Try grilled filet of John Dory or whatever was brought in as the catch of the day. The chef, Alfredo, also does excellent marinated meats, followed by a good selection of Asturian Cabrales cheese.

BOHEMIA, Gran Vía, 53. Tel. 87-76-49.
Cuisine: ASTURIAN. **Reservations:** Recommended.
$ **Prices:** Appetizers 650–950 ptas. ($6.10–$8.95); main dishes 1,200–1,900 ptas. ($11.30–$17.85). AE, MC, V.
Open: Lunch daily 1–4pm; dinner daily 8:30pm–midnight.
This establishment in the center of town is owned by the same people who operate the Hotel Marina (tel. 86-01-57) next door to the restaurant, the best hotel within the

town. Of the 44 rooms (all with bath), singles go for 4,000 pesetas ($37.60), doubles for 6,500 pesetas ($61.10), with breakfast costing 300 pesetas ($2.80) extra. Meals are taken here at the Bohemia, where the regional food is well prepared and competently served, and the portions are large. Specialties include warm hors d'oeuvres, monkfish stuffed with onions, and halibut cooked in cider sauce.

---

9. GIJÓN (XIXÓN)

294 miles N of Madrid, 119 miles W of Santander, 18 miles E of Oviedo

GETTING THERE **By Plane** Gijón doesn't have an airport, but there is one at Ranón, 26 miles (42km) away, a facility it also shares with Oviedo-bound passengers.

By Train Gijón has good rail links and makes a good gateway into Asturias. Three trains a day run from Madrid (6½ to 8½ hours). León is a convenient rail hub for reaching Gijón, as Gijón is connected with León with 9 trains per day (2 to 3 hours). You can also take the narrow-gauge FEVE from Bilbao.

By Bus Six buses a day connect Gijón with Madrid (5½ hours), and 2 buses per day run to and from Santander (4½ hours). Four buses a day go to León (2 hours).

By Car From Santander in the east, continue west along the N-634. At Ribadesella, you can take the turnoff to the 632, which is the coastal road that will take you to Gijón. This is the scenic view. To save time, continue on the N-634 until you reach the outskirts of Oviedo, then cut north on the expressway highway to Gijón.

ESSENTIALS The area code for Gijón is 985. The Tourist Information Office is at Marqués de San Esteban, s/n (tel. 985/34-60-46).

The major port of Asturias and its largest city is not just that: It is also a summer resort and an industrial center rolled into one. As a port, Gijón (pronounced hee-HON) is said to predate the Romans. The Visigoths came through here, and in the 8th century the Moors also made some forays into the area, but none of those would-be conquerors seem to have made much impression on Gijón.

The best part of the city to explore is the barrio of **Cimadevilla,** with its maze of alleys and its leaning houses. This section, jutting into the ocean to the north of the new town, spills over an elevated piece of land known as Santa Catalina. Santa Catalina forms a headland at the west end of the **Playa San Lorenzo,** stretching for about 1½ miles; this beach has good facilities and is sandy. After time at the beach you can stroll through the **Parque Isabel la Católica** at its eastern end.

The most exciting time to be in Gijón is on **Asturias Day,** the first Sunday in August. This fiesta is celebrated with parade floats, traditional folk dancing, and lots of music. But summers here tend to be festive even without a festival. Vacationers are fond of patronizing the cider taverns (*chigres*), eating grilled sardines, and joining in sing-alongs in the portside tascas. Be aware that you can get as drunk on cider as you can on beer, maybe somewhat faster.

Gijón is short on major monuments. The city was the birthplace of Gaspar Melchor de Jovellanos (1744–1811), one of Spain's most prominent man of letters, as well as agrarian reformer and liberal economist. Manuel de Godoy, the notorious minister, ordered that Jovellanos be held prisoner for seven years in Bellver Castle on Majorca. In Gijón his birthplace has been restored and turned into the Museo-Casa Natal de Jovellanos, Plaza de Jovellanos, open Tuesday through Saturday from 10am to 2pm and 4 to 8pm. Admission is free.

WHERE TO STAY

HERNÁN CORTÉS, Fernández Vallin, 5, 33205 Gijón. Tel. 985/34-60-00. Fax 985/35-56-45. rms (all with bath) MINIBAR TV TEL

$ Rates: 6,500 ptas. ($61.10) single; 8,200 ptas. ($77.10) double. Breakfast 800 ptas. ($7.50) extra. AE, DC, MC, V.

About a block east of Plaza del 6 de Agosto, midway between the Playa San Lorenzo and the boat harbor, stands one of the finest accommodations in town. Although it was recently renovated, its bedrooms still retain a bit of the allure of yesteryear, as well as providing such thoughtful extras as shoeshine paraphernalia. Facilities include a disco on the premises, convention rooms, and ample parking. The hotel doesn't have a restaurant, but does offer a nighttime cafeteria for snacks and light meals.

BEGOÑA, Carretera de la Costa, 44, 33205 Gijón. Tel. 985/14-72-11. Fax 985/39-82-22. 165 rms (all with bath). TV TEL

$ Rates: 6,500 ptas. ($61.10) single; 8,800 ptas. ($82.70) double. Breakfast 500 ptas. ($4.70) extra. AE, V.

This functional modern hotel, with much-appreciated parking for your car, has rooms that are well furnished and comfortable, and efficient chamber service to keep everything clean. Regional and national dishes, with many seafood concoctions, are served in the Begoña's restaurant, where meals begin at 1,500 pesetas ($1.40). The hotel lies on the southern outskirts of the new town, 1 block north of the Avenida Manuel Llaneza, the major traffic artery funneling vehicles in from the southwest.

LA CASONA DE JOVELLANOS, Plaza de Jovellanos, 1, 33201 Gijón. Tel. 985/34-12-64. Fax 985/35-61-51. 13 rms (all with bath). TV TEL

$ Rates: 8,500 ptas. ($79.90) single; 10,500 ptas. ($98.70) double. Breakfast 500 ptas. ($4.70) extra. AE, V.

This venerable hotel stands on the rocky peninsula that was the site of the oldest part of fortified Gijón, a short distance south of the Parque Santa Catalina. It contains only a few bedrooms, so reservations are imperative. The rooms themselves are attractively furnished and well maintained. The building, established in 1794 by the writer Jovellanos as the Asturian Royal Institute of Marine Life and Mineralogy, was later transformed into a hotel lying within walking distance of the beach and yacht basin.

WHERE TO EAT

CASA JUSTO [CHIGRE ASTURIANU], Hermanos Felgueroso, 50. Tel. 15-22-44.

Cuisine: ASTURIAN. **Reservations:** Recommended.

$ Prices: Appetizers 350–750 ptas. ($3.30–$7.05); main dishes 900–1,500 ptas. ($8.45–$14.10). AE, V.

Open: Lunch daily 1–4pm; dinner daily 7pm–midnight.

Housed within a very old cider press, for years this place has been called Chigre Asturianu, but most locals still call it by its old designation. Renovations have added well-designed dining rooms and kitchens to what used to be a large and drafty building. The cuisine is based primarily on fish and shellfish, but with plenty of Asturian regional dishes as well. Try octopus with potatoes, grilled fresh John Dory, or veal chops. There is a full array of wines. Here, too, you can sample that Roquefort-like cheese, Cabrales, made in the Picos de Europa. The Casa Justo lies south of the old town near Campo Sagrada on the road to Pola de Siero.

CASA VICTOR, Carmen, 11. Tel. 35-00-93.

Cuisine: SEAFOOD. **Reservations:** Recommended.

$ Prices: Appetizers 450–750 ptas. ($4.25–$7.05); main dishes 1,000–1,800 ptas. ($9.40–$16.90). AE, MC, V.

Open: Lunch daily 1:30–3:30pm; dinner Mon–Sat 8:30–11:30pm. **Closed:** Thurs in Nov.

Owner and sometime chef Victor Bango is a bit of a legend. He oversees the buying and preparation of the fresh fish for which this place is famous locally. The successful young people of Gijón enjoy the tavernlike atmosphere here, as well as the imaginative dishes—a mousse made from the roe of sea urchins, for example, all the rage in Asturias these days. Well-chosen wines accompany such other menu items as octopus served with fresh vegetables, many different preparations of hake, and grilled steak. The Casa Victor is located by the dockyards.

CASA TINO, Alfredo Truán, 9. Tel. 34-13-87.
   Cuisine: ASTURIAN. **Reservations:** Recommended.
$ **Prices:** Appetizers 450–750 ptas. ($4.25–$7.05); main dishes 1,400–1,900 ptas. ($13.15–$17.85). AE, V.
   Open: Lunch Fri–Wed 1:30–3:30pm; dinner Fri–Wed 8:30–11:30pm. **Closed:** June 17 to July 20.

Quality combined with quantity—at reasonable prices—is the hallmark of this restaurant, located near the police station, north of Manuel Llaneza and west of the Paseo de Begoña. Each day the chef prepares a different stew—sometimes fish, sometimes meat. The place is packed with chattering diners every evening, many of them habitués. Sample the white beans of the region cooked with pork, stewed hake, or marinated beefsteak, perhaps finishing with one of the fruited tarts.

---

10. OVIEDO [UVIÉU]

126 miles W of Santander, 276 miles N of Madrid

GETTING THERE **By Air** Oviedo doesn't have an airport. The nearest one is at Ranón, 32 miles (51.5km) away, which it shares with Gijón-bound passengers.

By Train From Madrid, there are 2 trains per day.

By Bus From Santander, there are 2 buses per day (4½ hours); from Madrid, 6 buses per day (5½ hours).

By Car Take the N-634 across the coast of northern Spain.

ESSENTIALS The area code for Oviedo is 985. The Tourist Information Office is at Plaza de Alfonso II (tel. 985/21-33-85).

Oviedo is the capital of the province of Asturias on Spain's northern coast, laved by the Bay of Biscay. Despite its high concentration of industry and mining, the area has unspoiled scenery. Only 16 miles (26km) from the coast, Oviedo is very pleasant in summer, when much of Spain is unbearably hot. It also makes an ideal base for excursions along the "Green Coast."

A peaceful city today, Oviedo has had a long and violent history. Razed in the 8th century during the Reconquest, it was rebuilt in an architectural style known as "Asturian Pre-Romanesque," which predated many of the greatest achievements under the Moors. Remarkably, this architectural movement was in flower when the rest of Europe lay under the black cloud of the Dark Ages.

As late as the 1930s Oviedo was suffering violent upheavals. An insurrection in the mining areas on October 5, 1934, led to a seizure of the town by miners, who set up a revolutionary government. The subsequent fighting led to the destruction of many historical monuments. The cathedral was also damaged, and the university set on fire. Even more destruction came during the Spanish Civil War.

WHAT TO SEE & DO

Oviedo has been rebuilt into a modern city around the Parque de San Francisco. It still contains some historical and artistic monuments, however, the most important being the **cathedral** on the Plaza de Alfonso II, a Gothic building begun in 1348 and completed at the end of the 15th century (except for the spire, which dates from 1556). Inside is an altarpiece in the florid Gothic style, dating from the 14th and 15th centuries. The cathedral's 9th-century **Cámara Santa (Holy Chamber)** is famous for the Cross of Don Pelayo, the Cross of the Victory, and the Cross of the Angels, the finest specimens of Asturian art in the world. Admission to the cathedral is free, but admission to the Holy Chamber is 50 pesetas (45¢). The cathedral is open daily from 9am to 1pm and 3:30 to 6pm; the Holy Chamber is open daily from 10am to 1pm and 4 to 6pm.

Behind the cathedral, the **Museo Arqueológico,** San Vicente, 5, (tel. 21-54-05), in a former convent dating from the 15th century, houses prehistoric relics discovered in Asturias, Pre-Romanesque sculptures, a numismatic display, and old musical instruments. It's open Tuesday through Saturday from 10am to 1:30pm and 4 to 6pm, on Sunday from 11am to 1pm. Admission is free.

Standing above Oviedo, on Monte Naranco, are two of the most famous examples of Asturian Pre-Romanesque architecture, the churches of Santa María de Naranco (converted from a 9th-century palace) and San Miguel de Lillo (a once-royal chapel). These structures stand a mile northwest of the center.

Santa María de Naranco, originally a palace/hunting lodge of Ramiro I (842–52), offers views of Oviedo and the snowcapped Picos de Europa. Once containing baths and private apartments, it was converted into a church in the 12th century. Intricate stonework depicts hunting scenes, and barrel vaulting rests on a network of blind arches. The open porticoes at both ends were considered 200 years ahead of their time architecturally. The church is open April through September, daily from 10am to 1pm and 4 to 7pm; October through March, daily from 10am to 1pm.

Lying about 100 yards away is **San Miguel de Lillo.** It, too, was built by Ramiro I, and was no doubt a magnificent specimen of Asturian Pre-Romanesque until 15th-century "architects" marred its grace. The stone carvings that remain, however, are exemplary. Most of the sculpture has been transferred to the archeological museum in town.

San Miguel de Lillo keeps the same hours as Santa María de Naranco (see above). Ask at the tourist office for its 45-minute walking tour from the center of Oviedo to the churches. Also check that the churches will be open at the time of your visit.

WHERE TO STAY

CLARÍN, Caveda, 23, 33002 Oviedo. Tel. 985/22-72-72. Fax 985/22-80-18. 47 rms (all with bath). MINIBAR TV TEL
$ Rates: 7,000 ptas. ($65.80) single; 9,000 ptas. ($84.60) double. Breakfast 475 ptas. ($4.45) extra. AE, MC, V.
This recently built modern hotel in the old quarter is noted for its tasteful decor, with comfortable, inviting, and well maintained rooms. On the premises you'll find a cozy and well-managed cafeteria, but no restaurant. The hotel stands right in the middle of the "monumental zone," within walking distance of many of the attractions.

HOTEL LA GRUTA, Alto de Buenavista, s/n, 33000 Oviedo. Tel. 985/23-24-50. Fax 985/25-31-41. 55 rms (all with bath). TV TEL
Bus: 1.
$ Rates: 6,000 ptas. ($56.40) single; 9,000 ptas. ($84.60) double. Breakfast 600 ptas. ($5.65) extra. AE, DC, MC, V.
In this family-run hotel just outside the city limits, the rooms are comfortably furnished, and many have views of the surrounding countryside. There's a restaurant on the premises.

HOTEL PRINCIPADO, San Francisco, 6, 33000 Oviedo. Tel. 985/21-77-92. Fax 985/21-39-46. 66 rms (all with bath). MINIBAR TV TEL
$ Rates: 7,000 ptas. ($65.80) single; 9,000 ptas. ($84.60) double. Breakfast 475 ptas. ($4.45) extra. AE, DC, MC, V.
The well-managed Principado stands opposite the university. Guests have access to an underground parking garage, easing the problem of parking in the center of town. Rooms are comfortably furnished and well maintained. The dining room serves nonguests as well as guests.

WHERE TO EAT

CASA PEÑAS, Melquiades Alvarez, 24. Tel. 22-03-20.
   Cuisine: ASTURIAN. **Reservations:** Not required.
$ **Prices:** Appetizers 450–950 ptas. ($4.25–$8.95); main dishes 1,200–1,900 ptas.
   ($11.30–$17.85). AE, DC, MC, V.
   Open: Daily 10am–midnight.
Considered the most atmospheric place in town, the Casa Peñas, near the train station, is one of the few fast-food places that attract the gastronomes of Oviedo. At the dining room in the rear, diners perch on high stools placed around wood tables. They can begin with tapas before going on to order a *plato del día* (plate of the day). Deli-type cold cuts are featured, including boiled pork shoulder, and the huge steaks are often served with a cheese sauce.

CASA CONRADO, Argüelles, 1. Tel. 22-39-19.
   Cuisine: ASTURIAN. **Reservations:** Required. **Bus:** 1.
$ **Prices:** Appetizers 850–1,200 ptas. ($8.95–$11.30); main dishes 1,400–2,000
   ptas. ($13.15–$18.80); fixed-priced menu 1,800 ptas. ($16.90). AE, DC, MC, V.
   Open: Lunch Mon–Sat 1–4pm; dinner Mon–Sat 9pm–midnight. **Closed:** Aug.
Almost as solidly established as the cathedral nearby, this restaurants offers Asturian stews, seafood platters, seafood soups, several preparations of hake, escalopes of veal with champagne, and a full range of desserts.

TRASCORRALES, Plaza Trascorrales, s/n. Tel. 22-24-41.
   Cuisine: ASTURIAN. **Reservations:** Required.
$ **Prices:** Appetizers 650–1,100 ptas. ($6.10–$10.35); main dishes 1,500–2,700
   ptas. ($14.10–$25.40). No credit cards.
   Open: Lunch daily 1–4pm; dinner daily 9pm–midnight.
The cuisine of Fernando Martín, the leading restaurateur of Oviedo, has introduced many new dishes to Oviedo. In spite of the innovations, however, none of the plates have lost their original Asturian base. Each dish is based on ingredients purchased at local markets. Try his gratinée of seafood, bull's-tail stew, or the most expensive item on the menu, bass baked in cider sauce. The orange ice cream makes a good dessert. This timbered building, draped in ivy, rises two floors. It lies in the west central part of town, 3 blocks south of the cathedral and 2 blocks west of the busy Avenida Padre Suárez.

CASA FERMÍN, San Francisco, 8. Tel. 21-64-97.
   Cuisine: ASTURIAN. **Reservations:** Recommended.
$ **Prices:** Appetizers 600–1,500 ptas. ($5.65–$14.10); main dishes 1,600–2,000
   ptas. ($15.05–$18.80). AE, MC, V.
   Open: Lunch Mon–Sat 1–4pm; dinner Mon–Sat 8:30–11:30pm.
The chef here prepares the best regional cuisine in town. To order its most classic dish, ask for *fabada asturiana,* a bean dish with Asturian black pudding and Avilés ham. A tasty hake cooked in cider is another suggestion. In season (October to March), venison is the specialty. Try also the traditional Cabrales cheese of the province. The Casa Fermín lies directly east of the Parque de San Francisco.

EL RAITAN, Trascorrales, 6. Tel. 21-42-18.
   Cuisine: ASTURIAN. **Reservations:** Recommended.
$ **Prices:** Fixed-priced menu 2,800 ptas. ($26.30).
   Open: Lunch Mon–Sat 2–5pm.
This lunch-only place south of the cathedral, serving a set menu, bases all its dishes on regional ingredients, with meals accompanied by wines from La Rioja. A large array of choices is available for each course. El Raitan is run by the leading restaurateur of Oviedo, Fernando Martín, who owns the more prestigious Trascorrales, which stands around the corner. Each day he presents nine classic regional dishes; these change with the season. The place has a tavern setting with overhead beams—atmospheric and intimate.

IN THE ENVIRONS

If you're driving to La Coruña and Santiago de Compostela, you may want to stop in the little town of Cornellana (Salas), 24 miles (39km) west of Oviedo on the route to Luarca.

HOTEL LA FUENTE, Carretera N-634, 33876 Cornellana. Tel. 985/83-40-42. 21 rms (9 with bath). **Directions:** Take the N-634 west to Cornellana.
$ Rates: 1,800 ptas. ($16.90) single without bath; 2,800 ptas. ($26.30) single with bath; 2,800 ptas. ($26.30) double without bath; 4,500 ptas. ($42.30) double with bath. Breakfast 225 ptas. ($2.10) extra. V.

⑤ This nice little inn, located on the N-634, has a sitting room on each floor as well as a bath. Bedrooms are simply furnished but comfortable. In the dining room overlooking the garden, you can order a *menú del día* for 950 pesetas ($8.95), including three courses of attractively served food, along with bread and wine.

---

11. LUARCA

332 miles N of Madrid, 140 miles E of La Coruña, 63 miles W of Oviedo.

GETTING THERE   By Bus   From Oviedo, 6 buses leave daily for Luarca (2½ hours).

By Car   Take the N-634 northwest to the coast, which you reach on the eastern outskirts of Luarca.

ESSENTIALS   The area code for Luarca is 985. The Tourist Information Office is at Plaza Alfonso X el Sabio (tel. 985/564-00-83).

The major port of eastern Asturias, Luarca makes a good center for exploring the "Green Coast." Constructed around an S-shaped cove amid sheer cliffs, the town is a dramatic sight just now beginning to awaken to its possibilities as a tourist destination. It lies at the mouth of the winding Negro River, spanned by seven bridges, and has a sheltered fishing harbor. At the far side of a high cliff is a beach, but you'll find far better sands elsewhere.

You can spend about 2 hours making your way through the **old quarter,** with its labyrinth of cobblestoned streets, stone-built steps, and *chigres* (old-fashioned Asturian taverns selling cider by the glass).

The architecture of the town, graced with many glassed-enclosed balconies, is somewhat ostentatious. Many of the houses were built with gold from the New World.

A lighthouse, church, and cemetery are clustered at the end of an estuary, occupying a headland where an old fort once guarded the harbor from attack by pirates. The cemetery contains grandiose family tombs and marble burial niches. The lighthouse still casts its beam into the night.

WHERE TO STAY

GAYOSO, Paseo Gómez, 4, 33700 Luarca. Tel. 985/64-00-50. 30 rms (all with bath). TEL
$ Rates: 6,500 ptas. ($61.10) single; 9,300 ptas. ($87.40) double. Breakfast 425 ptas. ($4) extra. MC, V. **Closed:** Nov to Apr.
This three-star hotel, established some 120 years ago, is still directed and maintained by the family who launched it. Lying very close to the beach, it is the best place to stay in Luarca, with comfortable, well-equipped rooms and prices that are reasonable for the coast. Scalloped wooden balconies grace the façade of this very atmospheric hotel.

WHERE TO EAT

CASA CONSUELO, Carretera Santander—La Coruña, km 317, Otur. Tel. 64-02-89.

Cuisine: ASTURIAN. **Reservations:** Recommended.

$ **Prices:** Appetizers 450–750 ptas. ($4.25–$7.05); main dishes 1,000–1,700 ptas. ($9.40–$16).

Open: Lunch Tues–Sun 12:30–4pm; dinner Tues–Sun 8pm–midnight. **Closed:** Sept 17 to Oct 9.

A generous and well-prepared cuisine is served here, and the raw ingredients that go into it are of good quality. The owners introduce new menu items each season. Typical dishes include monkfish stuffed with shellfish, a ragoût of fish roe, and a delectable pepper steak. This roadside dining tavern 4 miles (6.5km) west of town is well known throughout the area, and it's been in the same family for six generations. You can also rent one of their 26 comfortably furnished but simple bedrooms, costing from 3,800 pesetas ($35.70) for a single, rising to 5,000 pesetas ($47) for a double, with breakfast going for another 250 pesetas ($2.35).

LEONÉS, Alfonso X El Sabio, 1. Tel. 64-09-95.

Cuisine: ASTURIAN. **Reservations:** Recommended.

$ **Prices:** Appetizers 550–950 ptas. ($5.15–$8.95); main dishes 1,700–2,500 ptas. ($16–$23.50). AE, DC, MC, V.

Open: Lunch daily 1–4pm; dinner daily 7:30–11:30pm.

This is a cozy restaurant near the Plaza de la Feria, its interior decorated with wood paneling in a rustic tavern style. Wrought-iron chandeliers and farm artifacts add to the decor, a proper backdrop for the home-cooked Asturian meals served here. It's a favorite place with the locals: One couple "wouldn't think of dining anywhere else." Depending on availability at the market, a good selection of fish and meat dishes is presented. Almost everyone finishes off with the apple sherbet for dessert. If you're lunching light, try the garlic-flavored spinach and shrimp scrambled with eggs. Around the corner you'll find a second Leonés, this one at El Parque (tel. 64-00-54), with the same hours and prices. It is also furnished in a rustic style, with antiques as well as ox bells hanging from the walls.

GALICIA

Set atop Portugal in the northwest corner of Spain, Galicia is a rainswept land of green and granite, much of its coastline gouged out by fjord-like inlets. It is a land steeped in Celtic traditions, and in many areas its citizens, called *gallegos,* speak their own language, which they insist is not a dialect of Spanish, but a combination of Portuguese and Spanish. Often tossed by Atlantic storms, Galicia consists of four provinces: La Coruña (including Santiago de Compostela), Pontevedra, Lugo, and Orense.

The Romans, who arrived late, after having conquered practically everything else in Europe, made quite an impression on the monuments of the land. The Roman walls around the city of Lugo and the Tower of Hercules at La Coruña are part of their legacy. The Moors came this way too, and did a lot of damage along the way. But finding the natives none to friendly and other battlefields more promising, they moved on.

Nothing did more to put Galicia on the tourist map than the Santiago Road. It is the oldest, most traveled, and most famous route on the old continent. To guarantee their place in heaven, pilgrims journeyed to the tomb of Santiago (St. James), patron saint of Spain. They came across the Pyrénées by the thousands, risking their lives along the way. The Pilgrims' Way to Santiago led to the development and spreading of Romanesque art and architecture. The pilgrimage to the shrine lasted until medieval culture itself declined.

SEEING GALICIA

GETTING THERE

The quickest way to reach Galicia from Madrid is to **fly** to Labacolla Airport, east of Santiago de Compostela. Iberia offers daily flights from Madrid, and also from Bilbao and Barcelona. La Coruña Airport has only one flight a week to Madrid, so it is inconvenient for most schedules.

The **train** run from Madrid to Galicia takes from 8 to 12 hours, depending on the train and what part of Galicia you have selected as your gateway to the province. The most popular train runs to Santiago de Compostela and La Coruña. A third line runs to Vigo, a port in the south of Galicia, closer to the Portuguese frontier. The Expreso Nocturno contains sleepers.

Bus connections to Galicia are also possible from Madrid. ALSA, a private bus company, serves the route, with connections from Madrid to all the major cities, including La Coruña and Santiago de Compostela.

To reach Galicia by **car** from Madrid, take the N-VI all the way to La Coruña. If Santiago is your goal, you can cut south before entering La Coruña, taking the expressway highway, the A-9, into Santiago.

WHAT'S SPECIAL ABOUT GALICIA

Beaches
- ☐ La Toja's La Lanzada beach, semi-wild and 5 miles long.
- ☐ La Coruña's two beaches: Riazor in town and—even better—Santa Cristina, a few miles outside.

Great Towns
- ☐ Santiago de Compostela, goal of medieval pilgrims, legendary site of tomb of St. James.
- ☐ La Coruña, oldtime Atlantic seaport and embarkation site of Spain's Invincible Armada.

Great Cathedrals
- ☐ Cathedral at Santiago de Compostela, one of the Christian world's most important, with its celebrated Romanesque Pórtico de la Gloria.

Ancient Monuments
- ☐ Town walls of provincial capital of Lugo, encircling it since Roman times.

Scenic Drives
- ☐ Rías Bajas, the lower country of Galicia—deep inlets from Muros to La Toja.
- ☐ Rías Altas, north-country inlets from Ribadeo to La Coruña—miles and miles of corniche road scenery.
- ☐ Mirador de la Curota—at 1,634 feet, offering panoramic view of four inlets comprising Rías Bajas.

Historic Districts
- ☐ Old town of Santiago de Compostela, where the Middle Ages live on.

A SUGGESTED ROUTE

If you're touring the northern coast of Spain, you'll enter Galicia at the border town of Ribadeo.

Day 1   Take the corniche road along the northwestern coast, exploring the Rías Altas, or fjord district, of Galicia. Spend the night at La Coruña.

Day 2   After visiting the Tower of Hercules in the morning, continue south to Santiago de Compostela, the goal of the medieval pilgrim. Stay overnight there after visiting the old town and the cathedral.

Day 3   Drive to Pontevedra, a provincial capital, for the night, but take the detour along the *rías* of the Rías Bajas country, which many consider the most dramatic fjord scenery in Galicia.

Day 4   Leave Pontevedra after seeing its old quarter and drive south to Vigo to explore its old quarter and attractions before spending the night.

Day 5   Head inland from Vigo to Orense and visit its old quarter before continuing on to another provincial capital, Lugo, for the night. After a visit the next morning to its old Roman walls, you will find yourself on the national highway (N-VI) leading back to Madrid.

1. RIBADEO

366 miles N of Madrid, 97 miles E of La Coruña, 56 miles NE of Lugo

GETTING THERE   By Train   FEVE trains include Ribadeo on their slow route between Oviedo and EL Ferrol in the west.

By Bus   Good connections are possible, as two buses a day run between Oviedo in the east and La Coruña in the west.

By Car   Ribadeo is a stop on the main coastal route, the N-634, across the north of Spain.

ESSENTIALS   The area code for Ribadeo is 982. The Tourist Information Office is at Plaza de España (tel. 982/11-06-89).

On an estuary of the Eo River, the coastal resort of Ribadeo stands on the border between Asturias and Galicia. On the opposite bank lies the Asturian town of Castropol. On the Plaza Mayor is the **Ayuntamiento (Town Hall)**, a building from the 1700s where the count of Sargadelos once lived, a major personality in the Spanish Enlightenment.

The town's major attraction is the **Church of Santa Cruz**, offering a panoramic vista of the ría. It stands on a hill opening onto the estuary, a 1½-mile hike from town. A *romería*, a picniclike pilgrimage, takes place here on the first Sunday in August, with bagpipe music and much traditional dancing. You can take another 1½-mile hike to the lighthouse near the Playa de Roca Blancas, where you'll find a nice but tiny beach. Here you can watch fishermen bringing in their catch.

The landmark on the town skyline is the 1905 Torre de los Moreno, with a copper dome held up by four female figures. After seeing the few monuments, wander into the fishermen's barrio, site of all the *pulperías* (octopus bars), serving seafood *tapas* of octopus and plenty of good Galician wine.

WHERE TO STAY

EO, Avenida de Asturias, 5, 27700 Ribadeo. Tel. 982/11-07-50. 24 rms (all with bath). TEL
$ Rates: 5,500 ptas. ($51.70) single; 6,000 ptas. ($56.40) double. Breakfast 350 ptas. ($3.30). AE, DC, MC, V.
From many of its rooms, this well-run April-to-September hotel in the center of town offers vistas of the River Eo, from which it takes its name. In summer its swimming pool is filled with seawater. Rooms on the ground floor have pleasant terraces, and all the bedrooms are comfortably furnished. The hotel does not have a restaurant.

PARADOR DE RIBADEO, Amador Fernández, s/n. Tel. 982/11-08-25. Fax 981/11-03-46. 47 rms (all with bath). MINIBAR TV TEL
$ Rates: 7,800 ptas. ($73.30); 9,500 ptas. ($89.30) double. Breakfast 900 ptas. ($8.45) extra. AE, DC, MC, V.
This government-run parador in the center of town, with views over the Eo and the mountains beyond, is often filled with passengers arriving or departing on the Plymouth-to-Santander ferry. Not the best parador in Galicia, it is nevertheless immensely popular. Its appealing breakfast buffet rates as one of the best in the region. There's an acceptable restaurant, serving a full-course meal for 2,800 pesetas ($26.30); other facilities include a garden, swimming pool, and garage. Rooms are furnished in a lackluster modern style.

WHERE TO EAT

O'XARDIN, Reinante, 20. Tel. 11-02-22.
Cuisine: SEAFOOD. **Reservations:** None.
$ Prices: Appetizers 550–950 ptas. ($5.15–$8.95); main dishes 1,500–2,100 ptas. ($14.10–$19.75). DC, MC, V.
Open: Lunch daily noon–4pm; dinner daily 8pm–midnight. **Closed:** Feb.
This family-run restaurant, launched generations ago, is in fact owned by *two* families, who work hard to serve well-composed meals in a lovely garden. Inside, you'll find an old-fashioned place, with wall tiles and a bar covered with marble. Try

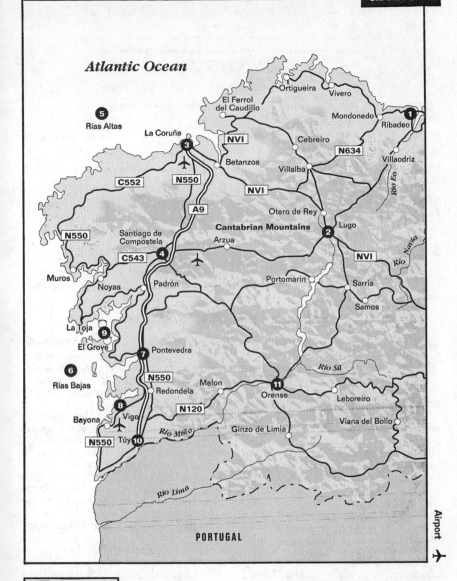

GALICIA

N

0 ┣━━━━┫ 15 mi
25.5 km

Atlantic Ocean

5 Rías Altas

La Coruña ✈ **3**

C552   **N550**

Betanzos

A9

N550

Santiago de Compostela

C543   **4**

Muros

Noyas

Padrón ✈

La Toja

9

El Grove

7 Pontevedra

6 Rías Bajas

N550

Redondela

8

Bayona ✈ Vigo

N550 Túy **10**

Río Miño

N120

Melon

Ginzo de Limia

Río Lima

PORTUGAL

El Ferrol del Caudillo

Ortigueira   Vivero

Mondonedo   Ribadeo **1**

Cebreiro   Villaodriz

N634

Villalba   *Río Eo*

Otero de Rey

Cantabrian Mountains

Arzua

Lugo **2**

Río Navia

NVI

Portomarin   Sarria

Samos

Río Sil

Orense **11**

Leboreiro

Viana del Bollo

NVI

NVI

Airport ✈

Galicia

★ Madrid

SPAIN

1 Ribadeo
2 Lugo
3 La Coruña
4 Santiago de Compostela
5 Rías Altas
6 Rías Bajas

7 Pontevedra
8 Vigo
9 El Grove & La Toja
10 Túy
11 Orense

the ragoût of mushrooms, the shrimp laced with saffron, the baked casserole of sole with oysters, or the fish stew.

2. LUGO

314 miles NW of Madrid; 60 miles SE of La Coruña

GETTING THERE   By Train   Lugo lies on the rail link with Madrid. Two trains a day arrive from La Coruña.

By Bus   Lugo has bus links with most of the major towns in the northwest, including Oviedo, 1 per day (5 hours), and Orense, 5 per day (2½ hours).

By Car   The N-VI connects Lugo with La Coruña as well as, at some distance, Madrid.

ESSENTIALS   The area code for Lugo is 982. The Tourist Information Office is at Plaza de España, 27 (tel. 982/23-13-61).

Lugo has known many conquerers. The former Celti-Iberian settlement fell to the Romans, and centuries later the Moors used the land and its people to grow crops for them. Today, Lugo is one of the four provincial capitals of Galicia. It is generally neglected by those taking the Pilgrims' Way to Santiago de Compostela. However, it makes a rewarding detour for a morning or afternoon of sightseeing.

WHAT TO SEE & DO

Lugo, split by the Miño River, is surrounded by a thick 1¼-mile **Roman wall,** the best preserved in the country. The wall is about 33 feet high and contains a total of 85 round towers; a sentry path can be approached by steps at the various town gates. Your best bet is to enter the old town at the Puerto de Santiago, the most interesting of the ancient gates, and begin a most impressive promenade— what may well be one of the highlights of your tour of Galicia.

Along the way you'll come to the **cathedral,** built in 1129 and notable for its trio of landmark towers. Standing at the Plaza Santa María, it has many Romanesque architectural features, such as its nave, but it was subsequently given a Gothic overlay. Further remodeling took place in the 18th century, when many features were added, such as the Chapel of the Wide-Eyed Virgin (Ojos Grandes) at the east end, with a baroque rotunda. The highlight of the cathedral is a 13th-century porch at the north end, which provides shelter for a Romanesque sculpted *Jesus Christ in His Majesty.* The figure rises over a capital and seems to hang in space. At the far end of the transept rise huge wood-built altarpieces in the Renaissance style.

As you wander about—and that is far preferable to going inside many monuments—you'll traverse the cobblestoned, colonnaded medieval streets and interesting squares of the old town, especially behind the cathedral. The 18th-century **Episcopal Palace**—called a *pazo* in Galicia—faces the north side of the cathedral and opens onto the Plaza Santa María. From the palace, old alleys behind it lead to a tiny nugget, the **Plaza del Campo,** one of the most charming squares of Lugo, flanked with ancient houses and graced with a fountain at its core.

Or from the bishop's palace at the Plaza Santa María, you can take the Calle Cantones to the Plaza de España, where you will be greeted with the **Ayuntamiento, (Town Hall),** built in a flowery rococo style.

From the Town Hall, follow the Calle de la Reina north to the **Iglesia de San Francisco,** a church said to have been founded by St. Francis upon his return from a pilgrimage west to the tomb of St. James. The cloister of the church, entered at the Plaza Soledad, has been turned into the **Museo Provincial.** Many artifacts, including sundials from Celtic and Roman days, are found in this museum, along with folkloric displays. It's open Monday through Friday from 9am to 1pm and 4 to 8pm. Admission is free.

WHERE TO STAY

PORTÓN DO RECANTO, La Campiña, 27923 Lugo. Tel. 982/22-34-55.
30 rms (all with bath). A/C TV TEL
$ Rates: 4,200 ptas. ($39.50) single; 5,500 ptas. ($51.70) double. Breakfast 300 ptas. ($2.80). DC, V.

⑤ If you're driving, this little hotel 2 miles (3.2km) north of town on the Carretera N-640 is one of your best bets, particularly if you're arriving from neighboring Asturias. The old building has a bit of charm, while the well-maintained bedrooms are filled with modern comforts. You can enjoy the scenery as you dine in the hotel restaurant, which serves regional fare; a complete meal costs 1,600 pesetas ($15.05).

MÉNDEZ NÚÑEZ, Reina, 1, 27002 Lugo. Tel. 982/23-07-11. 94 rms (all with bath). TEL
$ Rates: 5,500 ptas. ($51.70) single; 7,000 ptas. ($65.80) double. Breakfast 400 ptas. ($3.75) extra. No credit cards.

Just around the corner from the Plaza Mayor, this modern hotel rates as one of the best run in town. Owned by the same family since it was first established in 1888, it serves breakfast only; however, many restaurants and cafés are found within walking distance. It is convenient, too, for exploring the medieval streets of the old quarter. Rooms are well kept and comfortable.

WHERE TO EAT

CAMPOS, Rúa Nova, 4. Tel. 22-97-43.
Cuisine: GALICIAN. **Reservations:** Recommended.
$ Prices: Appetizers 550–950 ptas. ($5.15–$8.95); main dishes 1,200–2,700 ptas. ($11.30–$25.40); fixed-priced menu 1,400 ptas. ($13.15). AE, DC, MC, V.
Open: Lunch daily noon–4:30pm; dinner daily 8pm–midnight.

In the old quarter, immediately adjacent to the Plaza del Campo, this well-acclaimed restaurant is the creation of Amparo Yañez and his son, Manuel. Together, they offer imaginative combinations of fresh ingredients that are deftly prepared and much appreciated by their loyal clients. Seasonal game dishes, especially local pheasant, are featured along with fresh fish, such as grouper served with almonds. The best dessert is fresh local strawberries with honey and cream.

MESÓN DE ALBERTO, Cruz, 4. Tel. 22-83-10.
Cuisine: GALICIAN. **Reservations:** Recommended.
$ Prices: Appetizers 550–750 ptas. ($5.15–$7.05); main dishes 1,350–1,900 ptas. ($12.70–$17.85); fixed-priced menu 1,750 ptas. ($16.45). AE, DC, MC, V.
Open: Lunch Mon–Sat 1–4pm; dinner Mon–Sat 8pm–midnight.

Alberto García is the culinary star of Lugo, and with good reason. Ably assisted by his wife, Flor, he offers a well-chosen menu of imaginative fish and meat dishes and perhaps the best wine cellar in Lugo. The style of the place is that of a rustic tavern: a stand-up bar serving tapas, plus a handful of dining tables. The overflow is directed either to a somewhat more formal dining room beside the tavern or to the second floor. Try Alberto's salad with eel and an exotic vinegar, monkfish served with a mountain cheese (Cabrales from Asturias), or beefsteak for two, prepared with his "secret" sauce. The Mesón de Alberto stands 1 block north of the cathedral in the old quarter.

FERREIROS, Rúa Nueva, 1. Tel. 22-97-28.
Cuisine: GALICIAN. **Reservations:** Recommended.
$ Prices: Appetizers 650–950 ptas. ($6.10–$8.95); main dishes 1,500–2,100 ptas. ($14.10–$19.75); *menú clásico* 2,800 ptas. ($26.30). V.
Open: Lunch Thurs–Tues 1–5pm; dinner Thurs–Tues 7:30pm–midnight.

In business since the 1920s, this long-time favorite near the cathedral must be doing something right. In fact, it offers well-prepared and old-fashioned regional fare with a certain unpretentious flair. Portions are generous, and the food is fresh. The many shellfish dishes featured are the most expensive items on the menu. You can also order a big slab of rib or beef or else monkfish prepared in different ways.

---

3. LA CORUÑA

375 miles NW of Madrid, 96 miles N of Vigo.

GETTING THERE By Air   There is 1 flight a week from Madrid to La Coruña Airport.

By Train   From Madrid (via Orense and Zamora), there is twice-daily express service.

By Bus   From Santiago, there's frequent daily bus service leaving from the station on the Calle Caballeros (tel. 23-96-44). Four buses a day connect Madrid and La Coruña (9 hours).

By Car   La Coruña is reached from Madrid by the N-VI. You can also follow the coastal highway, the N-634, which runs all the way across the northern rim of Spain from San Sebastián in the east.

ESSENTIALS   The area code for La Coruña is 981. The Tourist Information Office is at Dársena de la Marina (tel. 981/22-18-22).

Despite the fact that La Coruña (Corunna in English and A Coruña in Galician) is an ancient city, it does not have a wealth of historical and architectural monuments. Celts, Phoenicians, and Romans all occupied the port, and it is another of the legendary cities that claims Hercules as its founder.

The great event in the history of La Coruña occurred in 1588, when Philip II's Invincible Armada sailed from here to England. Only half of the ships eventually got back to Spain. The following year, Sir Francis Drake and his ships attacked the port in reprisal.

WHAT TO SEE & DO

La Coruña's old town is ideal for strolling around and stopping at any of the historic churches and mansions. The **Plaza de María Pita**—named after the 16th-century Spanish Joan of Arc—divides the old town from the new. María Pita was a La Coruña housewife who is said to have spotted the approach of Drake's troops. Risking her own life, she fired a cannon shot to alert the citizens to an imminent invasion. For that act of heroism, she is revered to this day. Drake, on the other hand, is still a hated name in these parts.

You can take a pleasant stroll through the Jardines Méndez Núñez, lying between the harbor and Los Cantones (Cantón Grande and Cantón Pequeño). Facing the police station and overlooking the port, the gardens are in the very center of town and make for a restful interlude during your sightseeing.

The cobbled **Plazuela de Santa Bárbara** also merits a visit—a tiny tree-shaded plaza, flanked by old houses and the high walls of the Santa Barbara convent.

The **Jardín de San Carlos,** reached along the Paseo del Parrote, dates from 1843 and lies near the Casa de la Cultura. This garden grew up on the site of an old fortress that once guarded the harbor. It contains the tomb of General Sir John Moore, who fought unsuccessfully against the troops of Napoleon. He retreated with his British forces to La Coruña, where he was shot in a final battle. These gardens are an ideal picnic spot.

The city's major monument is the **Torre de Hércules,** a lighthouse more than a mile from the center of La Coruña. It overlooks the city and the sea, and was supposedly built by the emperor Trajan (restored in the 1700s). Admission to the tower (tel. 22-20-38) is free, and it's open daily from 10am to 1:30pm and 4 to 7:30pm. Take bus 9 or 13.

The **Iglesia de Santa María del Campo,** Calle de Santa María, is a church with an elaborately carved west door from the 13th century—modeled in the traditional Romanesque-Gothic style. Beneath its rose window you'll see a Gothic portal from the 13th or 14th century. The tympanum is carved with a scene depicting the Adoration of the Magi.

The Castillo de San Antón, a 16th-century fort is now the **Museo Arqueológico** (tel. 20-59-94), standing out in the bay on the southeast side of the peninsula. It is open June to September, daily from 10am to 2pm and 4 to 8pm. From October to May, hours are 10am to 2pm. Admission is 200 pesetas ($1.90). In addition to having a spectacular location on its own islet, it displays many unusual artifacts from La Coruña province.

The second-largest port in Spain, La Coruña is also a popular vacation resort, so it gets really crowded in July and August. Riazor Beach, right in town, is a good, fairly wide beach, but the best one is Santa Cristina, about 3 miles (4.8km) outside town. There's regular round-trip bus service. The best way to go, however, is via the steamer that plies the bay.

WHERE TO STAY

ALMIRANTE, Paseo de Ronda, 54, 15011 La Coruña. Tel. 981/25-96-00. 20 rms (all with bath). TV TEL **Bus:** 7, 14, or 19.
$ Rates: 4,200 ptas. ($39.50) double. Breakfast 325 ptas. ($3.05) extra. V.
There are few extra amenities here—just good, clean rooms, all doubles, at a real bargain price. There is no restaurant, but a continental breakfast will be served on order.

HOSTAL RESIDENCIA NAVARRA, Plaza de Lugo, 23, 15004 La Coruña. Tel. 981/22-54-00. 24 rms (12 with bath). TEL
$ Rates: 2,500 ptas. ($23.50) single without bath, 3,300 ptas. ($31) single with bath; 3,500 ptas. ($32.90) double without bath, 4,500 ptas. ($42.30) double with bath.

⑤ Welcoming and inexpensive, this family-run hotel just 5 minutes from the Playa Riazor is scattered over three floors of a modern apartment building in the commercial center of town. Its rooms are basic, but clean and comfortable. No breakfast is served, but many cafés are nearby.

HOTEL ESPAÑA, Juana de Vega, 7, 15004 La Coruña. Tel. 981/22-45-06. 84 rms (all with bath). TEL
$ Rates: 4,200 ptas. ($39.50) single; 6,000 ptas. ($56.40) double. Breakfast 325 ptas. ($3.05) extra. AE, DC, MC, V.

⑤ This pleasant hotel, just a few steps from the gazebos and roses of the Jardines de Méndez Núñez, has a narrow reception area, a comfortable series of long sitting rooms, and modern, simply furnished bedrooms. Breakfast is the only meal served.

RESIDENCIA RIAZOR, Avenida Barrie de la Maza, 29, 15004 La Coruña. Tel. 981/25-34-00. Fax 981/25-34-04. 176 rms (all with bath). TV TEL **Bus:** 5, 20, or 22.
$ Rates: 5,500 ptas. ($51.70) single; 8,000 ptas. ($75.20) double. Breakfast 400 ptas. ($3.75) extra. AE, DC, MC, V.
This 12-story modern hotel is right on the beach. It has a glass-enclosed lounge on the second floor and a snack bar–cafeteria. Rooms are functional and lack style, but they are clean and comfortable.

CIUDAD DE LA CORUÑA, Ciudad Residencial La Torre, s/n, 15002 La Coruña. Tel. 981/21-11-00. Fax 981/22-46-10. 131 rms (all with bath). A/C MINIBAR TV TEL **Bus:** 7, 13, or 14.

$ Rates: 7,000 ptas. ($65.80) single; 9,000 ptas. ($84.60) double. Breakfast 550 ptas. ($5.15) extra. AE, DC, MC, V.

On the northwestern tip of the peninsula, surrounded by sea grasses and dunes, this three-star establishment is cordoned off from the apartment-house complexes that surround it by a wide swath of green. Built in the early 1980s, the hotel features a swimming pool, a big-windowed bar, and a ground-floor restaurant. Each of the attractively modern bedrooms contains a kitchenette.

HOTEL ATLÁNTICO, Jardines de Méndez Núñez, s/n, 15006 La Coruña. Tel. 981/22-65-00. Fax 981/20-10-71. 200 rms (all with bath). TV TEL
$ Rates: 8,500 ptas. ($79.90) single; 10,500 ptas. ($98.70) double. Breakfast 500 ptas. ($4.70) extra. AE, DC, MC, V.

This convenient, comfortable hotel with a contemporary design contrasts with the lavishly ornate 19th-century park surrounding it. Crowds of Galicians promenade here in fine weather. The Atlantico is in the building that also houses the city's casino, a modern restaurant, and a disco. Bedrooms are well furnished, among the best in town.

WHERE TO EAT

Two or so blocks from the waterfront, there are several restaurants that specialize in Galician cuisine. It is customary to go window shopping for food here. The restaurants along two of the principal streets—the Calle de la Estrella and the Calle de los Olmos—have display counters in front of their establishments. Most of them charge comparable prices.

NAVEIRO, San Andrés, 129. Tel. 22-90-24.
   Cuisine: GALICIAN. **Reservations:** Recommended.
$ Prices: Appetizers 650–950 ptas. ($6.10–$8.95); main dishes 950–1,800 ptas. ($8.95–$16.90). No credit cards.
   Open: Lunch daily 12:30–4pm; dinner Mon–Sat 9–11:30pm. **Closed:** May 15 to June 15.

An easy walk from the Playa del Orzán in the center of town, Naveiro is perhaps the most typically Galician restaurant in the port. It offers inexpensive and tasty specialties, such as the classic green-and-white soup of the northwest known as *caldo gallego* (potatoes and greens). Hake is also available, prepared with peppers and potatoes. Spider crabs and oysters are other popular dishes, with octopus and red mullet occasionally featured. You'll also find beefsteak on the menu.

PIL-PIL, Paralela a Orillamar, s/n. Tel. 21-27-12.
   Cuisine: GALICIAN. **Reservations:** Recommended.
$ Prices: Appetizers 650–850 ptas. ($6.10–$8); main dishes 950–1,700 ptas. ($8.95–$16); fixed-priced menu 1,400 ptas. ($13.15). No credit cards.
   Open: Lunch Mon–Sat 1–4:30pm; dinner Mon–Sat 8pm–12:30am. **Closed:** Sept 15 to Oct 15.

In spite of its size, this small tavern has a fine culinary tradition and serves many elegant wines that are moderate in price. Host Luis Moya purchases fresh ingredients, often seafood, and handles them deftly in the kitchen. Try a clam omelet as an appetizer, followed by one of the main courses, perhaps grilled fish, concluding with a velvety-smooth chocolate mousse. The place is on the road leading to the Torre de Hércules.

EL CORAL, Estrella, 2. Tel. 22-10-82.
   Cuisine: GALICIAN. **Reservations:** Recommended. **Bus:** 1, 2, 5, or 17.
$ Prices: Appetizers 1,000–2,000 ptas. ($9.40–$18.80); main dishes 1,500–2,500 ptas. ($14.10–$23.50); fixed-priced menu 2,900 ptas. ($27.25). AE, DC, MC, V.
   Open: Lunch daily 1–4pm; dinner daily 9pm–midnight. **Closed:** Sun night in winter.

This is my favorite and one of the most popular dining spots at the port. In business since 1954, it offers polite service, cleanliness, and Galician cookery prepared with distinction. This two-fork restaurant specializes in shellfish, fish, meats, and Galician wines. The chef's specialty is *turbante de mariscos* (shellfish). You might also try the *calamares rellenos* (stuffed squid). A popular main course is *lubina* (sea bass) *al horno,* and the dessert specialty is a rich and fattening *filloas.* A pitcher (1 liter) of Ribero wine makes a good choice, and you can also order Condados and Ríoja wines.

4. SANTIAGO DE COMPOSTELA

391 miles NW of Madrid, 46 miles S of La Coruña

GETTING THERE **By Air** From Madrid, Iberia has daily flights to Santiago, and there are also daily flights from Barcelona. The only international airport in Galicia is east of Santiago de Compostela at Labacolla (tel. 981/59-44-62 for flight information).

By Train From La Coruña, there are 11 daily trains (2 hour). Three daily trains arrive from Madrid (8 to 12 hours, depending on the train).

By Bus Buses leave on the hour, connecting La Coruña with Santiago. Two buses arrive in Santiago daily from Madrid (10½ hours).

By Car Take the expressway highway (A-9/E-50) south from La Coruña to reach Santiago. From Madrid, the N-VI runs to Galicia. From Lugo, head south along the N-640.

ESSENTIALS The area code for Santiago de Compostela is 981. The Tourist Information Office is at Rúa del Villar, 43 (tel. 981/58-40-81).

All roads in Spain used to lead to this northwestern pilgrimage city. In addition to being the third-largest holy city of the Christian world, Santiago de Compostela is both a university town and a marketplace for Galician farmers.

But it was the pilgrims who made the city famous. A pilgrimage to the tomb of the beheaded apostle, St. James, was a high point for the faithful—peasant and prince alike—who journeyed here from all over Europe, often under difficult, sometimes life-threatening conditions.

Santiago de Compostela's link with legend began in A.D. 813, when an urn was discovered containing, it was believed, the remains of St. James. A temple was erected over the spot, but the poor saint wasn't allowed to remain in peace. Wars, a long and mysterious disappearance, and an equally mysterious "rediscovery" followed.

Aside from its religious connections, Santiago de Compostela, with its flagstoned streets, churches, and shrines, is one of the most romantic and historic of Spain's great cities and has been declared a national landmark. It also has the dubious distinction of being the rainiest city in Spain, but the showers tend to arrive and end suddenly. Locals claim that the rain only makes their city more beautiful.

WHAT TO SEE & DO

The highlight at Santiago de Compostela is undoubtedly the cathedral, and you should take at least two hours to see it. Afterward, take a stroll through this enchanting town, which has a number of other interesting monuments as well as many stately mansions along the Rúa de Villar and the Rúa Nueva.

⭐ The **cathedral,** Plaza del Obradoiro (tel. 58-35-48), begun in the 11th century, is thought by some to be the crowning achievement of Spanish Romanesque, even though it actually reflects a number of styles. Some of the architecture is spectacular. The Pórtico de la Gloria, carved by Mateo in the late 12th century, ranks among the finest produced in Europe at that time; the altar, with its blend of Gothic simplicity and baroque decor, is also extraordinary. The floor plan of the cathedral resembles a cross. It has three naves and several chapels and cloisters. You can visit the crypt, where a silver urn contains what are believed to be the remains of the Apostle St. James. A cathedral museum displays tapestries and archeological fragments. Next door, the **Palacio de Gelmírez,** an archbishop's palace built during the 12th century, is another outstanding example of Romanesque architecture. Admission to the cathedral is free; to the cloisters, 200 ptas. ($1.90); to the Palacio de Gelmírez, 100 ptas. (90¢). Hours are: cathedral, daily 10am–1:30pm and 4–7:30pm; museum, daily 10:30am–1:30pm and 4–6pm; Palacio de Gelmirez, July–Sept, daily 10:30am–1:30pm and 4–7pm.

Most of the other impressive buildings are also on the Plaza del Obradoiro, also called the Plaza de España. Next door to the cathedral is **Los Reyes Católicos,** now a parador (see "Where to Stay," below), formerly a royal hospital and, in the 15th century, a pilgrims' hospital. It was designed by Enrique de Egas, Isabella and Ferdinand's favorite architect. Tours (daily from 10am to 1pm and 4 to 7pm; tel. 58-22-00 for information) visit the cloistered courtyard with its beautiful 16th- to 18th-century fountains and the main chapel with its beamed ceiling.

The **Monasterio de San Martín Pinario,** Plaza de la Inmaculada, founded in 899 by monks and rebuilt in the 17th century, remains one of the most important monasteries in Galicia. Its large façade was built in the Compostela baroque style, with massive Doric columns. The interior has a richly ornamented Churrigueresque high altar and choir stalls that are truly works of art.

One of the most important squares in the old town is the **Plaza de la Quintana,** to the left of the cathedral's Goldsmith's Doorway. This is a favorite square with students, who often perch on the flight of broad steps that connect the rear of the cathedral to the walls of a convent. The square is dominated by the **Casa de la Canónica,** the former residence of the canon, which has wrought-iron window bars, lending it a rather severe appearance.

South of the square is the Renaissance-style **Plaza de las Platerías (Silversmiths' Square),** which has an elaborate fountain.

Farther afield, visit the Romanesque **Santa María del Sar,** on the Calle Castron d'Ouro, half a mile down the Calle de Sar, which starts at the Patio de Madre. This collegiate church is considered one of the architectural gems of the Romanesque style in Galicia. Its walls and columns are on a 15-degree slant, thought to be attributable to either a fragile foundation or an architect's fancy. Visit the charming cloister with its slender columns. The church is open Monday through Saturday from 10am to 1pm and 4 to 6:30pm. Admission is 50 ptas. (45¢).

Finally, cap off your day with a walk along the **Paseo de la Herradura,** the gardens southwest of the old town, from where you'll have a magnificent view of the cathedral and the old city.

WHERE TO STAY

DOUBLES FOR LESS THAN 9,500 PTAS. [$89.30]

HOSTAL RESIDENCIA ALAMEDA, San Clemente 32, 15705 Santiago de Compostela. Tel. 981/58-81-00. 20 rms (14 with bath). TV TEL

$ Rates: 2,000 ptas. ($18.80) single without bath; 2,800 ptas. ($26.30) single with bath; 3,800 ptas. ($35.70) double without bath, 4,800 ptas. ($45.10) double with bath. Breakfast 275 ptas. ($2.60) extra. AE, MC, V.

⑤ Located on the second floor of a building in the cathedral district, the Alameda has comfortable, immaculate rooms. The staff here is courteous and efficient. Ample parking is available, adjacent to the *hostal.* The Alameda serves reasonably priced luncheons and dinner Monday through Saturday for 1,200 pesetas ($11.30).

HOTEL MAYCAR, Doctor Teijeiro, 15, 15701 Santiago de Compostela. Tel. 981/56-34-44. 40 rms (all with bath). TEL **Bus:** 10 from train station.

$ Rates: 3,000 ptas. ($28.20) single, 4,800 ptas. ($45.10) double. Breakfast 250 ptas. ($2.35) extra. No credit cards.

This simple two-star hotel stands not far from the busy central Plaza de Galicia. The marble-trimmed lobby is unpretentious, and there is an elevator. The rooms are well-maintained but Spartan. Breakfast only.

HOTEL UNIVERSAL, Plaza de Galicia, 2, 15706 Santiago de Compostela. Tel. 981/58-58-00. 54 rms (all with bath). TEL
$ Rates: 3,000 ptas. ($28.20) single; 4,800 ptas. ($45.10) double. Breakfast 250 ptas. ($2.35) extra. AE, DC, MC, V.

Located south of the Fuente de San Antonio, just outside the center of the city, this is a pleasant and comfortable hotel despite its drab concrete façade. It has a modernized lobby, and there is a TV lounge on the premises. Rooms are furnished in a simple modern style. Breakfast only.

HOTEL GELMÍREZ, Hórreo, 92, 15702 Santiago de Compostela. Tel. 981/56-11-00. Fax 981/56-32-69. 138 rms (all with bath). TV TEL
$ Rates: 5,000 ptas. ($47) single; 7,000 ptas. ($65.80) double. Breakfast 350 ptas. ($3.30) extra. AE, DC, MC, V.

This soaring concrete structure near the train station is one of the largest hotels in the region. Built in the early 1970s, it has a comfortable and pleasant interior far more attractive than its plain façade suggests. On the premises are a café/bar and a dining room. Rooms are furnished in a functional modern style.

HOTEL COMPOSTELA, Hórreo, 1, 15702 Santiago de Compostela. Tel. 981/58-57-00. Fax 981/56-32-69. 100 rms (all with bath). MINIBAR TV TEL
$ Rates: 5,800 ptas. ($54.50) single; 9,500 ptas. ($89.30) double. Breakfast 450 ptas. ($4.25) extra. AE, DC, MC, V.

This hotel is conveniently located just a few short blocks from the cathedral, but it is also, unfortunately, close to the heavily trafficked city center. It has a grand granite façade, which belies the modern interior and bedrooms filled with clean, angular, machine-made furniture. A pleasant dining room and a café/bar are on the premises.

HOTEL DEL PEREGRINO, Avenida Rosalía de Castro, s/n, 15706 Santiago de Compostela. Tel. 981/59-18-50. Fax 981/59-67-77. 148 rms (all with bath). MINIBAR TV TEL **Bus:** 1 or 2.
$ Rates: 7,300 ptas. ($68.60) single; 10,500 ptas. ($98.70) double. Breakfast 675 ptas. ($6.35) extra. AE, DC, MC, V.

This four-star hotel at the edge of town off the main road is preferred by many people traveling to this remote part of Spain. It has a good restaurant, a bar and snack bar, and a rear garden with a swimming pool. The decor is restrained and tasteful; the bedrooms are modern and well furnished.

WORTH THE EXTRA BUCKS

HOSTAL DE LOS REYES CATÓLICOS, Plaza de España, 1, 15705 Santiago de Compostela. Tel. 981/58-22-00. Fax 981/56-30-94. 150 rms (all with bath). MINIBAR TV TEL
$ Rates: 14,200 ptas. ($133.50) single; 18,000 ptas. ($169.20) double. Breakfast 900 ptas. ($8.45) extra. AE, DC, MC, V.

This former 16th-century hospital, founded by Ferdinand and Isabella, has been turned into one of the most spectacular hotels in Europe. Next to the cathedral, it also served as a hospital and resting place for pilgrims visiting the tomb of St. James. Even if you don't stay here, you should stop in and see it, but only on a guided tour (see above).

The hotel has four huge open-air courtyards, each with its own covered walk, trees, gardens, and fountains. In addition, there are chapels, libraries, great halls, French grillwork, copies of paintings by Goya and El Greco, and a large collection of antiques. The Gothic chapel is the setting for weekly concerts.

There is a full range of accommodations, everything from Franco's former suite to monklike dormitories. Many of the palatial suites have ornate canopied beds draped in embroidered red velvet; hand-carved chests, gilt mirrors, and oil paintings enhance the air of luxury. A meal in the hostal's dining room goes for 3,000 pesetas ($28.20).

WHERE TO EAT

ALAMEDA, Puerta Fajera, 15. Tel. 58-66-57.
Cuisine: GALICIAN. **Reservations:** Recommended in summer.
$ Prices: Appetizers 450–1,000 ptas. ($4.25–$9.40); main dishes 1,500–2,200 ptas. ($14.10–$20.70); fixed-priced menu 1,600 ptas. ($15.05). AE, DC, MC, V.
Open: Lunch daily 1–4:30pm; dinner daily 8pm–12:30am.

⑤ The constant stream of diners, both foreign and local, indicates the popularity of this government-rated two-fork restaurant, located opposite a charming park. There is a stylish cafeteria/snack bar on the ground floor, handy for light meals and drinks; guests can sit at sidewalk tables in fair weather. Food includes many Galician specialties, and the chef is noted for his paella. Start with the caldo gallego (Galician soup) and follow with another regional specialty, *lacón con grelos* (hamhock with greens). The *necoras* (spider crabs) are also a real gourmet delight.

LA TACITA DE ORO, General Franco, 31. Tel. 56-32-55.
Cuisine: GALICIAN. **Reservations:** Recommended.
$ Prices: Appetizers 450–950 ptas. ($4.25–$8.95); main dishes 1,500–2,000 ptas. ($14.10–$18.80); fixed-priced menu 1,600 ptas. ($15.05). AE, DC, MC, V.
Open: Lunch Mon–Sat 12:30–4pm; dinner Mon–Sat 8pm–midnight. **Closed:** Dec.

A favorite place for business lunches, 5 minutes from the train station, this restaurant offers caldo gallego, fish soup, artichokes with ham, Basque-style eels, shellfish cocktail, and a wide array of fish platters. Two special meat courses: hamhock with greens and *fabada asturiana,* the famous stew of Asturias. Portions are generous, and service is attentive.

ANEXO VILAS, Avenida Villagarcía, 21. Tel. 59-83-87.
Cuisine: GALICIAN. **Reservations:** Required.
$ Prices: Appetizers 550–950 ptas. ($5.15–$8.95); main dishes 1,900–2,700 ptas. ($17.85–$25.40). AE, DC, MC, V.
Open: Lunch Tues–Sun 1–4pm; dinner Tues–Sun 8:30pm–midnight.

Although this restaurant is located at the edge of the old quarter, on a drab street off the Avenida de Donallo Romero, it's worth seeking out. It looks like a country tavern, and in fact, the *tasca* in front is one of the most popular in the area, especially with locals. It's a family-run place with conscientious service. A few of the Galician dishes served here are based on meat (the filet of beef with a sherry sauce is especially good), but the real specialties are seafood creations, such as fish soup, hake, and grilled shrimp.

RESTAURANT VILAS, Rosalía de Castro, 88. Tel. 59-10-00.
Cuisine: SEAFOOD. **Reservations:** Required.
$ Prices: Appetizers 900–1,800 ptas. ($8.45–$16.90); main dishes 2,000–3,000 ptas. ($18.80–$28.20). AE, DC, MC, V.
Open: Lunch daily 1–4pm; dinner Mon–Sat 8:30pm–midnight.

Located on the outskirts of the old town on the road to Pontevedra, this reliable Spanish tavern, housed in a three-story townhouse, has a devoted clientele, many from industry, politics, and the arts. Beyond the large bar near the entrance and display cases filled with fresh fish, you'll find the baronial stone-trimmed dining room. A wide variety of fish is available—fresh sardines, three different preparations of salmon, a *zarzuela* (seafood stew), and eels. Two different kinds of paella are served, and nonfish dishes such as partridge and rabbit also grace the menu. The restaurant was founded in 1915 as a little eating house. Back then, it was on the outskirts of town, but the place was enveloped by the city long ago. It stands on a street named after the illustrious poetess of Galicia. Today, the restaurant is run by the grandsons of the original founders.

5. RÍAS ALTAS

In Norway they're called fjords; in Brittany, *abers;* in Scotland, lochs; and in Galicia, *rías.* These are inlets cut into the Galician coastline by the turbulent Atlantic pounding against its shores. Rías Altas is a relatively modern name applied to all the estuaries on the northern Galicia coast, from Ribadeo (our gateway to Galicia on the border with Asturias) to La Coruña, the big Atlantic seaport of northwest Spain. The part that begins as Ribadeo—part of Lugo province—is also called Mariña Lucense. Four estuaries form the Artabro Gulf: La Coruña, Betanzoa, Ares, and Ferrol. All four converge on a single point where Marola crag rises.

FROM RIBADEO TO LA CORUÑA

150 miles; 4 hours minimum

From Ribadeo, take the corniche road west (N-634) until you reach the Ría de Foz. About 1½ miles (2.5km) south of the Foz–Barreiros highway, perched somewhat in isolation on a hill, stands the Iglesia de San Martín de Mondoñeda, part of a monastery that dates from 1112.

The little town of **Foz** itself is a fishing village and also a summer beach resort. Its beaches are separated by a cliff. You might stop here for lunch.

From Foz cut northwest along the coastal highway (C-642) going through **Burela,** another fishing village. You can make a slight detour south to **Sargadelos,** which is a ceramics center. You can purchase these famous Galician products here much more cheaply than elsewhere in Spain.

Back on the coastal road at Burela, continue west approaching Ría de Vivero and the historic village of **Vivero.** Part of its medieval walls and an old gate, the Puerta de Carlos V, have been preserved. The town has many old churches of interest, including the Gothic-style Iglesia San Francisco. Vivero is also a summer resort, attracting vacationers to its beach, the Playa Covas. Vivero also makes a good lunch stop.

The road continues northwest to **Vicedo,** passing such beaches as Xillo and Aerealong. Excellent vistas of the estuary greet you. Oxen can be seen plowing the cornfields.

Driving on, you'll notice the coastline becoming more sawtoothed. Eventually you reach **Ortigueira,** a major fishing village at the head of the ría from which it takes its name. A Celtic Folk Festival is staged here at the end of August.

From here you can continue south along the C-642 to **El Ferrol,** which used to be called El Caudillo, in honor of the late dictator, Francisco Franco, who was born here and who used to spend part of his summers in this area. El Ferrol is one of the major shipbuilding centers of Spain, and since the 18th century has also been a center of the Spanish navy. It's a grimy town, but it lies on one of the most beautiful rías. In spite of its parador, few tourists will want to linger at El Ferrol (also spelled O Ferrol).

From El Ferrol, the road continues south, passing through the small town of **Puentedeume** (also spelled Pontedeume), on the Rías Ares. Historically, it was the center of the counts of Andrade. The last remains of their 14th-century palace can be seen, along with the ruins of a 13th-century castle rising to the east.

Shortly below Betanzos, head west along the N-VI until you reach La Coruña.

WHERE TO EAT

NITO, Playa de Area, Vivero. Tel. 56-09-87.
   Cuisine: SEAFOOD. **Reservations:** Recommended.
$ Prices: Appetizers 350–950 ptas. ($3.30–$8.95); main dishes 1,400–2,200 ptas. ($13.15–$20.70); fixed-priced menu 2,200 ptas. ($20.70). AE, MC, V.
   Open: Lunch daily 1:15–4pm; dinner daily 8:30pm–midnight. **Closed:** Sun night in winter.
The decor here is simple, the better to allow visitors to enjoy the view overlooking the

sea. The restaurant maintains a balance between prices and the quality of its ingredients, and you get unpretentious but flavorful food. Shellfish, priced according to weight, is the specialty, but you can also order grilled sea bream, perhaps a house-style beefsteak. A full range of wines is also offered. Diners wishing to eat outside can sit on a garden-view terrace.

FROM LA CORUÑA TO CAPE FISTERRA

90 miles; 3 hours minimum

This next drive—called "to the end of the world"—takes you from La Coruña to Cape Fisterra (called Cabo Fisterra on most maps). For the ancients, Cape Fisterra was the end of the world as they knew it.

This route takes you along **A Costa da Morte** (also called La Costa de la Muerte—The Coast of Death), so called because of the numerous shipwrecks that occurred here.

Leaving La Coruña, take the coastal road west, heading first to the road junction of **Carballo,** a distance of 22 miles (35.5km). From this little town, many of the small coastal harbors will be within an easy drive. **Malpica,** to the northwest, is the most interesting, with its own beach. An offshore seabird sanctuary exists there, and Malpica itself was a former whaling port. From Malpica, continue to the tiny village of **Corme** at Punta Roncudo. This sheltered fishing village draws the summer beach fans, as there are many isolated sand dunes.

From Corme, continue along the circuitous roads to the whitewashed village of **Camariñas,** which stands on the ría of the same name. A road here leads all the way to the lighthouse at Cabo Vilán. Camariñas is known as a village of expert lacemakers, and you'll see the work for sale at many places.

The road now leads to **Mugia,** below which stands the lighthouse at Cabo Touriñan. Continue south to **Corcubion,** a village with a Romanesque church. From here, continue to the "end of the line," **Cabo Fisterra,** for a spectacular view. The sunsets from here are said to be among the most spectacular in the world. The Roman poet Horace said it all: "The brilliant skylight of the sun drags behind it the black night over the fruitful breasts of earth."

---

6. RÍAS BAJAS

⭐ From Cabo Fisterra you can continue south along the C-550 through Muros and Noya to the ✪ Rías Bajas, the four large estuaries facing the Atlantic from Cape Silleiro to Baiona to Point Louro in Muros. Two of these are in the province of Pontevedra, (Pontevedra and Vigo); one is in the province of La Coruña (Muros and Noya); and one (Arousa) divides its shores between the two provinces. The 20-mile Vigo estuary is the longest, stretching from *Ponte Sampasio* to Baiona.

FROM MUROS TO RIBEIRA

45 miles; 2½ miles

The seaside town of **Muros** has many old houses and a harbor, but **Noya** (also spelled Noia), to the southeast, is more impressive. If you don't have a car but would like to see at least one or two ría fishing villages, you can do so at either Noya or Muros: Both lie on a bus route connecting them with Santiago de Compostela. Eleven buses per day leave from Santiago heading for Noya and nine run to Muros. Some of the tiny little villages and beaches are also connected by bus routes.

Noya is known for its braided straw hats with black bands. It has a number of interesting, handsome old churches, including the 14th-century **Igrexa de Santa María** (with tombstones dating from the 10th century) and the **Igrexa de San Francisco.** A lot of good beaches lie on the northern bank of the ría near Muros. Noya might be your best bet for a lunch stop.

From Noya, the coast road continues west to **Porto do Son.** You can take a detour to Cabo de Corrubedo, with its lighthouse, before continuing on to **Ribeira** at the southern tip. Ribeira is a fishing port and a canning center. At Ribeira you'll see the **Ría de Arousa,** the largest and deepest of the inlets.

From Ribeira, continue east along the southern coastal road to **A Puebla de Caramiñal.** From here, take a signposted route 6 miles (9.6km) inland into the mountains, to admire the most magnificent panorama in all of rías country—the **Mirador de la Curota,** at 1,634 feet. The four inlets of the Ras Bajas can, under the right conditions, be seen from the belvedere. In clear weather you can also see Cape Fisterra.

Back on the C-550, drive as far as Padrón, where, it is claimed, the legendary sea vessel arrived bringing Santiago (St. James) to Spain. Padrón was also the home of romantic poet Rosalía de Castro (1837–85), sometimes called the Emily Dickinson of Spain. Her house, the **Casa Museo de Rosalía de Castro,** Carretera de Herbrón (tel. 981/81-12-04), is open to the public daily from 9am to 2pm and 4 to 8pm. Padrón also makes a good lunch stop.

From Padrón, follow the alleged trail of the body of St. James north along the N-550 to Santiago de Compostela, or take the N-550 south to Pontevedra.

WHERE TO STAY & EAT

CEBOLEIRO, Avenida de Galicia, 15, Noya. Tel. 82-05-31.
   Cuisine: SEAFOOD. **Reservations:** Not required.
$ **Prices:** Appetizers 450–900 ptas. ($4.25–$8.45); main dishes 900–1,700 ptas. ($8.45–$16). AE, MC, V.
   Open: Lunch daily 1:30–4pm; dinner daily 8:30–11:30pm. **Closed:** Dec 20 to Jan 15.

In the center of Noya is this family-run business presided over by the personable Nieves Fernández, assisted by his sons. This basic, no-frills place concentrates on its hearty food from the sea, including several preparations of hake. Other home-cooked items feature a few meat dishes and an apple tart for dessert. There are 35 simply furnished bedrooms attached to this place, costing 3,000 pesetas ($28.20) for a single and 4,000 pesetas ($37.60) for a double, with breakfast another 350 pesetas ($3.30).

CHEF RIVERA, Enlace Parque, 7, Padrón. Tel. 81-04-13.
   Cuisine: GALICIAN. **Reservations:** Recommended.
$ **Prices:** Appetizers 450–750 ptas. ($4.25–$7.05); main dishes 1,200–1,900 ptas. ($11.30–$17.85). AE, DC, MC, V.
   Open: Lunch daily 1–4pm; dinner daily 8pm–midnight.
The name of the owner, to everyone in town, is simply El Chef. The cuisine of Chef Rivera is innovative but also based on traditional recipes. His wife, Pierrette, attends to service in the dining room, which resembles an English pub with its dark, warm colors and leather upholstery. Try the shellfish soup or stew or the house-style monkfish. The restaurant is known for its *pimientos de Padrón.* Tiny green peppers are sautéed with garlic—nothing unusual about that. The trick is that about one in five of those peppers is hot. Finish with a lemon mousse. The couple also rent 17 simply furnished bedrooms, from 3,000 pesetas ($28.20) for a single and 3,800 pesetas ($35.70) for a double; breakfast is another 390 pesetas ($3.65).

---

7. PONTEVEDRA

36 miles S of Santiago de Compostela; 521 miles NW of Madrid

GETTING THERE   By Train   From Santiago de Compostela in the north, 8 trains a day run to Pontevedra (1½ hours).

By Bus Pontevedra has good links to major Galician cities. From Vigo in the south, the bus traveling time is only ½ hour if you take one of the 12 inland expresses leaving from Vigo daily. Less frequent bus service is also available from Santiago de Compostela in the north.

By Car From Santiago de Compostela, head south along the N-550 to reach Pontevedra.

ESSENTIALS The area code for Pontevedra is 986. The Tourist Information Office is at General Mola, 3 (tel. 986/85-08-14).

An aristocratic old Spanish town on the Lérez River and the capital of Pontevedra province, the city of Pontevedra still has vestiges of an ancient wall that once encircled the town. In medieval days, the town was called Pontis Veteris (Old Bridge).

Some of the best gallego seamen lived in Pontevedra in the Middle Ages. Sheltered at the end of the Pontevedra Ría, the city was a bustling port and foreign merchants mingled with local traders, seamen, and fishermen. It was the home of Pedro Sarmiento de Gamboa, the 16th-century navigator and cosmographer who wrote *Voyage to the Magellan Straits*. In the 18th century the Lérez delta silted up and the busy commerce moved elsewhere, mainly to Vigo. Pontevedra entered a period of decline, which may account for its significant old section. Had it been a more prosperous town, the people might have torn down the buildings to rebuild.

The old barrio—a maze of colonnaded squares and cobbled alleyways—lies between the Calle Michelena and the Calle del Arzobispo Malvar, stretching to the Calle Cobián and the river. The old mansions are called pazos, and they speak of former marine glory, since it was the sea that provided the money to build them. Seek out such charming squares as the Plaza de la Leña, the Plaza de Mugártegui, and the Plaza de Teucro.

WHAT TO SEE & DO

In the old quarter, the major attraction is the **Basílica de Santa María la Mayor,** Arzobispo Malvar, with its avocado-green patina, dating from the 16th century. This is a Plateresque church constructed with funds provided by the mariners' guild. Its most remarkable feature is its west front, which was carved to resemble an altarpiece. At the top is a depiction of the Crucifixion.

The **Museo Provincial,** Sarmiento, 51 (tel. 85-14-55), with a hodgepodge of everything from the Pontevedra attic, contains displays ranging from prehistoric artifacts to a still life by Zurbarán. Many of the exhibits are maritime-oriented, and there is also a valuable collection of jewelry. Hours are Tuesday through Sunday from 11am to 1:30pm and 5 to 8pm. Admission is 100 pesetas (95¢). The museum opens onto a major square in the old town, the Plaza de Leña (Square of Wood).

The **Iglesia de San Francisco,** Plaza de la Herrería, is another church of note. Its Gothic façade opens onto gardens. It was founded in the 14th century and contains a sculpture of Don Payo Gómez Charino, noted for his part in the 1248 Reconquest of Seville, when it was wrested from Muslim domination.

Directly south, the gardens lead to the 18th-century **Capilla de la Peregrina,** Plaza Peregrina, with a narrow half-moon façade connected to a rotunda and crowned by a pair of towers. It was constructed by followers of the cult of the Pilgrim Virgin, which was launched in Galicia some time in the 17th century.

WHERE TO STAY

HOTEL COMERCIO, Augusto González Besada, 3, 36001 Pontevedra. Tel. 986/85-12-17. 44 rms (all with bath). A/C TV TEL **Bus:** 14 or 20 from the train station.

$ Rates: 4,500 ptas. ($42.30) single; 6,000 ptas. ($56.40) double. Breakfast 400 ptas. ($3.75) extra. AE, DC, V.

This tall hotel, with its modern façade and art deco–inspired café and bar, is the most stylish in its price category in town. The bedrooms are comfortable. A restaurant serves lunches and dinners for 1,600 pesetas ($15.05).

HOTEL RÍAS BAJAS, Daniel de la Sota, 7, 36001 Pontevedra. Tel. 986/85-51-00. Fax 986/85-51-00. 100 rms (all with bath). TV TEL

$ Rates: 5,500 ptas. ($51.70) single; 8,000 ptas. ($75.20) double. Breakfast 450 ptas. ($4.25) extra. AE, DC, MC, V.

On a busy street corner near the Plaza de Galicia in the commercial center, this place is more comfortable than you might expect, judging from the outside. The largest hotel in town, it is often used for community political meetings and press conferences. The lobby, of stone and wood paneling, has been designed to look like an English club. Bedrooms are comfortable and well maintained. The hotel doesn't have a restaurant, but does offer a cafeteria.

HOTEL VIRGEN DEL CAMINO, Virgen del Camino, 55, 36001 Pontevedra. Tel. 986/85-59-00. Fax 986/85-09-00. 53 rms (all with bath). TV TEL

$ Rates: 5,500 ptas. ($51.70) single; 8,000 ptas. ($75.20) double. Breakfast 400 ptas. ($3.75) extra. AE, MC, V.

On a relatively quiet street off the C-531, at the edge of the suburbs, this balconied stucco hotel contains a comfortable English-style pub as well as spacious, comfortable sitting rooms. The bedrooms have wall-to-wall carpeting, and central heating in the winter. The more expensive doubles contain separate salons and sitting rooms. Breakfast only is served.

PARADOR NACIONAL CASA DEL BARÓN, Plaza de Maceda, s/n, 36002 Pontevedra. Tel. 986/85-58-00. Fax 986/85-21-95. 47 rms (all with bath). MINIBAR TV TEL

$ Rates: 8,000 ptas. ($75.20) single; 9,000 ptas. ($84.60) double. Breakfast 900 ptas. ($8.45) extra.

The parador is located in the old quarter of Pontevedra, in a well-preserved 16th-century palace near the Basílica de Santa María la Mayor. The interior has been maintained very much as the old pazo (manor house) must have looked. It includes a quaint old kitchen, or *lar* (literally "heart"), typical of Galician country houses and furnished with characteristic items. Off the vestibule is a courtyard dominated by a large old stone staircase. Many of the accommodations are large enough to include sitting areas; the beds are comfortable, the furnishings attractive. Many of the rooms overlook the walled-in formal garden. Both lunch and dinner can be had for 2,800 pesetas ($26.30). Most dishes, such as a casserole of shrimp with tomato sauce, are well prepared.

WHERE TO EAT

CASA ROMÁN, Augusto García Sánchez, 12. Tel. 84-35-60.
   Cuisine: SEAFOOD. **Reservations:** Not required.
$ Prices: Appetizers 800–1,200 ptas. ($7.50–$11.30); main dishes 1,400–2,500 ptas. ($13.15–$23.50). AE, DC, MC, V.
   Open: Lunch daily 1–4pm; dinner Mon–Sat 9pm–midnight. **Closed:** Sun night, except in July and Aug.

Known for the quality of its food, this well-established restaurant is on the street level of a brick apartment building in a leafy downtown development known as Campolongo, near the Plaza de Galicia. To reach the dining room, you pass through a tavern. In addition to lobster (which you can see in the window), a wide array of fish and shellfish dishes are served here, including sea bass, squid, sole, crab, lobsters, and tuna.

DOÑA ANTONIA, Soportales de la Herrería, 9. Tel. 84-72-74.

Cuisine: GALICIAN. **Reservations:** Required.
$ Prices: Appetizers 750–1,100 ptas. ($7.05–$10.35); main dishes 1,400–2,500 ptas. ($13.15–$23.50). AE, MC, V.
Open: Lunch Mon–Sat 1:30–4pm; dinner Mon–Sat 9–11:30pm. **Closed:** June 1–20.

Generally acknowledged as Pontevedra's best restaurant, Doña Antonia is located under a stone arcade on one of the town's oldest streets, east of the Jardines Vincenti. You climb one flight to reach the pink-and-white dining room. Menu items include baked suckling lamb, scaloppine with port, rolled filet of salmon, and kiwi sorbet.

---

8. VIGO

372 miles NW of Madrid; 17 miles S of Pontevedra; 96 miles S of La Coruña

GETTING THERE By Train Two trains a day connect Vigo with Madrid (8 to 11 hours). From Santiago de Compostela, there are 8 trains daily to Vigo (2½ hours).

By Bus From Santiago de Compostela in the north, there are 4 buses per day (2½ hours). From Madrid, there are two buses a day (9 hours).

By Car From Pontevedra, continue on the A-9, an express highway, south to Vigo.

ESSENTIALS The area code of Vigo is 986. The Tourist Information Office is at Jardines de las Avenidas, s/n (tel. 986/43-05-77).

Vigo is a modern city, possessing one of Spain's most important harbors. Sardine fishing is the major industry here, and many Vigo residents are involved in it in one way or another.

For a view of the truly beautiful setting—the harbor surrounded by cliffs dotted with old fortresses—go to the 400-foot-high **Castillo del Castro.**

The **Islas de Cíes** (the ancient Insulae Siccae), a rocky archipelago at the entrance to the bay, act as a breakwater, providing shelter and a spectacular scene, particularly at sunset. You can take a boat tour of these islands as Sir Francis Drake did when he captured Vigo—once in 1585 and again in 1589.

The old fishing village, the **Berbes Quarter,** is unusual and makes for a pleasant stroll. It is a port of call for many Dutch, British, and German vessels.

The day's catch is unloaded at 11pm, and that's the best time to go down to the harbor. If you're an early riser, it's also fun to go at 7am, when the wholesale merchants come down to purchase the catch from the night before.

The **Samil** and **Canido** beaches are easily reached by bus, about 15 minutes from the city.

WHERE TO STAY

HOTEL ESTORIL, Lepanto, 12, 36201 Vigo. Tel. 986/43-61-22. 40 rms (all with bath). TEL
$ Rates: 3,500 ptas. ($32.90) single; 5,000 ptas. ($47) double. Breakfast 150 ptas. ($1.40) extra. No credit cards.

This old-fashioned hotel near the train station is one of the best in Vigo, and a definite must for bargain hunters. It's a granite building on a street lined with 19th-century buildings. The dimly illuminated lobby exudes respectability, and the bench-lined TV lounge looks like the chapel of a monastery. The bedrooms are simple and clean, with slightly faded furniture. Breakfast is the only meal served.

HOTEL MÉXICO, Vía del Norte, 10, 36204 Vigo. Tel. 986/41-16-66. Fax 986/43-55-53. 112 rms (all with bath). TV TEL
$ Rates: 5,000 ptas. ($47) single; 7,800 ptas. ($73.30) double. Breakfast 480 ptas. ($4.50) extra. AE, DC, MC, V.

From its location on a steep embankment, guests have a sweeping view of the harbor from many of the balconied, comfortably furnished rooms. The hotel is modern and stylish, with ample use of handmade ceramic tiles and wooden furniture. There is a pleasant bar on the premises, plus a cafeteria, but no restaurant. You'll find it by the train station.

HOTEL ENSENADA, Alfonso XIII, 7, 36201 Vigo. Tel. 986/22-61-00. Fax 986/43-89-72. 109 rms (all with bath) A/C MINIBAR TV TEL **Bus:** 9.
$ Rates: 5,800 ptas. ($54.50) single; 8,000 ptas. ($75.20) double. Breakfast 525 ptas. ($4.95) extra. AE, DC, MC, V.
This hotel is in the center of both the commercial and the historic part of the city. Its in-house garage makes parking easy. If you're at the bar during one of the many civic functions held here, you may get to witness local community life in action. The hotel has both a cafeteria and a restaurant. Bedrooms are furnished in a functional modern style.

HOTEL IPANEMA, Vázquez Varela, 31-33, 36204 Vigo. Tel. 986/47-13-44. Fax 986/48-20-80. 60 rms (all with bath) TV TEL
$ Rates: 6,500 ptas. ($61.10) single; 8,000 ptas. ($75.20) double. Breakfast 500 ptas. ($4.70) extra. DC, MC, V.
Set at the top of a sloping commercial street east of the Plaza de España, this three-star hotel boasts an unusually elegant reception area decorated in reddish granite and furnished with plush sofas. Each of the comfortable modern bedrooms is functionally furnished. There's an English-styled wood-paneled pub, a favorite after-work meeting place, as well as a cafeteria (no restaurant).

WHERE TO EAT

LAS BRIDAS, Ecuador, 56. Tel. 43-13-91.
   Cuisine: GALICIAN. **Reservations:** Required.
$ Prices: Appetizers 500–2,000 ptas. ($4.70–$18.80); main dishes 800–2,000 ptas. ($7.50–$18.80). AE, DC, MC, V.
   Open: Lunch Mon–Sat 1:30–4pm; dinner Mon–Sat 8:30pm–midnight.
Popular and stylish, this restaurant off the Gran Vía occupies two adjoining storefronts on a commercial street in the center of town. A colorful bar/beer hall is in one section, the dining room in the other. The boisterous bar serves tapas. The adjoining restaurant, decorated with faintly equestrian trappings, offers fresh lobster from the tanks on the premises, baked Portuguese codfish, osso bucco with mushrooms, baked salmon, and a wide selection of fresh fish and shellfish.

PUESTO PILOTO ALCABRE, Avenida Atlántica, 98. Tel. 29-79-75.
   Cuisine: SEAFOOD. **Reservations:** Required. **Directions:** Take Avenida Beiramar 3 miles (4.8km) west from city.
$ Prices: Appetizers 600–1,600 ptas. ($5.65–$15.05); main dishes 1,200–2,000 ptas. ($11.30–$18.80); fixed-priced menu 1,600–2,000 ptas. ($15.05–$18.80); AE, DC, MC, V.
   Open: Lunch daily 1–3:30pm; dinner Mon–Sat 9pm–midnight. **Closed:** First two weeks in Nov.
One of Vigo's best-rated seafood restaurants, Puesto Piloto Alcabre features seafood soup, *chorizos* (sausages) with garbanzo beans, well-seasoned rice dishes, and a wide range of regional offerings. Several continental specialties are also on the menu, which is served in an attractive room.

EL MOSQUITO, Plaza de J. Villavicencio, 4. Tel. 43-35-70.
   Cuisine: SEAFOOD. **Reservations:** Required in summer.
$ Prices: Appetizers 800–1,200 ptas. ($7.50–$11.30); main dishes 1,500–2,000 ptas. ($14.10–$18.80); fixed-priced menu 2,850 ptas. ($26.80). AE, DC, MC, V.
   Open: Lunch Mon–Sat 1:30–4pm; dinner Mon–Sat 9:30–11:30pm. **Closed:** Religious holidays; mid-Aug to mid-Sept.
One of the oldest and best-established landmarks in a city filled with restaurants, El

Mosquito has a bar area in front and a rear dining room. The place will probably be crowded, since it's known for serving some of the best food in town, especially shellfish, grilled sole, and roast leg of kid.

---

9. EL GROVE & LA TOJA

395 miles NW of Madrid; 20 miles W of Pontevedra; 45 miles S of Santiago de Compostela

GETTING THERE   By Train   The train from Santiago de Compostela goes as far as Vilagarcía de Arousa; take the bus from there.

By Bus   From Pontevedra, buses heading for Ponte Vilagarcía de Arousa stop at La Toja.

By Car   From Pontevedra, take the 550 coastal road east via Sanxenxo. From Santiago de Compostela, take expressway A-9 to Caldas de Reis, turn off onto the 550, and head west to the coast.

ESSENTIALS   The area code for El Grove and La Toja is 986.

A summer resort and fishing village, **El Grove** is on a peninsula west of Pontevedra, with some 5 miles of beaches of varying quality. It juts out into the Ría de Arosa, a large inlet at the mouth of Ulla River. The village, sheltered from Atlantic gales because of its eastern position, has become more commercial than many visitors would like, but it is still renowned for its fine cuisine. A shellfish festival is held here every October.

   La Toja (A Toxa in Galician), an island linked to El Grove by a bridge, is a famous spa and the most fashionable resort in Galicia, known for its sports and leisure activities. The casino and the golf course are both very popular. The island is covered with pine trees and surrounded by some of the finest scenery in Spain.

   La Toja first became known for health-giving properties when, according to legend, the owner of a sick donkey left it on the island to die. The donkey recovered, and its cure was attributed to the waters of an island spring.

WHERE TO STAY IN EL GROVE

HOTEL AMANDI, Castelao, 94, 36989 El Grove. Tel. 986/73-19-42. Fax 986/73-16-43. 25 rms (all with bath). TEL
$ Rates: 6,000 ptas. ($56.40) single; 7,200 ptas. ($67.60) double. Breakfast 450 ptas. ($4.25) extra. AE, MC, V. **Closed:** Nov.
This stylish and tasteful hotel is a brisk 10-minute walk from the bridge that connects El Grove with La Toja. The rooms, most with TVs, are decorated with antique reproductions; the majority have tiny terraces with ornate cast-iron balustrades and sea views. Breakfast only is served.

WHERE TO EAT IN EL GROVE

LA POUSADA DEL MAR, Castelao, 202. Tel. 73-01-06.
   Cuisine: SEAFOOD. **Reservations:** Required in July and Aug.
$ Prices: Fixed-priced menu 1,700 ptas. ($16). Appetizers 295–650 ptas. ($2.75–$6.10); main dishes 800–1,700 ptas. ($7.50–$16). AE, DC, MC, V.
   Open: Lunch daily 1–4pm; dinner daily 8:30pm–midnight.
This warm, inviting place near the bridge leading to La Toja is the best dining spot

outside the hotels. At times you can watch women digging for oysters in the river in front of the restaurant. The chef, naturally, specializes in fish, including a wide selection of shellfish. Among the specialties are a savory soup, an outstanding shellfish paella, hake Galician style and fresh grilled salmon. For dessert, try the *flan de la casa*.

WHERE TO STAY IN LA TOJA

HOTEL LOUXO, 36991 Isla de la A Toxa. Tel. 986/73-00-00. Fax 986/73-02-00. 96 rms (all with bath). TV TEL
$ Rates (including continental breakfast): 10,000 ptas. ($94) single; 13,000 ptas. ($122.20) double. AE, DC, MC, V.
Set on flatlands a few paces from the town's ornate casino, is this modern white building, sheltered from the Atlantic winds. Open from late June until early October, it offers clean, stylish, modern accommodations. The many public rooms on the ground floor offer rows of comfortable seating areas and sweeping views over the nearby tidal flats. The hotel also serves an outstanding menu, with an emphasis on fresh fish. Meals cost from 2,300 pesetas ($21.60).

---

10. TÚY (TÚI)

18 miles S of Vigo; 30 miles S of Pontevedra

GETTING THERE By Train   Trains run daily from Vigo to Túy (1½ to 2 hours).

By Bus   From Vigo, buses run south to Túy hourly, taking 1 hour.

By Car   From Vigo, head south along the A-9 expressway until you see the turnoff for Túy.

ESSENTIALS   The area code for Túy is 986. The Tourist Information Office is at Puente Tripes, Avenida de Portugal (tel. 986/609-17-89).

A frontier town first settled by the Romans, Túy is a short distance from Portugal, located near the two-tiered road-and-rail bridge (over the Miño River) that links the two countries. The bridge was designed by Gustave Eiffel. For motorists coming from Portugal's Valenca do Minho, Túy will be their introduction to Spain.

WHAT TO SEE & DO

The winding streets of the old quarter lead to the **cathedral,** a national art treasure that dominates the *zona monumentale*. The acropolis-like cathedral-fortress, built in 1170, wasn't used for religious purposes until the early 13th century. Its principal portal, ogival in style, is exceptional. What is astounding about this cathedral is that later architects respected the original Romanesque and Gothic style and didn't make changes in its design. If you have time, you may want to visit the Romanesque-style **Church of San Bartolomé,** on the outskirts, and the **Church of Santo Domingo,** a beautiful example of Gothic style (look for the bas-reliefs in the cloister). The latter church stands next to the Parque de Santo Domingo. Walls built over Roman fortifications surround Túy.

WHERE TO STAY & EAT

PARADOR NACIONAL DE SAN TELMO, Avenida de Portugal, s/n, 36700 Túy. Tel. 986/60-03-09. Fax 986/60-21-63. 22 rms (all with bath). A/C TV TEL
$ Rates: 7,800–9,500 ptas. ($73.30–$89.30) double. Breakfast 900 ptas. ($8.45) extra. AE, DC, MC, V.
Advance reservations are essential if you want to stay in this elegant fortress-style hacienda located 4 streets north of the Miño River crossing. The inn, with its cantilevered roof, was designed to blend in with the architectural spirit of the

province, emphasizing local stone and natural woods. Brass chandeliers, paintings by well-known gallegos, and antiques combined with reproductions furnish the public rooms. In the main living room are a large inglenook fireplace, a tall banjo-shaped grandfather clock, hand-knotted rugs, 18th-century paintings, hand-hewn benches, and comfortable armchairs.

The bedrooms are sober in style, but comfortable, and offer views across a colonnaded courtyard to the river and hills. They are furnished with Castilian-style pieces, and the tiled baths are modern. The dignified dining room has a high wooden ceiling and tall windows that offer a fine view of the surrounding hills. Even if you are not a hotel guest, it is worth dining on the regional cuisine served here. The hors d'oeuvres alone consist of almost a dozen little dishes. The fish dishes are excellent, especially (when available) lamprey, as well as salmon, shad, and trout. Homemade cakes are offered for dessert. A complete meal costs 2,900 pesetas ($27.25).

11. ORENSE (OURENSE)

309 miles NW of Madrid, 63 miles E of Vigo

GETTING THERE By Train   Three trains a day connect Orense and Santiago de Compostela, with continuing service to Madrid. Trains also connect Vigo (our last stopover) with Orense at the rate of 5 per day. (45 minutes).

By Bus   Eight buses a day run from Vigo to Orense (2 hours). There are also 5 bus connections between Santiago de Compostela and Orense (4 hours).

By Car   Vigo and Orense are linked by the N-120, a good road. If you're driving from Madrid, take the N-VI past Ponferrada, cutting west at the junction with the N-120.

ESSENTIALS   The area code for Orense is 988. The Tourist Information Office is at Curros Enríquez, 1, Torre de Orense (tel. 988/23-47-17).

Capital of its own province, Orense dates from ancient times and takes its name from those legendary "mines of gold" believed to exist in the Miño Valley. Although surrounded by dull modern buildings, the old town is worth the drive here. A Roman bridge (**Puente Romano**) of seven arches crosses the Miño, taking passengers into the town center. In the 1200s the traffic across this bridge became so heavy with pilgrims bound for Santiago de Compostela that it had to be reconstructed.

Although a major industrial center of Galicia today, Orense has long been known for its springs, **Las Burgas,** which provide a medicinal drinking water. They reach temperatures of 150F. You can see a cloud of steam in the fountain near the Ayuntamiento (Town Hall) at the Plaza Mayor and at other places in the old town. A short walk away from the springs, along narrow twisting streets, is the old barrio.

WHAT TO SEE & DO

The major monument in Orense is the **cathedral,** northeast of the arcaded Plaza Mayor. It was founded in 572 and rebuilt in 1132–94. The elaborate 13th-century facade was disastrously restored in the 16th and 17th centuries. The main altar contains a Gothic retable from the 16th century by Cornelis de Holanda. The cathedral's most outstanding feature: the Romanesque tripled-arched Portico del Paraiso (Doorway to Paradise), which maintains its bright colors from the Middle Ages. Its central arch depicts the 24 Old Men of the Apocalypse. The cathedral is open daily from 10:30am to 1pm and 3:30 to 7:30pm.

The **Museo Provincial,** Plaza Mayor, housed in an episcopal palace from the 12th century, displays pottery, artifacts, ceramics, coins, and other items dating from prehistoric times to the Roman era, as well as some ecclesiastical art from the Middle Ages. It's open Tuesday through Sunday from 10am to 1pm and 5 to 8pm.

It's interesting to walk around the old quarter and discover hidden squares, including the **Plazuela de la Magdalena,** with its Iglesia de Santa María la Madre, dating from 1722. A stone Mary Magdalene weeps at the central cross in the square. The **Plaza del Trigo,** east of the Plaza Mayor, is a parvis to the south door of the cathedral. The **Plaza del Hierro** is graced with a fountain from Santa María la Real Osera, a 12th-century Cistercian monastery.

WHERE TO STAY

PADRE FEIJOÓ, Plaza Eugenio Montes, 1, 32005 Orense. Tel. 988/22-31-00. 71 rms (all with bath). TV TEL
$ Rates: 3,500 ptas. ($32.90) single; 5,000 ptas. ($47) double. Breakfast 475 ptas. ($4.45) extra. DC, MC, V.
Located near the old town in a neighborhood filled with many restaurants, this is one of the best places in town in the moderately priced category. Bedrooms are modestly furnished and well kept. The owner, also the resident manager, keeps an eye on things. Breakfast is the only meal served.

SILA, Avenida de La Habana, 61, 32003 Orense. Tel. 988/23-63-11. 64 rms (all with bath) TV
$ Rates: 3,800 ptas. ($35.70) single; 6,500 ptas. ($61.10) double. Breakfast 550 ptas. ($4.95) extra. AE, MC, V.
This hotel is capable of satisfying basic needs, offering a clean and safe environment for an overnight stay. Rooms are modestly but comfortably furnished. The hotel is near the Parque de San Lázaro, convenient to the major monuments of the old town. Its restaurant offers good Galician fare at 1,850 pesetas ($17.40) per meal.

WHERE TO EAT

MARTÍN FIERRO, Sáenz Diez, 65. Tel. 23-48-20.
   Cuisine: GALICIAN. **Reservations:** Recommended.
$ Prices: Appetizers 650–950 ptas. ($6.10–$8.95); main dishes 1,350–2,200 ptas. ($12.70–$20.70). AE, DC, MC, V.
   Open: Lunch Mon–Sat 1–4:30pm; dinner Mon–Sat 8pm–midnight.
Owner Ovidio Fernández Ojea respects the fresh fish he serves, but he prides himself especially on his beef. It comes directly from local granges, and the owner selects the cuts himself. He achieves a harmony between regional ingredients, tradition, and modern innovations in his cooking. Food is served with an impressive list of wines from his bodega. Try the vegetarian cannelloni, hake in a sauce of pine nuts, an array of grills, or beefsteak Martín Fierro with peppers. The place is air-conditioned and has a terrace. You'll find it north of the old quarter near the police station.

CARROLEIRO, San Miguel, 10. Tel. 22-05-66.
   Cuisine: GALICIAN. **Reservations:** Recommended.
$ Prices: Appetizers 450–750 ptas. ($4.25–$7.05); main dishes 1,200–1,500 ptas. ($11.30–$14.10); fixed-priced menu 2,200 ptas. ($20.70). AE, MC, V.
   Open: Lunch Tues–Sun 1–4pm; dinner Tues–Sun 8pm–midnight.
North of the cathedral and the Plaza Mayor is this agreeably decorated establishment, with an unwavering allegiance to a cuisine based on local ingredients and traditional recipes. Dishes are offered without complicated elaborations. Shellfish—the most expensive item on the menu—is priced according to weight. You can order several different preparations of beef, as well as *mero* (halibut). For dessert, try the flavorful caramel custard.

A. BASIC PHRASES & VOCABULARY

ENGLISH	SPANISH	PRONUNCIATION
Hello	**Buenos días**	bway-noss dee-ahss
How are you?	**Como está usted?**	koh-moh ess-tah oo-steth
Very well	**Muy bien**	mwee byen
Thank you	**Gracias**	gra-theeahss
Good-bye	**Adiós**	ad-dyohss
Please	**Por favór**	pohr fah-bohr
Yes	**Sí**	see
No	**No**	noh
Excuse me	**Perdóneme**	pehrdoh-neh-may
Give me	**Deme**	day-may
Where is?	**Donde está?**	dohn-day ess-tah
the station	**la estación**	la ess-tah-thyohn
a hotel	**un hotel**	oon-oh-tel
a restaurant	**un restaurante**	oon res-tow-rahn-tay
the toilet	**el servicio**	el ser-vee-the-o
To the right	**A la derecha**	ah lah day-ray-chuh
To the left	**A la izquierda**	ah lah eeth-kyayr-duh
Straight ahead	**Adelante**	ah-day-lahn-tay
I would like	**Quiero**	kyehr-oh
to eat	**comer**	ko-mayr
a room	**una habitación**	oo-nah ah-bee-tah-thyo-n
How much is it?	**Cuánto?**	kwahn-toh
The check	**La cuenta**	la kwen-tah
When	**Cuándo?**	kwan-doh
Yesterday	**Ayer**	ah-yayr
Today	**Hoy**	oy
Tomorrow	**Mañana**	mahn-yah-nah
Breakfast	**Desayuno**	deh-sai-yoo-noh
Lunch	**Comida**	co-mee-dah
Dinner	**Cena**	thay-nah

NUMBERS

1 **uno** (oo-noh)
2 **dos** (dose)
3 **tres** (trayss)
4 **cuatro** (kwah-troh)
5 **cinco** (theen-koh)
6 **seis** (sayss)
7 **siete** (syeh-tay)
8 **ocho** (oh-choh)
9 **nueve** (nway-bay)
10 **diez** (dyeth)
11 **once** (ohn-thay)
12 **doce** (doh-thay)
13 **trece** (tray-thay)

14 **catorce** (kah-tor-thay)
15 **quince** (keen-thay)
16 **dieciseis** (dyeth-ee-sayss)
17 **diecisiete** (dyeth-ee-sye-tay)
18 **dieciocho** (dyeth-ee-oh-choh)
19 **diecinueve** (dyeth-ee-nywaybay)
20 **veinte** (bayn-tay)
30 **trienta** (trayn-tah)

40 **cuarenta** (kwah-ren-tah)
50 **cincuenta** (theen-kween-tah)
60 **sesenta** (say-sen-tah)
70 **setenta** (say-ten-tah)
80 **ochenta** (oh-chen-tah)
90 **noventa** (noh-ben-tah)
100 **cien** (thyen)

B. MENU SAVVY

Alliolo Sauce made from garlic and olive oil

Arroz con costra Rice dish of chicken, rabbit, sausages, black pudding, chickpeas, spices, and pork meatballs—everything "hidden" under a layer of beaten egg crust

Arroz empedrado Rice cooked with tomatoes and cod and a top layer of white beans

Bacalao al ajo arriero Cod-and-garlic dish named after Leonese mule drivers

Bacalao al pil-pil Cod with garlic and chili peppers

Bacalao a la vizcaina Cod with dried peppers and onion

Bajoques farcides Peppers stuffed with rice, pork, tomatoes, and spices

Butifarra Catalonian sausage made with blood, spices, and eggs

Caldereta Stew or a stew pot

Caldereta extremña Kid or goat stew

Caldo gallego Soup made with cabbage, potatoes, beans, and various meat flavorings (ham, chorizo, spare ribs)

Chanfaina salmantina Rice, giblets, lamb sweetbreads, and pieces of chorizo

Chilindrón Sauce made from tomatoes, peppers, garlic, chorizo, and spicy sausage

Cochifrito navarro Small pieces of fried lamb

Cocido español Spanish stew

Cocido de pelotas Stew of minced meat wrapped in cabbage leaves and cooked with poultry, bacon, chickpeas, potatoes, and spices

El arroz amb fessols i naps Rice with beans and turnips

El caldillo de perro "Dog soup," made with onions, fresh fish, and orange juice

El cocido Madrileña Chickpea stew of Madrid, with potatoes, cabbage, turnips, beef, marrow, bacon, chorizo, and black pudding

El pato a la naranja Duck with orange, an old Valencian dish

Empanada Crusted pie of Galicia, with a variety of fillings

Escudella Catalan version of chickpea stew

Fabada White bean stew of Asturias

Habas a la catalana Stew of broad beans, herbs, and spices

Judías blancas Haricot beans

Judías negras Runner beans

Lacón con grelos Salted ham with turnip tops

La cassolada Potato-and-vegetable stew with bacon and ribs

La salsa verde Green sauce to accompany fish

Las magras con tomate Slices of slightly fried ham dipped in tomato sauce

La trucha a la navarra Trout fried with a piece of ham

Le pericana Cod, olive oil, dry peppers, and garlic

Mar y cielo "Sea and heaven," made with sausages, rabbit, shrimp, and fish

Merluza a la gallega Galician hake with onions, potatoes, and herbs

Merluza a la sidra Hake cooked with cider

Morcilla Black sausage akin to black pudding

Paella alicantina Rice dish with chicken and rabbit

Picada Sauce made from nuts, parsley, garlic, saffron, and cinnamon

Pilota Ball made of meat, parsley, bread crumbs, and eggs

Pinchito Small kebab

Pisto manchego Vegetable stew from La Mancha

Pollos a la chilindron Chicken cooked in a tomato, onion, and pepper sauce

Romesco Mediterranean sauce, with olive oil, red pepper, bread, garlic, and maybe cognac

Samfaina Sauce made from tomatoes, eggplant, onions, and zucchini

Sangría Drink made with fruit, brandy, and wine

Sofrito Sauce made from peppers, onions, garlic, tomatoes, and olive oil

Sopas castellanas Bread, broth, ham, and sometimes a poached egg and garlic

Sopa de ajo castellana Garlic soup with ham, bread, eggs, and spices

Tapas Small dishes or appetizers served with drinks at a tavern
Tortilla de patatas Spanish omelet with potatoes
Turrón Almond paste
Zarzuela Fish stew

C. GLOSSARY OF ARCHITECTURAL TERMS

Alcazaba Moorish fortress
Alcázar Moorish fortified palace
Ayuntamiento Town hall
Azulejo Painted glazed tiles, popular in Mudéjar work and later architecture, especially in Andalusia, Valencia, and Portugal
Barrio (Barri in Catalan) City neighborhood or district
Churrigueresque Floridly ornate baroque style of the late 17th and early 18th centuries in the style of Spanish sculptor and architect José Churriguera (1650–1725)
Ciudadela Citadel
Cortijo Andalusian country house or villa
Granja Farm or farmhouse
Isabelline Gothic Architectural style popular in the late 15th century, roughly corresponding to the English perpendicular
Judería Jewish quarter
Lonja Merchants' exchange or marketplace
Medina Walled center of a Moorish city, traditionally centered around a mosque
Mezquita Mosque
Mirhab Prayer niche in a mosque, by Koranic law facing Mecca
Mirador Scenic overlook or belvedere, or a glassed-in panoramic balcony sheltering its occupants from the wind
Mudéjar Moorish-influenced architecture, usually "Christianized" and adopted as Spain's most prevalent architectural style from the 12th to the 16th century
Plateresque Heavily ornamented Gothic style widely used in Spain and Portugal during the 16th century. Its name derives from the repoussé floral patterns hammered into 16th-century silver (*la plata*), which were imitated in low relief carvings in stone
Plaza de Toros Bullring
Plaza Mayor Square at the center of many Spanish cities, often enclosed, arcaded and enhanced with cafés and fountains
Puerta Portal or gate
Reja Iron grilles, either those covering the exterior windows of buildings or the decorative dividers in churches
Retablo Carved and/or painted altarpiece

D. THE METRIC SYSTEM

LENGTH

1 millimeter (mm)	= .04 inches (*or* less than $\frac{1}{16}$ in.)
1 centimeter (cm)	= .39 inches (*or* just under ½ in.)
1 meter (m)	= 39 inches (*or* about 1.1 yards)
1 kilometer (km)	= .62 miles (*or* about ⅔ of a mile)

To convert kilometers to miles, multiply the number of kilometers by .62. Also use to convert kilometers per hour (kmph) to miles per hour (m.p.h.).

To convert miles to kilometers, multiply the number of miles by 1.61. Also use to convert from m.p.h. to kmph.

CAPACITY

1 liter (l)	= 33.92 fluid ounces = 2.1 pints = 1.06 quarts
	= .26 U.S. gallons
1 Imperial gallon	= 1.2 U.S. gallons

To convert liters to U.S. gallons, multiply the number of liters by .26.
To convert U.S. gallons to liters, multiply the number of gallons by 3.79.
To convert Imperial gallons to U.S. gallons, multiply the number of Imperial gallons by 1.2.
To convert U.S. gallons to Imperial gallons, multiply the number of U.S. gallons by .83.

WEIGHT

1 gram (g)	= .035 ounces (*or* about a paperclip's weight)
1 kilogram (kg)	= 35.2 ounces
	= 2.2 pounds
1 metric ton	= 2,205 pounds (1.1 short ton)

To convert kilograms to pounds, multiply the number of kilograms by 2.2.
To convert pounds to kilograms, multiply the number of pounds by .45.

AREA

1 hectare (ha)	= 2.47 acres
1 square kilometer (km²)	= 247 acres = .39 square miles

To convert hectares to acres, multiply the number of hectares by 2.47.
To convert acres to hectares, multiply the number of acres by .41.
To convert square kilometers to square miles, multiply the number of square kilometers by .39.
To convert square miles to square kilometers, multiply the number of square miles by 2.6.

TEMPERATURE

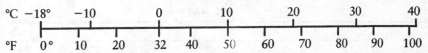

°C	−18°	−10		0		10		20		30		40
°F	0°	10	20	32	40	50	60	70	80	90	100	

To convert degrees Celsius to degrees Fahrenheit, multiply °C by 9, divide by 5, and add 32 (example: 20°C × 9/5 + 32 = 68°F).
To convert degrees Fahrenheit to degrees Celsius, subtract 32 from °F, multiply by 5, then divide by 9 (example: 85°F − 32 × 5/9 = 29.4°C).

E. SIZE CONVERSIONS

The following charts should help you to choose the correct clothing sizes in France. However, sizes can vary, so the best guide is simply to try things on.

WOMEN'S DRESSES, COATS, AND SKIRTS

American	3	5	7	9	11	12	13	14	15	16	18
Continental	36	38	38	40	40	42	42	44	44	46	48
British	8	10	11	12	13	14	15	16	17	18	20

WOMEN'S BLOUSES AND SWEATERS

American	10	12	14	16	18	20
Continental	38	40	42	44	46	48
British	32	34	36	38	40	42

WOMEN'S STOCKINGS

American	8	8½	9	9½	10	10½
Continental	1	2	3	4	5	6
British	8	8½	9	9½	10	10½

WOMEN'S SHOES

American	5	6	7	8	9	10
Continental	36	37	38	39	40	41
British	3½	4½	5½	6½	7½	8½

MEN'S SUITS

American	34	36	38	40	42	44	46	48
Continental	44	46	48	50	52	54	56	58
British	34	36	38	40	42	44	46	48

MEN'S SHIRTS

American	14½	15	15½	16	16½	17	17½	18
Continental	37	38	39	41	42	43	44	45
British	14½	15	15½	16	16½	17	17½	18

MEN'S SHOES

American	7	8	9	10	11	12	13
Continental	39½	41	42	43	44½	46	47
British	6	7	8	9	10	11	12

MEN'S HATS

American	6⅞	7⅛	7¼	7⅜	7½	7⅝
Continental	55	56	58	59	60	61
British	6¼	6⅞	7⅛	7¼	7⅜	7½

CHILDREN'S CLOTHNG

American	3	4	5	6	6X
Continental	98	104	110	116	122
British	18	20	22	24	26

CHILDREN'S SHOES

American	8	9	10	11	12	13	1	2	3
Continental	24	25	27	28	29	30	32	33	34
British	7	8	9	10	11	12	13	1	2

F. MILEAGE CHART

	Almería	Ávila	Barcelona	Cádiz	Córdoba	Coruña	Granada	MADRID	Málaga	Oviedo	Pamplona	Salamanca	San Sebastián	Toledo	Valencia	Zaragoza
Alicante	182	333	319	427	326	639	219	262	299	541	417	393	475	255	103	309
Almería		411	502	300	206	727	103	349	136	629	601	473	640	348	285	470
Ávila	411		445	383	283	334	331	71	399	231	328	60	295	85	290	259
Badajoz	374	197	634	212	169	479	272	249	270	381	468	142	451	228	444	450
Barcelona	502	445		774	563	693	532	385	618	559	271	482	328	429	216	184
Cádiz	300	383	774		163	665	208	411	164	567	663	371	702	361	501	613
Córdoba	206	283	563	163		617	103	248	116	528	500	328	539	194	338	450
Coruña	727	338	693	665	617		647	378	715	281	458	298	473	419	596	516
Cuenca	317	175	348	439	276	481	297	104	381	383	332	233	394	116	136	207
Gerona	564	507	62	858	625	755	600	447	680	621	333	544	390	491	278	246
Granada	103	331	538	208	103	647		269	80	549	521	391	560	264	322	471
León	556	158	486	494	454	207	472	206	544	73	250	122	268	243	425	308
MADRID	349	71	385	411	248	378	269		337	280	252	131	291	44	218	202
Málaga	136	399	618	164	116	715	80	337		617	590	469	628	314	402	539
Oviedo	629	231	559	567	528	211	649	280	617		287	195	262	316	498	374
Pamplona	601	328	663	500	458	458	521	252	590	287		273	57	296	314	109
Pontevedra	735	338	700	649	606	75	655	386	715	242	466	278	484	423	605	516
Salamanca	473	60	482	371	328	328	391	131	469	195	273		291	145	350	299
San Sebastián	640	295	328	702	539	473	560	291	628	262	57	291		325	368	166
Segovia	403	42	403	465	308	347	323	54	391	225	229	102	266	98	272	219
Seville	262	306	649	78	86	587	159	334	136	489	586	294	624	284	432	535
Toledo	348	85	429	361	194	419	264	44	314	316	296	145	335		231	246
Valencia	285	290	216	501	338	596	322	218	402	498	311	350	368	281		202
Valadolid	469	75	411	443	358	282	389	120	457	156	202	71	219	273	338	228
Zaragoza	470	259	184	613	450	516	471	202	539	374	109	299	166	246	202	

Distances are in miles.

INDEX

GENERAL INFORMATION

DESTINATIONS

KEY TO ABBREVIATIONS: * = Author's Favorites; $ = Special Value; B = Budget; E = Expensive; M = Moderately Priced

NOW, SAVE MONEY ON ALL YOUR TRAVELS!
Join Frommer's™ Dollarwise® Travel Club

Saving money while traveling is never a simple matter, which is why the **Dollarwise Travel Club** was formed 31 years ago. Developed in response to requests from Frommer's Travel Guide readers, the Club provides cost-cutting travel strategies, up-to-date travel information, and a sense of community for value-conscious travelers from all over the world.

In keeping with the money-saving concept, the annual membership fee is low —$20 for U.S. residents or $25 for residents of Canada, Mexico, and other countries—and is immediately exceeded by the value of your benefits, which include:

1. Any TWO books listed on the following pages.
2. Plus any ONE Frommer's City Guide.
3. A subscription to our quarterly newspaper, *The Dollarwise Traveler.*
4. A membership card that entitles you to purchase through the Club all Frommer's publications for 33% to 40% off their retail price.

The eight-page *Dollarwise Traveler* tells you about the latest developments in good-value travel worldwide and includes the following columns: **Hospitality Exchange** (for those offering and seeking hospitality in cities all over the world); **Share-a-Trip** (for those looking for travel companions to share costs); and **Readers Ask . . . Readers Reply** (for those with travel questions that other members can answer).

Aside from the Frommer's Guides and the Gault Millau Guides, you can also choose from our Special Editions. These include such titles as *California with Kids* (a compendium of the best of California's accommodations, restaurants, and sightseeing attractions appropriate for those traveling with toddlers through teens); *Candy Apple: New York with Kids* (a spirited guide to the Big Apple by a savvy New York grandmother that's perfect for both visitors and residents); *Caribbean Hideaways* (the 100 most romantic places to stay in the Islands, all rated on ambience, food, sports opportunities, and price); *Honeymoon Destinations* (a guide to planning and choosing just the right destination from hundreds of possibilities in the U.S., Mexico, and the Caribbean); *Marilyn Wood's Wonderful Weekends* (a selection of the best mini-vacations within a 200-mile radius of New York City, including descriptions of country inns and other accommodations, restaurants, picnic spots, sights, and activities); and *Paris Rendez-Vous* (a delightful guide to the best places to meet in Paris whether for power breakfasts or dancing till dawn).

To join this Club, simply send the appropriate membership fee with your name and address to: Frommer's Dollarwise Travel Club, 15 Columbus Circle, New York, NY 10023. Remember to specify which single city guide and which two other guides you wish to receive in your initial package of member's benefits. Or tear out the next page, check off your choices, and send the page to us with your membership fee.

FROMMER BOOKS
PRENTICE HALL PRESS
15 COLUMBUS CIRCLE
NEW YORK, NY 10023
212/373-8125

Date_____

Friends: Please send me the books checked below.

FROMMER'S™ GUIDES

(Guides to sightseeing and tourist accommodations and facilities from budget to deluxe, with emphasis on the medium-priced.)

☐ Alaska	$14.95	☐ Germany	$14.95
☐ Australia	$14.95	☐ Italy	$14.95
☐ Austria & Hungary	$14.95	☐ Japan & Hong Kong	$14.95
☐ Belgium, Holland & Luxembourg	$14.95	☐ Mid-Atlantic States	$14.95
☐ Bermuda & The Bahamas	$14.95	☐ New England	$14.95
☐ Brazil	$14.95	☐ New Mexico (avail. June '91)	$12.95
☐ Canada	$14.95	☐ New York State	$14.95
☐ Caribbean	$14.95	☐ Northwest	$15.95
☐ Cruises (incl. Alaska, Carib, Mex, Hawaii, Panama, Canada & US)	$14.95	☐ Portugal, Madeira & the Azores	$14.95
☐ California & Las Vegas	$14.95	☐ Scandinavia (avail. May '91)	$15.95
☐ Egypt	$14.95	☐ South Pacific	$14.95
☐ England & Scotland	$14.95	☐ Southeast Asia	$14.95
☐ Florida	$14.95	☐ Southern Atlantic States	$14.95
☐ France	$14.95	☐ Southwest	$14.95
		☐ Switzerland & Liechtenstein	$14.95

☐ USA $16.95

FROMMER'S $-A-DAY® GUIDES

(In-depth guides to sightseeing and low-cost tourist accommodations and facilities.)

☐ Europe on $40 a Day	$15.95	☐ Israel on $40 a Day	$13.95
☐ Australia on $40 a Day	$13.95	☐ Mexico on $35 a Day	$14.95
☐ Costa Rica; Guatemala & Belize on $35 a day (avail. Mar. '91)	$15.95	☐ New York on $60 a Day	$13.95
☐ Eastern Europe on $25 a Day	$15.95	☐ New Zealand on $45 a Day	$13.95
☐ England on $50 a Day	$13.95	☐ Scotland & Wales on $40 a Day	$13.95
☐ Greece on $35 a Day	$13.95	☐ South America on $40 a Day	$15.95
☐ Hawaii on $60 a Day	$14.95	☐ Spain on $50 a Day	$15.95
☐ India on $25 a Day	$12.95	☐ Turkey on $30 a Day	$13.95
☐ Ireland on $40 a Day	$14.95	☐ Washington, D.C. & Historic Va. on $40 a Day	$13.95

FROMMER'S TOURING GUIDES

(Color illustrated guides that include walking tours, cultural and historic sites, and other vital travel information.)

☐ Amsterdam	$10.95	☐ New York	$10.95
☐ Australia	$10.95	☐ Paris	$8.95
☐ Brazil	$10.95	☐ Rome	$10.95
☐ Egypt	$8.95	☐ Scotland	$9.95
☐ Florence	$8.95	☐ Thailand	$10.95
☐ Hong Kong	$10.95	☐ Turkey	$10.95
☐ London	$10.95	☐ Venice	$8.95

(TURN PAGE FOR ADDITONAL BOOKS AND ORDER FORM)

FROMMER'S CITY GUIDES
(Pocket-size guides to sightseeing and tourist accommodations and facilities in all price ranges.)

☐ Amsterdam/Holland	$8.95		☐ Minneapolis/St. Paul	$8.95
☐ Athens	$8.95		☐ Montréal/Québec City	$8.95
☐ Atlanta	$8.95		☐ New Orleans	$8.95
☐ Atlantic City/Cape May	$8.95		☐ New York	$8.95
☐ Barcelona	$7.95		☐ Orlando	$8.95
☐ Belgium	$7.95		☐ Paris	$8.95
☐ Berlin (avail. Mar '91)	$8.95		☐ Philadelphia	$8.95
☐ Boston	$8.95		☐ Rio	$8.95
☐ Cancún/Cozumel/Yucatán	$8.95		☐ Rome	$8.95
☐ Chicago	$8.95		☐ Salt Lake City	$8.95
☐ Denver/Boulder/Colorado Springs	$7.95		☐ San Diego	$8.95
☐ Dublin/Ireland	$8.95		☐ San Francisco	$8.95
☐ Hawaii	$8.95		☐ Santa Fe/Taos/Albuquerque	$8.95
☐ Hong Kong	$7.95		☐ Seattle/Portland	$7.95
☐ Las Vegas	$8.95		☐ St. Louis/Kansas City (avail. May '91)	$8.95
☐ Lisbon/Madrid/Costa del Sol	$8.95		☐ Sydney	$8.95
☐ London	$8.95		☐ Tampa/St. Petersburg	$8.95
☐ Los Angeles	$8.95		☐ Tokyo	$7.95
☐ Mexico City/Acapulco	$8.95		☐ Toronto	$8.95
☐ Miami	$8.95		☐ Vancouver/Victoria	$7.95

☐ Washington, D.C. $8.95

SPECIAL EDITIONS

☐ Beat the High Cost of Travel	$6.95		☐ Motorist's Phrase Book (Fr/Ger/Sp)	$4.95
☐ Bed & Breakfast—N. America	$14.95		☐ Paris Rendez-Vous	$10.95
☐ California with Kids	$15.95		☐ Swap and Go (Home Exchanging)	$10.95
☐ Caribbean Hideaways	$14.95		☐ The Candy Apple (NY with Kids)	$12.95
☐ Honeymoon Destinations (US, Mex &			☐ Travel Diary and Record Book	$5.95
Carib.)	$14.95		☐ Where to Stay USA (From $3 to $30 a	
☐ Manhattan's Outdoor Sculpture	$15.95		night)	$13.95

☐ Marilyn Wood's Wonderful Weekends (CT, DE, MA, NH, NJ, NY, PA, RI, VT) $11.95
☐ The New World of Travel (Annual sourcebook by Arthur Frommer for savvy travelers) $16.95

GAULT MILLAU
(The only guides that distinguish the truly superlative from the merely overrated.)

☐ The Best of Chicago	$15.95		☐ The Best of Los Angeles	$16.95
☐ The Best of France	$16.95		☐ The Best of New England	$15.95
☐ The Best of Hawaii	$16.95		☐ The Best of New Orleans	$16.95
☐ The Best of Hong Kong	$16.95		☐ The Best of New York	$16.95
☐ The Best of Italy	$16.95		☐ The Best of Paris	$16.95
☐ The Best of London	$16.95		☐ The Best of San Francisco	$16.95

☐ The Best of Washington, D.C. $16.95

ORDER NOW!

In U.S. include $2 shipping UPS for 1st book; $1 ea. add'l book. Outside U.S. $3 and $1, respectively.
Allow four to six weeks for delivery in U.S., longer outside U.S.

Enclosed is my check or money order for $_____

NAME_____

ADDRESS_____

CITY_____ STATE_____ ZIP_____

1290